THE LAW
OF
THE UNITED NATIONS

A Critical Analysis
of
Its Fundamental Problems

BY

HANS KELSEN

WITH SUPPLEMENT

Published under the auspices of
THE LONDON INSTITUTE OF WORLD AFFAIRS

THE LAWBOOK EXCHANGE, LTD.
Clark, New Jersey

ISBN 9781584770770 (hardcover)
ISBN 9781616192358 (paperback)

Lawbook Exchange edition 2000, 2011

The quality of this reprint is equivalent to the quality of the original work.

THE LAWBOOK EXCHANGE, LTD.
33 Terminal Avenue
Clark, New Jersey 07066-1321

Please see our website for a selection of our other publications and fine facsimile reprints of classic works of legal history:
www.lawbookexchange.com

Library of Congress Cataloging-in-Publication Data

Kelsen, Hans, 1881-1973.
The law of the United Nations: a critical analysis of its fundamental problems : with supplement / by Hans Kelsen.
p. cm.
"Published under the auspices of the London Institute of World Affairs."
Originally published: New York : F.A. Praeger, 1950. (Library of world affairs; no. 11).
Includes bibliographical references and index.
ISBN 1-58477-077-5 (cloth : alk. paper)
1. United Nations. Charter. 2. International law. I. London Institute of World Affairs.
II. Title. III. Library of world affairs ; no. 11.
KZ4991. K45 2000
341.23—dc21 00-025627

Printed in the United States of America on acid-free paper

THE LAW OF THE UNITED NATIONS

A Critical Analysis of Its Fundamental Problems

BY

HANS KELSEN

WITH SUPPLEMENT

Published under the auspices of
THE LONDON INSTITUTE OF WORLD AFFAIRS

FREDERICK A. PRAEGER, *Publisher*
NEW YORK

Published in the United States of America in 1950
by Frederick A. Praeger, Inc., Publisher
111 Fourth Avenue, New York 3, N.Y.

Fourth printing, 1964

Printed in the United States of America

CONTENTS

PART THREE

FUNCTIONS OF THE UNITED NATIONS

APPENDICES

PREFACE

ON INTERPRETATION

THIS book is a juristic—not a political—approach to the problems of the United Nations. It deals with the law of the Organisation, not with its actual or desired role in the international play of powers.

Separation of law from politics in the presentation of national or international problems is possible in so far as law is not an end in itself, but a means or, what amounts to the same, a specific social technique for the achievement of ends determined by politics. It stands to reason that in dealing with legal questions the elimination of the political issues involved is always relative, never absolute. In a merely juristic inquiry the political ends of the law-maker, in so far as they are ascertainable in an objective way, are taken for granted, and, hence, not subjected to a criticism, except to the degree that it may properly be restricted to the law as a means to these ends. ' Juristic ' in contradistinction to ' political ' has the connotation of ' technical.' It is not superfluous to remind the lawyer that as a ' jurist ' he is but a technician whose most important task is to assist the law-maker in the adequate formulation of the legal norms.

A study which does not content itself with a description of legal institutions as established by a social authority, but which aims at a critical analysis of the product of the law-making process, has to examine, in the first place, whether the legal instrument under consideration, be it a statute, a contract, or a treaty, is consistent in itself. Since the law is formulated in words and words have frequently more than one meaning, interpretation of the law, that is determination of its meaning, becomes necessary. Traditional jurisprudence distinguishes various methods of interpretation: the historical, in contrast to the grammatical, an interpretation according to the ' spirit,' in opposition to a literal interpretation keeping to the words. None of these methods can claim preference unless the law itself prescribes the one or the other. The different methods of interpretation may establish different meanings of one and the same provision. Sometimes, even one and the same method, especially the so-called grammatical interpretation, leads to contradictory results. It is incumbent upon the law-maker to avoid as far as possible ambiguities in the text of the law; but the nature of language makes the fulfilment of this task possible only to a certain degree.

Traditional jurisprudence is rarely inclined to admit that a legal norm has two or more meanings or, if such should be the case, that there is no juristic reason to prefer one of the various meanings to another. For it is considered to be the specific function of interpretation to find and establish the one, ' true ' meaning of a legal norm.

The view, however, that the verbal expression of a legal norm has only one, ' true ' meaning which can be discovered by correct interpretation is a fiction, adopted to maintain the illusion of legal security, to make the law-seeking public believe that there is only one possible answer to the question of law in a concrete case. Unfortunately, the contrary is true. That there is almost always a possible interpretation different from that adopted by the law-applying organ in a concrete case, is made clear by the practice of courts, such as the Permanent Court of International Justice, and the International Court of Justice, which publish both majority and dissenting opinions. In examining the decisions of these Courts one must inevitably conclude that in most cases the arguments of the dissenting judges are logically at least, equal in value to those which motivate the majority decision of the Court.

The true meaning of a legal norm is usually supposed to be the one which corresponds to the will of the legislator. But it is more than doubtful whether there exists at all such a thing as the ' will of the legislator,' especially where the law is the result of a complex procedure in which many individuals participate, such as the procedure through which a statute is adopted by a parliament or the procedure through which a multilateral treaty is negotiated and signed by many plenipotentiaries and ratified by many governments. The intention of the one or more who draft the text of a legal instrument is not at all identical with the will of the legislator, that is the will of those competent to make the draft a binding law, and who often fulfil this function without adequate knowledge of the text. In any event interpretation can take into consideration the intention of those who drafted the law or the will of the competent legislator only if intention or will is expressed in the terms of the law. However, the fact that the wording of a legal norm allows several interpretations proves that its actual framer or the competent legislator has not been able or willing to express his intention in a way excluding any interpretation not in conformity with his intention. In such a case, none of the several interpretations can be assumed to be the only one that corresponds to the intention of the framer or the will of the legislator. The ambiguity of a legal text moreover is sometimes not the unvoluntary effect of its unsatisfactory wording but a technique intentionally employed by the legislator, who, for some reason or another, could not decide between two or more solutions of a legal problem, and hence left the decision to the law-applying organs. If there are two or more possible interpretations, the law-applying organ has always the choice among them.

The fact that the legal norms as formulated in words having frequently more than one meaning is the reason why every legal instrument has its own life, more or less independent of the wishes and expectations of its begetters. That the law is open to more than one interpretation is certainly detrimental to legal security; but it has the advantage of making the law adaptable to changing circumstances, without the requirement of formal alteration.

The view that it is the function of interpretation to find the ' true ' meaning of the law, is based on an erroneous concept of interpretation. If interpretation is considered to be the determination of the true meaning of a legal norm, it must, by its very nature, be authentic, that is to say, it must have binding force. There are two kinds of authentic interpretation: a general and an individual one. The meaning of a legal norm may be determined by an act of the legislator in a general way and therefore be binding upon all law-applying organs; but the meaning of a legal norm may also be determined by an organ applying the norm to a concrete case, *e.g.*, by a court in its decision. The interpretation of the general norm, implied in the decision by which the norm is applied to a concrete case, is normally binding only for that case.

Authentic interpretation, whether general or individual, is a law-creating act. This is obvious in case of a general interpretation made by the legislator, But an act of individual interpretation has also a law-creating character. The decision of a judicial or administrative authority applying a general norm—which has several meanings—to a concrete case can correspond only to one of these meanings and must thus exclude the others. It is by the decision that one of several meanings of the applied norm becomes binding in the concrete case; and it is mainly, although not only with respect to its interpretative function that a judicial or administrative decision has a law-creating character.

The meaning of a legal norm which becomes binding by authentic —general or individual—interpretation is neither more nor less ' true ' than the other meanings, excluded by this interpretation. By authentic interpretation any meaning of the norm thus interpreted may become binding. Hence, the function of authentic interpretation is not to determine the true meaning of the legal norm thus interpreted, but to render binding one of the several meanings of a legal norm, all equally possible from a logical point of view. The choice of interpretations as a law-making act is determined by political motives. It is not the logically ' true,' it is the politically preferable meaning of the interpreted norm which becomes binding. Authentic interpretation may even attribute to a legal norm a meaning which a non-authentic interpretation could never dare to maintain. That is to say, by authentic interpretation a legal norm may be replaced by another norm of totally different content.

Interpretation as a legal function is possible only as authentic interpretation. Any other interpretation of a legal norm is an intellectual activity which may have great influence on the law-creating and law-applying function, but has no legal importance in itself. Interpretation as a legal function can be performed only by those whom the law authorises to interpret the law: the law-creating and law-applying organs. Non-authentic interpretation of the law, that is interpretation by persons not authorised by the law itself, is legally as irrelevant as the judgment of a private person on the guilt or innocence of an individual accused before a competent court of having committed a crime. A lawyer pleading the case of his client before a court, in interpreting the law, makes only suggestions to the law-applying organ. The task of a scientific commentary is first of all to find, by a critical analysis, the possible meanings of the legal norm undergoing interpretation; and, then, to show their consequences, leaving it to the competent legal authorities to choose from among the various possible interpretations the one which they, for political reasons, consider to be preferable, and which they alone are entitled to select. A scientific interpretation has to avoid giving countenance to the fiction that there is always but a single ' correct ' interpretation of the norms to be applied to concrete cases. This fiction, it is true, may have some political advantages. A party who sees his claim rejected by the legal authority may support this check more easily if he can be persuaded that another decision, another ' correct ' decision, was not possible. Especially in international law the states would perhaps be still less disposed to submit their disputes to international tribunals if they knew how much liberty of interpretation these tribunals possess even in applying written law, such as statutes or treaties. No political advantage, however, can justify the use of a legal fiction in a scientific commentary in order to declare an interpretation, which from one or another subjective point of view may be more desirable, as the only objectively ' correct ' one. This implies the fallacy of presenting a political convenience as a logical necessity. Besides, the scientific method of exhibiting on the basis of a critical analysis all possible interpretations of a legal norm, even those which are politically undesirable and those which permit the conjecture that they were not intended by the legislator, may have a practical effect which largely outweighs the advantage of the just mentioned fiction. Showing the legislator how far his product lags behind the goal of any law-making function, *i.e.* the unambiguous regulation of inter-individual or inter-state relations, may induce him to improve his technique.

These are the principles which directed the author in his critical analysis of the Charter of the United Nations. Since that instrument does not contain any provision concerning its interpretation, the organs and Members of the United Nations competent to apply the Charter are free to interpret the provisions to be applied by them according to their own discretion. Any meaning a provision of the Charter might possibly have can become the law in a particular case. Hence the author considered it necessary to present all the interpretations which according to his opinion might be possible, including those which he himself—if he were competent to apply the Charter—would reject as undesirable, and even those of which it could be presumed that they were not intended by the framers of the Charter. The author lays particular stress on the fact that in interpreting the Charter his main concern has been the problems of legal technique involved. He hopes that his study might be of some use not only to those who wish to understand, but also to those who will try to revise the law of the United Nations.

Finally, it should be noted that it is not the entire law of the Organisation that this book intends to cover; only the basic legal problems are analysed. This limitation to specifically legal problems may justify the fact that an essential function of the United Nations, the promotion of economic and social co-operation, is dealt with in this study only in connection with a general discussion of the purposes of the Organisation; for its importance lies rather in the political than in the legal field. This statement does not imply that the author under-estimates the value of the political activities of the United Nations; on the contrary, he is aware that the international community established at the San Francisco Conference is by its very nature a political phenomenon and that a merely juristic interpretation cannot do justice to it. The foregoing remarks concerning the separation of law from politics show his view that the former, as a means, is subordinate to the latter, as an end, and that political ends may be achieved by other means than by imposing obligations and conferring rights upon persons subjected to a strict law. But just as it would be foolish to underestimate the political aspect, it would be a serious mistake to ignore the importance of the task of improving, as far as possible, the law established to serve the purposes of the United Nations; which is exactly the ultimate goal of the critical analysis presented in this study.

HANS KELSEN.

Berkeley, California.
Spring, 1949.

PART ONE

THE PURPOSES OF THE UNITED NATIONS

CHAPTER 1

THE PREAMBLE

IT is usual to determine the purposes of an international organisation in the preamble of the treaty by which the organisation is constituted. The Preamble of the Charter of the United Nations refers to some, but not to all, purposes of the Organisation. It is in the first place Chapter I of the Charter which, under the heading ' Purposes and Principles,' deals with this problem. But to answer the question ' What are the purposes of the United Nations ? ' also other parts of the Charter must be taken into consideration. Some purposes of the Organisation; the registration of treaties and the protection of the peoples of non-self-governing territories (especially by the trusteeship system), are not even mentioned in the Preamble or in Chapter I.

1. TITLE OF THE INSTRUMENT AND NAME OF THE ORGANISATION

The Preamble of the Treaty signed at San Francisco on June 26, 1945, is preceded by the words ' Charter of the United Nations,' indicating the title of that legal instrument and the name of the Organisation constituted by it. ' Charter ' is certainly a more adequate designation of the constitution of an international community than ' Covenant,' the name which has been given to the statute of the League of Nations. The term ' Charter ' refers to the contents of the treaty whereas the term ' Covenant ' refers to the contractual form of the contents, which amounts to naming a treaty a treaty.

The name of the Organisation ' United Nations ' has been adopted ' in tribute to the memory of Franklin Delano Roosevelt '[1] who suggested it. It was taken from the ' Declaration by United Nations ' signed at Washington on January 1, 1942. By this treaty each contracting party assumed the obligations ' to employ its full resources, military or economic, against those members of the Tripartite Pact and its adherents with which such government is at war,' ' to co-operate with the governments signatory hereto, and not to make a separate armistice or peace with the enemies.'[2]

1 Cf. the Report of the Rapporteur of Committee I/1 of the United Nations Conference on International Organisation (U.N.C.I.O.) (Doc. 944, I/1/34 (1), p. 5).

2 The Report of the Rapporteur, Subcommittee I/1/A, Section 3, to Committee I/1 (U.N.C.I.O. Doc. 785, I/1/27) contains the following statement: ' Some members of the Subcommittee considered that United Nations is a very good name for the following reasons: (1) It is the name given by the late President Franklin Delano Roosevelt. In homage to his name and in acknowledgment of his efforts to create the Organisation, it would be appropriate to keep the name he first gave. (2) That name came to be widely known. It has already captivated the attention of the peoples of the world. The name should be the one by which our

The term 'United Nations,' taken literally, refers to states associated in some way or another, not to an organisation of states. In this literal meaning the term is used in the above mentioned Declaration. But in the Charter it is used to designate the international community constituted by the Charter. This ambiguity of the term is not very fortunate. But even as used in the Charter, the term has two different meanings. In the title of the Charter and in the text of the Preamble it is used to designate the total Organisation constituted by the Charter comprising, as an integral part, the Statute of the International Court of Justice. The signatures of the representatives of the Governments which participated in the San Francisco Conference

activity has been known and distinguished. (3) That though United Nations is not grammatically a title for an association or organisation, it becomes, what has already become by use, a proper noun and can be easily used that way.—All members share the wish to do due homage to Franklin Delano Roosevelt, but some thought that a name other than United Nations, which would indicate the existence of association or community or organisation, is in itself more fit.—The reasons can be given as follows: (1) The title United Nations will not designate the Organisation but its members. (2) When a dispute should occur among member nations they would no longer be united nations, and (3) the term "United Nations" in the historical sense refers to the nations that have taken this name in fighting the common enemy. In future years it would be difficult to admit some previous enemy states to take that name.'

Another argument against the name 'United Nations' was that 'it would be difficult to find an equivalent in certain languages' (*Report to the President on the Results of the San Francisco Conference by the Secretary of State.* Department of State, Publication No. 2349, Conference Series 71, Washington, 1945 [cited thereafter as: *Report to the President*], p. 32). The Summary Report of 14th Meeting of Committee I/1 (U.N.C.I.O. Doc. 856, I/1/32) contains the following statement: 'Delegates speaking in support of the term "The United Nations," who were far in the majority, pointed out that the principles for which the war had been fought and those which the Organisation would endeavour to carry forward into the peace were one and the same, and that this continuity should be reflected in the name of the Organisation. As for the doubts expressed as to the idea of collectivity in the term "The United Nations," it was pointed out that no one in referring to the United States thought of the American nation as 48 separate states but rather as a single, national entity. So, too, it was felt, would "The United Nations" designate a single organisation. As for the difficulty of eventually admitting to the membership of the Organisation those states with which members were now at war, these nations would not be given the privilege of membership until they had proved their faithful allegiance to the principles for which The United Nations stand. In looking back at some of the darkest moments of the war they saw that some particular good talisman had been attached to the name "United Nations." Under its banner the war had been fought through to complete victory. They now hoped that together under the same name the dream of President Roosevelt would be realised and peace maintained. As for the grammatical difficulties which might be encountered in translating "United Nations," many Delegates felt that each government should bear the responsibility of making a translation adapted to the needs of its language. Experience had shown that translations were frequently inaccurate and inevitably presented a bothersome and almost insurmountable problem. It was pointed out, in this case, that if a term such as "Union" or "Association" were added to "The United Nations" the stirring and unique breadth of the concept "United Nations" would be lost.'

are affixed at the end of the whole document containing the text of the Charter and the Statute of the International Court of Justice. The ' international organisation,' which according to the Preamble is ' to be known as the United Nations,' is the community constituted by the Charter comprising the Statute.

In the text of the Charter, however, the term ' United Nations ' is used in a narrower sense. When the Charter speaks of ' Members of the United Nations '—the term ' Member ' capitalised—it refers to the United Nations Organisation as constituted by the Charter not comprising the Statute. For ' Members of the United Nations ' are only the states which are parties to the Charter in this narrower sense of the term, not the states which are parties to the Statute but not parties to the Charter in this narrower sense. This results from Article 93 of the Charter according to which the ' Members of the United Nations ' are *ipso facto* parties to the Statute, whereas other states may become parties to the Statute only.

2. The Two Sentences of the Preamble

The text of the Preamble runs as follows:—

> We the peoples of the United Nations determined to save succeeding generations from the scourge of war, which twice in our lifetime has brought untold sorrow to mankind, and to reaffirm faith in fundamental human rights, in the dignity and worth of the human person, in the equal rights of men and women and of nations large and small, and to establish conditions under which justice and respect for the obligations arising from treaties and other sources of international law can be maintained, and to promote social progress and better standards of life in larger freedom, and for these ends to practice tolerance and live together in peace with one another as good neighbours, and to unite our strength to maintain international peace and security, and to ensure, by the acceptance of principles and the institution of methods, that armed force shall not be used, save in the common interest, and to employ international machinery for the promotion of the economic and social advancement of all peoples, have resolved to combine our efforts to accomplish these aims.
>
> Accordingly, our respective Governments, through representatives assembled in the city of San Francisco, who have exhibited their full powers found to be in good and due form, have agreed to the present Charter of the United Nations and do hereby establish an international organisation to be known as the United Nations.

The Preamble contains two sentences. In the first, it is declared that ' the peoples of the United Nations ' have resolved to combine their efforts to accomplish certain aims by certain means. In the second sentence it is declared that the Governments of these peoples have agreed to the Charter.

Originally Committee I/1 of the San Francisco Conference commended to the Co-ordination Committee the following phrasing of the introduction 'as the general sentiment of the Committee' with the request to examine the legal practicality of it: 'We the peoples of the United Nations . . . through our representatives assembled at San Francisco agree to this Charter.'[3] This text presented the Charter as an agreement of the peoples of the United Nations, in analogy to the Preamble of the Constitution of the United States 'We, the people of the United States . . . establish this constitution of the United States of America.' This formula expresses the idea of popular sovereignty[4] and has rather a political than a legal significance since it was not the people of the United States, but an assembly composed of representatives of the thirteen states of the Confederation which adopted the Constitution that came into force, and thus was 'established,' by the ratifications of the states forming the original confederation. The

[3] Cf. the Summary Report of 13th Meeting of Committee I/1 (U.N.C.I.O. Doc. 817, I/1/31).

[4] At the 1st meeting of Commission I of the San Francisco Conference, a member of the United States delegation declared that the opening words 'We the peoples of the United Nations' 'seem to us to express the democratic basis on which rests our new Organisation for peace and human welfare, achieved through the long agony of this peoples' war.' (U.N.C.I.O. Doc. 1,006, I/6). The democratic character of the Organisation is, in view of the privileged position of the five permanent members of the Security Council, very doubtful. The *Report to the President*, p. 34, contains the following statement: 'The opening words of the Preamble, and therefore of the Charter, are modelled upon the opening words of the Constitution of the United States—"We the peoples of the United Nations." The Delegation of the United States proposed these words which in our history express the democratic basis on which government is founded.' This is true with respect to the Government of the United States but not to the governments of all the states signatories to the Charter. The Charter does not impose on the Members of the Organisation the obligation to have a democratic form of government, nor is such form of government a condition for admission to the Organisation. At the *Hearings before the Committee on Foreign Relations, United States Senate, on the Charter of the United Nations*, United States Government Printing Office, Washington: 1945 (cited hereafter as: *Hearings*), pp. 227 ff., a Senator asked: 'Was there any sort of agreement or understanding about what "We the peoples of the United Nations" meant? Did they accept the idea of popular sovereignty?' Whereupon the representative of the Department of State answered: 'I think it was clearly understood that the phrase "We the peoples" meant that the peoples of the world were speaking through their governments at the Conference, and that it was because the peoples of the world are determined that those things shall be done which are stated in the preamble that the governments have negotiated the instrument.' Then the Senator asked: 'And that the governments represented at the Conference were actually the agents of the peoples of those countries represented there?' To this the answer was: 'I do not know that that question was discussed in that particular form, as a matter of political institutions. The document, being in the form of a treaty, had to be negotiated by governments.' Finally, the representative of the State Department declared: 'The phrase itself, "We the peoples" is borrowed from a well-known document.'

'people of the United States' could not be the author of the Constitution since the people of the United States, as a legal entity, was first constituted by the Constitution. The Charter is an international treaty concluded by states represented by their governments. These governments, not the 'peoples,' were represented at the San Francisco Conference.[5] Some of these states have a written or unwritten constitution which does not concede any essential influence on the conclusion of treaties to the people or does not imply the political ideology of popular sovereignty. In Committee I/1 of the San Francisco Conference the Netherlands delegate suggested 'that possibly there might be some constitutional difficulty at least as respected the Netherlands and possibly also with other states in using the phrasing proposed by the United States delegation: 'We the Peoples of the United Nations through our representatives assembled at San Francisco agree to this Charter.' In the Netherlands, sovereignty was not vested in the people under the Constitution, and the Crown, not the people, concluded treaties.'[6]

The text finally adopted marks only a partial improvement. The phrase 'We the Peoples of the United Nations determined to save . . . have resolved to combine our efforts to accomplish these aims,' implies the same political fiction as the phrase objected to by the Netherlands delegate. Not the 'peoples,' but the governments 'resolved' to combine their efforts to accomplish these aims. The resolution to combine the efforts of the United Nations to accomplish the aims determined in the Preamble is identical with the conclusion of the treaty called Charter of the United Nations; and the conclusion of this treaty is not a common act of the peoples of the United Nations but of their governments. Even the last phrase 'Accordingly, our respective Governments, through representatives . . . have agreed to the present Charter of the United Nations and do hereby establish an international organisation to be known as the United Nations' is legally not correct. For the governments are not organs of the peoples, but of the states, and by signing the text of the Charter their representatives assembled in San Francisco have not 'established' the Organisation; the Organisation has been 'established' by the coming into force of the Charter on October 24, 1945; and this was the effect of the ratifications made in accordance with Article 110 of the Charter, not of the signatures affixed to the text of the Charter in San Francisco on June 26, 1945.

The last sentence of the Preamble is incorrect also for another reason. The words: 'Our respective governments' refer to the 'peoples of the United Nations' mentioned at the beginning of the Preamble. The meaning of this term may be doubtful. The peoples whose governments established the United Nations became peoples of

[5] The Preamble of the Covenant of the League of Nations runs as follows: 'The High Contracting Parties . . . Agree to this Covenant of the League of Nations.'

[6] U.N.C.I.O. Doc. 817, I/1/31. Cf. also U.N.C.I.O. Doc. 926, I/1/36.

this Organisation, that means peoples of the states original Members of the Organisation, only after the Charter came into force. Prior to this date the peoples of the United Nations were the peoples of the states whose governments signed the Declaration of the United Nations of January 1, 1942. However, some states which became original Members of the United Nations constituted by the Charter have not signed the 'Declaration by the United Nations': Argentina, the Byelorussian Soviet Socialist Republic, Lebanon, Syria, the Ukrainian Soviet Socialist Republic; and one state which signed the Declaration did not attend the San Francisco Conference: Poland. The governments which through their representatives assembled in the City of San Francisco have agreed to the present Charter of the United Nations are neither identical with those who signed the Declaration nor with those who became original Members of the United Nations. If the words: 'We the peoples of the United Nations' at the beginning of the Preamble mean: the peoples of the states which will become the original Members of the United Nations, the last sentence of the Preamble is incorrect since the Government of Poland was not represented in the Conference at San Francisco.

The peoples whose governments, through representatives assembled in the city of San Francisco, have agreed to the present Charter of the United Nations are neither the peoples of the United Nations in the sense of the Declaration, nor in the sense of the Charter.

The meaning of the last sentence of the Preamble is that the Charter has been established as a treaty in conformity with the principle of general international law concerning the creation of rules legally binding upon states. Some provisions of the Charter contain also introductory formulas indicating the contractual character of the obligation stipulated by the provision, which implies that the obligation has been established by a treaty and hence has been assumed by the contracting parties. Thus, *e.g.*, Articles 25 and 74: 'The Members of the United Nations agree . . . ;' Article 43: 'All Members . . . undertake . . . ,' Article 94: 'Each Member . . . undertakes . . . ,' Article 56: 'All Members pledge themselves . . . ,' Article 73: 'Members . . . recognise the principle . . . and accept as a sacred trust the obligation . . . ' These formulas as well as the last sentence of the Preamble are technically superfluous. The statement of the fact that a norm belonging to a certain legal system has been created according to the procedure laid down by the constitution of this system for the creation of its norms, should not appear in the text of the norm in question, unless the constitution expressly requires that mention be made in the norm of the fact that it has been constitutionally established. The constitutions of some modern states prescribe that the statutes shall contain a reference to the decision of the parliament and the approval of the head of the state, that is to say the statement that the statute has been enacted in the way determined by the constitution. This is what is called the promulgatory clause.

However, the constitution of the international community established by general international law, *i.e.*, the rules concerning the creation of international law, especially the principles which govern the creation of contractual norms, has no provision of this kind. International treaties need not contain a promulgatory clause such as the second sentence of the Preamble although they often do. Neither need particular treaty provisions stipulating obligations of the contracting parties be introduced by formulas such as used in the above mentioned Articles of the Charter. Formulas such as: 'the members or parties agree,' 'pledge themselves,' 'undertake,' 'accept the obligation' and the like have no other meaning than the simple formula: the members or parties 'shall,' as used in other Articles of the Charter stipulating obligations.

3. Binding Force of the Preamble

The Preamble is part of the Charter. Consequently it has virtually the same legal validity, that is to say, the same binding force as the other parts of the Charter.[7] The binding force of a statement does actually depend not only on its being part of a statute or a treaty but also on its contents. Statutes and treaties often contain legally irrelevant elements. The contents of a statute or a treaty has binding force only if it has a normative character, that is to say, if its meaning is to establish by itself or in connection with other contents of the statute or treaty an obligation. A legal obligation to behave in a certain way is established if a sanction is attached to the contrary behaviour.[8] A statement whose meaning is to establish an obligation is a norm. A statement has normative character even if it may be used only for the purpose of interpreting other statements having the character of true norms.

The meaning of the Preamble is not to establish by itself obligations. As the *Report to the President on the Results of the San Francisco Conference by the Secretary of State of the United States* correctly says: 'the obligations of the Members are to be found in other portions of the text.'[9] The Preamble sets forth certain political ideals without guaranteeing their realisation by the sanctions stipulated by the Charter. Thus it has rather an ideological than a legal importance.[1] The *Report to the*

[7] At the *Hearings* (p. 229), a Senator asked: 'Legally speaking, would the preamble have legal force?' whereupon the representative of the Department of State answered: 'The position adopted at the Conference was that the preamble has the same force as the document itself; but the operating part of the document, of course, begins with the operating provisions.'

[8] Cf. *infra*, pp. 87 ff.

[9] *Report to the President*, p. 35.

[1] At the 1st meeting of Commission I (U.N.C.I.O. Doc. 1,006, I/6) the Rapporteur declared: 'It was . . . understood and clearly considered that the Preamble introduces the Charter and sets forth the declared common intentions which brought

President states: ' . . . the Conference did not doubt that the statements expressed in the Preamble constitute valid evidence on the basis of which the Charter may hereafter be interpreted.'[2] It is, however, doubtful whether the Preamble can be used as a means of interpretation. For its statements refer to objects which are regulated in a more detailed or in a different way, or are not mentioned at all in other parts of the Charter.

As a possible means of interpretation the first sentence of the Preamble comes into consideration. It determines the ' ends ' or ' aims ' of the United Nations and the means to accomplish them. The phrase which forms, as it were, the framework of the determination of the ends and means is not very satisfactory: ' We the peoples of the United Nations determined to . . . and for these ends to . . . have resolved to combine our efforts to accomplish these aims.' After it has been declared that the peoples are determined to do something for certain ' ends,' it is a superfluous repetition to say that these peoples have resolved to accomplish these aims. One of the means is formulated: ' to unite our strength to . . . ' To say: determined to unite our strength we have resolved to combine our efforts, is certainly not a masterpiece of style.

' Ends ' or ' aims ' means the same as ' purposes.' Article 1 of the Charter is especially devoted to the determination of the ' Purposes ' of the Organisation and also other Articles of the Charter refer to this subject. Consequently, repetitions—technically highly objectionable—were inevitable.[3] Sometimes the same idea is

us together in this Conference and moved us to unite our will and efforts, and to harmonise, regulate, and organise our international action to achieve our common ends.'

[2] *Report to the President*, p. 35.

[3] The Report of the Rapporteur of Committee 1 to Commission I (U.N.C.I.O. Doc. 944, I/1/34 (1)) contains the following statement: ' General Remarks. 1. It was very difficult, practically impossible, to draw a sharp and clear-cut distinction between what should be included under " Purposes," " Principles," or " Preamble." Given the nature of the substance we have in view, some single idea or norm of conduct could go into either of these divisions of the Charter without much difficulty. In fact, some questions were transferred during our deliberations from " Purposes " to " Principles " and found at last their final place in the " Preamble." It was, however, considered and clearly understood that: (*a*) The " Preamble " introduces the Charter and sets forth the declared common intentions which brought us together in this Conference and moved us to unite our will and efforts, and made us harmonise, regulate, and organise our international action to achieve our common ends. (*b*) The " Purposes " constitute the *raison d'être* of the Organisation. They are the aggregation of the common ends on which our minds met; hence, the cause and object of the Charter to which member states collectively and severally subscribe. (*c*) The chapter on " Principles " sets, in the same order of ideas, the methods and regulating norms according to which the Organisation and its members shall do their duty and endeavour to achieve the common ends. Their understandings should serve as actual standards of international conduct.—The " Purposes " and " Principles " constitute, in practice, the test for the effectiveness of the Organisation and the expected faithful compliance

expressed in the Preamble in other words than in another part of the Charter. The strangest thing is that the main ' Purpose ' of the Organisation: ' to maintain international peace and security ' (Article 1, paragraph 1) is presented in the Preamble not as an 'end,' but—on the second place only—as a means to achieve the ends of the Organisation in the phrase: ' to unite our strength to maintain international peace and security.' Another ' Purpose ': ' to bring about by peaceful means . . . settlement of international disputes ' (Article 1, paragraph 1) is not mentioned at all in the Preamble,

with the Provisions of the Charter.—Members of the Commission can see from what has been said that the distinction between the three parts of the Charter under consideration is not particularly profound. I hope, therefore, that we will all be tolerant in our individual wishes to see a given element of our thoughts go into one part rather than into another. 2. On the basis of the first general remark, I take leave to state the second.—The Provisions of the Charter, being in this case indivisible as in any other legal instrument, are equally valid and operative. The rights, duties, privileges, and obligations of the Organisation and its members match with one another and complement one another to make a whole. Each of them is construed to be understood and applied in function of the others.—It is for this reason, as well as to avoid undue repetition, that the Committee did not find it necessary to mention again in each paragraph relevant dispositions included in other paragraphs of the same chapter or other chapters. It was, nevertheless, unavoidable at times to make some repetition.—May the explanation given above dispel any doubts as to the validity and value of any division of the Charter, whether we call it " Principles," " Purposes," or " Preamble."—It is thus clear that there are no grounds for supposing that the Preamble has less legal validity than the two succeeding chapters. We found it appropriate to state the last remark, which could otherwise be taken for granted.'

[4] The Report of the Rapporteur of Subcommittee I/1/A of the San Francisco Conference (U.N.C.I.O. Doc. 785, I/1/27, p. 1) contains the following statement: ' The subcommittee . . . was intent upon doing two things: (*a*) To avoid in the Preamble undue repetition, in similar phraseology, of what had already gone into Principles, Purposes or other provisions of the Charter. (*b*) To give the Preamble a language and tone which leads its way to the hearts of men. The Preamble should introduce the Charter, and by so doing should have the harmony in ideas and words, and the light, which can awaken the imagination of the common man to the points at issue, kindle his feelings and move him.'

The final text of the Preamble has certainly not avoided undue repetitions of what had already gone into other parts of the Charter; but it must be emphasized that in a legal instrument a repetition is all the more undue the more its phraseology is changed. A critical analysis shows that there is, unfortunately, no harmony in the ideas of the Charter and the words of the Preamble. It is a difficult task to mould the language of a legal instrument in a way which leads to the hearts of common men and awakens their imagination. If it is possible at all it can be achieved not by well chosen words only, but by their meaning, by the real prospects they open. If the language of the Preamble remains far below the ideal formulated in the Report just quoted, it is not only because of its stylistic deficiency. It fails primarily because in the matter which evidently was supposed to appeal most to the hearts of the common man: the fundamental human rights, the Preamble can make no impressive declaration without being backed by substantial provisions of the Charter. Since the Charter completely fails in this respect, the words of the Preamble which particularly intend to kindle the feeling and move the heart of the common man remain empty phrases.

whereas the principle of good-neighbour policy, laid down in the Preamble, does not appear among the ' Purposes ' or ' Principles ' in Chapter I, but solely in Chapter XI (Article 74) dealing with non-self-governing territories. Some ideas are proclaimed in the Preamble that are not mentioned in other parts of the Charter, such as ' equal rights of men and women,' ' dignity and worth of the human person,' and ' to practice tolerance.'[4]

[4] See previous page.

Chapter 2

MAINTENANCE OF PEACE

The Preamble declares as an ' end ' of the United Nations ' to save succeeding generations from the scourge of war,' which is identical with what the Preamble declares as means for this end: ' to live together in peace with one another as good neighbours,' ' to maintain international peace and security,' and ' to ensure . . . that armed force shall not be used, save in the common interest.' All this corresponds to the ' Purposes ' determined in Article 1, paragraph 1: ' To maintain international peace and security, and to that end: to take effective collective measures for the prevention and removal of threats to the peace, and for the suppression of acts of aggression or other breaches of the peace . . .', and to the ' Principle ' laid down in Article 2, paragraph 4: ' All Members shall refrain in their international relations from the threat or use of force against the territorial integrity or political independence of any state, or in any other manner inconsistent with the Purposes of the United Nations.'

The formulas ' to maintain (or further) international peace and security' or ' maintenance of international peace and security' appear also in other Articles of the Charter (Articles 2, paragraph 6; 11, paragraphs 1 and 2; 43, paragraph 1; 47, paragraph 1; 48, paragraph 1; 51; 52, paragraph 1; 73 (c); 84; 99; 106). It is doubtful whether there is a difference between ' peace ' and ' security.' International security is guaranteed if international peace is maintained. It seems that the addition of the words ' and security ' is rather superfluous.

1. Prevention and Repression of Breaches of the Peace

To ' maintain ' international peace means to prevent a breach of the peace. If the peace has been broken, it cannot be maintained, but only restored. This terminological distinction is made in Articles 39 and 51, but not in the Preamble and Chapter 1. Article 1 distinguishes between ' prevention and removal of threats to the peace,' but speaks only of ' suppression '—not of prevention—' of acts of aggression and other breaches of the peace.' ' Prevention and removal of threats to the peace ' and ' suppression of acts of aggression and other breaches of the peace ' are presented as the purpose of ' effective collective measures ' to be taken for the ' Purpose ' to ' maintain international peace and security.' Peace can be maintained by removal or suppression of threats to the peace, but not by suppression of acts of aggression.

In Article 1, paragraph 1, obvious stress is laid on taking effective collective measures. They are mentioned in the first place. This is highly significant. The 'effective collective measures' form the centre of the political system which is at the basis of the Charter. By 'effective collective measures' the measures determined in Articles 41 to 50 are meant. They are enforcement measures not involving or involving the use of armed force (Articles 41 and 42). They are to be ordered by the Security Council and carried out by the Members determined by the Council (Article 48). In this respect Article 2, paragraph 5, is of importance which provides that 'All Members shall give the United Nations every assistance in any action it takes in accordance with the present Charter, and shall refrain from giving assistance to any state against which the United Nations is taking preventive or enforcement action.'

The reaction against a breach of the peace is formulated in Article 1, paragraph 1, as 'suppression of acts of aggression or other breaches of the peace.' The express mentioning of 'acts of aggression' is superfluous since these acts are included in the concept, 'breaches of the peace.'[1] The term 'aggression' has many different meanings, and no definition of the term has been inserted into the Charter. The reaction against threat to the peace is not characterised as 'suppression,' but as 'prevention and removal.' Removal means about the same as 'suppression.' In this connection the term 'prevention' is rather problematical. If 'effective collective measures' means enforcement measures determined by Articles 41 to 50, a threat to the peace cannot be 'prevented' by such action. For, according to Article 39, these measures shall be taken only if the 'existence' of a threat to the peace is determined by the Security Council. Then it is too late to 'prevent' it. What can be 'prevented' by an enforcement action as determined by Articles 41 to 50 is an actual breach of the peace. Since the Security Council is authorised by Article 39 to take enforcement measures in case it determines a mere threat to the peace, the enforcement measures taken by the Security Council may have not only a repressive but also a preventive character, in spite of the fact that Article 1, paragraph 1, speaks of 'prevention' only with reference to 'threats to the peace,' which, as pointed out, cannot be 'prevented' by enforcement actions. As enforcement actions may have a preven-

[1] The Report of Rapporteur, Subcommittee I/A to Committee I/1 (U.N.C.I.O. Doc. 723, I/1/A/19, p. 8) contains the following statement: 'A suggestion was made to consider "other breaches of the peace" coming after "aggression" as superfluous. But the subcommittee held that there may be breaches of the peace other than those qualified by present connotation as aggression and the subcommittee decided to keep "other breaches of the peace" as an all-inclusive term which implies the use of any means of coercion or undue external influence, which, through exertion or threat to security of a state, amounts to a breach of the peace.' The terms 'act of aggression' and 'breach of the peace' appear also in Article 39: 'The Security Council shall determine the existence of any threat to the peace, breach of the peace, or act of aggression. . . .' If 'breach of the peace' is the wider concept including that of 'act of aggression,' then the wording of Article 39 is obviously incorrect.

tive character, it is not correct to oppose—as Article 2, paragraph 5, Articles 5 and 50 do—preventive to enforcement actions (or measures).

The preventive function of ' maintaining ' peace is established by the provision of Article 1, paragraph 1, determining as a Purpose of the United Nations: ' to bring about by peaceful means, and in conformity with the principles of justice and international law, adjustment or settlement of international disputes or situations which might lead to a breach of the peace.' This purpose of the United Nations constitutes a function of the Organisation, to be carried out by the General Assembly, the Security Council, and the International Court of Justice. To this function of the Organisation corresponds an obligation of the Members, presented as a ' Principle ' in Article 2, paragraph 3: ' All Members shall settle their international disputes by peaceful means in such a manner that international peace and security, and justice, are not endangered.'

2. The Function of the Organisation and the Obligation of the Members

The obligation of the Members as formulated in Article 2, paragraph 3, is not quite in harmony with the corresponding function of the Organisation as formulated in Article 1, paragraph 1. The Members are obliged only to settle their international disputes, whereas the Organisation shall bring about also adjustment of situations which have not the character of disputes. The Members are obliged to settle all their international disputes by peaceful means, whereas the Organisation shall bring about only adjustment or settlement of international disputes or situations ' which might lead to a breach of the peace.' In Article 33, where the obligation of the Members is specified, only disputes ' the continuance of which is likely to endanger the maintenance of international peace and security ' are referred to. Under Article 2, paragraph 3, the Members are obliged to settle their international disputes in such a manner ' that international peace and security, and justice,' are not endangered. Under Article 1, paragraph 1, the Organisation shall bring about adjustment or settlement of disputes and situations ' in conformity with the principles of justice and international law.'

3. Law and Justice

In the Preamble, justice and international law are referred to in the provision determining as an end of the United Nations ' to establish conditions under which justice and respect for the obligations arising from treaties and other sources of international law can be maintained.' This phrase is probably modelled after the formula used in the Preamble of the Covenant: ' to promote international co-operation and to achieve international peace and security . . . by the firm establishment of the understandings of international law as the actual rule of conduct among Governments, and by the maintenance of justice and a scrupulous respect for all treaty obligations in the dealings of organised peoples with one another.' The Preamble of the Charter does not proclaim —as the Preamble of the Covenant does—the ' maintenance ' of justice and respect for international obligations, but: the establishment of ' conditions under which ' such is possible. The long phrase: ' obligations arising from treaties and other sources of international law ' could easily be replaced by two words: ' international obligations.' To lay particular stress on the respect for treaty obligations is rather problematical in view of the fact that the provision of Article 14 authorising the General Assembly to recommend measures for the peaceful adjustment of any situation regardless of origin, which it deems likely to impair the general welfare or friendly relations ' among nations ' has been interpreted to include the possibility of recommendations for the revision of treaties.[2] In Article 1, paragraph 1, the observance of justice and international law is expressly restricted to a special function of the Organisation: to bringing about adjustments or settlements of disputes and situations which might lead to a breach of the peace. Conformity with the principles of justice and international law is not required for other functions of the Organisation, especially not for taking ' effective collective measures for the prevention and removal of threats to the peace, and for the suppression of acts of aggression or other breaches of the peace,' the first Purpose of the Organisation mentioned in Article 1, paragraph 1. The terms ' in conformity with the principles of justice and international law ' were intentionally placed in the second, and not in the first part of this paragraph.[3] To proclaim the maintenance of justice

[2] At the 17th meeting of Committee II/2 (U.N.C.I.O. Doc. 748, II/2/39, p. 2) the delegate of the United States explained: ' . . . that, although he had originally contemplated a specific allusion in the Charter to the question of revision of treaties, he had foregone this in favour of the broad version of paragraph 6 of Section (B), Chapter V, put forward by the four sponsoring governments and France. It was inconsistent to launch an international Organisation based on international integrity and at the same time to intimate any lack of respect for the instruments through which international integrity functions, namely, treaties. He recognised the objections to identifying treaties as such with this paragraph and held that the concern of the Assembly was not with treaties *per se*, but with adjusting conditions which might impair peace and good relations between nations. Considerations of the general welfare may call for a recommendation that a treaty be respected rather than revised. He submitted that it was wiser not to connect the broad version of paragraph 6 with any specific definition regarding treaty revision. The phrase " the peaceful adjustment of any situations, regardless of origin," in his view, should not be interpreted to mean that the subject of treaty revision was foreclosed to the Assembly. If treaties gave rise to situations which the Assembly deemed likely to impair the general welfare or friendly relations among nations, it could make recommendations in respect of these situations.'

[3] Cf. the Report of Rapporteur of Committee I/1 (U.N.C.I.O. Doc. 944, I/1/34 (1), pp. 7 f.). At the 1st meeting of Commission I (U.N.C.I.O. Doc. 1,006, I/6) the President of the Commission (the representative of Belgium) declared in the

and—at the same time—the respect for international law is highly problematical. If justice is identical with international law, one of the two terms is superfluous. If, which is more probable, they are

discussion of the Preamble and Article 1 of the Charter: ' With regard to peace we feel the need to emphasise that our first object was to be strong to maintain peace, to maintain peace by our common effort and at all costs, at all costs with one exception—not at the cost of justice. ' (p. 2). And the representative of Panama stated: ' . . . we will not maintain peace and security at the cost of justice; that is to say, sacrificing the right of any nation. ' (p. 16). At the same meeting, the Rapporteur made the following statement: ' For the sake of discussion, paragraph 1 may be taken as composed of two parts: First, to maintain international peace and security, and the second part would be the rest of the paragraph after the semicolon as it has been read to you.—Dealing with the first part, a motion was made at first to add " justice " after " security "—" to maintain international peace, security, and justice."—A second motion was made to add after " security," the very motion that we have before us now, " in conformity with the principles of justice and international law." —Both motions received a bare majority vote in the Committee, but they did not attain the two-thirds majority necessary for a decision. It may seem, at first sight, that some members of the Committee who took the move to oppose the first two motions were trying to oppose justice itself. On the contrary, all those who took the floor to oppose the two motions were agreed that the concept of justice is a norm of fundamental importance; and all affirmed that peace, real and endurable, cannot be based on anything other than on justice. They held, however, that adding " justice " after " peace and security," as in the present motion, brings in at that juncture of the text a notion which lacks in clarity and welds it together with the more clear and almost tangible notion of peace and security. The resultant concept in this case does not remain sufficiently clear to be realisable. It tends, then, to provide a loophole for questioning any specific action of the Organisation, and a possibility for delaying measures and procedure while discussing abstract definitions.—The situations that may arise may be conceived this way. Peace is threatened by disputes, or by situations that may lead to a breach of the peace. A breach of the peace may ensue. At the first stage, the Organisation should insist and take measures that states do not threaten, or cause a breach of the peace. If they do, the Organisation should, at the second stage, promptly stop any breach of the peace, or remove it. After that, it can proceed to find an adjustment or settlement of that dispute or situation. When the Organisation has used the power given to it, and the force at its disposal to stop war, then it can find the latitude to apply the principles of justice and international law, or can assist the contending parties to find a peaceful solution.—The concept of justice and international law can thus find a more appropriate place in context with the last part of the paragraph dealing with disputes and situations. There it can find a more real scope to operate, and a more precise expression, and a more practical field of application. There was no intention, and this was made clear, to let this notion of justice and international law lose any of its weight and strength as an over-ruling arm of the whole Charter.—The Committee had before it the amendment of the four sponsoring governments which ran this way: " To deal with international disputes, with due regard to the fundamental principles of justice and international law." The Committee decided unanimously to change the words " with due regard to the fundamental principles of justice and international law " into " in conformity with the principles of justice and international law." And the Committee, by its final vote, gave that place to this notion which you find in the text before you ' (pp. 10 ff.).

At the same meeting the delegate of the United Kingdom made the following statement (p. 14): ' . . . . All of us, of whatever delegation, are naturally anxious to see justice carried out, and to see the alliance between justice and order

not identical and consequently may be in opposition to each other, the question arises whether, in case of conflict, the one or the other shall be maintained. Since the Charter gives no answer to this question and no definition of the concept of justice, the organ of the United Nations which has to apply the provision of the Charter has the choice between justice, that is to say what this organ considers to be justice in the case at hand, and positive international law; which practically means that the Charter does not strengthen but weaken the respect for the obligations of international law.

The postulate of Article 1, paragraph 1, to conform with the principles of justice and international law is directed at the same person as is the norm ' to take effective collective measures,' namely at the Organisation, not the individual Members. However, in Article 2, proclaiming the ' Principles ' of the United Nations, the Members, in settling their international disputes by peaceful means, are obliged only to observe ' that international peace and security, and justice, are not endangered '—only ' justice,' not ' international law,' although Article 2 says that the Members shall act in accordance with the Principles " in pursuit of the Purposes.' It is hardly understandable why the Organisation shall bring about adjustment or settlement of international disputes or situations which might lead to a breach of the peace in conformity with the principles of justice and international law, whereas the Members—in pursuit of this Purpose—shall settle all their international disputes, but not ' situations,' in conformity with ' justice ' but not with ' international law.' It is hardly understandable why the obligation of the Members is a ' Principle ' whereas the function of the Organisation is a ' Purpose.' As regards the conformity with justice and international law, there is no concordance between Article 1, paragraph 1, and Article 2, paragraph 3, nor between both Articles and the Preamble. [4]

on which the future of our work must depend. And the only issue raised by this amendment is the place, the actual place in the draft, where these words should be inserted. As I understand it, the present placing of these words as they have emerged from the Committee, insures in the first place that the actual business of maintaining peace and of preventing the guns beginning to go off, should not, in any circumstances, be delayed. That is the vital duty of the Security Council to prevent that thing beginning. And secondly, the placing of these words as proposed by the Committee does, I suggest to my colleague who moved the amendment, in fact secure that settlements and adjustments of any disputes should be in conformity with justice. I rather think that he, himself, used the illustration of the policeman or the gendarme who is concerned with dealing with a wrong that he sees arising. He does not stop at the outset of what he does to inquire where exactly lies the precise balance of justice in their quarrel. He stops it, and then, in order to make adjustment and settlement, justice comes into its own.' At the 15th meeting of Committee I/1 (U.N.C.I.O. Doc. 926, I/1/36, p. 2) the delegate of Panama said: ' . . . . He felt that the phrase " in conformity with the principles of justice and international law " applied only to the settlement of international conflicts and not to the other parts of the paragraph, and the report should make this clear.'

4 At the *Hearings* (p. 229) a Senator stated: ' It has seemed to me that the matters of the preamble are largely duplicated in the succeeding Chapter I and Chapter II, and I

4. International Peace

The peace the maintenance or restoration of which is a purpose of the United Nations is characterised as ' international ' peace. In ordinary use of language, ' international peace ' is a condition of absence of force in the relations among states. ' International ' peace is to be distinguished from ' internal ' peace, peace within one and the same state. Hence it is not the purpose of the United Nations to maintain or restore internal peace by interfering in a civil war within a state. This interpretation may be confirmed by the provision of Article 2, paragraph 7, forbidding any intervention on the part of the Organisation ' in matters which are essentially within the domestic jurisdiction of any state.' However, a civil war, as any other situation within a state, may be interpreted by the competent organ of the United Nations as a threat to international peace, in which case intervention on the part of the Organisation is not prohibited according to the express provision of Article 2, paragraph 7. Hence it is doubtful whether the restriction implied in the term ' international ' peace is of any importance.[5]

The purpose of the United Nations to maintain or restore peace is not restricted to the relations among the Member states. There is no provision of the Charter stipulating such restriction. Article 2, paragraph 6, expressly provides that the Organisation shall ensure that states which are not Members of the United Nations act in accordance with the Principles laid down in Article 2 of the Charter ' so far as may be necessary for the maintenance of international peace and security.' Hence the Principles formulated as obligations of Members: to settle international disputes by peaceful means and to refrain from threat or use of force, apply also to non-member states. The Preamble in establishing as an end of the United Nations ' to save succeeding generations from the scourge of war,' refers to ' mankind.' The purpose of the United Nations is world peace.

have been somewhat curious as to the reason for that.' Whereupon the representative of the Department of State declared: ' That is of course true. The basic ideas are the same. They are stated in the preamble as a motivation and in Chapter I as rules of conduct.' Then another Senator asked: ' It would scarcely be expected that they would be in conflict, would it? ' To this the answer was: ' No. They certainly cannot be in conflict. The question is how much is to be gained by reinforcing the expression of these thoughts by having them appear in one form in the preamble and in another form in the Chapter on purposes and principles.' The statement that the Preamble does not conflict with other parts of the Charter can hardly be confirmed by a critical analysis of the text.

[5] Cf. *infra*, pp. 769 ff.

Chapter 3

INTERNATIONAL CO-OPERATION

1. Political Co-operation

To bring about by peaceful means adjustment or settlement of international disputes or situations, is not the only preventive function of the Organisation. The other function, the purpose of which is to prevent a breach of the peace, is to promote international co-operation. In Article 13, dealing with competences of the General Assembly, a distinction is made between 'international co-operation in the political field,' and 'international co-operation in the economic, social, cultural educational, and health fields.' This distinction appears neither in the Preamble, nor in Article 1 determining the purposes of the United Nations, nor in Chapters IX and X especially devoted to international co-operation. In the Preamble the term international co-operation is not used at all. It is not very clear what is meant by 'international co-operation in the political field.' The term 'international' is superfluous since by a treaty only international co-operation of states can be established. Article 11, paragraph 1, speaks of 'co-operation' without using the adjective 'international.' If the term 'international' does not express the idea that it is a co-operation of states based on an international agreement, but refers to the field in which the co-operation shall be achieved, it is not correct to speak only of 'international' co-operation. For states may co-operate in the field of international as well as in the field of national politics. The provisions of the Preamble 'to reaffirm faith . . . in the equal rights . . . of nations large and small,' 'to establish conditions under which justice and respect for the obligations arising from treaties and other sources of international law can be maintained;' 'to live together in peace with one another as good neighbours,' 'to ensure by the acceptance of principles and the institution of methods, that armed force shall not be used, save in the common interest;' the provision of Article 1, paragraph 2, determining as a 'purpose' of the United Nations 'to develop friendly relations among nations based on respect for the principle of equal rights and self-determination of peoples, and to take other appropriate measures to strengthen universal peace;' the provision of Article 11, paragraph 1, conferring upon the General Assembly the competence to consider, and to make recommendations on, 'the general principles of co-operation in the maintenance of international peace and security, including the principles governing disarmament and the regulation of armaments' and the provision of Article 26 authorising the Security Council to formulate 'plans to be submitted to the Members of the United Nations for the establishment of a system for the regulation of armaments ' ' with the least diversion for armaments of the world's human and economic resources,' refer to co-operation in the field of international politics. But also the peaceful settlement of disputes and adjustment of other situations, as provided for in Article 1, paragraph 1, and specified in Chapter VI, may be classified as a function of the Organisation for the co-operation in the field of international politics.[1] ' Encouraging the progressive development of international law and its codification ' provided for in Article 13, paragraph 1(a) as a competence of the General Assembly might very well be considered as a function for co-operation in the field of international politics. It seems, however, that this function is not recognised by the Charter as ' promoting international co-operation in the political field,' since it is mentioned in addition to the latter. Nor is it considered to belong to ' co-operation in the economic, social, cultural, educational, and health fields ' (Article 13, paragraph 1(b)) since it is mentioned in the preceding paragraph and is not referred to in Chapters IX and X. Perhaps ' encouraging the progressive development of international law and its codification ' is supposed to promote co-operation in the legal field, as distinct from the political and economic and social fields.[2]

The various provisions of the Charter concerning human rights seem to establish a function of the Organisation for co-operation in the field of national politics, since it is in the first place national legislation by which these rights are to be guaranteed. However, in Article 13, paragraph 1(b) ' assisting in the realisation of human rights . . .' is mentioned as different from promoting international co-operation in the political field as well as from promoting international co-operation in the economic, social, cultural, educational, and health fields; but ' promoting and encouraging respect for human rights . . .' is presented in Article 1, paragraph 3, as one of the means to achieve ' international co-operation,' and to promote ' universal respect for,

1 In its resolution of November 13, 1947, paragraph 2 (*c*), the General Assembly instructed the Interim Committee: ' To consider, as it deems useful and advisable, and report with its conclusions to the General Assembly on methods to be adopted to give effect to that part of Article 11 (paragraph 1), which deals with the general principles of co-operation in the maintenance of international peace and security, and to that part of Article 13 (paragraph 1 (*a*)), which deals with the promotion of international co-operation in the political field.' (Resolutions adopted by the General Assembly, Doc. A/519, p. 15.)

In the Preliminary Report of Subcommittee 2 of the Interim Committee dealing with the implementation of paragraph 2 (*c*) of the General Assembly Resolution of November 13, 1947, pp. 3/4, it is stated that ' the pacific settlement of disputes between states . . . is recognised by the Charter as an important aspect of international co-operation in the political field . . . ' (Doc. A/AC.18/48, pp. 3 f.)

2 The Study on Article 11, paragraph 1, and Article 13, paragraph 1 (*a*), of the Charter prepared by the Secretariat for the Interim Committee (Doc. A/AC.18/33, p. 9) contains the statement: ' The word " political " is given no explanation, but it is set off as against legal development in the same clause, and as against economic, social and other fields, which were transferred to the following clause.'

and observance of, human rights . . .', referred to in Article 55, is one of the functions determined in the Chapter on 'International Economic and Social Co-operation' and one of the competences of the Economic and Social Council (Article 62, paragraph 2). Also 'promoting international co-operation in the economic, social, cultural, educational, and health fields' is a function for the promotion of co-operation in the field of national politics. But it is classified in Article 13, paragraph 1(b) as different from co-operation in the political field (Article 13, paragraph 1(a)); and Article 13, paragraph 2 stipulates:

> The further responsibilities, functions, and powers of the General Assembly with respect to matters mentioned in paragraph 1(b) above are set forth in Chapters IX and X.

Only paragraph 1, clause (*a*), not paragraph 1, clause (*b*), of Article 13 refers to co-operation in the political field. Hence the functions determined in Chapters IX and X are not to be considered as concerning co-operation 'in the political field.' It is, however, hardly possible to separate the political from the economic and social fields. If the maintenance of peace is a political purpose, then any co-operation for this purpose is a co-operation in the political field; and the co-operation referred to in Article 13, paragraph 1 (*b*) has certainly the purpose to maintain peace.[3] It seems that the formula 'co-operation in the political field' as used in Article 13, paragraph 1, clause (*a*), in contradistinction to 'co-operation in the economic, social, cultural, educational, and health fields' in clause (*b*), was intended to refer only to co-operation in the field of international politics. All the matters which could be characterised as being the objects of co-operation in the field of national politics are dealt with in the Chapter on 'economic and social co-operation.' 'To develop friendly relations among nations based on respect for the principle of equal rights and self-determination of peoples' referred to in Article 1, paragraph 2, is certainly a matter of co-operation in the field of international politics. But in Article 55 'peaceful and friendly relations among nations based on respect for the principle of equal rights and self-determination of peoples' are declared as the purpose of the economic and social co-operation, which, in Article 13, is distinguished from the co-operation in the political field.

2. Economic and Social Co-operation

As pointed out, the term 'international co-operation' does not appear in the Preamble. But that part of the Charter contains provisions

[3] The Report of Rapporteur of Committee II/3 (U.N.C.I.O. Doc. 861, II/3/55(1), p. 6) contains the statement 'that assisting in the realisation of human rights and basic freedoms for all and encouraging the development of international law are independent objectives along with promoting international co-operation in the political, economic, social, cultural, educational, and health fields.'

which refer to economic and social co-operation. 'To promote social progress and better standards of life in larger freedom' is proclaimed as an 'end' of the United Nations; and a 'means' to this end shall be 'to employ international machinery for the promotion of the economic and social advancement of all peoples.' Since 'social progress and better standards of life' is about the same as 'economic and social advancement,' how can the one be a means for the achievement of the other as an end? Neither the one nor the other is mentioned among the Purposes in Article 1. As a 'Purpose' of the United Nations the function concerned is determined in Article 1, paragraph 3 as follows: 'To achieve international co-operation in solving international problems of an economic, cultural, or humanitarian character.' The main organ for the performance of this function is the General Assembly assisted by the Economic and Social Council. The competence of the General Assembly is determined in Article 13, paragraph 1 (*b*): 'The General Assembly shall initiate studies and make recommendations for the purpose of . . . promoting international co-operation in the economic, social, cultural, educational, and health fields.' It is difficult to understand why the purpose of the Organisation is to achieve international co-operation in solving international problems (by 'international' co-operation only 'international' problems can be solved[4]), whereas the function of the competent organ is: 'to initiate studies and make recommendations for the purpose of promoting international co-operation' in certain 'fields,' which are not identical with the 'problems.' No 'field' referred to in Article 13, paragraph 1 (*b*), corresponds to the 'humanitarian' problems in Article 1, paragraph 3, and no 'problem' in Article 1, paragraph 3, corresponds to the educational and health fields in Article 13, paragraph 1 (*b*). The term 'educational' is superfluous, since the matter is covered by the term 'cultural.'[5] Chapter IX,

[4] The Report of the Rapporteur of Committee I/1 (U.N.C.I.O. Doc. 944, I/1/34(1), p. 10) contains the following statement: 'A suggestion was made that we should eliminate the word "international" coming before "problems." The word was kept on the understanding that some problems, though at first sight they look national, could be considered essentially international, owing to the interdependence of nations in our civilisation, and fall within the purview of this paragraph. Moreover it was not desired to impose consideration of internal national problems on the Organisation.—It was understood likewise that such problems can be considered by the Organisation only when the nation or state concerned with such problems brings them to the collective attention.'

[5] The Dumbarton Oaks Proposals, Chapter V, Section B, paragraph 6 and Chapter IX, Section A, paragraph 1, did not mention cultural and educational matters. In a Memorandum of the Delegation of Venezuela (U.N.C.I.O. Doc. 746, II/3/45, pp. 1 f.) it is contested that the word 'cultural' includes 'educational.' 'Culture signifies the product of human, conscious activity as opposed to nature, which creates spontaneously and without man's direction. *The pyramids of Egypt*—that is culture; *the Sequoia gigantea of California*—that is a wonder of nature.—To Latins culture means the material products of human activity—buildings and bridges, for example—and, together with civilisation, implies also the spiritual products of the

especially devoted to functions referred to in Articles 1, paragraph 3, and 13, paragraph 1 (*b*), deals—according to its heading—only with ' international economic and social co-operation;' and the name of the special organ established to discharge this function ' under the authority of the General Assembly ' (Article 60) also refers only to ' economic and social ' co-operation.

After ' international co-operation ' as a Purpose of the United Nations has been determined in Article 1, paragraph 3, Article 55 determines, again, the same purpose of the Organisation in a different way. It runs as follows:

> With a view to the creation of conditions of stability and well-being which are necessary for peaceful and friendly relations among nations based on respect for the principle of equal rights and self-determination of peoples, the United Nations shall promote—
>
> (*a*) higher standards of living, full employment, and conditions of economic and social progress and development;
>
> (*b*) solutions of international economic, social health, and related problems; and international cultural and educational co-operation; and
>
> (*c*) universal respect for, and observance of, human rights and fundamental freedoms for all without distinction as to race, sex, language, or religion.

The introductory clause is superfluous for it only explains and justifies the substantial provisions of the Article. The latter are supposed to refer to the same matter as Article 1, paragraph 3, and Article 13, paragraph 1 (*b*). But only clauses (*b*) and (*c*) of Article 55, parallel Article 1, paragraph 3, and Article 13, paragraph 1 (*b*). There are, it is true, slight differences in the wording: Problems of

same human activity—art, music, religion.—To Germans the contrary was true. " Kultur " meant the twisted, spiritual, human activity—or was it inhuman—which they wished to impose upon the world. Civilisation for them meant simply material achievements.—Culture, therefore, is something that man creates both in the spiritual and the material terrain.—Education, on the other hand, in its social concept denotes an attempt on the part of the adult members of the human society to transmit its culture.—The carpenter is not the workshop any more than education is culture. Education in other aspects is " something intangible, unpredictable. Education comes from within, it is a mans' own doing, or, rather, it happens to him, sometimes because of the teaching he has had, sometimes in spite of it.—Education is the hope of the world—only in the sense that there *is* something better than bribery, lies, and violence for righting the world's wrongs." (Jacques Barzun in *Teacher in America*).—Therefore, I suppose that the words " educational " and " cultural " be used separately and neither should be used as synonymous with the other.' The argument of the Venezuelan Memorandum is not convincing. It can hardly be denied that education is an essential element of ' culture ' whatever meaning this word may have.

'humanitarian character' are mentioned only in Article 1, paragraph 3; 'educational' and 'health' matters only in Article 13, paragraph 1 (*b*), and Article 55 (*b*). As far as human rights are concerned, under Article 55 the United Nations shall promote 'universal respect for, and observance of,' whereas under Article 1, paragraph 3, the United Nations has the purpose to achieve co-operation in 'promoting and encouraging respect for,' not observance of, human rights, and under Article 13, the General Assembly shall initiate studies and make recommendations for the purpose of 'assisting in the realisation of' these rights. Besides, as pointed out, in Article 13, paragraph 1 (*b*), the function of the Organisation with respect to human rights is characterised as not comprised in the function of promoting economic and social co-operation. However, these differences, although better avoided, are relatively harmless. Clause (*a*) of Article 55: 'promote higher standards of living, full employment, and conditions of economic and social progress and development,' has no counterpart in Article 1 or Article 13; but in the Preamble, as pointed out, we find the formula 'to promote social progress and better standards of life in larger freedom' and the phrase 'promotion of the economic and social advancement of all peoples.' It is not very clear what the difference is between 'social progress' and 'economic and social advancement,' and why the Preamble speaks only of 'progress' and 'advancement,' Article 55 (*a*) of 'progress and development'; 'progress' implies 'development,' and promotion of 'development' not constituting 'progress' is evidently not intended. It is difficult to understand why 'larger freedom' is placed only in the Preamble, and 'full employment' only in Article 55 (*a*), and what the meaning of the phrase 'in larger freedom' is. Political freedom in the sense of democracy, or economic freedom in the sense of liberalism? But according to Article 2, paragraph 7, nothing contained in the Charter shall authorise the Organisation to intervene in matters which are essentially within the domestic jurisdiction of any state; and the degree of political or economic freedom is certainly a domestic affair. The provision of Article 55 (*a*): the United Nations shall promote higher standards of living, full employment, and conditions of economic and social progress and development, is a specification of the provision of its clause (*b*): that the United Nations shall promote solutions of international economic and social problems. It is not very logical to mention first the particular and then the general.[6] In Article 55 (*b*), a distinction is made between promoting 'solutions of international

[6] The Drafting Subcommittee of Committee II/3 (U.N.C.I.O. Doc. 684, II/3/38, p. 2) made the following comments on clause (*b*) of Article 55: '1. The Subcommittee understands that the language of subparagraph (*b*) includes international co-operation in the suppression of traffic in, and abuse of, opium and other narcotics and dangerous drugs. 2. The committee wishes to emphasise that the "economic" field is comprehensive and includes, for instance, international trade, finance, and communications and transport.' The Report of the Rapporteur of Committee

economic, social, health and related problems' and promoting 'international cultural and educational co-operation.' But the solution of the problems indicated in the first sentence is an element of international co-operation; and the international co-operation indicated in the second sentence implies the solution of cultural and educational problems.[7]

The functions of the United Nations determined in Article 55 are, according to Article 60, to be performed by the General Assembly, and, under the authority of the General Assembly, by the Economic and Social Council. In Chapter X, dealing with the Economic and Social Council, under the heading 'Functions and Powers,' Article 62 provides:—

> 1. The Economic and Social Council may make or initiate studies and reports with respect to international economic, social, cultural, educational, health, and related matters and may make recommendations with respect to any such matters to the General Assembly, to the Members of the United Nations, and to the specialised agencies concerned.
>
> 2. It may make recommendations for the purpose of promoting respect for, and observance of, human rights and fundamental freedoms for all.
>
> 3. It may prepare draft conventions for submission to the General Assembly, with respect to matters falling within its competence.
>
> 4. It may call, in accordance with the rules prescribed by the United Nations, international conferences on matters falling within its competence.

Since Article 60 stipulates that all the functions set forth in Chapter IX shall be performed by the Economic and Social Council, it was super-

II/3 (U.N.C.I.O. Doc. 861, II/3/55 (1), p. 3) contains the following statement: 'The Committee agreed that the word "economic" is comprehensive in its import and should be *interpreted* to include, for instance, international trade, finance, communications and transport, and the vast problems of reconstruction. In this connection, it was also agreed that the international problems of raw materials and capital goods should be considered by the Economic and Social Council. The Committee further agreed that the language of A, 1 (*b*), should be understood to include international co-operation in the control of traffic in, and the suppression of the abuse of, opium and dangerous drugs.'

7 *The Report to the President*, pp. 113 f., explains this differentiation in the wording of Article 55, clause (*b*), as follows: 'The United States Delegation . . . felt that whereas the members individually and in co-operation could work toward *solutions* of international economic and social problems, the same language was not equally applicable to the cultural and educational fields. In those fields it was not the solutions of international problems that was sought, but the advancement of international *co-operation* as a means of promoting mutual understanding and good will among the peoples of the world. Stated in that way, it would also remove any basis for misapprehension that the Organisation was in any way designed to interfere in the domestic educational systems of any of the member nations.'

fluous to repeat in Article 62 a determination of these functions. But if repeated, why not completely, but only partly, repeated? Why is the function determined in Article 55, clause (*b*), but not the function determined in Article 55, clause (*a*), mentioned in Article 62? Why are, in the formula concerning the promotion of respect for human rights, the words 'without distinction as to race, sex, language, or religion.'—carefully maintained in Articles 55, 13, 1—dropped in Article 62? There is hardly a satisfactory answer to these questions.

An interpretation of the inconsistent provisions of the Charter concerning so-called economic and social co-operation results in the statement that one of the essential functions of the United Nations is to bring about through specific activities of the General Assembly and the Economic and Social Council co-operation of the Member states in the social field in general, and in particular in the fields of economy, of culture, education included, and of health. Co-operation in the social field implies promoting social progress and especially promoting respect for, and observance of, human rights (including fundamental freedoms) for all without distinction as to race, sex, language, or religion. Co-operation in the economic field implies promoting higher standards of life, full employment, and conditions of economic progress.

3. Human Rights

The Preamble stipulates as an end of the Organisation: 'to reaffirm faith in fundamental human rights, in the dignity and worth of the human person, in the equal rights of men and women and of nations large and small' and as a means to this end: 'to practice tolerance.' Partly corresponding provisions are to be found in Article 1, establishing as Purposes of the United Nations:—

> 2. To develop friendly relations among nations based on respect for the principle of equal rights and self-determination of peoples, and to take other appropriate measures to strengthen universal peace;
>
> 3. To achieve international co-operation in solving international problems of an economic, social, cultural, or humanitarian character, and in promoting and encouraging respect for human rights and for fundamental freedoms for all without distinction as to race, sex, language, or religion; and
>
> 4. To be a centre for harmonising the actions of nations in the attainment of these common ends;

in Article 13, paragraph 1 (*b*), where the General Assembly is authorised to initiate studies and make recommendations for the purpose of 'assisting in the realisation of human rights and fundamental freedoms for all without distinction as to race, sex, language, or religion; further in Article 55:—

> With a view to the creation of conditions of stability and well-being which are necessary for peaceful and friendly relations among nations based on respect for the principle of equal rights and self-determination of peoples, the United Nations shall promote—
>
> (*a*) . . .
>
> (*b*) . . .
>
> (*c*) Universal respect for, and observance of, human rights and fundamental freedoms for all without distinction as to race, sex, language, or religion;

in Article 62, paragraph 2, conferring upon the Economic and Social Council the power to 'make recommendations for the purpose of promoting respect for, and observance of, human rights and fundamental freedoms for all'; and in Article 68 authorising the Economic and Social Council to set up a commission 'for the promotion of human rights.' Finally, Article 76 (*c*) stipulates as one of the basic objectives of the trusteeship system: 'to encourage respect for human rights and for fundamental freedoms for all without distinction as to race, sex, language, or religion . . .'

These provisions refer to two different kinds of rights: human rights, that is rights of human beings, and rights of states. As pointed out, the function of the United Nations with respect to human rights is not very consistently determined in the Charter. In Article 1, paragraph 3, 'encouraging respect for human rights,' etc., is provided for as a means of 'achieving international co-operation; but in Article 13, paragraph 1 (*b*), 'assisting in the realisation of human rights,' etc., is presented as a matter different from promoting co-operation in the political as well as in the economic and social fields. In Article 55 (*c*), promoting respect for and observance of these rights is listed under the heading 'international economic and social co-operation,' but as a function different from 'solutions of international economic, social, health, and related problems; and international cultural and educational co-operation' (Article 55 (*b*)). In Article 62, paragraph 2, making recommendations relative to human rights is stipulated as a competence of the Economic and Social Council, the special organ for the achievement of economic and social co-operation. But in contradistinction to other matters—as for instance 'international cultural and educational co-operation' (Article 55 (*b*)) —the function of the Economic and Social Council with respect to human rights is not expressly characterised in Chapters IX and X as promoting 'co-operation.'

In the Preamble, determining the 'ends' of the United Nations, the Charter speaks of 'fundamental human rights,' but in Article 1, determining the purposes of economic and social co-operation, in Articles 13 and 62, determining the competence of certain organs, it speaks of ' human rights ' and ' fundamental freedoms for all.' The formula ' human rights and fundamental freedoms ' is incorrect, since ' freedoms ' are human rights, rights to be free from restrictions imposed by the government; and it is highly problematical to refer in a legal instrument to rights without referring to the corresponding duties, since legally there exists no right of an individual without a corresponding duty of another individual; and if the right is a ' freedom,' not without a corresponding duty of the government. In the Preamble, only the equal rights of men and women, that is to say, the principle of making no distinction as to sex, is proclaimed, whereas in Article 1, paragraph 3, and in other Articles also the principle of making no distinction as to race, language, or religion is established; and in Article 62, paragraph 2, the formula ' without distinction as to race, sex, language, or religion ' is completely dropped. It is difficult to understand why this principle in one case refers to ' rights,' in others to ' freedoms '; and why ' the dignity and worth of the human person ' and ' to practice tolerance ' are mentioned only in the Preamble, but not among the Purposes or in any other connection. There is no sufficient reason for determining the same purpose or function of the Organisation in the Preamble as ' to reaffirm faith ' in the fundamental human rights, in Article 1, paragraph 3, as ' promoting and encouraging respect for,' in Article 13, paragraph 1 (*b*), as ' assisting in the realisation,' in Article 55 (*c*), as to ' promote . . . universal respect for, and observance of ' these rights.

These inconsistencies, however, are without any legal importance since the Charter does not impose upon the Members a strict obligation to grant to their subjects the rights and freedoms mentioned in the Preamble or in the text of the Charter. The language used by the Charter in this respect does not allow the interpretation that the Members are under legal obligations regarding the rights and freedoms of their subjects. All the formulas concerned establish purposes or functions of the Organisation, not obligations of the Members, and the Organisation is not empowered by the Charter to impose upon the governments of the Member states the obligation to guarantee to their subjects the rights referred to in the Charter. The fact that the Charter, as a treaty, refers to a matter is in itself not a sufficient reason for the assumption that the Charter imposes obligations with respect to this matter upon the contracting parties.[8] Besides, the Charter does

[8] The Report of Rapporteur, Subcommittee I/1/A of the San Francisco Conference (U.N.C.I.O. Doc. 723, I/1/A/19, p. 10) contains the following statement referring to Article 1, paragraph 3: ' The subcommittee held that assuring or protecting such fundamental rights is primarily the concern of each state. If, however, such rights and freedoms were grievously outraged so as to create conditions which threaten peace or to obstruct the application of provisions of the Charter, then they cease to be the sole concern of each state.' If ' assuring and protecting fundamental human

in no way specify the rights and freedoms to which it refers. Legal obligations of the Members in this respect can be established

rights is the concern of each state, it is certainly a matter which is 'essentially within the domestic jurisdiction' of the state; and Article 2, paragraph 7, forbids intervention of the Organisation in such matters, except in case of threat to the peace and breach of the peace, that is to say, under Article 39. Only if this Article is interpreted to mean that the Security Council may declare the conduct of a state as a threat to, or a breach of, the peace, even if this conduct does not constitute a violation of an obligation expressly imposed upon the state by the Charter, action of the Organisation against the state is possible which does not grant to its subjects fundamental human rights. Since these rights are not defined in the Charter, it is upon the Security Council to determine them according to its discretion. Such interpretation of Article 39 is not impossible; but it amounts to a complete abolishment of the prohibition of intervention in domestic matters.

The question as to whether the provisions of the Charter concerning human rights and fundamental freedoms constitute obligations of the Members was discussed in the case of the treatment of Indians in the South African Union. At the 1st meeting of the joint first and sixth Committee, the representative of the South African Union declared: Up to the present 'there did not exist any internationally recognised formulation of such rights, and the Charter itself did not define them. Member states, therefore, did not have any specific obligations under the Charter, whatever other moral obligations might rest upon them.' (Journal of the United Nations, No. 40: Suppl. Nos. 1 and 6—A/C.1 & 6/1, p. 4.) The representative of India, however, maintained that the treatment of Indians by the Union of South Africa constituted a violation of the provisions of the Charter concerning human rights (p. 2). Also other representatives expressed the opinion that these provisions of the Charter established obligations of the Members. Thus, for instance, the representative of the Philippine Republic declared: 'The Indian question fell squarely in the field of obligations incurred by membership in the United Nations. Signature of the Charter involved the observance of the principle that there should be no distinction as to race, sex, language, or religion. This was one of the fundamental principles of the Charter. Any Member could call upon another to account before any appropriate organ of the United Nations for alleged infringement of that obligation.' (*Ibid.* No. 44: Suppl. Nos. 1 and 6—A/C.1 & 6/9, p. 31.) The representative of Colombia proposed to suggest to the General Assembly to request the International Court of Justice to give an advisory opinion on the following questions: '(*a*) Whether the Members of the United Nations, in accordance with the Preamble and Article 1, paragraph 3, of the Charter, are under obligation to amend immediately their internal legislation when it establishes racial discrimination incompatible with the text of the Charter? (*b*) Whether the Members of the United Nations are entitled in the future to enact internal legislation embodying racial discrimination? (*c*) Whether laws of racial discrimination constitute, or may be alleged by states to constitute, matters of internal jurisdiction on which the General Assembly is debarred from making recommendations to the state or states concerned, to the Security Council or to the Economic and Social Council?' (*Ibid.*, No. 46: Suppl. Nos. 1 and 6—A/C.1 & 6/13, p. 37.) This suggestion was not accepted. The resolution, adopted by the Assembly at its 52nd meeting, runs as follows:

The General Assembly,

Having taken note of the application made by the Government of India regarding the treatment of Indians in the Union of South Africa, and having considered the matter:

1. States that, because of that treatment, friendly relations between the two Member states have been impaired and, unless a satisfactory settlement is reached, these relations are likely to be further impaired;

only by an amendment to the Charter or by a convention negotiated under the auspices of the United Nations and ratified by the

> 2. Is of the opinion that the treatment of Indians in the Union should be in conformity with the international obligations under the agreements concluded between the two Governments and the relevant provisions of the Charter;
>
> 3. Therefore requests the two Governments to report at the next session of the General Assembly the measures adopted to this effect. (Doc. A/64/Add.1, p. 69.)

According to the wording of praagraph 2 of this resolution it is doubtful whether the General Assembly was of the opinion that the treatment of Indians should be in conformity ' with the international obligations under . . . the relevant provisions of the Charter,' that is to say, whether the Assembly did or did not interpret the ' relevant provisions of the Charter ' as constituting ' international obligations.'

On the initiative of the representative of Chile the sixth Committee suggested to the General Assembly to adopt the following resolution:

> The General Assembly,
>
> Considering the item proposed by Chile on ' violation by the Union of Soviet Socialist Republics of fundamental human rights, traditional diplomatic practices and other principles of the Charter,' which violation has consisted in preventing the Soviet wives of citizens of other nationalities from leaving their country with their husbands or in order to join them abroad, even when they are married to persons belonging to foreign diplomatic missions, or to members of their families or retinue;
>
> Considering that in the preamble to the Charter of the United Nations all the signatory countries resolved ' to re-affirm faith in fundamental human rights, in the dignity and worth of the human person and in the equal rights of men and women ';
>
> Considering that Article 1, paragraph 3, of the Charter binds all Members to encourage 'respect for human rights and for fundamental freedoms for all without distinction as to race, sex, language or religion,' and that in Article 55 (c) of the Charter the Members undertook to ' promote universal respect for, and observance of, human rights and fundamental freedoms for all without distinction as to race, sex, language, or religion ';
>
> Considering that, finally, the Economic and Social Council, in pursuance of the powers conferred upon it by Article 62, paragraph 2, of the Charter, in its resolution 154 (VII) D, dated August 23, 1948, deplored the ' legislative or administrative provisions which deny to a woman the right to leave her country of origin and reside with her husband in any other ' and that the draft International Declaration of Human Rights, in its Articles 14 and 17 respectively, provides that everyone has the right to leave any country including his own and that men and women of full age have the right to marry without any limitation due to race, nationality or religion;
>
> Declares that the measures which prevent or coerce the wives of citizens of other nationalities from leaving their country of origin with their husbands or in order to join them abroad, are not in conformity with the Charter; and that when those measures refer to the wives of persons belonging to foreign diplomatic missions, or of members of their families or retinue, they are contrary to courtesy, to diplomatic practices and to the principle of reciprocity, and are likely to impair friendly relations among nations;
>
> Recommends the Government of the Union of Soviet Socialist Republics to withdraw the measures of such a nature which have been adopted. (Doc. A/787.)

The statement ' that Article 1, paragraph 3, of the Charter binds all Members to

Members.[9] The Charter does not confer upon the individuals the legal possibility to appeal to an international court and especially to the 'principal judicial organ' of the United Nations, the International Court of Justice, in case one of the rights or freedoms proclaimed in the Preamble or referred to in the text of the Charter is violated. The Statute of the Court stipulates expressly in Article 34 that 'only states

encourage, etc.' is not quite in conformity with the wording of this provision which only declares that it is a purpose of the Organisation to achieve international co-operation in promoting and encouraging respect for human rights, etc. The statement that certain measures taken by the Soviet Union 'are not in conformity with the Charter' does not necessarily mean that these measures constitute the violation of an obligation imposed upon the Soviet Union as a Member of the United Nations.

[9] The Report of Rapporteur of Committee 1 to Commission I (U.N.C.I.O. Doc. 944, I/1/34 (1), p. 11) contains the following statement: '. . . a suggestion was made to draft or to include an already drafted bill of rights of nations and of individuals. The committee received the idea with sympathy, but decided that the present Conference, if only for lack of time, could not proceed to realise such a draft in an international contract. The Organisation, once formed, could better proceed to consider the suggestion and to deal effectively with it through a special commission or by some other method. The committee recommends that the General Assembly consider the proposal and give it effect.' At the first part of the first session of the General Assembly, the representative of Cuba submitted a proposal that the Assembly discuss the matter of a Declaration of Fundamental Human Rights and the Rights and Duties of Nations. The Cuban representative thought that if the principles embodied in the Charter were to become a reality it was necessary for the Assembly to adopt such a Declaration. But at its 7th meeting the General Assembly voted not to include the Cuban proposal in its agenda. Later, at its 55th meeting, the Assembly adopted two resolutions, one concerning a Declaration on Rights and Duties of states, and another on a Declaration on Fundamental Human Rights and Freedoms. The last mentioned resolution runs as follows:

> The General Assembly,
>
> Whereas the Economic and Social Council has established a Commission on Human Rights and has resolved that the work of the Commission shall be directed towards submitting proposals, recommendations and reports to the Council concerning an international bill of rights;
>
> Resolves therefore to refer the draft Declaration on Fundamental Human Rights and Freedoms to the Economic and Social Council for reference to the Commission on Human Rights for consideration by the Commission in its preparation of an international bill of rights; and
>
> Expresses the hope that the question will be referred back to it in order that it may be included in the agenda of the second regular session of the General Assembly. (Doc. A/64/Add.1, p. 68.)

Another resolution referred to the political rights of women. It runs as follows:

> The General Assembly,
>
> Whereas in the Preamble of the Charter the peoples of the United Nations have reaffirmed faith in the equal rights of men and women, and in Article 1 it is stated that the purposes of the United Nations are, among others, to achieve international co-operation in promoting and encouraging respect for human rights and for fundamental freedoms for all without distinction as to sex, and to be a centre for harmonising the actions of nations in the attainment of these common ends;

may be parties in cases before the Court.' No other subject matter is so often referred to in the Charter as the human rights and freedoms. They were not mentioned at all in the Dumbarton Oaks Proposals. Nevertheless there is, from a strictly legal point of view, no difference between the two documents with respect to this subject matter.

The General Assembly adopted at its 183rd meeting on December 10, 1948, a 'Universal Declaration of Human Rights.' The resolution runs as follows:—

PREAMBLE

Whereas recognition of the inherent dignity and of the equal and inalienable rights of all members of the human family is the foundation of freedom, justice and peace in the world,

Whereas disregard and contempt for human rights have resulted in barbarous acts which have outraged the conscience of mankind, and the advent of a world in which human beings shall enjoy freedom of speech and belief and freedom from fear and want has been proclaimed as the highest aspiration of the common people,

Whereas it is essential, if man is not to be compelled to have recourse, as last resort, to rebellion against tyranny and oppression, that human rights should be protected by rule of law,

Whereas it is essential to promote the development of friendly relations between nations,

Whereas certain Member states have not yet granted to women, political rights equal to those granted to men,

Therefore:

(*a*) Recommends that all Member states, which have not already done so, adopt measures necessary to fulfil the purposes and aims of the Charter in this respect by granting to women the same political rights as to men;

(*b*) Invites the Secretary General to communicate this recommendation to the Governments of all Member states. (*Ibid.* p. 90.)

The Economic and Social Council in a resolution adopted on June 21, 1946, stated that:

Pending the adoption of an international bill of rights, the general principle shall be accepted that international treaties involving basic human rights, including to the fullest extent practicable treaties of peace, shall conform to the fundamental standards relative to such rights set forth in the Charter. (Journal of the Economic and Social Council, first year, No. 29, p. 521.)

Finally the Economic and Social Council decided by a resolution adopted on August 26, 1948:

to transmit to the General Assembly the Draft International Declaration of Human Rights submitted to the Council by the Commission on Human Rights in the report of its third session (Doc. E/800), together with the remainder of this report and records of the proceedings of the Council at its seventh session on this subject. (Doc. E/1046.)

Whereas the peoples of the United Nations have in the Charter reaffirmed their faith in fundamental human rights, in the dignity and worth of the human person and in the equal rights of men and women and have determined to promote social progress and better standards of life in larger freedom,

Whereas Member states have pledged themselves to achieve, in co-operation with the United Nations, the promotion of universal respect for and observance of human rights and fundamental freedoms,

Whereas a common understanding of these rights and freedoms is of the greatest importance for full realisation of this pledge,

Now, Therefore,

The General Assembly

Proclaims this Universal Declaration of Human Rights as a common standard of achievement for all peoples and all nations, to the end that every individual and every organ of society, keeping this declaration constantly in mind, shall strive by teaching and education to promote respect for these rights and freedoms and by progressive measures, national and international, to secure their universal and effective recognition and observance, both among the peoples of Member states themselves and among the peoples of territories under their jurisdiction.

Article 1

All human beings are born free and equal in dignity and rights. They are endowed with reason and conscience and should act towards one another in a spirit of brotherhood.

Article 2

Everyone is entitled to all the rights and freedoms set forth in this declaration without distinction of any kind, such as race, colour, sex, language, religion, political or other opinion, national or social origin, property, birth or other status.

Furthermore, no distinction shall be made on the basis of the political, jurisdictional or international status of the country or territory to which a person belongs, whether it be independent, trust, non-self-governing or under any other limitation of sovereignty.

Article 3

Everyone has the right to life, liberty and security of person.

Article 4

No one shall be held in slavery or servitude; slavery and the slave trade shall be prohibited in all their forms.

ARTICLE 5

No one shall be subjected to torture or to cruel, inhuman or degrading treatment or punishment.

ARTICLE 6

Everyone has the right to recognition everywhere as a person before the law.

ARTICLE 7

All are equal before the law and are entitled without any discrimination to equal protection of the law. All are entitled to equal protection against any discrimination in violation of this declaration and against any incitement to such discrimination.

ARTICLE 8

Everyone has the right to an effective remedy by the competent national tribunals for acts violating the fundamental rights granted him by the constitution or by law.

ARTICLE 9

No one shall be subjected to arbitrary arrest, detention or exile.

ARTICLE 10

Everyone is entitled in full equality to a fair and public hearing by an independent and impartial tribunal, in the determination of his rights and obligations and of any criminal charge against him.

ARTICLE 11

1. Everyone charged with a penal offence has the right to be presumed innocent until proved guilty according to law in public trial at which he has had all guarantees necessary for his defence.

2. No one shall be held guilty of any penal offence on account of any act or omission which did not constitute a penal offence, under national or international law, at the time when it was committed. Nor shall a heavier penalty be imposed than the one that was applicable at the time the penal offence was committed.

ARTICLE 12

No one shall be subjected to arbitrary interference with his privacy, family, home or correspondence, nor to attacks upon his honour and reputation. Everyone has the right to the protection of the law against such interference or attacks.

Article 13

1. Everyone has the right to freedom of movement and residence within the borders of each state.

2. Everyone has the right to leave any country, including his own, and to return to his country.

Article 14

1. Everyone has the right to seek and to enjoy in other countries asylum from persecution.

2. This right may not be invoked in the case of prosecutions genuinely arising from non-political crimes or from acts contrary to the purposes and principles of the United Nations.

Article 15

1. Everyone has the right to a nationality.

2. No one shall be arbitrarily deprived of his nationality nor denied the right to change his nationality.

Article 16

1. Men and women of full age, without any limitation due to race, nationality or religion, have the right to marry and to found a family. They are entitled to equal rights as to marriage, during marriage and at its dissolution.

2. Marriage shall be entered into only with the free and full consent of the intending spouses.

3. The family is the natural and fundamental group unit of society and is entitled to protection by society and the state.

Article 17

1. Everyone has the right to own property alone as well as in association with others.

2. No one shall be arbitrarily deprived of his property.

Article 18

Everyone has the right to freedom of thought, conscience and religion; this right includes the freedom to change his religion or belief, and freedom, either alone or in community with others and in public or private, to manifest his religion or belief in teaching, practice, worship and observance.

Article 19

Everyone has the right to freedom of opinion and expression; this right includes freedom to hold opinions without interference and to seek, receive and impart information and ideas through any media and regardless of frontier.

ARTICLE 20

1. Everyone has the right to freedom of peaceful assembly and association.

2. No one may be compelled to belong to an association.

ARTICLE 21

1. Everyone has the right to take part in the government of his country, directly or through freely chosen representatives.

2. Everyone has the right of equal access to public service in his country.

3. The will of the people shall be the basis of authority of government; this will shall be expressed in periodic and genuine elections which shall be by universal and equal suffrage and shall be held by secret vote or by equivalent free voting procedures.

ARTICLE 22

Everyone, as a member of society, has the right to social security and is entitled to realisation, through national effort and international co-operation and in accordance with the organisation and resources of each state, of the economic, social and cultural rights indispensable for his dignity and the free development of his personality.

ARTICLE 23

1. Everyone has the right to work, to free choice of employment, to just and favourable conditions of work and to protection against unemployment.

2. Everyone, without any discrimination, has the right to equal pay for equal work.

3. Everyone who works has the right to just and favourable remuneration, insuring for himself and his family an existence worthy of human dignity, and supplemented, if necessary, by other means of social protection.

4. Everyone has the right to form and to join trade unions for the protection of his interests.

ARTICLE 24

Everyone has the right to rest and leisure, including reasonable limitation of working hours and periodic holidays with pay.

ARTICLE 25

1. Everyone has the right to a standard of living adequate for the health and well-being of himself and of his family, including food, clothing, housing and medical care and necessary social

services, and the right to security in the event of unemployment, sickness, disability, widowhood, old age or other lack of livelihood in circumstances beyond his control.

2. Motherhood and childhood are entitled to special care and assistance. All children, whether born in or out of wedlock, shall enjoy the same social protection.

Article 26

1. Everyone has the right to education. Education shall be free, at least in the elementary and fundamental stages. Elementary education shall be compulsory. Technical and professional education shall be made generally available, and higher education shall be equally accessible to all on the basis of merit.

2. Education shall be directed to the full development of human personality and to the strengthening of respect for human rights and fundamental freedoms. It shall promote understanding, tolerance and friendship among all nations, racial or religious groups, and shall further the activities of the United Nations for the maintenance of peace.

3. Parents have the prior right to choose the kind of education that shall be given to their children.

Article 27

1. Everyone has the right freely to participate in the cultural life of the community, to enjoy the arts and to share in scientific advancement and its benefits.

2. Everyone has the right to the protection of the moral and material interests resulting from any scientific, literary or artistic production of which he is the author.

Article 28

Everyone is entitled to a social and international order in which the rights and freedoms set forth in this declaration can be fully realised.

Article 29

1. Everyone has duties to the community in which alone the free and full development of his personality is possible.

2. In the exercise of his rights and freedoms, everyone shall be subject only to such limitations as are determined by law solely for the purpose of securing due recognition and respect for the rights and freedoms of others and of meeting the just requirements of morality, public order and the general welfare in a democratic society.

3. These rights and freedoms may in no case be exercised contrary to the purposes and principles of the United Nations.

ARTICLE 30

> Nothing in this declaration may be interpreted as implying for any state, group or person any right to engage in any activity or to perform any act aimed at the destruction of any of the rights and freedoms set forth herein.

This resolution has probably the character of a recommendation, although it does not present itself expressly as such. The General Assembly only ' proclaims ' this Declaration, ' as a common standard of achievement for all peoples and all nations.' If this proclamation is to be interpreted as a recommendation, the question arises to whom this recommendation is made. It is significant that it is not addressed to the ' Members,' or to ' states,' or to the ' governments.' The Declaration is intended to be a common standard of achievement for ' all peoples and all nations;' and the proclamation is made ' to the end that every individual and every organ of society . . . shall strive to . . . ' Thus the General Assembly recommends to ' every individual and every organ of society ' to do something with respect to the human rights laid down in the Declaration. The governments of the Member states may or may not be considered to be ' organs of society;' the term ' society ' is sometimes used as including the concept of state, sometimes in opposition to the concept of state.

Human rights, that is to say rights of individuals, are of legal importance only if the corresponding legal obligations—obligations of other individuals and especially obligations of the state—are established by state legislation or international agreements. But the resolution of the General Assembly does not or at least not expressly recommend legislative acts or international agreements. The General Assembly recommends that ' every individual and every organ of society ' shall constantly keep in mind the declaration and shall strive ' by teaching and education ' to promote respect for the rights and freedoms formulated in the Declaration. Respect for rights and freedoms—' freedoms ' are not mentioned in the title of the Proclamation—can be ' promoted ' only after the rights and freedoms are legally established. But ' every individual and every organ of society ' is not only invited to strive to promote by teaching and education respect for the rights and freedoms, but also ' by progressive measures, national and international, to secure their universal and effective recognition and observance, both among the peoples of Member states themselves and among the peoples of territories under their jurisdiction.' If by ' progressive measures, national and international ' also state acts of legislation and international agreements are to be understood, it must be remembered that neither ' every individual ' nor ' every organ of society ' can take such measures, that only the governments of the Member states are the authorities to which a recommendation of this kind should be directed. It seems that the General Assembly by using vague formulas such as 'peoples' and 'nations' instead of 'states,' 'organ of society' instead of 'government,' 'progressive measures, national and international' instead of 'legislation' and 'international agreements,' intentionally avoided to make recommendations of definite legal measures to the Members of the United Nations. As far as 'international' measures are concerned it is significant that the General Assembly did not adopt a draft convention on human rights to be submitted to the Members for ratification.[1] It stands to reason that the resolution of the General Assembly on Human Rights has no legal effect whatever.[2] It cannot be considered as authentic interpretation of the provisions of the Charter referring to human rights.[3] An authentic interpretation is possible only by an amendment to the Charter.

As to the legislative technique of the Declaration of Human Rights adopted by the General Assembly two remarks seem to be not superfluous. The first concerns Article 1 of the Declaration which contains the statements that 'all human beings are born free and equal,' and that they are 'endowed with reason and conscience.' As theoretical statements they should not be inserted into the text of an instrument which, if issued as a national law or concluded as an international agreement, would assume a legal character. Besides, the statement that all human beings are endowed with reason and conscience is, in view of the differences which exist with respect to the degree in which human beings are endowed with reason and conscience, meaningless. The statement that all human beings are born free and equal, is a specific natural-law doctrine, and this doctrine is far from being generally accepted.[4] If the question is under consideration how

[1] The text of a Draft Covenant on Human Rights prepared by the Drafting committee on an International Bill of Human Rights (Doc. E/800, pp. 15–20) was transmitted to the General Assembly by the above mentioned resolution of the Economic and Social Council.

[2] At the 218th meeting of the Economic and Social Council the representative of the United Kingdom stated: 'The United Kingdom Government felt strongly that the Covenant should be the core of the Bill, and that it should be a precise legal document without escape clauses. Only such a document would provide an effective safeguard of human rights and freedoms. The Declaration was a statement of ideals, to which it was hoped all peoples would aspire, but not an instrument legally imposing obligations on any state. It fell far short of being an adequate Bill of Rights for the purposes of the United Nations.' (Doc. E/SR. 218, p. 8.)

[3] 'Some delegations considered that it [the Declaration of Human Rights] should be treated as an authentic interpretation of the principles expressed in the Charter of the United Nations.' Statement made by the representative of Poland at the 215th meeting of the Economic and Social Council. (Doc. E/SR. 215, p. 10.)

[4] At the 215th meeting of the Economic and Social Council the representative of Brazil made the following statement with respect to Article 1: 'his delegation appreciated that it was attractive to adopt formulas to impress public opinion. Nevertheless, it saw no reason why a Declaration on Human Rights should be introduced by philosophical postulates taken from outdated theories of natural law. His delegation considered that the Declaration on Human Rights might profitably omit Article 1 altogether and begin with Article 2.' (Doc. E/SR. 215, p. 9.)

human beings are ' born,' which is a question of biology and psychology, no scientist can give another answer than that human beings are born neither free nor equal. But from the point of view of a bill of rights, it is not the question how human beings are born, but the question how human beings shall be treated by the law, regardless of how they actually are born, and regardless of the great differences which actually exist between them. It is not very fortunate that the Declaration of Human Rights starts with a problematical statement and thus places the whole document under the sway of a highly disputed doctrine.

Another characteristic feature of the Declaration of Human Rights is the fact that it contains no provision concerning international legal remedies to be employed in case of violations of the rights. No right in a legal sense of the term exists if there is no possibility for the subject of the so-called right to put into motion the coercive machinery of the state or—in case of an international bill of rights—the coercive machinery of an international organisation, if the subject has no access to a national or international court. An international bill of human rights is almost worthless if it does not establish or at least recommend to establish an international court to which the human beings whose rights are stipulated have direct access and which has the competence to render decisions binding upon the states which have violated, or not prevented the violation of, these rights. Article 8 of the Declaration, it is true, provides that ' Everyone has the right to effective remedy by competent national tribunals for acts violating fundamental rights granted him by a constitution or by law.' It is not correct to speak of a ' right to effective remedy,' because the legal possibility of employing such a remedy constitutes the right the violation of which is in question; and the rights can be violated only by acts of state or by the omission of the necessary acts of state. The rights stipulated in the Decalaration are rights the individual has to a certain conduct of the state. This is the reason why only an international bill of rights can effectively guarantee these rights, since only by international law an individual can effectively be protected against his own state. Such protection can be established only by the jurisdiction of an international Court.[5] But in this respect the Declaration of Human Rights provides only in

[5] At the 218th meeting of the Economic and Social Council the representative of Australia ' pointed out that under the English legal system the remedy was equal in importance to the right, for without the remedy there was no right. He was aware that other legal systems differed in that, but measures should be taken to ensure that the human rights laid down by the United Nations should not become dead letters as soon as they were infringed. . . . In the Charter an obligation was laid upon the Assembly to promote the realisation, to enforce, human rights. There must be an international tribunal for such enforcement. The General Assembly itself was a kind of international tribunal at which Member Governments might raise for adjudication cases of alleged infringement of the rights laid down in the Charter; but there must be an international tribunal before which individuals, or groups of individuals who could not obtain the backing of governments, might bring cases of infringement of their rights.' (Doc. E/SR. 218, pp. 5/6.)

Article 28 that ' Everyone is entitled to a social and international order in which the rights and freedoms set forth in this declaration can be fully realised.' This vague formula falls far short of recommending an effective remedy for violations of the rights set forth in the Declaration.

The protection of a special human right, the right of the individual to live as member of a national, ethnical, racial or religious group, is the purpose of the Convention on the Prevention and Punishment of the Crime of Genocide, the text of which was prepared by the Economic and Social Council under Article 62, paragraph 2, of the Charter and adopted by the General Assembly at its 179th meeting on December 9, 1948.[6]

Following is the text of the Convention:—

> The Contracting parties, Having considered the declaration made by the General Assembly of the United Nations in its Resolution 96 (I) dated December 11, 1946, that genocide is a crime under international law, contrary to the spirit and aims of the United Nations and condemned by the civilised world;
>
> Recognising that at all periods of history genocide has inflicted great losses on humanity; and

[6] Doc. A/P.V. 178, 179. This resolution of the General Assembly was preceded by a resolution adopted at its 55th meeting on December 11, 1946, which runs as follows:—

> Genocide is a denial of the right of existence of entire human groups, as homicide is the denial of the right to live of individual human beings; such denial of the right of existence shocks the conscience of mankind, results in great losses to humanity in the form of cultural and other contributions represented by these human groups, and is contrary to moral law and to the spirit and aims of the United Nations.
>
> Many instances of such crimes of genocide have occurred when racial, religious, political and other groups have been destroyed, entirely or in part.
>
> The punishment of the crime of genocide is a matter of international concern.
>
> The General Assembly, therefore,
>
> Affirms that genocide is a crime under international law which the civilised world condemns, and for the commission of which principals and accomplices—whether private individuals, public officials or statesmen, and whether the crime is committed on religious, racial, political or any other grounds—are punishable;
>
> Invites the Member states to enact the necessary legislation for the prevention and punishment of this crime;
>
> Recommends that international co-operation be organised between states with a view to facilitating the speedy prevention and punishment of the crime of genocide, and, to this end,
>
> Requests the Economic and Social Council to undertake the necessary studies, with a view to drawing up a draft convention on the crime of genocide to be submitted to the next regular session of the General Assembly. (Doc. A/64/Add. 1, pp. 188 f.)

At its 123rd meeting on November 21, 1947, the General Assembly adopted a resolution reaffirming its resolution of December 11, 1946. (Doc. A/519, pp. 129 f.)

Being convinced that, in order to liberate mankind from such an odious scourge, international co-operation is required;

Hereby agree as hereinafter provided:

ARTICLE 1

The contracting parties confirm that genocide, whether committed in time of peace or in time of war, is a crime under international law which they undertake to prevent and to punish.

ARTICLE 2

In the present convention genocide means any of the following acts committed with intent to destroy, in whole or in part, a national, ethnical, racial or religious group, as such:

(A) Killing members of the group;

(B) Causing serious bodily or mental harm to members of the group;

(C) Deliberately inflicting on the group conditions of life calculated to bring about its physical destruction in whole or in part;

(D) Imposing measures intended to prevent births within the group;

(E) Forcibly transferring children of the group to another group;

ARTICLE 3

The following acts shall be punishable:

(A) Genocide;

(B) Conspiracy to commit genocide;

(C) Direct and public incitement to commit genocide;

(D) Attempt to commit genocide;

(E) Complicity in genocide.

ARTICLE 4

Persons committing genocide or any of the other acts enumerated in Article 3 shall be punished, whether they are constitutionally responsible rulers, public officials or private individuals.

ARTICLE 5

The contracting parties undertake to enact, in accordance with their respective constitutions, the necessary legislation to give effect to the provisions of the present convention and, in particular, to provide effective penalties for persons guilty of genocide or any of the other acts enumerated in Article 3.

Article 6

Persons charged with genocide or any of the other acts enumerated in Article 3 shall be tried by a competent tribunal of the state in the territory of which the act was committed, or by such international penal tribunal as may have jurisdiction with respect to those contracting parties which shall have accepted its jurisdiction.

Article 7

Genocide and the other acts enumerated in Article 3 shall not be considered as political crimes for the purpose of extradition.

The contracting parties pledge themselves in such cases to grant extradition in accordance with their laws and treaties in force.

Article 8

Any contracting party may call upon the competent organs of the United Nations to take such action under the Charter of the United Nations as they consider appropriate for the prevention and suppression of acts of genocide or any of the other acts enumerated in Article 3.

Article 9

Disputes between the contracting parties relating to the interpretation, application or fulfilment of the present convention, including those relating to the responsibility of a state for genocide or any of the other acts enumerated in Article 3, shall be submitted to the International Court of Justice at the request of any of the parties to the dispute.

Article 10

The present convention, of which the Chinese, English, French, Russian and Spanish texts are equally authentic, shall bear the date of December 9, 1948.

Article 11

The present convention shall be open until December 31, 1949, for signature on behalf of any Member of the United Nations and of any non-member state to which an invitation to sign has been addressed by the General Assembly.

The present convention shall be ratified, and the instruments of ratification shall be deposited with the Secretary-General of the United Nations.

After January 1, 1950, the present convention may be acceded to on behalf of any Member of the United Nations and of any non-member state which has received an invitation as aforesaid.

Instruments of accession shall be deposited with the Secretary-General of the United Nations.

ARTICLE 12

Any contracting party may at any time, by notification addressed to the Secretary-General of the United Nations, extend the application of the present convention to all or any of the territories for the conduct of whose foreign relations that contracting party is responsible.

ARTICLE 13

On the day when the first twenty instruments of ratification or accession have been deposited, the Secretary General shall draw up a proces-verbal and transmit a copy of it to each Member of the United Nations and to each of the non-member states contemplated in Article 11.

The present convention shall come into force on the ninetieth day following the date of deposit of the twentieth instrument of ratification or accession.

Any ratification or accession effected subsequent to the latter date shall become effective on the ninetieth day following the deposit of the instrument of ratification or accession.

ARTICLE 14

The present convention shall remain in effect for a period of ten years as from the date of its coming into force.

It shall thereafter remain in force for successive periods of five years for such contracting parties as have not denounced it at least six months before the expiration of the current period.

Denunciation shall be effected by a written notification addressed to the Secretary-General of the United Nations.

ARTICLE 15

If, as a result of denunciations, the number of parties to the present convention should become less than sixteen the convention shall cease to be in force as from the date on which the last of these denunciations shall become effective.

ARTICLE 16

A request for the revision of the present convention may be made at any time by any contracting party by means of a notification in writing addressed to the Secretary-General.

The General Assembly shall decide upon the steps, if any, to be taken in respect of such request.

Article 17

The Secretary-General of the United Nations shall notify all Members of the United Nations and the non-member states contemplated in Article 11 of the following:

(A) Signatures, ratifications and accessions received in accordance with Article 11;

(B) Notifications received in accordance with Article 12;

(C) The date upon which the present convention comes into force in accordance with Article 13;

(D) Denunciations received in accordance with Article 14;

(E) The abrogation of the convention in accordance with Article 15;

(F) Notifications received in accordance with Article 16.

Article 18

The original of the present convention shall be deposited in the archives of the United Nations.

A certified copy of the convention shall be transmitted to all Members of the United Nations and to the non-member states contemplated in Article 11.

Article 19

The present convention shall be registered by the Secretary-General of the United Nations on the date of its coming into force.

The Convention imposes upon the contracting parties the obligation to prevent and to punish the crime of genocide as defined in Article 2, and, in addition, to punish certain acts related to genocide, as determined in Article 3. This obligation is specified by the obligation, stipulated in Article 5, to give effect to the provisions of the convention, in particular to provide effective penalties for persons guilty of genocide or any of the other acts enumerated in Article 3.

The obligation of the governments to punish individuals for having committed the crime of genocide or the other crimes defined in the convention implies the obligation of the individuals to refrain from performing the acts constituting these crimes. These crimes may be committed by private individuals or by a state, that is to say by individuals in their capacity as organs of a state, especially as members of the government. For, Article 4 provides that persons committing genocide or any other acts enumerated in Article 3 shall be punished 'whether they are constitutionally responsible rulers, public officials or private individuals'; and Article 9 refers to the 'responsibility of a state for genocide or any other acts enumerated in Article 3.' That means that the Convention imposes not only upon individuals as private persons but also upon states, that is to say, upon individuals in their capacity as organs of a state, the obligation to refrain from performing the acts punishable under the Convention. In providing for punishment of individuals for having committed the crimes, determined in the convention, in their capacity as organs of a state, the Convention establishes individual criminal responsibility for acts of state constituting violations of an international agreement. In this respect the Convention follows the pattern first applied by Article 227 of the Peace Treaty of Versailles establishing individual criminal responsibility of William II for violations of international law committed in his capacity as head of the German Reich, and later by the London Agreement for the Prosecution of the War Criminals of the European Axis Powers, establishing individual criminal responsibility for acts of state constituting crimes against peace and especially crimes against humanity as determined by this agreement. But in contradistinction to the Peace Treaty of Versailles and the London Agreement, the Convention on Genocide does not establish individual criminal responsibility for acts of state with retroactive force. Genocide and related crimes are punishable under the Convention only if committed after the Convention has come into force. The Convention has not the character of an *ex post facto* law.

It is hardly possible that individuals as private persons can commit the crime of genocide. No isolated individual, only an organised body of individuals can kill members of a group or cause serious bodily or mental harm to members of a group with the intent to destroy, in whole or in part, the group as such (Article 2, (A), (B); and this only at the command or with the authorisation or, at least, with the toleration of the government of a state. If so, the acts concerned are to be imputed to the government and hence are to be considered as acts of state. The acts determined in Article 2, (C), (D) and (E), can hardly be performed in any other way than directly by the government of a state. The mass murders of Jews, Poles, Catholics and members of other groups in Nazi Germany, which induced the General Assembly to adopt the draft convention on genocide, were acts of the German government or the Nazi Party which, actually as well as legally, was an organ of the German state. The crimes determined by the Convention, in so far as they actually could be committed by private individuals in a way not imputable to the state, constitute crimes which under the criminal law of all the states of the world are severely punishable. To protect mankind against these crimes, no international agreement is necessary.

The essential achievement of the Convention on Genocide is the obligation imposed upon states, and that means upon their governments, to refrain from genocide, and the individual criminal responsibility established for acts of state constituting this crime. Hence from the point of view of legal technique, the decisive question is: how to provide in an effective way for the punishment of genocide. Only by appropriate provisions concerning the punishment, the crime may be prevented. In this respect, Article 6 of the Convention stipulates that persons charged with genocide or any other acts enumerated in Article 3 'shall be tried by a competent tribunal of the state in the territory of which the act was committed, or by such international penal tribunal as may have jurisdiction with respect to such contracting parties as shall have accepted the jurisdiction of such tribunal.'

Genocide as an act of state may be committed in the territory of the state responsible for the crime or in the territory of another state. Genocide as an act of one state can hardly be committed in the territory of another state in time of peace. It may be committed in the territory of another state in time of war by the government of the occupant power. In this case, punishment of the guilty persons by the courts of the occupied state, that is by the courts of the state in the territory of which the act was committed, is possible only after the occupant army has withrawn and only if the state in the territory of which the crime was committed was victorious and the state responsible for the crime vanquished. That means that in this case under the Convention the victor is the judge over the vanquished state. It is this very fact which gave rise to the most serious objections against the war crime trials based on the London Agreement of August 8, 1945.

In case genocide, as act of state, is committed in the territory of the state responsible for the crime, the state is, under the Convention, obliged to punish itself. There can be little doubt that if a government, in violation of its international obligation, commits genocide, it will be inclined also to violate its obligation to punish the persons who in their capacity as organs of the state have committed the crime. Only in case the government responsible for the crime is overthrown in a civil war, there is a certain chance that the new government will fulfil its obligation to punish the guilty persons. But then the situation is quite similar to that where the government of a victorious state establishes itself as the judge over acts of a vanquished state.

The only effective way to punish genocide committed as acts of state, and thus to prevent this crime, is the establishment of an international criminal court and the execution of its judgments by an internationally organised power.[7] In this respect the Convention on

7 At the 218th meeting of the Economic and Social Council, the representative of New Zealand stated: 'Since large-scale acts of genocide could hardly take place under modern conditions without at least the complicity of the government of the territory concerned, it might not be sufficient to rely on the jurisdiction of national courts, and some form of international tribunal working in conjunction with the United Nations would appear to be necessary.' (Doc. E/SR. 218, p. 43.) At the 219th meeting of the Economic and Social Council, the representative of France declared that: 'his delegation regarded genocide as a crime committed, encouraged or tolerated by the Government of a State and, hence as an international crime

Genocide only refers to the possibliity of the establishment of an international penal tribunal. The Convention does not establish such a tribunal, and the attitude maintained by some Members of the United Nations during the discussion of this problem shows that the establishment of such court is, at least for the time being, hardly possible.[8]

Article 8 of the Convention authorises the contracting parties to call upon the competent organs of the United Nations to take such

which should be dealt with by an international court. Various objections had been raised to that idea but his delegation considered that it would be unwise to have recourse to national courts and requested that the latter be deprived of their place in the present draft. Only an international court could try a crime of genocide committed by a Government.' (Doc. E/SR. 219, p. 9.)

8 The Report of the Ad Hoc Committee on Genocide (Doc. E/794, p. 29) contains the following statements: 'For some representatives the granting of jurisdiction to an international court was an essential element of the Convention. They claimed that in almost every serious case of genocide it would be impossible to rely on the courts of the states where genocide had been committed to exercise effective repression because the Government itself would have been guilty, unless it had been, in fact, powerless. The principle of universal repression having been set aside for the reasons indicated below the absence of an international court would result, in fact, in impunity for the offenders. The supporters of an international court merely requested that the international jurisdiction be expressly provided for by the Convention without the latter setting up the actual organisation of the court. The members opposing this proposal first declared that the intervention of an international court would defeat the principle of the sovereignty of the state because this court would be substituted for a national court. Secondly, they claimed that mere reference in the Convention to an international court would have no practical value. What would this court be? There is for the moment no international court with criminal jurisdiction. It would be necessary either to create a new court or to add a new criminal chamber to the International Court of Justice and all the members of the Committee had agreed that they had neither the authority nor the time necessary for settling these problems.'

The representative of Poland declared : 'The inclusion in the Convention of the principle of an international criminal tribunal constitutes an obligation of the parties to this Convention, the contents of which are wholly unknown to them. The creation of an international criminal court whose jurisdiction could only be compulsory and not optional, is contrary to the principles on which the International Court of Justice and its Statute are based.' The representative of the Soviet Union declared: 'The representative of the Union of Soviet Socialist Republics considers that the decision of a majority of the Committee to place cases of genocide under the jurisdiction of a competent international court is wrong, since the establishment of an international court would constitute intervention in the internal affairs of states and a violation of their sovereignty, an important element of which is the right to try all crimes without exception, committed in the territory of the state concerned. The representative of the Union of Soviet Socialist Republics considers that Article 7 of the Convention should be drafted as follows: 'The High Contracting Parties pledge themselves to punish any offender under this Convention within any territory under their jurisdiction, the case to be heard by the national courts in accordance with the domestic legislation of the country.' Cf. also the declarations made by the representative of the Soviet Union at the 219th meeting of the Economic and Social Council (Doc. E/SR. 219, p. 6) and at the 178th meeting of the General Assembly (Doc. A/PV. 178, pp. 21 ff)

action under the Charter as they consider appropriate for the prevention and suppression of acts of genocide or any of the other acts enumerated in Article 3. But the only organ of the United Nations competent under the Charter to take effective action is the Security Council; and the Security Council can take such action only under Article 39 of the Charter, that is to say, if the act of genocide or any of the other acts enumerated in Article 3 of the Convention constitutes a threat to, or breach of, the peace. Besides, an enforcement action taken by the Security Council in such a case is based on the principle of collective responsibility of the state guilty of the threat to, or breach of, the peace, and not on the principle of individual responsibility proclaimed by the Convention on Genocide.

4. Rights of States

The provisions concerning the fundamental rights of states are presented, neither in the Preamble nor in Article 1, as matters of international co-operation. They are dealt with in paragraph 2 of Article 1; but only paragraph 3 of this Article refers expressly to international co-operation. However, in the introduction to Article 55 it is stated that ' conditions of stability and well-being . . . are necessary for peaceful and friendly relations among nations based on respect for the principle of equal rights and self-determination of peoples.' It is ' with a view to the creation ' of these conditions, referred to in the introduction, that according to Article 55 the United Nations shall establish international co-operation by performing the functions determined in this Article. The formula concerning the equal rights of the states as used in this Article is an almost literal repetition of the one used in Article 1, paragraph 2. The only difference is that Article 1, paragraph 2, speaks of ' friendly ' relations whereas Article 55 speaks of ' peaceful and friendly relations.' The addition of ' peaceful ' is superfluous since if a relation between two states is friendly it is necessarily peaceful. However, the repetition of the whole formula in Article 55 is, as pointed out, superfluous. It serves here as an explanation of the purpose of the Organisation to create ' conditions of stability and well-being.' If such explanation is deemed to be necessary at all, it has been given already in Article 1 proclaiming the purposes of the Organisation. Here ' to develop friendly relations . . . ' is declared a purpose of the United Nations, whereas the purpose proclaimed in Article 55: ' creation of conditions of stability and well-being ' does not appear in Article 1, where it belongs according to the system of the Charter.

Whereas Article 1, paragraph 2, and Article 55, speak of ' equal rights and self-determination of peoples,' the Preamble declares as an end of the United Nations to reaffirm faith in the ' equal rights . . . of nations large and small.' However, Article 2 formulates the first

Principle in accordance with which the Organisation and its Members shall act: ' The Organisation is based on the principle of the sovereign equality of all its Members.' The ' sovereign ' equality is not identical with the equality formulated in the Preamble as the ' equal rights ' of nations. It is worth noting that the principle of sovereignty is not mentioned in the Preamble. As to the ' equality ' of the states, the privileges conferred in Articles 27, 108 and 109, upon the states which are permanent members of the Security Council are incompatible with the principle of ' equal rights of nations large and small ' as well as with the principle of ' sovereign equality ' of the Members.[9] The principle of ' equal rights of nations large and small ' cannot be used to interpret the provisions of the Charter conferring privileges upon certain Members. Nor can the Purpose laid down in Article 1, paragraph 2: ' to develop friendly relations among nations based on respect for the principle of equal rights and self-determination of peoples ' be interpreted on the basis of the just mentioned statement of the Preamble. The term ' nations ' in the formula of the Preamble means probably states; the term ' peoples ' in Article 1, paragraph 2, may have a different meaning; for in its connection with ' self-determination ' it may mean not the state, but one of the elements of the state: the population. Self determination of the people usually designates a principle of internal policy, the principle of democratic

[9] At the 7th meeting of Committee I/1 (U.N.C.I.O. Doc. 382, I/1/19) one delegate felt that under the Dumbarton Oaks Proposals—which in this point are identical with Article 2, paragraph 1, of the Charter—' . . . states Members of the World Organisation would not receive equal treatment, and that therefore the words " sovereign equality " in paragraph 1 of Chapter 2 were somewhat ironic; it was suggested that the word " sovereign " be deleted.' At the 8th meeting of Committee I/1 (U.N.C.I.O. Doc. 423, I/1/20) several delegates ' expressed disapproval of the phrase " sovereign equality " and suggested replacing it by " juridical equality " or some similar term. It was pointed out that other parts of the Charter would not be consistent with the concept of equal sovereignty . . . ' The Report of the Rapporteur of Committee 1 to Commission I (U.N.C.I.O. Doc. 944, I/1/34 (1), p. 12) contains the following statement: ' The Committee voted to use the terminology " sovereign equality " on the assumption that it includes the following elements: (1) that states are juridically equal; (2) that each state enjoys the right inherent in full sovereignty; (3) that the personality of the state is respected, as well as its territorial integrity and political independence; (4) that the state should, under international order, comply faithfully with its international duties and obligations.' If the states are ' equal ' in spite of the fact that some have privileges which others have not, the term ' equal ' has lost its original sense. ' Juridical ' equality means ' equality before the law,' and that means that everybody has the duties and rights which the law confers upon him, or that everybody shall be treated as the law provides; which is an empty tautology. The second point of the interpretation given by Committee I/1 is meaningless as long as the term ' sovereignty ' is not defined. Point 3 does not result from Article 2, paragraph 1, but from Article 3, paragraph 4. Point 4 has nothing to do with the sovereign equality of the Members. It formulates the truism that legal obligation shall be complied with.

government. However, Article 1, paragraph 2, refers to the relations among states. Therefore the term ' peoples,' too—in connection with ' equal rights '—means probably states, since only states have ' equal rights ' according to general international law. That the Purpose of the Organisation is to develop friendly relations among states based on respect for the principle of self-determination of ' peoples,' does not mean that friendly relations among states depend on democratic form of government and that the purpose of the Organisation is to favour such form of government. This would not be compatible with the principle of ' sovereign equality ' of the Members, nor with the principle of non-intervention in domestic affairs established in Article 2, paragraph 7. If the term ' peoples ' in Article 1, paragraph 2, means the same as the term ' nations ' in the Preamble, then ' self-determination of peoples ' in Article 1, paragraph 2, can mean only ' sovereignty ' of the states.

The principle of ' equal rights,' that is the principle of the equality of states, and the principle of self-determination, that is the principle

1 At the San Francisco Conference the Belgian delegation made the following critical remarks on the text of Article 1, paragraph 2: ' 1. The amendment of the sponsoring governments mentions the equality of the rights of peoples, including that of self-determination. There seems to be some confusion in this: One speaks generally of the equality of states; surely one could use the word " peoples " as an equivalent for the word " states," but in the expression " the peoples' right of self-determination " the word " peoples " means the national groups which do not identify themselves with the population of a state. As for the word " nations " used at the beginning of this article, it is not possible to determine whether it is used in the first or in the second meaning of the word " peoples." 2. The second criticism on the text proposed by the amendment of the sponsoring governments is that it would be dangerous to put forth the peoples' right of self-determination as a basis for the friendly relations between the nations. This would open the door to inadmissable interventions if, as seems probable, one wishes to take inspiration from the peoples' right of self-determination in the action of the Organisation and not in the relations between the peoples.' (U.N.C.I.O. Doc. 374, I/1/17.) The Report of the Rapporteur of Committee 1 to Commission I (U.N.C.I.O. Doc. 944, I/1/34 (1), p. 10) contains the following statement: ' The Committee understands that the principle of equal rights of peoples and that of self-determination are two complementary parts of one standard of conduct; that the respect of that principle is a basis for the development of friendly relations and is one of the measures to strengthen universal peace; that an essential element of the principle in question is a free and genuine expression of the will of the people, which avoids cases of the alleged expression of the popular will, such as those used for their own ends by Germany and Italy in later years.'

As to the meaning of the term ' sovereign equality ' the Report of Rapporteur of Committee 1 to Commission I (p. 12) contains the following statement: ' The Committee voted to use the terminology " sovereign equality " on the assumption that it includes the following elements: (1) that states are juridically equal; (2) that each state enjoys the right inherent in full sovereignty; (3) that the personality of the state is respected, as well as its territorial integrity and political independence; (4) that the state should, under international order, comply faithfully with its international duties and obligations.'

of the sovereignty of states, are two different principles. But Article 1, paragraph 2, refers to 'the principle,' and not to the 'principles,' of equal rights and self-determination of peoples. This seems to indicate that the formula of Article 1, paragraph 2, has the same meaning as the formula of Article 2, paragraph 1, in which the principles of sovereignty and equality are combined in a rather problematical way into one principle: that of 'sovereign equality.'[1]

[1] See previous page.

PART TWO

ORGANISATION OF THE UNITED NATIONS

Chapter 4

MEMBERSHIP

1. Original Membership

The provisions of the Charter regulating membership are as follows:—

Article 3

The original Members of the United Nations shall be the states which, having participated in the United Nations Conference on International Organisation at San Francisco, or having previously signed the Declaration by United Nations of January 1, 1942, sign the present Charter and ratify it in accordance with Article 110.

Article 4

1. Membership in the United Nations is open to all other peace-loving states which accept the obligations contained in the present Charter and, in the judgment of the Organisation, are able and willing to carry out these obligations.

2. The admission of any such state to membership in the United Nations will be effected by a decision of the General Assembly upon the recommendation of the Security Council.

The Charter distinguishes between original and subsequent Members of the Organisation.[1] Original Members are the states which signed and ratified the Charter. According to Article 110, paragraph 1, the Charter shall be ratified by the signatory states 'in accordance with their respective constitutional processes.' An unconstitutional ratification is not valid; and a valid ratification is the essential condition of original membership. But who was competent to decide the question as to whether the ratification was in accordance with the constitutional process of the state concerned? The Charter did not expressly answer this question. According to general international law, it is the legitimate government of the state concerned

[1] The Report of the Rapporteur of Committee I/2 on Chapter III (Membership) (U.N.C.I.O. Doc. 1178, I/2/76 (2), p. 2) contains the following statement: 'It will be noted that a distinction is made between original Members and future Members. As regards original Members their participation in the Organisation is considered as acquired by right, while that of future Members is dependent on the fulfilment of certain conditions. It was, however, clearly understood that this distinction did not imply any discrimination against future Members but that normal course of events required it. Before new Members can be admitted the Organisation must exist, which in turn implies the existence of original Members.'

which is competent to interpret, in its relations to other states, its own constitution. Normally, an international treaty does not contain an express provision to the effect that its ratification shall be in accordance with the constitution of the ratifying government. Hence the interpretation of this constitution may be left to the government concerned. The Charter, however, expressly prescribes observance of the respective constitutional processes. Hence, the constitutional problem was not a merely internal matter; it was also a concern of the Organisation. The question as to whether a concrete ratification was in accordance with the constitution of the ratifying government was implied in the application of Article 110 of the Charter. Consequently, the authority which had to apply this Article was competent to decide the constitutional question.

Paragraph 2 of Article 110 provides that 'the ratifications shall be deposited with the Government of the United States of America which shall notify all signatory states of each deposit as well as the Secretary-General of the Organisation when he has been appointed.' This provision may be interpreted to mean that the government of the United States, acting in the service of the Organisation, had to accept the deposit of a ratification only if the latter was in conformity with the provision of paragraph 1 of Article 110 and, consequently, had to decide on behalf of the Organisation whether or not the ratification fulfilled the requirements of this paragraph when this question became doubtful.

According to Article 110, paragraph 3, the Charter of the United Nations (including the Statute of the International Court of Justice, which, according to Article 92 of the Charter, is an integral part of the latter) shall come into force 'upon the deposit of ratifications by the Republic of China, France, the Union of Soviet Socialist Republics, the United Kingdom of Great Britain and Northern Ireland, and the United States of America, and by a majority of the other signatory states. A protocol of the ratifications deposited shall thereupon be drawn up by the Government of the United States of America which shall communicate copies thereof to all the signatory states.' The states mentioned by name are those which have permanent seats in the Security Council.[2]

2 The *Report to the President* contains on p. 172 f. the following statement: 'In the case of multipartite treaties involving mutual rights and obligations, it is of great importance to determine which of the signatories and how many of them must give their approval before the treaty becomes binding. Otherwise, a small number of the signatories might find themselves bound by obligations which were drafted in the expectation that there would be many partners in the enterprise and which would be impossible of fulfilment in the absence of certain of the states which were also signatories of the treaty.—In the case of the Charter this difficulty would obviously arise unless a provision were inserted to guard against it. The whole discussion of the Charter in this Report reveals that the functioning of the United Nations as an organisation depends upon the participation and co-operation of the Five Powers

It stands to reason that the Charter has come into force only for the states which have ratified it, although this is not expressly stipulated. The process of ratification implies deposit of the ratification document with the government of the United States. The Charter does not prescribe a certain period of time within which ratification shall take place. Since the Charter has come into force before all signatories had ratified it, ratification was possible even after the Charter had come into force. In this case the coming into force of the Charter coincided with the deposit of the ratification. This is implied in paragraph 4 of Article 110 which provides that ' the states signatory to the present Charter which ratify it after it has come into force will become original Members of the United Nations on the date of the deposit of their respective ratifications.' The statement that the signatories which ratify the Charter after it has come into force, under paragraph 3 of Article 110, will become original Members of the United Nations is superfluous, because this was the effect of Article 3, providing that all signatories which have ratified the Charter shall become original Members of the United Nations. Also the states which ratified the Charter before it has come into force became original Members of the United Nations, without Article 110 containing a special provision to this effect. What paragraph 4 of Article 110 should expressly stipulate, but what its text only implies, is: that for signatories which ratify the Charter after it has come into force under Article 110, paragraph 3, the Charter comes into force at the date of the deposit of their ratification instruments.

The Charter does not contain a clause permitting signature or ratification under reservations.

Ratification of the Charter in accordance with the constitutional process of the state concerned is a condition of original membership; as to the act by which a state adheres to the Charter under Article 4 and thus becomes a subsequent Member, the Charter does not prescribe compliance with its constitutional process.

According to the wording of Articles 3 and 4 only ' states ' can be or become Members of the United Nations.[3] However, among the communities which signed and ratified the Charter were some whose

which will have permanent seats in the Security Council and upon the co-operation with them of other states. Accordingly, Article 110 provides that the ratifications of the United States, the United Kingdom, the Soviet Union, China, and France, and of a majority of the other signatory states, must be deposited before the Charter takes effect.' Since there are 51 signatories the Charter came into effect when it was ratified by the five powers that are permanent members of the Security Council and by twenty four other signatories. This was the case on October 24, 1945.

[3] In this respect there exists a difference between the Charter and the Covenant. Article 1, paragraphs 1 and 2, of the Covenant read as follows:—

> 1. The original Members of the League of Nations shall be those of the signatories which are named in the Annex to this Covenant and also such of those other states named in the Annex as shall accede without reservation

character as ' states ' in the sense of international law was doubtful, since they had not the degree of independence from other states which is required by international law, thus, for instance, India, the Philippine Commonwealth, the Byelorussian, and the Ukrainian Soviet Socialist Republic. According to the wording of Article 3 (which corresponds to the suggestion of Chapter III of the Dumbarton Oaks Proposals: ' Membership of the Organisation should be open to all peace-loving states '), a community which is not a ' state ' cannot be an original Member of the United Nations, even if it has signed and ratified the Charter. Also other provisions of the Charter speak of the Members as of ' states,' such as Article 2, paragraph 7; Article 11, paragraph 2; Articles 50, 79, 80, 110, 111 of the Charter and Articles 34 and 35 of the Statute of the International Court of Justice. Chapter XIX of the Charter refers five times to the signatory ' states.' It is doubtful whether the intention of those who drafted and accepted the text of Article 3 was to exclude from membership communities which are not ' states.' This problem was discussed at the San Francisco Conference. At the 4th meeting of Committee I/2 ' The delegate from the Philippines explained that his Government preferred the word " nation " to " state " inasmuch as the term " state " would not allow the Philippines to become a member of this Organisation at this time '[4] In the Report of the Rapporteur of Committee I/2 the following statement is made: ' It was pointed out to the Committee that Chapter III of the Dumbarton Oaks Proposals referred to membership of states. This reference, it was explained, might exclude from membership those nations participating in the Conference which had not yet achieved full statehood. The Committee felt that all nations participating in this Conference should be included as initial members of the Organisation.—A subcommittee on Chapter III was established on May 10 and recommended an English text for Chapter III, which the Committee adopted unanimously on May 12 (the French text was prepared a few days later). The English text as adopted by the Committee reads as follows: " Members of the Organisation are the

to this Covenant. Such accessions shall be effected by a Declaration deposited with the Secretariat within two months of the coming into force of the Covenant. Notice thereof shall be sent to all other Members of the League.

2. Any fully self-governing state, Dominion or Colony not named in the Annex may become a Member of the League if its admission is agreed to by two-thirds of the Assembly, provided that it shall give effective guarantees of its sincere intention to observe its international obligations, and shall accept such regulations as may be prescribed by the League in regard to its military, naval and air forces and armaments.

According to the wording of paragraph 1 (' also such of those other states ') it is supposed that all original Members are ' states,' although some of them—*e.g.*, India—were not. According to the wording of paragraph 2 not only states but also dominions or colonies could become Members of the League.

[4] Summary Report of the 4th meeting of Committee I/2 (U.N.C.I.O. Doc. 242, I/2/11).

signatories of the Charter whose ratification has become effective in accordance with Chapter XIX." '[5] This text was presented to Commission I. In another Report of the Rapporteur of Committee I/1 it is stated with reference to the suggested text (using the term ' signatories ' instead of ' states '): ' the definition adopted would serve to calm the fears of certain nations participating in our deliberations which, properly speaking, are not *states* and which for this reason might be denied the right of membership in the Organisation.'[6] In spite of this express recognition that some signatories were not ' states,' the term ' state ' was inserted into the finally adopted text of Article 3.

2. Subsequent Membership

Subsequent Members are those states—and only ' states ' can become subsequent Members—which are admitted to membership by a decision of the General Assembly adopted ' on the recommendation of the Security Council.' Admission of a state to membership is a matter within the common competence of the General Assembly and the Security Council. In this respect there exists a difference between the Charter and the Covenant of the League of Nations which in Article 1, paragraph 2, authorises exclusively the Assembly to decide about admission to the League. As to the functions which the General Assembly and the Security Council have to perform in the procedure by which a state is admitted to membership in the United Nations, the wording of Article 4, paragraph 2, is ambiguous. It may be—and, as a matter of fact, it has been—argued that the Security Council has only an advisory function, since it is the General Assembly which—according to the wording of paragraph 2 of Article 4—has to take the decision by which the admission is effected, and the Security Council has only the power to make a ' recommendation.' This term is used in other parts of the Charter, as *e.g.*, in Chapter VI, to designate a mere advice, an act which has no legal effect. The Security Council may make a recommendation favourable or unfavourable to the admission of the applicant state; but the General Assembly is not bound by such a recommendation. The Assembly may decide to admit a state which the Council recommended not to admit; and the Assembly may decide not to admit a state which the Council recommended to admit. The Charter provides only that the Assembly shall act ' upon ' the recommendation of the Council, which means: after the Council has made a favourable or unfavourable recommendation.[7]

5 Report of the Rapporteur of Committee I/2 on Chapter 3 (U.N.C.I.O. Doc. 606, I/2/43, p. 2.).

6 Report of the Rapporteur of Committee I/2 on Chapter 3 (U.N.C.I.O. Doc. 1178, I/2/76 (2).).

7 At the 41st meeting of the Security Council the delegate of Australia said: ' It is clear from the Article [4] that the General Assembly is the body which admits the Member to the Organisation. We interpret this to mean that the General Assembly

Although it must be admitted that this interpretation is not excluded by the wording of the Article 4, paragraph 2, it is not very likely that it was the intention of those who drafted the Charter to

is the only body which, acting on behalf of the Organisation, can make the final and the binding decision on the subject of admission.' (Journal of the Security Council, 1st year, No. 34, p. 654.) In a statement of the delegation of Costa Rica, it is declared: 'Under the Charter, the Security Council was only authorised to consider and recommend; but not to pronounce a final judgment. . . . The Security Council merely expressed a preliminary opinion. . . . The Assembly could accept or disregard the Council's recommendation or disapprove of applicant states . . . ' (Journal of the United Nations, No. 35, Suppl. No. 1–A/C. 1/54, pp. 79 ff.) At the 6th meeting of the Ad Hoc Political Committee of the General Assembly (Doc. A/AC.24/SR. 6, pp. 10 ff.) the representative of Argentina stated: 'Article 4 of the Charter laid down that admission of states which accepted the requisite conditions would be effected by the recommendation of the Security Council followed by a decision of the General Assembly. Thus, if the decision rested with the General Assembly, the recommendation of the Security Council had no compulsory character for the Assembly. Nevertheless, the Security Council had hitherto accepted the practise that if its permanent members did not achieve unanimity, the application for admission under review was not transmitted to the General Assembly. By doing so, the Security Council was assuming powers which it did not possess, since the General Assembly alone could decide to admit states which had requested admission. The Security Council's view was not indicated by a legal interpretation of the Charter. . . . It was true that the Charter did not stipulate that the Security Council must give a "favourable" recommendation; it had simply to make some kind of recommendation before the General Assembly took its decision. . . . The only thing that the Council might not do was to prevent the General Assembly from making use of the powers which it possessed in virtue of Article 4 of the Charter.' At the 11th meeting of the Ad Hoc Committee (Doc. A/AC.24/SR. 11, p. 8 f.) the representative of Argentina stated that the word 'recommendation' in Article 4, paragraph 2, of the Charter did not mean only a 'favourable recommendation': 'In political or legal questions a recommendation could be positive or negative, favourable or unfavourable. . . . Article 4 of the Charter only referred to a recommendation, without qualifying it. The interpretation approved by the very persons who had drafted the law was that the recommendation of the Security Council could be favourable or unfavourable and that the General Assembly could accept or reject it, whichever it was.' He referred to the Second Report of the Rapporteur of Committee II/1 of the San Francisco Conference (U.N.C.I.O. Doc. 1092, II/1/39) which contained the following statement with respect to Article 4, paragraph 2: 'The Committee was advised that the new text did not, in the view of the Advisory Committee of Jurists, weaken the right of the Assembly to accept or reject a recommendation for the admission of a new member, or a recommendation to the effect that a given state should not be admitted to the United Nations. The Committee agreed that this interpretation should be included in its minutes as the one that should be given to this provision of the Charter, and on this basis approved the text as suggested by the Co-ordination Committee.'

The representative of Argentina proposed the following resolution:—

> Whereas the admission of new Members into the United Nations should be governed strictly by the terms of the Charter, which provides that the decision will be effected by the General Assembly upon the recommendation of the Security Council; and
>
> Whereas, irrespective of whether such recommendation is favourable or not, the application for membership should be considered by the Assembly so that it may adopt a suitable resolution;

assign to the Security Council such a subordinate role in a matter of political importance. It is probable that the intended meaning of Article 4, paragraph 2, is: that the admission of a new Member shall be effected by a favourable decision of the Security Council followed by a concurrent decision of the General Assembly.[8] It is regrettable that this intention was not expressed in this way. For the formula 'upon the recommendation of the Security Council'—used also in Articles 5, 6 and 97 of the Charter and in Article 4, paragraph 3 and Article 69 of the Statute of the International Court of Justice—is misleading. The function conferred upon the Security Council in the procedure for admission of new Members, and in all other procedures where the General Assembly is authorised to take a decision only 'upon recommendation of the Security Council,' is not to make a mere 'recommendation' to the Assembly. The term 'recommendation' in Article 4, paragraph 2, Articles 5, 6 and 97 of the Charter, Article 4 paragraph 3 and Article 69 of the Statute has not the same meaning as it has—or may be interpreted to have—in other Articles of the Charter, for instance in Articles 10, 11, 14, 36, 37, 38: a mere advice, without legal effect because not binding upon those to whom the 'recommendation' is directed. The 'recommendation' of the Security Council stipulated in Article 4, paragraph 2, is a decision which has the same legal effect as the decision of the General Assembly stipulated in that provision. In spite of the wording of Article 4, paragraph 2, according to which only the General Assembly seems to be authorised to decide upon the admission of new Members, the decision of the Security Council is equally necessary to bring about the 'admission' of a state to membership. This is the consequence of the provision that the General Assembly can effect admission of a state to membership only upon the so-called recommendation of the Security Council, which implies: not without such 'recommendation'; and this 'recommendation' must be favourable. If the Security Council

> Now therefore the General Assembly decides as follows:
>
> 1. Applications for membership shall be submitted to the consideration of the Assembly when the Security Council has reached its decision; and the Security Council's decision shall be deemed to be a recommendation in favour of admission if the application has received seven or more affirmative votes, even if one or more permanent members have cast a negative vote.
>
> 2. The General Assembly may both reject an application for admission with a favourable recommendation and grant an application with an unfavourable recommendation, always provided that such a decision is supported by a two-thirds majority of its Members present and voting. (Doc. A/AC. 24/15.)

The Committee did not vote on this proposal since it was withdrawn.

8 At the 42nd meeting of the Security Council the delegate of the Soviet Union declared 'that the decision to admit a new Member to the Organisation can only be taken if corresponding decisions are taken by the two most important organs of the Organisation; the Security Council and the General Assembly.' (Journal of the Security Council, 1st year, No. 35, p. 678.)

is not in favour of the admission of an applicant state, it need not make any recommendation at all. Then the General Assembly is not in a position to take a decision by which the applicant state is admitted to membership. The Assembly is not bound to accept the recommendation of the Council; it may refuse to admit a state to membership though recommended by the Council. But the Assembly can decide to admit a state only if it has been 'recommended.' Hence the affirmative decision of the Security Council, called recommendation, must precede the decision of the General Assembly, even if the application for admission to membership is addressed to the Assembly. It seems that this interpretation of Article 4, paragraph 2, is actually presupposed by the Rules of Procedures of the General Assembly and of the Security Council. Rule 123 of the Rules of Procedure of the General Assembly and Rule 58 of the Rules of Procedure of the Security Council provide that 'any state which desires to become a Member of the United Nations shall submit an application to the Secretary-General.' The next step is determined by the Rules of Procedure of the Security Council as follows:—

RULE 59

The Secretary-General shall immediately place the application for membership before the representatives on the Security Council. Unless the Security Council decides otherwise, the application shall be referred by the President to a committee of the Security Council upon which each member of the Security Council shall be represented. The committee shall examine any application referred to it and report its conclusions thereon to the Council not less than thirty-five days in advance of a regular session of the General Assembly or if a special session of the General Assembly is called, not less than fourteen days in advance of such session.

RULE 60

The Security Council shall decide whether in its judgment the applicant is a peace-loving state and is able and willing to carry out the obligations contained in the Charter, and accordingly whether to recommend the applicant state for membership.

If the Security Council recommends the applicant state for membership, it shall forward to the General Assembly the recommendation with a complete record of the discussion.

If the Security Council does not recommend the applicant state for membership or postpones the consideration of the application, it shall submit a special report to the General Assembly with a complete record of the discussion.

> In order to ensure the consideration of its recommendation at the next session of the General Assembly following the receipt of the application, the Security Council shall make its recommendation not less than twenty-five days in advance of a regular session of the General Assembly, nor less than four days in advance of a special session.
>
> In special circumstances, the Security Council may decide to make a recommendation to the General Assembly concerning an application for membership subsequent to the expiration of the time limits set forth in the preceding paragraph.

Rule 124 of the Rules of Procedure for the General Assembly provides:

> The Secretary General shall send for information a copy of the application to the General Assembly, or to the Members of the United Nations if the General Assembly is not in session.

A decision by which the applicant state is admitted to membership can be taken by the Assembly—according to Rule 125—only after the Council has recommended the applicant state for membership.[9] Rule 125 provides:

> If the Security Council recommends the applicant state for membership, the General Assembly shall consider whether the applicant is a peace-loving state and is able and willing to carry out the obligations contained in the Charter, and shall decide, by a two-thirds majority of the Members present and voting, upon its application for membership.

If the General Assembly is in favour of the admission of an applicant state, not recommended by the Security Council, or if the Security Council has postponed the consideration of the application, the General Assembly may request the Security Council to re-open its procedure in this case. Rule 126 of the Rules of Procedure of the General Assembly provides:

> If the Security Council does not recommend the applicant state for membership or postpones the consideration of the application, the General Assembly may, after full consideration of the special report of the Security Council, send back the application to the Security Council, together with a full record of the discussion in the Assembly, for further consideration and recommendation or report.

[9] The interpretation advocated by the representative of Australia in the 43rd plenary meeting of the General Assembly, 1st session (Journal of the United Nations, No. 19, p. 197) ' that the initiative in regard to the admission of new Members lies with the General Assembly and the appropriate procedure would be for applications to be transmitted first to the General Assembly, which would decide whether or not the applications were admissible ' has no basis in the wording of Article 4, paragraph 2.

The decision by which the General Assembly admits a state to membership in the United Nations requires—according to the express provision of Article 18, paragraph 2—a two-thirds majority of the members present and voting. The decision of the Security Council by which the admission of an applicant state is ' recommended ' to the General Assembly shall be made, in conformity with Article 27, paragraph 3, by an affirmative vote of seven members including the concurring votes of the permanent members. Since the decision does evidently not concern a procedural matter, the rule of unanimity of the permanent members applies. Hence no state can be admitted to membership against the will of one of the five great Powers.[1]

The applicability of the veto right of the permanent members of the Security Council to the admission of new members is not consistent with the provision that membership in the United Nations is ' open ' to all states which fulfil the conditions laid down in Article 4, paragraph 1. This provision expresses a certain tendency towards

[1] The Interim Committee of the General Assembly recommended that decisions of the Security Council on the admission of a state to membership in the United Nations ' should be adopted by the vote of any seven members of the Security Council ' whether this decision is considered procedural or non-procedural (Doc. A/578 pp. 4, 9). The report of the Interim Committee contains the following statements with respect to this recommendation: ' In the opinion of the representative of Australia, this decision is procedural. In the opinion of the representatives of Argentina, Greece and Iraq, the question of admission of new Members is within the specific powers of the General Assembly, and the recommendation of the Security Council is not therefore covered by a privileged voting procedure, which the Charter has clearly designed for questions within the specific jurisdiction of the Security Council ' (p. 9). The opinion of the representative of Australia has no basis in the Charter. The same holds of the opinion expressed by the representative of Argentina (cf. the Summary Records of 6th and 11th meetings of the *Ad Hoc* Committee of the General Assembly on November 22 and 24, 1948) that the unanimity rule was not applicable to recommendations of the Security Council under Article 4, paragraph 2. The representative stated: ' The Charter had established the rule of the unanimity of the five permanent members of the Security Council only in respect of decisions taken within the Council and only if such decisions had as their object the maintenance of international peace and security. In all other fields, the unanimity rule was not applicable, for it would be contrary to one of the basic principles of the Charter, namely, the sovereign equality of all Member States ' (Doc. A/AC.24/SR 6, p. 11). With reference to the above quoted statement in the Second Report of the Rapporteur of Committee II/1 of the San Francisco Conference (U.N.C.I.O. Doc. 1092, II/1/39) he maintained that the San Francisco Conference ' had laid down in the case of the admission of new Members that the recommendation of the Security Council, whether favourable or unfavourable, must be sent to the General Assembly for the latter to decide ' (Doc. A/AC.24/SR 11, p. 9). But he admitted that ' in the case of the election of the Secretary-General, the Conference of San Francisco had expressly decided that the rule of unanimity had to be applied.' Under Article 97, the Secretary General shall be appointed by the General Assembly ' upon the recommendation of the Security Council.' The function of the Security Council in this case is exactly the same as its function in the case of admission of new Members. Hence the interpretation of Article 27 that the unanimity rule applies only to ' decisions ' concerning the maintenance of international peace and security has neither a basis in the Charter nor in the San Francisco Conference. Cf. *infra*, pp. 239 ff.

universality of the Organisation. There is, however, still another fact which is quite incompatible with this idea: Admission to membership is left to the discretion of both the Security Council and the General Assembly. The conditions for admission are: 1. to accept the obligations contained in the Charter; 2. to be a peace-loving state; 3. to be able and willing to carry out the obligations contained in the Charter. The fulfilment of the first condition is objectively ascertainable. Rule 123 of the Rules of Procedure of the General Assembly and Rule 58 of the Rules of Procedure of the Security Council provide that the application of a state for membership 'shall contain a declaration, made in a formal instrument, that it accepts the obligations contained in the Charter.' This application containing the formal instrument implies the adherence of the applicant to the Charter; when accepted by the General Assembly's decision approving its application, the applicant state becomes a Member of the United Nations. Rule 127 of the Rules of Procedure of the General Assembly stipulates:

> The Secretary-General shall inform the applicant state of the decision of the General Assembly. If the application is approved, membership will become effective on the date on which the General Assembly takes its decision on the application.[2]

The fulfilment of the second and third condition is not objectively ascertainable. The answer to the questions as to whether a community applying for admission is a peace-loving state, whether it is able and willing to carry out the obligations contained in the Charter, depends on the discretion of the Security Council and of the General Assembly; for Article 4, paragraph 1, provides that a peace-loving state in order to be admitted to membership must be able and willing to carry out the obligations contained in the Charter: 'in the judgment of the Organisation.' In the procedure for the admission of new Members the Organisation is represented by the Security Council and the General Assembly. According to the wording of the provision 'the judgment of the Organisation,' *i.e.*, the judgment of the Security Council and the General Assembly, seems to refer only to the question as to whether the applicant state is able and willing to carry out the

[2] Originally the text of Rule 117 (then 116) provided that 'membership will become effective on the date on which the applicant presents to the Secretary-General an instrument of adherence.' Consequently, in the letter of the Secretary-General to the President of the General Assembly concerning membership of Afghanistan, Iceland and Sweden (Journal of the United Nations, No. 37: Suppl. A–A/P.V./48, p. 307) it is stated: 'On 19 November, 1946, representatives duly habilitated of Afghanistan, the Republic of Iceland and Sweden presented to me the instrument of adhesion to the United Nations. According to Article 116 of the Provisional Rules of Procedure of the General Assembly, Afghanistan, the Republic of Iceland and Sweden must therefore be considered as Members of the Organisation as from that date.'

obligations contained in the Charter. But since the applicant community must be a peace-loving state, this condition, too, is subject to the 'judgment of the Organisation.' Both Security Council and General Assembly have to decide upon the same questions, and may decide them in different ways. Rule 60 of the Rules of Procedure of the Security Council stipulates: 'The Security Council shall decide whether in its judgment the applicant is a peace-loving state and is able and willing to carry out the obligations contained in the Charter,[3] Rule 125 of the Rules of Procedure of the General Assembly contains an analogous provision with respect to the Assembly.[4] The requirement that the applicant must be a peace-loving state contains two conditions: 1. the community which asks for admission must be a 'state' and, 2. this state must be 'peace-loving.' That only 'states' can be Members of the United Nations is stipulated also by Article 3. In order to be admitted to the Organisation under Article 4, the community must be, in the judgment of the Organisation, a state. This point is of importance if the admission of a new state is at issue, which has not yet been recognised as such by all, or some, of the Members. The non-recognition by a Member of a community as a new state may manifest itself by the fact that no diplomatic relations exist between this Member of the United Nations and the applicant community. Since general international law does not institute an objective authority to decide whether a community is a state in the

[3] The Committee on the Admission of New Members, established by the Security Council, adopted the following two resolutions:—

> 1. The Committee will consider written statements of facts from any of the applicant states or from any Member of the United Nations bearing on the applications which the Committee has been instructed to examine.
>
> 2. The Committee considers that it has the right to ask information from governments of Member states on applicants bearing upon the applications before the Committee.

The Security Council confirmed the validity of these resolutions at its meeting of August 7, 1946. (Security Council, Official Records, 1st year, 2nd series, No. 3, p. 28; Suppl. No. 4, p. 55.)

[4] In a draft resolution submitted to Committee 1 by the Australian delegation (Doc. A/C.1/23/Rev.1) the following principles have been established:—

> (*a*) The admission of new Members is a corporate act.
>
> (*b*) The General Assembly has primary and final responsibility in the process of admission.
>
> (*c*) The Security Council, not having been given any general power covering all matters within the scope of the Charter, its recommendation for the admission of an applicant to membership should be based solely on the judgment of the Council that the applicant state is able and willing to carry out its obligations under those sections of the Charter which come within the competence of the Security Council.

Cf. also the statement of the delegate of Australia at the 41st meeting of the Security Council 'that the recommendation which the Security Council can make on the subject of admission of a new Member can only concern matters in relation to security.' (Journal of the Security Council, 1st year, No. 34, p. 654.)

sense of international law, it depends upon each member of the Security Council and of the General Assembly to answer this question according to its own discretion.[5]

As to the second condition of the requirement 'peace-loving state,' it must be noted that the term 'peace-loving' is very vague.[6] That all original Members are peace-loving is an assumption made by

[5] Poland refused to vote for the admission of the Hashemite Kingdom of Transjordan because Poland did not consider the latter 'a sovereign state' (Security Council, Official Records, 1st year, 2nd series; Suppl. No. 4, p. 136); the United States refused to vote for admission of the Mongolian People's Republic because 'the United States Government had yet to receive information which convinced it that the Mongolian People's Republic was in fact an independent state' (Security Council, Official Records, 2nd year, Special Suppl. No. 3, p. 11). The representative of Australia made the statement that states occupied by foreign troops (such as Austria, Hungary, Italy, Roumania, Bulgaria) 'could not be regarded as sovereign or independent' (Ibid., pp. 20, 52.) At a meeting on July 14, 1948, of the Security Council Committee on the Admission of New Members, the representative of the Soviet Union suggested that the Committee postpone consideration of the application of Ceylon pending receipt of information from the Ceylon Government establishing its position as a sovereign and independent state (Doc. S/C.2./S.R.26).

During the examination of the applications of Hungary, Italy, Austria, Roumania, and Bulgaria the question arose whether states which were legally at a state of war with Members of the United Nations are admissible for membership. The representative of the Soviet Union proposed to postpone consideration of these applications until the peace treaties with ex-enemy countries had entered into force and the treaty with Austria had been concluded and entered into force. The representative of the United States declared: 'It is not possible to find a single word in the Charter which imposes upon us the obligation to postpone consideration of membership applications from ex-enemy states until the completion of ratification and the entry into force of the peace treaties.' (Security Council, Official Records, 2nd year, Special Suppl. No. 3, pp. 18, 43.) The latter statement is correct. But it is doubtful whether the legal status of war in the relation of a state to Members of the United Nations is compatible with the obligations imposed and the rights conferred upon this state as a Member of the United Nations, especially in view of the provisions of Articles 107 and 53. The fact that these provisions—according to their wording—apply to ex-enemy states also after the coming into force of the peace treaties, makes it doubtful whether the admission of a state 'which during the Second World War has been an enemy of any signatory of the present Charter' is compatible with the spirit of the Charter at all; even after the legal state of war has been terminated. It is hardly possible to apply Articles 107 and 53 against Members of the United Nations. Cf. *infra*, pp. 805 ff.

[6] The Report of the Rapporteur of Committee I/2 (U.N.C.I.O. Doc. 1178, I/2/76 (2), p. 3) contains the following statement: 'The term "all peace-loving states," generally deemed insufficient, was retained, while the qualifications for membership were elaborated. To declare oneself "peace-loving" does not suffice to acquire membership in the Organisation. What nation has ever professed any other sentiments? It is also necessary to prove two things: that a nation is ready to accept and fulfil the obligations of the Charter and that it is able to accept and fulfil them.' The opinion that the term 'peace-loving' refers to the future, not to the past (advocated by the representative of Syria at the Committee on the Admission of New Members) (Security Council, Official Records, 2nd year, Special Suppl. No. 3, p. 2) has no basis in the Charter. During the discussion of the application of the Outer Mongolian People's Republic in the Security Council, the delegate of China declared that his Government was forced to conclude from certain coincidents that

the Charter in using in Article 4 the formula: all 'other' peace-loving states.

The discretion of the Security Council and the General Assembly in answering the question as to whether an applicant community is a peace-loving state and whether it is able and willing to carry out the obligations contained in the Charter implies the discretion of the members of these two organs, voting for or against the admission. Their discretion is not limited by the Charter. For the Charter does not establish an authority competent to ascertain whether the positive or negative decision of the General Assembly or of the Security Council or the vote of an individual member of these bodies, regarding the question as to whether an applicant state fulfils the conditions laid down in Article 4, was right or wrong. Article 4, paragraph 1, may be interpreted to determine these conditions in an exhaustive way. But an interpretation according to which the provision concerned constitutes only a minimum, that the General Assembly or the Security Council may refuse to admit a state to membership in spite of the fact that it admittedly fulfils the conditions laid down in Article 4, paragraph 1, is not excluded by the wording of this paragraph.[7] But even if this provision is interpreted to be exhaustive, the fact that a

the applicant was not a peace-loving state within the terms of the Charter (Doc. S/479, pp. 39–46).

[7] The Report of the Rapporteur of Committee I/2 of the San Francisco Conference (U.N.C.I.O. Doc. 1160, I/2/76 (1), p. 3) contains the following statement referring to Article 4: 'It was clearly stated that the admission of a new Member would be subject to study, but the Committee did not feel it should recommend the enumeration of the elements which were to be taken into consideration. It considered the difficulties which would arise in evaluating the political institutions of states and feared that the mention in the Charter of a study of such a nature, would be a breach of the principle of non-intervention, or if preferred, of non-interference. This does not imply, however, that in passing upon the admission of a new Member, considerations of all kinds cannot be brought into account.'

At the 15th meeting of the First Committee, the delegate of the Soviet Union, in interpreting Article 4, declared that 'the most important factor was the applicant's conduct during the second world war; . . . the determining element was the applicant's contribution to the cause of the United Nations in their fight against fascism and for freedom, independence and civilisation.' (Journal of the United Nations, No. 27; Suppl. No. 1–A/C.1/39, p. 25.) When, during a discussion in the Security Council Committee on the admission of new Members, the delegate of Poland suggested that the four criteria for membership were: 1. whether an applicant was peace-loving; 2. whether it accepted the obligations contained in the Charter; 3. whether it was able to carry out these obligations; and 4. whether it was willing to do so, the representative of the Soviet Union stated that there was a fifth condition: the attitude of an applicant state toward Nazi aggression in World War II. (Doc. S/C.2/S.R. 16, pp. 1 f.)

In the discussion of the applications for membership of Ireland and Portugal the delegate of the Soviet Union stated that his Government could not support these applications since these countries had no diplomatic relations with the Soviet Union. (Doc. S/177.) After the peace treaties with Hungary, Italy, Rumania, and Bulgaria had come into force, the Security Council reconsidered the applications of these states for membership. In addition, the Security Council had before it the applica-

decision of the General Assembly or the Security Council, or a vote of an individual member of these bodies is not in conformity with this provision has no legal effect. The Charter does not provide for a sanction in case an applicant state which fulfils the conditions laid down in Article 4, paragraph 1, is not admitted to membership, and especially not for a procedure by which a positive or negative decision of the General Assembly or the Security Council or the vote of a member of these bodies, can be annulled because of non-conformity with the Charter. Hence under Article 4, paragraph 1, neither the General Assembly nor the Security Council is legally bound to admit to membership a state which fulfils the conditions laid down in this provision, nor is there a legal obligation of the members of these bodies to vote for a proposal to admit such a state. Consequently no state has a legal right to be admitted to membership.[8] There exists even no legal remedy in case the Security Council or the General Assembly, or both, do not act at all in case of an application for membership.

The provision of Article 4, paragraph 1, is a typical example of an insufficient legal technique. If it was really intended to 'open' the United Nations to all states which fulfil certain conditions, and to prevent that states which do not fulfil these conditions are not admitted, if it was the intention to establish a legal right to be admitted to the Organisation, then it was not enough to formulate the conditions for admission; then it was necessary to guarantee that the provision of the Charter concerning admission to membership be respected by the organs concerned. Such guarantee could consist in conferring, in case of a negative decision of the Organisation upon the applicant state, and in case of a conflict between the General Assembly and the Security Council in a question of membership, upon both of them, the right of appeal to the International Court of Justice. If, however, it was

tion of Finland. During the discussion the delegate of the Soviet Union declared that his government was willing to vote for the admission of Italy, but only on condition that all the other states—Bulgaria, Roumania, Hungary and Finland—are admitted as well. (Doc. S/P.V. 204.) To vote against the admission of a state because of its unsatisfactory behaviour during World War II or because there are no diplomatic relations between this state and the Member concerned, or to make voting for the admission of a state dependent on the admission of other states is not contrary to the provisions of Article 4 if the conditions laid down in this Article are interpreted to be not exhaustive.

8 In a telegram dated October 12, 1948 (Doc. A/687) the Government of the Mongolian People's Republic stated with reference to the fact that its application for membership had not been accepted: 'The Mongolian People's Republic, as a democratic, peace-loving and sovereign state, which made its fullest possible contribution to the common cause of the United Nations in the past war, cannot accept the rejection of her application for membership in the United Nations. Developing on a democratic basis, consistently following out a policy of peace and collaboration with all peoples, and also adhering to the principles set forth in the United Nations Charter, the Mongolian People's Republic has every justification and right to be a Member of the United Nations.' This statement has no basis in the Charter.

considered as not desirable to place, in the question of admission of new members, the Assembly and the Council under the legal control of another organ, then no conditions for admission should have been laid down in the Charter and Article 4 restricted to the provision of its paragraph 2. To impose upon the members of the General Assembly and the Security Council a legal obligation to vote in conformity with the provision of the Charter, is, from a technical point of view highly problematical. Such obligation could be established only by providing for a procedure the purpose of which is to annul a vote because of its non-conformity with the Charter. But non-conformity with the Charter can be constituted only by the motives of the vote, and the motives are subject to control only if the voting is not secret and if the reasons of the vote are expressly announced by the voting member. Such control can easily be evaded by simply not announcing the reason for one's vote.[9]

[9] At its meeting on November 17, 1947, the General Assembly adopted five resolutions concerning the applications of Ireland, Portugal, Transjordan, Italy and Finland requesting the Security Council to reconsider these applications. Each of these resolutions contained the statement that the opposition to the above mentioned application was based on grounds not included in Article 4 of the Charter. This statement implied the opinion of the General Assembly that the enumeration of conditions in Article 4 was exhaustive. At the same meeting, the General Assembly adopted a resolution to the effect of requesting the International Court of Justice for an advisory opinion on the following question:—

> Is a Member of the United Nations which is called upon, in virtue of Article 4 of the Charter, to pronounce itself by its vote, either in the Security Council or in the General Assembly, on the admission of a state to membership in the United Nations, juridically entitled to make its consent to the admission dependent on conditions not expressly provided by paragraph 1 of the said Article? In particular, can such a Member, while it recognises the conditions set forth in that provision to be fulfilled by the state concerned, subject its affirmative vote to the additional condition that other states be admitted to membership in the United Nations together with that state? (Doc. A/471; A/P.V. 118.)

In its opinion the Court declared that the conditions stated in Article 4, paragraph 1, are exhaustive in character. Some dissenting judges, however, adopted the other interpretation that the conditions enumerated in Article 4, paragraph 1, are 'essential' but not necessarily 'sufficient'; from this interpretation they concluded that Members are legally bound not to admit a state which fails to possess the conditions required in Article 4, paragraph 1, but are not legally bound to admit the applicant state if the conditions are fulfilled, and that a Member does not act contrary to the Charter if it bases its vote on considerations foreign to the qualifications specified in Article 4, paragraph 1, especially if it makes its vote for admission of an applicant state dependent on conditions not expressly stipulated in Article 4, paragraph 1. They based this opinion on the fact that the General Assembly and the Security Council are 'political organs' and that, consequently, their members are entitled to base their votes upon 'political considerations.' Considerations 'foreign to the qualifications specified in paragraph 1 of Article 4' were supposed to be 'political.' From the fact that the General Assembly and the Security Council are 'political' organs does not follow that their members are entitled to base their votes upon considerations foreign to the conditions specified in Article 4, paragraph 1. But their function under Article 4 may be characterised as 'political'

When the Security Council, after examining the applications for membership submitted by Albania, Mongolia, Transjordan, Ireland and Portugal, did not make any recommendations, the General Assembly adopted in the 49th plenary meeting a resolution to the effect to

if their members are authorised by the Charter to base their votes not only on considerations expressly determined in Article 4, paragraph 1, but also on others, not expressly determined in the Charter. The function of an organ acting under national or international law has a ' political ' character if the law confers upon the organ a relatively great amount of discretion in the performance of the function. But it is ' political ' within the framework of the law, and hence at the same time ' legal.' In the dissenting opinion the decisive question was quite correctly formulated as the question whether the members of the General Assembly and the Security Council were ' legally entitled ' to base their votes on considerations foreign to the conditions specified in Article 4, paragraph 1; and this question must, in conformity with Article 96 of the Charter, be a ' legal ' question if the Court shall be competent to answer it by an advsiory opinion.

In another dissenting opinion a judge stated that a Member of the United Nations was entitled ' to declare during the discussion and before the vote that it takes into account in voting: 1. the legal criteria prescribed in paragraph 1 of said Article [4], and 2. political considerations consistent with the Purposes of the United Nations.' This distinction is hardly possible. The question is whether the Charter authorises the members of the General Assembly and the Security Council to make their votes dependent only on the conditions expressly stipulated in the Charter or also on other conditions. If this question is to be answered in the affirmative, these other conditions are as ' legal ' as those stipulated expressly in the Charter; and the latter are—at the same time—as ' political ' as the former. ' Legal ' and ' political ' are not qualities inherent in a fact and do not exclude one another. The ' legal ' quality of a fact consists in its relation to legal norms, the political quality in its relation to other principles. Both relations may exist simultaneously. For a legal instrument may delegate political norms, that is to say, other norms than those expressly formulated in this instrument. Then these norms are political and legal at the same time. The law may regulate ' political ' matters; especially international law, regulating relations among states, refers to ' political ' matters. Being regulated by international law (especially by treaties) these matters assume a legal character without loosing their political character. The constitution of a community may authorise an organ to decide a matter according to political principles. These principles, determining a concrete decision, assume the character of legal principles, because delegated by the law; and a question concerning the competence of the organ is a legal question.

The Court adopted, by nine votes to six, the following opinion: that

> a Member of the United Nations which is called upon, in virtue of Article 4 of the Charter, to pronounce itself by its vote, either in the Security Council or in the General Assembly, on the admission of a state to membership in the United Nations, is not juridically entitled to make its consent to the admission dependent on conditions not expressly provided by paragraph 1 of the said Article;
>
> and that in particular a Member of the Organisation cannot while it recognises the conditions set forth in that provision to be fulfilled by the state concerned, subject its affirmative vote to the additional condition that other states be admitted to membership in the United Nations together with that state.

If the statement that a Member of the United Nations is juridically not entitled to make its consent to the admission dependent on conditions not expressly provided by paragraph 1 of Article 4 means that the Member is obliged not to vote in this way,

recommend 'that the Security Council re-examine the applications for membership in the United Nations of the above-mentioned states on their respective merits as measured by the yardstick of the Charter, in accordance with Article 4.' Since by Article 10, the General Assembly is authorised to make recommendations to the Security Council on any matter within the scope of the Charter or relating to the powers and functions of any organs provided for in the Charter, the just quoted recommendation was certainly within the competence of the Assembly. But the Council was not bound to accept such a recommendation, for the Assembly is not an institution of appeal for the decisions of the Security Council.[1] Finally, the above quoted Rule 126 was adopted on November 21, 1947, by the General Assembly, and the Security Council, on December 9, 1947, inserted

the statement has no basis in the Charter even if the enumeration of the conditions for admission is interpreted to be exhaustive. If the statement 'a Member cannot . . . subject its affirmative vote to the additional condition, etc.' means that a Member is obliged not to subject its affirmative vote to an additional condition, this statement, too, has no basis in the Charter. There is no legally effective restriction on the voting of the members of the General Assembly or the Security Council. This becomes manifest by the fact that even if the General Assembly or the Security Council accepts the interpretation of the Court that the enumeration of the conditions in Article 4, paragraph 1, is exhaustive, neither a vote of a Member not in conformity with this interpretation, nor a decision of the General Assembly or the Security Council based on such votes, could be declared null and void.

Without any basis in the Charter is also the dissenting opinion of a judge who declared that a state which fulfils the conditions laid down in Article 4, paragraph 1, has a 'right' to membership. Cf. International Court of Justice. Reports of Judgements, Advisory Opinions and Orders: Admission of a state to Membership in the United Nations. (Article 4 of the Charter.) Advisory Opinion of May 28, 1948, pp. 57 ff.).

1 Cf. the discussion at the 81st meeting of the Security Council (Official Records, 1st year, 2nd series, No. 23, pp. 508 ff.)

At its 152nd meeting the Security Council decided to instruct the Committee on Admission of new Members to re-examine the applications for membership in the United Nations of Albania, Mongolia, Transjordan, Ireland, Portugal. (Official Records, 2nd year, Special Suppl. No. 3, p. 4.) In conformity with Article 10 of the Charter authorising the General Assembly to make recommendations 'relating to the powers and functions of any organs provided for in the present Charter' not only to the Security Council but also to the Members of the United Nations, the General Assembly adopted on November 17, 1947, the following resolution:—

> The General Assembly,
>
> Whereas pursuant to the provisions of Article 4, paragraph 2, of the Charter, admission to membership in the United Nations will be effected by a decision of the General Assembly upon the recommendation of the Security Council, and
>
> Whereas no new recommendation to the General Assembly by the Security Council with regard to admission has been made;
>
> Decides to recommend to the permanent members of the Security Council to consult with a view to reaching agreement on the admission to membership of the applicants which have not been recommended hitherto, and to submit their conclusions to the Security Council. (Doc. A/519, p. 18.)

in Rule 60 of its own Rules of Procedure the provisions which form now the paragraphs 2 and 3 of this Rule, quoted above.

In view of the fact that the admission of new Members depends on the discretion of both the Security Council and the General Assembly and that the unanimity rule applies to the procedure in the Security Council, it is hardly possible to maintain that the principle of universality is realised by the Charter.[2] In spite of the wording of Article 4, membership in the United Nations is not ' open ' to all peace-loving states. Membership would be ' open ' only if any state could become a Member of the United Nations by a unilateral declaration to the effect that it adheres to the Charter.

3. Compulsory Membership?

During the discussion of the question of membership at the San Francisco Conference some delegates suggested to base the Organisation on the principle of universality and to insert into the text of the Charter the provision that all states are automatically, *ipso facto*, Members of the Organisation without an express act of accession or admission being necessary. The Report of the Rapporteur of Committee I/2 on Chapter III (Membership) contains the following statement with reference to the position taken by the delegation of Uruguay and other delegations. ' Faithful to the principle of the universality of the Organisation it arrives at the conclusion that all communities should be Members of the Organisation and that their participation is obligatory, that is to say that it will not be left to the choice of *any nation* whether to become a Member of the Organisation or to withdraw from it; thus the question of expulsion will not be raised.—Other delegations believed that universality in this sense was an ideal toward which it was proper to aim, but which was not practicable to realise at once.'[3] The idea of compulsory membership of states not contracting parties to the Charter has not been accepted. It was certainly not in conformity with general international law as it existed at the moment the question has been discussed at the San Francisco Conference. However, Article 2, paragraph 6, of the Charter authorises the Organisation to ' ensure that states which are not Members of the United Nations act in accordance with the Principles laid down in the Charter so far as may be necessary for the maintenance of international peace and security.' Principle 2 prescribes fulfilment of all obligations imposed upon the Members. Hence, the provision of Article 2,

2 At the 53rd meeting of the Security Council the Secretary-General stated: ' the founding Members of the United Nations and all the Great Powers which form part of our Organisation have agreed, on numerous occasions, that the United Nations must be as universal as possible.' (Official Records, 1st year, 2nd series, No. 4, p. 44.)

3 Report of the Rapporteur of Committee I/2 of the San Francisco Conference (U.N.C.I.O. Doc. 1178, 1/2/76 (2), pp. 2–3). Cf. also the Verbatim Minutes of the Third Meeting of Commission I (U.N.C.I.O. Doc. 1167, I/10, p. 7).

paragraph 6, may be interpreted to mean that the Charter imposes at least the most important obligations of the Members also upon non-members, and that means that the Charter claims to have the character of general international law. It remains to be seen whether this claim will obtain general recognition. If so, the idea of compulsory membership has not entirely been rejected.

4. Membership and Form of Government

It is significant that among the conditions of membership—be it original or subsequent—there is no reference to the form of government. The Charter does not require a democratic form of government as a condition of being or becoming a Member of the Organisation,[4] nor does it allow intervention of the Organisation for the purpose of promoting a democratic form of government in a state where another form of government is established or about to be established, as long as the form of government is considered to be a matter which is within the domestic jurisdiction of the state. Article 2, paragraph 7, expressly prohibits such intervention, except in case the situation implies, in the opinion of the Security Council, a threat to the peace, breach of the peace, or act of aggression (Article 39). Then intervention through the enforcement measures provided for in Chapter VII, even against a non-member state, is permitted.

On the motion of the Mexican delegation, Commission I of the San Francisco Conference decided to insert in the records of the Commission the following statement: 'It is the understanding of the Delegation of Mexico that Par. 2 of Chapter III [Article 4 of the Charter] cannot be applied to the states whose regimes have been established with the help of military forces belonging to the countries which have waged war against the United Nations, as long as those regimes are in power.'[5] This statement is directed against the

[4] Report of the Rapporteur of Committee I/2 of the San Francisco Conference contains the following statement: 'two principal tendencies were manifested in the discussions. On the one hand, there were some who declared themselves in favour of inserting in the Charter specific conditions which new Members should be required to fulfil especially in matters concerning the character and policies of governments. On the other hand, others maintained that the Charter should not needlessly limit the Organisation in its decisions concerning requests for admission . . . It was clearly stated that the admission of a new Member would be subject to study, but the Committee did not feel it should recommend the enumeration of the elements which were to be taken into consideration. It considered the difficulties which would arise in evaluating the political institutions of states and feared that the mention in the Charter of a study of such a nature would be a breach of the principle of non-intervention, or if preferred, of non-interference. This does not imply, however, that in passing upon the admission of a new Member, considerations of all kinds cannot be brought into account.' (U.N.C.I.O. Doc. 1074, I/2/76, p. 3.)

[5] Verbatim Minutes of 3rd meeting of Commission I (U.N.C.I.O. Doc. 1167, I/10, pp. 20–29).

admission of Spain under the Franco regime. It has political, not legal, importance. But as its 26th meeting, the General Assembly adopted the following resolution:

> 1. The General Assembly recalls that the San Francisco Conference adopted a resolution according to which paragraph 2 of Article 4 of Chapter II of the United Nations Charter 'cannot apply to states whose regimes have been installed with the help of armed forces of countries which have fought against the United Nations so long as these regimes are in power.'
>
> 2. The General Assembly recalls that at the Potsdam Conference the Governments of the United Kingdom, the United States of America and the Soviet Union stated that they would not support a request for admission to the United Nations of the present Spanish Government 'which, having been founded with the support of the Axis powers, in view of its origins, its nature, its record and its close association with the aggressor states, does not possess the necessary qualifications to justify its admission.'
>
> 3. The General Assembly, in endorsing these two statements, recommends that the Members of the United Nations should act in accordance with the letter and spirit of these statements in the conduct of their future relations with Spain.[6]

At its 59th meeting the General Assembly adopted a resolution[7] in which it recommended 'that the Franco Government of Spain be debarred from membership in international agencies established by or brought into relationship with the United Nations, and from participation in conferences or other activities which may be arranged by the United Nations or by these agencies, until a new and acceptable government is formed in Spain; . . . that if, within a reasonable time, there is not established a government which derives its authority from the consent of the governed, committed to respect freedom of speech, religion and assembly and to the prompt holding of an election in which the Spanish people, free from force and intimidation and regardless of party, may express their will, the Security Council consider the adequate measures to be taken in order to remedy the situation; that all Members of the United Nations immediately recall from Madrid their Ambassadors and Ministers plenipotentiary accredited there; . . . that the states Members of the Organisation report to the Secretary-General and to the next session of the Assembly what action they have taken in accordance with this recommendation.' These recommendations are justified in the preamble of the resolution as follows—

> The General Assembly recalls that, in May and June, 1946, the

6 Resolutions adopted by the General Assembly, Doc. A/64, p. 39.

7 Resolutions adopted by the General Assembly, Doc. A/64/add. 1, pp. 63 ff.

Security Council conducted an investigation of the possible further action to be taken by the United Nations. The Subcommittee of the Security Council charged with the investigation found unanimously:

'(*a*) In origin, nature, structure and general conduct, the Franco regime is a fascist regime patterned on, and established largely as a result of aid received from, Hitler's Nazi Germany and Mussolini's Fascist Italy.

'(*b*) During the long struggle of the United Nations against Hitler and Mussolini, Franco, despite continued Allied protests, gave very substantial aid to the enemy Powers. First, for example, from 1941 to 1945, the Blue Infantry Division, the Spanish Legion of Volunteers and the Salvador Air Squadron fought against Soviet Russia on the Eastern front. Second, in the summer of 1940, Spain seized Tangier in breach of international statute, and as a result of Spain maintaining a large army in Spanish Morocco large numbers of Allied troops were immobilised in North Africa.

'(*c*) Incontrovertible documentary evidence establishes that Franco was a guilty party with Hitler and Mussolini in the conspiracy to wage war against those countries which eventually in the course of the world war became banded together as the United Nations. It was part of the conspiracy that Franco's full belligerency should be postponed until a time to be mutually agreed upon.

The General Assembly, Convinced that the Franco Fascist Government of Spain, which was imposed by force upon the Spanish people with the aid of the Axis Powers and which gave material assistance to the Axis Powers in the war, does not represent the Spanish people, and by its continued control of Spain is making impossible the participation of the Spanish people with the peoples of the United Nations in international affairs; . . .

5. Re-entering the Organisation

Since the Charter provides for expulsion from the Organisation and—according to an interpretation adopted by Commission I of the San Francisco Conference—voluntary withdrawal from the Organisation is possible, the case may occur that a state, which for one or another reason has ceased to be a Member of the United Nations, wishes to re-enter the Organisation. The only provision applicable to this case is Article 4. It refers only to states which have not participated in the San Francisco Conference or have not signed the Declaration by United Nations of January 1, 1942. This is the consequence of the wording of paragraph 1: Membership 'is open to all *other* peace-loving states,' and of paragraph 2: 'the admission of any *such* state . . .' By this wording the states mentioned in Article 3 are excluded.[8] According to the wording of Articles 3 and 4 only states which were not original Members can re-enter the Organisation after having been expelled or having withdrawn. This is certainly the unintentional effect of a technical insufficiency in the text of the Charter. One of the arguments by which the provision concerning expulsion has been justified in the discussion of Committee I/2 of the San Francisco Conference was that expulsion 'could not be an obstacle to subsequent re-admittance if this were justified by circumstances.'[9] This argument fails with respect to the fifty-one original Members of the Organisation. In this point the text of the Charter is no better formulated than that of the Covenant whose Article 1, paragraph 2, made re-admittance of states named in the Annex to the Covenant legally impossible.[1]

6. Admittance of Non-Recognised States

The question may arise whether a community which claims to be a state but is not recognised as such by all the Members of the United Nations can be admitted in conformity with Article 4. The question may be answered in the affirmative since it is possible to interpret Article 4 to mean that the decision by which the General Assembly upon recommendation of the Security Council admits a community to membership in the Organisation implies the recognition of this community as a state and that by ratifying the Charter or adhering to it in joining the Organisation, a state transfers this competence to recognise a community as a state upon the Organisation.[2]

7. Membership in the Judicial Community of the United Nations under Article 93 of the Charter

In conformity with Article 92 of the Charter it is necessary to distinguish between the Charter in a narrower and the Charter in a wider sense comprising the Statute of the International Court of Justice as an 'integral part of the present Charter.' Consequently, it is necessary to distinguish also between the Organisation constituted by the Charter in the narrower sense and the Organisation constituted by the Charter in a wider sense of the term. The Organisation in the wider sense of the term, that is to say, the total community, is composed

8 At its 15th meeting Committee 1 of Commission II of the San Francisco Conference approved the following text which would have avoided the undesirable consequences mentioned above: 'The admission of any state to membership in the United Nations will be effected by a decision of the General Assembly upon the recommendation of the Security Council.' (U.N.C.I.O. Doc. 1094, II/1/40.)

9 Cf. *infra*, pp. 710 ff.

1 Since the Annex to the Covenant of the League of Nations contains the names of the states which had signed the Covenant (Part I of the Peace Treaty) the United States which had signed but not ratified the Covenant could not have entered the League in accordance with the provisions of the Covenant.

2 The same interpretation of Article 1, paragraph 2, of the Covenant was possible.

of two partial communites: the one is formed by states which are contracting parties to the Charter, that is to say, by the states which have ratified the Charter under Article 3 or have adhered to the Charter by being admitted under Article 4; these are the states which, according to Article 9, are represented in the General Assembly. This community is called the 'United Nations,' the term used in a narrower sense. For only the members of this community are called in Article 93 'Members of the United Nations.' The other partial community is formed by the states which are parties to the Statute constituting a judicial community whose organ is the International Court of Justice. According to Article 93 the members of this community may—but not necessarily need—be 'Members of the United Nations.' The Charter comprising the Statute of the International Court of Justice is called 'Charter of the United Nations,' and the Preamble declares that by this Charter 'an international Organisation to be known as the United Nations' is established. That means that the total community, too, is called 'United Nations.'

That the Charter, in distinguishing between parties to the Charter and parties to the Statute, calls only the former 'Members of the United Nations' is not quite correct. The statement that physical or juristic persons are 'members' of an organisation or community is a figurative expression. Its meaning is that these persons are subjected to the legal order which constitutes the organisation or community by regulating the mutual behaviour of these persons. If the legal order has the character of a treaty, the persons whose behaviour is regulated by it are—as a rule—the states which are contracting parties to the treaty. Since the Statute according to Article 92 forms an integral part of the Charter (in the wider sense of the term), all the states parties to the Statute are 'Members' of the United Nations, this term used in a wider sense designating the total community comprising the judicial community whose organ is the Court.

As pointed out, there are states which are members of the judicial community and consequently Members of the Organisation in the wider sense of the term without being Members of the Organisation (the 'United Nations') in the narrower sense of the term and states which are Members of both the 'United Nations' (in the narrower sense) and the judicial community. But there are no states which are only Members of the 'United Nations' in the narrower sense of the term and not at the same time members of the judicial community, for Article 93 stipulates:—

> 1. All Members of the United Nations are *ipso facto* parties to the Statute of the International Court of Justice.
>
> 2. A state which is not a Member of the United Nations may become a party to the Statute of the International Court of Justice on conditions to be determined in each case by the General Assembly upon the recommendation of the Security Council.

This Article constitutes a striking difference between the Charter and the Covenant. Membership in the League of Nations was not necessarily combined with membership in the judicial community constituted by the Statute of the Permanent Court of International Justice, which Statute did not form an integral part of the Covenant but was a treaty different from it. The Statute was an Annex to the Protocol of Signatures of the Statute of the Permanent Court of International Justice of December 16, 1920. Not all the Members of the League were parties to the Statute of the Permanent Court of International Justice, that is to say, of the Protocol of December 16, 1920. Some Members did not ratify this Protocol, thus, for instance, Argentina, Mexico, the Soviet Union. The Protocol was ' open for signature ' not only to Members of the League but also to states which were not Members of the League, but mentioned in the Annex to the Covenant. But not all these states ratified the Protocol, thus for instance the United States. Consequently not all the Members of the League were necessarily members of the judicial community constituted by the Statute of the Permanent Court of International Justice; but the judicial community constituted by the Statute of the International Court of Justice necessarily comprises all the Members of the ' United Nations ' (this term taken in its narrower sense) and as a possibility other states, which are parties to the Statute without being parties to the Charter in the narrower sense of the term. Membership in the judicial community and hence in the wider organisation is possible without membership in the narrower organisation, called the ' United Nations.'

The provision of Article 93, paragraph 1, that ' all Members of the United Nations are *ipso facto* parties to the Statute of the International Court of Justice ' is superfluous since this is the necessary consequence of the provision of Article 92 that the Statute ' forms an integral part of the present Charter.' What is necessary is to determine the conditions by which a state not a Member of the ' United Nations ' (in the narrower sense) is admitted to membership in the judicial community and hence in the wider organisation. Paragraph 2 of Article 93 does not contain such provision, but delegates the General Assembly, upon the recommendation of the Security Council, to determine ' in each case ' the conditions on which a state not a Member of the United Nations may adhere, that is ' become a party ' to that part of the Charter which is the Statute of the Court. The conditions by which a state may become a (subsequent) ' Member of the United Nations ' are determined in Article 4 of the Charter. They are different from the conditions by which a state, not a ' Member of the United Nations,' may become a member of the judicial community of the United Nations (in the wider sense of this term). The former are directly determined by the Charter; the determination of the latter is left to the Security Council and the General Assembly.

The conditions, determined by the General Assembly, on which Switzerland was admitted as a party to the Statute shall be discussed later.[3]

8. Membership in the Judicial Community of the United Nations under Article 35 of the Statute

The essential effect of the membership in the judicial community is that the Court is open to the members. For the members are not obliged to submit their disputes to the Court. They are merely authorised to do so. Only in case the state has submitted a dispute to the Court is it obliged to comply with the Court's decisions.

If the main contents of membership in the judicial community of the United Nations Organisation is to have access to the Court, there is still another way to become a member of this community than that determined in Article 93, paragraph 2, of the Charter. Article 35 of the Statute stipulates:—

> 1. The Court shall be open to the states parties to the present Statute.
>
> 2. The conditions under which the Court shall be open to other states shall, subject to the special provisions contained in treaties in force, be laid down by the Security Council, but in no case shall such conditions place the parties in a position of inequality before the Court.
>
> 3. When a state which is not a Member of the United Nations is a party to a case, the Court shall fix the amount which that party is to contribute towards the expenses of the Court. This provision shall not apply if such state is bearing a share of the expenses of the Court.

Paragraph 2 of this Article delegates the Security Council to lay down the conditions under which states which are neither Members of the United Nations (in the narrower sense of the term) nor parties to the Statute (without being Members of the 'United Nations') may obtain access to the Court, *i.e.*, may be authorised to submit their disputes to the Court. At its 76th meeting on October 15, 1946, the Security Council adopted a resolution concerning the conditions under which the Court shall be open to states which are not parties to the Statute. These conditions shall be analysed in another connection.[4] Whereas under Article 93, paragraph 2, of the Charter a state which is not a Member of the 'United Nations' can become only a permanent member of the judicial community, under Article 35, paragraph 2, a state can become either a permanent or a temporary member of the judicial community. In conformity with Article 35, paragraph 2, the

[3] Cf. *infra*, pp. 489 ff.
[4] Cf. *infra*, pp. 491 ff.

Security Council may determine the conditions under which the Court in a general way or only for a special case shall be open to a state not 'party to the Statute.' If the state is in a general way and under the same conditions as the 'parties to the Statute' permitted to submit its disputes to the Court, it is a permanent member of the judicial community. If the state is permitted only to submit one special case to the Court, it becomes a temporary member of the judicial community.

It follows that members of the United Nations in the wider sense of the term comprising also the judicial community whose organ is the Court are not only the so-called 'Members of the United Nations' but also the states which, without being 'Members of the United Nations,' are 'parties to the Statute' in the sense of Article 93, paragraph 2, of the Charter, and the states to which, without being parties to the Statute in the sense of Article 93, paragraph 2, the 'Court is open' under Article 35, paragraph 2, of the Statute.

9. Temporary Membership in the United Nations under Articles 32 and 70 and Indirect Membership under Article 52 of the Charter

There is also a kind of temporary membership with respect to the settlement of disputes under consideration by the Security Council. Under Article 32 'any state which is not a Member of the United Nations, if it is a party to a dispute under consideration by the Security Council, shall be invited to participate, without vote, in the discussion relating to the dispute. The Security Council shall lay down such conditions as it deems just for the participation of a state which is not a Member of the United Nations.' If the dispute is brought before the Security Council by the non-member state, party to the dispute, the latter must accept, according to Article 35, paragraph 2, of the Charter, 'in advance, for the purposes of the dispute, the obligations of pacific settlement provided in the present Charter.' But also in case the dispute comes before the Security Council in another way, the Council can hardly lay down other conditions than those stipulated in Article 35, paragraph 2, namely: to accept the obligations of pacific settlement.

The provision of Article 32 is modelled after Article 17, paragraph 1, of the Covenant of the League of Nations which provided that:

> In the event of a dispute between a Member of the League and a state which is not a member of the League, or between states not members of the League, the state or states not members of the League shall be invited to accept the obligations of membership in the League for the purposes of such dispute, upon such conditions as the Council may deem just.

Under this provision the non-member state was to be invited to accept 'the obligations of membership,' but none of the rights of membership was to be conferred upon the state which accepted the obligations. Article 32 of the Charter constitutes a remarkable improvement by providing that the non-member state, after having accepted the conditions laid down by the Security Council, shall be invited to participate in the discussion relating to the dispute. When invited, the non-member state becomes a temporary member of the Security Council and, as member of the Security Council, a member of the United Nations. But the state becomes only a temporary member and its obligations and rights of membership are restricted. It has only the obligations as laid down by the Security Council, and only the right to participate in the discussion of the dispute 'without vote.' The words 'without vote' were not contained in the corresponding provision of the Dumbarton Oaks Proposals (Chapter VI, Section D, paragraph 5.) They have been added at the San Francisco Conference.[5] Other aspects of Article 32 shall be discussed in connection with the organisation and procedure of the Security Council.[6]

A provision similar to Article 32 is Article 70 which runs as follows:—

> The Economic and Social Council may make arrangements for representatives of the specialised agencies to participate, without vote, in its deliberations and in those of the commissions established by it, and for its representatives to participate in the deliberations of the specialised agencies.

The agreements by which the specialised agencies have been brought into relationship with the United Nations (Article 57 of the Charter) contain provisions concerning representation of these agencies in the Economic and Social Council. The specialised agencies are international communities. Under Article 70 of the Charter these international communities may become members of the United Nations with restricted rights determined in this Article, and for the period of time the agreements are in force by which the specialised agencies are authorised to be represented in the Economic and Social Council of the United Nations.

Rule 13 of the Rules of Procedure for the Trusteeship Council provides:—

> Representatives of specialised agencies shall be invited to attend meetings of the Trusteeship Council and to participate, without vote, in its deliberations in the circumstances indicated in the respective agreements between the United Nations and the specialised agencies.

The constitutionality of this Rule is doubtful. Article 91 of the Charter authorises the Trusteeship Council only to 'avail itself of the assistance' of the specialised agencies in regard to matters with which

[5] U.N.C.I.O. Doc. 2, G/29, pp. 3 f.

[6] Cf. *infra*, pp. 222 ff.

they are concerned. The Charter does not empower the Trusteeship Council—as it empowers the Economic and Social Council in Article 70—to make arrangements 'for representatives of the specialised agencies to participate, without vote, in its deliberations, etc.'

Article 52 of the Charter authorises the Members of the United Nations to enter into regional arrangements and to establish regional agencies. These regional arrangements and regional agencies may—according to Article 53—even be utilised by the Security Council for enforcement action to be carried out by the regional organisation under the authority of the Security Council. The wording of Articles 52 and 53 does not exclude that Members may conclude regional arrangements with non-members.[7] If this interpretation is accepted, and a regional organisation, established in conformity with Chapter VIII, is considered to be an organ of the United Nations, then a non-member state party to a regional arrangement is, in its capacity as a member of a regional organisation, indirectly a Member of the United Nations. Its rights and duties are determined by the regional arrangement.

The result of the foregoing analysis is that it is necessary to distinguish membership in the United Nations in the narrower sense of the term, that is the sense in which the term is used in the Charter, implying representation in the General Assembly, from membership in a wider sense of the term, including also the relations in which states which are not Members in the narrower sense, stand to the Organisation under Articles 32, 52, 70, 93, paragraph 2, of the Charter and Article 35, paragraph 2, of the Statute of the Court.

10. The Relations of Non-members to the Organisation

Membership in a legal community means to be the subject of specific obligations and rights established by the legal order constituting the community. It is usual to lay stress upon the rights and to ignore the obligations when the concept of membership is defined. This is incorrect since the primary function of a legal order is to establish obligations. Rights are secondary phenomena. No right of a subject is possible without another subject's obligation. If membership in the United Nations is examined with respect to the obligations established by the Charter, it must be taken into consideration that there hardly exists any essential difference between Members and non-members; provided that Article 2, paragraph 6, is interpreted to mean that all the obligations imposed upon the Members for the purpose

[7] For instance, the League of Arab States which is considered to be a regional organisation within the meaning of Article 52 of the Charter. Transjordan, not a Member of the United Nations, is a member of this League. Cf. U.N.C.I.O. Doc. 72, III/4/1, and the statements of the representative of Syria in the Security Council, Official Records, 3rd year, No. 70, p. 20, No. 71, p. 13. The North Atlantic Treaty signed in Washington on April 4, 1949, is a regional arrangement to which two non-members, Italy and Portugal, are contracting parties.

of maintaining international peace and security—and almost all the obligations of the Members may be considered to be necessary for the maintenance of international peace and security—are also imposed upon the states which are not Members of the United Nations. Even the obligation of Member states established by Article 48 to carry out enforcement measures decided upon by the Security Council might be considered to be imposed by Article 2, paragraph 6, upon non-members. Enforcement measures are to be taken, according to Article 39, to maintain or restore international peace and security, and Article 50 presupposes the possibility of non-member states carrying out enforcement measures taken by the Security Council. There are also rights conferred upon non-members by the Charter. The one established by Article 32 and Article 35, paragraph 2, has already been discussed. Another important right established by the Charter is the one stipulated by Article 2, paragraph 7: the right to be exempt from any intervention on the part of the United Nations ' in matters which are essentially within the domestic jurisdiction.' This right is conferred upon ' any state,' not only upon Members. Under Article 50 of the Charter any state, ' whether a Member of the United Nations or not,' has the right to consult the Security Council with regard to the solution of special economic problems arising from the carrying out of preventive or enforcement measures taken by the Security Council. Finally, according to Article 81, a state which is not a Member of the United Nations may become an administering authority of a territory placed under the trusteeship system of the United Nations.

CHAPTER 5

THE OBLIGATIONS OF THE MEMBERS AND NON-MEMBERS

1. THE OBLIGATION TO FULFIL ALL OBLIGATIONS (ARTICLE 2, PARAGRAPH 2)

THE fundamental obligations of the Members are presented in Article 2 as 'Principles.' The introduction to this Article provides: 'The Organisation and its Members, in pursuit of the Purposes stated in Article 1, shall act in accordance with the following Principles.' According to this wording, all principles stipulated in paragraphs 1 to 7 constitute obligations of the Organisation as well as of the Members. But only paragraphs 2 to 5 stipulate obligations of Members.[1] Paragraph 1: 'The Organisation is based on the principle of the sovereign equality of all its Members,' is a theoretical statement about the basic idea of the Organisation; a statement which in view of the actual provisions of the Charter is rather problematical. If it is supposed to have any legal effect at all, it constitutes an obligation of the Organisation to respect the sovereign equality of the Members and, hence, a right, not an obligation, of the Members. Paragraph 6 confers a competence upon the Organisation in relation to non-members. Paragraph 7 imposes a restriction upon the competence of the Organisation, implying a right, not an obligation, of the Members.

According to the wording of the introduction to Article 2 the Organisation and its Members shall act not only in accordance with the Principles laid down in paragraphs 1 to 7, but also 'in pursuit of the Purposes stated in Article 1.'[2] But—as pointed out—the Purposes of the United Nations are formulated in Article 1 not in complete conformity with the Principles laid down in Article 2.

The first provision of Article 2 imposing an obligation upon the Members is paragraph 2, which runs as follows:—

All Members, in order to ensure to all of them the rights

[1] At the 8th meeting of Committee I/1 (U.N.C.I.O. Doc. 423, I/1/20) it was pointed out that paragraphs 2 to 6 of Article 2 'did not contain statements of principles but were statements of obligations to be assumed by the Members.' It was suggested that these paragraphs might be grouped separately so that certain Articles would deal exclusively with principles and rules of conduct while others would deal with obligations.

[2] The Report of Rapporteur of Committee I/1 (U.N.C.I.O. Doc. 944, I/1/34 (1), p. 11) contains the following statement referring to the introduction to Article 2: '(1) "In pursuit" does not indicate, as was made clear in the Committee, any purely idealistic approach. It definitely indicates the resolve of the Organisation and its members to give practical and effective application to both purposes and principles. (2) The keynote of collectivity is common to what precedes and follows this phrase, the text clearly indicating, "The Organisation and its Members."'

> and benefits resulting from membership, shall fulfil in good faith the obligations assumed by them in accordance with the present Charter.

This paragraph contains nothing but a superfluous, tautological statement that the Members are obligated to fulfil their obligations.[3] It presupposes as self-evident which are the obligations of the Members. The Charter, however, makes it difficult to answer this question, since it furnishes two different criteria, which are not consistent with each other. The one is that a certain conduct of the Members is characterised in the Charter by terms expressing the idea of obligation, such as: 'The Members shall,' 'the Members agree,' etc. The other is that a conduct is connected in the Charter with a measure which has the character of a sanction. Then, the opposite conduct is the contents of an obligation. However, there are provisions in the Charter of which it is doubtful whether they intend to impose an obligation on the Members. On the other hand, the Charter provides certain enforcement measures whose character as sanctions is problematical, and attaches these measures to a conduct of Members the opposite of which is not characterised by the Charter as obligatory.[4] Consequently, in some instances contradictory answers are possible to the question as to whether the Charter establishes a true obligation of the Members. An affirmative answer is certain only when both criteria are present: the conduct of a Member prescribed in terms expressing the idea of obligation, and a sanction, *i.e.*, enforcement action to be taken by the Organisation in case of contrary conduct.

The phrase of Article 2, paragraph 2, 'in order to ensure to all of them the rights and benefits resulting from membership' is a superfluous justification of the self-evident fact that obligations must be fulfilled in order that the corresponding rights may be ensured. The

[3] The Report above mentioned contains the following statement: 'To some members of the Committee, paragraph 2, seemed superfluous at first, but after consideration, that opinion was foresaken even by those who first held it. Why did we keep it, and why did we give it the new tenor in which it is presented to you? Paragraph 2 was kept to emphasise that rights and privileges in this Charter match with duties and obligations. That emphasis was deemed necessary in view of past experience, where states, especially in the period between the two wars, had come to place more emphasis on their rights than on their duties, and the practice had developed of subscribing blithely to certain obligations and then forgetting them in a moment of international crisis, or under the urge of a state's own interests. Furthermore, the Dumbarton Oaks Proposals became familiar to people, and if that paragraph should be cut out, some might be found in the future to affirm that the change had been made for sinister motives. But there is still a more important reason for keeping such a text as paragraph 2. The paragraph does not merely mean that one member which fulfils its duties and obligations may exercise certain privileges and rights, but it means also that if all members of the Organisation fulfil their obligations, all members receive the benefit. Thus, the non-fulfilment of the duties and obligations by one state deprives not only that state, but all the others, of some of the benefits. So much for the reasons for retaining this paragraph' (pp. 12–13).

[4] Cf. *infra*, pp. 706 ff.

phrase is incorrect in so far as the rights (this term taken in the broader sense including ' benefits ') resulting from membership of one state do not correspond to the obligations of the others, but rather to the obligations of the respective organs of the Organisation. Thus, in the first place, the main rights of all Members to participate in the discussion and voting in the General Assembly, and to be elected members of the Security Council and other organs of the United Nations; the privileges of the five great powers to be permanent members of the Security Council, their veto right under Article 27, paragraph 3, Articles 108, 109, paragraph 2; then the right (or benefit), stipulated in Article 31, of the Members which are not members of the Security Council to participate in the discussion of any question brought before the Security Council whenever the latter considers that the interest of the Member is especially affected; or the right stipulated in Article 32 to participate in the discussion relating to a dispute to which the Member is a party; or the right stipulated in Article 35 to bring any dispute to the attention of the Security Council; or the right of a Member not represented on the Security Council to be invited to participate in the decisions of the Council concerning the employment of contingents of that Member's armed forces, stipulated in Article 44; or the right of a Member which finds itself confronted with special economic problems arising from the carrying out of preventive or enforcement measures taken by the Security Council, to consult the Council according to Article 50; or the right of a Member to be invited to participate in the deliberations of the Economic and Social Council on any matter of particular concern to this Member according to Article 69; or the right of states which have become Members of the United Nations that their territories shall not be placed under the trusteeship system stipulated in Article 78; or the right of a Member, party to a case decided by a judgment of the International Court of Justice, to have recourse to the Security Council in case the other party fails to perform the obligations incumbent upon it under the judgment; and, last but not least, the ' inherent right of self defence ' referred to in Article 51, which is equivalent to the obligations of the Organisation to consider an act of self defence not as a violation of the obligation to refrain from the threat or use of force, or as a threat to the peace, breach of the peace, or act of aggression.

The words ' in good faith ' in Article 2, paragraph 2, too, are superfluous for it is impossible to ' fulfil ' an obligation in bad faith.[5]

[5] The words ' in good faith ' which are not used in the corresponding provision of the Dumbarton Oaks Proposals (Chapter II, paragraph 2) have been added on a motion of the delegation of Colombia. The intention was to insert a moral element into the text of the Charter. Cf. the discussion at the second meeting of Committee I (U.N.C.I.O. Doc. 1123, I/8). In this discussion the delegate of Panama stated that it is customary to use the phrase ' in good faith ' when reference is made to the observance of treaties. This is true. But it does not prove that the phrase implies a legally relevant meaning.

It would be more correct to say that the obligations of the Members are 'imposed' upon them by the Charter instead of that they are 'assumed' by them in accordance with the Charter. That the Charter is a treaty concluded by the Members is not essential to the obligation to obey the norms created by the treaty. Besides, the Charter, in Article 2, paragraph 6, may be interpreted to impose obligations also upon states which are not contracting parties to the treaty and consequently have no 'assumed' obligations according to the Charter.

Finally, it must be noted that the phrase 'present Charter' used in this and other Articles of the Charter is misleading. It might be understood to mean only the text of the Charter as adopted by the San Francisco Conference and ratified by the states, and not the text of the Charter as amended in accordance with Articles 108 or 109. Even in Article 108 the phrase 'Amendments to the present Charter, etc.' is incorrect, since the provisions concerning amendments refer not only to the 'present' Charter as the text which came into force on October 24, 1945, but also to a text which, as a result of any amendment, will come into force in accordance with Article 108 or 109, or in accordance with an amended amendment procedure.[6] The true meaning of the phrase 'present Charter' wherever it is used would be better expressed if the word 'present' had been dropped.[7]

2. The Obligation of Pacific Settlement of Conflicts (Article 2, Paragraphs 3 and 4)

The Principles stipulated in paragraphs 3 and 4 of Article 2 constitute the main obligations of the Members: to refrain from the threat and use of force and to settle their disputes by peaceful means. They run as follows:—

> 3. All Members shall settle their international disputes by peaceful means in such a manner that international peace and security, and justice, are not endangered.

[6] The same if true with respect to the phrase, 'the present Statute,' in Article 69 of the Statute of the International Court of Justice.

[7] At the *Hearings* (pp. 244 f.) the phrase 'present Charter,' which is used in Article 2, paragraph 2, and in other Articles of the Charter, has been criticised. A Senator asked: 'Does that mean that it excludes the amended Charter and that every time it is amended, it is necessary to go back to those places and say that it is the amended Charter? . . . If there is an amendment to the Charter, you must be very careful to make sure that it applies everywhere you want it to apply, otherwise it will be expressly excluded in every place where you say "present Charter"?' To this the representative of the Department of State answered: 'I can only venture a personal interpretation, of course, but I imagine that if an amendment is made to the Charter, then the new Charter becomes the present Charter as of that time.' Another Senator asked: 'You think, then, that the term "present Charter" does not have any more significance than the term "this Charter"?' The answer was: 'We took this to be the exact equivalent of the phrase "this Charter."' Finally, a Senator said: 'But the customary language is: "This Constitution and all amendments thereto." But that is not important, I am not arguing the point. The words "present Charter" are an unfortunate usage.'

> 4. All Members shall refrain in their international relations from the threat or use of force against the territorial integrity or political independence of any state, or in any other manner inconsistent with the Purposes of the United Nations.

These obligations shall be discussed later.[8]

3. The Obligation to Assist the Organisation (Article 2, Paragraph 5)

The Principle laid down in Article 2, paragraph 5, reads as follows:—

> All Members shall give the United Nations every assistance in any action it takes in accordance with the present Charter, and shall refrain from giving assistance to any state against which the United Nations is taking preventive or enforcement action.

The first part is not clear. 'Any action' taken by the United Nations may be interpreted to refer to any resolution adopted by any organ of the United Nations, also to mere recommendations; and by giving 'every assistance' to such action a conduct may be understood by which the Member complies with the resolution. This interpretation, however, would deprive Article 25 of the Charter imposing upon the Members the obligation to comply with certain decisions of the Security Council—not with the decisions of other organs—of any specific meaning. Hence it is probable that by 'action' only enforcement actions taken by the Organisation are meant. Enforcement actions may be taken by the Security Council under Article 39, or, with the authorisation of the Security Council, by a regional organisation under Article 53, or, under Article 106, as a joint action taken by the five great powers 'on behalf of the Organisation' and that means, by the United Nations. Hence the first part of Article 2, paragraph 5, may be interpreted to impose upon the Members the obligation to comply with any decision of the competent organ of the United Nations referring to enforcement actions.

At the 12th meeting of Committee I/1 of the San Francisco Conference the delegate of Norway stated with reference to Chapter II, paragraph 5 ,of the Dumbarton Oaks Proposals (which corresponds to Article 2, paragraph 5, first sentence of the Charter) that the word 'Organisation [which in Article 2, paragraph 5, of the Charter has been replaced by the term United Nations] referred to the Security Council.' This was, the delegate stated, 'the only organ of the Organisation having authority to take action. This would exclude any regional agency and also the five great powers acting on behalf of the Organisation in virtue of Chapter XII (Transitional Arrangements). He felt also that action taken under this paragraph comprised both action taken by the Council

[8] Cf. *infra*, pp. 359 ff.

to enforce its decisions and injunctions issued to parties to a dispute or situation.' [9] It may be doubted whether this interpretation is correct. Regional agencies, expressly admitted by Article 52, may, if acting in conformity with the Purposes and Principles of the United Nations, be described as delegated Organs of the United Nations. They may take action—Article 52, paragraph 1, refers expressly to 'regional action'—and, if authorised by the Security Council in conformity with Article 53, paragraph 1—even enforcement action. The 'joint action' taken by the five great powers according to Article 106 (Chapter XII of the Dumbarton Oaks Proposals) is as pointed out an action taken 'on behalf of the Organisation' and may consequently be considered as an action of the United Nations.

Whereas the first part of Article 2, paragraph 5—according to its wording—refers to 'any action' of the United Nations, the second part refers only to 'preventive or enforcement action' of the Organisation. But it seems that paragraph 5 should be interpreted to refer in both sentences to the same actions, namely, enforcement actions taken by the Organisation. The formula 'preventive or enforcement action' is problematical; for enforcement actions may have a repressive as well as a preventive character. The 'effective collective measures' referred to in Article 1, paragraph 1, are certainly the enforcement measures to be taken under Chapter VII the heading of which reads: 'Action with Respect to Threats to the Peace, Breaches of the Peace, and Acts of Aggression.' Article 1, paragraph 1, provides that these effective collective measures shall be taken 'for the prevention and removal of threats to the peace, and for the suppression of acts of aggression or other breaches of the peace.' That means that the enforcement measures may be preventive actions. Hence it is incorrect to speak of 'preventive *or* enforcement' action. [1]

[9] U.N.C.I.O. Doc. 810, I/1/30, pp. 5 f.

[1] At the 18th meeting of Committee III/3 (U.N.C.I.O. Doc. 782, III/3/41, p. 4) during the discussion of Chapter VIII, Section B, 'The Norwegian Delegate raised the drafting point as to whether enforcement action covered coercive action, both preventive and repressive.—The Chairman asked whether the Delegate of Norway wished to submit a formal motion to amend the existing text. The Norwegian Delegate replied that if enforcement action were construed as implying both preventive and repressive action, he supported that interpretation and, hence, would make no motion opposing it.—The Delegate of the United Kingdom said he considered that there was no conflict in words because action to enforce Council decisions included action to prevent aggression. The Australian Delegate strongly supported the viewpoint of the United Kingdom Delegate. The Norwegian Delegate withdrew his objection in light of this interpretation.'

At the 12th meeting of Committee I/1 (U.N.C.I.O. Doc. 810, I/1/30, p. 6) the delegate of Norway said with reference to Chapter II, paragraph 6, of the Dumbarton Oaks Proposals which corresponds to the second part of Article 2, paragraph 5, of the Charter: 'that some clarification was needed of the word "preventive." He noted that in Committee III/3, in a discussion of Chapter VIII, B. 6, there had been an interpretation of "enforcement action." This had been interpreted to mean action both to prevent and to suppress aggression, that is,

As a mere ' preventive ' action may be considered the action which is provided in Article 40: ' In order to *prevent* an aggravation of the situation the Security Council may, before making the recommendations or deciding upon the measures provided for in Article 39, call upon the parties concerned to comply with such provisional measures as it deems necessary or desirable.' If the ' provisional measures ' taken to ' prevent an aggravation of the situation ' were meant by the term ' preventive action ' used in Article 2, paragraph 5, then the formula ' preventive or enforcement action ' would be correct; for the provisional measures are—in themselves—not enforcement measures. But it is hardly possible to interpret ' preventive action ' referred to in Article 2, paragraph 5, to mean the ' provisional measures ' of Article 40. For in Article 5, where the formula ' preventive or enforcement action ' is also used, it is provided that a Member against which such action is taken may be ' suspended from the exercise of the rights and provileges of membership.' Article 40, however, provides that ' such provisional measures shall be without prejudice to the rights, claims, or position of the parties concerned.' All the parties involved in a situation whose aggravation the Security Council wishes to prevent, may be called upon—according to Article 40—to comply with provisional measures, and not only the party which is responsible for a threat to, or breach of, the peace. Hence it seems that the ' provisional measures ' of Article 40 are not a ' preventive action ' referred to in Article 5. If the formula used in Article 5 has the same meaning as the same formula used in Article 2, paragraph 5, the term ' preventive action ' can not be interpreted to mean actions taken under Article 40. Besides, the provisional measures provided for in this Article have not the character of actions taken by the Organisation ' against ' a state. They are measures recommended or ordered by the Security Council to be complied with by the states involved in a dangerous situation. The term ' preventive action ' in Article 2, paragraph 5, can hardly have another meaning than an enforcement action taken for the purpose to prevent a breach of the peace. That is an enforcement action taken in case the Security Council has determined, in conformity with Article 39, the existence of a threat to the peace. In Article 50, too, the formula ' preventive or enforcement measures '

action to remove a threat to the peace as well as action to suppress a breach of the peace. He felt that " preventive " as used here and in Chapter V, B. 3, meant admonitory action in the form, say of recommendations or injunctions addressed by the Security Council under Chapter VIII, B, to a party or parties, whether the measure involved (for example, the lifting of a blockade) was provisional or otherwise, and whether the admonitory action was accompanied or not by " enforcement " action. He felt the meaning of the text should be made clear by the Rapporteur in his report.' The Rapporteur, however, did not make clear the meaning of the text in his report. The interpretation of the Nowegian delegate that ' preventive ' means here and in Article 5 ' admonitory ' has no foundation in the text of the Charter.

may be interpreted to mean: enforcement actions taken to prevent or to react against a breach of the peace.

It is, of course, possible to consider even a recommendation made by the Security Council according to Article 36, paragraph 2, Article 37, paragraph 2, Articles 38 or 39, as a 'preventive action' since the purpose of such recommendations is certainly to prevent a breach of the peace. But it is hardly probable that Article 2, paragraph 5, refers to such action; especially because recommendations may be made to both parties to a conflict and not only to a party to which no assistance should be given. Only a Member that violated the Charter should be deprived of any assistance on the part of the other Members.

The Report of Rapporteur of Subcommittee to Committee I/1 of the San Francisco Conference,[2] contains the following statement referring to paragraphs 5 and 6 of Chapter II of the Dumbarton Oaks Proposals which correspond to paragraph 5 of Article 2 of the Charter: 'The French Delegation proposed to add to paragraph 5 of Chapter II the following phrase which was conceived in the French text as follows: "sans qu'un Etat puisse, pour s'y soustraire, invoquer un statut de neutralité." The French Delegate explained that what he meant by "statut de neutralité" was that of permanent neutrality. From the discussion that ensued, it was understood in subcommittee that the statute of permanent neutrality is incompatible with the principles declared in paragraphs 5 and 6 of Chapter II, in that no state can avail itself of the statute of permanent neutrality to be freed from the obligations of the Charter. The subcommittee, on that understanding, tacitly accepted that the vote taken on paragraphs 5 and 6 covers the French amendment.'

4. Financial Obligations (Articles 17 and 19)

There are other obligations of the Members which are not registered in the Charter as 'Principles' of the United Nations:

The obligation stipulated in Articles 17 and 19 to bear the expenses of the Organisation as apportioned by the General Assembly (to pay the Members' financial contributions to the Organisation). Article 17, paragraph 2 stipulates:

> The expenses of the Organisation shall be borne by the Members as apportioned by the General Assembly.

There is a special sanction provided by Article 19 for the violation of this obligation. This provision shall be discussed in the chapter on sanctions.

[2] U.N.C.I.O. Doc. 739, I/1/A/19 (*a*), p. 6.

5. The Obligation to Carry Out the Decisions of the Security Council (Articles 25, 48, 49)

One of the important obligations is stipulated in Article 25: 'The Members of the United Nations agree to accept and carry out the decisions of the Security Council in accordance with the present Charter.'' The formula 'The Members of the United Nations agree' means: the Members 'shall' or 'ought to.' It expresses the idea that the Members are 'obliged' to carry out the decisions of the Security Council. The words 'to accept' are superfluous. If the Members are obliged to carry out the decisions of the Security Council they need not 'accept' them. The phrasing of Article 25 emphasises the contractual character of the obligation established by this provision. But all the obligations established by the Charter have this character; and, as pointed out, it is superfluous to characterise in the text of a treaty a particular obligation established by this treaty as contractual, especially if other obligations established by the same treaty are not presented in this way.

The term 'decision' as used in Article 25 is ambiguous. Since the Security Council is a collegiate organ, any act of this organ requires a 'decision' meaning a resolution taken by a majority vote. It seems, however, as if Article 25 does not mean that the Members are obliged to carry out all decisions of the Security Council since, according to its wording, they agree to accept and carry out the decisions of the Security Council 'in accordance with the present Charter.' It is not clear whether the last mentioned words refer to 'the decisions of the Security Council,' or to the phrase 'to accept and carry out.'[3] However, in both cases the meaning of Article 25 is that the Members are obliged to carry out only those decisions which the Security Council has taken in accordance with the Charter; and the Charter characterises certain decisions of the Security Council in a way which permits the interpretation that they are not intended to be binding upon the Members, as, for instance, 'recommendations' (Articles 36, 37, 38, 39) or 'plans' (Article 26). Consequently Article 25 may be interpreted to mean: the Members are obliged to carry out all resolutions of the Security Council which the Security Council is authorised by the Charter to issue with the intention to bind the Members at whom they are directed; that is to say, all resolutions

[3] At the 14th meeting of Committee III/1 of the San Francisco Conference (U.N.C.I.O. Doc. 597, III/1/30, p. 3) the Australian delegate 'suggested that the language of paragraph 4 [of Chapter VI, Section B of the Dumbarton Oaks Proposals, corresponding to Article 25 of the Charter] was unsatisfactory. It was not clear whether the phrase "in accordance with the provisions of the Charter" referred only to the obligations to carry out the Council's decisions or referred to the decisions as well.' At the same meeting the proposal of the Belgian delegate to restrict the obligation of the Members to decisions of the Security Council taken under Chapters VI, VII and VIII of the Charter (corresponding to Chapter VIII of the Dumbarton Oaks Proposals) was not accepted (pp. 1 ff.).

which the Charter does not characterise in a way which permits the interpretation that they shall not have a binding force, such as 'recommendations' or 'plans.'[4] In this respect, however, the wording of the Charter is not always clear. Thus, for instance, the term 'call' as used in Article 33, paragraph 2, means probably only a recommendation; but the same term as used in Article 43: the 'call' by which a Member is requested to make available armed forces to the Security Council in accordance with a special agreement, is certainly intended to be binding upon the Members concerned. On the other hand, in order to establish a legal obligation to behave in a certain way it does not suffice, as pointed out, that the behaviour is prescribed in terms expressing the idea that the persons concerned 'shall' or 'ought to' or 'agree to' behave in this way, and the like. In order to establish a legal obligation a sanction must be attached to the contrary behaviour. And if a sanction is attached to a certain behaviour, the contrary behaviour is the contents of an obligation even if it is not prescribed in terms expressing the idea of an obligation. A decision of the Security Council takes on a binding quality, that is to say, constitutes a true obligation if noncompliance with the decision is under a sanction provided by the Charter. Under Article 39 the Security Council may consider noncompliance with its recommendation or 'call,' or 'plan' submitted to the Member, to be a threat to the peace and take enforcement action. If such enforcement action is interpreted to be a sanction, then it must be assumed that the Members are under the obligation to comply with a 'recommendation,' of a 'call' of the Security Council, or a 'plan' submitted by the Council to them. And then any 'decision' of the Security Council, the term 'decision' taken in its widest sense, may take on a binding quality.

As pointed out, the answer to the question as to whether a concrete 'decision' of the Security Council is legally binding upon the Members, may be doubtful. Who is competent to decide this question? The Security Council itself. But the introductory formula 'The Members of the United Nations agree' may have the unintentional effect to make possible the interpretation that also the Members concerned are competent to decide whether a concrete decision of the Security Council is 'in accordance with the present Charter' binding upon

[4] *The Report to the President*, p. 79, states: 'Decisions of the Security Council take on binding quality only as they relate to the prevention or suppression of breaches of the peace. With respect to the pacific settlement of disputes, the Council has only the power of recommendation.' The first sentence of this statement has certainly no basis in Article 25 of the Charter. The second sentence is incorrect in so far as decisions of the Security Council taken under Article 34 concerning the investigation of any dispute or any situation which might lead to international friction or give rise to a dispute, may be binding upon the Members concerned. Cf. *infra*, pp. 387 f. Besides, the actions which the Security Council is authorised to take with respect to the settlement of disputes also relate to the prevention of breaches of the peace. As to the interpretation of Article 25, cf. also *infra*, pp. 293 ff.

them. This possibility, however, is of minor importance since application of Article 39 is certainly independent of the interpretation of the Members.

The obligation of the Members stipulated in Article 25 is a specification of the general obligation of the Members stipulated in Article 2, paragraph 5: to give the United Nations every assistance in any action it takes in accordance with the present Charter. Provided that the term ' action ' as used in the first part of this paragraph does not mean only ' enforcement action,' any decision of the Security Council is an action of the United Nations and to give assistance to such action includes to carry out the decision.

If this interpretation is accepted there is no difference between ' recommendations ' and other decisions of the Security Council with respect to their binding character.

The obligation established by Article 25 is specified by the provisions of Articles 48 and 49 with respect to decisions of the Security Council taken under Articles 41 and 42 involving enforcement action.

Article 48 runs as follows:

> 1. The action required to carry out the decisions of the Security Council for the maintenance of international peace and security shall be taken by all the Members of the United Nations or by some of them, as the Security Council may determine.
>
> 2. Such decisions shall be carried out by the Members of the United Nations directly and through their action in the appropriate international agencies of which they are Members.

It is not clear what is meant by the ' appropriate international agencies.' It can only be international agencies which are in relationship with the United Nations. For if a Member of the United Nations is a Member of an international agency that has no relationship with the United Nations, its action in this agency is determined by the constitution of the agency, not by the Charter of the United Nations. The agencies referred to in Article 48, paragraph 2, can only be the ' specialised agencies ' referred to in Article 57 and only after they have been brought into relationship with the United Nations in conformity with Article 57 and 63.

Article 49 runs as follows: 'The Members of the United Nations shall join in affording mutual assistance in carrying out the measures decided upon by the Security Council.' This provision completes that of Article 25 in that it obligates the Members to afford mutual assistance in carrying out the decisions of the Security Council.

If Article 25 referred only to decisions of the Security Council concerning enforcement action under Articles 41 and 42, that is to say, if only these decisions would take on binding quality, as the *Report to the President* maintains, Article 25 would be superfluous since this effect is reached by Articles 48 and 49. Whereas the obligation established by Article 2, paragraph 5, may be interpreted to imply the obligation to give assistance also to a joint action of the five powers referred to in Article 106, and hence the obligation to carry out decisions of the five powers taken under this Article (the joint action under Article 106 being an action of the United Nations) the obligations established by Articles 25, 48 and 49 are restricted to decisions of the Security Council.

6. The Obligations with Respect to the Seat of the Organisation

The Charter does not determine directly the seat of the Organisation and consequently does not impose expressly upon the Members an obligation to permit establishment of the seat of the Organisation in their respective territories. There is, especially, no provision concerning the place where the General Assembly shall hold its meetings. This may be interpreted to mean that the obligation of a Member to permit the Organisation to establish its seats on the territory of the Member must be constituted by an agreement between the Organisation and the Member concerned. But the interpretation is not excluded that, since the Organisation must have a seat, all Members are obliged to permit the Organisation to establish its seat on their territories, without any special agreement being necessary.[5] Article 28, paragraph 3 provides: 'The Security Council may hold meetings at such places other than the seat of the Organisation as in its judgment will be to facilitate its work.' This provision implies the obligation of the Members to permit the Security Council to hold meetings in their territories.

7. The Obligations with Respect to Enforcement Actions (Articles 43, 44, 45, 48)

Highly important obligations with respect to enforcement actions to be taken by the Security Council are established in Chapter VII: the obligations stipulated in Articles 43 and 45, to make available to the Security Council armed forces, assistance and facilities including rights of passage, and to hold immediately available national air force contingents for combined international enforcement action; the obligation stipulated in Article 48, to take the action required by the Security Council to carry out the Council's decisions for the maintenance of international peace and security. These provisions shall be discussed in the chapter on sanctions.[6]

[5] Cf. *infra*, pp. 329 ff.
[6] Cf. *infra*, pp. 706 ff.

8. The Obligation with Respect to the Exercise of the Right of Self-Defence (Article 51)

Article 51 stipulates that any Member shall immediately report to the Security Council measures taken in the exercise of the right of self-defence and to cease to exercise this right as soon as the Security Council has taken the measures necessary to maintain international peace and security. This provision will be discussed in the chapter dealing with the limitations on the functions of the Organisation.[7]

9. The Obligations in case of Regional Arrangements (Article 54)

Article 54 stipulates: 'The Security Council shall at all times be kept fully informed of activities undertaken or in contemplation under regional arrangements or by regional agencies for the maintenance of international peace and security.' This provision imposes upon the Members parties to a regional arrangement or members of a regional agency, the obligation to keep the Security Council at all times fully informed of the activities referred to in this Article.

10. The Obligation with Respect to Economic and Social Co-operation (Article 56)

In the field of economic and social co-operation the Organisation, acting through the General Assembly and the Economic and Social Council, has only the power to make recommendations which are legally not binding upon the Members. But Article 56 provides: 'All Members pledge themselves to take joint and separate action in co-operation with the Organisation for the achievement of the purposes set forth in Article 55.' This Article is one of the most obscure provisions of the Charter. 'All Members pledge themselves' means that all Members are obligated. But what obligation does Article 56 impose upon the Members? To take some action in co-operation with the Organisation for the achievement of the purposes set forth in Article 55. To take action in co-operation with the Organisation means: to co-operate with the Organisation by taking action. The purposes set forth in Article 55 are to bring about economic and social co-operation; co-operation among the Members. Hence Article 56 provides: the Members shall co-operate with the Organisation in order to bring about co-operation among themselves. This is an empty tautology if the Charter does not determine precisely what is meant by 'co-operation with the Organisation.' The only effective way to co-operate with the Organisation would be to comply with the recommendations made by the Organisation with respect to the economic and social co-operation of the Members. But just this is not provided by the Charter, and it is at least doubtful whether such a provision would be compatible with Article 2, paragraph 7, prohibiting the Organisation to intervene in matters

[7] Cf. *infra*, pp. 769 ff.

which are essentially within the domestic jurisdiction of any state.[8] If there are any matters essentially within the domestic jurisdiction of the states, it is the matters for which the Charter provides ' economic and social co-operation.' Even non-obligatory recommendations may be interpreted as an intervention, not consistent with Article 2, paragraph 7. If the provisions of the Charter authorising the Organisation to make recommendations with respect to economic and social co-operation are to be interpreted as restricting the scope of Article 2, paragraph 7, such interpretation seems to be possible only in so far as these recommendations are not obligatory and, hence, that Article 56 does not impose any obligation upon the Members. Instead of obliging the Members to comply with the recommendations of the General Assembly or the Economic and Social Council the Charter provides for ' joint and separate action.' Who has to determine this action? Since the Charter does not authorise an organ of the United Nations to prescribe the actions by which the Members fulfil their obligations to co-operate with the Organisation, it is upon the Members to decide which joint or separate action is appropriate under the provision of Article 56. This Article can hardly be interpreted to mean that the Members are obliged to take joint or separate action determined in some way or another by the Organisation. Its meaning probably is: the Members shall take such joint or separate action they think appropriate to make effective the economic and social co-operation to be brought about by the Organisation. This is not a true obligation. Article 56 does not make the recommendations of the General Assembly or the Economic and Social Council obligatory. Legally, Article 56 is meaningless and redundant.[9]

[8] Cf. *infra*, pp. 769 ff.

[9] At the 12th meeting of Committee II/3 (U.N.C.I.O. Doc. 599, II/3/31, pp. 1 f.) the drafting subcommittee suggested the following text of Article 56: ' All Members pledge themselves to take separate and joint action and to co-operate with the Organisation and with each other to achieve these purposes.' The delegate of Australia said: ' that the sense of the paragraph was clear. The pledge means not only that nations should co-operate but also that each country will pursue the objectives of paragraph A—1 [of Chapter IX, Section A of the Dumbarton Oaks Proposals] by its own action in its own way and without interference in its domestic affairs by the International Organisation.' The matter was referred back to the subcommittee which recommended, at the 14th meeting of Committee II/3 (U.N.C.I.O. Doc. 684, II/3/38, p. 4) the following text: ' All Members undertake to co-operate jointly and severally with the Organisation for the achievement of these purposes.' At the 15th meeting of Committee II/3 (U.N.C.I.O. Doc. 699, II/3/40, pp. 1 f.) ' The Delegate of Australia contended that a major question of substance had been omitted in the redraft from the text originally referred to the Subcommittee. He said that the original pledge contained both a pledge to co-operate and a pledge to take separate action. The latter had been omitted from the revised draft. He suggested that a text which would meet the sense of the Committee would be as follows:

> In order that these purposes may be widely realised, all members pledge themselves to co-operate with the Organisation and with each other and to

To make recommendations of the Organisation obligatory may be the effect of an application of Article 39. But it is not very likely that non-compliance with a recommendation of the General Assembly or the Economic and Social Council with respect to economic and social co-operation will be considered by the Security Council as a threat to the peace and lead to enforcement action.

> take such independent action as they deem appropriate to achieve these purposes within their own territories.
>
> The Delegate of the United States said that the United States had abstained from voting at the previous meeting because it was not clear what principle the Committee was approving. The United States could not agree with the pledge as interpreted by the Australian Delegate since such pledges are inappropriate for the present Charter. She did support the pledge in its present form. The Delegate of Belgium agreed with the Australian Delegate that the Subcommittee had exceeded the limit of its mandate. He said that separate action means that national action should be taken to give effect to international purposes. Separate action might imply interference with domestic affairs but adequate protection is given elsewhere in the Charter. He contended that the present wording was too vague and nothing more than a statement of principle. He therefore supported the new Australian suggestion. The Delegate of the United Kingdom said that there was no doubt in his mind that the Committee had approved a threefold pledge—for separate action, for joint action, and for co-operation with the Organisation. He then went on to say that co-operation implies joint and separate action. He argued, however, that one essential principle had been omitted from the present draft. The Delegate of the United States said that the report of the Subcommittee was in entire accord with the general spirit of the Charter. It was to provide for collective action. He contended that the Delegate of the United Kingdom had proved the Subcommittee to be right when he stated that co-operation implied separate action. If in addition to pledging co-operation, the pledge adds separate action, that means something more than co-operation. Such an addition might imply that the International Organisation could intervene in domestic affairs. He said that the safeguarding clause in Chapter II is not sufficient since a pledge of the type adopted by Australia would make internal affairs matters of international concern. He said that the United States was eager to co-operate and eager to pursue policies consistent with international well-being, but attempts to impose these things from without would not be likely to be effective. He, therefore, asked the Committee to adopt the Subcommittee's report. The Delegate of New Zealand said that he anticipated no political difficulties about the pledge in New Zealand, but he thought it was essential to devise a wording that would create difficulties for no Member. He could not agree that the drafting committee had carried out its instructions. He suggested further discussion in order to reach agreement. The Delegate of the Soviet Union argued that the drafts before the Committee had contained no essential differences in substance. In fact, he thought that signing the Chater alone would be the equivalent of the pledge. He emphasised the importance of getting unanimity in the Committee, since lack of it might implicate that some countries do not want to fulfil the purposes of the Organisation. He moved that the question be referred back to the Subcommittee to evolve a formula which could be accepted unanimously. This motion was seconded by the Delegate of New Zealand. He thought that the English language was rich enough to find words that would satisfy all parties, and if that proved not to be so, he offered to draft a pledge in Russian.'

The matter was again referred back to the drafting subcommittee, which finally suggested the text which became Article 56 of the Charter. The discussion in Committee II/3 shows at least this—that even the Australian delegate was in favour of a provision which allowed the Members to pursue the purposes of the Organisation with respect to economic and social co-operation, ' by its own action in its own way

11. The Obligations with Respect to Non-Self-Governing and Trust Territories (Articles 73, 74, 76, 84, 87, 88)

The obligations imposed upon the Members by the provisions of the Charter concerning non-self-governing territories (Chapter XI) and the trusteeship system (Chapters XII and XIII) shall be discussed in the chapter on the protection of non-self-governing peoples.[1]

12. The Obligation with Respect to the Secretariat (Article 100)

Article 100 provides:

> 1. In the performance of their duties the Secretary-General and the staff shall not seek or receive instructions from any government or from any other authority external to the Organisation. They shall refrain from any action which might reflect on their position as international officials responsible only to the Organisation.
>
> 2. Each Member of the United Nations undertakes to respect the exclusively international character of the responsibilities of the Secretary-General and the staff and not to seek to influence them in the discharge of their responsibilities.

The obligation imposed by this Article upon the Members shall be discussed in the chapter on the Secretary-General.[2]

13. The Obligation to Bring All Treaties to Registration (Article 102)

The obligation imposed by Article 102 upon the Members to bring all their treaties to registration shall be discussed in connection with the corresponding function of the Organisation[3] and in the chapter on sanctions.[4]

14. The Obligations with Respect to the Legal Status of the Organisation, Its Officials and the Representatives of Its Members (Articles 104, 105)

According to Article 104, the Members are obliged to grant to the Organisation such legal capacity as may be necessary for the exercise

and without interference in its domestic affairs by the International Organisation,' or by action 'as they deem appropriate.' As to the interpretation of Article 56, the statement of the delegate of the United States is important that 'attempts to impose these things from without would not be likely to be effective.'

The *Report to the President*, p. 115, contains the following statement referring to Article 56: 'It pledges the varous countries to co-operate with the organisation by joint and separate action in the achievement of the economic and social objectives of the organisation without infringing upon their right to order their national affairs according to their own best ability, in their own way, and in accordance with their own political and economic institutions and processes.'

[1] Cf. *infra*, pp. 550 ff.
[2] Cf. *infra*, pp. 296 ff.
[3] Cf. *infra*, pp. 696 ff.
[4] Cf. *infra*, pp. 706 ff.

of its functions and the fulfilment of its purposes; according to Article 105, they are obliged to grant to the Organisation as such, as well as to the representatives of the Members and the officials of the Organisation, the necessary privileges and immunities. The provisions of the two Articles shall be discussed in the chapter on the legal status of the Organisation.[5]

15. The Obligations of Members and Other Parties to the Statute with Respect to the Court

Article 94, paragraph 1, of the Charter stipulates: 'Each Member of the United Nations undertakes to comply with the decision of the International Court of Justice in any case to which it is a party.' The obligation to comply with the decisions of the Court is only a conditional one. For the Members of the United Nations are not obliged to submit their disputes to the Court. They are obliged to comply with the decisions—not only with 'the decision'—of the Court if they have submitted their dispute to the Court. This, however, is not only an obligation of the Members of the United Nations but of all parties to the Statute which are not Members of the United Nations and even of the states to which the Court is open under Article 35, paragraph 2, of the Statute.

There are provisions in the Statute of the International Court of Justice which may be interpreted to impose obligations on the Members of the Organisation and on the states parties to the Statute but not Members of the Organisation. Article 19 stipulates that 'the Members of the Court, when engaged on the business of the Court, shall enjoy diplomatic provileges and immunities'; Article 42, paragraph 3, provides that 'the agents, counsel, and advocates of parties before the Court shall enjoy the privileges and immunities necessary to the independent exercise of their duties'; and Article 32, paragraph 8, stipulates that the salaries, allowances and compensation of the Members of the Court and the Registrar determined by paragraphs 1 to 7 'shall be free of all taxation.' Since the Organisation itself has no territorial sovereignty and hence is not in a position to grant diplomatic or similar privileges and immunities, and since the Organisation is not authorised to levy taxes, the provisions of Article19, Article 32, paragraph 8, and Article 42, paragraph 3, are applicable only to the states parties to the Statute. They are obliged to grant to the Members of the Court, the agents, counsel, and advocates of the parties before the Court, the privileges and immunities determined in these provisions, and not to impose taxes on the persons referred to in Article 32 with respect to that part of their income which falls under the categories determined in paragraph 8

[5] Cf. *infra*, pp. 329 ff.

Article 22, paragraph 1, of the Statute stipulates: 'The seat of the Court shall be established at The Hague. This, however, shall not prevent the Court from sitting and exercising its functions elsewhere whenever the Court considers it desirable.' This provision imposes upon the Netherlands as a party to the Statute the obligation to permit the seat of the Court to be established at The Hague and upon any state party to the Statute to permit the Court to exercise its functions elsewhere. A similar obligation is established by Article 28 of the Statute which stipulates: 'The chambers provided for in Articles 26 and 29 may, with the consent of the parties, sit and exercise their functions elsewhere than at the Hague.' All these provisions shall be discussed in the chapter on the judicial settlement of disputes.[6]

16. No Obligation of Disarmament

It is one of the most characteristic features of the Charter that it does not impose upon the Members the obligation to reduce their armaments. This is the consequence of the fact that the most important function of the Organisation is 'to take effective collective measures' for the maintenance of peace, and that this function can be exercised only through the armed forces of the Members. The Covenant of the League of Nations too, it is true, did not establish a strict obligation of the Members to disarm. But Article 8, the first Article in that part of the Covenant dealing with the obligations of the Members, stipulates: 'The Members of the League recognise that the maintenance of peace requires the reduction of national armaments to the lowest point consistent with national safety and the enforcement by common action of international obligations.'[7]

[6] Cf. *infra*, pp. 463 ff.

[7] The other paragraphs of Article 8 run as follows:

> 2. The Council, taking account of the geographical situation and circumstances of each state, shall formulate plans for such reduction for the consideration and action of the several Governments.
>
> 3. Such plans shall be subject to reconsideration and revision at least every 10 years.
>
> 4. After these plans shall have been adopted by the several Governments, the limits of armaments therein fixed shall not be exceeded without the concurrence of the Council.
>
> 5. The Members of the League agree that the manufacture by private enterprise of munitions and implements of war is open to grave objections. The Council shall advise how the evil effects attendant upon such manufacture can be prevented, due regard being had to the necessities of those Members of the League which are not able to manufacture the munitions and implements of war necessary for their safety.
>
> 6. The Members of the League undertake to interchange full and frank information as to the scale of their armaments, their military, naval and air programmes, and the condition of such of their industries as are adaptable to warlike purposes.

The Charter does not recognise that the maintenance of peace requires disarmament. It contains, however, two Articles which deal with this problem. The one is Article 11, paragraph 1, which authorises the General Assembly to 'consider the general principles of co-operation in the maintenance of international peace and security, including the principles governing disarmament and the regulation of armaments' and to 'make recommendations with regard to such principles to the Members or to the Security Council or to both.' The other is Article 26 which runs as follows:

> In order to promote the establishment and maintenance of international peace and secruity with the least diversion for armaments of the world's human and economic resources, the Security Council shall be responsible for formulating, with the assistance of the Military Staff Committee referred to in Article 47, plans to be submitted to the Members of the United Nations for the establishment of a system for the regulation of armaments.

The Charter recognises that a certain relationship exists between peace and disarmament, but only in so far as the maintenance of peace should be promoted with the 'least diversion for armaments of the world's human and economic resources.' Consequently, it provides in the same sentences in which it refers to disarmament for the establishment of principles or the formulation of plans for the regulation of armaments.

Nevertheless, an interpretation of the Charter is possible according to which the Members of the United Nations may be subjected to much stricter obligtaions with respect to their disarmament than the Members of the League were. The latter could be obliged to disarm only by the 'plan' formulated by the Council under Article 8, paragraphs 3 and 4. That is to say, the obligation of a Member to reduce its own armaments could be established only with its consent. The same seems to be true with respect to Article 26 of the Charter. The 'plans' formulated by the Security Council 'for the establishment of a system for the regulation of armaments' may provide for reduction of armaments; they must be 'submitted to the Members of the United Nations.' That means that they are binding upon them only if accepted by them. The obligation is established by a treaty concluded by the Member with the Organisation. Article 26, it is true, does not, as does Article 8, paragraph 4, of the Covenant, provide expressly for the 'adoption' of the plan by the Member. But if the plan of the Security Council is to be submitted to the Members, it can be only for the purpose to be adopted by them.

According to Article 26—if interpreted as an isolated provision of the Charter—the Members are free to accept or not accept the plan formulated by the Security Council and submitted to them. The situation appears in a different light if Article 39 is taken into consideration. The fact that a Member refuses to accept the plan providing for a reduction of its armament may, in the opinion of the Security Council, constitute a threat to the peace and consequently lead directly or indirectly (through the intermediate stage of a non-accepted recommendation of the Security Council) to an enforcement action. If this measure is interpreted as a sanction and if the obligation to behave in a certain way is considered to be constituted by a sanction to be executed in case of contrary behaviour, the Security Council, in submitting the plan referred to in Article 26 to a Member, may impose upon it the obligation to act in conformity with this plan; in other terms, the Security Council has the power to enforce its plans for the establishment of a system for the regulation of armaments, which may provide for disarmament.

The same interpretation may be applied to Article 11, paragraph 1. According to the wording of this provision, the Members are free to accept or not accept the ' recommendations ' made to them by the General Assembly with regard to the principles governing disarmament and the regulation of armaments. But, under Article 39, the Security Council may determine that the refusal to accept the recommendation of the General Assembly is a threat to the peace and may enforce this ' recommendation.'

Such enforcement of disarmament plans of the Council was impossible under the Covenant.

17. Obligations of Non-Members (Article 2, Paragraph 6)

Article 2, paragraph 6, provides: ' The Organisation shall ensure that states which are not Members of the United Nations act in accordance with these Principles so far as may be necessary for the maintenance of international peace and security.'

This provision is a consequence of the fact that the purpose of the United Nations—as pointed out—is not only to maintain peace within the Organisation but within the whole international community, that is to say: to maintain world peace. In order to fulfil this purpose the Charter imposes directly obligations only upon the Members of the Organisation; but indirectly also upon all the states which are not Members of the United Nations.

This is the import of Article 2, paragraph 6, provided it may be interpreted to mean that the Organisation is authorised to react against a non-Member state which does not act in conformity with the principles laid down in Article 2 with a sanction provided for by the Charter. There can be little doubt that such interpretation is possible at least with respect to the enforcement measures determined in Chapter VII of the Charter. According to the wording of the Articles concerned, these enforcement measures are not restricted to

Members. They can be executed, it is true, only through the Members upon the directions given by the Security Council; but they may be applied not only against Members but also against non-members and on the same conditions as against Members.[8] The Charter establishes a true legal obligation of Members to behave in a certain way only if it attaches to the contrary behaviour a sanction. If the Charter attaches a sanction to a certain behaviour of non-Members, it establishes a true obligation of non-Members to observe the contrary behaviour.

As to the question which obligations the Charter imposes upon non-Members, Article 2, paragraph 6, allows two interpretations, a restrictive and an extensive one. The Organisation is certainly authorised to ensure that non-member states shall act in conformity with the principles laid down in Article 2, paragraphs 3, 4 and 5; that is to say, that non-Member states are obliged by the Charter, just as Members are, to settle their disputes by peaceful means, to refrain in their relation to other states from the threat or use of force, to give the United Nations every assistance in any action it takes in accordance with the Charter, and to refrain from giving assistance to any state against which the United Nations is taking preventive or enforcement action.

We shall see later that, in conformity with Article 2, paragraph 6, the provisions of Chapter VI, concerning the pacific settlement of disputes, are, according to their wording, not restricted to Members, and that especially the Security Council is authorised by the Charter to intervene in disputes and other situations in which not only Members but Members and non-members, and even only non-Members are involved. Any non-member may, according to Article 35, bring to the attention of the Security Council or of the General Assembly any dispute to which it is a party. But this right is made dependent upon the condition ' if it accepts in advance, for the purpose of the dispute, the obligations of pacific settlement provided in the present Charter.' This provision is superfluous if Article 2, paragraph 6, is interpreted to mean that non-member states are under the obligation to act in conformity with Article 2, paragraph 3, that is, the obligation to settle disputes by peaceful means.

[8] At the 39th meeting of the Security Council the delegate of Poland, expressly referring to Article 2, paragraph 6, proposed to take enforcement measures under Articles 39 and 41 (severance of diplomatic relations) against Spain, a non-member, because ' the existence and activities of the Franco regime in Spain have led to international friction and endangered international peace and security.' He declared, after quoting Article 2, paragraph 6: ' The fascist regime in Spain does not act in accordance with the principles of the United Nations, nor has it ever given any evidence that it intends to do so. It endangers the maintenance of international peace and security. It is, therefore, the duty of our Organisation to ensure that any nation, whether a Member or not, does not endanger international peace and security.' (Journal of the Security Council, 1st year, No. 28, pp. 548 f.)

The question as to whether this is a true obligation of the Members in so far as its fulfilment is guaranteed by a sanction, especially by the enforcement measures provided by Chapter VII, shall be discussed later on. Here the statement suffices that if the peaceful settlement of disputes is a true obligation of the Members, it is also an obligation of the non-members provided that Article 2, paragraph 6, may be interpreted to mean that the Charter intends to impose certain obligations not only on Members but also on non-Members.

The provision of Article 2, paragraph 4—to refrain from the threat or use of force—constitutes certainly a true obligation of the Members since the enforcement measures of Chapter VII are primarily intended to be applied as reaction against the threat or use of force in violation of Article 2, paragraph 4. It is certainly the main purpose of Article 2, paragraph 6, to extend the most important function of the Organisation: to maintain peace by taking 'effective collective measures' to the relation between Members and non-members as well as to the relation between non-members and thus to impose upon them the obligation stipulated in Article 2, paragraph 4.

As to the obligations stipulated by Article 2, paragraph 5, it has already been pointed out that it makes the status of neutrality incompatible with membership in the Organisation. If by Article 2, paragraph 6, the obligation of paragraph 5 is imposed also on non-members, no non-member state can with reference to its duties of neutrality or its status of permanent neutralisation refuse to give assistance to an enforcement action taken by the United Nations against a Member or non-member state.

Among the obligations of the Members presented as principles of the Organisation Article 2, paragraph 2, stipulates that all Members shall fulfil the obligations imposed upon them by the Charter. The question arises whether the principles referred to in paragraph 6 comprise also the principles stipulated in paragraph 2. According to the wording of paragraph 6, this question may be answered in the affirmative. Then all obligations of the Members are obligations of the non-members; and there is a difference between the status of a Member and that of a non-member only in so far as the latter has all the obligations but not the rights of a Member. It has only the rights which the Charter expressly confers upon it, especially the right to bring 'questions' or 'disputes' before the General Assembly or the Security Council according to Article 11, paragraph 2, and Article 35, paragraph 2, and the right to be invited to participate without vote in the discussions relating to a dispute under consideration by the Security Council if the non-member is a party to the dispute, the Security Council being authorised to lay down such conditions as it deems just for the participation of a non-member state (Article 32).

However, there are some obligations of the Members which hardly can be imposed upon non-members: for instance, the obligation to bear the expenses of the Organisation as apportioned by the General Assembly (Articles 17 and 19); nor can the special sanction provided in Article 19 for the non-fulfilment of this obligation, suspension of the right of voting in the General Assembly, refer to non-members since the latter have no such right. The same holds true for the general sanction stipulated by Article 6 for the persistent violation of the principles contained in the Charter: expulsion from the Organisation; it can not refer to non-members. For this reason it is possible to interpret Article 2, paragraph 6, in a restrictive sense by attributing to the phrase ' in accordance with these principles ' the meaning: in accordance with the principles stipulated in paragraphs 3, 4 and 5. Violations of these principles may lead to the application of the enforcement measures provided in Chapter VII if the Security Council considers such violations as a threat to or a breach of the peace. Consequently these measures may work as sanctions and constitute true obligations. This holds, it is true, also with respect to the violation of other provisions of the Charter on the part of Members, so that the inapplicability of the sanctions stipulated in Articles 6 and 19 to non-members is not a decisive reason to restrict the obligations imposed upon non-members to those stipulated in paragraphs 3, 4 and 5 of Article 2. But it is doubtful whether the intention of the Charter goes so far as to authorise the Organisation to ensure that non-member states shall act in every respect as Members are obliged to act. If this is not the intention of the Charter the most plausible restriction is that which results from the interpretation of the term ' principles ' just mentioned.

It may seem that this interpretation finds some support in the fact that paragraph 6 authorises the Organisation to ensure that non-member states shall act in accordance with the principles of the Charter only ' so far as may be necessary for the maintenance of international peace and security.' This argument, however, is not correct. For the purpose of all the obligations imposed upon the Members is—directly or indirectly—the maintenance of international peace and security; and especially the enforcement measures of Chapter VII, the most important sanctions of almost all obligations (in so far as their violation is considered to be a threat to or breach of the peace) are to be taken only, according to Article 39, ' to maintain or restore international peace and security.'

In Article 2, paragraph 6, the Charter shows the tendency to be the law not only of the United Nations but also of the whole international community, that is to say, to be general, not only particular, international law. The Covenant of the League of Nations had the same tendency especially in its Articles 17 and 18, but to a much smaller extent. The League, however, had no opportunity to realise this tendency which is in contradiction to one of the fundamental principles of existing international law, that an international treaty can impose duties and confer rights only upon the contracting parties, that is to say, that an international treaty which is not concluded by all the states of the world does create particular, not general, international law. From the point of view of existing international law, the attempt of the Charter to apply to states which are not contracting parties to it must be characterised as revolutionary. Whether it will be considered as a violation of the old, or as the beginning of a new international law, remains to be seen.[9]

[9] The Report of Rapporteur of Subcommittee I/1/A to Committee I/1 of the San Francsico Conference which was occupied with Article 2 (U.N.C.I.O. Doc. 739, I/1/A/19 (*a*), p. 6) does not interpret paragraph 6 as imposing obligations upon non-Members. It contains with respect to the text of this paragraph the following statement: 'The vote was taken on the understanding that the association of the United Nations, representing the major expression of the international legal community, is entitled to act in a manner which will insure the effective co-operation of non-Member states with it, so far as that is necessary for the maintenance of international peace and security.' However, in the discussion of this paragraph at the 12th meeting of Committee I/1 (U.N.C.I.O. Doc. 810, I/1/30, p. 7) 'The Delegate of Uruguay asked for a clarification of the meaning of this paragraph. He asked how a non-Member could be brought within the sphere of the Organisation and how the Organisation could impose duties upon non-Members. The Rapporteur replied that the paragraph was intended to provide a justification for extending the power of the Organisation to apply to the actions of non-Members, but that the wording might have to be reconsidered if it were not clear. The Delegate of Belgium stated that he considered this a most important provision, for the Organisation should not be paralysed by having a state invoke provisions such as the Hague Agreements, neutrality agreements, etc. He felt that the Organisation could ignore the claim made by non-Members because it would be the authorised expression of the international legal community. The Australian Delegate agreed that this was a difficult provision to enforce but that it was an essential one. The Organisation would have to see that everything possible would be done to suppress an aggressor.'

At the *Hearings*, p. 233, the representative of the Department of State interpreted Article 2, paragraph 6, to mean that it imposes 'the obligations' to live up to the responsibilities of the Members upon the non-Member states. A Senator who had been a Member of the United States delegation to the San Francisco Conference chose the formula (p. 237): non-Member states 'are subject to the organisation's discipline,' which amounts to the same.

CHAPTER 6

CONFLICT OF OBLIGATIONS

1. DIFFERENCE BETWEEN THE CHARTER AND THE COVENANT OF THE LEAGUE OF NATIONS

LIKE the Covenant, the Charter contains a provision concerning conflicts between the obligations of the Members under the legal order of the Organisation and other obligations of these states. But the provisions of the Charter concerning such conflicts differ from those of the Covenant. Article 20 of the Covenant stipulates:

> 1. The Members of the League severally agree that this Covenant is accepted as abrogating all obligations or understandings *inter se* which are inconsistent with the terms thereof, and solemnly undertake that they will not hereafter enter into any engagements inconsistent with the terms thereof.
>
> 2. In case any Member of the League shall, before becoming a Member of the League, have undertaken any obligations inconsistent with the terms of this Covenant, it shall be the duty of such Member to take immediate steps to procure its release from such obligations.

Article 103 of the Charter runs as follows:

> In the event of a conflict between the obligations of the Members of the United Nations under the present Charter and their obligations under any other international agreement, their obligations under the present Charter shall prevail.

The first difference between Article 20 of the Covenant and Article 103 of the Charter is that the latter refers only to conflicts between treaty obligations, whereas the wording of the former could be interpreted to refer to conflicts between obligations under the Covenant and obligations assumed under treaties or other legal instruments.[1] In this respect the text of Article 103 of the Charter is clearer than that of Article 20 of the Covenant. It is not superfluous to note that Article 103 correctly uses the term 'international agreement' meaning all kinds of treaties, whereas the immediately preceding Article 102 makes a distinction between 'treaty' and 'international agreement.'[2]

1 The French text of Article 20 refers only to conflicts between treaty obligations. Cf. Hans Kelsen, *Legal Technique in International Law*, Geneva Studies, Vol. X, No. 6 (1939), pp. 148 ff.

2 Cf. *infra*, p. 696.

The second difference is that Article 103 of the Charter contains only one provision, and this provision corresponds to the first part of Article 20, paragraph 1, of the Covenant. The provisions of the second part of paragraph 1 and paragraph 2 of Article 20 of the Covenant have no equivalent in the Charter. However, it is just the first part of paragraph 1 of Article 20 which, if separated from the other parts of this Article, becomes highly problematical from the point of view of existing international law.

2. Conflicts between Treaty Obligations to which Article 103 Refers

As far as conflicts between treaty obligations are concerned, conflicts in two kinds of cases must be distinguished: (1) cases in which all the parties to two treaties are identical, (2) cases in which some, but not all, of the parties to two treaties are identical. If two treaties are concluded by totally different parties, no conflict of obligations is possible. At least one party must be common to both treaties. If the conflicting treaties are concluded by the same contracting parties, according to general international law the rule *lex posterior derogat priori* applies. The later treaty abrogates the earlier treaty. It is, however, possible that a treaty establishes the contrary principle: *lex prior derogat posteriori*, that is to say, that a later treaty (concluded by the same parties) shall be null and void if incompatible with the first treaty. This, *e.g.*, is the meaning of a treaty concluded forever or, what amounts to the same, a treaty declared as unchangeable and not annulable, or as 'eternal.' This is certainly not the meaning of Article 103 of the Charter. Intentionally it does not refer to a conflict between the Charter and an international agreement having the character of an amendment to the present Charter in the sense of Articles 108 and 109.

The wording of Article 103, however, does not correspond to its intention. Here the use of the term 'present' Charter shows one of its undesirable effects. If literally interpreted, it makes any amendment impossible. For an amendment to the 'present Charter' is an international agreement other than the 'present' Charter, that is the Charter as it came into force in conformity with its Article 110. With the exception of amendments to the Charter, Article 103 refers to international agreements concluded by states contracting parties to the Charter, that is to say, by two or more or by all the states which are contracting parties to the Charter, or by one or more states contracting parties to the Charter on the one hand and a non-Member state or non-Member states on the other hand. It refers to such treaties whether they have been concluded before or after the Charter has come into force.

3. Conflicts between Obligations under the Charter and Obligations Established by Treaties Concluded between Members

As to treaties concluded between Member states the provision of Article 103 is superfluous. For according to general international law, such treaty, if concluded before the Charter has come into force, is abrogated by the Charter; and if concluded after the Charter has come into force, the treaty inconsistent with the Charter is null and void under other provisions of the Charter. For such a treaty is an attempt to amend or abolish the Charter or parts of it in the relation of the Members, parties to this treaty. Such effect, however, can be reached only by an amendment to the Charter the procedure of which is determined in Articles 108 and 109. In no other way can the obligations and rights of the Members stipulated by the Charter be changed or abolished.

In contradistinction to the first part of Article 20, paragraph 1, of the Covenant, Article 103 of the Charter does not state that, in the event of a conflict between the obligations of the Members under the Charter and their obligations under another treaty, the latter is to be considered as 'abrogated' by the former, but that the obligations under the Charter shall 'prevail.' Whatever may be the meaning of the phrase 'the obligations under the Charter shall prevail,' it has no importance with respect to treaties concluded between Member states. For those treaties—if inconsistent with the Charter—are abrogated by the latter, according to general international law, when concluded before the Charter has come into force, and they are null and void under Articles 108 and 109 of the Charter when concluded after the Charter has come into force.

4. Conflicts between Obligations under the Charter and Obligations Established by Treaties Concluded between Members and Non-members.

Totally different is the case of a treaty concluded by Members of the United Nations and non-members. Some writers on international law maintain that the conclusion of a treaty inconsistent with a previous treaty concluded by, partly, the same states is an illegal act on the part of the state which is a party to both treaties; and since an illegal act cannot create the legal effects intended by it, such treaty is null and void. According to this doctrine the Charter would be non-valid in relation to Member states which had concluded with non-members a treaty inconsistent with the subsequently concluded Charter; whereas in case Members enter into an inconsistent treaty with non-members after the Charter has come into force, the first mentioned treaty would be null and void.

However, the doctrine in question is untenable. It is doubtful whether a state in concluding a treaty inconsistent with a treaty previously concluded with another party violates its obligation under international law and that the conclusion of such treaty is an illegal act on the part of this state. The state may conclude the later treaty with the sincere intention to procure release from the earlier one. This is exactly what Article 20, paragraph 2, of the Covenant presupposes. Otherwise, the situation to which this provision refers would imply that the state commits an illegal act in ratifying or adhering to the Covenant if the latter is inconsistent with a previously concluded treaty, and that, consequently, the Covenant is null and void in relation to this state. Article 20, paragraph 2, of the Covenant does certainly not share this view. According to general international law, it is not the act of concluding a treaty inconsistent with a previous treaty, but the nonfulfilment of this or the other treaty which is illegal. The act of concluding a treaty inconsistent with a previous treaty is illegal only if the state has assumed in that treaty the obligation not to conclude a treaty inconsistent with it. Such an obligation is stipulated in Article 20, paragraph 1, of the Covenant, but not in the Charter. Further, it is certainly not correct that the subsequent treaty is null and void. The nullity of the subsequent treaty can be based only on the principle *ex injuria jus non oritur*, which is not an absolute principle of positive law and which has many exceptions in national as well as in international law. Besides, even if the conclusion of a treaty inconsistent with a previous treaty is an illegal act, it is so only on the part of a state which is a contracting party to both treaties, not on the part of the state which is a contracting party only to the subsequent treaty. If the nullity of this treaty is to be considered as a sanction, such sanction is not justifiable in so far as it is inflicted upon the latter.

It is hardly possible to refute the view that, according to general international law, both treaties inconsistent with each other are valid and that the state contracting party to both violates the one if it fulfils the other. The objection that this interpretation presupposes the validity of two legal norms which logically exclude each other, a situation which is incompatible with the unity of the law, does not hold. The rule of law by which the obligation to fulfil a treaty is established stipulates, if correctly formulated: if a state party to a treaty does not fulfil this treaty, the sanctions provided by the law may or shall be directed against it. If two inconsistent treaties are valid, the law provides that sanctions may be directed against the state in both cases: when it, in fulfilling the one, does not fulfil the other, and *vice versa*; so that the state cannot avoid being liable to sanctions. This is an unsatisfactory situation, but it does not imply a logical contradiction within the system of the law.

5. The Obligation Not to Assume Inconsistent Treaty Obligations and the Obligation to Take Steps for Release from Inconsistent Treaty Obligations

By a treaty a previous or subsequent inconsistent treaty may be declared null and void. But since a treaty is valid only for the contracting parties, such a provision cannot apply to a state which is not a party to the treaty containing this provision.

In so far as the second part of Article 20, paragraph 1, of the Covenant refers to treaties concluded by Members of the League with non-members after the Covenant has come into force, its provision that the Members are obliged not to enter into such engagements inconsistent with the Covenant is correct. The same is true with respect to the provision of paragraph 2 obligating the Members to take steps to procure their release from obligations inconsistent with the Covenant if assumed before the latter has come into force. This provision does certainly not presuppose that the Covenant, if inconsistent with a treaty previously concluded by a Member of the League, is non-valid in relation to this Member because by ratifying the Covenant this Member performed an illegal act. Article 20, paragraph 2, evidently presupposes that the two treaties in conflict with each other are valid.

Article 103 of the Charter does neither stipulate the obligation of the Members to refrain from entering into inconsistent engagements nor the obligation to take steps to procure their release from previously assumed obligations inconsistent with the Charter.[3] With respect to treaties inconsistent with the Charter concluded by Members with non-members before or after the Charter has come into force,

[3] The Report of the Rapporteur of Committee IV/2 (U.N.C.I.O. Doc. 933, IV/2/42 (2), p. 6) contains the following statement: 'Concerning the second rule of Article 20 of the Covenant, by which the Members undertook not to enter thereafter into any engagement inconsistent with the terms thereof, the Committee has thought it to be so evident that it would be unnecessary to express it in the Charter, all the more since it would repeat in a negative form the rule expressed in paragraph 2 of Chapter 2 of the Charter.—The Committee has also considered the desirability of including the third type of provision which is found in Article 20 of the Covenant, namely, the provision that parties are under a duty to take steps to free themselves from "inconsistent obligations" in treaties with non-member states.—The Committee has considered that in the event of an actual conflict between such obligations and the obligations of Members under the Charter, particularly in matters affecting peace and security, the latter may have to prevail. The Committee is fully aware that as a matter of international law it is not ordinarily possible to provide in any convention for rules binding upon third parties. On the other hand, it is of the highest importance for the Organisation that the performance of the Members' obligations under the Charter in specific cases should not be hindered by obligations which they may have assumed to non-member states. The Committee has had these considerations in view when drafting the text. The suggested text is accordingly not limited to pre-existing obligations between Members.'

Article 103 provides exactly the same as it provides for inconsistent treaties concluded between Members: that the obligations under the Charter shall prevail. As pointed out, this phrase differs from that of the first part of Article 20, paragraph 1, of the Covenant, where the term 'abrogate' is used.[4] Is there a difference between the formula: a treaty obligation 'prevails' over another treaty obligation inconsistent with the former, and the formula: a treaty establishing an obligation 'abrogates' an inconsistent obligation established by another treaty? If in case of two norms or, what amounts to the same in case of two obligations inconsistent with each other, only one, 'prevails,' the other cannot be considered as valid; that means that the norm or obligation which does not 'prevail' must be considered as 'abrogated' by the treaty stipulating the obligation which 'prevails.' The term 'abrogate' usually refers only to the subsequent norm. If a preceding norm has the effect of invalidating a subsequent norm—as for instance a constitution an unconstitutional statute—one does not say the preceding norm 'abrogates' the subsequent norm; one prefers to say the preceding norm 'prevails,' meaning that only this norm is valid whereas the subsequent norm inconsistent with the preceding one is not valid. However, the legal effect of the preceding norm which 'prevails' in relation to the subsequent norm is exactly the same as the legal effect of a subsequent norm 'abrogating' the preceding norm. Besides the principle *lex posterior derogat priori*, there exists, as pointed out, an opposite principle: *lex prior derogat posteriori*.

It may be that the term 'prevail' instead of 'abrogate' has been chosen to cover both the invalidation by the Charter of inconsistent, preceding as well as subsequent, treaty obligations. If so, Article 103, superfluous with respect to inconsistent treaties concluded between Members, is highly problematical with respect to inconsistent treaties concluded between Members and non-members. Under existing general international law, a treaty has not the legal capacity of invalidating another treaty concluded not by the same parties. Only if the Charter, in view of Article 2, paragraph 6, is considered to constitute a new general international law, that is to say, if the law of the United Nations is recognised to be valid for, and applicable to, all the states of the world, the provision of Article 103 as relating to treaties between Members and non-members is not at variance with existing law. But in this case it is superfluous with respect to these treaties, too.[5]

[4] The Summary Report of the 6th meeting of Committee IV/2 (U.N.C.I.O. Doc. 419 IV/2/19, p. 1) contains the statement that some Members of the Committee 'felt that the word "abrogation" was too strong or that no mention of abrogation should appear in the text.'

[5] At the 12th meeting of Committee IV/2 (U.N.C.I.O. Doc. 873, IV/2/37 (1), p. 2) the Australian delegation refused to accept the suggested text of Article 103 '(1) because it had come to the conclusion . . . that on the whole it was not necessary to insert any express provision in the Charter and that the matter could

6. Solution of Treaty Conflicts by the Principle of Priority of Execution of the Preceding Treaty

In order to solve the conflict between two inconsistent treaties concluded partly by the same parties in a more adequate way than that provided for by general international law, it has been suggested that the state which has concluded two inconsistent treaties should be bound to perform only the first concluded treaty and to make reparation for the damage caused by the illegal non-performance of the subsequently concluded treaty. Both treaties remain valid, but a priority of execution is established with respect to the previously concluded one. If those who drafted Article 103 of the Charter had this solution in mind when they chose the term ' prevail ' instead of ' abrogate,' their intention has not been expressed in a correct way. The provision that of two inconsistent norms or obligations one shall ' prevail ' is not identical with the provision that the execution of one shall take priority over the execution of the other; especially if it is intended to establish by the last mentioned provision an obligation to execute only the previously concluded treaty.

7. No ' Automatic ' Abrogation

The Report of the Rapporteur of Committee IV/2 of the San Francisco Conference [6] contains the following statement relating to Article 103: ' . . . the Committee has concluded that it is necessary to incorporate in the Charter a provision regarding inconsistency between the obligations of Members under other treaties and under the Charter itself, if only because the omission of such a provision could give rise to inaccurate interpretations. Moreover, it has decided that it would be inadvisable to provide for the automatic abrogation by the Charter of obligations inconsistent with the terms thereof.' The last sentence seems to indicate the intention to have an obligation inconsistent with the Charter abrogated by the latter; only an ' automatic ' abrogation by the Charter should be avoided. [7] Abrogation should ' depend upon and be linked with the case of a conflict between the two categories of obligations.' This statement is difficult to understand. If two obligations are inconsistent with each other they are in ' conflict '; and non-automatic as well as automatic abrogation (or ' exclusion ') of one by the other is possible only in case of conflict. Perhaps it was

probably be left to the ordinary customary law of nations; (2) because in the text proposed by the Subcommittee, obligations between Members and non-members were dealt with on the same footing as obligations between Members themselves —a course for which there seemed at first sight to be insufficient legal warrant.'

6 U.N.C.I.O. Doc. 933, IV/2/42 (2), p. 5.

7 The Summary Report of the 4th meeting of Committee IV/2 (U.N.C.I.O. Doc. 270, IV/2/14, p. 1) contains the following statement: ' The sentiment was general that obligations between Members inconsistent with the Charter should be abrogated, although some delegations felt that the abrogation should not be automatic.'

intended that Article 103 should operate only in case a concrete conflict arises, that is to say, not only a conflict between obligations, but a conflict between two states with respect to the execution of the conflicting obligations.[8] According to the first statement of the Report of Committee IV/2, quoted above, Article 103 has been inserted into the Charter in order to avoid 'automatic' abrogation of obligations inconsistent with those under the Charter. But, by inserting Article 103 abrogation is made the 'automatic' effect of this Article, instead of the automatic effect of a rule of general international law. Abrogation is 'automatic' if it is the direct effect of a general rule of law; it is not 'automatic' if it is the effect of the decision of an authority competent to apply the general rule of law to a concrete conflict of obligations, that is to say, competent to ascertain the inconsistency and to declare the obligation inconsistent with the Charter obligation as null and void. Just this result cannot be derived from the text of Article 103. Its provision may be applied directly by the Members for themselves. No special organ is authorised in this respect. Only if a dispute arises to be settled by an organ of the United Nations, is this organ competent to apply Article 103.

8. The Meaning of the Term 'Obligations of the Members'

The application of Article 103 may encounter certain difficulties with respect to the meaning of the term 'obligations under the present Charter.' As pointed out in another chapter of this study,[9] the text of the Charter is far from giving a clear answer to the question: which are the obligations of the Members?

Article 103 deals with possible conflicts between treaty obligations of the Members of the United Nations. Hence it refers to the Members in their capacity as parties to the Charter. The term 'Members of the United Nations' usually means the parties to the Charter in the narrower sense of the term, not comprising the Statute of the International Court of Justice. According to Article 93 of the Charter 'All Members of the United Nations are *ipso facto* parties to the Statute,' that is to say, not only parties to the Charter in the narrower sense of the term, but also parties to the Statute. But a non-member 'may

[8] The Report of the Rapporteur of Committee IV/2 (U.N.C.I.O. Doc. 933, IV/2/42 (2), pp. 5 f.) states: 'It has been deemed preferable to have the rule depend upon and be linked with the case of a conflict between the two categories of obligations. In such a case, the obligations of the Charter would be pre-eminent and would exclude any others.—The nature of such a conflict has not been defined, but it would be enough that a conflict should arise from the carrying out of an obligation of the Charter. It is immaterial whether the conflict arise because of intrinsic inconsistency between the two categories of obligations or as a result of the application of the provisions of the Charter under given circumstances: *e.g.*, in the case where economic sanctions were applied against a state which derives benefits or advantages from previous agreements contrary to said sanctions.'

[9] Cf. *supra*, pp. 87 ff.

become a party to the Statute ' without becoming a party to the Charter or—what amounts to the same—a ' Member of the United Nations ' represented in the General Assembly. Article 103 applies only to the obligations of the parties to the Charter, not to the obligations of the parties to the Statute not being parties to the Charter (in the narrower sense of the term). In case of a conflict between the obligation which a Member of the United Nations has under the Statute and the obligation under any other treaty, Article 103 applies on the condition that the terms ' the present Charter ' in Article 103 are interpreted to mean: Charter in the wider sense of the term, comprising the Statute. In case of a conflict between the obligation which a non-member party to the Statute has under the Statute and any other treaty obligation, the principles of general international law relating to such conflicts apply. There was no sufficient reason to exclude from the rule that obligations under the Charter shall prevail over other treaty obligations, the obligations of non-member parties to the Statute. In drafting the text of Article 103 the existence of these obligations has probably been overlooked.[1]

9. The Charter and the Pact of Paris

A treaty concluded by all the Members of the United Nations prior to the coming into force of the Charter with states that are not Members is the General Treaty for the Renunciation of War signed at Paris on August 27, 1928. A comparison of the contents of these two treaties shows that no conflict exists between the obligations imposed upon the contracting parties by the Pact of Paris and those imposed by the Charter upon the Members. In fulfilling its obligations under the Charter a state cannot violate an obligation under the Pact of Paris since the former goes even farther than the latter. Whereas the Pact of Paris obliges the parties not to resort to war as an instrument of national policy and expressly permits war against a state which has violated the Pact—which implies the case of individual and collective self-defence—

[1] In case a non-member state becomes a party to the Statute under Article 93, paragraph 2 of the Charter or in case the Court is open to a state not a party to the Statute under Article 35, paragraph 2, of the Statute, the application of Article 103 of the Charter to conflicts of obligations under the Charter (including the Statute) to be accepted by the state in order to become a party to the Statute or to have access to the Court, and obligations of this state under other international agreements, may be desirable. The Committee of Experts of the Security Council stated in its report concerning the conditions on which Switzerland might become a party to the Statute of the International Court of Justice with respect to the condition: ' acceptance of all the obligations of a Member of the United Nations under Article 94 of the Charter ' that the obligations of a Member of the United Nations under Article 94 included the ' complementary obligations ' arising under Article 103 (and Article 25). (Resolutions adopted by the General Assembly, Doc. A/64/Add. 1, p. 184.) It may be doubted whether Article 103 stipulates an obligation of the Members. It does so only if it is interpreted to obligate the Members to execute only the obligations established by the Charter.

the Charter obliges them to refrain from any threat or use of force and permits—in principle—the use of armed forces only as an enforcement action taken by the Organisation as reaction against a threat to, or breach of, the peace and in case of individual or collective self-defence. The Charter, it is true, restricts this right in permitting its exercise only as long as the Security Council does not take the measures necessary to restore the peace. But this does not imply a conflict between the obligations under the Charter and those under the Briand Kellogg Pact. Whereas this Pact obliges the parties only to seek pacific settlement of their disputes, the Charter obliges them not only to seek such settlement, but also to submit their disputes, if not settled by means of their own choice, to an international agency endowed with the power to settle them.

The obligation to refrain from the use of force, however, is restricted by Articles 107 and 53 of the Charter with respect to enemy states, that is to say, any state which during the Second World War has been an enemy of any signatory to the Charter. The Charter permits enforcement action against any such state. In so far as these enforcement actions have the character of war, they are hardly compatible with the Briand Kellogg Pact. It may be argued that the former enemy states have violated the Pact and are, in accordance with the Preamble of the Pact, denied the benefits furnished by it. This argument holds only if the provision of the Preamble is interpreted as the affirmation of the rule that a contracting party is entitled to cancel a treaty violated by the other contracting party. If, however, the provision of the Preamble is interpreted to be a sanction, the situation is different. This sanction actually has been applied by resorting to war against the enemy states, which have violated the Pact, and once applied all provisions of the Pact are again applicable to all the contracting parties. The Pact has never ceased to be valid for all contracting parties. If a multilateral treaty is concluded with the intention to create an everlasting condition of things and if it provides special sanctions for its violation, its violation on the part of one or the other of the contracting parties does not entitle the other to cancel the treaty. Violation of the treaty has no other consequences but those provided for by the treaty itself. This interpretation of the Briand Kellogg Pact seems to be more adequate than the one according to which a violation of the Pact may lead to releasing the violator from its obligations under the Pact and to outlawing this state until it adheres again to the Pact in conformity with its provisions.[2]

[2] If violation of the Pact of Paris is interpreted to lead to possible cancellation of the Pact, such cancellation terminates the validity of the Pact only in the relationship between the state which cancels the Pact and the state responsible for the violation which is the cause of the cancellation. Resorting to war against the violator may be interpreted to imply cancellation. But the Pact remains in force in the relationship between the violator and the neutral states which do not cancel the Pact in relation to the former. Violation of the treaty does not *ipso facto* terminate its binding

If it is assumed that the Briand Kellogg Pact is still in force in relation to the former enemy states, it does not follow that Article 103 of the Charter applies, that is to say, that Articles 107 and 53 of the Charter prevail over the prohibition of the Pact. For Article 103 is applicable only in the event of conflict between ' obligations ' of the Members, and Articles 107 and 53 do not impose obligations but only confer rights upon the Members. The latter may or may not exercise these rights, and may, by obligations under other engagements, be prevented to exercise them. Article 103 does not provide that the ' Charter ' prevails; it stipulates only that the ' obligations ' under the Charter do prevail. Hence, the Pact of Paris may be interpreted to constitute a restriction to the rights conferred upon the Members by Articles 107 and 53.

force; it only gives the other party or parties to the treaty the opportunity to cancel the treaty on this ground. The question as to which of the states involved in a war has violated the Pact and which has applied the provision of the Preamble may be answered in different ways, not only by the belligerents but also by the neutrals. The doctrine that violation of the Pact entitles the other contracting parties to cancel the Pact leads to absurd consequences.

That the violation of the Pact—even if it could be objectively ascertained—terminates automatically the validity of the Pact in the relationship between the violator and all other contracting parties is the least possible interpretation, although sometimes maintained. The consequences of this doctrine are not less absurd than those of the previously mentioned one. The violator ceases to be a contracting party. But in conformity with Article 3 of the Pact which is open for adherence, it can immediately become again a party by a unilateral act of adherence, except if it is one of the original contractants: Germany, the United States, Belgium, France, Great Britain, the British Dominions, Italy, Japan, Poland, Czechoslovakia. For, according to the wording of Article 3, the Pact is open for adherence only ' by all the *other* Powers of the world.'

According to another doctrine, outbreak of war terminates automatically the validity of the Pact as between the belligerents only. Then the Pact may, after peace is restored, be put into force again by special agreements between the former enemies. But the Pact belongs just to that category of treaties which are not terminated by the outbreak of war: treaties concluded especially for war.

A relatively well-founded view is that the Pact of Paris has altogether lost its binding force for all contracting parties since the outbreak of the second World War has proved its complete lack of effectiveness. But even this doctrine is problematical because the Pact can be considered as non effective only with respect to those states which have violated it by an act of aggression. This, however, holds true only with the Axis powers which represent a small minority as compared with the United Nations, which resorted to war in full compliance with the Pact.

Chapter 7

WITHDRAWAL FROM THE ORGANISATION

1. The Commentary of Committee I/2 of the San Francisco Conference

Membership may be terminated against the will of the Member by expulsion in conformity with Article 6 of the Charter. Can it be terminated voluntarily by withdrawal from the Organisation? In contradistinction to the Covenant of the League of Nations, the Charter does not contain provisions for withdrawal. Neither did the Dumbarton Oaks Proposals contain such provisions. The subcommittee of Committee I/2 of the San Francisco Conference was of the opinion that the Dumbarton Oaks Proposals deliberately omitted provisions for withdrawal in order to avoid the weakness of the League Covenant.[1] The Dumbarton Oaks Proposals intended to establish a really permanent organisation. 'The subcommittee was strongly of the opinion that withdrawal should be impossible.' It was argued among others that the possibility of withdrawal would give recalcitrant Members the opportunity of securing concessions from the Organisation by threatening to leave it.[2] Committee I/2 voted on the question whether withdrawal should be expressly provided for in the Charter. Nineteen states voted affirmatively; twenty-two states, negatively. Finally the Committee decided that no withdrawal clause should be inserted in the Charter but 'that its idea could be expressed by the following text' which it was decided by thirty-eight votes to insert in the report: 'The Committee adopts the view that the Charter should not make express provision either to permit or to prohibit withdrawal from the Organisation. The Committee deems that the highest duty of the nations which will become Members is to continue their co-operation within the Organisation for the preservation of international peace and security. If, however, a Member because of exceptional circumstances feels constrained to withdraw, and leave the burden of maintaining international peace and security on the other Members, it is not the purpose of the Organisation to compel that Member to continue its co-operation in the Organisation.—It is obvious, particularly, that withdrawals or some other forms of dissolution of the Organisation would become inevitable if, deceiving the hopes of humanity, the Organisation was revealed to be unable to maintain peace or could do so only at the expense of law and justice.—Nor would a Member be bound to remain in the Organisation if its

[1] Cf. U.N.C.I.O. Doc. 314, I/2/17, and the Report on the United Nations Conference by the New Zealand Delegation, Wellington, 1945, p. 32.

[2] Cf. U.N.C.I.O. Doc. 1074, I/2/76.

rights and obligations as such were changed by Charter amendment in which it has not concurred and which it finds itself unable to accept, or if an amendment duly accepted by the necessary majority in the Assembly or in a general conference fails to secure the ratification necessary to bring such amendment into effect.—It is for these considerations that the Committee has decided to abstain from recommending insertion in the Charter of a formal clause specifically forbidding or permitting withdrawal.' [3] This commentary was included in the report of Commission I to the plenary session of the Conference.

2. THE 'EXCEPTIONAL CIRCUMSTANCES'

According to this commentary any Member has the right of withdrawing from the Organisation 'because of exceptional circumstances.' Who is competent to decide the question as to whether 'exceptional circumstances' exist? Since the Charter does not confer this competence upon a special organ, any Member is authorised to decide this question for itself. That means that any Member has—according to the commentary given by Committee I/2—the right to withdraw from the Organisation whenever it deems it necessary to withdraw. It is true that the commentary tries to explain somehow the vague term 'exceptional circumstance' in illustrating its meaning by some examples. The first of such exceptional circumstances is that 'the Organisation was revealed to be unable to maintain peace or could do so only at the expense of law and justice.' Again the question arises as to who is competent to decide that the Organisation was unable to maintain peace, etc., and again the answer is that any Member has the right to decide this question. The other example of exceptional circumstances is that a Member's 'rights and obligations as such were changed by Charter amendment in which it has not concurred.' This is in open contradiction to Articles 108 and 109 of the Charter, according to which amendments to the Charter shall come into force 'for all Members of the United Nations' when they have been adopted by a vote of two-thirds of the members of the General Assembly or recommended by a two-thirds vote of the General Conference and ratified in accordance with their respective constitutional processes by two-thirds of the Members of the United Nations, including all the permanent members of the Security Council. The amendment is binding not only upon the Members which have voted for it or recommended it and ratified it, but also upon all the other Members. A Member has no better right to withdraw because it is unable to accept the amendment than to withdraw because it does no longer accept any provision of the original Charter. That a Member withdraws from the Organisation means—if not expressed in this figurative term—that a state terminates, in relation to itself, by a unilateral act the binding

3 Report of the Rapporteur of Committee I/2 on Chapter III (U.N.C.I.O. Doc. 1178, I/2/76 (2), pp. 5 f.).

force of a treaty. According to the text of the Charter, there is no difference between the binding force of the provisions of the original Charter and the binding force of the provisions of an amendment duly accepted in accordance with Article 108 or Article 109.

The third example: that 'an amendment duly accepted by the necessary majority in the Assembly or in the General Conference fails to secure the ratification necessary to bring such amendment into effect,' is difficult to understand. If the amendment does not come into effect the legal situation is unchanged. A Member which votes for or recommends an amendment because it considers it desirable may wish to withdraw if the amendment fails to secure the necessary ratification;[4] but the commentary of Committee I/2 does not restrict the right of withdrawal to Members which voted for or recommended the amendment and ratified it. After an amendment adopted by the General Assembly in conformity with Article 108 or recommended by the General Conference in conformity with Article 109 has failed to secure the ratifications necessary to bring such amendment into effect, every Member has—according to the wording of the interpretation of Committee I/2—the right to withdraw. The question is only when this right comes into existence. Since the Charter does not prescribe a certain period of time within which an amendment is to be ratified, and does not exclude the possibility of ratifying an amendment even years after its acceptance by the General Assembly or the General Conference, it is hardly possible to fix a certain moment of time when an amendment has failed to secure the necessary ratifications.

3. The Right of Withdrawal and Article 2, Paragraph 6

The Commentary of Committee I/2, according to which any Member of the Organisation has the right of withdrawing by a unilateral act, is not quite consistent with the Principles of the Charter. For the purpose of such withdrawal is to get rid of the obligations imposed upon the Member by the Charter, especially those imposed by an amendment in which the Member has not concurred. This purpose, however, cannot be reached by withdrawal since, according to Article 2, paragraph 6, non-members are under the obligations established by the Charter or an amendment to the Charter just as Members are. If the Security Council considers withdrawal of a Member to be a threat to the peace it may, according to Article 39, recommend to the Member to forbear from withdrawing, and, in case of non-compliance with this recommendation, take enforcement measures; or take enforcement measures without previous recom-

[4] In this sense the commentary of Committee I/2 has been interpreted in the *Hearings* p. 240. To the question of a Senator: 'If the United States proposed an amendment which was vital and it was not adopted, would that be ground for withdrawal?' the representative of the Department of State answered in the affirmative.

mendations, that is to say, the Security Council may compel the state to remain a Member. The statement of the commentary, 'it is not the purpose of the Organisation to compel that Member to continue its co-operation in the Organisation,' is incompatible with the possibilities established by the wording of Article 39 of the Charter.

4. The Right of Withdrawal as Consequence of the Principles of Democracy and Sovereignty

When the Report of Commission I embodying the commentary of Committee I/2 was presented in the 9th Plenary Session of the Conference, on June 25, 1945, the delegate of the Soviet Union placed on record its dissent from the commentary. He declared: 'the opinion of the Soviet Delegation is that it is wrong to condemn beforehand the grounds on which any state might find it necessary to exercise its right of withdrawal from the Organisation. Such right is an expression of state sovereignty and should not be reviled, in advance, by the International Organisation—May I cite as an example of unconditional acknowledgment of this right of sovereign states Article 17 of the Constitution of U.S.S.R., which reads as follows: "To every Union Republic is reserved the right freely to secede from U.S.S.R." It is common knowledge that this right is a most striking manifestation of democracy on which the organisation of the Soviet State is founded. The U.S.S.R. is formed on the basis of voluntary accession.—It would be still less justifiable to condemn in advance the reasons for a state's withdrawing from the International Organisation, which is also founded on voluntarily participation of sovereign states. To deny or to revile such a right would be a violation of principles of democracy and sovereignty.'

According to the opinion of the delegate of the Soviet Union, the right of withdrawal is a consequence of the principle of democracy as well as of the principle of sovereignty. This seems not to be the opinion of Committee I/2, which in its commentary does not deduce the right of withdrawal from the sovereignty of the Members. The commentary speaks only of withdrawal under 'exceptional circumstances.' But the Rapporteur of Commission I in the meeting of the Commission on June 23, 1945, introduced the commentary by saying: 'The Commission does not recommend any text on withdrawal for inclusion in the Charter. However, the absence of such a clause is not intended to impair the right of withdrawal, which each state possesses on the basis of the principle of the sovereign equality of the Members.'[5] The principle of 'equality' of Members is in no

[5] Verbatim Minutes of 5th meeting of Commission I, U.N.C.I.O. Doc. 1187, I/13. At the 28th meeting of Committee I/2 of the San Francisco Conference also, the delegate of the United States declared 'that in an organisation of sovereign states it was clear that all Members would possess the faculty of withdrawal. He contrasted such an organisation with a federal union, the Members of which did not have

way impaired if all the Members, large and small, do not have the right of withdrawing from the Organisation by a unilateral act. The same is true with respect to the principle of democracy in so far as the principle of democracy in the relationship among states is identical with that of equality. Only if the concept of democracy is identified with anarchy (liberalism), that is to say, if only freedom is supposed to be the basic principle of democracy, such interpretation is possible. If Soviet Russia is a democracy, this democracy's basic principle is certainly not freedom, but—perhaps—equality.

The statement of the delegate of the Soviet Union that the right of withdrawal is the expression of the Member's sovereignty is not confirmed by his reference to Article 17 of the Constitution of U.S.S.R. The fact that the Constitution of U.S.S.R. contains an express provision conferring upon the members the right to secede is an argument against the doctrine that this right is an expression of sovereignty. If it were, no express provision conferring such right would be necessary; that the provision of Article 17 has been inserted into the Constitution of U.S.S.R. shows that the authors of the Constitution were of the correct opinion that such an express provision is necessary in order that the Members have the right to secede. This right is not a consequence of their sovereignty; the Members have it because it is conferred upon them by the Constitution to which they are subjected and, consequently, are as parts of a state, not sovereign. In Committee I/2 of the San Francisco Conference, the delegate of the Soviet Union declared to be in favour of ' a frank statement in the Charter ' concerning the right of withdrawal.[6] Such a statement is superfluous if the right of withdrawal is a consequence of sovereignty and the Members are, in spite of their submission to the Charter, as states, ' sovereign.'

If sovereignty implies the inalienable right of withdrawing from the organisation established by an international treaty to which a state is the contracting party, then sovereignty means that a sovereign state is bound by a treaty to which it is a party only as long as it pleases. Sovereignty in this unrestricted sense of the term is incompatible with any idea of international law binding upon the states. If the concept of unrestricted sovereignty, as advanced by the delegate of the Soviet Union, were really at the basis of the Charter, none of its provisions would have binding force upon the contracting parties. It can hardly be denied that it is an essential function of the international

the faculty to withdraw. The Charter should state what rights the Organisation possessed. It need not state what rights the Members possessed. If it were felt to be desirable that a statement be made on the subject of withdrawal, this statement should be in the Committee's report and should make it clear that withdrawal would be only for a substantial reason and that states were not being invited to leave at will.' (U.N.C.I.O. Doc. 1086, I/2/77, p. 4.)

[6] *Ibid.*

Organisation established by the Charter to restrict the 'sovereignty' of the Members and thus to eliminate the idea of an unrestricted sovereignty, in spite of the wording of Article 2, paragraph 1, proclaiming 'sovereign equality' of the Members as a principle of the Organisation.

5. Legal Importance of the Commentary of Committee I/2

The Commentary on withdrawal included in the report of Commission I is of no legal importance. In order to get legal effect, that is to say, in order to have the character of an authentic interpretation of the Charter, the principles expounded in the commentary were to be inserted into the text of the Charter or be made the substance of another treaty concluded by all the states contracting parties to the Charter, especially of a so-called additional protocol, or be formulated as a reservation attached to the signature or to the ratification. None of these procedures was adopted.[7] At the plenary session during which the report of Commission I was presented to the Conference, the leaders of the delegations were invited to vote on the Charter, the Statute of the International Court of Justice, and the Interim Arrangements, not on the report of Commission I embodying the commentary on withdrawals. Besides, one Member of the Conference declared expressly its dissent.[8] The agencies competent to apply and to interpret the Charter will not be bound by the commentary embodied in the report of Commission I. Hence, they will answer the question as to the right of withdrawal according to general international law.

[7] As to the attempt to consider the right of withdrawal from the Organisation as a multilateral reservation known to all the signatories before the exchange of ratifications, it should be noted that neither in the discussion at the San Francisco Conference nor in the text of the Charter an agreement has been expressed to the effect that the states participating in the Conference were allowed to sign or ratify the Charter with reservations. Since the Charter is a treaty open to accession, a reservation, in order to be valid for subsequent Members of the United Nations, would have to be attached to the accession. None of the states which were admitted to the United Nations under Article 4 of the Charter made a reservation concerning the right of withdrawal.

[8] After the delegate of the Soviet Union had expressed his dissent from certain statements of the Report of the First Commission concerning the right of withdrawal, the presiding officer declared that 'the statement that the delegate of the Soviet Union has made will, of course, be attached as he requests to the record of the plenary session.' Then he continued: 'Are there any other observations? There being none, the Report is approved.' (*The United States and the Peace.* Part 2. Verbatim Record of the Plenary Sessions of the United Nations Conference on International Organisation. San Francisco April-June, 1945, p. 82.) There was no voting on the Report. If it is to be considered as tacitly approved, it was not approved unanimously. Besides, even if unanimously approved by the San Francisco Conference, the Report of the First Commission concerning the right of withdrawal, not being a part of the Charter, would have no legal effect.

6. The Right of Withdrawal and the *Clausula Rebus Sic Stantibus*

It is a generally accepted opinion that an international treaty which is concluded with the purpose of setting up an everlasting condition of things cannot be denounced by a contracting party if this treaty does not provide for the possibility of unilateral withdrawal. The only exception to this rule admitted by some writers (but not by all) is the application of the *clausula rebus sic stantibus*. The question as to whether this *clausula* is a part of positive international law is much discussed. If this question is answered in the affirmative, the meaning of the *clausula* is supposed to be only that 'a vital change of circumstances may be of such kind as to justify a party in demanding to be released from the obligations of an unnotifiable treaty.[9] 'Vital change of circumstances' means that the obligations stipulated in the treaty imperil the existence of the party which demands to be released. When a state is of the opinion that a vital change of circumstances has occurred, it must first request the other party or parties to abrogate the treaty. If such abrogation together with the suggestion to submit the case to an international court is refused, the state may declare itself to be no longer bound by the treaty. In case a Member of the United Nations should intend to withdraw from the Organisation because of a vital change of circumstances, it must request from the Organisation to be released from Membership, and if this request is refused the dispute should be submitted to the principal judicial organ of the Organisation, the International Court of Justice. But there is no provision in the Charter which authorises the Security Council or the General Assembly to release a state from Membership, and the International Court of Justice has no jurisdiction in a dispute between the Organisation and a Member. The Member that wishes to withdraw has to address its request to all the other Members of the Organisation; and is allowed to exercise its right of withdrawal only after it has waited a reasonable period of time for an answer, unless the other Members suggest that the case be submitted to the decision of an international tribunal. This tribunal may be the International Court of Justice if the dispute is presented as a dispute between states, not as a dispute between the Organisation as such and its Members. In case the tribunal does not decide that a vital change of circumstances has occurred, no right of withdrawal exists.

This analysis shows that the *clausula rebus sic stantibus* does neither confer upon the Members the right of withdrawal as an expression of their 'sovereignty,' nor a right to withdraw under 'exceptional circumstances' as referred to in the commentary of Committee I/2. 'Exceptional circumstances' are not at all identical with 'vital change of circumstances.' Especially the fact that an amendment has been made without the consent of a Member, or the fact that an

[9] Cf. L. Oppenheim, *International Law*, I (Sixth Ed. 1947), pp. 843 ff.

amendment voted for by a Member has not been made, cannot be interpreted as a vital change of circumstances of such a kind to justify that a party be released from Membership. For the change involved by these facts has been foreseen by the Charter whose function it is to establish legal stability in spite of such changes.[1]

[1] The problem of withdrawal has circumstantially been discussed at the *Hearings*. In open contradiction to the opinion of the subcommittee of Commission I/2, mentioned above, one of the chief official advisers of the United States delegation to the San Francisco Conference declared as witness at the *Hearings* before the Committee: 'It was my view from the beginning, and I so advised the United States delegation, that under the original Dumbarton Oaks proposals, where there was no provision either to allow withdrawal or to veto withdrawal, it followed, as a matter of law, that there was a right of withdrawal, the reason being that the agreement was not of a type which in any sense merged the Member states into a new government or under which they give up any of their independence. That being so, the arrangement was in the nature of a joint adventure, you might say, and not one whereby the Member states lost their independence of action in any respect by merging it and creating a new government, as was done under the Constitution of the United States. So it was and is my view that, quite apart from any interpretation, there is a general right of withdrawal.' Although this expert did not use the term 'sovereignty,' his opinion amounts to the same as that of the delegate of the Soviet Union: that the right of withdrawal is an expression of the Members' sovereignty. He referred to 'the original statement on withdrawal,' made by a member of the United States Delegation, 'in a form which had previously been agreed upon with the American Delegation . . . : "It is the position of the United States delegation that there should be no amendment prohibiting withdrawal from the Organisation. The memorandum of the repertoire of the drafting subcommittee on membership, read on May 14, suggests that if there is no prohibition of withdrawal, and if the Charter remains silent on this matter, any possibility of lawful withdrawal is eliminated. That is not my view. It is my opinion that if the Charter is silent on withdrawal, the possibility of withdrawal would have to be determined in any particular case in the light of the surrounding circumstances at the time"' (pp. 647 f.). This statement shows that there was at the Conference a remarkable disagreement of opinions with respect to the legal effect the silence of the Charter will have on the right of withdrawal.

At the *Hearings*, the representative of the Department of State read the text on the commentary of Committee I/2. Then a Senator stated: 'The implication is that a Member-Nation would not have the absolute right of withdrawal because he must make application justifying the request for withdrawal; is that right?' In reply to this question the representative of the State Department called the attention of the Committee to Article 2, paragraph 6 (of the Charter); he said: 'There flows from that the proposition that withdrawing from the Organisation does not relieve a state of the obligation to live up to its responsibilities stated in paragraph 6. The right of withdrawal of course remains . . . but it has to be justified before the community of nations.' The representative of the State Department confirmed the interpretation that the commentary of Committee I/2 does not admit an 'absolute right of withdrawal' because the Member 'must make application justifying the request for withdrawal.' Then a Senator reminded the Committee: 'Was not the unlimited right of withdrawal omitted, among other reasons, because in the experience of the League of Nations that was the escape clause which prospective aggressors always embraced?'; whereupon the representative of the State Department answered: 'This is absolutely true,' confirming the Senator's statement that 'the unlimited right of withdrawal' was 'omitted' (pp. 232 f.).

7. Withdrawal from the Judicial Community

The Commentary of Committee I/2 refers only to the withdrawal of ' Members ' from the Organisation, the term ' Members ' meaning members of the community constituted by the Charter in the narrower sense of the term, the states represented in the General Assembly. There is, however—as pointed out—an organisation constituted by the Charter in the wider sense of the term, comprising as an integral

To the question of another Senator: ' What would be the procedure, and who would determine whether the right to withdraw had been justified ?' the representative of the State Department answered: ' It would be like any other procedure in the relationship between a Member state and the Organisation,' that is to say, he did not specify the procedure, but he admitted that a certain procedure must be followed to effectuate withdrawal. Then the Senator asked: ' Would it be decided by the Security Council or how would it be decided ? What body would pass on it ? Assume some nation made application to withdraw; who would determine whether the reasons given were justified or not ?'; whereupon the representative of the State Department answered: ' You see, there is no sanction in the Organisation to hold a state as a Member. There is a power in the Organisation to say whether or not the reasons which are advanced by the state are good and sufficient reasons.' This means that the Organisation has the power to decide whether a Member has or has not in a concrete case the right of withdrawal. Finally, the representative of the State Department declared: ' The question of mechanics, as to which body would handle that particular question and in what way, was not discussed. That was left for future determination. But I did want to call attention to the fact that in all matters relating to membership, the two organs act concurrently.' At that moment, the Chairman of the Committee intervened and propounded an opinion in direct opposition to the one until now advocated by the representative of the State Department. This part of the *Hearings* is so important that it shall be quoted at length.

The Chairman: ' Let me ask you a question right there: Is it not true that there is no application required if a nation desires to withdraw ? Moreover, there is no specific procedure to be followed. The theory of the whole withdrawal proposal, as I understand it, was that the nation affected would have to be the judge of the circumstances which it claimed had altered its position, and the penalty would be simply a mobilisation of world opinion as to whether its cause was a just one or an unjust one.'

The representative of the State Department: ' That is quite right.'

The Chairman: ' And that there was no compulsive power to keep a nation within the League if it desired to withdraw ?'

The representative: ' That is right.'

The Chairman: ' It was simply a question of leaving the world to judge whether they had adequate causes for withdrawal. They were the ones, however, to determine whether or not their circumstances had so changed as to make withdrawal justifiable.'

The representative: ' That is right.'

Later, a Senator asked: ' In the absence of a surrender of the right of withdrawal, would not a sovereign state retain that right ?'

The representative: ' That is right.'

The Chairman: ' That was the theory we proceeded upon, was it not ?'

The representative: ' That is right.'

The Chairman: ' We proceeded upon that theory in drafting this report of the committee.'

part the Statute of the International Court of Justice. This is the total community of the United Nations, which is composed of two partial communities: the United Nations in a narrower sense, and the judicial community constituted by the Statute. A state may be a member of the judicial community of the United Nations (in the wider sense of the term) without being a Member of the United Nations (in the narrower sense of the term). The problem of withdrawal may arise also for states which are only members of the judicial community.

The representative: 'That is right.'
The Chairman: 'I sat in with the committee when that report was prepared.'
A Senator to the representative: 'Then is it your answer that the Member state has an absolute right to withdraw?'
The representative: 'Yes, Senator.'
The Senator: 'Absolute?'
The representative: 'Yes.'
The Senator: 'Unqualified?'
The representative: 'Yes. But it is on notice that it will have to justify it.'
The Senator: 'You mean that it might incur the displeasure of the peace-minded people of the earth?'
The representative: 'Yes, Senator.'

At this point of the discussion the representative of the Department of State admitted an absolute right of withdrawal as consequence of the Members' sovereignty. Next the effect of Article 39 of the Charter on the right of withdrawal was discussed. A Senator asked: 'If the Security Council found that a projected withdrawal threatened the peace and security of the world, what would happen so far as the nation is concerned that wanted to withdraw; would it be compelled to stay in or would it be allowed to withdraw and suffer the penalties that any other nation might suffer if it threatened the peace and security of the world?', whereupon the answer was: 'That would depend upon the decision of the Security Council.' That means that the Security Council has the power to compel the state to remain a Member, or to allow it to withdraw and take enforcement action against it as a non-member; which is the only correct interpretation of Article 39. The consequence of this interpretation is, of course, that on behalf of Article 39 there cannot be an absolute right of withdrawal. This was exactly the conclusion drawn by the Senator, who said: 'May it be fairly inferred from what you have said that there is no such thing as a unilateral withdrawal without action by the Security Council?' And later: 'And it follows from that that the Security Council could bring coercive measures to stop the withdrawal?' The astonishing answer to this question was: 'No; it could not bring coercive measures to stop the withdrawal. What it could do is to say that, "Since you are no longer a Member and since some action of yours threatens the peace, you have got to put a stop to that action." That it has a right to do irrespective of whether a state is one which used to be a Member and withdraws or never was a Member, so long as it is a non-Member.' Then the Senator asked: 'In other words, the probable decree of the Security Council would be to come back into the Organisation?' Whereupon the representative of the State Department answered: 'Not necessarily' (pp. 234 f.). Not necessarily; but possibly. Later, he declared: 'I cannot imagine that a sanction of forcing a state against its will, contrary to the official interpretation which I have just read, would be a measure adopted by the Security Council.' But he admitted that 'if the fact of withdrawal itself, in the opinion of the Security Council, resulted in a threat to peace,' it would be treated 'like any other incident that threatened the peace without respect to membership or whether the state came back in or whether it did not.' That means that the Security Council may make

It has been completely ignored in the discussion on withdrawal at the San Francisco Conference. The answer to the question as to whether states which are members of the judicial community of the United Nations, but not 'Members of the United Nations,' may withdraw from the judicial community depends in the first place on the contents of the conditions determined under Article 93, paragraph 2, of the

any recommendation whatever especially a recommendation to refrain from withdrawal, or take enforcement measures against the Member with the effect to compel the Member to remain within the Organisation. Finally, he answered to the question of a Senator: 'No resolution or action that the Council or the Assembly could take could prevent the Member's withdrawal?'—'That would be my view' (p. 326).

On the question of withdrawal also the legal adviser of the Department of State was heard by the Committee on Foreign Relations. He advocated the opinion that any Member has the right to withdraw for certain reasons. His first statement was this: 'I think that the very fact that the matter was discussed and it was decided not to incorporate a provision in the Charter with respect to withdrawal, and the further fact that the working committee, and later, the full Commission, approved a statement that is was not the purpose of the Organisation to compel Members to continue in co-operation with it, shows that the Conference recognised that a state should have the right to withdraw from the Charter. I do not think that there is any question about the authority of a State to withdraw under the circumstances indicated.' That means that the Members have a right to withdraw under certain circumstances. But finally he declared: 'I do not think that this provision [the commentary of Committee I/2] places any inhibition upon a state with respect to withdrawal' (p. 347).

In reply to the question as to the legal effect of the commentary on withdrawal inserted into the Report of the Rapporteur, the legal adviser made the following statement: 'I say that for the reason that very frequently when treaties are entered into, the parties interpret their provisions in separate documents. Sometimes they place their interpretation in protocols annexed to the treaty. At other times they make them in other ways, as by exchange of notes and so forth. So that here you have, it seems to me, something that would stand on substantially an equal footing with the Charter itself, because that question was raised and was discussed and it was decided not to include anything in the Charter; but they agreed upon this formula which was approved by the working committee and by the Commission. I do not think that there is any question that any court of law would regard that as a legal interpretation of the right of a party to withdraw.'

Then a Senator asked: 'Whether it has not occurred to the judge that unless some state in the process of advising ratification of this treaty expressly dissents to that provision, that provision is a part of the agreement.' Thereupon the legal adviser answered: 'I think that is a correct statement' (p. 347).

The fact that the working committee, later, the full Commission, and finally, the Conference (without voting) 'approved' the commentary on withdrawal is not equivalent to an international treaty on this subject, all the less as the delegate of the Soviet Union formally expressed his dissent. If "the Conference recognised that a state should have a right to withdraw from the Charter,' it is difficult to understand why a clear provision was not inserted in the Charter, as the delegate of the Soviet Union suggested. Such provision was the more necessary as there was evidently no agreement of opinions with respect to the legal effect of the silence of the Charter. At the *Hearings*, a Senator asked: 'Might I suggest that what you [the delegation of the United States at the San Francisco Conference] attempted to do was that, whereas you did not prevent withdrawal, you did not wish to put in

Charter by the General Assembly on recommendation of the Security Council, and of the conditions laid down under Article 35, paragraph 2, of the Statute by the Security Council. Those ' conditions ' may or may not confer upon the state becoming a member of the judicial community the right of withdrawal from the community. If the conditions referred to in Article 93, paragraph 2, of the Charter and Article 35, paragraph 2, of the Statute do not confer the right of withdrawal from the judicial community upon the states which are only Members of this community, no such right exists, since neither the Charter nor the Statute stipulates such right. However, if the interpretation of Committee I/2 is accepted, the principles laid down in this commentary may—by analogy—be applied also to the withdrawal from the judicial community constituted by the Statute.

language that would encourage withdrawal without sufficient reason ?' The answer was: ' That is correct' (p. 647). If the rule concerning withdrawal formulated by the commentary is not an encouragement there was no reason not to insert this rule in the Charter.

Hackworth, in his *Digest of International Law*, vol. V (1943), p. 299, dealing with the question of withdrawal from a treaty, quotes the following passage from a memorandum transmitted by Assistant Secretary Olds to Senator Lenroot in connection with the question of the Permanent Court of International Justice: ' . . . There is no implied right in any one party to a treaty to withdraw at will in the absence of specific provision for such withdrawal by denunciation or otherwise or unless another party to the treaty has violated it so substantially as to justify its termination. While there can be no question that the United States would have the power to withdraw from the Permanent Court at any time, still distinction between the power to take such action and the propriety thereof can be clearly drawn. I feel, therefore, that to avoid the possibility of future misunderstanding, and particularly to strengthen the regard which should be had for international agreements, an appropriate reservation should be incorporated in the resolution by which the United States adheres to the Statute of the Permanent Court, recognising and reserving the right of the United States to withdraw from the Court '; and the following passage from J. L. Brierly, *Law of Nations* (2nd Ed., 1936), p. 201: ' . . . There is certainly no general right of denunciation of a treaty of indefinite duration; there are many such treaties in which the obvious intention of the parties is to establish a permanent state of things,—for example, the Pact of Paris—but there are some which we may fairly presume were intended to be susceptible of denunciation, even though they contain no express term to that effect. A *modus vivendi* is an obvious illustration; treaties of alliance and of commerce are probably in the same case.'

There can be little doubt that according to the opinion expressed in these passages and especially in the statement quoted from Brierly's *Law of Nations*, a right of withdrawal from the United Nations would require an express provision in the Charter. The Charter of the United Nations does certainly intend to establish a no less permanent state of things than the Pact of Paris which does not contain a provision on withdrawal. There is probably no expert in international law who would admit that any contracting party to the Pact of Paris has a right of withdrawal. But to the question of a Senator: ' I do not believe that there has been anything that you have said which conflicts with it [the above quoted statement] in any way,' the legal adviser answered: ' No, nothing at all' (p. 348). This answer could be correct only if the commentary on withdrawal inserted in the Report of the Rapporteur were an authentic interpretation of the Charter. This, however, is not the case.

According to Article 93, paragraph 1, the 'Members of the United Nations' are *ipso facto* parties to the Statute and hence members of the judicial community. Any such state is a member of two communities: of the United Nations as constituted by the Charter in the narrower sense of the term, and of the judicial community constituted by the Statute. Provided the 'Members of the United Nations' have the right of withdrawal in conformity with the commentary of Committee I/2, may this right be exercised only with respect to membership in the total community or also with respect to each of the partial communities of which the total community is comprised? Is it possible to withdraw as a 'Member of the United Nations,' but not at the same time as a member of the judicial community, and *vice versa?* The same question with respect to the League of Nations and the judicial community constituted by the Protocol of December 16, 1920, was to be answered in the affirmative, at least in so far as withdrawal from the League was possible without withdrawal from the judicial community. If withdrawal from the judicial community was possible at all, it was certainly possible without withdrawal from the League. But neither the Protocol nor the adjoined Statute provided for the possibility of withdrawal. The mutual independence of membership in the two communities was the consequence of the fact that the Statute of the Permanent Court of International Justice was not an integral part of the Covenant and the League was an international community different from that constituted by the Statute. However, the Statute of the International Court of Justice, although an integral part of the Charter, is nevertheless a relatively independent instrument. It is subject to an amendment procedure not identical with that to the Charter. It is especially the fact that membership in the community constituted by the Statute is possible without membership in the 'United Nations' which makes the interpretation possible that a Member of the United Nations may withdraw from the judicial community only or from the United Nations (in the narrower sense), remaining a party to the Statute. That it may become party to the Statute after having withdrawn from the United Nations cannot be doubted. If the right of withdrawal is considered to be a consequence of the Member's sovereignty, it is hardly possible to deny that a state may restrict the exercise of this right to any extent it likes. The 'extraordinary circumstances' referred to in the commentary of Committee I/2 may concern only the United Nations in the narrower sense, not the judicial community and *vice versa*. This is particularly true of the two examples of extraordinary circumstances mentioned in the Commentary. The 'Organisation' may be unable to maintain peace, but the Court may work satisfactory or the Court may become an instrument of power policy instead of law and justice, but the 'Organisation' in the narrower sense may maintain peace in a satisfactory way. The amendment, whose acceptance or non-acceptance according to the commentary, may be a cause of withdrawal, may be an amendment to the Charter in the narrower sense or to the Statute, a fact which has been ignored by the commentary.

If the states ' Members of the United Nations ' and at the same time members of the judicial community constituted by the Statute have a right of withdrawal at all, this right may be exercised with respect to each of the two partial communities separately.

CHAPTER 8

THE ORGANS OF THE UNITED NATIONS (GENERAL REMARKS)

1. 'THE PRINCIPAL' AND 'SUBSIDIARY' ORGANS

CHAPTER III of the Charter comprising Articles 7 and 8 reads as follows:

> ARTICLE 7
>
> 1. There are established as the principal organs of the United Nations: a General Assembly, a Security Council, an Economic and Social Council, a Trusteeship Council, an International Court of Justice, and a Secretariat.
>
> 2. Such subsidiary organs as may be found necessary may be established in accordance with the present Charter.
>
> ARTICLE 8
>
> The United Nations shall place no restrictions on the eligibility of men and women to participate in any capacity and under conditions of equality in its principal and subsidiary organs.

The two Articles contain some general statements concerning the organs of the United Nations. These statements have rather a theoretical than a legal character. Article 7 pretends to give a classification of all the organs, those which are already established by the Charter and those which may be established in the future, and an enumeration of the former. Two kinds of organs are distinguished: 'principal' and 'subsidiary' organs. This distinction is supposed to be exhaustive. It appears also in other Articles, such as Articles 8, 22, 29. As 'principal' organs are designated: the General Assembly the Security Council, the Economic and Social Council, the Trusteeship Council, the International Court of Justice, and the Secretariat. The statement of Article 7, paragraph 1, that the 'Secretariat' is an organ of the United Nations, is not in conformity with the provisions of the Charter which does not organise the Secretariat as a collegiate body able to act, like the General Assembly, the three Councils, or the International Court. The organ designated by the term 'Secretariat' is the Secretary-General. It is upon the Secretary-General, not upon the Secretariat, that the Charter confers definite functions. Article 102, it is true, provides that treaties shall 'be registered with the Secretariat and published by it.' But the functions determined by this Article are functions of the Secretary-General, who alone is responsible for them. The Secretariat is the office of the Secretary-General just as the 'Ministry' is the office of a cabinet minister. The members of the staff of the Secretariat (Articles 97 and 101) are organs of the United Nations but subordinate to the Secretary-General, just as the employees of a ministry are organs of the state but subordinate to the cabinet minister.

The structure and procedure for the creation of the organs mentioned in Article 7, paragraph 1, are determined in other Articles of the Charter. Their establishment by election or appointment is mandatory. The wording 'There *are* established as the principal organs of the United Nations . . . ' is not quite correct. For these organs are to be established in accordance with the provisions of the Charter by acts of Members and by acts of organs established by acts of Members. Thus, *e.g.*, the General Assembly, which according to Article 9, paragraph 1, consists of all the Members of the United Nations, is to be established by the Members appointing their representatives in accordance with Article 9, paragraph 2; or the Security Council, which consists according to Article 23 of five members which have a permanent seat, and six members elected by the General Assembly for a term of two years. It is to be established by the five permanent members appointing their representatives in accordance with Article 23, paragraph 3, by the election of the six non-permanent members by the General Assembly in accordance with paragraphs 1 and 2, and by the appointment of the representatives of the non-permanent members in accordance with paragraph 3.

The Charter distinguishes between principal and subsidiary organs. What is the meaning of the term 'subsidiary'? The Charter does not define this term. But in Articles 22 and 29 the General Assembly and the Security Council are authorised each to establish 'such subsidiary organs as it deems necessary for the performance of its functions.' That means that 'subsidiary' organs are auxiliary organs established for the purpose to assist the organ competent to establish them. If an organ is competent to establish a 'subsidiary' organ, it may establish it for the performance of some or of all its functions; but only for the performance of 'its' functions, that is to say, the functions assigned to it by the Charter.[1]

[1] During the discussion on the establishment of the Interim Committee as a subsidiary organ of the General Assembly, the question was raised in the First Committee whether the Interim Committee could rightly be deemed a 'subsidiary' organ in view of the general character of its terms of reference. 'In support of the view that the Interim Committee could not rightly be created as a subsidiary organ, the contention was advanced that a subsidiary body is "any organ created by a principal organ whose purpose is to assist the principal organ in undertaking, under its particular terms of reference, the examination of a determined question, and present a report thereon to the principal organ." This view was countered with the contention that the character of a body as a subsidiary organ under Article 7, paragraph 2, of the Charter is determined by the limitation of its authority, not by precise definition of the subject matter referred to it' (Doc. A/AC.18/SC.4/3, p. 2). The latter definition is correct, provided that by 'limitation of its authority' is meant that the competence of the subsidiary organ does not go beyond the competence of the organ by which it has been established and that the function of the subsidiary organ is to assist the organ establishing it in the performance of the functions assigned to the latter.

In contradistinction to the ' principal ' organs, whose establishment is mandatory, the ' subsidiary ' organs to which Article 7, paragraph 2, refers, is optional. They ' may be established ' ' as may be found necessary.' Nothing substantial is said in Article 7, paragraph 2, about the procedure through which they may be established. The words ' in accordance with the present Charter ' refer to the provision of other Articles. That means that Article 7, paragraph 2, is not a general authorisation granted to all principal organs to establish subsidiary organs. Subsidiary organs may be established only by acts of definite organs or Members for the purposes determined in other provisions of the Charter, and only if those competent to establish them find it necessary. Only two other Articles refer expressly to ' subsidiary ' organs: Articles 22 and 29—the one authorising the General Assembly, the other the Security Council to ' establish such subsidiary organs as it deems necessary for the performance of its functions.' No other ' subsidiary ' organs are expressly referred to in the Charter. Hence it may be assumed that only the organs established by the General Assembly under Article 22 and by the Security Council under Article 29 are ' subsidiary organs ' within the meaning of Article 7, paragraph 2. But it is also possible to interpret the term ' subsidiary organ ' to refer to any kind of auxiliary organ. Then not only the organs established under Articles 22 and 29 but also organs established under other Articles of the Charter may be considered to be ' subsidiary organs ' within the meaning of Article 7, paragraph 2.

As to the structure of these subsidiary organs neither Article 7, paragraph 2, nor Articles 22 and 29 contain provisions. Hence the General Assembly and the Security Council are free in this respect. They may establish collegiate organs or appoint a single individual as ' subsidiary ' organ, and the collegiate organs may be composed of members of the General Assembly or the Security Council respectively, or in any other way. They may be called ' commission ' or ' committee ' or ' group ' or otherwise.[2]

As pointed out, there are provisions of the Charter authorising organs other than the General Assembly and the Security Council to set up auxiliary organs not designated as ' subsidiary ' organs. Article 68 provides:

> The Economic and Social Council shall set up Commissions in economic and social fields and for the promotion of human rights, and such other commissions as may be required for the performance of its functions.

Article 47, paragraph 4, stipulates:

> The Military Staff Committee, with the authorisation of the Security Council and after consultation with appropriate regional agencies, may establish regional subcommittees.

[2] Cf. *infra*, p. 141.

If the term ' subsidiary ' organs in Article 7, paragraph 2, is interpreted to mean simply auxiliary organs, the commissions to be set up by the Economic and Social Council under Article 68 and the subcommittee to be established by the Military Staff Committee under Article 47, paragraph 4, may also be considered to be subsidiary organs within the meaning of Article 7, paragraph 2, though they are not expressly designated by the Charter as ' subsidiary.' The Military Staff Committee itself is also an auxiliary organ, for Article 47, paragraph 1, provides:

> There shall be established a Military Staff Committee to advise and assist the Security Council on all questions relating to the Security Council's military requirements for the maintenance of international peace and security, the employment and command of forces placed at its disposal, the regulation of armaments, and possible disarmament.

The wording: ' There shall be established . . . ' is not consistent with the provision of paragraph 2 of Article 47 according to which ' the Military Staff Committee shall consist of the Chiefs of Staff of the permanent members of the Security Council or their representatives.' This organ cannot be established by acts of another organ or by acts of the Members. For it is directly established by the Charter. The persons appointed by the governments of the United States, the United Kingdom, France, China, the Soviet Union as Chiefs of Staff form the Military Staff Committee without any act of making them members of this organ being necessary or possible. Nor does the establishment of the Military Staff Committee depend on the fact that it is found to be necessary by the governments concerned or by the Security Council. Hence the wording of Article 7, paragraph 2, is not applicable to the Military Staff Committee, which cannot be considered as subsidiary organ within the meaning of this provision.

According to Article 101, paragraph 1, of the Charter, the staff of the Secretariat ' shall be appointed by the Secretary-General under regulations established by the General Assembly.' Members of the staff are auxiliary organs, of the United Nations. If the term: subsidiary organs, in Article 7, paragraph 2, is understood in its wider sense, meaning auxiliary organs, the members of the Staff of the Secretariat are subsidiary organs within the meaning of this provision.

Article 21, paragraph 2, of the Statute of the International Court of Justice provides:

> The Court shall appoint its Registrar and may provide for the appointment of such other officers as may be necessary.

Provided that the term Charter in Article 7, paragraph 2, is interpreted to mean Charter in the wider sense, comprising the Statute, the Registrar and the other officers of the Court are subsidiary organs in the wider sense of this term.

Article 50 of the Statute stipulates:

> The Court may, at any time, entrust any individual, body,

bureau, commission or other organisation that it may select, with the task of carrying out an enquiry or giving an expert opinion.

The individuals or bodies, bureaux, commissions or other organisations referred to in this Article are working as auxiliary organs of the Court and, consequently, as auxiliary organs of the United Nations.

The Rules of Procedure of the General Assembly, of the Security Council, of the Economic and Social Council and of the Trusteeship Council authorise these organs to set up committees and commissions as auxiliary organs. The Rules of Procedure are established by the collegiate bodies concerned in conformity with provisions of the Charter conferring upon them the power to adopt their own rules of procedure (Articles 21, 30, 72, paragraph 1, 90, paragraph 1). Does this power imply the competence to create auxiliary organs? This question may be answered in the negative as well as in the affirmative. The negative answer may be based on the consideration that Rules of Procedure of a collegiate body refer to the transactions within the body; they cannot confer upon the body a power which is not conferred upon it by its basic constitution. This interpretation may be confirmed by the fact that the Articles authorising the General Assembly and the three Councils to adopt their rules of procedure (21, 30, 72 (1), 90 (1)) contain also special provisions empowering these bodies to elect presidents. If the president of a collegiate body is an organ of this body and the rules of procedure authorise the body to establish auxiliary organs, the provisions of the Charter concerning the election of presidents of the General Assembly and the three Councils would be superfluous. So would be also the provisions of Articles 22 and 29 of the Charter conferring upon the General Assembly and the Security Council the power to create subsidiary organs, and of Article 68 conferring upon the Economic and Social Council the power to establish commissions. However, if it is assumed that the power to adopt rules of procedure does not imply the power to create auxiliary organs, the provision of Rule 27 of the Rules of Procedure of the General Assembly authorising this body to elect seven vice-presidents has a basis in the Charter only if the vice-presidents are considered to be subsidiary organs within the meaning of Article 22. If the rules of procedure cannot provide for the establishment of auxiliary organs the creation of which is not authorised by the Charter, Rule 66 of the Rules of Procedure of the Trusteeship Council authorising this body to set up committees, and Rule 22 of the Rules of Procedure of the Economic and Social Council authorising this body to set up committees (composed of members of the Council) in addition to the commissions (not necessarily composed of members of the Council) referred to in Rule 68 are unconstitutional. For the Economic and Social Council and the Trusteeship Council are not authorised by the Charter to establish ' subsidiary organs.' If ' committees ' are considered to be ' subsidiary organs ' and if it is assumed that only the General Assembly and the Security Council are authorised to establish such organs, the committees established by these two Councils have no basis in the Charter. They are constitutional only if the provisions of the Charter authorising a collegiate body to adopt its own rules of procedure are interpreted to confer upon these bodies the power to create auxiliary organs, especially so-called ' committees.'

' Committee ' in a specific sense of the term, in contradistinction to ' commission,' may be defined as collegiate organ composed of members of the body by which it is established. Since the members of the General Assembly and the three Councils are states, the committees to be established by these bodies should be composed of states, provided that the term ' committee ' as used in the Rules of Procedure has a specific sense. But only the Rules of Procedure of the Economic and Social Council provide that the Committees which this Council is authorised to set up, shall be composed of members of the Council (Rule 22), whereas no such restriction is imposed upon the ' commissions ' which the Council may establish in conformity with Article 68 of the Charter. The Rules of Procedure of the other organs do not contain an analogous provision. The Rules concerning the Committee on Contributions and the Advisory Committee on Administrative and Budgetary Questions of the General Assembly may be interpreted to mean that these committees shall be composed, exclusively or partly, not by states, but by individuals elected for this purpose by the General Assembly. Rule 147 designates the Committee on Contributions as an ' expert ' committee and Rule 148 provides that the members of this committee shall be selected, *inter alia*, on the basis of ' personal qualifications and experience,' and that ' no two of the members shall be nationals of the same state.' Rule 145 contains analogous provisions concerning the composition of the Advisory Committee on Administrative and Budgetary Questions, and Rule 144 provides that the members of this Committee shall include ' at least two financial experts of recognised standing.' No state can fulfil the requirements laid down in these provisions. Only individuals can fulfil these requirements. They may or may not be, at the same time, representatives of Member states. The term ' committee ' is not used in these Rules of Procedure in a specific sense.[3]

If the interpretation is accepted that the provisions of the Charter authorising the General Assembly and the three Councils to adopt their own rules of procedure confer upon these bodies the power to create auxiliary organs, the committees established by these bodies in accordance with their rules of procedure may be considered to be organs different from the ' subsidiary organs ' referred to in Article 7,

[3] As to the question whether the presidents of the General Assembly and the three Councils are states represented by individuals to be designated by their governments, or individuals to be designated by the collegiate organs of the United Nations, cf. *infra*, pp. 156 f.

paragraph 2. It seems that this is the interpretation of the Charter presupposed by the Rules of Procedure of the General Assembly. After having authorised the General Assembly to establish special committees—such as the 'General Committee' (Rule 33), the 'Credential Committee' (Rule 24)—the Rules of Procedure provide in Rule 88:

> The General Assembly may set up such committees as it deems necessary for the performance of its functions.

Rule 90 provides for the establishment of the six 'Main Committees,' Rule 144 for the appointment of an 'Advisory Committee on Administrative and Budgetary Questions,' and Rule 147 for the appointment of a 'Committee on Contributions.' Quite independently from these provisions, the Rules of Procedure deal in Chapter XII with the 'Subsidiary Organs' of the General Assembly. In Rule 150, Article 22 of the Charter is reproduced, and, in addition, it is provided: 'The rules relating to the procedure of committees of the General Assembly as well as Rules 38 [concerning the participation of the Secretary-General in the meetings of the committees] and 55 [concerning publicity of the meetings] shall apply to the procedure of any subsidiary organ, unless the General Assembly or the subsidiary organ decides otherwise.' Hence it must be assumed that 'committees' within the meaning of these Rules of Procedure are not 'subsidiary organs' within the meaning of Article 7, paragraph 2. The establishment of these committees by the General Assembly is not based on Article 22, but on Article 21 of the Charter.

The Provisional Rules of Procedure of the Security Council do not differentiate 'committees' and 'subsidiary organs.' The only Rules referring to this matter are Rules 28 and 59. Rule 28 reads:

> The Security Council may appoint a commission or committee or a rapporteur for a specific question.

Rule 59 provides for the appointment of a committee for the purpose to examine the applications of states for admission to Membership. As a matter of fact, the Security Council established also other committees, such as the Committee of Experts, the Committee of Good Offices on the Indonesian Question, the Commission on Kashmir.[4]

An organ can create an auxiliary organ only by delegating its power, or part of it, to the auxiliary organ. No organ can legally delegate power to another organ without being authorised by the constitution to do so. The provisions of the Charter authorising certain organs to establish other organs must be interpreted to imply the authorisation to delegate power. It stands to reason that an organ can delegate only the power conferred upon it by the constitution. But how far does the authorisation to delegate power go? May the

[4] Cf. *infra*, pp. 391 ff.

General Assembly, empowered by Article 22 to establish subsidiary organs for the performance of its functions, authorise such an organ to make recommendations to the Members, or to the Security Council or to any other person, which the General Assembly itself may make under Article 10 or any other Article of the Charter? May the Security Council authorise a subsidiary organ established by it under Article 29 to perform any function conferred upon the Council by the Charter? The wording of Articles 22 and 29: 'for the performance of its functions' may be interpreted to mean: for the performance of the functions by the General Assembly or by the Security Council respectively. But it may also be interpreted to mean: for the performance of its function by the auxiliary organ. The first mentioned interpretation may be confirmed by the meaning of the term 'subsidiary' organ. If this interpretation is accepted, the General Assembly and the Security Council may confer upon a subsidiary organ only functions to be performed in relation to the principal organ by which the former was established; no functions to be performed in relation to Members or other organs of the United Nations or states or organisations outside the United Nations. If the other interpretation is accepted, no such restriction applies. As a matter of fact, the General Assembly and the Security Council have conferred upon subsidiary organs established by them functions to be performed in relation to Members and non-member states, as, *e.g.*, the United Nations Mediator for Palestine and the Committee of Good Offices in the Indonesian question.[5] As to organs created under the Rules of Procedure the same interpretations apply.

A special question is whether auxiliary organs established under the Charter are authorised to create other auxiliary organs. As to subsidiary organs established under Articles 22 and 29, again a negative as well as a positive answer is possible. The negative answer may be based on the fact that the provisions authorise only the General Assembly and the Security Council, not other organs, to establish subsidiary organs. A positive answer may be based on an interpretation according to which the two Articles authorise the two organs to establish not only directly but also indirectly subsidiary organs, and that consequently the General Assembly and the Security Council may authorise a subsidiary organ, established by them, to set up another subsidiary organ. As to the committees established under the Rules of Procedure of the General Assembly and the three Councils, the situation is somewhat different. If the provisions of the Charter authorising these bodies to adopt their own rules of procedure are interpreted to confer upon them the power to create auxiliary organs, the Rules of Procedure may authorise the committees to set up subcommittees. Hence the provision of Rule 93 of the Rules of

[5] Cf. *infra*, pp. 289, 395 ff.

Procedure of the General Assembly that ' each committee may set up sub-committees ' is covered by Article 21 as well as by Article 22 of the Charter. But the Security Council may, by a resolution taken under Article 29 of the Charter, authorise a committee or a commission to set up a sub-committee or a sub-commission as a ' subsidiary organ.' [6] The Rules of Procedure of the Economic and Social Council provide for committees (Rule 24), but not for sub-committees. Rule 64 providing for the establishment of the commissions referred to in Article 68 of the Charter, provides also: ' The Council may authorise commissions to set up subsidiary bodies.' This provision as well as the provision of Rule 63 ' authorising the commissions and subsidiary bodies to adopt their own rules of procedure ' is not covered by Article 68 of the Charter which empowers the Economic and Social Council only to set up ' commissions.' Although according to Rules 24 and 64 the Economic and Social Council may have as auxiliary organs: ' committees,' ' commissions ' and ' subsidiary bodies ' set up by commissions, Rule 28 authorises the Secretary-General or his deputy to make statements only upon the invitation of the President of the Council or the chairmen ' of committees of the Council and subsidiary bodies,' not upon the invitation of the chairmen of ' commissions '; and Rule 52 providing for the distribution of the summary records and relevant documents of private meetings of the Council refers only to ' committees and subsidiary bodies,' not to commissions. It seems that in Rules 28 and 52 the term ' subsidiary body ' includes ' commissions.' Rule 66 of the Rules of Procedure of the Trusteeship Council authorises this Council only to ' set up such committees as it deems necessary ' and to ' define their composition and terms of reference.' There is no express provision authorising these committees to set up sub-committees. But Rule 23 refers to ' committees, sub-committees and such subsidiary bodies as may be established by it [the Trusteeship Council].' Also Rules 25 and 26 refer to these sub-committees and subsidiary bodies as established by the Trusteeship Council. Hence the establishment of ' sub-committees ' and ' subsidiary bodies ' may be considered as authorised by the Rules of Procedure. But ' sub-committees ' are usually committees established by a committee, not by the main body itself; and according to the wording of the Rules 23, 25, 26 and 66, only the Trusteeship Council itself, not its committees are authorised to set up sub-committees. The term ' subsidiary bodies ' can hardly mean something different from committees and sub-committees. For the Trusteeship Council is not authorised—as the General Assembly and the Security Council—to establish ' subsidiary ' organs (in a specific sense of the term) or—as the Economic and Social Council—' commissions ' (in contradistinction to ' committees '). With respect to the establishment of auxiliary organs the legislative technique of the Charter as well as of the instruments implementing the Charter is anything but satisfactory.

[6] Cf. *infra*, pp. 399 f.

Is there a difference between ' principal ' and ' subsidiary ' organs? A ' subsidiary ' organ is an auxiliary organ, and the function of an auxiliary organ is to furnish assistance to another, the principal organ. However, among the organs designated in paragraph 1 of Article 7 as ' principal ' organs are some which have, at least partly, the character of auxiliary organs. This holds with respect to the Social and Economic Council which, according to Article 60, is an auxiliary organ of the General Assembly, and the Trusteeship Council which, according to Article 83, is an auxiliary organ of the Security Council and, according to Article 87, of the General Assembly. This holds especially with respect to the Secretary-General who—at least in principle—is an auxiliary organ of all the principal organs of the United Nations. Not all the organs designated in Article 7, paragraph 1, as ' principal ' organs are principal, in the true sense of the term, or supreme organs, meaning organs not subordinated to other organs. An organ is subordinated to another organ if it is legally or politically bound by commands of that organ. Only the General Assembly, the Security Council, and the International Court of Justice are supreme organs of the United Nations.

Hence the characterisation of the organs enumerated in Article 7, paragraph 1, as ' principal ' organs has no specific meaning. A legal document such as a statute or a treaty should contain only legal provisions, that is, statements by which obligations, rights, competences, functions and the like are determined; it should not contain theoretical statements such as a classification of the legal effects of the instrument. Such classifications are the task of commentaries. As contents of a legal instrument they are superfluous and, if not correct, misleading.

2. The Organs not referred to in Chapter III of the Charter

The classification of the organs of the United Nations made in Article 7 is incorrect not only because the so-called ' principal ' organs are—in truth—partly auxiliary organs, but also because the classification presented as exhaustive is evidently not exhaustive. It follows from previous statements that there are organs which are neither ' principal ' organs enumerated in Article 7, paragraph 1, nor ' subsidiary ' organs in the narrower sense, meaning organs established by the General Assembly under Article 22 or by the Security Council under Article 29. But there are organs of the United Nations which are neither ' principal ' organs enumerated in Article 7, paragraph 1, nor ' subsidiary ' organs in the wider sense of the term, that is to say auxiliary organs which ' may be found necessary ' and hence ' may be established in accordance with the present Charter.' The Military Staff Committee, as pointed out, is an auxiliary organ of the Security Council, but not a subsidiary organ within the meaning of Article 7, paragraph 2.

Articles 52 and 53 of the Charter refer to regional agencies which may be considered to be—at least indirectly—organs of the United

Nations in so far as the Members of the United Nations are authorised by the Charter to constitute such agencies for purposes of the United Nations, especially to organise collective self-defence in accordance with Article 51, and ' to achieve pacific settlement of local disputes '; and the Security Council shall ' encourage the development of pacific settlement of local disputes . . . by such regional agencies,' and even ' utilise ' such regional agencies for enforcement action ' under its authority.' Regional agencies are neither principal nor subsidiary organs within the meaning of Article 7.

Chapters IX and X refer to ' specialised agencies.' The Charter, it is true, does not recognise these agencies as ' organs ' of the United Nations. For Article 96, authorising in paragraph 1 the General Assembly and the Security Council to request the International Court of Justice to give an advisory opinion on legal questions, states in paragraph 2: ' Other organs of the United Nations and specialised agencies, which may at any time be so authorised by the General Assembly, may also request advisory opinions of the Court on legal questions . . . ' The phrasing ' other organs *and* specialised agencies ' indicates that the latter, although treated in matters referred to in Article 96 on the same level as organs, are not considered to be ' organs.' However, they may be characterised at least as indirect organs of the United Nations. For these agencies established by intergovernmental agreements and having international responsibilities in the fields of international economic and social co-operation which is a purpose of the United Nations, shall, according to Article 57, be brought into relationship to the United Nations. According to Articles 58 and 63, the activities of these specialised agencies may be ' co-ordinated ' by the Economic and Social Council upon recommendations on the part of the Organisation. According to Article 64, the Economic and Social Council may take appropriate steps to ' obtain regular reports from the specialised agencies.' According to Article 59, the Organisation shall even initiate the creation of ' new specialised agencies required for the accomplishment of the purposes set forth in Article 55.' Under Article 70 the Economic and Social Council may make arrangements for reciprocal representation of the agencies in the Council and of the Council in the agencies, which implies that these international communities may become temporary Members of the United Nations with restrictive rights. Article 91 empowers the Trusteeship Council to avail itself of the assistance of the specialised agencies in regard to matters with which they are concerned.[7] According to Article 17, paragraph 3, the General Assembly is authorised to ' consider and approve ' the financial and budgetary arrangements to be made with the specialised agencies and to ' examine the administrative budgets ' of the specialised agencies with a view ' to making recommendations ' to them.

[7] Cf. *infra*, p. 684.

What is the meaning of the term 'organ' as used in Article 96, paragraph 2? If it means only the 'organs' referred to in Article 7 of the Charter, the General Assembly cannot authorise the Military Staff Committee referred to in Article 47, or the regional agencies referred to in Article 52, or other organs of the United Nations, of which we shall speak later, to request advisory opinions from the Court. Such restriction is hardly justifiable. It is, however, not impossible to interpret the term 'organ' as used in Article 96, paragraph 2, to mean any individual or state and any group of individuals or states authorised by the Charter to perform functions of the United Nations. It is, of course, upon the General Assembly in applying Article 96, paragraph 2, to interpret this provision.[8]

According to Article 81, the administration of territories placed under the trusteeship system of the United Nations may be conferred upon one or more states or upon the Organisation itself. If the administering authority is one or more states, this state, or states, are organs of the United Nations, insofar as they exercise functions of the trusteeship system established under the authority of the United Nations (Article 75). But they are neither principal nor subsidiary organs within the meaning of Article 7.[9]

There is an organ of the United Nations established by Article 106. This organ has to exercise the responsibilities of the Security Council under Article 42, 'pending the coming into force of such special agreements referred to in Article 43 as in the opinion of the Security Council enable it to begin the exercise of its responsibilities under Article 42.' The organ consists of the five powers which have permanent seats in the Security Council. The five powers, represented by their governments, form an organ of the United Nations since their 'joint action' is performed according to the express provision of Article 106 'on behalf of the Organisation for the purpose of maintaining international peace and security,' which is the main purpose of the United Nations.[1]

Also the General Conference to be held for the purpose of reviewing the Charter in conformity with Article 109 must be classed as an organ of the United Nations. The General Conference has to exercise a function which is normally conferred upon the General Assembly: to adopt amendments to the Charter. Although the function of the General Conference is exactly the same as the just mentioned function of the General Assembly it is designated by another term. Whereas the General Assembly has to 'adopt' amendments to the Charter, the General Conference has to 'recommend' 'alterations' of the Charter. This terminological difference has, however, no legal importance.

[8] Cf. *infra*, pp. 545 ff.

[9] Cf. *infra*, p. 692.

[1] Cf. *infra*, pp. 756 ff.

There are some important organs of the United Nations established by the Statute of the International Court of Justice.

According to Article 4, paragraph 1, of the Statute the members of the Court shall be elected by the General Assembly and by the Security Council from a list of persons nominated by the national groups in the Permanent Court of Arbitration. These ' national groups ' exercise an essential function in the procedure through which a principal organ of the United Nations is created. They are established by Article 44 of the Hague Convention for the Pacific Settlement of International Disputes of 1907. They are organs of the United Nations by delegation. Since some Members of the United Nations are not represented in the Permanent Court of Arbitration, Article 4, paragraph 2, of the Statute provides that the governments of these Members shall appoint national groups ' under the same conditions as those prescribed for members of the Permanent Court of Arbitration by Article 44 of the Hague Convention.' These ' national groups ' are established as organs of the United Nations directly by the Charter (in the wider sense of the term).[2]

In case the ordinary procedure for the election of members of the International Court of Justice, determined in Articles 4–11 of the Statute, does not have the result that all seats are filled, Article 12 of the Statute provides for the appointment of a ' joint conference ' consisting of six members, three elected by the General Assembly, three by the Security Council. The joint conference has to choose one name for each seat still vacant and to submit it to the General Assembly and the Security Council for their respective acceptance. The ' joint conference,' too, is an organ of the United Nations, but is neither one of the principal organs enumerated in Article 7, paragraph 1, nor a subsidiary organ within the meaning of Article 7, paragraph 2.

Finally, there may be organs of the United Nations established or to be established by international agreements entered into by the United Nations. Thus, according to Article 11 of the Permanent Statute of the Free Territory of Trieste, which is an Annex (VI) to the Peace Treaty with Italy and has been approved by the Security Council, the latter has to appoint the Governor of Trieste. The Council also has the power to suspend and to dismiss the Governor who, according to Article 17 of the Statute, is ' the representative of the Security Council.' There can be little doubt that the Governor of the Free Territory of Trieste is an organ of the United Nations. But he is neither a principal nor a subsidiary organ within the meaning of Article 7 of the Charter. The legal basis of its establishment is Article 11 of the Statute of Trieste, not Article 29 of the Charter which authorises the Security Council to establish subsidiary organs for the performance ' of its functions '; which probably means: for the performance of the functions conferred upon the Council by the Charter.[3]

[2] Cf. *infra*, pp. 466 ff.

[3] Cf. *infra*, pp. 825 ff.

3. ' ORGAN ' AND ' MEMBER '

The term ' organ ' as used in Chapter III of the Charter refers to the concept of organ in a specific and narrower sense meaning an individual or a body of individuals exercising the function of a community according to the principle of division of labour. The term is used to differentiate ' organ ' and ' member.' However, in a wider sense of the term, any member of a community is its organ meaning an individual or a body of individuals determined by the legal order, constituting the community, to execute or to create the norms of this order. Thus, *e.g.*, any Member of the Organisation is an organ of the United Nations in so far as it participates in the amendment procedure determined in Articles 108 and 109 by ratifying the decision adopted by the General Assembly or the General Conference; the United States of America, in receiving, under Article 110, paragraph 2, the ratifications of the Charter deposited with its Government by the other signatories and notifying them and the Secretary-General of each deposit, in drawing up a protocol of the ratifications deposited under paragraph 3 of Article 110, and communicating copies thereof to all other signatories, acted as an organ of the United Nations; any state which, authorised by Article 31 of the Statute of the Court, chooses a person to take part as a judge in the deliberation and decision of the International Court of Justice in a particular case, is an organ of the United Nations, for it participates in the creation of one of its principal organs. Any Member of the United Nations is an organ of this organisation when it participates in an enforcement action taken by the Security Council under Article 41 or 42. However, the Charter in referring to functions of the Organisation or ' its organs ' does not refer to the acts of its Members. If a Member state or non-Member state, invited under Article 31, 32 or 44, participates in the discussion or decision of the Security Council, it functions as an organ of the United Nations, although the Charter does not characterise its function in this way.

4. STATES AND INDIVIDUALS AS ORGANS (INDIRECT AND DIRECT INTERNATIONAL ORGANS)

Since Article 7, paragraph 1, has a purely theoretical character and paragraph 2 of this Article is in itself not applicable, Article 8 seems to be the only provision of Chapter III which has a legal effect. This Article provides that the Organisation ' shall place no restrictions on the eligibility of men and women to participate in any capacity and under conditions of equality in its principal and subsidiary organs.' In interpreting this provision we must take into consideration that there are two different kinds of international organs: organs which are states or composed of states, and organs which are individuals or composed of individuals. An organ of the United Nations which is a state is, *e.g.*, the administering authority of a trust territory according to Article 81; organs of the United Nations which are composed of states are, *e.g.*, the General Assembly, the three Councils, the

Military Staff Committee. Organs of the United Nations which are individuals are, *e.g.*, the Secretary-General, the Members of the staff of the Secretariat, the Registrar of the International Court of Justice and the other officials of the Court; organs of the United Nations which are composed of individuals are, *e.g.*, the International Court of Justice. The subsidiary organs to be established by the General Assembly under Article 22 and by the Security Council under Article 29, the commissions to be set up by the Economic and Social Council under Article 68, the committees to be set up by the General Assembly, the Security Council and the Trusteeship Council under their Rules of Procedure, the regional subcommittees to be established by the Military Staff Committee under Article 47, paragraph 4, may be composed of states or of individuals. Since all social functions are acts of individual human beings and can be performed only by individuals, the functions determined by international law, too, can be performed only by individuals. The statement that an international organ is a state, or is composed of states, means that the creation of the organ is to be carried out in two stages; the first stage is to designate a state or several states for a certain function. This stage is directly determined by general or particular (contractual) international law. The second stage is to designate the individual or the individuals who are to represent the state or states in performing the function. As a rule, this stage is not directly, but indirectly, determined by international law. The designation of the individual or individuals by whom the states are to be represented is, normally, delegated by international law to these states, that is to say, to their national legal order. This is the case, *e.g.*, with respect to the representation of the Members on the General Assembly or the Security Council. But exceptionally the individual who has to perform the function determined by international law, that is to say, to function as international organ, may be directly determined by international law. This is the case, *e.g.*, with respect to the appointment of the Secretary-General and the members of the staff, the election of the members of the Court, the appointment of the Registrar and the other officers of the Court.

The statement that an international organ is a state, not an individual, means that international law only indirectly determines the individual who is to perform the function as an organ. Only individuals can be organs of national or international law or—what amounts to the same—organs of a community constituted by law. That individuals may be direct or indirect organs of an international community means, if correctly formulated, that individuals are normally indirect, and exceptionally only direct, organs of international communities. This is the consequence of the general principle that states are subjects of international law, which principle really means that international law only indirectly determines the individuals whose behaviour is the contents of the duties and rights established by international law, in delegating the states, that is the national legal orders, to determine these individuals. However, subjects of law are not only subjects of the duties and rights, but also subjects of the competences established by the law. Subjects of competences are organs. Just as the principle that subjects of international duties and rights are states has exceptions, that is to say, that there are exceptionally norms of international law which directly determine the individuals whose behaviour forms the contents of the duties and rights established by international law, so there are exceptions to the principle that international organs are states. There are rules of international law by which the individuals who are to perform an international function are directly determined so that it is not necessary to have them designated by acts of the states authorised to this effect. This can be done by indicating the name of the individual in the text of the treaty by which the international organisation is established. No act of appointment or election on the part of an already established international organ is necessary. In this way the first Secretary-General of the League of Nations was appointed (Annex II to the Covenant of the League of Nations). In case international organs are to be created by other international agencies, already established, these agencies may be authorised by the treaty, constituting the international organisation, to designate directly individuals as organs. In contradistinction to the Covenant of the League of Nations, the Charter authorises in Article 97 the General Assembly to appoint, on the recommendation of the Security Council, the first, and all subsequent, Secretaries-General. An individual directly appointed or elected by an international organisation (through its organ) for the purpose to function as its organ is not the representative of a member state in its capacity as partial organ of the community and thus only indirectly an organ of the international community; it is directly an organ of this community. The correct characterisation of the two kinds of international organs is not: organs which are states, and organs which are individuals, but: individuals who are indirect, and individuals who are direct international organs.

If the members of a collegiate organ are states represented by individuals to be designated by the governments of these states, it may happen that not all the states members of the collegiate organ designate their representatives. Then the question arises whether the organ can work constitutionally. The answer to this question depends on the way in which the composition of the organ is determined. If the membership of definite states is mandatory, the fact that one of the members does not designate its representative has the effect that the organ concerned is not constitutionally established. But the membership of all or some of the states which compose the organ may be only optional. Then the fact that a state whose membership is optional does not designate a representative has no effect on the constitutionality of the organ.[4]

[4] Cf. *infra*, pp. 165, 174, 176.

5. The Scope of Article 8

Article 8 lays down a prohibition: to place no restrictions on the eligibility of men and women to participate in the organs of the United Nations. To place restrictions on the eligibility of individuals means to stipulate by a law-making act that individuals of a certain kind are not eligible. Article 8 refers to a law-making function of the Organisation, to the establishment, by the organs of the United Nations, of rules concerning the election or appointment of other organs.[5] Article 8, it is true, refers only to the 'principal and subsidiary organs' of the United Nations and hence may be interpreted to apply only to organs mentioned in Article 7, paragraph 1, and the 'subsidiary organs' to be established by the General Assembly under Article 22 and by the Security Council under Article 29, since no other 'subsidiary' organs are referred to in the Charter. If, however, the term 'subsidiary organs' in Article 8 is interpreted to mean any auxiliary organ, then Article 8 may apply to all the organs of the United Nations.

The rules of the Charter concerning the composition of the organs established by, or to be established in accordance with, the Charter such as the provisions concerning the composition of the General Assembly, the Security Council, the Economic and Social Council, the Trusteeship Council, the Military Staff Committee, the International Court of Justice, and the rules concerning the appointment of the Secretary-General do not contain any restriction of the kind prohibited in Article 8. Such restrictions to be operative in the creation of these organs could be established only by amendments to the Charter. Only by an amendment to Article 9, paragraph 2, or Article 23, paragraph 3, for instance, could women be excluded from representing a Member in the General Assembly or in the Security Council. The General Assembly, in adopting its rules of procedure—even without the prohibition of Article 8—has not the power to restrict the representation of Members elected by the General Assembly for non-permanent membership in the Security Council to males. Besides, the question as to by whom a state is to be represented in the General Assembly or the Security Council is no concern of the Organisation but of the states. According to the Charter, states, not individuals, are members of these two organs; the same is true of the Economic and Social Council and the Trusteeship Council. For this reason, the provision of Article 8 does not apply to the representation on these organs. The provision is not binding upon the Members, but upon the Organisation. It reads: 'The United Nations shall

[5] For instance Regulation 10 of the Provisional Staff Rules, Annex II to the Resolution of the General Assembly concerning the Organisation of the Secretariat (Doc. A/64, p. 18), which runs as follows:

> Men and women are equally eligible for all posts in the Secretariat.

place no restrictions etc.' The term 'United Nations' is ambiguous and may mean, not the Organisation, but its Members. But in Article 8, the 'United Nations' to which the words 'its principal and subsidiary organs' refer can mean only the Organisation, since these organs are organs of the Organisation.

Members of the Military Staff Committee, too, are states, but the Charter determines that these states must be represented by their Chiefs of Staff or their representatives. A state excluding by a legislative act women from this function would not violate Article 8 of the Charter. The 'subsidiary organs' to be established under Article 22 by the General Assembly, under Article 29 by the Security Council, the commissions to be set up under Article 68 by the Economic and Social Council, the committees to be set up by the General Assembly, the Security Council and the Trusteeship Council under their Rules of Procedure and the regional subcommittees to be established by the Military Staff Committee under Article 47, paragraph 4, may be composed of states or of individuals to be determined by the bodies competent to create these organs. If the members of these organs are states Article 8 does not apply. Individuals are to be appointed or elected by organs of the United Nations as Secretary-General, members of the staff of the Secretariat, members of the International Court of Justice, as Registrar or other officers of the Court. The rules determining the appointment of the Secretary-General are laid down directly in Article 97 of the Charter; the rules concerning the election of the members of the Court in the Statute. To guarantee men and women equal access to these functions, Article 8 was not necessary since only by a change of the rules laid down in the Charter or the Statute a restriction on eligibility could be established, and such change is possible only by an amendment to the Charter or the Statute. Such amendments however are not excluded by Article 8, since Article 8 itself can be amended in accordance with the provisions of Articles 108 and 109 of the Charter.

The prohibition of Article 8 is applicable only to the adoption, by the organs of the United Nations, of rules regulating the designation of individuals as direct organs of the United Nations. These are the provisions to be laid down in the Rules of Procedure of the General Assembly and of the three Councils concerning the establishment of committees, the provisions to be laid down in the Rules of Procedure of the Economic and Social Council concerning the establishment of commissions referred to in Article 68, the regulations to be established by the General Assembly for the appointment of the staff of the Secretariat referred to in Article 101, and the rules to be laid down by the International Court of Justice concerning the appointment of the Registrar and other officers of the Court in conformity with Article 21, paragraph 2, of the Statute. In establishing all these rules the organs of the United Nations are bound by the prohibition of Article 8.

6. Competence of an Organ as Right or as Duty

The competence of an organ may be established by a legal order in two different ways: the organ may be authorised to exercise the function determined by the legal order so that it depends on the organ's discretion to exercise or not to exercise the function; or the organ may be obliged to exercise the function. It might seem at first sight that the Charter applies both methods to confer competences upon the organs of the United Nations, in stipulating one time the organ 'may,' the other time, the organ 'shall' perform a certain function. But the function determined by the legal order is the content of a legal obligation only if the legal order provides a sanction for the non-performance of the function. Such sanctions are practically impossible if supreme organs or collegiate organs are involved, especially organs composed of states such as the General Assembly or the various Councils of the United Nations. As a matter of fact the Charter does not provide sanctions to be directed against any organ of the United Nations, whether state or individual. Hence it makes no legal difference whether the Charter stipulates that an organ 'may' or that an organ 'shall' perform a definite function. In both cases the organ is legally only authorised, not obliged (in the strict sense of the term) to act as determined by the Charter. The same is true with respect to the terms 'responsibility' and 'duty' by which the Charter sometimes designates the functions conferred upon organs, as for instance in Article 13, paragraph 2, and Articles 24, 60, 73, 100.

That the use of the terms in question does not constitute a legal obligation of the organ to perform the function does not mean that it may have no effect at all. In case the Charter stipulates that an organ 'shall' perform a certain function, the organ will certainly consider itself to be morally and politically bound to act as prescribed by the Charter; and if it is an auxiliary organ and the function is to be performed for the benefit of a principal organ, as for instance, to submit a report to the latter, it may be assumed that the principal organ is authorised to order the auxiliary organ to perform the function. Such order again, it is true, does constitute only a moral-political, not a legal, obligation; but the use of the term 'shall in determining the function of an auxiliary organ may be interpreted to imply the power of the principal organ to issue such an order. In case the Charter merely stipulates that the auxiliary organ 'may' perform a function for the benefit of a principal organ, it could be doubted whether the latter is authorised to order its performance (as for instance, the General Assembly with respect to reports of the Economic and Social Council on certain observations referred to in Article 64, paragraph 2).

Chapter 9

THE GENERAL ASSEMBLY

1. Organisation

Article 9 of the Charter runs as follows:

> 1. The General Assembly shall consist of all the Members of the United Nations.
>
> 2. Each Member shall have not more than five representatives in the General Assembly.

Members of the General Assembly are states, but states represented by individuals. Consequently the General Assembly consists of the representatives of the Members of the United Nations. In this respect the text of Article 3, paragraph 1, of the Covenant: 'The Assembly shall consist of Representatives of the Members of the League,' is more adequate than that of Article 9, paragraph 1, of the Charter. To say: The General Assembly consists of representatives of the Members of the United Nations amounts to the same as to say: the General Assembly consists of the representatives of *all* the Members of the United Nations. The word 'all' in paragraph 1 of Article 9 is redundant.

In the General Assembly the principle of equality of the Members is strictly observed. According to Article 18, paragraph 1, each Member—great or small—has only one vote, and each vote has the same weight. Each Member may have not more than five representatives. In the Assembly of the League of Nations the Members were allowed to have only three representatives.[1] The Charter does not provide for alternates or advisers of the representatives. But the Member states may replace at any time the individual, appointed representative, by another individual in conformity with Article 9, paragraph 2. The Member state may appoint alternates and advisers, but only the representatives are organs of the United Nations and at the same time organs of the Member state. Alternates and advisers are not organs of the United Nations though organs of their states.

Since a Member may be represented by five individuals but has only one vote, organisation of its representatives as an acting body is

[1] At the 2nd meeting of Committee II/1 of the San Francisco Conference 'it was maintained the number of delegates in the Assembly should be limited to one for each member in order to make the General Assembly less cumbersome, and to protect the small nations who could not properly afford to send three or four delegates to the Assembly but might feel obliged to do so for reasons of prestige. In support of the view that each country should have several delegates, it was argued that this would enable members to obtain the advantages of consultation and division of work, and also to have in their representation in the Assembly various shades of political opinion.' (U.N.C.I.O. Doc. 211, II/1/6.)

necessary. Such organisation may be achieved by authorising one of them to act on behalf of all—as a chairman, for instance—especially in case of voting. That the text of the Charter does not contain such provision is all the more regrettable as it is doubtful whether the authorisation of the General Assembly to adopt its own rules of procedure (Article 21) implies the power of the General Assembly to authorise the Member states to appoint, as organs of the United Nations, alternates and advisers, and to designate as chairman one of the representatives referred to in Article 9, paragraph 2. This has actually been done by the Rules of Procedure of the General Assembly. These Rules run as follows:

RULE 21

> The delegation of a Member shall consist of not more than five representatives and five alternate representatives, and as many advisers, technical advisers, experts and persons of similar status as may be required by the delegation.

RULE 22

> An alternate representative may act as representative upon designation by the Chairman of the delegation.

RULE 23

> The credentials of representatives, and the names of members of a delegation shall be submitted to the Secretary-General if possible not less than one week before the date fixed for the opening of the session. The credentials shall be issued either by the Head of the State or Government or by the Minister for Foreign Affairs.

Since the General Assembly is a body of individuals it must have organs. In this respect the Charter provides in Article 21: that the General Assembly shall have a President elected by the General Assembly for each session. This provision is very vague. Must the President be elected from among the members of the General Assembly or is the General Assembly free to elect any personality whatever, as it is free in the appointment of a Secretary-General? If the President must be elected from among the members of the General Assembly, is the latter authorised to elect a certain individual, representative of a Member in the General Assembly, or have the words 'elect its President' the same meaning as the provision that the General Assembly shall elect members of the Security Council, or of other collegiate organs of the United Nations, namely that the General Assembly shall determine the state whose representative shall perform the function of President during one session, the government of this state being authorised to determine the individual, as it is authorised to determine the individuals by whom it is to be represented in the

General Assembly, Security Council and other collegiate organs of the United Nations? If so, is the government entitled to nominate for the function of President of the General Assembly any individual it pleases or is the government bound to nominate only one of those by whom it is represented in the General Assembly, so that the individual who performs the function of President is included in the five individuals by whom a Member may be represented in the General Assembly? May the government of the state on which the Presidency is conferred for the term of a session replace its representative during the term as it may do so with its representative in the General Assembly or in another collegiate organ of the United Nations? All these questions are not answered by the provision of Article 21 of the Charter. They may be answered by the Rules of Procedure of the General Assembly which the latter is authorised by the same Article to adopt. The Rules of Procedure of the General Assembly provide:

RULE 27

> The General Assembly shall elect a President and seven Vice-Presidents, who shall hold office until the close of the session at which they are elected. The Vice-Presidents shall be elected, after the election of the Chairmen of the six Main Committees referred to in Rule 90, on the basis of ensuring the representative character of the General Committee.

In authorising the General Assembly to elect seven Vice-Presidents the Rules of Procedure go beyond the Charter, which authorises the Assembly only to elect a President. The question as to whether Article 21 or Article 22 of the Charter confers upon the General Assembly the power of establishing the office of Vice-President has been discussed in another connection.[2] The provision that the Vice-Presidents shall be elected after the election of the Chairmen of the six Main Committees on the basis of ensuring the representative character of the General Committee, can be understood only in connection with the provision of Rule 33, which runs as follows:

> The General Committee shall consist of fourteen members no two of whom shall be members of the same delegation, and shall be so constituted as to ensure its representative character. It shall comprise the President of the General Assembly, who shall preside, the seven Vice-Presidents and the Chairmen of the six Main Committees.

To the question whether the election of a President refers to a Member state or to a definite individual, the Rules of Procedure give no direct answer. But Rule 26 stipulates:

> At the opening of each session of the General Assembly the Chairman of that delegation from which the President of the

[2] Cf. *supra*, p. 140.

> previous session was elected shall preside until the General Assembly has elected a President for the session.

This provision presupposes that the President is to be elected ' from a delegation.' However, the Rules of Procedure do not contain an express provision to this effect; nor a provision that only the chairman of a delegation can be elected President. But Rule 32 provides:

> The President, or Vice-President acting as President, shall not vote but shall appoint another member of his delegation to vote in his place.

This Rule presupposes that only that member of a delegation who is empowered by his government to cast the vote of the Member state he represents, and to authorise other members of his delegation to exercise this function, may be elected President or Vice-President. It is probably the chairman of a delegation who has this power. Instead of providing it expressly, the Rules of Procedures only presuppose that a Member state is to be elected to the Presidency or Vice-Presidency by electing the chairman of its delegation to this function.[3]

The main functions of the President are determined by Rule 31:

> In addition to exercising the powers which are conferred upon him elsewhere by these rules, the President shall declare the opening and closing of each plenary meeting of the session, shall direct the discussions in plenary meeting, ensure observance of these rules, accord the right to speak, put questions and announce decisions. He shall rule on points of order, and, subject to these rules, shall have complete control of the proceedings at any meeting and over the maintenance of order thereat.

The Rules of Procedure stipulate further:

RULE 28

> If the President finds it necessary to be absent during a meeting or any part thereof, he shall appoint one of the Vice-Presidents to take his place.

[3] Even before adopting the Provisional Rules of Procedure the General Assembly, at its 1st meeting on January 10, 1946, elected a President. In this election the Provisional Rules, not yet adopted by the General Assembly, were applied. One of the representatives of Belgium was elected President of the Assembly; but the minutes of the meeting do not show that he was elected in his capacity as a representative of a member of the General Assembly. At its 3rd meeting the General Assembly elected seven Vice-Presidents. The representative of the Netherlands proposed ' that the first delegates of the following countries be elected Vice-Presidents: China, France, the Union of South Africa, the Union of Soviet Socialist Republics, the United Kingdom, the United States of America, and Venezuela.' The proposal made by the representative of the Netherlands was adopted by acclamation. In this case it was clear that not individual persons but representatives of members of the General Assembly were elected. (Journal of the General Assembly, No. 3, pp. 54 ff.)

RULE 29

A Vice-President acting as President shall have the same powers and duties as the President.

RULE 30

If the President is unable to perform his functions, a new President shall be elected for the unexpired term.

Pursuant to Articles 21 and 22 of the Charter, the Rules of Procedure provide:

RULE 88

The General Assembly may set up such committees as it deems necessary for the performance of its functions.

RULE 93

Each committee may set up sub-committees, which shall elect their own officers.

According to the Rules of Procedure there are two kinds of Committees: Main Committees and other Committees. Rules 90 and 91 stipulate:

RULE 90

The Main Committees of the General Assembly are:

(1) Political and Security Committee (including the regulation of armaments);

(2) Economic and Financial Committee;

(3) Social, Humanitarian and Cultural Committee;

(4) Trusteeship Committee (including Non-Self-Governing Territories);

(5) Administrative and Budgetary Committee; and

(6) Legal Committee.

RULE 91

Each Member may be represented by one person on each Main Committee and on any other committee that may be constituted upon which all Members have the right to be represented. It may also assign to these committees advisers, technical advisers, experts or persons of similar status.

RULE 92

Upon designation by the Chairman of the delegation, advisers, technical advisers, experts or persons of similar status may act as members of committees. Persons of this status shall not, however, unless designated as alternate representatives

> be eligible for appointment as Chairmen, Vice-Chairmen or Rapporteurs of committees or for seats in the General Assembly.

An important committee of the General Assembly, the General Committee mentioned above, is not among the Main Committees. Its function is determined as follows:

> RULE 35
>
> The General Committee shall at the beginning of each session consider the provisional agenda, together with the supplementary list, and shall make a report thereon to the General Assembly. It shall consider requests for the inclusion of additional items in the agenda and shall report thereon to the General Assembly. It shall assist the President and the General Assembly in drawing up the agenda for each plenary meeting, in determining the priority of its items, and in the co-ordination of the proceedings of all committees of the General Assembly. Finally, it shall assist the President in the general conduct of the work of the General Assembly which falls within the competence of the President. It shall not, however, decide any political question.
>
> RULE 36
>
> A Member of the General Assembly which has no representative on the General Committee, and which has requested the inclusion of an item in the agenda, shall be entitled to attend any meeting of the General Committee at which its request is discussed, and may participate, without vote, in the discussion of that item.
>
> RULE 37
>
> The General Committee may revise the resolutions adopted by the General Assembly, changing their form but not their substance. Any such changes shall be reported to the General Assembly for its consideration.

A committee not mentioned among the Main Committees is the Credentials Committee, regarding which Rule 24 stipulates:

> A Credentials Committee shall be appointed at the beginning of each session. It shall consists of nine members, who shall be appointed by the General Assembly on the proposal of the President. The Committee shall elect its own officers. It shall examine the credentials of representatives and report without delay.

Two other committees to be established by the General Assembly, according to the Rules of Procedure, are the Advisory Committee on

Administrative and Budgetary Questions, and the Committee on Contributions.[4]

RULE 144

The General Assembly shall appoint an Advisory Committee on Administrative and Budgetary Questions (hereinafter called the 'Advisory Committee'), with a membership of nine, including at least two financial experts of recognised standing.

RULE 145

The members of the Advisory Committee, no two of whom shall be nationals of the same State, shall be selected on the basis of broad geographical representation, personal qualifications and experience, and shall serve for three years corresponding to three financial years, as defined in the regulations for the financial administration of the United Nations. Members shall retire by rotation and shall be eligible for reappointment. The two financial experts shall not retire simultaneously. The General Assembly shall appoint the members of the Advisory Committee at the regular session immediately preceding the expiration of the term of office of the members, or, in the case of vacancies, at the next session.

RULE 146

The Advisory Committee shall be responsible for expert examination of the budget of the United Nations, and shall assist the Administrative and Budgetary Committee of the General Assembly. At the commencement of each regular session it shall submit to the General Assembly a detailed report on the budget for the next financial year and on the accounts of the last financial year. It shall also examine on behalf of the General Assembly the administrative budget of specialised agencies and proposals for financial and budgetary arrangements with such agencies. It shall perform such other duties as may be assigned to it under the regulations for the financial administration of the United Nations.

RULE 147

The General Assembly shall appoint an expert Committee on Contributions, consisting of ten members.

[4] As to the composition of these committees, cf. *supra*, p. 141. When a member of these two committees, who was a representative of Czechoslovakia, was dismissed by his government from this office, the question arose whether as a result of this act he also lost his quality as member of the two committees. By a decision of the General Assembly adopted at its 151st meeting the question was decided in the negative. Cf. United Nations Bulletin, Vol. 5, pp. 874 f.

RULE 148

The members of the Committee on Contributions, no two of whom shall be nationals of the same State, shall be selected on the basis of broad geographical representation, personal qualifications and experience, and shall serve for a period of three years corresponding to three financial years, as defined in the regulations for the financial administration of the United Nations. Members shall retire by rotation and shall be eligible for reappointment. The General Assembly shall appoint the members of the Committee on Contributions at the regular session immediately preceding the expiration of the term of office of the members, or, in case of vacancies, at the next session.

RULE 149

The Committee on Contributions shall advise the General Assembly concerning the apportionment, under Article 17, paragraph 2, of the Charter, of the expenses of the Organisation among Members, broadly according to capacity to pay. The scale of assessments when once fixed by the General Assembly shall not be subject to a general revision for at least three years, unless it is clear that there have been substantial changes in relative capacities to pay. The Committee shall also advise the General Assembly on the assessments to be fixed for new Members, on appeals by Members for a change of assessments, and on the action to be taken with regard to the application of Article 19 of the Charter.

At its first session the General Assembly established a commission to deal with the problems raised by the discovery of atomic energy and other related matters. According to the resolution adopted by the Assembly on January 24, 1946:

'The Commission shall be composed of one representative from each of those States, represented on the Security Council, and Canada when that State is not a member of the Security Council. Each representative on the Commission may have such assistance as he may desire . . . The Commission shall proceed with the utmost despatch and enquire into all phases of the problem, and make such recommendations from time to time with respect to them as it finds possible. In particular, the Commission shall make specific proposals: (*a*) for extending between all nations the exchange of basic scientific information for peaceful ends; (*b*) for control of atomic energy to the extent necessary to ensure its use only for peaceful purposes; (*c*) for the elimination from national armaments of atomic weapons and of all other major weapons adaptable to mass destruction; (*d*) for effective safeguards by way of inspection and other means to protect complying States against the hazards of violations and evasions.—The work of the Commission should proceed by separate stages, the successful completion of each of which will develop the necessary confidence of the world before the next stage is undertaken. The Commission shall not infringe upon the responsibilities of any organ of the United Nations, but should present recommendations for the consideration of those organs in the performance of their tasks under the terms of the United Nations Charter.'

As to the relationship of the Commission with the organs of the United Nations the resolution provides:

'(*a*) The Commission shall submit its reports and recommendations to the Security Council, and such reports and recommendations shall be made public unless the Security Council, in the interest of peace and security, otherwise directs. In the appropriate cases the Security Council should transmit these reports to the General Assembly and the Members of the United Nations, as well as to the Economic and Social Council and other organs within the framework of the United Nations. (*b*) In view of the Security Council's primary responsibility under the Charter of the United Nations for the maintenance of international peace and security, the Security Council shall issue directions to the Commission in matters affecting security. On these matters the Commission shall be accountable for its work to the Security Council.' [5]

During its second session, the General Assembly adopted a resolution[6] providing for the establishment of an International Law Commission, and containing the statute of the Commission. The Commission, created to promote the progressive development of international law and its codification, consists of 15 members 'who shall be persons of recognised competence in international law,' elected by the Assembly for three year terms from a list of candidates nominated by the Members of the United Nations. The Commission is also empowered to: (1) draft multilateral conventions submitted by Members of the United Nations, by organs of the United Nations or the specialised agencies; (2) survey the field of international law in order to select topics for codification and make recommendations thereon to the Assembly; and (3) consider ways to make 'evidence of customary international law more readily available' through the collection and publication of pertinent documents and of decisions of national and international tribunals.

During its second session the General Assembly also established for the period between the closing of this session and the opening of the next regular session a so called Interim Committee on which each

[5] Resolutions adopted by the General Assembly, Doc. A/64, p. 9.

[6] Resolutions adopted by the General Assembly, Doc. A/519, pp. 105 ff.

member of the General Assembly was authorised to appoint one representative. The resolution of the General Assembly by which the Interim Committee was established (November 13, 1947) determined the competence of this committee as follows:—

> The Interim Committee, as a subsidiary organ of the General Assembly established in accordance with Article 22 of the Charter, shall assist the General Assembly in the performance of its functions by discharging the following duties:
>
> (*a*) To consider and report, with its conclusions, to the General Assembly on such matters as have been referred to it by the General Assembly;
>
> (*b*) To consider and report with its conclusions to the General Assembly on any dispute or any situation which, in virtue of Articles 11 (paragraph 2), 14 or 35 of the Charter, has been proposed for inclusion in the agenda of the General Assembly by any Member of the United Nations or brought before the General Assembly by the Security Council, provided the Committee previously determines the matter to be both important and requiring preliminary study. Such determination shall be made by a majority of two-thirds of the members present and voting unless the matter is one referred by the Security Council under Article 11 (paragraph 2), in which case a simple majority will suffice;
>
> (*c*) To consider, as it deems useful and advisable, and report with its conclusions to the General Assembly on methods to be adopted to give effect to that part of Article 11 (paragraph 1) which deals with the general principles of co-operation in the maintenance of international peace and security, and to that part of Article 13 (paragraph 1 *a*) which deals with the promotion of international co-operation in the political field;
>
> (*d*) To consider, in connection with any matter under discussion by the Interim Committee, whether occasion may require the summoning of a special session of the General Assembly and, if it deems that such session is required, so to advise the Secretary-General in order that he may obtain the views of the Members of the United Nations thereon;
>
> (*e*) To conduct investigations and appoint commissions of enquiry within the scope of its duties, as it may deem useful and necessary, provided that decisions to conduct such investigations or enquiries shall be made by a two-thirds majority of the members present and voting. An investigation or enquiry elsewhere than at the headquarters of the United Nations shall not be conducted without the consent of the State or States in whose territory it is to take place;

> (*f*) To report to the next regular session of the General Assembly on the advisability of establishing a permanent committee of the General Assembly to perform the duties of the Interim Committee as stated above with any changes considered desirable in the light of experience.

The resolution provided further:

> In discharging its duties the Interim Committee shall at all times take into account the responsibilities of the Security Council under the Charter for the maintenance of international peace and security as well as the duties assigned by the Charter or by the General Assembly or by the Security Council to other Councils or to any committee or commission. The Interim Committee shall not consider any matter of which the Security Council is seized.

Whereas the General Assembly by Article 12 of the Charter is only forbidden to make recommendations on disputes or situations while the Security Council is exercising in respect of these matters the functions assigned to it, the Interim Committee was prohibited even to 'consider' matters (not only disputes and situations) of which the Security Council is seized.

The representatives of the Soviet Union, the Ukrainian and the Byelorussian Republics, Poland, Czechoslovakia, and Yugoslavia declared the establishment of the Committee as unconstitutional and refused to take part in its activity. Consequently these governments did not appoint representatives. The delegates of Australia and the Philippines declared that this non-participation constituted a violation of the Charter. This view is hardly tenable. The Charter does not obligate the Members to participate in a committee established under Article 22 of the Charter. The only question is whether the non-participation made the activity of the committee illegal. This question must be answered in the negative. For the resolution of the General Assembly, which was the legal basis of the activity of the committee, expressly provided that 'each member of the General Assembly shall have the right to appoint one representative,' which means that each member may or may not be represented on this committee.[7]

As to the constitutionality of the Interim Committee itself, there are only two points regarding which it could be doubted whether the establishment of the Committee was in conformity with the Charter. The first point concerns the question as to whether the General Assembly is authorised to establish under Article 22 a subsidiary organ competent to work during the period between two sessions of the Assembly. Nothing in Article 22 prevents the Assembly to establish a committee with such an assignment. It is true that the General

[7] Resolutions adopted by the General Assembly, Doc. A/519, pp. 15 ff.; Doc. A/454; Doc. A/P.V. 110, 111.

Assembly, as we shall see later, in contradistinction to the Security Council is not intended by the Charter to function continuously. The Charter provides in Article 20 for ' regular annual ' and for ' special sessions '; and a ' special ' session is possible only if the ' regular ' session of the General Assembly lasts only part of the year. But Article 20 does not expressly establish such limitation, and special sessions are provided for only ' as occasion may require.' The General Assembly is not bound to limit the duration of its regular session so that a special session in the same year be possible. A regular session may, without any violation of the Charter, last a whole year if the agenda of the Assembly so requires; to convoke a special session for a special item is a question of mere convenience. And so is the organisation of annual sessions. It is the same Assembly, composed of the same members, that meets in all regular and special sessions. To allow a committee established by a collegiate body in one session to work only for this and not for the next session—a restriction which the Charter does not stipulate—is justifiable only if the composition of the collegiate body is not the same in each session, if its members are to be elected or appointed anew for each session. This is not the case with the members of the General Assembly.[8] Hence the establishment of a committee for the period between two regular sessions is not incompatible with Article 22 nor with the spirit of the Charter.

The second point concerns the question as to whether the General Assembly is competent to authorise the Interim Committee ' to conduct investigations and appoint commissions of enquiry.' It is true that the Charter expressly confers only upon the Security Council, in Article 34, the power to investigate ' any dispute, or any situation which might lead to international friction or give rise to a dispute.' But Article 22 authorises the General Assembly to establish subsidiary organs ' as it deems necessary for the performance of its functions.' Hence the Assembly has the power to instruct such subsidiary organ to do any work which the Assembly deems necessary for the performance of its functions. There can be no doubt that the General Assembly may not be able to perform a function conferred upon it by the Charter without an investigation of the matter to which the function refers. The same interpretation of Article 29, authorising the Security Council to establish subsidiary organs for the performance of its functions, is possible; it is even necessary since Article 34 confers the power of investigation upon the Security Council only with respect to disputes and certain situations, and only for the purpose to determine

[8] At the 21st meeting of the Fourth Committee, the Belgian delegate observed ' that in his opinion Article 22 permitted the establishment of subsidiary bodies only for the duration of one session of the General Assembly and not for the work of the next session.' The delegate of the United Kingdom ' associated himself with the interpretation of Article 22 given by the representative of Belgium.' (Journal of the United Nations, No. 55: Suppl. No. 4–A/C.4/74, p. 79.)

the dangerous character of these disputes and situations within the procedures of pacific settlement regulated in Chapter VI of the Charter.[9]

Different from the question as to whether the General Assembly is competent to undertake investigations is the question as to whether the Members are obliged to permit on their territory such investigations. In this respect an essential difference exists between the power of the General Assembly and that of the Security Council. Whereas the Members, under Article 25, are obliged to permit an investigation ordered by a decision of the Security Council, the General Assembly has not the power to enforce upon the Members an investigation to be carried out on their territory. But the resolution by which the General Assembly established the Interim Committee stipulates, in conformity with the Charter: 'An investigation or enquiry elsewhere than at the headquarters of the United Nations shall not be conducted without the consent of the State or States in whose territory it is to take place.'

The question as to whether the General Assembly was competent to confer upon the Interim Committee the power to appoint a commission is implied in the general problem of delegation of power by one organ to another. This problem has been discussed in another connection.[1]

At its 29th meeting, the Interim Committeee agreed unanimously to recommend to the General Assembly that the Interim Committee

[9] During the discussion on the establishment of the Interim Committee in the First Committee it was maintained that Article 13, paragraph 1: 'The General Assembly shall initiate studies . . . ' confers upon the General Assembly the power to make investigations. The statement of the delegate of the Soviet Union 'that Article 13 dealt with the General Assembly's right to initiate studies and not investigations of the kind which might be conducted by the Security Council under Article 34' is correct. (Doc. A/C.1/SR.94, p. 7.) The delegate of the United Kingdom justified the power of the General Assembly to set up a commission of inquiry as follows: 'Surely it would be nonsense if the Assembly were empowered to consider disputes (Article 35) to discuss situations (Article 11 (2)) and to make recommendations, without being able to verify its premises. Such power would be implicit were it not clear that Article 35 attracted, in so far as the General Assembly was concerned, the jurisdiction and functions of the Security Council contained in Article 34. There could in fact be no doubt that the Assembly could conduct investigations as required.' (Doc. A/C.1/SR.96, p. 5.)

[1] Cf. *supra*, p. 142. The Interim Committee set up various sub-committees without being especially authorised to this effect by the resolution of the General Assembly. During its 2nd special session on May 15, 1948, the General Assembly adopted a resolution by which it 'empowers a United Nations Mediator in Palestine, to be chosen by a Committee of the General Assembly composed of representatives of China, France, the Union of Soviet Socialist Republics, the United Kingdom, and the United States of America . . . ' (United Nations Bulletin, Vol. 4, No. 11, p. 433.) On May 20, 1948, the committee composed of these five Members appointed by a unanimous vote the Mediator. In this case, too, the General Assembly delegated to a committee its power to establish subsidiary organs, conferred by Article 22 on the General Assembly.

should be continued for a further period to be determined by the General Assembly.

At its 169th meeting the General Assembly decided to re-establish the Interim Committee until the next regular session.[2] The resolution runs as follows:

The General Assembly,

Having taken note of the report submitted to it by the Interim Committee on the advisability of establishing a permanent committee of the General Assembly (A/606),

Affirming that, for the effective performance of the duties specifically conferred upon the General Assembly by the Charter in relation to matters concerning the maintenance of international peace and security (Articles 11 and 35), the promotion of international co-operation in the political field (Article 13), and the peaceful adjustment of any situation likely to impair the general welfare or friendly relations among nations (Article 14), it is necessary to continue the Interim Committee for the purpose of considering such matters further and reporting with conclusions to the General Assembly,

Recognising fully the primary responsibility of the Security Council for prompt and effective action for the maintenance of international peace and security (Article 24),

Resolves that

1. There shall be re-established for the period between the closing of the present session and the opening of the next regular session of the General Assembly an Interim Committee on which each Member of the General Assembly shall have the right to appoint one representative;

2. The Interim Committee, as a subsidiary organ of the General Assembly established in accordance with Article 22 of the Charter, shall assist the General Assembly in the performance of its functions by discharging the following duties:

(*a*) To consider and report with its conclusions to the General Assembly on such matters as may be referred to the Committee by or under the authority of the General Assembly;

(*b*) To consider and report, with conclusions, to the General Assembly on any dispute or any situation which, in virtue of Articles 11 (paragraph 2), 14 or 35 of the Charter, has been proposed for inclusion in the agenda of the General Assembly by any Member of the United Nations, or by any non-member State under Articles 11 (paragraph 2) or 35, or has been brought before the General Assembly by the Security Council, provided the Committee previously determines

[2] Doc. A/740; Doc. A/P.V.169, pp. 2 ff.; Doc. A/810, pp. 28 ff.

the matter to be both important and requiring preliminary study. Such determination shall be made by a majority of two-thirds of the members present and voting, unless the matter is one referred to the General Assembly by the Security Council, in which case a simple majority will suffice;

(*c*) To consider systematically, using as a starting point the recommendations and studies of the Interim Committee contained in document A/605, the further implementation of that part of Article 11 (paragraph 1) relating to the general principles of co-operation in the maintenance of international peace and security, and of that part of Article 13 (paragraph 1 *a*) which deals with the promotion of international co-operation in the political field, and to report with conclusions to the General Assembly;

(*d*) To consider, in connexion with any matter under discussion by the Interim Committee, whether occasion may require the summoning of a special session of the General Assembly and, if the Committee deems that a session is required, so to advise the Secretary-General in order that he may obtain the views of the Members of the United Nations thereon;

(*e*) To conduct investigations and appoint commissions of inquiry within the scope of the Committee's duties, as it may deem useful and necessary, provided that decisions to conduct such investigations or inquiries shall be made by a two-thirds majority of the members present and voting. An investigation or inquiry elsewhere than at the headquarters of the United Nations shall not be conducted without the consent of the State or States in whose territory it is to take place;

(*f*) To report to the next regular session of the General Assembly on any changes in the Committee's constitution, its duration or its terms of reference which may be considered desirable in the light of experience;

3. The Interim Committee is hereby authorised to request advisory opinions of the International Court of Justice on legal questions arising within the scope of the Committee's activities;

4. In discharging its duties, the Interim Committee shall at all times take into account the responsibilities of the Security Council under the Charter for the maintenance of international peace and security as well as the duties assigned by the Charter or by the General Assembly or by the Security Council to other Councils or to any committee or commission. The Interim Committee shall not consider any matter of which the Security Council is seized and which the latter has not submitted to the General Assembly;

> 5. The rules of procedure governing the proceedings of the Interim Committee and such sub-committees and commissions as it may set up shall be those adopted by the Interim Committee on January 9, 1948, with such changes and additions as the Interim Committee may deem necessary, provided that they are not inconsistent with any provision of the present resolution or with any applicable rule of procedure of the General Assembly. The Interim Committee shall be convened by the Secretary-General, in consultation with the Chairman elected during the previous session of the Committee or the head of his delegation, to meet at the headquarters of the United Nations not later than January 31, 1949. At the opening meeting, the Chairman elected during the previous session of the Committee, or the head of his delegation, shall preside until the Interim Committee has elected a Chairman. The Interim Committee shall meet as and when it deems necessary for the conduct of its business. No new credentials shall be required for representatives who were duly accredited on the Interim Committee during its previous session;
>
> 6. The Secretary-General shall provide the necessary facilities and assign appropriate staff as required for the work of the Interim Committee, its sub-committees and commissions.

The most important changes in the competence of the Interim Committee made by this resolution are that the Committee is authorised to request advisory opinions from the International Court of Justice (paragraph 3), and that to the provision of the resolution of November 13, 1947: 'The Interim Committee shall not consider any matter of which the Security Council is seized,' the words are added: 'and which the latter has not submitted to the General Assembly' (paragraph 4).

The Special Committee which the General Assembly on May 15, 1947, at its first special session, set up in the Palestine question.[3] The text of the resolution runs as follows:

> Whereas the General Assembly of the United Nations has been called into special session for the purpose of constituting and instructing a Special Committee to prepare for the consideration at the next regular session of the Assembly a report on the question of Palestine, the General Assembly resolves that:
>
> 1. A Special Committee be created for the above-mentioned purpose consisting of the representatives of Australia, Canada, Czechoslovakia, Guatemala, India, Iran, Netherlands, Peru, Sweden, Uruguay and Yugoslavia;
>
> 2. The Special Committee shall have the widest powers to

[3] Doc. A/309; Official Records of the Second Session of the General Assembly; Suppl. No. 11, pp. 2 f.

ascertain and record facts, and to investigate all questions and issues relevant to the problem of Palestine;

3. The Special Committee shall determine its own procedure;

4. The Special Committee shall conduct investigations in Palestine and wherever it may deem useful, receive and examine written or oral testimony, whichever it may consider appropriate in each case, from the mandatory Power, from representatives of the population of Palestine, from Governments and from such organisations and individuals as it may deem necessary;

5. The Special Committee shall give most careful consideration to the religious interests in Palestine of Islam, Judaism and Christianity;

6. The Special Committee shall prepare a report to the General Assembly and shall submit such proposals as it may consider appropriate for the solution of the problem of Palestine;

7. The Special Committee's report shall be communicated to the Secretary-General not later than September 1, 1947, in order that it may be circulated to the Members of the United Nations in time for consideration by the Second Regular Session of the General Assembly;

The General Assembly,

8. Requests the Secretary-General to enter into suitable arrangements with the proper authorities of any state in whose territory the Special Committee may wish to sit or to travel, to provide necessary facilities, and to assign appropriate staff to the Special Committee;

9. Authorises the Secretary-General to reimburse travel and subsistence expenses of a representative and an alternate representative from each government represented on the Special Committee on such basis and in such form as he may determine most appropriate in the circumstances.

The Commission set up with regard to the future government of Palestine, for the implementation of the Plan of Partition with Economic Union, adopted by the General Assembly in its resolution of November 29, 1947.[4] The resolution provides:

A Commission shall be set up consisting of one representative of each of five Member states. The Members represented

[4] Resolutions adopted by the General Assembly, Doc. A/519, p. 133. At the 254th meeting of the Security Council, the delegate of Syria declared that the Palestine Commission was illegally constituted because its members were appointed by the President of the General Assembly in violation of Rule 84 of the Rules of Procedure of the General Assembly which provides: 'All elections shall be held by secret ballot.' (Doc. S/PV.254, pp. 21, 39.) However, in his annual report

on the Commission shall be elected by the General Assembly on as broad a basis, geographically and otherwise, as possible.

The Special Committee established in the Greek question. The text of the resolution adopted on October 21, 1947, runs as follows:[5]

1. Whereas the peoples of the United Nations have expressed in the Charter of the United Nations their determination to practise tolerance and to live together in peace with one another as good neighbours and to unite their strength to maintain international peace and security; and to that end the Members of the United Nations have obligated themselves to carry out the purposes and principles of the Charter,

2. The General Assembly of the United Nations, having considered the record of the Security Council proceedings in connection with the complaint of the Greek Government of December 3, 1946, including the report submitted by the Commission of Investigation established by the Security Council resolution of December 19, 1946, and information supplied by the Subsidiary Group of the Commission of Investigation subsequent to the report of the Commission;

3. Taking account of the report of the Commission of Investigation which found by a majority vote that Albania, Bulgaria and Yugoslavia had given assistance and support to the guerillas fighting against the Greek Government;

4. Calls upon Albania, Bulgaria and Yugoslavia to do nothing which could furnish aid and assistance to the said guerillas;

5. Calls upon Albania, Bulgaria and Yugoslavia on the one hand and Greece on the other to co-operate in the settlement of their disputes by peaceful means, and to that end recommends:

(1) That they establish normal diplomatic and good neighbourly relations among themselves as soon as possible;

(2) That they establish frontier conventions providing for effective machinery for the regulation and control of their common frontiers and for the pacific settlement of frontier incidents and disputes;

(3) That they co-operate in the settlement of the problems arising out of the presence of refugees in the four

on the work of the Organisation (July 1, 1947—June 30, 1948) the Secretary-General stated that at the 128th plenary meeting of November 29, 1947, 'the General Assembly elected Bolivia, Czechoslovakia, Denmark, Panama and the Philippines as members of the United Nations Palestine Commission charged with implementing the resolution.' (Official Records of the General Assembly, 3rd Session, Suppl. No. 1 (A/565), p. 3.)

5 Resolutions adopted by the General Assembly, Doc. A/519, pp. 12 ff.

States concerned through voluntary repatriation wherever possible and that they take effective measures to prevent the participation of such refugees in political or military activity;

(4) That they study the practicability of concluding agreements for the voluntary transfer of minorities;

6. Established a Special Committee:

(1) To observe the compliance by the four Governments concerned with the foregoing recommendations;

(2) To be available to assist the four Governments concerned in the implementation of such recommendations;

7. Recommends that the four Governments concerned co-operate with the Special Committee in enabling it to carry out these functions;

8. Authorises the Special Committee, if in its opinion further consideration of the subject matter of this resolution by the General Assembly prior to its next regular session is necessary for the maintenance of international peace and security, to recommend to the Members of the United Nations that a special session of the General Assembly be convoked as a matter of urgency;

9. Decides that the Special Committee

(1) Shall consist of representatives of Australia, Brazil, China, France, Mexico, the Netherlands, Pakistan, the United Kingdom and the United States of America, seats being held open for Poland and the Union of Soviet Socialist Republics;

(2) Shall have its principal headquarters in Salonika and with the co-operation of the four Governments concerned shall perform its functions in such places and in the territories of the four States concerned as it may deem appropriate;

(3) Shall render a report to the next regular session of the General Assembly and to any prior special session which might be called to consider the subject matter of this resolution, and shall render such interim reports as it may deem appropriate to the Secretary-General for transmission to the Members of the Organisation; in any reports to the General Assembly the Special Committee may make such recommendations to the General Assembly as it deems fit;

(4) shall determine its own procedure, and may establish such sub-committees as it deems necessary;

(5) Shall commence its work within thirty days after the final decision of the General Assembly on this resolution,

and shall remain in existence pending a new decision of the General Assembly.

10. The General Assembly requests the Secretary-General to assign to the Special Committee staff adequate to enable it to perform its duties, and to enter into a standing arrangement with each of the four Governments concerned to assure the Special Committee, so far as it may find it necessary to exercise its functions within their territories, of full freedom of movement and all necessary facilities for the performance of its functions.

The delegates of the Soviet Union and of Poland declared that their government refused to take part in the establishment and the work of the committee.[6] However, the attitude of the two states did not affect the legality of the committee's activity, since according to the basic resolution of the General Assembly representation of the two members in the committee was optional: 'seats being open for Poland and the Union of Soviet Socialist Republics.'

The United Nations Temporary Commission on Korea. The two resolutions adopted in this respect on November 14, 1947,[7] run as follows:

A. Inasmuch as the Korean question which is before the General Assembly is primarily a matter for the Korean people itself and concerns its freedom and independence, and recognising that this question cannot be correctly and fairly resolved without the participation of representatives of the indigenous population, The General Assembly,

1. Resolves that elected representatives of the Korean people be invited to take part in the consideration of the question;

2. Further resolves that in order to facilitate and expedite such participation and to observe that the Korean representatives are in fact duly elected by the Korean people and not mere appointees by military authorities in Korea, there be forthwith established a United Nations Temporary Commission on Korea, to be present in Korea, with right to travel, observe and consult throughout Korea.

B. The General Assembly, recognising the urgent and rightful claims to independence of the people of Korea; believing that the national independence of Korea should be re-established and all occupying forces then withdrawn at the earliest practicable date; recalling its previous conclusion that the freedom and independence of the Korean people cannot be correctly and fairly resolved without the participation of

[6] Doc. A/P.V.100.

[7] Resolutions adopted by the General Assembly, Doc. A/519, pp. 16 ff.

representatives of the Korean people, and its decision to establish a United Nations Temporary Commission on Korea (hereinafter called the ' Commission ') for the purpose of facilitating and expediting such participation by elected representatives of the Korean people,

1. Decides that the Commission shall consist of representatives of Australia, Canada, China, El Salvador, France, India, Philippines, Syria, Ukrainian Soviet Socialist Republic;

2. Recommends that the elections be held not later than March 31, 1948, on the basis of adult suffrage and by secret ballot to choose representatives with whom the Commission may consult regarding the prompt attainment of the freedom and independence of the Korean people and which representatives, constituting a National Assembly, may establish a National Government of Korea. The number of representatives from each voting area or zone should be proportionate to the population, and the elections should be under the observation of the Commission;

3. Further recommends that as soon as possible after the elections, the National Assembly should convene and form a National Government and notify the Commission of its formation;

4. Further recommends that immediately upon the establishment of a National Government, that Government should, in consultation with the Commission: (*a*) constitute its own national security forces and dissolve all military or semi-military formations not included therein: (*b*) take over the functions of government from the military commands and civilian authorities of north and south Korea, and (*c*) arrange with the occupying Powers for the complete withdrawal from Korea of their armed forces as early as practicable and if possible within ninety days;

5. Resolves that the Commission shall facilitate and expedite the fulfilment of the foregoing programme for the attainment of the national independence of Korea and withdrawal of occupying forces, taking into account its observations and consultations in Korea. The Commission shall report, with its conclusions, to the General Assembly and may consult with the Interim Committee (if one be established) with respect to the application of this resolution in the light of developments;

6. Calls upon the Member States concerned to afford every assistance and facility to the Commission in the fulfilment of its responsibilities;

> 7. Calls upon all Members of the United Nations to refrain from interfering in the affairs of the Korean people during the interim period preparatory to the establishment of Korean independence, except in pursuance of the decisions of the General Assembly; and thereafter, to refrain completely from any and all acts derogatory to the independence and sovereignty of Korea.

At the 84th meeting of the First Committee, the representative of the Ukrainian Republic declared that he must decline to participate in the work of the Commission as representatives of Korea had not been invited to attend the debate.[8] According to the resolution adopted by the General Assembly, membership of the Ukrainian Republic in the Commission was mandatory: 'The commission shall consist of representatives of . . . Ukrainian Soviet Socialist Republic.' Hence the constitutionality of the work of the Commission is doubtful.

2. PROCEDURE

A. *Sessions*

As to the procedure of the General Assembly, Article 20 of the Charter provides:

> The General Assembly shall meet in regular annual sessions and in such special sessions as occasion may require. Special sessions shall be convoked by the Secretary-General at the request of the Security Council or of a majority of the Members of the United Nations.

The Charter distinguishes between 'regular annual' and 'special' sessions of the Assembly. 'Annual' session means: one session a year. As pointed out, the duration of the regular session is not expressly determined by the Charter, nor do the Rules of Procedure contain a provision to this effect. They only determine the day of the year on which the regular session shall begin. That the regular session shall take only a part of the year could be concluded from the fact that the Charter presupposes special sessions to be possible in addition to the annual session. However, as pointed out, the convocation of special sessions is not mandatory, but only a matter of convenience. Nothing in the Charter prevents the General Assembly to continue a regular session if its agenda so require, until the beginning of the next regular session and thus practically to function continuously. Rule 5 of the Rules of Procedure provides 'that the General Assembly may decide at any session to adjourn temporarily and resume its meetings at a later date'; which facilitates a long duration of a regular session. The fact that the Charter expressly provides only that

[8] Doc. A/C./SR. 94, p. 3.

the Security Council shall 'function continuously' (Article 28, paragraph 1) does not imply that a regular session of the General Assembly must not last a whole year. Such duration of a regular session was probably not intended by the legislator. But the wording of the Charter is not in conformity with this intention.

Article 20 does not determine the way in which the regular annual sessions of the General Assembly shall be convoked. According to the Rules of Procedure no formal convocation is necessary, since Rule 1 provides: 'The General Assembly shall meet every year in regular session commencing on the third Tuesday in September.' But Rule 4 stipulates: 'The Secretary-General shall notify the Members of the United Nations, at least six days in advance, of the opening of a regular session.'

Only special sessions are to be convoked by the Secretary-General. In convoking a special session of the General Assembly, the Secretary-General does not act on his own initiative, but only at the request of the Security Council or of a majority of the Members. Since the convocation of a special session of the Assembly is a procedural matter the decision of the Security Council may be adopted, according to Article 27, paragraph 2, of the Charter, by an affirmative vote of any seven members. As to the special sessions, the Rules of Procedure stipulate:

RULE 6

The General Assembly may fix a date for a special session.

RULE 7

Special sessions of the General Assembly shall be held within fifteen days of the receipt by the Secretary-General of a request for such a session from the Security Council, or of a request from a majority of the Members of the United Nations, or of the concurrence of a majority of Members as provided in Rule 8.

RULE 8

Any Member of the United Nations may request the Secretary-General to summon a special session. The Secretary-General shall immediately inform the other Members of the United Nations of the request and inquire whether they concur in it. If within thirty days of the date of the communication of the Secretary-General a majority of the Members concur in the request, a special session of the General Assembly shall be summoned in accordance with Rule 7.

RULE 9

The Secretary-General shall notify the Members of the United Nations, at least fourteen days in advance, of the opening of a special session summoned at the request of the Security Council, and, at least ten days in advance, in the case of a request by a majority of the Members or the concurrence of a majority in the request of any Member.

The Charter does not contain a provision guaranteeing that the sessions of the General Assembly be public. Committee II/1 of the San Francisco Conference[9] 'discussed a proposal that the principle of free access to the sessions of the General Assembly by the public and press of the world be included in the Charter. This proposal was supported by a number of delegations on the ground that the Assembly as an organ of world opinion should, from the moment of its establishment, declare its will to maintain with this world public opinion the most constant and close bonds. While expressing full agreement with the principle underlying this proposal, other delegations expressed the view that the question of open sessions should be dealt with as a procedural matter by the General Assembly itself.' The Revised Report of the Rapporteur of Commission II[1] contains the following statement: 'Commission II has not thought it wise to specify in the Charter that these sessions shall be public, but it has provided that the Assembly shall fix its own rules of procedure and it recommends that the following statement be made a part of the official record of this Conference: "The Conference is of the opinion that regulations to be adopted at the first session of the General Assembly shall provide that, save in exceptional cases, the sessions of the General Assembly shall be open to the public and the press of the world."' The Rules of Procedure of the General Assembly contain the following provisions:

RULE 55

The meetings of the General Assembly and its Main Committees shall be held in public unless the body concerned decides that exceptional circumstances require that the meeting be held in private. Meetings of other committees and sub-committees shall also be held in public unless the body concerned decides otherwise.

RULE 56

All decisions of the General Assembly taken at a private meeting shall be announced at an early public meeting of the General Assembly. At the close of each private meeting of the Main Committees, other committees and sub-committees, the Chairman may issue a communiqué through the Secretary-General.

Whereas the Charter in Article 28, paragraph 3, at least indirectly, provides that the Security Council, as a rule, shall hold its meetings

[9] U.N.C.I.O. Doc. 1092, II/1/39, p. 1.
[1] U.N.C.I.O. Doc. 1180, II/18 (1), p. 2.

at the seat of the Organisation (by authorising this organ to hold meetings exceptionally at other places, as in its judgment will facilitate its work), no such provision with respect to the General Assembly is made. This may be interpreted to mean that the General Assembly is bound to hold its meetings only at the seat of the Organisation, since the authorisation of Article 28, paragraph 3, refers not to the General Assembly; or that the General Assembly is not bound to hold its meetings at the seat of the Organisation, since no rule with respect to the place of the meetings of the Assembly is laid down in the Charter. The latter interpretation is accepted in the Rules of Procedure which stipulate:

RULE 2

> Sessions shall be held at the headquarters of the United Nations unless convened elsewhere in pursuance of a decision of the General Assembly at a previous session or at the request of a majority of the Members of the United Nations.

Pursuant to this Rule, the General Assembly on November 15, 1947, voted to hold its third session in Europe.

As to the languages to be used in the discussions of the General Assembly, the Rules of Procedure provide:

RULE 44

> Chinese, English, French, Russian and Spanish shall be the official languages of the General Assembly, its committees and sub-committees. English and French shall be the working languages.

On December 7, 1948, the General Assembly resolved that Spanish be included as a working language.

RULE 45

> Speeches made in either of the working languages shall be interpreted into the other working language.

RULE 46

> Speeches made in any of the other three official languages shall be interpreted into both working languages.

B. *Voting*

The voting procedure is regulated by Article 18 of the Charter as follows:

> 1. Each member of the General Assembly shall have one vote.
>
> 2. Decisions of the General Assembly on important

questions shall be made by a two-thirds majority of the members present and voting. These questions shall include: recommendations with respect to the maintenance of international peace and security, the election of the non-permanent members of the Security Council, the election of the members of the Economic and Social Council, the election of members of the Trusteeship Council in accordance with paragraph 1 (*c*) of Article 86, the admission of new Members to the United Nations, the suspension of the rights and privileges of membership, the expulsion of Members, questions relating to the operation of the trusteeship system, and budgetary questions.

3. Decisions on other questions, including the determination of additional categories of questions to be decided by a two-thirds majority, shall be made by a majority of the members present and voting.

The provision of paragraph 1 that each member of the General Assembly shall have one vote, means that each Member state as member of the General Assembly shall have one vote. Members of the Assembly are not the individuals representing the Member states in the Assembly, but the Member states represented in the Assembly. Systematically, the provision of paragraph 1 of Article 18 belongs to Article 9 immediately after the provision of paragraph 2 of this Article that ' Each Member shall have not more than five representatives in the General Assembly.' Neither the Charter nor the Rules of Procedure determine which of the several representatives of a Member is authorised to cast the vote of the Member. This is legally an important question. Strange as it may seem, the Rules of Procedure which provide for a chairman of the delegation, do not indicate among his functions the competence to exercise the right of voting of the Member or to decide conflicts which may arise among the representatives of a Member with respect to the representation of their government. Rule 22 only provides that the Chairman of the delegation may designate an alternate representative to act as representative; and Rule 32, presupposing that only Chairmen of delegations may be elected President or Vice-President, provides that the President, or Vice-President acting as President, shall not vote but shall appoint another member of his delegation to vote in his place; which presupposes that the Chairman of the delegation is authorised to cast the vote of the Member state which the members of the delegation represent.

As to the voting procedure in the General Assembly, the Charter distinguishes between ' important questions ' (Article 18, paragraph 2), and ' other questions ' (paragraph 3) which, since they are not labelled ' important ' must be considered to be unimportant. This is not a very fortunate terminology. If the General Assembly is dealing with a question at all, this question can hardly be considered as unimportant.[2] The intention was to differentiate decisions which require a two-thirds majority and decisions which require only a simple majority. Since paragraph 2 enumerates the matters on which decisions must be made by a two-thirds majority it was superfluous to qualify these matters as 'important.' It had sufficed to say: Decisions on the following questions shall be made by a two-thirds majority, etc.

Also for other reasons paragraphs 2 and 3 of Article 18 are not satisfactorily formulated. According to the wording of paragraph 2, the enumeration of 'important questions' seems to be not exhaustive. The first sentence may be interpreted to mean that all 'important questions' are subjected to the vote of a two-thirds majority, so that the following sentence: These questions shall 'include . . .' may refer only to certain matters the importance of which is determined directly by the Charter, but does not exclude other important matters. However, in view of paragraph 3: 'Decisions on other questions, etc.' the interpretation that the enumeration of paragraph 2 is exhaustive, is possible, too.[3]

The words 'other questions' are ambiguous. They may mean questions other than important ones, that is to say unimportant questions, the enumeration of paragraph 2—in conformity with the wording of this paragraph—being not exhaustive. But they may also mean: questions other than those enumerated in paragraph 2. Then this enumeration is exhaustive. If the first interpretation is accepted, three different problems may arise. 1. It may be doubtful whether a concrete matter falls within the categories enumerated in paragraph 2; 2. it may be doubtful whether a matter about which there is no doubt that it does not fall within one of these categories, is 'important'; and 3. the question may arise whether a new category should be added to the categories enumerated in paragraph 2. If the enumeration is not exhaustive, all three questions may be decided, in accordance with paragraph 3, by decisions made by a simple majority.[4]

If the enumeration of paragraph 2 is considered to be exhaustive, only two problems are possible: it may be doubtful whether a concrete

[2] At the 52nd meeting of the General Assembly during the discussion of the case of the treatment of Indians in the Union of South Africa, the question arose whether the decision the Assembly was about to adopt in the matter required a two-thirds or a simple majority. The President of the Assembly formulated the question as follows: 'I would like to have your opinion as to whether you consider this matter an important matter requiring a two-thirds majority.' The delegate of India quite correctly stated: 'Every question that the Assembly discusses is important. We do not waste our time discussing unimportant questions.' (Journal of the United Nations, No. 55; Suppl. A–A/P.V./52, pp. 392, 394.)

[3] In the discussion of the treatment of Indians in South Africa the delegate of India interpreted the enumeration in paragraph 2 of Article 18 to be exhaustive. (*Ibid.*)

[4] At the 105th meeting of the General Assembly in the course of the discussion of the suggestion of the Fourth Committee that the Assembly should recommend to the Union of South Africa to place the former mandated territory of South West

matter falls within the categories enumerated; or whether a matter about which there is no doubt that it does not fall within these categories, falls within a category which should be added to those enumerated in paragraph 2. If the enumeration of 'important' questions is exhaustive, the question as to whether the decision on a concrete matter requires a two-thirds majority can be answered only by deciding that the question does, or does not, fall within the categories enumerated in paragraph 2, or, if there is no doubt that the concrete question does not fall within these categories, by deciding that the category within which this concrete question falls shall be added. Both questions are to be decided, according to paragraph 3, by a simple majority. But, if the enumeration of paragraph 2 is exhaustive, it is not possible to determine that the decision on a concrete matter which does not fall within the enumerated categories, requires a two-thirds majority (because it is important), without determining, at the same time, that the category within which this matter falls shall be added to those enumerated in paragraph 2.[5]

Africa under the trusteeship system, the question arose whether a decision to this effect required a two-thirds majority. The representative of Iraq expressed the view that a simple majority was sufficient, although Article 18, paragraph 2, expressly provides that decisions on 'questions relating to the operation of the trusteeship system' shall be made by a two-thirds majority. The President stated: 'The issue before us is whether this subject which we have been discussing does or does not require a two-thirds majority. The decision as to whether a two-thirds majority is or is not necessary will be decided by a simple majority.' (Official Records of Second Session of the General Assembly, Plenary Meetings, Vol. I, pp. 638 f.) He formulated the question as follows: 'We will have to decide whether this is a matter of importance requiring a two-thirds majority, and we will take a vote in this respect.' The official record contains the statement: 'The proposal that the matter was one of importance requiring a two-thirds majority was accepted by 22 votes to 18, with 5 abstentions' (p. 666). The question as to whether the suggested recommendation to place the former mandated territory of South West Africa under the trusteeship system falls under the category of questions enumerated in Article 18, paragraph 2: 'questions relating to the operation of the trusteeship system' was not put to the vote.

[5] This was probably the opinion of the delegate of Saudi Arabia, who in the discussion of the treatment of Indians in South Africa declared: 'What is mentioned in paragraph 3, after paragraph 2 has mentioned these exceptional cases [where a two-thirds majority is required], is not questions but categories of questions.' He maintained that 'when the Charter was drafted, it was never thought of putting individual questions before us . . . So if you like to put this as an important question, it must be preceded by another vote, to add as a category all questions . . . We must then add a category in which this question of the Indians in South Africa enter. We then vote on the category and the question will come afterward. But, by calling it an individual question, we shall never finish . . . we cannot vote for individual questions but we vote for categories of questions.' (*Ibid.*, p. 395.) This opinion is correct only under the supposition that the enumeration in paragraph 2 is exhaustive. If not, by 'decisions on other questions' in paragraph 3 also a decision may be understood by which an individual matter is declared important. It is not clear under what presupposition the General Assembly acted in voting on the question placed before it by the President.

During the discussion of the resolution concerning Transmission of Information

The decision by which a new category of ' important questions ' is added to those enumerated in paragraph 2 constitutes an amendment to Article 18, paragraph 2. The procedure of this amendment, provided by paragraph 3, constitutes an exception to the provisions of Chapter XVIII regulating the amendment procedure. Then the question arises whether an amendment by which an amendment to Article 18, paragraph 2, adopted under Article 18, paragraph 3, is to be repealed, must be adopted in conformity with the provisions of Chapter XVIII, or in the way determined in Article 18, paragraph 3. Since Article 18, paragraph 3, authorises the General Assembly only to increase the number of categories of important matters, not to reduce it, the amendment procedure of Chapter XVIII is required for the repeal of an

under Article 73 (*e*) of the Charter, at the 64th meeting of the General Assembly, the delegate of Cuba asserted the question under discussion was not ' important ' within the meaning of Article 18, and consequently, could be decided by a simple majority. ' To apply the two-thirds rule, it would be necessary to have resort to Article 79 [of the provisional Rules of Procedure, identical with Article 18, paragraph 3, of the Charter] and create a new category. The two-thirds majority would be necessary for the creation of this category.' (Journal of the United Nations, No. 63: Suppl. A–A/P.V./64, pp. 719 f.) The delegate probably interpreted the enumeration in Article 18, paragraph 2, to be exhaustive. His statement that the creation of an additional category requires a two-thirds majority is evidently erroneous.

Among the matters enumerated in paragraph 2 of Article 18 as ' important questions ' there is not the appointment of the Secretary-General under Article 97. The decision by which the Security Council has to make the necessary recommendation to the Assembly requires an affirmative vote of seven members including the concurring votes of the permanent members. If the enumeration in paragraph 2 is exhaustive, the decision by which the Assembly appoints a Secretary-General requires only a simple majority; unless the Assembly, by a simple majority, determines to add to the categories enumerated a new category: the appointment of the Secretary-General. If the enumeration is not exhaustive, the Assembly may decide that the appointment of the Secretary-General in general, or in a particular case is an important question and, hence, requires a two-thirds majority.

In a resolution concerning the terms of the appointment of the Secretary-General and its salary, adopted by the General Assembly at its 21st meeting, the following statement was made: ' From the provisions of Articles 18 and 27 of the Charter, it is clear that, for the nomination of the Secretary-General by the Security Council, an affirmative vote of seven members, including the concurring votes of the permanent members, is required; and that for his appointment by the General Assembly, a simple majority of the members of that body present and voting is sufficient, unless the General Assembly itself decides that a two-thirds majority is called for. The same rules apply to a renewal of appointment as to an original appointment; this should be made clear when the original appointment is made.' (Resolutions adopted by the General Assembly, Doc. A/64, p. 14.) It is not said that the appointment of the Secretary-General by the General Assembly requires a simple majority, unless an additional category concerning the appointment of the Secretary-General is determined by that body. Hence the statement may be interpreted to mean that the General Assembly may decide that the appointment of the Secretary-General in a concrete case is an ' important question ' and therefore requires a two-thirds majority, without adding a new category to those enumerated in paragraph 2; which presupposes that the enumeration is not exhaustive.

amendment adopted under Article 18, paragraph 3.[6] It stands to reason that the amendment procedure of Chapter XVIII is necessary for the elimination of any category mentioned in the original text of Article 18, paragraph 2.

The decision by which an additional category of important questions is determined requires only a simple majority. This provision has a rather paradoxical consequence. If in a case which does not fall within one of the categories of paragraph 2, a simple majority is in favour of a certain proposal and if members of the minority object that the matter is ' important ' and—under the presupposition that the enumeration in paragraph 2 is exhaustive—ask for a decision by which the category under which the case at hand falls, be added to those enumerated in paragraph 2, the simple majority, by voting for such addition, deprives itself of the power to decide the case. To retain this power, the majority must vote against the addition.

If the enumeration of categories in paragraph 2 is interpreted to be not exhaustive, a concrete case which does not fall within these categories may be considered as being an ' important question ' and consequently a two-thirds majority may be considered to be necessary even when the General Assembly does not adopt a decision by which the category within which the concrete case falls is added to the list of paragraph 2. The question as to whether the concrete matter is ' important ' is to be decided by a simple majority. Hence a member

[6] This question has been answered in the *Hearings*, p. 257, in a different way. A Senator asked: ' Assume that a category of such questions were established, requiring a two-thirds majority, and the Assembly decided to reduce or wipe out that category: Would it take a two-thirds vote or a majority vote ?' The Senator took it for granted that the General Assembly has the power ' to reduce or wipe out ' by its decision a category which it had added to the list of Article 18, paragraph 2, by a decision adopted under Article 18, paragraph 3. He only doubted whether the first mentioned decision may be adopted, just as the second, by a simple majority, or by a two-thirds majority. The representative of the Department of State answered the question of the Senator first as follows: ' I do not know. I suppose that a simple majority might suffice; but that would be a rule of procedure that would have to be established by the Assembly '; and later: ' I think that would be settled by future determination by the Assembly itself.' If the—very questionable —interpretation is accepted that the power conferred upon the General Assembly by Article 18, paragraph 3, to add, by a decision, categories of important questions to the list of Article 18, paragraph 2, implies the power to ' wipe out ' this category, then the decision to repeal can be adopted in the same way as the amendment was adopted: by simple majority. The interpretation that the repeal of an amendment to Article 18, paragraph 2, adopted under Article 18, paragraph 3, may likewise be adopted under this provision, is hardly compatible with its wording; though yet it is more acceptable than the opinion that the question may be decided by the rules of procedure of the General Assembly to be adopted under Article 21. If the power to repeal an amendment adopted under Article 18, paragraph 3, is implied in this provision, the procedural question: simple or two-thirds majority, is decided by Article 18, paragraph 3. If this provision does not confer upon the General Assembly the power to repeal its amendment to Article 18, paragraph 2, the repeal falls under the provisions of Chapter XVIII.

of the General Assembly who is against a proposal concerning the matter and assumes that he will be with his opinion in the minority, has good reason to be in favour of a decision by which the matter is declared to be 'important'; whereas a member who is in favour of the proposal but assumes that there will be a simple majority in favour of the proposal should vote against the 'importance' of the matter.

The decision by which the General Assembly requires the International Court of Justice to give an advisory opinion is not among the decisions enumerated in paragraph 2 of Article 18. When the General Assembly has to vote, under Article 96, on a proposal to ask the Court for an advisory opinion on a matter to be decided by the Assembly, and when the question of 'importance,' and hence of the kind of majority required, arises, it is necessary to distinguish clearly between two different items: shall asking the Court for an opinion be declared important and hence the decision to ask the Court be adopted by a two-thirds majority? or shall the matter on which the Court is to be asked for an opinion be declared to be important and—later on—be decided by a two-thirds majority? It may be argued that if the matter on which the Court is to be asked for an opinion is 'important' and hence requires to be decided by a two-thirds majority, also the decision by which the Court is asked for an opinion on this matter is important and requires a two-thirds majority. But it may also be argued as follows: the fact that the matter on which the Court is asked for an opinion is important and hence to be decided by a two-thirds majority does not imply that the decision by which the Court is asked for an opinion on this matter requires a two-thirds majority. If the enumeration in Article 18, paragraph 2, is interpreted to be exhaustive, the concrete decision by which the Court is asked for an opinion can be declared important only by a decision by which a new category of questions is added to those enumerated in Article 18, paragraph 2. This category may be determined as: requiring the International Court of Justice to give an advisory opinion on legal questions, or requiring the International Court of Justice to give an advisory opinion on legal questions provided the legal question concerns an important matter.[7]

[7] In the case of the treatment of Indians in South Africa two different resolutions were suggested. The one, by the delegation of the South African Union, to the effect of requesting an advisory opinion from the International Court of Justice; the other by the Joint first and sixth Committee, to the effect of stating that by the treatment of Indians in South Africa the friendly relations between the two Members have been impaired and expressing the opinion that the treatment of Indians in the Union should be in conformity with the international obligations. In asking the General Assembly to decide whether the question was important and hence required a two-thirds majority the President did not separate the two questions to which the two resolutions respectively referred. He finally formulated the subject matter of the voting as follows: 'does the Assembly consider that a two-thirds majority is required in respect of decisions taken as to the matter reported on in document A/205?' (Journal of the United Nations, No. 55: Suppl. A–A/P.V./52, p. 403.) The Assembly answered this question in the affirmative by a simple majority vote

The first matter designated in Article 18, paragraph 2, as 'important' question is 'recommendations with respect to the maintenance of international peace and security.' What does this phrase mean? Since it refers expressly to 'recommendations,' decisions of the Assembly which do not constitute a recommendation, such as a decision under Article 22 by which a subsidiary organ is established, do not fall within this category. But the phrase 'recommendations with respect to the maintenance of international peace and security' may mean all the recommendations which the General Assembly is authorised to make, since they all serve, directly or indirectly, the maintenance of international peace and security, which is the purpose of the Organisation. However, a more restricted interpretation is not excluded. There are decisions of the General Assembly, as, for instance, those concerning matters referred to in Chapter XI, which do not directly concern the maintenance of peace and of which it may be very doubtful whether they fall within this

(29 yes, 24 no). Then the suggested resolution to request an advisory opinion of the Court was rejected as it did not obtain a two-thirds, but only a simple majority (31 against 21 votes), and the resolution suggested by the Committee was adopted by a two-thirds majority (pp. 402 f.).

In its voting on the importance of the matter the Assembly did not determine an additional category of important questions. It decided only upon the importance of a concrete question. But the meaning of the decision is not clear. It may mean that the General Assembly declared the concrete question—that is the question of the treatment of Indians in South Africa—as an important question although it did not fall within one of the categories enumerated in paragraph 2 of Article 18. If so, the Assembly acted under the presupposition that this enumeration is not exhaustive, that by the formula 'other questions' used in paragraph 3 also an individual question, not falling within a category mentioned in paragraph 2, is to be understood. But the meaning of the decision might also be that the individual question to which the two suggested resolutions referred, did fall within one of the categories enumerated in paragraph 2. This interpretation of the decision may be supported by the fact that the President, in agreement with the opinion expressed by the delegate of Saudi Arabia, declared that according to paragraph 3 of Article 18 it was 'a question of category of matters and not of individual questions which we are called upon to add to the list in paragraph 2'; and at the same time approved the opinion of the delegate of Uruguay who had said: 'the important question is to know whether the subject matter before us is one that falls within the category contemplated in Article 18 which states: " . . . recommendations with respect to the maintenance of international peace . . . " (p. 397). If the President was of this opinion, he should have formulated the question concerning the importance of the matter separately for each of the two votings: Does the Assembly consider that requesting the International Court of Justice to give an advisory opinion on the treatment of Indians in South Africa is a question which falls within the category 'recommendations with respect to the maintenance of international peace and security'? Does the Assembly consider that the question to which the resolution suggested by the joint first and sixth Committee refers, falls within the category 'recommendations with respect to the maintenance of international peace and security'? It is evident that requesting an advisory opinion of the Court under Article 96 of the Charter is not at all a 'recommendation.' As to the resolution finally adopted by the Assembly, it did not—at least not expressly—contain any recommendation either. Cf. *infra*, pp. 455 f.

category.[8] The phrase may mean only the recommendations referred to in Article 11, paragraph 1: recommendations with regard to principles of co-operation in the maintenance of international peace and security; or the recommendations referred to in Article 11, paragraph 2: recommendations with regard to any questions relating to the maintenance of international peace and security brought before the General Assembly by any Member of the United Nations, or by the Security Council, or by a state which is not a Member of the United Nations in accordance with Article 35, paragraph 2; and in Article 14: recommendations for the peaceful adjustment of any situation, regardless of origin, which the Assembly deems likely to impair the general welfare or friendly relations among nations, including situations resulting from a violation of the provisions setting forth the Purposes and Principles of the United Nations. These may be recommendations in case of threat or use of force, consequently, recommendations with respect to the maintenance of international peace and security. The phrase may mean exclusively the recommendations referred to in Article 11, paragraphs 1 and 2, since there the words ' maintenance of international peace and security ' are used. Finally, the phrase ' recommendations with respect to the maintenance of international peace and security ' in Article 18, paragraph 2, may be interpreted to mean only the recommendations referred to in Article 11, paragraph 2, since only this paragraph speaks of ' recommendations with regard to ' ' any questions relating to the maintenance of international peace and security,' which formula is—although not entirely, but almost—identical with that of Article 18, paragraph 2. If this restrictive interpretation is accepted it could, for instance, be argued that recommendations under Article 14 (' measures for the peaceful adjustment of any situation, etc.') may be made by a simple majority vote (as long as the matters referred to in Article 14 do not belong to a category of questions added to those enumerated in Article 18, paragraph 2, by a decision of the General Assembly), whereas recommendations made with regard to any questions relating to the

[8] Before the voting on the resolution concerning Regional Conferences of Representatives of Non-Self-Governing Territories at the 64th meeting of the General Assembly, the President asked the Assembly whether a two-thirds majority was required. The resolution has the character of a recommendation. Referring to a passage in the text of the resolution which reads: ' Recognising the importance of the declaration contained in Chapter XI of the Charter . . . ', the President declared: ' I therefore conclude that the authors of this resolution have taken these words directly from Article 18 of the Charter. I therefore believe that we are confronted by an important question and that a two-thirds majority is required.' (Journal of the United Nations, No. 63: Suppl. A–A/P.V./64, pp. 707 f.) Since the resolution contains a recommendation it would have been more correct to vote on the question whether the proposed resolution concerns an important matter. Since this was the question on which the voting took place, the General Assembly assumed that the enumeration of important matters in paragraph 2 of Article 18 is not exhaustive.

maintenance of international peace and security, especially a dispute, brought before the General Assembly under Article 11, paragraph 2, must be made by a two-thirds majority vote. Although any distinction between recommendations of the General Assembly made ' with respect to the maintenance of international peace and security ' and other recommendations of the General Assembly is very artificial since the maintenance of international peace and security is—as pointed out —the general purpose of all the activities of the Organisation, a tendency to interpret the formula of Article 18, paragraph 2, as restrictively as possible would be quite understandable. For such interpretation facilitates one of the most important functions of the General Assembly by allowing this organ to make as many recommendations as possible by a simple majority vote.[9]

According to Article 18, paragraph 2, the election of members of all three Councils of the United Nations are declared ' important questions ' and hence require a two-thirds majority. According to Article 10, paragraph 1, of the Statute of the International Court of Justice, the election of the judges of this Court by the General Assembly (as well as by the Security Council) requires only ' an absolute majority of votes.' The election of the judges of the Court is certainly as ' important ' as the election of the members of one of the three Councils. But, in virtue of the special provision of Article 10 of the Statute, no two-thirds majority is required. This, too, is in favour of the interpretation according to which the enumeration in Article 18, paragraph 2, is to be considered as exhaustive. Another decision of the General Assembly for which a simple majority is expressly required is the one referred to in Article 109, paragraph 3, concerning the holding of a General Conference for reviewing the Charter. In this provision the required majority is not specified by the words ' of the members present and voting ' (the formula used in Article 18, paragraphs 2 and 3); consequently the majority of all the members (the votes of more than half of the members) is required. Also Article 10, paragraph 1, of the Statute does not stipulate a majority of the members present and voting; its wording is: ' an absolute majority of votes in the General Assembly and in the Security Council.' The identical provision in the Statute of the Permanent Court of International Justice has been interpreted to mean: a majority of the members present. But this interpretation was possible since Article 5 of the Covenant provided that decisions of the Assembly and the Council require either ' agreement of all the Members of the League repre-

[9] At the *Hearings* (p. 257), the representative of the Department of State stated that recommendations for peaceful adjustment—in contradistinction to recommendations for adjustment by enforcement measures—do not necessarily require merely a simple majority, as a Senator erroneously assumed. The representative expressed the view that a recommendation for peaceful adjustment, although not mentioned in Article 18, paragraph 2, may concern an important question and hence require a two-thirds majority.

sented at the meeting ' or ' a majority of the Members of the League represented at the meeting.' The Statute of the International Court of Justice forms an integral part of the Charter. Consequently, Article 10 of this Statute must be interpreted in consideration of the provisions of the Charter concerning decisions of the General Assembly and the Security Council. Since the Charter makes a distinction between a majority of the members present and voting, and a majority vote of the members, Article 10, paragraph 1, of the Statute may be interpreted to mean: majority of votes of all the members of the General Assembly and of the Security Council, and not only a majority of those present and voting. But another interpretation is not absolutely excluded, since Article 10, paragraph 1, of the Statute speaks of a majority of votes ' in the General Assembly and in the Security Council,' not of a majority or a majority vote ' of the members ' (as does Article 109, paragraph 3). A majority ' in the General Assembly ' or ' in the Security Council ' may mean a majority of the members present and voting. A two-thirds majority is expressly required for the adoption of amendments to the Charter in Article 108 and for the decision fixing the date and place of the General Conference in Article 109, paragraph 1. In these provisions, too, the words ' present and voting ' do not appear. Consequently a vote of two thirds of all the members is required. Rule 78 of the Rules of Procedure interprets the phrase ' Members present and voting ' to mean: ' Members casting an affirmative or negative vote. Members which abstain from voting are considered as not voting.'

The Charter does not determine the number of members who must be present in order to enable the General Assembly to transact business (quorum). In this respect the Rules of Procedure provide:

RULE 60

A majority of the Members of the General Assembly shall constitute a quorum.

As to the form of voting the Rules of Procedure provide:

RULE 79

The General Assembly shall normally vote by show of hands or by standing, but any representative may request a roll-call. The roll-call shall be taken in the English alphabetical order of the names of the Members, beginning with the Member whose name is drawn by lot by the President. The name of each Member shall be called in any roll-call and one of its representatives shall reply ' Yes,' ' No ' or ' Abstention.' The result of the voting shall be inserted in the record in the English alphabetical order of the names of the Members.

RULE 84

All elections shall be held by secret ballot. There shall be no nominations.[1]

The Charter does not contain a provision concerning the procedure to be applied in case the majority prescribed by the Charter is not reached. In this respect the Rules of Procedure stipulate:

RULE 85

When only one person or Member is to be elected and no candidate obtains in the first ballot the majority required, a second ballot shall be taken which shall be restricted to the two candidates obtaining the largest number of votes. If in the second ballot the votes are equally divided, and a majority is required, the President shall decide between the candidates by drawing lots. If a two-thirds majority is required, the balloting shall be continued until one candidate secures two-thirds of the votes cast; provided that, after the third inconclusive ballot, votes may be cast for any eligible person or Member. If three such unrestricted ballots are inconclusive, the next three ballots shall be restricted to the two candidates who obtained the greatest number of votes in the third of the unrestricted ballots, and the following three ballots thereafter shall be unrestricted, and so on until a person or Member is

[1] The last sentence of Rule 84: 'There shall be no nominations,' was the result of an amendment adopted at the 18th meeting of the General Assembly on the recommendation of the Sixth Committee. (Journal of the General Assembly, First Session, No. 16, pp. 319–336.) The proposal of the Ukrainian representative 'that all candidatures, both of states and persons, should be brought forward at meetings and that discussion should take place before a vote was taken, except in cases in which the Assembly unanimously decided to proceed to a vote by acclamation' was rejected. 'In favour of the Ukrainian proposal requiring nominations it was argued that representatives coming from all over the world were not well acquainted with one another. Qualified candidates of small countries particularly might not be generally known. Nominations and discussion would place the representatives in possession of sufficient information to vote for the most suitable candidate. It would further avoid the risk of persons or states being elected who did not wish to serve. The General Assembly during the present session had usually voted on the basis of nominations. Everyone had accepted this procedure as natural and in most cases the committees had been able to make elections of officers by unanimous vote. To forbid nominations was undemocratic. It was the basic right of every Member of the Organisation to make proposals on every matter within the competence of the General Assembly. To except the matter of elections would be a breach of the spirit of the Charter of the United Nations. To avoid frank discussion at the General Assembly's meetings would lead to lobbying, intrigues and discussion behind the scenes. Nominations would, on the contrary, tend to discourage the formation of blocs within the General Assembly. In favour of no nominations it was maintained that only in this way could absolute freedom and independence of voting be ensured. Discussion of the qualifications of candidates might easily lead to embarrassment and might impair the prestige of countries nominated or making nominations.' (*Yearbook of the United Nations*, 1946–47, pp. 62 f.)

elected. These provisions shall not prejudice the application of Rules 132, 133, 135 and 137.

RULE 86

When two or more elective places are to be filled at one time under the same conditions, those candidates obtaining in the first ballot the majority required shall be elected. If the number of candidates obtaining such majority is less than the number of persons or Members to be elected, there shall be additional ballots to fill the remaining places, the voting being restricted to the candidates obtaining the greatest number of votes in the previous ballot, to a number not more than twice the places remaining to be filled; provided that, after the third inconclusive ballot, votes may be cast for any eligible person or Member. If three such unrestricted ballots are inconclusive, the next three ballots shall be restricted to the candidates who obtained the greatest number of votes in the third of the unrestricted ballots, to a number not more than twice the places remaining to be filled, and the following three ballots thereafter shall be unrestricted, and so on until all the places have been filled. These provisions shall not prejudice the application of Rules 132, 133, 135 and 137.

RULE 87

If a vote is equally divided on matters other than elections, a second vote shall be taken at a subsequent meeting which shall be held within forty-eight hours of the first vote, and it shall be expressly mentioned in the agenda that a second vote will be taken on the matter in question. If this vote also results in equality, the proposal shall be regarded as rejected.

With respect to the procedure in the Committees of the General Assembly the Rules of Procedure stipulate:

RULE 94

Each committee shall elect its own Chairman, Vice-Chairman and Rapporteur. These officers shall be elected on the basis of equitable geographical distribution, experience and personal competence. These elections shall be held by secret ballot.

RULE 93

Each committee may set up sub-committees, which shall elect their own officers.

RULE 98

A majority of the members of a committee shall constitute a quorum.

RULE 114

Decisions in the committees of the General Assembly shall be taken by a majority of the members present and voting.

A principle of importance is laid down in Rule 58:

The General Assembly shall not, unless it decides otherwise, make a final decision upon any item on the agenda until it has received the report of a committee on that item.

C. *Differences between the Procedure of the General Assembly and that of the Security Council*

The procedure of the General Assembly differs from that of the Security Council in so far as in the latter there is no distinction between ordinary matters to be decided by a simple majority vote and 'important' matters to be decided by a two-thirds majority vote, but between 'procedural' matters to be decided by an affirmative vote of seven (from the eleven) members, and other matters to be decided by an affirmative vote of seven members including the concurring votes of the permanent members (Article 27, paragraphs 2 and 3). No member of the General Assembly has a veto right. In its procedure the principle of equality is strictly observed.

The General Assembly is authorised by Article 21—just as the Security Council by Article 30—to adopt its own rules of procedure. Since the decision concerned refers certainly to procedural matters, the provision of Article 27, paragraph 2, certainly applies to the decision of the Security Council. But it is doubtful whether the decision by which the General Assembly adopts its own rules of procedure is to be made by a simple or by a two-thirds majority vote. The matter is not mentioned among those enumerated in Article 18, paragraph 2. But, according to one of the interpretations mentioned above, this does not necessarily mean that the matter is not an 'important question' requiring a two-thirds majority, even if the adoption of the rules of procedure has not been added to the list of Article 18, paragraph 2, by a decision under paragraph 3. Yet a minority cannot prevent a simple majority from adopting the rules of procedure of the General Assembly.

The procedure of the General Assembly differs from that of the Security Council not only in so far as no member of the General Assembly has a veto right but also in so far as no member, if party to a dispute under consideration by the Assembly, is excluded from voting, whereas Article 27 provides that in decisions of the Security Council under Chapter VI and under paragraph 3 of Article 52, a party to a dispute shall abstain from voting.[2] Another difference between

[2] At its 9th meeting, Committee 1 of Commission II of the San Francisco Conference (U.N.C.I.O. Doc. 494, II/1/23, pp. 1 f.) 'discussed a proposal submitted by the Delegation of Costa Rica that members to whom acts of aggression were attributed

the procedure of the General Assembly and that of the Security Council is that under Article 32 'any state which is not a Member of the United Nations, if it is a party to a dispute under consideration by the Security Council, shall be invited to participate, without vote, in the discussion relating to the dispute,' whereas if a dispute to which a non-member is a party is under consideration by the General Assembly, the non-member neither shall nor can be invited to participate in the discussion. It is difficult to understand why the principles laid down in Article 27, paragraph 2, and Article 32, for the procedure of the Security Council do not apply in the procedure of the General Assembly. With respect to participation of non-members in the discussion, there exists also a difference between the procedure in the General Assembly and the procedure in the Economic and Social Council which, under Article 70 of the Charter, may allow 'representatives of the specialised agencies to participate, without vote, in its deliberations and in those of the commissions established by it.' Under the Charter, only states Members of the United Nations are allowed to participate in the discussion and the voting in the General Assembly.[3]

3. Competence (General Remarks)

A. *Legal and Political Competence*

Functions are conferred upon the General Assembly either directly by the Charter or indirectly by international agreements, being delegated by the Charter. The Charter determines the competence of the General Assembly by a general clause laid down in Article 10, and by special provisions referring to particular matters. The functions conferred upon the General Assembly may be designated as legal functions if

should not vote in their own cases. The Delegate of the United Kingdom, with the support of other delegates, expressed the view that questions relating to a determination of acts of aggression were to be decided on by the Security Council. They were therefore outside the competence of the Committee. The Costa Rica amendment was supported by a Delegate from Bolivia on the ground that it dealt merely with the form and manner of voting in the Assembly in the event of a state being charged with aggression. The Committee rejected by a vote of 20 to 5 the principle that delegates of states to which acts of agression are attributed should abstain from voting in the corresponding decision in the General Assembly.' The Committee also 'considered the principle embodied in proposals submitted by the Delegation of Chile that parties to disputes being considered in the Assembly should not vote in their own cases. The Delegate of the United Kingdom expressed the opinion that this principle fell in the same category as the one just decided and should, therefore, not be dealt with by this Committee. The Chilean Delegate pointed out that in some cases the Assembly might be called upon to consider disputes and that therefore the question of voting under those circumstances should be specified in the Charter. By a vote of 21 to 7, the Committee rejected the principle that parties to a dispute being considered by the Assembly should abstain from voting.'

[3] Cf. *infra*, p. 460.

the acts which the General Assembly is empowered to perform have legal effects, that is to say, if they constitute obligations, rights or competences, as for instance the admission of new Members under Article 4, or the participation in the amendment procedure under Article 108. They may be designated as political functions if they have no such effects, though they may actually influence the conduct of Members or non-members or the activity of other organs of the United Nations.

The legal functions may be performed by unilateral acts of the General Assembly or by participating in the conclusion of an international agreement or a contract under national law.[4] The legal functions may have a general or individual character, that is to say, the acts to be performed by the General Assembly may create general legal norms binding upon those whose conduct is regulated by them. These are legislative functions in the wider sense of the term, comprising not only unilateral acts, as for instance the adoption of the Rules of Procedure under Article 21, but also participation in the conclusion of treaties establishing general legal norms, as for instance the approval of trusteeship agreements under Article 85. The acts of the General Assembly may create only individual norms, that is to say, only an individual obligation, right or competence. These are administrative and quasi-judicial functions, as for instance the appointment of the Secretary-General under Article 97, or a decision under Article 19 by which the General Assembly permits a Member to vote; or they may have the character of legal transactions under national law, as for instance the approval of the agreement between the United Nations and the Carnegie Foundation concerning the use of the premises of the Peace Palace at the Hague. There is, however, no absolute difference between acts by which general, and those by which individual legal norms (obligations, rights, competences) are created; there are intermediate forms.[5] In case the United Nations should assume under Article 81 the function of an administering authority of a trust territory and exercise this function through the General Assembly, this

[4] As to the competence of the United Nations to conclude agreements under international and contracts under national law, cf. *infra*, pp. 329 ff.

[5] At its 50th meeting on December 7, 1946, the General Assembly adopted a resolution to the effect that a certain design 'shall be the emblem and distinctive sign of the United Nations and shall be used for the official seal of the Organisation.' (Doc. A/64/Add.1, pp. 185 f.); at its 96th meeting, a resolution to the effect 'that the flag of the United Nations shall be the official emblem adopted by the General Assembly under the terms of its resolution 92 (I) of December 7, 1946, centred on a light blue ground'; at the 101st meeting a resolution by which it declared 'that October 24, the anniversary of the coming into force of the Charter of the United Nations, shall henceforth be officially called "United Nations Day" and shall be devoted to making known to the peoples of the world the aims and achievements of the United Nations and to gaining their support for the work of the United Nations.' (Doc. A/519, p. 91.) These resolutions intend to have legal effects on the organs and Members of the United Nations. They are more than mere recommendations. As such they have no basis in the Charter.

organ would have legislative, administrative and judicial powers with respect to this territory.[6]

Political functions within the meaning determined above are: to 'discuss' matters within the scope of the Charter (Article 10); to 'consider' principles or reports (Articles 11, 15, 24, 87); to 'accept' or 'receive' reports, recommendations, or observations (Articles 15, 62, 64), but this only in order to 'consider' or 'discuss' them; to 'initiate' studies or negotiations (Articles 13, 59). The most important political function of the General Assembly is to make 'recommendations' (Articles 10, 11, 13, 14, 58, 64, 105). Such recommendations may be made to the Members of the United Nations (Articles 10, 11), to non-member states (Article 11, paragraph 2), or to the Security Council (Articles 10, 11); Article 13 authorises the Assembly to make recommendations in the field of international co-operation and Article 14 authorises the Assembly to recommend measures for the peaceful adjustment of any situation which it deems likely to impair the general welfare or friendly relations among nations, without any restriction as to the persons or authorities to which the recommendations may be made.[7] Recommendations, by their very

[6] Cf. *infra*, pp. 651 ff.

[7] The resolution of the General Assembly regarding the future government of Palestine, adopted at its 128th meeting on November 29, 1947, is based on Article 14 of the Charter, for it contains the following passage: 'The General Assembly . . . considers that the present situation in Palestine is one which is likely to impair the general welfare and friendly relations among nations.' The formula 'likely to impair the general welfare or friendly relations among nations' appears only in Article 14. In this resolution the General Assembly 'recommends to the United Kingdom, as the mandatory Power for Palestine, and to all other Members of the United Nations the adoption and implementation, with regard to the future government of Palestine, of the Plan of Partition with Economic Union set out below.' In addition, the General Assembly 'calls upon the inhabitants of Palestine to take such steps as may be necessary on their part to put this plan into effect'; and 'appeals to all Governments and all peoples to refrain from taking any action which might hamper or delay the carrying out of these recommendations . . .' The 'call' and the 'appeal' are to be interpreted as 'recommendations' within the meaning of Article 14 which authorises the Assembly only to 'recommend' measures for the peaceful adjustment of situations, not to 'call' or 'appeal.' That the General Assembly in this resolution makes recommendations not only to Members of the United Nations but to 'all Governments and all peoples' and to 'the inhabitants of Palestine,' is quite in conformity with Article 14 which—in contradistinction to Articles 10 and 11—does not restrict the circle of persons or authorities to whom recommendations may be made. It is, however, doubtful whether the resolution of the Assembly did not go beyond mere recommendations. It provided, under the heading 'Steps Preparatory to Independence':

> 1. A Commission shall be set up consisting of one representative of each of five Member states. The Members represented on the Commission shall be elected by the General Assembly on as broad a basis, geographically and otherwise, as possible.
>
> 2. The administration of Palestine shall, as the mandatory Power withdraws its armed forces, be progressively turned over to the Commission, which shall act in conformity with the recommendations of the General

nature, do not constitute a legal obligation to behave in conformity with them.[8] This is of particular importance with respect to recommendations made by the General Assembly to the Security

> Assembly, under the guidance of the Security Council. The mandatory Power shall to the fullest possible extent co-ordinate its plans for withdrawal with the plans of the Commission to take over and administer areas which have been evacuated.
>
> In the discharge of this administrative responsibility the Commission shall have authority to issue necessary regulations and take other measures as required.
>
> The mandatory Power shall not take any action to prevent, obstruct or delay the implementation by the Commission of the measures recommended by the General Assembly.

Since at the time the resolution was adopted the territory of Palestine was, if not under the sovereignty, so at least under the exclusive administration, of the United Kingdom, the General Assembly was competent under Articles 10 and 14 to recommend to the Government of the United Kingdom to establish an Arab and a Jewish state with economic union on the former mandate territory, but the Assembly was hardly competent to transfer the administration of Palestine to a commission established by the General Assembly. In view of the fact that the United Kingdom refused to have part in the implementation of the United Nations Plan of Partition, the resolution of the General Assembly restricted itself in the annexed ' Plan of Partition with Economic Union ' to recommend to the United Kingdom not to take any action ' to prevent, obstruct or delay the implementation by the Commission of the measures recommended by the General Assembly.' Hence the provision of the resolution: ' The administration of Palestine shall . . . be . . . turned over to the Commission . . . ' actually means that the commission shall take over the administration of Palestine. This is not a recommendation. This is a decision of the General Assembly to administer, on behalf of the United Nations, through a commission established by the General Assembly, a territory abandoned by its legitimate government. Even if the phrase ' The administration of Palestine shall, as the mandatory Power withdraws its armed forces, be progressively turned over to the Commission ' is interpreted to mean that the United Kingdom shall turn over to the Commission the administration of Palestine, the resolution of the General Assembly implies the decision that in case the United Kingdom accepts this recommendation the United Nations, through a commission appointed by the General Assembly, shall administer Palestine. The resolution provides expressly that the commission shall ' take over and administer areas which have been evacuated ' by

---

8 The Soviet Union refused to comply with the recommendations made by the General Assembly in its resolution concerning the independence of Korea (cf. *supra*, pp. 174 ff., and Annual Report of the Secretary-General, Doc. A/565, p. 31). At the 128th meeting of the General Assembly the delegates of Saudi Arabia, Pakistan, Iraq, Syria and Yemen declared that they did not consider their governments bound by the recommendations made in the resolution of the General Assembly regarding future government of Palestine. (Doc. A/P.V.128.) During the discussion of the Palestine question in the Security Council (starting with the 253rd meeting on February 24, 1948), the representative of the United Kingdom declared that his government was unwilling to take any part in the implementation of the General Assembly's resolution regarding future government of Palestine as long as there existed objection to it by either Arab or Jewish authorities. The representatives of Syria, Egypt and Lebanon denied expressly that the recommendations of the General Assembly had any binding force upon the Members. (Doc. S/P.V.254, p. 21; S/P.V.255, p. 16; S/P.V.267, pp. 12 f.)

Council. The latter may or may not accept and carry out such a recommendation.[9]

Under Article 62, paragraph 3, the Economic and Social Council 'may prepare draft conventions for submission to the General

the mandatory power, according to plans co-ordinated with the plans of the commission. To decide that the United Nations shall administer a territory for the purpose to establish on it two new states is hardly within the competence of the General Assembly or any other organ of the United Nations. At the meeting, on November 25, 1947, of the General Assembly's *ad hoc* committee on the Palestine question, the representative of Iraq argued that the partition proposal went beyond 'recommendations'; the representatives of Pakistan and of Lebanon contended that the proposed commission would have administrative and legislative powers in Palestine, and that the Assembly was not competent to establish such body. (Cf. United Nations Weekly Bulletin, Vol. III, No. 23, pp. 742 f.) At the 128th meeting of the General Assembly the delegate of Cuba pointed out that the General Assembly was empowered only to make recommendations, but that the partition plan was more than a recommendation. (*Ibid.*, No. 24, p. 775.) At the 120th meeting of the First Committee of the General Assembly on April 21, 1948, the representative of Syria stated: 'According to the Charter, the General Assembly could make only recommendations and had no power to implement decision. Article 14 was clearly so limited and so were the provisions of Chapter VI.' He referred to precedents of 'Assembly recommendations rejected by various states.' (Doc. A/C.1/SR. 120, pp. 1 f.) These arguments are, from a strictly legal point, correct. (As to the text of the resolution of the General Assembly of November 29, 1947, regarding the future government of Palestine, cf. Resolutions adopted by the General Assembly, Doc. A/519, pp. 131 ff.).

---

9 In its resolution regarding future government of Palestine (cf. note 7) the General Assembly 'requested' that:

> (*a*) The Security Council take the necessary measures as provided for in the plan for its implementation;
>
> (*b*) The Security Council consider, if circumstances during the transitional period require such consideration, whether the situation in Palestine constitutes a threat to the peace. If it decides that such a threat exists, and in order to maintain international peace and security, the Security Council should supplement the authorisation of the General Assembly by taking measures, under Articles 39 and 41 of the Charter, to empower the United Nations Commission, as provided in this resolution, to exercise in Palestine the functions which are assigned to it by this resolution;
>
> (*c*) The Security Council determine as a threat to the peace, breach of the peace or act of aggression, in accordance with Article 39 of the Charter, any attempt to alter by force the settlement envisaged by this resolution;

These 'requests' are to be interpreted as 'recommendations' within the meaning of Article 14 on the basis of which the resolution of the General Assembly has been adopted. At the 253rd meeting of the Security Council the representative of the United States suggested that the Security Council resolve to accept, subject to the authority of the Council under the Charter, the requests addressed to it by the General Assembly in paragraphs (*a*), (*b*) and (*c*) of its November resolution. (Doc. S/P.V.253.) The suggestion to accept the requests of the Assembly in paragraphs (*a*), (*b*) and (*c*) of its resolution was not approved by the Security Council, which implies that the Council did not consider itself bound by the 'requests.' At the 254th meeting of the Security Council the delegate of Syria stated: 'The Security Council is an independent organ of the United Nations with complete liberty to

Assembly, with respect to matters falling within its competence.' This implies the competence of the General Assembly to approve these draft conventions. Such approval has a legal effect in so far as only a draft convention approved by the Assembly can be submitted to ratification by the Members.

B. *Competence under Article* 10

Article 10 establishes the competence of the General Assembly in a general way as follows:

> The General Assembly may discuss any questions or any matters within the scope of the present Charter or relating to the powers and functions of any organs provided for in the present Charter, and except as provided in Article 12, may make recommendations to the Members of the United Nations or to the Security Council or to both on any such questions or matters.

The wording of this Article is technically defective. There is no reason to differentiate between ' questions ' and ' matters ' since the one term can be used in exactly the same sense as the other. The ' scope of the present Charter ' is identical with the competence of the United Nations as determined in the Charter.[1] Since this competence is to be exercised by the various organs of the United Nations, the competence of the General Assembly to discuss any matter within the scope of the Charter includes the competence to discuss matters ' relating to the powers and functions of any organs provided for in the present Charter.' By Article 10 the General Assembly is competent not only to discuss any matter within the competence of the United Nations but also to make recommendations on any such matter. This is a political, not a legal, competence in the sense defined above. Since the Charter determines as purpose of the United Nations to maintain and restore international peace and security by preventive and repressive measures (Preamble, Articles 1 and 2), there is hardly

act within the provisions of the Charter, irrespective of any recommendations or instructions given to it by any other body.' (Doc. S/P.V.254, p. 11.) At the 277th meeting of the Security Council the delegate of Belgium declared that ' the Security Council was free to accept or not to accept ' the request of the General Assembly. (Doc. S/P.V.277, p. 12–15.) As to the question, whether the Assembly was competent to recommend under Article 14 to the Security Council to take enforcement measures within the meaning of Article 39, cf. *infra*, pp. 208 ff.

[1] Committee II/2 (U.N.C.I.O. Doc. 686, II/2/34) suggested to confer upon the General Assembly the power to discuss any matter ' within the sphere of international relations.' The finally adopted text: ' within the scope of the Charter ' is not essentially different. Any matter within the sphere of international relations may be interpreted to be within the scope of the Charter since any such matter may be in some relation to international peace and security. At the 4th meeting of Commission II (U.N.C.I.O. Doc. 1151, II/17, p. 19) the Australian delegate interpreted the words ' within the scope of the present Charter ' as follows: ' That scope will include every aspect of the Charter, everything contained in it and everything

any international matter which the General Assembly is not competent to discuss and on which it is not competent to make recommendations.[2] But it is important to note that the main competence of the Assembly, as determined by Article 10, has a political, not a legal character. The intention was to establish the General Assembly as 'town meeting of the world,' the 'open conscience of humanity,' that is to say, as a

covered by it. It will include the Preamble of the Charter, the great purposes and principles embodied in it, the activities of all its organs; and the right of discussion will be free and untrammelled and will range over that tremendous area.'

[2] After the breakdown of negotiations in the Joint Commission on Korea (United States and Soviet Union) in August, 1947, the Government of the United States of America, on September 17, 1947, submitted the problem of the independence of Korea to the Secretary-General for inclusion in the agenda of the 2nd regular session of the General Assembly. On September 23, the General Assembly, on the recommendation of the General Committee, decided to place this item on its agenda and referred it to the First Committee for consideration and report. (Annual Report of the Secretary-General, Doc. A/565, p. 29.) The General Assembly finally adopted two resolutions quoted *supra*, pp. 174 ff.

In the discussions of the First Committee some delegates denied the competence of the United Nations to deal with the problem of the independence of Korea. (Doc. A/C.1/S.R.87–94.) The main argument was that this problem was connected with the peace treaties and the United Nations was not competent to deal with problems of the peace treaties. The only provision of the Charter on which this view could be based is Article 107 which authorises the Members of the United Nations to take action, especially enforcement action, in relation to any state which during the Second World War has been an enemy to any signatory to the Charter. Since Korea was not an enemy, it is doubtful whether Article 107 applies at all. But even if Korea was considered to be part of the territory of a former enemy state, it could hardly be argued that Article 107 excludes the competence of the General Assembly to discuss the problem of the independence of Korea and make recommendations in this respect, provided that this problem is a question within the scope of the Charter; and it is within the scope of the Charter if it has anything to do with the maintenance of international peace. At the 87th meeting of the First Committee, the representative of Australia stated 'that Article 107 of the Charter did not preclude examination of this question by the United Nations, since the General Assembly had the necessary competence to recommend if not to carry out measures. Since the Allied Powers had been unable to conclude the peace treaties speedily, it devolved on the United Nations to deal with the question. Nevertheless, such questions should only be brought before the General Assembly as a last resort, because its function was not to intervene in the preparation of the peace treaties but to see that peace was maintained once the treaties had been signed.' (Doc. A/C.1/S.R.87, p. 5.) The view that questions to be solved by the peace treaties are excluded from the competence of the United Nations and devolve on this Organisation only if the peace treaties are not speedily concluded, has no basis in the Charter. The wording of Article 107 does not prevent the General Assembly to discuss problems to be solved by the peace treaties and make recommendations on such problems. The fact that the General Assembly discusses and recommends an action in relation to a former enemy state does not imply invalidation or preclusion of any other action, even an action contrary to the one recommended by the General Assembly. At the 91st meeting the representative of India quite correctly stated 'that Article 107 of the Charter was only permissive in effect and did not prevent the Assembly from considering such matters.' (Doc. A/C.1/S.R.91, p. 8.) Cf. *infra*, pp. 805 ff.

deliberative and criticising organ.[3] Hence, legal functions of the Assembly are to be considered as exceptions and require special provisions in the Charter. As a matter of fact, the Assembly has assumed legal functions not expressly conferred upon it by the Charter. Thus, for instance, the above mentioned approval of the agreement with the Carnegie Foundation has no basis in the Charter; nor is there a provision in the Charter authorising the General Assembly to adopt on behalf of the United Nations, certain functions of the League of Nations, which actually was done by resolutions of the General Assembly adopted at its 49th and 65th meetings. The Charter, unfortunately, does not contain a provision authorising a definite organ of the United Nations in a general way to perform the legal functions which may be necessary to achieve the purpose of the Organisation, but which are not stipulated by a special provision of the Charter.

C. *Competence under Article* 11

In addition to Article 10, Chapter IV of the Charter contains other provisions referring to the competence of the General Assembly to discuss matters and make recommendations on such matters, which are technically superfluous because covered by Article 10. Article 11 stipulates:

> 1. The General Assembly may consider the general principles of co-operation in the maintenance of international peace and security, including the principles governing disarmament and the regulation of armaments, and may make recommendations with regard to such principles to the Members or to the Security Council or to both.
>
> 2. The General Assembly may discuss any questions relating to the maintenance of international peace and security brought before it by any Member of the United Nations, or by the Security Council, or by a state which is not a Member of the United Nations in accordance with Article 35, paragraph 2, and, except as provided in Article 12, may make recommendations with regard to any such questions to the state or states concerned or to the Security Council or to both. Any such question on which action is necessary shall be referred to the Security Council by the General Assembly either before or after discussion.
>
> 3. The General Assembly may call the attention of the Security Council to situations which are likely to endanger international peace and security.
>
> 4. The powers of the General Assembly set forth in this Article shall not limit the general scope of Article 10.

[3] *Yearbook of the United Nations*, 1946–47, p. 51.

Paragraph 1 of this Article is completely covered by Article 10 since ' the general principles of co-operation in the maintenance of international peace and security, including the principles governing disarmament and the regulation of armaments,' are—according to Article 1 of the Charter—within the scope of the Charter. That Article 11, paragraph 1, authorises the General Assembly to ' consider ' whereas Article 10, to ' discuss,' does not constitute a difference in the meaning of the two Articles. It is only an inconsistency in the terminology of the Charter.[4] But whereas the competence of the General Assembly to make recommendations under Article 10 is restricted by the reference to Article 12, the provision of this Article does not apply to recommendations of the General Assembly made under Article 11, paragraph 1.

The competence of the General Assembly to make recommendations with regard to principles governing disarmament and the regulation of armaments to the Members of the United Nations is—at least partly—concurrent with the competence of the Security Council under Article 26 to formulate plans ' for the establishment of a system for the regulation of armaments ' to be submitted to the Members of the United Nations. Since these plans are to be ' submitted ' to the Members which are not obligated to accept them, there is hardly an essential difference between the power of the General Assembly to make recommendations and that of the Security Council to formulate and submit plans.

The first sentence of paragraph 2, too, is almost completely

[4] The Second Report of Subcommittee 3 of Committee II/2 (U.N.C.I.O. Doc. 677, II/2/B/9) contains the following statement (referring to the use of the term ' discuss ' in Article 10: ' The Subcommittee was of the view that the right to " consider " encompasses the right to " discuss ".' At the *Hearings*, p. 246, the representative of the Department of State stated: ' The right of the Assembly to discuss, consider, and debate any question relating to the maintenance of international peace and security is absolute. Nobody can stop it.' As to the use of the term ' discuss ' in Article 10 and Article 11, paragraph 2, in contradistinction to the term 'consider' in Article 11, paragraph 1, a Senator asked (p. 242): ' Is there any reason for using those two words differently? ' The representative of the State Department answered: ' Perhaps the word " consider " is more comprehensive than the word " discuss," because the word " consider " may have an implication of leading to some sort of action—recommendation, for example.' Whereupon the Senator asked: ' Then, you did use the words deliberately.' Answer: ' Oh, yes; they were used deliberately.' Senator: ' When you discuss, you do not consider?' Answer: ' When you consider, you certainly discuss; and when you discuss, you consider. But you consider perhaps with a view to doing something about it ' . . . Senator: ' But there is a real difference, then, between the two words?' Answer: ' We thought when we were drafting these particular provisions that the use of the two words would reinforce the concept of free discussion and free consideration.' The statement that the word ' consider ' is more comprehensive and may have the implication of leading to recommendation does not conform with the terminology of the Charter which in Article 10, as well as in Article 11 confers expressly on the Assembly the power of making recommendations, although it uses in one Article the term ' discuss ' and in the other the term ' consider.'

covered by Article 10. 'Questions relating to the maintenance of international peace and security' in whatever way they may have been brought before the General Assembly are 'questions within the scope of the present Charter.' After Article 10 has authorised the General Assembly to discuss any questions relating to the maintenance of international peace and security (being within the scope of the Charter) and to make recommendations on any such question, regardless of the way in which such question has been brought before the Assembly, Article 11, paragraph 2, restricts the competence of the General Assembly to discuss such questions only if brought before the Assembly 'by any Member of the United Nations, or by the Security Council, or by a state which is not a Member of the United Nations in accordance with Article 35, paragraph 2.' If the Assembly prefers to act under Article 10 instead of under Article 11, it is not hampered by this restriction. But the restriction established by the reference to Article 12: not to make recommendations on disputes or situations while the Security Council is dealing with them, applies whether the General Assembly acts under Article 10 or Article 11, paragraph 2. Since Article 12, referred to in Article 10, deals with 'any dispute or situation' the 'questions' referred to in Article 10 include 'disputes' and 'situations.' The 'questions' referred to in Article 11, paragraph 2, may even be considered to be identical with disputes or situations, since the only provision of the Charter which authorises Members and non-Members to bring 'questions' before the General Assembly is Article 35, and the only provision of the Charter which authorises the Security Council to bring a question before the Assembly is Article 12, paragraph 1. Both provisions refer only to disputes or (other) situations. Article 35, paragraph 1, authorises the Members to 'bring any dispute, or any situation of the nature referred to in Article 34, to the attention' of the General Assembly. This phrase may be interpreted to mean that the Members of the United Nations are authorised to bring to the attention of the General Assembly 'any dispute,' but situations (not having the character of a dispute) only if they are of the nature referred to in Article 34. Article 34, however, refers to situations of different nature. It authorises the Security Council to investigate any dispute, or any 'situation which might lead to international friction or give rise to a dispute, in order to determine whether the continuance of the dispute or situation is likely to endanger the maintenance of international peace and security.' Hence Article 35, paragraph 1, may be interpreted to mean that any Member of the United Nations is authorised to bring to the attention of the General Assembly situations 'which might lead to international friction or give rise to a dispute' or situations the continuance of which 'is likely to endanger the maintenance of international peace and security.' Both interpretations are possible.

Article 35, paragraph 2, authorises any non-Member to 'bring to the attention' of the General Assembly only a dispute to which it is a party, not a ' situation '; and Article 12, paragraph 1, authorises the Security Council to request the General Assembly to make a recommendation on a dispute or (other) situation in respect to which the Security Council exercises the functions assigned to it. The Charter assigns to the Security Council functions in respect to any dispute, but only in respect to situations which might lead to international friction or give rise to a dispute (Article 34). It may be assumed that the words: to ' bring to the attention of the General Assembly ' in Article 35, paragraphs 1 and 2, and the words: ' request the General Assembly ' in Article 12, paragraph 1, have the same meaning as ' bring before the General Assembly ' in Article 11, paragraph 2. If it were possible to interpret Article 11, paragraph 2, to mean that the purpose of this provision is to authorise Members of the United Nations and the Security Council to bring any question relating to the maintenance of international peace and security before the General Assembly, then the term ' questions ' as used in Article 11, paragraph 2, could be interpreted not to be identical with disputes or situations. This interpretation might be supported by the fact that Article 11, paragraph 2, refers only to Article 35, paragraph 2, authorising non-Members to bring disputes to the General Assembly, but does not refer to Article 35, paragraph 1, authorising Members to bring disputes and other situations before the General Assembly, nor to Article 12, paragraph 1, authorising the Security Council to bring disputes and other situations before the General Assembly. But it is possible that the words of Article 11, paragraph 2: ' brought before it by any Member of the United Nations, or by the Security Council ' mean: brought before the General Assembly in conformity with other provisions of the Charter authorising the Members or the Security Council to this effect. However that may be, under Article 10 the General Assembly is competent to make recommendations only to Members or to the Security Council, whereas under Article 11, paragraph 2, also to non-Member states. If the General Assembly intends to make recommendations to non-Members, it must act under Article 11, paragraph 2, not under Article 10.

On the other hand, Article 11, paragraph 2, contains a restriction which Article 10 does not. Article 10 refers only to the provisions of Article 12, not to the provision of Article 11, paragraph 2, that any ' questions ' relating to the maintenance of international peace and security brought before the General Assembly by a Member of the United Nations, or by the Security Council, or by a state which is not a Member of the United Nations in accordance with Article 35, paragraph 2, ' shall be referred to the Security Council by the General Assembly either before or after discussion ': if ' action is necessary.' That means that the General Assembly—acting under Article 11, paragraph 2—may discuss such question, but must not make recommendations. It must refer the question to the Security Council; even if the question has been brought before the Assembly—under Article 11, paragraph 2—by the Security Council itself. Recommendation is excluded not only when the 'question' is a dispute or (other) situation and dealt with by the Security Council (Article 12, paragraph 1) but also when the question is of such nature that action is necessary. If the General Assembly acts under Article 11, paragraph 2, it is under three restrictions of which only one applies if it acts under Article 10. If it acts under Article 10, only the restriction applies that no recommendation must be made with respect to a dispute or situation dealt with by the Security Council. By referring only to Article 12, Article 10 establishes no other restriction. If the General Assembly acts under Article 11, paragraph 2, also the restrictions apply that the question must have been brought before the Assembly in the way determined in Article 11, paragraph 2, and that the question must be referred to the Security Council before any recommendation has been made, if action is necessary.

The phrase 'if action is necessary' is not very clear. The term 'action' may mean any act of the Organisation: discussion, call, recommendation, enforcement measure; or only enforcement measure. The term is used in the Charter with different meanings. In Article 37, paragraph 2, *e.g.*, 'action' means recommendations of procedures or methods of adjustment; in Article 48, it means enforcement action. In Article 11, paragraph 2, the term 'action' can hardly mean 'discussion' and 'recommendation by the General Assembly,' or only 'recommendation by this body.' For if the term 'action' includes 'discussion' and 'recommendation by the General Assembly' the previous sentence is meaningless. Article 11, paragraph 2, cannot authorise the General Assembly to discuss questions and make recommendations with regard to them, and, at the same time, stipulate that these questions shall be referred to the Security Council if discussion or recommendation is necessary. The same is true with respect to investigation. Provided that the General Assembly has the power to investigate—and it must have this power if it is competent to discuss and to make recommendations[5]—there is no sufficient reason for providing that the Assembly shall refer a question to the Security Council if investigation is necessary. Neither can 'action' mean discussion, investigation and recommendation by the Security Council. If the General Assembly deems that a question brought before it should for some reason or another be dealt with by the Security Council it can recommend to the Security Council to do so under Article 10 or under Article 11, paragraph 2, first sentence. 'Action' can only mean 'enforcement action.' This is the specific

[5] Cf. *infra*, pp. 391, 456 f. The question as to whether the term 'action' in Article 11, paragraph 2, means also investigation was raised during the discussion on the establishment of the Interim Committee of the General Assembly in the First Commission. Cf. Doc. A/AC.18/SC.4/3, pp. 11 f.

function which is reserved to the Security Council. In this case, and in this case only, the General Assembly shall make no recommendation but refer the case to the Security Council.

The question as to whether ' action ' is necessary is to be decided by the General Assembly, for the latter shall refer a question to the Security Council only if action is necessary. But such decision is hardly possible ' before ' discussion.

It is rather strange that the General Assembly is authorised by Article 11, paragraph 2, to decide that in a question relating to the maintenance of international peace and security, brought before it by a Member, a non-Member or the Security Council, enforcement action is necessary and is bound to ' refer ' this question to the Security Council, but is not authorised to ' recommend ' to the Council to take enforcement action. For referring a question to the Security Council as a question in which enforcement action is necessary implies recommending to the Security Council to take enforcement action. It is difficult to understand why the General Assembly under Article 10 may make any recommendation whatever and, therefore, may recommend enforcement action to the Security Council with respect to any question within the scope of the Charter, but under Article 11, paragraph 2, is not allowed to recommend enforcement action to the Security Council concerning questions which also are within the scope of the Charter.

After the General Assembly has decided that ' action ' is necessary and then has referred the case to the Security Council, the latter has to deal with it. Is the Security Council bound by the General Assembly's decision that ' action ' is necessary? That is to say is the Security Council bound to execute the decision of the General Assembly? Since the Charter does not impose upon the Security Council any such obligation, the question must be answered in the negative. The Security Council is free in its decision with respect to the case referred to it under Article 11, paragraph 2. It may come to the conclusion that no action, especially no enforcement action, is necessary; which constitutes a conflict between the General Assembly and the Security Council. Such conflict is almost inevitable if the General Assembly refers to the Security Council, under Article 11, paragraph 2, a question which the Security Council itself, under the same Article and paragraph, has brought before the General Assembly. For the Security Council will probably bring a question before the General Assembly only if it does not consider that action on this question is necessary.

Paragraph 3 of Article 11 authorises the General Assembly to ' call the attention ' of the Security Council to situations which are likely to endanger international peace and security. The concept ' situation ' covers also ' dispute,' for a dispute is a ' situation,' whereas a situation is not necessarily a dispute. Paragraph 2 of Article 11 obliges the

General Assembly to ' refer ' questions on which action is necessary to the Security Council. As pointed out, the ' questions ' referred to in paragraph 2 of Article 11 include disputes and situations of the nature referred to in Article 34 brought before the General Assembly by a Member of the United Nations, disputes brought before the General Assembly by non-Members (under Article 35, paragraph 2) and disputes and other situations brought before the General Assembly by the Security Council (under Article 11, paragraph 2). What is the difference between ' referring ' such disputes or other situations to the Security Council as provided by paragraph 2 and ' calling the attention ' of the Security Council to a situation (including disputes) which is likely to endanger international peace and security, as provided by paragraph 3? To ' refer ' the case to the Security Council is obligatory only if enforcement action is necessary; to ' call the attention ' of the Security Council is possible also if no such enforcement action is necessary. The provision of paragraph 2 to refer the question to the Security Council is applicable only after the case has been discussed, although, according to the text of the provision, also before discussion. In any case the General Assembly is supposed to ' refer ' to the Security Council only situations (including disputes) which have been brought before it by a Member or the Security Council itself, and disputes brought before it by non-Members. But the General Assembly may call the attention of the Security Council to a situation which has not been brought before the General Assembly by a Member, non-Member or the Security Council. The situation, however, must have been brought before the General Assembly in some way; for the latter may call the attention of the Security Council only to situations ' which are likely to endanger international peace and security ' and this fact must be established by the General Assembly. If Article 11, paragraph 2, in connection with Article 35, paragraph 1, and Article 34, is interpreted to mean that the Assembly may discuss ' situations ' likely to endanger the maintenance of international peace and security brought before it by a Member (under Article 35, paragraph 1), then the Assembly may call the attention of the Security Council—under Article 11, paragraph 3—to all situations brought before the Assembly by a Member (referred to in Article 11, paragraph 2). If the situation has been brought before the Assembly by the Security Council (under Article 11, paragraph 2) it is superfluous to call the attention of the latter to the situation. If a situation brought before the Assembly by a Member is ' likely to endanger international peace and security ' it may well constitute a ' threat to the peace ' which, according to Article 39 may make an enforcement action necessary. In that case the Assembly must ' refer ' the situation to the Security Council under paragraph 2, not ' call its attention ' to it under paragraph 3, of Article 11. If the Assembly calls the attention of the Security Council to a situation under Article 11, paragraph 3, and if the Security Council, in following the call of the Assembly, deals with this case, the General Assembly deprives itself of the possibility to make recommendations; the same effect occurs if the Assembly refers a 'question' to the Security Council in case the former considers enforcement action necessary. There can be little doubt that the second sentence of paragraph 2 and of paragraph 3 of Article 11 overlap each other at least partly.

The provision of paragraph 4 that the powers of the General Assembly set forth in Article 11 shall not limit the general scope of Article 10 is problematical; for Article 10 confers upon the General Assembly evidently more powers than does Article 11. As the powers conferred upon the Assembly by the provisions of Article 11 are included in the competence conferred upon the Assembly in Article 10, the scope of the latter cannot be limited by the former. In so far paragraph 4 is superfluous. However, the second sentence of paragraph 2, as pointed out, contains a restriction of the competence of the General Assembly which Article 10 does not contain: to refer questions on which action is necessary to the Security Council. If the function of referring a question to the Security Council is considered to be a 'power' of the General Assembly, the statement of paragraph 4, that the powers of the General Assembly set forth in Article 11 shall not limit the general scope of Article 10, confirms the interpretation, presented above, that the General Assembly acting under Article 10 is not restricted by the provision of Article 11, paragraph 2: that, if action is necessary, the question must, before any recommendation is made, be referred to the Security Council. The same result has the interpretation that paragraph 4 of Article 11 simply means that the scope of Article 10 shall not be restricted by the provisions of Article 11. Then the restriction established by the second sentence of paragraph 2 does not apply to the General Assembly if acting under Article 10. If, however, paragraph 4, taken literally, is interpreted to refer only to the 'powers' of the General Assembly, not to the restriction established by paragraph 2, second sentence, then paragraph 4 does not prevent an interpretation according to which the restriction of the power of the Assembly established by paragraph 2 constitutes a limit of the general scope of Article 10. Then the Assembly is not authorised by Article 10 to recommend to the Security Council enforcement action. Such interpretation is, indeed, not impossible; but, in view of the fact that Article 10 does not refer to Article 11, less plausible than the one presented above.[6]

[6] In its resolution concerning the future government of Palestine, the General Assembly recommended to the Security Council to 'consider, if circumstances during the transitional period require such consideration, whether the situation in Palestine constitutes a threat to the peace. If it decides that such a threat exists, and in order to maintain international peace and security, the Security Council should supplement the authorisation of the General Assembly by taking measures, under Articles 39 and 41 of the Charter . . .' (Doc. A/519, p. 131.)

D. *Competence under Article* 14

If Article 11, paragraph 2 applies to situations of the nature referred to in Article 34, Article 14 is—at least partly—covered by Article 11, paragraph 2, and by Article 10. Article 14 runs as follows:

> Subject to the provisions of Article 12, the General Assembly may recommend measures for the peaceful adjustment of any situation, regardless of origin, which it deems likely to impair the general welfare or friendly relations among nations, including situations resulting from a violation of the provisions of the present Charter setting forth the Purposes and Principles of the United Nations.

It stands to reason that the peaceful adjustment of any situation referred to in this Article is a matter within the scope of the Charter, and that consequently any recommendation for the peaceful adjustment of such situation is within the power conferred upon the General Assembly by Article 10. Just as in Article 10, the competence of the General Assembly to make recommendations is restricted in Article 14 by reference to the provision of Article 12. As compared with Article 11, paragraph 2, Article 14 seems to differ in so far as Article 11, paragraph 2, authorises the General Assembly to make recommendations with regard to certain 'questions,' whereas Article 14 gives to this organ only the power to recommend measures for the peaceful adjustment of certain 'situations.' If the 'questions' referred to in Article 11, paragraph 2, are disputes or (other) situations—which is the most plausible interpretation of this term—the recommendations referred to in Article 11, paragraph 2, must be recommendations of measures for the peaceful settlement or adjustment of disputes or situations. For, if action is necessary, the General Assembly is not authorised to make recommendations but is bound to 'refer' the question to the Security Council. Article 14 seems to go a little further than Article 11, paragraph 2, provided this paragraph refers to disputes of all kinds but to other situations only if they are of the nature referred to in Article 34; that is to say, to situations which might lead to international friction or give rise to a dispute, or, according to another interpretation, to situations the continuance of which is likely to endanger international peace and security. Article 14 refers to situations 'likely to impair the general welfare or friendly relations among nations, including situations resulting from a violation of the present Charter setting forth the Purposes and Principles of the United Nations.' A situation may be likely to impair the general welfare, without leading to international friction or giving rise to a dispute or without being a situation the continuance of which is likely to endanger international peace and security. There is, however, hardly a clear difference between a situation likely to impair friendly relations among nations and a situation which might lead to international friction or give rise to a dispute or a situation the continuance of which is likely to endanger international peace and security. Since violations of the Charter on the part of Members more than any other facts lead to situations likely to impair friendly relations among nations, the words: 'including situations resulting from a violation of the provisions of the present Charter, etc.' are superfluous. They are, in addition, highly questionable. For the provisions of the Charter setting forth the Purposes of the United Nations cannot be violated by the Members, since Article 1 establishes functions of the Organisation, not obligations of the Members; and some violations of the 'Principles,' as for instance the use of force by one Member against another Member, result in a situation where enforcement action by the Security Council is so evidently necessary that the General Assembly will hardly come in a position to make recommendations since the Security Council will probably exercise in respect to this situation the functions assigned to it in the Charter (Article 12). If, however, Article 12 does not apply, the General Assembly may make recommendations under Article 14; but this Article restricts the General Assembly to recommend measures for the 'peaceful' adjustment of any situation. Hence, the General Assembly under Article 14 cannot recommend that the Security Council take enforcement action, even in case of a 'violation of the provisions of the present Charter setting forth the Purposes and Principles of the United Nations.' Under Article 10 the General Assembly is not restricted to the recommendation of means of 'peaceful' adjustment.[7] In contradistinction to

[7] At the *Hearings* (p. 252), a Senator asked: 'Does the General Assembly have any power to recommend measures for the forcible adjustment of any situation?' The representative of the Department of State answered: 'No. The General Assembly has no such power.' Then the Chairman intervened: 'I think perhaps you misunderstood. He means: has the Assembly any authority to recommend to the Security Council?' The representative of the State Department: 'The Assembly may recommend to the Security Council any measure that it wishes to recommend, but the Security Council is bound by its own terms of reference when it deems that the continuance of the situation is likely to endanger international peace and security.' The Senator: 'There is no limitation on the nature of the recommendation which the Assembly may make to the Council?' The representative: 'Oh, no.' The Senator: 'It may be a recommendation for a peaceful adjustment or for a violent adjustment?' The representative: 'The Assembly can make any recommendation that it wishes to. The Security Council is obligated to act within the framework of its authority and its functions.' Another Senator asked: 'Article 14 says "the General Assembly may recommend measures for the peaceful adjustment of any situation, regardless of origin, which it deems likely to impair the general welfare or friendly relations among nations." It does not say anything else. Therefore, is it not limited?' Then the representative of the State Department declared: 'Article 14 relates to those situations which do not involve a possible violation or possible impairment of international peace and security. Article 14 relates to the situations which involve impairment of general welfare or friendly relations among nations. Situations which involve the possible impairment of international peace and security are dealt with in the earlier Articles; that is, Articles 11 and 12, and particularly in numbered paragraph 2 of Article 11,

Articles 10 and 11, Article 14 does not provide for 'discussion' of the situation for which the General Assembly is authorised to make recommendations although such recommendations are hardly possible

where the General Assembly can make recommendations regarding situations which involve the maintenance of international peace and security, but only under the conditions which are described in Article 12 and subject to the provisions that questions on which action is necessary should be referred to the Security Council.'

The statement that Article 14 relates only to those situations which do not involve a possible violation or possible impairment of international peace and security, is hardly compatible with the wording, 'including situations resulting from a violation of the provisions of the present Charter setting forth the Purposes and Principles of the United Nations.' Later, a Senator asked: 'Suppose that the Assembly has taken under discussion and consideration a situation which it believes is inimical to the general welfare or threatens friendly relations, and comes to the conclusion that it has developed to the point where the Security Council should take jurisdiction. Is the Assembly free to recommend that the Council take action and, if so, can it make any recommendations as to kind or character of action to be taken?' Answer: 'Senator, as long as the Security Council is not handling the situation . . .' The Senator: 'I am assuming it is not, because I stated that the Assembly was considering it.' The representative: 'Then the Assembly is free to make any kind of recommendation it wants to. If the Assembly comes to the conclusion that the situation which it is handling is developing badly, it itself is really under an obligation to ask the Security Council to look at it, because this Article says that the General Assembly may call the attention of the Security Council to situations which are likely to endanger international peace and security.' The question of the Senator referred evidently to Article 14, whereas the answer of the representative of the State Department to Article 11, paragraph 3, which provision is not referred to in Article 14. Finally, a Senator said: 'Notwithstanding the fact that Article 14 seems to limit the Assembly to making recommendations for the peaceful adjustment of situations which might not be interpreted forcible adjustment of the situation, is it not true that Article 10 is much broader than that and is not limited by Article 14'; and, after quoting Article 10, 'that seems to give the General Assembly the right to consider any question that is brought within the functions of any of these various organisations set up in the Charter, and is not limited by Article 14 which seems to limit the functions to the peaceful adjustment of the situation. Is that a proper interpretation?' The representative: 'Yes, Senator.'

The resolution of the General Assembly on the future government of Palestine, as pointed out, may be assumed to have been adopted under Article 14 of the Charter. But in the same resolution the General Assembly recommended to the Security Council 'to consider, if circumstances . . . require such consideration, whether the situation in Palestine constitutes a threat to the peace' and if it decides that such a threat exists, to maintain international peace and security 'by taking measures, under Articles 39 and 41 of the Charter . . .' In making this recommendation the General Assembly could not act under Article 14, but it could act under Article 10. The argument advanced by the representative of Syria at the 254th meeting of the Security Council (Doc. S/P.V.254, pp. 22 f.) against the resolution of the General Assembly on the future government of Palestine (cf. *supra*, p. 195) to the effect that the Assembly is not competent to recommend to the Security Council enforcement measures, is correct only in so far as it refers to Article 14. Cf. also Doc. S/P.V.260, pp. 13 ff.

In the Spanish case the General Assembly adopted at its 59th meeting a resolution by which it 'recommends that all Members of the United Nations immediately recall from Madrid their Ambassadors and Ministers plenipotentiary accredited

without previous discussion, and only discussion is possible if Article 12 applies.[8]

Just as Article 10 and Article 11, paragraph 2, Article 14 subjects the power it confers upon the General Assembly to the provision of Article 12. But, as Article 10, Article 14 does not stipulate that the General Assembly shall refer the situation on which it intends to make recommendations, either before or after discussion, to the Security Council if on such situation 'action is necessary,' as it is stipulated in Article 11, paragraph 2; and, as pointed out, 'action' will frequently be necessary on situations resulting from a violation of the Charter. Since, however, the General Assembly under Article 14 cannot recommend such 'action' (only recommendations of peaceful adjustment being possible) it is of no importance that Article 14 does not contain the restriction to refer the case to the Security Council if action is necessary. If action is necessary, Article 14 is not applicable.

Another difference between Article 14 and Article 11, paragraph 2, consists in that the way in which the situation has been brought before the General Assembly, while determined by Article 11, paragraph 2, is indifferent under Article 14.

Finally, it must be pointed out that under Article 14, the General Assembly may make recommendations to whatever persons or authorities it deems it necessary, whereas under Article 10, only to Members and to the Security Council, and under Article 11 to Members, non-Member states and the Security Council.

E. *Revision of Treaties*

The Charter does not contain a provision analogous to Article 19 of the Covenant concerning the revision of treaties. At the San Francisco Conference suggestions to insert into the Charter such provisions were made, but without success. At the 17th meeting of

there.' (Resolutions adopted by the General Assembly, Doc. A/64/Add.1, p. 64.) This resolution was opposed for the reason that the measure recommended by the General Assembly constituted a kind of enforcement action similar to that determined in Article 41, and that the General Assembly was not competent to recommend coercive measures. This criticism is not justified. Article 41 provides for 'the severance of diplomatic relations.' This measure can be taken only by the Security Council. But the General Assembly did not recommend severance of diplomatic relations, but a measure short of it. Under Article 10 the General Assembly may recommend to the Security Council to order severance of diplomatic relations in conformity with Article 41, and to the Members to take measures short of those determined by Article 41.

[8] At the 90th meeting of the General Assembly during the discussion of the situation in Korea, the Australian delegate justified 'the right of the Assembly to discuss the matter,' by referring to Article 14 of the Charter. He stated: 'it is quite immaterial how the situation has arisen. . . . The United States delegation is calling the attention of the Assembly to a situation which has arisen in Korea and which is likely to impair the general welfare or friendly relations among nations.' (Official Records of the Second Session of the General Assembly, Plenary Meetings, Vol. I, pp. 280 f.)

Committee II/2 the delegate of the United States declared with reference to paragraph 6 of Section B, Chapter V, of the Dumbarton Oaks Proposals as amended by a proposal of the four sponsoring powers[9] (which provision became Article 14 of the Charter): 'that, although he had originally contemplated a specific allusion in the Charter to the question of revision of treaties, he had foregone this in favour of the broad version of paragraph 6 of Section B, Chapter V, put forward by the four sponsoring governments and France. It was inconsistent to launch an international Organisation based on international integrity and at the same time to intimate any lack of respect for the instruments through which international integrity functions, namely, treaties. He recognised the objections to identifying treaties as such with this paragraph and held that the concern of the Assembly was not with treaties *per se*, but with adjusting conditions which might impair peace and good relations between nations. Considerations of the general welfare may call for a recommendation that a treaty be respected rather than revised. He submitted that it was wiser not to connect the broad version of paragraph 6 with any specific definition regarding treaty revision. The phrase "the peaceful adjustment of any situations, regardless of origin," in his view, should not be interpreted to mean that the subject of treaty revision was foreclosed to the Assembly. If treaties gave rise to situations which the Assembly deemed likely to impair the general welfare or friendly relations among nations, it could make recommendations in respect of these situations.'[1] Such recommendations may be made by the General Assembly not only under Article 14 but also under Article 10, since recommendation to revise a treaty which gives rise to a situation which is likely to impair the general welfare or friendly relations among nations amounts to the adjustment of a situation which—in the last instance—might lead to a breach of the peace. This is a 'Purpose' of the United Nations. Hence the recommendation to revise the treaty refers to a matter within the scope of the Charter.

Recommendations for the adjustment of situations may be recommendations for the revision of treaties even if the 'situations' are not especially characterised as situations 'regardless of origin.' Article 1 of the Charter speaks of 'adjustment' of 'situations' meaning any possible situations, whether they arise from treaties or from any other fact.

[9] Cf. U.N.C.I.O. Doc. 203, II/2/8.

[1] U.N.C.I.O. Doc. 748, II/2/39, pp. 2 f. At the 90th meeting of the General Assembly the Australian delegate stated, with reference to the words 'regardless of origin' in Article 14: 'That phrase . . . was emphasised over and over again at San Francisco for the very purpose of enabling this General Assembly in the future, as time goes on, to take up a situation that may originate in a treaty, to express its opinion on the matter and, after discussion, to make an appropriate recommendation.' (Official Records of the Second Session of the General Assembly, Plenary Meetings, Vol. I, p. 281.)

The argument brought forth against the insertion of a revision clause into the Charter: that the revision of treaties is incompatible with the principle of respect for treaties expressly stipulated in the Preamble of the Charter, is not correct. This principle can mean only that treaties shall be observed as long as they are not abrogated in a legal procedure. A revision clause only provides for such a legal procedure.[2] It is fully compatible with the principle of respect for treaties even if it confers upon an international agency the legal power to abrogate a treaty without the consent of all the contracting parties, that is to say a genuine legislative function.

No such power was conferred upon the Assembly by Article 19 of the Covenant. It only authorised the Assembly to 'advise' from time to time 'the reconsideration by Members of the League of treaties which have become inapplicable and the consideration of international conditions whose continuance might endanger the peace of the world.'[3] In authorising the General Assembly to recommend measures for the peaceful adjustment of situations which it deems likely to impair the general welfare or friendly relations among nations, the Charter does not lag behind Article 19 of the Covenant. For a decision of the Assembly under Article 19 of the Covenant unanimity was required; a decision of the General Assembly under Article 14 of the Charter as a recommendation 'with respect to the maintenance of international peace and security,' is to be made by a two-thirds majority of the Members present and voting (Article 18, paragraph 2, of the Charter). The omnipresence of Article 39 within the scope of the Charter makes even an interpretation possible according to which the Charter goes far beyond the Covenant as far as treaty revisions are concerned. The fact that a state refuses to comply with the 'recommendation' of the General Assembly to revise a treaty may be considered by the Security Council as a threat to the peace and lead —directly or indirectly—to enforcement action. That means that

[2] At the 17th meeting of Committee II/2 (U.N.C.I.O. Doc. 748, II/2/39, p. 3). 'The delegate of Belgium declared on behalf of his Delegation that, in this important debate, the voice of his country was wholly disinterested. Belgium was not seeking alterations to any of its treaty relationships and its attitude was wholly objective and conciliatory. He explained his unqualified support for the principle of respect for treaty obligations, with the corollary that treaties must never be revised by force. But this principle did not imply the immutability of treaties. All forms of legal enactment fall out of date with the passage of time and with changing circumstances, and this applies to treaties as much as to municipal law. The problem of compatibility between treaty revision and respect for treaties might lead to a discussion in a vicious circle.'

[3] It was not very fortunate that Article 19 of the Covenant recognised the possibility of treaties becoming 'inapplicable.' If a treaty is 'inapplicable,' it ceases to be binding, and hence its 'reconsideration' is not necessary. This, however, was not the intended meaning of Article 19. The phrase 'treaties which have become inapplicable' probably meant: treaties the application of which has become difficult.

the revision of treaties—under Article 2, paragraph 6, also of treaties of non-Members—may be enforced by the Organisation in order to maintain peace.[4]

F. *Competence under Article* 13

Article 13 provides:

1. The General Assembly shall initiate studies and make recommendations for the purpose of:

(*a*) promoting international co-operation in the political field and encouraging the progressive development of international law and its codification;

(*b*) promoting international co-operation in the

[4] At the *Hearings* (pp. 251 ff.) a Senator, formerly a member of the United States delegation to the San Francisco Conference, made the following statement with respect to Article 14: 'When this Article was originally written it specifically included reference to the revision of treaties. There was objection to the specific identification of revision of treaties lest it seem to be an invitation to take apart these international contracts, the integrity of which necessarily goes to the very roots of sound international relationships. Properly the objection was made that the reference to the revision of treaties might seem to be an invitation for the revision of the peace treaties with our enemies. Therefore, since the objective was not the revision of treaties, but the revision of conditions, this substitute language was agreed upon, referring to the peaceful adjustment of any situations, regardless of origin, "which it deems likely to impair the general welfare or friendly relations among nations," and so forth.—In other words, we said what we meant. We did not mean to put the emphasis upon the revision of treaties; we meant to put the emphasis upon the revision of conditions. Those conditions may arise out of any source, regardless of origin. They may arise out of the failure to enforce a treaty. They may arise out of the onerous conditions of a treaty. There may be many other reasons besides the revision of treaties which are responsible for these conditions which impair the general welfare. The revision of treaties is not identified, because when it was identified it seemed to be the sole objective of the Article. On the contrary, the objective is to review conditions and revise conditions which are deemed likely to impair the general welfare, and those conditions can be examined regardless of origin, which obviously includes treaties.' To the question of another Senator: 'As I understand you, the Article is intended to give authority to review and correct conditions even though those conditions might arise out of or be dealt with in a treaty?' The answer was: 'That is correct. Of course, the power is solely one of recommendation.' In the following discussion, a Senator asked: 'Is it true that there is no sanction involved in the execution of Article 14, and that its validity and vitality rest upon the self-discipline of the nations involved?' Whereupon the representative of the State Department answered: 'There is no sanction there except a moral sanction.' But he added later: 'Sanction is provided only for breaches of the peace or threats to peace.' And finally, he made this statement: 'I should say . . . that so far as situations which are referred to in Article 14 are concerned, so long as they arise out of conditions which are likely to impair the general welfare and friendly relations among nations and are not deemed to be a threat to international peace and security, there is no authority in the Charter for any forcible measures. If those same situations became transformed or aggravated in such a way that it became possible for the Organisation—and in this case, the Security Council—to determine that a situation like that is of such a nature that its continuance may threaten the peace, the Organisation still has no power to take forcible action. It is only when the Security Council determines that an actual threat to the peace exists

economic, social, cultural, educational, and health fields, and assisting in the realisation of human rights and fundamental freedoms for all without distinction as to race, sex, language, or religion.

2. The further responsibilities, functions, and powers of the General Assembly with respect to matters mentioned in paragraph 1 (*b*) above are set forth in Chapters 9 and 10.

Just as Article 14, Article 13 authorises the General Assembly to make recommendations without determining to whom these recommendations shall or may be made, which—as pointed out—has the consequence that the General Assembly may make the recommendations referred to in Article 13 to any person or authority involved in the matter to which the recommendations refer.

The competence conferred upon the General Assembly by this Article, too, is covered by Article 10; for international co-operation and especially the realisation of human rights and fundamental freedoms for all are matters which—according to Article 1—are within the scope of the Charter. 'Progressive development of international law and its codification' are not expressly mentioned in Article 1 of the Charter but they are 'measures to strengthen universal peace' proclaimed as a Purpose of the United Nations in paragraph 2 of this Article.[5] Article 13, paragraph 1, it is true, authorises the General Assembly to 'initiate studies' and to 'make recommendations' whereas Article 10 authorises the General Assembly to 'discuss' and 'to make recommendations.' Since 'studies' of a matter may be necessary to make recommendations on it, the competence to 'initiate studies' may be considered as being included in the competence to make recommendations.

G. *Exclusive, Common, Concurrent Competence*

The competence of the General Assembly is an exclusive one if the effect of the function can be brought about solely by an act of the

or that a breach of the peace has occurred, that the Organisation has the right to take forcible action.'

The decisive point is that the Security Council may consider non-compliance with a recommendation of the General Assembly made under Article 14 as a 'threat to the peace' and hence take enforcement action. Consequently, there is not only a moral sanction involved in the execution of Article 14.

[5] Article 15 of the Statute of the International Law Commission, adopted by the resolution of the General Assembly at its 123rd meeting (Doc. A/519, p. 107) provides:

> In the following Articles the expression 'progressive development of international law' is used for convenience as meaning the preparation of draft conventions on subjects which have not yet been regulated by international law or in regard to which the law has not yet been sufficiently developed in the practice of States. Similarly, the expression 'codification of international law' is used for convenience as meaning the more precise formulation and systematisation of rules of international law in fields where there already has been extensive state practice, precedent and doctrine.

General Assembly, no act of another organ being necessary and no other organ being competent to exercise the function concerned, as for instance the authorisation of certain organs and specialised agencies to request advisory opinions of the International Court of Justice under Article 96, paragraph 2.

The competence is common to the General Assembly and another organ if the act of the General Assembly can bring about its specific effect only together with the act of the other organ, as for instance the expulsion of a Member under Article 6 or the election of the members of the International Court of Justice under Article 4 of the Statute, both functions being common to the General Assembly and the Security Council. In case of a common competence, the acts of the organs concerned are partial functions and the organs partial organs, the total function being performed by a total organ composed of the organs within whose common competence the total function is placed.

There is a concurrent competence if the same function can be exercised not only by the General Assembly but also by another organ of the United Nations, especially by the Security Council. Such concurrent competence exists, *e.g.*, with respect to the settlement of disputes and adjustment of other situations, which function is within the competence of the General Assembly under Articles 11 and 35 as well as within the competence of the Security Council under Articles 34 to 38. Conflicts between the concurrently competent organs are possible, and provisions necessary to avoid or solve such conflicts. The Charter tries to avoid conflicts between the General Assembly and the Security Council in the field of their concurrent competence by the provision of Article 12, paragraph 1, which reads as follows:

> While the Security Council is exercising in respect of any dispute or situation the functions assigned to it in the present Charter, the General Assembly shall not make any recommendation with regard to that dispute or situation unless the Security Council so requests.

By this provision the competence of the General Assembly is restricted only with respect to making recommendations, not with respect to discussing matters or taking resolutions concerning these matters which have not the character of recommendations[6]; and it is restricted only with respect to recommendations concerning disputes and situations (not having the character of disputes). It is restricted only with regard to concrete cases actually dealt with by the Security Council. The restriction of the competence of the General Assembly is valid only during the time the Security Council is dealing with the dispute or situation; that means that the Assembly has the power to make recommendations with respect to disputes or other situations with which the Council has not yet dealt or with which it has ceased

[6] In the Palestine question the General Assembly and the Security Council dealt at the same time with the same situation, the situation in Palestine.

to deal.[7] The words ' while the Security Council is exercising . . . the functions . . . ' may be interpreted to mean: while a dispute or situation is still on the agenda of the Council. But it may also be interpreted to mean: while the Security Council is actually exercising its functions; so that when the Council because of the exercise of the veto right is reduced to inaction, it should not be considered as ' exercising ' its functions. Article 12, paragraph 1, does not prevent the General Assembly to make a recommendation after the Security Council has made a recommendation in the same case. The competence of the Assembly to make recommendations is restricted only temporarily. The Council may lift this restriction by requesting the General Assembly to make a recommendation. Thus the purpose of this restriction, to avoid conflicts between the General Assembly and the Security Council, is not completely assured.

In pursuance of this purpose, paragraph 2 of Article 12 provides:

> The Secretary-General, with the consent of the Security Council, shall notify the General Assembly at each session of any matters relative to the maintenance of international peace and security which are being dealt with by the Security Council and shall similarly notify the General Assembly, or the Members of the United Nations if the General Assembly is not in session, immediately the Security Council ceases to deal with such matters.

The wording of paragraph 2 is not quite consistent with that of paragraph 1. The latter refers to ' any dispute or situation '; the former, to ' any matters relative to the maintenance of international peace and security.' If the ' matter ' is not a ' dispute ' or a ' situation,' the General Assembly's competence to make recommendations is not restricted.[8] It is restricted until the Security Council has adopted a decision to the effect that it has ceased to deal with the

[7] At the 9th meeting of Committee II/2, the delegate of Belgium declared: ' It should be understood that the power of the General Assembly to make recommendations applies not only to the questions which the Security Council has not yet considered but also to questions the consideration of which it has concluded.' (U.N.C.I.O. Doc. 1008, II/2/52, p. 3.)

[8] The *Report to the President*, pp. 62 f., contains the following statement referring to Article 12: ' In order to avoid a situation in which a dispute might be kept on the agenda of the Security Council without being actively considered, a provision was added to the Charter requiring the Secretary-General, with the consent of the Security Council, to notify the Assembly as soon as the Security Council has ceased to deal with such matters.—A clause was also written into Article 12, paragraph 2, of the Charter providing that the Secretary-General, with the consent of the Security Council, must notify the General Assembly at each session of any matters relative to the maintenance of international peace or security which are being dealt with by the Security Council. These provisions were supported as a means of ensuring that the General Assembly would be kept informed if the Security Council failed to settle a dispute or wished to request a recommendation from the General Assembly. They were also supported on the ground that since all Members of the

matter. This decision may or may not be considered as concerning a procedural matter within the meaning of Article 27, paragraph 2.[9]

Whereas the General Assembly is prohibited from making recommendation with regard to a dispute or a situation while the Security Council is exercising in respect to this dispute or situation the functions assigned to it in the Charter, the Security Council is not subjected to an analogous prohibition of making recommendations with regard to disputes or situations in respect to which the General Assembly is exercising the functions assigned to it in the Charter. The Security Council may take under its consideration a dispute or a situation with which the General Assembly is dealing, with the effect of bringing into operation the prohibition of Article 12, paragraph 1.

The *Report to the President* states: 'Perhaps the basic difference between the constitutional arrangement of the United Nations and that of the League of Nations is that instead of the Assembly and the Council having identical functions, as was the case under the League, the General Assembly and the Security Council will each have different functions assigned to it.'[10] This statement is not quite correct. Under the Charter the General Assembly and the Security Council have concurrent competences in some highly important matters. Article 10 of the Charter confers upon the General Assembly the competence to discuss and make recommendations on all matters which are within the competence of the Security Council. It is practically only the taking of enforcement action under Articles 39, 41, 42, from which the General Assembly is excluded.

Special competences of the General Assembly will be discussed in the chapters dealing with the functions of the United Nations.

Organisation are responsible for assisting in enforcement measures, they are entitled to full information about action that is contemplated or has been taken.'

At the *Hearings* (p. 247), a Senator asked with reference to Article 12: 'I am not indicating the likelihood of anything of this kind, but the Security Council could block off all "hot" subjects and thus keep them out of the jurisdiction of the General Assembly.' Whereupon the representative of the Department of State answered: 'The language here is:

> While the Security Council is exercising in respect of any dispute or situation the functions assigned to it in the present Charter . . .'

The Senator: 'The duty would be on the Council to exercise its function?' Answer: 'That is right.' The Senator: 'But that could be . . . a very slow race. I am not implying the likelihood of anything of that kind, but it would be within the power of the Security Council to give very slow consideration to any subject it wanted to keep from the consideration of the Assembly.' Answer: 'That is right, but it would not prevent the Assembly from discussing and debating that question, and it would not prevent the Assembly from calling the attention of the Security Council to a situation which it considers as likely to endanger international peace and security.'

9 Cf. *infra*, p. 268.

10 *Report to the President*, p. 60.

Chapter 10

THE SECURITY COUNCIL

1. Organisation

A. *Permanent and Non-Permanent Membership*

Article 23 of the Charter runs as follows:

> 1. The Security Council shall consist of eleven Members of the United Nations. The Republic of China, France, the Union of Soviet Socialist Republics, the United Kingdom of Great Britain and Northern Ireland, and the United States of America shall be permanent members of the Security Council. The General Assembly shall elect six other Members of the United Nations to be non-permanent members of the Security Council, due regard being specially paid, in the first instance, to the contribution of Members of the United Nations to the maintenance of international peace and security and to the other purposes of the Organisation, and also to equitable geographical distribution.
>
> 2. The non-permanent members of the Security Council shall be elected for a term of two years. In the first election of the non-permanent members, however, three shall be chosen for a term of one year. A retiring member shall not be eligible for immediate re-election.
>
> 3. Each member of the Security Council shall have one representative.

Just as the members of the General Assembly, the members of the Security Council are states. States can act only through their organs, that is to say, through individuals representing them. The Security Council consists of the representatives of the states which are the 'members' of this body only in so far as these states are authorised to be represented on the Security Council by certain individuals. These individuals are to be appointed by the states, that is to say, by other organs of the states competent to make the appointment according to their respective constitutions. They are not to be appointed by the United Nations as, for instance, the Secretary-General or the members of the International Court of Justice. The representatives are bound to act in conformity with the instructions given to them by the competent organs of their states. Hence the text of Article 4, paragraph 1, of the Covenant of the League of Nations, 'The Council shall consist of Representatives of, etc.,' is more adequate than that of Article 23: 'The Security Council shall consist of eleven Members of the United Nations.'

The number of the states whose representatives form the Security Council, as compared with the number of the members of the Council of the League of Nations, is relatively small; in spite of the fact that the number of members of the Council as determined directly in the Covenant was only nine: five permanent and four non-permanent members. But this number could be, and as a matter of fact was, increased by a decision of the Council with the approval of the Assembly. In contradistinction to the Covenant, the Charter does not provide the possibility of increasing the number of the Security Council's permanent or non-permanent members.[1] This implies another difference between the Charter and the Covenant: under the Covenant two kinds of permanent members of the Council were to be distinguished: those directly determined by Article 4, paragraph 1, of the Covenant, and those named in addition to the former by the Council with the approval of the Assembly in conformity with Article 4, paragraph 2. Under the Charter only the five states directly determined in Article 23 are permanent members of the Security Council.

Whereas the term of office of the non-permanent members of the Council and the conditions of their re-eligibility were left by Article 4, paragraph 2, *bis* of the Covenant to rules to be adopted by the Assembly, rules dealing with the election of the non-permanent members, the Charter does not authorise the General Assembly to adopt such rules,

[1] At the 2nd meeting of Committee III/1 of the San Francisco Conference (U.N.C.I.O. Doc. 120, III/1/3, p. 2) 'The Soviet delegate stated that one of the characteristics of the Organisation was that actions should be fast and effective. Increasing the members of the Security Council would not meet this objective. The Dumbarton Oaks Proposals have created a Council of quantitative and qualitative composition that will insure attainment of this objective. He pointed to the disastrous effects of the suddenness of enemy action during the present war and recommended approval of Chapter VI, Section A, of the Dumbarton Oaks Proposals [corresponding to Article 23 of the Charter].' The Summary Report of the 5th meeting of Committee III/1 (U.N.C.I.O. Doc. 263, III/1/11, p. 2) contains the following statement: 'Those delegates who spoke in favour of the Dumbarton Oaks text providing for eleven members emphasised the following points: (1) that the number of eleven had been fixed, not merely for purposes of speed and efficiency, but also to provide a proper balance in the Council between five permanent and six non-permanent members; (2) that other sections of the Dumbarton Oaks text, particularly those concerning the powers and functions of the Council and its relationship to the Assembly, were of greater importance to the smaller nations than the number of non-permanent seats on the Council; (3) that the smaller nations were represented in the Assembly on a basis of full equality with the great powers; (4) that the representation of non-member interests in the work of the Council would be assured effectively by Section D, paragraph 4; (5) that since the smaller nations could not provide effectively for their own security, the composition of the Council, proposed in the Dumbarton Oaks text, would meet their needs far better than a mere increase in membership which might weaken the Council as an organ of defence against aggression; and (6) that the interest of great and small powers in peace and security rested fundamentally upon the ability of the great powers to work together, and that this would not be guaranteed by any increase in Council membership.'

but determines directly that the non-permanent members of the Security Council shall be elected for a term of two years, and that the retiring member shall not be eligible for immediate re-election. Since the Covenant of the League of Nations did not exclude immediate re-eligibility there were members of the Council which were not *de jure* but *de facto* permanent by actually being re-elected. Such *de facto* permanent membership is excluded by the Charter. With respect to the election of the non-permanent members of the Security Council, the General Assembly is authorised, by the general provision of Article 21, only to adopt rules dealing with the procedure of this election.[2] In order to avoid a complete renewal of all the non-permanent members in each second year, the Charter provides that in the first election of the non-permanent members three only shall be chosen for the term of two years, and three for the term of one year only.

Whereas the Assembly of the League of Nations was free in the election of the non-permanent members, bound only by the rules the Assembly itself adopted for this election, the General Assembly is bound by the provision of the Charter to pay due regard ' in the first instance to the contribution of Members of the United Nations to the maintenance of international peace and security and to the other purposes of the Organisation, and also to equitable geographical distribution.' It is upon the General Assembly to interpret and apply this provision. The individual Member has no legal means to contest the election of non-permanent members of the Security Council on the ground that the General Assembly has not paid due regard to the circumstances determined in Article 23, paragraph 1. No Member has a right to be elected, the term ' right ' taken in a technical sense; but, if elected, it has a right to sit on the Council as its member, that is to say, to be represented on this body.

To the election of non-permanent members of the Security Council the following general provisions of the Rules of Procedure of the General Assembly apply:

RULE 128

> Except as provided in Rule 136 [referring to elections of members of the Trusteeship Council] the term of office of members of Councils shall begin on January 1 following their election by the General Assembly, and shall end on 31 December following the election of their successors.

The Charter contains no provision for the case that a non-permanent member ceases to be a member of the Security Council before its

[2] At the 8th meeting of Committee III/1 (U.N.C.I.O. Doc. 380, III/1/17) the Canadian delegate proposed ' that the General Assembly should adopt rules for the election of non-permanent members of the Security Council in accordance with the principles set forth in the amendments of the four sponsoring governments. The proposed amendment was defeated.'

term expires because it ceases to be a Member of the United Nations. It authorises the General Assembly to elect non-permanent members only for a full term and only after the full term of the previously elected members has expired. It is doubtful whether the Assembly is authorised by Article 21 to adopt among its own Rules of Procedure a rule providing for such filling of vacancies. But Rule 129 stipulates:

> Should a member cease to belong to a Council before his term of office expires, a by-election shall be held separately at the next session of the General Assembly to elect a member for the unexpired term.

The number of the permanent as well as the non-permanent members of the Security Council as determined by Article 23 of the Charter may be changed by an amendment to the Charter in conformity with Article 108 or 109; the number of the permanent members also by a permanent member ceasing to exist as a state and by withdrawal of a permanent member from the Organisation, provided that withdrawal is considered to be possible. Since expulsion of a permanent member is possible only with the consent of this member, it is not very likely that the number of the permanent members will be changed in this way.

The question arises whether suspension from the exercise of the rights and privileges of membership under Article 5 includes suspension of the right to sit as a permanent or elected non-permanent member on the Security Council. This question is practical only with respect to the right of the elected members since the veto right of the permanent members applies to the measure of suspension. If it is assumed that the right to sit as an elected member on the Security Council is a corollary of the right of membership in the Organisation, since only a Member of the United Nations can be elected a non-permanent member of the Security Council, the question must be answered in the affirmative. The Member whose rights of membership are suspended under Article 5 remains a non-permanent member of the Security Council, but the exercise of this right, too, is suspended. That means that, if the exercise of its right of membership is restored before its term as a non-permanent member of the Security Council expires, it may resume the exercise of this right.

B. *Temporary Membership*

A temporary increase of the members of the Security Council is possible under Articles 31, 32 and 44. Articles 31 and 32 run as follows:

ARTICLE 31

> Any Member of the United Nations which is not a member of the Security Council may participate, without vote, in the

> discussion of any question brought before the Security Council whenever the latter considers that the interests of that Member are specially affected.
>
> ARTICLE 32
>
> Any Member of the United Nations which is not a member of the Security Council or any state which is not a Member of the United Nations, if it is a party to a dispute under consideration by the Security Council, shall be invited to participate, without vote, in the discussion relating to the dispute. The Security Council shall lay down such conditions as it deems just for the participation of a state which is not a Member of the United Nations.

Article 31 has been modelled after Article 4, paragraph 5, of the Covenant which runs as follows:

> Any Member of the League not represented on the Council shall be invited to send a Representative to sit as a member at any meeting of the Council during the consideration of matters specially affecting the interests of that Member of the League.

The difference between the two provisions is: that under Article 31 of the Charter the Member of the United Nations which is not a member of the Security Council has no right to be invited; it 'may' be invited and its invitation depends on the fact that the Security Council 'considers that the interests of that Member are specially affected.' That means that the invitation depends on the discretion of the Security Council.[3] Under Article 4, paragraph 5, of the Covenant, a Member of the League which is not a member of the Council had a right to be invited—it 'shall' be invited, if the matter under consideration by the Council specially affected the interests of that Member. This difference, however, is not of great importance. For the question as to whether the matter under consideration by the Council did or did not specially affect the Member could—finally—be decided only by the Council in spite of the fact that this was not expressly provided by the Covenant. If there was a conflict of opinion in this respect between the Council and the Member the latter had no legal means to enforce its claim to be invited upon the Council. Article 31 of the

[3] At the 12th meeting of Committee III/1 (U.N.C.I.O. Doc. 531, III/1/26) the delegate of Canada referred to the suggestion of the Canadian delegation 'to delete the phrase "whenever the Security Council considers." This phraseology, he stated, would discourage a non-member of the Council from bringing its special interests in a matter to the Council's attention. The question of whether a state's interests were especially affected would in any case have to be determined by the Security Council.' The delegate of the Philippines 'raised a question as to whether the phrase "specially affected" referred to the interests of a particular country or to those of other countries which might be bound to it by regional arrangements. The answer to the question would determine his position on the proposed amendments.' The answer to this question depends on the Security Council's consideration.

Charter differs not only from Article 4, paragraph 5, of the Covenant, but also from Article 32 of the Charter, which provides that Members and non-Member states, if parties to a dispute under consideration by the Security Council, ' shall ' be invited to participate in the discussion relating to the dispute. Under this provision the invitation depends much less on the discretion of the Council than under Article 4, paragraph 5, of the Covenant. For the fact that a state is party to a dispute can be objectively ascertained, which is not the case with the fact that interests of a state are specially affected.

The state invited under Article 31 or 32 of the Charter is entitled to participate in the discussion only, not in the voting. The Member of the League invited under Article 4, paragraph 5, of the Covenant was entitled to participate also in the voting, except if the matter under consideration was a dispute and the Member invited was a party to it (Article 15, paragraphs 6 and 7). Article 4, paragraph 5, stipulated that the Member shall be invited to send a representative ' to sit as a member '—that is to say as a member of the Council. Although Articles 31 and 32 of the Charter do not use this formula (Article 31 does not expressly provide for an ' invitation ' of the Member) and in spite of the fact that the states invited under these Articles are entitled only to participate in the discussion of the question, not in the voting about it, the meaning of Articles 31 and 32, too, is that the states concerned may or shall send a representative to sit ' as a member ' at the meetings of the Security Council when the question or the dispute is discussed. During its participation in the discussion the state invited under Article 31 or 32 of the Charter is a member of the Security Council, but it is only a temporary member with restricted rights. It may exercise all functions of a member with respect to the matter under discussion, except voting. It may participate in the discussion not only of substantial but also of procedural questions in so far as these questions, in the opinion of the Council, affect its interests.[4] Rules 37 and 38 of the Provisional Rules of Procedures of the Security Council stipulate:

Rule 37

> Any Member of the United Nations which is not a member of the Security Council may be invited, as the result of a decision of the Security Council, to participate, without vote, in the discussion of any question brought before the Security Council when the Security Council considers that the interests of that Member are specially affected, or when a Member brings a matter to the attention of the Security Council in accordance with Article 35 (1) of the Charter.

[4] At the 27th meeting of the Security Council the representative of Iran was invited under Article 31 to participate in the discussion concerning the postponement of the discussion of the case, which evidently was a procedural matter. (Journal of the Security Council, 1st year, No. 21, pp. 424, 428 f.)

RULE 38

Any Member of the United Nations invited in accordance with the preceding Rule or in application of Article 32 of the Charter to participate in the discussions of the Security Council may submit proposals and draft resolutions. These proposals and draft resolutions may be put to a vote only at the request of a representative on the Security Council.

If the matter is not a ' dispute ' but a ' situation ' in which a state which is not a member of the Council and a state which is a member of the Council are involved, and the former is invited to participate in the discussion under Article 31 of the Charter, the invited state—but not the member—is excluded from voting. The rule of Article 27, paragraph 3, excluding members of the Council from voting, applies only to disputes, not to other situations, and only to decisions under Chapter VI and Article 52, paragraph 3; not, *e.g.*, to decisions taken under Article 39. This constitutes an important difference between Article 31 and Article 32 which expressly refers to disputes only. But if the Security Council is dealing with a dispute between a member and a non-member of the Council under Article 39, and the non-member is invited under Article 32 to participate in the discussion without vote, the other party, member of the Council, is not excluded from voting in the decision adopted under Article 39. In this case there is no difference between the application of Article 31 to a ' situation ' and that of Article 32 to a ' dispute ' with respect to the inequality of the position in which an ordinary (permanent or non-permanent) member and a temporary member of the Council are placed regarding the right of voting.[5]

[5] At the San Francisco Conference the Canadian delegation proposed the following text of paragraph 5, Section D, Chapter VI, of the Dumbarton Oaks Proposals (corresponding to Article 32 of the Charter): ' Any Member of the Organisation not having a seat on the Security Council, if it is party to a dispute under consideration by the Security Council, shall be invited to participate in the discussion relating to the dispute and shall enjoy the same position with regard to discussion and voting as the other party to the dispute. In the case of a non-Member of the Organisation, the Security Council shall lay down such conditions as it may deem just for the participation of such a non-Member in the discussion of a dispute to which it is a party.' Cf. Summary Report of the 21st meeting of Committee III/1 (U.N.C.I.O. Doc. 975, III/1/50, p. 2). The Canadian delegate justified this proposal as follows: ' It was not desirable that a member of the Security Council, when a party to a dispute, could be a judge in its own cause, while the other party to the dispute was not accorded the same voting rights. The amendment would apply only to Section B of Chapter VIII, since neither party to a dispute would have the right to vote when procedures of pacific settlement were employed. As regards the slight change relating to states not Members of the Organisation, he felt that it was unreasonable and unfair to place states which had not accepted the obligations and responsibilities of membership in the same position as those who had.'

' The delegate of the Netherlands emphasised that as a matter of elementary justice both parties to a dispute should have equality in voting status. He indicated his willingness to accept the modifications of his amendment introduced by the

Under Article 32 of the Charter not only a Member, but also a non-Member state party to a dispute under consideration by the Security Council shall be invited to participate in the discussion of the dispute. But Rule 38 of the Rules of Procedure refers only to Members of the United Nations invited in application of Article 32 of the Charter, and confers only on these Members the right to submit proposals and draft resolutions, not on non-Member states invited in application of Article 32; an inequality of treatment which is hardly justifiable, and probably only the unintentional result of defective drafting.

There can be no doubt that under Article 32 of the Charter only 'states' can be invited to participate in the discussion of the Security Council. If the character of a community as a 'state' is disputed, and the Security Council decides to invite this community to participate in its discussion under Article 32 of the Charter, the Council recognises this community as a 'state' within the meaning of Article 32. It is, however, upon the Security Council to interpret the term 'state' as used in Article 32. The Security Council may be of the opinion that a community, even if not 'sovereign' in the usual sense of the term, is a 'state' within the meaning of Article 32.[6] The invitation

delegate of Canada. The United States representative objected to the amendment on the grounds that it would alter the composition of the Security Council. It would give a party to a dispute, not a member of the Council, greater privileges than other Members of the Organisation, and would accord to it the right of veto if it were involved in a dispute with a permanent Member. The delegate of the United Kingdom also pointed out that the amendment would give a party to a dispute the right of veto if it were involved in a dispute with a permanent Member, thus placing it in a more favourable position than the elected members of the Security Council. If a non-Member were involved in a dispute with a non-permanent Member, its vote would reduce the power of the other non-permanent Members. The delegate of the U.S.S.R. argued that the amendment would destroy the principle of the permanent composition of the Security Council and would undermine the voting formula agreed upon. The delegates of Canada and Australia indicated that there was no intention of granting the right of veto to non-Member states, and that this should be made clear in the final text if the amendment were adopted.' (*Ibid.*, p. 3.)

At the 12th meeting of Committee III/1 (U.N.C.I.O. Doc. 531, III/1/26, p. 4) the delegate of Norway 'called attention to the lack of precision in this paragraph concerning failure to include, among those invited to participate in the Council's discussion, states which, though they might not be parties to the dispute, might be able, nevertheless, to contribute an essential element in settling it. Possession of information, or any number of other circumstances, might make the participation of such states desirable. He did not propose to put them on the same footing as Member states, but suggested that it would be wise to make clear that the Council was expected to call upon all third parties.'

6 In the Indonesian question the delegate of Australia suggested to invite the government of Indonesia to participate in the discussion of the question in the Security Council under Article 32 (Official Records of the Security Council, 2nd Year, No. 67, pp. 1618, 1627). The representative of the Netherlands objected that Indonesia was not a sovereign state (pp. 1619 ff., S/P.V. 181, p. 33). The representative of India expressed the view that under Article 32 a 'state without full

may be made on the initiative of the Security Council, without an application made by the state concerned.[7]

According to Article 15, paragraph 6 of the Covenant, unanimity was required for decisions of the Council referring to the settlement of disputes; but the votes of the representatives of the parties to the dispute were not counted. This rule applied also to those Members of the League which, under Article 4, paragraph 5, of the Covenant, were invited to send a representative to sit as a member at the meeting of the Council during the consideration of the dispute to which they were parties; and to non-member states, parties to a dispute, in case the Council deemed it just, under Article 17, paragraph 1, to grant them the same position as Members of the League in the procedure for the settlement of disputes. Article 4, paragraph 5, of the Covenant

sovereignty' may be invited 'for the purpose of Chapter VII of the Charter' (S/P.V. 181, pp. 42–45). The representative of Belgium called attention to the fact that an invitation of a community under Article 32 might be interpreted as an 'indirect recognition' (p. 71). As a matter of fact the Security Council at its 181st meeting decided to invite Indonesia. At this meeting the President of the Security Council declared: 'The discussion is now over, and we have to proceed to a vote on this point—that is, whether the representative of the Indonesian Republic should be invited to participate in the discussion in the Security Council of the question now before it.

As to the determination or definition of sovereignty and the degree of sovereignty which the Indonesian Republic possesses now, I think that is beyond our discussion. We have nothing to do with that. We are not defining sovereignties now. Sovereignty has several prerogatives. I think the Indonesian Republic may be enjoying some of them and may not be enjoying others. However, the invitation to participate in this discussion and to study the problem now presented to the Security Council does not necessitate that this State enjoy all the prerogatives and exercise all the qualifications of a sovereignty. The word "State" which appears in Article 32 does not indicate what type of state is being referred to.

There is the United States of America and there is the State of Michigan. The latter has a certain amount of sovereignty. It has sovereignty in legislation. For instance, the State of Michigan has laws, taxation, and other sovereign rights. But in regard to currency or foreign representation, it does not have sovereign right....

I should like to add that an invitation to the representatives of the Indonesian Republic to participate in this discussion would not bind any state to recognise the independence or sovereignty of the Indonesian Republic. The invitation would be extended simply in connection with the work of the Security Council.' (S/P.V. 181, pp. 108–111.)

But the representative of the Netherlands stated 'that the decision was taken without prejudice of any sort and that the resolution was not based on Article 32 of the Charter or Rule 39 of the Rules of Procedure.' (p. 112). It is not clear under what provision of the Charter or the Rules of Procedure the decision of the Security Council was taken. The representative of the United Kingdom who supported the view expressed by the representative of the Netherlands that Indonesia was not a sovereign state, maintained that the invitation of Indonesia was a violation of Article 32 of the Charter (S/P.V. 184, pp. 38–40).

[7] At the 181st meeting of the Security Council the President declared during the discussion of the Indonesian question that there was 'no necessity for a special application to be made by the nation which is not a Member if it is a party to the dispute under consideration.' (S/P.V. 181, p. 32.)

referred only to the Council, not to the Assembly. But the rule that the votes of the representatives of parties to a dispute shall not be counted applied, according to Article 15, paragraph 10, also to decisions of the Assembly. The Charter, however, restricts this rule to decisions of the Security Council under Chapter VI and Article 52, paragraph 3, so that not only the important decisions of the Security Council taken under Article 39, if they relate to disputes, but also all decisions of the General Assembly relating to disputes, especially recommendations with respect to the settlement of disputes (Articles 10, 11, 35), are not subjected to the rule. This is especially critical in case a dispute between a Member of the United Nations and a non-Member state is under consideration by the General Assembly. For Article 32, providing for invitation of the non-Member, refers only to the disputes under consideration by the Security Council; the non-Member has no right under the Charter to be invited to participate in the discussion of a dispute to which it is a party if the discussion takes place in the General Assembly, whereas its opponent, if it is a Member of the United Nations, participates in the discussion as well as in the voting.

Article 4, paragraph 5, of the Covenant referred to any possible matter under consideration by the Council regardless of the way in which the matter has come to the Council. Article 31 of the Charter refers to ' any question brought before the Security Council.' This formula could be interpreted to mean: questions brought before the Security Council from the outside, since the term ' bring before ' is used in Article 11, paragraph 2, in this sense. But it is possible also to interpret the formula to mean any question under consideration by the Security Council—a formula used in Article 32—whether the question has been brought before the Security Council from the outside or by the Security Council itself, that is to say, by a member of this body under its rules of procedure. The latter interpretation is preferable since there is no reason to restrict the scope of Article 31 to questions brought before the Security Council from the outside.

Article 4, paragraph 5, of the Covenant referred to any matter, including disputes and military enforcement action. If literally interpreted, the formula of Article 31 of the Charter ' any question brought before the Security Council ' has the same scope as Article 4, paragraph 5, of the Covenant. Then, Article 31 is overlapping, partly, Article 32 regulating invitation of states not members of the Security Council in case of ' disputes,'[8] and Article 44 regulating

[8] In the Syrian and Lebanese case the Council invited the two Members to participate in the discussion under Article 31, although the two states had brought the case before the Council as a ' dispute.' The President of the Security Council declared at the 19th meeting that ' it is not necessary at this stage for us to decide whether Article 32 applies. Syria and Lebanon, no matter whether a dispute in the technical sense exists or not, are manifestly states whose interests are specially affected by the discussion of the question which is now before the Council. There-

invitation of Members of the United Nations not represented on the Security Council to participate in decisions concerning the employment of contingents of the Member concerned. But another interpretation is not excluded and even more adequate. Article 31 may be interpreted to refer not to disputes, since another Article: Article 32, refers especially to this matter; and it may be interpreted not to refer to the decisions of the Security Council concerning the employment of contingents of a Member not represented on it, since Article 44 refers especially to this matter. Article 4, paragraph 5, of the Covenant, however, was the only provision of the Covenant providing for the invitation of a state not a member of the Council to send a representative to sit as a member at the meetings of the Council.

A question may be brought before the Security Council in different ways. Under Article 35, paragraph 1, a Member may bring any dispute or a situation which might lead to international friction or give rise to a dispute to the attention of the Council. The question arose whether, under Article 31, this Member is to be invited to participate in the discussion of the matter brought by it to the attention of the Council. In conformity with the wording and spirit of Article 31, the Member which brought the question, under Article 35, paragraph 1, before the Council is to be invited to participate in the discussion only if the Council considers that the interests of that Member are specially affected. The interests of the Member may or may not be specially affected, since Article 35, paragraph 1, does not prescribe that a Member may bring a dispute or a situation to the attention of the Council only if the Member's interests are specially affected by the dispute or the situation. A Member may bring to the attention of the Council a dispute to which it is not a party; if it is a party, it is doubtful whether Article 35, paragraph 1, is applicable at all. A Member may bring to the attention of the Council a situation without being involved in it in any way. The 'special' interest to which Article 31 refers is different from the general interest any Member may have in the maintenance of the peace of the world.[9]

fore I suggest that we should exercise our own powers under Article 31 of the Charter, and should invite Syria and Lebanon, as we did in the case of Iran and Greece, to participate, without vote, in our discussion of this question.' This suggestion was accepted by the Council. (Journal of the Security Council, 1st Year, No. 15, pp. 265–274.)

[9] At its 2nd meeting the Security Council adopted a resolution to the effect 'that the States which have presented complaints should be invited to participate in the work, in the sittings of the Security Council.' (Journal of the Security Council, 1st Year, No. 3, p. 25.) This resolution was not in conformity with the Charter. In the Indonesian case the Ukrainian Republic, which brought the case before the Council under Article 35, paragraph 1, has been invited to participate in the discussion without a formal decision of the Council that the interests of the Ukraine are specially affected. The President of the Security Council stated that the Council acted by general consent according to the principle 'that any state which makes a claim before the Council has a right to come to the Council and be heard.' He declared 'that it is clearly within the competence of the Council, if it so desires,

However, Rule 37 of the Provisional Rules of Procedure of the Security Council stipulates that not only any Member of the United Nations which is not a member of the Security Council, especially interested in the question under discussion, but also any Member which brings a matter to the attention of the Security Council in accordance with Article 35 (1) of the Charter ' may be invited.' This provision constitutes an attempt to amend Article 31 of the Charter, which is not within the power conferred upon the Security Council by Article 30 of the Charter.[1]

If the question under consideration by the Security Council is the employment of the contingents which a Member not represented on the Security Council is obliged to make available to it under Article 43 or Article 45, Article 44 applies, which runs as follows:

> When the Security Council has decided to use force it shall,

to invite any non-member which has made a complaint to attend and state its case without any right to participate further in the Council's discussion except, of course, with the further permission of the Council.' This statement has no basis in the Charter. It is—as the President admitted—not based on Article 31 of the Charter, but ' on the general powers of the Council.' To the question of the delegate of the Netherlands: ' On what precisely are the general powers of the Council to which you have just referred, based,' the President answered, ' that the power under which the Council is acting in regard to the matter is a general power that is given to the Council to determine its own procedure.' (*Ibid.*, No. 13, pp. 225 ff.) This power is conferred upon the Council by Article 30. But this power must be exercised by the Council within the framework of the Charter which expressly determines the conditions under which a non-member may be invited to participate in the acting of the Council. The rule formulated by the President certainly goes beyond the limits laid down by the Charter.

In the Czechoslovak case the Government of Chile which brought this case to the attention of the Security Council under Article 35, paragraph 1, as a ' situation ' (in which Chile was not involved) requested to be invited to participate in the discussion of this matter in conformity with Article 31 (Doc. S/694). In the discussion of the case in the Security Council the representative of the Ukrainian Republic protested against the invitation of Chile (granted by the Security Council) stating that the fact that Chile is the author of the letter by which the matter has been brought to the attention of the Council is not a reason for inviting this state under Article 31. He stressed that there is only a ' remote relation between Chile and the events in Czechoslovakia.' (Doc. S/P.V. 268, p. 61.) The invitation was in conformity with Rule 37 of the Provisional Rules of Procedure of the Security Council.

[1] Rule 37 (originally 34) of the Provisional Rules of Procedure was adopted at the 41st meeting of the Security Council (Journal of the Security Council, 1st Year, No. 34, p. 652). At the 59th meeting of the Security Council the representative of the United States declared in the discussion of the Greek case: ' I have always understood that under Article 35 of the Charter, the Council's attention may be drawn to a situation, either orally or in writing, without the necessity of making any charges.' (Security Council, Official Records, 1st Year, 2nd Series, No. 7, pp. 175 f.) Article 35 cannot be interpreted to mean that the Council's attention may be drawn orally to a dispute or a situation and that, consequently, the state which brings a case to the attention of the Council must be invited to participate in the discussion. For such an interpretation is incompatible with the wording and the spirit of Articles 31 and 32.

> before calling upon a Member not represented on it to provide armed forces in fulfilment of the obligations assumed under Article 43, invite that Member, if the Member so desires, to participate in the decisions of the Security Council concerning the employment of contingents of that Member's armed forces.

The invitation of the Member under this Article is a right of the Member, in so far as it depends only upon the desire of the latter, not —as the invitation under Article 31—upon the discretion of the Security Council. The Member invited under Article 44 is entitled to participate in all the decisions of the Security Council concerning the employment of the contingents of that Member's armed forces. It may be assumed that this formula implies the Member's right to participate also in the discussions preceding the decisions, although the wording refers only to the decisions. If a restrictive interpretation is accepted, the participation of the Member in the discussions relating to the employment of its contingents may be considered to be covered by Article 31, and then depends on the discretion of the Security Council. If the Member is entitled to participate in discussion and voting, it is a temporary member of the Security Council with the unrestricted rights of a non-permanent member. In this case the Security Council is composed, at least, of twelve members (if the employment of the contingents of one Member only is to be decided upon), five permanent members and, at least, seven non-permanent members. The Member invited under Article 44 has no veto right and may be outvoted, since the rule of Article 27, paragraph 3, applies also to decisions under Article 44.[2] In this case a majority of seven votes (including the concurrent votes of the five permanent members) is opposed to a minority of five, not, as normally, of four votes. A Member of the League of Nations, invited under Article 4, paragraph 5, to send a representative to sit at the meeting of the Council during the consideration of the Council's recommendation to contribute to the armed forces to be used to protect the Covenants of the League, made under Article 16, paragraph 2, could not be outvoted, for, to this

[2] The Report of Rapporteur on Chapter VIII, Section B (of the Dumbarton Oaks Proposals, corresponding to Chapter VII of the Charter) (U.N.C.I.O. Doc. 881, III/3/46, p. 3) contains the following statement referring to Article 44: 'This supplementary paragraph takes into account the concern very vigorously expressed by many powers that the military forces put at the disposition of the Security Council by the special agreements might be used without the contributing nation having had a voice in the Council meetings where it is decided to use these forces. Henceforth, every Member not represented on the Council may participate, with the right of voting, in the deliberations of the Council when it is a question of the utilisation of its armed forces. To repeat a well-chosen expression of the Delegate of the Netherlands, the principle of "*no military action without representation*" was accepted by the Committee. This decision is of such a nature as to reassure, in large measure, the middle and small powers, which might otherwise have feared that they were giving *carte blanche* to the Council in the particularly serious domain of the utilisation of their military forces outside their national frontiers.'

decision the rule of Article 5, paragraph 1, of the Covenant, requiring agreement of all the Members represented at the meeting of the Council, applied.

When the Security Council is to invite a Member or non-member under Article 31, 32 or 44, to participate in the discussion or decision it must take a decision concerning the invitation. Then the question arises whether such decision refers to a procedural matter in the sense of Article 27, paragraph 2, and hence is not subjected to the veto right of the permanent members. There can be little doubt that the decisions concerned refer to substantive matters although two of them: the ones under Articles 31 and 32, are provided by Articles placed in the Charter under the heading 'Procedure.'[3] However, in the Statement of the Delegations of the Four Sponsoring Governments on Voting Procedure in the Security Council[4] it is declared that 'a procedural vote will govern the decisions made under the entire Section D of Chapter VI [or the Dumbarton Oaks Proposals corresponding to Articles 28—32 of the Charter]. This means that the Council will, by a vote of any seven of its members . . . invite a Member of the Organisation not represented on the Council to participate in its discussions when that Member's interests are specially affected; and invite any state when it is a party to a dispute being considered by the Council to participate in the discussion relating to that dispute.' The Statement does not refer to invitations under Article 44. Besides, it is not an authentic interpretation of Article 27 of the Charter. This Article, as well as the Statement, ignores the difference which exists between decisions which the Security Council is bound to take, such as the decisions under Articles 32 and 44, and

[3] At the 12th meeting of Committee III/1 (U.N.C.I.O. Doc. 531, III/1/26, p. 4) the delegate of Norway pointed out that paragraph 5, Chapter VI, Section D, of the Dumbarton Oaks Proposals—corresponding to Article 32 of the Charter—'did not deal with procedure but with a substantive matter. It established a right of Members of the Organisation not having a seat on the Council and for non-members of the Organisation.'

[4] U.N.C.I.O. Doc. 852, III/1/37 (1), p. 1. Cf. *infra*, pp. 249 ff. At the 50th meeting of the Security Council, in the course of the discussion of a report of the Atomic Energy Commission the delegate of Australia suggested to invite, under Article 31, Canada to participate in the discussion. The motion was adopted against the vote of a permanent member (Soviet Union). The representative of the Soviet Union declared: 'that an invitation to participate in a meeting of the Security Council, even without a decisive vote, is undoubtedly not a question of procedure but one of substance. For this reason, the results of the voting show that this question was not decided today in the affirmative but in the negative.' But the President of the Security Council declared: 'I consider it is a question of procedure under the Charter, and so I invite the representative of Canada to take his place at the Council table.' (Official Records of the Security Council, 1st Year, 2nd Series, No. 1, p. 4.) To support the statement of the President the delegate of Australia referred to the Statement of the Four Sponsoring Powers on Voting Procedure in the Security Council. But he also declared that this statement did not bind Powers who did not participate in making it (p. 5).

decisions which are more or less within its discretion, such as a decision under Article 31 or decisions under Article 39. In case the Security Council fails to invite the Member or non-member in spite of the fact that the latter fulfils the conditions determined in Article 32 or 44, neither the Member nor the non-member has a legal possibility of enforcing its claim to be invited upon the Security Council. Such a situation involves a dispute between the Member or non-member and the Organisation and the Charter does not provide any procedure for the settlement of such disputes.

Articles 31, 32 and 44 of the Charter, and Rules 37 and 38 of the Rules of Procedure, constitute temporary membership of states in the Security Council. Rule 39 of the Rules of Procedure has a different character. It runs as follows:

> The Security Council may invite members of the Secretariat or other persons, whom it considers competent for the purpose, to supply it with information or to give other assistance in examining matters within its competence.

Persons invited under this Rule are not representatives of states and are not entitled to submit proposals and draft resolutions. They may only supply the Security Council with information they are asked for or give other assistance in conformity with the requests of the Council.[5]

C. *Representation*

According to Article 23, paragraph 3, each member of the Security Council shall have one representative. This rule applies not only to the ordinary (permanent and non-permanent) but also to the temporary members of the Council (Articles 31, 32, 44) and applies—according to its wording—to all meetings of the Council. Article 28, paragraph 2, provides that at the 'periodic' meetings of the Council

[5] In the discussion of the Palestine question the Security Council invited the Governments of Egypt and Lebanon under Article 31 of the Charter, and Rule 37 of the Rules of Procedure, to participate in the discussion, but the Jewish Agency for Palestine, a non-governmental organisation, under Rule 39 of the Rules of Procedure, 'to have its representative to sit during the deliberations of the Security Council on the Palestine question, for the purpose of supplying such information and rendering such assistance as the Security Council may require.' (Doc. S/P.V. 253, pp. 2 ff. Cf. also Official Records of the Security Council, 3rd Year, No. 57, p. 22.)

In the Czechoslovak case, the representative of Chile which brought the case to the attention of the Security Council and was invited to participate in the discussion (cf. *supra*, p. 230) suggested to invite the former representative of Czechoslovakia under Rule 39 of the Rules of Procedure. After the President of the Council had stated that—according to Rule 38—the representative of Chile (not a Member of the Security Council) could not make proposals, that such proposals could be put to vote only at the request of a representative on the Security Council, the representative of Argentina supported the proposal of Chile, whereupon the Security Council resolved to invite the former representative of Czechoslovakia under Rule 39. (Doc. S/P.V. 268, p. 91; S/P.V. 272, pp. 6, 11.)

' each of its members may, if it so desires, be represented by a member of the government or by some other specially designated representative.' Since the Charter does not speak of meetings of the Security Council other than its ' periodic ' meetings, this term could be interpreted to mean all meetings of the Security Council. Then the provision of Article 28, paragraph 2, would mean that the governments of the states which are members of the Security Council are not bound with respect to the designation of their representative on the Security Council. Such effect could be reached by omitting any provision relating to the designation of representatives on the part of the governments, authorised to be represented on the Security Council. No such provision relating to the representation on the General Assembly has been adopted; and the members of the General Assembly have exactly the same right with respect to their representation on this body as they have under Article 28, paragraph 2, with respect to the representation on the Security Council.

However, according to the intention of those who drafted the text of Article 28, paragraph 2, its provision does not refer to all the meetings of the Security Council, but only to special meetings at which each member may be represented not by its ordinary, but a special, delegate, member of the government or some other specially designated representative. Although the Charter does not clearly distinguish between ordinary and ' periodic ' (meaning: special) meetings, Article 28, paragraph 1, is intended to refer only to the representation at the ordinary meetings of the Security Council. It reads as follows:

> The Security Council shall be so organised as to be able to function continuously. Each member of the Security Council shall for this purpose be represented at all times at the seat of the Organisation.

If the intention of the legislator was to provide that the members of the Security Council shall be represented by a permanent delegate but that they may, at special meetings, be represented by a special delegate which may be a member of the government, the expression of this intention in Article 28 is far from being clear. Article 28, paragraph 1, speaks of being represented ' at the seat of the Organisation '; Article 28, paragraph 2, of being represented ' at the meetings.' Such a formula as ' to be represented at the seat of the Organisation ' normally refers to a diplomatic envoy sent by a state to the United Nations in exercise of the right of legation. That the United Nations, as a person of international law, has the active and passive right of legation, just as the League of Nations had this right, cannot be doubted. A member of the Security Council—just as any other state—may be permanently represented ' at the seat of the Organisation ' by a diplomatic envoy, different from the person representing the member ' at the meetings ' of the Security Council. The non-permanent members of the Security Council can permanently, that is,

' at all times,' be represented only ' at the seat of the Organisation ' by diplomatic envoys. They cannot be permanently represented ' at the meetings ' of the Security Council. Paragraph 1 of Article 28 stipulates that each member of the Security Council shall at all times be represented at the seat of the Organisation for a special purpose: to enable the Security Council ' to function continuously.' But why should a non-permanent member of the Security Council be represented at ' all times ' at the seat of the Organisation, as Article 28, paragraph 1, prescribes? In order to enable the Council to function continuously, it would be sufficient to oblige the non-permanent member to be represented at the seat of the Organisation during the term of two years for which it is elected. And why should a member of the Council be represented by a member of the government only at a special, that is, ' periodic,' meeting, since nothing in the Charter prevents a state, member of the Security Council, to appoint a member of its government as representative on the Council in accordance with Article 23, paragraph 3, whereupon this member of the government may represent the state at all meetings of the Council, not only at the ' periodic ' ones. Rule 13 of the Rules of Procedure referring to representation, does not differentiate between ordinary and special (periodic) meetings:

> Each member of the Security Council shall be represented at the meetings of the Security Council by an accredited representative. The credentials of a representative on the Security Council shall be communicated to the Secretary-General not less than twenty-four hours before he takes his seat on the Security Council. The Head of Government or Minister of Foreign Affairs of each member of the Security Council shall be entitled to sit on the Security Council without submitting credentials.

The provision that the members of the Security Council may be represented by an ordinary permanent and by an extraordinary special delegate is incompatible with the provision of Article 23, paragraph 3, that ' each member of the Security Council shall have *one* representative.' It is incompatible even if Article 23, paragraph 3, is interpreted to mean that each member shall have one representative at the meetings of the Security Council, but may have another—the permanent one—at the seat of the Organisation. That both, the ' permanent ' and the ' special ' represent the member at the same meeting is certainly not in conformity with Article 23, paragraph 3. Only one of them can be considered to be the representative of the member. The other may function as his advisor. It is not possible to consider him as a second representative both having one vote only, or as his alternate. With respect to the representation on the Security Council the Charter does not provide, as it provides with respect to the representation on the General Assembly, that the members may have more than one representative but that the representatives of one member shall have together only one vote. Nor does the Charter provide for alternates of the representatives.[6]

D. *Presidency*

As to the organisation of the Security Council, the Charter does not provide that this body shall have a President elected by its members, by a rule analogous to that of Article 21 concerning the Presidency in the General Assembly. The question as to the Presidency in the Security Council is answered only indirectly by Article 30:

> The Security Council shall adopt its own rules of procedure, including the method of selecting its President.

That means that the Charter authorises the Security Council to select a President in conformity with the rules of procedure which this body is likewise authorised by the Charter to adopt.

Rule 18 of the Provisional Rules of Procedure of the Security Council reads as follows:

> The Presidency of the Security Council shall be held in turn by the members of the Security Council in the English alphabetical order of their names. Each President shall hold office for one calendar month.

Rule 19 of the Provisional Rules stipulates:

> The President shall preside over the meetings of the Security Council and, under the authority of the Security Council, shall represent it in its capacity as an organ of the United Nations.

The provision that the President of the Security Council 'shall represent it in its capacity as an organ of the United Nations' implies that the President of the Security Council is authorised to represent the United Nations in its internal and external relations, in so far as functions of the Organisation are concerned, which are to be performed by the Security Council. This is of particular importance with respect to the conclusion of treaties.

Rule 20 provides:

> Whenever the President of the Security Council deems that, for the proper fulfilment of the responsibilities of the Presidency, he should not preside over the Council during the consideration of a particular question with which the member he represents is directly connected, he shall indicate his decision to the Council. The Presidential chair shall then devolve, for the

[6] The unsatisfactory drafting of Article 28, paragraphs 1 and 2 became manifest at the *Hearings* (pp. 267 ff). Under the impression of some critical questions concerning the meaning of Article 28, the representative of the Department of State admitted: 'It is a somewhat confusing position.'

> purpose of the consideration of that question, on the representative of the member next in English alphabetical order, it being understood that the provisions of this Rule shall apply to the representatives on the Security Council called upon successively to preside. This Rule shall not affect the representative capacity of the President as stated in Rule 19 or his duties under Rule 7.

The Charter does not authorise the Security Council to establish in its autonomous Rules of Procedure the institution of a vice-president. The Provisional Rules of Procedure adopted by the Security Council do not provide for such an organ.

2. Procedure

A. *Sessions*

Whereas the General Assembly shall meet only in regular annual sessions and in such special sessions as occasion may require (Article 20) the Security Council shall be in continuous session, or, as Article 28, paragraph 1, stipulates, 'function continuously.' The distinction between ordinary meetings and special (called 'periodic') meetings of the Security Council, that is to say, meetings at which the members are represented by their permanent representatives (Article 28, paragraph 1) and meetings at which they are represented by a special representative (member of the government or other specially designated person) (Article 28, paragraph 2), has already been mentioned.
The Provisional Rules of Procedure of the Security Council stipulate in this respect:

Rule 1

> Meetings of the Security Council shall, with the exception of the periodic meetings referred to in Rule 4, be held at the call of the President at any time he deems necessary, but the interval between meetings shall not exceed fourteen days.

Rule 2

> The President shall call a meeting of the Security Council at the request of any member of the Security Council.

Rule 3

> The President shall call a meeting of the Security Council if a dispute or situation is brought to the attention of the Security Council under Article 35 or under Article 11 (3) of the Charter, or if the General Assembly makes recommendations or refers any question to the Security Council under Article 11 (2), or if the Secretary-General brings to the attention of the Security Council any matter under Article 99.

RULE 4

> Periodic meetings of the Security Council called for in Article 28 (2) of the Charter shall be held twice a year, at such times as the Security Council may decide.

As to the place where the meetings of the Council shall be held, Article 28, paragraph 3, of the Charter stipulates:

> The Security Council may hold meetings at such places other than the seat of the Organisation as in its judgment will best facilitate its work.

The Rules of Procedure stipulate:

RULE 5

> Meetings of the Security Council shall normally be held at the seat of the United Nations.
>
> Any member of the Security Council or the Secretary-General may propose that the Security Council should meet at another place. Should the Security Council accept any such proposal, it shall decide upon the place, and the period during which the Council shall meet at such place.

The Charter does not prescribe that the meetings of the Council shall be public. But Rule 48 of the Provisional Rules provides:

> Unless it decides otherwise, the Security Council shall meet in public. Any recommendation to the General Assembly regarding the appointment of the Secretary-General shall be discussed and decided at a private meeting.

As to the languages to be used in the discussions of the Security Council, the following rules apply:

RULE 41

> Chinese, English, French, Russian and Spanish shall be the official languages of the Security Council, and English and French the working languages.

RULE 42

> Speeches made in either of the working languages shall be interpreted into the other working language.

RULE 43

> Speeches made in any of the three other official languages shall be interpreted into both working languages.

B. *Voting*

(*a*) The ' Concurring Votes of the Permanent Members ' (Veto Right)

As to the voting procedure in the Security Council, Article 27 stipulates:

> 1. Each member of the Security Council shall have one vote.
>
> 2. Decisions of the Security Council on procedural matters shall be made by an affirmative vote of seven members.
>
> 3. Decisions of the Security Council on all other matters shall be made by an affirmative vote of seven members including the concurring votes of the permanent members; provided that, in decisions under Chapter VI, and under paragraph 3 of Article 52, a party to a dispute shall abstain from voting.

Paragraph 1 of Article 27 provides with reference to the Security Council literally the same as Article 18, paragraph 1, with respect to the General Assembly: that each member of the body concerned shall have only one vote. Nevertheless the meaning of the two provisions is different. For the weight of the votes of members is equal in the General Assembly but not equal in the Security Council. This inequality of the votes is the consequence of the provision of paragraph 3 that decisions of the Security Council on non-procedural matters require a majority of seven votes including the concurring votes of the permanent members. Whereas a decision of the Council of the League of Nations required unanimity of all the members of the Council, a decision of the Security Council requires only unanimity of its permanent Members. This provision confers upon the permanent members the much discussed ' veto-right.'[7]

The first question which arises with respect to the interpretation of Article 27 is the question, what is the meaning of the phrase ' concurring votes of the permanent members?' Does it mean the concurring votes cast by the representatives of all the five permanent members, or only the concurring votes cast by the representatives of the five permanent members present and voting? This implies the question as to the effect of absence or abstention from voting on the part of representatives of the five permanent members of the Security Council in decisions on non-procedural matters. This question refers only to cases where the permanent member is entitled to vote, not to those cases where the member, in accordance with Article 27,

[7] At the 10th meeting of Committee III/1 (U.N.C.I.O. Doc. 459, III/1/22, p. 4) it was pointed out ' that the Committee was making a mistake by falling into the habit of using the word " veto " which was an ugly one and which aroused antagonism.' But at the 4th meeting of Commission III (U.N.C.I.O. Doc. 1149, III/11, p. 20) the delegate of Australia declared: ' Some objection was taken to using the name " veto," but the name is quite an accurate description of the right itself.'

paragraph 3, is obliged to abstain from voting because the resolution refers to a dispute in which the member is a party. The problem concerns the legal effect of voluntary absence or abstention from voting by a permanent member, not the obligatory abstention from voting by a permanent or a non-permanent member.

The wording of Article 27, paragraph 3, allows two different interpretations. The one is that a decision under Article 27, paragraph 3, requires the concurring votes of the representatives of all five permanent members. In case one or more of the representatives of the permanent members are not present at the voting or abstain from voting, no valid decision can be taken. A permanent member may exercise his veto right by being absent or by abstaining from voting. Abstention from voting by a permanent member in a decision on a non-procedural matter takes on the character of a veto even if the member does not intend to prevent by abstaining from voting a valid decision.[8] The wording of the provision concerned is not: including the concurring votes of the permanent members ' present and voting,' as it is in Article 18, paragraphs 2 and 3, relating to the voting procedure in the General Assembly. It is just the addition of the words ' present and voting ' which has the effect to prevent non-voting of one or the other member to invalidate a decision thus adopted. ' The ' permanent members of the Security Council are the five states designated in Article 23, paragraph 1. If the concurring votes of ' the ' permanent members are required, the votes of these five members are meant. The only exception to the rule requiring the concurring votes of all permanent members of the Security Council for non-procedural decisions is constituted by the provision that in decisions under Chapter VI and under paragraph 3 of Article 52 a party to the dispute shall abstain from voting. Since this rule applies also to the permanent members, decisions under Chapter VI and paragraph 3 of Article 52 require the concurring votes of the representatives of those permanent members only, which are not parties to the dispute. Consequently their absence from the voting procedure or abstention

[8] At the 20th meeting of Committee III/1 (U.N.C.I.O. Doc. 1105, III/1/48 (2)) ' The Canadian delegate explained that since the Yalta formula required an affirmative vote of seven out of the eleven members of the Council absence or abstention would be equivalent to a negative vote and the chances of a deadlock would thus be greatly increased. The frequence with which abstention from voting was likely to take place had been amply demonstrated both in the Council of the League of Nations and at this and other recent international conferences. During the discussions in the Committee much attention had been paid to the prospect that a permanent member of the Council would exercise a veto power through casting a negative vote, but it was more likely in practice that a permanent member who found himself in a very small minority would merely abstain from voting. It was easy to imagine situations in which both permanent and non-permanent members of the Council, while not anxious to impede effective action by the Council, would for good reasons not feel able to cast a positive vote for such action and would prefer to abstain.'

from voting does not prevent a decision under the just mentioned Articles of the Charter; except in the case that all five permanent members are parties to a dispute, for in this case no majority of seven votes is possible.

This is also the interpretation of Article 27 given by the Statement of the Four Sponsoring Powers on the voting procedure in the Security Council. As to the decisions on non-procedural matters the Statement declares that they ' will be governed by a qualified vote —that is the vote of seven members including the concurring votes of the five permanent members, subject to the proviso that in decisions under Section A and a part of Section C of Chapter VIII [of the Dumbarton Oaks Proposals] parties to a dispute shall abstain from voting.' At the *Hearings*, the Chairman stated that in all cases, except the case where a permanent member being a party to a dispute is excluded from voting, ' the votes of five permanent members are required.'[9]

However, the interpretation that non-presence or abstention from voting on the part of a permanent member of the Security Council in a non-procedural matter does not prevent a valid decision of the Council, is not excluded. It may be based on the fact that in Articles 108 and 109, where the ratification of an amendment by all five permanent members of the Council is required, the Charter expressly says: ' including all the permanent members of the Security Council.' Since Article 27, paragraph 3, does not require the concurring votes of ' all ' permanent members but only ' the concurring votes of the permanent members,' a valid decision of the Council in a non-procedural matter can be reached even in case one permanent member abstains from voting. This interpretation prevails in the practice of the Security Council. Abstention by a permanent member is not considered to have the effect of a negative vote and does not, therefore, defeat substantive decisions concurred in by seven members of the Security Council including the other permanent members voting on the decision.[1] If this interpretation of Article 27,

[9] *Hearings*, p. 265.

[1] During the discussion of the voting procedure in the Security Council which took place in the First Committee of the General Assembly, the representatives of several Members suggested various modifications in the application of the rule of unanimity of the permanent members of the Council. Among those suggested were: that abstention by or absence of a permanent member should not constitute a veto. Cf. *Yearbook of the United Nations*, 1946–47, p. 132.

At its 39th meeting the Security Council adopted a resolution by which it decided to appoint a ' subcommittee of five of its members ' and to instruct this subcommittee ' to examine the statements made before the Security Council concerning Spain, to receive further statements and documents, and to conduct such inquiries as it may deem necessary, and to report to the Security Council before the end of May.' (Journal of the Security Council, 1st Year, No. 32, p. 628.) The question as to whether this was a decision on a matter of substance or on a matter of procedure was not decided. The resolution was adopted by ten votes with the abstention of the Soviet Union. Before the voting took place, the delegate of the Soviet Union expressed his intention to abstain from voting and

paragraph 3, is accepted, the question arises: what is the effect if two or three permanent members abstain from voting? How many permanent members may abstain from voting without preventing a valid

declared: 'my abstention from voting on this matter may in no way be regarded as a precedent capable of influencing in any way the question of the abstention of permanent members of the Security Council' (p. 627). The delegate of the United States expressed his wish to reserve the position of the United States on the statement of the delegate of the Soviet Union; with that understanding, he declared to be prepared to agree that the abstention of the delegate of the Soviet Union 'should not create a precedent for the future' (p. 628).

In the Iranian case, the Security Council adopted at its 30th meeting a resolution by which it requested the Governments of Iran and the Soviet Union to report to the Council until May 6, 1946, 'whether the withdrawal of all Soviet troops from the whole of Iran has been completed . . . ' This resolution was adopted by nine votes, in the absence of the delegate of the Soviet Union. (*Ibid.*, No. 24, pp. 458, 466.)

At the 124th meeting of the Security Council, in the course of the discussion of the trusteeship agreement for the former Japanese mandated Islands submitted for the approval of the Council by the United States, the delegate of the United States declared not to be in a position to accept a certain amendment suggested by another member of the Security Council. But he stated: 'Here we are one of the parties to the agreement that we are proposing, and it does not seem ethical to us that we should exercise a veto on any question as a member of the Security Council.' At the same time he declared that if the amendment were adopted, his government would be compelled, 'in view of its responsibilities, to withdraw the tender of an agreement.' (Official Records of the Security Council, 2nd Year, No. 31, p. 665.) To withdraw the tender of an agreement would have had the same effect as the exercise of the veto right.

At its 230th meeting the Security Council adopted—in the India-Pakistan question—a resolution by which a commission was established and invested with the dual function of investigating the facts pursuant to Article 34 and exercising such mediatory influence as it could. The resolution was adopted by a majority vote, one permanent member—the Soviet Union—abstaining from voting. At the 232nd meeting, the representative of Argentina declared that his government regarded this decision as unconstitutional. He stated: 'We have here a decision of substance, and it falls under Paragraph 3 of Article 27 of the Charter. The Argentine delegation voted in favour of this resolution and these words do not modify our way of thinking in this connection. I consider it my duty, however, to place on record that this decision is invalid legally. I am sure that this is not the first time that this has occurred. It is, however, the first time that it has occurred since Argentina has been elected as a member of the Security Council. In order not to interrupt the debate on the agenda which took up all the time of the last meeting, I have delayed this statement until today. I wish to place on record, however, that I do not oppose the permanent members of the Security Council renouncing the use of their privilege if they consider it desirable, but when they do so, it should be done publicly. Abstention is a means of concealing the veto, either because it is not desired to vote affirmatively, in order to avoid establishing a harmful precedent from the point of view of contrary decisions in the future, or because it is not desired to vote in the negative, in order not to appear to oppose a good decision, or in order to diminish the size of the target which the privilege offers to those who combat it.' The representative of the United Kingdom made a reservation with regard to this declaration. He stated: 'Every written constitution is always developed by the practice of the institutional organs which have to work it. A process of development has, doubtless, begun in many

decision of the Security Council? To these questions there is no answer in the text of the Charter.[2] If Article 27, paragraph 3, is interpreted to mean that decisions on non-procedural matters require only the concurring votes of the permanent members present and voting, the majority of seven must be made up of the votes of these permanent members and the votes of a number of non-permanent members equivalent to the difference of seven and the number of permanent members present and voting. Since there are only six non-permanent members, at least one permanent member must be present and voting, in order to make a valid decision of the Council possible. It is doubtful whether such a situation has been anticipated by those who drafted Article 27.

If the concurring votes of all five permanent members are required for a substantive decision, affirmative votes of the representatives of only two non-permanent members are necessary. Hence absence or

most important and, as I think, most valuable ways in the General Assembly. Hitherto, as I understand it, the abstention by a permanent member of the Security Council in a vote on a matter of substance is, by practice and precedent in the Security Council, not considered a negative vote by that member, and I hope and trust that that understanding and practice will be adhered to.' The representative of France associated himself with the remark made by the British representative. He stated: 'The French delegation, both in the General Assembly and in the Security Council, has constantly taken the position that the abstention does not constitute a negative vote.' (Doc. S/P.V. 232, p. 1–12.)

In a Memorandum on Pacific Settlement by the Security Council, submitted by the Canadian Delegation to the First Committee (Doc. A/C. 1/91) the following suggestion was made: 'In order that a permanent member may not have to veto a proposal which it feels it cannot actively support, the right of a permanent member to refrain from supporting a proposal, without by so doing exercising the veto, should be formally recognised in the rules of procedure of the Security Council. The rules might provide that a permanent member which, before a vote is taken, makes a statement to the following effect should be held to have cast an affirmative vote within the meaning of Article 27 of the Charter: "While I am not prepared to support this proposal, I am not prepared to prevent its acceptance if that is the desire of the majority. I am willing, in the circumstances, to have my position considered as constituting the degree of concurrence necessary in order that a decision may be reached"' (pp. 3 f.). This suggestion aims at an amendment of the Charter. Insertion in the Rules of Procedure would not suffice.

2 One paragraph of the first resolution in the Indonesian question was adopted at the 173rd meeting of the Security Council on August 1, 1947, by a vote of 7 members, including the concurring votes of only 2 permanent members, 3 permanent members abstaining; another paragraph was adopted by a vote of 8 members, including the concurring votes of 3 permanent members, 2 permanent members abstaining. The representative of the United Kingdom declared: 'the United Kingdom does not wish its abstention to be treated as a veto, invalidating the resolution which has otherwise secured the necessary majority'; whereupon the President of the Council stated: 'It is now jurisprudence in the Security Council—and the interpretation accepted for a long time—that an abstention is not considered a veto, and the concurrent votes of the permanent members mean the votes of the permanent members who participate in the voting. Those who abstain intentionally are not considered to have cast a veto.' (Official Records of the Security Council, 2nd Year, No. 68, pp. 1700, 1703, 1711–12.)

abstention from voting on the part of representatives of one to four non-permanent members cannot prevent a valid decision under Article 27, paragraph 3, provided that the representatives of all five permanent members cast concurring votes.[3]

The most satisfactory solution of the question as to the effect of abstention from voting by a permanent member would be to leave it to the descretion of the member whether his abstention should or should not have the effect of a veto and, hence, to allow the member to make a statement to this effect before voting. But this solution has no basis in the Charter.[4]

(*b*) Quorum

The Charter does not provide a *quorum* for the voting procedure of the Security Council. Nor do the autonomous Rules of Procedure adopted by the Security Council under Article 30 of the Charter contain such a provision. If it is assumed that the decision on a non-procedural matter requires the concurring votes of all five permanent members, a provision concerning a *quorum* in case of such a decision could refer only to the number of representatives of non-permanent members whose presence is necessary to make the Council able to transact business. The rule concerning a *quorum* constitutes a restriction to the rule determining the number of the members of a collegiate organ. If there is no rule concerning a *quorum*, all members must be present in order to enable the organ to transact business. Since there is no special rule concerning the *quorum* for decisions of the Security Council, the presence of all members of the Council is required for the adoption of a resolution. However, in the practice of the Security Council absence of a member, even of a permanent member, does not prevent this body from adopting a

[3] At the 20th meeting of Committee III/1 (U.N.C.I.O. Doc. 967, III/1/48, p. 2; 1105, III/1/48 (2), pp. 1 f.) the delegate of the United States 'stated that when a permanent member of the Council was a party to a dispute, its enforced abstention would mean that the other four permanent members and three of the non-permanent members might reach a decision which involved a judgment concerning "the rightness or wrongness of a dispute."' The decision need not necessarily involve a judgment concerning 'the rightness or wrongness' of the dispute.

At the same meeting the Canadian delegate declared: 'Under the Yalta formula one could never be sure how many members of the Council would in fact be able to vote on any dispute which might come before the Council for pacific settlement, since this would depend on whether one or more members of the Council were involved in the dispute. To take action under Section 8, A, might require not seven out of eleven affirmative votes but seven out of some smaller number. Indeed situations might occur in which the Council might not be able to take any action at all. This would happen if five members of the Council were parties to a dispute such as might arise out of some multilateral treaty such as the Act of Algeciras.'

[4] This solution—a so-called 'optional veto'—has been suggested by the delegate of Canada. (Doc. A/C. 1/63, p. 3; A/C. 1/91, pp. 3 f.)

resolution. Absence of a permanent member is considered to be equivalent to abstention from voting.[5]

(*c*) The Vote of the Temporary Member under Article 44

Under Article 44 a Member of the United Nations which is not a member of the Security Council may participate in certain decisions of this body. Is the vote of this temporary member of the Security Council to be counted if it is one of seven votes cast for a proposition in the matter referred to in Article 44? If the answer is in the affirmative, the term 'member' in the phrase 'affirmative vote of seven members' as used in Article 27, paragraph 3, must be interpreted to mean: ordinary (permanent and non-permanent) as well as temporary members of the Security Council. If so, the affirmative vote of the temporary member paralyses the effect of the absence or abstention from voting of one ordinary non-temporary member. If the term 'member' as used in the above-mentioned phrase is interpreted to mean only ordinary permanent and non-permanent members of the Security Council, that is to say, that the affirmative vote of the temporary member is not to be counted among the seven votes constituting the majority as determined by Article 27, paragraph 3, the provision of Article 44 is deprived of any legal effect. The provision that a Member of the United Nations which is not a member of the Security Council shall be invited 'to participate in the decisions of the Security Council' concerning certain matters can hardly be interpreted in another way than that the vote of this Member shall be counted just as any vote of an ordinary non-permanent member of the Security Council. Then the Member invited under Article 44 is called by the Charter itself a 'member' of the Security Council.

(*d*) Procedural and Non-Procedural Matters

Whereas Article 18 of the Charter distinguishes between decisions of the General Assembly on 'important' and decisions on other questions, Article 27 distinguishes between decisions of the Security Council on 'procedural' and decisions on non-procedural or substantive matters. There can be little doubt that by 'decision' any resolution of the Security Council is to be understood, regardless of whether the resolution has the character of a decision binding upon the Members within the meaning of Article 25, or of a mere 'recommendation.'[6] The distinction between procedural and non-procedural

[5] When the Security Council at its 30th meeting adopted the above-mentioned resolution in the Iranian case only 10 members—4 permanent and 6 non-permanent—were present. Cf. *supra*, p. 242.

[6] Cf. *infra*, pp. 293 f. The opinion expressed by the representative of Argentina that the rule of unanimity of the permanent members applies only to decisions in the specific sense of Article 25 which have as their object the maintenance of international peace and security, consequently not to 'recommendations' made under

matters is of importance in so far as a majority of seven members, including the permanent members, is required only for decisions on non-procedural matters and in so far as the rule that a member of the Council which is party to a dispute under consideration by the Council shall abstain from voting, likewise applies only to decisions on non-procedural matters. The latter restriction follows from the fact that the rule constituting this restriction is, grammatically, part of the sentence by which the qualified majority is prescribed for decisions on non-procedural matters. But this conclusion is only possible, not necessary. The sentence: 'provided that, in decisions under Chapter VI, and under paragraph 3 of Article 52, a party to a dispute shall abstain from voting,' may also be interpreted to mean that in all decisions under Chapter VI—not only in non-procedural decisions under Chapter VI—a party to a dispute shall abstain from voting. This interpretation may be justified by the fact that the words 'decisions under Chapter VI' cover also procedural decisions, and that the decisions under Article 52, paragraph 3, too, may have procedural character.[7]

In the application of Article 27, paragraph 2, the most important question is: what is the meaning of the word 'procedural' as used in this paragraph. The distinction between 'procedural' and non-procedural matters is one of those distinctions which—such as 'formal' and 'material' or 'adjective' and 'substantive' (law)—have no fixed meaning, but change their significance according to the standpoint

Article 4 of the Charter (Doc. A/AC.24/SR. 6, p. 11) has no basis in Article 27. Cf. *supra*, pp. 61 ff.

[7] At the 3rd meeting of the Security Council the President made the following statement (in the Iranian case): 'If the Council should accept the view that there is a dispute, then under the terms of paragraph 3 of Article 27, as the Soviet Union is named as the other party to this dispute, it will not be possible for the delegate from the Soviet Union to exercise a vote, during the consideration of this particular debate, in any of the decisions referred to in that paragraph. This does not apply, of course, to decisions on procedure or matter under paragraph 2 of Article 27.' (Journal of the Security Council, 1st Year, No. 5, p. 58.)

During the discussion in the Security Council of the Corfu Channel case, the delegate of Australia suggested a resolution calling for the appointment of a subcommittee to examine the available evidence and to make a report on the facts of the case to the Council. Before the voting on this suggestion took place, the delegate of the United Kingdom declared: 'As a party to this dispute, I am deprived of my vote under Article 27, paragraph 3, of the Charter, when it is a matter of a decision under Chapter VI. I presume, though, that the vote which we are going to take is a purely procedural one and that I can exercise my vote.' (Official Records of the Security Council, 2nd Year, No. 21, p. 425.) As a matter of fact, the delegate participated in the voting, in spite of the fact that the delegate of the Soviet Union contended that the suggested resolution referred to a substantive, not a procedural matter. The President was of the opinion 'that the establishment of a subcommittee such as proposed by the Australian delegation was not one of the decisions mentioned in Chapter VI of the Charter' (p. 428). Thus, the question whether the rule that a party to a dispute shall abstain from voting refers only to non-procedural decisions under Chapter VI was not decided.

from which they are viewed. The same matter may be ' procedural ' from one point of view and ' substantive ' from another. More problematical than in any other field is the distinction between ' procedural ' and ' substantive ' matters in the field of law. For, in a certain sense, the entire law may be considered as a procedure, so that it is not possible to distinguish clearly procedural rules of law from substantive rules. If the concept of ' procedural matters ' in contra-distinction to non-procedural or substantive matters is employed in a legal instrument at all, it is indispensible to define as clearly as possible what is meant by these terms, or to enumerate the matters which are to be considered as ' procedural.'

The Charter, however, does neither the one nor the other. Subdivisions of Chapters IV, V, X, XIII of the Charter and Chapter III of the Statute of the International Court of Justice have the heading ' Procedure.' But it may be doubted whether some matters referred to in Articles placed under this heading are ' procedural ' matters in the sense of Article 27, paragraph 2. Thus for instance, the establishment of subsidiary organs by the General Assembly according to Article 22, and by the Security Council according to Article 29; or setting up commissions by the Economic and Social Council according to Article 68; or the invitation of a Member or non-member to participate in the discussion of the Security Council according to Articles 31 and 32; or the invitation of Members to participate in the deliberations of the Economic and Social Council according to Article 69. Significant in this respect is that the invitation of Members to participate in certain decisions of the Security Council is provided for in Article 44 which is not placed under a heading ' Procedure.' It may be doubted whether the decision of the Security Council under Article 28, paragraph 3, to hold meetings at places other than the seat of the Organisation, or the arrangements which the Economic and Social Council is authorised by Article 71 to make for consultation with non-governmental organisations, have a procedural character, in spite of the fact that the Articles concerned are within subdivisions titled ' Procedure.'[8]

On the other hand, some decisions of the Security Council concerning matters which are not referred to in subdivisions titled ' Procedure ' are, according to an express provision of the Charter to be taken by a majority vote of ' any seven members of the Security

[8] At the *Hearings* (p. 266), the representative of the Department of State stated that ' in the first place, the matters in the whole section on procedure, which includes Articles 28, 29, 30, 31 and 32, are regarded as procedural matters.' But in the Co-ordination Committee of the San Francisco Conference the representative of Canada rightly declared that ' the use of " Procedure " as a heading does not in any way qualify or lessen the substantive rights granted in the various Articles.' (U.N.C.I.O. Doc. WD 407, CO/169, p. 2.)

As to the practice of the Security Council concerning the establishment of subsidiary organs, cf. *infra*, pp. 391 ff.

Council,' as, for instance, the decision by which the Security Council (together with the General Assembly) under Article 109, paragraph 1, fixes the place and date of a General Conference, and its decision relating to the holding of a General Conference under paragraph 3 of the same Article. According to a special provision of Article 10 of the Statute of the International Court of Justice the election of the judges of the Court requires an absolute, *i.e.*, a simple, majority of votes in the General Assembly and in the Security Council, and any vote of the Security Council, whether for the election of judges or for the appointment of members of the joint conference envisaged in Article 12 of the Statute, shall take place 'without any distinction between permanent and non-permanent members of the Security Council.' Election of judges and appointment of members of the joint conference are certainly not procedural matters. Article 18 of the Charter mentions election of the non-permanent members of the Security Council, of the members of the Economic and Social Council and of the members of the Trusteeship Council among the 'important questions' to be decided by the General Assembly which decisions require a two-thirds majority. As pointed out in a previous chapter, election of the judges of the Court is certainly a matter as important as the election of the members of the three Councils of the United Nations. But Article 10, paragraph 1, of the Statute constitutes a restriction of the rules established by Article 18, paragraph 2, and likewise of the rule established by Article 27 of the Charter. In the last mentioned regard Article 10 of the Statute constitutes a restriction of Article 27 of the Charter, not only in so far as for a decision of the Security Council in a non-procedural matter the veto right of the permanent members is expressly abolished but also in so far as not a majority of seven but only of six members of the Security Council is required.

Since the Charter does not define the concept 'procedural matters' the organ which is to apply the provision of Article 27, paragraphs 2 and 3, that is to say, the Security Council, is competent to interpret the provision and thus to determine the meaning of the word 'procedural.' The question as to whether a matter is procedural or not may be disputed within the Security Council and the dispute settled by a decision of this body. A decision to the effect that the matter is procedural requires a majority of seven votes including the concurring votes of the permanent members because this decision itself refers to a non-procedural matter. In case the procedural character of a matter is disputed within the Security Council, the matter is to be considered as non-procedural as long as its procedural character is not decided upon by a decision taken under Article 27, paragraph 3. This interpretation follows from the fact that the provision of Article 27, paragraph 3, providing that decisions of the Security Council require a majority of seven affirmative votes including the concurring votes of the permanent members, is the rule and the provision of Article 27, paragraph 2, providing that decisions on procedural matters require a majority of seven members, the exception.[9]

(*e*) The Statement of the Four Sponsoring Powers on the Voting Procedure in the Security Council

Subcommittee III/1/B of the San Francisco Conference submitted on May 22, 1945, a questionnaire concerning the voting procedure in the Security Council to the four sponsoring powers. In response to this questionnaire, the following statement by the Delegations of the Four Sponsoring Powers on Voting Procedure in the Security Council was presented to the Subcommittee.[1]

Specific questions covering the voting procedure in the

[9] That the decision of the question whether a matter is procedural or substantive requires a qualified majority, is also the interpretation presented by the Statement of the Sponsoring Governments, paragraph 2 of Part II (cf. *infra*, p. 253). At the 49th meeting of the Security Council the President declared that 'if it is to be decided whether a question is one of procedure or substance, it is necessary to accept one or another alternative by seven votes, but the five permanent members must concur.' (Journal of the Security Council, 1st Year, No. 42, p. 841.) Cf. also the statement of the delegate of the Soviet Union at the 19th meeting of the Council. (*Ibid.*, No. 15, p. 273.) At the 202nd meeting of the Security Council the delegate of the United States suggested a resolution to the effect that the Security Council should, pursuant to Article 12 of the Charter, 'request' the General Assembly to consider the dispute between Greece and her three northern neighbours and make 'any recommendations with regard to that dispute which it deems appropriate under the circumstances.' The resolution was approved by a vote of 9 to 2, with the Soviet Union and Poland voting in the negative. The ruling of the President that the resolution was substantive and failed to pass because of the negative vote of the Soviet Union was challenged by the representative of the United States. The vote of whether the resolution was procedural—itself a substantive vote—was 9 in favour to 2, the U.S.S.R. and Poland opposed. The United States original resolution was, therefore, substantive and had failed of passage through the veto of the Soviet Union (Doc. S/P.V./202).

During the discussion of the Czechoslovak case the representative of the United States declared with respect to the statement of the Four Sponsoring Powers, Part II, paragraph 2: 'Part II, paragraph 2 of the Four-Power Statement was to be used only as stated therein, in cases where the Charter itself did not provide an indication as to whether a given decision was procedural. . . . It is quite obvious that it would be a misuse of the Four-Power Statement to resort to the preliminary determination under Part II, paragraph 2, for the express purpose of evading the provisions of Part I of the same statement. To hold otherwise is to make ridiculous Part I. Also, the effect of such a contention is to minimise the area governed by procedural votes under Article 27, paragraph 2, of the Charter. This section of the Charter has no meaning if it is possible for a permanent member of the Security Council to prevent utilisation of the voting procedure contemplated in this connection on any question without regard to the usual meaning of the word "procedural," and without regard to the clear indications in the Charter of those matters which were intended to be procedural. Under such an interpretation, Article 27, paragraph 2, might just as well have been omitted.' (Official Records of the Security Council, 3rd Year, No. 63, pp. 24–25.)

[1] U.N.C.I.O. Doc. 852, III/1/37 (1). The Statement is dated June 7, 1945.

Security Council have been submitted by a Subcommittee of the Conference Committee on Structure and Procedures of the Security Council to the Delegations of the four Governments sponsoring the Conference—the United States of America, the United Kingdom of Great Britain and Northern Ireland, the Union of Soviet Socialist Republics, and the Republic of China. In dealing with these questions, the four Delegations desire to make the following statement of their general attitude towards the whole question of unanimity of permanent members in the decisions of the Security Council.

I

1. The Yalta voting formula recognises that the Security Council, in discharging its responsibilities for the maintenance of international peace and security, will have two broad groups of functions. Under Chapter VIII, the Council will have to make decisions which involve its taking direct measures in connection with settlement of disputes, adjustment of situations likely to lead to disputes, determination of threats to the peace, removal of threats to the peace, and suppression of breaches of the peace. It will also have to make decisions which do not involve the taking of such measures. The Yalta formula provides that the second of these two groups of decisions will be governed by a procedural vote—that is, the vote of any seven members. The first group of decisions will be governed by a qualified vote—that is, the vote of seven members, including the concurring votes of the five permanent members, subject to the proviso that in decisions under Section A and a part of Section C of Chapter VIII parties to a dispute shall abstain from voting.

2. For example, under the Yalta formula a procedural vote will govern the decisions made under the entire Section D of Chapter VI. This means that the Council will, by a vote of any seven of its members, adopt or alter its rules of procedure; determine the method of selecting its President; organise itself in such a way as to be able to function continuously; select the times and places of its regular and special meetings; establish such bodies or agencies as it may deem necessary for the performance of its function; invite a Member of the Organisation not represented on the Council to participate in its discussions when that Member's interests are specially affected; and invite any state when it is a party to a dispute being considered by the Council to participate in the discussion relating to that dispute.

3. Further, no individual member of the Council can alone prevent consideration and discussion by the Council of a dispute or situation brought to its attention under paragraph 2,

Section A, Chapter VIII. Nor can parties to such dispute be prevented by those means from being heard by the Council. Likewise, the requirement for unanimity of the permanent members cannot prevent any member of the Council from reminding the Members of the Organisation of their general obligations assumed under the Charter as regards peaceful settlement of international disputes.

4. Beyond this point, decisions and actions by the Security Council may well have major political consequences and may even initiate a chain of events which might, in the end, require the Council under its responsibilities to invoke measures of enforcement under Section B, Chapter VIII. This chain of events begins when the Council decides to make an investigation, or determines that the time has come to call upon states to settle their differences, or makes recommendations to the parties. It is to such decisions and actions that unanimity of the permanent members applies, with the important proviso, referred to above, for abstention from voting by parties to a dispute.

5. To illustrate: in ordering an investigation, the Council has to consider whether the investigation—which may involve calling for reports, hearing witnesses, dispatching a commission of inquiry, or other means—might not further aggravate the situation. After investigation, the Council must determine whether the continuance of the situation or dispute would be likely to endanger international peace and security. If it so determines, the Council would be under obligation to take further steps. Similarly, the decision to make recommendations, even when all parties request it to do so, or to call upon parties to a dispute to fulfil their obligations under the Charter, might be the first step on a course of action from which the Security Council could withdraw only at the risk of failing to discharge its responsibilities.

6. In appraising the significance of the vote required to take such decisions or actions, it is useful to make comparison with the requirements of the League Covenant with reference to decisions of the League Council. Substantive decisions of the League of Nations Council could be taken only by the unanimous vote of all its members, whether permanent or not, with the exception of parties to a dispute under Article 15 of the League Covenant. Under Article 11, under which most of the disputes brought before the League were dealt with and decisions to make investigations taken, the unanimity rule was invariably interpreted to include even the votes of the parties to a dispute.

7. The Yalta voting formula substitutes for the rule of complete unanimity of the League Council a system of qualified

majority voting in the Security Council. Under this system non-permanent members of the Security Council individually would have no ' veto.' As regards the permanent members, there is no question under the Yalta formula of investing them with a new right, namely, the right to veto, a right which the permanent members of the League Council always had. The formula proposed for the taking of action in the Security Council by a majority of seven would make the operation of the Council less subject to obstruction than was the case under the League of Nations rule of complete unanimity.

8. It should also be remembered that under the Yalta formula the five major powers could not act by themselves, since even under the unanimity requirement any decisions of the Council would have to include the concurring votes of at least two of the non-permanent members. In other words, it would be possible for five non-permanent members as a group to exercise a ' veto.' It is not to be assumed, however, that the permanent members, any more than the non-permanent members, would use their ' veto ' power wilfully to obstruct the operation of the Council.

9. In view of the primary responsibilities of the permanent members, they could not be expected, in the present condition of the world, to assume the obligation to act in so serious a matter as the maintenance of international peace and security in consequence of a decision in which they had not concurred. Therefore, if majority voting in the Security Council is to be made possible, the only practicable method is to provide, in respect of non-procedural decisions, for unanimity of the permanent members plus the concurring votes of at least two of the non-permanent members.

10. For all these reasons, the four sponsoring Governments agreed on the Yalta formula and have presented it to this Conference as essential if an international organisation is to be created through which all peace-loving nations can effectively discharge their common responsibilities for the maintenance of international peace and security.

II

In the light of the considerations set forth in Part I of this statement, it is clear what the answers to the questions submitted by the Subcommittee should be, with the exception of Question 19.[2] The answer to that question is as follows:

1. In the opinion of the Delegations of the Sponsoring

[2] Question 19: ' In case a decision has to be taken as to whether a certain point is a procedural matter, is that preliminary question to be considered in itself as a procedural matter, or is the veto applicable to such preliminary question ?'

Governments, the Draft Charter itself contains an indication of the application of the voting procedures to the various functions of the Council.

2. In this case, it will be unlikely that there will arise in the future any matters of great importance on which a decision will have to be made as to whether a procedural vote would apply. Should, however, such a matter arise, the decision regarding the preliminary question as to whether or not such a matter is procedural must be taken by a vote of seven members of the Security Council, including the concurring votes of the permanent members.

This Statement has not the character of an authentic interpretation of the Charter. It expresses the opinion of four Members of the United Nations.[3] It is even doubtful whether these four states are

[3] At the 4th meeting of Commission III (U.N.C.I.O. Doc. 1149, III/11, p. 21) the delegate of Australia declared with reference to the Statement: 'What happened was this: the Subcommittee submitted a questionnaire to the sponsoring governments, and, after considerable time a general reply was given and that document is embodied in that report. I want to stress that that reply has not in any sense been endorsed either by the Subcommittee or by the Committee. It has merely been incorporated in the records and made an annex to the Rapporteur's report.' At the 70th meeting of the Security Council the delegate of Australia declared with reference to the Statement of the Sponsoring Powers: 'Of course that document has no binding force on this Council or on any other part of the United Nations.' (Official Records of the Security Council, 1st Year, 2nd Series, No. 16, p. 411. Cf. also the statement of the delegate of the Netherlands at the 49th meeting of the Council, Journal of the Security Council, 1st Year, No. 42, p. 842.) Similar statements were made by the representative of Argentina at the 288th meeting (Official Records of the Security Council, 3rd Year, No. 63, p. 27); the representative of Canada at the 300th meeting (*ibid.*, No. 71, p. 40); the representatives of Syria, Belgium, the United States at the 303rd meeting of the Security Council (Doc. S/P.V. 303). At the 288th meeting the representative of Argentina suggested to apply to the decision of the question whether a matter is procedural the same principle which, according to Article 18, applies to the decision of the General Assembly concerning the question as to whether a question is important. He stated: 'Article 18 of the Charter states that when the General Assembly is in doubt as to whether a question is important or not (a majority of two-thirds being required in the former case and a simple majority in the latter) the decision shall be made by a simple majority. This is good sense, for otherwise, if a two-thirds majority were necessary even to decide whether a question is important or not, the Assembly would never reach a decision in these cases. Now Article 18 is a part of the Charter, even though it is not mentioned in the statement of the four great Powers. It is a part of the legal document that binds all States Members of the United Nations. Consequently, I maintain that if there is any doubt as to whether paragraph 2 or paragraph 3 of Article 27 is applicable, the majority required to settle that doubt is only any seven votes, so that there may be some conformity between the provisions governing the Security Council and these governing the General Assembly.' (Official Records of the Security Council, 3rd Year, No. 63, p. 27.) An analogous application of Article 18, paragraph 2, to decisions of the Security Council has no basis in the Charter. As to the interpretation of Article 18, paragraph 2, cf. *supra*, pp. 180 ff.

obliged *inter se* to maintain the opinion they have expressed in the Statement, since the Statement seems not to be the content of a treaty.[4]

The Statement cannot even be considered as an interpretation of the distinction between decisions on procedural and decisions on non-procedural matters; for it attempts to substitute for this distinction a totally different one, namely the distinction between decisions 'which involve direct measures in connection with settlement of disputes, adjustment of situations likely to lead to disputes, determination of threats to the peace, removal of threats to the peace, and suppression of breaches of the peace,' on the one hand and decisions 'which do not involve the taking of such measures.' There can be no doubt that among the decisions which do not involve the measures determined in the Statement there may be decisions on matters which have no procedural character at all. This is shown by most of the decisions which the Statement in paragraph 2 of Part I indicates as examples for 'procedural votes.' It is consequently misleading that the 'affirmative vote of seven members' referred to in Article 27, paragraph 2, is characterised in the Statement as 'procedural vote.' And it is difficult to understand why the sponsoring governments did not suggest to insert into the text of Article 27 the formula of the Statement instead of the formula of the Yalta Agreement.[5] The procedural character of all the decisions referred to in paragraph 2 of Part I of the Statement is at least doubtful. But they may be decisions which do not involve the taking of 'direct measures' in connection with settlement of disputes, etc. It is not clear whether paragraph 3 of Part I of the Statement is intended to indicate only examples of 'considerations and discussion.' Its wording and the first words of paragraph 4: 'Beyond this point' are rather in favour of a negative answer to this question. If this interpretation of paragraph 3 is correct, only the decision that a dispute or situation brought to the attention of the Security Council under Article 35, paragraphs 1 and 2, shall be discussed or considered requires a simple majority of any

[4] At the 300th meeting of the Security Council, the representative of the Soviet Union stated: 'The San Francisco Declaration deals precisely with the interpretation of the Charter. It is not an agreement under which the Five Powers have assumed obligations in addition to those assumed under the Charter.' (Official Records of the Security Council, 3rd Year, No. 71, p. 42.) But the question is whether this interpretation is binding upon the sponsoring Powers. Later the Soviet delegate said: 'that the delegation of the Soviet Union will not digress one single iota from the obligations assumed under the San Francisco Declaration' (p. 43).

[5] At the 4th meeting of Commission III (U.N.C.I.O. Doc. 1149, II/11, p. 24) the delegate of Australia declared: 'In our view, the interpretation given to the phrase "procedural matters" in the joint reply leaves the position uncertain and confused, and sooner or later we think that the International Court of Justice should be asked to give its opinion upon the question of interpretation involved. If not, and if the veto power is used improperly or unfairly, it will be necessary subsequently to ask for an amendment of the Charter and that is a slow and difficult process.'

seven members; the decision of the questions as to whether a dispute or situation brought before the Security Council on its own initiative under Article 33, paragraph 2, Articles 34, 36, or under Articles 37 and 38, or by the General Assembly under Article 11, paragraph 3, shall be discussed or considered requires the qualified majority of seven members including the concurring votes of the permanent members, so that the discussion and consideration of such disputes or situations can be blocked by the veto of one permanent member.[6]

The difference between 'discussion' and 'consideration' is not very clear. At the 4th meeting of Commission III[7] the delegate of Australia said that the words 'consideration and discussion' 'are used in a limited sense . . . there can be a hearing,' that is to say, a discussion in which the parties to the dispute participate in conformity with Article 32. In the Statement 'consideration' means hardly more than 'discussion.' Consequently the delegate of Australia correctly interpreted the Statement in declaring finally: 'the net effect of the joint statement is that consideration and discussion by the Council cannot be blocked, but in ordinary speech "consideration"

[6] *The Report to the President*, pp. 72 f., contains the following statement: 'In the course of the preparation of this statement there arose a point on which the Sponsoring Powers differed. They were at all times fully in agreement that the text of the Yalta formula must be approved without change and that the rule of unanimity of the permanent members should apply to decisions of the Security Council during the stage of peaceful settlement as well as during enforcement. However, a question of interpretation arose as to whether under the formula any one permanent member, not a party to a given dispute, could prevent the consideration and discussion of such dispute by the Council. The Department of State between the time of the Crimea Conference and San Francisco, had issued an official statement interpreting the Yalta voting formula in the sense that no one member could prevent such discussion. The United States delegation placed considerable importance upon this interpretation and its views were shared by the delegations of the United Kingdom, China and France. The Delegation of the Soviet Union expressed the opinion during the preparation of the joint statement that the discussion and consideration of a dispute in the Security Council should be considered a substantive, rather than a procedural, matter. In the exchange of views which occurred on this important point the United States Delegation stressed the imperative necessity of providing for full discussion and consideration of any situation brought before the Security Council before any one permanent member could prevent further action by the Security Council with respect to the dispute. After full deliberation the Delegation of the Soviet Union agreed to this viewpoint, and complete agreement was therefore reached among the great powers on this basic question.' The formula 'full discussion and consideration of any situation brought before the Security Council' seems to indicate that at least in the opinion of the United States Delegation a liberal interpretation of the rule laid down in the Statement of the Four Sponsoring Governments is adequate. The practice of the Security Council seems to be to place a question on its agenda by a procedural vote. In this way, *e.g.*, the Iranian case (Journal of the Security Council, 1st Year, No. 20, p. 385) and the Greek case (Official Records of the Security Council, 1st Year, 2nd Series, No. 7, p. 197) were placed on the agenda of the Council.

[7] Verbatim Minutes of the 4th meeting of Commission III (Doc. 1149, III/11, p. 22).

would include calling for reports, hearing witnesses, even appointing a commission of investigation. But clearly, under the reply of the sponsoring governments, the veto is applicable to a decision to use any of these last-mentioned procedures.'[8]

It is significant that the Charter does not mention a ' decision ' of the Security Council relating to the question as to whether a discussion or consideration of a dispute or situation shall take place. All acts of the Security Council which are mentioned in Chapter VI of the Charter: call upon the parties to settle their dispute by pacific means (Article 33, paragraph 2), investigate a dispute or situation and determine whether the continuance of it is likely to endanger the maintenance of peace (Article 34), recommendation of appropriate procedures or methods of adjustment (Article 36, paragraph 1, Article 37, paragraph 2), recommendations of terms of settlement (Article 37, paragraph 2, Article 38), require, according to the Statement, a qualified majority implying the veto right of each permanent Member. This is justified in the Statement by the fact that decisions and actions by the Security Council which go beyond ' discussion and consideration ' ' may well have major political consequences and may even initiate a chain of events which might in the end require the Council under its responsibilities to invoke measures of enforcement.' There can be little doubt that the discussion of disputes, especially when the parties participate in this discussion, may have the same political consequences as a call upon the parties to settle their dispute by peaceful means or an investigation of the dispute, or a recommendation of methods of

[8] U.N.C.I.O. Doc. 1149, III/11, p. 23. The Summary Report of the 9th meeting of Committee III/1 (U.N.C.I.O. Doc. 417, III/1/19, p. 1) contains the following statement: 'The delegate of one of the sponsoring governments, in response, expressed the view that a permanent member could not prevent the investigation by the Security Council of a dispute under the provisions of Chapter VIII, Section A.' This statement is not in conformity with Article 27, paragraph 2, since the decision to make an investigation is not a procedural matter, nor with the Statement by the Delegation of the Four Sponsoring Governments, of June 7, 1945. At the 18th meeting of Committee III/1 (U.N.C.I.O. Doc. 936, III/1/45, p. 2) the delegate of New Zealand ' expressed his regret that a more satisfactory reply had not been made to the questionnaire submitted to the sponsoring governments. The difference in interpretation which had existed among the sponsoring governments was a reason to press for a clarification of the voting procedure. The Statement had extended the " veto " right of the permanent members to situations in which certain delegates had thought it would not be operative. Those delegates had been strengthened in their belief that the right of " veto " was not applicable to a Council investigation by a statement made in a previous meeting by the Delegate of the United Kingdom. Although the Statement of the sponsoring governments represented a retrogression from this view, it was an advance over the interpretation that a permanent member could veto even the initiation of discussion in the Security Council.'

At the 10th meeting of Committee III/1 (U.N.C.I.O. Doc. 459, III/1/22, p. 5) the Czechoslovak representative declared that: 'In his view, the great powers were not free to do as they pleased under this voting formula because they were bound by the principles set forth in the Charter.' This statement has no basis in the text of the Charter.

adjustment or of terms of settlement. It is difficult to understand why—as the Statement asserts—the chain of critical events should begin ' when the Council decides to make investigation or determines that the time has come to call upon the states to settle their differences, or make recommendations to the parties,' and not when in the discussion of the dispute the parties accuse each other of having violated the Charter and apply for action on the part of the Security Council.[9]

It seems that, according to the Statement, only decisions relating to discussion and consideration of disputes or situations taken under Chapter VI, not under Chapter VII, are subject to mere ' procedural ' vote. If it is intended to determine the existence of a threat to, or a breach of, the peace under Article 39, a discussion of the dispute or situation involving the threat to, or breach of, the peace may precede the decision by which the existence of the threat to, or breach of, the peace is to be determined. If the decision of the question whether a discussion shall take place in case the Security Council acts or intends to act under Article 39 is subject to the veto right, whereas the decision relating to a discussion taken under an Article of Chapter VI is not, then it must be made clear under which Article of the Charter the Security Council is acting in discussing a dispute or situation before the decision can be taken relating to the question as to whether a discussion shall take place or not. Some members may be of the opinion that the dispute or the situation is in a state which requires action under Article 39 whereas others may think that the Security Council should act under the provisions of Chapter VI. Then this preliminary question must be decided. The problems concerned are completely ignored by the Statement.

Finally, it should be noted that the formula in Part II, paragraph 2, of the Statement, ' the decision regarding the preliminary question as to whether or not such a matter is procedural must be taken by a vote of seven members including the concurring votes of the permanent members,' is not very satisfactory. It implies that the proposal: the matter is procedural, or the proposal: the matter is non-procedural,

[9] At the 4th meeting of Commission III (U.N.C.I.O. Doc. 1149, III/11, pp. 23f) the delegate of Australia criticised the Statement of the Four Sponsoring Governments in this respect as follows: ' That is the argument: when a dispute comes into existence, a chain of events may follow from the moment the Security Council is required to adopt a course of procedure in the preliminary state, right through the various processes until the stage is reached when it might be decided by the Council that actual force shall be used in order to prevent any danger to international peace or security. Now that is all perfectly true and correct. It may. And, Mr. President, it is for that very reason that, in our submission, the exercise by one power of its right to block conciliation of the dispute—even where both disputants ask for conciliation could prevent the dispute from being composed at the earlier stage. By preventing the dispute from being settled and composed, the chain of events may go on until serious consequences in the way of a breach of the peace may occur.'

may be put to the vote. If the second proposal is put to the vote and does not obtain the qualified majority, and if such result is supposed to mean that the matter is to be considered as procedural, no permanent member of the Security Council can through the exercise of its veto right prevent a matter from being declared procedural. If, however, the first proposal is put to the vote and does not obtain the qualified majority, and if such result is supposed to mean that the matter is to be considered as non-procedural, each permanent member can through the exercise of its veto right prevent a matter from being declared procedural. If the fact that one of the two proposals does not obtain the qualified majority is not supposed to mean that the other is accepted and, consequently, that after the one has failed to obtain the qualified majority, the other is to be put to the vote, it is quite possible that neither of them will be accepted. To avoid these consequences, it would have been advisable to formulate the rule in question by determining which proposal: the negative or the affirmative, shall be put to the vote, and to stipulate that in case one proposal does not obtain the qualified majority, its opposite is to be considered as accepted. It is certainly in accordance with the spirit of Article 27 to assume that only a proposal affirming the procedural character of the matter concerned shall be put to the vote.

(*f*) Obligatory Abstention from Voting

The above-mentioned question as to under which Article the Council is acting is of particular importance in case the second part of Article 27, paragraph 3, providing that, in decisions under Chapter VI, and under paragraph 3, of Article 52, 'a party to a dispute shall abstain from voting,' is to be applied. If taken literally, this provision is not applicable at all, since neither the Articles of Chapter VI nor Article 53, paragraph 3, refer expressly to 'decisions' in the strict sense of the term as used in Article 25 imposing upon the Members the obligation to carry out the decisions of the Security Council. It is especially the 'recommendations' made under Chapter VI which are not 'decisions' in this sense of the term if they are considered to be not binding upon the parties. The same is true with respect to the 'call' referred to in Article 33, paragraph 2, and the 'encouraging' referred to in Article 52, paragraph 3. Article 37, paragraph 2, it is true, provides that the Security Council shall 'decide' whether to recommend procedures and methods of adjustment or terms of settlement. But the 'decision' by which it makes the one or the other recommendation is usually interpreted not to be binding upon the parties. If the provision excluding the parties to a dispute from voting shall be applicable at all, the term 'decision' as used in Article 27, paragraph 3, second part, must be interpreted to mean any resolution taken by the Security Council under Chapter VI, or Article 52, paragraph 3, whether or not it has the character of a

' decision ' in the sense of Article 25. Article 52, paragraph 3, provides:

> The Security Council shall encourage the development of pacific settlement of local disputes through such regional arrangements or by such regional agencies either on the initiative of the states concerned or by reference from the Security Council.

The rule excluding a member of the Security Council which is a party to a dispute from voting in the decision relating to this dispute seems to be applicable to decisions under Article 52, paragraph 3, only in so far as the Security Council, by this decision, refers a concrete dispute to a regional agency for pacific settlement.

The meaning of the words ' decisions under Chapter VI ' is doubtful not only because of the singificance of the term ' decision ' but also because it is not very clear what is meant by the words ' under Chapter VI.' These words may be interpreted in a restrictive or an extensive way. As decisions of the Security Council under Chapter VI may be considered only those taken to the effect of a call upon the parties to a dispute under Article 33, paragraph 2; an investigation under Article 34; recommendations under Article 36, paragraph 1, Article 37, paragraph 2, or Article 38. But a decision to establish a committee, even for the purpose to undertake an investigation within the meaning of Article 34, may be considered a decision taken under Article 29, and hence not a decision under Chapter VI but under Chapter V. The same is true with respect to a decision by which the International Court of Justice is requested to give an advisory opinion on a dispute with which the Security Council is dealing under Chapter VI, or on a decision by which the Council finds that a dispute with which it is dealing under Chapter VI concerns a matter essentially within the domestic jurisdiction of one of the parties. Such decisions are only indirectly taken under Chapter VI; they are directly taken under Chapter XIV or Chapter I. Likewise, a decision on the question whether a case has the character of a ' dispute ' or of a ' situation ' may be considered not to be a decision under Chapter VI, because such a decision is not expressly provided for in that Chapter. However, the words ' decisions under Chapter VI ' may also be interpreted to mean not only decisions expressly provided for in that Chapter but also decisions which are necessary in order to take those expressly provided for in Chapter VI.

It is doubtful whether the provision of the second part of Article 27, paragraph 3, applies to all decisions relating to disputes and taken under Chapter VI, or only to non-procedural decisions of this kind,[1] and, further, whether it applies only to decisions expressly provided for in that Chapter or also to those necessary to take these

[1] Cf. *supra*, p. 246.

decisions; but there is no doubt that the rule excluding parties to a dispute from voting does not apply to decisions relating to disputes, but taken under Chapter VII of the Charter. If the Security Council under Article 39 determines that a dispute constitutes a threat to or breach of the peace and adopts a decision to the effect to make recommendations to the parties to the dispute or to the effect to take enforcement measures against one or the other party to the dispute constituting a threat to or breach of the peace, the member of the Council which is a party to the dispute—whether permanent or non-permanent member—is not excluded from voting. In this case the Council is not, even not indirectly, dealing with the dispute under Chapter VI, but exclusively under Chapter VII.[2]

The application of the rule excluding a member of the Security Council which is a party to a dispute from voting depends entirely on the answer to the question under which Article the decision of the Council is to be taken. This is a strange consequence of the wording of Article 27, paragraph 3. A member of the Security Council, party to a dispute, is excluded from voting in case of a decision by which the Security Council under Article 34 determines that the continuance of the dispute is likely to endanger the maintenance of international peace and security; but the same member is not excluded from voting in case of a decision by which the Council under Article 39 determines that the dispute involves a threat to the peace, which is not very different from determining that the continuance of the dispute is endangering the peace. In order to determine under Article 39 the existence of a threat to the peace constituted by a dispute, the Security Council may need to investigate the dispute. If it has not yet investigated the dispute under Article 34, it may do so under Article 39, provided that the power conferred upon the Security Council by this Article implies also the power of undertaking an investigation in order to determine the existence of a threat to, or breach of, the peace. The decision of the Council to investigate the dispute in order to determine the existence of a threat to, or breach of, the peace—that is a decision under Article 39—is not subject to the rule excluding a party to a dispute from voting; but the decision to investigate a dispute in order to determine that its continuance endangers the maintenance of peace, that is a decision under Article 34, is subject to this rule. Under Article 29 the Council may establish a committee authorised to

[2] Committee 3 of Commission III at the San Francisco Conference interpreted the provision of Article 39, authorising the Security Council to make 'recommendations,' to mean that 'the action of the Council so far as it relates to the peaceful settlement of a dispute or to situations giving rise to a threat of war, a breach of the peace, or aggression, should be considered as governed by the provisions contained in Section A [corresponding to Chapter VI of the Charter].' (U.N.C.I.O. Doc. 881, III/3/46, p. 6.) That can only mean that the Council may make under Article 39 the same recommendations as under Chapter VI. But it cannot mean that the Council acts under Chapter VI when, after having determined the existence of a threat to or breach of the peace, it makes a recommendation referred to in Article 39.

investigate a dispute under consideration by the Council. If the decision is taken under this Article, but for the purpose laid down in Article 34, the rule of Article 27, paragraph 3, may or may not apply.[3] But if the investigation committee is established under Article 29 for the purpose of determining the existence of a threat to, or breach of, the peace within the meaning of Article 39, the rule excluding a party to the dispute from voting certainly does not apply. A member of the Security Council, party to a dispute, is excluded from voting in case of a decision by which the Security Council, after having determined under Article 34, or Article 37, paragraph 2, that the continuance of the dispute endangers the peace, makes, under Article 36, paragraph 1, or Article 37, paragraph 2, a recommendation to the parties either with respect to procedures or methods of adjustment or with respect to settlement. But the same member is not excluded from voting in case of a decision by which the Security Council, under Article 39, after having determined the existence of a threat to the peace, makes the same recommendations to the parties.[4] It is obvious that the provision of Article 27, paragraph 3, establishing one of the most fundamental principles of legal procedure: that nobody should be a judge in its own cause, can easily be eluded by choosing the procedure provided by Article 39, instead of a procedure provided by an Article of Chapter VI. And it does not need any trick of interpretation in order to eliminate this principle from the most important case in which it claims application: the case of taking enforcement action. For in this case the principle is eliminated directly by the Charter.

A highly problematical restriction of the principle in question is constituted by the fact that the rule established in the second sentence of Article 27, paragraph 3, refers only to 'disputes,' not to 'situations' which have not the character of a 'dispute.' The provisions of Chapter VI expressly distinguish between 'disputes' and 'situations.'[5]

[3] Cf. *supra*, p. 246.

[4] In the British Commentary on the Charter (Cmd. 6666 London, 1945), p. 16, we read: 'If any one of them [the Great Powers] is a party to a dispute, it has no vote in any judgment which the Security Council may pronounce. In such a case at least three elected states must concur in the judgment of the Security Council.' 'Only when enforcement action is necessary is the complete unanimity of the Great Powers always required.' These statements are not correct. Determination of the existence of a threat to, or breach of, the peace, as well as recommendations under Article 39, decisions which do not refer to enforcement action, require complete unanimity of the great powers, even in case the threat to, or breach of, the peace is involved in a dispute, and the recommendation refers to a dispute to which any of them is a party. Article 39 is under Chapter VII and the rule by which parties to a dispute are excluded from voting refers only to decisions under Chapter VI and under paragraph 3 of Article 52 (Chapter VIII).

[5] The proposal of the United States to apply the rule of Article 27, paragraph 3, concerning abstention from voting, to 'all parties involved in matters arising before the Security Council, whether technically they be deemed disputes or situations' (Doc. A/AC.18/SC.3/4, p. 2) is not compatible with the clear wording of Articles

If a member of the Security Council is involved in a situation which has not, or not yet, the character of a dispute, the member is not excluded from voting in case the Security Council decides under Article 34 to investigate the situation, or makes under Article 36 recommendations for the adjustment of the situation. Hence the question may arise: what is the difference between a situation which has the character of a dispute, and a situation which has not this character. 'Situations' are referred to three times in Chapter VI: in Article 34: a 'situation which might lead to international friction or give rise to a dispute'; in Article 35: any situation of the nature referred to in Article 34; and in Article 36, paragraph 1: 'a situation of like nature,' meaning of a nature like the nature of a dispute referred to in Article 33: 'the continuance of which is likely to endanger the maintenance of international peace and security.' Situations of such nature must always imply a possible or actual conflict between states, there must be always, at least, two states—directly or indirectly—involved in the situation; otherwise no danger to the peace could exist, and the 'situation' would be a matter of domestic jurisdiction excluding any

34, 35 and 36, of the Charter, which distinguish between 'disputes' and 'situations.' This distinction has been made already in the Dumbarton Oaks Proposals in Chapter VIII, Section A, paragraph 1 (corresponding to Article 34) and paragraph 2 (corresponding to Article 35). It does not appear, it is true, in Chapter VIII, Section A, paragraph 5, of the Dumbarton Oaks Proposals, which refers only to 'disputes,' not to 'situations.' But this provision was amended at the San Francisco Conference where it became Article 36 of the Charter. The above-mentioned Memorandum contains the following statement: 'At San Francisco, the provision of the Charter which later became Article 36 was enlarged to cover situations as well as disputes in order to prevent any technical claim (such as was made on occasions before the League of Nations) that the Council lacked jurisdiction because a matter could not be deemed a dispute. Unfortunately, Article 27 was never amended to conform to the new wording of Article 36. However, it is clear from the discussions in Committee III/2 (twelfth meeting) at San Francisco, that this amendment to Article 36 was never intended to be the basis of a distinction between the duty of States to abstain from voting in a dispute to which they are parties, and the absence of such a duty in the case of situations in which they are directly concerned.' The last statement may be correct. But in the discussion of Committee III/2 (twelfth meeting) the distinction between 'disputes' and 'situations' was considered to be of great importance. Article 35, paragraph 2, authorises a non-member state to bring to the attention of the Security Council only a dispute to which it is a party, not a 'situation,' and requires only that a non-member state, party to a dispute brought by it to the attention of the Security Council, accept in advance the obligations of pacific settlement. In the discussion of Committee III/2 (twelfth meeting) the question arose: 'Should a non-member, involved in a situation of the type referred to in this Article, be required to accept the obligations of pacific settlement of the Charter, if that non-member brings such situation to the attention of the Council or the Assembly? On this question, the delegate of Australia suggested that, since the Charter did not establish any obligations of pacific settlement in relation to situations, the insertion of "situations" in any redraft of the second sentence, as had been suggested, would be of doubtful validity.' (U.N.C.I.O. Doc. 992, III/2/27, p. 7.) It can hardly be concluded from this discussion that the term 'dispute' in Article 27, paragraph 3, may be interpreted to include 'situations' not having the character of disputes.

intervention on the part of the Organisation. Hence it may be difficult to distinguish between ' disputes ' and other ' situations.' In order to make the provision of Article 27, paragraph 3, second part, applicable the term ' dispute ' must be interpreted to mean: contending in argument. Then a ' dispute ' exists in the relation between two states only if the one has addressed a claim to the other state and if the latter has refused to comply with this claim. When a state attacks another state without previously having demanded anything from the attacked state and without this state having refused to comply with a demand of the other, there exists a conflict between the two states, but no ' dispute.' If a conflict of opinions arises within the Security Council with respect to the question as to whether a certain situation has the character of a dispute or is a situation other than a dispute, this preliminary question must be decided by the Security Council. In taking this decision the Security Council is not bound by the opinion of the parties, even if the parties agree that there is a ' dispute ' or that there is a situation not having the character of a dispute.[6] It may be doubted—as pointed out—whether such a decision is a ' decision under Chapter VI,' because it is not expressly provided for in that Chapter. If the question is answered in the negative, the rule excluding a party to a dispute from voting does not apply. Hence a permanent member may avoid the application of this rule by denying that a matter in which it is involved is a dispute and by provoking a decision of the Council in which this member participates, thus preventing the Council from declaring the case a ' dispute.'[7]

In order to be excluded from voting the Member of the Security Council must be a party to the dispute to which the decision refers.

[6] At the 19th meeting of the Security Council the delegate of the United Kingdom stated: ' If any accuser state says that there is a dispute, then there is a dispute; and if a state makes a charge against another state, and the state against which it is made repudiates it or contests it, then there is a dispute, and the Council can make its recommendation.' (Official Records of the Security Council, 1st Year, 1st Series, No. 1, p. 276.) But who has to decide whether the facts exist which, according to the definition formulated in the second sentence of this statement, constitute a dispute? If the Security Council has to decide this question, then the first sentence of the statement is not correct. At the same meeting the representative of the Netherlands stated: ' since the answer to the question whether that matter is a dispute or a situation has consequences, consequences namely with regard to the voting procedure, I do not think, in the final analysis, that it can be left to the parties to decide whether a matter is a dispute or a situation. That is a question that should be decided by the Council after having heard the development of the parties' statements ' (p. 277). The same opinion was expressed by the delegate of the Soviet Union (p. 279).

[7] In its Memorandum on Pacific Settlement by the Security Council (Doc. A/C.1/91, p. 6) the delegation of Canada stated: ' Under the proviso to paragraph 3 of Article 27 of the Charter, a party to a dispute is required to abstain from voting in decisions taken under Chapter VI. This proviso would be rendered of no effect if a permanent member of the Security Council could veto a decision that a dispute exists or that it is, itself, a party to a dispute. Therefore the Security Council should work out agreed procedures to ensure that no state is judge in its own cause.'

This is not clearly enough expressed by the second part of Article 27, paragraph 3.

The obligation to ' abstain from voting ' as it is formulated in the second part of Article 27, paragraph 3, may be violated. The representative of a member may cast its vote in spite of the fact that the Security Council is of the opinion that this member is excluded from voting. In this case the vote illegally cast by the representative must not be counted. Hence it would have been more appropriate to formulate the rule concerned as follows: In decisions regarding a dispute, if taken under Chapter VI and under Article 52, paragraph 3, the votes of the parties to the dispute must not be counted.

(*g*) Veto Right Outside the Procedure in the Security Council

Finally, it may be noted that the veto right of the five great powers does not only apply in the voting procedure of the Security Council. It works also in the amendment procedure regulated by Articles 108 and 109 of the Charter. Amendments to the Charter come into force only when ratified by ' two-thirds of the Members of the United Nations, including all the permanent members of the Security Council.' [8]

(*h*) Voting on Obligatory and non-Obligatory Functions

Competences are conferred upon the Security Council by the Charter in two different ways. Some Articles stipulate: the Security Council ' shall ' perform certain functions; others: the Security Council ' may,' etc. As pointed out in a previous chapter of this study, [9] it may be doubted whether any clear intention of the legislator is behind this difference of the wording. If there is any intention the use of the word ' shall ' does not in any case constitute a legal obligation in the strict sense of the term, since the Charter does not provide sanctions to be inflicted upon the Security Council in case it does not perform the function which it ' shall ' perform. But the term ' shall,' as pointed out, may be interpreted to constitute a moral obligation, that is to say, the difference in the wording of the provision by which competences are conferred upon the Security Council could be interpreted to mean that—according to the intention of the legislator —the Security Council should not consider itself to be free to perform or not to perform the function if the Charter says that the Council ' shall,' whereas in case the word ' may ' is used, the Security Council is authorised to assume that the function is placed within its discretion.

[8] At the 17th meeting of Committee III/1 (U.N.C.I.O. Doc. 922, III/1/44, p. 4) the delegate of Peru declared that ' when circumstances changed the Charter ought to be improved, and that if it were necessary to retain the veto in the amending process it would be necessary to recognise the right of powers to withdraw from the Organisation.'

[9] Cf. *supra*, p. 154.

To impose a legal or moral obligation upon a collegiate organ is always problematical in so far as the action by which the obligation is to be fulfilled requires a decision of the organ, and hence a voting procedure. Voting, however, implies the possibility of a negative result, which is in contradiction to the legal or moral obligation imposed upon the organ. To avoid such contradiction, the legal order may provide that functions conferred upon a collegiate body by a formula using the word ' shall ' are to be performed by the presiding officer on behalf of the body without previous decision taken by a majority vote. In case this is not feasible for some reason or another, the possibility of a negative result may be restricted by making the decision as easy as possible, that is to say, by providing that decisions relating to functions which ' shall ' be performed by the collegiate organ are to be taken by simple majority vote of the members present and voting; whereas decisions relating to functions which the collegial organ ' may ' perform may be taken by a qualified majority. It would have been quite understandable if the Charter had provided that only decisions relating to functions which the Security Council according to the Charter ' may ' perform are subject to the veto right of each permanent member, whereas decisions relating to functions which the Security Council—according to the Charter ' shall ' perform require an affirmative vote of any seven members. However, as pointed out, the voting procedure as established by Article 27 completely ignores the difference which the wording of the Charter makes between quasi-obligatory and discretionary functions of the Security Council.[1]

(*i*) Incapacity of the Security Council to Reach a Decision

The inevitable effect of the voting procedure conferring the right of veto upon each of the permanent members must be that no decision of any importance can be taken against the will of one of the privileged states even if this state is involved in the matter to which the decision refers. For, as pointed out, the rule excluding interested parties from that decision does apply only to disputes, not to other ' situations ' and does not apply at all to decisions concerning enforcement actions. Even recommendations relating to disputes, if taken under Article 39, are not subject to the rule. Finally, a permanent member of the Security Council may use its veto right not only in its own interest but also in the interest of other states parties to a dispute or involved in another situation likely to endanger the peace. Consequently the Security Council sometimes will not be able to exercise its most important functions, especially those referred to in Article 39. This

[1] At the 4th meeting of Commission III (U.N.C.I.O. Doc. 1149, III/11, p. 23) the Australian delegate declared: ' In our view, wherever the Council's power is associated with a duty to exercise it, the decision of the Council is limited to questions of time and method, and could, and should, fairly be treated as procedural and therefore not subject to the veto. However, the joint statement plainly treats all these decisions as subject to the veto.'

Article, and that means the entire Chapter VII which forms the core of the Charter, is practically inapplicable if directed against a permanent member of the Security Council, or a state protected by a permanent member. What does the Charter provide in case that the Security Council cannot reach a decision under Article 27?

(*aa*) Transfer of Competence to the General Assembly

If the decision refers to a matter which is within the concurrent competence of the Security Council and the General Assembly, the matter may be taken over by the General Assembly. In this respect Article 11, paragraph 2, and Article 12, come into consideration.[2] According to paragraph 2 of Article 11, the Security Council may bring before the General Assembly 'any questions relating to the maintenance of international peace and security'; and the General Assembly may make recommendations with regard to this question. Since Article 11, paragraph 2, stipulates: 'Any such question on which action is necessary shall be referred to the Security Council by the General Assembly either before or after discussion,' it may be assumed that the Security Council is not authorised to bring before the General Assembly under Article 11, paragraph 2, a question on which—according to its own opinion—enforcement action is necessary. If, according to the opinion of the General Assembly, enforcement action is necessary—which evidently cannot be decided by the Assembly 'before discussion'—reference to the Council is meaningless if the question has been brought before the Assembly because the Council was unable to act. According to Article 12, paragraph 1, the Council may 'request' the Assembly to make recommendations in respect of a 'dispute or a situation' while the former is exercising in respect to this matter the functions assigned to it in the Charter. This is an exception to the rule of Article 12, paragraph 1, that the Assembly shall not make any recommendation with respect to a dispute or situation while the Council is exercising in respect to this dispute or situation the functions assigned to it in the Charter. May the Council 'request' the Assembly to make recommendations on a dispute or a situation under Article 12, paragraph 1, even if—according to the Council's opinion—enforcement action is necessary? An affirmative as well as a negative answer is possible. The affirmative answer may be based on the fact that the provision concerning the Council's 'request' follows the provision binding the Assembly to refer to the Council questions on which action is necessary, and hence may be interpreted to be a restriction to that provision. The negative answer may be based on the argument that no such restriction is intended since, if enforcement action is necessary, the competence of the Council is exclusive, the Assembly having no power of taking enforcement action. If in such a case the Council is unable to act, no action

[2] Cf. *supra*, pp. 193 ff.

on the part of the Organisation is possible. Can the Council request the Assembly under Article 12, paragraph 1, to make a recommendation in case of a threat to the peace, breach of the peace, or act of aggression? This question must be answered in the affirmative only if it is assumed that the Assembly is competent to determine the existence of a threat to, or breach of, the peace. It seems that the Assembly has not this competence, which is expressly conferred only upon the Council in Article 39. But if the Assembly is not competent to determine the existence of a threat to, or breach of, the peace, how can the Assembly decide that enforcement action is necessary and then refer the case to the Council in accordance with Article 11, paragraph 2? That the Security Council cannot transfer to the General Assembly the competence to decide upon enforcement action under Article 39, is evident.[3]

It is not very likely that the Security Council will bring a question before the General Assembly under Article 11, paragraph 2, or 'request' under Article 12, paragraph 1, the General Assembly to make recommendations in respect to a 'dispute or situation' if the Security Council itself is able and willing to make a recommendation in the matter concerned. Provisions authorising the Security Council to refer a matter to the General Assembly seem to be especially appropriate for the case that the Security Council's decision is blocked by the veto right of one of its permanent members. But the decision by which the Security Council brings a question before the General Assembly under Article 11, paragraph 2, and especially the decision by which the 'request' referred to in Article 12, paragraph 1, is to be made, may hardly be considered to be procedural matters since they constitute an individual transfer of competence; if so, they are subject to the veto right of the permanent members. Then it is not very likely that the Security Council will by such a qualified majority decision refer to the General Assembly a matter which could not be decided in substance by the Security Council itself since the latter was not able to reach the qualified majority.

The matter, however, may be brought before the General Assembly not by the Security Council but on the General Assembly's own initiative, under Article 10, or on the initiative of any Member of the United Nations or by a state which is not a Member of the United

[3] The subcommittee appointed by the Security Council at its 39th meeting, in the Spanish case, suggested, *inter alia*, that the Council should make a recommendation to the General Assembly 'that unless the Franco regime is withdrawn . . . a resolution should be passed by the General Assembly recommending the termination of diplomatic relations with the Franco regime by each Member of the United Nations . . . ' (Journal of the Security Council, 1st Year, No. 38, p. 743.) There is no provision of the Charter authorising the Security Council to make 'recommendations' to the General Assembly; and the Assembly is certainly not competent to recommend the termination of diplomatic relations, since this is an enforcement action determined in Article 41, the application of which is reserved to the Council by Article 39. The suggestion of the subcommittee was not adopted by the Council.

Nations under Article 11, paragraph 2, and Article 35, paragraph 2; and the General Assembly may make a recommendation in the matter under the condition that the Secretary-General, under Article 12, paragraph 2, has notified the General Assembly or, if the General Assembly is not in session, the Members of the United Nations, that the Security Council has ceased to deal with the matter. It is doubtful whether this notification to be made by the Secretary-General requires the consent of the Security Council, which Article 12, paragraph 2, prescribes for the analogous notification by the Secretary-General of the matters which are being dealt with by the Security Council. The wording: the Secretary-General shall 'similarly' notify the General Assembly, etc., and especially the fact that only the Security Council itself can decide whether or not it has ceased to deal with a matter are rather in favour of an affirmative answer to this question. If the Secretary-General is authorised to notify the General Assembly or the Members that the Security Council has ceased to deal with the matter concerned only with the consent of the Security Council the question arises whether the decision of the Security Council by which this consent is to be given is or is not a procedural matter. If it is considered to be a non-procedural matter, the member which by its veto blocked the decision of the Security Council may also block the decision concerning the notification in order to prevent the General Assembly from taking a decision which it considers to be not compatible with its interests.[4]

Another interpretation of Article 12, however, is not excluded. It is not expressly stipulated that the General Assembly must consider the Security Council as dealing with a matter relative to the maintenance of peace or exercising its functions in respect to a dispute or situation as long as the Secretary-General has not notified the General Assembly or the Members of the United Nations that the Security Council has ceased to deal with the matter. It may be argued that the question as to whether the Security Council is still dealing with a matter or exercising its functions in respect to it is to be decided by

[4] By a resolution taken under Article 12, paragraph 2, by the Security Council at its 79th meeting, the Spanish case was turned over to the General Assembly. The resolution runs as follows: 'The Security Council resolves that the situation in Spain is to be taken off the list of matters of which the Security Council is seized, and that all records and documents of the case be put at the disposal of the General Assembly. The Security Council requests the Secretary-General to notify the General Assembly of this decision.' (Official Records of the Security Council, 1st Year, 2nd Series, No. 21, p. 498.) This resolution was carried unanimously. In this case the notification of the General Assembly by the Secretary-General, provided for by Article 12, paragraph 2, was consented to by the Security Council. At its 202nd meeting the Security Council adopted a resolution to the effect that the Greek question 'be taken off the list of matters of which the Security Council is seized,' and that the Secretary-General be instructed to place all records and documents in the case at the disposal of the General Assembly. (Doc. S/P.V. 202.) The resolution was considered to refer to a procedural matter and hence approved in spite of a permanent member—the Soviet Union—voting against it.

the General Assembly and may be decided in the negative even without a formal notification on the part of the Secretary-General. Further, as pointed out, it is doubtful whether the consent of the Security Council is required for the notification that the Security Council has ceased to deal with the matter. For the phrase ' with the consent of the Security Council ' in Article 12, paragraph 2, refers directly only to the provision that the Secretary-General ' shall notify the General Assembly at each session of any matters relative to the maintenance of international peace and security which are dealt with by the Security Council.'

The possibility, however, that a matter which cannot be decided by the Security Council (becuase of its voting procedure) be taken over by the General Assembly is no absolute guarantee of its being positively settled. For the decision of the General Assembly requires—as a rule—a two-thirds majority of the members present and voting; and it may be impossible to reach such a majority. Besides, the General Assembly is competent only to make recommendations not binding upon the states parties to a dispute or involved in another situation.

(*bb*) Self-Help

As long as the Security Council does not reach a decision by which the existence of an act of aggression is determined or the ' necessary measures ' are taken as a reaction against such act of aggression, Article 51 of the Charter applies, conferring upon the Members the right of self-defence.[5] But this Article applies only in case of an armed attack. The right of self-defence must not be exercised in case of any other violation of the legally protected interests of a Member. In case the right of a Member which has been violated in another way than by an armed attack, is to be enforced against the guilty state which refuses to repair the wrong it has done, and if the Security Council does not take the necessary enforcement action, the Charter prevents any other possibility of enforcing the violated right. The delinquent state which is in actual possession of the illegal advantage is protected by the Charter against any enforcement action other than that taken by the Security Council. For the Charter forbids any use of force on the part of the individual Members except for the exercise of the right of self-defence against armed attack (and against ex-enemy states under Articles 107 and 53.)

In this respect the Covenant of the League of Nations differs from the Charter. The Covenant reserved to the Members the right of self-help in all cases in which the League was proved unable to settle the dispute. Article 15, paragraph 7, of the Covenant provides:

> If the Council fails to reach a report which is unanimously agreed to by the members thereof other than the Representatives

[5] Cf. *infra*, pp. 791 ff.

> of one or more of the parties to the dispute, the Members of the League reserve to themselves the right to take such action as they shall consider necessary for the maintenance of right and justice.

And paragraph 6 of this Article, which prohibits resort to war against a state which complies with the recommendations of the Council unanimously agreed to, does not prohibit war against the party which does not comply with the recommendation of the Council.

At the San Francisco Conference the delegate of France proposed the following amendment: 'Should the Council not succeed in reaching a decision, the Members of the Organisation reserve to themselves the right to act as they may consider necessary in the interest of peace, right and justice.'[6] This proposition was not accepted.

If the constitution of an international organisation abolishes or restricts the principle of self-help established by general international law, it must fulfil two requirements. It must guarantee first that any dispute not settled by agreement of the parties will be settled by the Organisation; and second that, to the same extent as the individual Member is deprived of its right of self-help, enforcement action of the Organisation will actually take place. Otherwise the Organisation constitutes, instead of an improvement, a dangerous deterioration of the legal status under general international law. The Charter fulfils neither the first nor the second requirement. The Charter does not exclude the possibility that disputes the continuance of which is likely to endanger the peace remain unsettled, and that violated rights remain unenforced.[7]

[6] U.N.C.I.O. Doc. 2, G/7 (o), Part II, pp. 2–3. The first part of the French proposition reads as follows: 'To maintain and to restore international peace and security, the Security Council shall have recourse, according to circumstances, to "recommendations" or "decisions." "Recommendations" shall be approved by an (unqualified) two-thirds majority vote of the members of the Council. "Decisions" shall be approved by a qualified two-thirds majority vote (including the concurring votes of the permanent members).'

[7] In the British Commentary on the Charter, p. 17, the following statement is made: 'Thus the successful working of the United Nations depends on the preservation of the unanimity of the Great Powers; not, of course, on all the details of policy, but on its broad principles. If this unanimity is seriously undermined no provision of the Charter is likely to be of much avail. In such a case the Members will resume their liberty of action.' The last sentence is certainly not correct; at least not from a legal point of view. It is certainly true that without unanimity the Organisation cannot work; but from a political point of view the Organisation is superfluous as long as the Great Powers agree.

The Report to the President, p. 66, characterises the political idea underlying the Organisation of the Security Council as follows: 'There were theoretically two alternative means of preserving this unity. The first was through the formation of a permanent alliance among the great powers. This method might have been justified on narrow strategic grounds, but it would have been repugnant to our traditional policy. It also would have contained elements of danger becuase it

(cc) Public Opinion

At the 20th meeting of Committee III/1[8] of the San Francisco Conference the delegate of the United States suggested that, in case the veto right exercised by a permanent member would block a decision of the Security Council, 'a solution might be forthcoming from the discussion, without the necessity of decision.' This is true, provided that discussion cannot be prevented by a permanent member exercising his veto right, which can hardly be maintained on the basis of the Charter, and which can be maintained on the basis of the Statement of the Four Sponsoring Governments only with respect to discussions under Chapter VI. As pointed out, it is very doubtful whether the Statement extends the exclusion of the veto right to discussions of matters regulated by provisions of Chapter VII of the Charter. That solution may result from mere discussion holds only under the condition that the discussion proves to be a channel of public opinion, and this is the case only if the discussion is public. The Charter does not contain provisions by which publicity of discussion in the General Assembly or the Security Council is guaranteed. The autonomous Rules of Procedure of these bodies provide for publicity; but publicity may be excluded by a simple majority in the General Assembly and by a majority of any seven members in the Security Council.[9]

(dd) Solution Outside the Security Council

The fact that a decision of the Security Council is blocked by the veto of a permanent member does not mean that, if the decision shall refer to a dispute, this dispute will not be dealt with in some way. 'It does mean,' as the Australian delegate said at the San Francisco Conference[1] 'that it will be dealt with outside the Security Council; dealt with perhaps by two, perhaps by three, perhaps by four only of the great powers. In other words, it will not have that examination in accordance with the consistent principle of just settlement of disputes which will, I am sure, characterise all the proceedings of the Security Council itself. It would be a step backwards to the occasions

might well have been interpreted as a menace by nations not party to it. Accordingly, this method was rejected. The second method was through the establishment of a general security system based upon the principle of sovereign equality of all peace-loving states and upon the recognition of the predominant responsibility of the great powers in matters relating to peace and security. This was the policy adopted by this Government as reflected in the Moscow Declaration of October 30, 1943 . . . ' The difference between the 'formation of a permanent alliance among the great powers' and the policy adopted in the Charter is not very great, for the Organisation can work only on the basis of a permanent alliance of the great powers.

8 U.N.C.I.O. Doc. 967, III/1/48, pp. 2 f.

9 Cf. *supra*, p. 238.

1 U.N.C.I.O. Doc. 1149, III/11, p. 25.

before the Great War in which settlements of disputes were often made outside the League of Nations altogether and in which the processes of the League were not utilised. There were, side by side, the League with its principles, its procedures, and its jurisdiction, and parallel to it and in rivalry with it, arrangements made for settlement which did not, as we know, conform to the great principles of the League of Nations.'

C. *The 'Primary Responsibilities' of the Great Powers as justification of Their Veto Right*

The privileged position which the Charter grants the five great powers in conferring upon each of them a permanent seat in the Security Council and the veto right is justified in the Statement of the Four Sponsoring Powers by their 'primary responsibilities.' In the discussions of the San Francisco Conference great stress was laid on these special responsibilities of the five powers. The Summary Report of the 10th meeting of Committee III/1 [2] contains a statement of the delegate of the Soviet Union, in which 'it was admitted that the right of "veto" would put the permanent members of the Council in a special position but it was pointed out that this corresponded to the responsibilities and duties that would be imposed upon them.' At the 11th meeting of Committee III/1 [3] the representative of Yugoslavia, in defending the voting procedure in the Security Council as proposed by the sponsoring governments, declared 'that the responsibility of the permanent members undoubtedly far surpassed that of the non-permanent'; and even the Cuban representative who was against the veto right of the permanent members of the Security Council admitted 'that the responsibility of the great powers surpassed that of the other powers.'[4] This may be true from a political point of view. Legally the five privileged powers have no other duties or responsibilities than all the other Members of the United Nations. The Charter confers 'primary responsibility for the maintenance of international peace and security' upon the Security Council (Article 24, paragraph 1), not upon its permanent members.[5] Article 106, it is true, authorises the

[2] U.N.C.I.O. Doc. 459, III/1/22, p. 1.

[3] U.N.C.I.O. Doc. 486, III/1/24, p. 5.

[4] *Ibid.*, p. 5.

[5] The Summary Report of the 7th meeting of Committee III/1 (U.N.C.I.O. Doc. 338, III/1/14, pp. 1 f) contains the following statement: 'In opposition to the Mexican proposal [to change the designation of permanent seats on the Council to semi-permanent, which would give the Assembly an opportunity at the end of an eight-year period to reconsider the allocation of seats in this category] the comment was made that states designated as permanent members would not have the sole responsibility for the maintenance of peace. The five governments had been made permanent members because they formed a necessary and sufficient nucleus of power, but every member, great or small, would have the same obligation to do all within its power to preserve peace. The opinion was voiced that while it was possible to refer to the primary responsibility of the Security Council it was

five great powers to take such joint action on behalf of the Organisation as may be necessary for the purpose of maintaining international peace and security. This responsibility, however, is imposed upon them only ' pending the coming into force of such special agreements as in the opinion of the Security Council enable it to begin the exercise of its responsibilities under Article 42,' that is to say, only for the transitional period during which the Security Council cannot take enforcement action involving the use of armed force. Hence the responsibility of the five great powers under Article 106 cannot jusitfy their privileged position within the Security Council.

D. *Progress as Compared with the Covenant?*

The Statement of the Four Sponsoring Powers justifies the voting procedure in the Security Council further in maintaining that it represents a progress in two respects, as compared with the Covenant of the League of Nations. First, the rule excluding parties to a dispute from voting in a decision relating to the dispute has a wider scope in the Charter than it had in the Covenant. It is true that this rule, according to the wording of Article 15, paragraphs 6 and 7, of the Covenant, was restricted to recommendations made for the settlement of a dispute. But, according to Article 15, paragraph 10, the rule applied not only to recommendations made by the Council, but also to recommendations made by the Assembly. Under the Charter the rule applies only to decision of the Security Council, not of the General Assembly. The practice of the League went further than the wording of the Covenant. There was an outspoken tendency to consider the principle that nobody should be at the same time judge and party a universally recognised rule of law. But first of all this principle was expressly accepted in Article 16, paragraph 4, of the Covenant, according to which in the decision of the Council concerning the expulsion

juridically impossible to invest member states with different degrees of responsibilities.' *The Report to the President*, too, stresses the ' predominant ' or ' special ' responsibilities of the great powers for the maintenance of peace. On page 67 we read: ' The provisions for the Security Council recognise the special responsibilities of the great powers for maintaining the peace and the fact that the maintenance of their unity is the crucial political problem of our time.' But the *Report* recognises that it is the Security Council which is 'charged with the principal responsibility' for the maintenance of peace. In view of the fact that the majority of the members of the Security Council are smaller powers it is hardly possible to identify the Security Council with the great powers. It is even more problematical to say that the Security Council is so organised as to 'afford full opportunity for the great powers to maintain . . . this essential unity,' if on the next page it stated: 'The prestige of the Security Council, its influence in world affairs generally, and its success in the maintenance of peace and security will depend upon the degree to which unity is achieved among the great powers.' The organisation of the Security Council presupposes, but does not ' afford ' the unity of the great powers.

of a member the representative of a state to be expelled was excluded from voting. This is not the case under the Charter. The second point in which, according to the Statement of the Four Sponsoring Governments, the voting procedure in the Security Council constitutes a progress as compared with the Covenant is that a majority of seven from eleven votes, even if it has to include the concurring vote of five permanent members, makes the operation of the Council less subject to obstruction than was the case under the Covenant's rule of complete unanimity.

This is only to a certain extent true. For the veto right of the five permanent members of the Security Council may block essential action of the Organisation in cases where the principle of complete unanimity of the Covenant could not have this effect. The decentralisation of the procedure for the execution of sanctions, so characteristic of the Covenant and generally recognised as one of its greatest insufficiencies, made it yet possible that sanctions could be directed even against a great power, permanent member of the Council. This was especially true of economic sanctions. Their performance did not require any action of the Council. Under Article 16, paragraph 1, of the Covenant, it was upon the individual Member state to decide whether the Covenant has been violated by another state, and to apply to that state the economic measures determined in this paragraph. No decision of the Council was necessary for this purpose. Even military sanctions to be directed against a great power were not excluded under the Covenant. According to Article 16, paragraph 2, the Council was authorised 'to recommend' to the several governments concerned what effective military, naval or air force the members of the League should severally contribute to the armed forces to be used to protect the covenants of the League. Such 'recommendations,' it is true, required a unanimous vote of all members of the League represented at the meeting of the Council. But such recommendations had no legally binding force; they had only a moral or political importance. Hence there was no essential difference between a decision of the Council adopted by a unanimous and that adopted by a majority vote. The latter had no legal effect; but in this respect it did not differ from the former, which, too, was of a certain moral or political importance. Under the Charter, no enforcement action, especially no economic enforcement action, is possible except through the Security Council. Hence the veto right of the great powers works in every case and, consequently, enforcement action against a great power is excluded.[6] Strange as it may seem, the centralisation of the procedure for the

[6] The statement made by the representative of the United States at the 44th meeting of the General Assembly, 'The permanent members are bound legally and morally in the same degree as all other Members of the United Nations . . . ' (Journal of the United Nations, No. 20: Suppl. A–A/P.V./44, p. 243) is not quite correct, since the sanctions which constitute the legal obligations are applicable only to Members which are not permanent members of the Security Council.

execution of enforcement measures, a great progress of the Charter in one respect, turns out to be a regrettable regress in another respect. It is a progress only in so far as the enforcement measures are to be directed against states not permanent members of the Security Council; it is a regress in so far as they actually cannot be directed against a great power.

The veto right of the five permanent members has also other effects which make it doubtful whether the majority principle combined with the privilege of veto right conferred only on the five great powers is preferable to the rule of complete unanimity.

A permanent member of the Security Council may exercise its veto right not only in its own affairs but also in the interest of another state. Hence the members which have no such right may be induced to secure for themselves the friendship and protection of one of the five great powers. Since the Security Council is not bound strictly to comply with existing law, it is more important for a state not a permanent member of the Security Council to have a friend or protector among the five great powers than carefully to fulfil its obligations under the Charter. If a state can rely upon one of the five powers no action can be taken against it, even in case of open violation of the law. The veto right of the five permanent members of the Security Council may lead to a political system of more or less open clientage,[7] that is to say, to

[7] It is significant that the delegate of Czechoslovakia in defending the veto right of the five great powers on which the delegate of Soviet Russia so energetically insisted, declared at the 17th meeting of Committee III/1 (U.N.C.I.O. Doc. 922, III/1/44, p. 1): 'The veto, far from being an instrument directed against the small powers, might very well be exercised in the interests of smaller nations. Appreciation of this possibility was important, for it would prevent the impression that might arise from the debates here of a struggle between large and small powers.' At the 11th meeting of Committee III/1 (U.N.C.I.O. Doc. 486, III/1/24, p. 4) the delegate of Norway declared: 'the Yalta unanimity rule [meaning the unanimity of the five great powers] meant that each nation might be reasonably sure that there would be no intervention in domestic affairs. Thus, unanimity might be regarded as a safeguard to the smaller nations.' This statement hardly means anything else but: the veto right gives a great power the possibility of protecting a small power against intervention on the part of the Organisation. At the same meeting (p. 6) the Cuban delegate declared: 'The right of "veto" was very dangerous because if a conflict arose between two small nations, one of them might obtain the support of a great power in order to continue its war and thus again involve the whole world.'

At the 45th meeting of the General Assembly the delegate of the Ukrainian Republic declared that an abolishment of the veto right of the great Powers is 'aimed against small and medium nations. Let us imagine for a moment the situation in which small and medium nations would find themselves if Article 27 were abolished and if a bloc of one group of certain nations were to dominate the Security Council completely. There cannot be the smallest doubt that such a situation would react most painfully against the interest of medium and small nations which would be compelled to accept any decision thrust on them by some monopolistic bloc.' (Journal of the United Nations, No. 20: Suppl. A–A/P.V./45, p. 260.)

a dismemberment of the Organisation into five groups of states each of them taking advantage of the privilege of its patron. The principle of complete unanimity does not create such a tendency.

The Statement of the Four Sponsoring Governments stresses that the five permanent members of the Security Council cannot act by themselves since even a non-procedural decision requires 'the concurring votes of at least two of the non-permanent members.' The political dependence of the smaller states on the great powers established by the voting procedure of Article 27 will make it not too difficult for the five permanent members to get two non-permanent members to vote for their agreement. By the fact that five of the eleven members of the Security Council are permanent and have a veto right, this body is actually divided into two groups, an upper and a lower house, as it were. It is useless to submit a non-procedural matter to the lower house (the six non-permanent members), before the upper house (the five permanent members) has reached a unanimous decision on that matter. In the lower house even no majority is required. Two concurring votes suffice. If the real structure of the Security Council is taken into consideration it is not correct to say —as the Statement does—that 'at least' the votes of two non-permanent members are required for a valid decision of the Security Council. It is more correct to say that the consent of *no more* than two permament members suffices to transform a unanimous decision of the five permanent members into a valid decision of the Security Council.

The unanimity rule laid down in the Covenant for the decision of the Council was of relatively little importance since the decisions of the Council in the most serious matters, namely under Article 10 and Article 16, had only the character of 'advice' or 'recommendation.' The members of the League not represented on the Council were not obliged to carry out the decisions of the Council in these matters. The machinery of the League was from the very beginning intended to operate—in conformity with the usual type of international organisation—on a contractual basis and—in this sense—laid hold of all members to the same extent. The Charter, however, establishes an obligation of all the members to carry out the majority vote decisions of the Security Council, especially with respect to the enforcement action to be taken by the Council. The machinery of the United Nations goes far beyond the usual international type of organisation: it approaches the national type. The Security Council has almost the character of a governmental body. Hence the political measurements used for forms of government are applicable to it. The question of democracy and of autocracy becomes unavoidable. The veto right of the five permanent members of the Security Council, which places the privileged powers above the law of the United Nations, establishes their legal hegemony over all the other members of the Organisation and thus stamps on it the mark of an autocratic or aristocratic regime.

This is all the more critical as the United Nations presents itself ideologically as the crowning of a war waged for a victory not only of arms but of ideals, especially of the ideal of democracy. If the Security Council by its voting procedure was to be elevated to the rank of a government at all, only a democratic form of government, that is to say, the majority vote principle without veto rights of privileged members, was adequate. For only such an organisation could avoid the resentful resistance of all the non-privileged states which became manifest already at the San Francisco Conference.

One of the essential elements of democracy is the principle of equality. It may be doubted whether the principle of democratic equality is applicable to subjects other than human individuals. But if an international community composed of states can be established under a democratic constitution at all, the principle of equality must refer to the states as members of the community. This is the reason why the Charter proclaims as its first principle the sovereign equality of all its members. There is an open contradiction between the political ideology of the United Nations and its legal constitution. And this contradiction may completely paralyse the great advantage that the Charter tried to gain over the Covenant by conferring upon the Security Council a power almost equal to that of a government.

E. *Revision of the Veto Right of the Permanent Members of the Security Council*

The paralysing effect of the rule requiring unanimity of the permanent members of the Security Council for non-procedural decisions has led to a strong movement for a revision of Article 27, paragraph 3. In view of the actual attitude of the permanent members of the Council, especially the Soviet Union, it is not very likely that this movement will result in an amendment of the Charter. All that has been reached, until now, are some resolutions of the General Assembly which have no legal effect. A resolution adopted at its 61st meeting on December 13, 1946, runs as follows:

> The General Assembly, mindful of the Purposes and Principles of the Charter of the United Nations, and having taken notice of the divergencies which have arisen in regard to the application and interpretation of Article 27 of the Charter:
>
> Earnestly requests the permanent members of the Security Council to make every effort, in consultation with one another and with fellow members of the Security Council, to ensure that the use of the special voting privilege of its permanent members does not impede the Security Council in reaching decisions promptly;
>
> Recommends to the Security Council the early adoption of practices and procedures, consistent with the Charter, to assist

in reducing the difficulties in the application of Article 27 and to ensure the prompt and effective exercise by the Security Council of its functions; and

Further recommends that, in developing such practices and procedures, the Security Council take into consideration the views expressed by Members of the United Nations during the second part of the first session of the General Assembly.[8]

At its 123rd meeting on November 21, 1947, the General Assembly adopted the following resolution:

The General Assembly, in the exercise of its power to make recommendations relating to the powers and functions of any organs of the United Nations (Article 10 of the Charter),

Requests the Interim Committee of the General Assembly, in accordance with paragraph 2 (*a*) of resolution 111 (II) of the General Assembly of November 13, 1947, establishing that Committee, to:

1. Consider the problem of voting in the Security Council, taking into account all proposals which have been or may be submitted by Members of the United Nations to the second session of the General Assembly or to the Interim Committee;

2. Consult with any committee which the Security Council may designate to co-operate with the Interim Committee in the study of the problem;

3. Report, with its conclusions, to the third session of the General Assembly, the report to be transmitted to the Secretary-General not later than July 15, 1948, and by the Secretary-General to the Member States and to the General Assembly;

Requests the permanent members of the Security Council to consult with one another on the problem of voting in the Security Council in order to secure agreement among them on measures to ensure the prompt and effective exercise by the Security Council of its functions.[9]

The Interim Committee of the General Assembly resolved at its 19th meeting on July 9, 1948, to make a series of recommendations on the problem of voting in the Security Council, including the following: That members of the Security Council recognise 36 items in a list of possible decisions as procedural, and conduct business accordingly—that is, take decisions on them by the vote of any seven members. These are (*a*) 'all decisions of the Security Council adopted in application of provisions which appear in the Charter under the heading "Procedure"'; (*b*) 'all decisions which concern the relationship between the Security

[8] Resolutions adopted by the General Assembly, Doc. A/64/Add. 1, p. 64.

[9] Resolutions adopted by the General Assembly, Doc. A/519, p. 23.

Council and other organs of the United Nations, or by which the Security Council seeks the assistance of other organs of the United Nations, relate to the internal procedure of the United Nations'; (*c*) 'all decisions of the Security Council which relate to its internal functioning and the conduct of its business'; (*d*) 'certain decisions of the Security Council, which bear a close analogy to decisions included under the above-mentioned criteria'; (*e*) 'certain decisions of the Security Council . . . which are instrumental in arriving at or in following up a procedural decision.' The Interim Committee recommended further that the permanent members agree to adopt the simple seven-vote rule for a number of other items—whether these are considered procedural or non-procedural. In effect, this would mean that the permanent members would agree to drop the 'veto' in cases involving: peaceful settlement of disputes; application for membership in the United Nations; and the so-called 'double veto' decisions on whether a question is substantive and therefore subject to the 'veto' or not; that wherever possible, the permanent members of the Council consult among themselves concerning important decisions to be taken; and to consult, before a vote is taken, if their unanimity is required to enable the Security Council to function effectively; if there is no unanimity, the minority of the permanent members would only exercise their 'veto' only when they consider the question of vital importance to the United Nations as a whole; the 'veto' would not be exercised simply because a proposal does not go far enough to satisfy the permanent members. After approving these proposals for submission to the General Assembly, the Interim Committee also recommended that the Assembly consider at its coming session whether the time had come or not to call a General Conference to amend the Charter.[1]

3. Competence

A. *General Determination of the Competence of the Security Council (Article 24)*

The competence of the Security Council coincides to a great extent with the competence of the entire Organisation; for the performance of almost all legally important functions of the United Nations is conferred upon the Security Council either exclusively or together with the General Assembly.

The competence of the Security Council is determined in a general way by Article 24, paragraphs 1 and 2:

> 1. In order to ensure prompt and effective action by the United Nations, its Members confer on the Security Council primary responsibility for the maintenance of international peace and security, and agree that in carrying out its duties under this responsibility the Security Council acts on their behalf.

[1] Doc. A/578.

> 2. In discharging these duties the Security Council shall act in accordance with the Purposes and Principles of the United Nations. The specific powers granted to the Security Council for the discharge of these duties are laid down in Chapters VI, VII, VIII and XII.

Paragraph 1 of Article 24 contains three statements: 1. that the Members of the United Nations ' confer on the Security Council primary responsibility for the maintenance of international peace and security '; 2. that the purpose of conferring upon the Security Council primary responsibility for the maintenance of international peace and security is: ' to ensure prompt and effective action by the United Nations '; 3. that the Members ' agree that in carrying out its duties under this responsibility the Security Council acts on their behalf.'

Only the first and second statements have legal importance. The third statement is a theoretical characterisation of the function of the Security Council, which, as such, is legally irrelevant and, in addition, incorrect. The Security Council is an organ of the United Nations, as Article 7, paragraph 1, of the Charter correctly—though superfluously—states. As an organ of the United Nations the Security Council acts on behalf of the United Nations, not on behalf of its Members. ' On behalf ' of the Members means: as their agent or representative; which is evidently not the case since not all Members are represented in the Security Council and the latter may act on the basis of a majority vote decision, that is to say, against the will of certain Members. Under Article 25, the Members are obliged to carry out the decisions of the Security Council. Hence they are subordinated to this organ, a relationship which is incompatible with the statement that this organ acts on their behalf. Since the Security Council acts on behalf of the United Nations and not on behalf of its Members, any act of the Security Council is—as the first words of Article 24 correctly state—' action by the United Nations,' and not action by the Member states. Acts of the Council, that is to say, acts performed in accordance with the rules of the Charter regulating the functions of the Security Council, are—as are the acts of any organ of the United Nations—to be imputed to the Organisation, not to its Members. To disregard this imputation to the Organisation to make the Organisation disappear behind its Members is the tendency of the sovereignty-dogma which is incompatible with the idea of a legal order binding upon the states, and especially with the idea of states being members of an international organisation imposing obligations upon its members.

The same dogma induced the formula: ' the Members agree that . . .' by which the contractual character of the functions conferred upon the Security Council is stressed. It has been pointed out in another chapter of this study[2] that this formula has the same character as the

[2] Cf. *supra*, p. 8.

so-called promulgatory clauses used in statutes to testify that the statute has been issued in conformity with the Constitution; and that in treaties promulgatory clauses, that is to say, clauses declaring that the rules laid down in the treaty have been created by an agreement of states, are superfluous. Nevertheless, that treaties usually contain such clauses not only as a general introduction to the entire text of the treaty, as a preamble, but also as an introduction to particular provisions, is the result of the tendency to lay stress on the principle of sovereignty, to express the idea that the provisions of the treaty are not imposed upon the states obligated by the treaty, but the result of their free will, that they are bound by the provisions of the treaty only because they have consented to them. Whether this doctrine is or is not correct, inserted into the text of an international treaty it is superfluous, and has no more authority than it has if advocated in a textbook.

It is the sovereignty-dogma which also leads to the incorrect formula: 'the Members confer on the Security Council, etc.' It is not the Members, it is the Charter, which confers responsibilities on the Security Council. The formula cannot be justified by stating that the Charter is a treaty concluded by the Members; for the Charter is not a treaty concluded by the 'Members,' but by states which became 'Members' only through the Charter, after this treaty came into force.

The meaning of the phrase: 'In order to ensure prompt and effective action by the United Nations,' is not clear, since the term 'action' is ambiguous. As pointed out, this term is used in the Charter with different meanings.[3] It sometimes designates any act whatever, sometimes enforcement action. In Article 37, paragraph 2, it designates 'recommendation'; in Article 11, paragraph 2, probably, enforcement action. Enforcement action, as determined in Chapter VII, is the specific action reserved to the Security Council. No other organ of the United Nations (except the five great powers during the transition period, under Article 106) and no Member (except in case of self-defence under Article 51 or acting against an ex-enemy state under Article 53, paragraph 3, and Article 107) is authorised by the Charter to take such action. Article 1, paragraph 1, of the Charter, declares that the first Purpose of the United Nations is to maintain international peace and security and to that end to take 'effective collective measures,' etc. By 'effective' measures enforcement action is meant. Hence the 'effective' action by the United Nations referred to in Article 24, paragraph 1, might be interpreted to mean enforcement action. This interpretation, however, is not consistent with the statement of Article 24: that in order to ensure prompt and effective action by the United Nations 'primary responsibility for the maintenance of international peace and security' is conferred upon the Security Council. Peace and security are to be maintained under the Charter not only by enforcement action but also by other actions. Article 1, paragraph 1, of the Charter, in determining

[3] Cf. *supra*, pp. 91 f., 204 f.

the actions which the Organisation may take in order to maintain international peace and security mentions not only 'effective measures for the prevention and removal of threats to the peace, and for the suppression of acts of aggression or other breaches of the peace,' meaning the enforcement actions specified in Articles 39, 41 and 42, but also: 'adjustment or settlement of international disputes or situations which might lead to a breach of the peace' to be brought about 'by peaceful means, and in conformity with the principles of justice and international law.' Enforcement action and adjustment or settlement of disputes and specific situations by peaceful means are the actions which the Organisation may take in order to achieve the Purpose of the United Nations 'to maintain international peace and security,' as formulated in Article 1, paragraph 1, of the Charter. The other Purposes laid down in Article 1—it is true—shall also serve the maintenance of peace; one of these Purposes is even formulated 'to take appropriate measures to strengthen universal peace.' But by the term 'maintenance of international peace and security' as used in Article 24, the Purpose determined in Article 1, paragraph 1, that is to say the maintenance of peace in this narrower sense may be meant. If so, in conferring on the Council 'primary responsibility for the maintenance of international peace and security,' Article 24 restricts the competence of this organ to the actions determined in Article 1, paragraph 1. Article 24, paragraph 2, expressly provides that the Security Council in discharging its duties 'shall act in accordance with the Purposes and Principles of the United Nations,' that means: in accordance with the provisions of Articles 1 and 2 of the Charter. The provision directly applying to the 'responsibility for the maintenance of international peace and security' is that of Article 1, paragraph 1, referring to the Purpose 'to maintain international peace and security.'

That the words 'the maintenance of international peace and security' in paragraph 1 of Article 24 have the same meaning as the words 'to maintain international peace and security' as used in Article 1, paragraph 1, to characterise a specific Purpose of the United Nations, is a very plausible interpretation and probably corresponds to the intention of those who drafted Article 24;[4] but it is not the only possible one in view of the wording. For paragraph 2 of Article 24, dealing with the duties (meaning, the functions) which the Security Council has under the responsibility for the maintenance of international peace and security, says: 'The specific powers granted to the Security Council for the discharge of these duties are laid down in Chapters VI, VII, VIII and XII.' Chapters VI, VII and VIII, determine functions of the Council corresponding to the means which Article 1, paragraph 1, authorises the Organisation to take for the purpose to maintain international peace and security. Chapters VI and VIII deal with the settlement of disputes and the adjustment of other situations, Chapter VII with enforcement actions. But Chapter XII refers to the trusteeship system, and the functions conferred

[4] Cf. Note 6.

upon the Council in this Chapter are different from those conferred by Article 1, paragraph 1, upon the Organisation for the maintenance of international peace and security, in the narrower and specific sense of this term. If the trusteeship functions of the Security Council are duties which the Council has under its responsibility for the maintenance of international peace and security, this term must be used in paragraph 1 of Article 24 in a wider sense than in paragraph 1 of Article 1. Besides, the Charter confers functions (or 'duties') upon the Council not only in Chapters VI, VII, VIII and XII, but also in other parts,[5] especially in the Statute of the International Court. Hence, the formula 'responsibility for the maintenance of international peace and security' may be interpreted to mean about the same as the statement of the Preamble, that the peoples of the United Nations unite their strength 'to maintain international peace and security,' defining thus the universal purpose of the Organisation, without implying any specific functions. Then, Article 24, paragraph 1, means nothing else but that the Charter confers upon the Security Council primary responsibility for the achievement of the general purpose of the United Nations. As to the means by which the Security Council shall discharge this responsibility, Article 24 says nothing. The actions which the Council is authorised to take are determined in other Articles of the Charter (and the Statute). Article 24 only stipulates that, in taking these actions or—what amounts to the same—in fulfilling the functions conferred upon it by the Charter, the Security Council shall act in accordance with the provisions of Articles 1 and 2 of the Charter. It may be that paragraph 1 of Article 24 was intended only to stress the political importance of the Council, not to establish a positive legal effect. If this interpretation is accepted, Article 24, paragraph 1, is not, as it would seem, a general determination of the competence of the Security Council. This competence is determined in other provisions of the Charter, not in a general way but by conferring on the Council particular functions in different fields.

The maintenance of international peace and security, this term taken in a narrower or a wider sense, is not only a responsibility of the Security Council but also of the General Assembly. But only the Security Council is authorised by the Charter to maintain international peace and security by enforcement actions. It may be that the term 'primary' responsibility is used in Article 24 in order to justify that only the Council is competent to take enforcement measures for the maintenance of peace. The term 'primary' is only a theoretical description of the responsibility conferred upon the Security Council by the Charter. Whether this description is correct depends on these provisions as compared with those which confer responsibilities for the maintenance of international peace

[5] At the 36th meeting of the Security Council the delegate of Mexico stated that Article 24, paragraph 2, first sentence, 'invests the Council with implied powers wider in scope than the specific powers laid down in Chapters VI, VII, VIII and XII, to which the second sentence of the same paragraph and Article refers.' (Journal of the Security Council, 1st Year, No. 30, p. 594.)

and security upon other organs of the United Nations, especially on the General Assembly. As a matter of fact, the Charter confers upon the Security Council more important responsibilities, or—correctly formulated—more effective powers for the maintenance of peace, than upon any other organ of the United Nations.

Article 24, paragraph 1, may be interpreted to confer on the Security Council the competence to maintain peace by the means determined in Article 1, paragraph 1, of the Charter; or to confer no particular or general competence upon the Council. But it can hardly be interpreted to confer on the Council the competence to maintain peace and security —in the widest possible sense—by any means that the Council may choose. Such interpretation is incompatible with the statement of Article 24, paragraph 2, that the powers granted to the Council for the discharge of the duties which it has under the responsibility for the maintenance of peace are laid down in Chapters VI, VII, VIII and XII. For even if it must be admitted that this enumeration is incomplete since the Charter confers powers upon the Security Council also in other Chapters and in the Statute, an extensive interpretation cannot go further than to the assumption that the powers of the Council referred to in the last sentence of paragraph 2 are those granted to the Council by the Charter (including the Statute), and not only those granted by the Chapters mentioned in that sentence.

It is impossible to interpret Article 24 to mean that it confers upon the Council powers not conferred upon it in other Articles of the Charter (or the Statute).[6] The first sentence of paragraph 2 refers to the ' duties '

[6] When the question arose whether the Security Council was competent to approve the Annexes VI, VII and VIII of the Peace Treaty with Italy and thus to assume the functions conferred upon it by this treaty, the Secretary-General submitted to the Security Council a statement in which he interpreted Article 24 to confer upon the Security Council powers limited only by ' the fundamental principles and purposes found in Chapter I of the Charter.' (Official Records of the Security Council, 2nd Year, No. 3, pp. 44 f.) The Secretary-General tried to prove in his statement that the intention of the Charter to confer upon the Security Council the general competence to maintain peace and security and to restrict this competence only by the provisions establishing the Purposes and Principles of the United Nations (that is, Articles 1 and 2), results from the records of the San Francisco Conference. He referred to U.N.C.I.O. Doc. 597, III/1/30. But this document does not refer to a discussion of Article 24 (Chapter VI, Section B, paragraph 1 of the Dumbarton Oaks Proposals) but to a discussion of Article 25 (Chapter VI, Section B, paragraph 4, of the Proposals). It was a discussion on an amendment suggested by the delegate of Belgium to add in paragraph 4 (Article 25 of the Charter) after the words 'Security Council' the words: 'taken under Chapter VIII (of the Dumbarton Oaks Proposals, corresponding to Chapters VI, VII and VIII of the Charter). The representative of the United Kingdom spoke against this amendment; he suggested that the phrase ' in accordance with the provisions of the Charter ' in Article 25 (definitive text: in accordance with the present Charter) ' sufficiently met the point raised by the Belgian delegate. . . . He had no objection to the Belgian amendment provided it was certain that no decisions relating to other parts of the Charter would thereby be excluded.' The delegate of the Soviet Union likewise declared to be against the Belgian amendment; but he expressly stated: ' Paragraph 4

which the Council has under the responsibility conferred upon it for the maintenance of peace. If the interpretation of paragraph 1 is accepted that ' maintenance of international peace ' is a reference to the general purpose of the Organisation and not identical with the particular purpose of the United Nations as determined in Article 1, paragraph 1, the ' duties under this responsibility ' include all the ' duties ' conferred upon the Council by other Articles of the Charter. If the other interpretation is accepted, the duties of the Council under the responsibility for the maintenance of peace are only the duties conferred upon it for the settlement of disputes, the adjustment of situations and the enactment of enforcement measures. The wording of the last sentence of paragraph 2 is neither compatible with the one nor with the other interpretation. This sentence says either too much (by mentioning Chapter XII) or too little (by not referring to other Chapters of the Charter and to the Statute). Besides, as pointed out,[7] the term ' duties ' is not correct. Since there is no provision for a sanction which might be executed against the Security Council—or any other organ of the United Nations—the Charter does not impose ' duties ' upon these organs but confers functions or powers upon them. The heading under which Article 24 is presented reads ' Functions and Powers,' not duties.

Under Articles 10, 11, 13 and 14, the General Assembly is authorised to make recommendations; in accordance with express provisions of Articles 10 and 11, such recommendations may be made to the Security Council; since Articles 13 and 14 do not determine to whom the General Assembly may make recommendations, under these Articles too, the Assembly may make recommendations to the Security Council. Then the question arises whether the General Assembly is authorised to recommend to the Security Council any action whatever with respect to

did not give unlimited powers to the Security Council.' The representative of Canada stated that: ' since paragraph 4 [Article 25 of the Charter] immediately followed paragraph 3 [Article 24, paragraph 2, of the Charter], in which it was stated that the specific powers conferred upon the Security Council were laid down in Chapter VIII [Chapters VI, VII and VIII, of the Charter], paragraph 4 should be interpreted also as referring exclusively to Chapter VIII.' This discussion at the San Francisco Conference shows that some delegates were of the opinion that the Security Council was not restricted to the specific powers set forth in Chapters VI, VII and VIII (Chapter XII was not yet inserted into the text of the Charter). But it does not show a generally accepted opinion that the powers conferred upon the Council by Article 24 are limited only by being ' subject to the purposes and principles of the United Nations,' as the Secretary-General maintained in his statement.

A Working Paper prepared by the Secretariat in the Palestine question (Doc. A/AC.21/13, p. 6) contains the statement that the Security Council by its decision approving the Annexes VI, VII and VIII to the Peace Treaty with Italy, ' recognised the principle that it has sufficient power, under the terms of Article 24 of the Charter, to assume new responsibilities, on condition that they relate directly or even indirectly to the maintenance of international peace and security, and that in discharging these duties, the Security Council acts in accordance with the purposes and principles of the United Nations (Article 1 and 2 of the Charter).'

7 Cf. *supra*, p. 154.

matters referred to in Articles 10, 11, 13 and 14, or only actions which the Security Council is competent to perform according to other provisions of the Charter determining its powers. As pointed out in another connection, the Security Council is not bound to carry out the recommendations made to it by the Assembly under Articles 11, 12, 13 or 14.[8] But is the Security Council allowed to perform an action recommended to it by the General Assembly although no other provision of the Charter confers upon the Council the competence to perform it? An affirmative as well as a negative answer is possible. If the first mentioned interpretation is accepted, the General Assembly has under Articles 10, 11, 13 and 14, the power to enlarge the competence of the Security Council as established by other provisions of the Charter. Although the wording of the Charter does not exclude this interpretation, it was probably not intended by those who drafted the Charter;[9] for it implies a certain superiority of the Assembly over the Council, which is not in conformity with the general idea of the relationship between the two organs prevailing at the San Francisco Conference. If, in conformity with this view, the other interpretation is accepted, the Security Council can not be authorised by a recommendation made to it by the General Assembly under Articles 10, 11, 13 or 14, to perform an action which is not within its power as determined by other Articles of the Charter.[1]

[8] Cf. *supra*, pp. 196 f. In the discussion of the Palestine question in the Security Council in February, 1948, the representative of the United States stated: 'The recommendations of the General Assembly have great moral force which applies to all members regardless of the view they hold or the votes which they may have cast on any particular recommendation. Similarly the Security Council, although not bound under the Charter to accept and carry out General Assembly recommendations, is nevertheless expected to give great weight to them.' (U.S. Mission to the United Nations, Press Release 394, February 24, 1948, p. 1.) At the meeting of the Security Council on April 1, 1948, the representative of Belgium stated that the Security Council was under no obligation to comply with the request the General Assembly made in its resolution of November 29, 1947. (Official Records of the Security Council, 3rd Year, No. 52, p. 4.) Cf. the following Note.

[9] At the 254th meeting of the Security Council the representative of Syria declared with respect to the resolution of the General Assembly concerning the future government of Palestine (cf. *supra*, pp. 195 ff.) that it 'cannot be of any effect on the Security Council in the exercise of its duties, since the functions of the Security Council are limitatively defined in the Charter. The resolution of the General Assembly may not in any way add to, delete from or modify those functions.' (Doc. S/P.V. 254, p. 11.) At the 327th meeting of the Security Council the representative of Argentina stated in the discussion of the Spain question: 'I was not aware of the fact that the General Assembly was in a position to grant powers to the Security Council; until now I have always believed that both the Security Council and the General Assembly itself derive their powers from the Charter.' (Official Records of the Security Council, 3rd Year, No. 90, p. 6.)

[1] Acting under Article 14 of the Charter, the General Assembly at its 128th meeting adopted a resolution regarding the future government of Palestine (cf. *supra*, pp. 195 ff.) in which it requested that:

(*a*) The Security Council take the necessary measures as provided for in the plan for its implementation;

(*b*) The Security Council consider, if circumstances during the transitional

According to the first sentence of Article 24, paragraph 2, the Security Council shall act in accordance with the provisions of Article 1 and Article 2 of the Charter—determining the Purposes and Principles of

period require such consideration, whether the situation in Palestine constitutes a threat to the peace. If it decides that such a threat exists, and in order to maintain international peace and security, the Security Council should supplement the authorisation of the General Assembly by taking measures, under Articles 39 and 41 of the Charter, to empower the United Nations Commission, as provided in this resolution, to exercise in Palestine the functions which are assigned to it by this resolution;

(*c*) The Security Council determine as a threat to the peace, breach of the peace or act of aggression, in accordance with Article 39 of the Charter, any attempt to alter by force the settlement envisaged by this resolution.

In the same resolution the General Assembly placed the Commission destined to administer Palestine after the withdrawal of the mandatory power 'under the guidance of the Security Council,' which implies the recommendation to the Security Council to direct the administration of Palestine through the Commission. Was the Security Council competent to carry out these recommendations of the General Assembly, without regard to the question as to whether the General Assembly was competent to establish a commission with the power to take over the administration of Palestine? As to the measures for the implementation of the Plan of Partition, not having the character of enforcement measures, two provisions of the Charter come into consideration: Article 36, paragraph 1, and Article 39. Under Article 36, paragraph 1 (referring to Article 33, paragraph 1) the Security Council is authorised to 'recommend appropriate procedures or methods' for the 'adjustment' of a situation the continuance of which is likely to endanger the maintenance of international peace and security. This Article was hardly applicable; first of all because the term 'appropriate procedure or methods of adjustment' must be interpreted to mean not substantive 'terms of settlement' as referred to in Article 37, paragraph 2, but only measures of a procedural character. (Cf. *infra*, p. 402.) The implementation of the Partition Plan, implying the establishment, by a commission of the General Assembly, of two new states, is much more than 'procedures or methods of adjustment.' Besides, the situation in Palestine as considered by the General Assembly was different from that authorising the Security Council to intervene under Article 36, paragraph 1. In its resolution regarding the future government of Palestine, the General Assembly 'considers that the present situation in Palestine is one which is likely to impair the general welfare and friendly relations among nations,' which is not identical with a situation 'the continuance of which is likely to endanger the maintenance of international peace and security.' Even if Article 36, paragraph 1, should be interpreted to authorise the Security Council to carry out the recommendations of the General Assembly, the Council could proceed under this Article only after having investigated the situation in Palestine under Article 34 of the Charter and after having determined that the continuance of the situation was likely to endanger the maintenance of international peace and security. The other provision conferring upon the Security Council the competence of intervening in a situation is that of Article 39. It authorises the Council to make recommendations of any kind whatsoever, or to take enforcement measures, regarding a situation which constitutes a threat to the peace, breach of the peace, or act of aggression. Under this Article the Security Council was certainly competent to carry out the recommendation of the General Assembly to take the necessary measures for the implementation of the Partition Plan; but only under the condition that the Security Council—as expressly provided for by Article 39—determined that the situation in Palestine constituted a threat to, or breach of, the peace; a possibility anticipated in the resolution of the General

the United Nations—in discharging all its ' duties ' (more correctly: its powers or functions). Since the Security Council has not true ' duties,' but only functions or powers, the phrasing of the second sentence: the

Assembly (clauses (*b*) and (*c*)). In recommending to the Security Council to decide whether the situation in Palestine constitutes a threat to the peace and in case the Council adopted such decision, to take the measure provided for in Articles 39 and 41, the General Assembly recommended nothing that was not within the competence of the Security Council. The same is true with respect to the recommendation to determine as a threat to the peace, breach of the peace, or act of aggression any attempt to alter by force the settlement envisaged by the resolution of the General Assembly. For it is within the discretion of the Security Council to determine what constitutes a threat to, or breach of, the peace. The argument advanced at the 267th meeting of the Security Council (Doc. S/P.V. 267) by the representative of Lebanon against the competence of the Security Council to deal with the Palestine question: that there existed no threat to international peace because the situation in Palestine interested and concerned only Palestine itself, is without foundation in the Charter. The interpretation suggested by the representative of the United States at the 253rd meeting of the Security Council, that under the Charter the Council was authorised to remove a threat to international peace, whether it arose from outside or inside Palestine, was correct. But his statement: that the Charter did not empower the Council to enforce a political settlement and therefore the Council was not competent to enforce the partition suggested by the General Assembly, is hardly in conformity with the Charter. If the Security Council considered the partition as suggested by the General Assembly as necessary for the maintenance of international peace, that is to say if the Council considered non-implementation of the partition plan as a threat to international peace, the Council was authorised by the Charter to take the measures referred to in Articles 39, 41, 42, for the purpose to maintain or restore peace by enforcing the partition plan.

As a matter of fact the Security Council took a series of measures regarding the situation in Palestine. But it did so without immediately determining that this situation was of the nature referred to in Article 35, paragraph 1, authorising the Council to recommend methods of peaceful adjustment, and without determining that the situation in Palestine constituted a threat to, or breach of, the peace within the meaning of Article 39, authorising the Council to make recommendations of any kind or take enforcement measures. Suggestions made by the representative of the United States (May 15, 1948) and later by the representative of the Soviet Union (May 27, 1948) failed of approval by the Council (cf. Annual Report of the Secretary-General on the Work of the Organisation. July 1, 1947–30, June, 1948. General Assembly, Official Records, Third Session: Suppl. No. 1, A/565, pp. 9, 10). Only on July 15, 1948, in view of the notorious state of war which existed in the relation between Arab states and the newly established state of Israel recognised by the United States and the Soviet Union, the Security Council adopted a resolution determining ' that the situation in Palestine constitutes a threat to the peace within the meaning of Article 39 of the Charter.' (Cf. United Nations Bulletin, Vol. V, p. 596.) The measures taken by the Security Council (until June 30, 1948) regarding the situation in Palestine were as follows: ' On March 5, 1948, the Council adopted a resolution calling upon the permanent members to consult and inform the Council regarding the situation with respect to Palestine, and to make recommendations to it regarding the guidance and instructions which the Council might usefully give to the Palestine Commission with a view to implementing the resolution of the General Assembly. The Council also appealed to all Governments and peoples to take all possible action to prevent or reduce disorders occurring in Palestine.' (Report of the Secretary-General, p. 5.) On April 1, 1948, the Security Council adopted a resolution calling for a truce in Palestine and a resolution

specific powers granted to the Security Council for the discharge of these duties (' duties ' meaning ' powers ' or ' functions '), is rather problematical. It amounts to the statement that specific powers are granted to

requesting the Secretary-General to convoke a special session of the General Assembly to consider further the question of the future government of Palestine (p. 6). On April 17, the Council adopted a resolution calling ' upon all persons and organisations in Palestine, especially the Arab Higher Committee and the Jewish Agency for Palestine, to cease all activities of a military or para-military nature, as well as acts of violence, terrorism and sabotage,' and also ' requested ' the United Kingdom Government, as long as it remained the Mandatory Power, to use its best efforts to bring all those concerned in Palestine to accept these measures. All Governments, and particularly those of the countries neighbouring upon Palestine, were asked to assist in the implementation of this resolution. On April 23, the Council established a Truce Commission for Palestine composed of representatives of those members of the Security Council which had career consular officers in Jerusalem, namely Belgium, France and the United States of America (Syria having indicated that it was not prepared to serve on the Commission), ' to assist the Security Council in supervising the implementation by the parties of the Council's resolution of April 17, 1948.' (p. 6.) On May 12, the Council ' authorised the President to advise the Truce Commission that it should explore and adopt such means of assistance as it might require in the performance of its functions.' (p. 6.) On May 18, the Council ' addressed a number of questions to the Governments of Egypt, Iraq, Lebanon, Saudi Arabia, Syria, Transjordan and Yemen, also to the Arab Higher Committee and the Jewish Authorities in Palestine, for the purpose of clarifying the situation subsequent to the armed intervention of the Arab States in Palestine. The Council requested replies to these questions within forty-eight hours as from noon, May 19, 1948, New York Standard Time.' (p. 9.) On May 22, the Council adopted a resolution calling ' upon all Governments and authorities to abstain from any hostile military action in Palestine and to issue a cease-fire order to their military and para-military forces to become effective thirty-six hours after midnight, May 22, New York Standard Time. At the request of the Arab States, the Council at its meeting on May 24, 1948, granted an extension of forty-eight hours ending May 26, 1948, noon, New York Standard Time.' (p. 10.) On May 29, the Council adopted a resolution calling ' for the cessation of hostilities in Palestine for a period of four weeks and instructing the United Nations Mediator for Palestine, appointed in virtue of the General Assembly resolution of May 14, to make contact with both parties, as soon as the cease-fire was in force, with a view to making recommendations to the Security Council about an eventual settlement for Palestine.' (p. 10.) The resolution also provided ' that, should the resolution be rejected, repudiated or violated by either party or both, the situation in Palestine would be reconsidered with a view to action under Chapter VII of the Charter.' (p. 10.) In this resolution, the Council instructed the Mediator, ' in concert with the Truce Commission, to supervise the observance of the truce. It decided also that they should be provided with a sufficient number of military observers.' (p. 12.) At the request of the Mediator, the states Members of the Truce Commission put at the disposal of the Mediator a number of military observers and a few patrol vessels and planes. (p. 12.) On June 2, the Council instructed the United Nations Mediator in Palestine ' to arrange, in consultation with the two parties and the Truce Commission, for the effective date of the cease-fire. The Council added that the cease-fire should be arranged as quickly as possible, taking into account the considerations attendant upon the problem of control.' (p. 11.)

These measures, insofar as they refer directly to the states involved in the situation in Palestine and the population of this territory, have the character of recommendations. In the main, these recommendations aimed at the establishment

the Security Council for the discharge of these powers. What is meant by ' specific powers ' is not clear. Are these powers ' specific ' because they are granted only to the Security Council, or are they ' specific ' in

of a truce, which means a substantive adjustment of the situation in Palestine. They were not mere recommendations of ' procedures or methods.' Recommendations of substantive terms of adjustment of a situation (not dealt with as a dispute referred to the Security Council under Articles 37 or 38) are possible only under Article 39. Such recommendations must be preceded by a decision of the Council determining the existence of a threat to, or breach of, the peace. In the resolution of July 15, 1948, the Security Council, after having determined that the situation in Palestine constituted a threat to the peace within the meaning of Article 39, did not make recommendations under Article 39, but applied Article 40, which authorises the Council to take ' provisional measures ' ' in order to prevent an aggravation of the situation ' referred to in Article 39, ' before making the recommendations or deciding upon the measures provided for in Article 39.' In applying Article 40 the Security Council may ' call upon the parties concerned to comply with such provisional measures as it deems necessary or desirable.' In its resolution of July 15, 1948, the Security Council ' ordered ' the parties to conduct themselves in a certain way. The resolution provides: The Security Council—

> Orders the Governments and authorities concerned, pursuant to Article 40 of the Charter of the United Nations, to desist from further military action and to this end to issue cease-fire orders to their military and para-military forces, to take effect at a time to be determined by the Mediator, but in any event not later than three days from the date of the adoption of this resolution;
>
> Declares that failure by any of the Governments or authorities concerned to comply with the preceding paragraph of this resolution would demonstrate the existence of a breach of the peace within the meaning of Article 39 of the Charter requiring immediate consideration by the Security Council with a view to such further action under Chapter 7 of the Charter as may be decided upon by the Council;
>
> Calls upon all Governments and authorities concerned to continue to co-operate with the Mediator with a view to the maintenance of peace in Palestine in conformity with the resolution adopted by the Security Council on May 29, 1948;
>
> Orders as a matter of special and urgent necessity an immediate and unconditioned cease-fire in the City of Jerusalem to take effect 24 hours from the time of the adoption of this resolution, and instructs the Truce Commission to take any necessary steps to make this cease-fire effective;
>
> Instructs the Mediator to continue his efforts to bring about the demilitarisation of the City of Jerusalem, without prejudice to the future political status of Jerusalem, and to assure the protection of and access to the Holy Places, religious buildings, and sites in Palestine;
>
> Instructs the Mediator to supervise the observance of the truce and to establish procedures for examining alleged breaches of the truce since June 11, 1948, authorises him to deal with breaches so far as it is within his capacity to do so by appropriate local action, and requests him to keep the Security Council currently informed concerning the operation of the truce and when necessary to take appropriate action;
>
> Decides that, subject to further decision by the Security Council or the General Assembly, the truce shall remain in force, in accordance with the present resolution and with that of May 29, 1948, until a peaceful adjustment of the future situation of Palestine is reached;

contradistinction to other powers granted to the Council? If they are granted—as it is stated—for the discharge of the same ' duties ' as those referred to in paragraph 1, they could be ' specific ' only in so far as other organs have no such powers. But this is true only with respect to the power laid down in Chapter VII: the power to take enforcement action.

It is difficult to understand why the second sentence of paragraph 2 has been considered to be necessary at all. To tell the reader of the Charter in which Chapters he can find the provisions conferring powers upon the Security Council is certainly not the task of the Charter, but of a commentary to it. The enumeration of the Chapters in which the specific powers are granted to the Council is not only superfluous, it is—as formulated in the last sentence of paragraph 2—evidently not complete, as has been pointed out.

Some important powers are conferred upon the Security Council in Chapters IV, V and XIV, and in the Statute of the International Court of Justice which is an integral part of the Charter. Among these powers the one conferred upon the Council by Article 94, paragraph 2 (Chapter XIV), is certainly ' specific,' if this term has any sense at all. It is a power which the Council has under its responsibility for the maintenance of peace, the term taken in its narrower sense; for it concerns the settlement of disputes. The first sentence of Article 24, paragraph 2, providing that the Council, in discharging the duties which it has under the responsibility for the maintenance of peace, shall act in accordance with the Purposes and Principles of the United Nations, refers to the same duties as the second sentence of this paragraph refers to. Hence, according to the wording of paragraph 2, the Council is bound to conform with the Purposes and Principles of the United Nations only in discharging its functions under Chapters VI, VII, VIII and XII, not under other Chapters; especially not in applying Article 94, paragraph 2, when it makes recommendations or decides upon measures to be taken to give effect to a judgment of the International Court of Justice with which a party fails to comply. Article 1, paragraph 1, of the Charter, states that a Purpose of the United Nations is to bring about peaceful settlement of disputes ' in conformity with the principles of justice and international

Reiterates the appeal to the parties contained in the last paragraph of its resolution of May 22 and urges upon the parties that they continue conversations with the Mediator in a spirit of conciliation and mutual concession in order that all points under dispute may be settled peacefully;

Requests the Secretary-General to provide the Mediator with the necessary staff and facilities to assist in carrying out the functions assigned to him under the resolution of the General Assembly of May 14, and under this resolution; and

Requests that the Secretary-General make appropriate arrangements to provide necessary funds to meet the obligations arising from this resolution. (United Nations Bulletin, Vol. V, p. 596.)

As to the question whether the Security Council is competent to issue ' orders ' under Article 40, cf. *infra*, pp. 739 ff.

law.' According to the wording of Article 24, paragraph 2, this provision does not apply to the power which the Council has under Article 94, paragraph 2. Hence it is hardly possible to take the last sentence of Article 24, paragraph 2, literally.[2]

The enumeration of the 'specific powers granted to the Security Council' in paragraph 2 of Article 24 is incomplete also for the reason that important powers may be granted to the Council by international agreements entered into by the United Nations.

[2] The Records of the San Francisco Conference do not contain any essential contribution to the interpretation of Article 24. Paragraph 1 of Article 24 corresponds to Chapter VI, Section B, paragraph 1, of the Dumbarton Oaks Proposals, which runs as follows:

> In order to ensure prompt and effective action by the Organisation, members of the Organisation should by the Charter confer on the Security Council primary responsibility for the maintenance of international peace and security and should agree that in carrying out these duties under this responsibility it should act on their behalf.

The term 'maintenance of international peace and security' as used in this provision can hardly have another meaning than the words 'to maintain international peace and security' in Chapter I, paragraph 1, of the Dumbarton Oaks Proposals determining the first purpose of the Organisation and stipulating that this purpose shall be achieved by 'effective collective measures for the prevention and removal of threats to the peace and the suppression of acts of aggression or other breaches of the peace' and by 'adjustment or settlement of international disputes which may lead to a breach of the peace.' There is nothing in the Dumbarton Oaks Proposals that corresponds to the Preamble of the Charter and its words: 'to unite our [the United Nations'] strength to maintain international peace and security.' That the term 'maintenance of international peace and security' in Chapter VI, Section B, paragraph 1, of the Dumbarton Oaks Proposals means: maintenance of international peace and security by the measures determined in Chapter I, paragraph 1, results also from the fact that paragraph 2 of Chapter VI, Section B, prescribes:

> In discharging these duties the Security Council should act in accordance with the purposes and principles of the Organisation,

and that paragraph 3 stipulates:

> The specific powers conferred on the Security Council in order to carry out these duties are laid down in Chapter VIII.

Chapter VIII contains the provisions concerning settlement of disputes by the Security Council and enforcement actions to be taken by the Council, which are the means determined by Chapter I, paragraph 1, for the maintenance of peace and security by the Organisation.

Paragraph 3 of Chapter VI, Section B, of the Dumbarton Oaks Proposals has its counterpart in the last sentence of Article 24, paragraph 2. Chapters VI, VII and VIII, of the Charter, referred to in that sentence, correspond to Chapter VIII of the Dumbarton Oaks Proposals. Chapter XII of the Charter (Trusteeship system) has probably been added, because the Dumbarton Oaks Proposals did not contain provisions of trusteeship. Those who drafted Article 24 evidently overlooked that also Chapter XIV of the Charter contains a provision—not contained in the Dumbarton Oaks Proposals—by which an important power relating to settlement of disputes is conferred upon the Security Council and that also the Statute of the Court—not contained in the Dumbarton Oaks Proposals—grants important powers to the Council in this respect. This explains the inconsistency of the last sentence of Article 24, paragraph 2, with paragraph 1, of that Article.

The particular competences of the Security Council shall be discussed in connection with the functions of the Organisation.

B. *Legal Effect of the Acts of the Security Council* (*Article* 25)

As to the legal effect which the Charter attributes to the acts of the Security Council, Article 25 stipulates:

> The Members of the United Nations agree to accept and carry out the decisions of the Security Council in accordance with the present Charter.

This provision has been analysed in a previous part of this study.[3] As pointed out, the term ' decisions ' may be interpreted to mean any resolution adopted by the Security Council; or only decisions which, in accordance with the provisions of the Charter under which they are adopted, are binding upon the Members.

If the latter interpretation is accepted, ' recommendations ' made under Chapter VI or under Article 39 are, in themselves, not ' decisions ' within the meaning of Article 25.[4] But, as pointed out, decisions of the Security Council which, in accordance with the Charter, are not binding upon the Members, such as a mere recommendation, may nevertheless assume a binding character if the Security Council, under Article 39, considers non-compliance with its decision as a threat to the peace and takes enforcement action against the recalcitrant Member. Provided that such enforcement action is interpreted to be a sanction, the conduct of the state against which this sanction is directed must be interpreted as violation of an obligation.

[3] Cf. *supra*, pp. 95 ff., and *infra*, pp. 444 ff.

[4] In the case of the Corfu Channel Incident the Government of the United Kingdom stated (in an application made to the International Court of Justice) that the decision by which the Security Council on April 9, 1947, under Article 36, paragraph 3, of the Charter recommended the government of the United Kingdom and the government of Albania, both involved in a dispute before the Council, to refer the case to the International Court of Justice, was binding upon the parties since Albania had accepted in the present case all obligations which a Member of the United Nations would have to assume in a similar case, and Article 25 of the Charter imposes upon the Members the obligation to accept and to carry out the decisions of the Security Council. (International Court of Justice, Distr. 151, 1947. General List No. 1, p. 5.) In a letter dated July 2, 1947, the government of Albania denied that the resolution of the Security Council of April 9, 1947, had a binding character, and contended that Article 25 of the Charter ' does not apply to recommendations made by the Council with reference to the pacific settlement of disputes.' In its judgment delivered on March 25, 1948, the International Court of Justice did not pass upon the contradictory interpretations of Article 36, paragraph 3, of the Charter, presented by the contesting parties. But seven judges, and the national judge (appointed by the Albanian government) in their separate opinions rejected the view that a decision of the Security Council by which a recommendation is made under Article 36, paragraph 3, of the Charter, has a binding character. (Cf. the text of the letter and the separate opinions, published in the *International Law Quarterly*, Vol. 2, No. 1, 1948, pp. 70 ff., 78 ff.)

Enforcement action, taken under Article 39, is the only way to enforce decisions of the Security Council and by taking such action the Security Council may enforce not only its own decisions (whether they have in themsleves a binding character or not) but also decisions of any other organ of the United Nations.[5] Decisions of the Court, too, can be enforced according to Article 94, paragraph 2, only by the Security Council which has the exclusive power to enforce decisions of all organs of the United Nations. But the difference between the enforcement of decisions of the International Court of Justice and the enforcement of decisions of other organs of the United Nations consists in that the Security Council is authorised to take enforcement measures under Article 39 only after it has determined the existence of a threat to, or breach of, the peace constituted by non-compliance with a decision of the Council itself, of the General Assembly or another organ of the United Nations, whereas Article 94, paragraph 2, may be interpreted to authorise the Security Council to give effect to a judgment of the International Court of Justice without determining that non-compliance with the judgment constitutes a threat to, or breach of, the peace.[6] Article 94, paragraph 2, is the only provision of the Charter which expressly refers to the enforcement of decisions of an organ of the United Nations. Enforcement of decisions of organs other than the Court is only indirectly provided for in Article 39, as a reaction against a threat to, or breach of, the peace. The purpose of the enforcement action taken under Article 39 is not directly—as that of an action taken under Article 94, paragraph 2—to give effect to the decision the non-compliance with which constitutes a threat to, or breach of, the peace, but ' to maintain or restore international peace and security.' If non-compliance with the decision of an organ of the United Nations constitutes a threat to, or breach of, the peace, the Security Council may continue the enforcement action taken under Article 39 against the recalcitrant state until the latter has complied with the decision concerned, in so far as only then—in the opinion of the Security Council—international peace and security are maintained or restored.

The Charter does not provide that the decisions—except those of the International Court of Justice—in order to be enforceable must be in conformity with the law which exists at the time they are adopted. The purpose of the enforcement action under Article 39 is not: to maintain or restore the law, but to maintain, or restore peace, which is not necessarily identical with the law. In taking enforcement actions under Article 39, the Security Council is bound to act ' in accordance with the Purposes and Principles of the United Nations ' (Article 24, paragraph 2).

[5] The statement made by the representative of Syria during the discussion of the Palestine question in the First Committee of the General Assembly that Chapter VII ' empowered the Security Council to enforce only its own decisions ' (Doc. A/C.1/SR/120, p. 2) is not correct. Article 39 does not impose such restriction on the Security Council

[6] Cf. *infra*, pp. 541 f.

But Article 1, paragraph 1, of the Charter, determining the Purposes, restricts the rule to act ' in conformity with the principles of justice and international law ' to the function of ' bringing about by peaceful means adjustment or settlement of international disputes or situations ' (*i.e.*, the functions of the Security Council under Chapter VI) and thus excludes this rule from the function of taking ' effective collective measures for the prevention and removal of threats to the peace, and for the suppression of acts of aggression and other breaches of the peace ' (*i.e.*, the functions of the Security Council under Chapter VII, especially Article 39). The statement of the Preamble: that the peoples of the United Nations are determined ' to establish conditions under which justice and respect for the obligations arising from treaties and other sources of international law can be maintained,' is hardly applicable to an enforcement action under Article 39; and even if applicable, and even if the formula ' in conformity with the principles of justice and international law ' in Article 1, paragraph 1, were not restricted to the function of adjustment or settlement of disputes and other situations by peaceful means but would refer also to the effective collective measures for the maintenance or restoration of peace, the Security Council would not be bound to maintain or restore the existing law. For the Council would be empowered to establish justice if it considered the existing law as not satisfactory, and hence to enforce a decision which it considered to be just though not in conformity with existing law. The decision enforced by the Security Council may create new law for the concrete case.

CHAPTER 11

THE SECRETARY-GENERAL

1. ELECTION

As pointed out in the analysis of Article 7, the ' Secretariat ' which is designated in that Article as one of the principal organs of the United Nations, is not organised as a collegiate body able to act as a unity; consequently it cannot be an organ of the United Nations. The organ which is meant in Article 7 is the Secretary-General. The ' Secretariat ' is his office; and the members of its staff are, as organs of the United Nations, subordinate to the Secretary-General. Article 97 of the Charter provides:

> The Secretariat shall comprise a Secretary-General and such staff as the Organisation may require. The Secretary-General shall be appointed by the General Assembly upon the recommendation of the Security Council. He shall be the chief administrative officer of the Organisation.

The Secretary-General is elected by the Security Council and the General Assembly. The terminology of Article 97 is not correct. The Secretary-General is not ' appointed ' but ' elected ' by the General Assembly just as the members of the International Court of Justice are ' elected ' and not 'appointed,'[1] and the ' recommendation ' of the Security Council, in this case, too, is not a mere suggestion but an essential part of the procedure by which an important organ of the United Nations is created. This ' recommendation ' has the same character as the election of a member of the Court by the Security Council. The Rules of Procedure

[1] Chapter X, paragraph 1, of the Dumbarton Oaks Proposals correctly stipulated: ' He [the Secretary-General] should be elected by . . . ' At the San Francisco Conference the delegate of the Netherlands proposed ' that the word " appointed " be substituted for " elected " in order to emphasise the administrative nature of the Secretary-General's office. The Committee adopted, with only one negative vote, the Netherlands motion . . . ' (U.N.C.I.O. Doc. 1155, I/2/74 (2), p. 4.) An administrative organ may be ' elected ' as well as ' appointed.' The difference between ' election ' and ' appointment ' lies in the first place in the character and, in the second place, in the legal position of the organ which has the function to create another organ. An organ is ' elected ' by a collegiate organ, and ' appointed ' by an individual organ. If an individual organ is competent to ' appoint ' another organ, it is, as a rule, superior to the appointed organ. Hence the term ' appointed ' has the connotation of creating an inferior organ. This is the reason why it is possible to say that a collegiate organ ' appoints ' another organ if this organ is subordinated to the creating collegiate organ. The Secretary-General, however, is subordinated to the General Assembly only with respect to certain of his functions. With respect to the function determined in Article 99 of the Charter, or Article 5 of the Statute, *e.g.*, he is not subordinated to the General Assembly. Nor are all his functions of an administrative nature.

of the General Assembly, under the heading ' Election of the Secretary-General ' provide:

RULE 130

> When the Security Council has submitted its recommendation on the appointment of the Secretary-General, the General Assembly shall consider the recommendation and vote upon it by secret ballot in private meeting.

A resolution of the General Assembly adopted at its 17th meeting[2] contains the following statements:

> From the provisions of Articles 18 and 27 of the Charter, it is clear that, for the nomination of the Secretary-General by the Security Council, an affirmative vote of seven members, including the concurring votes of the permanent Members, is required; and that for his appointment by the General Assembly, a simple majority of the members of that body present and voting is sufficient, unless the General Assembly itself decides that a two-thirds majority is called for. The same rules apply to a renewal of appointment as to an original appointment; this should be made clear when the original appointment is made.
>
> It would be desirable for the Security Council to proffer one candidate only for the consideration of the General Assembly, and for debate on the nomination in the General Assembly to be avoided. Both nomination and appointment should be discussed at private meetings and a vote in either the Security Council or the General Assembly, if taken, should be by secret ballot.

The just mentioned resolution of the General Assembly also provides:

> 1. The terms of the appointment of the Secretary-General shall be such as to enable a man of eminence and high attainment to accept and maintain the position.
>
> 2. The Secretary-General shall receive a salary of an amount sufficient to bring him in a net sum of $20,000 (U.S.), together with representation allowance of $20,000 (U.S.), per annum. In addition, he shall be provided with a furnished residence, the repairs and maintenance of which, excluding provision of household staff, shall be borne by the Organisation.
>
> 3. The first Secretary-General shall be appointed for five years, the appointment being open at the end of that period for a further five-year term.
>
> 4. The following observations contained in paragraphs 18–21 of Section 2, Chapter VIII, of the Preparatory Commission's Report be noted and approved:
>
> (*a*) There being no stipulation on the subject in the Charter, the General Assembly and the Security Council are

[2] Resolutions adopted by the General Assembly, Doc. A/64, p. 14.

free to modify the term of office of future Secretaries-General in the light of experience.

(*b*) Because a Secretary-General is a confidant of many governments, it is desirable that no Member should offer him, at any rate immediately on retirement, any governmental position in which his confidential information might be a source of embarrassment to other Members, and on his part a Secretary-General should refrain from accepting any such position. [3]

It is evident that the Secretary-General is not able to perform all the functions conferred upon him by the Charter personally. He needs deputies and assistants. As to the assistants the Charter provides for a staff of the Secretariat which, according to Article 101, paragraph 1, shall be appointed by the Secretary-General. At the San Francisco Conference the sponsoring powers proposed to insert into the Charter the provision that there should be four Deputy Secretaries-General; but this proposi-

[3] The Report of Rapporteur (General) of Committee I/2 (U.N.C.I.O. Doc. 1155, I/2/74 (2), p. 3 f.) contains the following statement on this subject: 'The Dumbarton Oaks Proposals contained no provision for these questions, but an amendment of the sponsoring governments provided that the term of office of the Secretary-General should be three years and that he should be eligible for re-election. Several delegates opposed any reference in the Charter to the term of office. They argued that the Organisation should not be bound by the Charter in this matter, but should be free to determine the length of office as conditions warranted.—Delegates answering these views held that the three-year term associated with the eligibility of the incumbent Secretary-General for re-election provided an adequate method of attracting outstanding candidates for the position and at the same time protecting the Organisation from the lengthy tenure of an unsuitable Secretary-General.—The Committee voted in favour of a provision for the eligibility of the Secretary-General for re-election and for a three-year term of office.—Subsequent to these decisions, the Committee was advised that the vote of Committee II/1 on the election of the Secretary-General had been referred by the Steering Committee to Committee III/1, and that the latter Committee had reversed the decision of Committee II/1 and had accepted the original text of the Dumbarton Oaks Proposals, namely, that the Secretary-General should be elected by the General Assembly, on recommendation of the Security Council, that is, including the unanimous vote of the permanent members.—In view of this new situation affecting the election of the Secretary-General, the delegate of the Netherlands, supported by the delegates of New Zealand and Belgium, proposed that the earlier decisions of the Committee adopting a three-year term of office be rescinded and that the Committee accept the original Dumbarton Oaks text, that is, the third sentence of paragraph 1, with the exception of the clause "for such term and under such conditions as are specified in the Charter." He stated that the necessity of unanimous agreement of the permanent members of the Security Council for the re-election of the Secretary-General every three years would either deprive him of his independence or force him to leave his office at a time when his experience would be most useful to the Organisation. If there was hesitation on this point in the Committee, he suggested that the determination of the term of office might be left as a matter of later agreement between the Security Council and the General Assembly. It was understood by the Committee that the unanimity of the permanent members would be required in the decision of the Security Council on this matter.'

tion was not accepted.[4] At its 31st meeting the General Assembly adopted a resolution concerning the 'Organisation of the Secretariat,'[5] which under Section 1, paragraph 3, stipulates:

> The Secretary-General is authorised to appoint Assistant Secretaries-General and such other officials and employees as are

[4] The Report of Rapporteur (General) of Committee I/2 (U.N.C.I.O. Doc. 1155, I/2/74 (2), pp. 4 ff.) contains the following statement: 'The Dumbarton Oaks Proposals made no reference to deputy secretaries-general. The sponsoring governments, however, proposed an amendment to Chapter X providing that there should be four deputies to be elected by the General Assembly on recommendation of the Security Council for a period of three years.—The debate on this matter revolved about two questions: First, whether provision should be made in the Charter for deputy secretaries-general; and Second, if provision were made for deputy secretaries-general, whether the number of such officers should be specified in the Charter.—The delegates opposing specific reference to deputies stated that it was impossible at this time to foresee the needs of the Organisation with regard to deputies. They explained that the Assembly would be in a better position to estimate these needs at subsequent times. They felt that the number of deputies would depend upon the distribution of functions within the Secretariat.—The delegate of the Soviet Union, in order to meet one of the objections raised, proposed that the amendment of the sponsoring governments should be revised to provide five deputies instead of four. Opponents of the amendment contended that adoption of the number four and the mode of election of the deputies might jeopardise the international character of the Secretariat. Some delegates also indicated that they favoured the appointment of the deputies by the Secretary-General instead of their election by the Assembly upon the nomination of the Security Council. They felt that the method proposed by the sponsoring governments might render difficult the proper relationship between the Secretary-General and the deputies and might not be conducive to the efficient functioning of the Secretariat.—Those who supported the amendment of the sponsoring governments argued that five deputies would be needed—one to act as alternate to the Secretary-General and one to serve each of the four principal organs. They stated that the international character of the Secretariat would be protected by the method of election of the deputies, which would parallel the method of election of the Secretary-General. Those delegates also explained that the method of election would give considerable prestige to the deputies.—The Committee voted 15 in favour to 13 opposed on the question of referring specifically in the Charter to deputy secretaries-general. The Chairman ruled that since provisions of the text of the Charter require a two-thirds majority to be adopted, this vote was not sufficient for adoption.—Following this vote the Steering Committee requested Committee I/2 to reconsider the matter of deputies, and to vote on specific proposals. The Committee then by a vote of 20 in favour to 19 against, failed to adopt the proposal of the Soviet Union to provide in the Charter for five deputies. The Committee also failed by a vote of 22 in favour to 18 against to adopt the amendment of the sponsoring governments to provide for four deputies. The Committee then adopted by a vote of 40 in favour to 1 against, the first two sentences of paragraph 1, Chapter X, of the Dumbarton Oaks Proposals, as noted above in this report.—The delegate of the Soviet Union subsequently proposed that the first and third sentences of paragraph 1 be modified, so as to include reference to deputies but without specification as to number. His amendment would have made the paragraph read as follows: "There shall be a secretariat comprising a Secretary-General, *deputies*, and such staff as may be required. The Secretary-General shall be the chief administrative officer of the Organisation. The Secretary-General *and his deputies* shall be elected by the General Assembly, on recommendation of the Security Council."' This motion was rejected.

[5] Resolutions adopted by the General Assembly, Doc. A/64, pp. 14 ff.

> required and to prescribe their responsibilities and duties. Assistant Secretaries-General shall have responsibility for and supervision of Departments and Services. There shall always be one Assistant Secretary-General designated by the Secretary-General to deputise for him when he is absent or unable to perform his functions.

As to the substitution of the Secretary-General the Rules of Procedure of the General Assembly provide in Rule 38 that he 'may designate a member of the staff to act in his place' at the meetings of the General Assembly, its committees and subcommittees; and in Rule 63, that he may designate a member of the Secretariat to make 'as his representative,' oral or written statements to the General Assembly concerning any question under consideration by it. Rule 101 contains an analogous provision with respect to the committees and subcommittees of the Assembly. The Provisional Rules of Procedure of the Security Council stipulate in Rule 21: 'The Secretary-General may authorise a deputy to act in his place at meetings of the Security Council'; Rule 22 confers not only on the Secretary-General but also on 'his deputy acting on his behalf' the right to make oral or written statements to the Security Council concerning questions under consideration by it. The Rules of Procedure of the Economic and Social Council (Rules 23, 26) and of the Trusteeship Council (Rules 23, 26) contain analogous provisions. The power of the Secretary-General to designate a deputy for the performance of functions conferred by the Charter on him, which implies a transfer of power, should be established by the Charter itself.[6] It is more than doubtful whether the Charter authorises the General Assembly, the Security Council and the other Councils to adopt by a resolution provisions to this effect. Article 21 of the Charter authorises the General Assembly, Article 30 the Security Council, Article 72 the Economic and Social Council, and Article 90 the Trusteeship Council only to adopt their own rules of procedure, not to confer upon the Secretary-General the power to transfer functions, conferred upon him, to a deputy.

As to the appointment of the staff, Article 101 provides:

> 1. The staff shall be appointed by the Secretary-General under regulations established by the General Assembly.
>
> 2. Appropriate staffs shall be permanently assigned to the Economic and Social Council, the Trusteeship Council, and, as required, to other organs of the United Nations. These staffs shall form a part of the Secretariat.

[6] During the discussion of Article 98 of the Charter in Committee I/2 of the San Francisco Conference (U.N.C.I.O. Doc. 1155, I/2/74 (2), p. 6), it was agreed 'that the Secretary-General could depute these duties should occasion require.' The report of the Preparatory Commission states on page 86: 'Many of the Secretary-General's duties will naturally be delegated, in greater or lesser degree, to members of his staff and particularly to his higher officials. But the execution of these duties must be subject to his supervision and control; the ultimate responsibility remains his alone.'

> 3. The paramount consideration in the employment of the staff and in the determination of the conditions of service shall be the necessity of securing the highest standards of efficiency, competence, and integrity. Due regard shall be paid to the importance of recruiting the staff on as wide a geographical basis as possible.

The provision of Article 101, paragraph 2, that ' appropriate staffs shall be permanently assigned to the Economic and Social Council, the Trusteeship Council and, as required, to other organs of the United Nations ' is not quite consistent with the provision that these staffs shall form a part of the Secretariat. The first provision seems to aim at the establishment of separate Secretariats for the various organs; the second provision establishes the unity of one Secretariat for the whole Organisation. Instead of ' permanent ' staffs assigned to various organs of the United Nations, the ' Organisation of the Secretariat,' adopted by the General Assembly at its 31st meeting on February 13, 1946, provides for the following special departments of the Secretariat: (*a*) Department of Security Council Affairs; (*b*) Department of Economic Affairs; (*c*) Department of Social Affairs; (*d*) Department for Trusteeship and Information from Non-Self-Governing Territories; (*e*) Department of Public Information; (*f*) Legal Department; (*g*) Conference and General Services; (*h*) Administrative and Financial Services. Rule 39 of the Rules of Procedure of the General Assembly stipulates:

> The Secretary-General shall provide and direct the staff required by the General Assembly and any committees or subsidiary organs which it may establish.

Rule 24 of the Provisional Rules of Procedure of the Security Council stipulates:

> The Secretary-General shall provide the staff required by the Security Council. This staff shall form a part of the Secretariat.

Rule 26 of the Rules of Procedure of the Economic and Social Council runs as follows:

> The Secretary-General shall provide and direct the staff required by the Council, its committees and such subsidiary bodies as may be established by it.

Rule 25 of the Rules of Procedure for the Trusteeship Council reads:

> The Secretary-General shall provide and direct the staff required by the Trusteeship Council and such committees, subcommittees and other subsidiary bodies as it may establish.

None of these provisions prescribes that the staffs shall be ' permanently ' assigned to the organs concerned.[7]

[7] ' In the discussions of the Executive Committee of the Preparatory Commission there were two schools of thought. The majority recommended that the Secretariat should be organised functionally, each administrative unit being at the

2. Competence

As to the functions of the Secretary-General, Article 98 of the Charter provides:

> The Secretary-General shall act in that capacity in all meetings of the General Assembly, of the Security Council, of the Economic and Social Council, and of the Trusteeship Council, and shall perform such other functions as are entrusted to him by these organs. The Secretary-General shall make an annual report to the General Assembly on the work of the Organisation.

According to Article 97, the Secretary-General shall be the chief 'administrative' officer of the Organisation and 'in that capacity' he shall, under Article 98, act in all meetings of the General Assembly, the Security Council, the Economic and Social Council, and the Trusteeship Council. However, not all functions of the Secretary-General have an 'administrative' character. Under Article 98 the General Assembly and the three Councils may entrust him with administrative as well as other, that is to say, political, functions.[8] The Charter and the Rules of Procedure of the General Assembly and of the three Councils confer upon the Secretary-General numerous functions which have a merely administrative character. But it is certainly not an 'administrative' function which Article 99 of the Charter determines in providing:

> The Secretary-General may bring to the attention of the Security Council any matter which in his opinion may threaten the maintenance of international peace and security.

disposal of any organ of the United Nations for the performance of work falling within its competence. A minority view held that each of the principal organs should have its own Secretariat. The majority view prevailed and the General Assembly decided that the Secretariat should be divided into eight principal units, each under an Assistant Secretary-General.' (U.N. Department of Public Information, Background Paper, No. 44, p. 7.)

[8] The Draft Report of Sub-committee I/2/D (U.N.C.I.O. Doc. 720, I/2/D/1, p.1) contains the following statement: 'The Sub-committee was in general agreement that the language of paragraph 2 [of Chapter X of the Dumbarton Oaks Proposals, corresponding to Article 98 of the Charter] should be kept sufficiently broad to cover all functions of the Secretariat, political as well as administrative, and that no attempt should be made to enumerate therein specific functions which are provided in other chapters of the Charter.' At the 17th meeting of Committee I/2 (U.N.C.I.O. Doc. 732, I/2/50, p. 1, 'The Delegate of the Netherlands pointed out that in the explanatory statement on paragraph 2 [Article 98 of the Charter], contained in the draft report, reference was made to political as well as to administrative functions of the Secretariat. He declared that the Secretariat would have only administrative functions and would not have any political functions.'—In the Report of Rapporteur (General) of Committee I/2 (U.N.C.I.O. Doc. 1155, I/2/74 (2), p. 6) the words 'political as well as administrative' are omitted. The Report states: 'Paragraph 2 [Article 98 of the Charter] was considered by the sub-committee on the Secretariat. The sub-committee considered a proposal made by the Delegate of Mexico that registration of treaties and other agreements made between members of the Organisation should be included among the main functions of the Secretariat, and a

It is of importance to note that Article 99 does not impose upon the Secretary-General an obligation to bring to the attention of the Security Council any matter which in his opinion may threaten the maintenance of peace. The function determined in Article 99 is to be exercised at the discretion of the Secretary-General. It is difficult to understand why the Charter does not expressly authorise the Secretary-General to perform an analgous function in relation to the General Assembly.[9] In exercising his power under Article 99 the Secretary-General must first determine that the matter which he intends to bring to the attention of the Security Council threatens the maintenance of international peace and security. Is this possible without a previous

similar amendment submitted by the Delegation of the Philippine Commonwealth. The recommendation of the sub-committee that, since the Charter would provide elsewhere for the registration of treaties, it was unnecessary to include enumeration of this function in Chapter X, was agreed to by the full Committee. The Committee likewise accepted the sub-committee's recommendation that the language of paragraph 2 should be kept sufficiently broad to cover all of the functions of the Secretariat, and that no attempt should be made to enumerate therein specific functions which are provided in other chapters of the Charter.'

[9] The Report of Rapporteur (General) of Committee I/2 (U.N.C.I.O. Doc. 1155, I/2/74 (2), p. 7 f.) contains the following statements with respect to Article 99: 'It was agreed that the authority to bring to the attention of the Security Council any matter which in his opinion might threaten international peace and security should be exercised at the discretion of the Secretary-General and should not be imposed upon him as a duty. The Committee agreed to this recommendation.' 'The sub-committee and the Committee considered an amendment to paragraph 3 [Article 99 of the Charter] proposed by Venezuela which would permit the Secretary-General to bring to the attention of the General Assembly, as well as to the Security Council, any matter which in his opinion might threaten international peace and security. The Venezuelan Delegate explained that his amendment was intended to give the Secretary-General discretionary power to bring certain matters to the attention of either the General Assembly or Security Council. He contended that this function did not place too great a burden on the Secretary-General. Its advantage was to keep the General Assembly informed of certain situations which states themselves might not bring to the attention of the Assembly.—Some delegates in opposing the Venezuelan amendment discussed the difficulty in which the Secretary-General might be placed in having to decide between the General Assembly and the Security Council in presenting matters concerning peace and security. It was argued further that the Secretary-General would be exercising powers which are not even possessed by the member states. The Committee rejected the Venezuelan amendment by a vote of 18 to 11.—The Delegate of Uruguay proposed to amend paragraph 3 by providing that in addition to matters which in his opinion might threaten international peace and security, the Secretary-General could bring to the attention of the Security Council any matters which constitute an infringement or violation of the principles of the Charter. The Delegate of Uruguay contended that the Secretary-General should take into account matters which would not necessarily threaten international peace but which would constitute violations of the principles of the Charter. He suggested that there should be some provision by which infringements or violations of the principles of the Charter by the member within its own country should be brought to the attention of the Organisation. Delegates opposing this amendment argued that as in the case of the Venezuelan amendment, it would place too heavy a burden upon the Secretary-General. This amendment was rejected by a vote of 16 to 13.'

investigation, and has the Secretary-General the power of investigating the matter? In the Greek case the representative of the United States suggested in the Security Council to establish a commission of investigation. In the course of the discussion at the 70th meeting the Secretary-General made the following statement: 'Just a few words to make clear my own position as Secretary-General and the rights of this office under the Charter. Should the proposal of the United States representative not be carried, I hope that the Council will understand that the Secretary-General must reserve his right to make such enquiries or investigations as he may think necessary, in order to determine whether or not he should consider bringing any aspect of this matter to the attention of the Council under the provisions of the Charter.'[1] This view presupposes that not only the Security Council but also other organs of the United Nations have the right of investigating a matter if investigation is necessary to exercise the power conferred upon the organ concerned with respect to the matter.[2] Consequently, if the Security Council would refuse to investigate a matter under Article 34, the Secretary-General could make such investigation under Article 99. It might be doubted whether this interpretation corresponds to the intention of the framers of the Charter.

A function which has no 'administrative' character in the technical sehse of the term is conferred upon the Secretary-General by Rules 63 and 101 of the Rules of Procedure of the General Assembly.

Rule 63

> The Secretary-General or a member of the Secretariat designated by him as his representative, may at any time make either oral or written statements to the General Assembly concerning any question under consideration by it.

Rule 101

> The Secretary-General or a member of the Secretariat designated by him as his representative may, at any time, make oral or written statements to any committee or subcommittee concerning any question under consideration by it.

A similar provision is contained in Rule 22 of the Provisional Rules of Procedure of the Security Council:

> The Secretary-General, or his deputy acting on his behalf, may make either oral or written statements to the Security Council concerning any question under consideration by it.

Analogous functions of the Secretary-General are established by the

[1] Official Records of the Security Council, 1st Year, 2nd Series, No. 16, p. 404.

[2] On this view the practice of the General Assembly is based, which makes investigations without being expressly authorised to do so by the Charter. Cf. *supra*, p. 166 f.

Rules of Procedure of the two other Councils. Rule 28 of the Rules of the Economic and Social Council provides:

> The Secretary-General or his deputy may at any time, upon the invitation of the President of the Council or of the Chairman of committees of the Council and subsidiary bodies, make either oral or written statements concerning any question under consideration.

Rule 26 of the Rules of Procedure for the Trusteeship Council stipulates:

> The Secretary-General, or his deputy acting on his behalf, may at any time, upon the invitation of the President or of the chairman of a committee or a subsidiary body of the Trusteeship Council, make oral or written statements concerning any question under consideration.

The difference between the provisions of the Rules of Procedure of the General Assembly and the Security Council on the one hand and the analogous provisions of the two other Rules of Procedure is striking. Whereas the Secretary-General is authorised to make statements in the meetings of the Economic and Social Council and the Trusteeship Council and their committees and subsidiary bodies only upon the invitation of the President of the Council or the chairman of a committee or subsidiary body, he may make such statements to the General Assembly and its committees and subcommittees and to the Security Council at his own initiative.

Other functions that have more than an ' administrative ' character are established by Rules 11, 12, 13 and 17, of the Rules of Procedure of the General Assembly. Under these provisions the Secretary-General has the power to draw up the provisional agenda for a regular session of the General Assembly, to include all items ' which he deems it necessary to put before the General Assembly,' and to request the inclusion of supplementary items in the agenda of a regular as well as of a special session. Under Rule 23 of the Provisional Rules of Procedure of the Security Council the Secretary-General may be appointed by the Security Council ' as rapporteur for a specified question.'

The Charter confers functions upon the Secretary-General not only in Chapter XV. Under Article 12, paragraph 2, the Secretary-General, with the consent of the Security Council, shall notify the General Assembly at each session of any matters relative to the maintenance of international peace and security which are being dealt with by the Security Council and shall similarly notify the General Assembly, or the Members of the United Nations if the General Assembly is not in session, immediately the Security Council ceases to deal with such matters;

Under Article 20, the Secretary-General shall convoke special sessions of the General Assembly at the request of the Security Council or of a majority of the Members of the United Nations;

Under Article 102, the Secretary-General shall, as soon as possible, register and publish every treaty and every international agreement entered into by any Member of the United Nations submitted to it for this purpose.

Under Article 5, paragraph 1, of the Statute, of the International Court of Justice, the Secretary-General, at least three months before the date of the election of the members of the Court, shall address a written request to the members of the Permanent Court of Arbitration belonging to the states which are parties to the Statute, and to the members of the national groups appointed under Article 4, paragraph 2, of the Statute, inviting them to undertake, within a given time, by national groups the nomination of persons in a position to accept the duties of a member of the Court;

Under Article 7 of the Statute, the Secretary-General shall prepare a list in alphabetical order of all the persons nominated by the national groups and shall submit this list to the General Assembly and to the Security Council;

Under Article 13, paragraph 4, of the Statute, the President of the Court shall transmit to the Secretary-General any resignation of a member of the Court addressed to the President. It is the notification to the Secretary-General which makes the place vacant;

Under Article 14 of the Statute, the Secretary-General shall, within one month of the occurrence of a vacancy in the Court, proceed to issue the invitations provided for in Article 5;

Under Article 36, paragraph 4, of the Statute, the declaration by which a state recognises as compulsory *ipso facto* and without special agreement in relation to any other state accepting the same obligation the jurisdiction of the Court in legal disputes, shall be deposited with the Secretary-General, who shall transmit copies thereof to the parties to the Statute and to the Registrar of the Court;

Under Article 40, paragraph 3, of the Statute, the Registrar of the Court shall notify the Members of the United Nations through the Secretary-General of cases brought before the Court under Article 40, paragraph 1;

Under Article 67 of the Statute, the Court shall give notice to the Secretary-General of advisory opinions to be delivered in open Court;

Under Article 70 of the Statute, the Court, when proposing amendments to the Statute, shall do so through written communications to the Secretary-General.

Under the Financial Regulations adopted by the General Assembly, the Secretary-General is responsible for preparing the budget, for allocating funds, for controlling expenditures, for collecting contributions from Members and for the custodianship of all funds.[3]

Some important functions are conferred upon the Secretary-General by treaties entered into by the United Nations.[4]

3. Legal Status of the Members of the Secretariat

A. *International Character*

In order to guarantee the international character of the Secretariat and to make the Secretary-General as well as the members of his staff independent of any authority external to the Organisation, Article 100 provides:

> 1. In the performance of their duties the Secretary-General and the staff shall not seek or receive instructions from any government or from any other authority external to the Organisation. They shall refrain from any action which might reflect on their position as international officials responsible only to the Organisation.
>
> 2. Each Member of the United Nations undertakes to respect the exclusively international character of the responsibilities of the Secretary-General and the staff and not to seek to influence them in the discharge of their responsibilities.

In the discussion of Committee I/2 of the San Francisco Conference[5] the question was raised as to whether Article 100 'covered the risk which might be faced by a member of the Secretariat as the result of taking an oath of allegiance to the Organisation. In answer to this question it was pointed out that the experience of the League of Nations demonstrated that there was no practical difficulty in this matter except in the case of the Fascist states.' The question also was raised whether Article 100 'covered the risk which might be faced by a member of the Secretariat who participated in the preparation of military plans for possible use against his own state. It was pointed out that if a member of the Secretariat were to become aware of such military plans, he might be liable to heavy penalty under the laws of his own state for failure to reveal them to his own government . . . It was felt by members of the subcommittee that the question of the liability of members of the Secretariat for military service to their own states would be settled by administrative arrangements when the problem arose.' A Member of the United Nations, in assuming the

[3] Cf. the resolutions of the General Assembly adopted at its 31st meeting on February 10, 1946 (Doc. A/64, o. 21), at its 55th meeting on December 11, 1946 (Doc. A/64/Add. 1, p. 144), at its 121st meeting on November 20, 1947 (Doc. A/519, pp. 68 f.). Cf. also Background Paper No. 44, pp. 5 ff.

[4] Cf. *infra*, p. 351.

[5] Cf. Report of Rapporteur (General) of Committee I/2 (U.N.C.I.O. Doc. 1155, I/2/74 (2), p. 9).

obligation established by Article 100, paragraph 2, 'to respect the exclusively international character of the responsibilities of the Secretary-General and the staff' is bound to exempt its nationals from any obligation otherwise imposed upon them by the national legal order, incompatible with the obligations of a member of the Secretariat. It would be a violation of the obligation stipulated in Article 100, paragraph 2, if the government or the Courts of a Member state would inflict upon a person, member of the Secretariat, a penalty for having not revealed to his government a military plan of which the person concerned became aware in his capacity as member of the Secretariat. Besides, the members of the Secretariat, as 'officials of the United Nations' are also protected by Article 105, paragraph 2, which imposes upon the Members the obligation to grant them such privileges and immunities as are necessary for the independent exercise of their functions in connection with the Organisation.

The resolution of the General Assembly on the terms of appointment of the Secretary-General contains the following statement:

> Because a Secretary-General is a confidant of many governments, it is desirable that no Member should offer him, at any rate immediately on retirement, any governmental position in which his confidential information might be a source of embarrassment to other Members, and on his part a Secretary-General should refrain from accepting any such position.

The 'Provisional Staff Regulations' (Annex II of the Resolution of the General Assembly on the Organisation of the Secretariat) contain the following Regulations:

> REGULATION 1
>
> The Secretary-General and all members of the staff of the Organisation are international civil servants, and their responsibilities are not national but exclusively international. By accepting appointment, they pledge themselves to discharge their functions and to regulate their conduct with the interests of the United Nations only in view. In the performance of their duties they shall not seek nor receive instructions from any government or from any other authority external to the Organisation. All members of the staff are subject to the authority of the Secretary-General, and are responsible to him in the exercise of their functions.
>
> REGULATION 2
>
> Upon accepting their appointment, all members of the staff shall subscribe to the following oath or declaration:
>
> > 'I solemnly swear (undertake, affirm, promise) to exercise in all loyalty, discretion, and conscience the functions entrusted to me as a member of the international

service of the United Nations to discharge those functions and regulate my conduct with the interests of the United Nations only in view, and not to seek or accept instructions in regard to the performance of my duties from any government or other authority external to the Organisation.'

Regulation 3

The oath or declaration shall be made orally by the Secretary-General and Assistant Secretaries-General at a public meeting of the General Assembly, and by the other higher officers in public before the Secretary-General or his authorised deputy.

Regulation 4

The immunities and privileges attaching to the United Nations by virtue of Article 105 of the Charter are conferred in the interests of the Organisation. These privileges and immunities furnish no excuse to the staff members who enjoy them for non-performance of their private obligations or failure to observe laws and police regulations. In any case where these privileges and immunities arise, the staff member concerned shall immediately report to the Secretary-General, with whom alone it rests to decide whether they shall be waived.

Regulation 5

Members of the staff shall exercise the utmost discretion in regard to all matters of official business. They shall not communicate to any person any unpublished information known to them by reason of their official position except in the course of their duties or by authorisation of the Secretary-General.

Regulation 6

Members of the staff shall avoid any action. and in particular any kind of public pronouncement or activity which may adversely reflect on their position as international civil servants. They are not expected to give up their national sentiments or their political and religious convictions; but they shall at all times bear in mind the reserve and tact incumbent upon them by reason of their international status.

Regulation 7

No member of the staff shall accept, hold, or engage in any office or occupation which in the opinion of the Secretary-General is incompatible with the proper discharge of his duties with the United Nations.

Regulation 8

Any member of the staff who becomes a candidate for a public office of a political character shall resign from the Secretariat.

Regulation 9

No member of the staff shall accept any honour, decoration, favour, gift or fee from any Government or from any other source external to the Organisation during the period of his appointment, except for war services.

Regulation 10

Men and women are equally eligible for all posts in the Secretariat.

Regulation 11

So far as practicable, appointments to posts in the Secretariat shall be made on a competitive basis.

Regulation 12

Persons appointed to permanent posts in the Secretariat shall serve such probationary period as may be prescribed by the Secretary-General.

Regulation 13

The Secretary-General shall provide facilities to train members of the staff in subjects relating directly or indirectly to their duties. This training shall apply particularly to members on probation whose earlier educational opportunities have been inadequate or whose language qualifications are deficient.

Regulation 14

With due regard to the maintenance of the staff on as wide a geographical basis as possible and without prejudice to the inflow of fresh talent at the various levels, vacancies shall be filled by promotion of persons already in the service of the United Nations in preference to appointments from outside. This consideration shall also be applied, on a reciprocal basis, to the specialised agencies brought into relationship with the Organisation.

Regulation 15

The Secretary-General shall provide machinery through which members of the staff may participate in the discussion of questions relating to appointment and promotion.

B. *Relationship between the Secretary-General and the Members of the Staff*

The Charter does not contain a provision regulating the relationship between the Secretary-General and the members of the staff. The subordination of the latter to the former is established by Regulation 1 of the Provisional Staff Regulations which provides: 'All members of the staff are subject to the authority of the Secretary-General and are responsible to him in the exercise of their functions.' In this respect also Regulation 19 of the Provisional Staff Regulations is important:

> The Secretary-General may impose disciplinary measures on members of the staff whose conduct or work is unsatisfactory. He may discharge a member of the staff who persistently fails to give satisfactory service. He may summarily dismiss a member of the staff for serious misconduct.

Regulation 29 authorises the Secretary-General to implement the Staff Regulations by issuing 'Staff Rules.' The following Staff Rules refer to disciplinary measures:[6]

RULE 140

> (*a*) The Secretary-General may impose disciplinary measures on staff members whose conduct is unsatisfactory.
>
> (*b*) Disciplinary measures include written censure, suspension without pay, transfer to an inferior post, dismissal with regular notice, or summary dismissal.

RULE 141

> No staff member shall be subjected to a disciplinary measure without being given a prior opportunity to state his case in writing.

RULE 142

> If a charge of serious misconduct is made against a staff member and the Secretary-General considers that the charge is *prima facie* well founded and that the staff member's continuance in office pending an investigation of the charge would prejudice the service, the staff member may be suspended with or without pay from his functions pending investigation, the suspension being without prejudice to the rights of the staff member.

Regulation 23 of the Provisional Staff Regulations stipulates

> The Secretary-General shall establish administrative machinery for inquiry and appeal in disciplinary and termination cases. This machinery shall provide for staff participation.

In this respect the Staff Rules provide:

RULE 135

> A Staff Committee, elected by staff members to represent their views, shall be consulted on general questions relating to

[6] United Nations Administrative Manual, Vol. 2, pp. 416–431.

staff administration and welfare. This shall not apply in emergency situations.

RULE 145

(*a*) An Appeals Board shall be established for the purpose of advising the Secretary-General, with whom the final decision will rest, with regard to the following appeals by staff members:

(i) Appeals against any decision regarding the application of the Staff Rules or of established administrative practices to the termination of appointments;

(ii) Appeals alleging non-observance of agreed terms of appointment;

(iii) Appeals against disciplinary action;

(iv) Claims for allowances;

(v) Appeals of such other character as the Secretary-General may specify.

(*b*) The Appeals Board may render advisory opinions on questions submitted to it by the Secretary-General or by the Staff Committee with the Secretary-General's approval.

RULE 146

(*a*) The Appeals Board shall consist of five members having equal votes, appointed as follows:

(i) A Chairman appointed by the Secretary-General after consultation with the Staff Committee. One or more alternate chairmen may be appointed in the same manner;

(ii) Two members appointed by the Secretary-General;

(iii) Two members representing the staff.

(*b*) The two members representing the staff ((iii) above) shall be drawn from a panel organised in three groups . . .

(*c*) A Secretary, having no vote, shall be appointed by the Secretary-General to the Appeals Board.

RULE 147

Unless the staff member appealing to the Board objects, the Staff Committee shall have the right to have a representative present at all sessions of the Board at which the representatives of the parties interested in the case may be present.

RULE 148

(*a*) The Secretary-General shall prescribe the procedure for filing appeals.

(*b*) The Appeals Board shall regulate its own procedure.

C. *Contractual Character*

The relationship between the Organisation and the members of the Secretariat has the character of a contract. This is expressly provided for in Chapter 7 of the Resolution of the General Assembly on the Organisation of the Secretariat with respect to the members of the staff. But it is true also with respect to the relationship between the Secretary-General and the Organisation.

As to the members of the staff, Staff Rule 63 provides:

> Upon appointment every staff member shall receive a letter of appointment signed by the Secretary-General or his authorised representative.

The letter of appointment shall have full force and effect when it has been signed by the staff member.[7] The rules laid down in the Charter, the Staff Regulations and Staff Rules, determining the relationship between the United Nations on the one hand, the Secretary-General and the members of his staff on the other hand (including the provisions concerning disciplinary measures) must be implied in the contract entered into with these officials in order to be binding upon the contracting parties. The United Nations has not the power to establish, by a unilateral act, duties and rights of individuals in their relation to the United Nations.

A contract is a legal transaction, and the duties and rights created by this transaction are legal duties and legal rights only if the contract is concluded under a positive legal order which provides for enforcement of the contract. The Charter, which is part of international law, authorises certain organs of the United Nations to enter into contracts with private individuals; but neither the Charter nor general international law provides for enforcement of these contracts in case of non-fulfilment on the part of one of the contracting parties. These contracts are legally enforceable only if concluded on the basis of a national legal order.

In this respect Article 104 of the Charter applies. This Article imposes upon the Members the obligation to confer upon the Organisation 'such legal capacity as may be necessary for the exercise of its functions and the fulfilment of its purposes.' At its 31st plenary meeting, the General Assembly adopted a resolution by which the text of a general Convention on the privileges and immunities of the United Nations was approved, to be concluded with the Member states on the basis of Articles 104 and 105 of the Charter.[8] According to Article 1 of this Convention, the United Nations shall possess juridical personality. It shall have the capacity to contract and to institute legal proceedings. That a Member state confers upon the United Nations the legal capacity to contract means that it confers upon the Organisation

[7] United Nations Administrative Manual, Vol. 2, p. 184.

[8] Resolutions adopted by the General Assembly (Doc. A/64, pp. 25 ff.).

the capacity to enter into contracts under the Member state's national law. The Headquarters Agreement between the United Nations and the United States of America, signed at Lake Success, June 26, 1947,[9] provides in Article 3, Section 7, that 'the federal, state and local law of the United States of America shall apply within the headquarters district.' To the contracts concluded by the United Nations with the members of the Secretariat on the territory of a Member state, and especially on the territory of the United States, the national law of this state is—in principle—applicable. But another question is to what extent the jurisdiction of the national courts and enforcement through the executive power of the territorial state is restricted by the immunities this state is obliged to grant to the Organisation and its officials under Article 105 of the Charter.

D. *Privileges and Immunities*

Under Article II, Section 2, of the Convention on the privileges and immunities of the United Nations the Organisation, its property and assets wherever located and by whomsoever held 'shall enjoy immunity from every form of legal process except in so far as, in any particular case, it has expressly waived its immunity. It is, however, understood that no waiver of immunity shall extend to any measure of execution.' Consequently, the Organisation is not suable at all, except its immunity has been waived. But which organ of the United Nations is competent to waive the immunity of the Organisation? The Charter does not answer this question. As to the officials, Article 5 of the Convention on the privileges and immunities of the United Nations provides:

> SECTION 17
>
> The Secretary-General will specify the categories of officials to which the provisions of this Article and Article 7 shall apply. He shall submit these categories to the General Assembly. Thereafter these categories shall be communicated to the Governments of all Members. The names of the officials included in these categories shall from time to time be made known to the Governments of Members.[1]

[9] Resolutions adopted by the General Assembly (Doc. A/519, pp. 92 ff.).

[1] At its 50th meeting on December 7, 1946, the General Assembly adopted the following resolution:

> The General Assembly
>
> Having considered the proposal of the Secretary-General that, in accordance with Section 17 of Article 5 of the Convention on the Privileges and Immunities of the United Nations, the categories of officials to which the provisions of Articles 5 and 7 shall apply should include all members of the staff of the United Nations, with the exception of those who are recruited locally and are assigned to hourly rates;
>
> Approves the granting of the privileges and immunities referred to in Articles 5 and 7 of the Convention on the Privileges and Immunities of the

SECTION 18

Officials of the United Nations shall:

(*a*) be immune from legal process in respect of words spoken or written and all acts performed by them in their official capacity;

(*b*) be exempt from taxation on the salaries and emoluments paid to them by the United Nations;

(*c*) be immune from national service obligations;

(*d*) be immune, together with their spouses and relatives dependent on them, from immigration restrictions and alien registration;

(*e*) be accorded the same privileges in respect of exchange facilities as are accorded to the officials of comparable ranks forming part of diplomatic missions to the government concerned;

(*f*) be given, together with their spouses and relatives dependent on them, the same repatriation facilities in time of international crisis as diplomatic envoys;

(*g*) have the right to import free of duty their furniture and effects at the time of first taking up their post in the country in question.

SECTION 19

In addition to the immunities and privileges specified in Section 18, the Secretary-General and all Assistant Secretaries-General shall be accorded in respect of themselves, their spouses and minor children, the privileges and immunities, exemptions and facilities accorded to diplomatic envoys, in accordance with international law.

SECTION 20

Privileges and immunities are granted to officials in the interests of the United Nations and not for the personal benefit of the individuals themselves. The Secretary-General shall have the right and the duty to waive immunity of any official in any case where, in his opinion, the immunity would impede the course of justice and can be waived without prejudice to the interests of the United Nations. In the case of the Secretary-General, the Security Council shall have the right to waive immunity.

SECTION 21

The United Nations shall co-operate at all times with the appropriate authorities of Members to facilitate the proper

United Nations, adopted by the General Assembly on 13 February, 1946, to all members of the staff of the United Nations, with the exception of those who are recruited locally and are assigned to hourly rates. (Doc. A/64/Add. 1, p. 139.)

administration of justice, secure the observance of police regulations, and prevent the occurrence of any abuse in connection with the privileges, immunities and facilities mentioned in this Article.

Only the Secretary-General and all Assistant Secretaries-General shall enjoy full diplomatic immunities.[2] In case of disputes arising out of employment contracts they are suable only if their immunity is waived. Other members of the Secretariat are suable; the wording of Section 18 (*a*) does not apply to employment contracts since the conclusion of such contract is not an act which the appointee performs in his official capacity; it is the basis of its official capacity.

Article 8, Section 29, provides:

> The United Nations shall make provisions for appropriate modes of settlement of:
>
> (*a*) disputes arising out of contracts or other disputes of a private law character, to which the United Nations is a party;
>
> (*b*) disputes involving any official of the United Nations who by reason of his official position enjoys immunity, if immunity has not been waived by the Secretary-General.

The provisions of this Section are not very clear. Does clause (*a*) refer to disputes arising out of employment contracts with officials,

[2] Article 7 provides:

> SECTION 24
>
> The United Nations may issue United Nations *laissez-passer* to its officials. These *laissez-passer* shall be recognised and accepted as valid travel documents, by the authorities of Members, taking into account the provisions of Section 25.
>
> SECTION 25
>
> Applications for visas (where required) from the holders of United Nations *laissez-passer*, when accompanied by a certificate that they are travelling on the business of the United Nations, shall be dealt with as speedily as possible. In addition, such persons shall be granted facilities for speedy travel.
>
> SECTION 26
>
> Similar facilities to those specified in Section 25 shall be accorded to experts and other persons who, though not the holders of United Nations *laissez-passer*, have a certificate that they are travelling on the business of the United Nations.
>
> SECTION 27
>
> The Secretary-General, Assistant Secretaries-General and Directors travelling on United Nations *laissez-passer* on the business of the United Nations shall be granted the same facilities as are accorded to diplomatic envoys.
>
> SECTION 28
>
> The provisions of this Article may be applied to the comparable officials of specialised agencies if the agreements for relationship made under Article 63 of the Charter so provide.

that is to say, are these contracts and consequently the disputes arising out of them considered to be of a private law character? If they are supposed to be of a public law character, does clause (*b*) refer to them? Clause (*b*) refers only to disputes involving officials whose immunity can be waived by the Secretary-General. Why does clause (*b*) not refer to disputes involving the Secretary-General if his immunity has not been waived by the Security Council?

Another question is whether the provision of Section 29, clause (*a*), intends to substitute for the jurisdiction of the territorially competent national Courts the jurisdiction of agencies established by the United Nations for the settlement of the disputes referred to in Section 29; that is to say, whether Section 29, clause (*a*), imposes upon the contracting states the obligation to recognise the exemption of these disputes from their jurisdiction? If the provision of Section 29, clause (*a*), shall not have this effect, why should it be inserted into a treaty between the United Nations and the Member states? As to the disputes referred to in Section 29, clause (*b*), the same question arises. If immunity of the official involved in the dispute is not waived, the jurisdiction of the Member state concerned is excluded. Why insert this provision into a treaty with Member states if by this provision no obligation is imposed and no right is conferred upon the Member state? Besides, it should be noted that immunity of an official for acts that he performs in his official position is immunity for acts imputable to the Organisation, and hence not a privilege of the official but a privilege of the United Nations, established by Article 2, Section 2, of the Convention.

Under the Covenant of the League of Nations an Administrative Tribunal was established[3] competent to decide on 'complaints alleging non-observance, in substance or form, of the terms of appointment of officials of the Secretariat or of the International Labour Organisation, and of such provisions of the Staff Regulations as are applicable to the case.' Its activity was generally recognised as satisfactory. Paragraph 11 of the Resolution of the General Assembly concerning the Organisation of the Secretariat authorises the Secretary-General to appoint a small advisory committee, possibly including representatives of the staff, to draft a 'Statute for an administrative Tribunal' to be submitted to the Second Part of the First Session of the General Assembly. This advisory committee prepared a draft Statute which was submitted to the Assembly, which, however, resolved to postpone the decision in this matter. Afterwards the above-mentioned Appeals Board was established. The Board has the power 'of advising the Secretary-General, with whom final decision will rest,' with regard to appeals by members of the

[3] The Statute of the Administrative Tribunal was adopted by the Assembly of the League of Nations at its 8th ordinary session by a resolution of September 26, 1927. Official Journal, 927, Special Supplement, No. 53, p. 28.

staff 'alleging non-observance of agreed terms of appointment' (Rule 145 (*a*) (ii)).

E. *Private or Public Law?*

The question whether the relationship between an international organisation and its official, established by an employment contract, is of private or public law character has been examined with respect to the League of Nations by a Committee of Jurists appointed by the Council of the League in 1925. The Committee declared the relation, 'being connected with public employment,' 'cannot be judged purely according to the principles of private law and civil legislation but must be considered mainly in the light of the principles of public law and administrative legislation.'[4] The differentiation between public and private law is highly problematical and justified only in so far as based on positive provisions of a legal order. Contracts of public law are considered to differ from contracts of private law because one party to the contract, the state, is at the same time the maker of the law under which the contract is concluded. But a difference actually exists only in so far as the law treats certain (not all) contracts to which the state is a party in another way than contracts to which only private persons are parties. Since an international organisation, such as the United Nations, has no legislative power with respect to employment contracts, contracts to which such an international organisation is a party can be classified as contracts of public law only by analogy. The Committee of Jurists appointed by the Council of the League of Nations stated: 'Relations connected with public employment are always governed by the exigencies of the public interest, to which the private and personal interests of the officials must necessarily give way.' It may be that the national legal order under which an employment contract with the United Nations has been concluded, contains such a provision with reference to employment contracts to which the state is a party. But there is no provision in the Charter or the regulations established on the basis of the Charter determining the relation between the United Nations and its officials, which—as implied in the employment contract—justifies an interpretation according to which the interest of one contracting party—namely, the official—must always give way to that of the other party, the United Nations.

[4] Official Journal, 925, p. 1443.

CHAPTER 12

REGIONAL ARRANGEMENTS

1. REGIONAL ORGANISATION

A. *Arrangements and Agencies*

JUST as the Covenant in Article 21 authorised the Members of the League to enter ' regional understandings ' ' for securing the maintenance of the peace,'[1] the Charter permits in Article 52 ' regional arrangements ' for dealing with matters ' relating to the maintenance of international peace and security.' Like the League of Nations, the United Nations does not claim to be the only and exclusive organisation of its Members for the maintenance of peace. For this purpose the states, Members of the United Nations, are authorised by the Charter to establish regional organisations which may work as organs of the total organisation.[2]

Article 52, paragraph 1, stipulates:

> Nothing in the present Charter precludes the existence of regional arrangements or agencies for dealing with such matter relating to the maintenance of international peace and security as are appropriate for regional action, provided that such arrangements or agencies and their activities are consistent with the Purposes and Principles of the United Nations.

Regional arrangements are treaties which have a regional character. Regional agencies are international agencies established by regional arrangements. The phrase ' regional arrangements *or* agencies ' is not quite correct. Regional agencies can be established only by regional arrangements. What is meant by the phrase is: regional arrangements by which regional action is provided for to be performed through special agencies, and regional arrangements by which regional action is not provided for to be performed by special agencies but by the contracting states themselves. Literally interpreted, the term ' regional ' means: pertaining to a ' region,' that is to say, to a certain territory. Regional arrangements are treaties concluded by states which are in a relation of geographical propinquity. As used in Chapter VIII of the Charter which bears the heading: ' Regional Arrangements ' (without reference to regional ' agencies '), the term ' regional ' has also the connotation of ' partial,' that is to say, treaties

[1] Article 21 of the Covenant runs as follows:

> Nothing in this Covenant shall be deemed to affect the validity of international engagements, such as treaties of arbitration or regional understandings like the Monroe doctrine, for securing the maintenance of peace.

[2] Cf. *supra*, p. 145.

concluded only by a part of the Members of the United Nations, and, hence, constituting only partial communities as compared with the total community: the United Nations. It stands to reason that such treaties are concluded to satisfy certain common interests of the contracting parties. The community of interests may—but need not necessarily be—based on their geographical propinquity. There is good reason to assume that, according to the intention of the framers of the Charter, the meaning of the term 'regional arrangements' is wider than that of treaties concluded by neighbouring states.[3] In Article 53 the term is used to cover any treaty concluded by some Members for action against enemy states under Article 107 or against renewal of aggressive policy on the part of any enemy state, without regard to geographical situation of the states parties to the treaty. The intended meaning of the term 'regional arrangements' is treaties concluded by some, not by all, Members of the United Nations.

It might seem that the regional arrangements referred to in Chapter VIII are intended to mean treaties concluded only by Members of the United Nations. For paragraph 2 of Article 52 expressly refers to Members of the United Nations. But the wording of paragraph 1 does not exclude treaties concluded by Members with non-members. This provision refers to 'regional arrangements,' not to regional arrangements 'among Members.'[4]

B. *Matters Appropriate for Regional Action*

Article 52, paragraph 1, refers to regional arrangements for dealing with matters 'relating to the maintenance of international peace and

[3] At the 5th meeting of Committee 4 to Commission III of the San Francisco Conference the following amendment suggested by the Egyptian delegation was discussed: 'There shall be considered as regional arrangements organisations of a permanent nature grouping in given geographical area several countries which, by reason of their proximity, community of interests or cultural, linguistic, historical or spiritual affinities, make themselves jointly responsible for the peaceful settlement of any disputes which may arise between them and for the maintenance of peace and security in their region, as well as for the safeguarding of their interests and the development of their economic and cultural relations.' The Egyptian delegate 'observed that regional arrangements are not intended solely to guard against aggression but to serve wider purposes also, such as the promotion of social and economic co-operation. In the Egyptian view it was of the essence of a regional arrangement that it should be of a permanent nature.' The delegate of the United States replied: 'that the question of defining the term "regional arrangement" had already been fully debated, and the decision had been reached that reliance should be placed upon the general terms of the Charter. While the language submitted by the delegate of Egypt clearly defined obvious legitimate and eligible factors for a regional arrangement, it was probable that it failed to cover all the situations which might be embraced by regional arrangements. The attempt to enter into definitions would entail indefinite discussion and interminable delays.' (U.N.C.I.O. Doc. 889, III/4/12, p. 1; 553, III/4/A/9, p. 3.)

[4] The Arab League and the North Atlantic Treaty are regional arrangements to which also non-Members are parties. Cf. *supra*, p. 85.

security,' that means treaties which have the same purpose as the Charter. But not to all such arrangements; only to those for dealing with ' such matters ' relating to the maintenance of international peace and security ' as are appropriate for regional action.' Here the question arises: who is competent to decide the appropriateness of a regional action? Since the Charter does not authorise a special organ of the United Nations, the Members concerned seem to have the power of deciding this question. However, some regional actions are recognised as appropriate by the Charter itself: pacific settlement of disputes, in Article 52, paragraphs 2 and 3; enforcement action under the authority of the Security Council; measures against enemy states under Article 107 and action against the renewal of aggressive policy on the part of any enemy state in Article 53, paragraph 1. But the language of Article 52 does not exclude the interpretation that also other purposes are appropriate for regional action, and that regional arrangements which provide for other actions than those referred to in Chapter VIII are covered by the provision of paragraph 1.[5]

C. *Compatibility of Regional Arrangements with the Charter*

Article 52, paragraph 1, stipulates that the validity of the regional arrangements determined in this paragraph is not precluded by the

[5] The Drafting Sub-committee II/3/A of the San Francisco Conference considered ' whether specific provision should be included in the Charter for making regional forms of co-operation in social, economic, and related fields consistent with the purposes of economic and social co-operation set forth in Chapter IX. It had been considered, however, in view of the paragraph [Article 56] pledging the members of the Organisation to take joint and separate action in co-operation with the Organisation for the achievement of these purposes, that it would be unnecessary to include any specific provision of this sort.' (U.N.C.I.O. Doc. 780/II/3/53, p. 3.)

A regional arrangement not only for the purposes expressly determined in Chapter VIII of the Charter is the Five Power Pact, signed at Brussels March 17, 1948, by Belgium, France, Luxembourg, the Netherlands, and Great Britain. The preamble determines the purposes of the treaty as follows:

> To reaffirm their faith in fundamental human rights, in the dignity and worth of the human person and in other ideals proclaimed in the Charter of the United Nations;
>
> To fortify and preserve the principles of democracy, personal freedom and political liberty, the constitutional traditions and the rule of law which are their common heritage;
>
> To strengthen, with these aims in view, the economic, social and cultural ties by which they are already united;
>
> To co-operate loyally and to co-ordinate their efforts to create in Western Europe a firm basis for European economic recovery;
>
> To afford assistance to each other, in accordance with the Charter of the United Nations, in maintaining international peace and security and in resisting any policy of aggression;
>
> To take such steps as may be held necessary in the event of a renewal by Germany of a policy of aggression;
>
> To associate progressively in the pursuance of these aims other states inspired by the same ideals and animated by the like determination:

Charter provided that such arrangements are consistent with the terms of Articles 1 and 2 of the Charter. This is, correctly formulated, the meaning of the phrase: ' Nothing in the present Charter precludes the

> Desiring for these purposes to conclude a treaty for collaboration in economic, social and cultural matters and for collective self-defence . . .

Articles 1, 2 and 3, provide:

> ARTICLE 1
>
> Convinced of the close community of their interests and of the necessity of uniting in order to promote the economic recovery of Europe, the high contracting parties will so organise and co-ordinate their economic activities as to produce the best possible results, by the elimination of conflict in their economic policies, the co-ordination of production and development of commercial exchanges.
>
> The co-operation provided for in the preceding paragraph, which will be effected through the consultative council referred to in Article 7 as well as through other bodies, shall not involve any duplication of, or prejudice to, the work of other economic organisations in which the high contracting parties are or may be represented but shall on the contrary, assist the work of those organisations.
>
> ARTICLE 2
>
> The high contracting parties will make every effort in common, both by direct consultation and in specialised agencies, to promote the attainment of a higher standard of living by their peoples and to develop on corresponding lines the social and other related services of their countries. The high contracting parties will consult with the object of achieving the earliest possible application of the recommendations of immediate practical interest relating to social matters, adopted with their approval in the specialised agencies. They will endeavour to conclude as soon as possible conventions with others in the sphere of social security.
>
> ARTICLE 3
>
> The high contracting parties will make every effort in common to lead their peoples toward better understanding of the principles which form the basis of their common civilisation and to promote cultural exchanges by conventions between themselves or by other means.

Also the Charter of the Organisation of American States, established at Bogota Conference March 30—May 2, 1948, is a regional arrangement within the meaning of Article 52 of the Charter. Article 1 of this Charter provides:

> The American States establish by this Charter the international organisation that they have developed to achieve an order of peace and justice, to promote their solidarity, to strengthen their collaboration, and to defend their sovereignty, their territorial integrity and their independence. Within the United Nations, the Organisation of American States is a regional agency.

The purposes of this regional arrangement are defined in Article 4:

> The Organisation of American States, in order to put into practice the principles on which it is founded and to fulfil its regional obligations under the Charter of the United Nations, proclaims the following essential purposes:
>
> (*a*) To strengthen the peace and security of the continent;
>
> (*b*) To prevent possible causes of difficulties and to ensure the pacific settlement of disputes that may arise among the Member States;
>
> (*c*) To provide for common action on the part of those States in the event of aggression;
>
> (*d*) To seek the solution of political, juridical and economic problems that may arise among them; and

existence of regional arrangements or agencies . . . provided that such arrangements or agencies and their activities are consistent with the Purposes and Principles of the United Nations.' Provisions of a treaty, such as the Charter, are norms and norms can 'preclude' only the 'existence,' that is the validity of other norms, especially of other treaty provisions, including provisions by which agencies are established and authorised to perform certain activities; but norms cannot preclude the existence of facts such as agencies or their actual activities. The term 'existence' probably has been chosen in order to cover not only regional arrangements entered into after the Charter has come into force but also regional arrangements which were in existence before this date, as the treaty constituting the League of the Arab States which was signed at Cairo on March 22, 1945, and which came into 'existence' on May 10, 1945.

What does it mean that the provisions of the Charter do not preclude the validity of certain regional arrangements provided that they are consistent with certain provisions of the Charter? If the meaning of this statement is only that such arrangements are not invalidated by the Charter, it is superfluous. That the validity of treaties concluded by parties to the Charter is not affected by the Charter if these treaties are consistent with the Charter stands to reason and does not need an express provision in the Charter. The meaning of Article 52, paragraph 1, however, may be that the Members of the United Nations are authorised to conclude the regional arrangements referred to in this Article. Such authorisation was necessary only if the Charter would contain a general provision by which the Members are prohibited to enter into treaties for the maintenance of international peace and security, that is to say, if the Charter would establish a monopoly of the United Nations for the maintenance of international peace and security, excluding any other treaty concluded by Members for this purpose. Then, a special provision establishing a restriction to this monopoly in permitting certain regional arrangements for the maintenance of international peace and security was necessary. The Charter, however, does not establish such monopoly of the United Nations. It even does not forbid the Members to conclude treaties inconsistent with the Charter. In contradistinction to the Covenant of the League of Nations which obligates the Members not to enter into future engagements inconsistent with the Covenant and to take steps to procure their release from previously assumed

> (*e*) To promote, by co-operative action, their economic, social and cultural development.

Consistency with the Charter of the United Nations is emphasised in Article 102:

> None of the provisions of this Charter shall be construed as impairing the rights and obligations of the Member States under the Charter of the United Nations.

As to regional arrangements for the purpose of defence against armed attack, cf. *infra*, pp. 791 ff.

obligations, Article 103 of the Charter only provides that in case of conflict between obligations under the Charter and other obligations of the Members the former shall prevail.[6] Hence an authorisation to conclude regional arrangements consistent with the Charter or with special provisions of the Charter is completely redundant.

However, the provision that certain arrangements if consistent with Articles 1 and 2 of the Charter are not precluded may have not only a negative but also a positive meaning. Although it probably does not correspond to the intention of the legislator, Article 52, paragraph 1, might be interpreted to mean that the regional arrangements referred to in Article 52, paragraph 1, if inconsistent with the terms of Articles 1 and 2, are precluded by the Charter, that is to say, are to be considered as invalidated by the Charter, whether they have been entered into before or after the Charter has come into force. If interpreted in this way, Article 52, paragraph 1, would be not quite consistent with Article 103. The former would have in a certain respect a narrower, in another respect a wider, scope than the latter. Article 52, paragraph 1, refers only to Articles 1 and 2 of the Charter (Purposes and Principles); Article 103, to the whole Charter; Article 52, paragraph 1, to all terms of Articles 1 and 2; Article 103, only to those establishing obligations. If this interpretation is accepted, Article 52, paragraph 1, invalidates not only regional arrangements entered into for the maintenance of 'international peace and security' inconsistent with the terms of Articles 1 and 2 of the Charter, but also regional arrangements which deal with matters relating to the maintenance of international peace and security not appropriate for regional action, even if not inconsistent with the terms of Articles 1 and 2 of the Charter. Then, and only then, the question becomes important: who is competent to decide the appropriateness of regional action as provided by regional arrangements?

2. Special Competence of the Regional Organisations

A. *Settlement of Local Disputes*

The Charter confers certain functions upon regional organisations, that is to say, upon the regional community constituted by the regional arrangement or upon the special organ (agency) established by the regional arrangement. In this respect Article 52, paragraphs 2 to 4, comes into consideration:

> 2. The Members of the United Nations entering into such arrangements or constituting such agencies shall make every effort to achieve pacific settlement of local disputes through such regional arrangements or by such regional agencies before referring them to the Security Council.

[6] Cf. *supra*, pp. 111 ff.

> 3. The Security Council shall encourage the development of pacific settlement of local disputes through such regional arrangements or by such regional agencies either on the initiative of the states concerned or by reference from the Security Council.
>
> 4. This Article in no way impairs the application of Articles 34 and 35.

The phrases in paragraphs 2 and 3: ' . . . entering into such arrangements or constituting such agencies . . . ', and ' . . . through such regional arrangements or by such regional agencies . . . ' show the same defect as the analogous formulas in paragraph 1. Regional agencies can be constituted only by regional arrangements and if a dispute is settled through a regional agency it is—indirectly—also settled through the arrangement by which the agency has been constituted.

Paragraphs 2, 3 and 4, of Article 52, confer upon regional organisations the function of pacific settlement of local disputes. According to the wording of these paragraphs it is a function conferred upon all regional arrangements.[7] This is not consistent with paragraph 1

[7] The Five Power Pact of Brussels provides with respect to settlement of local disputes:

> Article 8
>
> In pursuance of their determination to settle disputes only by peaceful means, the high contracting parties will apply to disputes between themselves the following provisions:
>
> The high contracting parties will, while the present treaty remains in force, settle all disputes falling within the scope of Article 36, paragraph 2, of the Statute of the International Court of Justice, by referring them to the court, subject only, in the case of each of them, to any reservation already made by that party when accepting this clause for compulsory jurisdiction to the extent that that party may maintain the reservation.
>
> In addition, the high contracting parties will submit to conciliation all disputes outside the scope of Article 36, paragraph 2, of the Statute of the International Court of Justice. In the case of a mixed dispute involving both questions for which conciliation is appropriate and other questions for which judicial settlement is appropriate, any party to the dispute shall have the right to insist that the judicial settlement of the legal questions shall precede conciliation. The preceding provisions of this article in no way affect the application of relevant provisions or agreements prescribing some other method of pacific settlement.

The Charter of the Organisation of American States contains the following provisions concerning settlement of local disputes:

> Article 20
>
> All international disputes that may arise between American States shall be submitted to the peaceful procedures set forth in this Charter, before being referred to the Security Council of the United Nations.
>
> Article 21
>
> The following are peaceful procedures: direct negotiation, good offices, mediation, investigation and conciliation, judicial settlement, arbitration,

which authorises the establishment of regional arrangements for other purposes than for the settlement of local disputes. According to paragraph 2, the Members of the United Nations which are members of a regional organisation ' shall,' *i.e.*, are obliged to ' make every effort to achieve pacific settlement of local disputes ' through their regional organisation. This provision and the provisions of paragraphs 3 and 4 are paralleled by the provisions of Chapter VI of the Charter. The relationship between Article 52 and Chapter VI of the Charter shall be discussed in the chapter of this study dealing with the settlement of disputes.[8]

B. *Enforcement Actions*

Regional organisations may act as organs of the United Nations not only in settling local disputes, but also in taking enforcement action under the authority of the Security Council. In this respect Article 53 stipulates:

> 1. The Security Council shall, where appropriate, utilise such regional arrangements or agencies for enforcement action under its authority. But no enforcement action shall be taken under regional arrangements or by regional agencies without the authorisation of the Security Council, with the exception of measures against any enemy state, as defined in paragraph 2 of this Article, provided for pursuant to Article 107 or in regional arrangements directed against renewal of aggressive policy on the part of any such state, until such time as the Organisation may, on request of the Governments concerned, be charged with the responsibility for preventing further aggression by such a state.

and those which the parties to the dispute may especially agree upon at any time.

ARTICLE 22

In the event that a dispute arises between two or more American States which, in the opinion of one of them, cannot be settled through the usual diplomatic channels, the Parties shall agree on some other peaceful procedure that will enable them to reach a solution.

ARTICLE 23

A special treaty will establish adequate procedures for the pacific settlement of disputes and will determine the appropriate means for their application, so that no dispute between American States shall fail of definitive settlement within a reasonable period.

Some regional arrangements, as *e.g.*, the North Atlantic Treaty, do not contain provisions concerning the settlement of local disputes. The provision of Article 1 of this Treaty: ' The Parties undertake, as set forth in the Charter of the United Nations, to settle any international disputes in which they may be involved by peaceful means in such a manner that international peace and security, and justice, are not endangered, and to refrain in their international relations from the threat or use of force in any manner inconsistent with the purposes of the United Nations,' is only a repetition of the provisions of Article 2, paragraph 3 and 4, of the Charter.

[8] Cf. *infra*, pp. 433 ff.

> 2. The term enemy state as used in paragraph 1 of this Article applies to any state which during the Second World War has been an enemy of any signatory of the present Charter.

To ' utilise regional arrangements or regional agencies for enforcement action ' means to utilise the states parties to a regional arrangement and hence members of a regional organisation either directly, or indirectly in utilising the agency constituted by a regional arrangement, for enforcement action. A regional arrangement is a treaty and as such cannot be utilised for enforcement action.

The provision that the Security Council shall utilise regional arrangements or agencies for enforcement action presupposes the provision of Article 25 obligating the Members to carry out the decisions of the Security Council, of Article 48 obligating the Members to carry out the decisions of the Security Council concerning enforcement action directly and through their action in the appropriate international agencies of which they are members, and of Article 49 obligating the Members to join in affording mutual assistance in carrying out the measures decided upon by the Security Council. The Security Council can utilise regional arrangements or regional agencies for enforcement action insofar as the states parties to such arrangements are bound by the Charter to execute the decisions of the Security Council.

The enforcement action referred to in Article 53, paragraph 1, may be taken to maintain or restore peace within the regional community, that is to say, against a party to the regional arrangement which is guilty of a threat to the peace or breach of the peace in relation to another party to this arrangement. But the wording of Article 53, paragraph 1, does not restrict the Security Council to utilise the members of a regional organisation or their agency only for enforcement action taken to maintain or restore peace within this organisation. It may utilise especially regional agencies for enforcement action taken to maintain or to restore peace wherever a threat to the peace or a breach of the peace makes such action necessary.

Without authorisation of the Security Council, enforcement actions under a regional arrangement, and especially by a regional agency, are permissible in three cases: (*a*) Enforcement action as a measure against any enemy state provided for pursuant to Article 107. This Article permits action in relation to any enemy state taken or authorised as a result of the Second World War by the Governments having responsibility for such action.[9] The provision of Article 53 referring to such action is superfluous. It is covered by Article 107. (*b*) Enforcement action provided for in regional arrangements directed against renewal of aggressive policy on the part of any enemy state until such time as the Organisation may, on request of the Governments concerned, be charged with the responsibility for preventing

[9] Cf. *infra*, pp. 805 ff.

further aggression by such a state. This provision is a remarkable extension of the rule laid down in Article 107 by which Members of the United Nations are released from the obligation to refrain from the threat or use of force and to settle their disputes by peaceful means. These provisions shall be discussed in another connection.[1] (*c*) Enforcement action in the exercise of collective self-defence under Article 51 of the Charter. This case is not mentioned in Article 53. But there can be no doubt that the provision of Article 51 authorising collective self-defence constitutes a restriction of the rule laid down in Article 53 that no enforcement action shall be taken under regional arrangements or by regional agencies without the authorisation of the Security Council. Article 51 provides: 'Nothing in the present Charter shall impair the inherent right of . . . collective self-defence . . . ', and the right of collective self-defence implying the right of using force may be organised by regional arrangements.

Article 54 provides:

> The Security Council shall at all times be kept fully informed of activities undertaken or in contemplation under regional arrangements or by regional agencies for the maintenance of international peace and security.

This provision imposes upon the Members of the United Nations in their capacity as parties to regional arrangements and upon the regional agencies as—indirect—organs of the United Nations the obligation to inform the Security Council of their activities undertaken or in contemplation for the maintenance of international peace and security. This provision is paralleled by the provision of Article 51 that measures taken by Members in the exercise of the right of self-defence shall be immediately reported to the Security Council. But the provision of Article 54, goes beyond that of Article 51. It refers not only to measures taken in the exercise of collective self-defence organised by regional arrangements, but also to other measures taken under regional arrangements for the maintenance of peace. On the other hand the provision of Article 51 refers expressly only to Members, whereas Article 54 refers also to non-members which are parties to a regional organisation.[2]

[1] Cf. *infra*, pp. 809 ff.

[2] Cf. Article 5 of the Inter-American Treaty of Reciprocal Assistance, *infra*, pp. 793 f. and Article 5 of the Brussels Five Power Treaty, *infra*, pp. 794 f. Article 5, paragraph 2, of the North Atlantic Treaty (cf. *infra*, pp. 795 f.) in conformity with Article 51 of the Charter contains a provision to the effect that all measures taken as a result of an armed attack shall immediately be reported to the Security Council. But the Treaty does not contain an express provision that the Security Council, in conformity with Article 54, shall be fully informed of other measures taken under this regional arrangement, especially of the measures stipulated in Article 3 (mutual aid for the development of the capacity to resist armed attack).

CHAPTER 13

LEGAL STATUS OF THE ORGANISATION

1. GENERAL REMARKS

THE United Nations possesses juridical personality in the field of international law as well as in the field of the national law of the Member states. Juridical personality means the capacity of being a subject of legal duties and legal rights, of performing legal transactions and of suing and being sued at law. An international community possesses juridical personality in the field of international law if the treaty constituting the community confers upon its organs the competence to exercise certain functions in relation to the members and especially the power to enter into international agreements establishing duties, rights and competences of the community. These duties, rights and competences are, it is true, the duties, rights and competences of the members; but in a collective way because to be carried out or exercised through the organs of the community in accordance with the constituent treaty. Hence the duties, rights and competences are those of the community and as such different from the duties, rights and competences which the members have individually. Such differentiation, however, is possible only if the community is centralised, that is to say, if the constituent treaty establishes special organs competent to carry out the duties and exercise the rights and competences of the community. In carrying out the duties and exercising the rights and competences of the community the organs act on behalf of the community, not on behalf of the members. This is the reason why—as pointed out in another connection—the wording of Article 24, paragarph 1, of the Charter, providing that in carrying out its duties the Security Council acts on behalf of the Members of the United Nations, is not correct.

The constituent treaty need not expressly confer upon the international community juridical personality. The latter is—or is not—implied in the substantial provisions of the constituent treaty. Committee IV/2 of the San Francisco Conference considered it superfluous to make the international juridical personality of the Organisation the subject of a text. It assumed that 'it will be determined implicitly from the provisions of the Charter taken as a whole.'[1]

However, if the constituent treaty does not contain a provision conferring expressly upon the community international juridical

[1] Report of the Rapporteur of Committee IV/2 (U.N.C.I.O. Doc. 933, IV/2/42 (2), p. 8).

personality, that is to say unrestricted legal capacity under international law, the community has only those special capacities as conferred upon it by particular provisions. This is of practical importance for the legal capacity of concluding treaties, especially treaties with single states or other international persons, by which the Organisation assumes specific functions not conferred upon it by its constitution; and for the legal capacity of suing and being sued before international tribunals. At the San Francisco Conference the Belgian delegation proposed to insert into the Charter the following provision: 'The Parties to the present Charter recognise that the Organisation they are setting up possesses international status, together with the rights this involves.'[2] If this proposal had been accepted the Organisation would have the power to conclude any treaty whatever, especially treaties by which the Organisation accepts functions not conferred upon it by the Charter. If the constitution of an international organisation authorises this organisation in a general way to enter into international agreements with other persons of international law, the constitution must also contain a provision determining the organ competent to conclude, on behalf of the organisation, the agreements. The Charter of the United Nations neither contains a general provision authorising the Organisation to enter into international agreements nor a provision determining the organ competent to conclude on behalf of the United Nations such agreements. Consequently the United Nations has legally only the power to enter into those international agreements which it is authorised by special provisions of the Charter to conclude; and these agreements are to be concluded, on behalf of the Organisation, through the organs determined by these special provisions.

A treaty by which the United Nations assumes functions not conferred upon it by the Charter is equivalent to an amendment to the Charter. If the United Nations concludes such a treaty not authorised by the Charter its constitutionality is highly problematical.

The provisions of the Charter authorising the United Nations to enter into international agreements are presented in the following section.

2. International Agreements to be Concluded by the United Nations (Juridical Personality of the Organisation under International Law)

Article 26 of the Charter provides that the Security Council shall formulate 'plans to be submitted to the Members of the United Nations for the establishment of a system for the regulation of armaments.' When these plans are accepted by the Members to whom they are submitted, a treaty is established between the United Nations, represented by the Security Council, and the Member state concerned;

[2] U.N.C.I.O. Doc. 524, IV/2/26; cf. also Summary Report of 10th meeting of Committee IV/2 (U.N.C.I.O. Doc. 554, IV/2/28).

Article 43, paragraph 3, authorises the Security Council to conclude on behalf of the United Nations with Members or 'groups of Members' the agreements referred to in Article 43, paragraphs 1 and 2, governing the 'numbers and types of forces' to be made available to the Security Council, 'their degree of readiness and general location, and the nature of the facilities and assistance to be provided.' Paragraph 3 of this Article, it is true, provides that these agreements shall be concluded 'between the Security Council and Members or between the Security Council and groups of Members'; but, since the Security Council is not a juridical person, but merely the organ of the United Nations as a juridical person, the agreements can be concluded only between the United Nations, through the Security Council, and Members or groups of Members. If the 'groups of Members' are not organised and hence have no juridical personality, the agreement concerned can be concluded only between the United Nations, through the Security Council, on the one hand, and several Members, forming an unorganised group. Paragraph 3 expressly provides that these agreements shall be subject to ratification by the signatory states in accordance with their respective constitutional processes. These agreements, too, represent treaties concluded between the Organisation and its Members;

Article 53, paragraph 1, authorises the Members of the United Nations which are parties to a regional arrangement, and especially to a regional arrangement by which regional agencies are established, to take enforcement action against any enemy state as defined in paragraph 2 of this Article, without the authorisation of the Security Council in so far as the regional arrangements are directed against renewal of aggressive policy on the part of any enemy state 'until such time as the Organisation may, on the request of the governments concerned, be charged with the responsibility for preventing further aggression by such a state.' The Organisation must accept the request of the governments concerned, in order to be charged with the function of preventing further aggression by the enemy state. Acceptance of the request constitutes a treaty. It is by such a treaty concluded between the Organisation and the Member state concerned that the function referred to in Article 53, paragraph 1, is transferred to the Organisation. The Charter does not determine the organ of the United Nations competent to accept the request; but as no organ other than the Security Council is competent to take enforcement action, it is the Security Council through which the Organisation has to conclude this agreement;

Article 57, paragraph 1, provides that specialised agencies shall be brought into relationship with the United Nations, and Article 63, paragraph 1, authorises the Economic and Social Council to 'enter into agreements with any of the agencies referred to in Article 57, defining the terms on which the agency concerned shall be brought into relationship with the United Nations. Such agreements shall be subject to approval by the General Assembly.' These agreements are treaties concluded between the United Nations, represented by the Economic and Social Council and the General Assembly on the one hand, and the international organisations whose agencies are brought into relationship with the United Nations by these agreements, on the other hand;

Article 64, paragraph 1, authorises the Economic and Social Council to take appropriate steps to obtain regular reports from the specialised agencies, and to make arrangements with the Members of the United Nations and with the specialised agencies to obtain reports on the steps taken to give effect to its own recommendations and to recommendations on matters falling within its competence made by the General Assembly. The 'appropriate steps' and the 'arrangements' referred to in this paragraph may have the character of international agreements;

Article 17, paragraph 3, provides that the General Assembly shall consider and approve any financial and budgetary arrangements with specialised agencies referred to in Article 57. These arrangements, too, may have the character of international agreements concluded between the United Nations and the international organisation whose organ the specialised agency is. The Charter does not determine the organ of the United Nations competent to make the financial and budgetary arrangements to be approved by the General Assembly. Upon the analogy of Article 63, paragraph 1, it may be assumed that, according to the intention of the Charter, the Economic and Social Council is competent to make these financial and budgetary arrangements; they may even be included in the agreements referred to in Article 63. The same is true with respect to the arrangements which the Economic and Social Council is authorised by Article 70 to make 'for representatives of the specialised agencies to participate, without vote, in its deliberations and in those of the commissions established by it, and for its representatives to participate in the deliberations of the specialised agencies';

Articles 75, 77 and 79, provide for so-called trusteeship agreements by which certain territories may be placed under the trusteeship system of the United Nations. These trusteeship agreements are treaties concluded by the United Nations on the one hand, and the states competent to dispose of these territories on the other hand.[3] The Charter characterises the function of the United Nations with respect to these trusteeship agreements as 'approval.' Under Article 83, the terms of trusteeship agreements, their alteration or amendment shall be approved by the Security Council if the trusteeship agreements refer to strategic areas; under Article 85, the terms of trusteeship agreements, their alteration or amendment shall be

[3] Cf. *infra*, pp. 578 ff.

approved by the General Assembly if these agreements refer to areas not designated as strategic. The United Nations, in approving the trusteeship agreements through the Security Council or the General Assembly, becomes a party to these treaties. The Charter authorises the United Nations to enter into such agreements, and by entering into these agreements to assume the functions determined by the agreements;

Article 105, paragraph 3, authorises the General Assembly to 'propose conventions to the Members of the United Nations' for the purpose to determine the details of the application of paragraphs 1 and 2 of this Article concerning the privileges and immunities which the Organisation shall enjoy in the territory of each of its Members, and the privileges and immunities which the representatives of the Members of the United Nations and the officials of the Organisation shall enjoy as far as such privileges and immunities are necessary for the independent exercise of their functions in connection with the Organisation. It is not expressly stipulated, but it may be assumed, that these conventions are to be concluded between the United Nations and the Member states and that the General Assembly is the organ through which these conventions are to be concluded on behalf of the Organisation.

The Charter (including the Statute) contains certain provisions by which the participation of non-member states in the procedure for the settlement of disputes by the Security Council or by the General Assembly, their adherence to the Statute of the Court, their participation in the election of the members of the Court and in the procedure for the amendment of the Statute, is made dependent on certain conditions, determined either directly by the Charter or by an organ of the United Nations. Thus, Article 32 of the Charter provides that the Security Council shall lay down such conditions as it deems just for the participation of a state which is not a Member of the United Nations in the discussion of the Security Council of a dispute to which the non-member state is a party. Only if the non-member state accepts these conditions, can it be invited. If these conditions are laid down, not in a general way, but in a concrete case for a particular dispute with respect to a definite non-member state, the acceptance of these conditions is an agreement between the non-member state concerned and the Organisation. If the conditions are laid down in a general way, they constitute legal rules to be applied to a special case in the same way as a statute is applied. The non-member state can be invited under Article 32 only if it complies with these objective rules.

Article 35, paragraph 2, provides that a state which is not a Member of the United Nations may bring to the attention of the Security Council or of the General Assembly any dispute to which it is a party 'if it accepts in advance, for the purposes of the dispute, the obligations of pacific settlement provided in the present Charter.'

The condition under which the non-member state may bring to the attention of the Organisation a dispute is directly determined by the Charter; its acceptance on the part of the non-member state is not to be interpreted as entering into an agreement with the United Nations, but as compliance with an objective rule of law.

Article 93, paragraph 2, provides that a state which is not a Member of the United Nations may become a party to the Statute of the International Court of Justice on conditions to be determined ' in each case ' by the General Assembly upon the recommendation of the Security Council. If this provision is applied in accordance with its wording, the conditions must be determined individually with respect to a definite state which wishes to accede to the Statute. In accepting the conditions determined by the General Assembly upon the recommendation of the Security Council, the state concerned enters into an agreement with the United Nations.

Article 4, paragraph 3, of the Statute, provides that the conditions under which a state which is a party to the present Statute but is not a Member of the United Nations may participate in electing the members of the Court ' shall, in the absence of a special agreement, be laid down by the General Assembly upon recommendation of the Security Council.' The provision refers expressly to the possibility of a special agreement between a definite state and the Organisation. If, however, the General Assembly upon recommendation of the Security Council lays down in a general way the conditions under which a non-member state party to the Statute may participate in electing the members of the Court, the rules concerned form a part of the law of the United Nations, and the state, in fulfilling these conditions, does not enter into an agreement with the United Nations. If the conditions referred to in Article 4, paragraph 3, of the Statute, are laid down individually, they may be included in the conditions determined under Article 93, paragraph 2, of the Charter.

Article 69 of the Statute provides that the General Assembly upon recommendation of the Security Council may adopt provisions concerning the participation in the amendment procedure of states which are parties to the Statute but are not Members of the United Nations. It seems that by ' provisions ' general rules are meant, not individual conditions determined for the participation of an individual state in the amendment procedure. Compliance with these provisions has not the character of entering into an agreement.

Article 28, paragraph 3, of the Charter, provides:

> The Security Council may hold meetings at such places other than the seat of the Organisation as in its judgment will best facilitate its work.

This provision certainly implies an obligation of any Member of the United Nations to permit the Security Council to hold meetings on any Member's territory. Should the Security Council decide to hold meetings on the territory of a non-member state, an agreement between the United Nations represented by the Security Council and the state concerned is necessary. Article 28, paragraph 3, may be interpreted to authorise the United Nations to conclude such a treaty through the Security Council. An analogous interpretation of Articles 22 and 28 of the Statute is possible in case the Court, or one of its chambers, should decide to sit and exercise its functions elsewhere than on the territory of a state party to the Statute.

As a matter of fact the United Nations has entered into international agreements not authorised by one of the just mentioned provisions of the Charter; as for instance the agreement concerning the execution of the transfer to the United Nations of certain Assets of the League of Nations, signed on July 19, 1946, and the Protocol concerning the execution of various operations in the transfer to the United Nations of certain Assets of the League of Nations, signed on August 1, 1946, with the League of Nations;[4] the Interim Agreement on the Privileges and Immunities of the United Nations concluded with the Swiss Federal Council,[5] and the Agreement concerning the Ariana Site concluded with the Swiss Confederation;[6] the Headquarter Agreement, signed on June 26, 1947, with the United States of America;[7] the agreement concluded with the contracting parties to the peace treaty with Italy by the Security Council's approval of Annexes VI, VII and VIII, of this treaty, on January 10, 1947.[8]

As the United Nations is an international juridical person, it may have the right of active and passive legation. The Charter, however, does not contain a provision stipulating the exercise of this right.[9]

[4] Resolutions adopted by the General Assembly (Doc. A/64/Add. 1, pp. 139 ff.).

[5] Resolutions adopted by the General Assembly (Doc. A/64/Add. 1, p. 194; A/175, pp. 16 ff.). This agreement has no basis in Articles 104 and 105 of the Charter which refer only to Members of the United Nations. Switzerland is not a Member. By the resolution of December 14, 1946, the General Assembly approved also certain arrangements formulated in a letter of October 22, 1946, from the Head of the Swiss Federal Political Department which contains *inter alia* under point 5 the following provision:

> It is understood, further, that military operations, in case of conflict between States Members of the United Nations, or between the United Nations and a third State, will in no case be directed from Swiss Territory. (Doc. A/175, p. 3.)

There is no basis in the Charter for assuming such an obligation.

[6] Resolutions adopted by the General Assembly (Doc. A/64/Add. 1, p. 194; A/175, pp. 26 ff.).

[7] Resolutions adopted by the General Assembly (Doc. A/519, pp. 91 ff.). Cf. *infra*, pp. 350 ff.

[8] Cf. *infra*, pp. 825 ff.

[9] The practice has developed of establishing at the seat of the Organisation permanent missions of Member states. At its 169th meeting the General Assembly adopted the following resolutions:

A

The General Assembly,

Considering that, since the creation of the United Nations, the practice

3. Juridical Personality of the Organisation under the National Law of the Members

If the United Nations shall possess juridical personality not only in the field of international but also in the field of national law, the latter capacity must be conferred upon the Organisation by the law of the states concerned. For this purpose Article 104 provides:

> The Organisation shall enjoy in the territory of each of its Members such legal capacity as may be necessary for the exercise of its functions and the fulfilment of its purposes.

The wording of this provision refers to 'legal capacity' without any restriction to the field of national law. But it is only with respect to the legal capacity under national law that Article 104 is necessary, and has been adopted. The Report of Rapporteur of Committee IV/2 of the San Francisco Conference[1] contains the following statement with respect to Article 104: 'It is to be noted that this provision is

> has developed of establishing, at the seat of the Organisation, permanent missions of Member States,
>
> Considering that the presence of such permanent missions serves to assist in the realisation of the purposes and principles of the United Nations and, in particular, to keep the necessary liaison between the Member States and the Secretariat in periods between sessions of the different organs of the United Nations,
>
> Considering that in these circumstances, the generalisation of the institution of permanent missions can be foreseen and that the submission of credentials of permanent representatives should be regulated,
>
> Recommends
>
> 1. That the credentials of the permanent representatives shall be issued either by the head of the State or by the head of the Government or by the Minister of Foreign Affairs, and shall be transmitted to the Secretary-General;
>
> 2. That the appointments and changes of members of the permanent missions other than the permanent representative shall be communicated in writing to the Secretary-General by the head of the mission;
>
> 3. That the permanent representative in case of temporary absence shall notify the Secretary-General of the name of the member of the mission who will perform the duties of head of the mission;
>
> 4. That Member States desiring their permanent representatives to represent them on one or more of the organs of the United Nations should specify the organs in the credentials transmitted to the Secretary-General;
>
> Instructs the Secretary-General to submit, at each regular session of the General Assembly, a report on the credentials of the permanent representatives accredited to the United Nations.
>
> B
>
> The General Assembly
>
> Instructs the Secretary-General to study all questions which may arise from the institution of permanent missions, including permanent missions to the European Office of the United Nations, and, if necessary, to report on this subject to the next regular session of the General Assembly. (Doc. A/P.V. 169, pp. 32 ff.)

[1] U.N.C.I.O. Doc. 933, IV/2/42 (2), p. 8.

conceived in very general terms. It is confined to a statement of the obligation incumbent upon each member State to act in such a way that the Organisation enjoys in its territory a juridical status permitting it to exercise its functions. The Organisation should be capable, in effect, as regards internal law, of performing the juridical acts required to put its capacities into operation. The Organisation must be able, in its own name, to contract, to hold movable and immovable property, to appear in court. These are only examples. The Committee has preferred to express no opinion on the procedures of internal law necessary to assure this result. These procedures may differ according to the legislation of each member State. It is possible that among the majority of them it may be indispensable that the Organisation be recognised as a juridical personality.'

Article 104 imposes upon the Members the obligation to grant to the Organisation the legal capacity referred to in this Article. But —according to its wording—it does not confer upon the Organisation the power to exercise this capacity by performing definite legal transactions. An express provision to this effect was not superfluous. Since the framers of the Charter probably did not intend to authorise the United Nations to perform any legal transaction whatever, it was necessary to determine what legal transaction under national law the Organisation shall be entitled to perform. It was probably intended to authorise the Organisation to perform all legal transactions necessary to achieve its purposes. If so, it was advisable to insert such a provision into the Charter.

The 'Convention on the Privileges and Immunities of the United Nations' adopted by the General Assembly in its resolution of February 13, 1946,[2] provides in Article 1, Section 1:

> The United Nations shall possess juridical personality. It shall have the capacity:
>
> (*a*) to contract;
>
> (*b*) to acquire and dispose of immovable and movable property;
>
> (*c*) to institute legal proceedings.

4. Privileges and Immunities

The Charter imposes upon the Members not only the obligation to grant to the Organisation juridical personality in the field of national law, but also the obligation to grant to the Organisation, to the representatives of its Members, and to the officials of the Organisation certain privileges and immunities. Article 105 provides:

> 1. The Organisation shall enjoy in the territory of each of its Members such privileges and immunities as are necessary for the fulfilment of its purposes.

[2] Resolutions adopted by the General Assembly (Doc. A/64, pp. 25 ff.).

> 2. Representatives of the Members of the United Nations and officials of the Organisation shall similarly enjoy such privileges and immunities as are necessary for the independent exercise of their functions in connection with the Organisation.
>
> 3. The General Assembly may make recommendations with a view to determining the details of the application of paragraphs 1 and 2 of this Article or may propose conventions to the Members of the United Nations for this purpose.

In this respect there exists a difference between the Charter and the Covenant of the League of Nations which in Article 7, paragraphs 4 and 5 stipulated:

> 4. Representatives of the Members of the League and officials of the League when engaged on the business of the League shall enjoy diplomatic privileges and immunities.
>
> 5. The buildings and other property occupied by the League or its officials or by Representatives attending its meetings shall be inviolable.

The Covenant provided for ' diplomatic privileges and immunities,' whereas the Charter only for ' such privileges and immunities as are necessary ' with respect to the Organisation: ' for the fulfilment of its purposes,' with respect to its officials and the representatives of its Members: ' for the independent exercise of their functions in connection with the Organisation.' The Covenant obligated the Members of the League to grant diplomatic privileges and immunities to the representatives of the Members and the officials of the League; as to the League as such, the Covenant required only inviolability of the buildings and other property occupied by the League. The Charter provides that the necessary privileges and immunities shall be granted: 1. to the Organisation as such; and 2. to the representatives of its Members and to its officials. By the ' Organisation ' referred to in Article 105, paragraph 1, all organs of the United Nations are to be understood. The Report of the Rapporteur of Committee IV/2[3] states that the provision of paragraph 1 ' covers all the agencies of the Organisation, that is, the agencies or authorities established by the Charter, as well as the other bodies and organisms which might subsequently be established by virtue of the powers conferred by the Charter.' But the Report adds: ' those agencies not belonging to the Organisation, although they may have been brought into connection or relation with the Organisation through application of the Charter ' are excluded from the provision. These are the ' specialised agencies ' referred to in Article 57 of the Charter. This interpretation of paragraph 1 is correct only if the specialised agencies brought into relationship with the Organisation are not considered to be organs of

[3] U.N.C.I.O. Doc. 933, IV/2/42 (2), p. 2.

the United Nations. As pointed out,[4] they may be conceived of as indirect organs of the United Nations, and hence they may claim the privileges and immunities referred to in Article 105, paragraph 1, whose wording does not exclude such interpretation. However, the Convention on the Privileges and Immunities of the United Nations, adopted by the General Assembly, does not refer to the specialised agencies. With respect to these agencies the General Assembly adopted at its 31st meeting a Resolution on the Co-ordination of the Privileges and Immunities of the United Nations and the Specialised Agencies,[5] and at its 123rd meeting, a Convention on the Privileges and Immunities of the Specialised Agencies 'for acceptance by the specialised agencies and for accession by all Members of the United Nations and by any other State member of a specialised agency.'[6]

Insofar as by the 'privileges and immunities' referred to in Article 105, paragraph 1, exemption of the United Nations from the jurisdiction of the Member states is to be understood, it should be noted that such exemption as privilege of a juristic person necessarily means exemption of the acts of this juristic person from the jurisdiction of the states legally bound to grant this privilege. For a juristic person manifests its legal existence through its acts, and its acts are performed by individuals in their capacity as organs of the juristic person. These acts are acts of the juristic person insofar as they are imputed to the juristic person. Hence exemption of the United Nations from the jurisdiction of the Member states coincides with exemption of individuals from the jurisdiction of the Member states with respect to acts performed by these individuals in their capacity

[4] Cf. *supra*, p. 146.

[5] Resolutions adopted by the General Assembly (Doc. A/64, p. 33). This resolution contains the statement: 'the General Assembly considers that the privileges and immunities of the United Nations should be regarded, as a general rule, as a maximum within which the various specialised agencies should enjoy such privileges and immunities as the appropriate fulfilment of their respective functions may require, and that no privileges and immunities which are not really necessary should be asked for.'

[6] Resolutions adopted by the General Assembly (Doc. A/519, pp. 112 ff.). In this resolution the General Assembly declared that it is 'desirable that any specialised agency which is hereafter brought into relationship with the United Nations in accordance with Article 63 of the Charter should derive its privileges and immunities exclusively from the said General Convention, with such modifications as may be necessary to meet the particular requirements of that agency to be contained in an annex.'

If it is assumed that the specialised agencies are not organs—at least indirect organs—of the United Nations, the question arises as to whether the General Assembly was competent to deal with the privileges and immunities of these international organisations. The provisions of Articles 58 and 60 authorising the Assembly to make recommendations 'for the co-ordination of the policies and activities of the specialised agencies' are a rather problematical basis; for the privileges and immunities to be granted to the specialised agencies can hardly be considered as 'policies' or 'activities' of these agencies.

as organs of the United Nations. Paragraph 2 of Article 105 refers to the privileges and immunities of individuals in their capacity as ' representatives of the Members of the United Nations ' and ' officials of the Organisation.' In both capacities these individuals are direct or indirect organs of the United Nations. But paragraph 2 does not restrict the privileges and immunities to be granted to the individuals concerned to the acts which they perform in their capacity as organs of the United Nations. ' Functions in connection with the Organisation ' are, it is true, in the first place functions of the Organisation, that is to say functions performed by the individuals concerned in their capacity as organs of the United Nations. But in order to exercise these functions independently, privileges and immunities, especially exemption from the jurisdiction of the Member states may be necessary with respect to acts which have not the character of acts of the Organisation, but which are in connection with the official functions of the individuals concerned. These acts, too, although not imputable to the Organisation, are covered by the wording of Article 105, paragraph 2. Acts performed by representatives of Members or officials of the Organisation in their capacity as private persons which are in no connection with the Organisation, and that means: in no connection with the official functions of the individuals as organs of the United Nations, are not covered by the privileges and immunities referred to in Article 105, paragraph 2.

' Diplomatic privileges and immunities ' in the usual sense of this term, that is to say the privileges and immunities to be granted under general international law to diplomatic envoys by the receiving state, imply in the first place exemption from the jurisdiction of the receiving state with respect to acts performed by the diplomatic envoy in his capacity as private person. Acts performed in his capacity as organ of his state are exempt from the jurisdiction of the receiving state according to another principle of general international law, the rule that no state has jurisdiction over another state, which necessarily means: over the acts of another state, whether these acts are performed by diplomatic envoys or by other organs of the state. Article 7, paragraph 4, of the Covenant, prescribes that representatives of the Members and officials of the League shall enjoy ' diplomatic privileges and immunities ' when engaged on the business of the League. That may mean, that, in the first place, acts performed by these persons in their capacity as organs of the League shall be exempt from the jurisdiction of the Member states, and only in the second place also private acts performed by them ' when ' *i.e.*, during the time they were engaged on the business of the League. By granting exemption from the jurisdiction of the Member states to the official acts of the representatives of the Members and officials of the League, this exemption was granted to the League as such, although the Covenant did not contain an express provision to this effect. Since the ' diplomatic privileges and immunities ' referred to in Article 7, paragraph 4, were intended to cover not only the private acts of the representatives and officials but also their acts performed in their capacity as organs of the League, the term had another than its usual meaning. Besides the privileges and immunities granted to representatives of the Members and officials of the League could not be ' diplomatic ' since these persons did not exercise diplomatic functions.

In this respect the text of the Charter is more appropriate than that of the Covenant.

The Charter, however, is not consistent in this point. With respect to the members of the Court, who are ' officials ' of the Organisation—whereas the members of the Permanent Court of International Justice were not officials of the League—Article 19 of the Statute—an integral part of the Charter—stipulates that they ' shall enjoy diplomatic privileges and immunities.' This inconsistency may be explained by the fact that Article 19 of the Statute is a literal copy of the same Article of the old Statute. Article 42, paragraph 3, of the new Statute, which has no counterpart in the old Statute, referring to ' the agents, counsel, and advocates of parties before the Court, stipulates, in conformity with the formula of Article 105 of the Charter, that they ' shall enjoy the privileges and immunities necessary to the independent exercise of their duties.'

The formula: ' such privileges and immunities as are necessary ' for certain purposes requires an authority to determine what is necessary. The Report of the Rapporteur of Committee IV/2 contains the following statement:[7] ' The draft article proposed by the Committee does not specify the privileges and immunities respect for which it imposes on the member states. This has been thought superfluous. The terms *privileges* and *immunities* indicate in a general way all that could be considered necessary to the realisation of the purposes of the Organisation, to the free functioning of its organs and to the independent exercise of the functions and duties of their officials: exemption from tax, immunity from jurisdiction, facilities for communication, inviolability of buildings, properties, and archives, etc. It would moreover have been impossible to establish a list valid for all the member states and taking account of the special situation in which some of them might find themselves by reason of the activities of the Organisation or of its organs in their territory. But if there is one certain principle it is that no member state may hinder in any way the working of the Organisation or take any measures the effect of which might be to increase its burdens, financial or other.' However, this interpretation of the phrase ' such privileges and immunities as are necessary ' is not authentic, and the Charter does not answer the question as to who is competent to decide what is ' necessary.' But Article 105, paragraph 3, provides for ' recommendations ' to be made by the General Assembly ' with a view to determining the details of

[7] U.N.C.I.O. Doc. 933, IV/2/42, p. 3.

the application of paragraphs 1 and 2 of this Article ' of for ' conventions ' to be concluded between the Members and the Organisation for this purpose. ' Recommendations ' are not binding, but ' conventions ' are. By conventions ratified by Members the ' necessary ' privileges and immunities may be determined; and ' diplomatic.' privileges and immunities may be considered to be necessary. It must be pointed out that even without any such convention the Members are obliged by Article 105 to grant to the Organisation, its officials, and the representative of its Members the ' necessary ' privileges and immunities. If no convention exists there is no possibility of imposing upon a Member a definite interpretation of the provisions of Article 105, paragraphs 1 and 2.

The conventions referred to in Article 105, paragraph 3, shall deal —as expressly stipulated—with the privileges and immunities referred to in Article 105, paragraphs 1 and 2, not with the legal capacity to be granted to the Organisation under Article 104. But the Convention on Privileges and Immunities deals not only with the privileges and immunities referred to in Article 105, paragraphs 1 and 2, but also in Article 1, Section 1, quoted above, with the legal capacity to be granted to the Organisation under Article 104.

Although the members, the Registrar, and the other officers of the International Court of Justice—' the principal judicial organ of the United Nations ' (Article 92)—are ' officials of the Organisation,' the Convention does not refer to these persons, whose privileges and immunities are regulated by other legal instruments. They will be discussed in the chapter on Judicial Settlement of Disputes. As to the privileges and immunities of the Organisation the Convention stipulates:

ARTICLE 2

PROPERTY, FUNDS AND ASSETS

SECTION 2

> The United Nations, its property and assets wherever located and by whomsoever held, shall enjoy immunity from every form of legal process except in so far as in any particular case it has expressly waived its immunity. It is, however, understood that no waiver of immunity shall extend to any measure of execution.

SECTION 3

> The premises of the United Nations shall be inviolable. The property and assets of the United Nations, wherever located and by whomsoever held, shall be immune from search, requisition, confiscation, expropriation and any other form of interference, whether by executive, administrative, judical or legislative action.

SECTION 4

The archives of the United Nations, and in general all documents belonging to it or held by it, shall be inviolable wherever located.

SECTION 5

Without being restricted by financial controls, regulations or moratoria of any kind,

(*a*) The United Nations may hold funds, gold or currency of any kind and operate accounts in any currency;

(*b*) The United Nations shall be free to transfer its funds, gold or currency from one country to another or within any country and to convert any currency held by it into any other currency.

SECTION 6

In exercising its rights under Section 5 above, the United Nations shall pay due regard to any representations made by the Government of any Member in so far as it is considered that effect can be given to such representations without detriment to the interests of the United Nations.

SECTION 7

The United Nations, its assets, income and other property shall be:

(*a*) exempt from all direct taxes; it is understood, however, that the United Nations will not claim exemption from taxes which are, in fact, no more than charges for public utility services;

(*b*) exempt from customs duties and prohibitions and restrictions on imports and exports in respect of articles imported or exported by the United Nations for its official use. It is understood, however, that articles imported under such exemption will not be sold in the country into which they were imported except under conditions agreed with the Government of that country;

(*c*) exempt from customs duties and prohibitions and restrictions on imports and exports in respect of its publications.

SECTION 8

While the United Nations will not, as a general rule, claim exemption from excise duties and from taxes on the sale of movable and immovable property which form part of the price to be paid, nevertheless, when the United Nations is making important purchases for official use of property on which such duties and taxes have been charged or are chargeable, Members will, whenever possible, make appropriate administrative arrangements for the remission or return of the amount of duty or tax.

Article 3

Facilities in Respect of Communications

Section 9

The United Nations shall enjoy in the territory of each Member for its official communications treatment not less favourable than that accorded by the Government of that Member to any other Government, including its diplomatic mission, in the matter of priorities, rates and taxes on mails, cables, telegrams, radiograms, telephotos, telephone and other communications; and press rates for information to the press and radio. No censorship shall be applied to the official correspondence and other official communications of the United Nations.

Section 10

The United Nations shall have the right to use codes and to despatch and receive its correspondence by courier or in bags, which shall have the same immunities and privileges as diplomatic couriers and bags.

As to the privileges and immunities of the representatives of the Members the Convention stipulates:

Article 4

The Representatives of Members

Section 11

Representatives of Members to the principal and subsidiary organs of the United Nations and to conferences convened by the United Nations, shall, while exercising their functions and during their journey to and from the place of meeting, enjoy the following privileges and immunities:

(*a*) immunity from personal arrest or detention and from seizure of their personal baggage, and, in respect of words spoken or written and all acts done by them in their capacity as representatives, immunity from legal process of every kind;

(*b*) inviolability for all papers and documents;

(*c*) the right to use codes and to receive papers or correspondence by courier or in sealed bags;

(*d*) exemption in respect of themselves and their

spouses from immigration restrictions, aliens registration or national service obligations in the State they are visiting or through which they are passing in the exercise of their functions;

(*e*) the same facilities in respect of currency or exchange restrictions as are accorded to representatives of foreign governments on temporary official missions;

(*f*) the same immunities and facilities in respect of their personal baggage as are accorded to diplomatic envoys, and also;

(*g*) such other privileges, immunities and facilities, not inconsistent with the foregoing, as diplomatic envoys enjoy, except that they shall have no right to claim exemption from customs duties on goods imported (otherwise than as part of their personal baggage) or from excise duties or sales taxes.

SECTION 12

In order to secure for the representatives of Members to the principal and subsidiary organs of the United Nations and to conferences convened by the United Nations, complete freedom of speech and independence in the discharge of their duties, the immunity from legal process in respect of words spoken or written and all acts done by them in discharging their duties shall continue to be accorded, notwithstanding that the persons concerned are no longer the representatives of Members.

SECTION 13

Where the incidence of any form of taxation depends upon residence, periods during which the representatives of Members to the principal and subsidiary organs of the United Nations and to conferences convened by the United Nations are present in a State for the discharge of their duties shall not be considered as period of residence.

SECTION 14

Privileges and immunities are accorded to the representatives of Members not for the personal benefit of the individuals themselves, but in order to safeguard the independent exercise of their functions in connection with the United Nations. Consequently a Member not only has the right but is under a duty to waive the immunity of its representative in any case where in the opinion of the Member the immunity would impede the course of justice, and it can be waived without prejudice to the purpose for which the immunity is accorded.

SECTION 15

The provisions of Sections 11, 12 and 13, are not applicable as between a representative and the authorities of the State of which he is a national or of which he is or has been the representative.

SECTION 16

In this article the expression 'representatives' shall be deemed to include all delegates, deputy delegates, advisers, technical experts and secretaries of delegations.

Article 5, dealing with the privileges and immunities of officials has been quoted in the chapter on the Secretary-General. In this connection it should be noted that according to Section 19 of Chapter 5 of the Convention 'the Secretary-General and all Assistant Secretaries-General shall be accorded in respect to themselves, their spouses and minor children, the privileges and immunities, exemptions and facilities accorded to diplomatic envoys, in accordance with international law.' The formula 'the privileges . . . accorded to diplomatic envoys in accordance with international law' is more correct than the formula used in the Covenant and the old Statute: 'diplomatic privileges and immunities.' But the provision of Section 19 seems to go farther than Article 105, paragraph 2, of the Charter, which provides that officials of the Organisation (not their spouses and children) shall enjoy such privileges and immunities as are necessary for the independent 'exercise of their functions in connection with the Organisation.' The 'privileges and immunities . . . accorded to diplomatic envoys' imply exemption from the jurisdiction of the Member states with respect to all private acts of the persons concerned, also those which have nothing to do with the 'exercise of their functions in connection with the Organisation.' On the other hand, the officials referred to in Section 18 of the Convention shall be immune only 'from legal process in respect of words spoken or written and all acts performed by them in their official capacity,' not with respect to other acts, even if in connection with their official functions. If exemption from jurisdiction is restricted to acts performed by individuals in their capacity as organs of the United Nations, the question arises who is competent to decide whether an act is or is not of this character. Since the Convention does not contain a provision in this respect two interpretations are possible: the Member state the jurisdiction of which is restricted, through its competent organ; or the United Nations represented, in case of a representative of a Member, by the organ to which the representative belongs, in case of an official, by the Secretary-General. The principle of 'national discrimination,' that is the rule that exemption from jurisdiction does not apply in the relation between a state and its own nationals, stipulated in Article 4, Section 15, with respect to representatives of

Members, is not recognised in Article 5 of the Convention with respect to officials of the Organisation.

Article 6 of the Convention deals with: 'Experts on Missions for the United Nations.' It runs as follows:

SECTION 22

Experts (other than officials coming within the scope of Article 5) performing missions for the United Nations shall be accorded such privileges and immunities as are necessary for the independent exercise of their functions during the period of their missions, including the time spent on journeys in connection with their missions. In particular they shall be accorded:

(*a*) immunity from personal arrest or detention and from seizure of their personal baggage;

(*b*) in respect of words spoken or written and acts done by them in the course of the performance of their mission, immunity from legal process of every kind. This immunity from legal process shall continue to be accorded notwithstanding that the persons concerned are no longer employed on missions for the United Nations;

(*c*) inviolability for all papers and documents;

(*d*) for the purpose of their communications with the United Nations, the right to use codes and to receive papers or correspondence by courier or in sealed bags;

(*e*) the same facilities in respect of currency or exchange restrictions as are accorded to representatives of foreign governments on temporary official missions;

(*f*) the same immunities and facilities in respect of their personal baggage as are accorded to diplomatic envoys.

SECTION 23

Privileges and immunities are granted to experts in the interests of the United Nations and not for the personal benefit of the individuals themselves. The Secretary-General shall have the right and the duty to waive the immunity of any expert in any case where, in his opinion, the immunity would impede the course of justice and it can be waived without prejudice to the interests of the United Nations.

Under Article 5 of the Headquarters Agreement the United States of America grants privileges and immunities 'as it accords to diplomatic envoys accredited to it' to permanent representatives to the United Nations. This agreement is discussed in the following section.

5. Legal Status of the Seat of the United Nations

The United Nations possesses the legal status of a person of international law, but it does not possess sovereignty over the territory on which its seat is to be established.

In contradistinction to the Covenant of the League of Nations, the Charter, as pointed out, does not determine the seat of the Organisation. Article 7, paragraphs 1 and 2, of the Covenant, expressly provide:

> 1. The Seat of the League is established at Geneva.
>
> 2. The Council may at any time decide that the Seat of the League shall be established elsewhere.

Such a provision imposes upon the state on whose territory the seat of the organisation, determined directly or indirectly by its constitution, is to be established the obligation to permit the establishment of the seat of the organisation on its territory, provided that this state is a party to the treaty constituting the organisation. If the constitution of the international organisation does not contain a provision determining the seat of the organisation, the question arises as to whether and on what conditions a definite state is obliged to permit establishment on its territory of the seat of the organisation. If the treaty constituting the organisation provides for special organs which can exercise their functions only if the organisation has a seat on the territory of a definite member state, it may be argued that each state party to the constituent treaty is under such obligation. But, as pointed out, it may also be argued that this obligation must be stipulated by a special treaty concluded by the organisation and the state concerned. Even it is assumed that this obligation is imposed directly by the constitution of the organisation upon each member state, a treaty is necessary to implement it. In any case, the constitution of the organisation should determine which of its organs is competent to conclude such a treaty.

The only provisions of the Charter referring to the 'seat of the Organisation' are contained in Article 28. Paragraph 2 of this Article provides that each member of the Security Council shall be represented at all times 'at the seat of the Organisation'; and paragraph 3 provides that the Security Council may hold meetings 'at such places other than the seat of the Organisation as in its judgment will best facilitate its work.' However, where the seat of the Organisation shall be established is not determined by the Charter. Nor does the Charter confer upon any of its organs the power to decide this question.

It is true that the Interim Arrangements Concluded by the Governments Represented at the United Nations Conference on International Organisation, signed at San Francisco on June 26, 1945, contain the provision that the Preparatory Commission of the United Nations established by the Interim Arrangements 'shall make studies and prepare recommendations concerning the location of the permanent headquarters of the Organisation.' It may be assumed that the phrase 'location of the permanent headquarters of the Organisation' has the same meaning as that used in Article 28 of the Charter: 'seat of the Organisation.' But the Interim Arrangements do not determine to whom the Preparatory Commission shall make the recommendations relating to the location of the permanent headquarters of the Organisation, nor does this treaty confer any competence in this matter upon any organ of the United Nations.

As a matter of fact, the Preparatory Commission adopted the following decision:[8]

> The Preparatory Commission recommends that:
>
> 1. the permanent headquarters of the United Nations should be located in the United States of America;
>
> 2. the site of the permanent headquarters should be in the east of the United States of America;
>
> 3. the specific site should be determined by the First Part of the First Session of the General Assembly on the basis of recommendations to be prepared by the Interim Committee established by the Preparatory Commission (Section 2 of this Chapter); and
>
> 4. the agreement to be entered into between the competent authorities of the United States of America and the Secretary-General of the United Nations should be negotiated with reference to the general principles set forth in the Draft Convention on Privileges and Immunities and in the Draft Treaty with the United States of America, which are transmitted as working papers for consideration by the General Assembly in Appendices B and C of Chapter VII.

The Preparatory Commission took it for granted that the General Assembly is competent to determine the seat of the Organisation. This supposition, however, has no basis in the Charter.

On the recommendations made by the Preparatory Commission, the General Assembly actually assumed the competence to determine the seat of the Organisation. At its 18th meeting the General Assembly appointed the Permanent Headquarters Committee, and, upon recommendation of this Committee, at its 33rd meeting resolved that 'The Permanent headquarters of the United Nations shall be established in Westchester (New York) and/or Fairfield (Conn.) counties, *i.e.*, near to New York City' and that 'the interim headquarters of the United Nations shall be located in New York City.'[9] At its 31st meeting the General Assembly authorised the Secretary-

[8] Report of the Preparatory Commission of the United Nations, 1945, p. 114.

[9] Resolutions adopted by the General Assembly (Doc. A/64, p. 37).

General 'to negotiate with the competent authorities of the United States of America the arrangements required as a result of the establishment of the seat of the United Nations in the United States of America' and approved a draft convention 'for use in these negotiations as a basis of discussion.'[1] This convention should be concluded on behalf of the United Nations by the Secretary-General. The General Assembly is authorised by Article 98 of the Charter to confer upon the Secretary-General such function.

On June 26, 1947, the Headquarters Agreement between the United Nations and the United States of America was signed at Lake Success.

In the Headquarters Agreement the area destined to be the seat of the Organisation is called 'headquarters district.'[2] According to Article 3, Section 7 (*a*), of the agreement, 'the headquarters district shall be under the control and authority of the United Nations as provided in this agreement.' But 'the control and authority' to be exercised by the United Nations under this agreement is very restricted.

First of all, the district remains under the law and judicial jurisdiction of the United States. Article 3, Section 7, provides:

> (*b*) Except as otherwise provided in this agreement or in the General Convention, the federal, state and local law of the United States shall apply within the headquarters district.
>
> (*c*) Except as otherwise provided in this agreement or in the General Convention, the federal, state and local courts of the United States shall have jurisdiction over acts done and transactions taking place in the headquarters district as provided in applicable federal, state and local laws.
>
> (*d*) The federal, state and local courts of the United States, when dealing with cases arising out of or relating to acts done or transactions taking place in the headquarters district, shall take into account the regulations enacted by the United Nations under Section 8.

The United Nations is authorised to exercise a limited legislative power. Section 8 provides:

> The United Nations shall have the power to make regulations, operative within the headquarters district, for the purpose of establishing therein conditions in all respects necessary for the full execution of its functions. No federal, state or local law or regulation of the United States which is inconsistent with a regulation of the United Nations authorised by this section shall, to the extent of such inconsistency, be applicable within the headquarters district. Any dispute, between the United

[1] *Ibid.*, pp. 27 f.
[2] Resolutions adopted by the General Assembly (Doc. A/519, pp. 91 ff.).

> Nations and the United States, as to whether a regulation of the United Nations is authorised by this section or as to whether a federal, state or local law or regulation is inconsistent with any regulation of the United Nations authorised by this section, shall be promptly settled as provided in Section 21. Pending such settlement, the regulation of the United Nations shall apply, and the federal, state or local law or regulation shall be inapplicable in the headquarters district to the extent that the United Nations claims it to be inconsistent with the regulations of the United Nations. This section shall not prevent the reasonable application of fire protection regulations of the appropriate American authorities.

The authority competent to settle the disputes referred to in Section 8 is an arbitral tribunal whose composition and jurisdiction shall be discussed in another connection.[3] The regulations referred to in Section 8 have the character of administrative law. In so far as they are to be applied by courts of the United States, they are American law whose creation is delegated by an international agreement entered into by the United States and the United Nations. Which organ of the United Nations is competent to exercise this legislative power? To this question the Charter has no answer.

The Headquarters Agreement confers upon the Secretary-General a limited authority in the field of police. Article 6, Section 16 (*b*), stipulates:

> If so requested by the Secretary-General, the appropriate American authorities shall provide a sufficient number of police for the preservation of law and order in the headquarters district, and for the removal therefrom of persons as requested under the authority of the United Nations. The United Nations shall, if requested, enter into arrangements with the appropriate American authorities to reimburse them for the reasonable cost of such services.

The police force placed at the disposal of the Secretary-General is not a police force of the United Nations. It remains a police force of the United States which authorises the Secretary-General to dispose of it for definite purposes and under definite conditions. Article 3, Section 10, stipulates:

> The United Nations may expel or exclude persons from the headquarters district for violation of its regulations adopted under Section 8 or for other cause. Persons who violate such regulations shall be subject to other penalties or to detention under arrest only in accordance with the provisions of such laws or regulations as may be adopted by the appropriate American authorities.

[3] Cf. *infra*, pp. 486 f.

Expulsion or exclusion referred to in Section 10 may be ordered by the competent organ of the United Nations—probably the Secretary-General. If employment of force is necessary, the American police at the disposal of the Secretary-General is to be used. Detention under arrest and penalties other than expulsion or exclusion are to be ordered only by American authorities and under American law established by American authorities.

The police force to be used within the headquarters district is different from that to be used to protect the district from the outside. In this respect Section 16 (*a*) of Article 6 provides:

> The appropriate American authorities shall exercise due diligence to ensure that the tranquillity of the headquarters district is not disturbed by the unauthorised entry of groups of persons from outside or by disturbances in its immediate vicinity and shall cause to be provided on the boundaries of the headquarters district such police protection as is required for these purposes.

As far as police protection from the outside is concerned, the United Nations has no authority at all. It is the United States which is obliged by the Headquarters Agreement to afford this protection. The same is true with respect to public services such as electricity, water, gas, and the like. Article 7 stipulates:

> SECTION 17
>
> (*a*) The appropriate American authorities will exercise, to the extent requested by the Secretary-General, the powers which they possess [with respect to the supplying of public services] to ensure that the headquarters district shall be supplied on equitable terms with the necessary public services, including electricity, water, gas, post, telephone, telegraph, transportation, drainage, collection of refuse, fire protection, snow removal, et cetera. In case of any interruption or threatened interruption of any such services, the appropriate American authorities will consider the needs of the United Nations as being of equal importance with the similar needs of essential agencies of the Government of the United States, and will take steps accordingly, to ensure that the work of the United Nations is not prejudiced.
>
> (*b*) Special provisions with reference to maintenance of utilities and underground construction are contained in Annex 2.
>
> SECTION 18
>
> The appropriate American authorities shall take all reasonable steps to ensure that the amenities of the headquarters district are not prejudiced and the purposes for which the district is required are not obstructed by any use made of the

land in the vicinity of the district. The United Nations shall on its part take all reasonable steps to ensure that the amenities of the land in the vicinity of the headquarters district are not prejudiced by any use made of the land in the headquarters district by the United Nations.

The United Nations has no sovereignty over the territory called the headquarters district. The legal relationship concerned is ownership under the law of the United States. In this respect Article 2, Section 3, of the Agreement, stipulates:

> The appropriate American authorities shall take whatever action may be necessary to assure that the United Nations shall not be dispossessed of its property in the headquarters district, except as provided in Section 22 in the event that the United Nations ceases to use the same, provided that the United Nations shall reimburse the appropriate American authorities for any costs incurred, after consultation with the United Nations, in liquidating by eminent domain proceedings or otherwise any adverse claims.

Article 9, Sections 22 and 23, stipulate:

SECTION 22

> (*a*) The United Nations shall not dispose of all or any part of the land owned by it in the headquarters district without the consent of the United States. If the United States is unwilling to consent [to a disposition which the United Nations wishes to make of all or any part of such land], it shall buy the land in question from the United Nations at a price to be determined as provided in paragraph (*d*) of this section.
>
> (*b*) If the seat of the United Nations is removed from the headquarters district, all right, title and interest of the United Nations in and to real property in the headquarters district or any part of it shall, on request of either the United Nations or the United States be assigned and conveyed to the United States. In the absence of such a request, the same shall be assigned and conveyed to the sub-division of a state in which it is located or, if such sub-division shall not desire it, then to the state in which it is located. If none of the foregoing desire the same, it may be disposed of as provided in paragraph (*a*) of this section.
>
> (*c*) If the United Nations disposes of all or any part of the headquarters district, the provisions of other sections of this agreement which apply to the headquarters district shall immediately cease to apply to the land and buildings so disposed of.
>
> (*d*) The price to be paid for any conveyance under this

section shall, in default of agreement, be the then fair value of the land, buildings and installations, to be determined under the procedure provided in Section 21.

SECTION 23

The seat of the United Nations shall not be removed from the headquarters district unless the United Nations should so decide.

The United Nations is authorised to establish on its property radio broadcasting facilities and an aerodrome.

ARTICLE 2

SECTION 4

(*a*) The United Nations may establish and operate in the headquarters district:

(1) its own short-wave sending and receiving radio broadcasting facilities, including emergency link equipment, which may be used on the same frequencies (within the tolerances prescribed for the broadcasting service by applicable United States Regulations) for radio-telegraph, radio-teletype, radio-telephone, radio-telephoto, and similar services;

(2) one point-to-point circuit between the headquarters district and the office of the United Nations in Geneva (using single sideband equipment) to be used exclusively for the exchange of broadcasting programmes and inter-office communications;

(3) low power, micro wave, low or medium frequencies, facilities for communication within headquarters buildings only, or such other buildings as may temporarily be used by the United Nations;

(4) facilities for point-to-point communications to the same extent and subject to the same conditions as permitted under applicable rules and regulations for amateur operations in the United States, except that such rules and regulations shall not be applied in a manner inconsistent with the inviolability of the headquarters district provided by Section 9 (*a*);

(5) such other radio facilities as may be specified by supplemental agreement between the United Nations and the appropriate American authorities.

(*b*) The United Nations shall make arrangements for the operation of the services referred to in this section with the International Telecommunication Union, the appropriate agencies of the Government of the United States and the appropriate agencies of other affected Governments with regard to all frequencies and similar matters.

(*c*) The facilities provided for in this section may, to the extent necessary for efficient operation, be established and operated outside the headquarters district. The appropriate American authorities will, on request of the United Nations, make arrangements, on such terms and in such manner as may be agreed upon by supplemental agreement, for the acquisition or use by the United Nations of appropriate premises for such purposes and the inclusion of such premises in the headquarters district.

SECTION 5

In the event that the United Nations should find it necessary and desirable to establish and operate an aerodrome, the conditions for the location, use and operation of such aerodrome and the conditions under which there shall be entry into and exit therefrom shall be the subject of a supplemental agreement.

The United Nations shall enjoy a privilege similar to the immunity of domicile granted to diplomatic envoys by general international law. Article 3, Section 9, provides:

(*a*) The headquarters district shall be inviolable. Federal, state or local officers or officials of the United States, whether administrative, judicial, military or police, shall not enter the headquarters district to perform any official duties therein except with the consent of and under conditions agreed to by the Secretary-General. The service of legal process, including the seizure of private property, may take place within the headquarters district only with the consent of and under conditions approved by the Secretary-General.

(*b*) Without prejudice to the provisions of the General Convention or Article 4 of this agreement, the United Nations shall prevent the headquarters district from becoming a refuge either for persons who are avoiding arrest under the federal, state, or local law of the United States or are required by the Government of the United States for extradition to another country, or for persons who are endeavouring to avoid service of legal process.

In addition to the obligation to guarantee inviolability to the headquarters district, the United States assumes certain obligations, stipulated in Article 4, concerning Communications and Transit. Article 5 contains the following provisions concerning permanent representatives to the United Nations:

SECTION 15

(1) Every person designated by a Member as the principal permanent representative to the United Nations of such Member

or as a permanent representative with the rank of ambassador or minister plenipotentiary;

(2) Such resident members of their staffs as may be agreed upon between the Secretary-General, the Government of the United States and the Government of the Member concerned;

(3) Every person designated by a member of the specialised agency, as defined in Article 57, paragraph 2 of the Charter, as its principal permanent representative, with the rank of ambassador or minister plenipotentiary at the headquarters of such agency in the United States; and

(4) Such other principal permanent representatives of members of a specialised agency and such resident members of the staffs of representatives of a specialised agency as may be agreed upon between the principal executive officer of the specialised agency, the Government of the United States and the Government of the Member concerned,

Shall, whether residing inside or outside the headquarters district, be entitled in the territory of the United States to the same privileges and immunities, subject to corresponding conditions and obligations, as it accords to diplomatic envoys accredited to it. In the case of Members whose governments are not recognised by the United States, such privileges and immunities need be extended to such representatives, or persons on the staffs of such representatives, only within the headquarters district, at their residences and offices if outside the district, in transit between the district and such residences and offices, and in transit on official business to or from foreign countries.

PART THREE

FUNCTIONS OF THE UNITED NATIONS

CHAPTER 14

QUASI-JUDICIAL SETTLEMENT OF DISPUTES AND ADJUSTMENT OF OTHER SITUATIONS

1. THE GENERAL PROVISIONS

ACCORDING to Article 1, paragraph 1, of the Charter, it is a Purpose—and that means a function—of the United Nations ' to bring about by peaceful means, and in conformity with the principles of justice and international law, adjustment or settlement of international disputes or situations which might lead to a breach of the peace.' To this function of the Organisation corresponds the obligation of the Members laid down in Article 2, paragraph 3: ' All Members shall settle their international disputes by peaceful means in such a manner that international peace and security, and justice, are not endangered.' Whereas the function of the Organisation refers to adjustment and settlement of international disputes or situations, the obligation of the Members refers only to the settlement of international disputes. Whereas the Organisation's function is to bring about adjustment or settlement of international disputes or situations ' which might lead to a breach of the peace,' the Members are obliged to settle all their international disputes. Whereas the Organisation shall bring about adjustment or settlement of disputes or situations ' by peaceful means, and in conformity with the principles of justice and international law,' the Members are obliged to settle their disputes ' by peaceful means in such a manner that international peace and security, and justice, are not endangered.' The provision concerning the function of the Organisation is evidently not consistent with that concerning the obligation of the Members.

It is not clear what difference exists between ' adjustment ' and ' settlement ' of disputes or situations. In the general usage of language both terms mean the same.[1] In Article 36, paragraph 1, the Security Council is authorised to recommend ' appropriate procedures or methods of adjustment '; in Article 37, paragraph 2, to recommend ' terms of settlement.' The ' procedures or methods of adjustment ' referred to in Article 36, paragraph 1, are—as far as they refer to disputes—the ' peaceful means ' by which a ' solution ' shall be sought by the parties according to Article 33, paragraph 1. ' Solution ' of the dispute is identical with ' settlement of the dispute.' The heading of Chapter VI is ' Pacific Settlement of Disputes ' (although some Articles of this Chapter deal with ' adjustment ' and ' situations '); in Article 14, the phrase ' peaceful adjustment of any situation ' is

[1] Webster's New International Dictionary of English Language (1944): ' adjustment . . . the bringing of a thing or things into proper or exact position or condition; arrangement; settlement . . . '

used. To speak of settlement of disputes and adjustment of situations seems to correspond mostly to the terminology of the Charter. The legal effect of the Charter, however, would probably not be affected if its text would speak only of 'settlement,' not of 'adjustment,'[2] with reference both to disputes and situations.

The distinction between 'disputes' and 'situations' appears not only in Article 1, paragraph 1, and in Chapter VI.[3] Article 12, paragraph 1, speaks of the Security Council 'exercising in respect of any dispute or situation the functions assigned to it. It would be correct to speak of 'disputes and other situations,' since any dispute is a situation whereas not every situation is a dispute.[4] A 'dispute' exists if one party makes a claim against another party and the other party rejects the claim.[5] Not every conflict is a dispute; a state may

[2] The Report of Rapporteur, Subcommittee I/1/A to Committee I/1 of the San Francisco Conference (U.N.C.I.O. Doc. 723, I/1/A/19, pp. 7 f.) contains the following statement: 'Suggestions were made to rule "adjustment" out and explanations for its meaning were asked and made.—One of the English-speaking delegates said that adjustment meant solution of a dispute in a just manner. Another English-speaking delegate sought to explain it by the French word "amenagement."—Some held that "settlement" ought to be considered adequate because it carries with it the conception of a juridical solution or proper arbitration and was more clear. It was argued that "settlement" also implies something final, while "adjustment" stands there to make possible solutions of a preparatory nature which may be deemed necessary in the course of a settlement. It was further argued that the principles of justice and international law rule adjustments as well as settlements.—On the understanding of these reasons and their general acceptance the subcommittee decided to keep "adjustment" in the text.'

[3] Chapter I, paragraph 1, of the Dumbarton Oaks Proposals which corresponds to Article 1, paragraph 1, of the Charter does not distinguish between disputes and situations; it speaks only of 'adjustment or settlement of international disputes which may lead to a breach of the peace.' Report of Rapporteur of Committee 1 to Commission I (U.N.C.I.O. Doc. 944, I/1/34 (1), p. 9) contains the following statement: 'A suggestion was made to rule out "adjustment" on the plea that "settlement" is sufficient, but in case "adjustment" is kept, the word "situations" should be added after "disputes."—"Settlement" was not found adequate because it implies something final, while "adjustment" stands there to make possible solutions of a preparatory nature. Such solutions may be found necessary in the course of settlement.—The word "situations" was added after "disputes" as a more inclusive term to match with "adjustment."—It was clear in any case of adjustment or settlement of disputes or situations, that the solution should be made in conformity with justice and international law.'

[4] At the 3rd meeting of the Security Council, during the discussion of the Iranian case, the representative of Iran declared, 'the only course for the Iranian Government was to bring the dispute to the attention of the Security Council as a situation which might lead to international friction.' (Journal of the Security Council, 1st Year, No. 5, p. 49.)

[5] At the 84th meeting of the Security Council the President of the Council considered the case under discussion to be a dispute (and hence Article 32 applicable) because 'Charges have been made against these Governments [Albania and Bulgaria, by Greece] and these Governments have contested these charges and made counter-charges.' (Official Records of the Security Council, 1st Year, 2nd Series, No. 26, p. 607.)

attack another state without any previous dispute. Sometimes the Charter speaks only of 'situations,' comprising in this term disputes too; thus, in Article 11, paragraph 3, or in Article 14. The difference between disputes and other situations is of great importance, since some rules of the Charter refer only to disputes, not to other situations; such as the provisions of Article 27, paragraph 3, concerning the abstention from voting in the Security Council, and others.

It seems that the Charter imposes obligations upon the Members only with respect to 'disputes,' not with respect to 'situations.' Where obligations of the Members are dealt with, only disputes are mentioned—for instance in Article 2, paragraph 3, and Articles 33 and 37. The Organisation, on the other hand, is authorised to intervene not only in disputes but also in other situations, and this not only according to Article 1, paragraph 1, but also according to other provisions. Thus, the General Assembly may discuss, according to Articles 10, 11 and 12, disputes or other situations and make recommendations for their settlement or adjustment. Article 11, paragraph 3, authorises the General Assembly to call the attention of the Security Council to 'situations,' including disputes, 'which are likely to endanger international peace and security'; Article 14, to recommend measures for the peaceful adjustment of 'any situation which it deems likely to impair the general welfare or friendly relations among nations.' Under Chapter VI, the Security Council has the power to investigate disputes as well as other situations (Article 34), to recommend procedures or methods of adjustment with respect to disputes as well as other situations (Article 36, Article 37, paragraph 2), but to recommend terms of settlement only with respect to disputes (Article 37, paragraph 2, Article 38).

As to the nature of the disputes and the other situations in which the Organisation is authorised to intervene, the various provisions of the Charter are not very consistent. First of all, it should be pointed out that Article 1, paragraph 1, authorises the Organisation to bring about adjustment of settlement of disputes and other situations only if they 'might lead to a breach of the peace';[6] and under the provisions of Articles 36 and 37, the Security Council is authorised to make recommendations only with respect to disputes or other situations the

[6] The Report of Rapporteur of Committee 1 to Commission I (U.N.C.I.O. Doc. 944, I/1/34 (1), p. 9 f.) contains the following statement: 'Another suggestion considered the words "which may lead to a breach of the peace" at the end of the paragraph, either unnecessary or detrimental to the solution of other disputes. That consideration was held to be mistaken, as it was remarked that "other breaches of the peace" refers to the taking of collective measures where the Organisation can act *ex officio*.—Other disputes should find a solution in conformity with the principles of justice and international law but do not necessarily entail taking collective measures. The Organisation should not be in principle burdened with minor disputes which do not endanger peace between the parties.'

The suggestion to drop the words 'which may lead to a breach of the peace' was quite justifiable; the way in which the Report explains the refutation of this suggestion is, at least partly, understandable.

continuance of which is likely to endanger the peace. But the Security Council may, under Article 38, make recommendations with respect to, and, under Article 34, investigate ' any dispute ' whatever, although it may investigate only a situation ' which might lead to international friction or give rise to a dispute.' Under Article 35, any Member of the United Nations may bring ' any dispute ' whatever, but only ' any situation of the nature referred to in Article 34 ' to the attention of the Security Council or of the General Assembly; and under Article 35, paragraph 2, a state which is not a Member of the United Nations may bring to the attention of the Security Council or of the General Assembly ' any dispute ' whatever to which it is a party, but not a situation which has not the character of a dispute. The General Assembly, under Article 10, may discuss any dispute or other situation whatever if it is a question or matter ' within the scope of the present Charter,' and make recommendations on any such dispute or other situation. Under Article 11, paragraph 2, the General Assembly may discuss any dispute or other situation whatever as a ' question relating to the maintenance of international peace and security ' brought before it by any Member or by the Security Council and a dispute brought before it by a non-member, provided the non-member is a party to the dispute, and make recommendations on these disputes or situations.

Another inconsistency is implied in the different ways the Charter determines the dangerous character of the dispute or other situation in which the Organisation is authorised to intervene. Article 1, paragraph 1, refers to disputes or situations ' which might lead to a breach of the peace '; Article 11, paragraph 3, refers to situations ' which are likely to endanger international peace and security '; Article 14, to any situation ' which it [the General Assembly] deems likely to impair the general welfare or friendly relations among nations '; Article 33, paragraph 1, obligates the parties to seek solution, by means of their own choice, of disputes ' the continuance of which is likely to endanger the maintenance of international peace and security;' Article 34 authorises the Security Council to investigate ' any dispute, or any situation which might lead to international friction or give rise to a dispute,' the phrase beginning with ' which ' relating only to ' situation,' not to ' dispute '; but the purpose of the investigation is to determine ' whether the continuance of the dispute or situation is likely to endanger the maintenance of international peace and security '; Article 35, paragraph 1, authorises any Member of the United Nations to bring ' any dispute, or any situation of the nature referred to in Article 34, to the attention of the Security Council or of the General Assembly '; but Article 34 refers to situations ' which might lead to international friction or give rise to a dispute ' and to situations the continuance of which is ' likely to endanger international peace and security.' Article 36, paragraph 1, confers upon the Security Council the power to make certain recommendations ' at any stage of a dispute of the nature referred to in Article 33 or of a situation of like nature,' that is to say: a dispute or situation 'the continuance of which is likely to endanger the maintenance of international peace and security'; the same clause is used to characterise the disputes as to which the Security Council is authorised by Article 37, paragraph 2, to make recommendations. It is difficult to understand why under Article 1, paragraph 1, the disputes and other situations with respect to which the Organisation shall bring about adjustment or settlement are characterised as such 'which might lead to a breach of the peace,' whereas the disputes and other situations with respect to which the Security Council is authorised by Article 36, paragraph 1, and Article 37, paragraph 2, to make certain recommendations as such 'the continuance of which is likely to endanger the maintenance of international peace and security'; and the situations with respect to which the General Assembly is authorised, by Article 14, to recommend measures for the peaceful adjustment, as such 'which the General Assembly deems likely to impair the general welfare or friendly relations among nations'; why in Article 11, paragraph 3, the formula 'which are likely to endanger international peace and security,' whereas in Articles 33, 34 and 37, the formula 'the continuance of which is likely to endanger, etc.' is used; why the General Assembly may, under Article 11, paragraph 3, call the attention of the Security Council to 'situations which are likely to endanger international peace and security,' whereas under Article 34, the Security Council may investigate any situation 'which might lead to international friction or give rise to a dispute.' There is hardly any essential difference between the nature of the disputes and other situations characterised by the different formulas, and there was no reason to use another formula than the one used in Article 1, paragraph 1: 'which might lead to a breach of the peace.' Even the phrase 'likely to impair the general welfare or friendly relations among nations' (Article 14) has hardly another meaning than that of Article 1, paragraph 1; for the intervention of the General Assembly provided for in Article 14, like any action of the Organisation, has the purpose to maintain or restore peace, and a situation likely to impair the general welfare or friendly relations among nations is to be adjusted by means recommended by the General Assembly only because such a situation might finally lead to a breach of the peace.

As pointed out, Article 2, paragraph 3, obligates the Members to settle all their international disputes by peaceful means. But Articles 33 and 37, which specify this obligation,[7] provide that only the parties

[7] At the 5th meeting of Committee III/2 (U.N.C.I.O. Doc. 356, III/2/11) the delegate of France noted 'that it would be desirable to avoid the repetition of the idea in Chapter II, paragraph 3 [of the Dumbarton Oaks Proposals corresponding to Article 2, paragraph 3, of the Charter], which is caused by the present form of Chapter VIII, Section A, paragraph 3' [corresponding to Article 33, paragraph 1, of the Charter]. The latter provision, however, is not exactly a repetition of the former; it is rather a specification.

to a dispute 'the continuance of which is likely to endanger the maintenance of international peace and security' shall seek a solution of such dispute by peaceful means; and that they shall refer only such dispute to the Security Council when they fail to settle it by means of their own choice. The Security Council under Article 34 has to determine whether the continuance of the dispute is likely to endanger the maintenance of international peace and security; and only if the Council deems that the dispute is of such dangerous character, may it, under Articles 36 or 37, recommend appropriate procedures for the adjustment of the dispute or terms of settlement. But if the parties to the dispute fulfil their obligation under Article 2, paragraph 4, to refrain in their international relations from the threat or use of force, the dispute cannot endanger the peace. In restricting the obligation of the parties to settle their disputes by peaceful means of their own choice, and the function of the Security Council to intervene in disputes which constitute a danger to the peace, the framers of the Charter show little confidence in the effectiveness of their own work.

The obligation established by Article 2, paragraph 3, refers only to 'international' disputes. We shall see later[8] that, according to Article 2, paragraph 7, disputes arising out of matters which are essentially within the domestic jurisdiction of one party might be considered not to have the character of 'international' disputes and not to be under the obligation of the Members to submit them to settlement under the Charter. Exempt from this obligation are, under Article 107, also disputes with ex-enemy states which are the result of the Second World War, and, under Article 53, paragraph 2, disputes between a party (or parties) to a regional arrangement and an ex-enemy state in so far as the dispute concerns the renewal of aggressive policy on the part of the ex-enemy state and the regional arrangement provides for enforcement measures directed against such renewal.[9] It should be pointed out that international disputes are not exclusively disputes between states. At that San Francisco Conference, it is true, on the initiative of the Sponsoring Powers, the word 'international' (in the sentence of Article 2, paragraph 3: All Members shall settle their international disputes) was added to make it clear 'that the Organisation would concern itself only with disputes *among* the nations.'[1] But by the formula 'international disputes' other disputes than those among states are not at all excluded. For, also a dispute between a state and a private individual may have an international character when it arises out of a relation between the state and the individual regulated by international law: for instance, by an international treaty protecting certain rights of the individual. Are the 'international disputes' referred to in Article 2, paragraph 3,

[8] Cf. *infra*, pp. 781 f.

[9] Cf. *infra*, pp. 805 ff.

[1] *Report to the President*, p. 40. The above quoted sentence continues: 'A conclusion stated more explicitly in the seventh principle.'

only disputes between states or does the term include also international disputes between a state and an individual? International disputes are possible not only between states, and between states and individuals, but also between states and international organisations such as the League of Nations or the United Nations, and between international organisations. A civil war which takes place within a state Member of the United Nations is certainly not an international dispute within the meaning of Article 2, paragraph 3. When the Indonesian question came before the Security Council the representative of the Netherlands maintained that Indonesia was no sovereign state and, consequently, he opposed any action by the Security Council on the ground that what happened in Indonesia was a matter of domestic jurisdiction.[2] It seems that the Security Council did not share the view of the Netherlands delegate; for the Council invited a representative of the Indonesian Republic to participate in the discussion of the case. Under Article 32 only ' states ' can be invited. If a representative of Indonesia was invited, the invitation was made under Article 32, and this implies an indirect recognition of the Indonesian Republic as a ' state ' by the Security Council.[3]

According to Article 34, paragraph 1, of the Statute of the International Court of Justice, only disputes between states may be brought before the Court. But the wording of Article 2, paragraph 3, of the Charter, does not restrict the obligation of the Members to settle their international disputes by peaceful means to disputes between states. Only in so far as this obligation is in correspondence with the obligation to refrain from the threat or use of force—the term ' force ' meaning non-peaceful means—the dispute between a state and a private individual may be considered as not to be included in the disputes referred to in Article 2, paragraph 3, since in such disputes non-peaceful means of settlement are out of the question. Nevertheless, the continuance of such a dispute may endanger the maintenance of peace and security and become a dispute between states. But the text of the Articles concerned goes beyond this intention and may lead to unforeseen difficulties.

According to Article 1, paragraph 1, the Organisation shall bring about adjustment or settlement of international disputes or other situations which might lead to a breach of the peace not only by peaceful means but also ' in conformity with the principles of justice and international law.' This is a postulate directed at all the organs of the United Nations which are competent, according to the Charter, to perform the function of the United Nations determined in Article 1, paragraph 1, second part. These organs are the General Assembly, the Security Council, and the International Court of Justice, ' the principal judicial organ of the United Nations ' (Article 92). As far as the Court is concerned, the postulate to conform with the principles of

[2] Cf. *infra*, p. 440.

[3] Cf. *supra*, pp. 226 f.

justice and international law is not consistent with the provision of Article 38, paragraph 1, of the Statute, according to which the Courts' function is to decide disputes 'in accordance with international law,' not in accordance with the principles of justice.

Since the principles of justice are not identical with, and sometimes in opposition to, the rules of positive international law, it may be impossible to comply with the postulate to conform with both, justice and international law. The General Assembly, as well as the Security Council, in making recommendations for the settlement of disputes, if justice is in conflict with positive international law, can only apply the one or the other, not both at the same time. Hence they have the choice between the two principles. The—probably not intended—effect of the formula in question is that the organs of the United Nations which act under the provision of Article 1, paragraph 1, second part, may refuse to apply the rules of existing international law if they consider them to be unsatisfactory, and apply principles which they consider to be 'just.' Since the Charter does not and cannot define the concept of justice, any settlement of a dispute or adjustment of another situation, recommended by the General Assembly or the Security Council is in conformity with the postulate in question. For the organ which makes the recommendation will certainly not admit that its decision is not in conformity with justice if it is not in conformity with positive law; and it is upon the organ to decide this question. The effect of the formula 'in conformity with the principles of justice and international law' is to leave the settlement of disputes and the adjustment of other situations to the discretion of the Organisation.

The function of the Organisation to bring about settlement of disputes and the obligation of the Members to settle their disputes are to a great extent in such close correlation that it is difficult to understand why the former shall be 'in conformity with the principles of justice and international law,' whereas the latter shall not be performed in exactly the same way, but 'in such a manner that international peace and security, and justice, are not endangered.'

The demand not to endanger justice in settling a dispute is directed at the Members of the United Nations, the latter being obliged to settle their disputes by peaceful means.[4] The peaceful means to settle a dispute are: agreement of the parties brought about either directly by negotiation or mediation, or indirectly by accepting the recommendation of a conciliation commission; or by submitting the

[4] Report of Rapporteur of Committee I/1 (U.N.C.I.O. Doc. 944, I/1/34 (1), p. 13) contains the following statement relating to Article 2, paragraph 3: 'The Committee felt, in the light of past experience of some unjust adjustments or settlements, that it is not sufficient to assure that peace and security are not endangered. It added "justice."'

dispute to the decision of an international tribunal. If the dispute is settled directly by agreement between the parties, the requirement of justice seems to be of no use at all. For in this case, justice can mean only what the parties consider to be just; and if they voluntarily reach an agreement with respect to the settlement it may be supposed that they both consider the settlement to be just. To question the justice of an agreement entered into by the parties concerned is certainly not proper; but it is not excluded, at least according to the wording of Article 2, paragraph 3. After having entered into the agreement, one party may try to contest its validity under Article 2, paragraph 3, by maintaining that it endangers justice. This is certainly not in conformity with the principle of ' respect for the obligations arising from treaties ' proclaimed in the Preamble.

Under Article 33, paragraph 1, the parties may submit the dispute to a conciliation commission or to an international tribunal. What effect has the provision of Article 2, paragraph 3, obliging the Members not to endanger justice in settling their disputes, in this respect? Are the parties obliged to bind, in the instrument establishing the conciliation commission or the tribunal, the authority thus established to apply principles of justice not rules of existing international law, if they are in conflict with the former? It does not seem that this is the intention of Article 2, paragraph 3. If so, what is the use of obliging the Members not to endanger justice in settling their disputes? May a party refuse to comply with the recommendation of a conciliation commission or the decision of an international tribunal on the ground that the recommendation or the decision endangers justice? This is possible with respect to the recommendation of a conciliation commission, even without the provision of Article 2, paragraph 3, that the settlement of a dispute shall not endanger justice. Not to comply with the decision of the tribunal is a violation of the obligation assumed by the parties in the treaty by which the dispute has been submitted to the decision of the tribunal.

Under Article 33, paragraph 1, the parties may submit the dispute to the International Court of Justice. Article 36, paragraph 3, even provides ' that legal disputes should as a general rule be referred by the parties to the International Court of Justice in accordance with the provisions of the Statute of the Court.' The Statute, as pointed out, does not authorise the Court to decide disputes according to principles of justice. Under Article 38, the Court is bound ' to decide in accordance with international law.' Only if the parties agree thereto, the Court may decide the dispute *ex aequo et bono*, which is not identical with ' principles of justice.' May a party refuse to comply with a decision of the Court on the ground that the decision endangers justice, because Article 2, paragraph 3, obliges the Members not to endanger justice in settling their disputes? If Article 2, paragraph 3, should be interpreted in this way, it would be in open conflict with the obligation of the Member laid down in Article 94, paragraph 1, of the Charter, 'to comply with the decision of the International Court of Justice in any case to which it is a party.'

Under Article 37, paragraph 2, the Security Council, and, under Article 10 or Article 11, paragraph 2, the General Assembly may make recommendations for the settlement of a dispute. Referring to its obligation under Article 2, paragraph 3, a party may refuse to comply with the recommendation on the ground that the latter, although in conformity with positive international law, endangers justice. In so far as the recommendation is considered not to be binding upon the parties, such refusal is possible, but not consistent with the provision of Article 1, paragraph 1, second part, according to which, as pointed out, the organs of the United Nations—except the Court—have the choice between justice and positive law when the latter is in conflict with the former. Besides, under Article 37, paragraph 2, the Security Council is authorised 'to recommend such terms of settlement as it may consider appropriate.' It is not said: as it may consider 'just'; it is said: 'appropriate' and that may be interpreted as 'politically' appropriate. No other kind of action of a body composed of representatives of governments is possible.

Article 2, paragraph 3, obligates the Members not only not to endanger 'justice' but also 'international peace and security' in settling their disputes by peaceful means. How can international peace—and that implies international security—be endangered if the dispute is settled 'by peaceful means'? In the Report of the Rapporteur of Committee I/1 of the San Francisco Conference the following commentary was given to this provision: 'Controversies are to be settled likewise in such a way that international peace and security are not endangered. Therefore, no condition should be created by which parties endanger the peace of others.'[5] It is not very likely that the settlement of a dispute between two states if established by peaceful means, will endanger the peace of a third state. Still such possibility is not excluded. The obligation not to endanger the peace of another state with which there is not yet a dispute is covered by Article 2, paragraph 4. The provision of Article 2, paragraph 3, refers to the relation between the parties to a dispute; a prohibition to endanger the peace of others certainly does not belong in the text of this provision.

[5] Cf. Report of Rapporteur of Committee I/1 (U.N.C.I.O. Doc. 944, I/1/34 (1), p. 13. The Report says further, pp. 13 ff.: 'Going further not to the text of paragraph 3 itself, but to its relation with other parts of the Charter, it is clear that the paragraph provides the conditions governing the *ex officio* intervention of the Organisation in the settlement of disputes. The Organisation and its Members are bound to abide by this principle.—If, however, a dispute of a minor nature arises, there would be nothing in this paragraph to prejudice the right or duty of members to bring their dispute before the Organisation in the manner provided for by the Charter.'

According to the just-quoted commentary, the words ' in such a manner that international peace and security . . . are not endangered ' have been inserted in Article 2, paragraph 3, with the intention to prevent conditions by which the parties to the dispute endanger the peace of others. This intention, however, is not expressed. The wording refers to a danger to the peace of anybody, also to the peace of the parties. Hence, the words may have a rather undesirable effect. If it is possible that a dispute is settled by peaceful means and, nevertheless, peace is endangered by the settlement, a party to the dispute may declare not to be bound by the settlement because it endangers international peace and security and consequently is not in conformity with Article 2, paragraph 3. The fact that the settlement has been brought about by an agreement of the parties does not exclude that one of them may appeal to the clause in question in contesting the settlement, since the formula of Article 2, paragraph 3, includes the possibility that any peaceful settlement whatever may endanger international peace and security. Besides, the party may declare that it has given its consent to the settlement under pressure, or that it has not foreseen its consequences, and the like.

The settlement of disputes referred to in Article 2, paragraph 3, includes settlement by a decision of the International Court of Justice. May a party refuse to comply with the decision of the Court by arguing that it is obliged to settle its dispute by this means only in so far as the decision of the Court does not endanger international peace and security, and that the decision concerned does not comply with this condition ? All this is certainly not intended, since in open contradiction to the ' respect for the obligations arising from treaties,' proclaimed in the Preamble, and with the obligation ' to comply with the decision of the International Court of Justice,' laid down in Article 94, paragraph 1. But the wording of Article 2, paragraph 3, makes such interpretation not impossible.

Finally, the question arises as to whether the provisions of the Charter concerning the pacific settlement of disputes and adjustment of other situations apply only to disputes between Members and to situations in which only Members are involved, or also to other ' disputes and situations.' The function of the Organisation determined in Article 1, paragraph 1 as: bringing about by peaceful means adjustment or settlement of international disputes or situations which might lead to a breach of the peace, is not restricted to disputes between Members or situations in which only Members are involved. This is quite consistent with the fact that the Organisation aims at world peace, not only at peace among the Members. The Purpose proclaimed at the first place: ' to maintain international peace and security,' (Article 1, paragraph 1) is formulated in such a general way that it is hardly possible to interpret it as being restricted to the relationship among Members.

The obligation to settle disputes by peaceful means, as laid down in Article 2, paragraph 3, however, is expressly imposed only upon 'Members.' This may be interpreted to constitute no true inconsistency in relation to Article 1, paragraph 1, since Article 2, paragraph 6, authorises the Organisation to ensure that states which are not Members of the United Nations act in accordance with the Principles laid down in Article 2 so far as may be necessary for the maintenance of peace and security. If there is a Principle the accordance with which is necessary for the maintenance of peace, it is the Principle laid down in Article 2, paragraph 3: to settle disputes by peaceful means. Hence the obligation stipulated in Article 2, paragraph 3, may be considered to be imposed also upon non-members.

This interpretation may be confirmed by the wording of the provisions of Chapter VI, dealing with the pacific settlement of disputes and the adjustment of other situations. All the provisions of this Chapter refer to disputes or other situations in general, without containing a restriction to disputes between Members or situations in which only Members are involved. According to Article 33, paragraph 1, 'the parties to any dispute,' not only 'Members,' shall seek a solution by peaceful means of their own choice, and shall, under Article 37, paragraph 1, refer the dispute to the Security Council if they fail to settle it by such means. According to Article 33, paragraph 2, the Security Council shall call upon 'the parties' to settle their disputes by means of their own choice, without being restricted to call only upon Members as parties to a dispute. According to Article 34, the Security Council may investigate 'any dispute or any situation,' not only disputes or situations in which Members are involved; and according to Article 35, paragraph 1, any Member may bring 'any dispute or any situation' to the attention of the Security Council or of the General Assembly, not only disputes or situations in which Members are involved; Article 36, paragraphs 1, and 2, in authorising the Security Council to recommend procedures or methods of adjustment 'at any stage of a dispute . . . or of a situation,' contains nothing which indicates that this provision refers only to disputes or situations in which Members are involved; and the same is true with respect to the provisions of Article 37, paragraph 2, authorising the Security Council to make recommendations for the disputes referred to it.

Article 36, paragraph 3, stipulates that the Security Council in making recommendations should take into consideration that legal disputes should as a general rule be referred by the parties to the International Court of Justice. This provision, too, does not necessarily apply only to disputes between Members since, according to Article 93 of the Charter, and Article 35, paragraph 2, of the Statute of the Court, the Court may be open to non-members, even to states which are not parties to the Statute.

Article 35, paragraph 2, of the Charter, provides that a non-member may bring to the attention of the Security Council or of the General Assembly a dispute if it is a party to it and if it accepts in advance, for the purposes of the dispute, the obligations of pacific settlement provided in the present Charter. In this respect, there exists a difference between Members and non-members. A Member may bring to the attention of the Security Council or of the General Assembly—according to Article 35, paragraph 1—any dispute, also a dispute to which the Member is not a party, and any other situation if dangerous to the peace. If Article 33, paragraph 1, and Article 37, paragraph 1, in conformity with their wording, are interpreted to mean that parties to any dispute, Members as well as non-members, shall ' first of all ' seek a solution by peaceful means of their own choice, and only if they fail to settle it in this way, refer it to the Security Council, Article 35, paragraph 2, does not seem to be consistent with the provisions of Article 33, paragraph 1, and Article 37, paragraph 1. For, under Article 35, paragraph 2, non-member states are allowed to bring a dispute to which they are parties immediately before the Security Council, without seeking ' first of all ' to settle it by peaceful means of their own choice. If Article 33, paragraph 1, and Article 37, paragraph 1, are interpreted to apply only to disputes to which Members are parties, there is no inconsistency between these Articles and Article 35, paragraph 2. Yet an inconsistency exists in the relation between Article 33, paragraph 1, and Article 37, paragraph 1, on the one hand, and Article 35, paragraph 1, on the other hand, with respect to Member states. If Member states are obliged ' first of all ' to seek a solution of their disputes by peaceful means of their own choice and, only if they fail to settle them in this way, to refer them to the Security Council, it is inconsistent to authorise any Member, also a Member which is a party to a dispute, to bring that dispute immediately, and without any attempt to settle it by the means indicated in Article 33, paragraph 1, before the Security Council. Hence, the inconsistency which exists between Article 35, paragraph 2, referring to disputes to which non-members are parties, and Article 33, paragraph 1, and Article 37, paragraph 1, referring to any dispute whatever, is no reason for interpreting the latter provisions, in spite of their wording, to mean that they apply only to disputes between Members.

Article 38 authorises ' the parties to any dispute,' not only Members, to request the Security Council to make recommendations with a view to a pacific settlement. Non-members are not excluded.

Finally, attention should be called to Article 32. Without referring to the provision of Article 35, paragraph 2, that a non-member may bring to the attention of the Security Council a dispute to which it is a party only if it accepts in advance, for the purposes of the dispute, the obligations of pacific settlement provided in the Charter, Article 32 stipulates that any state which is not a Member of the United Nations—

just as a Member state—' if it is a party to a dispute under consideration by the Security Council,' shall be invited to participate, without vote, in the discussion relating to the dispute. It is further stipulated that ' the Security Council shall lay down such conditions as it deems just for the participation of a state which is not a Member of the United Nations.' Nothing in this Article indicates that disputes to which non-members are parties shall be under consideration by the Security Council only if brought to its attention under Article 35, paragraph 2. Article 32 may be interpreted to presuppose that the jurisdiction of the Security Council with respect to the settlement of disputes refers to disputes to which Members as well as non-members are parties.

If the provisions of Articles 33, 34, 36, 37 and 38, and the statement in Article 1, paragraph 1, concerning the Purpose of the United Nations to bring about by peaceful means settlement of disputes, were intended to refer only to disputes between members, this intention was certainly not expressed in a way by which an opposite interpretation is excluded.

2. The Procedures for the Quasi-Judicial Settlement of Disputes and the Adjustment of Other Situations

Settlement of disputes or adjustment of other situations which might lead to a breach of the peace may be brought about by the Security Council or by the General Assembly; settlement of disputes also by the International Court of Justice.

Chapter VI of the Charter, which bears the heading ' Pacific Settlement of Disputes,' is particularly devoted to this subject; but it deals also with the adjustment of other situations, and does not contain all provisions concerning settlement of disputes and adjustment of other situations. Chapter XIV and the Statute of the International Court of Justice deal especially with the function of this agency which is the ' principal judicial organ of the United Nations ' and whose main function is to settle disputes. The jurisdiction of the General Assembly with respect to disputes and other situations is determined in Chapter IV. The provisions of Chapter VI refer mainly to the jurisdiction of the Security Council, but some refer also to the General Assembly and the International Court of Justice. Important provisions are to be found also in Chapters V, VII, VIII and XV.

A. *Settlement by the Security Council*

There are various procedures for the settlement of disputes and the adjustment of other situations by the Security Council. Two are instituted by the parties to the dispute, the others by the Security Council itself, one on its own initiative, the others on the initiative of

Members, non-members, the General Assembly, or the Secretary-General.[6]

(*a*) Procedures instituted by the parties

The first of the two procedures to be instituted by the parties to the dispute is regulated by Article 33, paragraph 1, and Article 37. These Articles refer only to disputes, not to other situations. Article 33, paragraph 1, runs as follows:

> The parties to any dispute, the continuance of which is likely to endanger the maintenance of international peace and security, shall, first of all, seek a solution by negotiation, enquiry, mediation, conciliation, arbitration, judicial settlement, resort to regional agencies or arrangements, or other peaceful means of their own choice.

The intention of this provision is to impose an obligation[7] upon the parties to a dispute: the obligation 'first of all' to seek a solution of the dispute by peaceful means of their own choice. 'First of all' means: before referring the dispute to the Security Council under

[6] According to the usual interpretation, the Charter establishes only one procedure for the settlement of disputes, and this procedure has four stages. During the first three stages, it is a procedure of pacific settlement. In the first stage, the Security Council does not appear (Article 33, paragraph 1); in the second stage, the Security Council may recommend procedures; and in the third stage it may recommend terms of settlement (Articles 33, paragraph 2, to 38). The fourth stage is under Article 39. At this stage, the procedure ceases to be one of pacific settlement.—This interpretation is not compatible with the text of the Charter. To assume four stages would be possible only if the Charter would fix a chronological order so that the second stage had to be preceded by the first, the third by the second, and the fourth by the third stage. This, however, is not at all the case. At one and the same stage the Security Council may recommend procedures or terms of settlement (Article 37, paragraph 2); it may recommend procedures 'at any stage' according to Article 36, paragraph 1; and the Council may apply Article 39 even before the first stage is terminated. Hence the view that there is only one procedure of settlement divided into three or four stages, is untenable.

In contradistinction to the Charter, the Covenant of the League of Nations provided only one procedure for the settlement of disputes by the Council, the one regulated in Article 15. This procedure had three clearly distinguished stages. The first stage was referred to in paragraph 1: submission, by one party, of the dispute to the Council; the second stage was the attempt of the Council to bring about settlement by an agreement of the parties, referred to in paragraphs 2 and 3. If the dispute could not be settled in this way, the procedure entered into its third stage regulated by paragraphs 4 to 8. At this stage, the Council was authorised to make recommendations which it 'deemed just and proper' in regard to the dispute. Paragraphs 9 and 10 concerned the possibility of referring the dispute to the Assembly.

[7] At the 3rd meeting of Commission III (U.N.C.I.O. Doc. 1088, III/8) the delegate of Australia made the following statement with respect to the effect of Article 33, paragraph 1, on the parties to a dispute: 'They are under a duty.'

Article 37, paragraph 1.[8] It may be doubted whether non-compliance with this provision can be considered to be the condition of a sanction, since the formula 'to seek a solution' is too vague and the parties to the dispute are not bound in case one of the means indicated in this paragraph fails, to try another and finally to apply the one which alone guarantees a settlement, namely, arbitration or judicial decision.[9] Nothing in the wording of Article 33, paragraph 1, allows the inter-

[8] The provision that the parties shall 'first of all' seek a solution by peaceful means of their own choice is taken over from paragraph 3 of Chapter VIII, Section A, of the Dumbarton Oaks Proposals. At the San Francisco Conference the delegate of Ethiopia proposed the omission of the words 'first of all.' He explained that the purpose of this amendment was 'to allow the Security Council to intervene in or to be seized of a dispute even before recourse to other means of settlement were exhausted, if it appeared likely that the continued employment of such means would not result in a peaceful solution of the dispute. The delegate of the United States stated that he considered the Ethiopian amendment would entail an undesirable modification of the purpose of paragraph 3, and gave the following interpretation of the action of the Security Council under the Dumbarton Oaks Proposals in the circumstances envisaged by the amendment: It was very desirable that the parties to a dispute should endeavour to settle the dispute by the use of conciliation or other ordinary methods of peaceful settlement. If, however, those methods were not successful, and a threat to the peace or an act of aggression occurred, the Security Council should not delay, but should act immediately as provided by Chapter VIII, Section B. He considered that the Council should and must intervene in any dispute which threatened world peace, but that it should not possess such power with regard to all disputes, since its competence would then be unduly and unnecessarily expanded. He assured the delegate of Ethiopia that if a serious situation arose, the Security Council, acting under Section B, need not wait for the completion of preliminary procedures; it was, in fact, obligated to act, and a country which was a victim of aggression could call on it for immediate assistance. The Ethiopian delegate stated that, in view of this clarification, he would withdraw his amendment, it being understood that one of the parties to a dispute had the right to request that Council to intervene during the course of preliminary peaceful negotiations.' (U.N.C.I.O. Doc. 356, III/2/11, p. 2.) If the statement of the delegate of the United States expressed the intention of those who drafted Article 33, paragraph 1, it would have been correct to accept the proposal of the Ethiopian delegate and to omit the words 'first of all.'

[9] At the 6th meeting of Committee III/2 (U.N.C.I.O. Doc. 383, III/2/13, p. 2) 'the delegate of the Union of Soviet Socialist Republics noted that paragraph 3 [Article 33 of the Charter] did not place any limitation on the choice of peaceful procedures, either on the parties to the dispute or on the Security Council.'—At the *Hearings* (p. 272) a Senator asked: 'Why, may I ask right there, if the parties to a dispute adopt one of these methods enumerated in Article 33, have they not performed their full obligations, or could they be required to try another additional method?' Whereupon the representative of the Department of State answered: 'They are required, Senator, I should say, under Article 33 to exhaust all of these methods or those that may be applicable to a particular situation, because there is an obligation laid on them later on in this chapter in Article 37, that if the parties to a dispute of the nature referred to in Article 33 fail to settle it by the means indicated in that article, they shall refer it to the Security Council. Therefore, if they refer a dispute to the Security Council, the chances are that the first thing that the Security Council would do would be to say to them, "Have you exhausted the means enumerated in Article 33 and any other means that you could think of for

pretation that the parties are obliged to exhaust all possible means of pacific settlement. The parties shall seek a solution by one or the other means indicated. If one party suggests one of these means, the other is not obliged to accept it. There must be an agreement between the parties with respect to the means of settlement, and there can be no legal obligation to come to an agreement. If one party enters into negotiation without any serious intention to come to an agreement or suggests one of the other means indicated in this paragraph, knowing that the other party will reject it, it may maintain to have complied with the prescription 'to seek a solution.' The importance of the provision concerned does not lie in the possibility of a sanction in case of non-compliance, but in the non-application of Article 37: If the means by which a solution of the dispute shall be sought under Article 33, paragraph 1, are not properly tried by one party, the other may object to refer the dispute to the Security Council under Article 37, paragraph 1, on the ground that the requirement of Article 33, paragraph 1, to seek 'first of all' a solution by the means indicated in this paragraph is not yet fulfilled, and that the fulfilment of this requirement is a condition of the application of Article 37; and the Security Council may, for the same reasons, refuse to act under Article 37, paragraph 2, in case a party refers the dispute to the Council under Article 37, paragraph 1. It is one of the main principles underlying the system of norms adopted by the Charter for the settlement of disputes that the Security Council should intervene in a dispute only after the parties themselves have tried to settle it by peaceful means of their own choice.[1] It is especially in this respect

settling this dispute?"' The statement that the parties are obliged to exhaust all methods indicated in Article 33, paragraph 1, has certainly no basis in the Charter. The Interim Committee of the General Assembly, at its 11th meeting on March 2, 1948, appointed a sub-committee to study the proposals which had been or might be submitted to the committee for the implementation of paragraph 2 (*c*) of the General Assembly resolution of November 13, 1947, and to formulate recommendations to the Interim Committee. Paragraph 2 (*c*) called upon the Interim Committee 'to consider . . . methods to be adopted to give effect to that part of Article 13 [of the Charter] . . . which deals with co-operation in the political field.' The Report of the Sub-committee contains the following passage: 'The words "first of all" in Article 33, paragraph 1, do not mean that all the methods enumerated must be tried before the Council can become concerned with the dispute. Some of the methods of settlement are similar in character, *e.g.*, mediation and conciliation, arbitration and judicial settlement; to attempt all these methods would be an unduly prolonged process, particularly for a dispute the continuance of which is likely to endanger peace.' (Doc. A/A.C.18/73, pp. 7 f.) As to the effect of Article 37, cf. *infra*, pp. 377 f.

1 In his report to Committee III/2 of the San Francisco Conference, the Rapporteur of the drafting sub-committee stated. 'The most important idea of the text was the principle that members of the Organisation should undertake to settle their disputes by peaceful means, and this provision accordingly had been placed at the beginning of the Chapter.' (U.N.C.I.O. Doc. 992, III/2/27, p. 1.) At the *Hearings*, the representative of the Department of State presented the following interpretation of Article 33, paragraph 1 (p. 270): 'Any countries which are

that the Charter differs from the Covenant, which did not contain a provision similar to that of Article 33, paragraph 1.

Article 33, paragraph 1, refers to 'any' dispute the continuance of which is likely to endanger the maintenance of international peace and security. But some disputes of this kind do not fall under this provision: disputes which arise out of matters which are essentially within the domestic jurisdiction of one of the states parties to the dispute. Under Article 2, paragraph 7, the members are not obliged to submit such disputes to settlement under the Charter, and the Organisation is excluded from intervention. But the contention of one party that the dispute refers to a matter which is essentially within its domestic jurisdiction may be contested by the other. Then the question arises whether Article 37 is applicable. It shall be discussed later.

Under Article 33, paragraph 1, the parties are not obliged to seek first of all adjustment of a situation, which has not the character of a dispute, by means of their own choice; they are obliged only to seek first of all a solution of their disputes; not of all disputes, but only of disputes 'the continuance of which is likely to endanger the maintenance of international peace and security.' Who has to decide the question as to whether a situation in which more than one state is involved, is a 'dispute,' and, if so, whether the dispute is of the nature referred to in Article 33, paragraph 1? As long as the Security Council does not intervene, these questions can be decided only by the parties themselves, that is to say, by agreement. But if there is no agreement with respect to these questions, if one party does, but the other does not, consider the situation to be a dispute,[2] or the dispute to be dangerous to the peace, Article 33, paragraph 1, is not applicable. This, again, is of importance with respect to the application of Article 37, which we shall discuss later.

The enumeration of the peaceful means for the solution of the dispute: 'negotiation, enquiry, mediation, conciliation, arbitration, judicial settlement, resort to regional agencies or arrangements,' is exhaustive. There are no other means of peaceful settlement.[3]

parties to any such disputes obligate themselves by the terms of the Charter, first of all, before coming to the Council and before invoking any of the machinery of the Organisation, to seek a solution of their difficulties by negotiation, enquiry, mediation, conciliation, arbitration, judicial settlement, resort to regional agencies or arrangements, or any other peaceful means of their own choice. That is, they are expected to resort to these means of their own choice and to exhaust them as fully as possible in an attempt to reach a pacific settlement of their dispute.'

[2] The conflict between Syria and Lebanon on the one hand, and France and Great Britain on the other, was brought before the Security Council by Syria and Lebanon as a 'dispute'; but the French Government denied that the case was a 'dispute.' (Journal of the Security Council, 1st Year, No. 8, p. 139; No. 16, pp. 303, 343.)

[3] Some writers distinguish between 'mediation' and 'good offices'; the latter being the attempt of a third power to bring about negotiations between the parties in conflict, the former consisting in direct conduct of negotiations between the

Hence, either the preceding enumeration or the reference to ' means of their own choice ' is superfluous. The question may arise whether the parties may choose under Article 33, paragraph 1, as a kind of ' conciliation,' submission of the dispute to the Security Council or the General Assembly. The question as to whether the parties are authorised by Article 33, paragraph 1, to submit this dispute to the Security Council should be answered in the negative since Article 37, paragraph 1, provides that a dispute shall be referred to the Council only after the parties have failed to settle it by the means indicated in Article 33. But the wording of Article 33 does not exclude another interpretation. Somewhat different is the question as to whether submitting the dispute to settlement by the General Assembly is among the means of the parties' ' own choice ' referred to in Article 33, paragraph 1. The General Assembly is competent to settle disputes by making recommendations under Articles 10 and 11, and Members as well as non-members are entitled to bring disputes before the General Assembly under Article 35. The wording of none of the Articles concerned does exclude submitting the dispute to the Assembly under Article 33, paragraph 1. But it may be doubted whether this was intended by the legislator.

The means by which the parties to a dispute shall seek the solution must be ' means of their own choice,' that is to say means which they themselves have chosen without any interference on the part of the Organisation. When the Security Council or the General Assembly has intervened in the dispute by recommending definite means for its solution, and the parties have accepted this recommendation, the means applied by them are not means ' of their own choice ' within the meaning of Article 33, paragraph 1. For the means to which this provision refers are means chosen prior to the intervention of the Organisation.

After the parties to the dispute have complied with the provisions of Article 33, paragraph 1, and have failed to settle their dispute by the means indicated in this paragraph, Article 37 applies. This Article is in close connection with Article 33, paragraph 1. The two provisions belong together; they form integral parts of one and the same procedure. The fact that three other Articles, establishing procedures different from that regulated by Article 33, paragraph 1, and Article 37, are inserted between these Articles is very confusing.

Article 37 runs as follows:

> 1. Should the parties to a dispute of the nature referred to in Article 33 fail to settle it by the means indicated in that Article, they shall refer it to the Security Council.

parties on the basis of proposals made by the mediator. But in practice it is hardly possible to separate the one from the other. The term ' mediation ' in Article 33, paragraph 2, may be interpreted to include ' good offices.'

> 2. If the Security Council deems that the continuance of the dispute is in fact likely to endanger the maintenance of international peace and security, it shall decide whether to take action under Article 36 or to recommend such terms of settlement as it may consider appropriate.

The wording of paragraph 1 does not allow any doubt that the parties to any dispute the continuance of which is likely to endanger the maintenance of international peace and security, after having failed to settle the dispute in accordance with Article 33, paragraph 1, have no choice among the various procedures provided for the settlement of disputes in the other Articles of Chapter VI of the Charter. The only way they have to follow is the one determined by Article 37: they must refer the dispute to the Security Council under paragraph 1 of that Article. Whether the competence of the Security Council under Article 37 is established in case one party refers the dispute to the Council or whether there must be an agreement of the parties to refer the dispute to the Council is not very clear. The wording of Article 37, paragraph 1: '*they* shall refer it to the Security Council,' allows both interpretations. But at the 7th meeting of Committee III/2 of the San Francisco Conference the interpretation was given 'that if one party to a dispute should violate its obligation to refer the dispute to the Security Council, such failure would in no case effect the right of the other party so to refer it, and the Security Council would then be wholly seized of the dispute.'[4] This interpretation has certainly a most desirable tendency, but it is not the only possible interpretation of Article 37, paragraph 1, providing that 'the parties' shall refer the dispute to the Security Council. It is regrettable that the text of the Charter has not been adapted to this interpretation. Article 15, paragraph 1, of the Covenant, expressly provided that 'any party to the dispute' may submit the dispute to the Council; no agreement was necessary to constitute the competence of the Council to settle a dispute. But the Council had no power under Article 15 to intervene in a dispute on its own initiative. Since the Security Council has this power under Articles 34 and 36 of the Charter, it would be understandable if the Charter required agreement of the parties to establish the competence of the Security Council in a procedure instituted by the parties. Such agreement seems to be necessary in so far as the parties are obliged to refer the case to the Security Council only if it is a 'dispute' not excluded by Article 2, paragraph 7, from settlement under Article 33, if its continuance is likely to endanger the maintenance of international peace and security, and if their attempt to settle it by peaceful means of their choice has failed. If one party is of the opinion that the case is of this nature, whereas the other party is not, and hence refuses to refer it to the Security Council under Article 37, paragraph 1, it is doubtful whether

[4] U.N.C.I.O. Doc. 433, III/2/15, p. 1.

this paragraph applies. But Article 37, paragraph 2, provides that the Security Council, after a dispute has been referred to it, shall first decide whether the continuance of it is in fact likely to endanger the maintenance of international peace and security. This implies the decision whether the matter referred by one party to the Security Council is a ' dispute,' and especially whether the dispute concerns a matter which is essentially within the domestic jurisdiction of the other party[5] in case this party makes such objection. The decision of the Security Council that the continuance of the dispute is ' in fact ' likely to endanger the maintenance of international peace and security is adequate only in case there is no agreement of the parties with respect to the question as to whether the condition of Article 33, paragraph 1: that the continuance of the dispute is likely to endanger the peace, is fulfilled. If both parties agree that the dispute is a danger to the peace it seems to be very strange to allow the Security Council to decide that the dispute is no danger to the peace and that therefore there is no reason to interfere. This competence of the Security Council is justifiable only in case that one party alone refers the dispute to the Council because the other party is not of the opinion that the continuance of the dispute is likely to endanger the peace. Then, and only then, is it understandable that the Security Council has to examine whether this is ' in fact ' the case.

There may be disagreement between the parties with respect to the application of Article 37, paragraph 1, not only on the ground that one, but not the other, party considers the matter to be a ' dispute,' or a dispute not excluded by Article 2, paragraph 7; or the dispute to be dangerous to the peace; but also on the ground that only one party, but not the other, is of the opinion that they have failed to settle their dispute by the means indicated in Article 33, paragraph 1. One party might, in opposition to the other, think that there is not yet a reason to assume that the means applied by them to settle their dispute will not succeed, or that another means, not yet tried, might succeed. May the Security Council decide this question as it may decide the questions whether the case is a ' dispute ' not concerning a matter of domestic jurisdiction, or whether the continuance of the dispute is likely to endanger the peace? Article 37, paragraph 2, expressly authorises the Security Council to decide only the last question. But it is not excluded to argue that the fulfilment of the provision of Article 33, paragraph 1, is a condition of the application of Article 37, establishing the jurisdiction of the Security Council, and that consequently the Security Council has to decide whether this condition is fulfilled. If the Security Council deems that the parties have not yet fulfilled the requirement of Article 33, paragraph 1, it may refuse to intervene

[5] As to the question whether the Security Council is competent to decide this issue, cf. *infra*, pp. 783 f.

under Article 37, paragraph 2.[6] The Security Council may also indirectly decide the disputed question as to whether the requirement of Article 33, paragraph 1, is fulfilled. It may in applying Article 37, paragraph 2, decide that the continuance of the dispute endangers the peace and recommend to the parties to continue the procedure they have adopted for the settlement of the dispute or to adopt another procedure indicated in Article 33, paragraph 1. If, however, the parties agree that it is of no use to continue to act under Article 33, paragraph 1, the Security Council should not refuse to intervene under Article 37, paragraph 2, that is to say, to examine the question as to the nature of the dispute and, if it deems it dangerous, to make one of the two recommendations referred to in that paragraph. For at the stage of the dispute to which Article 37, paragraph 1, refers, that is before an investigation of the dispute by the Security Council, the question as to whether the parties have complied with the provision of Article 33, paragraph 1, can be decided in no other way than by agreement of the parties.

After the dispute has been referred to the Security Council under Article 37, paragraph 1, the question arises whether the Security Council is bound to deal with the matter, or whether it is within its discretion to place or not to place the matter on its agenda. The wording of Article 37, paragraph 2, is not clear. It is not expressly stipulated that the Security Council, in case a dispute is referred to it under Article 37, paragraph 1, ' shall ' decide whether the continuance of the dispute is in fact likely to endanger the peace; it is only said: ' If the Security Council deems . . . '. But the fact that this provision is stipulated in the same Article as the provision that the parties to the dispute ' shall ' refer it to the Security Council in case their attempts to settle it by means of their own choice under Article 33, paragraph 1, have failed, allows the assumption that the intended

[6] In the case of the Mavrommatis Palestine Concessions, the jurisdiction of the Permanent Court of International Justice depended—*inter alia*—upon the fulfilment of the condition laid down in Article 26 of the Mandate for Palestine that the dispute ' cannot be settled by negotiation.' In its judgment the Court stated: ' Negotiations do not of necessity always presuppose a more or less lengthy series of notes and despatches; it may suffice that a discussion should have been commenced, and this discussion may have been very short; this will be the case if a deadlock is reached, or if finally a point is reached at which one of the Parties definitely declares himself unable, or refuses, to give way, and there can therefore be no doubt that *the dispute cannot be settled by diplomatic negotiation.*' ' The Court realises to the full the importance of the rule laying down that only disputes which cannot be settled by negotiation should be brought before it. It recognises, in fact, that before a dispute can be made the subject of an action at law, its subject matter should have been clearly defined by means of diplomatic negotiations. Nevertheless, in applying this rule, the Court cannot disregard, amongst other considerations, the views of the States concerned, who are in the best position to judge as to political reasons which may prevent the settlement of a given dispute by diplomatic negotiation.' (Publications of the Permanent Court of International Justice, Series A, No. 2, pp. 13, 15.)

meaning of Article 37, paragraph 2, is: that the Security Council in case a dispute has been referred to it under Article 37, paragraph 1, is bound to apply Article 37, paragraph 2, and that only if a dispute has been referred to the Council under Article 37, paragraph 1, the procedure of Article 37, paragraph 2, has to take place. If this interpretation is accepted the procedure of the Security Council regulated in Article 37, paragraph 2, is not a procedure *ex officio*; it is a procedure which depends on the parties to the dispute.

The first step of this procedure is the examination by the Security Council of the questions whether the matter is a 'dispute,' whether the parties have complied with the provision of Article 33, paragraph 1, whether the jurisdiction of the Council is not excluded by Article 2, paragraph 7, if contended by one party, and whether the continuance of the dispute is likely to endanger the maintenance of international peace and security.[7] The opinion of the parties involved about the nature of the case: whether it is a dispute or not,

[7] At the 125th meeting of the Security Council in the course of the discussion of the dispute between the United Kingdom and Albania concerning the incidents in the Corfu Channel, the delegate of Brazil stated: 'Albania and the United Kingdom had not exhausted such means when they referred their case to the United Nations, on October 29, 1946, and on January 10, 1947, respectively. In my opinion, consequently, the provisions of the Charter had not been observed when the Council decided to consider this dispute before the parties had exhausted the resources set forth in our constitutional document. . . . I feel I should make clear the error of this precedent in order to avoid a repetition which might be highly detrimental to our authority and functions. The Council apparently made use of the ample faculty conferred upon it by Article 34, through which it may investigate any dispute or any situation, combining it with Articles 35 and 36, wherein is stated the manner of recommending appropriate procedures or methods of adjustment. But these articles are applicable only, first, when the requirements of Article 33, calling for peaceful adjustment, have been complied with, and secondly, when the dispute or situation is likely to endanger the maintenance of international peace and security. . . . In the examination of disputes and situations, the Council is not restricted, as a court or tribunal would be, to the consideration of proofs, facts, circumstances, and laws. Our function is political, not judicial. Our consideration of a dispute or situation should limit itself to that part of the one or the other which may endanger the maintenance of international peace and security. Our attributions, therefore, preclude the consideration of any other disputes or situations, under penalty of the enlargement of our competence beyond the limits fixed by the Charter. . . . The hope of the Brazilian delegation is, therefore, that in the future the Council will admit for consideration, after the peaceful resources recommended in Article 33 are exhausted, only those disputes whose continuance is likely to endanger international peace and security, provided such menace is ascertained by previous investigation.' (Official Records of the Security Council, 2nd Year, No. 32, pp. 687 f.) The practice of the Security Council does not conform to this interpretation. At the 127th meeting the President of the Council declared with respect to the statement of the Brazilian delegate: 'His statement contained a very restrictive interpretation—part of it seemed to me unduly restrictive—of the competence of the Security Council.' (*Ibid.*, No. 34, p. 728.) The statement of the Brazilian delegate that the Security Council shall admit for consideration disputes only after the peaceful resources recommended in Article 33 are exhausted, has no basis in the wording of Chapter VI.

whether it refers to a matter essentially within the domestic jurisdiction of one party, and whether its continuance endangers the peace, is not binding upon the Council. In establishing its jurisdiction in the case, the Council has to decide for itself whether the requirements of the Charter are fulfilled. This implies an investigation which the Council is authorised to make by Article 34. The provision of Article 37, paragraph 2: that the Council before taking action under Article 36 or recommending terms of settlement shall decide whether the continuance of the dispute endangers the peace, presupposes that the Council has not yet investigated the dispute under Article 34 and hence not yet determined whether it is of the nature referred to in Article 37, paragraph 2. The result of the Council's examination may be negative or positive. In the first case, the Security Council is not allowed to intervene; in the second case, 'it shall decide whether to take action under Article 36 or to recommend such terms of settlement as it may consider appropriate.' That means that the Security Council has the choice between the two different measures indicated here. 'To take action under Article 36' means 'to recommend appropriate procedures or methods of adjustment.' The words 'to take action' as used in contradistinction to 'recommend such terms, etc.,' are not well chosen. The term 'action' is used in the Charter to designate enforcement action. But the 'action' referred to in Article 37, paragraph 2, is only a 'recommendation'; a mere recommendation of procedures for the settlement of the dispute, not a recommendation of terms of settlement. The Charter emphasises the distinction between these two kinds of recommendations, of which only the second one goes into the merits of the case. It is very doubtful whether at this stage of the dispute, after the parties have tried in vain to settle their dispute by the means indicated in Article 33, paragraph 1, and, for this reason, have both referred the dispute to the Security Council, it is appropriate for the latter to recommend to the parties to try again one of these means. As pointed out, only in case the parties do not agree with respect to the question as to whether attempts to settle their dispute under Article 33, paragraph 1, should be continued, a recommendation of procedures or methods is justified. However, such recommendation is hardly compatible with the Security Council's decision that the continuance of the dispute is likely to endanger the maintenance of international peace and security. If the situation implies a danger to the peace, only recommendations of terms of settlement seem to be appropriate. The provision of Article 37, paragraph 2, may probably be explained by the general tendency to confer upon the Security Council the greatest possible amount of discretion, to avoid any strict determination of its function.

It stands to reason that no decision of the Security Council can be taken without previous discussion. But Chapter VI of the Charter does not contain a provision expressly authorising the Council to discuss a dispute or a situation not having the character of a dispute, similar to Articles 10 and 11 referring to discussion of matters by the General Assembly. Hence it must be assumed that the power conferred upon the Council by Article 37, paragraph 2, to determine the dangerous character of a dispute and to make recommendations, as any power conferred upon the Council by other provisions of Chapter VI, implies the power to discuss (or consider) the matter which the Council is expressly empowered to deal with in some way or another.[8]

The second procedure instituted by the parties is regulated by Article 38, which runs as follows:

> Without prejudice to the provisions of Articles 33 to 37, the Security Council may, if all the parties to any dispute so request, make recommendations to the parties with a view to a pacific settlement of the dispute.

The wording of this Article allows two contradictory interpretations. Since it refers to 'any' dispute, it may be interpreted to mean that, if the parties to a dispute—whether or not of the nature referred to in Article 33, paragraph 1—agree the dispute may be brought before the Council for settlement, without any previous attempt by the parties themselves to settle it according to Article 33, paragraph 1. The formula 'without prejudice to the provisions of Articles 33 to 37' may be interpreted to mean that these Articles apply if there is no agreement of the parties to refer the dispute immediately for settlement to the Council. However, this formula may be interpreted to mean —and this interpretation is more plausible—that Article 38 refers only to disputes which are not of the nature referred to in Article 33. If the parties are of the opinion that their dispute is not likely to endanger the peace, they may by agreement submit the dispute directly to the Security Council. The competence of the Security Council cannot be established—as it can under Article 37, paragraph 1—by one party referring the dispute to the Council. Whereas under Article 37,

[8] According to the interpretation of Article 27 of the Charter by the Four Sponsoring Powers (cf. *supra*, pp. 249 ff.) 'no individual member of the Council can alone prevent consideration and discussion by the Council of a dispute or situation brought to its attention under paragraph 2, Section A, Chapter VIII [Dumbarton Oaks Proposals, corresponding to Article 35 of the Charter].' With reference to this interpretation the Australian delegation to the San Francisco Conference declared in a statement: 'It is important to understand that the words "consideration and discussion" are used in the joint statement in a much narrower sense than they ordinarily bear. In ordinary speech "consideration" of a dispute would include calling for reports, hearing witnesses, or even the appointment of a commission of investigation. The joint statement, however, treats the veto as applicable to a decision to use any of those procedures. It is only "consideration and discussion" of a very preliminary and restricted character that is to be free of the veto. It may be said that, without veto, the Council can only discuss whether a dispute can be discussed, and can only investigate whether it should be investigated.' (U.N.C.I.O. Doc. 897, III/1/42, p. 10.)

paragraph 2, the Security Council 'shall' make a recommendation, under Article 38 it 'may' do so. It may make recommendations to the parties with a view to a pacific settlement of the dispute; but it may also refuse to make such recommendations. Under Article 37, paragraph 2, after having determined the dangerous character of the dispute, the Council has the choice between two different measures: either recommendation of 'appropriate procedures or methods of adjustment' or of 'such terms of settlement as it may consider appropriate'; but it 'shall' make the one or the other; provided that the dispute has been referred to it under Article 37, paragraph 1; just as the Security Council can 'make recommendations to the parties with a view to a pacific settlement of the dispute' only if all the parties to the dispute so request under Article 38. The procedure under Article 38, as the procedure under Article 37, paragraph 2, is not a procedure *ex officio*; it depends on the parties.

Article 37, paragraph 2, and Article 38, are the only provisions of Chapter VI of the Charter by which the Security Council is authorised to recommend terms of settlement.[9] They refer to disputes only, not to other situations, and only to disputes brought before the Council by the parties themselves; not to disputes in a procedure instituted by the Council *ex officio*. This is evident as far as Article 38 is concerned. That the provision of Article 37, paragraph 2, authorising the Council to recommend appropriate procedures, etc., or terms of settlement, refers only to disputes which the parties, under Article 37, paragraph 1, after having failed to settle them by means of their own choice, are obliged to bring before the Council, results from the fact that the provision of paragraph 2 is combined with the obligation of paragraph 1 in one and the same Article.[1]

[9] Originally the Dumbarton Oaks Proposals conferred upon the Security Council no power to recommend terms of settlement. If this was due to the idea that to recommend terms of settlement was incompatible with the sovereignty of the state, it was not consistent to confer—in the Dumbarton Oaks Proposals as well as in the Charter—upon the General Assembly the power to make recommendations without any restriction to their contents. Cf. *infra*, pp. 457 f.

[1] In the Dumbarton Oaks Proposals, the provisions laid down in paragraphs 1 and 2 of Article 37 of the Charter were placed in one paragraph: paragraph 4 of Chapter VIII, Section A. The text of this paragraph was amended by the addition of the sentence beginning with the words: 'or whether . . .' and by the amendment (Doc. 2, G/29, p. 4) presented by the sponsoring Powers to Committee III/2. It read as follows:

> If, nevertheless, parties to a dispute of the nature referred to in paragraph 3 above fail to settle it by the means indicated in that paragraph, they should obligate themselves to refer it to the Security Council. If the Security Council deems that the continuance of the particular dispute is in fact likely to endanger the maintenance of international peace and security, it shall decide whether to take action under paragraph 5 *or whether itself to recommend such terms of settlement as it may consider appropriate.*

The intention of this paragraph was interpreted at the 2nd meeting of Committee III/2 (U.N.C.I.O. Doc. 188, III/2/3, p. 2) to be 'that in case of a dispute not

' The dispute ' of which paragraph 2 speaks can be only the dispute mentioned in paragraph 1. It is possible that this was not intended by the framers of the Charter. But if the provision of paragraph 2 authorising the Security Council to recommend procedures or terms of settlement was intended to refer to all disputes with which the Council may deal, it was a mistake to place it together with the one concerning the obligation of the parties to refer unsettled disputes to the Council, in the same Article. In its practice, the Security Council seems to consider itself authorised to act under Article 36 or to recommend terms of settlement regardless of the way in which the case—as a dispute or as a situation—was brought before it.[2]

The terms of settlement recommended by the Security Council under Article 37, paragraph 2, or Article 38, need not necessarily be in conformity with international law. Article 37, paragraph 2, authorises the Security Council to recommend such terms of settlement ' as it may consider appropriate.' Article 38 does not contain even this restriction with respect to the content of the recommendation. It is true that Article 24, paragraph 2, expressly provides that the Security Council in discharging its duties ' shall act in accordance with the Purposes and Principles of the United Nations.' But Article 1, paragraph 1, stipulates as a Purpose of the United Nations ' to bring about by peaceful means, and in conformity with the principles of justice and international law, adjustment or settlement of international disputes or situations.' That means, as pointed out, that the Security Council is authorised to recommend a settlement which might involve an infringement upon the rights which the one or the other party has under existing international law, if the Security Council considers such settlement as ' just ' or, under Article 37, paragraph 2, as ' appropriate.' There is hardly any difference between the two terms, since it is upon the Security Council to decide what is ' just ' or ' appropriate,' and it may always consider a recommendation which it thinks ' appropriate ' as ' just.' In case of a territorial dispute, for

settled by the terms of paragraph 3 [corresponding to Article 33, paragraph 1, of the Charter], or by recommendations of the Security Council under paragraph 5 [corresponding to Article 36, paragraph 1, of the Charter], the parties should be obligated to refer it to the Security Council with the object of obtaining a peaceful settlement. The Council then might recommend the employment of one or more of the procedures of paragraph 3, or it might itself take cognizance of the dispute and recommend the solution which it deemed appropriate.' According to this interpretation, the Council might make the recommendations referred to in Article 37, paragraph 2, only when the parties have referred the dispute to it under Article 37, paragraph 1. The statement that the parties should refer the dispute to the Council not only in case of a dispute not settled by the terms of paragraph 3 (corresponding to Article 33, paragraph 1) but also in case of a dispute not settled ' by recommendations of the Security Council under paragraph 5 ' (corresponding to Article 36, paragraph 1) has no basis in the wording or paragraph 4 of Chapter VIII, Section A, neither in its original nor in its amended text.

[2] Cf. notes, pp. 403, 416, 420, 421 f.

instance, the Security Council might recommend as appropriate that one party shall cede a part of the disputed territory to the other party, regardless of whether the latter has any legally justifiable claim to this territory.

In the procedures instituted by the parties, that is the procedure under Article 37 in connection with Article 33, paragraph 1, and the procedure under Article 38, the competence of the Security Council, as pointed out, is established by the parties referring the dispute to the Council. Consequently the Council ceases to be competent in the matter as soon as the parties agree to withdraw the dispute from the Council. In this case the matter is automatically removed from the agenda of the Security Council. However, such withdrawal is not of great importance since the Security Council may restore its jurisdiction by instituting an *ex officio* procedure on its own initiative under Article 34 and Article 36.

That the parties have the power to terminate the jurisdiction of the Council by withdrawing the case, seems to be self-evident in the procedure under Article 38. In the procedures regulated by Articles 33, paragraph 1, and 37, the parties may withdraw their dispute from the Security Council, either because they have succeeded in settling the dispute by means of their own choice after it has been referred to the Security Council, or because they agree to continue their efforts to settle the dispute under Article 33, paragraph 1; at least they may withdraw the dispute before the Council has determined, under Article 37, paragraph 2, its dangerous character. But even after the Security Council has determined the dangerous character of the dispute, withdrawal of the dispute from the jurisdiction of the Council may be considered to be possible, as long as the Security Council has not made a recommendation under Article 37, paragraph 2. This follows from the fact that the competence of the Security Council under Article 37 depends on the parties and the parties are obliged to refer the dispute to the Council only if they believe, or at least if one party believes, that there is no hope to settle it by peaceful means of their own choice. In this procedure no other authority can decide these two questions before the dispute is referred to the Council. After it is referred to the Council, the latter, it is true, becomes competent to decide that the dispute is dangerous to the peace. But this decision loses any importance if the parties afterwards reach an agreement, either with respect to the settlement or with respect to the continuance of their attempts to settle it. As pointed out, one of the basic ideas of Chapter VI is to encourage pacific settlement of disputes by the parties themselves and to allow interference of the Security Council only after it is clear that the first way does not lead to a settlement. If it is assumed that the procedure of Article 37, paragraph 2, has to take place only if a dispute is referred by the parties to the Security Council under Article 37, paragraph 1, this procedure cannot be continued if the parties have withdrawn the dispute from the Council.

(*b*) Procedures Instituted by the Security Council

The principle that the Security Council shall interfere in a dispute only after the parties have tried in vain to settle it by means of their own choice, is not consistently maintained in the Charter. There are other procedures for the settlement of disputes which are determined by the opposite principle. First of all, the procedure to be instituted by the Security Council itself on its own initiative; it is regulated by Article 34, Article 33, paragraph 2, and Article 36.

Article 34 runs as follows:

> The Security Council may investigate any dispute, or any situation which might lead to international friction or give rise to a dispute, in order to determine whether the continuance of the dispute or situation is likely to endanger the maintenance of international peace and security.

The provision of this Article is ambiguous. It may mean that the Security Council is authorised to make investigations if the Council—in the course of the procedures regulated in the other Articles of Chapter VI, for instance in applying Article 37, paragraph 2—deems such investigation necessary, the term 'investigation' taken in a specifically technical sense. But Article 34 may also be interpreted to mean that the Council is authorised to intervene in any dispute or any situation of the nature determined in that Article on its own initiative by undertaking an investigation. This interpretation of the provision regarding investigation may be supported by the fact that Article 34 precedes all the other Articles regulating the procedures of the Security Council for the settlement of disputes and adjustment of other situations.[3] If Article 34 were not intended to establish a special procedure but only to refer to a phase within other procedures, it would have been placed after the Articles regulating these procedures. If the interpretation is accepted that Article 34 regulates a special procedure of the Security Council, the latter is authorised to intervene *ex officio* in any dispute—and any other situation of the nature determined in this Article—even before the parties had any opportunity of settling the dispute by peaceful means of their own choice or of adjusting, by themselves, the situation. This intervention must be carried out as an 'investigation.' If Article 34 is interpreted to establish an *ex officio* procedure of the Security Council, the term 'investigation' must be interpreted in a broader than a mere technical sense. It must include all preliminary steps leading to a technical investigation, especially the decision of the

[3] In the Dumbarton Oaks Proposals the corresponding provision (Chapter VIII, Section A, paragraph 1) was even placed at the top of Chapter VIII, Section A, dealing with Pacific Settlement of Disputes (corresponding to Chapter VI of the Charter).

Council to deal with a dispute or another situation *ex officio*, that is to place the matter on its agenda, without which no investigation of the dispute or situation can be decided upon. That Article 34 is interpreted to establish an *ex officio* procedure of the Security Council does not exclude the possibility of applying Article 34 to investigations necessary in the course of procedures regulated in other Articles of the Charter.[4] But it should be noted that such investigation is not obligatory according to the wording of Article 34. The Council may ' investigate ' a dispute or another situation by examining and discussing written or oral statements by the parties to the dispute or by those involved in the situation. The Council may undertake investigation through a special organ appointed for this purpose by the Council. The special organ may be a commission authorised to carry out the investigation on the territory of the state party to the dispute or involved in the situation. The Members must permit such investigation since they are obliged by Article 25 to ' carry out the decisions of the Security Council in accordance with the present Charter.'[5]

Article 34 refers not only to disputes but also to situations not having the character of disputes. Whereas a ' dispute ' can exist only in the relationship between two or more definite states, a ' situation '

[4] Since the Security Council—except under Article 38—has the power to make the recommendations provided for in Chapter VI only with respect to disputes or other situations which are likely to endanger the peace, none of these recommendations can be made without some kind of preliminary investigation the purpose of which is to determine the nature of the dispute or situation. Hence Article 34 should be applied in all procedures under Chapter VI (except that under Article 38). But the practice of the Security Council does not conform to this principle.

[5] At the *Hearings* (pp. 319 f.) the question was raised as to ' how much the Organisation can investigate inside of a country ?' To this question, the representative of the Department of State first made the following statement: ' Obviously it can do what the governments themselves are willing for it to do.' That probably means that there is no obligation of the Members to permit investigations and that the investigations have to be carried out through the governments themselves. But the following discussion led to another result. A Senator called attention to Article 2, paragraph 5: ' All Members shall give the United Nations every assistance in any action it takes in accordance with the present Charter, and shall refrain . . . ' Another Senator stated: ' Then it would be a violation of the Charter if any nation did not permit investigations to be made within its borders that had been ordered by the Assembly or the Council; is that correct ?' Whereupon the representative of the State Department declared: ' It would be judged by the Organisation itself as to whether or not such an action constitutes failure to live up to the commitment to give every assistance in any action taken in accordance with this Charter.'

The obligation of the Members to permit an investigation decided upon by the Security Council under Article 34 is based on Article 25, not on Article 2, paragraph 5. (Cf. *supra*, p. 91.) Hence no obligation of the Members is constituted by a resolution of the General Assembly to investigate a situation. Cf. *infra*, p. 457. In the course of the discussion of the Greek case the delegate of Australia quite correctly stated at the 162nd meeting of the Security Council that the resolution of the Council to investigate a dispute or situation ' is a decision, and not a recommendation; therefore, Article 25 does apply.' (Official Records of the Security Council, 2nd Year, No. 61, p. 1420.)

may have a more general character, not being restricted to definite states and not being confined to a definite territory. But it is not impossible to interpret the term ' situation ' to mean a concrete situation in which definite states are involved, a situation which might lead to friction or to a dispute between definite states.[6]

Under Article 34, the Security Council has the power to investigate ' any dispute,' but ' situations ' only ' if they might lead to international

[6] At the 57th meeting of the Security Council the delegate of the Soviet Union proposed that ' the Security Council should adopt a resolution requiring States Members of the United Nations to submit the following information to the Security Council within two weeks: (1) At what points on the territory of Members of the United Nations or other States, with the exception of former enemy territories, and in what number are armed forces of other Members of the United Nations stationed? (2) At what points in the above-mentioned territories are air and naval bases situated and what is the size of their garrisons belonging to the armed forces of other Member States of the United Nations.' (*Ibid.*, 1st Year, 2nd Series: Suppl. No. 5, Annex 9.) At the 71st meeting he declared: ' The question raised in this statement is one concerning a situation, and therefore, on the basis of Articles 34 and 35 of the Charter of the United Nations, the Security Council not only can, but in the opinion of my Government, must take a decision in regard to this question.' (*Ibid.*, 1st Year, 2nd Series, No. 17, p. 424.) Later he specified his statement by referring to a number of definite countries (pp. 430 ff.); and stated that the situation to which he referred ' may lead to serious international friction.' ' The situation mentioned in the Soviet statement falls entirely within the scope of Articles 34 and 35 of the United Nations Charter. . . . I have considered it necessary to give this explanation in order to show that the investigation by the Security Council of the question raised in my statement is called for by the United Nations Charter ' (pp. 437 f.). In the course of the discussion of the question whether the Soviet proposal should be placed on the agenda of the Security Council the delegate of Australia declared to be against admission of this item to the agenda because the situation to which the Soviet proposal referred could be described only as a ' world situation. . . . We are face to face with a general proposition and not with a particular matter, the general proposition being that if foreign troops are in the territory of any ex-enemy State, there is a danger to peace. . . . A situation of the kind described in Article 34 seems to us to be a particular situation, not a general world situation or even a continental situation. . . . we should be told exactly what spot the representative of the U.S.S.R. has in mind which constitutes a danger to peace or a possible cause of friction. Then, and then only, can this Council decide procedurally whether or not there is something which needs to be examined at greater length ' (p. 426). But the delegate of France declared that in spite of the fact ' that we are no longer dealing with a definite case comparable to a clearly outlined dispute, the geographical boundaries of which have been definitely fixed. . . . the question at issue does not for this reason fail to come under the terms of Article 34. I do not think that this Article ought to be understood only in the sense of a very definite and specific situation concerning a given country. It seems to me that a " situation," in the sense of Article 34, may be a state of affairs which extends, as in the case before us, to several countries; or, shall we say, that it is not because the question raised by the U.S.S.R. delegation is broader in scope than those which we usually examine, that it does not, for that reason, constitute a " situation " and that, if it threatens the peace of the world, we ought to abstain from dealing with it. An excessively narrow interpretation of the Charter in regard to this matter would involve a dangerous limitation of the powers of the Security Council and would not in reality correspond to the duties incumbent upon us according to the terms of the Charter.' (*Ibid.*, No. 18, p. 445.)

friction or give rise to a dispute.' It is quite reasonable that the Security Council is authorised to investigate any dispute ' in order to determine whether the continuance of the dispute . . . is likely endanger the maintenance of international peace and security.' But it amounts to a vicious circle to provide that the Council may investigate only a situation ' which might lead to international friction or give rise to a dispute ' in order to find out whether this situation is a danger to the peace. To determine that the situation might lead to international friction or give rise to a dispute is possible only after an investigation of the situation, by whatever means this investigation may be carried out.[7] In order to avoid this vicious circle Article 34 must be interpreted to mean: the Security Council may investigate . . . any situation which *prima facie* might lead to international friction, etc.[8] That means that the Security Council may investigate any situation which it deems advisable to investigate. There was no sufficient reason not to authorise the Security Council to investigate any situation without restriction—as it is authorised to investigate any dispute, since this body will actually not decide to investigate a situation if it does not deem it necessary to do so.

It is important to note that the investigation referred to in Article 34 is limited to a definite purpose: it must be undertaken in order to determine whether the continuance of the dispute or situation under consideration by the Council ' is likely to endanger the maintenance of international peace and security.' It is an investigation within the framework of the procedures laid down in Chapter VI. The

7 At the 16th meeting of the Security Council, during the discussion of the Indonesian case, the representative of the United States declared: ' . . . because the right of investigation is so important the United States Government feels that investigations should not be lightly undertaken. In determining whether or not a situation warrants investigation the Security Council must have reason to believe from all the circumstances before it that the continuance of the situation is likely to endanger international peace.' (Journal of the Security Council, 1st Year, No. 13, p. 233.) This statement is not quite in conformity with Article 34. It is just the purpose of the investigation to determine whether the continuance of the situation is ' likely to endanger international peace.' But it would be possible to say that the Security Council in determining whether or not a situation warrants investigation must have reason to believe that the situation ' might lead to international friction or give rise to a dispute.' The representative of the United States probably did not see any essential difference between this formula and the one he used. If he was right, the text of Article 34 contains the vicious circle mentioned above.

8 In the course of the discussion of the above-mentioned Soviet proposal to investigate under Article 34 the situation constituted by the presence of armed forces of Members on the territories of other Members, the delegate of the Netherlands declared to be against admission of this item to the agenda of the Security Council because no ' sufficient *prima facie* case has been made to justify placing this matter on the Council's agenda.' (Official Records of the Security Council, 1st Year, 2nd Series, No. 17, p. 439.) Also in the Czechoslovak question the representative of Chile interpreted the phrase ' situation which might lead to international friction or give rise to a dispute ' to mean that ' there must be proof which constitutes *prima facie* evidence that peace is in danger . . . ' (Doc. S/P.V. 268, p. 91.)

investigation may be conducted by the Security Council itself or by an auxiliary organ established by the Council for this purpose. The decision of the Council to undertake such an investigation concerns—according to the interpretation of Article 27 by the four Sponsoring Powers—a substantive, not a procedural matter and hence requires a majority of seven members including the concurring votes of the permanent members. However, investigations may be necessary for other purposes than those determined in Article 34—for instance in order to determine, under Article 39, the existence of facts which constitute a ' threat to the peace, breach of the peace, or act of aggression,' which is different from a dispute or situation ' likely to endanger . . . peace . . . ';[9] and an investigation may be necessary not only by the Security Council but also by the General Assembly, the latter being competent, too, to deal with disputes and other situations dangerous to the peace. Nevertheless, Article 34 is the only provision of the Charter expressly providing for investigations. Hence the interpretation is possible that investigations are authorised by the Charter only for the purpose determined in Article 34 and that only the Security Council is authorised to undertake such investigations. Although it is likely that this was indeed the original intention of those who drafted the Charter, such interpretation would lead to absurd consequences. The Organisation cannot properly intervene in a situation without an investigation by which the facts constituting the situation are ascertained. Hence it may be assumed that the Charter conferring upon the General Assembly and the Security Council the function to intervene in various situations (this term taken in its broadest sense) authorises these organs to undertake the investigations necessary to fulfil their functions. That no such express provision has been inserted into the Charter is highly regrettable. The lack of such a provision has the effect that the opposite interpretation is not excluded, so that no other investigation than the one authorised by Article 34 may be considered as constitutional.

The decision by which an investigation is instituted should be distinguished from the decision by which a special organ is established to carry out the investigation. For the former is certainly substantive in character whereas the latter may, perhaps, be considered to be procedural. As to the establishment of special organs for the purpose of an investigation, Articles 29 and 22 apply. These Articles confer upon the Security Council and the General Assembly the power to establish such subsidiary organs as they deem necessary for the performance of their functions. If the General Assembly or the Security Council decides to investigate a situation, and if they deem it necessary, they may establish a committee or a commission or any

[9] Cf. the statement which the President made in the discussion of the Spanish case at the 44th meeting of the Security Council (Journal of the Security Council, 1st Year, No. 37, pp. 731 f.).

other kind of organ and authorise it to conduct the investigation. Articles 22 and 29 do not confer upon the two agencies the power to investigate, but only the power to establish organs for this purpose, provided that they have the power of investigation. But this is, as pointed out, certain only as far as Article 34 applies. If it is assumed that the Charter authorises the General Assembly and the Security Council to make the investigations necessary for the performance of the functions expressly conferred upon them, Article 34 is superfluous. The difference between an investigation instituted by the General Assembly and the one ordered by the Security Council is that in the first case the Members are not obliged to permit the investigation, since Article 25 refers only to decisions of the Security Council, not to decisions of the General Assembly. It is doubtful whether Article 34 authorises the Security Council not only to investigate disputes and other situations, but also to establish a special organ for this purpose. If the Article is interpreted to empower the Security Council to establish special organs of investigation, Article 34 is partly overlapping Article 29. But there may exist an important difference in the application of the two provisions. The establishment by the Security Council of a subsidiary organ under Article 29 concerns, according to the interpretation by the Sponsoring Powers, a procedural, not a substantive matter.[1] If this interpretation is accepted, the decision concerned is not subject to the veto right of the permanent members of the Security Council.[2] But there is no sufficient reason to assume that a decision taken under Article 34 has a procedural character. This view is confirmed by the interpretation of Article 27 by the Sponsoring Powers. A decision to the effect to investigate a situation has certainly not a merely procedural character. If the decision establishing a special organ to carry out an investigation is taken under Article 34 without being separated from the decision by which the investigation is instituted, it can hardly be considered as procedural; and even if it is a separate decision, if taken under Article 34, the authority of the interpretation by the Sponsoring Powers cannot be invoked to defend the view that such a decision is procedural. Then the veto right of the permanent members applies. Further, the decision by which a subsidiary organ under Article 29 is established is not a 'decision under Chapter VI'; hence the provision of Article 27, paragraph 3, that 'a party to a dispute shall abstain from voting,' does not apply. Finally, under Articles 22 and 29, a subsidiary organ may be established not only for the purpose of investigation, but for any

[1] Article 5, paragraph 2, of the Covenant of the League of Nations expressly declared 'the appointment of Committees to investigate particular matters' as a matter of procedure; decisions of the Assembly or the Council establishing such committees required a simple majority. Article 5, paragraph 2, was the only provision of the Covenant dealing with investigation.

[2] Cf. the discussion of the Greek case (Ukrainian complaint) at the 70th meeting of the Security Council (Official Records, 1st Year, 2nd Series, No. 16, pp. 410 f.).

other purpose within the competence of the General Assembly or the Security Council, and may be composed of representatives of the members of the organs establishing it or in any other way.[3] In the

[3] In the Greek question the representative of the United States proposed at the 147th meeting of the Security Council to establish ' a commission as a subsidiary organ ' composed of a representative of each of the states members of the Security Council, and to authorise this commission not only to make certain investigations but also to ' use its good offices ' for the settlement of controversies arising out of the situation which existed in the relationship between Greece and its neighbours. (Official Records of the Security Council, 2nd Year, No. 51, p. 1125.) This proposition was opposed because it intended to confer upon the commission powers going beyond those determined by Article 34. The delegate of Australia quite correctly referred to Article 29 of the Charter authorising the Security Council to establish subsidiary organs for other purposes than investigation. (*Ibid.*, No. 61, p. 1420.) In the Indonesian question, the Security Council adopted on August 25, 1947, a resolution by which it requested ' the Governments members of the Council who have career consular representatives in Batavia to instruct them to prepare jointly for the information and guidance of the Security Council reports on the situation in the Republic of Indonesia following the Resolution of the Council of August 1, 1947, such reports to cover the observance of the " cease fire " orders and the conditions prevailing in areas under military occupation or from which armed forces now in occupation may be withdrawn by agreement between the parties ' and requested ' the Governments of the Netherlands and of the Republic of Indonesia to grant to the representatives referred to in paragraph 5 all facilities necessary for the effective fulfilment of their mission.' (Doc. S/P.V. 194.) The commission composed of the career consuls of the members of the Security Council in Batavia may be considered to be a subsidiary organ established under Article 29; such an organ could not be created under Article 34. On August 22, 1947, the Council also resolved ' to tender its good offices to the parties in order to assist in the pacific settlement of their dispute in accordance with paragraph (*b*) of the Resolution of the Council of August 1, 1947. The Council expresses its readiness, if the parties so request, to assist in the settlement through a committee of the Council consisting of three members of the Council, each party selecting one, and the third to be designated by the two so selected.' (Doc. S/514.) The Committee of Good Offices consisted of Australia, selected by the Republic of Indonesia, Belgium named by the Netherlands, and the United States chosen by Australia and Belgium. The question arises whether the Security Council is competent to intervene in a dispute by offering and exercising its ' good offices.' If this function consists in the attempt of inducing the parties to re-assume negotiations, the Security Council may, under Article 36, paragraph 1, offer and exercise its good offices. Under the same provision or under Article 37, paragraph 2, the Security Council may act as mediator, if by mediation, in contradistinction to good offices, is understood to make substantive or procedural proposals to the parties concerning the settlement of their dispute. If the Security Council is competent to exercise good offices and to act as mediator, it may establish under Article 29, not under Article 34, subsidiary organs for these purposes.

A commission of mediation was established in the India-Pakistan question by the resolution of the Security Council of January 20, 1948, which runs as follows:

> The Security Council,
>
> Considering that it may investigate any dispute or any situation which might, by its continuance, endanger the maintenance of international peace and security; that, in the existing state of affairs between India and Pakistan, such an investigation is a matter of urgency;
>
> Adopts the following resolution:
>
> A. A Commission of the Security Council is hereby established composed

practice of the Security Council, the decision by which an investigation is instituted, and the decision by which a special organ for this purpose is established, are not clearly distinguished and Article 34 is interpreted to authorise the Council to establish investigation organs.[4]

of representatives of three Members of the United Nations, one to be selected by India, one to be selected by Pakistan, and the third to be designated by the two so selected. Each representative on the Commission shall be entitled to select his alternates and assistants.

B. The Commission shall proceed to the spot as quickly as possible. It shall act under the authority of the Security Council and in accordance with the directions it may receive from it. It shall keep the Security Council currently informed of its activities and of the development of the situation. It shall report to the Security Council regularly, submitting its conclusions and proposals.

C. The Commission is invested with a dual function:

(1) to investigate the facts pursuant to Article 34 of the Charter;

(2) to exercise, without interrupting the work of the Security Council, any mediatory influence likely to smooth away difficulties, to carry out the directions given to it by the Security Council, and to report how far the advice and directions, if any, of the Security Council have been carried out.

D. The Commission shall perform the functions described in clause C:

(1) in regard to the situation in the Jammu and Kashmir State set out in the letter of the representative of India addressed to the President of the Security Council, dated January 1, 1948, and in the letter from the Minister of Foreign Affairs of Pakistan addressed to the Secretary-General, dated January 15, 1948; and

(2) in regard to other situations set out in the letter from the Minister of Foreign Affairs of Pakistan addressed to the Secretary-General dated January 15, 1948, when the Security Council so directs.

E. The Commission shall take its decision by majority vote. It shall determine its own procedure. It may allocate among its members, alternate members, their assistants, and its personnel such duties as may have to be fulfilled for the realisation of its mission and the reaching of its conclusions.

F. The Commission, its members, alternate members, their assistants, and its personnel, shall be entitled to journey, separately or together, wherever the necessities of their tasks may require, and, in particular, within those territories which are the theatre of the events of which the Security Council is seized.

G. The Secretary-General of the United Nations shall furnish the Commission with such personnel and assistance as it may consider necessary.' (Doc. S/654.)

It seems that the commission referred to in this resolution has been established under Article 34 of the Charter since the preamble evidently uses the words of this Article. But under this Article only one of the functions determined in clause C of the resolution could be conferred upon the commission: 'to investigate the facts,' not the other: 'to exercise . . . mediatory influence.'

At its 286th meeting on April 21, 1948, the Security Council adopted a resolution in which it instructed the commission, established by its resolution of January 20, 1948, to 'place its good offices and mediation at the disposal of the Governments

4 For note see p. 396.

If an investigation undertaken by the Security Council under Article 34 has the result that the Council determines the dangerous

of India and Pakistan with a view to facilitating the taking of the necessary measures, both with respect to the restoration of peace and order and to the holding of a plebiscite by the two Governments, acting in co-operation with one another and with the Commission and further instructs the Commission to keep the Council informed of the action taken under the Resolution.' To this end the Security Council recommended to the Government of India *inter alia* that 'The Government of India should undertake that there will be established in Jammu and Kashmir a Plebiscite Administration to hold a Plebiscite as soon as possible on the question of the accession of the State to India or Pakistan.' (Doc. S/726.)

At the 287th meeting of April 23, 1948, the Security Council adopted the following resolution in the Palestine question:

> 'Referring to its resolution of April 17, 1948, calling upon all parties concerned to comply with specific terms for a truce in Palestine,
>
> The Security Council,
>
> Establishes a truce commission for Palestine composed of representatives of those members of the Security Council which have career consular officers in Jerusalem, noting, however, that the representative of Syria has indicated that his Government is not prepared to serve on the Commission. The function of the Commission shall be to assist the Security Council in supervising the implementation by the parties of the resolution of the Security Council of April 17, 1948;
>
> Requests the Commission to report to the President of the Security Council within four days regarding its activities and the development of the situation, and subsequently to keep the Security Council currently informed with respect thereto.
>
> The Commission, its members, their assistants and its personnel shall be entitled to travel, separately or together, wherever the Commission deems necessary to carry out its tasks.
>
> The Secretary-General of the United Nations shall furnish the Commission with such personnel and assistance as it may require, taking into account the special urgency of the situation with respect to Palestine.' (Doc. A/620, p. 85/86.)

Only Article 29, not Article 34, can be the legal basis to establish such a Truce Commission.

At its 135th meeting on May 14, 1948, the General Assembly adopted a resolution providing for the appointment of a United Nations Mediator in Palestine. The resolution:

> Empowers a United Nations Mediator in Palestine, to be chosen by a committee of the General Assembly composed of representatives of China, France, the Union of Soviet Socialist Republics, the United Kingdom and the United States of America, to exercise the following functions:
>
> (*a*) To use his good offices with the local and community authorities in Palestine to:
>
> (i) Arrange for the operation of common services necessary to the safety and well-being of the population of Palestine;
>
> (ii) Assure the protection of the Holy Places, religious buildings and sites in Palestine;
>
> (iii) Promote a peaceful adjustment of the future situation of Palestine.

character of the dispute or the situation, the Council may apply Article 33, paragraph 2, or Article 36.

> (*b*) To co-operate with the Truce Commission for Palestine appointed by the Security Council in its resolution of April 23, 1948.
>
> (*c*) To invite, as seems to him advisable, with a view to the promotion of the welfare of the inhabitants of Palestine, the assistance and co-operation of appropriate specialised agencies of the United Nations such as the World Health Organisation, of the International Red Cross, and of other governmental or non-governmental organisations of a humanitarian and non-political character. (Doc. A/552.)

China and the United States submitted to Sub-committee 2 of the Interim Committee of the General Assembly some suggestions concerning the elaboration of the procedures for pacific settlement mentioned in Article 33 of the Charter; among the suggested methods were mediation through ' officers of the principal organs of the United Nations,' and ' tender of good offices ' by ' officers of principal organs of the United Nations in their official capacity.' (Doc. A/AC. 18/SC 2/2, p. 3.)

[4] In the Spanish case the Security Council adopted on April 29, 1946, at the suggestion of the Australian delegate a resolution to the effect to create a ' sub-committee ' under Article 29, instead of an investigation commission under Article 34, and instructed this sub-committee ' to examine the statements made before the Security Council concerning Spain, to receive further statements and documents, and to conduct such inquiries as it may deem necessary, and to report to the Security Council as soon as possible.' The function of this sub-committee evidently was to investigate, though it has not been called by this term. The purpose of the sub-committee's investigation was—according to the resolution on which it was established—to enable the Security Council to decide whether the situation in Spain ' has led to international friction and endangers international peace and security.' (Journal of the Security Council, 1st Year, No. 31, p. 622; No. 32, p. 628.) The Australian delegate in order to explain his suggestion declared: ' I have cut out the idea of a formal investigation under Article 34 so as to enable the proposed body to be brought in under Article 29 as a subisidiary organ; and I call it a sub-committee instead of a committee.' (*Ibid.*, No. 31, p. 603.) But if the Security Council wishes to undertake an investigation under Article 34, and if it wishes to make this investigation by a special committee, can such a committee be established under any other provision than that of Article 29? Whether it is called committee, or sub-committee, or commission is of no importance.

In the Greek question, the representative of the United States proposed at the 70th meeting of the Security Council on September 20, 1946, a resolution to the effect—

> That the Security Council, acting under Article 34 of the Charter, establish a commission of three individuals to be nominated by the Secretary-General, to represent the Security Council on the basis of their competence and impartiality, and to be confirmed by the Security Council;
>
> That the Security Council instruct the commission:
>
> (1) to investigate the facts relating to the border incidents along the frontier between Greece on the one hand and Albania, Bulgaria and Yugoslavia on the other;
>
> (2) to examine the statements submitted to the Security Council concerning these incidents and such further information from other sources as it deems necessary; and
>
> (3) to submit to the Security Council as soon as practicable a report on the facts disclosed by its investigation;

Article 33, paragraph 2, stipulates:

> The Security Council shall, when it deems necessary, call upon the parties to settle their dispute by such means.

> That the commission shall have authority to conduct its investigation in the area and to call upon Albania, Bulgaria, Greece and Yugoslavia for information relevant to its investigation:
>
> That the Security Council request the Secretary-General to communicate with appropriate authorities in the countries involved, in order to obtain permission for the commission to conduct its investigation in these countries. (Official Records of the Security Council, 1st Year, 2nd Series, No. 16, p. 412.)

In spite of the fact that Article 34 was expressly referred to in the text of the resolution, the delegate of France declared: ' This motion, the intention of which is merely to establish a committee of investigation, is not a motion of substance, but rather of procedure. Permit me to add that, in my opinion, this motion comes under the provisions of Article 29 of the Charter ' (p. 410). Such interpretation is possible only if one ignores that the decision to undertake an investigation is implied in the decision to establish a committee of investigation. The President declared the resolution as not adopted although 8 members voted in the affirmative, because one permanent member (Soviet Union) voted in the negative (p. 412). That means that the resolution was considered to concern a non-procedural matter. At its 87th meeting on December 19, 1946, the Security Council adopted in the Greek question unanimously a resolution to the effect ' that the Security Council, under Article 34 of the Charter, establish a commission of investigation to ascertain the facts relating to the alleged border violations along the frontier between Greece on the one hand and Albania, Bulgaria, and Yugoslavia on the other.' (*Ibid.*, No. 28, p. 676.) The decision to investigate the facts and the decision to establish a commission for this purpose were combined in one and the same act. The purpose of the investigation as determined by the resolution of the Council was not in conformity with the wording of Article 34: to determine whether the continuance of the dispute or situation is likely to endanger the maintenance of international peace and security. But it may be assumed that the commission had to ascertain the facts in order to enable the Council to determine the nature of the dispute or situation.

In the Corfu Channel Incidents case the Australian delegate again suggested to appoint a ' sub-committee ' ' to examine all the available evidence concerning the above-mentioned incidents and to make a report to the Security Council.' (Official Records of the Security Council, 2nd Year, No. 18, p. 118.) The representative of the United Kingdom asked the President: ' As a party to this dispute, I am deprived of my vote under Article 27, paragraph 3, of the Charter, when it is a matter of a decision under Chapter VI. I presume, though, that the vote which we are going to take is a purely procedural one and that I can exercise my vote. Is that the case?' (*Ibid.*, No. 21, p. 425.) This statement implies three different questions: 1. whether the decision to establish a sub-committee is to be taken under Chapter VI; 2. whether the decision concerns a procedural matter; 3. whether the rule excluding parties to a dispute from voting applies to all decisions under Chapter VI or only to decisions on non-procedural matters. That the rule requiring unanimity of the permanent members of the Security Council applies only to non-procedural decisions, was not questioned. But it seems that the representative of the United Kingdom was of the opinion that even if the decision was to be taken under Chapter VI he was not excluded from voting, since the decision was procedural. (Cf. *supra*, p. 246.) The representative of the Soviet Union expressed the view that ' a decision on the establishment of such a

The wording ' The Security Council shall . . . ', in contradistinction to ' The Security Council may . . . ', is used when the legislator

committee cannot be considered as procedural, particularly in the light of previous decisions of the Security Council and of precedents [he referred to the decision by which an investigation commission was established in the Greek case], and in the light of the well-known statement of the four Great Powers at San Francisco ' (p. 425). The President of the Security Council declared that the resolution proposed by the Australian delegate did not institute an investigation under Chapter VI: ' there is no question in this case of undertaking an investigation. . . . In so far as it sanctions an exception to the voting order, Article 27, paragraph 3, must, where applicable, be interpreted strictly; it cannot be stretched to cover cases which are not mentioned in Chapter VI of the Charter. If we study the various Articles of Chapter VI we shall see that the establishment of a sub-committee, such as that proposed by the Australian resolution, is not amongst the decisions and recommendations mentioned in that Chapter ' (p. 426). The President did not declare under which Article of the Charter the proposed resolution to establish a sub-committee was to be taken. But the representative of the United States stated: ' Clearly the Council itself can, as a matter of procedure, make enquiries about any question, and it follows that it can authorise a sub-committee of its own creation, drawn from its own members, to do the same thing if it finds that that is a convenient method of conducting its business. I must join issue with the representative of the Soviet Union when he compares the sub-committee proposed by the representative of Australia to the Commission set up by the Council to conduct an investigation in Greece. The two things are entirely different, in my opinion. To adopt the view which has been expressed by the representative of the Soviet Union would mean that the Council could never, without the consent of every one of the five permanent members, set up any agency for the conduct of its business. I think that is, in fact, contrary to Article 29 of the Charter, which states: " The Security Council may establish such subsidiary organs as it deems necessary for the performance of its functions." That is all we propose to do by setting up this sub-committee ' (pp. 430/1). According to this interpretation the Council is authorised by the Charter ' to make enquiries about any question.' The representative of Syria stated that the resolution was not to be taken under Article 34. For ' the proposed sub-committee will not be created in order to find out whether the existing situation between these two States in question would be likely to endanger the maintenance of international peace and security, but simply to clarify certain ambiguities in the statements which we have heard from both parties. For this reason, I consider that the parties to this dispute are not obliged to abstain from voting under Chapter VI of the Charter ' (p. 430). The delegate of Colombia declared that the investigation to be made by the sub-committee ' is not the technical investigation mentioned in Article 34 of the Charter.' ' Article 34 uses the word " investigation " in a much more restricted and technical sense ' (p. 429). The question as to whether the decision concerned a procedural or substantive matter was not expressly decided; neither the question as to whether the rule excluding the parties to a dispute from voting applies only to non-procedural decisions adopted under Chapter VI. The resolution to establish a sub-committee was adopted by eight votes with three abstentions among which there was one permanent member (Soviet Union). The representative of the United Kingdom participated in the voting, which implies that the decision was not taken under Chapter VI (p. 432).

In the Czechoslovak question, at the 288th meeting of the Security Council the delegate of Argentina proposed the following resolution (suggested by Chile, not a member of the Security Council):

> Whereas the attention of the Security Council has been drawn by a Member of the United Nations, in accordance with Articles 34 and 35 of the

intends to make a certain function of the Council mandatory. By adding the words ' when it deems necessary,' Article 33, paragraph 2,

> Charter, to the situation in Czechoslovakia, which may endanger international peace and security; and the Security Council has been asked to investigate this situation; and
>
> Whereas, during the debate which took place in the Council, the existence of further testimonial and documentary evidence in regard to such situation has been announced;
>
> Whereas the Security Council considers it advisable that such further testimonial and documentary evidence should be heard,
>
> Therefore, to this end and without prejudice to any decisions which may be taken in accordance with Article 34 of the Charter,
>
> The Security Council resolves to appoint a sub-committee of three members and instructs this sub-committee to receive or to hear such evidence, statements and testimonies, and to report to the Security Council at the earliest possible time.

The representative of the Soviet Union declared that he considered this draft resolution as ' not of a procedural nature ' and proposed first to decide ' whether or not this is a procedural matter ' (Official Records of the Security Council, 3rd Year, No. 63, p. 19). The representative of the United States expressed the view that ' to establish a sub-committee is clearly a procedural decision. It is a decision under Article 29 of the Charter, not under Chapter VI ' (p. 19). This view was supported by the Canadian delegate (p. 21). At the 300th meeting, the representative of the Soviet Union stated that the proposed sub-committee was ' an organ for the purpose of investigation. . . . Consequently, a decision regarding the establishment of such an organ must be taken by a non-procedural vote.' (*Ibid.*, No. 71, p. 41.) This view is certainly correct if the decision to institute an investigation within the meaning of Article 34 and the decision to establish an organ for this purpose are combined in one resolution to be taken under Article 34. At the 303rd meeting of the Security Council the President suggested first to decide upon the preliminary question: whether the proposed resolution to establish a sub-committee was procedural. Eight votes were cast in the affirmative, with 2 against, and one abstention. One permanent member (Soviet Union) voted against. Referring to the interpretation by the four Sponsoring Powers the President declared the matter as substantive. In his statement he rejected the interpretation according to which the term ' investigation ' in Article 34 applied only to investigations on the spot. He referred to Part 1 (5) of the Statement of the four Sponsoring Powers which said that an investigation under Article 34 ' may involve calling for reports hearing witnesses. . . . ' This proved that the term ' investigation ' in Article 34 was to be understood in the widest sense and to be applicable to the motion before the Council (Doc. S/P.V. 303).

In the Greek case, the Security Council by a resolution adopted at its 131st meeting, authorised the investigation commission created at its 87th meeting to establish ' a subsidiary group, composed of a representative of each of the members of the Commission, to continue to fulfil such functions as the Commission may prescribe in accordance with its terms of reference.' (Official Records, 2nd Year, No. 37, pp. 796, 800.) In pursuance of this resolution the commission established the subsidiary group. At the 133rd meeting of the Security Council, the delegate of the Soviet Union maintained that the commission was not entitled to delegate its own functions to the Subsidiary Group. (*Ibid.*, No. 39, p. 829.) In the following discussion the delegate of Yugoslavia attacked the Security Council's decision by which the commission of investigation was authorised to establish a

obliterates this effect and, at the same time, gets in conflict with the principle that the Security Council shall not intervene before the parties have tried to settle the dispute by means of their own choice.[5]

Subsidiary Group as contrary to the Charter, since the Charter nowhere recognised 'the legal institution of the delegation of power.' (*Ibid*, No. 40, p. 846.) The arguments of the delegates of the Soviet Union and of Yugoslavia are not correct. It is true that delegation of power conferred on an organ by a constitution is legal only if the constitution permits such delegation. But the Charter authorises the Security Council and the General Assembly in Articles 22 and 29 to confer, to a certain extent, their powers on subsidiary organs, since these organs are to be established 'for the performance of [the General Assembly's and the Security Council's] functions.' To interpret Article 34 as authorising the Security Council to establish a commission of investigation implies the interpretation according to which the Security Council is authorised to delegate its power of investigation to such commission. It is true that a commission established by the Council is not entitled to establish on its own initiative a subsidiary organ and to confer upon it functions conferred upon the commission by the Council. Rule 28 of the Rules of Procedure of the Security Council based on Articles 29 and 30 of the Charter authorises the Security Council 'to appoint a commission or committee'; but there is no Rule authorising such a commission or committee to set up sub-committees, as Rule 93 of the Rules of Procedure of the General Assembly provides with respect to committees established by the Assembly under Rule 88. But Article 29 of the Charter may be interpreted to empower the Security Council to establish subsidiary organs not only directly, but also indirectly by authorising a subsidiary organ to establish another subsidiary organ. (Cf. *supra*, p. 143.) The Subsidiary Group was appointed by the commission of investigation, set up by the Security Council in the Greek case on the basis of a resolution of the Security Council adopted within the limits of Articles 29 and 34.

5 Originally, Committee III/2 of the San Francisco Conference adopted the text: 'The Security Council may call upon the parties to settle their dispute by such means.' The word 'may' has been preferred to the word 'shall' as Report of the Rapporteur of Committee III/2 (U.N.C.I.O. Doc. 1027, III/2/31 (1), p. 3) states, 'to make it clear that the parties to a dispute should not wait until the Security Council calls upon them to perform their obligations.' At the 12th meeting of Committee III/2 (U.N.C.I.O. Doc. 992, III/2/27, p. 5) the Australian delegate 'proposed the maintenance of "shall" and the insertion immediately thereafter of the words "whenever necessary."' At the 3rd meeting of Commission III (U.N.C.I.O. Doc. 1088, III/8, p. 8) he declared with respect to the above statement that the parties should not wait, etc., 'that is obviously a very important point and a very sound point. But what is to be the position if the parties do not take action in accordance with paragraph 3 and do not endeavour to settle their dispute by peaceful means? That is the crux or the position. Is the Security Council merely to retain the power to call upon them to settle their disputes by such means, or should it not, after a reasonable time has elapsed, be obligated to call upon the parties to settle their disputes by such means? It might appear a technical point but it is not, because the Security Council's main work will, we hope, lie in the peaceful conciliation of parties to important disputes, and it should not merely be a matter of discretion with the Security Council to act or not to act as it thinks fit. . . . We think that it is of great importance that, after a certain time has elapsed when the parties to the dispute have failed to conciliate between themselves, the Security Council should say, should be obligated to say, to the parties: "You have to settle; you should settle your dispute by means of peaceful conciliation, because that is your duty under the Charter. It is your duty so to settle your dispute, and it is our duty as a Security Council to tell you to do so."'

The means referred to in this paragraph are the peaceful means of the own choice of the parties indicated in Article 33, paragraph 1. Article 33, paragraph 2, is applicable only to disputes, not—as Articles 34 and 36—also to other situations. It seems as if the ' call ' referred to in Article 33, paragraph 2, is supposed to be possible without the investigation referred to in Article 34. The ' call ' shall be made when the Security Council deems it necessary. This provision precedes Article 34 providing for investigation. If, however, Article 33, paragraph 2, authorises the Security Council only to call upon the parties to settle disputes referred to in paragraph 1 of this Article, that is to say, disputes the continuance of which is likely to endanger the peace, the Council can exercise this function only if it has determined the dangerous character of the dispute, which seems to be possible only after the investigation referred to in Article 34. Investigation under Article 34 is the means prescribed by the Charter by which the Security Council has to determine whether the continuance of the dispute or situation is likely to endanger the maintenance of international peace and security.

Article 36 stipulates:

> 1. The Security Council may, at any stage of a dispute of the nature referred to in Article 33 or of a situation of like nature, recommend appropriate procedures or methods of adjustment.
>
> 2. The Security Council should take into consideration any procedures for the settlement of the dispute which have already been adopted by the parties.
>
> 3. In making recommendations under this Article the Security Council should also take into consideration that legal disputes should as a general rule be referred by the parties to the International Court of Justice in accordance with the provisions of the Statute of the Court.

The formula ' appropriate procedures or methods of adjustment ' in paragraph 1 refers both to disputes and other situations. As to disputes, recommending ' procedures or methods of adjustment ' is a measure different from recommending ' terms of settlement ' stipulated in Article 37, paragraph 2. That the recommendation referred to in Article 36, paragraph 1, is not a recommendation of

According to this interpretation, the Security Council shall ' call upon the parties ' under Article 33, paragraph 2, if the parties have failed to apply one of the means indicated in Article 33, paragraph 1. That means that Article 33, paragraph 2, belongs to a procedure different from that regulated by Article 33, paragraph 1, and Article 37. If so, there can be no doubt that the parties must not wait to act under Article 33, paragraph 1, until the Security Council calls upon them to perform their obligation, regardless of Article 33, paragraph 2, being formulated: the Security Council ' shall,' or ' may,' call upon the parties to settle their disputes by the means indicated in Article 33, paragraph 1.

'terms of settlement' results from the fact that according to Article 37, paragraph 2, the Security Council has to make a choice between these two kinds of recommendations. As to other situations, too, recommending 'procedures or methods of adjustment' must be different from recommending terms of adjustment. Recommendations made under Article 36, paragraph 1, can not have a substantive, but only a procedural character. Under Article 36, paragraph 1, the Security Council may recommend a specific way which according to its opinion might lead to the settlement of a dispute or the adjustment of another situation; but the Council must not recommend a definite settlement or adjustment.[6] Hence, as far as disputes are concerned, to recommend 'appropriate procedures or methods of adjustment,' as provided by Article 36, paragraph 1, seems to be the same as to call upon the parties to settle their dispute by the peaceful means of their own choice, as provided by Article 33.[7] These 'means' comprise all possible 'procedures or methods of adjustment,' or of 'solution' as Article 33, paragraph 1, says. Since 'procedures' are 'methods,' and *vice versa*, one of the two terms is superfluous. Apart from the fact that the provision of Article 33, paragraph 2, refers only to disputes whereas the provision of Article 36, paragraph 1, also to other situations, the two provisions are different only in so far as Article 33, paragraph 2, is interpreted to mean that the Security Council may remind in general terms the parties of their obligation under Article 33, paragraph 1, whereas under Article 36, paragraph 1, it may recommend a definite

6 The sub-committee established by the Security Council at its 39th meeting in the Spanish case suggested that the Council should take, under Article 36, paragraph 1, the following actions: '(*a*) The endorsement by the Security Council of the principles contained in the declaration by the Governments of the United Kingdom, the United States and France, dated March 4, 1946. (*b*) The transmitting by the Security Council to the General Assembly of the evidence and reports of this sub-committee, together with the recommendation that unless the Franco regime is withdrawn and other conditions of political freedom set out in the declaration are, in the opinion of the General Assembly, fully satisfied, a resolution be passed by the General Assembly recommending that diplomatic relations with the Franco regime be terminated by each Member of the United Nations. (*c*) The taking of appropriate steps by the Secretary-General to communicate these recommendations to all Members of the United Nations and all others concerned.' (Doc. S/75, p. 15.) There can be little doubt that the actions referred to under (*a*) and (*b*) are by no means compatible with Article 36, paragraph 1, authorising the Security Council to recommend appropriate procedures or methods of adjustment. Cf. the critical remarks of the delegate of the United Kingdom at the 40th meeting of the Security Council. (Journal of the Security Council, 1st Year, No. 39, p. 762.)

7 At the 5th meeting of Committee III/2 (U.N.C.I.O. Doc. 356, III/2/11, p. 3) the delegate of France pointed out that there existed at present in paragraph 5 of Chapter VIII, Section A, of the Dumbarton Oaks Proposals (corresponding to Article 36, paragraph 1, of the Charter) a repetition of an idea in paragraph 3 of the same Section (corresponding to Article 33, paragraph 2, of the Charter).

procedure for the settlement of the dispute or the adjustment of the situation.[8]

According to the wording of Article 36, paragraph 1, the Security Council may make these recommendations ' at any stage ' of a dispute or a situation. As far as disputes are concerned, this provision is as inconsistent with the provision of Article 33, paragraph 1, as is Article 34; for it authorises the Security Council to intervene in a dispute before the parties have attempted to solve it by means of their own choice. That the Council has the power to make recommendations ' at any stage ' of a dispute or a situation is problematical also because this implies the right of the Council to make the recommendations referred to in Article 36, paragraph 1, even before Article 34 has been applied. But it is difficult to interpret paragraph 1 of Article 36 literally. For the Council is authorised by this paragraph expressly to make certain recommendations, not with respect to all disputes or situations, but only with respect to those ' of the nature

[8] At the *Hearings* (pp. 270 f.), the representative of the Department of State made the following statement with respect to Article 33, paragraph 2: ' The Security Council at this stage is expected, under paragraph 2 of Article 33, to watch the situation, and when it deems it necessary or useful, to call upon the parties to such disputes to settle the disputes by means of their own choice. In other words, to remind them of their obligation to do so.' According to this interpretation, the ' call ' referred to in Article 33, paragraph 2, is to be made at that ' stage ' of the dispute to which Article 33, paragraph 1, refers, that is, possibly, before investigation. A Senator asked with reference to Article 33, paragraph 2: ' Is that a general direction or would the Security Council have the authority to tell the party to settle, for example, by arbitration?' Whereupon the representative of the State Department answered: ' No; I think this definitely means to call upon the parties to settle a dispute by means of their own choice. The other power comes at a somewhat later stage. Or it may come at this stage if the Council wishes to do so, but it is not necessarily so.' But when the Senator asked: ' But you would say the Security Council does not have the right to order the parties to accept a particular method of peaceful settlement?', the representative of the State Department answered: ' No; it has not.'

It seems that the Security Council applied Article 33, paragraph 2, in the Indonesian question which was brought before the Council under Article 35, paragraph 1. At its 173rd meeting the Council adopted the following resolution:

> The Security Council
>
> Noting with concern the hostilities in progress between the armed forces of the Netherlands and the Republic of Indonesia, calls upon the parties:
>
> (*a*) to cease hostilities forthwith, and
>
> (*b*) to settle their disputes by arbitration or by other peaceful means and keep the Security Council informed about the progress of the settlement. (Official Records of the Security Council, 2nd Year, No. 68, pp. 1702 f.)

Only clause (*b*) of the resolution can be interpreted as an application of Article 33, paragraph 2; to ' cease hostilities ' as recommended in clause (*a*) is not a means within the meaning of Article 33; nor is clause (*a*) a recommendation within the meaning of Article 36, paragraph 1.

referred to in Article 33,' and that means disputes or situations the continuance of which is likely to endanger the maintenance of international peace and security. Consequently the Security Council cannot make a recommendation under Article 36, paragraph 1, 'at any stage' of a dispute or situation, but only after it has determined that the continuance of the dispute or situation is likely to endanger international peace and security. This is exactly the purpose of the investigation to be made under Article 34. Without such investigation, there is no sufficient reason to consider the dispute or situation as being 'of the nature referred to in Article 33.' Consequently Article 36 can properly be applied only after Article 34 has been applied. But such investigation can be made quite informally by the Council itself, without appointing a special commission of investigation. As pointed out, Article 37, paragraph 2, too, can be applied only after an investigation under Article 34 has led the Security Council to the conclusion that the continuance of the dispute is in fact likely to endanger the peace.[9] Hence, Article 34 and Article 33, paragraph 2, or Article 34 and Article 36 belong together, just as Article 33, paragraph 1 and Article 37 do. Article 34—except if applied in the procedure regulated by Articles 33, paragraph 1, and 37—represents the first stage of the *ex officio* procedure instituted by the Security

[9] At the 7th meeting of Committee III/2 (U.N.C.I.O. Doc. 433, III/2/15, p. 2) 'the delegate of Canada proposed that the sub-committee on drafting should consider whether the Security Council should not be given explicit authority to investigate a dispute, under paragraph 4 [corresponding to Article 37 of the Charter], in order to assist in securing a peaceful solution.' This proposition has not been carried out.

Article 37, paragraph 2, is the only provision by which the Security Council is expressly bound to examine, before making recommendations, whether a dispute is likely to endanger the maintenance of international peace and security. As to 'situations' no express provision to this effect exists; nor does the Charter contain an express provision binding the General Assembly to examine whether a dispute or a situation brought before it is likely to endanger the peace. The Memorandum on Pacific Settlement by the Security Council, submitted by the delegation of Canada to the First Committee (Doc. A/C.1/91, p. 5) contains the following statements: 'Apart from the special jurisdiction which may be conferred on it under Article 38 by all the parties to any dispute, the Security Council's jurisdiction is restricted to international disputes and situations which are likely to endanger the maintenance of international peace and security. The preliminary question to be settled therefore when a dispute or a situation is brought to the attention of the Security Council is whether the Council has jurisdiction to deal with the matter, that is to say whether the continuance of the dispute or situation is likely to endanger the maintenance of international peace and security. Therefore the Security Council should work out agreed procedures to ensure that the early stages of the consideration of a dispute or situation by the Security Council are directed towards settling the preliminary question whether the continuance of the dispute or situation is likely to endanger the maintenance of international peace and security. It may be necessary for the Council in these early stages to discuss the facts of the case and the claims and the counter-claims, but the purpose of this initial examination should be, not to arrive at a recommendation on the settlement or adjustment of the dispute or situation, but to decide the preliminary question of jurisdiction.'

Council on its own initiative. After the investigation made under Article 34 has brought a positive result, in case of a dispute the Security Council has the choice between Article 33, paragraph 2, and Article 36. It may apply the one or the other, or first Article 33, paragraph 2, and then Article 36. In case of situations which have not the character of a dispute, the Security Council can apply only Article 36, not Article 33, paragraph 2.

The competence of the Security Council in the procedure under Article 34, Article 33, paragraph 2, and Article 36—in contradistinction to its competence in the procedure under Article 33, paragraph 1, and Article 37, and the procedure under Article 38—does not depend on the parties to the dispute. When the Security Council, on its own initiative, has under Article 34 placed on its agenda and investigated the dispute and has determined its dangerous character, the parties cannot withdraw the dispute from the Council. The Council may keep the matter on its agenda as long as it deems necessary. Even if the parties declare that they have settled the dispute and hence, a 'dispute' in the sense of Article 33 no longer exists, the Security Council may remain seized with the matter as with a 'situation' likely to endanger the maintenance of the peace.

In open contradiction to the principle underlying the procedure regulated by Article 33, paragraph 1, and Article 37, the Security Council may under Article 34 investigate a dispute in spite of the fact that the parties have already begun to settle their dispute by negotiation, inquiry, mediation, conciliation, arbitration, judicial settlement, resort to regional agencies or arrangements, or other peaceful means of their own choice. The Security Council, after having determined the dangerous nature of the dispute, may recommend appropriate procedures or methods of adjustment ('adjustment' probably meaning also 'settlement'), even if the parties have submitted the dispute to an international tribunal of arbitration or the International Court of Justice. The wording of Article 36, paragraph 1, does not exclude such possibility.[1] Paragraphs 2 and 3 of this Article, it is

[1] At the San Francisco Conference, the Turkish Government proposed to add after paragraph 5 of Chapter VIII, Section A, of the Dumbarton Oaks Proposals [corresponding to Article 36, paragraph 1, of the Charter] the following sentence: 'Nevertheless, recommendations made by the Security Council must not interfere with legal procedure in the case of a dispute which has already been submitted for legal settlement.' (U.N.C.I.O. Doc. 2, G/14 (e) (1), p. 2.)

At the 10th meeting of Committee III/2 (U.N.C.I.O. Doc. 530, III/2/20, pp. 1 f.) 'the delegate of Turkey explained that the purpose of this amendment was to insure that the Security Council would not intervene in a case which was being heard by the International Court of Justice. If the dispute developed into a threat to the peace during proceedings before the Court, then the Council might intervene, but otherwise it should be clear that there would be no interference with judicial proceedings. This view was supported by the delegate of Peru. The delegate of

true, provide that the Security Council 'should' (not 'shall') 'take into consideration any procedures for the settlement of the dispute' —nothing is said with respect to 'situations'—'which have already been adopted by the parties,' and 'that legal disputes should as a general rule be referred by the parties to the International Court of Justice in accordance with the provisions of the Statute of the Court.' Whatever these provisions mean, their wording does not bind the Security Council to wait with its recommendations until the procedure adopted by the parties themselves has failed, and to refrain from any interference if the dispute has been submitted by the parties to the Court or another international tribunal. It is, for instance, not incompatible with the wording of Article 36 that the Security Council may recommend that the parties refer the dispute, already submitted to an international conciliation commission, to the Court, because the Security Council considers the dispute to be a legal, and not a political, one; or recommend that the parties refer the dispute, already submitted to an international tribunal of arbitration or to the International Court of Justice, to the Security Council, because the Council considers the dispute to be a political and not a legal one. If this was not the intention of the legislator—which is probable—he has formulated paragraphs 2 and 3 of Article 36 in a most unsatisfactory way. The wording of these provisions, however, is clear enough to ascertain that the Security Council has no power by itself to refer the dispute to the International Court of Justice. This can be done only 'by the parties.'[2]

the Union of South Africa said he thought there was no intention implied in the paragraph that the Council should intervene unless there were a threat to the peace. The delegate of the United Kingdom took a similar view, and suggested the reference of the amendment to the drafting committee in order that this might be made clear.—The delegate of the United States said that as he understood the situation, paragraph 5, which had just been approved, referred only to a dispute of the nature referred to in paragraph 3 of the same Section, namely, a dispute which was likely to endanger peace and security. He understood also that the Turkish amendment did not purport to place any restrictions on the action of the Security Council in such a case, but that it meant that if a dispute were being satisfactorily handled by the Court and there was no threat to the peace, then there should be no interference by the Council.—The delegate of Turkey agreed with this interpretation and indicated he would be satisfied if the Turkish amendment and this interpretation were referred to the drafting committee.' In consideration of the Turkish suggestion, paragraph 2 of Article 36 has been adopted. Its text does not exclude, however, the possibility against which the Turkish amendment was directed.

The Summary Report of the 12th meeting of Committee III/2 (U.N.C.I.O. Doc. 992, III/2/27, p. 4) contains the following statement with respect to Article 36, paragraph 2: 'According to this Article, the Security Council, in making recommendations in accordance with the first sentence, must determine whether or not the parties had already adopted pacific procedures. If so, the Council would not ordinarily call upon them to adopt such procedures, or make recommendations for the employment of other designated procedures.' It may be that the Security Council, in case the parties had already adopted certain procedures

Since Article 36 refers not only to disputes between Members but also to disputes between Members and non-members and even to disputes between non-members, it may happen that the Security Council is dealing with a dispute between two states of which one, or both, are not parties to the Statute of the International Court of Justice. According to the wording of Article 36, paragraph 3, of the Charter, the Security Council may recommend even in such a case to the parties to refer the dispute—if it is a legal dispute according to the opinion of the Council—to the International Court of Justice. But the state which is not a party to the Statute can refer its dispute to the

for the settlement of their dispute, ' would not ordinarily ' call upon them to adopt such procedures or recommend others. But the question is whether the Charter prohibits such intervention on the part of the Council. This question cannot be answered in the affirmative. There is, in particular, nothing in the wording of Article 36, paragraph 2, that restricts the intervention of the Council in a dispute which was being heard by the International Court of Justice or any other authority, to the case where the Security Council, under Article 39, has determined the existence of a threat to the peace.

The Summary Report of the 14th meeting of Committee III/2 (U.N.C.I.O. Doc. 1029, III/2/33, p. 4) contains the following statement with reference to Article 36, paragraph 3: ' The Secretary, after reading the Article, noted that the Sub-committee, on the motion of the delegate of Norway, had added the words " by the parties " after the word " referred."—The delegate of China reported that the Sub-committee had not considered it desirable to accept the amendment, proposed by the delegate of Australia at the previous meeting, and providing for the substitution of the words " act upon the rule " for the words " take into consideration." It had been felt that the original text was sufficiently clear, and that it had given adequate expression to the intent of the Committee. The Sub-committee had accepted the addition of the words " by the parties " in order to make it perfectly clear that the Security Council had no right or duty to refer justiciable disputes to the International Court of Justice.'

At the 13th meeting of Committee III/2 (U.N.C.I.O. Doc. 1016, III/2/29, pp. 1 f.) ' Judge Manley O. Hudson, of the Permanent Court of International Justice, said that he assumed that it was implicit in the provisions of the Article that the Security Council, in making recommendations, would take account of obligations which states may have assumed with respect to the jurisdiction of the International Court of Justice. He thought the phrase " should normally be referred " contained a slight suggestion that the Security Council might fail to take account of the compulsory jurisdiction which a state or states might have assumed under Article 36 of the Statute of the Court.—The delegate of the United Kingdom explained that if both parties to a dispute had accepted the optional clause, there was no scope for a recommendation by the Security Council. Either party, in that case, could institute procedures before the Court. A difficulty might arise only if neither of two signatories to the optional clause should start proceedings before the Court. In that case, however, the delegate of the United Kingdom felt that the Security Council would, no doubt, take into account the fact that both parties had signed the clause.'—At the *Hearings* (pp. 333 f.) a Senator asked whether ' the Council can act notwithstanding there is pending an issue in the Court.' The representative of the Department of State answered: ' Oh, yes, quite so.' He also stated: ' There is no way whatsoever by which the Council can force litigants into the Court.'—But the Council may ' recommend ' to submit the dispute to the Court and consider non-compliance with its recommendation as a threat to the peace with all the consequences determined in Article 39.

Court only if it fulfils the requirements of Article 35, paragraph 2, of the Statute.[3]

Although the wording of Article 36, paragraph 1, implies the possibility of the Security Council's recommending to refer the dispute to the Council itself, it is doubtful whether the Council can settle the dispute referred to it in compliance with such a recommendation. For, as pointed out, the Council is authorised to recommend terms of settlement only under Article 37, paragraph 2, and Article 38, that is

[3] At its 127th meeting the Security Council, in the Corfu Channel case, recommended under Article 36, paragraph 3, 'that the United Kingdom and the Albanian Governments should immediately refer the dispute to the International Court of Justice in accordance with the provisions of the Statute of the Court.' (Official Records of the Security Council, 2nd Year, No. 34, pp. 726 f.) The Council did not adopt a formal decision to the effect that it considered the dispute to be a legal one. The Australian delegate, who suggested reference to the Court, incidentally said: '. . . and this is now a legal dispute . . .' (p. 723.) The fact that Albania is not a party to the Statute was not mentioned in the discussion. But the Australian delegate made the following statement, in order to justify the jurisdiction of the Court: 'Under Article 25 of the Charter a Member agrees ". . . to accept and carry out the decisions of the Security Council . . .". Under Article 36, "the Security Council may . . . recommend appropriate procedures or methods of adjustment" of a dispute. And under the same Article, the general rule is stated ". . . that legal disputes"—and this is now a legal dispute—"should . . . be referred by the parties to the International Court of Justice in accordance with the provisions of the Statute of the Court." That reference implies an acceptance of jurisdiction. Furthermore, in the letter of invitation sent by this Council to the Government of Albania, there is one vital condition laid down: ". . . to participate without a vote in the proceedings with regard to this dispute on condition that Albania accepts, in the present case, all the obligations which a Member of the United Nations would have to assume in a similar case." Therefore, any decision, any recommendation that we may make binds the United Kingdom and also binds Albania. In addition, Article 36 of the Statute of the International Court of Justice provides for the jurisdiction of the Court as follows: ". . . comprises all . . . matters specially provided for in the Charter of the United Nations . . .". Consequently, we arrive at this conclusion: under provisions of both the Charter of the United Nations and the Statute of the Court, the Security Council is clearly entitled to make such a recommendation . . .'

This interpretation of the Charter and the Statute is rather problematical. First of all, it is doubtful whether a recommendation made by the Security Council under Article 36 of the Charter is a decision binding upon the Members according to Article 25. If it is a mere 'recommendation,' it might not be considered to be a binding 'decision.' Only if Article 25 is interpreted to refer also to 'recommendations' made by the Security Council, the fact that Albania has accepted 'in the present case all the obligations which a Member of the United Nations would have to assume in a similar case,' constitutes an obligation of Albania to comply with the recommendation of the Council to refer the dispute to the Court. The case was brought before the Court by a unilateral application addressed by Great Britain to the Registrar of the Court under Article 40, paragraph 1, of the Statute. (International Court of Justice, Distr. 151, 1947, General List No. 1, pp. 3 f.) The application of the British Government is based on the arguments brought forward by the Australian delegate mentioned above. As to the legal aspects of the case brought before the Court, cf. *infra*, pp. 501, 517, 536 f.

to say, in case the dispute has been referred to it under these Articles. In case of a situation which has not the character of a dispute and whose dangerous nature has been determined under Article 34, the Council is not bound to take into consideration any procedure which had already been adopted by the parties concerned for its adjustment, nor is the Council authorised to recommend terms of adjustment.

After the Security Council has, on its own initiative or on the initiative of any other authority except the parties themselves, investigated a dispute, determined its dangerous character under Article 34, and recommended appropriate procedures or methods of adjustment under Article 36, paragraph 1, and after the parties have failed to settle the dispute by the means recommended to them by the Security Council, the question arises whether Article 37, paragraph 1, applies, that is to say, whether the parties are obliged to refer such dispute to the Council. Strange as it may seem, the answer to this question is according to the wording of Article 37, paragraph 1, in the negative. For the provision of this paragraph refers expressly to disputes which the parties fail to settle by the means indicated in Article 33, paragraph 1. These are means ' of their own choice,' not means recommended to them by the Security Council under Article 36, paragraph 1. The, probably unintentional, effect of the wording of Article 37, paragraph 1, is that a dispute which the parties fail to settle cannot be shifted from the procedure regulated by Article 34, Article 33, paragraph 2, and Article 36, to the procedure regulated by Article 33, paragraph 1, and Article 37, the only procedure (except the one under Article 38) that can be terminated by a recommendation of terms of settlement by the Security Council.[4]

[4] As pointed out, the Dumbarton Oaks Proposals in Chapter VIII, Section A, under the heading ' Pacific Settlement of Disputes ' did not confer upon the Council the power to recommend terms of settlement. The idea was to leave the settlement of the dispute to the parties, to authorise the Security Council only to recommend appropriate procedures or methods of adjustment, even in case the parties, after failing to settle the dispute by means of their own choice, have referred it to the Security Council. The power to make other recommendations than those of ' procedures or methods ' is conferred upon the Security Council only in Section B of Chapter VIII, under the heading ' Determination of Threats to the Peace or Acts of Aggression and Action with respect Thereto.' Paragraph 2 of this Section runs as follows:

> In general the Security Council should determine the existence of any threat to the peace, breach of the peace or act of aggression and should make recommendations or decide upon the measures to be taken to maintain or restore peace and security.

This provision corresponds to Article 39 of the Charter.—The Charter maintains the idea of the Dumbarton Oaks Proposals to leave settlement of disputes in principle to the parties and allow the Security Council to intervene only if the parties fail. But the Charter confers upon the Council not only the power to recommend ' procedures or methods ' but also ' terms of settlement.' However, the provision conferring upon the Council this power has been inserted into Articles 37 and 38 only, dealing with disputes referred to the Security Council by

The procedure regulated by Article 34, Article 33, paragraph 2, and Article 36, may be instituted on the initiative of others rather than of the Security Council itself.

Article 35 stipulates:

> 1. Any Member of the United Nations may bring any dispute, or any situation of the nature referred to in Article 34, to the attention of the Security Council or of the General Assembly.
>
> 2. A state which is not a Member of the United Nations may bring to the attention of the Security Council or of the General Assembly any dispute to which it is a party if it accepts in advance, for the purposes of the dispute, the obligations of pacific settlement provided in the present Charter.
>
> 3. The proceedings of the General Assembly in respect of matters brought to its attention under this Article will be subject to the provisions of Articles 11 and 12.

Like Article 34, Article 35, paragraph 1, refers to any dispute, but only to situations (not having the character of a dispute) of the nature referred to in Article 34. Under Article 35, paragraph 1, a procedure for settlement of disputes by the Security Council may be initiated by 'any Member of the United Nations.' The wording comprises also the Members which are parties to a dispute, and thus—as pointed out—is not consistent with Articles 33 and 37, which obligate the parties first to seek a solution by peaceful means of their own choice and to go to the Security Council—under Article 37, paragraph 1—only after they have tried in vain to settle it in this way. It might be objected that fulfilling this obligation is not incompatible with bringing the dispute to the attention of the Security Council, since this is different from 'referring' the dispute to the Council under Article 37, paragraph 1. However, to bring a dispute to the attention of the Security Council can have no other purpose than to give the Council the opportunity of dealing with the dispute under Article 35, paragraph 1, to investigate it under Article 34 and to make recommendations under Article 36; that is to say, to enable the Security Council to start an *ex officio* procedure under Article 34 and Article 33, paragraph 2, or Articles 34 and 36. This results especially from paragraph 2 of Article 35, where a non-member is authorised 'to bring to the attention of the Security Council or of the General Assembly' any dispute to which it is a party 'if it accepts in advance,

the parties. To authorise the Security Council to recommend terms of settlement also in case the dispute has been brought before it in another way and also in case of situations which have not the character of a dispute, has been omitted because in Chapter VI of the Charter the procedure regulated by Article 33, paragraph 1, and Article 37, is mixed up with the other procedures provided for in this Chapter.

for the purposes of the dispute, the obligations of pacific settlement provided in the present Charter.' This condition would be superfluous if the meaning of the formula ' to bring to the attention ' were not: to give the Council the opportunity of instituting *ex officio* the procedure finally leading to recommendations under Article 36.[5] However, to bring a dispute (or another situation) to the attention of the Security Council under Article 35, paragraphs 1 or 2, differs from referring a dispute to the Council under Article 37, paragraph 1, in so far as a state party to a dispute may bring, in accordance with the wording of Article 35, paragraph 1, the dispute before the Security Council without having sought a solution in accordance with Article 33, paragraph 1. For if this provision is applied, the dispute has to be brought before the Council under Article 37, paragraph 1, not under

[5] At the 12th meeting of Committee III/2 (U.N.C.I.O. Doc. 992, III/2/27, pp. 7 f. [Corrigendum Doc. 1045, III/2/27 (1), June 17, 1945]) the delegate of Ethiopia wished to receive ' a clarification of the meaning of the phrase "bring . . . to the attention of the Security Council or the General Assembly" appearing in Article 3 [corresponding to Article 35 of the Charter], in the light of the phrase "they shall refer it to the Security Council" contained in Article 6 [corresponding to Article 37 of the Charter].' The delegate of China explained that according to Article 3, ' any state could bring any kind of dispute to the attention of the Council. This Article, however, did not provide for or define the nature of the action which the Council might take. By Article 6, the Council may take action, provided it first decides that the continuance of the dispute is likely to endanger international peace and security, and if the Council is satisfied that the parties have failed to settle the dispute by pacific means of their own choice. Although a party may bring a dispute to the attention of the Council in accordance with Article 3, the Council may, nevertheless, act immediately under Article 6, provided the required conditions have been fulfilled.' This explanation is not quite in accordance with the Articles referred to. It is true that Article 3 [corresponding to Article 35, paragraphs 1, and 2 of the Charter] did not provide for or define the nature of the action which the Council might take. But from the text of the second paragraph of Article 3 [corresponding to Article 35, paragraph 2, of the Charter] it must be concluded that a dispute is brought to the attention of the Security Council for the purpose of settlement. As to the nature of the action which the Council might take, Article 4 of the provisions discussed in Committee III/2 applies, which corresponds to Article 36, paragraph 1, of the Charter, providing that the Council may ' at any stage of a dispute or a situation ' ' recommend appropriate procedures or methods of adjustment.' The difference between ' bringing a dispute to the attention of the Security Council ' under Article 35, and ' referring ' a dispute to the Security Council under Article 37, paragraph 1, is not that in the first case the action to be taken by the Council is not determined by the Charter, whereas in the second case it is determined; the difference, as far as the action of the Council is concerned, is that in the first case the Council is authorised to recommend only procedures or methods, whereas in the second case the Council is authorised to recommend also terms of settlement.

If a party brings a dispute to the attention of the Security Council under Article 3 (Article 35 of the Charter), the Council cannot ' act immediately under Article 6 ' (Article 37 of the Charter). For the Council can act under Article 6 only if the dispute has been referred to it under this Article, that is to say under conditions precisely determined in this Article and different from those determined in Article 3.

Article 35, paragraphs 1 or 2. According to the wording of the Charter, the provision of Article 33, paragraph 1, applies only to the procedure regulated by this Article in connection with Article 37; and this procedure applies only to disputes, not to other situations.[6]

[6] During the discussion of the Greek case, which was brought to the attention of the Security Council by Greece as a 'situation' under Article 35, paragraph 1—but was declared by the President of the Council to be a dispute (cf. p. 415)—the delegate of Poland stated: 'that since, by implication, we have decided that the case before us is in the nature of a dispute, before we take further decisions we must comply with Article 33 of the Charter, which says that in case of disputes the parties shall seek all methods of adjustment before they call upon the Security Council to take a decision.' (Official Records of the Security Council, 1st Year, 2nd Series, No. 28, p. 652.)

During the discussion of the Corfu Channel Incident case, which was brought to the attention of the Security Council by Great Britain as a party to the dispute under Article 35, paragraph 1 (Official Records, 2nd Year, Suppl. No. 3, Annex 8, p. 36), and decided by the Council under Article 36, the delegate of the Soviet Union declared to be against the proposal for inclusion of the case in the agenda of the Security Council, because Great Britain did not comply with the provisions of Article 33, paragraph 1. The representative of Great Britain in spite of the fact that his Government had brought the dispute with Albania to the attention of the Security Council under Article 35, paragraph 1, asserted that Great Britain had complied with the provision of Article 33, paragraph 1. (*Ibid.*, No. 6, pp. 115 f.; No. 18, pp. 366, 376.) But at the same time he referred to Article 36, paragraph 1, which says: 'The Security Council may, at any stage of a dispute of the nature referred to in Article 33, or of a situation of like nature, recommend appropriate procedures or methods of adjustment'; that is to say, he called the attention of the Council to the fact that Article 36 is in conflict with Article 33, paragraph 1. The delegate of Brazil maintained that Articles 35 and 36 of the Charter 'are applicable only, first, when the requirements of Article 33, calling for peaceful adjustment, have been complied with, and secondly, when the dispute or situation is likely to endanger the maintenance of international peace and security.' (*Ibid.*, No. 32, p. 687.) As to the second condition, the statement is correct; but the statement that Article 35, paragraph 1, and Article 36, apply only when the requirements of Article 33, paragraph 1, have been complied with, has no basis in the Charter.

The Memorandum on Pacific Settlement by the Security Council, submitted by the Canadian delegation to the First Committee (Doc. A/C.1/91) contains the following statement: 'All the Members of the United Nations have under Article 33 of the Charter undertaken that, if they are parties to any disputes the continuance of which is likely to endanger the maintenance of international peace and security, they will first of all seek a solution by negotiation, inquiry, mediation, conciliation, arbitration, judicial settlement, resort to regional agencies or arrangements, or other peaceful means of their own choice. The spirit of this undertaking applies to situations which might lead to international friction or give rise to a dispute. Therefore, the rules of procedure of the Security Council should provide that, when a state brings a dispute or a situation to the attention of the Security Council, it should submit in writing a preliminary statement setting forth the steps which have been taken by the states concerned to carry out their obligation under the Charter to seek a solution by peaceful means of their own choice before coming to the Security Council.' The present Charter does not provide that a state may bring to the attention of the Security Council a dispute or a situation—these are the words of Article 35—only after the states involved in the dispute or the situation have taken the steps to carry out their obligation to seek a solution by

Consequently, if Article 35, paragraph 1, is interpreted—according to its wording—to apply also to Members which are parties to the dispute, it is more convenient to the party to the dispute to bring it before the Security Council under Article 35, paragraph 1, than under Article 37, paragraph 1.[7] But if a party brings a dispute before the Council under

peaceful means of their own choice. This obligation is stipulated in Article 33, paragraph 1, which applies only to disputes, not to 'situations,' and which is in connection with Article 37 obligating the parties to the dispute to 'refer' it to the Security Council, but in no connection with Article 35 which provides for bringing 'to the attention of the Security Council or the General Assembly' disputes and 'situations.' The Canadian suggestion amounts to an amendment of the Charter. It could not be constitutionally adopted by an amendment to the Rules of Procedure.

[7] As a matter of fact, most disputes and situations considered by the Security Council have been brought before it by Members under Article 35, paragraph 1. It is significant that in a Memorandum concerning 'the methods and procedures which have been employed by the United Nations for the pacific settlement of disputes and peaceful adjustment of situations,' prepared by the Secretariat for the Interim Committee of the General Assembly (Doc. A/AC.18/61, p. 4), among the Articles under which a dispute or situation may be brought before the Security Council Article 37, paragraph 2, is not mentioned. According to the interpretation presented in this memorandum 'a dispute or situation may be brought to the attention of the Security Council' only: '(*a*) By the General Assembly under Article 11 or 12 of the Charter; (*b*) By a Member under Article 35, paragraph 1; (*c*) By a State not a Member of the United Nations party to the dispute under Article 35, paragraph 2; (*d*) By the Secretary-General under Article 99.' The Memorandum states that the following cases have been brought before the Security Council under Article 35, paragraph 1:

Iranian Question—brought by Iran (letters dated January 19, 1946, Journal of the Security Council, page 13, and March 18, 1946, S/15);

Greek Question—brought by U.S.S.R. (letter dated January 21, 1946, Journal of the Security Council, page 14);

First Indonesian Question—brought by Ukrainian S.S.R. (letter dated January 21, 1946, Journal of the Security Council, page 15);

Syrian and Lebanese Question—brought by Syria and Lebanon (letter dated February 4, 1946, S/5);

Spanish Question—brought by Poland (letters dated April 8 and 9, 1946, S/32 and S/34);

Ukrainian Complaint against Greece—brought by Ukrainian S.S.R. (telegram dated August 24, 1946, S/137);

Greek Frontier Incidents Question—brought by Greece (letter dated December 3, 1946, S/203);

Incidents in the Corfu Channel—brought by United Kingdom (letter dated January 10, 1947, S/247);

Egyptian Question—brought by Egypt (letter dated July 8, 1947, S/410);

Second Indonesian Question—brought by India (letter dated July 30, 1947, S/447); (Australia, then a member of the Security Council, raised the question under Article 39—letter dated July 30, 1947, S/449);

India Pakistan Question—brought by India (letter dated January 1, 1948, S/628);

Czechoslovak Situation—brought by Chile (letter dated March 12, 1948, S/694).

Article 35, paragraph 1, it cannot—according to the wording of Chapter VI—expect that the Council will act under Article 37.

The following ' disputes ': the Iranian case, the Syria and Lebanon case, and the Corfu Channel Incidents case have been brought before the Security Council by a Member, party to the dispute, under Article 35, paragraph 1. In the Syrian and Lebanon case the delegates of the two states, in a letter to the Secretary-General of February 4, 1946, stated that they, ' acting on the instructions of their Governments, have the honour, in accordance with Article 34 of the Charter, to bring this dispute to the attention of the Security Council and to request it to adopt a decision recommending the total and simultaneous evacuation of the foreign troops from the Syrian and Lebanese territories.' (Journal of the Security Council, 1st Year, No. 8, p. 139.) Under Article 34, no dispute or situation can be brought before the Council. But the words ' bring this dispute to the attention of the Security Council ' are a quotation of Article 35, paragraph 1. At the 19th meeting of the Security Council the President declared: ' By the letter of February 4 these two delegations have exercised their right as Members of the United Nations under paragraph 1 of Article 35 of the Charter, to bring to the attention of the Council a certain matter.' (*Ibid.*, No. 15, p. 265.) The request made in the letter that the Security Council should recommend the evacuation of the foreign troops, is a request to recommend terms of settlement; which is possible neither under Article 34 nor under Article 35, paragraph 1, but only if the dispute is referred to the Security Council under Article 37.

In the Memorandum of the Secretariat (A/AC.18/61, p. 3) it is stated: ' In certain instances States have made reference to the peaceful means of their own choice to which they have resorted, pursuant to Article 33, paragraph 1, of the Charter, before a question is brought to the attention of the Security Council: (*a*) In their initial communication bringing the question to the attention of the Security Council; (*b*) And/or in their initial statements before the Security Council.' In all the instances referred to in the memorandum the case has been brought before the Security Council under Article 35, paragraph 1. ' In two instances objection has been raised to the inclusion of a dispute or situation in the agenda of the Security Council on the grounds that peaceful means of settlement had not been exhausted by the parties (Iranian Question—25th meeting, Journal of the Security Council, pages 367 and following), or that they were still in progress and had been, or would be, successful (Incidents in the Corfu Channel, Official Records, 2nd Year, pages 115 and following). In these instances the decision of the Council was to include these questions in the agenda (26th meeting, Journal of the Security Council, page 385 and 95th meeting, Official Records, 2nd Year, page 117)' (p. 5).

A dispute between Hyderabad, not a Member of the United Nations, and India, a Member of the United Nations, was brought before the Security Council under Article 35, paragraph 2. On August 21, 1948, the Secretary to the Government of the Nizam of Hyderabad and Berar addressed a cablegram to the President of the Security Council which contained the following statements: ' The Government of Hyderabad, in reliance on Article 35 (2) of the Charter of the United Nations, requests you to bring to the attention of the Security Council the grave dispute which has arisen between Hyderabad and India, and which, unless settled in accordance with international law and justice, is likely to endanger the maintenance of international peace and security . . . Hyderabad, a State not a Member of the United Nations, accepts for the purposes of the dispute the obligations of pacific settlement provided in the Charter of the United Nations. It is understood that the submission of the present complaint to the Security Council does not prejudice the submission of the dispute to the General Assembly.' (Doc. S/986.) At its 357th meeting the Security Council placed the communication of the government of Hyderabad on its agenda without prejudging the question of its competence in paragraph 2. For the Council can act under Article 37, paragraph 2, only if the dispute is referred to it under paragraph 1 of that Article. When invoked under Article 35, paragraph 1, the Council can act only under Articles 35, 34 and 36, that is to say, the Council can make only recommendations of procedures or methods of adjustment, not recommendations of terms of settlement. Besides, since any dispute is a situation, a Member party to a dispute may evade the provisions of Article 33, paragraph 1, and Article 37, paragraph 1, by bringing a case which in fact is a dispute, as a ' situation ' to the attention of the Security Council under Article 35, paragraph 1.[8] The practice of the

the case. Representatives of the governments of Hyderabad and of India were invited to participate in the discussion. The representative of India denied the competence of the Security Council on the ground that Hyderabad was not an independent state. He declared that in his government's view ' Hyderabad is not competent to bring any question before the Security Council; that it is not a State; that it is not independent; that never in all its history did it have the status of independence; that neither in the remote past nor before August, 1947, nor under any declaration made by the United Kingdom, nor under any act passed by the British Parliament, has it acquired the status of independence which would entitle it to come in its own right to present a case before the Security Council. . . . If, therefore, I deny the competence of any area to come before the Security Council on a matter like this, it is because my Government and I are convinced that if the Articles of the Charter are not properly read, appreciated and respected, if opportunity is given to any particular area which does not possess the characteristics of a State to lay what it considers its grievances before the Security Council, the utility of the United Nations will be considerably impaired and great damage will be done to the cause of peace itself.' (Official Records of the Security Council, 3rd Year, No. 109, pp. 18 f.) At the 359th meeting, he stated that the use of force by the government of India was necessary: ' to maintain law and order which had completely broken down in several parts of Hyderabad.' The decisive point was that the government of India considered the dispute as concerning a matter within the domestic jurisdiction of India: ' we maintain the domestic character of the dispute.' (*Ibid.*, No. 111, pp. 6 f.)

[8] This was the case when Greece brought to the attention of the Security Council the conflict with Yugoslavia, Bulgaria and Albania, under Article 35, paragraph 1, as a ' situation which is leading to friction with her neighbours.' (Official Records of the Security Council, 1st Year, 2nd Series; Suppl. No. 10, Annex 16, pp. 169 f.) But the Security Council, through its President, declared the case to be a dispute. (*Ibid.*, No. 26, p. 607; cf. also No. 28, p. 652.) In spite of the fact that the dispute was brought to the attention of the Security Council by Greece under Article 35, paragraph 1, not referred to the Council under Article 37, paragraph 1, the delegate of the United States proposed a resolution by which the Council was to make recommendations far beyond those determined in Article 36, paragraph 1. The resolution suggested by the representative of the United States followed closely the text of the proposals made by the commission of investigation established by the Security Council in the Greek case. The commission proposed to the Council among others ' that it should recommend to the Governments of Greece on the one hand and Albania, Bulgaria and Yugoslavia on the other, to do their utmost to establish normal good-neighbourly relations, to abstain from all action direct or indirect which is likely to increase or maintain the tension and unrest in the border areas, and rigorously to refrain from any support, overt or covert, of elements in neighbouring countries aiming at the overthrow of the lawful governments of those countries. . . . ' (*Yearbook*, p. 371.) The delegate of the United

Security Council, as pointed out, is not in conformity with the wording of Chapter VI. In the actual procedure it makes no difference whether a case is brought before the Council under Article 35 or under Article 37.[9]

Another difference which exists between bringing a dispute before the Security Council under Article 35, paragraph 1, and bringing a dispute before the Council under Article 37, paragraph 1, is that in the first case the procedure of the Council is an *ex officio* procedure, whereas in the second case the procedure of the Council is depending on the parties to the dispute. To ' bring to the attention ' of the Security Council (or of the General Assembly) a matter, does not mean to bind the Council (or the Assembly) to intervene. Everybody may bring to the attention of the Council (or of the Assembly) anything. Nothing in the text of Article 35 allows the interpretation that the Council (or Assembly) is bound to deal with a dispute or a situation brought to its attention under Article 35. The positions of the Security Council under Article 35 is not different from that under Article 34: it is upon the Council to decide at its discretion, whether it will place the dispute or the situation on its agenda and thus institute

States proposed that the Security Council should resolve: ' The Security Council adopts the proposals made by the majority of the Members of the Commission. . . . ' (*Ibid.*, p. 374.) By such a resolution the Security Council would have recommended ' terms of settlement,' possible only under Article 37, paragraph 2, not mere ' procedures or methods of adjustment.' But the proposition of the delegates of the United States was not adopted by the Council, although nine members voted in favour of it. Since the Soviet Union voted against it, the resolution failed to pass. (Doc. S/P.V. 170.) (Official Records, 2nd Year, No. 66, p. 1612.)

[9] The Memorandum on Pacific Settlement by the Security Council submitted by the delegation of Canada to the First Committee (Doc. A/C.1/91, pp. 5 f.) contains the following statement: ' The primary responsibility of the Security Council for the maintenance of international peace and security was conferred on it by the Members of the United Nations to ensure prompt and effective action by the United Nations. The rules and practices of the Security Council should therefore be based on a recognition of the fact that the Security Council is under an obligation to deal with disputes and situations when it has decided that they come within its jurisdiction. Every member of the Security Council is under an obligation to see that prompt and effective action is taken by the Council. These obligations of the Council as a whole and of its members individually can be discharged only if the Council without delay pursues one or more of the three courses of action set forth in the relevant provisions of the Charter (paragraph 2 of Article 24, paragraph 2 of Article 33, paragraph 1 of Article 36, and paragraph 2 of Article 37). It may pursue these courses in any order it sees fit. The three courses of action are (*a*) to remind the parties to a dispute of their undertaking to settle it by peaceful means of their own choice; (*b*) to call upon the states parties to a dispute or directly involved in a situation to adopt such particular peaceful means or methods of adjustment as the Council considers most likely to succeed; (*c*) to recommend terms of settlement to the parties to a dispute.' The practice of the Security Council actually corresponds to the principle laid down in the Canadian suggestion: that the Security Council may pursue the three courses of action ' in any order it sees fit.' But this principle is certainly not laid down in the present Charter.

the *ex officio* procedure which ultimately leads to recommendations under Article 36. This procedure does not depend—as does the procedure under Article 37, paragraph 2—upon the parties; under Article 35, paragraph 1, a Member that is not at all a party to the dispute or involved in the situation, may bring the matter to the attention of the Security Council. Hence the state which has brought a dispute (or another situation) to the attention of the Security Council under Article 35, paragraph 1, cannot withdraw the matter from the attention of the Council; whereas the parties which have referred a dispute to the Council under Article 37, paragraph 1, may do so.[1]

[1] The question as to the effect of the withdrawal of a case from the Security Council arose during the consideration of the dispute between Iran and the Soviet Union. In a letter from the Iranian Ambassador to the Secretary-General, dated April 9, 1946, the statement was made ' that the Iranian Government has complete confidence in the word and pledge of the Soviet Government, and for this reason withdraws its complaint from the Security Council.' (Journal of the Security Council, 1st Year, No. 26, p. 498.) Previously the delegate of the Soviet Union had requested that the Iranian case should be removed from the agenda of the Security Council.

With respect to the question as to whether the matter could properly be retained on the agenda of the Council, the Secretary-General addressed to the President of the Council a memorandum which contains the following statements:

> Under Article 33 the Council may call upon the parties to a dispute to settle it by negotiations, inquiry, et cetera. Under Article 34 it may investigate any dispute or situation which might lead to international friction or give rise to a dispute. Under Article 36 it may recommend appropriate procedures for the settlement of a dispute under Article 33 or of a situation of like nature. Under Article 37 the Council may decide to take action under Article 36 if it deems that the continuance of a dispute is in fact likely to endanger the maintenance of international peace and security. And finally, under Article 38 it may, if all the parties to any dispute so request, make recommendations to the parties with a view to pacific settlement.
>
> It is to be noted that the Security Council can be seized of a dispute or situation in one of three ways. (1) under Article 35 by a State; (2) under Article 34 by the Security Council itself, and (3) under Article 99 by the Secretary-General.
>
> In the present case Article 99 is obviously not applicable. The Security Council has taken no action under Article 34; that is, it has not ordered an investigation, which is the only action possible under that Article. It is therefore not applicable at this time and cannot become applicable until an investigation is ordered.
>
> The Council was originally seized of the dispute under Article 35, paragraph 1. Now that Iran has withdrawn its complaint the Council can take no action under Article 33, Article 36, Article 37, or Article 38, since the necessary conditions for applying these Articles, namely a dispute, between two or more parties, do not exist. The only Article under which it can act at all is Article 34. But that Article, as has already been said, can only be invoked by a vote to investigate, which has not been taken or even suggested in this case.
>
> It is therefore arguable that, following withdrawal by the Iranian representative, the question is automatically removed from the agenda

In order to reconcile the provision of Article 35, paragraph 1, that any Member may bring a dispute to the attention of the Security

> unless: (*a*) the Security Council voted investigation under Article 34, or (*b*) a Member brings it up as a situation or dispute under Article 35, or (*c*) the Council proceeds under Article 36, paragraph 1, which would appear to require a preliminary finding that a dispute exists under Article 33, or that there is a 'situation of like nature.' (Journal of the Security Council, 1st Year, No. 27, pp. 522 f.)

If it is assumed that the Iranian case was under consideration by the Security Council as a dispute brought to the attention of the Council under Article 35, paragraph 1, it is hardly correct to speak of a 'complaint,' as did the Iranian ambassador in his letter of April 9, 1946, and the Secretary-General in his communication to the Security Council. Under Chapter VI of the Charter, no state can make a 'complaint' against another state; and consequently no state can withdraw a 'complaint' from the Council. This applies especially in case a dispute or situation has been brought to the attention of the Council under Article 35, paragraph 1. According to this provision a Member may bring to the attention of the Security Council a dispute to which it is not a party and, hence, has no complaint at all in the matter.

Although a state which has brought a dispute or situation to the attention of the Council under Article 35, paragraph 1, cannot withdraw a complaint, because it has not made a complaint, it could make a declaration to the effect that it withdraws the dispute or situation from the attention of the Council. But such an act could not have any effect, since the Council may give its attention to the matter even if it had not been brought to its attention by the state which now wishes to withdraw the case. Such a declaration is particularly without effect when the Council has already given its attention to the matter, as in the case of the dispute between Iran and Soviet Russia; and this even before the Council has undertaken an investigation under Article 34. The Council can deal with a matter, it can discuss it, without making an investigation. It must discuss it before adopting a decision under Article 34. Hence the Secretary-General's statement that the only Article under which the Security Council can act at all is Article 34, is not correct. It may act under Article 35, paragraph 1, in discussing the dispute or the situation; or even under Article 36, paragraph 1, in making recommendations. To make a recommendation without formally investigating the matter is certainly not proper; but it is not illegal, since the Charter does not stipulate that recommendations must not be made without previous investigation. The argument that if a party to the dispute has withdrawn its 'complaint' no dispute exists and, hence, Article 36 cannot be applied, is not convincing. For, whether a dispute still exists or not, is upon the Security Council to decide, and even if no dispute existed—according to the opinion of the Security Council—the latter could deal with the case as with a 'situation.'

Totally different is the situation in case a dispute has been 'referred' to the Security Council under Article 37, paragraph 1, by the parties. The parties who refer a dispute to the Council can withdraw this dispute from the Council, because in this case the Council's jurisdiction is based on the action of the parties, whereas in case a dispute has been brought to the attention of the Council under Article 35, paragraph 1, the jurisdiction of the Council is based on its own decision to deal with the matter.

At its 33rd meeting the Security Council decided to refer to the Committee of Experts for examination and report the memorandum of the Secretary-General. The Committee was not able to formulate a common opinion on the question put to it by the Security Council. However, the majority were of the opinion: 'The Security Council may hold that, even after an agreement has been reached between the parties, circumstances may continue to exist (for example the conditions under

Council, with the provision of Articles 33 (1) and 37 (1), that the parties shall refer the dispute to the Council only after having tried to settle it by means of their own choice, it would be advisable to interpret Article 35, paragraph 1—in conformity with the spirit of Chapter VI, though not with the wording of Article 35, paragraph 1—to mean that only Members which are not parties to a dispute may bring the dispute to the attention of the Security Council, whereas to Members which are parties to the dispute Article 33, paragraph 1, and Article 37, apply. If this interpretation is accepted, then Article 35, paragraph 1, establishes a procedure for the settlement of disputes different from that regulated by Article 33, paragraph 1, and Article 37[2] and that regulated by Article 38, in so far as the first

which the agreement has been negotiated) which might still leave room for fears regarding the maintenance of peace and which justify the maintenance of the question in the list of matters with which it is concerned. (Doc. S/42.) At its meeting on April 23, 1946, the Security Council rejected the motion of the representative of the Soviet Union (amended by the representative of France) that the Iranian question should be removed from the agenda of the Security Council. This decision was correct under the assumption that the Iranian question was under consideration by the Council under Article 35, paragraph 1, of the Charter.

2 The conflict between Iran and the Soviet Union, the first dispute dealt with by the Security Council, was brought before the latter by a note from the Iranian delegation of January 19, 1946, which enclosed the following statements: 'Owing to interference of the Soviet Union, through the medium of their officials and armed forces, in the internal affairs of Iran, a situation has arisen which may lead to international friction. In accordance with Article 33 of the Charter of the United Nations the Iranian Government have repeatedly tried to negotiate with the Government of the Soviet Union, but have met with no success. Accordingly, the Iranian Delegation to the General Assembly of the United Nations, on behalf of the Iranian Government, have the honour to request you, in accordance with the terms of Article 35 (1) of the Charter, to bring the matter to the attention of the Security Council so that the Council may investigate the situation and recommend appropriate terms of settlement.' The Iranian note did not refer to a dispute but to a 'situation,' and brought the matter under Article 35, paragraph 1, to the attention of the Council. On the other hand, the Iranian Government maintained to have fulfilled the requirements of Article 33, which presupposes the existence of a dispute, and requested the Council not only to make an investigation—which is consistent with Article 35, paragraph 1—but also to recommend terms of settlement, which is possible only if the matter is a dispute and if it is referred to the Security Council under Article 37, paragraph 1. In a second note of January 26, 1946 (Journal of the Security Council, No. 4, p. 37), the Iranian delegation again referred to Article 35 (in the text published in the Journal of the Security Council, Article 25 is referred to, which is probably a misprint) and asked to investigate the 'dispute.'

The representative of the Soviet Union argued that there was no foundation for consideration by the Security Council of the substance of the Iranian communication. His main argument was that the provision of Article 33, paragraph 1, was not yet complied with. (*Ibid.*, No. 5, pp. 53 ff.) The Security Council discussed the dispute and adopted in its meeting of January 30, 1946, the following resolution:

> The Security Council, having heard the statements by the representatives of the Soviet Union and Iran in the course of its meetings of January 28 and 30, and

mentioned procedure is initiated by any Member of the United Nations, whereas the second and third ones by the parties to the dispute.[3]

> Having taken cognisance of the documents presented by the Soviet and Iranian delegations and those referred to in the course of the oral debates;
>
> Considering that both parties have affirmed their readiness to seek a solution of the matter at issue by negotiations; and such negotiations will be resumed in the near future,
>
> Requests the parties to inform the Council of any results achieved in such negotiations. The Council in the meanwhile retains the right at any time to request information on the progress of the negotiations. (*Ibid.*, No. 6, pp. 82 f.)

In adopting this resolution the Security Council took none of the measures expressly mentioned in Chapter VI of the Charter. It did not call upon the parties under Article 33, paragraph 2, nor make an investigation under Article 34, nor make recommendations under Articles 36, 37 or 38. But the resolution was interpreted by the representatives of the United Kingdom and the Soviet Union to mean a recommendation, made by the Security Council under Article 36, paragraphs 1 and 2 to the parties to settle their dispute by direct negotiation. (Cf. *ibid.*, No. 19, p. 370; No. 20, p. 386.)

The second phase of the Iranian-Russian affair was initiated by a note of the Iranian Ambassador to the Secretary-General of the United Nations of March 18, 1946, which enclosed the following statement: 'Pursuant to Article 35, paragraph 1, of the Charter of the United Nations, Iran brings to the attention of the Security Council a dispute between Iran and the Union of Soviet Socialist Republics, the continuance of which is likely to endanger the maintenance of international peace and security. This dispute has arisen by reason of new developments since the adoption of the Security Council of the resolution of January 30, 1946, relating to the earlier dispute between the U.S.S.R. and Iran.' (*Ibid.*, No. 17, p. 352.) By this note the dispute was brought to the attention of the Security Council under Article 35, paragraph 1. But in its declaration before the Security Council on April 2, 1946, the representative of Iran said: 'I regret to inform the Council that to my knowledge no positive results [of the negotiations with the Soviet Union] have been achieved. I am instructed by the Government of Iran to refer the dispute to the Council for decision in accordance with the powers and duties of the Council.' (*Ibid.*, No. 21, p. 428.) And in its letter to the Secretary-General of April 2, 1946, the Iranian ambassador stated: 'In closing permit me to repeat that in referring these disputes to the Council, the Iranian Government . . . [hopes] that the Council will find a just solution which will promote friendly relations in the future.' (*Ibid.*, No. 23, p. 453.) To 'refer' a dispute for 'decision' or 'just solution' to the Security Council after attempts to solve it have not achieved positive results, is possible only under Article 37, paragraph 1. Hence it may be doubted under which Article the dispute has been under consideration by the Security Council. In view of the first note of the Iranian Government addressed to the Security Council in the first phase of the dispute and of its declaration before the Security Council in the second phase, it might be assumed that the dispute was referred to the Council under Article 37, paragraph 1. But since this government expressly quoted Article 35, paragraph 1, it may also be assumed that this Article applies. That a party brings its own dispute to the attention of the Security Council under Article 35, paragraph 1, is certainly compatible with the wording of that provision but inconsistent with the obligation under Article 33, paragraph 1, 'first of all' 'to seek a solution by means of their own choice' and only after this attempt has failed to refer the dispute under Article 37, paragraph 1, to the Security Council.

[3] For note, see p. 422.

The procedure initiated by any Member under Article 35, paragraph 1, however, can lead only to an *ex officio* procedure under Articles 34

The conflict which arose between the Soviet Union and the Security Council with respect to the question as to whether the Council should deal with the dispute, was, at least partly, due to this inconsistency. In its declaration made at the 4th meeting of the Security Council (on January 30, 1946) the representative of the Soviet Union rightly referred to the clear provisions of Article 33, paragraph 1, and Article 37. (*Ibid.*, No. 5, pp. 56 f.)

At its 30th meeting the Security Council adopted a resolution to the effect ' that the Council defer further proceedings on the Iranian appeal until May 6, at which time the Soviet Government and the Iranian Government are requested to report to the Council whether the withdrawal of all Soviet troops from the whole of Iran has been completed and at which time the Council shall consider what, if any, further proceedings on the Iranian appeal are required.' (*Ibid.*, No. 24, pp. 458, 466.) This was an indirect recommendation of withdrawing the Soviet troops from Iran. It is an—indirect—recommendation of terms of settlement, which is possible under the Charter only when a dispute is referred to the Council under Article 37, paragraph 1.

The India-Pakistan question was brought before the Security Council by a letter from the representative of India addressed to the President of the Security Council dated January 1, 1948. In this letter, the Government of India referred to Article 35 of the Charter and characterised the case as a ' situation.' It requested the Security Council ' to ask the Government of Pakistan: (1) to prevent Pakistan Government personnel, military and civil, from participating or assisting in the invasion of the Jammu and Kashmir State; (2) to call upon other Pakistan nationals to desist from taking any part in the fighting in the Jammu and Kashmir State; (3) to deny to the invaders: (*a*) access to and use of its territory for operations against Kashmir, (*b*) military and other supplies, (*c*) all other kinds of aid that might tend to prolong the present struggle.' (Doc. S/628, pp. 5 f.) This is a request for terms of settlement within the meaning of Article 37, paragraph 2. The Government of Pakistan, in its ' reply to the complaint preferred by India against Pakistan under Article 35 of the Charter of the United Nations,' dated January 15, 1948, brought to the attention of the Security Council under Article 35 of the Charter ' disputes which have arisen between India and Pakistan and which are likely to endanger the maintenance of international peace and order.' It requested the Security Council: ' (1) to call upon the Government of India (*a*) to desist from acts of aggression against Pakistan; (*b*) to implement without delay all agreements between India and Pakistan . . . ; (*c*) to desist from influencing or putting pressure directly or indirectly on the Reserve Bank of India in regard to the discharge of its functions and duties towards Pakistan; (2) to appoint a Commission or Commissions (*a*) to investigate the charges of mass destruction of Muslims . . . (*e*) to arrange for the cessation of fightings . . . ' (Doc. S/646, pp. 1, 9 f.) This, too, is a request for terms of settlement within the meaning of Article 37, paragraph 2, although the case was brought as a dispute to the attention of the Security Council under Article 35.

On January 17, 1948, the Security Council adopted a resolution which called upon the two governments ' to take immediately all measures within their power (including public appeals to their people) calculated to improve the situation and to refrain from making any statements and from doing or causing to be done or permitting any acts which might aggravate the situation; and further requests each of these Governments to inform the Council immediately of any material change in the situation which occurs or appears to either of them to be about to occur while the matter is under consideration by the Council, and consult with the Council thereon. . . . ' (Doc. S/651.) On April 21, 1948, the Security Council adopted a resolution in which it declared ' that the continuation of the dispute is

and 33, paragraph 2, or Articles 34 and 36 (or, as we shall see later, under Article 39).

Whereas a Member may, under Article 35, paragraph 1, bring ' any dispute ' whatever to the attention of the Security Council, only ' situations ' ' of the nature referred to in Article 34 ' are subjected to this rule. Article 34 refers to situations ' which might lead to international friction or give rise to a dispute ' and to situations the continuance of which is ' likely to endanger the maintenance of international peace and security.' These two qualifications are supposed to be not identical If so, does Article 35, paragraph 1, refer to the one or to the other? Both interpretations are possible, as far as the Member state is concerned which wants to know what kind of situation it is authorised to bring to the attention of the Security Council or the General Assembly. But the action a Member state takes

likely to endanger international peace and security.' The Council requested *inter alia* Pakistan to secure the withdrawal of non-resident tribesmen and Pakistani from Jammu and Kashmir, and India to withdraw its troops from these territories. (Doc. S/726.) These requests are evidently not recommendations of ' procedures or methods of adjustment ' within the meaning of Article 36, paragraph 1, but recommendations of ' terms of settlement ' within the meaning of Article 37, paragraph 2, in spite of the fact that the case has not been brought before the Council under Article 37, paragraph 1.

Whereas the India-Pakistan case was brought to the attention of the Security Council under Article 35, as ' situation ' by one party and as ' dispute ' by the other party, both involved in the conflict, the Czechoslovakian question was brought to the attention of the Council under Article 35, paragraph 1, as a ' situation ' constituting a ' threat to international peace and security ' by the government of Chile, which was not involved in the situation. According to information originating from the former representative of Czechoslovakia ' the political independence of Czechoslovakia, a Member of the United Nations, has been violated by the threat of the use of force by another Member of the United Nations, the Union of the Soviet Socialist Republics.' The government of Chile requested the Security Council to investigate the situation under Article 34. (Doc. S/694.) The Soviet Union voted against placing the case on the agenda of the Security Council (but was outvoted). (Doc. S/P.V. 268.) The government of Czechoslovakia, invited under Article 31 to participate without vote in the discussion of the case under consideration by the Security Council, rejected the invitation. In a letter of April 18, 1948, the Government declared: ' The discussion of internal matters before the Security Council is in contradiction to the provisions of the Charter. Such matters are exclusively within the domestic jurisdiction of any state. The Czechoslovak Government therefore rejects with indignation the unfounded complaint which has been put before the Security Council.' (Doc. S/718.)

[3] In a letter dated July 8, 1947, the Prime Minister and Minister of Foreign Affairs of Egypt charged that a dispute existed between Egypt and the United Kingdom, which the Security Council should consider under Articles 35 and 37 of the Charter. (Doc. S/410.) According to the wording of the Charter a dispute can be brought before the Security Council either under Article 35 *or* Article 37. In this case, the Security Council was not able to make any recommendation whatever. At the 201st meeting, the President stated: ' The Security Council has been unable to adopt any decision on the Egyptian question so far . . . of course the Egyptian question remains on the agenda of the Security Council.' (Doc. S/P.V. 201, p. 101.)

under Article 35, paragraph 1, has the purpose to initiate a procedure of the Security Council or of the General Assembly. A procedure leading to recommendations by the Security Council can refer only to situations which—according to the opinion of the Security Council—' might lead to international friction or give rise to a dispute.' For only such situations can be investigated by the Security Council in accordance with Article 34. And only if the Security Council has determined that the continuance of the situation is ' likely to endanger the maintenance of internal peace and security,' this organ of the United Nations may make recommendations under Article 36, paragraph 1. The opinion which the Member state, acting under Article 35, paragraph 1, has about the nature of the situation is without any importance; hence the restriction imposed upon Member states with respect to situations they are authorised to bring to the attention of the Security Council, is quite superfluous.

As to ' situations ' not having the character of disputes—in contradistinction to ' disputes '—no differentiation between Members which are and those which are not involved in the situation is necessary. For Chapter 6 does not contain a provision referring to states involved in a ' situation ' analogous to the provision of Article 33, paragraph 1, referring to states parties to a dispute. Members involved in a situation which might lead to international friction, or give rise to a dispute, or in a situation the continuance of which is likely to endanger international peace and security, are not obliged first to seek by means of their own choice a solution. They, as well as any other Member, may immediately bring the situation to the attention of the Security Council, which may proceed under Articles 34 and 36.

Article 35, paragraph 2, refers only to disputes and only to non-members parties to the dispute. Non-members are not authorised to bring ' situations ' not having the character of disputes or disputes to which they are not parties, to the attention of the Security Council or of the General Assembly.[4] The relation of Article 35,

[4] At the 14th meeting of Committee III/2 (U.N.C.I.O. Doc. 1029, III/2/33, p. 2), the delegate of France explained the provision excluding a non-member from bringing to the attention of the Security Council or the General Assembly ' situations ' or disputes to which the non-member is not a party, as follows: ' The reasons for this exclusion were of a highly practical order. If all the members of the Organisation, the Security Council itself, and the Secretary-General were unanimously of the opinion that a dispute should not be brought before the Security Council, why should a non-member, not a party to the dispute, be able to bring it to the attention of that body? The delegate of France thought it inadmissible to confer such a right in these circumstances; the proper functioning of the Organisation would be disturbed, and difficulties would be placed in the way of the Security Council. The silence of the text in this respect had been unanimously approved by the members of the Sub-committee. One additional hypothesis, continued the delegate of France, was deserving of mention. This involved the case to which reference had been made in the earlier debate, in which a non-member might desire to bring to the attention of the Security Council, not a dispute, but

paragraph 2, to Article 33, paragraph 1, is highly problematical. For the latter, referring to ' any ' dispute, may be interpreted, as pointed out, to mean that it refers not only to disputes between Members, but also to disputes between Members and non-members, and between non-members. If Article 33, paragraph 1, and Article 37, paragraph 1, are interpreted in accordance with their wording, to apply also to disputes to which non-members are parties, then Article 35, paragraph 2 is even more inconsistent with Article 33, paragraph 1, than is Article 35, paragraph 1. Article 35, paragraph 2, authorises non-members to bring to the attention of the Security Council disputes to which they are parties, even before they have tried to settle them by means of their own choice. However, a non-member, party to a dispute, has to act under the Charter in the same way as a Member: first in conformity with Article 33, paragraph 1; then in conformity with Article 37, paragraph 1. If it brings the dispute to the attention of the Security Council before having sought a solution under Article 33, it violates this provision.

It may be objected that even if the just presented interpretation is considered to be correct, the provision of Article 35, paragraph 2, is necessary according to which the non-member has to accept in advance, for the purposes of the dispute the obligations of pacific settlement provided in the Charter. However, if, under Article 2, paragraph 6, states which are not Members of the United Nations are obliged to act in accordance with the Principles of the Charter, especially in accordance with the Principles laid down in Article 2, paragraphs 3 and 4, it is superfluous to demand that a non-member accept for the purposes of the dispute the obligations of pacific settlement provided in the Charter. These obligations are implied in Article 2, paragraph 6. Besides, in this respect the text of

a situation likely to create friction or endanger the maintenance of international peace and security. On the basis of such hypothesis, no obligations could be imposed on the non-member involved in such a situation, since Article 1 of the text placed obligations of peaceful settlement only upon the parties to disputes. Further, the term " situations " referred to problems less acute than did the term " disputes." If a situation developed into a dispute, then a non-member which was a party to the dispute which had previously been no more than a situation, could bring it to the attention of the Security Council.'

At the San Francisco Conference the delegation of Greece proposed to insert after Chapter VI, Section A, paragraph 2, of the Dumbarton Oaks Proposals [corresponding to Article 35, paragraphs 1 and 2] the following provision: ' It is understood that the enemy states in this war shall not have the right of recourse to the Security Council before the entry into effect of the treaties putting an end to the war.' (U.N.C.I.O. Doc. 321, III/2/9, p. 3.) This proposal was not accepted. But Committee 3 to Commission III voted unanimously to insert into the report the following text: ' It is understood that the enemy states in this war shall not have the right of recourse to the Security Council or the General Assembly before the Security Council grants them this right.' (U.N.C.I.O. Doc. 1095, III/3/50, p. 4.) This interpretation has no basis in the Charter.

Article 35, paragraph 2, is problematic also for another reason. According to its wording, it is the bringing to the attention of the Security Council or of the General Assembly which is conditioned by the acceptance of the obligations of pacific settlement. Such a provision cannot have any effect. A non-member cannot be prevented to bring to the attention of the Organisation any matter whatever. What could be conditioned by the acceptance of the obligations of pacific settlement on the part of the non-member is only: that the Organisation may deal with the dispute brought to its attention. To deal with disputes to which non-members are parties, the Organisation, and especially the Security Council, is not bound by the fact that the dispute has been brought to its attention under Article 35, even if in case of a dispute to which a non-member is a party the non-member has accepted in advance, for the purposes of the dispute, the obligations of pacific settlement provided in the Charter. When the Security Council has, at its discretion, taken up the dispute, it has, under Article 32, to invite the non-member to participate, without vote, in the discussion relating to the dispute. Then the Council has to lay down such conditions as it deems just for the participation of the non-member. This is the right moment to require that the non-member, in order to participate, should accept the obligations of pacific settlement.

As to the conditions to be laid down under Article 32, the Security Council will hardly formulate other conditions than those stipulated in Article 35, paragraph 2: to accept in advance for the purposes of the dispute the obligations of pacific settlement provided in the Charter. But according to the wording of Article 32, the Security Council may lay down quite different conditions. If the Council does so, and the non-member state which brought the dispute to the attention of the Council does not accept the conditions laid down by the Council under Article 32, the state may not be invited to participate in the discussion of the dispute although it has, in conformity with Article 35, paragraph 2, accepted in advance, for the purposes of the dispute, the obligations of pacific settlement provided in the Charter. It was certainly not consistent to authorise in Article 32 the Security Council to lay down whatever conditions it deems just for the participation of the non-member state, and to require in Article 35, paragraph 2, the non-member state to fulfil a definite condition: namely, to accept the obligations of pacific settlement.[5] The fact that a state which is not a Member of the

[5] When the question arose in the Security Council to invite, under Article 32, the non-member states Albania and Bulgaria to participate in the discussion of a dispute which had not been brought before the Council by these states under Article 35, paragraph 2, the Council laid down the following condition: 'that Albania and Bulgaria should accept in advance, for the purposes of the case, the obligations of pacific settlement provided in the Charter.' (Official Records of the Security Council, 1st Year, 2nd Series, No. 26, pp. 608, 613.) In the Corfu Channel case,

United Nations can not be invited by the Security Council to participate in the discussion of the dispute to which it is a party because it did not accept the conditions laid down by the Council under Article 32, does not necessarily prevent the Council from proceeding in the matter. The same is true if a Member state, for some reason or another, does not accept the invitation issued to it by the Council under Article 32 or 31.[6]

The formula of Article 35, paragraph 2, 'obligations of pacific settlement provided in the present Charter' is not very clear. What are these obligations? There can be no doubt that the obligations laid down in Article 2, paragraphs 3 and 4 are included. But Chapter VI dealing with the 'Pacific Settlement of Disputes' contains provisions which do not constitute obligations in the strict sense of the term. If it is assumed that Article 33, paragraph 1, in connection with Article 37, paragraph 1, establishes an obligation of the parties to the dispute to seek first of all a solution by means of their own choice and to refer the dispute to the Security Council only after they have made serious efforts to this effect, it is hardly possible to require the non-member state to accept 'in advance' this obligation at the moment it brings

Albania was invited by the Council on the condition 'that Albania accepts, in the present case, all the obligations which a Member of the United Nations would have to assume in a similar case.' (Official Records, 2nd Year, No. 6, p. 123; No. 7, p. 131.) The practice of the Security Council as to the conditions to be laid down under Article 32 is described in the Memorandum of the Secretariat (Doc. A/AC 18/61, p. 6) as follows: 'The Security Council has decided, by extension of Article 35, paragraph 2, that those conditions should be the acceptance in advance, for the purposes of the dispute, of the obligations of pacific settlement provided in the Charter.' The Memorandum refers to the following decisions: 'Decision in the Greek Frontier Incidents Question (Official Records, 1st Year, 2nd Series, No. 26, p. 613); decision in the Corfu Channel Incidents Question (Official Records, 2nd Year, No. 6, pp. 123-124); decision in the Second Indonesian Question (S/P.V. 181, pp. 22-25, and 111).'

[6] At its 287th meeting the Security Council resolved to invite the government of Czechoslovakia to participate without vote in the discussion of the Czechoslovak case. The question as to whether this invitation was made under Article 31 or 32 was not decided. (Official Records of the Security Council 3rd Year, No. 53, pp. 3 ff.) The Czechoslovak Government rejected the invitation referring to Article 2, paragraph 7, of the Charter. In its letter dated April 8, 1948, the Government declared: 'The discussion of internal matters before the Security Council is in contradiction to the provisions of the Charter. Such matters are exclusively within the domestic jurisdiction of any state. The Czechoslovak Government therefore rejects with indignation the unfounded complaint which had been put before the Security Council. . . . Since the discussion of internal matters of Czechoslovakia in the Security Council is contrary to the basic principles of the Charter, inspired by the aim of protecting the sovereignty and independence of states, the Czechoslovak Government does not find it possible to take in any way part in such discussion.' (Doc. S/718.) In spite of the refusal of the Czechoslovak Government to participate in the discussion the Security Council continued to deal with the case. (Cf. Official Records of the Security Council, 3rd Year No. 56,, pp. 1 ff.)

the dispute before the Council. There is no obligation to comply with the recommendations made by the Security Council under Chapter VI, except Article 25 is interpreted to apply also to mere ' recommendations ' of the Council, which is very doubtful. There is certainly an obligation of the Members to comply with a decision of the Security Council adopted under Article 34 to the effect to investigate a dispute; but this obligation is based on Article 25 and the obligation established by Article 25 is not a particular ' obligation of pacific settlement.' What is meant by the formula ' to accept the obligations of pacific settlement ' is probably: to submit to the provisions of the Charter concerning the settlement of disputes, whether these provisions establish strict obligations or not.[7]

Although it is not expressly stipulated in Article 35, paragraph 2, the acceptance of the obligations of pacific settlement must be communicated to the organ to whose attention the dispute is brought.

The provision of Article 35, paragraph 2, that a non-member state must accept in advance, for the purposes of the dispute, the obligations of pacific settlement provided in the Charter, applies only to disputes brought to the attention of the Security Council or of the General Assembly by this non-member, and only to this state. However, under Article 35, paragraph 1, a Member state may bring to the attention of the Security Council or the General Assembly a dispute between a Member and a non-member, or a dispute between two non-members. In these cases, under Article 35 the non-member states need not accept in advance the obligations of pacific settlement provided in the Charter. Under Article 35, paragraph 2, a non-member state may bring to the attention of the Security Council or of the General Assembly not only a dispute to which this non-member and a Member are parties, but also a dispute to which the other party (which does not bring the dispute to the attention of the Security Council) is also a non-member. In this case, under Article 35, only the non-member which brings the dispute before the Organisation, not the other non-member, has to accept in advance, for the purposes of the dispute, the obligations of pacific settlement provided in the Charter. Since such acceptance can be required only in order to justify the application of the provisions of the Charter concerning the pacific settlement of disputes to non member states, it is—at least—inconsistent to restrict the acceptance of the obligations concerned to the non-member which brings the dispute before the Organisation.

[7] At the 84th meeting of the Security Council the Australian delegate declared: ' To our delegation, it seems that one of the most important obligations of a Member in this case [meaning: obligations of pacific settlement] is the one contained in Article 25.' (Official Records of the Security Council, 1st Year, 2nd Series, No. 26, p. 611.) The opposite opinion, advocated by the Mexican and Soviet Russian delegates (pp. 612 f.) has no basis in the Charter. As to the question whether to comply with a recommendation of the Security Council under Article 36, paragraph 3, is an obligation of pacific settlement, cf. *infra*, pp. 444 ff.

However, under Article 32, the Security Council may require acceptance of the obligations of pacific settlement from any non-member party to a dispute under consideration by the Council, whether the non-member has, or has not, brought the dispute to the attention of the Council.[8] Although disputes to which non-members are parties may be also under consideration by the General Assembly, there is no provision in the Charter analogous to Article 32 referring to these disputes.[9]

As pointed out, under Article 35, paragraph 2, a non-member state may bring only a dispute to which it is a party, not a ' situation ' in which it is involved, before the Security Council or the General Assembly, although the Security Council as well as the General Assembly is competent to deal with situations (not having the character of a dispute) in which non-member states are involved. This results from Article 34 authorising the Council to investigate ' any dispute, or any situation which might lead to international friction or give rise to a dispute,' Article 35 authorising any Member

[8] At the 14th meeting of Committee III/2 (U.N.C.I.O. Doc. 1029, III/2/33, p. 3) the delegate of the Union of South Africa asked ' whether it would be desirable or feasible to provide that a non-member State, which was a defendant in a dispute brought to the attention of the Security Council, might be invited to accept the obligations of pacific settlement of the Charter for the dispute in question.—The delegate of the United States made reference to the provisions of Chapter VI, Section D, paragraph 5, and to the unnumbered paragraph of Chapter II of the Dumbarton Oaks Proposals, as being applicable to the question raised by the delegate of the Union of South Africa.—The delegate of the United Kingdom said that this question had been discussed at length in both sessions of the Sub-committee, and that a unanimous decision had been reached not to provide for an " invitation " in a case of this kind. The reason which had carried most weight with him was that a defendant state was in quite a different position from a plaintiff state; the former could not be required to accept the relevant obligations of the Charter, and the Security Council could not, for purposes envisaged in this Chapter, utilise other methods than those of persuasion to achieve its ends. Further, if it were provided that the Security Council should " invite " a non-member, and the invitation were refused, the task of the Council might be made more difficult than if no such provision existed. The Security Council and General Assembly could in any case proffer an invitation if no express authorisation were included in the Charter. For all these reasons, the Sub-committee had felt it preferable to leave the Organisation as unhampered as possible in the choice of methods for dealing with disputes involving non-member States.' According to the wording of Article 32 of the Charter, as it has been finally accepted at the San Francisco Conference, the Security Council shall invite any non-member state party to a dispute under consideration by the Council to participate in the discussion of the dispute and lay down conditions for this participation, regardless of whether the non-member state is a plaintiff of a defendant, that is to say, whether it has or has not brought the dispute before the Council; and the conditions laid down by the Council may be in all these cases: to accept the obligations of pacific settlement. But under Article 35, paragraph 2, only the non-member state which is the plaintiff that is to say, which brings the dispute before the Council, is required to accept the obligations of pacific settlement.

[9] Cf. *infra*, p. 460.

of the United Nations to bring 'any dispute, or any situation of the nature referred to in Article 34, to the attention of the Security Council or of the General Assembly,' and Article 36, paragraph 1, authorising the Council to recommend appropriate procedures or methods 'at any stage of a dispute of the nature referred to in Article 33 or of a situation of like nature.' In all these provisions the jurisdiction of the Security Council is not restricted to disputes to which only Members of the United Nations are parties or situations in which only Members are involved. The Council may, especially, deal with a situation not having the character of a dispute in which a Member and a non-member are involved. Then Article 31 applies. This Article does not expressly refer to 'situations,' but to 'any question brought before the Security Council,' which implies disputes as well as situations not having the character of disputes. Since Article 32 applies especially to disputes, only Article 31 is applicable if a 'situation' which has not the character of a dispute is brought before the Security Council. If in such a situation a Member and a non-member are involved and if the Council considers the interests of the Member as well as of the non-member to be specially affected, the Council is authorised to invite the Member to participate in the discussion, but not the non-member. This is certainly an unjustifiable defect of the Charter. To overcome, at least partly, this difficulty, the Security Council may, in applying Article 34, investigate the situation and in the course of this investigation ask the non-member to answer questions in order to get the necessary information. The non-member state may be asked to make written statements, but it is doubtful whether it may even be invited to send a representative authorised to make oral statements in the meeting of the Council. In any case the non-member state cannot be invited to participate—on an equal footing with the Member state—in the discussion.[1] The

[1] The case of the Ukrainian complaint against Greece was discussed in the Security Council under the presupposition that it did not constitute a 'dispute' but a 'situation.' In this situation Albania—a non-member state—was, according to the opinion of the Security Council, involved. The Council decided 'to invite the representative of Albania to come to the table for the purpose of making a factual statement.' The President of the Council declared 'that this does not imply the right to participate in the discussion.' The delegate of Australia advocated the opinion that Albania could be invited to make statements in the course of an investigation established under Article 34. But the decision of the Council was adopted on the proposition of the delegate of Mexico who declared that there existed a 'general principle, in accordance with the spirit of the Charter, according to which every time a question of great interest to a particular State is discussed in the Council, the State in question should be heard at the Council table.' He also expressed the opinion that the question under discussion (the complaint of the Ukrainian Republic against Greece concerning its relation to Albania) 'has the character of a dispute [between Greece and Albania].' The first statement of the Mexican delegate has no basis in the Charter; the second was only his personal opinion, not the opinion of the Security Council. It is not clear under which Article the decision of the Council has been adopted. No decision to

Council is competent to deal with disputes and other situations and even with ' questions ' which are neither disputes or other situations,

investigate the situation was taken. The Australian delegate abstained from voting and explained this abstention by the statement: ' We do not regard this as the correct moment or the correct procedure for hearing the representative of Albania.' The President expressed the opinion that a representative of Albania could be invited to supply information under Rule 39 of the Rules of Procedure of the Council. This provision refers, however, to persons who, in their capacity as experts, may be invited by the Council to support this organ with information, not to states, as the Chinese and Dutch representatives correctly stated. (Cf. Official Records of the Security Council, 1st Year, 2nd Series, No. 9, pp. 249 ff.; No. 10, pp. 260 ff.)

Under Article 35, paragraph 1, the Greek Government brought to the attention of the Security Council a situation in which Greece, Yugoslavia, Bulgaria and Albania were involved. (Cf. *ibid.*, Suppl. No. 10, Annex 16, pp. 169 ff.) At its 82nd meeting the Security Council adopted the following resolution:

> The Security Council resolves:
>
> 1. That the representatives of Greece and of Yugoslavia are invited to participate in the discussion without vote.
>
> 2. That the representatives of Albania and Bulgaria will be invited to enable the Security Council to hear such declaration as they may wish to make.
>
> Should the Security Council find at a later stage that the matter under consideration is a dispute, the representatives of Albania and Bulgaria will be invited to participate in the discussion without vote. (*Ibid.*, No. 24, pp. 556 f.)

The first paragraph of the resolution is based on Article 31. The legal basis of the second paragraph is not clear. The Council did not consider the case of the Greek complaint as a ' dispute ' and did not invite Albania and Bulgaria to make statements in the course of an investigation established under Article 34. It was probably based on the ' spirit of the Charter,' just as the invitation of Albania in the case of the Ukrainian complaint against Greece.

At the 84th meeting of the Security Council, in the discussion of the Greek complaint, the President of the Council declared: ' It seems clear, from the statements we have heard, that the case before the Council is of a nature which makes it appropriate for the Council to invite Albania and Bulgaria to participate, without vote, in our future discussions on the matter. Charges have been made against these Governments, and these Governments have contested these charges and made counter-charges. It seems to me that the principle contained in Article 32 of the Charter is clear—namely, that when non-members of the United Nations are contesting charges made against them before the Security Council, equity and sound practice require that they " be invited to participate without vote in the discussion " of the Council. I suggest that the case before us comes within the spirit and meaning of Article 32, whether or not it is technically labelled a situation or a dispute.—I propose that, in accordance with the spirit of that Article and with the spirit of justice with which the Charter is inspired, we invite Albania and Bulgaria to participate, without vote, during the remainder of this discussion, in order to assist the members of the Council in reaching an appropriate settlement of the case. I earnestly hope the Council will agree to such an invitation, without feeling it necessary to enter upon a technical debate concerning the basis of its action.' (*Ibid.*, No. 26, pp. 607 ff.) The interpretation of Article 32 according to which a non-member state is to be invited to participate in the discussion ' whether or not the case is technically labelled a situation or a dispute,' is by no

and not only with those affecting the interests of Members. Members and, according to Article 2, paragraph 6, also non-members, are under the jurisdiction of the Organisation. Consequently there was no reason to restrict the legal possibility of non-members to bring questions before the Organisation, to ' disputes ' to which they are parties (Article 35, paragraph 2); and especially no reason to restrict the power conferred upon the Council by Article 31, to Members, and its power under Article 32 to Members and non-members parties to a dispute. The restriction of Article 32 is the more regrettable as the distinction between ' disputes ' and ' situations ' is highly artificial, and superfluous difficulties may arise when it is doubtful whether the case under consideration is a ' dispute ' or another ' situation.' It is certainly upon the Council to decide this question; and in deciding it the Council is not bound by the opinion of the one or other party.[2]

The question as to whether a case has, or has not, the character of a dispute—decisive for the question as to whether Article 32 is applicable—is a substantive, not a procedural, matter.[3] This evidently increases the difficulties caused by the restrictions established in Articles 31, 32 and 35, paragraph 2. It may be that the question as to whether a case is or is not a ' dispute ' can be decided by the Security Council only after having heard the parties involved. If the party is a Member, Article 31 is applicable since the application of this Article does not require a decision about the nature of the case.[4] But if the party is a non-member, Article 31 is not applicable and to apply Article 32, in order to decide whether this Article is applicable, constitutes a vicious circle.[5]

(*c*) Procedures Initiated by the General Assembly and by the Secretary-General

The procedure for settlement of disputes and adjustment of other situations regulated by Article 34, Article 33, paragraph 2, and

means compatible with the clear text of this Article which authorises invitation of a non-member state only if it is a party to a dispute. Hence, before inviting a non-member under Article 32, the Council should—directly or indirectly—consider the case to be a dispute. The proposal of the President to invite Albania and Bulgaria to participate in the discussion, was adopted.

[2] Cf. the discussion at the 19th meeting of the Security Council (Journal of the Security Council, 1st Year, No. 15, pp. 265 ff.).

[3] This view has been advocated by the delegate of the Soviet Union at the 19th meeting of the Security Council. (*Ibid.*, p. 273.)

[4] In the Syrian and Lebanese question the Security Council decided to invite the representatives of the two states to participate in the discussion without having decided whether the case was a dispute or not and, consequently, whether the invitation was made under Article 31 or Article 32. (*Ibid.*, p. 274.) This was possible because both states were Members of the United Nations.

[5] At the 19th meeting of the Security Council (*ibid.*, p. 273) the Mexican delegate declared: ' A decision between a situation and a dispute can only be made after a party exercised his right to be heard.'

Article 36, may be initiated not only by the Security Council itself and by Members and non-members, but also by the General Assembly and the Secretary-General.

Under Article 10, the General Assembly may recommend to the Security Council to investigate, in accordance with Article 34, a dispute or another situation and the Security Council may comply with such recommendation. Under Article 11, paragraph 3, 'the General Assembly may call the attention of the Security Council to situations which are likely to endanger international peace and security.' Since the term 'situation' is not used in connection with 'disputes,' it may be interpreted to include the latter. After the attention of the Security Council has been called by the General Assembly to a situation, the Council may, under Article 34, make an investigation of the situation. The purpose of this investigation is —as pointed out—to determine whether the continuance of the situation is likely to endanger the maintenance of international peace and security. If the investigation has a positive result, the Security Council may apply Article 36. The investigation, however, may have a negative result. The Security Council may determine that the situation is not likely to endanger international peace and security and consequently take no action at all. Then there exists a conflict of opinions between the Security Council and the General Assembly. In this case, the General Assembly itself may take action with respect to the situation under Article 10 or Article 11, paragraph 2, that is to say, it may discuss the situation and make recommendations with regard to it. The General Assembly, it is true, is not expressly authorised by the Charter to investigate the situation; but in order to fulfil the function conferred upon it by Article 11, paragraph 3, and determine that the situation is likely to endanger international peace and security, the Assembly may examine the situation in discussing it, in asking for written statements of the parties involved and even in establishing, under Article 22, a special organ authorised to examine the situation and to report to the Assembly. But the Members are not obliged to permit such examination, especially not on their own territory, since, as pointed out, there is no provision referring to decisions of the General Assembly analogous to that of Article 25, by which the Members are obliged to accept and carry out the decisions of the Security Council.

If a state—Member or non-member—has brought before the General Assembly a dispute or another situation under Article 35, paragraph 1, the Assembly may discuss it and make recommendations with regard to it. But if 'action is necessary' with respect to the dispute or the situation, the Assembly, under Article 11, paragraph 2, 'shall' refer it to the Security Council 'either before or after discussion.' In order to determine that 'action is necessary' the General Assembly may apply the same methods as those that are at its disposal for determining that a situation is likely to endanger the peace. When a dispute or another situation has been referred by the Assembly to the Council under Article 11, paragraph 2, the latter may with respect to the dispute or situation apply Article 34 and 36, or—as we shall see later—Article 39. But the Council may decide that no action is necessary. Then, again, a conflict of opinions exists between the two organs. In this case, however, the General Assembly cannot take the action which it deems necessary. For 'action' means here—as pointed out[6]—enforcement action, which can be taken only by the Security Council.

Article 99 provides:

> The Secretary-General may bring to the attention of the Security Council any matter which in his opinion may threaten the maintenance of international peace and security.

Under this Article, the Secretary-General may bring to the attention of the Security Council—but not of the General Assembly[7]—any dispute or any other situation of the nature referred to in this Article, and the Council may open the procedure regulated by Article 34, Article 33, paragraph 2, and Article 36, or apply Article 39.

(*d*) Procedure for Settlement of Local Disputes

A special procedure seems to be established by Article 52 for the settlement of so-called 'local disputes,' that is to say, disputes between states which are parties to a regional arrangement. Article 52 runs as follows:

> 1. Nothing in the present Charter precludes the existence of regional arrangements or agencies for dealing with such matters relating to the maintenance of international peace and

[6] Cf. *supra*, pp. 204 f.

[7] The Report of Rapporteur of Committee I/2 of the San Francisco Conference contains the following statement concerning paragraph 3 of Chapter X of the Dumbarton Oaks Proposals [corresponding to Article 99 of the Charter]: 'The sub-committee and the committee considered an amendment to paragraph 3 proposed by Venezuela which would permit the Secretary-General to bring to the attention of the General Assembly, as well as to the Security Council, any matter which in his opinion might threaten international peace and security. The Venezuelan delegate explained that his amendment was intended to give the Secretary-General discretionary power to bring certain matters to the attention of either the General Assembly or the Security Council. He contended that this function did not place too great a burden on the Secretary-General. Its advantage was to keep the General Assembly informed of certain situations which states themselves might not bring to the attention of the Assembly. Some delegates in opposing the Venezuelan amendment discussed the difficulty in which the Secretary-General might be placed in having to decide between the General Assembly and the Security Council in presenting matters concerning peace and security. It was argued further that the Secretary-General would be exercising powers which are not even possessed by the member states. The Committee rejected the Venezuelan amendment by a vote of 18 to 11.' (U.N.C.I.O. Doc. 1155, I/2/74 (2), p. 7.)

> security as are appropriate for regional action, provided that such arrangements or agencies and their activities are consistent with the Purposes and Principles of the United Nations.
>
> 2. The Members of the United Nations entering into such arrangements or constituting such agencies shall make every effort to achieve pacific settlement of local disputes through such regional arrangements or by such regional agencies before referring them to the Security Council.
>
> 3. The Security Council shall encourage the development of pacific settlement of local disputes through such regional arrangements or by such regional agencies either on the initiative of the states concerned or by reference from the Security Council.
>
> 4. This Article in no way impairs the application of Articles 34 and 35.

Paragraph 2 of Article 52 is paralleled by Article 33, paragraph 1, providing that ' the parties to any dispute, the continuance of which is likely to endanger the maintenance of international peace and security, shall, first of all, seek a solution by negotiation, enquiry, mediation, conciliation, arbitration, judicial settlement, resort to regional agencies or arrangements, or other peaceful means of their own choice.' The two provisions, however, are not quite consistent. According to Article 33, paragraph 1, the parties to a dispute, even if parties to a regional arrangement, have the choice among the means of settlement indicated in this Article. According to Article 52, paragraph 2, states which enter into a regional arrangement referred to in paragraph 1 ' shall ' make every effort to achieve pacific settlement of local disputes, that is to say, disputes between parties to the regional arrangements, through such regional arrangements, and if the arrangements establish a special agency, through this agency. That means that—according to the wording of Article 52, paragraph 2—Members of the United Nations, if they enter into regional arrangements referred to in Article 52, paragraph 1, are obliged to insert into the text of the arrangement, provisions for the pacific settlement of disputes arising between them, and, if the arrangement constitutes a special agency, to confer upon this agency the competence to settle such disputes. Under Article 52, paragraph 2, the parties to a local dispute do not have the choice among the means of pacific settlement which states have under Article 33, paragraph 1. Under Article 52, paragraph 2, Members of the United Nations, if they have entered into a regional arrangement, are obliged ' to make every effort to achieve pacific settlement ' of all local disputes; whereas according to Article 33, paragraph 1, states are obliged to seek peaceful settlement by means of their own choice not for all disputes, but only for disputes the continuance of which is likely to endanger the maintenance of international peace and security.

The inconsistency between Article 33, paragraph 1, and Article 52, paragraph 2, raises the question whether Article 33, paragraph 1, must be interpreted as being restricted by Article 52, paragraph 2. This question may be answered in the affirmative, since Article 52, paragraph 4, contains a reference to the provision of Chapter VI in providing that Article 52 'in no way impairs the application of Articles 34 and 35.' From the fact that Article 33 is not referred to it might be concluded that the application of this Article is impaired by Article 52, paragraph 2, so that to parties of local disputes Article 33, paragraph 1, is to be applied only in so far as consistent with Article 52, paragraph 2. This interpretation, however, is possible, but not necessary, the fact that only Articles 34 and 35 are mentioned in Article 52, paragraph 4, does not necessarily mean that Article 52 impairs the application of the non-mentioned Articles of Chapter VI.

Still less consistent with the provisions of Chapter VI concerning the pacific settlement of disputes is paragraph 3 of Article 52. In addition, this paragraph is hardly consistent with paragraph 2 of Article 52. It is difficult to understand how the Security Council shall encourage the development of pacific settlement of local disputes through regional arrangements, after paragraph 2 has imposed upon the Members parties to a regional arrangement the strict obligation to make every effort to achieve pacific settlement of all local disputes through such regional arrangements. It is difficult to understand how such encouragement could be afforded on the initiative of the states concerned if the states concerned are under the obligation of paragraph 2. And it is not completely understandable how the Security Council in conformity with the procedure laid down in Chapter VI can 'refer' a dispute for settlement to the parties of the regional arrangement or to the agency established by this arrangement. Under the provisions of Chapter VI, the Security Council can only recommend appropriate procedures or methods of adjustment (Article 36, paragraph 1, and Article 37, paragraph 2) or terms of settlement (Article 37, paragraph 2, and Article 38). In case a local dispute is before the Security Council the latter may, under Article 36, paragraph 1, recommend to the parties to settle the dispute by resort to their regional arrangement or the regional agency if such agency is established by the arrangement. It is even doubtful whether in such a case a 'recommendation' is appropriate in view of the strict obligation established by Article 52, paragraph 2. It is also doubtful whether the Security Council, if allowed to make any recommendation at all, may recommend any other method of adjustment than that through the regional arrangement or the regional agency, provided that the Council's power is considered to be restricted by Article 52, paragraph 2. In any case, under Chapter VI the Council cannot 'refer' the dispute to such agency. To 'refer' a dispute to a regional agency or directly to the parties to the regional arrangement if no regional agency is established, means to refer the settlement of the dispute to these authorities. This is certainly incompatible with the provisions of Chapter VI dealing with the settlement of disputes which are not settled by the parties themselves, that is to say, with Articles 37 and 38, according to which only the Security Council itself has the competence to recommend terms of settlement. It may be that the term 'reference from the Security Council' means—according to the intention of the legislator—only a recommendation to be made under Article 36, paragraph 1; that is to say, the Security Council shall recommend in case of local disputes resort to regional arrangements or regional agencies. If this was the intention of the legislator, it is certainly not properly expressed. But this interpretation, too, involves a restriction of the power conferred upon the Security Council by Article 36, paragraph 1. Be that as it may, 'reference from the Security Council' as provided for in Article 52, paragraph 3, is possible only if, in case of local disputes, Article 52, and not the procedures laid down in Chapter VI apply; or if the latter apply, only in so far as they are consistent with Article 52. As pointed out, the provision of Article 52, paragraph 4, may, but need not necessarily, be interpreted in this way. However, if it was intended to restrict the provisions of Chapter VI by the provisions of Article 52, that is to say, to organise the procedure for the pacific settlement of local disputes in a way different from that for the settlement of other disputes, it was necessary to insert into Chapter VI a clause to this effect. For, the provisions of Chapter VI precede those of Article 52 and are formulated in general terms covering all disputes, local disputes included.

If the formula 'reference from the Security Council' as used in Article 52, paragraph 3, means that the Security Council shall refer the settlement of local disputes brought before it to the states parties to a regional arrangement or to the regional agency established by this arrangement, paragraph 3 of Article 52 is hardly compatible with the provision of paragraph 2 of this Article according to which—in connection with Article 37, paragraph 1—the parties to a local dispute are obliged to refer the dispute, and that means the settlement of the dispute, to the Security Council after they have made every effort to achieve pacific settlement through the regional arrangement or by the regional agency, and these efforts have failed. How can the Security Council refer a local dispute to the regional authorities if the parties to the local dispute are obliged to refer it to the Security Council? Such 'reference from the Security Council' is possible only before the parties to the local dispute have made any effort to achieve pacific settlement in conformity with Article 52, paragraph 2. But at this stage the Security Council, if it has to respect the provision of Article 52, paragraph 2, can only remind the parties of their obligation under this paragraph; it cannot 'refer' the dispute; that is to say, the Security Council cannot transfer its competence to settle it.

Article 52, paragraph 4, refers to the relation between the procedure for the pacific settlement of local disputes laid down in Article 52 and the procedure (or procedures) for the pacific settlement of all disputes laid down in Chapter VI. As pointed out, it is not clear why Article 52, paragraph 4, mentions only the application of Articles 34 and 35 as not impaired by Article 52. But Article 52, paragraph 4, makes it sure that also local disputes may be investigated under Article 34 by the Security Council and may be brought to the attention of the Security Council or the General Assembly under Article 35, paragraph 1, by any Member of the United Nations, and under Article 35, paragraph 2, by a non-member if it is a party to such local dispute. In case the local dispute is brought to the attention of the Security Council under Article 35 the Security Council may investigate the dispute. If the investigation—whether initiated by the Council itself under Article 34 or by a Member or non-member under Article 35—has the result that the dispute is determined by the Security Council to be likely to endanger international peace and security, the Security Council may make recommendations under Article 36, paragraph 1, especially the recommendation to seek solution of the dispute by resort to the regional arrangement or the regional agency. If it is assumed that not Article 36 but Article 52, paragraph 3, does apply in such case, the Security Council shall 'refer' the settlement of the dispute to the parties of the regional arrangement or to the regional agency under Article 52, paragraph 3. If, in spite of this reference, the local dispute cannot be settled by regional arrangements, the parties may refer the dispute back to the Security Council under Article 52, paragraph 2. It may, however, be argued that reference of a local dispute from the Security Council to regional arrangements excludes reference of such dispute from the parties to the Security Council. If this interpretation is accepted, Article 52, paragraph 2 (in connection with Article 37, paragraph 1) obliging the parties to refer the dispute to the Security Council, applies only if the dispute has not been referred to the regional authorities by the Security Council under Article 52, paragraph 3. All this shows how confused the situation of local disputes is under the combined provisions of Chapters VI and VIII of the Charter.

(*e*) Settlement under Article 39

The Security Council has competence with respect to the settlement of disputes and adjustment of other situations not only under Chapters VI and VIII, but also under Chapter VII. Article 39 states:

> The Security Council shall determine the existence of any threat to the peace, breach of the peace, or act of aggression and shall make recommendations, or decide what measures

shall be taken in accordance with Articles 41 and 42, to maintain or restore international peace and security.

Since this Article provides not only for enforcement measures but also authorises the Security Council, after having determined the existence of a threat to, or breach of, the peace (including act of aggression), 'to make recommendations' of any kind, consequently also recommendations of the kind referred to in Articles 33 (2), 36 or 37, this provision establishes another procedure for the peaceful settlement of disputes or adjustment of situations, provided the dispute or the situation constitutes a threat to the peace or a breach of the peace. It is important to note that the Security Council under Chapter VII need not necessarily take enforcement measures. It may not only make recommendations under Article 39, but also under Article 40, call upon the parties concerned to comply with provisional measures; and these measures may have the character of mere recommendations if not ordered by the Security Council under the sanctions referred to in Article 39. Under Article 39, a dispute or another situation constituting a threat to, or breach of, the peace may be settled by the Security Council not only by peaceful means but also by the use of force as determined in Articles 41 and 42. How can a dispute or another situation be brought before the Security Council under Article 39, that is to say, as a case constituting a threat to, or breach of, the peace? Certainly by the Security Council itself, on its own initiative. That means that any member of the Security Council may ask to put such a case on the agenda of the Security Council. It is doubtful whether 'any Member of the United Nations' under Article 35, paragraph 1, and a non-member under Article 35, paragraph 2, may bring to the attention of the Security Council a dispute or another situation in order to be dealt with under Article 39, because it may be argued that this Article applies only within a procedure conducted under Chapter VI.[8] As to situations not having

[8] The first case brought before the Security Council under Article 39 was the conflict between the Netherlands and Indonesia. In a letter dated July 30, 1947, to the Secretary-General, the representative of the Government of Australia, at this time member of the Security Council, stated: 'The Australian Government considers that these hostilities constitute a breach of the peace under Article 39 and urges that the Council take immediate action to restore International Peace and Security. In order to prevent an aggravation of the situation the Australian Government proposes that the Security Council, as a provisional measure, and without prejudice to the rights, claims, or position of the parties concerned, should call upon the Governments of the Netherlands and of the Republic of Indonesia to cease hostilities forthwith and to commence arbitration in accordance with Article 17 of the Linggadjati Agreement between the Netherlands and the Government of the Republic of Indonesia signed at Batavia on March 25, 1947.' The representative of Australia requested the Secretary-General 'to call immediately a meeting of the Security Council for the consideration of this communication and that the Provisional Agenda, including this item, be communicated to the representatives on the Security Council simultaneously with the notice of the meeting.' (Doc. S/449.) The case was brought before the Security Council also by the Government

the character of a dispute, Article 35, paragraph 1, expressly applies only to those which are of the nature referred to in Article 34, which is different from the nature referred to in Article 39; and Article 35, paragraph 2, provides that the non-member must accept for the purposes of the dispute the ' obligations of pacific settlement ' which implies that the dispute may be brought to the attention of the Security Council only for pacific settlement. Such pacific settlement, as pointed out, is possible also under Article 39, but this is not the main purpose of this Article. In conformity with Article 11, paragraph 2, the General Assembly may refer to the Security Council a dispute or other situation which constitutes a threat to, or breach of, the peace, in so far as it is a question on which action is necessary. However, under whatever Article of the Charter a dispute or other situation has been brought before the Security Council, the latter may always apply Article 39, by determining *ex officio* the existence of a threat to, or breach of, the peace. The Council may take this step without regard to whether, in case of a dispute, the parties have or have not complied with the provision of Article 33, paragraph 1. But a decision by which the existence of a threat to, or breach of, the peace is determined, must be taken in order to establish the competence of the Security Council to take the measures referred to in Articles 39

of India, which at that time was not a member of the Security Council, by a letter dated July 30, 1947, to the President of the Security Council. In this letter the Government of India referred to Article 35, paragraph 1, of the Charter, and stated: ' In the opinion of the Government of India this situation endangers the maintenance of international peace and security which is covered by Article 34 of the Charter. The Government of India therefore requests the Security Council to take the necessary measures provided by the Charter to put an end to the present situation.' (Doc. S/447.) At the invitation of the President of the Security Council the representatives of the Netherlands and of India participated in the discussion of the Council. At the 171st meeting of the Security Council the representative of Australia declared: ' the Australian Government has drawn the attention of the Council under Article 39 of the Charter of the United Nations to the situation in Indonesia. . . . However, although the parties to any dispute are bound to seek a solution by mediation and negotiation under Article 33, all attempts to bring the parties together have failed, and it is felt that further delay is not justified because of the loss of life being sustained.' (Official Records of the Security Council, 2nd Year, No. 67, p. 1622.) The representative of India stated: ' India has asked for action under Chapter VI, which relates to disputes the continuance of which is likely to endanger the maintenance of international peace and tranquility. Australia has applied under Chapter VII, which relates to actual threats to the peace. There is really no difference of opinion between Australia and India in this matter. We did not, however, invoke the more urgent provisions of Chapter VII, for we felt that, not being a member of the Security Council, we were not entitled to do so. We rejoice that Australia has taken up this matter under the provisions of Chapter VII, and we are most grateful for this action. We warmly associate ourselves with the Australian proposal pending careful consideration of ours.' (p. 1620). The representative of Australia thought it necessary to refer to Article 33, paragraph 1, of the Charter. The representative of India expressed the view that only a member of the Security Council may bring a case under Article 39 before the Security Council.

and 40 of the Charter.[9] The procedure under Article 39 differs from the procedure under Article 37 in that Article 33, paragraph 1, does

[9] In the Indonesian question, the representative of Australia proposed, at the 171st meeting of the Security Council, the following resolution:

> The Security Council,
>
> Noting with concern the hostilities in progress between the armed forces of the Netherlands and of the Republic of Indonesia, and
>
> Having determined that such hostilities constitute a breach of the peace under Article 39 of the Charter of the United Nations,
>
> Calls upon the Governments of the Netherlands and of the Republic of Indonesia, under Article 40 of the Charter of the United Nations, to comply with the following measures, such measures to be without prejudice to the rights, claims, or position of either party:
>
> (*a*) to cease hostilities forthwith, and
>
> (*b*) to settle their disputes by arbitration in accordance with Article 17 of the Linggadjati Agreement, signed at Batavia on March 25, 1947. (Official Records of the Security Council, 2nd Year, No. 67, p. 1626.)

The representative of the Netherlands denied the competence of the Security Council, arguing that there was no threat to, or breach of, international peace, since there was no conflict between two sovereign states, Indonesia not being a sovereign state, and that the situation was a matter essentially within the domestic jurisdiction of the Netherlands: 'The Charter was designed, I think, to operate between sovereign States. Article 2, paragraph 1 of the Charter says, "The Organisation is based on the principle of the sovereign equality of all its Members." I beg to observe that no State which is not a sovereign State is eligible for membership. Let me add that Committee 1 of the San Francisco Conference, in its report to Commission 1, stated that sovereign equality includes the following element: " . . . (2) that each State enjoys the right inherent in full sovereignty." There is on the side of the Republic of Indonesia no question of full sovereignty. The sovereign Power—and I think this has never been disputed yet—is the Netherlands, whose Government has difficulties with one of its constituent elements, not with an external element. We therefore contend: First, the Charter is not applicable to what is now happening in Java and Sumatra; and Secondly, that while it seems to us that that contention is adequate to rule out action of any kind, including an affirmative vote on the Australian draft resolution now before us, we consider, in addition, that this is a matter essentially within the domestic jurisdiction of the Netherlands. . . . Assuming purely and simply for argument's sake that the Charter is applicable—which I deny—to what is now taking place in Java and Sumatra, where then, I ask, is there any danger to international peace and security, let alone breaches of the peace or acts of aggression in the sense of the Charter? In what countries outside the Netherlands' territory are there any signs of danger to peace caused by this action?' (p. 1645). Doubts about the competence of the Security Council were expressed by the delegates of Belgium, the United Kingdom and France. (*Ibid.*, No. 68, pp. 1653 ff., 1676 f.) The representative of the United Kingdom declared: 'I shall only say that so far we have not heard any really convincing arguments to persuade us that this is a war between two sovereign States.' The representative of the United States submitted an amendment to the Australian resolution to the effect to eliminate from its text the invocation of Articles 39 and 40 which raises 'very complex and serious questions of law.' The amendment reads as follows:

> The Security Council,
>
> Noting with concern the hostilities in progress between the armed forces of the Netherlands and of the Republic of Indonesia,

not apply, so that a dispute may be brought before the Security Council before the parties have tried to solve it by means of their own

> Calls upon the parties,
>
> (*a*) to cease hostilities forthwith, and
>
> (*b*) to settle their disputes by arbitration or by other peaceful means.

The representative of the United States declared: 'My delegation believes that if we can pass that simple statement quickly, we may then go into the legal issues involved at a subsequent time, when our various delegations on this Council will have had the time to study and to think of all of the indications which might follow our adopting any one of the juridical principles.' (pp. 1658 f). The Australian delegate accepted the United States amendment. He declared: 'we should avoid long juridical and technical arguments. To meet those objections, we eliminated from our original resolution those references to the Charter which might have raised difficulties regarding the competence of this Council.' (p. 1694). The representative of China approved the United States amendment. He stated: 'I think it would be dangerous to talk too much about legalities. I thought it wise of the Australian representative to avoid those dangers, and I appreciate the improvement, from that point of view, of the United States amendment, which also avoids legalities. In discussing a question of this type, if we pay too much attention to legalities, we shall become involved. As the representative of a country in that part of the world with which we are now concerned, I should like to report to this Council that emphasis on legalities might have very serious and undesirable political consequences. What does this legality involve? It is said that the Council has no competence because there is no threat to international peace, as this is not international war. In any event it is war. It is not civil war; it is not international war. What is it? It is a colonial war. What then are you upholding? You are upholding the freedom to wage colonial war as you please. You say that when a colonial war is being waged, this Council has no right to interfere. Legally you may be right, but that kind of legality does not go far. It may create more troubles and more problems in this world. If legality is emphasised, the other side will counter with revolutionary slogans such as "Down with imperialism," "Away with the old regime." Therefore you create more trouble in that way; and we are getting away from that.' (p. 1685). This is a strange way of applying the Charter. The statement of the Chinese representative means that if the Charter does not confer competence upon the Security Council to deal with the Indonesian question it is advisable not to 'emphasise legality,' which implies to act without authorisation by the Charter. The representative of France even proposed to insert into the text of the resolution suggested by Australia and amended by the United States the formula:

> Reserving entirely the question of the Council's competence as regards the application of the Charter but prompted by a wish to see the cessation of bloodshed in the two islands. . . . (p. 1678).

How can the question of the Council's competence in the Indonesian case be 'reserved' if the Council by a resolution intervenes in the conflict?

At its 173rd meeting on August 1, 1947, the Security Council adopted the resolution proposed by Australia and amended by the United States and Poland to add in paragraph (*b*) the sentence: 'and keep the Security Council informed of the progress of the settlement.' The French amendment was rejected. Already before the rejection of the French amendment the President declared: 'We are not saying that the Security Council is or is not competent to deal with the question . . .' (p. 1701); and to a question of the French delegate he answered: 'I do not consider that the question [of the competence of the Security Council]

choice;[1] it differs from all procedures under Chapter VI in that members of the Security Council, parties to the dispute, are not

has been settled, but that it has been left in abeyance.' (p. 1702). With reference to this declaration the French delegate stated at the end of the meeting: 'I wish to say most emphatically, however, that the decision we have just taken, in regard to which the Council has not cleared up the question of its competence in so serious a matter, seems to me regrettable. Nevertheless, I welcome your statement, Mr. President, that the question of competence is not settled by this resolution. That is an important statement and I take note of it once again.' (p. 1713).

There can be hardly any doubt that the Security Council, by adopting the resolution declared itself competent to intervene in the conflict between the Netherlands and Indonesia, although it did not make an express statement about its competence and although it did not indicate the Articles of the Charter under which it was acting. The representative of the United Kingdom correctly stated: 'in the view of my delegation, the resolution before us, even as it is redrafted by the United States delegation, does not avoid entirely the difficulty to which I have referred. It does, on the contrary, prejudge the legal position, because to call on parties to cease fighting is definitely to imply that Article 2, paragraph 7, of the Charter does not apply.' (p. 1674). And the representative of the Soviet Union said with reference to the French amendment, that he could not agree with the suggestion 'to mention in our resolution that the Security Council, although it adopts this decision, is still not certain that it has the right to do so or that the question comes within its jurisdiction. In the first place, this would reduce the weight of such a decision, and in the second place, it would create an undesirable precedent for the future, as it would mean that the Security Council might consider a particular question though it was not certain that the question came within its jurisdiction.' (p. 1692). As a matter of fact, in spite of the elimination of any reference to Articles 39 and 40 of the Charter from the text of the resolution, the delegate of Australia after its adoption declared that the Security Council was examining the case under the Articles of Chapter VII (p. 1708); the representative of Poland said at the 181st meeting of the Security Council that the Indonesian question was taken under discussion under Article 39 of the Charter (Doc. S/P.V. 181, p. 51) and, at the 185th meeting, that by admitting the case under Article 39 of the Charter the Security Council 'recognised the competence of the Security Council to deal with the case. Although the resolution did not expressly mention Article 39, it is quite clear that under this Article, and only under this Article, the case can be dealt with here, and measures provided by the Charter can be applied.' (Doc. S/P.V. 185, p. 46.) Even the representative of the United States declared at the 193rd meeting of the Security Council that paragraph (*a*) of the resolution of August 1, 1947, was 'a provisional measure under Article 40' (Doc. S/P.V. 193, p. 71); and at the 195th meeting, the Australian delegate maintained that by the resolution of August 1, 1947, 'action was taken under Article 40' (Doc. S/P.V. 195, pp. 32–35). At the 185th meeting the delegate of the Philippines argued that Article 2, paragraph 7, did not apply because the Security Council acted under Article 39 (Doc. S/P.V. 185, p. 76). On August 26, 1947, the Security Council adopted the following resolution:

The Security Council

Taking into consideration that military operations are being continued on the territory of the Indonesian Republic:

1. Reminds the Government of the Netherlands and the Government of the Indonesian Republic of its resolution of August 1, 1947, concerning the 'cease fire order' and peaceful settlement of their dispute;

For note [1] see p. 443.

excluded from voting in the decision by which the existence of the threat to, or breach of, the peace is determined, nor from the

2. Calls upon the Government of the Netherlands and the Government of the Indonesian Republic to adhere strictly to the recommendation of the Security Council of August 1, 1947. (Doc. S/521.)

To interpret the 'call' of the resolution of August 1, 1947, an 'order' implies that this resolution was adopted under Chapter VII of the Charter; for under Chapter VI no 'order' can be issued. (Cf. *infra*, p. 740.) It is, however, very doubtful under what provision the Security Council acted. For measures taken under Articles 39 and 40 require the preliminary determination by the Security Council of the existence of a threat to, or breach of, the peace. The passage in the original draft resolution: 'having determined that such hostilities constitute a breach of the peace under Article 39 of the Charter of the United Nations' has intentionally been eliminated. The formula 'Noting the hostilities in progress . . .' in the preamble of the resolution of August 1, 1947, is not equivalent to determining the existence of a threat to the peace, breach of the peace, or act of aggression' as prescribed by Article 39. If this is correct, the resolution of August 1, 1947, cannot be considered as a provisional measure under Article 40 and certainly not as a cease fire 'order.' It could be only a 'recommendation' under Chapter VI. However, since the case came not before the Security Council under Article 37 or 38, the only recommendations legally possible under the Charter were recommendations of 'appropriate procedures or methods of adjustment' in accordance with Article 36, paragraph 1. The so-called cease fire order is certainly not such a recommendation. But the Security Council, to use the words of the representative of China, quoted above, preferred to 'avoid legalities.'

[1] The conflict between the United States of America, the United Kingdom and France on the one hand, and the Soviet Union on the other, which had arisen as the result of the imposition by the Soviet government of restrictions on transport and communications between the western zones of occupation in Germany and Berlin, was brought before the Security Council by identical notifications from the three first-mentioned powers to the Secretary-General, dated September 29, 1948 (Doc. S/1020). In their letter the three governments characterised the case as a dispute between them and the Soviet Union that had arisen out of actions of the Soviet Union which they considered to 'create a threat to the peace within the meaning of Chapter VII of the Charter.' They expressly referred to 'their obligations under the Charter to settle their disputes by peaceful means' and affirmed that they 'have made every effort to resolve their differences directly with the Soviet Government.' At the 361st meeting of the Security Council the representative of the United States stated: 'In accordance with our obligations under Article 33 of that Charter, the Government of the United States, in agreement with the Governments of France and the United Kingdom has made every effort to remove the threat to the peace created by the U.S.S.R., through direct discussions with the Government of the Soviet Union'; and at the 363rd meeting, he declared: 'The Charter requires that, in such a situation, a Member shall first of all seek to exhaust the peaceful procedures indicated in Article 33 and, if these fail, resort to the Security Council. That is why the United States, in agreement with France and the United Kingdom, has brought the U.S.S.R. blockade measures in Berlin to the attention of the Security Council.' (Official Records of the Security Council, 3rd Year, No. 113, p. 21; No. 115, p. 4.) Although the dispute was brought to the Council not under Article 37, but under Article 39 (as a case of threat to the peace), the states which brought the dispute before the Council considered themselves bound by Article 33, paragraph 1. But according to the wording of the Charter, Article 33, paragraph 1, applies only in connection with Article 37, not in connection with Article 39.

decision by which a recommendation is made or enforcement measures are taken or, under Article 40, the parties are called upon to comply with provisional measures.

(*f*) Settlement under Article 94

Under Article 94, paragraph 2, of the Charter, the Security Council is competent to make recommendations in case a party fails to perform the obligations incumbent upon it under a judgment rendered by the International Court of Justice, and the other party has recourse to the Council. This competence of the Council shall be discussed in the chapter on Judicial Settlement of Disputes.

(*g*) Legal Effect of Recommendations of the Security Council

As pointed out in a previous part of this study,[2] the legal effect of a recommendation made by the Security Council under Chapter VI or under Article 39 is doubtful. The term 'recommendation' seems to indicate the intention of the legislator not to attach to the act of the Security Council any binding force.[3] On the other hand, Article 25 stipulates the obligation of the Members 'to accept and carry out the decisions of the Security Council in accordance with the present Charter.' If this provision is interpreted to refer to all decisions of the Security Council and if the term 'decision' is understood to mean any resolution adopted by the Council, the recommendations made by the Security Council—since made by 'decisions'—are not mere 'recommendations' but orders binding upon those whom they

[2] Cf. *supra*, pp. 293 ff.

[3] At the 7th meeting of Committee III/2 (U.N.C.I.O. Doc. 433, III/2/15, p. 2) 'the delegate of Belgium requested an interpretation from the sponsoring governments of the legal effects of the word "recommend" ("recommander") as used in paragraph 4. The delegate of the United States expressed the view that the recommendation of a settlement under paragraph 4 [corresponding to Article 37 of the Charter] was not obligatory unless the dispute involved a threat to the peace, as envisaged under Chapter VIII, Section B, paragraph 1 [corresponding to Article 39 of the Charter]. It was only if the failure to settle a dispute, or to carry out a recommendation of the Security Council, constituted a threat to the peace that the Security Council could "take any measures necessary for the maintenance of international peace and security," and then it must act "in accordance with the purposes and principles of the Organisation" '.

At the 9th meeting of Committee III/2 (U.N.C.I.O. Doc. 498, III/2/19, p. 2) 'the delegate of Belgium requested a more precise answer to his previously posed question as to whether the term "recommend" ("recommander") in Chapter VIII, Section A, [of the Dumbarton Oaks Proposals corresponding to Chapter VI of the Charter] entailed obligations for states, parties to a dispute, or whether it meant only that the Council was offering advice which might or might not be accepted.— The delegate of the United States expressed agreement with the views of the delegate of the United Kingdom, and said he had intended to make it clear that in Section A no compulsion or enforcement was envisaged.' (Cf. also U.N.C.I.O. Doc. 1027, III/2/31 (1), p. 4.)

concern.[4] But also another interpretation is possible according to which the term ' decisions ' in Article 25 means only resolutions by which binding norms are to be created. Decisions of the Security Council taken under Article 34 referring to an investigation, have certainly not the character of ' recommendations,' and hence are in any case ' decisions ' in the narrower sense of the term, as used in Article 25, and as such binding upon the states concerned. But ' recommendations ' made under Articles 36, 37, 38 or 39, or a ' call ' made under Article 33, paragraph 2, have—according to this interpretation—no binding force.[5] However, under Article 39, the Security Council may consider non-compliance with its recommendation a threat to the peace and resort to enforcement action against the recalcitrant state.[6] If such enforcement action is

[4] At the 127th meeting of the Security Council the Australian delegate interpreted a recommendation made by the Council under Article 36 as binding upon the parties, in referring to Article 25 according to which the Members have to accept and carry out the decisions of the Security Council. (Official Records of the Security Council, 2nd Year, No. 34, pp. 723, 726.)

[5] During the discussion of the Greek case the delegates of Yugoslavia and the Soviet Union, supporting a view expressed by the representative of Bulgaria, asserted that under Chapter VI including Article 34 the Security Council could make only recommendations, not decisions binding upon the parties. (Cf. Official Records of the Security Council, 2nd Year, No. 57, p. 1280; No. 59, pp. 1371, 1383; No. 64, pp. 1536, 1541.) To justify this interpretation the delegate of Yugoslavia referred to Article 2, paragraph 7, which he interpreted to mean that ' the Charter restricts the sovereignty of states only in the case of the measures provided for in Chapter VII. . . . The authors of the Charter clearly established a distinction between two kinds of procedure: that provided for by Chapter VI and that provided for by Chapter VII. In drawing up the measures contained in Chapter VI, they took special care not to restrict the sovereignty of States. It was only in connection with a serious situation that they thought fit to restrict this soverignty.' (*Ibid.*, No. 63, pp. 1520 f.) The statement that the Charter restricts the sovereignty of states only by provisions of Chapter VII is untenable. Any provision of the Charter imposing—directly or indirectly—obligations upon the Members is a restriction of their ' sovereignty '; and the Charter imposes obligations evidently not only in Chapter VII.

During the same discussion the representative of Australia, supported by other delegates, stated that a resolution by which the Security Council institutes an investigation under Article 34 ' is a decision, and not a recommendation; therefore, Article 25 does apply.' He further stated that ' whether it is a decision or a recommendation that is involved—and we have indicated that we can make both under Chapter VI—we cannot make either until we have determined that the continuation of the situation does endanger international peace and security.' (*Ibid.*, No. 61, p. 1420.)

[6] The Dumbarton Oaks Proposals contained in Chapter VIII, Section B (1), the provision:

> Should the Security Council deem that a failure to settle a dispute in accordance with procedures indicated in paragraph 3 of Section A [corresponding to Article 33 of the Charter], or in accordance with its recommendations made under paragraph 5 of Section A [corresponding to Article 36, paragraph 1], constitutes a threat to the maintenance of international peace and security, it should take any measures necessary for

interpreted to be a sanction, a recommendation of the Security Council may constitute the obligation to comply with the recommendation, that is to say, the so-called 'recommendation' may have the same character as a 'decision' of the Security Council, binding upon the Members under Article 25.[7] This is of great importance in case of a recommendation of terms of settlement. As pointed out, since such a recommendation may not conform with positive law and thus imply an infringement upon the rights of one or the other party, the Security Council having the power to enforce its recommendations may create new law in the relation between the contesting parties; a power which is not conferred upon the principal judicial organ of the United Nations, the International Court of Justice.[8]

> the maintenance of international peace and security in accordance with the purposes and principles of the Organisation.

The Charter does not contain this provision; but the same result may be achieved by the application of Article 39.

[7] It is not in this sense that the term 'decide' in Article 37, paragraph 2, is used. It means here the same as 'consider.' At the 7th meeting of Committee III/2 (U.N.C.I.O. Doc. 433, III/2/15, pp. 1 f.) the delegate of the Union of South Africa raised 'the question whether changing the word "decide" ("decidera") to "consider" or another suitable term would change the procedure.—It was pointed out that the term "decision" appeared to be used in slightly different senses in different parts of the Dumbarton Oaks Proposals, and it was suggested that this matter might be referred to the proposed sub-committee on drafting. The Committee, after receiving the report of the sub-committee, might then suggest to the Co-ordination Committee the desirability of bringing all parts of the Charter into harmony in this matter.' This has not been done.

[8] With reference to the fact that a recommendation of the Security Council might infringe upon the rights of a party to a dispute, the delegate of Belgium suggested at the San Francisco Conference the following amendment: 'Any state party to a dispute brought before the Security Council shall have the right to ask the Permanent Court of International Justice [International Court of Justice] whether a recommendation or a decision made by the Council or proposed in it infringes on its essential rights. If the Court considers that such rights have been disregarded or threatened, it is for the Council either to reconsider the question or to refer the dispute to the Assembly for decision.' (U.N.C.I.O. Doc. 2, G/7 (*k*) (1), p. 2; cf. also U.N.C.I.O. Doc. 461, III/2/16.) At the 7th meeting of Committee III/2 (U.N.C.I.O. Doc. 433, III/2/15, pp. 2 ff.) 'the delegate of Belgium stated that if, as appeared to be the case, the power of the Security Council to "recommend" ("recommander") involved the possibility that a Member of the Organisation might be obliged to abandon a right granted to it by positive international law as an essential right of statehood, the delegation of Belgium wished formally to present its amendment to the Committee. The purpose of the amendment was, in case a party to a dispute considered that a recommendation of the Security Council infringed on its essential rights, to allow the state to request an advisory opinion on the question by the International Court of Justice. If the Court found such rights to be infringed or threatened, then the Security Council would be required either to reconsider the question or to refer the dispute to the General Assembly for a decision. It was not in any sense the purpose of this amendment to limit the legitimate powers of the Security Council. It would, however, be desirable to strengthen the juridical basis of the decisions of the Security Council. The delegate of the Union of Soviet Socialist Republics expressed the opinion that the Belgian

It may be doubted only whether non-compliance with a recommendation made under Article 38 can be considered by the

Amendment should not be adopted by the Committee. He felt that the Security Council should receive the full confidence of the Members of the Organisation. There should be no question in the minds of any delegates that the Security Council might wish in any way to infringe the rights of a sovereign state. Furthermore, he considered that the Belgian Amendment would have the effect of weakening the authority of the Council to maintain international peace and security. If it were possible for a state to appeal from the Council to the International Court of Justice, and if there were the further possibility of an ultimate reference of the dispute to the General Assembly, the Council would find itself handicapped in carrying out its functions. In such circumstances, the Council might even be placed in a position of being a defendant before the Court. The Organisation must be based upon confidence in its constituent bodies. The delegate of the United States emphasised the importance of the requirement that the action of the Security Council in dealing with a dispute involving a threat to the peace be taken " in accordance with the purposes and principles of the Organisation." He referred to Chapter I, paragraph I, as amended by the sponsoring governments, which states that one of the purposes of the Organisation is to bring about the peaceful settlement of disputes " with due regard for principles of justice and international law " (Doc. 2, G/29, p. I). He did not interpret the Proposals as preventing any state from appealing to the International Court of Justice at any time on any matter which might properly go before the Court. On the whole, he did not consider the acceptance of the Belgian Amendment advisable, particularly since he believed that the Security Council was bound to act in accordance with the principles of justice and international law. The delegate of France declared that, while he viewed with great sympathy the ideas in the Belgian Amendment, he was doubtful that it would be effective in obtaining its desired end, especially since it involved a dispersal of responsibilities in the Organisation. He supported the views expressed by other delegates as to the advisability of clarifying the meaning of the words " decisions " and " recommendations " in paragraph 4. He pointed out that in practice, and particularly for a small state, the difference between the political authority of a recommendation and the legal force of a decision might not be great. He suggested that the subcommittee on drafting should endeavour to give the most complete guarantees possible that the Security Council accomplish its task according to law and justice. The delegate of Colombia expressed his warm support of the Belgian Amendment. He believed that the confidence generally felt in the Security Council should not exclude confidence in the International Court of Justice. Noting that the Dumbarton Oaks Proposals provided that justiciable disputes should normally be referred to the Court, he suggested that no question was more eminently legal than one concerning the essential rights of a state. The Belgian Amendment, therefore, was in full conformity with the terms of the Charter. Concerning possible procedural difficulties raised by the Amendment, the delegate of Colombia stated that in his opinion such difficulties would be the result, rather, of inadequacies in the formulation of Chapter VIII, Section A.'

At the 9th meeting of Committee III/2 (U.N.C.I.O. Doc. 498, III/2/19, pp. I f.) ' the delegate of the United Kingdom stated he thought the adoption of the Belgian amendment would be prejudicial to the success of the Organisation. The amendment would, in his opinion, result in the decision by the Court of International Justice of political questions in addition to legal questions. The performance of this function by the Court, he felt, would seriously impair the success of its role as a judicial body. Further, the procedures proposed by the amendment would cause delay, at a time when prompt action by the Security Council was most desirable. A powerful weapon would thus be placed in the hands of a state

Security Council to be a threat to the peace, since this recommendation refers to disputes the continuance of which is not deemed by the

contemplating aggression, and the Council would not be able to play the part in maintaining peace which was intended for it. Finally, he considered it necessary that the Council possess the trust and confidence of all states; its majority would be composed of small states, and it would be obligated to act in a manner consistent with the purposes and principles of the Organisation.—The delegate of South Africa supported this position, emphasising the importance of the act of faith which the small states were making in the acceptance of paragraph 4. He thought it fair to assume that decisions representing agreement among the great powers would be reasonable, since they would be influenced not only by their own interests but also by the interests of those countries with which they have close relationships, and also by world public opinion.—The delegate of the Byelo-Russian Soviet Socialist Republic expressed the opinion that the Belgian amendment should not be adopted by the Committee, laying particular emphasis on the view that the reference of disputes to the Court would weaken the position of the Council in maintaining peace.' 'The delegate of the United States expressed agreement with the views of the delegate of the United Kingdom, and said he had intended to make it clear that in Section A no compulsion or enforcement was envisaged. He noted that he had earlier expressed opposition to the second sentence of the Belgian amendment to paragraph 3, which concerned this point (Doc. 2, G/7 (*k*), p. 2). The delegate of Belgium stated that since it now was clearly understood that a recommendation made by the Council under Section A of Chapter VIII did not possess obligatory effect, he wished to withdraw the Belgian amendment. The withdrawal was accepted by the Chairman.'

The Report of the Rapporteur of Committee III/2 (U.N.C.I.O. Doc. 1027, III/2/31 (1), p. 4) contains the following statement with respect to Article 37: 'In the course of discussion on an amendment offered by the delegation of Belgium, the delegates of the United Kingdom and the United States gave assurance that such a recommendation of the Security Council possessed no obligatory effect for the parties.'

The Report to the President (p. 84) contains the following statement with respect to Article 37, paragraph 2: 'The parties are not obligated at this stage of a dispute to accept the terms of settlement recommended by the Security Council, any more than they are obligated to accept the Council's other recommendations. If, however, their failure to do so results in a threat to the peace, then the enforcement provisions of Chapter VII come into play.' With reference to this statement a Senator asked at the *Hearings* (pp. 274 f.) the question: 'Is it true that you accomplished the combination of the authority to pass upon the merits of an issue and to enforce it by arms—that combination in the Security Council?' Then the Chairman interjected 'that the recommendation carries no compulsion whatever.' Later (p. 277 f.) the Senator formulated his question in a more general way: 'I would like to ask whether anybody in this Conference having to do with this treaty regarded this reference to Chapter VII, that is the application of the enforcement provision of Chapter VII, to have anything to do with the recommendation beyond the point of preventing the use of armed force between them?' To this question, the representative of the Department of State answered: '. . . what the Council does under Chapter VI in no way affects its powers under Chapter VII, because Chapter VII deals with a situation based on a different set of facts from the set of facts on which the powers of the Security Council are based under Chapter VI.' During the continued discussion the Senator stated: 'In effect I gather from what you say that this provision or application of Chapter VII that is referred to in the report by the Secretary of State to the President on page 84 does not apply to this situation and ought not to be there. This provision reads: 'If however, their

Security Council to be likely to endanger the maintenance of international peace and security.

If non-compliance with a recommendation made under Article 36, paragraph 1, by which the Security Council calls upon the parties to accept a definite procedure or method for the settlement of their dispute, may be considered, under Article 39, by the Security Council as a threat to the peace, the parties may be supposed to be obliged to accept this procedure. If the Security Council recom-

failure to do so results in a threat to the peace, then the enforcement provisions of Chapter VII come into play.' Whereupon the representative of the Department of State declared: ' But that is absolutely correct. If their failure to accept this recommendation results in a situation which is determined by the Security Council to constitute a threat to the peace, it is no longer a situation the continuance of which may threaten the peace, but it is a situation which itself represents a threat to the peace . . . '

There is hardly an objectively ascertainable difference between a ' situation the continuance of which may threaten the peace ' and a ' situation which itself represents a threat to the peace,' or, as the representative of the State Department said on another occasion (p. 285), between a situation which ' may result in a threat to the peace ' and a situation which is ' an actual threat to the peace '; especially if the Security Council is completely free in determining the existence of a threat to the peace, and may consider a situation the continuance of which may threaten the peace or ' result in a threat to the peace ' as a ' threat to the peace.' Besides, the question is not whether Article 39 refers to another situation than Article 37, but whether the Security Council may consider non-compliance with its recommendation a threat to the peace. And this question must be answered in the affirmative. The consequence of this is that the statement in the *Report to the President* (p. 84) that if the parties to a dispute fail to accept the Council's recommendation and the Council considers such failure as a threat to the peace, ' the enforcement provisions of Chapter VII come into play,' is correct. That means that, in the *Report*, action under Chapter VII is coupled with the action under Chapter VI. This is exactly what the Senator maintained. He said with respect to the last-quoted statement of the representative of the State Department: ' They are coupled there. You say they ought not to be coupled, that they are not related to each other. Can you say, then, that the use of military authority which is granted by Chapter VII, is not intended by this treaty to be used to enforce in this indirect way, that is spoken of here on page 84, the recommendation of the Security Council, but is used only for the purpose of preventing hostilities?' Whereupon the representative of the State Department answered: ' I would say that; certainly.' This answer led the Senator to the following statement: ' All right. Let us have the record rest there. That is where I thought it ought to be left. It is not my disposition in asking these questions to develop the fact that this expansion of the authority of the Security Council was intended to combine in the Security Council both the powers of judgment and the powers of execution of the judgment. I think that would be a grave mistake and a step backward instead of forward.' Whereupon the Chairman declared: ' With all due respect to the Secretary and to you, the report to the President could in no wise control the text of the Charter. If there is any conflict, the text of the Charter would govern.'

There can be little doubt that the statement in the *Report to the President*, but not the interpretation of Article 39 by the Senator, with which the representative of the Department of State finally agreed, is in accordance with the text of this Article, and that this Article indeed confers upon the Security Council both the power of judgment and the power of execution of the judgment.

mends submission of the dispute to the International Court, its so-called recommendation has, in view of the possible application of Article 39, almost the same effect as an act by which the Security Council refers the dispute to the Court.[9]

B. *Settlement by the General Assembly*

In Chapter VI of the Charter dealing with the pacific settlement of disputes and the adjustment of other situations, the Security Council is presented as the main non-judicial organ for the performance of the function which the Organisation has in this respect. The General Assembly is mentioned only incidentally in Article 35. But the powers conferred upon the General Assembly in Chapter IV include important functions of that body in this field.

The procedure leading to settlement of disputes or adjustment of other situations by intervention of the General Assembly may be instituted on the initiative of a Member (Article 35 (1)) or a non-member (Article 35 (2)),[1] or on the initiative of the General Assembly itself (Articles 10, 11 (2)), or of the Security Council (Articles 11 (2), 12 (1)); but not on the initiative of the Secretary-General. The answer to the question as to whether states—Members or non-members—in their capacity as parties to a dispute are authorised to bring their dispute before the General Assembly

[9] At the *Hearings* (p. 271) the representative of the Department of State made the above-quoted statement that the Security Council has not the right to order the parties ' to accept a particular method of peaceful settlement.' This statement does not take into consideration the possible application of Article 39. In this respect the following discussion at the *Hearings*, p. 272, is highly illustrative: the Chairman stated: ' Lest there be some misapprehension, somebody spoke about the authority of the Council to compel the states to do something. The suggestion that they adopt these peaceful methods only arises because of their obligation and their promise to do so, but there is no compulsion to make them do these things. Of course, if they don't, and a situation develops which threatens world peace, the quarrel then goes to the Security Council.' The representative of the State Department: ' That is right. The quarrel goes to the Security Council, and even so the Security Council can only recommend at this stage.' The Chairman: ' Oh, yes, it cannot compel them, though.' The representative of the State Department: ' Senator, there is a very important distinction to be kept in mind here. At this stage, the determination of the Security Council is on the subject of whether or not a dispute or a situation is of such a character that its continuance may lead to a threat to the peace or a breach of the peace. At a later stage, or at the next stage to which I will come in a minute, the determination of the Council will be as to whether or not a particular dispute or situation in fact represents a threat to the peace or a breach of the peace, and then the whole action is different. But as long as we are in the stage of determination by the Council as to whether or not the continuance of the situation is likely to lead to a threat to the peace or a breach of the peace that stage involves only the procedures described in Chapter VI under which the Security Council may make various recommendations.'

[1] Until now no case has been brought under Article 35 before the General Assembly. This Article has been used only to bring disputes or other situations before the Security Council.

under Article 33, paragraph 1, depends on the interpretation of this provision discussed above. The answer is in the affirmative it it is assumed that submitting the dispute to the Assembly may be one of the means of the parties' own choice referred to in Article 33, paragraph 1.[2] Such interpretation is possible according to the wording of Article 33, paragraph 1. If it is accepted, then the parties are obliged under Article 37, paragraph 1, to refer the dispute to the Security Council if the action of the General Assembly does not result in a settlement of the dispute; which would amount to an appeal from the General Assembly to the Security Council. It is, however, doubtful whether this interpretation corresponds to the intention of those who drafted the Charter. The idea underlying Article 33, paragraph 1, probably was that the Organisation, not only the Security Council, should not intervene in a dispute before the parties have tried to solve it by means of their own choice (except submission to the Security Council or the General Assembly). Then the obligation to seek first of all solution by means of their own choice refers also to the case that the dispute is brought before the General Assembly. But this interpretation is not quite compatible with Article 37, according to which the parties, if they fail to settle their dispute under Article 33, paragraph 1, are bound to refer it to the Security Council and are not allowed to bring it before the General Assembly. Hence it is hardly possible to maintain that parties to a dispute, before submitting it to the Assembly, must comply with the provision of Article 33, paragraph 1. This provision applies only to disputes brought before the Security Council. Intervention of the General Assembly may be brought about immediately after a dispute has arisen.[3] Nor is an obligation imposed upon the parties to a

[2] In the study on Article 11, paragraph 1, and Article 13, paragraph 1 (*a*), of the Charter, prepared by the Secretariat for the Interim Committee of the General Assembly (Doc. A/AC 18/33, p. 11), it is stated that 'a dispute, or situation, might be put before it [the General Assembly] under Article 33, as a "means of their own choice".' But Article 33 refers only to 'disputes,' not to 'situations.' In the Memorandum concerning the Use by Organs of the United Nations of Measures and Procedures of Pacific Settlement, prepared by the Secretariat for the Interim Committee (Doc. A/AC 18/61, p. 15), Article 33 is not mentioned among the Articles of the Charter under which a question may be brought before the General Assembly.

[3] The Memorandum of the Secretariat (Doc. A/AC 18/61, p. 15) contains the following statement: 'In certain instances reference has been made to peaceful means of settlement which have been adopted before resort to the General Assembly. (i) Treatment of Indians in the Union of South Africa: Second part of the first session (A/68, A/68/Add. 1, A/68/Add. 2, A/149, A/167 and A/167/Add. 1) (*Negotiations*). Second session (A/373 and A/387) (*Negotiations*). (ii) The problem of the independence of Korea: Second session (A/C.1/218 and A/C.1/SR 88) (*Negotiations*). (iii) Relations of Members of the United Nations with Spain: Second part of the first session (A/177, A/C.1/24 and A/C.1/128) (*Consideration by the Security Council*). Second session (A/C.1/SR. 104 and A/C.1/SR 105) (*Consideration by the Security Council*). (iv) Threats to the political independence

29 (2)

dispute—Members or non-members—to refer the dispute in case they fail to settle it by the means indicated in Article 33, paragraph 1, to the Assembly. Article 37, paragraph 1, applies only to the Security Council, not to the General Assembly.

Under Article 35, paragraph 2, only non-members may as parties to a dispute bring this dispute to the attention of the General Assembly. Under Article 35, paragraph 1, a Member of the United Nations may bring to the attention of the General Assembly any dispute and hence also a dispute to which it is a party. In the same way, a Member may bring to the attention of the General Assembly any situation which might lead to international friction or give rise to a dispute, even a situation in which it is itself involved. That a Member or non-member may bring a dispute under Article 35 before the General Assembly is not consistent with the obligation of the parties to the dispute to refer the case, if they are not able to settle it by means of their own choice, to the Security Council and not to the General Assembly; even if it is assumed that the parties themselves may, as a means of their own choice, bring the dispute before the General Assembly under Article 33, paragraph 1.

The provision of Article 35 authorising Members to bring any dispute and other ' situations ' of a dangerous nature, and authorising non-members to bring disputes to which they are parties, to the attention of the General Assembly is paralleled by the provision of Article 11, paragraph 2: ' The General Assembly may discuss any questions relating to the maintenance of international peace and security brought before it by any Member of the United Nations, or by the Security Council, or by a state which is not a Member of the United Nations in accordance with Article 35, paragraph 2.' ' Questions relating to the maintenance of international peace and security ' comprise certainly disputes as well as other situations.[4] In Article 11, paragraph 2, only Article 35, paragraph 2 is referred to, authorising non-members to bring disputes to which they are parties to the attention of the General Assembly; not Article 35, paragraph 1, authorising Members to bring disputes and situations of a dangerous nature to the attention of the Assembly. This may be interpreted to mean that non-members may bring before the Assembly not only disputes and situations of a dangerous nature under Article 35,

and territorial integrity of Greece: Second session (A/C.1/191, A/C.1/SR. 60, A/C.1/SR. 61 and A/C.1/SR. 62) (*Consideration by the Security Council*). Only the cases mentioned under (i) and (ii) are of interest in this connection.

[4] At the *Hearings*, p. 246, the representative of the State Department, said with reference to the meaning of the term ' questions ' in Article 11, paragraph 2: ' These questions, as will be seen from a later article, relate not only to actual disputes, but they relate also to situations the continuance of which may threaten the peace. may lead to disputes, or may lead to international friction. Any such question can be brought to the attention of the General Assembly, and the General Assembly may discuss any such question.'

paragraph 1, but also other ' questions relating to the maintenance of international peace and security,' especially situations which are not of the nature referred to in Article 34. These other ' questions ' may be brought by Members before the General Assembly, not under Article 35, paragraph 1, but directly under Article 11, paragraph 2, since no other provision of the Charter authorises Members to bring such matters before the General Assembly.[5]

Article 11, paragraph 2, authorises also the Security Council to bring ' questions relating to the maintenance of international peace and security ' before the General Assembly. This provision is paralleled by the provision of Article 12, paragraph 1, authorising the Security Council to ' request ' the General Assembly to make recommendations with regard to any dispute or situation in respect of which the Council is exercising ' the functions assigned to it in the present Charter.' These are the functions determined in Chapter VI of the Charter. That the authorisation of the Security Council laid down in Article 11, paragraph 2, is different from the authorisation laid down in Article 12, paragraph 1, may be assumed because the latter is not referred to in the former. Article 12, paragraph 1, refers only to disputes and other situations with respect to which the Security Council is exercising its jurisdiction; Article 11, paragraph 2, refers to all ' questions relating to the maintenance of international peace and security.' Under Article 12, paragraph 1, the Security Council may only bring a dispute or another situation before the General Assembly ' while ' the Council is exercising in respect to this dispute or situation the functions assigned to it in the Charter, and only in requesting the General Assembly to make recommendations with regard to the dispute or situation. Under Article 11, paragraph 2, the Security Council may bring before the Assembly, disputes and situations in respect to which it is not actually exercising the functions

[5] The conflict between India and the Union of South Africa concerning the treatment of Indians was brought before the General Assembly by a letter of the Indian delegation to the Secretary-General, dated June 22, 1946, requesting ' that the question of the treatment of Indians in the Union of South Africa be included in the provisional agenda for the second part of the first session of the General Assembly.' (Doc. A/149.) At the 19th meeting of the General Committee the delegate of India declared: ' The delegation of India did not call upon the Assembly to intervene in a dispute arising out of the treatment of Indians in South Africa; it insisted that the question should be discussed by the Assembly.' (Journal of the United Nations, No. 15; Suppl. B-A/BUR/35, p. 6.) This statement was made to meet the argument of the representative of the Union of South Africa that the matter was essentially within the domestic jurisdiction of that state and hence Article 2, paragraph 7, applicable, according to which the Members are not required ' to submit such matters to settlement under the present Charter.' The statement of the Indian delegate presupposes that matters to be submitted to settlement under the Charter must be disputes. (Cf. *supra* p. 452). The Indian delegate also maintained that the matter was not a question ' that concerned two countries only ' but ' a world problem,' and that it was ' not a legal ' but a ' political ' question. (Journal of the United Nations, No. 40; Suppl. Nos. 1 & 6-A/C 186/1, p. 3.)

assigned to it by the Charter, and other questions of the nature determined in Article 11, paragraph 2, not being disputes or 'situations'; and under this provision the Security Council may bring before the Assembly, disputes and other situations without requesting the Assembly to make recommendations.

The procedure leading to settlement of disputes or adjustment of situations may be instituted not only on the initiative of Members and non-members and of the Security Council; but also on the initiative of the General Assembly itself. This is possible under Articles 10 and 14.

Article 10 authorises the General Assembly to discuss 'any questions or any matters within the scope of the present Charter' and to make recommendations 'on any such questions or matters.' That these 'questions or matters' include 'disputes' and other 'situations' may be concluded not only from the fact that in Article 11, paragraph 2, by the term 'questions,' without any doubt, 'disputes' and 'situations' are meant; but also from the fact that Article 10 restricts the power of the General Assembly to make recommendations on the 'questions or matters' by referring to Article 12, which deals with the settlement of disputes and adjustment of situations by the Security Council. Since Article 10 does not restrict the power of the General Assembly to discuss questions or matters within the scope of the Charter to those brought before the Assembly from the outside, the latter may, under this Article, discuss any dispute or any other situation brought before it on its own initiative and make recommendations on such dispute or situation.

The wording of Article 14 may be interpreted in the same way, namely, 'subject to the provisions of Article 12' (which deals with the settlement of disputes and adjustment of other situations), 'the General Assembly may recommend measures for the peaceful adjustment of any situation, regardless of origin'; 'any situation' includes 'disputes,' and making recommendations includes discussion. The nature of the situation is characterised by the formula, 'which it [the General Assembly] deems likely to impair the general welfare or friendly relations among nations, including situations resulting from a violation of the provisions of the present Charter setting forth the Purposes and Principles of the United Nations.' Situations of this nature certainly include 'situations which might lead to international friction or give rise to a dispute,' which the Security Council under Article 34 is authorised to investigate. Like Article 10, Article 14 does not determine the way in which the situation is to be brought before the General Assembly in order that the Assembly may discuss it and make a recommendation on it. Hence the General Assembly may take the action determined in Article 14 on its own initiative.[6]

[6] At the *Hearings*, p. 253, the representative of the Department of State advocated the following interpretation of Article 14: 'Article 14 relates to those situations which do not involve a possible violation or possible impairment of international

What action is the General Assembly authorised to take with respect to disputes and other situations which are, in accordance with Articles 10, 11 or 14, under its consideration? It has the power to discuss these disputes and situations and to make recommendations on them.[7] As pointed out, the Charter does not confer upon the

peace or security. Article 14 relates to the situations which involve impairment of the general welfare or friendly relations among nations. Situations which involve the possible impairment of international peace and security are dealt with in the earlier articles; that is, Articles 11 and 12, and particularly in numbered paragraph 2 of Article 11, where the General Assembly can make recommendations regarding situations which may involve the maintenance of international peace and security, but only under the conditions which are described in Article 12 and subject to the provisions that questions on which action is necessary should be referred to the Security Council.' According to this interpretation, the phrase 'impair the general welfare or friendly relations among nations' does not comprise 'endanger international peace and security' or 'threat to the peace.' But how can Article 14 in relating to situations which involve impairment of the general welfare or friendly relations among nations, not relate to 'situations which involve the possible violation or possible impairment of international peace and security,' if it expressly stipulates that situations 'likely to impair the general welfare or friendly relations among nations' include 'situations resulting from a violation of the provisions of the present Charter setting forth the Purposes and Principles of the United Nations,' among which the obligation is established to refrain from threat of use of force? Is 'threat or use of force' not an impairment or violation of peace and security?

[7] The resolution adopted by the General Assembly at its 52nd plenary meeting, in the case of the treatment of Indians in South Africa, runs as follows:

> The General Assembly, having taken note of the application made by the Government of India regarding the treatment of Indians in the Union of South Africa, and having considered the matter:
>
> 1. States that, because of that treatment, friendly relations between the two Member States have been impaired and, unless a satisfactory settlement is reached, these relations are likely to be further impaired;
>
> 2. Is of the opinion that the treatment of Indians in the Union should be in conformity with the international obligations under the agreements concluded between the two Governments and the relevant provisions of the Charter;
>
> 3. Therefore requests the two Governments to report at the next session of the General Assembly the measures adopted to this effect. (A/64/Add. 1, p. 69.)

It is doubtful whether the formulation of this resolution is in conformity with the Charter, which authorises the General Assembly to make recommendations, not to express an 'opinion' or to 'request' something.

The Greek question, after having been taken off the list of matters with which the Council was seized (cf. *supra*, pp. 249, 268) was placed on the agenda of the General Assembly. The item was submitted by the delegation of the United States as 'threats to the political independence and territorial integrity of Greece.' (Doc. A/344.) At its 167th meeting on November 27, 1948, the General Assembly adopted the following resolution:

> The General Assembly,
>
> 1. Having considered the reports of the Special Committee established by General Assembly resolution 109 (II),

General Assembly by a special provision, analogous to that of Article 34, the power of investigating the disputes or other situations with respect

2. Having noted the conclusions of the Special Committee and, in particular, its unanimous conclusion that, despite the aforesaid resolution of the General Assembly, 'the Greek guerillas have continued to receive aid and assistance on a large scale from Albania, Bulgaria and Yugoslavia, with the knowledge of the Governments of those countries' and that the Greek guerillas in the frontier zones have, as found by the Special Committee:

(1) 'Been largely dependent on external supply. Great quantities of arms, ammunition and other military stores have come across the border, notably during times of heavy fighting. Strongly held positions of the guerillas have protected their vital supply lines from Bulgaria, Yugoslavia and, in particular, from Albania. In recent months, there has been less evidence of receipt of supplies from Yugoslavia by the guerillas.

(2) Frequently moved at will in territory across the frontier for tactical reasons, and have thus been able to concentrate their forces without interference by the Greek Army, and to return to Greece when they wished.

(3) Frequently retired safely into the territory of Albania, Bulgaria and Yugoslavia when the Greek Army exerted great pressure.'

3. Having noted further the conclusions of the Special Committee that a continuation of this situation 'constitutes a threat to the political independence and territorial integrity of Greece and to peace in the Balkans' and 'that the conduct of Albania, Bulgaria and Yugoslavia has been inconsistent with the purposes and principles of the Charter of the United Nations';

4. Having noted the recommendations submitted by the Special Committee;

5. Considers that the continued aid given by Albania, Bulgaria and Yugoslavia to the Greek guerillas endangers peace in the Balkans, and is inconsistent with the purposes and principles of the Charter of the United Nations;

6. Calls upon Albania, Bulgaria and Yugoslavia to cease forthwith rendering any assistance or support in any form to the guerillas in fighting against the Greek Government, including the use of their territories as a base for the preparation or launching of armed action;

7. Again calls upon Albania, Bulgaria and Yugoslavia to co-operate with Greece in the settlement of their dispute by peaceful means in accordance with the recommendations contained in resolution 109 (II);

8. Calls upon Albania, Bulgaria and Yugoslavia to co-operate with the Special Committee in enabling it to carry out its functions, in particular the functions of being available to assist the Governments concerned in accordance with paragraph 10 (*c*) of this resolution, and upon Greece to continue to co-operate toward the same end;

9. Recommends to all Members of the United Nations and to all other States that their Governments refrain from any action designed to assist directly or through any other Government any armed group fighting against the Greek Government;

10. Approves the reports of the Special Committee, continues it in being with the functions conferred upon it by resolution 109 (II) and instructs it;

(*a*) To continue to observe and report on the response of Albania, Bulgaria and Yugoslavia to the General Assembly injunction not to

to which it is authorised to make recommendations. But some kind of investigation is necessary in order to make such recommendations under Articles 10, 11 or 14, and to ascertain, under Article 10, whether the dispute or other situation is 'within the scope of the present Charter'; under Article 11, paragraph 2, whether there is a relation of the dispute or the other situation to the maintenance of international peace and security or whether action is necessary on the dispute or the situation; and under Article 14, whether the situation is likely to impair the general welfare or friendly relations among nations, especially whether the situation results from a violation of the provisions of the Charter setting forth the Purposes and Principles of the United Nations. Under Article 22 the General Assembly may even establish a subsidiary organ, a special committee for instance, authorised to examine the matter under consideration by the Assembly and to report to the latter. But the power of the Assembly does not go so far as does the power of the Security Council under Article 34, for the decisions of the Assembly are not binding upon the Members. As pointed out, the Charter does not contain a provision referring to decisions of the General Assembly analogous to the one of Article 25, referring to the decisions of the Security Council.

As to the content of the recommendations to be made with

> furnish aid to the Greek guerillas in accordance with the General Assembly resolution 109 (II) and the present resolution;
>
> (*b*) To continue to utilise observation groups with personnel and equipment adequate for the fulfilment of its task;
>
> (*c*) To continue to be available to assist the Governments of Albania, Bulgaria, Greece and Yugoslavia in the implementation of resolution 109 (II) and of the present resolution; and for this purpose, in its discretion to appoint, and utilise the services and good offices of, one or more persons whether or not members of the Special Committee;
>
> 11. Decides that the Special Committee shall have its principal headquarters in Greece, and with the co-operation of the Government or Governments concerned, shall perform its functions in such places as it may deem appropriate for the fulfilment of its mission;
>
> 12. Authorises the Special Committee to consult, in its discretion, with the Interim Committee (if it is continued) with respect to the performance of its functions in the light of developments;
>
> 13. Requests the Secretary-General to provide the Special Committee with adequate staff and facilities to enable it to perform its functions. (Doc. A/728, pp. 11 ff.; A/P.V./167, pp. 91 f.)

In so far as paragraph 3 of this resolution amounts to the determination of a threat to the peace, its constitutionality is doubtful. It is the Security Council, and not the General Assembly, which is authorised by Article 39 of the Charter to determine the existence of a threat to the peace. In paragraphs 6, 7 and 8, the General Assembly 'calls upon' Albania, Bulgaria and Yugoslavia, but in paragraph 9 'recommends' to 'all Members of the United Nations.' If by 'calling upon' a function is to be understood which shall have more legal effect than a 'recommendation,' the paragraphs 6, 7 and 8, of the resolution, are hardly compatible with the provisions of the Charter determining the competence of the General Assembly.

respect to the disputes or other situations under its consideration, the General Assembly is less restricted than the Security Council. The Council is authorised in Chapter VI to recommend terms of settlement only with respect to disputes, not with respect to other situations, and with respect to disputes only when they have been referred to it by the parties under Article 37 or Article 38, and in case of Article 37 if it deems that the continuance of the dispute is likely to endanger the peace. In all other cases the Security Council has only the power to recommend ' appropriate procedures or methods of adjustment ' and this under the condition that the continuance of the dispute or of the other situation is likely to endanger the peace. The power of the Security Council is unrestricted with respect to the content of its recommendations only with respect to recommendations made under Article 39, after having determined the existence of a threat to, or breach of, the peace. The General Assembly, however, may recommend terms of settlement or adjustment with respect to any dispute and any other situation which is under its consideration, especially with respect to disputes or other situations for which the Security Council is not authorised to make recommendations. Except under Article 38, the Security Council may make recommendations only for disputes or other situations the continuance of which is likely to endanger the maintenance of the peace (Article 36, paragraph 1, Article 37, paragraph 2). The General Assembly may make recommendations even if the continuance of the dispute or situation is not likely to endanger the maintenance of the peace. If the General Assembly acts under Article 10, the only requirement is that the dispute or the situation is within the scope of the Charter, and almost any dispute and any situation may be considered from one or another angle as being within the scope of the Charter. If the General Assembly acts under Article 14, the situation (including disputes) must be ' likely to impair the general welfare or friendly relations among nations.' Under this Article the Assembly is authorised only to ' recommend measures for the peaceful adjustment.' This restriction does not apply if the Assembly acts under Article 10. Under this Article the General Assembly may recommend to the Security Council to take enforcement measures. But if the Assembly acts under Article 11, paragraph 2, its power to make recommendations is restricted by the provision that, if the dispute or the situation is of a nature to make action necessary, the Assembly shall refer it to the Security Council either before or after discussion. It may discuss the dispute or the situation, but it must not make any recommendation on it. The meaning of the term ' action ' has been discussed in another connection.[8]

In another respect the power of the General Assembly to make recommendations for the settlement of disputes or the adjustment of

[8] Cf. *supra*, pp. 204 f.

other situations, as compared with the same power of the Security Council, is restricted in so far as the Assembly is authorised to make recommendations under Article 10 or Article 11, paragraph 2, only to the states concerned (Members under Article 10; Members and non-members under Article 11, paragraph 2), or to the Security Council, or to both, whereas the Charter contains no restriction with respect to the addressee of the recommendations to be made by the Security Council. As far as the General Assembly itself is supposed to settle the dispute or to adjust the situation by its recommendations, only recommendations to the states concerned—parties to the dispute or involved in the situation not having the character of a dispute—come into consideration. Hence the restriction is of no importance. Besides, it does not apply to recommendations the General Assembly may make under Article 14.

The legal effect of the recommendations made by the General Assembly is the same as that of the recommendations made by the Security Council. They are not binding unless the Security Council considers non-compliance with a recommendation made by the Assembly as a threat to the peace under Article 39. There is a difference only in so far as the General Assembly has not the power which the Security Council does have: to enforce its own recommendations. In case the General Assembly has made a recommendation with a view to the settlement of a dispute and the parties do not comply with the recommendation, they remain under the obligation of Article 33, paragraph 1, to seek solution by means of their own choice, and if they fail to settle their dispute in this way to refer it, under Article 37, paragraph 1, to the Security Council. The question as to whether the parties may submit their dispute under Article 33, paragraph 1, to the General Assembly, has been discussed in another connection.

It is rather strange that if a Member or non-member brings a dispute before the General Assembly under Article 35, the latter may recommend terms of settlement, but if the Member or non-member brings the same dispute before the Security Council, the latter can only recommend procedures or methods. The same difference exists between a procedure instituted by the General Assembly on its own initiative, and a procedure instituted by the Security Council on its own initiative. It may be doubted whether these differences have been deliberately established or are the unintentional effect of the wording of the Articles concerned.

Other differences between the procedure in the General Assembly and that in the Security Council are: that in making recommendations the latter, but not the former, has to 'take into consideration any procedures for the settlement of the dispute which have already been adopted by the parties,' and 'that legal disputes should as a general rule be referred by the parties to the International Court of Justice.'

For Article 36, paragraphs 2 and 3, which contain these provisions, refer only to the Security Council, not to the General Assembly. This means that the General Assembly is even less prevented than the Security Council from intervening in a dispute for which the parties have already adopted a procedure for its settlement and from making recommendations for disputes which have a legal character.

An important difference consists in that if a non-member state is a party to a dispute under consideration by the General Assembly, it is not entitled to be invited to participate in the discussion relating to the dispute. There is no provision analogous to that of Article 32 referring to the Security Council that applies to the General Assembly. But when a non-member under Article 35, paragraph 2, brings to the attention of the General Assembly a dispute to which it is a party, it must accept in advance, for the purposes of the dispute, the obligations of pacific settlement provided in the Charter. This is all the more regrettable as, if it is a dispute between a Member and a non-member, the former is represented on the General Assembly and may participate not only in the discussion but also in the voting. For Article 27, paragraph 3, excluding the parties to a dispute from voting, applies only to the procedure in the Security Council, not to that in the General Assembly; which is the most striking difference in the procedures of the two bodies for the settlement of disputes.[9]

[9] At its 91st meeting on September 23, 1947, the General Assembly referred the question of 'Threat to the political independence and territorial integrity of Greece,' submitted by the delegation of the United States, to the First Committee for consideration and report. (Doc. A/409.) In letters addressed to the Secretary-General, the government of Bulgaria asked to be granted a hearing in the General Assembly, the government of Albania to be invited to participate in all the debates of the General Assembly on the Greek question. (Doc. A/C.1/190, 192.) In a letter dated September 25, 1947 (Doc. A/C.1/193) the President of the General Assembly advised the First Committee 'to allow representatives of Bulgaria and Albania to be heard on the question of "Threats to the Political Independence and Territorial Integrity of Greece," since this question has been referred to the First Committee for its consideration and report to the General Assembly.' Pursuant to this advice, the First Committee adopted at its 60th meeting on September 25, 1947, the following resolution: 'The First Committee enquires of the representatives of Albania and Bulgaria if their Governments are prepared to accept the principles and provisions of the Charter in the settlement of the Greek question.' (Doc. A/C. 1/194). In their answers the governments of Bulgaria and Albania declared that although they in general were willing to respect the principles of the Charter, they refused to make a declaration to this effect as a condition of their invitation to participate in the discussion of the Greek question. Thereupon the First Committee adopted at its 62nd meeting the following resolution: 'The Governments of Albania and Bulgaria having failed to furnish a satisfactory reply to the request made to them by the First Committee, the latter has decided to hear the statements of the Bulgarian and Albanian delegations on the Greek question and requests them to place themselves at the disposal of the Committee in order to reply to any questions which may be put to them.' (Doc. A/C.1/200.) After the two Governments accepted the invitation, they were invited to state their views at the 64th meeting of the First Committee. (Doc. A/409, p. 1.)

Another provision concerning the procedure in the Security Council, which has no analogy in the procedure of the General

The constitutionality of the decision of the First Committee, adopted at its 60th meeting, by which an attempt was made to apply by analogy the provision of Article 32 referring to the procedure in the Security Council to the procedure in the First Committee of the General Assembly, is highly problematical. Less problematical is the constitutionality of the decisions adopted in the 62nd meeting of the First Committee, although it has no legal basis in the Charter or in the Rules of Procedures of the General Assembly. It implies the application, by analogy, of Rule 39 of the Rules of Procedure of the Security Council.

In the Palestine question, the representative of Poland proposed a resolution of the General Assembly to the effect 'to invite representatives of the Jewish Agency for Palestine to appear before the plenary meeting of the General Assembly for the purpose of stating their views on this question.' He justified his proposal as follows: 'We do not find anywhere in the rules of procedure, nor especially in the Charter, any rule to prohibit the hearing of the Jewish Agency or any other representatives before any organs of the General Assembly. The lack of such a prohibition would be quite sufficient to justify the adoption of the resolution proposed by the Polish delegation, as amended by the Czechoslovak delegation. However, the Charter goes much further. Articles 71 and 80 allow the hearing of representatives of non-governmental bodies whenever that may be required, and the hearing may take place before the General Assembly.' The principle: what is not prohibited is permitted, applies to subjects, not to organs of a community which are allowed to do only what they are authorised to do. Article 71 authorises the Economic and Social Council 'to make suitable arrangements for consultation with non-governmental organisations.' It is doubtful whether 'consultation' includes the appearing of representatives before the meeting of the Council. In any case, the fact that the Charter confers expressly upon the Economic and Social Council a power which it does not confer upon the General Assembly leads to a conclusion just contrary to that of the Polish delegate. The representative of the United States quite correctly stated: 'How many times have we heard that there is no authority expressed in the Charter and no prohibition expressed in the Charter to permit the discussion of issues in this Assembly by non-members? Therefore, it has been maintained that, since it is not prohibited, we can invite anybody we desire and give them the same privileges, the same duties which Member States have under the Charter. The Charter does not grant that.' He added: 'I think we are agreed on the premise that there is nothing in the Charter that expressly or implicitly prohibits, and nothing in the Charter that expressly or implicitly authorises the reception of witnesses in the General Assembly, the invitation to guests to appear in this, the greatest parliamentary body in all the world. We are agreed upon that.' Even the reception of witnesses or the 'invitation to guests to appear' in the General Assembly has no basis in the Charter. Finally the General Assembly adopted at its 75th meeting the following resolution: '(1) that the First Committee grant a hearing to the Jewish Agency for Palestine on the question before the Committee; (2) To send to that same Committee for its decision those other communications of a similar character from the Palestinian population which have been received by this special session of the General Assembly or may later be submitted to it.' (Official Records of the First Special Session of the General Assembly, Vol. I, pp. 70–115.) The First Committee proposed to the President of the General Assembly to consider the following resolution: 'That the First Committee grant a hearing to the Arab Higher Committee on the question before the Committee,' whereupon the General Assembly at its 76th meeting adopted the resolution: 'The General Assembly affirms that the decision of the First Committee to grant a hearing to the Arab Higher Committee gives a correct

Assembly, is that of Article 24, paragraph 2: that the Security Council, in discharging its duties, shall act in accordance with the Purposes and Principles of the United Nations. It is the provision of Article 1, paragraph 1, to bring about 'in conformity with the principles of justice and international law' adjustment or settlement of international disputes or situations, which refers to the duties here in question. This difference is hardly of any importance, since the provision of Article 1, paragraph 1, applies to the functions of the General Assembly as well as to those of the Security Council without any other special provision being necessary, and its application is, as pointed out, of problematical value.

Finally it may be noted that the General Assembly has no power analogous to that conferred upon the Security Council by Article 94, paragraph 2, to make recommendations for a dispute in case the latter has been decided by a judgment of the International Court of Justice and one party fails to perform the obligations incumbent upon it under the judgment, whereupon the other party has recourse to the Security Council. No such recourse to the General Assembly is possible.

The jurisdictions which the General Assembly and the Security Council have with respect to the settlement of disputes and the adjustment of other situations are, to a great extent, concurrent. To avoid conflicts between the two organs of the United Nations is the purpose of the provision laid down in Article 12, which has been analysed in a previous part of this study.[1]

interpretation of the Assembly's intention.' (*Ibid.*, pp. 115–116.) It is doubtful whether the General Assembly is authorised to confer upon one of its committees a power the Assembly itself does not have.

During the discussion of the problem of Korean independence, the delegate of the Soviet Union proposed that elected representatives of the Korean people should take part in the discussion of the question in the First Committee and in the General Assembly. (Doc. A/C.1/S.R.87, p. 4; A/C.1/229.) Other delegates supported this proposition, referring to the precedent in the Palestinian question. (Doc. A/C.1/S.R.88, p. 1; A/C.1/S.R.89, p. 5.) The reasons why the First Committee did not accept the Soviet propositions were not constitutional considerations, but the practical impossibility to find true representatives of the Korean people. (Statements of the delegate of the United Kingdom (Doc. A/C.1/S.R.88, p. 2), of the United States delegate (Doc. A/C.1/S.R.89, p. 4).)

[1] Cf. *supra*, pp. 216 ff.

CHAPTER 15

JUDICIAL SETTLEMENT OF DISPUTES (THE INTERNATIONAL COURT OF JUSTICE)

1. GENERAL REMARKS

THERE are in principle two different ways to settle an international dispute; agreement of the parties to the dispute, or decision by an international agency. Negotiation, enquiry, mediation, and conciliation, referred to in Article 33, paragraph 1, of the Charter, lead to the settlement of a dispute only if they bring about an agreement of the parties. Such agreement may be constituted by the fact that both parties accept the recommendation made by a commission of conciliation with respect to the settlement of the dispute. If the recommendation, which is not binding upon the parties, is not accepted by both of them, the dispute remains unsettled.

It is by its binding force that the decision of an international agency, to which the parties have submitted their dispute, is distinguished from other procedures for the settlement of disputes. These agencies have the character of tribunals if their members have the character of judges. They are judges only if they are independent, that is to say, if they are not bound by instructions from—and consequently are not representatives of—the states—or any other authority—by which they are appointed. They are bound only by the law which they are to apply according to the treaty by which the tribunal has been established, or by which the disputes are submitted to the tribunal. The latter may apply other norms than those of positive international law only if it is expressly authorised to do so. It is a typical element of an international tribunal that its decisions, binding upon the parties, are to be taken by a majority vote if the tribunal is composed of more than two members.

Article 33, paragraph 1, of the Charter, distinguishes between 'arbitration' and 'judicial settlement.' This was the terminology of Articles 12 and 13 of the Covenant of the League of Nations. There, 'judicial settlement' meant settlement by the Permanent Court of International Justice, whereas 'arbitration' meant settlement by other international tribunals. Since the words 'arbitration' and 'judicial settlement' in Article 33, paragraph 1, are taken over from the Covenant of the League, and under the Charter the Permanent Court of International Justice is substituted by the International Court of Justice, 'judicial settlement' in Article 33, paragraph 1, of the Charter, may be interpreted to mean—according to the intention of those who drafted this paragraph—decisions of the International Court of Justice, whereas 'arbitration' decisions by other international tribunals. This terminology is not correct. ' Arbitration,' too, has the character of ' judicial settlement,' that is to say, settlement by a judge or a body of judges binding upon the parties. The differentiation between arbitration and judicial settlement, as made in the Covenant and in the Charter, is not intended to refer to the function of the tribunals but to their organisation. By arbitration usually the decision of a tribunal is understood which is established, at least partly, by the parties to a dispute, only for the settlement of this single dispute, and only after this dispute has arisen. Judicial settlement, in the specific sense of the term as used in the Covenant, signified the decision of a tribunal established not, or not directly, by the parties, and not only for a single dispute after it has arisen, but for an unlimited number of future disputes—either all disputes or a certain category of disputes—and, hence, for an unlimited or relatively lasting period of time. Such a permanent or relatively permanent tribunal may or may not be a collegiate organ, and may or may not be called a ' court.' As a matter of fact, the only tribunal of this kind during the period of the League was the Permanent Court of International Justice. But the Charter does not prevent the Members from establishing, by treaties, true permanent courts other than the International Court of Justice and from submitting their disputes to such courts. Article 95 expressly authorises the Members to entrust the solution of their differences to tribunals other than the International Court of Justice. If according to the intention of the legislator, ' judicial settlement ' in Article 33, paragraph 1, is to be interpreted to mean decisions by the International Court of Justice, by ' arbitration ' are to be understood not only decisions of *ad hoc* tribunals or arbitration but also decisions of true permanent courts, provided such courts are actually established by Members of the United Nations. Hence the differentiation between arbitration and judicial settlement in Article 33, paragraph 1, is hardly justifiable.

Between the type of an *ad hoc* tribunal of arbitration and the type of a true permanent court there are some intermediate types—just as there are intermediate types between tribunals of arbitration and commissions of conciliation—such as a body composed not of judges but of true representatives of the appointing states, whose decisions are binding upon the parties which have submitted their dispute to that body.

In so far as the recommendations of terms of settlement made by the Security Council or by the General Assembly are not binding upon the parties to the dispute, the function of the two bodies has the character of conciliation. In so far as these recommendations are considered to be binding because non-compliance may entail enforcement action, the function of the Security Council, as well as that of the General Assembly, lies midway between conciliation and arbitration. Neither the Council nor the Assembly, in settling a dispute by a decision, even if binding upon the parties, has the character of an international tribunal, because the individuals who, in their capacity as representatives of the Members of the United Nations, form the two bodies, are not ' judges '; and they are not judges because they are not independent but bound by instructions of their governments.

The permanent tribunal established by the Charter under the name of International Court of Justice, is an organ of the United Nations; the Statute of the Court forms an integral part of the Charter (Article 92). Consequently, all Members of the United Nations are parties to the Statute, since they are parties to the Charter. The express provision of Article 93, paragraph 1: ' All Members of the United Nations are *ipso facto* parties to the Statute of the International Court of Justice,' is superfluous. The Members would be parties to the Statute also without this provision.

In this respect there exists a difference between the Charter and the Covenant. The latter only authorised the Council to prepare the statute of a court; and this Statute was an international agreement different from the Covenant: the Protocol of Signature of the Statute of the Permanent Court of International Justice, Geneva, December 16, 1920, to which the Statute of the Court was adjoined. Consequently, parties to the Covenant were not necessarily parties to the Statute; and parties to the Statute were not necessarily Members of the League of Nations. The Permanent Court of International Justice, created under the auspices of the League of Nations, was legally not an organ of this organisation, but of another organisation, different from the League though in connection with it; the Permanent Court of International Justice was the only organ of the community constituted by the Protocol of Signature of December 16, 1920.

The Statute of the International Court of Justice is an almost literal copy of the Statute of the Permanent Court of International Justice. Article 92 of the Charter states expressly that the Statute of the International Court of Justice ' is based upon the Statute of the Permanent Court of International Justice.' This statement of a fact is superfluous, since the fact has no legal consequences.[1]

[1] The Summary Report of the 13th meeting of Committee IV/1 (U.N.C.I.O. Doc. 615, IV/1/45, p. 1) contains the following statement with respect to the phrase of Article 92 indicating that the Statute of the International Court of Justice is based on the Statute of the Permanent Court of International Justice: ' The view was expressed that the proposal merely states a historical fact and might give rise to confusion. Others thought that in view of the general desire to perpetuate the jurisprudence of the old Court, and of the number of delegations which favoured legal continuity of the old Court, the paragraph was desirable.' The new Court is certainly not bound to interpret provisions of the new Statute identical with those of the old Statute, in the same way as the Permanent Court did. It may do so; but this possibility exists also without the statement that the new Statute is based upon the old one.

As the legal problems resulting from the Statute of the International Court of Justice are, to a great extent, identical with those of the Statute for the Permanent Court of International Justice on which an abundant literature exists, in the following only those provisions are discussed in detail which are new or which give cause to criticism.

2. The Organisation of the Court

A. *The Election of the Judges*

The organisation of the International Court of Justice is almost the same as that of the Permanent Court of International Justice. Only a few unimportant changes have been made. It may be doubted whether the new title is better than the old one. Since justice is not identical with law, it is misleading to call a tribunal a court of ' justice ' if the tribunal is bound by its statute to decide the disputes submitted to it ' in accordance with international law '; an express provision of Article 38, paragraph 1, of the new Statute, not contained in the old one. A tribunal is international because it has been established by an international agreement and has to apply international law. Hence it may be called an international tribunal as well as a tribunal of international law. It is, however, an improvement that the word ' permanent ' has been dropped. By being called ' permanent ' the old Court could not be prevented to exist only during the short period between two world wars.

The new Court shall consist, just as the old one, of fifteen judges under a President and a Vice-President, elected by the members of the Court from their midst (Articles 3, 21). The members of the Court are elected by the Security Council and the General Assembly of the United Nations, just as the members of the Permanent Court of International Justice were elected by the Council and the Assembly of the League of Nations. Each candidate must obtain an absolute majority of votes in the General Assembly and in the Security Council (Article 10, paragraph 1). In electing the judges, the permanent members of the Security Council have no right of veto (Article 10, paragraph 2); but the states represented on the Security Council have a double vote since they are also represented on the General Assembly. The members of the Court shall be elected from a list of persons nominated in the same way as the candidates were nominated under the old Statute. It is a list of persons nominated by the ' national groups ' in the Permanent Court of Arbitration, established by the Hague Convention of 1907. In this respect, Article 44 of the Convention for the Pacific Settlement of International Disputes, signed at The Hague, October 18, 1907, stipulates:

> Each contracting power selects four persons at the most, of known competence in questions of international law, of the highest moral reputation, and disposed to accept the duties of arbitrator.

> The persons thus selected are inscribed, as members of the court, in a list which shall be notified to all the contracting powers by the bureau.
>
> Any alteration in the list of arbitrators is brought by the bureau to the knowledge of the contracting powers.
>
> Two or more powers may agree on the selection in common of one or more members.
>
> The same person can be selected by different powers.
>
> The members of the court are appointed for a term of six years. These appointments are renewable.
>
> Should a member of the court die or resign, the same procedure is followed for filling the vacancy as was followed for appointing him. In this case the appointment is made for a fresh period of six years.

Since not all Members of the United Nations are parties to the Convention for the Pacific Settlement of International Disputes of 1907, Article 4, paragraph 2, of the Statute provides:

> In the case of Members of the United Nations not represented in the Permanent Court of Arbitration, candidates shall be nominated by national groups appointed for this purpose by their governments under the same conditions as those prescribed for members of the Permanent Court of Arbitration by Article 44 of the Covention of the Hague of 1907 for the pacific settlement of international disputes.

The so-called ' national groups ' were originally persons appointed by the governments for the purpose of becoming eligible as judges in the tribunals to be formed under the Hague Convention for the Pacific Settlement of International Disputes. The old, as well as the new, Statute confers upon these persons the function to nominate the candidates for the election of the members of the Court. Article 5 of the Statute provides:

> 1. At least three months before the date of the election, the Secretary-General of the United Nations shall address a written request to the members of the Permanent Court of Arbitration belonging to the states which are parties to the present Statute, and to the members of the national groups appointed under Article 4, paragraph 2, inviting them to undertake, within a given time, by national groups, the nomination of persons in a position to accept the duties of a member of the Court.
>
> 2. No group may nominate more than four persons, not more than two of whom shall be of their own nationality. In

> no case may the number of candidates nominated by a group be more than double the number of seats to be filled.

The invitation referred to in paragraph 1 is addressed to the members of the 'national groups.' Are the latter in making the nomination of the candidates bound by the instructions of their governments which have respectively appointed them? In making the nominations the members of the national groups are not independent judges, but administrative agencies. Hence, the first question may be answered in the affirmative, the second, in the negative. In any case, the Statute does not establish independence of the members of the national groups from their governments.

As to the number of candidates to be nominated, paragraph 2 stipulates only one limit: not more than four persons. The national groups may nominate less, even one single person. They can nominate four persons only if two or more seats are to be filled; if only one seat is to be filled, not more than two candidates are allowed to be nominated by one national group. In this case all candidates nominated by one group may be of the nationality of the nominating group. The very important rule providing for nomination of persons of a nationality other than that of the nominating group works only if the groups nominate more than two persons.

May a national group nominate a person who is a member of this group? The Statute does not forbid it. As a matter of fact, at least eight of the fifteen judges elected the first time under Articles 4 and 8 of the Statute were members of the national groups by which they were nominated as candidates for this election.[2]

It is difficult to understand why this method of establishing the list of candidates has been maintained. Since the members of the national groups are appointed by, and not independent from, the governments, and since they may nominate themselves, governmental influence on the nomination of the candidates is decisive.[3] Consequently it would

[2] Among the fifteen judges chosen at the first election, seven were members of the national groups by which they were nominated.

The following national groups nominated only their own members as candidates for election: Egypt, Iran, Mexico, Norway. The national groups of Mexico as well as of Norway nominated only one candidate; both have been elected judges. The national group of Ethiopia was composed of only two members who nominated themselves and a third candidate who was also nominated by another national group whose member he was. Cf. U.N. General Assembly, Doc. A/8, January 12, 1946, pp. 66 ff., and: Rapport du Conseil Administrative de la Cour Permanente d'Arbitrage, La Haye, 1946, pp. 10 ff.

[3] At the *Hearings*, pp. 337 f., the representative of the Department of State declared on the one hand that the question of the nomination of judges as dealt with in the Committee of Jurists 'was largely political.' On the other hand he justified the method accepted by the Charter as follows: 'On the nomination of judges it was felt that to allow the nominations to be made by the national groups of states parties to the Hague Convention of 1907 would be more likely to keep the nominations

have made no great difference to confer the nomination of the candidates directly upon the governments and eliminate the anachronistic 'national groups,' agents of a judicial organisation which no longer plays a role important enough to be conserved by this connection with the new Court. In order to guarantee political independence of the judges it was necessary to prevent as far as possible any influence of the governments on their nomination. This could be achieved by a provision according to which the judges were to be elected by the independent authorities which each national group—according to Article 6 of the Statute—'is recommended to consult' before making its nominations, namely, 'its highest court of justice, its legal faculties and schools of law, and its national academies and national sections of international academies devoted to the study of law.'[4] No such attempt has been made.

The new and the old Statute contain identical provisions referring to the case that it is not possible to carry out the necessary elections in one meeting of the electoral body. Article 11 stipulates:

> If, after the first meeting held for the purpose of the election, one or more seats remain to be filled, a second and, if necessary, a third meeting shall take place.

Article 12 provides:

> 1. If, after the third meeting, one or more seats still remain unfilled, a joint conference consisting of six members, three appointed by the General Assembly and three by the Security Council, may be formed at any time at the request of either the General Assembly or the Security Council, for the purpose of choosing by the vote of an absolute majority one name for each seat still vacant, to submit to the General Assembly and the Security Council for their respective acceptance.
>
> 2. If the joint conference is unanimously agreed upon any person who fulfils the required conditions, he may be included in its list, even though he was not included in the list of nominations referred to in Article 7.
>
> 3. If the joint conference is satisfied that it will not be successful in procuring an election, those members of the Court who have already been elected shall, within a period to be fixed by the Security Council, proceed to fill the vacant seats by selection from among those candidates who have obtained votes either in the General Assembly or in the Security Council.

free from political considerations. . . .' As pointed out above, more than half of the elected judges were members of their national groups appointed by their governments.

[4] Cf. H. Kelsen, *Peace Through Law* (1944), pp. 129 ff.

> 4. In the event of an equality of votes among the judges, the eldest judge shall have a casting vote.

During the first election of the members of the Court differences of opinion have arisen as to the meaning of the term 'meeting' in Articles 11 and 12 of the Statute. The President of the General Assembly was of the opinion that at one meeting only one ballot can take place, so that the term 'meeting' was equivalent to 'ballot'; whereas the representative of El Salvador, who had previously served as President of the Permanent Court of International Justice, maintained that 'meeting' should be interpreted to mean one day, and not just one ballot.[5] The interpretation advocated by the President of the Assembly has hardly a basis in the Statute which does not forbid taking more than one ballot during one meeting. But the General Assembly, at its 24th meeting, upheld the ruling of its President. In order to settle the disputed issue the Assembly decided to insert into its Rules of Procedure the following provision:

> RULE 140
>
> Any meeting of the General Assembly held in pursuance of the Statute of the International Court of Justice for the purpose of the election of members of the Court shall continue until as many candidates as are required for all the seats to be filled have obtained in one or more ballots an absolute majority of votes.

The Security Council adopted an analogous Rule (61).

Article 12 of the Statute does not determine whether the appointment of the members of the joint conference is—as the election of the members of the various Councils of the United Nations—the designation of Members or other states whose governments are authorised to designate the individuals to represent them in the conference, or whether individuals shall be directly appointed by the General Assembly and the Security Council and if so, whether the General Assembly and the Security Council are free in choosing these individuals or whether only those are eligible who represent Members in the General Assembly or the Security Council. All these interpretations are compatible with the wording of Article 12, paragraph 1, of the Statute. Article 12 of the Statute of the Permanent Court of International Justice, whose text is identical with that of Article 12 of the Statute of the International Court of Justice, has been interpreted by the Assembly of the League of Nations to mean that the Assembly is authorised to appoint three individuals. At the 13th meeting of the Second Assembly of the League of Nations three persons who were representatives of Members of the League in the Assembly were elected members of the Joint Conference.[6]

[5] Cf. Journal of the General Assembly, No. 25, pp. 441 f.

[6] Cf. Records of the Second Assembly, Plenary, p. 273. At the 12th meeting of the Assembly a representative of the British Empire suggested the following principles

Under the new Statute, as under the old one (Article 13), the members of the Court shall be elected for nine years and may be re-elected. In order to avoid that the entire Court be renewed every ninth year and thus the desirable continuity of judicature endangered, Article 13 of the new Statute provides ' that of the judges elected at the first election, the terms of five judges shall expire at the end of three years and the terms of five more judges shall expire at the end of six years. The judges whose terms are to expire at the end of the above-mentioned initial periods of three and six years shall be chosen by lot to be drawn by the Secretary-General immediately after the first election has been completed.'

B. *The Qualification of the Judges*

The qualifications of the judges required by the Statute of the International Court of Justice are the same as those required by the Statute of the Permanent Court of International Justice. Article 2 of the new Statute runs as follows:

> The Court shall be composed of a body of independent judges, elected regardless of their nationality from among persons of high moral character, who possess the qualifications required in their respective countries for appointment to the highest judicial offices, or are jurisconsults of recognised competence in international law.

The most important requirements are that the judges shall be ' independent ' and that they shall be ' elected regardless of their nationality.' But just as the old Statute, the new one does not guarantee the highest possible degree of independence, and does not respect its own postulate that the nationality of a person to be elected judge shall not be regarded.

The provisions of the Statute whose purpose it is to assure a certain impartiality and independence of the decisions of the Court are as follows: Article 16 stipulates:

> 1. No member of the Court may exercise any political or administrative function, or engage in any other occupation of a professional nature.
>
> 2. Any doubt on this point shall be settled by the decision of the Court.

Article 17 provides:

> 1. No member of the Court may act as agent, counsel, or advocate in any case.

concerning the election of the three members of the Joint Conference by the Assembly: 1. The Assembly shall not elect members of those states who are already on the Council; 2. the three persons to be elected by the Assembly should represent different systems of law; 3. that these persons should not be immediately concerned in the issue between the two members who were involved in the concrete case. (*Ibid.*, p. 258.)

> 2. No member may participate in the decision of any case in which he has previously taken part as agent, counsel, or advocate for one of the parties, or as a member of a national or international court, or of a commission of enquiry, or in any other capacity.
>
> 3. Any doubt on this point shall be settled by the decision of the Court.

Article 20 stipulates:

> Every member of the Court shall, before taking up his duties, make a solemn declaration in open court that he will exercise his powers impartially and conscientiously.

Article 24 states:

> 1. If, for some special reason, a member of the Court considers that he should not take part in the decision of a particular case, he shall so inform the President.
>
> 2. If the President considers that for some special reason one of the members of the Court should not sit in a particular case, he shall give him notice accordingly.
>
> 3. If in any such case the member of the Court and the President disagree, the matter shall be settled by the decision of the Court.

The—indirectly expressed—meaning of this Article is that a member of the Court may be excluded from taking part in the decision of a particular case or from sitting in a particular case (which is not the same, although both formulas seem to be used as being identical) either by agreement between the President and the member or, if no such agreement is brought about, by a decision of the Court.

In spite of these provisions the political independence of the judges is endangered by the influence the governments have on their nomination through the institution of the 'national groups'; and this influence is all the stronger as the judges are, according to the new, just as according to the old, Statute, elected for a period of only nine years and may, after their term has expired, be re-elected. There can be little doubt that appointment for life or with a certain age limit guarantees a higher degree of political independence than the method chosen by the Statute.

In contradiction to the proclaimed irrelevancy of nationality, the Statute stipulates in Article 3, paragraph 1, that no two judges may be nationals of the same state; and in Article 10, paragraph 3, that if more than one national of the same state obtains an absolute majority of votes both of the Security Council and the General Assembly, the eldest of these only shall be considered as elected. The old Statute contained only the rule laid down in Article 10, paragraph 3, not the rule laid down in Article 3, paragraph 1. Article 3, paragraph 2, of the new Statute—which has no counterpart in the old Statute—provides:

> A person who for the purposes of membership in the Court could be regarded as a national of more than one state shall be deemed to be a national of the one in which he ordinarily exercises civil and political rights.

Like the old Statute, the new one provides in Article 9 that in the Court as a whole 'the representation of the main forms of civilisation and of the principal legal systems of the world should be assured.' Since any great power represents a main form of civilisation and one of the principal legal systems of the world, the effect of this provision is that in fact each great power has a political claim to be represented in the Court by a judge of its nationality. This claim has been carefully respected by the League of Nations. It is hardly compatible with the principle that an independent judge is no representative of a state, or of a civilisation, or of a legal system, and it is certainly not in harmony with the principle that the judges shall be elected 'regardless of their nationality.'

The principle that nationality shall have no influence on the eligibility of the judges may be endangered by the provision of Article 2 of the Statute that the person to be elected judge of the Court shall possess either 'the qualifications required in his country for appointment to the highest judicial offices,' or be a 'jurisconsult of recognised competence in international law.' That the latter qualification is required only alternatively with the former is to be explained by the fact that the Court may deal with cases whose proper settlement presupposes the knowledge of law other than international, for instance, labour law. Article 26 provides even for the establishment of special chambers for dealing with such cases.[7] Hence it is quite understandable that a person need not necessarily be an expert in international law in order to be eligible for the Court. If the person is not an expert in international law, he must fulfil the other requirement: he must possess the qualifications required in his

[7] Article 26 provides:

> 1. The Court may from time to time form one or more chambers, composed of three or more judges as the Court may determine, for dealing with particular categories of cases; for example, labour cases and cases relating to transit and communications.
>
> 2. The Court may at any time form a chamber for dealing with a particular case. The number of judges to constitute such a chamber shall be determined by the Court with the approval of the parties.
>
> 3. Cases shall be heard and determined by the chambers provided for in this Article if the parties so request.

Article 29 provides: 'With a view to the speedy despatch of business, the Court shall form annually a chamber composed of five judges which, at the request of the parties, may hear and determine cases by summary procedure. In addition, two judges shall be selected for the purpose of replacing judges who find it impossible to sit.

country for appointment to the highest judicial offices. His country is the state whose national he is. The law of the state may request certain qualifications for appointment to the highest judicial offices which a person who would be highly qualified as a judge of the International Court of Justice might not fulfil. Then it is his nationality—indirectly—which excludes his eligibility for the Court.

The most evident restriction of the principle in question is the institution of national judges, taken over from the old Statute, by the new one. Article 31 stipulates:

> 1. Judges of the nationality of each of the parties shall retain their right to sit in the case before the Court.
>
> 2. If the Court includes upon the Bench a judge of the nationality of one of the parties, any other party may choose a person to sit as judge. Such person shall be chosen preferably from among those persons who have been nominated as candidates as provided in Articles 4 and 5.
>
> 3. If the Court includes upon the Bench no judge of the nationality of the parties, each of these parties may proceed to choose a judge as provided in paragraph 2 of this Article.
>
> 4. The provisions of this Article shall apply to the case of Articles 26 and 29. In such cases, the President shall request one or, if necessary, two of the members of the Court forming the chamber to give place to the members of the Court of the nationality of the parties concerned, and, failing such, or if they are unable to be present, to the judges specially chosen by the parties.
>
> 5. Should there be several parties in the same interest, they shall, for the purpose of the preceding provisions, be reckoned as one party only. Any doubt upon this point shall be settled by the decision of the Court.
>
> 6. Judges chosen as laid down in paragraphs 2, 3, and 4 of this Article shall fulfil the conditions required by Articles 2, 17 (paragraph 2), 20, and 24 of the present Statute. They shall take part in the decision on terms of complete equality with their colleagues.

Instead of providing that no judge of the nationality of one of the contesting parties shall have right to sit in the case before the Court, the Statute stipulates that, if the Court includes upon the bench no judge of the nationality of one or both parties, the party whose nationality is not represented in the Court may choose a person to sit as judge. The underlying idea is that the possible partiality of the one judge, who is a national or an otherwise reliable man of one party, shall be balanced by the possible partiality of another judge, national or an otherwise reliable man of the other party. This method is certainly not the most ideal solution of the problem to guarantee the impartiality of the Court and is, if it fulfils its purpose, superfluous, since the vote of one national judge will paralyse the vote of the other.

C. *The Seat of the Court*

Like the old Statute, the new one stipulates in Article 22 that the seat of the Court shall be established at The Hague. But the new Statute contains the additional provision: 'This, however, shall not prevent the Court from sitting and exercising its functions elsewhere whenever the Court considers it desirable.'

Article 22 imposes upon the Kingdom of the Netherlands, Member of the United Nations and party to the Statute, the obligation to permit the establishment of the seat of the Court on its territory and especially at The Hague. It obliges all the parties to the Statute, original parties or later adherents, to permit the Court to sit and exercise its functions on their territories whenever the Court adopts a decision to this effect. Under the Statute the Court can decide to sit and exercise its functions only on the territory of a state which is bound by the Statute. Hence the term 'elsewhere' in Article 22 goes too far. A state which is not bound by the Statute can be obliged to permit the Court to sit and exercise its functions on this state's territory only by a special agreement concluded with the Organisation. The decision of the Court is to be adopted, in accordance with Article 55, by a majority of the judges present. By a decision of the Court to sit and exercise its functions 'elsewhere' the seat of the Court, as determined by the Statute, is not changed. The seat of the Court as determined directly by the Charter remains at The Hague; whereto the Court may always return and has to return when its sitting and exercising its functions 'elsewhere' are no longer desirable. The Hague must be considered to be the permanent seat of the Court; but the Court may establish its temporary seat elsewhere. An analogous provision is stipulated in Article 28. It refers to the chambers which the Court is authorised to form by Articles 26 and 29. These chambers may, according to Article 28, 'with the consent of the parties, sit and exercise their functions elsewhere than at The Hague'; consequently also elsewhere than at any other place where the Court is sitting and exercising its functions in accordance with Article 22, paragraph 1. It is not clear whether the full Court or the chamber concerned is competent to adopt the decision regarding the place where the chamber shall sit and exercise its functions. Both interpretations are possible. An essential difference between Article 22 and Article 28 is that a chamber may sit and exercise its functions elsewhere than at The Hague only with the consent of the parties, whereas such consent is not necessary in case the full Court decides to sit and exercise its functions 'elsewhere.'[8]

[8] The Summary Report of the 11th meeting of the United Nations Committee of Jurists (U.N.C.I.O. Doc. Jurist 64, G/51, p. 7) contains the following statement:

Members of the Court or other persons may be engaged in the business of the Court elsewhere than at the permanent and temporary seat of the Court or its chambers. Under Article 44, paragraph 2, of the Statute the Court may take steps ' to procure evidence on the spot.' This may be at a place different from the seat of the Court or its chambers. Article 50 provides:

> The Court may, at any time, entrust any individual, body, bureau, commission, or other organisation that it may select, with the task of carrying out an enquiry or giving an expert opinion.

This provision is of particular importance with respect to the power of the Court to entrust persons with the task of carrying out an enquiry. The enquiry may be carried out elsewhere than at the seat of the Court or its chambers. The states upon which the Statute is binding are obliged to permit any activity of the Court administered under Article 44, paragraph 2, or Article 50.

D. *The Court as ' Principal Judicial Organ of the United Nations '*

According to Article 92 of the Charter, the International Court of Justice shall be ' the principal judicial organ of the United Nations.' The term ' United Nations ' means here the total community comprising the judicial community of which the Court is the organ. It has another meaning than in the formula ' Members of the United Nations ' as used in Article 93 of the Charter where it means the partial community composed only of states represented on the General Assembly. Members of the judicial community may be states parties to the Statute but not Members of the ' United Nations ' in the narrower sense, that is to say, states not represented on the General Assembly.[9]

If the term ' judicial organ ' in Article 92 means ' tribunal,' the International Court of Justice is not only the ' principal,' but also the only judicial organ of the Organisation, at least the only tribunal established directly by the Charter as an organ of the United Nations. The Security Council and the General Assembly, in so far as they, too, are competent to settle disputes, are only quasi-judicial organs of the United Nations. This is true even if the interpretation is accepted that recommendations made by the Security Council for the settlement

' The Chairman explained that Articles 22 and 28 were different in purpose. Article 22 was intended to permit the Court to hold sittings elsewhere, for example, in case it was prevented from sitting at The Hague, while Article 28 was intended to permit chambers to sit where it was desirable for the conduct of particular cases.' This interpretation is not quite consistent with the text of the two Articles. According to the wording of Article 22 the full Court, too, may decide to sit and exercise its functions ' where it is desirable for the conduct of particular cases.' Article 22 seems to apply to the conduct of ' particular cases,' since it does not authorise the Court to change its permanent or main seat, which is directly determined by the Statute to be at The Hague.

[9] Cf. *supra*, pp. 4 f., 79 ff.

of disputes under Articles 37, 38 or 39, are, as decisions of the Council in accordance with Article 25, binding upon the parties. The Security Council, as pointed out, is not a judicial organ because its members are not independent. But can the Security Council under Article 29 of the Charter establish a tribunal as a subsidiary organ 'for the performance of its functions'? If it is assumed that the Security Council has the function to settle disputes by decisions binding upon the parties the Council may establish a special tribunal for the settlement of disputes, provided that it confers upon the subsidiary organ independence. But as long as such tribunal is not established, the International Court of Justice is the only judicial organ of the United Nations. It is, as pointed out, not the only international tribunal and even not the only permanent court to which the Members are authorised to submit their disputes. Article 33 of the Charter expressly permits the Members to submit their disputes not only to 'judicial settlement,' *i.e.*, to the decisions of the International Court of Justice, but also to arbitration; and Article 95—repeating only what has been stipulated already in Article 33, paragraph 1 of the Charter—stipulates:

> Nothing in the present Charter shall prevent Members of the United Nations from entrusting the solution of their differences to other tribunals by virtue of agreements already in existence or which may be concluded in the future.

Hence the Members are allowed to submit their disputes in accordance with pre-existing or newly concluded treaties to *ad hoc* tribunals of arbitration or to establish—for instance by regional arrangements—another permanent court of justice. According to Article 33, paragraph 1, and Article 95, of the Charter, they may establish a special court with compulsory jurisdiction, excluding the jurisdiction of any other tribunal, even the jurisdiction of the International Court of Justice established by the Charter.

All this is not quite consistent with the provision of Article 36, paragraph 3, of the Charter, 'that legal disputes should as a general rule be referred by the parties to the International Court of Justice in accordance with the provisions of the Statute of the Court.' This provision, it is true, presents itself only as 'a general rule' permitting exceptions. But the provisions of Articles 33 and 95, that the Members may submit their disputes and consequently all their legal disputes to the judicial settlement of other tribunals, establish also a general 'rule' and do not refer to exceptions only.

3. Legal and Political Disputes

The Charter does not obligate the Members to submit legal disputes to a tribunal. It expresses only a wish that legal disputes be submitted to the International Court of Justice. Neither the Member nor the Security Council is bound to comply with this wish. If it deems it advisable, the latter may recommend that the parties settle a legal dispute by means other than those of arbitration or judicial settlement. It may even recommend that the parties submit a legal dispute to a permanent court other than the International Court of Justice in case such other court has been established by the parties. And if this court—according to its statute—has compulsory jurisdiction the parties may not be allowed to submit their dispute to another tribunal. But it is doubtful whether the Security Council has to respect such obligation.[1]

According to Article 36, paragraph 1, of the Statute, 'the jurisdiction of the Court comprises all cases which the parties refer to it.' That means that the parties may bring before the Court any dispute whatever. In so doing the parties make the dispute a legal dispute. According to the usual terminology 'legal' disputes are distinguished from non-legal, *i.e.*, 'political' disputes. The legal or non-legal, that is political, character of a dispute does not depend on its substance, *i.e.*, the subject matter with respect to which the parties are in conflict, but on the norms which are to be applied to it. The dispute is legal if it is to be decided according to norms of positive law; it is non-legal, *i.e.*, political, if it is to be decided according to other norms, especially according to principles of justice or equity. Whether legal or other norms are to be applied to a dispute depends on the parties, or on the authority competent to decide the dispute. Any dispute consists in that one party claims a certain conduct of the other party and the other party refuses to comply with this claim. If one party justifies its claim or its rejection of the other party's claim by referring to positive law, the dispute is—from the point of view of this party—a legal dispute. If a party justifies its claim or its rejection of the other party's claim by referring not to norms of positive law but to other norms, such as justice or equity, the dispute is—from the point of view of this party—a political dispute. If the parties submit their dispute to an agency for settlement the dispute is a legal dispute if this agency is authorised to settle it by applying to it rules of positive law; otherwise it is a political dispute. But if the agency concerned is authorised by a norm of international law, especially by an international agreement to decide a dispute according to principles of justice or equity and the like, these principles, delegated by international law, assume the character of international law in being applied by the agency. Its decision, binding upon the parties, has legal character. The agency—if independent: a tribunal—creates law for the concrete case. Hence the difference between so-called 'legal' and so-called 'political' disputes is only a difference between two kinds of legal disputes: disputes to be settled in accordance with pre-existent law, that is the law as it exists at the time the dispute arises, and disputes to be

[1] Cf. *supra*, pp. 405 f.

settled in accordance with the law to be created by the competent authority for the settlement of the dispute. The latter way may be chosen when the pre-existent law is considered to be not satisfactory.

That the existing law is considered by one or the other party, or even by both parties to the dispute, as unsatisfactory, does not mean that the dispute cannot be settled in accordance with this law. It is always possible to settle a dispute under the law as it actually exists at the time the dispute arises. For it is always possible to answer the question as to whether the claim of one party is justified and, consequently the rejection of this claim by the other party is unjustified under the existing law, or *vice versa*. In other terms: it is always possible to decide, in applying the existing law, which of the two parties is right and which is wrong. For there are always only two possibilities: either there exists a norm of existing law imposing upon one party the obligation to behave in the way claimed by the other party; then the latter is right and the former is wrong. Or there exists no such norm; then the one which rejects the claim is right and the one which makes the claim is wrong. A third possibility is logically excluded. If the fact that a dispute can be decided under existing law is expressed by the statement that the dispute is 'justiciable,' then all disputes are justiciable. However, though it is always logically possible to settle a dispute under existing law, it may not always be politically desirable to do so. Existing law as applied to a dispute may be, from one or the other point of view, unsatisfactory. Then one or the other party, or both, may wish to have the dispute settled—not by application of existing law and, if courts are authorised only to apply existing law, not by a court, but by another agency. Such disputes are called political, not 'legal,' disputes.

If it is correct that a dispute is legal if it is to be settled according to existing law, any attempt to define the concept of 'legal dispute' in contradistinction to that of 'political dispute' by referring to the subject matter of the dispute must fail. This is true even with respect to the definition of legal disputes as 'disputes with regard to which the parties are in conflict as to their respective rights . . . ', the well-known formula of the Locarno Treaties. As a definition of legal disputes this formula is of problematical value because it is not clear enough whether 'right' means right in the sense of positive law and whether both parties must justify their claim or counter-claim by referring to their 'right' under positive law, or whether it suffices that only one party does so whereas the other party may refer to a 'natural' right and the like; and, finally, because a dispute concerns in the first place not the rights, but the obligations of the parties; and the obligations as well as the corresponding rights are established by norms of positive law, so that the dispute, if it is a legal dispute, refers, in the last analysis, to the question whether a norm of existing law establishes the disputed obligation and, only secondarily, also the corresponding right.

Whereas the Charter (in the narrower sense of the term) uses the term ' legal disputes ' (in Article 36, paragraph 3) without defining this concept, the Statute contains a provision which, although it is not exactly a definition, tries to specify it. Article 36 of the Statute after stipulating in paragraph 1 that the jurisdiction of the Court comprises ' all cases which the parties refer to it '—which means: refer to it by agreement—provides in paragraph 2:

> The states parties to the present Statute may at any time declare that they recognise as compulsory *ipso facto* and without special agreement, in relation to any other state accepting the same obligation, the jurisdiction of the Court in all legal disputes concerning:
>
> (*a*) the interpretation of a treaty;
>
> (*b*) any question of international law;
>
> (*c*) the existence of any fact which, if established, would constitute a breach of an international obligation;
>
> (*d*) the nature or extent of the reparation to be made for the breach of an international obligation.

The declaration by which the ' compulsory ' jurisdiction of the Court is to be recognised in conformity with this paragraph shall be discussed later. In this connection only the concept of legal disputes as specified by the enumeration in clauses (*a*) to (*d*) is of interest.

First of all, it should be noted that, whatever the provision of Article 36, paragraph 2, of the Statute, concerning legal disputes may mean, it applies only in case a dispute is brought before the Court by parties which both have declared under Article 36, paragraph 2, that they recognise as ' compulsory ' the jurisdiction of the Court. Even in this case, however, the parties may refer to the Court any dispute whatever, since Article 36, paragraph 1, still applies. As long as they agree upon the jurisdiction of the Court, the dispute is a legal dispute since the Court is bound by Article 38, paragraph 1, to apply positive international law, unless both parties agree that the Court shall decide the dispute *ex aequo et bono* (Article 38, paragraph 2). In the latter case the dispute is not a legal, but a political, dispute, in spite of the fact that it is to be settled by the Court and in spite of the fact that it may concern one of the subjects enumerated in clauses (*a*) to (*d*) of Article 36, paragraph 2. The question as to whether or not the dispute concerns one of these subjects is of importance only when the jurisdiction of the Court is disputed for this reason; and it may be disputed also for the reason that the dispute, although concerning one of the subjects enumerated in clauses (*a*) to (*d*) of Article 36, paragraph 2, is not a legal dispute. This is possible; for the wording of the provision is not: the states recognise the jurisdiction of the

Court in all disputes concerning, etc., but: ' in all *legal* disputes concerning, etc. This implies that a dispute concerning one of the subjects enumerated in clauses (*a*) to (*d*) may not be a legal dispute; and that is the case if one of the parties does not justify its claim or counterclaim by referring to existing law. If, for instance, a state claims from another state a certain conduct, basing this claim on the interpretation of a treaty concluded with the other state, and the latter refuses to comply with this claim basing its refusal on the argument that the treaty provision referred to by the other party does not conform with the principles of justice, the dispute concerns the interpretation of a treaty—at least for one party—but is not a legal dispute from the point of view of the other party. The same is possible if the dispute concerns a ' question of international law ' or the ' breach of an international obligation ' or the ' nature or extent of the reparation to be made ' for such a breach. In all these cases only one party may refer to positive law, the other party to other norms. The wording of Article 36, paragraph 2, does not exclude the interpretation that, if only one party to a dispute concerning the subjects enumerated in clauses (*a*) to (*d*) bases its claim on positive law whereas the other on other norms, the dispute must not be considered as legal. If it had been the intention of the legislator that all disputes referred to in clauses (*a*) to (*d*) should be considered as legal disputes, the word ' legal ' should not have been used to characterise the disputes with respect to which the states declare to recognise the jurisdiction of the Court. These disputes assume the character of legal disputes just by being placed under the jurisdiction of the Court.

If the legal character of the dispute and hence the jurisdiction of the Court is disputed, paragraph 6 of Article 36 applies:

> In the event of a dispute as to whether the Court has jurisdiction, the matter shall be settled by the decision of the Court.

But how shall the Court decide the question as to whether the dispute is, as paragraph 2 requires, a ' legal ' dispute? Which criterion shall the Court choose? It is, of course, within the power of the Court to choose any criterion whatever. The Court may declare any dispute to be a legal dispute. Then paragraph 2, in connection with paragraph 6, of Article 36, is to be interpreted to mean that legal disputes are disputes which by the party referring the dispute to the Court and by the Court are deemed to be suitable for being decided according to existing law. But the Court may also declare a dispute to be a legal dispute only if both parties justify their claims and counterclaims by referring to positive international law. Then each party, in spite of having made the declaration referred to in Article 36, paragraph 2, and in spite of the fact that the dispute concerns one of the subjects enumerated in clauses (*a*) to (*d*), may withdraw such dispute from the jurisdiction of the Court by justifying its claim or rejection of the other party's claim not by positive law, but by other norms, that is to say, by declaring the dispute to be a political one.

The enumeration of disputes in paragraph 2 of Article 36 is identical with that of the corresponding Article 36 of the old Statute which has been taken over from Article 13 of the Covenant of the League of Nations. There the enumerated disputes are not characterised as 'legal' disputes but as 'those which are generally suitable for submission to arbitration or judicial settlement,' that is to say, as justiciable disputes. This is a theoretical statement without any legal importance. But the enumeration itself is, from a logical point of view, highly problematical. For the disputes of the categories referred to in clauses (*a*), (*c*) and (*d*), of Article 36, paragraph 2, are —or may be—disputes concerning questions of international law and hence are covered by clause (*b*). This is evident with respect to disputes concerning 'the interpretation of a treaty' referred to in clause (*a*). The question as to whether a fact constitutes 'a breach of an international obligation' is also a question of international law. For it is only by a rule of international law that an international obligation is established, and a fact constitutes a breach of this obligation only if it is not in conformity with this rule. Any question, if it is to be answered by a court on the basis of existing law is a question of law, even if it is a so-called 'question of fact'; for any fact is a legally relevant fact only in its relation to the law. If the Court has to decide disputes 'in accordance with international law'—as expressly provided in Article 38, paragraph 1 of the Statute—the question of the nature and extent of reparation must also be answered as a question of international law. Hence the clauses (*a*), (*c*) and (*d*) are superfluous. Their formulation was, to a certain extent, justified within the text of the Statute of the Permanent Court of International Justice, since its Article 36, paragraph 2, established jurisdiction of the Court 'in all or any of the classes of legal disputes' concerning the four different subject matters enumerated in clauses (*a*) to (*d*). Under Article 36 of the old Statute the jurisdiction of the Court could be restricted by the parties to one or the other of these classes of disputes. But in this respect, the text of Article 36, paragraph 2, of the new Statute is different. It authorises the parties only to accept 'the jurisdiction of the Court in all legal disputes concerning, etc.' According to the wording of this provision the parties have no choice among the four categories of disputes enumerated in clauses (*a*) to (*d*). Consequently there was no reason not to formulate Article 36, paragraph 2, as follows: The states . . . may declare that they recognise . . . the jurisdiction of the Court in disputes concerning any question of international law.

In order to avoid any doubt as to when the Court has to consider a dispute as concerning a question of international law and hence as a 'legal' dispute, it would have been advisable to formulate instead of 'disputes concerning any question of international law': disputes in which at least one party refers to international law. Any dispute between states concerns a question of international law if the dispute is to be settled according to international law and hence can be settled by a decision of the Court. A dispute concerns a question of international law only for one party if this party, not the other, refers to international law. Hence the essential point is whether a dispute which concerns a question of international law for one party, or only a dispute which concerns a question of international law for both parties, is within the jurisdiction of the Court under Article 36, paragraph 2. Only if the Court has jurisdiction in all disputes which for one party concern a question of international law, and that means in all disputes in which one party, and not necessarily also the other, refers to international law, the other party is not in a position to exclude the jurisdiction of the Court by refusing international law to be applied to the dispute and thus depriving the dispute of its legal character. That a party to a dispute refers to international law is implied in the fact that it refers the dispute to the Court which has to apply international law to it. Hence the declaration referred to in Article 36, paragraph 2, would have best achieved its purpose if formulated: the states declare that they recognise the jurisdiction of the Court . . . in all disputes in which one party refers the dispute to the Court. As pointed out, the Court may, under Article 36, paragraph 6, interpret the declaration of the parties made under Article 36, paragraph 2, in this way. But the wording of this Article does not exclude another interpretation of the term 'legal disputes.'

4. The Jurisdiction of the Court

A. *Only States Parties before the Court*

As to the question how a dispute may be brought before a tribunal of arbitration or a permanent court other than the International Court of Justice, the Charter contains no provision. The Members in establishing by treaties such tribunals of arbitration or permanent courts are free to regulate this topic at their discretion.

According to the Charter and the annexed Statute, disputes can be brought before the International Court of Justice only by states. Article 34, paragraph 1, of the Statute, expressly stipulates: 'Only states may be parties in cases before the Court.' Since at the time the Charter came into force, not all Members of the United Nations were 'states' in the strict sense of 'sovereign' communities subjected only to international law (India, *e.g.*) the text suggested by the United Nations Committee of Jurists (identical with the text of Article 34 of the old Statute) was more correct: 'Only states or Members of the United Nations may be parties in cases before the

Court.'[2] The intended meaning of Article 34 of the Statute is that only disputes between states shall be decided by the Court, not disputes between private individuals, between a state and a private individual, or between a state and a community of states, especially not disputes between a state and the United Nations, or disputes between international communities. All these disputes are excluded from the jurisdiction of the International Court of Justice. The fact that no private individual has access to the Court seems to be not consistent with the fact that the Charter—in contradistinction to the Covenant—contains provisions whose purpose is to protect the individual against the state.[3] However, as pointed out in another connection,[4] the Charter does not impose upon the Members the obligation to grant their citizens the rights and freedoms mentioned in the Preamble or in the text of the Charter, or 'equal rights of men and women,' mentioned only in the Preamble. Hence the Charter does not confer upon the individuals the legal possibility of appealing to the Security Council or an international tribunal, especially to the International Court of Justice in case one of the 'rights and freedoms' proclaimed in the Preamble or referred to in the text of the Charter is violated.

The exclusion of individuals from being parties in cases before the Court applies not only to cases where the individual is the plaintiff, but also to cases where the individual is the defendant, as, *e.g.*, in the trial of war criminals before the International Military Court established by the Agreement for the Prosecution and Punishment of European Axis War Criminals signed at London on August 8, 1945, or in a trial of persons guilty of a crime punishable under the Convention on Prevention and Punishment of the Crime of Genocide approved by the General Assembly on December 11, 1948. The international penal tribunal referred to in Article 6 of the Convention cannot be the International Court of Justice under its present Statute. Thus Article 34, paragraph 1, of the Statute, prevents the International Court of Justice from becoming the judicial instrument of individual responsibility for violations of international law of the kind as established by the just mentioned treaties. If the establishment of such individual responsibility for violations of international law is considered to be one of the most necessary improvements of the still primitive technique of collective responsibility in international law, then Article 34, paragraph 1, of the Statute, cannot be considered as a satisfactory achievement of the work of San Francisco.

[2] At the 5th meeting of the Committee of Jurists (U.N.C.I.O. Doc. Jurist 30, G/22, p. 10) the suggestion to strike out the words 'or Members' was not accepted. The Adviser of the United States pointed out 'that there had been controversy in this matter of defining a State and he felt that the present wording [states or Members of the United Nations] would do no harm.'

[3] Cf. *supra*, pp. 27 ff.

[4] Cf. *supra*, pp. 29 ff.

The rule according to which only states are admitted in cases before the Court is unsatisfactory also for a reason which is, so to speak, immanent in the Charter. The Charter requires or permits the conclusion of important treaties between the United Nations and Members of the Organisation or non-members. Disputes may easily arise out of such treaties; but these disputes, although 'legal' disputes according to Article 36, paragraph 2, of the Statute, as disputes 'concerning the interpretation of a treaty,' are excluded from the jurisdiction of the Court since one party at least is not a state, but a community of states. Also disputes between the United Nations and other international communities of states are excluded from the jurisdiction of the Court though their settlement by a decision of the Court would be highly desirable. The same is true with respect to conflicts between organs of the United Nations, regarding their jurisdiction.[5]

In disputes to which the United Nations is a party the Court, though not competent to settle them by its decision, may be asked for an advisory opinion by the General Assembly or the Security Council or other organs of the United Nations and specialised agencies authorised to this effect by the General Assembly (Article 96 of the

[5] At the 5th meeting of the Committee of Jurists (U.N.C.I.O. Doc. 30, G/22, p. 6) the Chairman stated that 'personally, he had doubts as to the desirability of allowing international organisations to be parties; any disputes in which they were engaged were really the disputes of the members, not of the international organisation.' At the San Francisco Conference, the delegation of Venezuela proposed the following text of Article 34 (U.N.C.I.O. Doc. 284, IV/1/24):

> 1. With the exception of the provisions in paragraph 2 of this Article, only States or Members of the United Nations may be parties in cases before the Court.
>
> 2. Upon request from any of the intergovernmental international organisations or offices dependent on The United Nations, the Court shall settle conflicts of jurisdiction which may arise among them. As a Court of Appeal, the Court shall have cognizance over such cases as are tried under original jurisdiction by other international administrative tribunals dependent upon The United Nations.
>
> 3. The Court, subject to and in conformity with its own Rules, may request of intergovernmental international organisations information relevant to cases before it, and shall receive such information presented by such organisations on their own initiative.

This proposition was not accepted. At the 18th meeting of Committee IV/7 (U.N.C.I.O. Doc. 801, IV/1/64, p. 2) the delegate of France declared 'that he could not approve the first part of the Venezuelan proposal, because (1) the prestige of the Court would be diminished by giving it jurisdiction over secondary matters; (2) the Court might become involved in conflicts between the Security Council and the General Assembly which would be dangerous; (3) the Assembly should be the final authority in such cases. Such matters had been satisfactorily handled in the past by consultation between the organisations and possibly by reference to the Assembly, the latter having the power to request advisory opinions from the Court.'

Charter; Article 65 of the Statute). Such opinion is, in itself, not binding upon the parties. But if the Organisation and the other party, in a special agreement, assume the obligation to consider the advisory opinion of the Court as binding the provision of the Statute which excludes the competence of the Court for disputes to which the Organisation is a party, may be eluded. This has been done in two important treaties: the General Convention on Privileges and Immunities of the United Nations (the text of which had been approved and proposed for accession by the General Assembly at its 31st meeting and which has been acceded by several states) and the Headquarters Agreement between the United Nations and the United States of America, signed at Lake Success, June 26, 1947. Section 30 of the General Convention on the Privileges and Immunities of the United Nations provides:

> All differences arising out of the interpretation or application of the present convention shall be referred to the International Court of Justice, unless in any case it is agreed by the parties to have recourse to another mode of settlement. If a difference arises between the United Nations on the one hand and a Member on the other hand, a request shall be made for an advisory opinion on any legal question involved in accordance with Article 96 of the Charter and Article 65 of the Statute of the Court. The opinion given by the Court shall be accepted as decisive by the parties.

The phrase 'The opinion given by the Court shall be accepted as decisive by the parties' probably means that the advisory opinion given by the Court shall be binding upon the parties. Section 21 of the Headquarters Agreement provides:

> (*a*) Any dispute between the United Nations and the United States concerning the interpretation or application of this agreement or of any supplementary agreement, which is not settled by negotiation or other agreed mode of settlement, shall be referred for final decision to a tribunal of three arbitrators, one to be named by the Secretary-General, one to be named by the Secretary of State of the United States, and the third to be chosen by the two, or, if they should fail to agree upon a third, then by the President of the International Court of Justice.
>
> (*b*) The Secretary-General or the United States may ask the General Assembly to request of the International Court of Justice an advisory opinion on any legal question arising in the course of such proceedings. Pending the receipt of the opinion of the Court, an interim decision of the arbitral tribunal shall be observed by both parties. Thereafter, the arbitral tribunal shall render a final decision, having regard to the opinion of the Court.

The phrase ' having regard to the opinion of the Court ' in clause *(b)* is not clear. It may mean only that the arbitral tribunal should take into consideration the opinion of the Court without being bound to accept it. But the phrase may also be interpreted to mean that the arbitral tribunal is bound to decide the case in conformity with the opinion of the Court. That the arbitral tribunal shall first issue an ' interim decision ' and, after the Court has given an ' advisory opinion,' a ' final decision,' whose function may or may not be to transform the advisory opinion of the Court—not binding in itself—into an award binding upon the parties, is indeed a very artificial detour. The unfortunate provision of Article 34, paragraph 1, of the Statute, that only states may be parties before the Court, made this detour necessary. If the arbitral tribunal shall be bound in its ' final decision ' by the opinion of the Court, it will be necessary to insert into the compromise a provision to this effect.

The exclusion of international organisations from being parties to cases before the Court is partly compensated by the provisions of paragraphs 2 and 3 of Article 34 of the Statute, which have no counterpart in the old Statute. They run as follows:

> 2. The Court, subject to and in conformity with its Rules, may request of public international organisations information relevant to cases before it, and shall receive such information presented by such organisations on their own initiative.
>
> 3. Whenever the construction of the constituent instrument of a public international organisation or of an international convention adopted thereunder is in question in a case before the Court, the Registrar shall so notify the public international organisation concerned and shall communicate to it copies of all the written proceedings.

Paragraph 2 was suggested by the Committee of Jurists. The first part of the paragraph authorizes the Court to request information of international organisations. ' Public ' international organisations probably means: organisations constituted by an agreement of international law, not by a contract of national law. An organisation is ' international ' in a legal sense of the term only if it is based on international law. The addition of the word ' public ' is superfluous. The term ' public ' has a specific meaning only in contradistinction to ' private '; there are no ' private ' international organisations,[6] for all international law is ' public ' law. Sometimes an organisation established on the basis of the national law of a state is called ' international ' because its members are citizens of various states or because it co-operates with organisations established for similar purposes in other states as, for instance, the so-called ' Third International.'

[6] At the 5th meeting of the Committee of Jurists (U.N.C.I.O. Doc. Jurist 30, G/22, p. 4) the delegate of Mexico stated that ' it was not clear what would be included in the term "public international organisations" '.

Used in this way, the term 'international' has a merely political, not a legal significance. The reference to the Rules of the Court in paragraph 2 may be explained by the fact that Article 44 of the Rules of the old Court required the Registrar to forward to the parties copies of all documents in the case.[7] At the 5th meeting of the Committee of Jurists,[8] the delegate of Australia inquired whether paragraph 2 of Article 34 meant that such information furnished by international organisations should be treated by the Court as evidence; and the delegate of New Zealand declared[9] that 'the Court must and could be trusted not to use information obtained under Article 34 in a manner prejudicial to the parties. He thought it safe to assume that the parties would be given an opportunity to refute such information if they desired.' With reference to these statements the Chairman called attention to Article 44 of the Rules of the old Court, and stated: 'Under such a rule there could be no question of the Court's considering information of which the parties were unaware.'[1]

The wording of the second part of paragraph 2 of Article 34 is rather problematical. It authorises the Court to receive information presented by international organisations on their own initiative. The words the Court 'shall' receive such information gives the impression that some obligation should be imposed upon the Court; which is not the case.[2]

Paragraph 3 of Article 34 has been proposed by the delegate of the United Kingdom, who stated 'that the proposed text is intended to provide necessary procedure to implement Article 34.'[3]

[7] Article 44 of the Rules of the International Court of Justice runs as follows:

> 1. The Registrar shall transmit to the judges and to the parties copies of the pleadings and documents annexed in the case, as and when he receives them.
>
> 2. The Court, or the President if the Court is not sitting, may, after obtaining the views of the parties, decide that the Registrar shall in a particular case make the pleadings and annexed documents available to the government of any Member of the United Nations or of any State which is entitled to appear before the Court.
>
> 3. The Court, or the President if the Court is not sitting, may, with the consent of the parties, authorise the pleadings and annexed documents in regard to a particular case to be made accessible to the public before the termination of the case.

Article 44 of the Rules of the Permanent Court was almost identical. Only slight changes have been made.

[8] U.N.C.I.O. Doc. Jurist 30, G/22, p. 3.

[9] *Ibid.*, p. 5.

[1] *Ibid.*, p. 6.

[2] Cf. the discussion of this subject at the 5th meeting of the Committee of Jurists, *ibid.*, pp. 3 ff. Article 26 of the old Statute included a provision authorising the International Labour Office 'to furnish the Court with all relevant information' in labour cases; 'for this purpose the Director of that Office shall receive copies of all the written proceedings.'

[3] U.N.C.I.O. Doc. 615, IV/1/45, May 26, 1945, p. 3.

B. *The States to Which the Court Is Open: The Members of the Judicial Community*

Not all states are entitled to be parties in cases before the Court or, to use an expression of the Statute, the Court is not open to all the states of the world. A court is ' open ' to a subject if the subject can appear before the Court either as a plaintiff or as a defendant. But the distinction between plaintiff and defendant is not quite applicable in the procedure before the International Court of Justice since a case can come before the Court only with the consent of the parties, *i.e.*, by a special or general agreement entered into by the parties to the case. Since the Court has no true compulsory jurisdiction no state can be summoned as a defendant by another state as the plaintiff. Both must submit the case to the Court and hence both parties are plaintiffs and defendants at the same time. In this sense the Court is open only to the members of the judicial community constituted by the Statute. The essential characteristic of this judicial community is just that the International Court of Justice is open to the members of the community. There are three categories of members. To the first category belong all ' Members of the United Nations.' Article 93, paragraph 1, of the Charter provides that ' all Members of the United Nations are *ipso facto* parties to the Statute of the Court of International Justice '; ' parties to the Statute ' means: members of the community constituted by the Statute.

The second category of members of the judicial community is referred to in Article 93, paragraph 2, of the Charter, which provides:

> A state which is not a Member of the United Nations may become a party to the Statute of the International Court of Justice on conditions to be determined in each case by the General Assembly upon the recommendation of the Security Council.

The possibility of becoming a party to the Statute and thus a member of the judicial community, without becoming a party to the Charter in the narrower sense of the term and thus a ' Member of the United Nations ' is rather problematical. For a state which is only a party to the Statute without being a party to the Charter (in the narrower sense) cannot be obligated by the Charter—provided Article 2, paragraph 6, is not applied—and cannot derive rights from the Charter. Article 94 of the Charter contains two important provisions concerning the Court, of which the one has not at all, the other only indirectly a counterpart in the Statute. Hence these provisions do not apply by themselves to parties to the Statute which are not Members of the United Nations and that means, not parties to the Charter in the narrower sense of the term. We shall return to this point later.

At its 56th meeting the General Assembly adopted—upon the recommendation of the Security Council—the following resolution concerning the conditions on which Switzerland may become a party to the International Court of Justice:[4]

> Switzerland will become a party to the Statute of the Court on the date of the deposit with the Secretary-General of the

[4] Resolutions adopted by the General Assembly (A/64/Add. 1, p. 183). The text of the resolution of the General Assembly has been suggested by the Committee of Experts of the Security Council. In the report of this committee it is stated:

> ' 3. The Committee decided that it is unnecessary to use in the first suggested condition the words in the Protocol of Signature of the Statute of the Permanent Court of International Justice (December 16, 1920, Series D, No. 1, 4th Edition, p. 7) whereby signatories declared acceptance of " the jurisdiction of the Court in accordance with the terms and subject to the conditions of" the Statute. In the opinion of the Committee, acceptance of the provisions of the Statute includes acceptance of any incidental jurisdiction exercisable by the Court under the provisions of the Statute.
>
> 4. The Committee desires to state that its intention in inserting the second suggested condition is the same as that which caused it to recommend the identical wording appearing in paragraph (1) of the resolution adopted by the Security Council on October 15, 1946, setting out the conditions under which the Court shall be open to States not parties to the Statute. The obligations imposed by Article 94 of the Charter upon a Member of the United Nations should, in the opinion of the Committee, apply equally to non-members of the United Nations which become parties to the Statute and to non-parties which are allowed access to the Court. In the opinion of the Committee, the obligations of a Member of the United Nations under Article 94 include the complementary obligations arising under Articles 25 and 103 of the Charter in so far as the provisions of those Articles may relate to the provisions of Article 94, and non-members of the United Nations which become parties to the Statute (and non-parties which have access to the Court) become bound by these complementary obligations under Articles 25 and 103 in relation to the provisions of Article 94 (but not otherwise), when they accept " all the obligations of a Member of the United Nations under Article 94." The French text of this latter phrase in the recommendation in this report differs from the French text of the Council resolution of October 15, 1946, relating to access to the Court. The Committee believes that the present text states the meaning more accurately.
>
> 5. On the third suggested condition—contributions to the expenses of the Court—the Committee noted that the last sentence of Article 35, paragraph 3, of the Statute contemplates a general contribution (*i.e.*, not one assessed in each case) towards the expenses of the Court by parties to the Statute which are not members of the United Nations. Although budgetary matters are within the competence of the Assembly, the obligation to contribute to the expenses of the Court must be imposed by the Assembly as a condition under Article 93, paragraph 2, upon the recommendation of the Security Council. The Committee therefore decided to recommend this condition.
>
> 6. The Committee desires to draw attention to the fact that under Article 93, paragraph 2, of the Charter, the conditions on which a State which is not a member of the United Nations may become a party to the Statute are to be determined *in each case* by the General Assembly upon the recommendation of the Security Council. Accordingly, the conditions recommended above as appropriate to the case of Switzerland are not intended to constitute a precedent to be followed either by the Security

United Nations of an instrument, signed on behalf of the Government of Switzerland and ratified as may be required by Swiss constitutional law, containing:

(*a*) Acceptance of the provisions of the Statute of the International Court of Justice;

(*b*) Acceptance of all the obligations of a Member of the United Nations under Article 94 of the Charter;

(*c*) An undertaking to contribute to the expenses of the Court such equitable amount as the General Assembly shall assess from time to time after consultation with the Swiss Government.

The third category of members of the judicial community

Council or by the General Assembly in any future case under Article 93, paragraph 2, of the Charter.

7. The Committee points out that when Switzerland becomes a party to the Statute by accepting the conditions determined by the General Assembly under Article 93, paragraph 2, of the Charter, Switzerland may, under Articles 4 and 69 of the Statute, participate in electing members of the Court and in making amendments to the Statute, on conditions which the Assembly may prescribe upon the recommendation of the Security Council. In this connection, it is noted that, while Article 93, paragraph 2, of the Charter, requires the setting of conditions of accession in each case, Articles 4 and 69 of the Statute permit the General Assembly, on the recommendation of the Security Council, to set generally applicable conditions on which non-member states parties to the Statute may participate in electing members of the Court and in the making of amendments to the Statute. The Committee advises that no special conditions on those matters should be prescribed in the case of Switzerland. It advises also that the Council should not now recommend to the Assembly generally applicable conditions under Articles 4 and 69 of the Statute, but should do so after Switzerland or some other non-member State has actually acceded to the Statute. At that time, the Council may wish to include in the generally applicable conditions provisions similar to those of Article 19 of the Charter in connection with the third condition of accession suggested in paragraph 2 above [text of the resolution recommended to the General Assembly] if the General Assembly prescribes that condition and Switzerland accepts it.' (*Ibid.*, pp. 184 f.)

On July 28, 1948, Switzerland became a party to the Statute of the International Court of Justice. On that date there was deposited with the Secretary-General a document containing the following declaration of the Swiss Government: 'The Swiss Federal Council . . . declares by these presents that the Swiss Confederation, in order to become a Party to the Statute of the International Court of Justice of June 26, 1945, accepts the three conditions laid down by the General Assembly of the United Nations in a resolution of December 11, 1946, to wit: (*a*) that it accepts the provisions of said Statute; (*b*) that it accepts all the obligations of a Member of the United Nations under Article 94 of the Charter of the United Nations of June 26, 1945; that it undertakes to contribute to the expenses of the International Court of Justice such equitable amount as the General Assembly of the United Nations shall assess from time to time after consultation with the Swiss Federal Council. Done at Berne, July 6, 1948.' (Doc. S/947.)

constituted by the Statute is referred to in Article 35, paragraph 2, of the Statute. This Article runs as follows:

> 1. The Court shall be open to the states parties to the present Statute.
>
> 2. The conditions under which the Court shall be open to other states shall, subject to the special provisions contained in treaties in force, be laid down by the Security Council, but in no case shall such conditions place the parties in a position of inequality before the Court.
>
> 3. When a state which is not a Member of the United Nations is a party to a case, the Court shall fix the amount which that party is to contribute towards the expenses of the Court. This provision shall not apply if such state is bearing a share of the expenses of the Court.

This Article is an almost literal copy of Article 35 of the old Statute, which runs as follows:

> The Court shall be open to the Members of the League and also to States mentioned in the Annex of this Covenant.
>
> The conditions under which the Court shall be open to other States shall, subject to the special provisions contained in treaties in force, be laid down by the Council, but in no case shall such provisions place the parties in a position of inequality before the Court.
>
> When a State which is not a Member of the League of Nations is a party to a dispute, the Court will fix the amount which that party is to contribute towards the expenses of the Court. This provision shall not apply if such State is bearing a share of the expenses of the Court.

Since the Covenant of the League of Nations did not contain provisions analogous to those of Article 93 of the Charter, that is to say, provisions concerning membership in the judicial community whose organ was the Permanent Court, Article 35 of the old Statute was the only provision concerning this subject—or what amounts to the same—concerning access to the Court. Article 93 of the Charter and Article 35 of the new Statute refer—by and large—to the same object, but the one uses a terminology different from that of the other. Article 93 of the Charter speaks of states being or becoming parties to the Statute; Article 35 of the Statute speaks of the Court being or becoming open to states. However, the essential legal effect of the fact that a state is a party to the Statute is that the Court is open to this state. According to Article 35, paragraph 2, of the Statute, the Court may become open to states which are not parties to the Statute; but—as we shall see—in fulfilling the conditions on which a state gets access to the Court under this paragraph the state becomes a party to the Statute, without being called so by the Statute.

Pursuant to Article 35, paragraph 2, of the Statute, the Security Council, at its 76th meeting on October 15, 1946, adopted the following resolution, by which the conditions were laid down on which the Court shall be open to states not parties to the Statute:

(1) The International Court of Justice shall be open to a State which is not a party to the Statute of the International Court of Justice, upon the following conditions, namely: that such State shall previously have deposited with the Registrar of the Court a declaration by which it accepts the jurisdiction of the Court, in accordance with the Charter of the United Nations and with the terms and subject to the conditions of the Statute and rules of the Court, and undertakes to comply in good faith with the decision or decisions of the Court and to accept all the obligations of a Member of the United Nations under Article 94 of the Charter.

(2) Such declaration may be either particular or general. A particular declaration is one accepting the jurisdiction of the Court in respect only of a particular dispute or disputes which have already arisen. A general declaration is one accepting the jurisdiction generally in respect of all disputes or of a particular class or classes of disputes which have already arisen, or which may arise in the future.

A State, in making such a general declaration, may, in accordance with Article 36, paragraph 2, of the Statute, recognise as compulsory, *ipso facto*, and without special agreement, the jurisdiction of the Court, provided, however, that such acceptance may not, without explicit agreement, be relied upon *vis-a-vis* States parties to the Statute, which have made the declaration in conformity with Article 36, paragraph 2, of the Statute of the International Court of Justice.

(3) The original declarations made under the terms of this resolution shall be kept in the custody of the Registrar of the Court, in accordance with the practice of the Court. Certified true copies thereof shall be transmitted, in accordance with the practice of the Court, to all States parties to the Statute of the International Court of Justice, and to such other States as shall have deposited a declaration under the terms of this resolution, and to the Secretary-General of the United Nations.

(4) The Security Council of the United Nations reserves the right to rescind or amend this resolution by a resolution which shall be communicated to the Court, and on the receipt of such communication and to the extent determined by the new resolution, existing declarations shall cease to be effective except in regard to disputes which are already before the Court.

(5) All questions as to the validity or the effect of a declaration made under the terms of this resolution shall be decided by the Court.[5]

There is hardly any essential difference between the conditions on which the Court, in accordance with Article 35, paragraph 2, of the Statute, shall be open to states which are not parties to the Statute and the conditions on which, in accordance with Article 93 of the Charter, a state which is not a Member of the United Nations—Switzerland—became a party to the Statute. Clause (*a*) of the resolution of the General Assembly concerning the conditions on which Switzerland may become a party to the Statute: 'acceptance of the provisions of the Statute of the International Court of Justice,' amounts to the same as the condition laid down in the resolution of the Security Council of October 15, 1946: acceptance of 'the jurisdiction of the Court, in accordance with the Charter of the United Nations and with the terms and subject to the conditions of the Statute and rules of the Court.' Clause (*b*) of the resolution of the General Assembly: 'Acceptance of all the obligations of a Member of the United Nations under Article 94 of the Charter,' is identical with the second and third conditions laid down by the Security Council: 'to comply in good faith with the decision or decisions of the Court and to accept all the obligations of a Member of the United Nations under Article 94 of the Charter.' The condition 'to accept all the obligations of a Member of the United Nations under Article 94 of the Charter' seems to be covered by the foregoing condition: 'to comply in good

[5] Official Records of the Security Council, 1st Year, 2nd Series, No. 19, pp. 466 ff. The text of this resolution is almost identical with that of the resolution which the Council of the League of Nations adopted on May 7, 1922, pursuant to Article 35, paragraph 2, of the old Statute. (The League of Nations, Official Journal (1922), p. 545.) In his oral report at the 76th meeting of the Security Council the Rapporteur made the following statement: 'The principles underlying the proposed resolution are: (1) To give the freest possible access to the Court to States not parties to the Statute. (2) Not to put any new obligations on the parties to the Statute. The parties to the Statute will have the advantage of bringing before their own Court any State not a party which is willing to appear, but under no condition can the parties to the Statute be forced to appear before the Court against their own will and consent.—The report of the Committee does not answer some questions raised in the Council when it discussed for the first time the matter now under consideration, in particular the question of how the resolution of the Council of the League of Nations had worked in practice. The Committee found that only two particular declarations had been made, both of them by Turkey and one the famous *Lotus* case, and general declarations have only been made on the following two occasions: on April 22, 1937, by the Principality of Monaco, and on March 22, 1939, by the Principality of Liechtenstein.' The delegate of Poland suggested the following resolution: 'In accordance with the spirit of the resolutions adopted by the General Assembly in London on February 9 and February 10, 1946, the above resolution does not apply to States whose regimes have been installed with the help of armed forces of countries which have fought against the United Nations so long as these regimes are in power.' This proposal was rejected. (pp. 468, 482.)

faith with the decision or decisions of the Court.' For Article 94 stipulates—in paragraph 1—only the obligation 'to comply with the decision of the International Court of Justice in any case to which it [each Member] is a party.' Paragraph 2 of Article 94 stipulates a right, not an obligation, the right of having recourse to the Security Council. But the Committee of Experts of the Security Council, in its Report and Recommendation concerning the conditions under which Switzerland may become a Party to the Statute[6] interpreted Article 94 as follows: 'the obligations of a Member of the United Nations under Article 94 include the complementary obligations arising under Articles 25 and 103 of the Charter insofar as the provisions of those Articles may relate to the provisions of Article 94, and non-members of the United Nations which become parties to the Statute (and non-parties which have access to the Court) become bound by these complementary obligations under Articles 25 and 103 in relation to the provisions of Article 94 (but not otherwise), when they accept "all the obligations of a Member of the United Nations under Article 94".' This interpretation is rather problematical. As pointed out, Article 25 may be interpreted to stipulate an obligation to comply with decisions of the Security Council only if they have not the character of mere recommendations; and Article 94, paragraph 2, refers to 'recommendations' of the Security Council. A decision of the Council 'to give effect to the judgment' of the Court may indeed constitute an obligation of the party concerned; but this is an obligation under Article 25 or 39, not under Article 94. As to Article 103, it is doubtful whether this provision stipulates an obligation of the Members.[7] It refers to a situation where there exists already an obligation under other provisions of the Charter in conflict with an obligation under an international agreement other than the Charter. In such a situation, the obligation under the Charter 'prevails.' That may mean that only the obligation under the Charter is valid or that execution of the obligation under the Charter has priority. If the obligation of a Member under Article 94, paragraph 1, or an obligation imposed upon a Member by a decision adopted by the Security Council under Article 94, paragraph 2, is in conflict with an obligation of this Member under another international agreement, the obligation under Article 94, paragraph 1, or the obligation imposed upon the Member by the decision of the Security Council prevails. If this principle shall apply also to states not Members of the United Nations, but parties to the Statute under Article 93, paragraph 2, or to states to which the Court is open under Article 35, paragraph 2, of the Statute, the application of Article 103 to these states must be made a condition under which a non-member state may become a party to the Statute (Article 93, paragraph 2, of

[6] Doc. A/64/Add. 1, p. 184.

[7] Cf. *supra*, pp. 111 ff.

the Charter) or a condition under which the Court shall be open to a state which is not a party to the Statute (Article 35, paragraph 2, of the Statute). Neither the conditions on which Switzerland became a party to the Statute (resolution of the General Assembly of December 11, 1946) nor the conditions on which the Court is open to states not parties to the Statute (resolution of the Security Council of October 15, 1946) indicate that Article 103 shall be applicable to these states. The condition: that these states accept the obligations of a Member, does not necessarily include the condition that Article 103 applies. Only if this Article is interpreted to mean that a Member is obliged to execute only its obligation under the Charter and not its obligation under another international agreement (if in conflict with the former obligation) does Article 103 stipulate an obligation of a Member. But this is an obligation under Article 103, not under Article 94.

According to clause (*c*) of the resolution of the General Assembly Switzerland shall undertake to 'contribute to the expenses of the Court such equitable amount as the General Assembly shall assess from time to time after consultation with the Swiss Government.' According to Article 35, paragraph 3, of the Statute, the Court shall fix in each case the amount which a state to which the Court is open under Article 35, paragraph 2, shall contribute to the expenses of the Court.

According to the resolution of the Security Council a state which is not a party to the Statute can get access to the Court not only by a particular declaration for a particular dispute or disputes which have already arisen, but also by a general declaration for all disputes or a particular class of disputes which have already arisen, or which may arise in the future. A state to which the Court is open not only for a particular dispute but for all disputes or a particular class of disputes, may even make a declaration under Article 36, paragraph 2, of the Statute, providing that 'the states parties to the present Statute may at any time declare that they recognise as compulsory *ipso facto* and without special agreement . . . the jurisdiction of the Court in all legal disputes . . . ' By making a declaration in conformity with the resolution of the Security Council on October 15, 1946, a state submits for a particular dispute or for a category of disputes or for all disputes to which it is a party—to the Statute of the Court and the provisions of the Charter concerning the Court. This state thus becomes a temporary or permanent party to the Statute or—what amounts to the same—a temporary or permanent member of the judicial community constituted by the Statute.[8] There is no essential

[8] At its 49th meeting the General Assembly adopted a resolution concerning the transfer to the United Nations of powers exercised by the League of Nations under the international agreements, conventions and protocols on narcotic drugs. By this resolution a Protocol was approved to be signed by the states who are parties

difference between the legal status of a state which under Article 35, paragraph 2, of the Statute, by a general declaration in conformity with the resolution of the Security Council of October 15, 1946, gets access to the Court for all its disputes and the legal status of the state which under Article 93, paragraph 2 of the Charter, in accordance with the resolution of the General Assembly of October 23, 1946, became a ' party to the Statute.'[9]

to these agreements, conventions and protocols. The Annex to the Protocol approved by the resolution of the General Assembly refers in Section 5 to the International Convention for the Suppression of Illicit Traffic in Dangerous Drugs, signed at Geneva on June 26, 1936. The resolution of the Assembly provides that for Article 17, second paragraph of this convention a paragraph shall be substituted which contains the following sentence: ' In the absence of agreement on the choice of another tribunal, the dispute shall, at the request of any one of the Parties, be referred to the International Court of Justice, if all the Parties to the dispute are Parties to the Statute, and, if any of the Parties to the dispute is not a Party to the Statute, to an arbitral tribunal constituted in accordance with the Hague Convention of October 18, 1907, for the Pacific Settlement of International Disputes.' (*Yearbook*, p. 268.) If a party to a dispute is not a ' party to the Statute ' in the sense of Article 35, paragraph 1, of the Statute, but a state to which ' the Court is open ' under Article 35, paragraph 2, especially on the basis of a ' general declaration,' there is no reason to refer the dispute to another tribunal than to the International Court of Justice. The only reasonable interpretation of the term ' party to the Statute ' in the above-quoted sentence is the one according to which also states to which the Court is open under Article 35, paragraph 2, are comprised.

9 At the 5th meeting of the Committee of Jurists (U.N.C.I.O. Doc. Jurist 30, G/22, pp. 12 f.), ' Judge Hudson explained that the Dumbarton Oaks Proposals [Chapter VII, paragraphs 4 and 5, corresponding to Article 93 of the Charter] treated the question of adherence to the Statute while Article 35 [of the Statute] dealt with access to the Court '; and ' that formal adhesion to the Court was different from access to the Court as a litigant.' But access to the Court under Article 35, paragraph 2, of the Statute, is possible for a state only if it fulfils the conditions laid down in the resolution of the Security Council of October 15, 1946; and these conditions require a declaration by which the state to which the Court shall be open ' accepts the jurisdiction of the Court in accordance with the Charter of the United Nations and with the terms and subject to the conditions of the Statute and rules of the Court . . . ' This declaration amounts to an adherence to the Statute, especially in case of a ' general declaration,' when access to the Court is granted ' in respect of all disputes . . . which have already arisen, or which may arise in the future.' The resolution of the Council of the League of May 17, 1922, required a declaration by which the state ' accepts the jurisdiction of the Court, in accordance with the Covenant of the League of Nations and with the terms and subject to the conditions of the Statute and Rules of Procedure of the Court . . . ' This formula is almost identical with the declaration by which the Members of the League and the states mentioned in the Annex to the Covenant of the League became parties to the Statute of the Permanent Court. The decisive phrase of the Protocol of Signature of the Statute of the Court, of December 16, 1922, runs as follows: ' They [the Members of the League of Nations] hereby declare that they accept the jurisdiction of the Court in accordance with the terms and subject to the conditions of the above-mentioned Statute.' The Protocol was open for signature by the Members of the League and by the states mentioned in the Annex to the Covenant. In signing and ratifying the Protocol a state made the above declaration and thus became a party to the Statute of the Court.

The difference between the two ways of becoming a member of the judicial community on the part of a state not a Member of the United Nations is that under Article 93, paragraph 2, of the Charter, the conditions are to be determined by the Security Council together with the General Assembly, whereas under Article 35, paragraph 2, of the Statute, the conditions are to be determined by the Security Council exclusively; and, further, that the conditions for being admitted as a 'party' to the Statute under Article 93, paragraph 2, of the Charter can be determined only 'in each case,'[1] that is to say, for a single state, whereas the conditions under which the Court is open to states not 'parties' to the Statute may be laid down not only for a single state, but in a general rule applicable to any state; as was actually done in the resolution of the Security Council of October 15, 1946. It may be doubted whether these differences are justifiable, especially with respect to cases of a 'general declaration' by which states, under Article 35, paragraph 2, accept the jurisdiction of the Court 'generally in respect of all disputes or of a particular class or classes of disputes which have already arisen, or which may arise in the future'—as the resolution of the Security Council of October 15, 1946, in conformity with the resolution of the Council of the League of Nations of May 17, 1922, provides.[2]

[1] The Report of Rapporteur of Committee IV/1 (U.N.C.I.O. Doc. 913, IV/1/74 (1), p. 5) contains the following statement referring to the formula 'in each case' in Article 93, paragraph 2, of the Charter: 'this will not preclude the adoption of uniform conditions as to a number of states.' This interpretation is hardly compatible with the wording of Article 93, paragraph 2.

[2] At the 5th meeting of the Committee of Jurists (U.N.C.I.O. Doc. Jurist 30, G/22, pp. 12 ff.) the delegate of Costa Rica 'pointed out that the Assembly was excluded from action under paragraph 2 of Article 35.' The delegate of the United Kingdom said: 'that there were really two questions involved here: The Assembly would decide what states might adhere to the Statute but the Security Council was given the right to decide who might be parties to cases, probably because it was in permanent session while the Assembly was not.' Then the delegate of Mexico 'suggested that paragraph 2 should be amended so that when the Assembly was in session it should have power to determine who should be parties to cases and the Council should have the right when the Assembly was not in session.' Later Judge Hudson 'explained that under paragraph 2 the Council [of the League] had not set conditions of access to the Court in particular cases. The matter was settled by a general resolution of the Assembly [?], which laid down conditions for access applicable in all cases.' This is probably a reference to the resolution of the Council of May 17, 1922. That the Security Council, but not the General Assembly is in permanent session, does not justify the exclusion of the latter from laying down general conditions for access to the Court on the part of states not parties to the Statute, since the General Assembly has the power under Article 93, paragraph 2, to determine 'in each case' the conditions of becoming a party to the Statute. The wording of Article 35, paragraph 2, it is true, does not exclude—as the delegate of Australia rightly pointed out—'*ad hoc* arrangements in particular cases.' But a general regulation such as established by the resolution of the Council of the League of May 17, 1922, and by the resolution of the Security Council of October 15, 1946, is likewise possible.

C. *Rights and Duties of the Members of the Judicial Community*

States which have accepted the conditions laid down by the Security Council under Article 35, paragraph 2, of the Statute, are parties to the Statute although the Statute does not use this term to designate their position, and in spite of the fact that the Statute establishes certain differences between them and the states which it expressly calls 'parties to the Statute.' As far as the main right and the main obligation are concerned there is no difference between the so-called and the not so-called parties to the Statute. Both are members of the judicial community, both have access to the Court without being obliged to submit cases to the Court, and both are obliged to comply with the decision of the Court if they have submitted a dispute to it. The Charter, it is true, seems to allow, in Article 95, only 'Members of the United Nations' 'to entrust the solution of their differences to other tribunals by virtue of agreements already in existence or which may be concluded in the future' and the Statute does not contain an analogous provision concerning the 'parties to the Statute' which are not 'Members of the United Nations.' The provision of Article 95, however, is not necessary in order to assume the legal possibility of submitting disputes to other tribunals. This possibility results from the fact that the Members of the United Nations as well as the other parties to the Statute are not obliged to submit their disputes or certain categories of their disputes to the International Court of Justice.[3] As to the obligation to comply with the decisions of the Court, the Charter seems to impose it only upon 'Members of the United Nations,' and not upon the states which are 'parties to the Statute' without being Members of the United Nations. For Article 94, paragraph 1, stipulates:

> Each Member of the United Nations undertakes to comply with the decision of the International Court of Justice in any case to which it is a party.

The wording of this provision is evidently too narrow, for just in the preceding Article the Charter provides that states which are not Members of the United Nations may become parties to the Statute. Should not these states also be under the obligation to comply with the decision of the Court in a case to which they are a party? But states which are not Members of the United Nations, that is to say, not parties to the Charter (in the narrower sense of the term) are not

[3] The Report of the Rapporteur of Committee IV/1 (U.N.C.I.O. Doc. 913, IV/1/74 (1), p. 5) contains the following statement: 'Even for states which are parties to the Statute, freedom will be reserved to entrust the settlement of their differences to tribunals of their own choice other than the International Court of Justice.' This is correct. But if an express provision guaranteeing this freedom was considered to be necessary with respect to the 'Members of the United Nations,' why was no such provision concerning the parties to the Statute not Members of the United Nations inserted in the Charter or the Statute?

bound by Article 94, paragraph 1, of this Charter if Article 2, paragraph 6, of the Charter is not interpreted to constitute an obligation of all non-member states to comply with the provision of Article 94, paragraph 1; and the application of Article 2, paragraph 6, in the case is indeed highly problematical. This is probably the reason why in the resolution of the General Assembly of December 11, 1946, concerning the conditions under which Switzerland may become a party to the Statute, clause (*b*) expressly stipulates: ' Acceptance of all obligations of a Member of the United Nations under Article 94 of the Charter ' and the conditions laid down by the resolution of the Security Council of October 15, 1946, contain an analogous provision. However, the obligation, established in Article 94, paragraph 1, only for Members of the United Nations, is indirectly established in the Statute for all members of the judicial community. It is implied in the provision of Article 38, paragraph 1, of the Statute, that the Court has the function ' to decide ' the disputes submitted to it; in the provision of Article 59 that the decision of the Court has ' binding force ' between the parties in respect to the particular case; and in the provision of Article 60 that the judgment is final and without appeal. All these provisions apply to all parties to the dispute. Thus Article 94, paragraph 1, of the Charter, is superfluous, since the effect at which it aims is established by the Statute not only for Members of the United Nations but for all the other members of the judicial community. It is significant that the wording of Article 94, paragraph 2, concerning the right of a party to a case to have recourse to the Security Council in the event that the other party fails to perform the obligations incumbent upon it under a judgment rendered by the Court, refers not to ' Members of the United Nations ' but to all parties to a case before the Court. But according to the rule that treaty provisions apply only to the parties of a treaty, Article 94, paragraph 2, can confer a right only upon Members of the United Nations.

The Statute does not contain an analogous provision. Among the conditions laid down by the General Assembly under which a non-member state (Switzerland) became a party to the Statute, and the conditions laid down by the Security Council under which a state not party to the Statute gets access to the Court, there is only acceptance of the ' obligations ' under Article 94; no reference is made to the right established in Article 94, paragraph 2, of the Charter. Consequently, states which are not Members of the United Nations have the right established in Article 94, paragraph 2, only if the Charter (in the narrower sense of the term) is generally recognised to be—with respect to this provision—a treaty *en faveur d'Etats tiers*, that is to say, in favour of states which, without being, as Members of the United Nations, contracting parties to the Charter (in the narrower sense of the term), become parties to the Statute under Article 93, paragraph 2, of the Charter, or get access to the Court under Article 35, paragraph 2, of the Statute; an exception to the rule that treaties confer rights only upon the contracting parties.

This interpretation is of particular importance for the provision of Article 35, paragraph 2, of the Statute, which provides that the Security Council in laying down the conditions under which the Court shall be open to a state which is not a party to the Statute, shall not place the parties 'in a position of inequality before the Court.' Such inequality before the Court certainly exists when one party has the right to have recourse to the Security Council under the condition determined in Article 94, paragraph 2, but the other party has no such right. If Article 94, paragraph 2, is interpreted to confer the right to have recourse to the Security Council only upon Members of the United Nations, that is to say, only upon states parties to the Charter (in the narrower sense of the term), in case of a dispute between a Member and a state which has access to the Court under Article 35, paragraph 2, of the Statute, a situation of inequality before the Court exists. For the resolution of the Security Council of October 15, 1946, does not confer upon the state which, though not a party to the Statute, gets access to the Court, the right stipulated in Article 94, paragraph 2. As pointed out, only the 'obligations of a Member of the United Nations under Article 94 of the Charter' are imposed upon the state. This omission is all the more regrettable as it constitutes a violation of the Statute. The provision of Article 35, paragraph 2, of the Statute, that the parties shall not be placed in a position of inequality before the Court, refers only to disputes in which a state is involved which is not a party to the Statute, but has access to the Court under this paragraph.[4] The Charter (in the narrower sense of the term) does not contain an analogous provision referring to disputes between Members (subjects of the right established in Article 94, paragraph 2) and states which are not Members (and hence not subjects of this right) but parties to the Statute under Article 93, paragraph 2, of the Charter. The fact that the resolution

[4] In the dispute concerning the Corfu Channel Incident between the United Kingdom and Albania, not a party to the Statute, the Albanian Government declared in a letter dated July 2, 1947, to the Registrar of the Court 'its acceptance of the Court's jurisdiction for this case,' and the Court interpreted this declaration as the fulfilment of the provision of Article 35, paragraph 2, of the Statute, and the resolution of the Security Council of October 15, 1946. By a decision adopted on January 20, 1947, the Security Council had invited the Albanian Government to participate, without vote, in the proceedings with regard to this dispute, on the condition 'that Albania accepts in the present case, all the obligations which a Member of the United Nations would have to assume in a similar case.' In a telegram dated January 24, 1947, the Albanian Government accepted the Security Council's conditions. Neither the acceptance of the Court's jurisdiction nor the acceptance of the conditions laid down by the Security Council for Albania's participation in the discussion of the case conferred upon Albania the right, stipulated in Article 94, paragraph 2, to have recourse to the Security Council in case the other party would fail to perform the obligations under a judgment rendered by the Court. Cf. *supra*, p. 293.

of the General Assembly of December 11, 1946, does not confer the right established in Article 94, paragraph 2, upon Switzerland, is regrettable but not in contradiction to the Charter or to the Statute; and consequently in a dispute between Switzerland and a Member of the United Nations inequality before the Court exists in the relation between the two parties. These paradoxical inconsistencies can be avoided only if Article 94, paragraph 2, is interpreted, in accordance with its wording, to establish a right of any party to a case, even if the party is not a Member of the United Nations, that is to say, as an exception to the rule that treaty rights are conferred only upon the parties to the treaty.[5]

The main obligation imposed upon the members of the judicial community, to comply with the decisions of the Court, is common to all of them in their capacity as parties to the Statute under Article 35, paragraph 1, or as states to which the Court is open under Article 35, paragraph 2, of the Statute. As to the obligation of contributing to the expenses of the Court, there are three provisions referring to this subject. Article 17, paragraph 2, of the Charter provides:

> The expenses of the Organisation shall be borne by the Members as apportioned by the General Assembly.

Since the International Court of Justice is an organ of the United Nations, the expenses of the Court are included in the 'expenses of the Organisation.' Under this provision, only the Members of the United Nations, not the parties to the Statute which are not 'Members of the United Nations,' are obliged to contribute towards the expenses of the Court.

A provision concerning the particular expenses of the Court is contained in Article 33 of the Statute which provides that:

> The expenses of the Court shall be borne by the United Nations in such a manner as shall be decided by the General Assembly.

The relation between this Article of the Statute and Article 17, paragraph 2, of the Charter, is not very clear. The decision of the General Assembly referred to in Article 33 of the Statute may or may not be identical with the decision by which the General Assembly apportions the expenses of the Organisation (including the expenses of the Court) among the Members under Article 17, paragraph 2, of the Charter. If identical, Article 33, of the Statute, does not say more than Article 17, paragraph 2, of the Charter does, and the Statute, too, imposes the obligation to contribute to the expenses of the Court only upon those parties to the Statute which are Members of the United Nations. This interpretation may be confirmed by the fact that Article 33 authorises the General Assembly to decide upon the manner by which the

[5] The inequality before the Court constituted by the fact that one party has a right of recourse to the Council whereas the other has not, could not exist under the Covenant of the League and the old Statute, because the Covenant did not stipulate such a right.

expenses of the Court shall be borne. This may indicate that only members of the General Assembly are supposed to share the expenses of the Court under Article 33 of the Statute, since the General Assembly—according to general international law—has not the power to impose obligations upon states which are not represented on this body.

However, since Article 17, paragraph 2, of the Charter, is not referred to in Article 33 of the Statute, it is, perhaps, not impossible to assume that the decision of the General Assembly referred to in Article 33 of the Statute is not identical with the decision referred to in Article 17, paragraph 2, of the Charter, that this Article concerns only the expenses of the United Nations in the narrower sense of the term, not including the judicial community of which the Court is the organ, and that the manner in which the expenses of the Court are to be borne shall be determined under Article 33 of the Statute—by a decision of the General Assembly different from the one referred to in Article 17, paragraph 2. If this interpretation should be accepted, the General Assembly could apportion the expenses of the Court among the parties to the Statute, including the states which are parties to the Statute without being Members of the 'United Nations,' in the narrower sense of this term. As parties to the Statute they are bound by the provision of this Statute according to which the General Assembly—in spite of the fact that they are not represented on this body—is authorised to impose upon them the obligation to contribute to the expenses of the Court.

This interpretation, however, is hardly compatible with the fact that Article 33 of the Statute is an almost literal copy of Article 33 of the old Statute, which runs as follows:

> The expenses of the Court shall be borne by the League of Nations, in such a manner as shall be decided by the Assembly upon the proposal of the Council.

In the old Statute this provision was not redundant since the Court was not an organ of the League in the strict sense of the term. Hence the provision of Article 6, paragraph 5, of the Covenant, 'The expenses of the League shall be borne by the Members of the League in the proportion decided by the Assembly,' did not cover the expenses of the Court. Under Article 33 of the old Statute the expenses of the Court were to be borne only by the Members of the League, regardless of their position as parties or non-parties to the Statute. Hence, an analogous interpretation of Article 33 of the new Statute is most plausible; and this all the more as the text of the old Article 33 has been changed only in so far as the term 'League of Nations' has been replaced by the term 'United Nations,' and the words 'by the Assembly upon the proposal of the Council' by the words 'by the General Assembly.' The last-mentioned alteration may have been made to adapt Article 33 of the new Statute to Article 17 of the

Charter, which confers budgetary power exclusively upon the General Assembly. As a matter of fact, the appropriation resolutions of the General Assembly for the financial years 1946 and 1947 contained in Part II appropriations for the expenses of the International Court of Justice, its Registry and common services.

The legal situation as to the expenses of the Court under the old Statute was rather strange. By an international treaty, the Protocol of December 16, 1920, different from the Covenant of the League, financial obligations were imposed upon the Members of the League even if not parties to the Statute (annexed to the Protocol). Only the Members of the League even if not parties to the Statute—not the parties to the Statute if not Members of the League—were obliged to contribute to the expenses of the Court, whereas parties to the Statute which were not Members of the League only voluntarily contributed to the expenses of the Court. This may be explained by the fact that the old Statute was drafted under the erroneous presupposition that the Court was an organ of the League. The new Court, it is true, is an organ of the United Nations, but non-members may be parties to the Statute. Instead of copying a highly problematical provision of the old Statute, it would have been advisable to provide that the expenses of the Court shall be borne by the parties to the Statute, that is to say, by the permanent members of the judicial community, in accordance with the decision of a body composed of these members, or in accordance with a decision of the General Assembly in which the parties to the Statute which are not Members of the United Nations are to be invited to participate.

That under Article 17, paragraph 2, of the Charter, as well as under Article 33 of the Statute the Members of the United Nations represented on the General Assembly, and not the parties to the Statute, are to contribute to the expenses of the Court may be concluded also from the wording of Article 35, paragraph 3, of the Statute, which runs as follows:

> When a state which is not a Member of the United Nations is a party to a case, the Court shall fix the amount which that party is to contribute towards the expenses of the Court. This provision shall not apply if such state is bearing a share of the expenses of the Court.

This paragraph refers to non-member states which are parties to the Statute under Article 93, paragraph 2, and to non-member states to which the Court has been opened under Article 35, paragraph 2, of the Statute. It evidently presupposes that all these states are not under the obligation to contribute to the expenses of the Court as established by Article 17, paragraph 2, of the Charter, and Article 33 of the Statute.

However, the resolution by which the conditions were determined under which Switzerland may become a party to the Statute provides that this state shall contribute to the expenses of the Court such an equitable amount as ' the General Assembly shall assess from time to time after consultation with the Swiss Government.' This provision is compatible with Article 35, paragraph 3, of the Statute, conferring upon the Court the competence to fix the amount which a state, not Member of the United Nations but party to a case, is to contribute towards the expenses of the Court, only because the second sentence of this paragraph provides that its first sentence ' shall not apply if such state is bearing a share of the expenses of the Court.' This provision has been taken over from Article 35, paragraph 3, of the old Statute; but there it had a meaning different from that it has now, in the new Statute.

Under the Covenant all Members of the League, even if not members of the judicial community, were obliged to contribute to the expenses of the Court. Parties to the Statute of the Permanent Court were under no obligation to contribute to the expenses of the Court. But they could voluntarily make such contributions.[6] To avoid double payment for the Court's expenses, the second sentence of Article 35, paragraph 3, of the Statute was added; it applied in case a state which was not a Member of the League but party to a case before the Court, had made voluntary contributions to the expenses of the Court.

Under the Charter all Members of the United Nations are parties to the Statute of the Court. Hence no Member has to contribute to the expenses of the Court, which is an organ of the United Nations, without being a party to the Statute. Switzerland, which is a party to the Statute without being a Member of the United Nations, is obliged to contribute to the expenses of the Court under clause (*c*) of the resolution of the General Assembly of December 11, 1946. Hence the first sentence of Article 35, paragraph 3, would not apply in case Switzerland should be a party to a case before the Court. The second sentence of this paragraph would apply; but not—as under the old Statute—because the state, not a Member of the Organisation, is voluntarily bearing a share of the expenses of the Court. In case other non-member states would be admitted to become parties to the Statute in accordance with Article 93, paragraph 2, of the Charter, under the same conditions as Switzerland, the first sentence of Article 35, paragraph 3, could apply only to states to which the Court is open under Article 35, paragraph 2, of the Statute. These states are obliged only to contribute to the expenses of the particular case to which they are parties as fixed by the Court, for the provision of Article 35, paragraph 3, refers only to the situation ' when a state . . . is a party to a case.' This is hardly appropriate if the state has access to the Court on the basis of a ' general declaration ' in the

[6] Cf. Manley O. Hudson, The Permanent Court of International Justice (1943) pp. 311 f.

sense of the resolution of the Security Council of October 15, 1946, that is to say, if the state is a permanent member of the judicial community. The question as to what 'the expenses of the Court' are in a particular case has to be decided by the Court at its discretion.

Provisions of the Statute confer certain privileges upon the members of the Court, the agents, counsel, and advocates of the parties, to which correspond obligations of the states which are bound by the Statute. These states are not only those which are parties to the Statute under Article 93 of the Charter, but also those which are subject to the Statute on the basis of a 'general declaration' made in accordance with the resolution of the Security Council under Article 35, paragraph 2, that is to say, all permanent members of the judicial community. States which submit to the Statute only by a 'particular declaration,' that is to say, states which are only temporarily subject to the Statute (or only temporary members of the judicial community) are bound by the provisions concerned only as long as they are subject to the Statute, and only if the obligations constituted by these provisions of the Statute permit temporary fulfilment. This is certainly the case with the obligations which correspond to the privileges established by Article 19 and Article 42, paragraph 3, of the Statute. Article 19 provides:

> The members of the Court, when engaged on the business of the Court, shall enjoy diplomatic privileges and immunities.

As a rule, the members of the Court are engaged on the business of the Court at the permanent or temporary seat of the Court or its chambers. According to Article 23, paragraph 3, of the Statute, members of the Court are bound, 'unless they are on leave or prevented from attending by illness or other serious reasons duly explained to the President, to hold themselves permanently at the disposal of the Court.' Though a member who is holding himself at the disposal of the Court is not directly 'engaged on the business of the Court' in the sense of Article 19, he does so in order to be ready to be engaged on the business of the Court. Hence Article 19 may be interpreted to apply also to a member of the Court holding himself at the disposal of the Court.

The obligation to confer upon the members of the Court the diplomatic privileges and immunities referred to in Article 19 is incumbent upon the states which are obliged to permit the Court or its chambers to have their seat on their territory. Exceptionally members of the Court may be engaged on the business of the Court outside the seat of the Court or its chambers. As pointed out, under Article 44, paragraph 2 of the Statute, the Court may take steps 'to procure evidence on the spot,' that is to say on the territory of any state upon which the Statute is binding, and the evidence may be procured by a member of the Court. Article 44 provides that in such a case the Court shall apply direct to the government of the state upon whose territory the evidence is to be procured. But the state, if subject to the Statute, is bound to permit the Court to procure the evidence on the spot and to grant to the members of the Court engaged on this business of the Court the privileges referred to in Article 19. Under Article 50, the Court may ' entrust any individual, body, bureau, commission, or other organisation that it may select, with the task of carrying out an enquiry.' The states which are subject to the Statute are obliged to permit such enquiry on their respective territories and, if the enquiry is to be carried out by a member of the Court, to grant him diplomatic privileges and immunities under Article 19. Finally, a member of the Court should be considered to be engaged on the business of the Court when travelling to and from the place where he has to fulfil his functions. All the states upon which the Statute is binding are under the obligation established by Article 19 of the Statute to grant diplomatic privileges and immunities to a member of the Court who, engaged on the business of the Court, is travelling through their territories. It is important to note that this Article does not exclude the home-state of the member of the Court.

Article 19 of the Statute is partly paralleled by the provision of Article 105, paragraph 2 of the Charter, that ' officials of the Organisation ' ' shall enjoy such privileges and immunities as are necessary for the independent exercise of their functions in connection with the Organisation.' Members of the Court are ' officials of the Organisation.' In so far Article 105, paragraph 2 of the Charter, is applicable to them. But Article 19 of the Statute, granting all the privileges and immunities which diplomatic envoys enjoy under general international law, and not only as far as such privileges ' are necessary ' for the exercise of the functions of the members of the Court, goes farther than Article 105, paragraph 2. The latter probably imposes the corresponding obligations only upon Members of the United Nations (in the narrower sense), not upon states which are not Members but upon which the Statute is binding. Hence only Article 19 of the Statute comes into consideration for members of the Court.[7]

Article 42, paragraph 3, of the Statute, provides:

> The agents, counsel, and advocates of parties before the Court shall enjoy the privileges and immunities necessary to the independent exercise of their duties.

This provision has no counterpart in the old Statute. The obligations, corresponding to these privileges and immunities are of the same scope as those established by Article 105, paragraph 2, of the Charter. Like the obligation established by Article 19 of the Statute, the obligation established by Article 42, paragraph 3, is incumbent only upon the states upon which the Statute is binding,

[7] Cf. *supra*, pp. 337 ff.

that is to say, upon all the members of the judicial community of which the International Court of Justice is the organ.

Article 105, paragraph 3, of the Charter authorises the General Assembly to make recommendations with a view to determining the details of the application of paragraph 2 (and 1) of this Article or may propose conventions to the Members of the United Nations for this purpose. As a matter of fact, the General Assembly, at its 31st meeting, adopted a resolution by which it approved the text of a convention on the privileges and immunities of the United Nations and proposed it for accession by each Member. The function of this convention cannot be to constitute the obligation of the Members to grant the privileges and immunities referred to in Article 105, paragraph 2; for these obligations are already established by this paragraph. The function of the conventions suggested by the General Assembly can only be to specify this obligation.

There is no provision analogous to that of Article 105, paragraph 3, referring to the privileges and immunities of the members of the Court established by Article 19 of the Statute. Nevertheless, the General Assembly at its 31st meeting adopted also a resolution on the privileges and immunities of the International Court of Justice. In this resolution the Assembly invited ' the members of the Court at their first session to consider this question and to inform the Secretary-General of their recommendations.' To give effect to this resolution the Court entered into negotiations with representatives of the Netherlands Foreign Ministry which led to an agreement on the following general principles that should govern the matter:

> 1. As concerns the privileges, immunities, facilities and prerogatives, within the territory of the Netherlands, of members and staff of the International Court of Justice of other than Dutch nationality:
>
> (*a*) The members of the Court will, in a general way, be accorded the same treatment as heads of diplomatic missions accredited to Her Majesty the Queen of the Netherlands.
>
> As regards the privileges, immunities and facilities above-mentioned, this provision applies also to the Registrar of the Court and to the Deputy Registrar when acting for the Registrar.
>
> (*b*) The Deputy Registrar of the Court will, in a general way, be accorded the same treatment as counsellors attached to diplomatic missions at The Hague.
>
> The higher officials of the Court—first secretaries and secretaries—will, in a general way, be accorded the same treatment as secretaries attached to diplomatic missions at The Hague.

(*c*) The other officials of the Court will be treated as officials of comparable rank attached to diplomatic missions at The Hague.

2. Members of the Court, the Registrar and higher officials of the Court who are of Netherlands nationality are not answerable to the local jurisdiction for acts performed by them in their official capacity and within the limits of their duties.

Netherlands nationals of whatever rank are exempt from direct taxation on the salaries allotted to them from the Court's budget.

3. The wives and unmarried children of members of the Court, the Registrar and the higher officials of the Court, when of non-Netherlands nationality shall receive the same treatment as the head of the family, if they live with him and are without profession. The household of the family (governesses, private secretaries, servants, et cetera) occupy the same position as is accorded in each case to the domestic staff of diplomatic persons of camparable rank.

4. Privileges and immunities are granted in the interests of the administration of international justice and not in the personal interest of the beneficiary.

As concerns officials of the Registry, the Registrar, with the President's approval, may withdraw their immunities, with due regard to the principle laid down in the previous paragraph. In the case of the Registrar, this duty shall rest with the Court.

5. The assessors of the Court and the agents, counsel and advocates of the Parties, shall be accorded such privileges, immunities and facilities for residence and travel as may be required for the independent exercise of their functions.

Witnesses and experts shall be accorded the immunities and facilities necessary for the fulfilment of their mission.[8]

On the basis of this agreement the Court submitted detailed recommendations to the General Assembly, which, at its 55th meeting, adopted the following resolution:

1. The General Assembly, Approves the agreements concluded between the International Court of Justice and the Netherlands Government, as recorded in the exchange of letters between the President of the Court and the Minister for Foreign Affairs of the Netherlands (Annex).

2. Recommends that if a judge, for the purpose of holding himself permanently at the disposal of the Court, resides in some country other than his own, he should be accorded

[8] Resolutions adopted by the General Assembly, Doc. A/64/Add. 1, p. 180 f.

diplomatic privileges and immunities during the period of his residence there.

3. Recommends that judges should be accorded every facility for leaving the country where they may happen to be, for entering the country where the Court is sitting, and again for leaving it. On journeys in connection with the exercise of their functions, they should, in all countries through which they may have to pass, enjoy all the privileges, immunities and facilities granted by these countries to diplomatic envoys.

This provision should also apply to the Registrar and to any officer of the Court acting as Registrar.

4. Recommends that:

(*a*) Officials of the Court should enjoy in any country where they may be on the business of the Court, or in any country through which they may pass on such business, such privileges, immunities and vacilities for residence and travel as may be necessary for the independent exercise of their functions.

The Registrar, and any officer of the Court acting as Registrar, should, while on the business of the Court, be accorded diplomatic privileges and immunities.

(*b*) Inasmuch as these privileges and immunities are granted to officials of the Court in the interests of the International Court of Justice, and not for the personal benefit of the individuals themselves, the Registrar of the Court, with the President's approval, should have the right and the duty to waive the immunity in any case where, in his opinion, the immunity would impede the course of justice, and can be waived without prejudice to the interests of the Court. In the case of the Registrar, the Court should have the right to waive immunity.

5. Recommends that:

(*a*) (i) The agents, counsel and advocates before the Court should be accorded, during the period of their missions, including the time spent on journeys in connection with their missions, the privileges and immunities provided for in Article 4, Sections 11, 12 and 13 of the Convention on the privileges and immunities of the United Nations under the conditions of Article 4, Section 15, of that Convention.

(ii) Assessors of the Court should be accorded, during the period of their missions, including the time spent on journeys in connection with their missions, the privileges and immunities provided for in Article 6,

Section 22, of the Convention on the privileges and immunities of the United Nations.

(iii) Witnesses, experts and persons performing missions by order of the Court should be accorded, during the period of their missions, including the time spent on journeys in connection with their missions, the privileges and immunities provided for in Article 6, Section 22, of the Convention on the privileges and immunities of the United Nations.

(*b*) Inasmuch as the privileges and immunities referred to above under (*a*) are granted in the interests of the good administration of justice and not for the personal benefit of the individuals themselves, the appropriate authority should have the right and the duty to waive the immunity in any case where, in its opinion, the immunity would impede, and can be waived without prejudice to, the course of justice.

For this purpose, the competent authority in the case of agents, counsel and advocates representing a State will be the State concerned. In other cases (including those of assessors of the Court, persons performing missions by order of the Court and witnesses or experts), the competent authority will be the International Court of Justice or, when the Court is not sitting, the President of the Court.

6. Recommends that:

(*a*) The authorities of members should recognise and accept United Nations *laissez-passer*, issued by the International Court of Justice to the members of the Court, the Registrar and the officials of the Court, as valid travel documents, taking into account the provisions of sub-paragraph (*b*).

(*b*) Applications for visas (where required) from the judges of the Court and the Registrar should be dealt with as speedily as possible. All other holders of *laissez-passer* should receive the same facilities when the applications for visas are accompanied by a certificate that they are travelling on the business of the Court. In addition, all holders of *laissez-passer* should be granted facilities for speedy travel.

(*c*) Similar facilities to those specified in sub-paragraph (*b*) should be accorded to experts and other persons who, though not the holders of United Nations *laissez-passer* delivered by the International Court of Justice, have a certificate that they are travelling on the business of the Court.[9]

The constitutionality of the procedure which led to this resolution is problematical; not only because the Charter does not contain a

[9] *Ibid.*, pp. 177 ff.

provision—analogous to that of Article 105, paragraph 3—authorising the General Assembly to make recommendations with a view to determining the details of the application of Articles 19 and 42 (3) of the Statute, but also because the Court is not competent to enter into an agreement with a state or to make recommendations with a view to the application of the above-quoted Articles to the General Assembly. As to the content of the resolution of the Assembly it should be noted that the approval of the Agreement with the Government of the Netherlands does not constitute the obligations of this government, which are established by the Statute and only specified by the agreement entered into with the Court and approved by the General Assembly; except for the provisions concerning the privileges and immunities granted to the Registrar, Deputy Registrar, and other officials of the Court. The Statute does not contain provisions concerning privileges and immunities of these organs of the Court, nor of the assessors to be appointed by the Court under Article 30. As to the difference made by the agreement between persons of Dutch and persons of other than Dutch nationality, it may be doubted whether it is in conformity with the Statute.

The other provisions of the resolution have the character of recommendations with respect to the application of Articles 19 and 42, paragraph 3 of the Statute, by the states concerned. Since the interpretation of these provisions of the Statute is within the competence of these states, the recommendations of the Assembly are not binding upon them. This is of particular importance with respect to the recommendations concerning the officials of the Court and the assessors of the Court, for whom—as pointed out—the Statute does not provide privileges and immunities. In contradistinction to the resolution adopted under Article 105, paragraph 3, of the Charter, the resolution dealing with the application of Articles 19 and 42 (3) of the Statute does not suggest the conclusion of agreements in conformity with the recommendations made in paragraphs 2 to 6 of the resolution. The only agreement is that with the Netherlands, approved in paragraph 1 of the resolution.

Article 32, paragraph 8, of the Statute provides that the salaries, allowances, and compensation of the members of the Court and the Registrar as determined in paragraphs 1 to 7 of this Article ' shall be free of all taxation.' This provision implies an obligation imposed upon states not to subject to taxation the salaries, allowances, and compensation of the members of the Court and the Registrar. It applies to the states upon which the Statute is binding: the members of the judicial community constituted by the Statute of the International Court of Justice.

Article 31, paragraph 2, of the Statute provides that if the Court includes upon the Bench a judge of the nationality of one of the parties, ' any other party may choose a person to sit as judge.' Since, this right to appoint a national judge is conferred by the Statute to ' any party,' it may be exercised not only by a party which is a Member of the United Nations, but also by a state which is a party to the Statute without being a Member, and by a state to which the Court is open under Article 35, paragraph 2, of the Statute.

Article 40, paragraph 3, of the Statute, stipulates that the Registrar of the Court shall ' notify the Members of the United Nations through the Secretary-General,' of any action by which a case has been brought before the Court under Article 40, paragraph 1; but it is added: ' and also any other states entitled to appear before the Court.' The text of Article 40 is almost identical with that of the analogous Article of the old Statute. The meaning of the phrase is not clear and it is hardly understandable why it has been taken over from the old Statute in spite of the fact that it has been severely criticised. Whatever its meaning may be, there can be no doubt that states to which the ' Court is open,' either under Article 35, paragraph 1, or Article 35, paragraph 2, are ' states entitled to appear before the Court.' With respect to the right to be notified under Article 40, there is no difference between the two categories of members of the judicial community. The same is true with respect to the right established by Article 66, paragraph 1, of the Statute, according to which the Registrar shall give notice of the request for an advisory opinion made under Article 65, ' to all states entitled to appear before the Court '; with respect to the right established by Article 66, paragraph 2, according to which the Registrar shall notify ' any state entitled to appear before the Court . . . as likely to be able to furnish information on the question, that the Court will be prepared to receive, within a time limit to be fixed by the President, written statements, or to hear, at a public sitting to be held for the purpose, oral statements relating to the question '; and with respect to the right established by Article 66, paragraph 3, stipulating that ' any state entitled to appear before the Court,' if it should have failed to receive the special communication referred to in paragraph 2 of Article 66, ' may express a desire to submit a written statement or to be heard.'

Article 67 of the Statute stipulates that the Court shall deliver its advisory opinions in open court ' notice having been given to the Secretary-General and to the representatives of Members of the United Nations, of other states and of international organisations immediately concerned.' The right to receive notice under this Article is the same whether states parties to the Statute under Article 35, paragraph 1, or states to which the Court is open under Article 35, paragraph 2, are immediately concerned.

The right to make an application for revision of a judgment, stipulated in Article 61 of the Statute, is conferred upon any party to a dispute decided by the Court. Hence no difference exists in this respect between parties to the Statute under Article 35, paragraph 1, and states to which the Court is open under Article 35, paragraph 2.

Article 36, paragraph 2, authorises only 'the states parties to the present Statute' to declare that they recognise as compulsory *ipso facto* and without special agreement in relation to any other state accepting the same obligation, the jurisdiction of the Court in all legal disputes' concerning certain matters determined in this Article. But according to the resolution adopted by the Security Council pursuant to Article 35, paragraph 2, also states which are not parties to the Statute in the sense of Article 35, paragraph 1, but to which the 'Court is open' under Article 35, paragraph 2, on the basis of a general acceptance of the Court's jurisdiction, may make the declaration referred to in Article 36.

There are, however, two rights which—according to the wording of the provisions concerned—are reserved to 'Members of the United Nations' and may be conferred, by a decision of the General Assembly upon recommendation of the Security Council, only upon states which are 'parties to the Statute' under Article 35, paragraph 1. The one is the right to participate in the electing of members of the Court stipulated in Article 4, paragraph 3; the other is the right to participate in the amendment procedure regulated in Article 69. As far as the first-mentioned provision is concerned, there is a difference between Article 4 of the new and the analogous Article of the old Statute. Article 4, paragraph 3, of the old Statute stipulated:

> The conditions under which a State which has accepted the Statute of the Court but is not a member of the League of Nations, may participate in electing the members of the Court shall, in the absence of a special agreement, be laid down by the Assembly on the proposal of the Council.

The formula 'a State which has accepted the Statute of the Court but is not a member of the League of Nations' taken literally, is applicable also to states which under Article 35, paragraph 2, in conformity with the resolution of the Council of May 17, 1922, accepted the jurisdiction of the Court by a 'general declaration.'[1] Article 4, paragraph 3, of the new Statute, however, stipulates:

> The conditions under which a state which is a party to the present Statute but is not a Member of the United Nations may participate in electing the members of the Court shall, in the

[1] The resolution of the Council of May 17, 1922, quoted above provided that: under Article 35, paragraph 2, the Court shall be open to a state which is not a Member of the League nor mentioned in the Annex to the Covenant upon the condition that such state shall previously have deposited with the Registrar of the Court a declaration 'by which it accepts the jurisdiction of the Court in accordance with . . . the terms and subject to the conditions of the Statute . . . of the Court.' The Drafting Committee of the Conference Regarding the Revision of the Statute of the Permanent Court of International Justice, Held at Geneva from

absence of a special agreement, be laid down by the General Assembly upon recommendation of the Security Council.

The formula ' a state which is a party to the present Statute but is not a Member of the United Nations ' does not cover Article 35, paragraph 2. The phrase ' a state which is a party to the Statute ' designates only states referred to in Article 35, paragraph 1, not the states referred to in Article 35, paragraph 2. Consequently states which, in acceptance of the conditions laid down by the Security Council under Article 35, paragraph 2, have submitted to the Statute, cannot obtain the right of participation in electing the members of the Court even if the Court has been opened to them on the basis of a ' general declaration ' to accept the jurisdiction of the Court in accordance with the terms and subject to the conditions of the Statute, so that they have become permanent members of the judicial community. The exclusion of this category of states parties to the Statute—although not called so by the Statute—is hardly justifiable.

Article 69 of the Statute, which has no counterpart in the old Statute, contains the same formula as the above-quoted Article 4, paragraph 3, in stipulating that the General Assembly upon recommendation of the Security Council may adopt provisions concerning the participation in the procedure for amendments to the Statute of ' states which are parties to the present Statute but are not Members of the United Nations.' There is no reason to exclude from this procedure states which are permanent members of the community constituted by the Statute under Article 35, paragraph 2. Besides, it must be borne in mind that even states which are ' parties to the Statute ' but not ' Members of the United Nations ' have no right,

September 4 to 12, 1929, originally suggested the following text of Article 4, paragraph 3, of the Statute:

> The conditions under which a state which is a party to the Protocol of Signature of the Statute of the Court of December 16, 1920, but is not a Member of the League of Nations may participate in electing the members of the Court shall, in absence of any special agreement on the subject, be laid down by the Assembly on the proposal of the Council.

At the 5th meeting of the Conference the words ' which is a party to the Protocol ' have been replaced by the words ' which has accepted the Statute of the Court,' because these were the words employed by the Protocol. (Cf. League of Nations Doc. C.514. M.173, 1929 V., pp. 50, 76.) In the Protocol the signatories ' declare their acceptance of the adjoint Statute of the Permanent Court of International Justice ' and ' consequently, they hereby declare that they accept the jurisdiction of the Court in accordance with the terms and subject to the conditions of the above-mentioned Statute.' The latter formula is used in the resolution of the Council of May 17, 1922.

The formula of Article 4, paragraph 3, of the old Statute: ' a state which has accepted the Statute of the Court but is not a Member of the League of Nations,' was probably intended to refer only to states parties to the Protocol but not Members of the League. But its wording allows it to be applied also to states which were neither Members of the League nor parties to the Protocol, but which had accepted the Statute under Article 35, paragraph 2, by a ' general declaration.'

directly stipulated by the Statute, to participate in electing the members of the Court and in the amendment procedure. They may only obtain these rights if the General Assembly upon recommendation of the Security Council confers upon them such rights. The two organs are delegated to issue the rules concerned in Article 4, paragraph 3, by the phrase: the provisions 'shall' be laid down by them, in Article 69, by the phrase: the organs 'may' adopt the provisions. It is not very likely that it was intended in the one case to oblige the two organs, in the other case only to entitle them, to issue the rules concerned. It is more likely that the terminological difference has no definite purpose.[2]

D. *Compulsory Jurisdiction?*

Disputes may be brought before the International Court of Justice only with the consent of the parties to the dispute. This results from Article 36, paragraph 1, of the Statute:

> The jurisdiction of the Court comprises all cases which the parties refer to it and all matters specially provided for in the Charter of the United Nations or in treaties and conventions in force.

In stipulating that the jurisdiction of the Court comprises all cases which 'the parties' refer to it, Article 36, paragraph 1, provides that the parties to a dispute must agree to refer the case to the Court

[2] As to the question of Switzerland's right to participate in the election of the members of the Court under Article 4, paragraph 3, of the Statute, and in the procedure for amendments to the Statute under Article 96, cf. point 7, of the Report and Recommendation of the Committee of Experts to the Security Council concerning the conditions on which Switzerland may become a Party to the Statute of the International Court of Justice, adopted by the Security Council on its 80th meeting on November 15, 1946, cf. *supra*, pp. 490 f.

At its 360th meeting on September 28, 1948, the Security Council resolved to recommend to the General Assembly:

> to determine as follows the conditions in which a State, a party to the Statute of the Court, but not a Member of the United Nations, may participate in electing the members of the International Court of Justice:
>
> 1. Such a State shall be on an equal footing with the Members of the United Nations in respect to those provisions of the Statute which regulate the nominations of candidates for election by the General Assembly;
>
> 2. Such a State shall participate, in the General Assembly, in electing the members of the Court in the same manner as the Members of the United Nations;
>
> 3. Such a State, when in arrears in the payment of its contribution to the expenses of the Court, shall not participate in electing the members of the Court in the General Assembly, if the amount of its arrears equals or exceeds the amount of the contribution due from it for the preceding two full years. The General Assembly may, nevertheless, permit such a State to participate in the elections, if it is satisfied that the failure to pay is due to conditions beyond the control of that State. (Doc. S/969.)

This recommendation was adopted by the General Assembly at its 150th meeting on October 8, 1948.

in order to establish its jurisdiction for that case.[3] As to 'matters specially provided for in the Charter,' the only provision which comes into consideration is that of Article 36, paragraph 3, of the Charter, 'that legal disputes should as a general rule be referred by the parties to the International Court of Justice in accordance with the provisions of the Statute of the Court.' In accordance with this provision, the Security Council may adopt a decision recommending to the parties of a dispute to refer this dispute to the Court. If Article 25 of the Charter is interpreted to apply also to recommendations of the Security Council, and consequently a recommendation to refer a dispute to the Court is interpreted to be binding upon the parties, Article 36, paragraph 3, of the Charter, constitutes a case where parties to a dispute are obliged to refer it to the Court and hence to recognise the jurisdiction of the Court, even without their voluntary agreement. But, as pointed out in a previous connection, this interpretation, according to which Article 36, paragraph 3, would provide a kind of compulsory jurisdiction of the Court, is doubtful.[4]

[3] The Permanent Court of International Justice in several cases recognised the principle that its jurisdiction was based on the consent of the parties. (Series A, No. 2, p. 16; No. 9, p. 32; No. 15, p. 22; No. 17, p. 37. Cf. Hudson, *op. cit.*, p. 410.)

[4] Cf. *supra*, pp. 444 ff. The Summary Report of the 19th meeting of Committee IV/1 (U.N.C.I.O. Doc. 828, IV/1/67, p. 3) contains the following statement: 'The French delegate proposed that the words "in the Charter of the United Nations or," be deleted in paragraph (1) of Article 36 since the Charter did not appear to confer jurisdiction in any case. However, another view was expressed that paragraph 6 of Chapter VIII A, of the Charter [?] related to compulsory references of cases to the Court by the Security Council. It was therefore, agreed that there should be no deletion.' Chapter VIII, Section A, paragraph 6, of the Dumbarton Oaks Proposals, corresponding to Article 36 of the Charter stipulated that 'justiciable disputes should normally be referred to the International Court of Justice.'

The case concerning the Incidents in the Corfu Channel was brought before the International Court of Justice by a letter, dated May 13, 1947, from the Government of the United Kingdom to the Registrar of the Court, in which the Government contended 'that the Court has jurisdiction under Article 36 (1) of its Statute as being a matter, which is one specially provided for in the Charter of the United Nations, on the grounds: (*a*) that the Security Council of the United Nations, at the conclusion of proceedings in which it dealt with the dispute under Article 36 of the Charter, by a Resolution, of which a copy forms Annex 2 to this Application [Resolution adopted on April 9, 1947] decided to recommend both the Government of the United Kingdom and the Albanian Government to refer the present dispute to the International Court of Justice; (*b*) that the Albanian Government accepted the invitation of the Security Council under Article 32 of the Charter to participate in the discussion of the dispute and accepted the condition laid down by the Security Council, when conveying the invitation, that Albania accepts in the present case all the obligations which a Member of the United Nations would have to assume in a similar case. (A copy of the invitation of the Security Council and of the Albanian Government's reply thereto form Annex 3 to the present Application); (*c*) that Article 25 of the Charter provides that the Members of the United Nations agree to accept and carry out the decisions of the Security

The reference in Article 36, paragraph 1, of the Statute to 'treaties and conventions in force' may be interpreted to mean treaties (the term 'conventions' is superfluous as conventions are treaties) which were in force at the moment the Charter (including the Statute) came into existence. Otherwise the addition of the words 'in force' would be redundant. At the moment the Charter came into existence no treaty could be in force by which a matter was referred to the International Court of Justice, since this Court did not exist prior to that date. However, the interpretation of this reference must take into consideration Article 37 of the Statute, which runs as follows:

> Whenever a treaty or convention in force provides for reference of a matter to a tribunal to have been instituted by the League of Nations, or to the Permanent Court of International Justice, the matter shall, as between the parties to the present Statute, be referred to the International Court of Justice.

The terms 'treaties and conventions in force' in Article 36, paragraph 1, may, however, also be interpreted to refer not only to international agreements which were in force when the Charter came into existence, but also to agreements to be concluded in the future.[5] Then this provision authorises the parties to any such treaty to confer upon the International Court of Justice, jurisdiction in matters not provided for in the Charter of the United Nations (in the wider sense of the term). In so far as these 'matters' are disputes the jurisdiction of the Court is based on the agreement of the parties to the dispute, which agreement is implied in the treaty conferring jurisdiction upon the Court. Since a treaty is binding only upon the contracting parties, the latter can confer upon the Court, jurisdiction only in disputes to which they are parties. Since according to Article 36, paragraph 1, of the Statute 'the jurisdiction of the Court comprises all cases which the parties refer to it,' the Statute need not authorise states to confer by treaties jurisdiction upon the Court in disputes to which they are

Council in accordance with the present Charter.' (International Court of Justice, Distr. 151, 1947, General List No. 1, pp. 3 f.)

In its letter of July 2, 1947, the Government of Albania denied that a recommendation made by the Security Council under Article 36, paragraph 3, of the Charter, had a binding character and that this provision constituted a compulsory jurisdiction of the Court. In its decision, delivered on March 25, 1948, the Court ignored this question; but in a separate opinion seven judges declared that the view maintained by the Albanian Government appeared to them well-founded and that they could not accept 'an interpretation according to which this Article [36, paragraph 3, of the Charter] without explicitly saying so, has introduced more or less surreptitiously a new case of compulsory jurisdiction.' (Cf. the text of the separate opinion, published in the *International Law Quarterly*, Vol. II, No. 1 (1948), pp. 78 f.)

[5] This was the interpretation of the identical phrase in Article 36 of the old Statute. (Cf. Records of the First Assembly of the League of Nations, Committees, I, p. 384, and Hudson, *op. cit.*, pp. 438 f.)

parties. However, by a treaty, states may not merely establish the jurisdiction of the Court but may assume the obligation to submit to the Court a particular dispute or a category of disputes or all possible disputes which might arise between them. By such a treaty a state may be obliged to recognise the jursidiction of the Court in any dispute which the other party, by a unilateral application made in conformity with Article 40, paragraph 1, of the Statute, refers to the Court. Even then, the jurisdiction of the Court in a concrete case is based on the agreement of the parties to the case, not on a special agreement referring to the particular case, but on the general agreement implied in the treaty establishing the obligation of the contracting parties to submit their disputes to the Court.

The wording of the provision of Article 36, paragraph 1, that the jurisdiction of the Court comprises 'all matters' specially provided for 'in treaties and conventions in force,' refers not only to disputes but to 'all matters,' and not only to international agreements entered into by states but to all possible agreements. Hence the question arises whether this provision may be interpreted to constitute an authorisation to confer upon the Court jurisdiction in cases to which not only states, but international organisations are parties. This question may be answered in the negative if it is assumed that such an extension of the jursidiction of the Court requires an amendment to the Statute which in Article 34, paragraph 1, expressly restricts this jurisdiction to cases to which states are parties. But an affirmative answer is not excluded by the wording of the Article 36, paragraph 1. It seems, however, that the General Assembly adopted the first mentioned interpretation. Otherwise there would have been no sufficient reason to provide in the Convention on the Privileges and Immunities of the United Nations and in the Headquarters Agreement, mentioned above, in case of conflict between the Organisation and the state concerned for advisory opinions of the Court, instead of stipulating that the case should be submitted to the decision of the Court.[6]

Jurisdiction in disputes between states can be conferred upon the Court only by treaties to which the states the disputes of which are to be submitted to the Court, are contracting parties. But some trusteeship agreements—concluded by the Organisation and the state designated as administering authority—contain a provision to the effect that disputes between the administering authority and another Member of the United Nations relating to the interpretation or application of the agreement shall be submitted to the International Court of Justice.[7] It is evident that such a provision in itself cannot

[6] Cf. *supra*, p. 486.

[7] Such clauses are contained in the Trusteeship agreements for British Togoland, British Cameroons, Tanganyika, French Togoland, French Cameroons, Ruanda-

establish the jurisdiction of the Court in case of a dispute between the administering authority and another Member of the United Nations. Such a dispute can be submitted to the Court only with the consent of the other party. If this party is willing to submit the dispute to the Court, the administering authority is bound by the trusteeship agreement to recognise the jurisdiction of the Court. In this respect the trusteeship agreement has the character of a treaty in favour of third states (*en faveur d'Etats tiers*).[8]

There are some instruments conferring upon the Court or its President an extrajudicial function, such as appointment of umpires, presidents of conciliation commissions, and the like. Thus, *e.g.*, the Agreement between the United Nations and the Swiss Confederation on the Ariana Site[9] contains the following provision:

> ARTICLE 13
>
> Any disputes which may arise with regard to the execution or interpretation of the present Agreement shall be referred to a tribunal composed of three arbitrators. The United Nations and the Swiss Federal Council shall each appoint an arbitrator. The third arbitrator, who will preside over the tribunal, shall be appointed by the President of the International Court of Justice.

An agreement between the Netherlands and the Indonesian Republic of March 25, 1947,[1] provides:

> The Netherlands Government and the Government of the Republic shall settle by arbitration any dispute which might arise from this Agreement, and which cannot be solved by joint consultation in a conference between the said delegations. In this case a chairman of another nationality, with a casting vote, shall be appointed by mutual consent between the delegations,

Urundi, and Western Samoa. Article 19 of the Trusteeship agreement for British Togoland reads as follows:

> If any dispute whatever should arise between the Administering Authority and another Member of the United Nations relating to the interpretation or application of the provisions of this Agreement, such dispute, if it cannot be settled by negotiation or other means, shall be submitted to the International Court of Justice, provided for in Chapter XIV of the United Nations Charter.

The clauses inserted in the other Trusteeship Agreements mentioned above are more or less identical. They have been taken over from the Mandates Agreements.

8 At the 12th meeting of Subcommittee 1 of the Fourth Committee during the discussion of the trusteeship agreement for Western Samoa, the representative of Australia quite correctly observed with respect to the provision concerned that the second party to a dispute would not be obligated by the terms of Article 16 [of the the trusteeship agreement] although the contrary seemed to be implied in the text. (Summary Records of Meetings of Subcommittee 1 of the Fourth Committee, November 15—December 10, 1946, p. 87.)

9 Doc. A/175, p. 29.

1 *International Court of Justice, Yearbook*, 1946–1947, p. 233.

or failing this, by the President of the International Court of Justice.

Article 36, paragraph 1, of the Statute, refers to 'the jurisdiction of the Court,' which probably means only the competence of the Court to render judicial decisions. Neither the Charter (in the narrower sense) nor the Statute contains a provision authorising the Court or its President to accept other functions conferred upon them by international agreements or other legal instruments. The constitutionality of the acceptance of such functions is especially doubtful in case of agreements or other legal instruments not approved by the United Nations.[2]

Article 36, paragraph 2, provides:

> The states parties to the present Statute may at any time declare that they recognise as compulsory *ipso facto* and without special agreement, in relation to any other state accepting the same obligation, the jurisdiction of the Court in all legal disputes concerning:
>
> (*a*) the interpretation of a treaty;
>
> (*b*) any question of international law;
>
> (*c*) the existence of any fact which, if established, would constitute a breach of an international obligation;
>
> (*d*) the nature or extent of the reparation to be made for the breach of an international obligation.

The declaration referred to in this paragraph makes a special agreement by which the dispute is to be brought before the Court, unnecessary. Under Article 36, paragraph 2, the Court has jurisdiction in a particular case only when both parties to the dispute have made the declaration referred to in this paragraph; and by this declaration a state recognises the jurisdiction of the Court only 'in relation to any other state accepting the same obligation.' The unilateral declaration of one state together with the unilateral declaration of another constitute an agreement. This agreement, it is true, has not the character of a 'special agreement' within the meaning of the term used in Article 36, paragraph 2. But it is a general agreement in so far as the states by

[2] 'At the request of the French Government the President of the Court nominated observers in connection with the plebiscite held in the districts of Tende-Brigue on the Franco-Italian frontier during October, 1947. The plebiscite was necessary to determine whether these territories should be attached to France, according to the terms of the Peace Treaty with Italy, since the French Constitution of 1946 provides that no territory may be added to the Republic without the consent of the population of the territory concerned.' (United Nations Department of Public Information, Background Paper 33, February 24, 1948, p. 15.) The appointment of observers in connection with a plebiscite has nothing to do with the jurisdiction of the Court as established by the Charter (in the wider sense of the term); and the President of the Court is not authorised by the Charter to accept and to exercise such a function in his capacity as organ of the Court on the basis of the request of the government of a state.

making the declaration referred to in Article 36, paragraph 2, in relation to one another, agree to recognise the jurisdiction of the Court in all legal disputes, in case one party brings the dispute before the Court. Hence the jurisdiction of the Court under Article 36, paragraph 2, is based on a general agreement of the parties to the dispute, just as under Article 36, paragraph 1, states by a treaty may assume the obligation to refer to the Court certain or all possible disputes which may arise between them.

No state can be forced into Court against its will. But that does not mean that a state can be party to a case before the Court only together with that state (or those states) with which it has—either specially or generally—agreed upon referring the case to the Court. For Articles 62 and 63 of the Statute provide:

> ARTICLE 62
>
> 1. Should a state consider that it has an interest of a legal nature which may be affected by the decision in the case, it may submit a request to the Court to be permitted to intervene.
>
> 2. It shall be for the Court to decide upon this request.
>
> ARTICLE 63
>
> 1. Whenever the construction of a convention to which states other than those concerned in the case are parties is in question, the Registrar shall notify all such states forthwith.
>
> 2. Every state so notified has the right to intervene in the proceedings; but if it uses this right, the construction given by the judgment will be equally binding upon it.

If the Court grants the request submitted by a state under Article 62, or if a state uses its right to intervene under Article 63, the state concerned becomes a party to the pending case although there exists no special or general agreement between this state and the other parties to the case.

The jurisdiction which the Court has under Article 36, paragraph 2, on the basis of the declarations referred to in this provision is not a 'compulsory' jurisdiction in the true sense of the word. In order to establish true compulsory jurisdiction of the International Court of Justice, the Statute would have to provide that any member of the judicial community, party to any case whatever, is obliged to recognise the jurisdiction of the Court if the other party refers the dispute to the Court.[3] But it provides only for the possibility of entering into

[3] The Draft Statute proposed by the Committee of Jurists contains two alternatives with respect to the text of Article 36, one of which accepts the optional clause of the old Statute; the other formulates the principle of compulsory jurisdiction. It runs as follows: 'The Members of the United Nations and States parties to the present Statute recognise as among themselves the jurisdiction of the Court as

agreements for the establishment of the jurisdiction of the Court, in advance and in a general way. It is significant that the provision of Article 36, paragraph 2, is characterised as ' optional clause ' in the practice of the states and the literature of international law.

The difference between the so-called ' compulsory ' jurisdiction as established by Article 36, paragraph 2, of the Statute and the provision of a genuine compulsory jurisdiction as formulated above is,

compulsory *ipso facto* and without special agreement in any legal dispute ' (follow the clauses (*a*) to (*d*) of Article 36, paragraph 2). The Report of Rapporteur on Draft of Statute of an International Court of Justice submitted by the Committee of Jurists to the Conference at San Francisco contains the statement ' that the majority of the Committee was in favour of compulsory jurisdiction, but it has been noted that, in spite of this predominant sentiment, it did not seem certain, nor even probable, that all the nations whose participation in the proposed International Organisation appears to be necessary were now in a position to accept the rule of compulsory jurisdiction, and that the Dumbarton Oaks Proposals did not seem to affirm it; some, while retaining their preferences in this respect, thought that the counsel of prudence was not to go beyond the procedure of the optional clause inserted in Article 36, which has opened the way to the progressive adoption, in less than 10 years, of compulsory jurisdiction by many States which in 1920 refused to subscribe to it. Placed on this basis, the problem was found to assume a political character, and the Committee thought that it should defer it to the San Francisco Conference.' (The International Court of Justice. *Selected Documents Relating to the Drafting of the Statute.* U.S. Government Printing Office, Washington, 1946, pp. 124 f.)

The subcommittee entrusted with the study of Article 36 of the Statute made the following declaration (U.N.C.I.O. Doc. 702, IV/1/55, p. 3): ' The desire to establish compulsory jurisdiction for the Court prevailed among the majority of the Subcommittee. However, some of these delegates feared that insistence upon the realisation of that ideal would only impair the possibility of obtaining general accord to the statute of the Court, as well as to the Charter itself.' The Summary Report of the 14th meeting of Committee IV/1 (U.N.C.I.O. Doc. 661, IV/1/50, pp. 2 and 4) contains the following statements: ' The delegate of China pronounced himself in favour of giving the Court complete jurisdiction over all legal disputes. This would result in decreasing the number of international disputes since mere threat of being brought before the Court would deter states from plainly illegal action. The adoption of this principle would present important advantages, and nothing prejudicial would result, since the only cases which could be brought before the Court would be within the four categories provided for in Article 6.' ' The delegate of the United Kingdom pointed out that his country had accepted compulsory jurisdiction of the Court by signing sixteen years ago the optional clause, and that Great Britain was still bound by it. His country was therefore not opposed to compulsory jurisdiction in principle, but the Committee must discuss the matter from a practical standpoint. Two countries, whose co-operation is essential, are not ready to accept compulsory jurisdiction. The same two countries had never acceded to the Statute of the Permanent Court of International Justice. They appear, however, ready to become members of the new Court. If the compulsory jurisdiction clause is introduced in the Statute, the Statute being a part of the Charter, the position of these two countries would be very difficult. He pointed out that the optional clause has been accepted by fifty-six states and produced satisfactory results. He thought it wise, therefore, to accept a solution and leave these two states time to consider the question of compulsory jurisdiction.' The delegate of France, too, was against compulsory jurisdiction of the Court.

it is true, only relative. Since the jurisdiction of an international tribunal can be established only by treaty concluded by the states to be subjected to the tribunal's jurisdiction, this jurisdiction is always based on the consent of all parties to the case over which the tribunal has jurisdiction. But it makes a remarkable difference whether the Statute of the tribunal obliges directly any party to any possible dispute to accept the jurisdiction of the tribunal if the other party to the dispute refers the case to the tribunal, or whether the Statute—as the Statute of the International Court of Justice does—only offers the possibility of establishing agreements the essence of which has just been characterised.

Paragraph 2 of Article 36 of the new Statute corresponds, on the whole, to paragraph 2 of Article 36 of the old Statute. Some changes have been made, but they are of minor importance, except the one already mentioned: the Statute of the Permanent Court of International Justice authorised the states to restrict the jurisdiction of the Court to the one or the other classes of disputes enumerated in clauses (*a*) to (*d*); whereas according to the Statute of the International Court of Justice, the states, if they make the declaration referred to in Article 36, paragraph 2, are authorised only to confer upon the Court jurisdiction in all legal disputes enumerated in clauses (*a*) to (*d*). They are not authorised to make in their declaration exceptions from the legal disputes enumerated in clauses (*a*) to (*d*). Paragraph 3 of Article 36—identical with the corresponding provision of the old Statute—allows only to make the declaration 'on condition of reciprocity on the part of several or certain states, or for a certain time.' Reservations excluding categories of disputes which fall within one of the clauses (*a*) to (*d*) are not, or not expressly, permitted. But under the old Statute, declarations have been made containing such reservations.[4] Some of these declarations are now in force under the new Statute[5] in accordance with paragraph 5 of Article 36 which runs as follows:

> Declarations made under Article 36 of the Statute of the Permanent Court of International Justice and which are still

[4] The Report of the Rapporteur of Committee IV/1 (U.N.C.I.O. Doc. 913, IV/1/74 (1), pp. 11 f.) quotes the following statement of the subcommittee's report: 'The question of reservations calls for an explanation. As is well known, the article has consistently been interpreted in the past as allowing states accepting the jurisdiction of the Court to subject their declarations to reservations. The subcommittee has considered such interpretation as being henceforth established. It has therefore been considered unnecessary to modify paragraph 3 in order to make express reference to the right of the states to make such reservations.'

[5] Thus, for instance, the declaration of the United Kingdom which is effective only with regard to disputes 'other than: (1) disputes in regard to which the parties to the dispute have agreed or shall agree to have recourse to some other method of peaceful settlement; (2) disputes with the government of any other Member of the League of Nations which is a member of the British Commonwealth of Nations, all of which disputes shall be settled in such manner as the parties have agreed or

> in force shall be deemed, as between the parties to the present Statute, to be acceptances of the compulsory jurisdiction of the International Court of Justice for the period which they still have to run and in accordance with their terms.

Also declarations recently made under the new Statute contain reservations excluding legal disputes from the jurisdiction of the Court, which is not in conformity with Article 36.[6] Nevertheless,

shall agree; (3) disputes with regard to questions which by international law fall exclusively within the jurisdiction of the United Kingdom; (4) subject to the condition that His Majesty's Government reserve the right to require that proceedings in the Court shall be suspended in respect of any dispute which has been submitted to and is under consideration by the Council of the League of Nations; (5) disputes arising out of events occurring at a time when His Majesty's Government in the United Kingdom were involved in hostilities.' Or the declaration of Iran which is effective only ' with the exception of: (1) disputes relating to the territorial status of Persia, including those concerning the rights of sovereignty of Persia over its islands and ports; (2) disputes in regard to which the parties have agreed or shall agree to have recourse to some other method of peaceful settlement; (3) disputes with regard to questions which, by international law, fall exclusively within the jurisdiction of Persia; (4) subject to the condition that Persia reserves the right to require that proceedings in the Court shall be suspended in respect of any dispute which has been submitted to the Council of the League of Nations.' (*Yearbook*, pp. 612, 610.)

[6] For instance the declaration of Guatemala, signed on January 27, 1947, effective until January 27, 1952, under the following conditions: ' Effective in relation to any other State accepting the same obligation in all legal disputes, except the dispute between England and Guatemala concerning the restoration of the territory of Belize, which the Government of Guatemala would agree to submit to the judgment of the Court, if the case were decided *ex aequo et bono* in accordance with Article 38, paragraph 2, of the Statute of the Court '; or the declaration of Turkey signed on May 22, 1947, effective until May 22, 1952, under the conditions: ' Effective without special agreement in relation to any other State accepting the same obligation in all disputes which will arise in the future concerning: (1) the interpretation of a treaty; (2) any question of international law; (3) the existence of any fact, which, if established, would constitute a breach of an international obligation; (4) the nature or extent of the reparation to be made for the breach of an international obligation; with the exception of: (1) situations previous to this declaration and differences which arise therefrom; (2) disputes for which it may be possible to apply, directly or indirectly, agreements and conventions concluded by Turkey providing for a different method of settling disputes '; or the declaration of France, signed on February 18, 1947, effective until five years after date of ratification and thereafter until notice of termination, under the conditions: ' Effective without special agreement in relation to any other State accepting the same obligation for all disputes which may arise in respect of facts or situations subsequent to ratification of the present declaration with the exception of: (1) disputes with regard to which the parties may have agreed or may agree to have recourse to another form of peaceful settlement; (2) differences relating to matters which are essentially within the national jurisdiction as understood by the Government of the French Republic '; or the declaration of the United States, signed on August 14, 1946, effective until August 14, 1951, and thereafter until the expiration of six months after notice may be given to terminate this declaration under the conditions: ' In all legal disputes arising after the date of signature of the declaration, except: (1) disputes the solution of which the parties shall entrust to other tribunals

they may be considered to be valid. Since the states are not obliged to make a declaration under Article 36, paragraph 2, they cannot be prevented from making a declaration that is more restrictive than provided for in Article 36. Hence the practical value of the provision concerning the content of the declaration which may be made under Article 36, paragraph 2, is problematical.[7]

When in a dispute between two states the declaration made by one of them under Article 36, paragraph 2, contains a reservation which the declaration made by the other under the same provision does not contain, the question arises whether this reservation applies also to the other. The answer depends on the interpretation of the phrase 'in relation to any other state accepting the same obligation' in paragraph 2 of Article 36. The words 'the same obligation' may mean: the obligation established by paragraph 2: to 'recognise as compulsory *ipso facto* and without special agreement . . . the jurisdiction of the Court.' The declaration made by one state under Article 36, paragraph 2, is binding upon this state, in conformity with its content, only in relation to another state which also has made a declaration under Article 36, paragraph 2; and this declaration is binding upon the state concerned, in conformity with its content although this content may differ from the content of the former. Consequently, if the declaration of one litigant contains a reservation excluding certain disputes, which the declaration of the other does

by virtue of agreements already in existence or which may be concluded in the future; or (2) disputes with regard to matters which are essentially within the domestic jurisdiction of the United States of America as determined by the United States of America; or (3) disputes arising under a multilateral treaty, unless (1) all parties to the treaty affected by the decision are also parties to the case before the Court, or (2) the United States of America specifically agrees to jurisdiction.' (*Yearbook*, pp. 609, 611, 612.)

[7] At its 113th meeting the General Assembly adopted the following resolution:

The General Assembly, Considering that, in virtue of Article 1 of the Charter, international disputes should be settled in conformity with the principles of justice and international law;

Considering that the International Court of Justice could settle or assist in settling many disputes in conformity with these principles if, by the full application of the provisions of the Charter and of the Statute of the Court, more frequent use were made of its services;

1. Draws the attention of the States which have not yet accepted the compulsory jurisdiction of the Court in accordance with Article 36, paragraphs 2 and 5, of the Statute, to the desirability of the greatest possible number of States accepting this jurisdiction with as few reservations as possible;

2. Draws the attention of States Members to the advantage of inserting in conventions and treaties arbitration clauses providing, without prejudice to Article 95 of the Charter, for the submission of disputes which may arise from the interpretation or application of such conventions or treaties, preferably and as far as possible to the International Court of Justice;

3. Recommends as a general rule that States should submit their legal disputes to the International Court of Justice.' (Doc. A/519, pp. 103 f.)

not contain, this reservation applies only to the one, not to the other. But the phrase ' in relation to any other state accepting the same obligation ' may be interpreted to mean that a declaration made under Article 36, paragraph 2, is binding upon the state which made the declaration only in relation to another state which also made a declaration under Article 36, paragraph 2, and only to the extent the declaration made by its opponent is binding upon the latter; so that a reservation made by the one applies also to the other, even if not contained in its own declaration. This interpretation has been accepted by the Permanent Court of International Justice.[8] Under such circumstances, it is hardly possible to speak of a ' compulsory ' jurisdiction of the Court.

Even if recognised as provided for in Article 36, paragraph 2, without any reservation, the jurisdiction of the Court is still restricted to a certain class, namely, to legal disputes. Since, as pointed out, the legal character of a dispute, in spite of the enumeration in paragraph 2 of Article 36, does not depend on the subject matter to which the dispute refers but on the norms to be applied to the dispute, a state—even after having made the declaration under Article 36, paragraph 2—may exclude a dispute concerning one of the enumerated subjects from the jurisdiction of the Court. For it may justify its claim or reject its opponent's claim not by rules of existing law but by principles of justice and thus declare the dispute to be a political one, not subjected to the jurisdiction of the Court under Article 36, paragraph 2; and if there is in this respect a dispute as to the jurisdiction of the Court, the latter may under Article 36, paragraph 6, decide in favour of the party which denies its jurisdiction. This is contrary to the true idea of compulsory jurisdiction under which no ' political ' dispute is possible. It is an essential consequence of the principle of compulsory jurisdiction that all disputes are to be considered as legal and justiciable.

Since the Statute of the International Court is—according to an express provision of Article 92 of the Charter—' an integral part of the present Charter ' and the Court—according to the same Article and Article 7 of the Charter—the ' principal judicial organ of the United Nations,' the provisions of the Statute may be considered to be provisions of the Charter. Consequently, Article 36 of the Statute may be considered as ' contained in the present Charter.' If so, Article 2, paragraph 7, of the Charter, refers also to the Statute of the International Court of Justice. It stipulates: ' Nothing contained in the present Charter shall authorise the United Nations to intervene in matters which are essentially within the domestic jurisdiction of any state or shall require the Members to submit such matters to settlement under the present Charter.' There can be little doubt that the decision of a dispute by the International Court of Justice in

[8] Cf. Hudson, *op. cit.*, p. 466.

accordance with Article 36 of the Statute is ' settlement under the present Charter,' even if the term ' Charter ' is taken in a narrower sense, not comprising the Statute. For Article 36, paragraph 3, of the Charter provides that legal disputes should as a general rule be referred by the parties to the Court. Consequently, a party which has recognised the jurisdiction of the Court in accordance with Article 36, paragraph 2, of the Statute, may, in case it considers that the dispute arises out of a matter which is within its domestic jurisdiction, refuse the jurisdiction of the Court with reference to Article 2, paragraph 7, of the Charter. A state may even in the in the declaration made under Article 36, paragraph 2, exclude from the jurisdiction of the Court disputes arising out of a matter which is essentially within the domestic jurisdiction of this state.[9] If the other party does not agree, claiming that the dispute does not arise out of a matter which is essentially within the domestic jurisdiction of the opponent, and hence the jurisdiction of the Court is disputed, Article 36, paragraph 6, of the Statute, applies. According to this provision, the matter shall be settled by the decision of the Court. But how shall the Court decide the question as to whether a dispute arises out of a matter which is essentially within the domestic jurisdiction of the state claiming such jurisdiction? One may argue that Article 36, paragraph 6, confers upon the Court the power to decide disputes concerning its jurisdiction, and for this purpose the Court has to apply and, consequently, to interpret Article 2, paragraph 7, of the Charter. That means that the Court has to determine which

[9] Some declarations now in force under Article 36, paragraph 5, as the above-quoted declarations of the United Kingdom and of Iran, exclude from the jurisdiction of the Court disputes with regard to questions which by international law fall ' exclusively ' within the jurisdiction of the state concerned. This is in conformity with Article 15, paragraph 8, of the Covenant of the League, which refers to matters which ' by international law ' are ' solely ' within the domestic jurisdiction of a state, whereas Article 2, paragraph 7, of the Charter, refers to matters which are ' essentially ' within the domestic jurisdiction of a state. Article 36, paragraph 5, expressly provides that these declarations shall be in force ' in accordance with their terms.' If such a clause is referred to in a case before the Court by the state which made the declaration with this reservation, the Court has to decide whether the matter which the dispute concerns falls, by international law, ' exclusively ' —not ' essentially '—within the jurisdiction of the state concerned.

The provision of Article 36, paragraph 5, that the declarations made under the old Statute which were in force when the new Statute came into force shall be deemed, as between the parties to the new Statute, to be acceptances of the compulsory jurisdiction of the new Court ' in accordance with their terms,' is—if taken literally—not applicable to the clause of the declaration of the United Kingdom (and similar declarations in force under Article 36, paragraph 5, of the new Statute) according to which the declaration is effective ' subject to the condition that His Majesty's Government reserve the right to require that proceedings in the Court shall be suspended in respect of any dispute which has been submitted to and is under consideration by the Council of the League of Nations.' The wording of Article 36, paragraph 5, does not allow to interpret this clause to mean that, now, the Security Council is to be substituted for the Council of the League.

matters are essentially within the domestic jurisdiction of a state, and the parties to the case are bound by this decision. But one may also argue: Since Article 2, paragraph 7, does not confer upon an organ of the United Nations the power to determine what matters are essentially within the domestic jurisdiction of a state, only the state concerned is authorised to decide this question, and that, consequently, the Court has to decide the dispute concerning its jurisdiction in favour of the party which claims the dispute to arise out of a matter which is essentially within its domestic jurisdiction. This interpretation is at the basis of the declarations made by France and the United States under Article 36, paragraph 2, of the Statute. These declarations exclude from the jurisdiction of the Court all disputes with regard to matters which are essentially within the domestic jurisdiction of France and the United States respectively, ' as understood by the Government of the French Republic ' and ' as determined by the United States of America.'[1] This interpretation of Article 36 of the Statute in connection with Article 2, paragraph 7, of the Charter, implies that a party to a dispute before the Court, in spite of its declaration to recognise as ' compulsory ' the jurisdiction of the Court in all legal matters, may withdraw any such dispute from the jurisdiction of the Court by declaring it as regarding a matter which is essentially within its domestic jurisdiction; which is just the contrary of compulsory jurisdiction.

If the parties to a multilateral treaty are parties to the Statute of the International Court of Justice and have made a declaration under Article 36, paragraph 2, of the Statute, recognising as compulsory the jurisdiction of the Court, the question may arise whether any of them is entitled to bring any violation of the treaty by another party as a ' case ' before the Court by a unilateral application in conformity with Article 40, paragraph 1, of the Statute, even if no direct interest of the applicant party is violated. If, for instance, a state party to the Convention on Genocide has failed to fulfil its obligation under Article 5 to enact the necessary legislation to give effect to the provisions of the Convention, may any other party to the Convention bring this case before the Court, provided that both have made a declaration under Article 36, paragraph 2? The question may be answered in the affirmative. Neither Article 36, nor Article 40, of the Statute, provide that a party may bring a case before the Court only if a direct interest has been violated by the other party. Any party to a multilateral treaty may be considered to be interested in the fulfilment by all other contracting parties of the obligations imposed upon them by the treaty. The existence of this interest is proved by the fact that the party concerned entered into the multilateral treaty. By concluding a treaty, whether bilateral or multilateral, each contracting party promises to all the others to fulfil the obligations

[1] Cf. *supra*, pp. 525 f.

established by the treaty. Consequently each contracting party may claim the fulfilment of these obligations on the part of all the others. Article 63 of the Statute recognises the legal interest which any party to a multilateral treaty has in the construction of that treaty. Article 36, paragraph 1, and Article 40, paragraph 1, do not even require that the case have the character of a ' dispute ' between the state which brings the case before the Court and the state against which the proceedings of the Court are to be instituted. Article 36, paragraph 2, it is true, refers to legal ' disputes.' But a dispute between two parties to a multilateral treaty exists already if one party asks the other to fulfil its obligations under the treaty and the other party refuses to comply or denies to have failed to fulfil its obligations

In its declaration made under Article 36, paragraph 2, the United States excluded jurisdiction of the Court in ' disputes arising under a multilateral treaty, unless (1) all parties to the treaty affected by the decision are also parties to the case before the Court, or (2) the United States of America specially agrees to jurisdiction.' This formula is not very clear. The words ' affected by the decision ' probably mean: affected by the decision of the Court. But do they refer to ' all parties ' or to ' the treaty ' ? They probably refer to ' all parties.' But the question as to which parties are affected by the decision of the Court can be answered only after the Court has assumed and exercised jurisdiction in the dispute concerned. The phrase is probably modelled after Article 62, paragraph 1, of the Statute, referring to ' an interest of a legal nature which may be affected by the decision in the case,' and hence means: all parties to the multilateral treaty which may be affected by the decision of the Court are also parties to the case before the Court. Taken literally, this clause authorises the United States, if a party to a multilateral treaty, in spite of its declaration under Article 36, paragraph 2, to refuse to appear before the Court in case another party to the treaty, which also made a declaration under Article 36, paragraph 2, brings a dispute before the Court which arises out of its contention that the United States has violated its obligations under the treaty, if not all other parties to this treaty which may be affected by the decision of the Court are parties to the case. It is upon the United States to decide which parties to the treaties may be affected by the decision of the Court; and the United States, with reference to Article 63 of the Statute, may very well maintain that all parties to the multilateral treaty may be affected by the decision. That means that the Court will hardly have jurisdiction under Article 36, paragraph 2, in a dispute to which the United States is a party in case the dispute has arisen under a multilateral treaty and the United States does not specially agree to the jurisdiction of the Court.

The situation is different if the multilateral treaty contains a provision to the effect that disputes between the contracting parties relating to the interpretation, application or fulfilment of the treaty shall be submitted to the International Court of Justice at the request of any of the parties to the dispute; a provision which, for instance, the Convention on Genocide actually contains in Article 9. If under a multilateral treaty containing such a clause a dispute arises in which one party to the treaty asserts that another party has violated the treaty and if one of these parties refers the dispute to the Court, the other is obliged to recognise its jurisdiction, whether the parties have or have not made declarations under Article 36, paragraph 2.

5. The Law to Be Applied by the Court

It is an essential characteristic of an international tribunal that it has to apply existing international law to the dispute submitted to it, unless the treaty by which the tribunal is established authorises it to apply other norms, such as rules of justice or equity, or the like. Article 38 of the Statute stipulates:

> 1. The Court, whose function is to decide in accordance with international law such disputes as are submitted to it, shall apply:
>
> > (*a*) international conventions, whether general or particular, establishing rules expressly recognised by the contesting states;
> >
> > (*b*) international custom, as evidence of a general practice accepted as law;
> >
> > (*c*) the general principles of law recognised by civilised nations;
> >
> > (*d*) subject to the provisions of Article 59 [restricting the binding force of the decision to the case at hand], judicial decisions and the teachings of the most highly qualified publicists of the various nations, as subsidiary means for the determination of rules of law.
>
> 2. This provision shall not prejudice the power of the Court to decide a case *ex aequo et bono*, if the parties agree thereto.

The provision of Article 38, paragraph 1—which does not appear in the corresponding Article of the Statute of the Permanent Court of International Justice—that it is the function of the Court to decide the disputes submitted to it 'in accordance with international law,'[2]

[2] The Report of the Rapporteur of Committee IV/1 (U.N.C.I.O. Doc. 913, IV/1/74 (1), p. 12) contains the following statement: 'The First Committee has adopted an addition to be inserted in the introductory phrase of this article referring to the function of the Court to decide disputes submitted to it in accordance with international law. The lacuna in the old Statute with reference to this point did not prevent the Permanent Court of International Justice from regarding itself as an organ of international law; but the addition will accentuate that character of the new Court.'

is probably superfluous; but it does no harm. There is certainly no objection to paragraph 2 of Article 38, authorising the Court 'to decide a case *ex aequo et bono*, if the parties agree thereto.' It is, however, very doubtful whether the treaty establishing the Court should indicate the various components of which international law consists and define these components. This is exactly what paragraph 1 of Article 38 of the new Statute tries to do. In this respect it follows the old Statute. Whereas, however, the old Statute simply says: 'The Court shall apply . . . ', the new Statute states: 'The Court, whose function is to decide in accordance with international law such disputes as are submitted to it, shall apply . . . ' Thus it is expressly declared that the following intends to be an authentic enumeration of the various components of existing international law to be applied by the Court. This enumeration, however, is problematical.

Only the norms referred to in clauses (*a*), (*b*) and (*c*), may be considered as parts of international law. The 'judicial decisions and the teachings of the most highly qualified publicists of the various nations,' referred to in clause (*d*) are not parts of the international law to be applied by the Court, in the same sense as the rules referred to in clauses (*a*), (*b*) and (*c*). These 'judicial decisions' and 'teachings' are—as clause (*d*) expressly says—merely subsidiary means for the determination of the rules of law referred to in clauses (*a*), (*b*) and (*c*). The rules of law determined in this way are included in the rules of law referred to in clauses (*a*), (*b*) and (*c*). It is doubtful whether by the enumeration of Article 38, paragraph 1, an order of successive application is established;[3] in any case there is no reason to give these 'judicial decisions' and 'teachings' the fourth place. Since the Court has to apply the rules of international law it will, if it thinks necessary, use 'judicial decisions' and 'teachings' as means to determine the rules of law which it is authorised to apply, in the first as well as in the second and the third place; and the Court will use not only these but also other means to determine the rules of law to be applied by it even if clause (*d*) were not stipulated. Clause (*d*) is incomplete and superfluous.

The formulation of clause (*a*) is evidently too narrow. If, for instance, a territorial dispute arises out of a treaty of cession and if the Court has to apply this treaty, no 'rule,' that is to say, no general norm, can be applied as clause (*a*) prescribes, since treaties of cession do not establish 'rules' expressly recognised by the contesting parties; they stipulate only the concrete obligation of one state to

[3] The Summary Report of the 5th meeting of Committee IV/1 (U.N.C.I.O. Doc. 240, IV/1/15, p. 2) contains the following statement referring to Article 38: 'It was questioned whether this Article, enumerating the sources of law to be applied by the Court, intends also to stipulate the order in which they are to be resorted to. The two observers for the Permanent Court of International Justice invited by the Chairman to comment, agreed that it did not.'

withdraw from a definite territory and the concrete right of another state to occupy this territory.

If an international convention establishes ' rules,' that is to say, general norms, these rules are binding only upon the contracting parties to the convention; and the Court can apply such convention to the contesting states only if they are parties to the convention. In concluding a convention a state does more than ' recognise ' the rules established by the convention; it participates in their creation. Hence the legally decisive fact as to the applicability of a convention is not that the contesting states have expressly recognised the rules established by the convention, but the fact that the contesting states are contracting parties to the convention. What clause (*a*) of Article 38 stipulates is simply that the Court shall apply treaties which impose duties and confer rights upon the contesting states.

The wording of clause (*b*) too, is unsatisfactory. It is not possible to apply ' international custom,' since ' custom ' is a habitual or usual course of action, and the course of action cannot be applied to a case. What is applicable to a dispute is a legal norm created by custom, a norm of customary international law. Since custom is itself a qualified practice of the states, custom can hardly be the ' evidence ' of a practice. According to a certain doctrine, custom in not a law-creating fact but only evidence of a pre-existing rule of law created in another, more or less mysterious, way. It was probably this doctrine: that custom is only evidence of a rule of law—not evidence of a ' practice '—which is at the basis of the formula used in clause (*b*) of Article 38, paragraph 1. The doctrine is most questionable and by no means generally accepted. As a mere theoretical statement it should not be inserted into the text of a legal instrument. What clause (*b*) actually stipulates is simply that the Court shall apply customary international law.

Regarding clause (*c*), it is doubtful whether such a thing as ' general principles of law recognised by civilised nations ' exists at all. It is not very likely that the fundamental antagonism which nowadays separates the civilised nations in the political as well as economic field, should not extend to the field of law. Besides, it is not clear whether the general principles referred to in clause (*c*) must be recognised by all, and if not by all, by how many civilised nations, in order to be applicable by the Court. It is more than doubtful whether such rules, if they exist, are part of international law, as it is presupposed according to the first sentence of Article 38. Clause (*c*) certainly confers upon the Court a good deal of discretion to decide all the questions which the vague formula of this clause leaves open; in particular the question how the Court shall decide a case, when a rule which the Court considers to be a ' general principle of law recognised by civilised nations ' is in conflict with a rule of customary or contractual international law referring to the case. According to the wording of Article 38, the Court has the choice between them.

It seems that clause (*c*) is supposed to be applied when neither a norm of customary nor of contractual international law (clauses (*a*) and (*b*)) is applicable to the case at hand, and there exists a general principle of law which refers to the case. Such a situation, however, is not possible. International law as actually composed of the norms of customary and contractual law, is—logically—always applicable to a concrete case. But the—logically possible—application may be, in the opinion of the law-applying authority, politically not satisfactory. Hence clause (*c*) may easily be interpreted to confer upon the Court the power to apply, instead of customary or contractual international law, a norm which the Court considers to be a 'general principle of law recognised by civilised nations,' if the Court deems this principle more satisfactory than the existing customary and contractual international law. Since the principle of *aequo et bono* is a principle recognised in some legal systems as a part of positive law, Article 38, paragraph 1, clause (*c*), may endanger the application of Article 38, paragraph 2, which requires the consent of the parties to the application of the *bonum et aequum* principle.

All these difficulties could have been avoided if the Statute had provided that the Court should apply existing international law unless the contesting parties agree that the case shall be decided *ex aequo et bono*, leaving it to the Court to determine which rules are international law and in what successive order they are to be applied. The transfer without change of Article 38, paragraph 1, clauses (*a*) to (*d*), of the old into the new Statute is no improvement of the Court's jurisdiction.

6. The Procedure of the Court

The procedure of the Court is regulated in exactly the same manner as that of the Permanent Court of International Justice, which has proved to be quite satisfactory. In the following only some of the principles shall be discussed.

Article 40, paragraph 1, of the Statute, provides:

> Cases are brought before the Court, as the case may be, either by the notification of the special agreement or by a written application addressed to the Registrar. In either case the subject of the dispute and the parties shall be indicated.

It is not very clear when a case is to be brought before the Court 'by the notification of the special agreement' and when 'by a written application addressed to the Registrar.' The most plausible interpretation seems to be that when the jurisdiction of the Court is based on a special agreement, and that is the case where there is no 'compulsory' jurisdiction within the meaning of Article 36, paragraph 2, of the Statute, the case must be brought before the Court by the notification of the special agreement; whereas when the Court has compulsory jurisdiction and consequently no special agreement is necessary according to Article 36, paragraph 2, the case may be brought before the Court by one of the parties to the case, the other being obliged to recognize the jurisdiction of the Court in accordance with its declaration made under Article 36, paragraph 2. But an interpretation is not excluded according to which a case may be brought before the Court by a written application also when no compulsory jurisdiction of the Court within the meaning of Article 36, paragraph 2, is established. Article 32, paragraphs 1 and 2, of the Rules of the Court provide:

> 1. When a case is brought before the Court by means of a special agreement, Article 40, paragraph 1, of the Statute, shall apply.
>
> 2. When a case is brought before the Court by means of an application, the application must, as laid down in Article 40, paragraph 1, of the Statute, indicate the party making it, the party against whom the claim is brought and the subject of the dispute. It must also, as far as possible, specify the provision on which the applicant founds the jurisdiction of the Court, state the precise nature of the claim and give a succinct statement of the facts and grounds on which the claim is based, these facts and grounds being developed in the Memorial, to which the evidence will be annexed.

The wording of paragraph 1 of this Article is not quite consistent with Article 40, paragraph 1, of the Statute. According to the latter, cases are brought before the Court not, as Article 32, paragraph 1, of the Rules provides ' by means of a special agreement,' but ' by the notification of the special agreement '; and Article 40, paragraph 1, of the Statute, applies not only when a case is brought before the Court by the notification of the special agreement, but also when a case is brought before the Court by a written application. But the meaning of Article 32, paragraph 1, of the Rules, is: when the jurisdiction of the Court is based on a special agreement, Article 40, paragraph 1, of the Statute, shall apply. Then, Article 40, paragraph 1, is interpreted to mean that the case may be brought before the Court either by the notification of the special agreement or by a written application, when its jurisdiction is based on a special agreement. That Article 32 of the Rules presupposes the interpretation of Article 40, paragraph 1, of the Statute, according to which a case may be brought before the Court by a written application not only when compulsory jurisdiction of the Court within the meaning of Article 36, paragraph 2, is established, may follow from the provision of Article 32, paragraph 2, of the Rules, that the application must ' as far as possible, specify the provision on which the applicant founds the jurisdiction of the Court.' If the case could be brought before the Court by a written application only when compulsory jurisdiction within the meaning of Article 36, paragraph 2, of the Statute, is established, the applicant could found the jurisdiction of the Court only on the declarations made by the parties to the case under Article 36, paragraph 2, of the Statute. The question as to the way in which a case is to be brought before the Court refers to one of the most important stages in the judicial procedure. It can hardly be denied that neither the Statute nor the Rules contain a clear answer to this question.[4]

[4] The Corfu Channel case was brought before the Court by the Government of the United Kingdom by a written application as a case of compulsory jurisdiction. In its letter of July 2, 1947, the Albanian Government declared that ' in the absence of an acceptance by Albania of Article 36 of the Court's Statute or of any other instrument of international law whereby the Albanian Government might have accepted the compulsory jurisdiction of the Court, the Government of the United Kingdom was not entitled to refer this dispute to the Court by unilateral application.' But in its decision on the preliminary objection of the Albanian Government the Court stated:

> The Albanian contention that the Application cannot be entertained because it has been filed contrary to the provisions of Article 40, paragraph 1, and of Article 36, paragraph 1, of the Court's Statute, is essentially founded on the assumption that the institution of proceedings by application is only possible where compulsory jurisdiction exists and that, where it does not, proceedings can only be instituted by special agreement. This is a mere assertion which is not justified by either of the texts cited. Article 32, paragraph 2, of the Rules does not require the Applicant, as an absolute necessity, but only " as far as possible," to specify in the application the provision on which he founds the jurisdiction of the Court. It clearly implies, both by its actual terms and by the reasons underlying it, that the institution of proceedings by application is not exclusively reserved for the domain of compulsory jurisdiction. In submitting the case by means of an Application, the Government of the United Kingdom gave the Albanian Government the opportunity of accepting the jurisdiction of the Court. This acceptance was given in the Albanian Government's letter of July 2, 1947. Besides, separate action of this kind was in keeping with the respective positions of the parties in proceedings where there is in fact a claimant, the United Kingdom, and a defendant, Albania.
>
> Furthermore, there is nothing to prevent the acceptance of jurisdiction, as in the present case, from being effected by two separate and successive acts, instead of jointly and beforehand by a special agreement. As the Permanent Court of International Justice has said in its Judgment No. 12, of April 26, 1928, p. 23: " The acceptance by a State of the Court's jurisdiction in a particular case is not, under the Statute, subordinated to the observance of certain forms, such as, for instance, the previous conclusion of a special agreement." The Security Council's recommendation has been relied upon to support opposite conclusions. But, in the first place, though this recommendation clearly indicates that the bringing of the case before the Court required action on the part of the parties, it does not specify that this action must be taken jointly, and, in the second place, the method of submitting the case to the Court is regulated by the texts governing the working of the Court as was pointed out by the Security Council in its recommendation. The Court cannot therefore hold to be irregular a proceeding which is not precluded by any provision in these texts. (Cf. *International Law Quarterly*, Vol. II (1948), pp. 75 f.)

The proceeding by which a dispute between a party to the Statute and a state not a party to the Statute is brought before the Court in conformity with Article 40, paragraph 1, of the Statute, is possible only after the state not a party to the Statute has made the declaration, which, in accordance with Article 35, paragraph 2, of the Statute and the resolution of the Security Council of October 15, 1946, is required

As the Charter, in its Article 40, provides for provisional measures to be taken by the Security Council, the Statute stipulates in Article 41:

> 1. The Court shall have the power to indicate, if it considers that circumstances so require, any provisional measures which ought to be taken to preserve the respective rights of either party.
>
> 2. Pending the final decision, notice of the measures suggested shall forthwith be given to the parties and to the Security Council.

in order that this state may appear before the Court. Article 36 of the Rules of Court provides in this respect:

> When a State which is not a party to the Statute is admitted by the Security Council, in pursuance of Article 35 of the Statute, to appear before the Court, it shall satisfy the Court that it has complied with any conditions that may have been prescribed for its admission: the document which evidences this compliance shall be filed in the Registry at the same time a the notification of the appointment of the agent.

In the Corfu Channel case, the Government of the United Kingdom submitted its dispute with Albania, not a party to the Statute, to the Court by an application dated May 13, 1947, and filed in the Registry of the Court on May 22, 1947, before Albania made the declaration required by Article 35, paragraph 2, and the resolution of the Security Council implementing this provision. As a matter of fact, Albania never made such a formal declaration. It only declared, in a letter dated July 2, 1947, filed in the Registry of the Court on July 23, 1947, to be prepared ' to appear before the Court ' notwithstanding ' the irregularity in the action taken by the Government of the United Kingdom ' which in the opinion of the Albanian Government consisted in having brought the case before the Court by a written application instead of by the notification of a special agreement. The Albanian Government emphasised ' that its acceptance of the Court's jurisdiction for this case cannot constitute a precedent for the future.' On July 31, 1947, the President of the Court, as the Court was not sitting, made an Order in which it was stated *inter alia*: ' . . . having regard to the Resolution of the Security Council of April 9, 1947 [by which the Council recommended that the parties should refer the dispute to the Court] the said note of the Albanian Government [of July 2, 1947] may be regarded as constituting the document mentioned in Article 36 of the Rules of Court.' (*Ibid.*, pp. 71 f.) It is very doubtful whether Albania's declaration to be prepared to appear before the Court and to accept its jurisdiction for this case, made in a letter the purpose of which was not to fulfil the condition laid down in Article 35, paragraph 2, and the resolution of the Security Council of October 15, 1946, but to present an objection against the way in which the United Kingdom had brought the case before the Court, can be considered as the fulfilment of the condition under which the Court is open to a state not a party to the Statute. In his separate opinion, the national judge chosen by Albania in accordance with Article 31, paragraph 2, of the Statute, stated quite correctly with reference to the resolution of the Council of the League of Nations of May 17, 1922, and the resolution of the Security Council of October 15, 1946: ' According to these resolutions, the acceptance of the jurisdiction of the Court is a *preliminary* condition to be able to appear before the Court. By this act (declaration) the competence of the Court is not of course yet established. The condition for the establishment of the competence of the Court is a special agreement (*compromis*) or the acceptance of the compulsory jurisdiction in treaties or conventions (Article 36 (1) and 36 (2) of the Statute).' (*Ibid.*, pp. 86 f.)

This ' power ' of the Court is not very clearly defined. The Court is not authorised to ' take ' or to ' order,' but only to ' indicate ' provisional measures ' which ought to be taken.' Paragraph 2 speaks only of measures ' suggested.'[5] This wording makes it difficult to interpret Article 41 to mean that the Court may impose upon the contesting parties the obligation to comply with provisional measures ordered by the Court

Other procedural provisions of the Statute are:

' The full Court shall sit except when it is expressly provided otherwise in the present Statute.' ' A quorum of nine judges shall suffice to constitute the Court.' (Article 25.) ' All questions shall be decided by a majority of the judges present. In the event of an equality of votes, the President or the judge who acts in his place shall have a casting vote.' (Article 55.) ' The judgment is final and without appeal. In the event of dispute as to the meaning or scope of the judgment, the Court shall construe it upon the request of any party.' (Article 60.) According to Article 61, revision of a judgment is possible only when some fact is discovered ' of such a nature as to be a decisive factor, which fact was, when the judgment was given, unknown to the Court and also to the party claiming revision, always provided that such ignorance was not due to negligence.' ' The official languages of the Court shall be French and English.' (Article 39.) ' The procedure shall consist of two parts: written and oral. The written proceedings shall consist of the communication to the Court and to the parties of memorials, counter-memorials and, if necessary, replies; also all papers and documents in support.' ' The oral proceedings shall consist of the hearing by the Court of witnesses, experts, agents, counsel, and advocates.' (Article 43.) ' The hearing in Court shall be public, unless the Court shall decide otherwise, or unless the parties demand that the public be not admitted.' (Article 46.) But: ' The deliberations of the Court shall take place in private and remain secret.' (Article 54, paragraph 3.) ' The Court may, at any time, entrust any individual, body, bureau, commission, or other organisation that it may select, with the task of carrying out an enquiry or giving an expert opinion.' (Article 50.) The Court is not bound by any rule regulating the means or the valuation of evidence. In case one of the parties does not appear before the Court or fails to defend its case, the other party may, according to Article 53, ' call upon the Court to decide in favour of its claim '; the Court, however, ' must, before doing so satisfy itself, not only that it has jurisdiction . . . but also that the claim is well founded in fact and law.'

[5] In the French, Spanish and Chinese texts of Article 41 of the Statute the term meaning ' indicate ' as used in paragraph 1 is also used in paragraph 2. Only the Russian text completely conforms with the English text.

7. Execution of Judicial Decisions

The Statute does not contain a provision guaranteeing the execution of the decisions of the Court against a recalcitrant state. But Article 94, paragraph 2, of the Charter, provides:

> If any party to a case fails to perform the obligations incumbent upon it under a judgment rendered by the Court, the other party may have recourse to the Security Council, which may, if it deems necessary, make recommendations or decide upon measures to be taken to give effect to the judgment.

This provision does not refer—as the analogous provision of Article 13, paragraph 4, of the Covenant,[6] does—to decisions of any international tribunal, but only to judgments of the International Court of Justice. It does not impose upon the Security Council the obligation to enforce the judgments of the Court against recalcitrant parties. It provides for a procedure of appeal in case of non-compliance with the judgment of the Court and makes the action of the Security Council to be taken as the result of the procedure dependent upon the Council's discretion by authorising this body to choose between two different actions: either to make recommendations or to decide upon measures to be taken to give effect to the judgment of the Court.

In case the Security Council chooses to make recommendations, it may recommend to comply with the judgment of the Court. But in making a recommendation under Article 94, paragraph 2, the Security Council is not bound to conform with the judgment of the Court with which the party concerned did not comply. The wording of Article 94, paragraph 2, it is true, allows an interpretation according to which not only the word ' decide,' but also the words ' make recommendations ' refer to the words ' upon measures to be taken to give effect to the judgment.' But the other interpretation, according to which the Security Council has the choice between any kind of recommendation and a decision to give effect to the judgment of the Court, is not only possible but, grammatically, more adequate. In accordance with this interpretation, the Security Council may recommend a solution of the dispute totally different from that decided by the Court.[7] If Article 25 of the Charter is interpreted to

[6] Article 13, paragraph 4, of the Covenant of the League of Nations, runs as follows:

> The Members of the League agree that they will carry out in full good faith any award or decision that may be rendered, and that they will not resort to war against a Member of the League which complies therewith. In the event of any failure to carry out such an award or decision, the Council shall propose what steps should be taken to give effect thereto.

[7] At the *Hearings* (p. 288) a Senator asked with reference to Article 94: ' If the matter is referred to the Council, the Council is not limited in its method of enforcement or adjustment to anything that happened in the Court, but it would have the same power, within the scope of its authority, that it would have had if the case had originally been brought before the Council.' Whereupon the

apply to recommendations of the Security Council, recourse to the Security Council under Article 94, paragraph 2, has the effect of an appeal to a higher authority. Even if it is assumed that recommendations made by the Security Council are not binding upon the parties, a recourse under Article 94, paragraph 2, may have the effect of an appeal. For the Council may consider non-compliance with a recommendation made under Article 94, paragraph 2, a threat to the peace and take enforcement action under Article 39 against the state which does not comply with the Council's recommendation. That means that the Security Council may enforce its recommendation instead of enforcing the Court's judgment. Article 94, paragraph 2, confers upon the Security Council the power to substitute its recommendation for the Court's judgment. This means, further, that the obligation imposed upon the Members by Article 94, paragraph 1, and by the Statute of the Court: to comply with the decisions of the Court, may be restricted by application of Article 94, paragraph 2.

representative of the Department of State answered: 'I think that is right, Senator.' Then the Senator asked: 'So it would not be limited in any way in its jurisdiction to adjust it merely because it had gone to the Court and one of the parties had refused to abide by the decision?' Answer: 'I think it would have to be considered as a case coming to the Council.' Then another Senator asked (p. 289): 'Is this not true: That in all matters considered and acted upon by the Council, no matter what those matters may have received by some other organisation or some branch of this organisation, the treatment by the Security Council is always *de novo*, so to speak? In other words, it never acts on an appeal or passes judgment on what some other organisation has done; it acts *de novo* on what has originated in the Council?' Whereupon the representative of the State Department answered: 'That is right.' Then a third Senator asked (p. 286): 'Is the Security Council the sheriff of the Court?' Whereupon the representative of the State Department answered: 'I think the explanation of this paragraph [Article 94, paragraph 2] is that when the Court has rendered a judgment and one of the parties refuses to accept it, then the dispute becomes political rather than legal. It is as a political dispute that the matter is referred to the Security Council. The Security Council then acts not as a judicial body, because the judicial body has already acted, but in its capacity as a political body in a dispute which is a political dispute or in a situation which is a political situation.' That means that the Council in making recommendations under Article 94 is not bound to conform with the decision of the Court.

It may be doubted whether this was the intention of those who suggested at the San Francisco Conference to insert the provision of Article 94, paragraph 2, into the text of the Charter. The Summary Report of the 20th meeting of Committee IV/1 (U.N.C.I.O. Doc. 864, IV/1/71, pp. 2 f.) contains the following statement: 'An addition to Chapter VII offered by Cuba (U.N.C.I.O. WD 187) provided that if a state should fail to comply with a decision of the Court, the Security Council should make recommendations or decide on the necessary measures for enforcement. In support of the proposal it was argued that the principle of respect for judgments of the Court was of highest importance to the new international order and ought to be expressly implemented by the Charter, that the Committee of Jurists in Washington had called attention to the problem and noted that it should be dealt with in the Charter, and that the Covenant of the League of Nations had contained a similar provision in paragraph 4 of Article 13.' If the intention was to guarantee 'respect for judgments of the Court,' this intention was certainly not satisfactorily expressed by the wording of Article 94, paragraph 2.

By having recourse to the Security Council under Article 94, paragraph 2, the party places the Court under the control of the Council. Since under the Charter self-help (except in case of an armed attack as self-defence) is prohibited, non-compliance with the Court's judgment may compel the other party to have recourse to the Security Council under Article 94, paragraph 2. Such recourse may have the effect of transforming a legal dispute, decided by the Court in accordance with existing law, into an issue to be settled anew by the Council according to political principles.

Recommendations or other decisions under Article 94, paragraph 2, require a majority of seven members including the votes of the permanent members. In case the party which does not comply with the decision of the Court is a member of the Security Council and the other party, not a member of the Council, has recourse to the Council under Article 94, paragraph 2, the party which is a member (and which has violated the obligation incumbent upon it under the judgment rendered by the Court) is not excluded from voting in the decision by which the Council makes a recommendation for the settlement of the dispute brought before it under Article 94, paragraph 2. The second sentence of Article 27, paragraph 3, does not apply to decisions of the Security Council taken under Article 94, paragraph 2. But the party which is not a member of the Council and whose right under the judgment of the Court has been openly violated, is excluded from voting. For under Article 32 it can be invited to participate in the discussion of the Security Council only 'without vote.' If the other party is a permanent member of the Security Council it can even prevent, by its veto, any recommendation of the Security Council not favourable to it.

In case the Security Council decides to give effect to the judgment of the Court, it has again a choice between two kinds of action; it may take enforcement measures or measures which have not this character. If the Council decides to take enforcement measures to give effect to the judgment of the Court, the question arises whether the Council can take enforcement measures other than those determined in Chapter VII of the Charter. Although an affirmative answer to this question is not excluded by the wording of Article 94, paragraph 2, it is more plausible to assume that a judgment of the Court can be enforced only by measures taken under Article 41 or 42. The Charter does not provide for other enforcement measures to be taken by the Security Council. If this interpretation is accepted, the question arises whether the Security Council can take enforcement measures to give effect to a judgment of the Court without applying Article 39, that is to say, without determining that the non-compliance with the judgment constitutes a threat to, or breach of, the peace. In view of the fact that the Charter, in the case of non-compliance with a judgment of the Court, institutes a procedure of appeal, it is hardly possible to consider such non-compliance as a threat to, or breach of, the peace. It is certainly not a threat or use of force constituting a violation of the obligation established in Article 2, paragraph 4. Article 94, paragraph 2, does not refer to Article 39. The Council is authorised to give effect to a judgment of the Court ' if it deems necessary,' that is to say, whenever the Council deems necessary to enforce a judgment of the Court against a recalcitrant party. Hence it is possible to interpret Article 94, paragraph 2, to mean that the Security Council may take enforcement measures to give effect to the judgment of the Court without determining under Article 39 that the non-compliance with the judgment of the Court constitutes a threat to, or breach of, the peace. That the Security Council may make recommendations under Article 94, paragraph 2, without applying Article 39, results from the fact that Article 94, paragraph 2, expressly authorises the Council to this effect. Only if the Security Council considers that non-compliance of a party with the judgment of the Court constitutes a threat to, or breach of, the peace, Article 39 applies; and in this case—and only in this case—the Security Council may make recommendations or take enforcement action without being invoked by a party, and even if invoked by a party, not necessarily for the purpose of giving effect to the judgment of the Court, but—in conformity with Article 39—' to maintain or restore international peace and security.' [8] Under Article 39, the Security Council may take enforcement action not only in case of non-compliance with a judgment of the International Court of Justice, but also in case of non-compliance with any other decision of the Court. [9]

As to the enforcement measures to be taken under Article 94, paragraph 2, the measures determined in Article 41 of the Charter come into consideration. Article 41 authorises the Security Council to take enforcement measures not involving the use of armed force ' to give effect to its decisions.' This may be interpreted to mean: to give effect not only to a decision taken under Article 39. But it is doubtful whether the Security Council may take enforcement measures involving the use of armed force without applying Article 39. For Article 42 provides that these enforcement measures must be taken ' to maintain or restore international peace and security.' This is the formula used in Article 39.

If it is assumed that the Security Council can take no other enforcement measures but those determined in Articles 41 and 42,

[8] If this interpretation is accepted, there exists in this respect a difference between enforcement measures taken under Article 94, paragraph 2, to give effect to a judgment of the Court, and an enforcement action taken under Article 51 by the Security Council, to restore peace broken by an armed attack. Action under Article 51 must be taken by the Security Council in conformity with Article 39. Cf. *infra*, p. 801.

[9] Cf. *infra*, pp. 724 ff.

and that Article 42 as well as Article 41 can be applied only after the Security Council has determined, under Article 39, the existence of a threat to, or breach of, the peace, the measures to be taken under Article 94, paragraph 2, to give effect to the judgment of the Court, can be enforcement measures only if the Security Council has determined under Article 39, that non-compliance with the judgment of the Court constitutes a threat to, or breach of, the peace. This interpretation is not excluded, but hardly in conformity with the text of Article 94, paragraph 2.[1] Whether the Council takes enforcement measures directly under Article 94, paragraph 2, or under Article 39,

[1] At the *Hearings* (pp. 286 ff.) the representative of the Department of State made the following statements with respect to the conditions under which the Security Council is authorised to act under Article 94, paragraph 2: 'Article 94 would have to be governed by the powers conferred upon the Council in the other parts of the Charter; that is, the language there would have to be governed by the powers which the Security Council possesses. If the Security Council possessed powers of imposing settlements, then this paragraph could be read in terms of enforcement action. But since it does not possess those powers, I think this paragraph must be read in terms of such powers as it does possess.' 'The Security Council may proceed to take action only within the scope of its powers, and the actual scope of its powers is such that the Council can act only after it makes certain determinations.' 'The Security Council would have to determine first of all, under Chapter VI, whether or not a continuance of that situation would be likely to threaten the peace, and then it could take the measures which are indicated under Chapter VI. Then, if the situation became aggravated, it would have to determine under Article 39 whether that particular situation actually represented a threat to the peace. If it is so determined it could act under Article 39; but its action under Article 39, for the purpose of maintaining international peace and security, would be for that purpose primarily.' 'The Council may proceed, I suppose, to call upon the country concerned to carry out the judgment, but only if the peace of the world is threatened, and if the Council has made a determination to that effect.'

When the legal advisor of the Department of State was heard, a Senator asked (p. 331): '. . . under Article 94, when we call upon the Security Council to take measures to give effect to the judgment of the Court, I understood . . . that that was limited to Article 39, and therefore when the Security Council is called in to act as a sheriff, as I suggested this morning, it must necessarily reach a decision before it acts that the case is one which involves a threat to the peace or a breach of the peace or active aggression or something of that sort endangering the maintenance of international peace and security, before it acts; and therefore it is optional with the Security Council as to whether it will carry out a decision of the Court, and that depends primarily upon whether it is one which threatens the peace of the world.' Whereupon the legal advisor answered: 'I think that this statement is absolutely correct.' However, finally, he declared: 'The Council would be entirely free to do what it might see fit.' If the Security Council is 'entirely free' in acting under Article 94, it is not bound—as it is under Article 39—to determine previously the existence of a threat to the peace. This is certainly in accordance with the wording of Article 94 which does not refer to Article 39. The Chairman asked the legal advisor (p. 332): 'In other words, your contention is that there was no desire or intention to increase the jurisdiction of the Council?' Whereupon he answered: 'That is absolutely correct, Mr. Chairman.' If it was the intention not to increase the jurisdiction of the Security Council, this intention was not expressed in the wording of Article 94.

the veto right of the permanent members applies to such decisions. Hence the judgment of the Court cannot be enforced against a permanent member of the Council.

In case a state does not comply with the decision of an international tribunal other than the Court of International Justice, no organ of the United Nations is charged with enforcing the judgment. Only Article 39 is applicable. This means that in this case the Security Council can intervene only if it determines the existence of a threat to, or a breach of, the peace. But in this case, too, the Security Council may make recommendations which do not conform with the decision of the tribunal. Article 39 gives no guarantee for the maintenance of existing law. If the Security Council, for some reason or another, does not give effect to the judgment of the International Court of Justice which is not complied with by a party, or does not take enforcement action against a state which refuses to carry out the decision of another international tribunal, there is no legal possibility of enforcing the law under the Charter of the Unted Nations. There can be no doubt that the situation of a state violated in its right by non-compliance with the decision of an international tribunal on the part of another state, is much worse under the Charter than it would be under general international law or than it was under the Covenant of the League of Nations. Under general international law, self-help by resorting to war or reprisals against the violator of the law is possible. Under the Covenant, Article 13, paragraph 4, applied, according to which the Council was bound (' shall ') to propose what steps should be taken to give effect to the judgment of the Permanent Court of International Justice or of any other international tribunal, and was not authorised to substitute its own decision for that of any tribunal. And self-help on the part of the state violated in its right was not excluded; this state was only obliged by Article 12 not to resort to war until three months after the decision of the tribunal. Even under the Briand-Kellogg Pact, war for the enforcement of the law as established by the decision of the international tribunal was not forbidden. For such a war could be interpreted to be not a means of national policy, but a means of international policy because a means of restoring international law. Reprisals, that is to say, the employment of force not involving the use of armed force, against a violator of the law were neither excluded by the Covenant, nor by the Briand-Kellogg Pact. If the constitution of an international community forbids self-help as reaction against a violation of the law not committed by the use of force, it should contain provisions guaranteeing the execution of judicial decisions rendered directly or indirectly under the constitution, by collective action of the community. It is one of the most regrettable technical defects of the Charter that it does not fulfil this requirement.

8. Advisory Opinions

International disputes may be settled indirectly by the International Court of Justice through advisory opinions given by the Court to the General Assembly and to the Security Council, which organs are competent to settle disputes directly by their recommendations. Article 96 of the Charter provides:

> 1. The General Assembly or the Security Council may request the International Court of Justice to give an advisory opinion on any legal question.
>
> 2. Other organs of the United Nations and specialised agencies, which may at any time be so authorised by the General Assembly, may also request advisory opinions of the Court on legal questions arising within the scope of their activities.

Under this Article only the General Assembly and the Security Council are directly authorised by the Charter to request advisory opinions of the Court, not only in case of a dispute, but also 'on any legal question.' Other organs of the United Nations are allowed to request advisory opinions of the Court only if authorised to do so by the General Assembly. Such authorisation may have an individual or a general character. At its 55th meeting the General Assembly adopted a resolution by which it authorised 'the Economic and Social Council to request advisory opinions of the International Court of Justice on legal questions arising within the scope of the activities of the Council,'[2] and at its 113th meeting an analogous resolution concerning the Trusteeship Council.[3] The specialised agencies referred to in paragraph 2 of Article 96 are those mentioned in Article 57 of the Charter. Most of the agreements concluded with the approval of the General Assembly under Article 63 of the Charter, in order to bring certain specialised agencies into relationship with the United Nations, contain provisions authorising these agencies to request advisory opinions of the International Court of Justice on legal questions arising within the scope of their activities. Excepted are questions concerning the mutual relationships of the specialised agencies concerned and the United Nations or other specialised agencies.[4] In its resolution adopted at its 169th meeting on

[2] Resolutions adopted by the General Assembly, Doc. A/64/Add. 1, p. 176.

[3] Resolutions adopted by the General Assembly, Doc. A/519, p. 103. The agreement with the Universal Postal Union (Doc. A/347) does not contain an authorisation to request advisory opinions of the International Court of Justice.

[4] For instance the agreements with the International Labour Organisation (Article 9, paragraph 2); the Food and Agricultural Organisation (Article 9, paragraph 2); the United Nations Educational, Scientific and Cultural Organisation (Article 11, paragraph 2); the International Civil Aviation Organisation (Article 10, paragraph 2); the International Bank for Reconstruction and Development (Article 8).

December 3, 1948, the General Assembly authorised the Interim Committee to request advisory opinions of the International Court of Justice on legal questions arising within the scope of its activities.[5]

The problem arising out of the interpretation of the term 'organ' as used in Article 96, paragraph 2, of the Charter, has been discussed in a previous chapter.[6] In this connection it should be mentioned only that, if the term 'organ' has the same meaning as in Chapter III entitled 'Organs,' and if by 'principal' organs only those enumerated in Article 7, paragraph 1, and by 'subsidiary' organs only those established under Articles 22 and 29 of the Charter are to be understood, some organs of the United Nations, not referred to in Chapter III of the Charter, cannot be authorised by the General Assembly to request advisory opinions from the Court; for instance, the Military Staff Committee referred to in Article 47, or the commissions set up by the Economic and Social Council under Article 68 of the Charter. The special commission 'for the promotion of human rights,' referred to in this Article, may well be in a position to need the opinion of the Court on a legal question. But also the regional agencies, referred to in Article 52 of the Charter, cannot be authorised by the General Assembly to request advisory opinions from the Court if Article 96, paragraph 2, is interpreted in this restricted way. This would be highly regrettable, as regional agencies may be established for the settlement of local disputes and these disputes may have a legal character.

The competence of requesting advisory opinions as established by Article 96, paragraph 2, in contradistinction to that established by Article 96, paragraph 1, is restricted in so far as the organs authorised by the General Assembly are permitted to request advisory opinions only on legal questions 'arising within the scope of their activities.' No such restriction is imposed upon the analogous competence of the General Assembly and of the Security Council in paragraph 1 of Article 96. Nevertheless, these organs, too, are competent to request advisory opinions on legal questions only if such questions arise within the scope of their activities, that is to say, within their jurisdiction. The determination of any organ's jurisdiction implies the norm not to act beyond the scope of its activity as determined by the legal instrument instituting the organ. It is not very likely that it was intended to enlarge, by Article 96, paragraph 1, the scope of the activity of the General Assembly and the Security Council determined by other Articles of the Charter. Hence the words 'arising within the scope of their activities' in paragraph 2 of Article 96 are redundant.

Advisory opinions of the Court given under Article 96 of the

[5] Cf. *supra*, p. 169.

[6] Cf. *supra*, pp. 146 f.

Charter are not binding upon the organs to which they have been given.[7]

Article 96 of the Charter is paralleled by Article 65, paragraph 1, of the Statute, which runs as follows:

> The Court may give an advisory opinion on any legal question at the request of whatever body may be authorised by or in accordance with the Charter of the United Nations to make such a request.

This provision confers upon the Court the power to give advisory opinions. This authorisation, however, is already implied in the provision of Article 96 of the Charter.[8] As to the question to whom advisory opinions may be given, Article 65 of the Statute is not quite in conformity with Article 96 of the Charter. Under Article 65 of the Statute the Court is authorised to give advisory opinions only to a 'body,' that is to say, to a collegiate organ, consequently not to the Secretary-General, who—under Article 96, paragraph 2, of the Charter—may be authorised by the General Assembly to request such advisory opinion of the Court.

Article 96 of the Charter as well as Article 65 of the Statute restrict the competence of the Court with respect to advisory opinions to 'legal questions.' By 'legal questions' also interpretations of general rules of customary or conventional international law may be understood. At the 113th meeting of the General Assembly the representatives of Poland and the Soviet Union denied that this term included interpretation of the Charter. According to their opinion the International Court of Justice was competent to give advisory

[7] The opinion expressed by the representative of the United Kingdom at the 9th meeting of the Ad Hoc Political Committee of the General Assembly on November 23, 1948, that the advisory opinion of the International Court of Justice on 'Admission of a State to the United Nations' (International Court of Justice. Advisory opinion of May 28, 1948, p. 57) had the character of an 'authoritative interpretation of one important part of the Charter' (Doc A/AC. 24/SR 9, p. 8) has no basis in the Charter.

[8] The Summary Report of the 16th meeting of Committee IV/1 (U.N.C.I.O. Doc. 714, IV/1/57, p. 2) contains the following statement referring to Article 65 of the Statute: 'It was observed that since the Charter provides for advisory opinions and since the Statute is a part of the Charter, it was unnecessary to have the same provision in the Statute. In reply to this observation, it was indicated that while the Statute was a part of the Charter, the Charter was not a part of the Statute.' The fact that the Charter is not a part of the Statute does not justify the repetition in the Statute of a provision laid down in the Charter. Some provisions laid down in the Charter (in the narrower sense), but not in the Statute, as *e.g.*, the provision of Article 94, paragraph 2, were better placed in the Statute, since they are intended to apply not only to Members of the United Nations, but also to states which are not Members, that is to say, not parties to the Charter (in the narrower sense), but parties to the Statute. The provision of Article 96, however, does not apply to states, but to organs of the United Nations. Its repetition in the Statute is, indeed, superfluous.

opinions only on 'specific legal disputes.'[1] This view can hardly be based on the wording of Article 96 of the Charter or Article 65 of the Statute. At the same meeting on November 14, 1947, the General Assembly adopted the following resolution:

> Considering that it is a responsibility of the United Nations to encourage the progressive development of international law;
>
> Considering that it is of paramount importance that the interpretation of the Charter of the United Nations and the constitutions of the specialised agencies should be based on recognised principles of international law;
>
> Considering that the International Court of Justice is the principal judicial organ of the United Nations;
>
> Considering that it is also of paramount importance that the Court should be utilised to the greatest practicable extent in the progressive development of international law, both in regard to legal issues between States and in regard to constitutional interpretation,
>
> Recommends that organs of the United Nations and the specialised agencies should, from time to time, review the difficult and important points of law within the jurisdiction of the International Court of Justice which have arisen in the course of their activities and involve questions of principle which it is desirable to have settled, including points of law relating to the interpretation of the Charter of the United Nations or the constitutions of the specialised agencies, and, if duly authorised according to Article 96, paragraph 2, of the Charter, should refer them to the International Court of Justice for an adivsory opinion.[2]

On November 17, 1947, the General Assembly adopted the resolution requesting the International Court of Justice to give an advisory opinion on the meaning of Article 4, paragraph 1, of the Charter.[3] In its opinion the Court stated that the question '. . . is a problem of interpretation and consequently a legal question. It has nevertheless been contended that the question put must be regarded as a political one and that, for this reason, it falls outside the jurisdiction of the Court. The Court cannot attribute a political character to a request which, framed in abstract terms, invites it to undertake an essentially judicial task, the interpretation of a treaty provision. It is not concerned with the motives which may have inspired this request, nor with the considerations which, in the concrete cases submitted for examination to the Security Council, formed the subject of the exchange of views which took place in that body. It is the duty of

[1] Doc. A/P.V. 113, p. 25.

[2] Resolutions adopted by the General Assembly, Doc. A/519, p. 103.

[3] Cf. *supra*, pp. 72 ff.

the Court to envisage the question submitted to it only in the abstract form which has been given to it; nothing which is said in the present opinion refers, either directly or indirectly, to concrete cases or to particular circumstances. It has also been contended that the Court should not deal with a question couched in abstract terms. That is a mere affirmation devoid of any justification. According to Article 96 of the Charter and Article 65 of the Statute, the Court may give an advisory opinion on any legal question, abstract or otherwise. Lastly, it has also been maintained that the Court cannot reply to the question put because it involves an interpretation of the Charter. Nowhere is any provision to be found forbidding the Court, "the principal judicial organ of the United Nations," to exercise in regard to Article 4 of the Charter, a multilateral treaty, an interpretative function which falls within the normal exercise of its judicial powers. Accordingly, the Court holds that it is competent, on the basis of Article 96 of the Charter and Article 65 of the Statute, and considers that there are no reasons why it should decline to answer the question put to it.'[4]

Under Article 65 of the Statute the Court is only authorised, not obliged, to give advisory opinions. The Court may, foı reasons completely within its descretion, refuse to give an advisory opinion requested in conformity with the Charter and the Statute.

The other provisions of the Statute concerning advisory opinions of the Court—Articles 65, paragraph 2: 66, 67, 68—deal with the procedure of the Court in this matter.

[4] International Court of Justice. Reports of Judgments, Advisory Opinions and Orders, Advisory Opinion of May 28, 1948, pp. 61 f.

CHAPTER 16

PROTECTION OF NON-SELF-GOVERNING PEOPLES (CHAPTERS XI, XII, XIII OF THE CHARTER)

1. NON-SELF-GOVERNING TERRITORIES NOT PLACED UNDER THE TRUSTEESHIP SYSTEM (CHAPTER XI)

THE Charter confers upon the Organisation functions regarding all territories 'whose peoples have not yet attained a full measure of self-government' provided that Members of the United Nations have or assume responsibility for the administration of such territories (Article 73). These territories may or may not be placed under the trusteeship system regulated in Chapters XII and XIII of the Charter. If they are not placed under this system, only Chapter XI applies to them.

Chapter XI contains two Articles which run as follows:

ARTICLE 73

> Members of the United Nations which have or assume responsibilities for the administration of territories whose peoples have not yet attained a full measure of self-government recognise the principle that the interests of the inhabitants of these territories are paramount, and accept as a sacred trust the obligation to promote to the utmost, within the system of international peace and security established by the present Charter, the well-being of the inhabitants of these territories, and, to this end:
>
> (*a*) to ensure, with due respect for the culture of the peoples concerned, their political, economic, social, and educational advancement, their just treatment, and their protection against abuses;
>
> (*b*) to develop self-government, to take due account of the political aspirations of the peoples, and to assist them in the progressive development of their free political institutions, according to the particular circumstances of each territory and its peoples and their varying stages of advancement;
>
> (*c*) to further international peace and security;
>
> (*d*) to promote constructive measures of development, to encourage research, and to co-operate with one another and, when and where appropriate, with specialised international bodies with a view to the practical achievement of the social, economic, and scientific purposes set forth in this Article; and

(*e*) to transmit regularly to the Secretary-General for information purposes, subject to such limitation as security and constitutional considerations may require, statistical and other information of a technical nature relating to economic, social, and educational conditions in the territories for which they are respectively responsible other than those territories to which Chapters XII and XIII apply.

ARTICLE 74

Members of the United Nations also agree that their policy in respect of the territories to which this Chapter applies, no less than in respect of their metropolitan areas, must be based on the general principle of good-neighbourliness, due account being taken of the interests and well-being of the rest of the world, in social, economic, and commercial matters.

These Articles stipulate obligations of Members; functions of the Organisation are provided for only in so far as by Article 73, clause (*e*), the Secretary-General is authorised to receive ' statistical and other information of a technical nature relating to economic, social, and educational conditions ' from the Members responsible for the administration of territories to which Chapter XI does apply, but not Chapters XII and XIII. This, however, is not the only function which the Organisation is authorised by the Charter to exercise with respect to the territories to which Chapter XI (but not Chapters XII and XIII) apply. Since the General Assembly under Article 10 is authorised to discuss any matter within the scope of the Charter and to make recommendations on such matters to the Members or to the Security Council, and since the administration of the territories to which Chapter XI applies is certainly a matter within the scope of the Charter, the Assembly may discuss the matters to which Articles 73 and 74 refer and make recommendations on these matters. If such a recommendation is considered to be an ' intervention,' the Assembly is competent to intervene in matters of the administration of the territories to which Chapter XI applies, except such administration is considered to be a matter essentially within the domestic jurisdiction of the state responsible for the administration, in spite of the fact that the latter is under international obligations in this respect. Such an interpretation of Article 2, paragraph 7, is not impossible, but makes the provisions of Chapter XI illusory. As a matter of fact, the General Assembly has discussed the matters regulated by Chapter XI and has made recommendations on them, which shall be discussed later.[1]

[1] During the discussion of a proposal that the General Assembly should request the Economic and Social Council to convoke a conference of non-self-governing peoples to which Chapter XI applies, it has been suggested ' that the General Assembly had not the power to recommend to Members the taking of measures regarding the administration of their territories [to which Chapter XI applies], on

The heading of Chapter XI ' Declaration regarding Non-Self-Governing Territories ' is rather strange and misleading. The

the ground that such recommendations would be an intervention into purely domestic affairs.' (Statement of the delegates of the Philippine Republic at the 25th meeting of the Sixth Committee. Journal of the United Nations No. 48: Suppl. No. 6-A/C.6/100, p. 78.) When the modified proposition: the General Assembly should recommend that the Economic and Social Council together with the administrative authorities of the territories to which Chapter XI applies organize the convocation of regional conferences of representatives of non-self-governing territories, was discussed at the 64th meeting of the General Assembly, the delegate of the United States declared, the difference between territories to which only Chapter XI applies and trust territories to which Chapters XII and XIII apply, consists in that with respect to the latter ' this General Assembly, with the help of the Trusteeship Council, shares authority with the administering Member state . . . '; with respect to non-self-governing territories which are not placed under trusteeship, ' the United Nations has no authority to intervene in such territories. That authority remains with their own national government.' (Journal of the United Nations, No. 63, pp. 683 f.) This formula goes further than the intention of the delegate of the United States. First, there is in the terminology of Article 2, paragraph 7, no intervention in a territory, but intervention in a ' matter.' Then the delegate probably did not intend to deny the competence of the General Assembly to make recommendations on matters to which Chapter XI refers, even if such recommendations were to be interpreted to be ' interventions ' in the administration of the territories to which Chapter XI applies. Another question is whether the Economic and Social Council is competent to convoke conferences of representatives of the peoples inhabiting these territories. This is a question of the interpretation of Article 62, paragraph 4. Cf. *infra*, p. 565.

During the same discussion the delegate of the United Kingdom declared: ' The Charter itself provides no organ for the supervision of application of Chapter XI.' (p. 688). This statement, too, goes too far. Under Article 10 the General Assembly may very well discuss the fact that a Member has not fulfilled its obligations under Chapter XI and make recommendations in this respect. The General Assembly—together with the Security Council—may even apply the sanction provided for in Article 6 in case a Member violates its obligations under Articles 73 and 74. If this is ' supervision ', the Charter indeed does provide organs for the supervision of application of Chapter XI. But the Trusteeship Council is not among these organs. Cf. *infra*, pp. 684 ff.

There is certainly a difference between the competence of the United Nations with respect to non-self-governing territories under trusteeship and those not under trusteeship. But the difference does not consist in that in the latter case the Organization has no right at all to interfere. During a debate in the Fourth Committee of the General Assembly in 1947, the representative of the United States spoke of a ' sharp ' and ' fundamental ' distinction made at San Francisco between Chapter XI on the one hand and Chapters XII and XIII on the other. He stated: ' It was realised then, and it remains true now, that in many non-self-governing territories sovereignty or jurisdiction vests in the administering states; and nothing was written into the Charter to change this fundamental fact. On the other hand, there are other non-self-governing territories—trust territories—where supervision lies in the hands of the United Nations; and in such territories the United Nations can and should hold the administering power to strict accountability. Chapter XI of the Charter dealt with the former; Chapters XII and XIII with the latter. . . . It seems to my Delegation of fundamental importance that this sharp differentiation made in the Charter between territories and peoples under the sovereignty or jurisdiction

provisions of Articles 73 and 74 are not a unilateral ' declaration ' of some states, but the content of the treaty to which all Members of the United Nations are contracting parties in spite of the fact that obligations are imposed by these Articles only upon Members which administer territories referred to in these Articles. The obligations established in Articles 73 and 74 do not differ in any way from other obligations imposed upon Members by the Charter. They are binding also upon states which did not participate in the San Francisco Conference but became, or will become later, Members of the United Nations. Article 73 expressly says: ' Members . . . which have or assume responsibilities . . . ' A persistent violation of the obligations stipulated in Chapter XI may lead to the sanction provided for in Article 6 of the Charter which, too, is an action by which the Organisation may intervene in matters regulated by Chapter XI.[2]

of an independent state and those which are not should be maintained. Chapters XII and XIII materially alter the status of the non-self-governing territories coming within their scope. Chapter XI does not. No effort should be made to blur this distinction.' (U.S. Mission to the United Nations, Press Release 251, October 6, 1947.) In view of the competence the General Assembly has with respect to non-self-governing territories not under trusteeship in accordance with Article 10 and (together with the Security Council) under Article 6, it is hardly possible to maintain that the United Nations has no jurisdiction over these territories. The difference between the relation of the United Nations to these territories and that to trust territories is not as sharp as the delegate of the United States assumed.

[2] The basis of the discussion at the San Francisco Conference which led to the adoption of Chapter XI was a Working Paper (U.N.C.I.O. Doc. 323, II/4/12) prepared on ' proposals submitted by delegations of Australia, China, France, the Soviet Union, the United Kingdom, the United States, together with suggestions made by other delegations . . . (Report of Rapporteur of Committee II/4, U.N.C.I.O. Doc. 1115, II/4/44 (1) (*a*), pp. 1 f.) Chapter XI corresponds to Section A of the Working Paper; and the heading of this Section was originally ' General Policy '. At the 11th meeting of Committee II/4 (U.N.C.I.O. Doc. 712, II/4/30, p. 2) ' it was said that this heading obscured the distinction between the scope of Section A and Section B ' (corresponding to Chapters 12 and 13 of the Charter). This was probably the reason why the words ' General Policy ' have been replaced by the word ' Declaration.' The Report of Rapporteur of Committee II/4 states with respect to the Articles of Chapters XI, XII and XIII proposed by Committee II/4 : ' These Articles are grouped into two sections: A. Declaration, and B. International Trusteeship System. The Committee makes the following recommendations to Commission II: *Declaration* (Section A, paragraphs 1 and 2).—The Committee recommends that a Declaration, Section A, paragraphs 1 and 2, be made by states Members of the United Nations having responsibilities for the administration of territories whose peoples have not yet attained a full measure of self-government. This Declaration would be applicable to all such territories . . . ' The meaning of this statement was not that a declaration apart from signing and ratifying the text of the Charter should be made. As a matter of fact, no such declaration has been made. And the provisions of Chapter XI are binding upon all Members concerned, without any special ' declaration ' made in addition to the act by which a state becomes a Member of the United Nations. The phrase in Article 73: Members . . . which have or assume responsibilities . . . ' recognise ' the principle that . . . has no other meaning than the phrase: Members ' agree ' in Articles 74 and 25, or the phrase: Members ' undertake ' in Articles 43 and 94, or the

There can be hardly any doubt that the provisions of Articles 73 and 74 constitute obligations of the Members concerned. This is expressly stipulated with respect to the provisions of Article 73, 'Members . . . accept . . . the obligation to . . . ' The resolution adopted by the General Assembly at its 27th meeting on Non-Self-Governing Peoples[3] states with respect to Chapter XI: the Members 'accept . . . the obligation to promote to the utmost the well-being of the inhabitants of these territories. To that end they accept certain specific obligations, including the obligation to develop self-government and to assist the inhabitants in the progressive development of free political institutions.' And: the General Assembly 'draws attention to the fact that the obligations accepted under Chapter XI of the Charter by all Members of the United Nations [not only by a 'declaration' made by some Members] are in no way contingent upon the conclusion of trusteeship agreements or upon the bringing into being of the Trusteeship Council and are, therefore, already in full

phrase: Members 'pledge themselves' in Article 56. As pointed out in a previous connection, the meaning of the phraseology: the contracting parties 'declare', 'agree', 'pledge themselves', 'recognise', 'accept', and the like, is only to stress the contractual character of the provisions, to maintain the idea of sovereignty according to which a state can be legally bound only by its own will; which, as formulation of treaty provisions, is completely superfluous since these provisions are, even without any such formula, binding only upon the contracting parties.

At the 64th meeting of the General Assembly the delegate of France declared: 'As regards Chapter XI particularly, I would remind you that this Chapter is not in the same form as the other provisions of the Charter. It is entitled: "Declaration". It contains a unilateral declaration by a certain number of states, and the Charter merely confines itself to recording it. This is absolutely clear; there can be no argument on this point.' (Journal of the United Nations, No. 63: Suppl. A-A/P.V./64, p. 703.) This statement is 'absolutely' erroneous; but it shows how misleading the title of Chapter XI is. The same is true of the statement made by the Australian delegate in a sub-committee appointed by the Fourth Committee: 'The three Chapters [XI, XII, XIII] had a common root. But Chapter XI was a unilateral declaration on the part of administering states, while Chapter XII represented an international multilateral contractual undertaking.' (Doc. A/C./4/68, p. 10.) Even if the content of Chapter XI originally were a unilateral declaration of certain states, by its insertion into the Charter it became an 'international multilateral contractual undertaking', to use the expression of the Australian delegate. And only as content of the Charter is it binding upon the states concerned. In this respect there is no difference between the provisions of Chapter XI and those of Chapters XII and XIII.

In his Annual Report on the work of the Organisation for the period July 1, 1947—January 30, 1948 (General Assembly, Official Records: Third Session, Suppl. No. 1 A/565, p. 102) the Secretary-General stated: 'The transmission to the Secretary-General of information on economic, social and educational conditions in non-self-governing Territories is an obligation specifically stipulated in the Charter under Article 73 (*e*). The other provisions of Article 73 are of a declaratory character.' This statement has no basis in the text of Article 73. The provisions of clauses (*a*), (*b*), (*c*) and (*d*) constitute obligations just as the provision of clause (*e*).

[3] Resolutions adopted by the General Assembly (Doc. A/64, p. 13.)

force.' That means that the Assembly considers not only the provision laid down in the preamble of Article 73 but also the provisions of clauses (*a*) to (*e*) as constituting obligations of the Members concerned.[4]

The most important question to be answered by an interpretation of Chapter XI is: what are the territories to which the provisions of this Chapter apply? The definition 'territories whose peoples have not yet attained a full measure of self-government' is highly ambiguous. First, because the term 'self-government' may be interpreted in very different ways; then, because the probably intended exclusion of peoples within metropolitan areas from the application of Chapter XI is not very clearly expressed. The people of the whole territory of a Member state may not yet have attained the full measure of self-government. Self-government, meaning a democratic form of government, is not a condition of being or becoming a Member of the United Nations. The obligation stipulated in clause (*b*) of Article 73 'to develop self-government' is not intended to be incumbent upon Member states which have no democratic form of government with respect to the whole people of that state, although the wording of Article 73 does not exclude such interpretation; for—taken literally—a Member state which has an autocratic form of government is a Member which has responsibility for the administration of a territory whose people has not yet attained a full measure of self-government. The formula 'non-self-governing territories' is usually interpreted to mean only non-self-governing colonies;[5] but the term 'colony' is no less ambiguous than the term 'non-self-governing.' Probably only

[4] At the 63rd meeting of the General Assembly the delegate of the United States declared: 'Chapter XI, like many other provisions of the Charter, depends at the present time essentially upon the voluntary action of the Member states.' (Journal of the United Nations, No. 63: Suppl. A-A/P.V./64, p. 685.) That cannot mean that the Members are not under obligation to act as Chapter 11 provides. At the 16th meeting of the Fourth Committee of the General Assembly the delegate of the Philippine Republic stated with reference to the obligations stipulated by Chapter XI: 'The obligations on the part of the administering nations also implied a corresponding right on the part of the inhabitants of the non-self-governing territories to ask for the due observance by the administering states of the obligations assumed by them under the Charter.' (Journal of the United Nations, No. 27: Suppl. No. 4-A/C.4/49, p. 28.) There is no provision in the Charter on which such a right could be based. The 'inhabitants of the non-self-governing territories' do not form an organised body endowed with juristic personality capable to exercise such a right.

[5] At the 15th meeting of the General Assembly the delegate of Australia said with respect to Chapters XI, XII and XIII: 'In a real sense, therefore, the Charter brings the Colonial world generally within the sphere of international responsibility.' (Journal of the General Assembly, No. 10, p. 249.) At the 27th meeting of the General Assembly the delegate of the United Kingdom spoke of the territories referred to in Chapter XI as of 'colonial territories', and said of Chapters XII and XIII: 'we are creating machinery perhaps specially designed for the well-being of the colonial or non-self-governing peoples . . .' (*Ibid*, No. 28, pp. 488, 489.)

territories were meant inhabited by relatively primitive aborigines with a backward civilisation. The formula of the Working Paper, which was the basis of the discussion at the San Francisco Conference, a formula taken over from Article 22 of the Covenant of the League of Nations: 'territories inhabited by peoples not yet able to stand by themselves,' expresses the intention of the legislator somewhat better than the formula used in Chapter XI.[6]

Who is competent to decide the question: What territories fall within the category 'non-self-governing' territories? If the General Assembly is competent to make recommendations on matters regulated by Chapter XI, and that means to apply its provisions, the Assembly may—in form of a recommendation—specify these territories. But a recommendation of the Assembly has no binding force; hence it depends finally on the Member states to decide which are the territories to which their obligations under Chapter XI refer. In its resolution

[6] The Summary Report of the 11th meeting of Committee II/4 at the San Francisco Conference (U.N.C.I.O. Doc. 712, II/4/30, pp. 2 f.) contains the following statement: '"Peoples not yet able to stand by themselves under the strenuous conditions of the modern world." It was said that these words did not clearly indicate what peoples were referred to. The words were outmoded, having been first drafted in the light of conditions prevailing 25 years ago. From the military point of view very few countries if any were now able to stand alone in protecting themselves. Similarly very few countries were economically self-sufficient. The words, moreover, might be objectionable to certain peoples. It was pointed out that among dependent peoples there were peoples that were undeveloped and peoples with a long heritage of civilisation. These two categories should be differentiated. On the other hand, it was urged that the words in question had come to have a special and generally recognised meaning through their embodiment in Article 22 of the Covenant and that the working out of an appropriate and generally acceptable substitute had proved to be a matter of great difficulty.' The question of the exact meaning of the term 'non-self-governing territories' was raised during a discussion in a sub-committee appointed by the Fourth Committee of the General Assembly. The report of the sub-committee (Doc. A/C.4/68, p. 3) contains the following statements: 'The Indian representative, while considering the Charter definition of Non-Self-Governing Territories as territories whose peoples had not yet attained a full measure of self-government sufficiently clear, gave his approval to the definition suggested by the United States Government in a letter to the Secretary-General, that Chapter XI would appear to apply to any territories administered by a Member of the United Nations which do not enjoy the same measure of self-government as the metropolitan area of that Member. The representative of the Union of Soviet Socialist Republics proposed that the definition should be: all possessions, protectorates and territories the people of which have not yet reached self-government and do not possess the right to elect local self-governing bodies, or to take part in the legislative bodies of the governing country on the same terms as the people of the governing country. The Egyptian representative suggested that a Non-Self-Governing People was one living in a non-metropolitan territory and differing from the metropolitan state in race, culture and language.—The Cuban, French and Australian representatives, however, deprecated any attempt at a formal definition. The United Kingdom's letter to the Secretary-General was to the same effect. It was, therefore, agreed to note the territories enumerated as subject to Chapter XI but not to attempt a definition for the time being.'

on Non-self-governing Peoples, adopted at its 27th meeting,[7] the General Assembly requested the Secretary-General ' to include in his annual report on the work of the Organisation, as provided for in Article 98 of the Charter, a statement summarising such information as may have been transmitted to him by Members of the United Nations under Article 73 (*e*) of the Charter . . . ' In a letter of June 29, 1946,[8] the Secretary-General drew the attention of the Members to this resolution and invited them, *inter alia*, to enumerate the non-self-governing territories subject to their jurisdiction. In its resolution on Transmission of Information under Article 73 (*e*) of the Charter, adopted at its 64th meeting, the General Assembly noted that information has been transmitted by governments which are enumerated in the Resolution, and also noted that certain governments enumerated in the Resolution ' have declared their intention of transmitting information.'[9] That means that the Assembly left it to the Members to determine which territories fall within the category of non-self-governing territories.

The obligations imposed upon the Members by Articles 73 and 74 are formulated in rather vague terms. The value of ' the principle that the interests of the inhabitants of these territories are paramount ' depends on the answer to the question as to who is competent to decide what are the interests of the inhabitants, and since the Charter does not provide anything in this respect, it is in the first place the administering government which is competent to decide this question. The same is true with respect to the obligation ' to promote . . . the well-being of the inhabitants.' In this respect the text of the Charter constitutes a certain progress as compared with the text of Article 22 of the Covenant: ' the principle that the well-being and development of such peoples form a sacred trust of civilisation.' The Charter is more precise, in determining ' the sacred trust ' as an ' obligation of the Members.' But, in contradistinction to the Covenant, the Charter restricts the obligation to promote the well-being of the inhabitants by the addition: ' within the system of international peace and security established by the present Charter.' This formula may be interpreted to mean that in case the obligation to promote the well-being of the inhabitants of the non-self-governing territories is in conflict with the obligations or rights of the administering state with respect to the maintenance or restoration of international peace and security, these obligations and rights prevail; in spite of the principle to be recognised by the administering state ' that the interests of the inhabitants of these territories are paramount.'

The—not very consistent—obligations to recognise the interests of the inhabitants as paramount and to promote their well-being only

[7] Doc. A/64, p. 13.

[8] *Yearbook of the United Nations*, 1946-47, p. 208.

[9] Doc. A/64/Add. 1, pp. 124 f.

within the system of international peace and security established by the Charter, are specified by the provisions of clauses (*a*) to (*e*).

The obligation of 'just treatment' under clause (*a*) is practically without any value in view of the almost absolute uncertainty of the meaning of 'justice.'[1] As to 'protection against abuses,' Article 22 of the Covenant was more specific. It stipulated with respect to so-called B Mandates 'the prohibition of abuses such as the slave trade, the arms traffic, and the liquor traffic,' not mentioned in Article 73 of the Charter.[2]

The obligation established in clause (*b*) 'to develop self-government' is practically identical with the obligation 'to take due account of the political aspirations of the peoples, and to assist them in the progressive development of their free political institutions.' The political aspirations of the peoples concerned are always directed at least towards self-government, which is also the tendency immanent in any 'free' political institution. But the value of these obligations of the administering authority is made highly problematical by the restriction: 'according to the particular circumstances . . .' Whether and to what extent the particular circumstances allow the development of self-government depends, at least in the first place, on the arbitrary decision of the administering government. And even if it is assumed that the General Assembly is competent under Article 10, to recommend to a Member to grant self-government to the people of a non-self-governing territory under its jurisdiction, such recommendation is not binding upon the Member concerned (except that non-compliance with the recommendation is considered by the

[1] Article 23 (*b*) of the Covenant of the League of Nations provided that the Members of the League 'undertake to secure just treatment of the native inhabitants of the territories under their control.' But all provisions of Article 23 were under the restriction laid down in the first sentence: 'subject to and in accordance with the provisions of international conventions existing or hereafter to be agreed upon.

[2] Annex B to Report of Rapporteur of Committee II/4 at the San Francisco Conference (U.N.C.I.O. Doc. 1115, II/4/44 (1) (*a*), p. 13): 'Questions asked by the delegate of the Netherlands of the delegate of the United States in regard to the interpretation of Section A of the Trusteeship Chapter [Chapter XI of the Charter]. The delegate of the Netherlands: "The questions are: 1. Do the purposes and obligations formulated in paragraph 1 imply that the states Members concerned should enact appropriate protection of the arable land of the non-self-governing peoples for whose administration they have responsibilities? 2. Do these purposes and obligations imply that such states members should abolish penal sanctions on contract labour, in accordance with existing and future labour conventions? 3. Does an obligation—at least a moral obligation—result from this Chapter and the Charter as a whole for the states Members concerned to eliminate, in the territories under consideration, all discrimination resulting from feelings of racial superiority and to combat such feelings by education and by all other adequate means?" The delegate of the United States: "In accordance with the provisions of Section A, I would consider it clear that the abuses you refer to are included in the abuses against which the people concerned are to be protected and the obligation referred to in paragraph 1 covers this situation."'

Security Council under Article 39 as a threat to the peace and a condition of enforcement action). It should be noted that Article 73 (*b*) stipulates only the obligation to develop self-government whereas Article 76 (*b*) determines as an objective of the trusteeship system 'to promote . . . progressive development towards self-government or independence.[3] In general usage of language the term 'self-government' is sometimes used as identical with 'independence.' The Charter, however, differentiates 'self-government' and 'independence,' independence meaning—in the Charter—'sovereignty.'

Whereas the obligations of the administering states stipulated in the preamble of Article 73 refer to the 'inhabitants' of the non-self-governing territories, the obligations stipulated in clauses (*a*) and (*b*) refer to the 'peoples' concerned. By 'inhabitants' not only the indigenous population but also immigrant settlers might be understood. But the term 'people' in clauses (*a*) and (*b*) includes probably only the indigenous population, which results from the content of the respective provisions.

The stipulation of the obligation 'to further international peace and security' (clause (*c*)) is superfluous because included in the 'system of international peace and security established by the present Charter,' mentioned in the preamble of Article 73. But it is significant that in an Article the main purpose of which seems to be to provide for protection of non-self-governing peoples, the promotion of international peace and security which may impair this protection, is referred to twice.

The obligation stipulated in clause (*d*) 'to promote constructive measures of development, to encourage research' is probably only a specification of the obligations stipulated in clauses (*a*) and (*b*); the obligation to co-operate with one another and with specialised bodies,

[3] The Report of the Rapporteur of Committee II/4 (U.N.C.I.O. Doc. 1115, II/4/44 (1) (*a*), p. 3) contains the following statement: 'In connection with this Declaration there was very lengthy discussion with regard to the objectives to be sought in the political development of the territories concerned. There was general agreement that self-government was a goal for such development. Some delegates desired in addition to include independence as an alternative goal, 'independence or self-government.' It was said that independence was an aim of many dependent peoples and that its attainment should not be excluded by the terms of the Charter. On the other hand, it was urged that since the section on the Declaration applied to all dependent 'territories' and not merely to those placed under trusteeship, the reference to independence should more properly be made in the section on Trusteeship.' Against the motion to formulate Article 73, clause (*c*) as follows: To promote development towards independence or self-government, etc.: it was argued, among others, that the word '"self-government" did not exclude the possibility of independence and represented a broad measure of agreement which it would be inexpedient to impair by the substitution of a more controversial wording.' (U.N.C.I.O. Doc. 404, II/4/17, pp. 2 f.)

is implied by Article 1, paragraph 3, and Chapters IX and X. Article 73 (*d*) goes, perhaps, a little further in so far as it provides for co-operation 'with specialised international bodies,' not only with specialised agencies referred to in Chapters IX and X. But this obligation is restricted by the formula 'where appropriate,' which to decide depends on the government administering the territory. In the resolution of the General Assembly on Transmission of Information under Article 73 (*e*) of the Charter it is stated: 'The value of the association of Non-self-governing Territories in the work of the specialised agencies as a means of attaining the objectives of Chapter XI of the Charter has been stressed.'[4]

The most important obligation is the one established by clause (*e*). For, information on the conditions in the territories to which the provisions of Chapter XI apply (territories placed under trusteeship are expressly excluded) may be the basis of that kind of supervision which has been mentioned above. But the obligation to transmit information is subject to serious restrictions. First of all, the information is 'to be transmitted to the Secretary-General for information purposes.' That information is to be transmitted for information purposes seems to be a meaningless tautology. But the phrase might be interpreted to mean that the reports made by the administering governments must not be used to any other purpose but to be kept in the archives of the Secretariat. The Charter does not provide what is to be done with the information the Secretary-General receives from the Members. But the interpretation is not excluded that nothing in the Charter prevents the General Assembly from using these informations received by its auxiliary organ, the Secretary-General, in exercising its competence under Article 10 with respect to the administration of non-self-governing territories. The Secretary-General himself, of course, has no such competence.[5] The second important restriction of the obligation to transmit information consists in that this information shall be only of a 'technical nature' and relate only to 'economic, social, and educational conditions' in the territories concerned, which means that the administering governments are not obliged to transmit information relating to the political conditions of the territories under their jurisdiction.[6]

[4] Resolutions adopted by the General Assembly (Doc. A/64/Add. 1, p. 125).

[5] At the 21st meeting of the Fourth Committee of the General Assembly the delegate of the United Kingdom stated with respect to Article 73 (*e*) 'that the Secretariat should not assume political responsibilities.' (Journal of the United Nations, No. 55: Suppl. No. 4-A/C.4/74, p. 77.)

[6] At the 15th meeting of the Fourth Committee of the General Assembly the delegate of India expressed the hope 'that, in accordance with Article 73 (*b*), information regarding the political progress of the population would be provided.' (Journal of the United Nations, No. 25: Suppl. No. 4-A/C.4/45, p. 15.) During the discussion in the sub-committee appointed by the Fourth Committee, the delegate of the Soviet Union argued 'that the United Nations was also interested in Articles 73 (*a*) and (*b*) in their reference to political advancement and that it would

Finally, the obligation to transmit information is restricted in so far as 'security and constitutional considerations may require' a 'limitation.' It is upon the administering governments to make such considerations. The 'security' referred to in this clause may be interpreted to mean the national security of the administering state, whereas the 'security' referred to in the preamble and clause (*e*) is certainly 'international' security.[7]

According to the express provision of Article 73, clause (*e*), trust territories are not under the obligation laid down in this paragraph. It is Article 88 which applies to trust territories in this respect. The reports which are to be transmitted to the General Assembly under Article 88 include information on 'the political . . . advancement of the inhabitants of each trust territory.' They are 'annual' reports, whereas Article 73 (*e*) provides only for 'regular' information.

In the Resolution on Transmission of Information under Article 73 (*e*) of the Charter, adopted at its 64th meeting, December 14, 1946,[8] the General Assembly :

> 1. Invites the Members transmitting information to send to the Secretary-General by June 30 of each year the most recent information which is at their disposal;
>
> 2. Recommends that the information transmitted in the course of 1947 by Members of the United Nations under Article 73 (*e*) of the Charter should be summarised, analysed and classified by the Secretary-General and included in his report to the second session of the General Assembly, in order that, in the light of the experience gained, the General Assembly may be able to decide whether any other procedure may be desirable for dealing with such information in future years;
>
> 3. Recommends that the Secretary-General communicate to the specialised agencies the information transmitted, with

be impossible to note any progress made unless information was transmitted on these matters.' 'The representative of Poland alluded to Article 73 (*d*) which referred to the scientific purposes set forth in the Article. He considered that information should be supplied on all conditions covered by this Article.' (Doc. A/C.4/68, p. 5.) The chairman, however, summarised the discussions 'as indicating that there was general agreement that, although not mandatory under Article 73 (*e*), information on political progress would be of great importance and was much to be desired.' (p. 6).

7 At the 14th meeting of the Fourth Committee of the General Assembly the delegate of the United Kingdom made the following statement: 'The obligation of Article 73 (*e*) was made by the Charter "subject to such limitations as security and constitutional considerations may require". Secondly, the material to be furnished was defined as "statistical and other information of a technical nature relating to economic, social and educational conditions". Thirdly, the material was to be transmitted to the Secretary-General for information purposes. Thus, the obligation under Chapter XI was entirely different from those of Chapter XII in that it conferred no supervision rights upon the United Nations.' (Journal of the United Nations, No. 23: Suppl. No. 4-A/C.4/44, p. 9.)

8 Resolutions adopted by the General Assembly. (Doc. A/64/Add. 1, pp. 125 ff.)

a view to making all relevant data available to their expert and deliberative bodies;

4. Invites the Secretary-General to convene, some weeks before the opening of the second session of the General Assembly, an *ad hoc* committee composed in equal numbers of representatives of the Members transmitting information under Article 73 (*e*) of the Charter and of representatives of Members elected, by the General Assembly at this session, on the basis of an equitable geographical distribution;

5. Invites the Secretary-General to request the Food and Agriculture Organisation, the International Labour Organisation, the United Nations Educational, Scientific and Cultural Organisation, and the World Health Organisation and the International Trade Organisation, when constituted, to send representatives in an advisory capacity to the meeting of the *ad hoc* committee;

6. Invites the *ad hoc* Committee to examine the Secretary-General's summary and analysis of the information transmitted under Article 73 (*e*) of the Charter with a view to aiding the General Assembly in its consideration of this information, and with a view to making recommendations to the General Assembly regarding the procedures to be followed in the future and the means of ensuring that the advice, expert knowledge and experience of the specialised agencies are used to the best advantage.[9]

The competence of the General Assembly to make the recommendations under paragraphs 1 to 5 is covered by Articles 10 and 98 of the Charter. The election of an *ad hoc* committee and its authorisation to examine the Secretary-General's summary and analysis of the information transmitted to him under Article 73 (*e*) is based on Article 22 of the Charter.[1]

9 At the 21st meeting of the Fourth Committee of the General Assembly the delegate of France denied the constitutionality of the establishment of the *ad hoc* Committee. The delegate of the United States stated: 'The establishment of new machinery in the form of an *ad hoc* committee would be a modification of the Charter.' But the delegate of Cuba quite correctly referred to Article 22 of the Charter. (Journal of the United Nations, No. 55: Suppl. No. 4-A/C./4/74, pp. 77 ff.)

1 At the 21st meeting of the Fourth Committee, the representatives of Belgium and the United Kingdom objected that Article 22 permitted the establishment of subsidiary bodies only for the duration of one session of the General Assembly and not for the work of the next session. (Official Records of the Second part of the first session of the General Assembly. Fourth Committee, Part I. Summary Record of Meetings November 1—December 12, 1946, p. 127.) The wording of Article 22 does not justify such interpretation. The proposal of the representative of China to confer upon the Trusteeship Council the function to examine the information transmitted under Article 73 (*c*). (Summary Records of meetings of Sub-Committee 2 of Fourth Committee November 16—

On November 3, 1947, the General Assembly adopted five resolutions concerning information transmitted under Article 73 (*e*) of the Charter.[2] The first resolution invited Members transmitting information under Article 73 (*e*) to undertake 'all necessary steps to render the information as complete and up to date as possible, in order to facilitate the completion of the Secretary-General's summaries and analyses of the information,' and recommended the use of a standard form for the guidance of members in the preparation of information.[3]

The second resolution dealt with the use of supplement information by the Secretary-General in analysing information from non-self-governing territories. It authorises the use of comparisons between conditions in such territories and in any autonomous countries.[4]

The third resolution concerned transmission of 'political' information from territories. It reads as follows:

> The General Assembly,
>
> Having noted that some Members responsible for the administration of Non-Self-Governing Territories already have voluntarily transmitted information on the development of self-governing institutions in the Non-Self-Governing Territories,
>
> Considers that the voluntary transmission of such information and its summarising by the Secretary-General are entirely in conformity with the spirit of Article 73 of the Charter, and should be therefore duly noted and encouraged.[5]

December 5, 1946, Annex 2 d, pp. 89 ff) has no basis in the Charter. Cf. *ibid*, pp. 22 ff.; Summary Record of Meetings of Fourth Committee, November 1—December 12, 1946, p. 273.

2 Resolutions adopted by the General Assembly. (Doc. A/519, pp. 48 ff.)

3 *Ibid*, p. 48.

4 *Ibid*, p. 55.

5 *Ibid*, p. 56. The Fourth Committee suggested that the General Assembly should recommend to Members administering non-self-governing territories to submit information of a political nature. The text of the resolution proposed by the Fourth Committee runs as follows:

> Considering that the Members of the United Nations responsible for the administration of territories, the populations of which have not yet attained a full measure of self-government, undertake the obligation under Article 73 b to develop self-government, to take due account of the political aspirations of the peoples, and to assist them in the progressive development of their free political institutions, according to the particular circumstances of each territory and its peoples and their varying stages of advancement,
>
> The General Assembly,
>
> Considers that the transmission of information relating to the results achieved in the matter of the participation of local populations in the work of local organs of administration is entirely in conformity with the spirit of Article 73 of the United Nations Charter and recommends those Members

The fourth resolution called for continued co-operation with the specialised agencies to enable the Secretary-General to fulfil the functions derived from Article 73 (*e*).[6]

The fifth resolution created a special committee to continue the work of the *ad hoc* committee and to provide the machinery to deal with information transmitted under Article 73 (*e*). It reads as follows:

> The General Assembly,
>
> 1. Invites the Fourth Committee to constitute a special committee to examine the information transmitted under Article 73 (*e*) of the Chartei on the economic, social and educational conditions in the Non-Self-Governing Territories, and to submit reports thereon for the consideration of the General Assembly with such procedural recommendations as it may deem fit, and with such substantive recommendations as it may deem desirable relating to functional fields generally but not with respect to individual territories;
>
> 2. Authorises this special committee for this purpose
>
> (*a*) to avail itself of the counsel and assistance of the specialised agencies in such manner as it may consider necessary or expedient;
>
> (*b*) to establish liaison with the Economic and Social Council;
>
> (*c*) to invite the Members to provide such supplemental information as may be desired within the terms of Article 73 (*e*); and
>
> 3. Considers that the special committee should be composed of the Members of the United Nations transmitting information and an equal number of Members elected by the Fourth Committee on behalf of the General Assembly on as wide a geographical basis as possible, the committee to meet as the General Assembly may decide.[7]

The provisions of Article 74 do not impose upon Members any obligation not covered by other provisions of the Charter.

> responsible for Non-Self-Governing Territories to transmit such information. (Doc. A/424, p. 14.)

The General Assembly did not accept this proposal. It adopted the above quoted resolution.

[6] *Ibid*, p. 56.

[7] *Ibid*, p. 57. The special Committee created by this resolution was to meet in Geneva on September 2, 1948 before the third session of the General Assembly to examine the summaries and analyses of information transmitted under Article 73 (*e*) of the Charter on conditions in Non-Self-Governing Territories and to submit reports thereon to the General Assembly. (Cf. Annual Report of the Secretary General on the Work of the Organization, July 1, 1947—June 30, 1948, p. 100.) The special Committee met in Geneva on September 2, 1948, but adjourned on September 17 without reaching agreement.

By a resolution adopted at its 64th meeting on Regional Conferences of Representatives of Non-Self-Governing Territories, the General Assembly directly intervened in the administration of these territories. The resolution runs as follows:

> The General Assembly,
>
> Considering that the resolution on Non-Self-Governing Peoples adopted during the first part of the first session of the General Assembly draws attention to the fact that the obligations accepted by Members of the United Nations under Chapter XI of the Charter are already in full force;
>
> Recognising the importance of the declaration contained in Chapter XI of the Charter especially as it concerns the peace and security of the world, and the political, economic, social and educational advancement of the peoples of Non-Self-Governing Territories as well as their just treatment and protection against abuses;
>
> Recommends all Members having or assuming responsibilities for the administration of Non-Self-Governing Territories to convene conferences of respresentatives of Non-Self-Governing Peoples chosen or preferably elected in such a way that the representation of the people will be ensured to the extent that the particular conditions of the territory concerned permit, in order that effect may be given to the letter and spirit of Chapter XI of the Charter and that the wishes and aspirations of the Non-Self-Governing Peoples may be expressed.[8]

The recommendation made by this resolution is within the competence of the General Assembly established by Article 10.[9]

[8] Resolutions adopted by the General Assembly. (Doc. A/64/Add. 1, pp. 126 f.)

[9] According to the originally proposed text of the resolution, the General Assembly should ' request the Economic and Social Council to convoke ' ' a Conference of non-self-governing peoples to which Chapter XI of the Charter applies.' Later this proposal was modified in so far as the Assembly should recommend ' that the Economic and Social Council, together with the administrative authorities concerned, organise the convokation of regional conferences of representatives of non-self-governing territories.' (Doc. A/C./468, pp. 19 ff.; A/251.) Against this proposal the delegates of the United Kingdom and France objected at the 64th meeting of the General Assembly, that it constituted a violation of Article 2, paragraph 7. (Journal of the United Nations, No. 63: Suppl. A/P.V./64, pp. 689, 698.) This is hardly correct. Administration of non self governing territories is not a matter which is essentially within the domestic jurisdiction of the states having responsibilities for the administration. For the states are with respect to this administration under international obligations imposed upon them by the Charter. The proposal was not in conformity with the Charter in so far as Article 62 authorises the Economic and Social Council only to call ' international conferences ', and that means conferences of state governments, and not conferences of representatives of the peoples or territories under the jurisdiction of states Members of the United Nations. The representative of India

2. The Trusteeship System

A. *Functions and Obligations*

(*a*) Trusteeship and Mandate

Article 75 of the Charter provides:

> The United Nations shall establish under its authority an international trusteeship system for the administration and supervision of such territories as may be placed thereunder by subsequent individual agreements. These territories are hereinafter referred to as trust territories.

If the term ' trusteeship system ' means a set of rules regulating trusteeship, then the trusteeship system referred to in Article 75 is already a part of the Charter, laid down in Articles 75 to 91 and need not be established by the United Nations, as Article 75 states. But the trusteeship system, laid down in the Charter, must be implemented by the trusteeship agreements to be concluded under the Charter. In the establishment of these agreements the United Nations only participates by ' approving ' the agreements concluded by the states directly concerned in accordance with Articles 79, 83 and 85.

The Charter does not define the concept of ' trustee ' although the term is not used in its original meaning: a person holding property in trust, that is to say, for the benefit of another. An institution of public, especially of international, not of private, law is intended. The term itself indicates merely a certain analogy to private trusteeship. The difference is that the trustee of the system established under the authority of the United Nations is not a private person but a state or an international organisation, and that what it is holding in trust is not property but the power of administering a territory. This administration must be exercised for the benefit of the population. For this purpose the administration is to be placed by the trusteeship agreement under the ' supervision ' of the United Nations.

Trusteeship as established by and under the Charter is about the same institution as the mandates of the Covenant of the League of Nations.

The mandate system of the League of Nations was the result of a compromise between the usual practice of victorious states to annex the colonial territories of the vanquished states and the proposition put forward after the First World War to place these territories under international administration.

stated (p. 691) that the proposed conference ' is a conference of peoples, or groups which ought to be nations, in self-governing territories. Therefore it is an international conference. . . . ' A conference of ' groups which ought to be nations ' is not an ' international conference ' within the meaning of Article 62, paragraph 4 of the Charter.

The purpose of the mandate system is laid down in paragraphs 1 and 2 of the Article 22 of the Covenant:

> 1. To those colonies and territories which as a consequence of the late war have ceased to be under the sovereignty of the States which formerly governed them and which are inhabited by peoples not yet able to stand by themselves under the strenuous conditions of the modern world, there should be applied the principle that the well-being and development of such peoples form a sacred trust of civilisation and that securities for the performance of this trust should be embodied in this Covenant.
>
> 2. The best method of giving practical effect to this principle is that the tutelage of such peoples should be entrusted to advanced nations who by reason of their resources, their experience or their geographical position can best undertake this responsibility, and who are willing to accept it, and that this tutelage should be exercised by them as Mandatories on behalf of the League.

The essence of the mandate system may be formulated as: administration on behalf of the League of Nations of territories inhabited by peoples not yet able to stand by themselves for the purpose of promoting the well-being and development of those peoples.

Under the Covenant three different categories of Mandates were established, ' according to the stage of the development of the people, the geographical situation of the territory, its economic conditions, and other similar circumstances ' (Article 22, paragraph 3). It was usual to characterise them as A, B and C, Mandates. The A Mandates were determined in paragraph 4 of Article 22 as follows:

> 4. Certain communites formerly belonging to the Turkish Empire have reached a stage of development where their existence as independent nations can be provisionally recognised subject to the rendering of administrative advice and assistance by a Mandatory until such time as they are able to stand alone. The wishes of these communities must be a principal consideration in the selection of the Mandatory.

As to the B Mandates paragraph 5 provided:

> 5. Other peoples, especially those of Central Africa, are at such a stage that the Mandatory must be responsible for the administration of the territory under conditions which will guarantee freedom of conscience and religion, subject only to the maintenance of public order and morals, the prohibition of abuses such as the slave trade, the arms traffic, and the liquor traffic, and the prevention of the establishment of fortifications or military and naval bases and of military training of the natives for other than police purposes and the defence of territory, and

> will also secure equal opportunities for the trade and commerce of other Members of the League.

Paragraph 6 referred to the C Mandates:

> 6. There are territories, such as Southwest Africa and certain of the South Pacific Islands, which, owing to the sparseness of their population, or their small size, or their remoteness from the centres of civilisation, or their geographical contiguity to the territory of the Mandatory, and other circumstances, can be best administered under the laws of the Mandatory as integral portions of its territory, subject to the safeguards above-mentioned in the interests of the indigenous population.

The difference between the three categories of Mandates consisted in the different degree of power conferred upon the mandatory state. In case of A Mandates the mandatory power was only entitled to render ' administrative advice and assistance '; in case of B Mandates the Mandatory government had full administrative power, with certain expressly stipulated restrictions; in case of C Mandates the territory could be administered under the laws of the Mandatory as integral portion of its territory.

The main principles of the trusteeship system are laid down in Article 76 as the ' basic objectives ' of this system. This Article runs as follows:

> The basic objectives of the trusteeship system, in accordance with the Purposes of the United Nations laid down in Article 1 of the present Charter, shall be:
>
> (*a*) to further international peace and security;
>
> (*b*) to promote the political, economic, social, and educational advancement of the inhabitants of the trust territories, and their progressive development towards self-government or independence as may be appropriate to the particular circumstances of each territory and its peoples and the freely expressed wishes of the peoples concerned, and as may be provided by the terms of each trusteeship agreement;
>
> (*c*) to encourage respect for human rights and for fundamental freedoms for all without distinction as to race, sex, language, or religion, and to encourage recognition of the interdependence of the peoples of the world; and
>
> (*d*) to ensure equal treatment in social, economic, and commercial matters for all Members of the United Nations and their nationals, and also equal treatment for the latter in the administration of justice, without prejudice to the attainment of the foregoing objectives and subject to the provisions of Article 80.

Only the objectives set forth in clause (*b*) are specific of the trusteeship system. The objective of clause (*a*) and the first of the two objectives in clause (*c*) coincide with general purposes of the United Nations laid down in Article 1 of the Charter. The stipulation of these objectives is superfluous since the preamble of Article 76 expressly provides that 'the basic objectives of the trusteeship system' shall be 'in accordance with the Purposes of the United Nations laid down in Article 1 of the present Charter.' Even this provision is not necessary since the purposes laid down in Article 1 are purposes 'of the United Nations' and consequently apply also to the trusteeship system established under the authority of the United Nations. Just as in Article 73 stress is laid on the furtherance of international peace and security, presented as the first objective of the trusteeship system although there is no, or no direct, relation between this purpose of the United Nations and the specific objective of the trusteeship system: to promote the advancement of the inhabitants of the trust territories and their development towards self-government or independence. The second objective of clause (*c*): 'recognition of the interdependence of the peoples of the world,' as well as the objective determined in clause (*d*): 'to ensure equal treatment . . . for all Members of the United Nations and their nationals, etc.,' refer more to the benefit of other peoples than those of the trust territories. The principle of the open door, laid down in clause (*d*), might even be injurious to the inhabitants of trust territories. Hence it was necessary to restrict this objective by adding: 'without prejudice to the attainment of the foregoing objectives,' among which to promote the advancement of the inhabitants and their development towards self-government or independence, is certainly the most important one. These objectives shall be discussed in connection with the trusteeship functions of the Organisation and the obligations of the administering authorities.[1]

According to the provisions of the Charter, trusteeship involves the following elements: (1) a territory placed under the trusteeship system, called 'trust territory' (Articles 75, 77); (2) an administering authority competent to exercise the administration of the trust territory. Such authority may be one or more states (not necessarily member states) or the Organisation itself (Article 81); (3) the Organisation, not as administering, but as supervising, authority (Article 75 distinguishes between 'administration' and 'supervision' of trust territories). In exercising its function of supervision the Organisation is represented by the General Assembly and the Security Council; both are assisted by a special organ, the Trusteeship Council (Chapter XIII).

What are the territories and by what procedure are they to be placed under the trusteeship system? Who determines the

[1] Cf. *infra*, pp. 609 ff., 631 ff.

administering authority? What are the obligations of the administering authority and the functions of the United Nations in its capacity as supervisor? How are these obligations and functions to be determined, altered, or terminated? Where does the sovereignty over trust territories rest?

(*b*) The territories to be placed under Trusteeship

The Covenant of the League of Nations provided in Article 22, paragraph 1, that 'those colonies and territories which as a consequence of the late war have ceased to be under the sovereignty of the states which formerly governed them and which are inhabited by peoples not yet able to stand by themselves' should be placed under the mandate system. The Charter of the United Nations does not, however, establish an obligation to place definite territories under trusteeship. Article 77 only indicates certain categories of territories which may, but need not necessarily, be placed under the trusteeship system of the Charter. It may be deduced from the 'objectives' of the trusteeship system, as determined in Article 76, clause (*b*), that only territories whose peoples have not yet attained 'self-government or independence' can be placed under the trusteeship system. For only with respect to such territories the provision of Article 76, clause (*b*), is applicable: to promote 'their progressive development towards self-government or independence.' The meaning of the terms 'self-government' and 'independence' is doubtful. As pointed out, the meaning of 'self-government' sometimes includes 'independence,' *i.e.*, external sovereignty. If, however, self-government is supposed to be something different from independence —as in the phrase of Article 76 (*b*): self-government 'or' independence—self-government probably means political self-determination, that is a democratic form of government; whereas independence means external sovereignty. Since independence in this sense has nothing to do with the form of government, the provisions of Article 76 are not applicable to a territory which is 'independent' although its form of government does not correspond to the principle of self-government. Hence a sovereign state cannot be placed under trusteeship even if its form of government is not democratic. And when a trust territory is made independent, that is to say, established as a sovereign state, the objective of Article 76 (*b*) is attained even if the form of government of this new state is not that of self-government. This is the consequence of the wording: self-government 'or' independence. Excluded from the trusteeship system are, according to the express provision of Article 78, the territories 'which have become Members of the United Nations.' It seems that only under these restrictions the provisions of Article 77 are to be understood.

To be placed under the trusteeship system is the effect of a special agreement. Article 75 expressly refers to 'subsequent individual agreements ' by which territories may be placed under the trusteeship system.[2] Article 77 stipulates:

> 1. The trusteeship system shall apply to such territories in the following categories as may be placed thereunder by means of trusteeship agreements:
>
> (*a*) territories now held under mandate;
>
> (*b*) territories which may be detached from enemy states as a result of the Second World War; and
>
> (*c*) territories voluntarily placed under the system by states responsible for their administration.
>
> 2. It will be a matter for subsequent agreement as to which territories in the foregoing categories will be brought under the trusteeship system and upon what terms.

The ' subsequent agreement ' referred to in paragraph 2 is probably identical with the ' trusteeship agreements ' mentioned in paragraph 1.[3]

It is of importance to note that the Charter does not impose upon the Members an obligation to place certain territories under the trusteeship system. Article 77, it is true, reads: The trusteeship system ' shall ' apply . . . , but its text continues: to such territories as ' may ' be placed thereunder ' by means of trusteeship agreements.' Since a territory can be placed under trusteeship only by agreement, the voluntary consent of the state which has the right to dispose of the territory is necessary.[4] The wording of Article 77, paragraph 1,

[2] During the discussion of the Working Paper in Committee II/4 the delegate for Egypt proposed to delete the words ' by subsequent individual agreements ' from paragraph B 1 of the Working Paper (corresponding to Article 75 of the Charter). ' He argued that the reference to individual agreements was a matter of detail which did not properly fall within a clause dealing with general principles; furthermore, its meaning was obscure.—In opposition to this, it was argued that the words it was proposed to delete were an essential element in the decision to establish a trusteeship system and could not be removed without creating confusion. The existing mandates had been brought under the mandatory system of the League of Nations by individual agreements, and the three types of territory which it was proposed to bring under the new trusteeship system could only be placed under this system by means of similar agreements. The words in dispute conveyed that no territory could be placed under trusteeship by any form of unilateral action.—Decision: The amendment was defeated and paragraph B 1 was then adopted by 31 votes to 1.' (U.N.C.I.O. Doc. 448, II/4/18.)

[3] During the discussion of Section B, paragraph 3 of the Working Paper, which corresponds to Article 77 of the Charter, it was pointed out ' that there were 2 references in paragraph 3 in different terms to subsequent agreements and that these references were ambiguous.' (U.N.C.I.O. Doc. 512, II/4/21.)

[4] At the 19th meeting of the Fourth Committee of the General Assembly the delegate of the South African Union correctly stated that there is nothing in the Charter to support the contention that a government ' could be compelled to enter into a trusteeship agreement even against its own views or those of the people concerned.' (Journal of the United Nations, No. 33: Suppl. No. 4-A/C.4/68, p. 51.) The Union of South Africa refused to place the former mandate territory of South West Africa under the trusteeship system of the United Nations.

clause (*c*), characterising only the territories mentioned in this clause as ' voluntarily ' to be placed under the trusteeship system, is misleading.[5] All the territories are voluntarily to be placed under the system;[6] the whole trusteeship system, in so far as it is established

The Fourth Committee of the General Assembly adopted in 1947 a resolution by which it recommended that the General Assembly urge the Government of the Union of South Africa to propose a trusteeship agreement for South West Africa. This resolution contained the statement that ' it is the clear intention of Chapter XII of the Charter of the United Nations that all territories previously held under mandate, until granted self-government or independence, shall be brought under the international trusteeship system.' (Doc. A/422.) The General Assembly, however, at its 105th meeting amended this resolution by striking out this statement and expressed only ' the hope that the Union Government may find it possible ' to propose a trusteeship agreement. (Resolutions adopted by the General Assembly Doc. A/519, pp. 47 f.) In the discussion preceding this resolution the representative of the United States declared ' that the conclusion of trusteeship agreements was to be a voluntary, and not a compulsory, process ' (Official Records of the Second Session of the General Assembly, Plenary Meetings, Vol. I, p. 578). To justify the opposite interpretation that Article 77 established an obligation to place the territories indicated in this Article under trusteeship, the representative of the Soviet Union advanced the argument that if there were no such obligation 'a situation might arise under which no country would place its territories under trusteeship ' (Summary Record of Fourth Committee November 1—December 12, 1946, p. 90, p. 188). This possibility exists; nevertheless, the Charter did not establish an obligation of the Members to place territories under trusteeship.

5 At the 105th meeting of the General Assembly the representative of China stated: ' Under Article 77 of the Charter, the Trusteeship System is applicable to three categories of territories, the first of which comprises territories now held under mandate. The requirement of a voluntary act is mentioned only in connection with the third category of territories and can hardly be held applicable to territories under mandate. Use of the word ' voluntarily ' in the third category conveys the sense of compulsion in regard to the other categories, particularly mandated territories which are specifically referred to and emphasised in Article 80, paragraph 2 of the Charter, which does not condone any delay or postponement of the negotiations and conclusion of agreements for placing mandated territories under the Trusteeship System. Therefore, I submit that there is a clear obligation on the part of the mandatory Power to place mandated territories under the Trusteeship System.' (Official Records of the Second Session of the General Assembly, Plenary Meetings, Vol. I, pp. 600 f.) The same view was expressed by the representative of Haiti (p. 608).

6 At the *Hearings* (p. 314) the Chairman inserted in the record a letter from the Secretary of the Navy which contains the following statement with reference to the chapter on the trusteeship system: ' This chapter has been a matter of particular concern to the Navy because of our recognition of the fact that undivided control of certain strategic areas in the Pacific wrested from the Japanese by our armed forces in this war, is essential to the security of this country. Our agreement that this Charter is in accord with the military interest of this country is conditioned by our understanding that the United States is not committed by this Charter or any provision thereof to place under trusteeship any territory of any character, and that if this country hereafter determines to place any territory under trusteeship this will be done only on such terms as it may then voluntarily agree to.'

In the course of the discussion the Chairman made the following statement: ' We signed the Charter on the theory that our interests in the Pacific and elsewhere were amply protected. The first thing to note is that no territory can be placed

by the trusteeship agreements, has a voluntary character; and without the trusteeship agreements by which territories are placed under the trusteeship system of the Charter, this system cannot work.[7] Besides, it is not only the coming under the trusteeship system of a definite territory, it is also the terms of the trusteeship which can be established only by a trusteeship agreement, according to the clear wording of Article 77, paragraph 2.[8] The wording of Article 77, paragraph 1, clause (*c*), is incorrect also because the territories referred to in clauses (*a*) and (*b*), too, can be placed under the trusteeship system only by states ' responsible for their administration '; and even this formula is not quite correct, since in order to place a territory under the trusteeship system of the United Nations it does not suffice to be ' responsible for the administration ' of the territory. The state or the states must have the right to dispose of the territory. If the wording of clause (*c*) was intended to authorise a state actually administering a territory without being the territorial sovereign, to place it under trusteeship, clause (*c*) is in conflict with general

under trusteeship without the consent of the nations affected. If we are in possession of an island in the Pacific our interests are sure to be affected, and it cannot be placed under trusteeship except with our consent. When territories are so placed the conditions under which they are placed under the trusteeship must be agreed to by the affected nations. In short, it was our attitude that if we are in possession of an island which we have conquered from Japan at the cost of blood and treasure we can remain in possession of it, if it is within a strategic area, until we consent to have it go under trusteeship; and when we do agree that it go under the trusteeship, we have the right to stipulate the terms upon which it will go there.' After a Senator said, ' We have very serious claims concerning land which, at the great cost of blood, we have taken from Japan,' the Chairman stated: ' Under our conception, all we have to do is to hold on to them until such time as we need to give them up. I do not think we would want to give them up if they are in strategic areas. If we did, we would give them up with strings on them which would guarantee . . . ' The Senator: ' Who would determine the strings? ' The Chairman: ' We would—the United States.' . . . The Chairman: ' . . . It is conceivable that there might be some territories within a strategic area, which would be large enough so that we might retain those portions necessary for military and naval purposes and yet put the other portions where the population resided under some qualified trusteeship.' . . . The Chairman: ' We would have to consent to the terms under which such territories would go in trusteeship, which means that we keep the control in our hands.'

7 At the 16th meeting of the Fourth Committee of the General Assembly the delegate of Belgium stated: ' The trusteeship agreements had no other purpose than to put the Charter into effect in a given territory.' (Journal of the United Nations, No. 27: Suppl. No. 4–A/C.4/49, p. 26.)

8 At the 124th meeting of the Security Council the delegate of the United States stated with reference to Article 77, paragraph 2: ' This clause, if my memory is correct, was regarded at the time of the negotiation of the Charter as a sort of joker . . . ' (Official Records of the Security Council 2nd Year, No. 31, p. 649.) As a matter of fact, the clause was already contained in the Working Paper (Doc. 323, II/4/12), which was the basis of the discussion in Committee II/4 of the San Francisco Conference and was only stylistically modified. Why should a clause considered to be a mere ' joker ' have been inserted into the final text of the Charter?

international law. If actual administration would suffice to entitle a state to place a territory under trusteeship, any territory under belligerent occupation could be disposed of in this way by the occupant power; which would evidently constitute a violation of general international law. Besides, it is hardly possible to derive the competence of placing a territory under trusteeship from Article 77. For the purpose of this Article is to determine the territories which may be placed under trusteeship, not the states by which trusteeship agreements may be concluded. This is the purpose of Article 79.

As pointed out, the Charter contains also a provision by which certain territories are positively excluded from being placed under the trusteeship system. It is Article 78 which provides: 'The trusteeship system shall not apply to territories which have become Members of the United Nations, relationship among which shall be based on respect for the principle of sovereign equality.'

According to Article 22 of the Covenant of the League of Nations, certain territories ' which as a consequence of the late war have ceased to be under the sovereignty of the States which formerly governed them ' have been placed under the ' tutelage ' of some of the victorious powers which were obliged to exercise this tutelage ' as Mandatories on behalf of the League.' The intention underlying the Charter is to place the territories which were under the mandate system of the Covenant, or some of them, under the trusteeship system of the Charter. An express exception is made by Article 78 which was intended to apply in the first place to Lebanon and Syria. Their territories were under the mandate system of the League but they became Members of the United Nations by being permitted to attend the San Francisco Conference and to sign and ratify the Charter. However, as far as these states are concerned, Article 78 is superfluous. No prohibition to place certain territories under the trusteeship system is necessary when this effect can be brought about only voluntarily, that is to say, with the consent of the state which has the right to dispose of the territory concerned. Since Syria and Lebanon are now independent states, they cannot be placed under the trusteeship system without the consent of their respective governments. It is even doubtful whether Article 78 is applicable at all to these states since they are not territories whose peoples have not yet attained self-government or independence. Besides, the text of Article 78 is not quite correct since only ' states,' and not ' territories,' can become Members of the United Nations. However, it was not possible to formulate the Article as follows: The trusteeship system shall not apply to territories of states which have become Members of the United Nations. For such provision would have had the effect to prevent the Members of the United Nations to place any territory, acquired by them, under the trusteeship system. Under general international law a state is entitled to place a territory under the trusteeship system of the United Nations only if it has sovereignty over this territory, that is to say, if it has the right to dispose of this territory. On the other hand, there are Members of the United Nations which were not yet ' independent ' when the Charter came into force, such as India and the Philippines. To the territories of these communities Article 78 was certainly applicable though this was not intended. But with respect to them, the statement of Article 78 ' relationship among which shall be based on respect for the principle of sovereign equality ' is more than problematical. For these communities were certainly neither ' sovereign ' nor ' equal ' as compared with other Members.

The first category of territories mentioned in Article 77 that may be placed under the trusteeship system are ' territories now [that means at the moment the Charter came into force] held under mandate.' As pointed out, the Charter does not impose upon the states entitled to dispose of the former mandated territories the obligation to place under the trusteeship system all these territories. The opposite opinion, advocated in the discussion of the Fourth Committee of the General Assembly,[9] has no basis in the Charter.

The trusteeship system of the United Nations is intended to be applied not only to territories formerly held under League mandate, but also to the territories which may be detached from enemy states (clause (*b*)), and other territories offered for this purpose by the states concerned (clause (*c*)). As pointed out, not only the last-mentioned territories but also those referred to in clauses (*a*) and (*b*) can only ' voluntarily ' be placed under the trusteeship system. This results, especially with respect to former mandated territories, also from Article 80, whose paragraph 1, stipulates:

> Except as may be agreed upon in individual trusteeship agreements, made under Articles 77, 79 and 81, placing each territory under the trusteeship system, and until such agreements have been concluded, nothing in this Chapter shall be construed in or of itself to alter in any manner the rights whatsoever of any states or any peoples or the terms of existing international instruments to which Members of the United Nations may respectively be parties.

[9] That the Members are obliged to place all former mandated territories which are under their jurisdiction under the trusteeship system of the Charter was maintained at the 5th meeting of the Fourth Committee of the General Assembly by the delegate of Brazil, at the 7th meeting by the delegate of India, at the 18th meeting by the delegate of the Soviet Union, and at the 19th meeting by the delegate of the Byelorussian Republic. (Journal of the General Assembly, No. 14; Suppl. No. 4–A/C./4/6, p. 18; No. 17; Suppl. No. 4–A/C.4/18, p. 27; Journal of the United Nations, No. 30; Suppl. No. 4/A/C.4/54, p. 37; No. 33; Suppl. No. 4–A/C.4/68, p. 56.) At the 4th meeting of the Fourth Committee the delegate of the Netherlands correctly maintained that Article 77 ' did not make the transfer of mandated territories to the trusteeship system absolutely obligatory.' (Journal of the General Assembly, No. 13; Suppl. No. 4–A/C.4/5, p. 11.)

If nothing in the Charter alters the rights of the states relating to territories under their jurisdiction 'except as may be agreed upon in individual trusteeship agreements . . . placing each territory under the trusteeship system, and until such agreements have been concluded,' the Charter cannot be interpreted to oblige states to place territories under the trusteeship system. But this, and that prior to the coming into force of the trusteeship agreements the Charter has no effect on the legal status of the territories to be placed under the system, is already the consequence of Articles 77 and 79. According to these provisions territories can be placed under the trusteeship system only by the trusteeship agreements which, as 'agreements,' can be entered into only voluntarily and which must determine the terms of trusteeship, so that all provisions of the Charter concerning trusteeship are applicable to a territory only after the agreement concerned has come into force,—most of the provisions of the Charter becoming binding only when inserted into the agreement. This holds true especially of the provision of Article 76, clause (*d*), according to which it is one of the basic objectives of the trusteeship system to 'ensure equal treatment in social, economic, and commercial matters for all Members of the United Nations and their nationals.' As long as a territory is not placed under the trusteeship system by a trusteeship agreement, this provision cannot apply. Hence, the formula of Article 76, clause (*d*), 'subject to the provisions of Article 80' is superfluous. It seems that the purpose of Article 80, paragraph 1, was to conserve rights established with respect to certain territories prior to the coming into force of Chapter XII of the Charter pending the making of trusteeship agreements. But the provisions of Chapter XII concerning the legal status of the territories referred to in this Chapter apply only after these territories have been placed under trusteeship, and that means: after the trusteeship agreements have come into force. Also without the provision of Article 80, paragraph 1, the rights concerned would not have been altered by the Charter. However, not only paragraph 1, but also paragraph 2, of Article 80, is quite redundant.[1] It runs as follows:

> Paragraph 1 of this Article shall not be interpreted as giving grounds for delay or postponement of the negotiation

[1] The original text contained in Section B, paragraph 5, of the Working Paper (U.N.C.I.O. Doc. 323, II/4/12, p. 5) which was the basis of the discussion in Committee II/4, read as follows: 'Except as may be agreed upon in individual trusteeship arrangements placing each territory under the trusteeship system, nothing in this chapter should be construed in and of itself to alter in any manner the rights of any state or any peoples in any territory.' At the 10th meeting of Committee II/4 (U.N.C.I.O. Doc. 580, II/4/24, p. 2) 'the delegate for the United States stated that paragraph B 5, was intended as a conservatory or safeguarding clause. He was willing and desirous that the minutes of this Committee show that it is intended to mean that all rights whatever they may be, remain exactly the same as they exist—that they are neither increased or diminished by the

> and conclusion of agreements for placing mandated and other territories under the trusteeship system as provided for in Article 77.

adoption of this Charter. Any change is left as a matter for subsequent agreements. The clause should neither add nor detract, but safeguard all existing rights, whatever they may be.' Since the Charter cannot change existing rights established by a treaty different from the Charter and not concluded by the same states, a clause excluding such change is superfluous. At the 13th meeting of Committee II/4 the delegate of the United States suggested an amendment which became Article 80 of the Charter (U.N.C.I.O. Doc. 877, II/4/35, p. 3).

In the discussion of Section B, paragraph 5, of the Working Paper, 'it was suggested, with reference to mandated territories, that the paragraph should include a specific reference to paragraph 4 of Article 22 of the Covenant of the League of Nations [the so-called A Mandates]. Objections to this suggestion were raised on the grounds that it would be inadvisable to refer, specifically, to any one international instrument to which all the United Nations were not parties. It was stated that the phrase " existing international instruments " was preferable.—The Committee accepted the interpretation that among the " rights whatsoever of any states or any peoples " . . . there are included any rights set forth in paragraph 4 of Article 22 of the Covenant of the League of Nations.' (Report of the Rapporteur of Committee II/4 (U.N.C.I.O. Doc. 1115, II/4/44 (1) (*a*), p. 5). The rights of the peoples of the mandated territories mentioned in paragraph 4, Article 22, of the Covenant, consists in that their wishes must be considered ' in the selection of the Mandatory.' This right could not be altered by the Charter but only by an amendment to the Covenant. But it does not imply a right with respect to the selection of the administering authority under the trusteeship system of the Charter. If Article 80, paragraph 1, has no other meaning than that it does not alter Article 22, paragraph 4 of the Covenant, it is superfluous. If it intends to confer upon the peoples of mandated territories referred to in Article 22, paragraph 4, of the Covenant, the right to participate in the selection of the administering authority under the trusteeship system of the Charter, its text is certainly insufficient. In this respect the wording suggested by the delegate for Iraq in the 13th meeting of Committee II/4 (U.N.C.I.O. Doc. 877, II/4/35, p. 3) was more adequate: '(*a*) In the event of any territory being placed under the trusteeship system, nothing in this Chapter should be construed in and of itself to alter in any manner the rights of any state in any territory or to diminish the rights of the people of that territory. (*b*) Notwithstanding anything contained in this Chapter, in the event of the transfer to the trusteeship system of any territory now administered on the basis of paragraph 4, of Article 22, of the Covenant of the League of Nations, such trusteeship shall not apply to such a territory save within the limits and for the purposes laid down in the aforementioned paragraph of the Covenant. In favour of the motion, it was said that, unless amended, paragraph B 5, would leave peoples coming under the trusteeship system at the mercy of those making the trusteeship arrangements, for no provision was included for consulting the desires of the peoples concerned. The paragraph should contain a guarantee that in drawing up trusteeship arrangements the rights of the peoples concerned should not be in any way reduced. While it was gratifying to have it recorded that the rights set forth in paragraph 4, of Article 22, of the Covenant, were included in paragraph B 5, it would be preferable to word paragraph B 5, so that there could be no doubt on this matter.' This motion was rejected on the following reasons: 'Against the amendment of the delegate of Iraq, it was said that the effect would be to cut off the rights of some peoples in some territories as the text of the amendment used the word " people " in the singular, whereas the paragraph [as suggested by the United States delegate] would safeguard all rights. Moreover, it was pointed out

Paragraph 1 cannot give grounds for delay or postponement of negotiation and conclusion of agreements for placing mandated and other territories under the trusteeship system since it has no specific effect at all. Besides, since there is no obligation whatsoever to place territories under the trusteeship system, any state may delay or postpone the negotiation and conclusion of the trusteeship agreement without violating the Charter.

(*c*) The Trusteeship Agreements

By whom shall the 'trusteeship agreements' be concluded? To this question the Charter has no direct answer. It provides only in Article 79:

> The terms of trusteeship for each territory to be placed under the trusteeship system, including any alteration or amendment, shall be agreed upon by the states directly concerned, including the mandatory power in the case of territories held under mandate by a Member of the United Nations, and shall be approved as provided for in Articles 83 and 85.

If it may be supposed that the agreements referred to in Article 79 are indentical with the trusteeship agreements referred to in Article 77 (which is not self-evident in view of the wording of the two Articles), these agreements are to be concluded by the 'states directly concerned.' But which states are 'directly concerned'?

The Charter does not contain a definition of the concept 'states directly concerned.' Such a definition, constituting an authentic interpretation of the Charter, that is to say, a general rule binding upon the Members and organs of the United Nations, is possible only by an amendment to the Charter. No organ of the United Nations is competent to define the terms concerned in this sense. But the Members and organs which are to apply Article 79 are competent to interpret the phrase 'states directly concerned' in the concrete case in which they apply Article 79.[2]

that not all of the United Nations were parties to the same international instruments, some for example being bound by the Covenant and some not. Account should be taken of the respective positions of all the United Nations in this respect.' The amendment suggested by the delegate of Iraq referred to the terms of trusteeship agreements. Its effect would have been that these agreements had to guarantee to the people of each trust territory the same rights as guaranteed to it by paragraph 4 of Article 22 of the Covenant. The amendment suggested by the delegate of the United States (which became Article 80 of the Charter) referred to the period 'until' the trusteeship agreements have been concluded, and expressly excepts these agreements from the principle not to alter the rights granted by the Covenant to the peoples of the mandated territories.

[2] At the San Francisco Conference attempts were made to insert into the Charter a definition of the 'states directly concerned'; but without success. The problem was discussed by the Fourth Committee of the General Assembly. Some delegates

Under general international law, a territory can be placed under trusteeship, whatever this term may mean, only by the authority which is entitled to dispose of the territory, to cede or lease it, and the like. The right to dispose of a territory is implied in the power which is usually called territorial sovereignty. The procedure by which a territory is placed under the trusteeship system of the United Nations has three main objectives: to place the territory under the administration of a definite authority, that is to say to determine the administering authority; to place the administration of this territory under the supervision of the Organisation; and to determine the terms under which the territory shall be administered. The Charter does not confer upon the Organisation the power to determine unilaterally the administering authority. This can be done only by the trusteeship agreement. Article 81 provides:

> The trusteeship agreement shall in each case include the terms under which the trust territory will be administered and designate the authority which will exercise the administration of the trust territory. Such authority, hereinafter called the administering authority, may be one or more states or the Organisation itself.

The agreement by which the administering authority is to be determined must be concluded between the power which is entitled to dispose of the territory and the power under whose trusteeship administration the territory is to be placed; which agreement has to be 'approved' by the Organisation. Under general international law no other 'states' but the territorial sovereign, *i.e.*, the state entitled to dispose of the territory, and the one under whose administration the territory is to be placed, are 'directly concerned.' These states may or may not be identical. The Charter cannot exclude them from the 'states directly concerned,' as the states competent to conclude the trusteeship agreement. They are the states which are legally concerned; and the term 'directly concerned' may be interpreted to mean only 'legally concerned.'[3] But it may

suggested a definition to be established by the Fourth Committee or by the General Assembly or by the Trusteeship Council. By definition they probably meant an authentic interpretation. But none of these organs is competent to offer an authentic interpretation of the Charter. Article 79 can be applied by the General Assembly and the Security Council without such a definition. This view has been expressed by the representative of the United States at the 6th meeting of the Fourth Committee on January 25, 1946 (Summary Records of Fourth Committee, January 11—February 7, 1946, p. 19) and by the Chairman of Sub-Committee 1 at its 27th meeting on December 9, 1946 (Summary Records of meetings of Sub-Committee 1, November 15—December 10, 1946, p. 207).

[3] At the 27th meeting of Sub-Committee 1 of the Fourth Committee the representative of Australia stated: 'Since, in a real sense, every state had an interest in the trusteeship agreement for each territory, the Charter had specified that a state's concern must be not only real and strong, but it must also be a "direct concern." Interest in the administration of a territory by another state could

be interpreted to mean also 'politically concerned.' Politically concerned is any state interested in the matter. But the authority competent to apply and, consequently, to interpret Article 79 may restrict the scope of the phrase to the Members of the United Nations, to the members of the Trusteeship Council or to the permanent members of the Security Council or in any other way. None of these interpretations is excluded by the Charter.[4] In case the formula 'states directly concerned' is interpreted to mean not only 'legally' but also 'politically concerned,' the Organisation, through its competent organ, has—at least indirectly—the power to decide which states, as the 'states directly concerned,' have to conclude the trusteeship agreement under consideration by the Organisation. It is true that the Organisation and the state entitled to place the territory under trusteeship may differ in their answer to the question as to which are the states directly concerned. But since the trusteeship agreement must be approved by the Organisation, the latter may refuse to approve an agreement to which not all the states or states other than those which in its opinion are directly concerned, are contracting parties. (This does not apply to the state entitled to dispose of the territory and the state which is to become the adminis-

not . . . be direct unless it was a juridical interest. That conclusion was reinforced by consideration of Article 77 (*c*) of the Charter, which provided for the voluntary submission to the trusteeship system of territories other than those held under mandates or taken from enemy states in the last war. It was improbable, in the case of such territories that the Charter required the consent of states other than the administering state, if there was nothing in their history to justify that consent being required. It was clear, therefore, that a direct juridical interest must exist in order that a state should be directly concerned. . . . ' (Summary Records of meetings of Sub-Committee 1, November 15—December 10, 1946, p. 206.)

[4] The representative of Poland expressed the view that the trusteeship Territories were the concern of all the United Nations as such (Summary Record of Meetings of Fourth Committee, November 1—December 12, 1946, p. 105). The representative of the Soviet Union submitted 'that among the states directly concerned should be counted the five great Powers, as they were permanent members of the Trusteeship Council. That special position emphasised their responsibility for trust territories. It should also be considered that the trust territories, according to Articles 76 and 84 of the Charter, were called upon to play their part in the attainment of international peace and security, within the general system of measures which were within the scope of the Security Council. That fact should obviously not be ignored when deciding the question of the states directly concerned.' (Summary Records of Sub-Committee 1, November 15—December 10, 1946, p. 174.) The delegation of Iraq proposed that the General Assembly should resolve: ' . . . among the prime and principal considerations for determining whether a state is directly concerned are the following: (i) Neighbourship and geographic adjacency of a state to the territory in question. (ii) Linguistic, cultural, economic, social and historical ties between a state and the territory in question.—The aforesaid considerations are not exhaustive. States which have other reasons to be considered as directly concerned may be entitled to participate in the negotiation of a given trusteeship agreement.' (Summary Record of meetings of Fourth Committee, January 11—February 7, 1946, p. 49.)

tering authority, which states—under general international law—must be recognised by the Organisation as 'states directly concerned.'

Hence it depends finally upon the Organisation to decide which states, in addition to the state which is entitled to dispose of the territory and the state which is to become the administering authority, are 'directly concerned.' Any state may claim to be 'directly concerned,' but if this claim is not recognised by the organ of the United Nations competent to approve the trusteeship agreement, it can have no effect.[5] The approval of a trusteeship agreement by the competent organ of the United Nations must be regarded as a definitive decision of the question as to which were the states entitled to be contracting parties to this concrete trusteeship agreement.[6]

[5] At the *Hearings* (p. 321) a Senator asked the following question with reference to Article 79: 'How is it to be determined whether a state is directly concerned in any of these trusteeship problems?' Whereupon the representative of the Department of State answered: 'I imagine that would be determined by negotiations among the states which claimed to be concerned.'—The Senator: 'Could any state come in and claim that it was concerned, under this language?' The representative: 'I imagine any state could claim that it is concerned, but there are certain guiding principles with respect to the particular categories with which we are dealing here. One category is formed by the mandates. The states concerned there are clearly the principal allied and associated powers of the last war, with the enemy states in this war substracted.'—The Senator: 'Outside of that category, take some of the territories which were not under the mandate system of the League. How would it be determined as to which states were directly concerned?' The representative: 'There would be only two other categories in addition to the mandates. One would be the territories detached from the enemy in the course of this war. And the states directly concerned would be determined by agreement among the United Nations or the nations at war with the particular enemy.'—The Senator: 'You mean then that it would come up, perhaps, in the Assembly, or would that be a matter of negotiation outside of the United Nations Organisation?'—The representative: 'That would be entirely outside of the Organisation.'—The Senator: 'So that if countries A and B claimed a direct interest, and country C claimed it, it would be a question of negotiation between the countries A and B and C?'—The representative: 'That is right.' The interpretation according to which the determination of the states directly concerned is a matter of negotiation 'entirely outside of the Organisation' ignores that under Article 79 the trusteeship agreement must be approved by the Organisation. Besides, 'negotiation' does not necessarily lead to 'determination,' except the interpretation advocated by the representative of the State Department implies that it is for the state competent to place a territory under trusteeship to decide which are the other states directly concerned and to reject the claim of any state which it does not recognise as directly concerned. But such interpretation can hardly be based on Article 79.

[6] At the 28th meeting of Sub-Committee 1 of the Fourth Committee the representative of India stated, regarding the interpretation of the phrase 'states directly concerned,' that 'it was for the General Assembly to decide on the question and to interpret the provision of the Charter accordingly. The interested party would then be able to accept the decision or to appeal to the Court.' (Summary Records of Meetings of Sub-Committee 1, November 15—December 10, 1946, p. 213.) Appeal to the Court is not possible since the case would be a dispute between the United Nations and a Member state, and under Article 34 of the Statute of the

Article 79 does not only provide that the 'states directly concerned' shall agree upon the terms of trusteeship but also upon 'any alteration or amendment.' The question arises whether the states directly concerned in the conclusion of the agreement by which a territory is placed under trusteeship, are identical with the states directly concerned in the alteration or amendment of this agreement. Under general international law a treaty can be altered or amended only by the contracting parties to the treaty, except the treaty contains special provisions in this respect. This principle can not be changed by the Charter. But the Charter could make the approval of alterations or amendments of the trusteeship agreements by the Organisation dependent not only on the consent of the states which, according to general international law must consent, but, in addition, on the consent of other states. If so, the states which the Organisation considered as directly concerned in the conclusion of the trusteeship agreement need not necessarily be identical with those the Organisation considers as directly concerned in the alteration or amendment of the agreement. The wording of Article 79 does not exclude such interpretation.[7]

International Court of Justice only states, not international organisations, may be parties in cases before the Court. Cf. *supra*, p. 483 ff.

During the discussion of the trusteeship for Tanganyika in Sub-Committee 1 of the Fourth Committee, India claimed to be recognised as a 'state directly concerned.' The preamble of the draft agreement submitted by the United Kingdom contained the phrase: The General Assembly 'in accordance with Article 85 of the said Charter, having satisfied itself that the requirements of Article 79 of the said Charter have been complied with' hereby resolves to approve, etc. The representative of India proposed either to include in the text of the trusteeship agreement 'a clause establishing the fact that the agreement would enter into force after the Government of India had signified its agreement with its terms,' or to delete the phrase just quoted. The representative of the United Kingdom declared that he was prepared to delete the reference to Article 79 in the preamble as requested by the Indian representative (Summary Records of Meetings of Sub-Committee 1, November 15—December 10, 1946, pp. 211 f, 214). The fact that the trusteeship agreement does, or does not, refer to Article 79 is of no importance as to the effect of the approval of the agreement by the Organisation. After the agreement is approved by the competent organ of the United Nations, no state can contest the validity of the agreement on the ground that it was a state directly concerned but did not participate in the conclusion of the agreement, whether the agreement did or did not contain a reference to Article 79.

7 Sub-Committee 1 of the Fourth Committee approved a proposal of the delegation of the United States to the effect that a recommendation be included in the report of the sub-committee which contained the following passage: 'There has . . . been no specification by the General Assembly of "States directly concerned" in relation to the proposed Trust Territories. Accordingly, the General Assembly in approving the terms of trusteeship does not prejudge the question of what States are or are not "directly concerned" within the meaning of Article 79. It recognises that no State has waived or prejudiced its right hereafter to claim to be such a "State directly concerned" in relation to approval of subsequently proposed trusteeship agreements and any alteration or amendment of those now approved,

There can be no doubt that according to the wording of Article 79, all ' states directly concerned ' have to be contracting parties to the trusteeship agreement in order to make the agreement suitable for approval by the Organisation; and there must be, at least, two states directly concerned so that an agreement can be submitted to the Organisation for approval. Article 79 speaks of ' states directly concerned ' in the plural and provides that these ' states ' must ' agree ' upon the terms of trusteeship before submitting the agreement to the Organisation.[8] The states directly concerned must be contracting

and that the procedure to be followed in the future with reference to such matters may be subject to later determination.' (Summary Records of Meetings of Fourth Committee, November 1—December 12, 1946, p. 302.) The statement that the General Assembly in approving the terms of a concrete trusteeship does not prejudice the question of what states are or are not directly concerned within the meaning of Article 79, is not quite correct. The question is prejudged in so far as the conclusion of this trusteeship agreement is concerned. The question is not prejudged only in relation to ' subsequently proposed trusteeship agreements,' as it is expressly formulated in the proposal of the United States. Hence the interpretation of the delegate of the United Kingdom, that the right of the state which claims to be a state directly concerned in the conclusion of a trusteeship agreement, but is not recognised as such in the approval of this agreement by the Organisation, would remain latent ' (Summary Records of Meetings of Sub-Committee 1, November 15—December 10, 1946, p. 214) is not correct. In this connection, the delegation of France made the following statement: ' (*a*) The French delegation considers that the approval by the General Assembly of the trusteeship agreements submitted by the French Government will necessarily imply recognition of the fact that these agreements comply with the conditions of Article 79 of the Charter of the United Nations. (*b*) Following approval of the draft trusteeship agreements by the General Assembly, the French Government would reject in advance any claim subsequently presented as regards these agreements by any State declaring itself to be directly concerned. (*c*) If in the future, any amendments or modifications should be proposed to the said agreements, the French Government reserves its right regarding any State which should claim to be directly concerned, to recognise it as such or not.' (Summary Record of Meetings of Fourth Committee, November 1—December 12, 1946, p. 302.) Regarding the proposal of the United States, the delegate of the Soviet Union declared that the decision of the Sub-Committee adopting the proposal ' was unlawful in the light of Article 79 of the Charter, and that consequently the trusteeship agreements would be invalid.' (Summary Records of Meetings of Sub-Committee 1, November 15—December 10, 1946, p. 209.) This view has no basis in the Charter.

[8] At the 16th meeting of the Fourth Committee, the representative of the United States expressed the opinion that ' " States " in Article 79 included the singular as well as the plural, and thus the Charter would be interpreted as though it read " the States or State directly concerned," depending upon the individual case. Hence, the fact that the plural form was used in the Charter did not mean that in every case several States must be found whose preliminary agreement would have to be obtained in order that the territory could be placed under trusteeship. Thus with respect to territories administered by a single State, its agreement was the only agreement required as a prelude to Assembly action.' (Summary Records of Meetings of Fourth Committee, November 1—December 12, 1946, pp. 75 f.) It may be that ' such interpretation of the Charter ' is—as the representative of the United States asserted—' the most workable and the fairest possible.' But it is certainly not ' legally proper.' A plural cannot be interpreted to mean the singular,

parties to the trusteeship agreement. Hence the provisions of Article 79 are not complied with if states directly concerned are only informed of the content of the trusteeship agreement, or consulted; [9] or if they participate as members of the General Assembly

and the ' agreement ' required by Article 79 is not the offer made by one state to the Organisation, which together with the ' approval ' of the latter would constitute the trusteeship ' agreement,' but an agreement of at least two states, brought about prior to the approval.

[9] Some Member states tried to interpret the provision of Article 79 that the terms of trusteeship ' shall be agreed upon by the states directly concerned,' to mean that these states need not be contracting parties to the agreement, that the provision is complied with if the state entitled to place the territory under the trusteeship system has informed or consulted with the states which it considers to be directly concerned. Some governments interpreted Article 79 to mean that a state, before submitting to the Organisation a draft trusteeship agreement, has to get the approval of the terms of the agreement from the state which the state submitting the agreement considers to be directly concerned, without being obliged to permit the latter to become a contracting party to the agreement. Pursuant the resolution of the General Assembly on Non-Self-governing Peoples, the Secretary-General addressed a letter to certain states administering former mandated territories, in which he asked them to inform him, *inter alia*, as to ' the progress of negotiations ' on the trusteeship agreements to be submitted to the Organisation (Summary Records of Meetings of Fourth Committee, November 1—December 12, 1946, pp. 193 ff.). In its answer to this letter, the Government of Australia stated that ' the terms of this agreement [for the territory of New Guinea] have been published and are now being discussed with the Governments of New Zealand, the United Kingdom, the United States, and France, with a view to submission to the General Assembly ' (p. 194). The Foreign Minister of Belgium stated that the draft agreement for Ruanda-Urundi ' has been submitted to the British Government, which my Government certainly regards as being directly concerned according to the provisions of Article . . . of the United Nations Charter. This draft trusteeship agreement has also been communicated, for their information, to the Governments of China, the United States of America, France and the Union of Soviet Socialist Republics.' He further stated: ' The British Government have signified their approval of the draft agreement . . . ' (p. 195). In the final document of this agreement the approval of the British Government does not appear. The French Government stated in its answer that the terms of trusteeship concerning the territories of Togoland and the Cameroons ' have been submitted for approval to the British Government which is considered by the French Government as a " state directly concerned " in accordance with the provisions of Article 79 of the Charter. The terms of trusteeship have further been communicated for information purposes to the other permanent members of the Security Council, and also to the mandatory Powers of Territories on the African Continent ' (p. 195). At the 20th meeting of the Fourth Committee the delegate of France declared: ' In order to work out draft trusteeship agreements, France had had to undertake exchanges with the states that she considered " directly concerned," although no definition of that term had been available. France undertook to communicate with the United Kingdom concerning Togoland and the Cameroons as a result of the resolution of the Supreme Council of May 7, 1919, and of the decision of the Council of the League of Nations of July 20, 1922.' (p. 111.) The approval on the part of the United Kingdom is not mentioned here. The Government of New Zealand, in its answer to the letter of the Secretary-General, stated that a draft trusteeship agreement in respect to the territory of Western Samoa had been prepared ' for submission to the other "states directly concerned" as required by Article 85 of the Charter

of the Security Council in the procedure by which the trusteeship agreement is approved by these organs of the United Nations.[1]

In case the Security Council has to approve the trusteeship agreement (Articles 79, 83), the states which the Council considers to be directly concerned may be, if they are Members of the United Nations, but not members of the Security Council, invited under

of the United Nations.' The New Zealand Government stated further: 'It is proposed, without prejudice to the ultimate interpretation of the phrase "states directly concerned" to regard the United Kingdom, Australia, the United States of America and France as "states directly concerned" in the conclusion of the agreement affecting Western Samoa. The draft has accordingly been submitted to those states for comment, but their final views have not as yet been received' (p. 196). It is not clear whether the New Zealand Government originally intended to recognise the states directly concerned as contracting parties to the agreement. In the final document New Zealand appears as the only state directly concerned. The Government of the United Kingdom referred in its answer to the Secretary-General only to 'negotiations with other Members of the United Nations' (p. 198). But the French Government stated in its answer: 'The British Government, for its own part, has submitted for approval by the French Government the terms of trusteeship regarding Togoland and the Cameroons under British mandate' (p. 195).

At the 16th meeting of the Fourth Committee the delegate of the United States stated that 'the Government of the United States was transmitting for information to certain other states a draft of a strategic-area trusteeship agreement [concerning the former Japanese mandated islands] which, at an early date, was to be submitted formally to the Security Council.' (Journal of the United Nations, No. 27; Suppl. No. 4–A/C.4/49, p. 19.) At the 113th meeting of the Security Council the delegate of the United States declared: 'The United States believes it has conformed to the requirements of Article 79 of the Charter, first, by transmitting copies of a draft trusteeship agreement for the former Japanese mandated islands to all Members of the United Nations, which, in the view of the Government of the United States, may have special interests in these islands and, now, by formally submitting the draft agreement to the Security Council for its approval.' (Official Records of the Security Council, 2nd Year, No. 20, p. 413.) It is not mentioned whether the states to which copies were transmitted have approved the terms of trusteeship as suggested by the United States. At the 116th meeting of the Security Council the delegate of the United States declared that 'in the spirit of the Charter' Article 79 provides only 'that all interested parties have a chance to be heard.' Consequently he maintained 'that the draft trusteeship agreement is in the nature of a bilateral contract between the United States, on the one hand, and the Security Council on the other.' (*Ibid.*, No. 23, pp. 475 f.) If the part which the states directly concerned have to perform in the conclusion of a trusteeship agreement is reduced to being heard, then the agreement is indeed a bilateral contract between the state submitting it and the United Nations approving it. But this is certainly not provided for by Article 79.

[1] At the 24th meeting of Sub-Committee 1 of the Fourth Committee the representative of Belgium stated that 'if the fifty-four United Nations [as represented in the General Assembly] agreed to accept the trusteeship agreements [by approving them under Articles 79 and 85] there could be no question that all the states directly concerned had given their consent.' (Summary Records of Meetings of Sub-Committee 1, November 15—December 10, 1946, p. 182.) This view is hardly compatible with Articles 79 and 85 which clearly distinguish between the agreement of the states directly concerned and the decision of the General Assembly by which this agreement is approved.

Article 31, as states whose 'interests are specially affected,' to participate without vote in the discussion of the matter. But this is certainly not enough to comply with the provision of Article 79 that the states directly concerned have to conclude the trusteeship agreement. The states directly concerned have to participate in that stage of the procedure which the Charter determines by providing that the states directly concerned shall 'agree' upon the terms of trusteeship (Article 79). This is the conclusion of the trusteeship 'agreement' on the part of the states directly concerned. It is—according to the Charter—a stage of the procedure for the placing of a territory under trusteeship which must precede the stage characterised by the Charter as 'approval' of the terms of trusteeship (Articles 79, 83 and 85).[2] This 'approval' of the terms of trusteeship agreed upon by the states directly concerned is an act of the Organisation. A state invited under Article 31 participates in this act of the Organisation, and only in its preparatory phase, since the invited state participates only in the discussion, not in the voting.[3] If the General

[2] At the 8th meeting of the Fourth Committee of the General Assembly the delegate of Belgium 'associated himself with the position taken by the delegation for the Netherlands that the United Nations would not participate during the first state of drawing up trusteeship agreements. Only when the agreements had been concluded would the General Assembly come into the picture.' (Journal of the General Assembly, No. 17; Suppl. No. 4–A/C.4/18, p. 27.) At the 119th meeting of the Security Council the delegate of Australia declared 'that it is necessary to make a mental distinction between the two acts which take place in the establishment of a trusteeship area under the United Nations Charter. First of all, the terms of the trusteeship agreement are to be agreed upon as provided in Article 79 and, second, in the case of strategic areas, the terms so agreed upon under Article 79 have to be approved by the Security Council under Article 83. They are in effect two separate acts.' (Official Records of the Security Council, 2nd Year, No. 26, p. 521.)

[3] At its 118th meeting the Security Council resolved under Article 31 of the Charter to invite the members of the Far Eastern Commission not represented on the Security Council to participate without vote in the discussion of the trusteeship agreement concerning the former Japanese mandated islands. At the 124th meeting the President of the Council ascertained that these states, namely Canada, India, the Netherlands, New Zealand and the Philippine Republic, 'have expressed their agreement that the United States should be the administering authority of the former Japanese mandated islands in the Pacific and that such islands should constitute a strategic Trust Territory.' (Official Records of the Security Council, 2nd Year, No. 31, p. 643.) It is doubtful whether a Member invited under Article 31 to participate 'without vote' in the discussion of the question whether the Council shall approve the terms of a trusteeship agreement, is entitled to express its agreement. Besides, consent to the designation of the United States as administering authority and of the territory as a strategic area is not equivalent to participating in the conclusion of the agreement, required by Article 79. At the same meeting, the delegate of Syria stated in the discussion on the trusteeship: 'I think that in the way we are proceeding we are not giving proper implementation or effect to Article 79 of the Charter, because we are paying no attention or consideration at all to the states directly concerned. In the Security Council, it was proposed that we should invite certain states whose interests we considered as specially affected.

Assembly or the Security Council considers not only the state entitled to dispose of the territory and the one to become the administering authority (the two being normally identical), but also another state as directly concerned and is willing to approve a trusteeship agreement only if this state is admitted by the other (or the two others) to participate in the conclusion of the agreement, this third state recognised by the Organisation as directly concerned is in a position to delay or even to prevent the placing under trusteeship of the territory. Hence the Organisation is not interested at all in recognising states other than those legally entitled to place the territory under trusteeship and those to become the administering authority as 'directly concerned.'[4]

We invited them, and we heard their statements and their remarks, but they did not take part in the vote.' But he added: 'However, it is something to show a certain respect for the states directly concerned as stipulated in Article 79. This constitutes formulation of an agreement made between the trustee state and the Security Council after consulting the states directly concerned.' (pp. 672 f.).

[4] At the 23rd meeting of Sub-Committee 1 of the Fourth Committee the representative of the United States 'expressed doubts concerning the view that all five great Powers should be counted among the States directly concerned in all cases, merely because they were permanent members of the Trusteeship Council and of the Security Council. The fact that their special position had been recognised by permanent status on the Trusteeship Council did not necessarily justify giving them a further special position. Such an interpretation would give a veto power over all the terms of the trusteeship agreements to each of the five great Powers, which, in his opinion, was not acceptable, at least at that moment.' (Summary Records of Meetings of Sub-Committee 1, November 15—December 10, 1946, p. 175.) Any state which in addition to the one which places the territory under trusteeship is recognised to be a state directly concerned is given a veto power over all the terms of the trusteeship agreement. At the 28th meeting of Sub-Committee 1 the representative of Belgium stated that if Article 79 would be interpreted to mean that in case of a trusteeship agreement concerning a former mandate territory not only the mandatory power but also other states are to be recognised as directly concerned and hence entitled to become contracting parties to the trusteeship agreement, Article 79 would provide 'for a virtual veto power for the "States directly concerned," but it could not have been the intention of the authors of the Charter to multiply the number of possibilities of veto which, in his opinion, should be understood in as limited sense as possible. Only states which had legal title to the Territories had the right to oppose the enforcement of trusteeship agreements.' (p. 212). The wording of Article 79 stipulating that the states directly concerned shall 'agree' upon the terms of trusteeship is too clear to allow the assumption that the authors of the Charter intended just the contrary.

Regarding the trusteeship agreement for Western Samoa, to which only the United Nations and New Zealand are the contracting parties, the representative of the latter declared at the 1st meeting of Sub-Committee 1 of the Fourth Committee that 'regarding the "States directly concerned" his government felt that the interests of the native population should not be subordinated to the interests of other States.' (*Ibid.*, p. 3.) In its letter to the Secretary-General (cf. *supra*, p. 585) the government of New Zealand proposed 'to regard the United Kingdom, Australia, the United States of America and France as the "States directly concerned" in the conclusion of the agreement affecting Western Samoa. The draft has accordingly been submitted to those States for comment. . . . ' Only for comment, not for participation in conclusion of the agreement. The view that the interests of a state

Only ' states ' are ' directly concerned ' and, if recognised as such, entitled to participate in the conclusion and in the alteration or amendment of the trusteeship agreement. The Charter does not confer upon the population of the territory to be placed under trusteeship any right whatsoever to take part in these transactions. Even if the population of the territory concerned is organised as a legal community at the time the territory is to be placed under trusteeship, this community has no claim under the Charter to be heard in the procedure by which the terms of the trusteeship agreement are stipulated. In this respect there exists a difference between the trusteeship system of the Charter and the mandate system of the Covenant which in Article 22, paragraph 4, concerning so-called A Mandates provided that the wishes of the ' communities ' formerly belonging to the Turkish Empire ' must be a principal consideration in the selection of the Mandatory.' Under Article 81, the trusteeship agreement shall ' designate the authority which will exercise the administration of the trust territory.' This designation is within the exclusive competence of the governments of the states directly concerned and the Organisation.[5]

if the latter is entitled to participate in the conclusion of the trusteeship agreement, may conflict with the interests of the native population, is correct.

[5] At the San Francisco Conference, the delegate for Egypt moved that the following words be added at the end of paragraph B. 6 of the Working Paper [corresponding to Article 81 of the Charter]: ' " . . . due regard being given to the wishes of the population in the selection of the trustee authority, in accordance with paragraph B. 2 above." (Paragraph B. 6 would then read as follows: " The Trusteeship agreement in each case shall include the terms under which the territory will be administered and designate the authority which shall exercise the administration of the trust territory. Such authority, hereafter called the administering authority, may be one or more states or the United Nations Organisation itself, due regard being given to the wishes of the population in the selection of the trustee authority in accordance with paragraph B. 2 above.")—In favour of the motion it was said that in the Covenant of the League of Nations provision was made for taking into consideration the wishes of the people in selecting the mandatory power in certain cases. It was to be hoped that the Charter now being drafted would go at least as far in this matter as the Covenant had done. Moreover, reference to " the freely expressed wishes of the peoples concerned " had been inserted in paragraph B. 2 [corresponding to Article 76 (*b*)] relating to the basic objectives of the trusteeship system, and for consistency a similar reference should be included in the paragraph relating to the conclusion of the trusteeship agreements. It was desirable to have an elastic phrase which would apply only in cases in which the peoples concerned were capable of forming an opinion on the question of selecting an administering authority. It was unfair to assign such peoples to the administration of a power without consulting their wishes. If greater consideration had been given to the wishes of the people concerned in connection with some of the mandates much trouble would have been avoided. Since the Committee proposed to give directions to the Assembly in such matters as the composition of the Trusteeship Council directions might also appropriately be given to the Assembly in this matter.—Against the motion it was said that if certain words from paragraph B. 2 were to be repeated in paragraph B. 6 all of paragraph B. 2 should for consistency likewise be repeated. The interests of the peoples concerned were protected by paragraph B. 5 as well as by paragraph B. 2,

Legally ' concerned ' is also the United Nations. For it is under the supervision of the United Nations that the administration of the trust territory is to be exercised; that means that the Organisation assumes the function of supervision with respect to the administration of the territory, which, too, is possible only by an agreement between the Organisation and the state entitled to place the territory under the trusteeship system. However, the Organisation itself may according to Article 81 become, under the terms of a trusteeship agreement, the administering authority.[6]

If only one state is entitled to dispose of the territory to be placed under trusteeship, an agreement to this effect may be concluded under general international law by this state and the United Nations, provided that this state or the Organisation is designated in the agreement as administering authority. If another state is to be made the administering authority, the agreement must be concluded by these two states and the United Nations. But Article 79 covers only the case that by an agreement between two or more states (as states directly concerned) and the United Nations (approving the agreement) a territory is placed under the trusteeship system. It does not cover the case that by an agreement between one state and the United Nations a territory is placed under the direct administration of the

and in addition the trust agreements would require approval by the General Assembly at which time ample opportunity for taking into consideration in so far as possible the wishes of the peoples concerned would be afforded. There would be evident practical difficulties in ascertaining the wishes of the peoples of very backward areas. The motion placed no limit upon the areas to which it should apply, while the reference in the Covenant to consulting the wishes of the people was restricted to "A" Mandates. It was quite probable that at the end of the war the allocation of territories would be determined by a number of considerations in addition to regard for the wishes of the inhabitants. Strategic considerations, for example, might be an important element in determining the choice of the trust power.

During the discussion general agreement was expressed with regard to the objectives sought by the motion but not with regard to the method by which these objectives were to be attained. After a motion by the delegate for Iraq that further discussion be postponed had failed of adoption, the delegate for India moved that the Egyptian amendment be amended by the insertion after the word " given " of the words " wherever conditions permit." (The Egyptian amendment as modified by the Indian motion would then read: " Due regard being given wherever conditions permit to the wishes of the population in the selection of the trustee authority, in accordance with paragraph B.2 above.")—The Committee rejected the amendment by the delegate for India to the amendment by the delegate for Egypt . . . rejected the motion by the delegate for Egypt by a vote of 8 for and 26 against.' Summary Report of 14th meeting of Committee II/4 (U.N.C.I.O. Doc. 1018, II/4/38, pp. 3 f.).

6 The Summary Report of 11th meeting of Committee II/4 (U.N.C.I.O. Doc. 712, II/4/30, p. 4) contains the following statement: ' Opposition to the provision for direct international administration was expressed, on the grounds both that this was likely to provide an unsatisfactory system in itself, and that the reference to it was out of harmony with the apparent intentions of the draft as a whole. But no motion in this sense was submitted.'

Organisation; nor the case that by an agreement between one state and the United Nations a territory is placed under the trusteeship administration of this state—no other state being contracting party to the agreement. Strange as it may seem, this is just the case with almost all the trusteeship agreements actually submitted to the General Assembly and the Security Council and approved by them. Only the trusteeship agreement for the territory of Nauru has been submitted by three states: Australia, New Zealand, and the United Kingdom, all three states being designated in the agreement as the joint administering authority.

It is by the trusteeship agreement that the territory is placed under the supervision of the United Nations. This is possible only with the consent of the Organisation. Hence the provision of Article 79 was necessary that the agreement entered into by the states directly concerned 'shall be approved as provided for in Articles 83 and 85,' that means by the Organisation through the Security Council or the General Assembly. As pointed out, the wording of Article 79 presupposes two stages in the process of placing a territory under the trusteeship system: first an agreement must be concluded by the 'states directly concerned,' and then this agreement must be approved by the Organisation. But such procedure is not possible if there is only one state directly concerned and this state, or the Organisation, is to be designated as the administering authority.

If the territory is under the joint sovereignty of two or more states, the trusteeship agreement may be concluded by these states with one another or with a third state, on the one hand, and the Organisation on the other. This may be the case especially under Article 77 paragraph 1 (*b*), if the territory detached from an enemy state has been ceded in the peace treaty to, or has been annexed in another way by, two or more of the victorious states.[7]

[7] Article 23 of the Peace Treaty with Italy provides:

> 1. Italy renounces all right and title to the Italian territorial possessions in Africa, *i.e.*, Libya, Eritrea and Italian Somaliland.
>
> 2. Pending their final disposal, the said possessions shall continue under their present administration.
>
> 3. The final disposal of these possessions shall be determined jointly by the governments of the Soviet Union, of the United Kingdom, of the United States of America, and of France within one year from the coming into force of the present Treaty, in the manner laid down in the joint declaration of February 10, 1947, issued by the said governments, which is reproduced in Annex XI.
>
> Annex XI provides:
>
> 1. The governments of the Union of Soviet Socialist Republics, of the United Kingdom of Great Britain and Northern Ireland, of the United States of America, and of France agree that they will, within one year from the coming into force of the Treaty of Peace with Italy bearing the date of February 10, 1947, jointly determine the final disposal of Italy's territorial

Articles 79, 83 and 85, authorise the Organisation only to 'approve' a trusteeship agreement submitted by the states directly concerned, especially by the state entitled to dispose of the territory. The initiative in the procedure for the placing of a territory under trusteeship has to be taken by these states, not by the Organisation. But under Article 10 the General Assembly may make recommendations to the Members of the United Nations on any question within the scope of the Charter; consequently the General Assembly may recommend to a Member, entitled to place a territory under trusteeship, to do so.[8]

> possessions in Africa, to which, in accordance with Article 23 of the Treaty, Italy renounces all right and title.
>
> 2. The final disposal of the territories concerned and the appropriate adjustment of their boundaries shall be made by the Four Powers in the light of the wishes and welfare of the inhabitants and the interests of peace and security, taking into consideration the views of other interested governments.
>
> 3. If with respect to any of these territories the Four Powers are unable to agree upon their disposal within one year from the coming into force of the Treaty of Peace with Italy, the matter shall be referred to the General Assembly of the United Nations for a recommendation, and the Four Powers agree to accept the recommendation and to take appropriate measures for giving effect to it.
>
> 4. The Deputies of the Foreign Ministers shall continue the consideration of the question of the disposal of the former Italian Colonies with a view to submitting to the Council of Foreign Ministers their recommendations on this matter. They shall also send out commissions of investigation to any of the former Italian Colonies in order to supply the Deputies with the necessary data on this question and to ascertain the views of the local population.

These provisions may be interpreted to mean that Italy has ceded the colonies referred to in Article 23 of the Peace Treaty to the four Powers named in that Article, that these Powers have assumed the obligation to dispose of the territories concerned in the way determined in Annex XI, and to permit that, pending their final disposal, the territories shall remain under the administration actually excerised when the Treaty came into force. The Peace Treaty does not stipulate an express obligation to place the territories referred to in its Article 23 under the trusteeship system of the United Nations.

[8] At the 271st meeting of the Security Council on March 19, 1948, the representative of the United States declared: 'My government believes that a temporary trusteeship for Palestine should be established under the Trusteeship Council of the United Nations to maintain the peace and to afford the Jews and Arabs of Palestine, who must live together, further opportunity to reach an agreement regarding the future government of that country. Such a United Nations trusteeship would, of course, be without prejudice to the character of the eventual political settlement, which we hope can be achieved without long delay. In our opinion, the Security Council should recommend the establishment of such a trusteeship to the General Assembly and to the mandatory power. This would require an immediate special session of the General Assembly, which the Security Council might call under the terms of the Charter.' (Doc. S/P.V. 271, pp. 32 f.) Article 20 of the Charter provides that 'special sessions [of the General Assembly] shall be convoked by the Secretary-General at the request of the Security Council or of a majority of the

As regards the territories held under mandate on behalf of the League of Nations, the situation is rather complex. The Charter presupposed that the League of Nations was legally still existent when the Charter came into force. For Article 77, paragraph 1 (*a*), speaks of territories 'now held under mandate'; and Article 79 requires that 'the mandatory power' in the case of 'territories held under mandate' by a Member of the United Nations shall be among the states directly concerned, which are entitled to conclude the trusteeship agreement. Hence the question arises: who was competent under the Covenant of the League of Nations to place a

Members of the United Nations.' On March 30, 1948, the Security Council adopted a resolution requesting the Secretary-General 'in accordance with Article 20 of the United Nations Charter, to convoke a special session of the General Assembly to consider further the question of the future government of Palestine.' The Security Council did not—as the representative of the United States originally suggested—recommend to the General Assembly and to the mandatory power a trusteeship for Palestine. Such a recommendation was hardly within the competence of the Security Council. It simply ordered the Secretary-General to convoke a special session of the General Assembly for the purpose 'to consider' the question of the future government of Palestine.

At the beginning of the special session of the General Assembly, the delegation of the United States presented a 'draft trusteeship agreement for Palestine' (Doc. A/C.1/277). According to the preamble of this paper, the General Assembly should resolve 'to approve the following terms of trusteeship for Palestine'; Article 2 of the draft-agreement provided: 'The United Nations, acting through the Trusteeship Council, is hereby designated as Administering Authority for Palestine.' Neither from the preamble nor from any Article of the draft agreement it was evident which were the states directly concerned and therefore entitled to submit the agreement to the General Assembly for approval. Actually it was the United States which presented the draft agreement to the General Assembly. But the United States was certainly not competent to submit a trusteeship agreement for Palestine to the Organisation, since the United States was not entitled to dispose of this territory. The idea probably was that the General Assembly should recommend to the United Kingdom, as the mandatory power, to submit this or a similar draft agreement to the General Assembly for approval. The part the General Assembly was to play in the first stage of the procedure was to take the initiative. At the 132nd meeting of the First Committee of the General Assembly on April 30, 1948, the representative of Sweden 'observed that the United States working paper took the form of a draft trusteeship agreement, the United Nations being the party on one side. He asked who would be the other party.' To this question the representative of the United States replied that 'he was not aware of any provisions in the Charter regarding the initiation of draft trusteeship agreements, but, in the case of previous trusteeship agreements which had been approved under Article 85, drafts had been submitted by mandatory powers. Certainly the case of Palestine was somewhat different, but he believed that if a temporary trusteeship were agreed upon, then the trusteeship agreement would be between the United Nations on the one hand and the present Mandatory Power on the other.' (Doc. A/C.1/SR 132, p. 3.) In view of Articles 79 and 10, the statement that the Charter does not contain provisions regarding the initiation of draft trusteeship agreements is hardly correct. The General Assembly has the power to initiate the procedure leading to the establishment of a trusteeship agreement because Article 10 authorises the General Assembly to recommend to Members to submit a draft trusteeship agreement.

territory held under mandate under the trusteeship system of the Charter?

The territories to which Article 22 of the Covenant referred were held under mandate on the legal basis of international agreements concluded by the Principal Allied and Associated Powers, to which these territories had been ceded by the Peace Treaty, the mandatory power and the League of Nations. Placing such a territory under trusteeship implies termination of the mandate. The Covenant did not contain provisions concerning termination of the mandate; only the mandate agreements concerning the former Turkish territories contained express provisions in this respect. Since the mandate for Syria and Lebanon had already been terminated when the Charter came into force, only the mandate agreement for Palestine came into consideration. Article 28 of this mandate agreement reads as follows:

> In the event of the termination of the mandate hereby conferred upon the Mandatory, the Council of the League of Nations shall make such arrangements as may be deemed necessary for safeguarding in perpetuity, under guarantee of the League, the rights secured by Articles 13 and 14, and shall use its influence for securing, under the guarantee of the League, that the Government of Palestine will fully honour the financial obligations legitimately incurred by the Administration of Palestine during the period of the mandate, including the rights of public servants to pensions or gratuities.

It is evident that in accordance with this provision the mandate could be terminated only by the establishment of an independent government of Palestine. This is in conformity with Article 22, paragraph 4, of the Covenant referring to the 'communities formerly belonging to the Turkish Empire.' As long as the mandate system was in force, Palestine could not be placed under the trusteeship system without violation of the Covenant and the mandate agreement for this territory. A modification of the mandate agreement to the effect of substituting the trusteeship system for the mandate system would hardly have been compatible with Article 22 of the Covenant; and even if compatible, it required—in conformity with Article 27 of the mandate agreement —the consent of the Council of the League of Nations.

The mandate agreements for the former German territories (B and C Mandates) did not contain express provisions concerning termination of the mandate. It is doubtful whether termination of these mandates was possible at all in conformity with the Covenant; or, if so, in another way than by establishing the independence of these territories. If it is assumed that these mandates, since constituted by international agreements, could be terminated by an agreement concluded by the same contracting parties, the consent of the Principal Allied and Associated Powers, the mandatory Power and the League of

Nations represented by the Council, was necessary in order to substitute the trusteeship system for the mandate system. If it is assumed that the Principal Allied and Associated Powers, by placing the territory concerned under the mandate system, had conferred all their rights regarding these territories upon the League of Nations, only the consent of the mandatory power and the League of Nations was necessary. As long as the League of Nations existed, the transformation of a League of Nations mandate into a United Nations trusteeship was—if at all—legally possible only with respect to B and C Mandates by an agreement between the League of Nations and the mandatory power on the one hand and the United Nations on the other.[9]

However, when the territories concerned were actually placed under the trusteeship system, the League of Nations had ceased to exist and its Covenant including the mandate system was no longer in force.

The dissolution of the League was decided at the 21st session of the Assembly on April 18, 1946, in the following terms:[1]

> The Assembly of the League of Nations,
>
> Considering that the Charter of the United Nations has created, for purposes of the same nature as those for which the League of Nations was established, an international organisation known as the United Nations to which all States may be admitted as Members on the conditions prescribed by the Charter and to which the great majority of the Members of the League already belong;
>
> Desiring to promote, so far as lies in its power, the continuation, development and success of international co-operation in the new form adopted by the United Nations;
>
> Considering that, since the new organisation has now commenced to exercise its functions, the League of Nations may be dissolved; and
>
> Considering that, under Article 3, paragraph 3, of the

[9] In the discussion of Section B, paragraph 3, of the Working Paper, which corresponds to Article 77, it was pointed out with reference to the territories now held under mandate that ' no private title to a mandated territory could lie with a mandatory power. It was for the League itself to pass title to such territories, perhaps by a general agreement with the new Organisation, and not for the mandatory power to undertake to do so by individual agreements. Questions concerning the protection of vested financial interests could be taken care of perhaps by an article in the agreement between the old League and the new Organisation, but in any case financial interests were of secondary concern as compared with the major question of the welfare of peoples. It would be evidently impossible for two parallel systems—the League system and the new trusteeship system—to continue to exist side by side.' (Summary Report of 8th meeting of Committee II/4, U.N.C.I.O. Doc. 512, II/4/21, p. 2).

[1] Series of League of Nations Publications. General 1946. 1, p. 97.

Covenant, the Assembly may deal at its meetings with any matter within the sphere of action of the League:

Adopts the following resolution:

DISSOLUTION OF THE LEAGUE OF NATIONS

1. (1) With effect from the day following the close of the present session of the Assembly, the League of Nations shall cease to exist except for the sole purpose of the liquidation of its affairs as provided in the present resolution. . . .

It is more than doubtful whether a dissolution of the League by a resolution of the Assembly was in conformity with the Covenant. Article 3, paragraph 3, of the Covenant, referred to in the resolution, does hardly authorise the Assembly to dissolve the League. The procedure for a dissolution of the League is not expressly provided for by the Covenant. As dissolution of the League means terminating the validity of the Covenant, such termination might be brought about by an amendment made under Article 26. If the term 'amendment' is interpreted to mean the establishment of rules which presuppose the continued validity of the Covenant, the only legal way of dissolving the League was the conclusion of treaties by which Part 1 of the four peace treaties which contain the Covenant of the League was abolished. Both ways were, for political reasons, excluded.

The League of Nations actually ceased to exist as consequence of the fact that its main organs ceased to work and that its Members actually ceased to consider themselves as bound by the Covenant.

With respect to the mandates the Assembly of the League of Nations adopted the following resolution:[2]

The Assembly,

Recalling that Article 22 of the Covenant applies to certain territories placed under mandate the principle that the well-being and development of peoples not yet able to stand alone in the strenuous conditions of the modern world form a sacred trust of civilisation:

(1) Expresses its satisfaction with the manner in which the organs of the League have performed the functions entrusted to them with respect to the mandates system and in particular pays tribute to the work accomplished by the Permanent Mandates Commission;

(2) Recalls the role of the League in assisting Iraq to progress from its status under an 'A' Mandate to a condition of complete independence, welcomes the termination of the mandated status of Syria, the Lebanon and Transjordan, which have, since the last session of the Assembly, become independent members of the world community;

[2] *Ibid.*, p. 73.

(3) Recognises that, on the termination of the League's existence, its functions with respect to the mandated territories will come to an end, but notes that Chapters XI, XII and XIII of the Charter of the United Nations embody principles corresponding to those declared in Article 22 of the Covenant of the League;

(4) Takes note of the expressed intention of the Members of the League now administering territories under mandate to continue to administer them for the well-being and development of the peoples concerned in accordance with the obligations contained in the respective mandates, until other arrangements have been agreed between the United Nations and the respective mandatory Powers.

The statement of paragraph (3) that 'on the termination of the League's existence, its functions with respect to the mandated territories will come to an end,' has only a declaratory character, but it is in conformity with the fact that the mandate system ceased to be in force. The statement that 'Chapters XI, XII and XIII, of the Charter of the United Nations embody principles corresponding to those declared in Article 22 of the Covenant of the League' is of no legal importance; it does not confer upon the United Nations any authority with respect to the former mandated territories.

The statement of paragraph (4) together with the corresponding declarations of the mandatory powers could, perhaps, be interpreted as constituting an agreement entered into by the League of Nations and these powers, and thence a contractual obligation of the latter. But apart from the question of whether the Assembly of the League of Nations was competent to enter into such agreement, the latter has ceased to be valid on the termination of the existence of the League as the other contracting party. Hence legally there existed no obligation of the former mandatory powers 'to continue to administer [the former mandate territories] for the well-being and development of the peoples concerned in accordance with the obligations contained in the respective mandates, until other arrangements have been agreed between the United Nations and the respective mandatory Powers.' Nor can the statement of paragraph (4) be interpreted to authorise the United Nations and the mandatory powers to make the arrangements referred to in this paragraph. The Assembly was not competent to confer upon the United Nations or upon mandatory powers the right to place the mandated territories under the trusteeship system. As far as the United Nations was concerned, an agreement between this organisation and the League was necessary; but no such agreement was established nor could be established in conformity with the Covenant. The trusteeship system did not automatically replace the mandate system, and the United Nations did not succeed to the rights of the League of Nations as to the former mandated territories. There is no legal continuity in the relation of these two systems. The one ceased to exist long before the other came into existence.[3]

The statement of paragraph (4) was hardly intended to authorise the mandatory powers to place the mandated territories under the trusteeship system of the United Nations. The Assembly only 'takes note' of the intention of the mandatory powers indicated in that paragraph. But the statement evidently presupposed that the Members which administered mandated territories were, after the termination of the League, entitled to dispose of these territories. This, however, is just the question. Besides, the statement refers only to Members,

[3] At the meeting of the Assembly of the League of Nations on April 18, 1946, the representative of Egypt correctly declared: 'It is the view of my Government that mandates have terminated with the dissolution of the League.' At the 116th meeting of the Security Council the delegate of the United States stated with respect to the former Japanese mandated islands: 'that Japan never did have sovereignty over these islands and that so far as the trusteeship is concerned, any interest of the *cestui que trust* was represented by the predecessor of the United Nations, namely, the League of Nations, and, as the successors of the League of Nations, it is in our hands. If there is any entity which can properly represent that aspect of the life of these islands, it is the United Nations.' (Official Records of the Security Council, 2nd Year, No. 23, pp. 471 f.) This seems to imply the view that the United Nations was the successor of the League of Nations to the sovereignty over the mandated areas. This view is legally untenable. At the 271st meeting of the Security Council the representative of the United States quite correctly stated: 'The United Nations does not automatically fall heir to the responsibilities either of the League of Nations or of the mandatory power in respect of the Palestine mandate. The record seems to us entirely clear that the United Nations did not take over the League of Nations mandate system.' (Doc. S/P.V. 271, p. 26.) A statement made to the Fourth Committee of the General Assembly by the representative of the Union of South Africa contains the following sentence: 'The trusteeship system embodied in the Charter . . . is not the successor of the Mandate system. . . .' (Summary Records of Meetings of Fourth Committee, November 1—December 12, 1946, p. 235.) At the 4th meeting of the Fourth Committee, the delegate of the Netherlands called attention 'to the gap in the administration of the mandated territories between the winding up of the League of Nations and their coming under the trusteeship system.' But he added: 'It should be made clear that the Trusteeship Council should have the power to deal with such territories in the interim period.' (Journal of the General Assembly, No. 13; Suppl. No. 4–A/C.4/5, p. 11.) How could the Trusteeship Council have the power to deal with the former mandated territories prior to the coming into force of the trusteeship agreements? At the 124th meeting of the Security Council, in the discussion of a proposal made by the delegate of Poland to insert into the preamble of the trusteeship agreement concerning the former Japanese mandated islands the clause: 'Whereas Japan has violated the terms of the above mandate of the League of Nations and has thus forfeited her mandate . . .', the delegate of the Soviet Union made the following statement: 'There is no continuity, either legal or otherwise, between the mandatory system of the League of Nations and the Trusteeship System laid down in the United Nations Charter. There is therefore nothing which might entitle the Security Council to discuss this question [Polish proposal], let alone take any decisions on it. The mandatory system of the League of Nations is distinct from the Trusteeship System which the United Nations is now trying to establish.' (Official Records of the Security Council, 2nd Year, No. 31, pp. 643, 648.)

not to the non-member which, then, actually administered such a territory.

At the moment the League of Nations ceased to exist, not only its Covenant but also the mandate agreements to which the League was a contracting party—and its existence was an essential condition—ceased to be valid. Hence the question as to who was competent to place the former mandated territories under the trusteeship system of the United Nations could be decided only in accordance with general international law and the Charter of the United Nations. The question as to who was entitled to dispose of the former mandated territories could be answered only according to general international law. And to this question three answers were possible: (*a*) the Principal Allied and Associated Powers, provided that the sovereignty over the territories concerned had been conferred upon them by the Peace Treaties and that they had retained their joint sovereignty under the League Covenant; (*b*) the Principal Allied and Associated Powers together with the former mandatory power; and (*c*) only the former mandatory power.

The second interpretation was possible only if it was assumed that the former mandatory power—which under the Covenant had no sovereignty over the territory since it exercised its administration according to Article 22, paragraph 2, only ' on behalf of the League '—on the termination of the League's existence established, in addition to the sovereignty of the Principal Allied and Associated Powers, its own sovereignty over the former mandated territories, so that these territories were under the joint sovereignty of the Principal Allied and Associated Powers and the former mandatory power. The third interpretation was possible only under the assumption that the Principal Allied and Associated Powers, by placing the territories under the mandate system conferred their sovereignty upon the League of Nations and that after the disappearance of the League only the state actually exercising the administration was in a position to extend its sovereignty over the territory concerned. Such an act, amounting to an annexation of the mandated territory by the former mandatory power, was certainly possible without any violation of the Covenant—which had ceased to be in force—or of the Charter. Prior to the coming into force of a trusteeship agreement only Chapter XI of the Charter was applicable to a formerly mandated territory; and annexation of this territory by the former mandatory power was compatible with the obligations imposed upon the Members by this part of the Charter. Under the Charter, the United Nations has no competence to consent, or to refuse to consent, to the annexation of a formerly mandated territory by the power actually exercising the administration.[4]

[4] The delegate of the Union of South Africa submitted to the General Assembly during the second part of the first session a proposal calling for approval by the Assembly

As pointed out, the Charter can neither establish nor abolish the right of a state to place a territory under trusteeship. But the Charter

of the annexation of the former mandated territory of South West Africa by the Union. Since the delegate of the Union declared at the 3rd meeting of the Fourth Committee of the General Assembly that according to the view of his government the Charter did not make the transfer of the mandates to the trusteeship system obligatory (Journal of the General Assembly, No. 12; Suppl. No. 4–A/C.4/4, p. 9) and since he declared at the 14th meeting of the Fourth Committee that the Union of South Africa was ' legitimately ' concerned in securing the annexation of that territory (Journal of the United Nations, No. 23; Suppl. No. 4–A/C.4/44, p. 5), it is probable that the Union brought the case before the General Assembly rather for political than for legal reasons. It was in this way that the delegate of the United Kingdom interpreted the step of the South African Government at the 19th meeting of the Fourth Committee when he stated: ' . . . the South African Government had thought it wise to bring the question before the United Nations. In doing so the South African Government paid a tribute to the standing of the United Nations. Consequently it was proper to give credit to the Government of the Union of South Africa for having offered the United Nations the opportunity to express its opinion about the political intentions of the South African Government.' (Journal of the United Nations, No. 33; Suppl. No. 4–A/C.4/68, p. 49.)

During the discussion of the South African proposal some delegates expressed the view that the annexation of a former mandated territory was incompatible with the obligations imposed upon the Members by the Charter. This view was partly based on the unfounded assumption that the Charter obligated the Members to place all former mandated territories under trusteeship, and partly on a hardly tenable interpretation of Articles 73 and 76 of the Charter. As to the latter point, the question is characteristic which was raised by the Czechoslovakian delegate with respect to the South African proposal at the 17th meeting of the Fourth Committee: ' Could our Organisation consider a proposal which, instead of dealing with a progressive evolution towards the independence and the autonomy of the inhabitants of a territory, was on the contrary designed to put an end to their political aspirations which had been reaffirmed by the Charter, by outright annexation of their territory ?' (Journal of the United Nations, No. 27; Suppl. No. 4–A/C.4/51, p. 33.) This question probably refers to both Articles 73 and 76. At the 18th meeting of the Fourth Committee the delegate of the Soviet Union declared that the South African proposal ' was a direct violation of the provisions and principles of the Charter which in Article 76 provided for the promotion of progressive development of trust territories towards full independence.' (*Ibid.*, No. 30; Suppl. No. 4-A/C.4/54, p. 37.) As to the obligations imposed by Article 73 upon the Members with respect to the administration of territories whose peoples have not yet attained a full measure of self-government, these obligations are all the more compatible with the annexation of the territories concerned as the provisions of Article 73 refer—if not only, so certainly also—to territories under the sovereignty of Members which have responsibilities for the administration. The fact that a territory inhabited by a people which has not yet attained a full measure of self-government is under the sovereignty of the administering authority does not affect the obligations of this authority stipulated by Article 73. As to the provisions of Article 76, they refer only to territories placed under trusteeship. It is true that if a Member refuses to place a territory under trusteeship, Article 76—in so far as it goes farther than Article 73 (*e.g.*, to promote development towards independence) —does not apply to this Member. But to consider annexation of a former mandated territory as incompatible with the objectives of the trusteeship system presupposes that the Members are legally obliged to place all former mandated territories under their administration under trusteeship of the Charter. This, however, does not hold.

may provide that the trusteeship agreement shall be concluded not only by the state which is—under general international law—entitled

At its 64th meeting the General Assembly adopted the following resolution:

The General Assembly,

Having considered the statements of the delegation of the Union of South Africa regarding the question of incorporating the mandated territory of South West Africa in the Union;

Noting with satisfaction that the Union of South Africa, by presenting this matter to the United Nations, recognises the interest and concern of the United Nations in the matter of the future status of territories now held under mandate;

Recalling that the Charter of the United Nations provides in Articles 77 and 79 that the trusteeship system shall apply to territories now under mandate as may be subsequently agreed;

Referring to the resolution of the General Assembly of February 9, 1946, inviting the placing of mandated territories under trusteeship;

Desiring that agreement between the United Nations and the Union of South Africa may hereafter be reached regarding the future status of the mandated territory of South West Africa;

Assured by the delegation of the Union of South Africa that, pending such agreement, the Union Government will continue to administer the territory as heretofore in the spirit of the principles laid down in the mandate;

Considering that the African inhabitants of South West Africa have not yet secured political autonomy or reached a stage of political development enabling them to express a considered opinion which the Assembly could recognise on such an important question as incorporation of their territory:

The General Assembly, therefore,

Is unable to accede to the incorporation of the territory of South West Africa in the Union of South Africa; and

Recommends that the mandated territory of South West Africa be placed under the international trusteeship system and invites the Government of the Union of South Africa to propose for the consideration of the General Assembly a trusteeship agreement for the aforesaid territory. (Doc. A/64/Add. 1, pp. 123 f.)

In declaring to be 'unable to accede to the incorporation of the territory of South West Africa in the Union of South Africa' and in recommending that the former mandated territory 'be placed under the international trusteeship system,' the General Assembly acted within its competence. The Assembly did not disapprove of the annexation, it declared only not to be able to approve it.

At the 19th meeting of the Fourth Committee the representative of the Union of South Africa declared that if the Assembly did not agree to the annexation, 'the Union Government could take no other course than to abide by the declaration it had made to the last Assembly of the League of Nations to the effect that it would continue to administer the territory as heretofore as an integral part of the Union, and to do so in the spirit of the principles laid down in the mandate.' He further declared that the Union would comply with Article 73 (*e*) of the Charter; and he made the statement, quoted in another connection, that no Member can be compelled by the Charter to enter into trusteeship agreements. (Journal of the United Nations, No. 33; Suppl. No. 4–A/C.4/68, p. 51.)

The last mentioned statement is certainly correct. But the Union, with or without annexation of South West Africa, is not only under the obligation stipulated

to dispose of the territory, but also by other states politically interested in the matter. It is under this assumption that the provision of Article 79 must be interpreted: that the terms of trusteeship for each territory to be placed under the trusteeship system shall be agreed upon by the states directly concerned, including the mandatory power in the case of territories held under mandate by a Member of the United Nations. Since the mandate system together with the League of Nations has ceased to exist, the term 'mandatory power' in Article 79 must be interpreted to mean: the state which formerly under the Covenant and the Mandate agreement had held the territory under mandate. This state, if a Member of the United Nations, was, according to Article 79, among the 'states directly concerned' and consequently was entitled to participate in the conclusion of the respective trusteeship agreement concerning the territority formerly under its mandate, whether it had or had not the power to dispose of the territory—that is to say whether it was legally or only politically concerned. According to Article 79, a state which was a former mandatory power but not a Member of the United Nations, was excluded from the mandatory powers which were to agree upon the terms of trusteeship. But Article 79 did not, and could not, exclude from the states directly concerned Japan in its capacity as a state entitled to dispose of the territory formerly held by it under mandate; provided that Japan—either alone or together with the Principal Allied and Associated Powers, or as one of the Principal Allied and Associated Powers, had the right to dispose of the territory formerly held by it under mandate. Japan was excluded only in its capacity as former mandatory power, not in its capacity as territorial sovereign

by Article 73 (*e*) but under all obligations stipulated by Articles 73 and 74. The obligation voluntarily assumed by the Union, to administer the territory in the spirit of the principles laid down in the mandate, does not imply that the territory will continue to have the status of a mandated territory. This would be legally impossible since the mandate system ceased to exist together with the League of Nations.

On September 25, 1947, the delegate of the South African Union stated in the General Assembly that while it did not intend to proceed with the incorporation of South West Africa, it considered itself under no legal obligation to propose a trusteeship agreement for that territory. The majority of inhabitants of South West Africa favoured incorporation, and the Union intended to maintain the *status quo*, and to transmit to the United Nations an annual report on the administration of that territory. After a considerable debate in the trusteeship committee, a resolution was approved which recommended that the General Assembly (1) take note of the decision of the Government of the Union of South Africa not to proceed with the incorporation of South West Africa; (2) maintain its recommendation that South West Africa be placed under the trusteeship system; (3) urge the Government of the Union to propose a trusteeship agreement for that territory; and (4) authorise the Trusteeship Council to examine the report on South West Africa submitted by the Union of South Africa and to submit its observations to the Assembly. (Doc. A/422.) As to the resolution of the General Assembly cf. *supra.*, p. 572.

—if it, alone or together with other states, possessed the sovereignty over the territory concerned. Just as any other state was not excluded from concluding the trusteeship agreement for a territory over which it was the sovereign and hence entitled to dispose of it. The former mandatory powers are not the only states directly concerned; except Japan, they are, according to the wording of Article 79 only ' included ' in the ' states directly concerned.'[5]

All trusteeship agreements concluded until now under Articles 79, 83 and 85, of the Charter, refer to former mandated territories. All mandated territories—except South West Africa—have been placed under trusteeship. Eight draft agreements have been submitted to the General Assembly, each only by one state, the former mandatory power designated in the agreement as administering authority. In approving these draft agreements, the General Assembly recognised only the former mandatory power as a state directly concerned. One draft agreement—that for Nauru—has been submitted by the governments of the United Kingdom, Australia and New Zealand, the former mandatory powers, which were designated in the agreement as administering authorities. In approving this agreement, the General Assembly recognised as states directly concerned only the three former mandatory powers. Only in this case the approval of the General Assembly was in conformity with Articles 79 and 85, since only in this case there were more than one state ' directly concerned.'[6]

5 At the 124th meeting of the Security Council during the discussion of the trusteeship agreement concerning the former Japanese mandated islands, the delegate of Syria interpreted Article 79 to mean that ' if the mandatory state is not a Member of the United Nations, it should not be considered any further as a mandatory state and should be totally ignored.' (Official Records of the Security Council, 2nd Year, No. 31, p. 652.) This statement certainly goes too far. Article 79 only provides that if a state is not a Member of the United Nations, it is, in its capacity as mandatory, not included within the ' states directly concerned.' If the state—Member or non-member—happens to be the sovereign over the former mandated territory, it is not excluded, in this capacity, from the states directly concerned. Literally interpreted, the phrase ' including the mandatory power, etc.' is inapplicable because after the dissolution of the League there was no ' mandatory power.'

6 Cf. *supra*, pp. 583 f. At the 62nd meeting of the General Assembly the delegate of the Soviet Union declared that the draft trusteeship agreements submitted to the Assembly for approval did not conform to Article 79 of the Charter because they ' did not receive from the States directly concerned that co-ordination of objectives which is laid down in Article 76 of the United Nations Charter. This Article [evidently Article 79 is meant], however, provides, that the conditions of trusteeship for each trusteeship territory shall be defined by agreements between the States directly concerned, including the mandatory Power, in cases where the territory is under the mandate of one of the Members of the United Nations.—During the entire period between the first and second parts of the first session of the General Assembly no attempt was even made to attain an agreement as to which States should be considered directly concerned. At the same time in certain cases the question as to which States were directly interested in one or the other of the mandated territories being included in the trusteeship system, was decided unilaterally and arbitrarily by the mandatory Powers themselves. Such a state of things is contrary

In placing the former mandated territories under the trusteeship system the states concerned did not claim to be entitled to dispose of the territories as the territorial sovereigns. These states, as well as the General Assembly in the decisions by which it approved the draft agreements, maintained the fiction that the mandate system still existed, that the states placing the territories concerned under the trusteeship system were still ' mandatory ' powers until the moment they became administering authorities under Article 81 of the Charter and the trusteeship agreements. Some trusteeship agreements—as, *e.g.*, those for Samoa and New Guinea—contain in their preamble the formula: The General Assembly approves the following terms of trusteeship ' in substitution for the terms of the mandate under which the territory has been administered,' as if the legal status of mandate had existed until the status of trusteeship has been established. This legal fiction is all the more objectionable as under the mandate system of the League of Nations the mandatory powers were certainly not entitled to dispose of the mandated territory, and the approval of the trusteeship agreements by the General Assembly was in conformity with general international law only under the assumption that the states which placed the territories under trusteeship by submitting draft agreements to the General Assembly were the territorial sovereigns and as such entitled to dispose of the territories. As mandatory powers they were certainly not the sovereigns. The other assumption that the Principal Allied and Associated Powers alone or together with the former mandatory power were the sovereigns, was practically excluded since two enemy states—Italy[7] and Japan—were among them.

to the provisions of Article 79 of the Charter.' As to its own interpretation of Article 79, the delegation of the Soviet Union declared ' that first of all the five great Powers should be included among the States directly concerned '; each of the five permanent members of the Security Council should have ' the right to declare itself a State directly concerned as regards the trusteeship territories. This, however, would not mean that each of these States should make such a declaration as regards all the trusteeship territories.' (Journal of the United Nations, No. 62; Suppl. A–A/P.V./62, pp. 630 f.). This is not an interpretation of Article 79 that necessarily follows from the text of this Article; it is a view which the General Assembly or the Security Council may or may not accept in approving a trusteeship agreement. The delegation of the Soviet Union proposed a resolution by which the General Assembly should reject the draft trusteeship agreements submitted to it for three reasons, the first of which was: ' The proposed draft trusteeship agreements for the above-mentioned territories cannot be considered as Trusteeship agreements, since Article 79 of the Charter provides that the terms of Trusteeship shall be agreed upon by the states directly concerned, whereas so far it has not been determined which countries are directly concerned.' (p. 632.) The Soviet proposal was rejected.

7 The Peace Treaty with Italy signed in Paris on February 10, 1947, which came into force after the General Assembly had approved the trusteeship agreements submitted to it (except that for Nauru), *i.e.*, after December 13, 1946, contains the following clause (Article 40): ' Italy hereby renounces all rights, titles and claims deriving from the mandate system or from any undertakings given in connection therewith, and all special rights of the Italian State in respect of any mandated territory.'

In the resolution on Non-Self-Governing Peoples adopted at its 27th meeting, the General Assembly invited ' the states administering territories now held under mandate to undertake practical steps, in concert with the other states directly concerned, for the implementation of Article 79 of the Charter (which provides for the conclusion of agreements on the terms of trusteeship for each territory to be placed under the trusteeship system), in order to submit these agreements for approval, preferably not later than during the second part of the first session of the General Assembly.'[8] This resolution did not only invite the mandatory powers to submit trusteeship agreements to the United Nations for approval; it referred to the ' states administering territories now held under mandate.' The phrase ' territories now held under mandate ' is used in Article 77 (*a*). It probably was intended to mean territories the legal status of which was determined by Article 22 of the Covenant and a mandate agreement, whether actually administered by the mandatory power or by another state. When the Charter came into force the Japanese mandated territory was not administered by the mandatory power, but—as a result of the war—by the United States. The resolution of the General Assembly certainly applied also to the United States as a state acutally administering a territory ' held under mandate.' Even if this phrase should be interpreted to mean: territories administered as mandates by the mandatory powers, the United States, actually administering the Japanese mandated territory was authorised by the Charter to place this territory under trusteeship. For Article 77 (*c*) refers to ' territories voluntarily placed under the [trusteeship] system by states responsible for their administration,' which are not necessarily the states entitled to dispose of the territory.

In conformity with the above-quoted resolution of the General Assembly and Article 77 (*c*) of the Charter, the United States submitted to the Security Council the draft of a trusteeship agreement for the former Japanese mandated Islands, in which the United States was designated as the administering authority, and the territory as strategic area. The Security Council approved the agreement at its 124th meeting on April 2, 1947, the United States being recognised as the only state directly concerned. The Preamble of this agreement refers to Article 77 (*a*): ' territories now held under mandate,' not to Article 77 (*c*), and expressly states that the Security Council has ' satisfied itself that the relevant Articles of the Charter have been complied with.' This statement is problematical in view of the wording of Article 79: ' states '—not ' state '—directly concerned; and it does not necessarily imply that the United States under general international law was entitled to place the former Japanese mandated territory under the trusteeship system of the United Nations.

[8] Resolutions adopted by the General Assembly, Doc. A/64, p. 13.

The only condition under which the United States was entitled to dispose of the territory concerned would have been: the establishment of its sovereignty over the islands. This was possible according to the rule of general international law concerning acquisition of a territory by subjugation. As a matter of fact, however, the United States did not claim to be the territorial sovereign at the moment she placed the territory under trusteeship. Hence the legality of the procedure remains doubtful.[9]

[9] As to the title of the United States to place the former Japanese mandated islands under the trusteeship system of the Charter, the delegate of the United States declared at the 16th meeting of the Fourth Committee of the General Assembly, on November 7, 1946, ' that the United States was prepared to place under trusteeship, with the United States as administering authority, Japanese islands for which it had assumed responsibility as a result of the Second World War. . . . ' (Journal of the United Nations, No. 27; Suppl. 4–A/C.4/49, p. 19.) By a letter dated February 17, 1947, addressed to the Secretary-General, the representative of the United States on the Security Council submitted a draft trusteeship agreement for the ' former Japanese mandated islands ' ' in accordance with Article 83 of the Charter ' (Doc. S/281). Neither in the letter nor in the text of the draft agreement (as finally approved by the Security Council) Article 79 was referred to. In the preamble to the draft agreement as well as in the finally approved text it is stated that ' Japan, as a result of the Second World War, has ceased to exercise any authority in these islands '; and in the preamble as well as in the Articles of the Agreement the territory is characterised as ' formerly ' held by Japan under mandate. That implies the view that Japan, as a result of the war, had ceased to be the mandatory power. But, on the other hand, the preamble expressly quotes Article 77 (*a*) referring to ' territories now held under mandate.'

At the 113th meeting of the Security Council the delegate of the United States justified the title of the United States to place the former Japanese mandated islands under the trusteeship system as follows: He referred to the resolution of the General Assembly on Non-self-governing Peoples (adopted at its 27th meeting) by which ' the states administering territories now held under mandate ' were invited to place these territories under trusteeship. He declared: ' Since the United States was, and is, occupying the territory formerly mandated to Japan, the United States desires to play its part in attaining the objectives of the General Assembly's resolution, so that trusteeship agreements for all former mandated territories should be concluded promptly and the trusteeship system organised as soon as possible.' (Official Records of the Security Council, 2nd Year, No. 20, p. 408.) As pointed out, the United States in placing the islands under trusteeship, acted certainly in conformity with the General Assembly's resolution and Article 77 (*c*); but neither the Charter nor a resolution of the General Assembly could confer upon the United States a title to dispose of a territory not under her sovereignty. The delegate declared further: ' As a result of the war, Japan has ceased to exercise, or to be entitled to exercise, any authority over these islands.' (p. 413.) That Japan, as a result of the war, has actually ceased to exercise any authority, is an undeniable fact; but whether she has thereby lost her title as a mandatory power, is doubtful. In this respect the delegate brought forward two reasons:

(*a*) ' Japan, by her criminal acts of aggression, forfeited the right and capacity to be the mandatory power of the islands.' (p. 413.) At the 116th meeting of the Security Council, he specified this argument as follows: ' These islands were entrusted to Japan, under mandate, in the League of Nations system, following the first world war. In utter disregard of the mandate, Japan used the territories for aggressive warfare, in violation of the law of nations, against the United States and

(*d*) The Approval of the Trusteeship Agreements

There are two different kinds of trusteeship: trusteeship with respect to areas designated in the trusteeship agreement as strategic areas

other Members of the United Nations. This, under international law, was a criminal act; it was an essential violation of the trust, and by it Japan forfeited the right and capacity to be the mandatory of the islands.' (*Ibid.*, No. 23, p. 472.) At the 124th meeting of the Security Council, he expressed the opinion that ' competent to declare a forfeiture of the mandate and establish a trusteeship in its place ' are ' first, the administering authority; secondly, the other interested states or parties; thirdly, the Security Council.' (*Ibid.*, No. 31, p. 650.) At the 116th meeting of the Security Council also the delegate of Poland declared that Japan by her violation of the mandate ' has forfeited her mandatory rights,' and proposed to insert into the preamble of the trusteeship agreement the phrase ' whereas Japan has violated the terms of the above mandate of the League of Nations and has thus forfeited her mandate. . . . ' (*Ibid.*, No. 23, p. 469); and at the 119th meeting the delegate of France declared: ' . . . Japan forfeited her mandate over the Pacific islands because she violated her obligations. As the League of Nations no longer exists, it is the duty of the United Nations to declare the mandate forfeited.' (*Ibid.*, No. 26, p. 539.) The question under what conditions a mandatory power forfeits its rights can be answered only on the basis of the Covenant of the League; and the Covenant does not provide that a violation of the terms of the mandate has as a consequence the forfeiture of the rights as a mandatory power. The view that the United Nations is competent to ascertain such violation and to decide that the rights of the mandatory power are forfeited, has no basis in the Charter. At the 124th meeting, the delegate of Australia correctly stated that ' a breach of a mandate in itself does not constitute forfeiture '; and at the same meeting the delegate of the Netherlands declared : ' I venture to differ . . . with those who hold that the mere fact of Japanese violation of the terms of the mandate is tantamount to forfeiture of their rights and I agree in that respect with the Australian representative.' (*Ibid.*, No. 31, pp. 645, 650.) And at the 116th meeting, the delegate of the United Kingdom stated that ' there is no provision in the Charter whereby the Security Council is empowered to deprive even an enemy state of its mandate.' (*Ibid.*, No. 23, p. 464.) The proposal of the Polish delegate was not accepted by the Security Council.

(*b*) The second reason advanced by the United States delegate to prove the termination of Japan's status as mandatory power was that Japan has accepted in the Instrument of Surrender the Cairo Declaration of 1943, subsequently reaffirmed in the Potsdam Declaration. (*Ibid.*, No. 20, p. 413.) At the 119th meeting of the Security Council, the delegate of the United States specified this argument by quoting the following passage of the Japanese surrender offer: ' The Japanese Government is ready to accept the terms enumerated in the Joint Declaration which was issued at Potsdam on July 26, 1945, by the heads of the Governments of the United States, Great Britain, and China, and later subscribed to by the Soviet Government, with the understanding that the said declaration does not comprise any demand which prejudices the prerogatives of His Majesty as a Sovereign Ruler.' He quoted further Section 8 of the Proclamation Defining Terms for Japanese Surrender, issued at Potsdam on July 26, 1945: ' The terms of the Cairo Declaration shall be carried out and Japanese sovereignty shall be limited to the Islands of Honshu, Hokkaido, Kyushu, Shikoku and such minor islands as we determine '; and the Cairo statement, released on December 1, 1943: ' . . . the Three Great Allies are fighting this war to restrain and punish the aggression of Japan. They covet no gain for themselves and have no thought of territorial expansion. It is their purpose that Japan shall be stripped of all the islands in the Pacific which she has seized or occupied since the beginning of the First World War in 1914, and that all the territories Japan

(Articles 82, 83), and trusteeship agreements with respect to areas not designated as strategic. It is in the agreement by which a

has stolen from the Chinese, such as Manchuria, Formosa, and the Pescadores, shall be restored to the Republic of China. Japan will also be expelled from all other territories which she has taken by violence and greed. . . . ' (*Ibid.*, No. 26, pp. 527 f.)

At the 113th meeting of the Security Council the delegate of the United States declared as the view of his government that, as a consequence of the fact that Japan's status as a mandatory power was terminated, ' the conclusion of a trusteeship agreement, pursuant to the Charter, for the former Japanese mandated islands clearly can take effect at this time and does not depend upon, and need not await, the general peace settlement with Japan.' (*Ibid.*, No. 20, p. 413.)

The Japanese Instrument of Surrender is an international agreement signed by the Japanese Government on the one hand and the Governments of the United States, the Republic of China, the United Kingdom, the Soviet Union, Australia, Canada, France, the Netherlands and New Zealand, on the other hand. The representatives of two of the contracting parties, namely the United Kingdom and Australia, declared—the one at the 119th meeting and the other at the 124th meeting of the Security Council—that they consider the terms of this agreement concerning the territorial changes imposed upon Japan not as final. The British delegate declared, ' we look forward to the terms of surrender being drawn up in their final form in the peace treaty.' (*Ibid.*, No. 26, p. 536); The Australian delegate stated that the instrument of surrender ' was provisional for those accepting the surrender in so far as they would later on and ultimately decide what to do with the rights surrendered . . . ' (*Ibid.*, No. 31, p. 651.) These statements are correct. By the surrender agreement Japan assumed the obligation to give up the territories determined in the Potsdam Declaration. But the question to whom these territories are to be ceded can only be decided by the peace treaty. Besides, the surrender agreement refers only to territories under the sovereignty of Japan. At the time the surrender agreement came into force, that is on September 2, 1945, the League of Nations was still legally existent and hence Japan, as mandatory power, had probably no sovereignty over the mandated islands and certainly no right to dispose of them. Consequently the surrender agreement had no effect on Japan's status as mandatory power. At the 116th meeting of the Security Council the delegate of the United Kingdom stated that, although ' the United States carries out the functions of government in the islands, the fact remains that the mandatory power is *de jure* Japan and that this situation cannot, strictly speaking, be changed except by means of provisions in the final peace treaty. (*Ibid.*, No. 23, p. 464.) In this connection he quoted Article 80, paragraph 1, of the Charter, which refers to ' the rights whatsoever of any states,' and which is consequently also applicable to the rights Japan holds as mandatory power. This Article expressly provides that nothing in the Chapter on International Trusteeship System shall be construed to alter in any manner these rights until the trusteeship agreements have been concluded. The Australian delegate declared at the same meeting that his government is ' in accord with the view that the United States should continue the *de facto* administration of those islands.' (p. 465.) However, he finally proposed to insert into the text of the trusteeship agreement a clause to the effect that ' this agreement will enter into force on the date on which the interim or final treaty of peace between Japan and the Allied Powers, victorious in war against Japan, becomes binding on Japan.' (*Ibid.*, No. 26, p. 521.) This proposal was not accepted by the Council. Japan has certainly lost her title as mandatory power, not because she actually ceased to exercise authority over the territory formerly under her mandate, but as the effect of the termination of the mandate system by the dissolution of the League of Nations. In this way all the mandatory powers lost

territory is placed under trusteeship that this territory (or part of it) is to be designated as strategic. That means that the 'states directly concerned,' that is at least the state entitled to place the territory under the trusteeship system and the state which is designated as administering authority, may make such designation a condition of their entering into the trusteeship agreement. The terms of the agreement for strategic areas shall be 'approved' by the Security Council; the terms of the agreement for non-strategic areas shall be approved by the General Assembly.

If the Organisation in its capacity as 'supervisor' has any function at all in relation to the trust territory, the agreement by which a territory is placed under the trusteeship system established under the authority of the United Nations means: to confer upon the Organisation the functions which according to the Charter are to be conferred upon the Organisation. This is possible only with the consent of the Organisation. In approving the terms of the trusteeship agreement by which a territory is placed under the trusteeship system, the Organisation, acting through the Security Council or the General Assembly, becomes a contracting party to the agreement, which, according to Article 79, can not be altered or amended without the approval of the Organisation. If the act called 'approval' is supposed to have any legal effect at all, it can only mean that the trusteeship agreement is not valid without such approval on the part of the Organisation. That the validity of a contract or treaty concluded by two parties, including its alteration or amendment, depends on the

their titles. The fact that Japan ceased to be a mandatory power did not justify that the United States disposed of the territory. The legal situation of the former Japanese mandated territory differs from the legal situation of the other former mandated territories only in so far as Japan was not in a position to extend its sovereignty over the territory concerned after the mandate system ceased to exist, since Japan as result of the war had completely lost its control of the territory. But Japan was—and is—still one of the Principal Allied and Associated Powers which according to an interpretation accepted by the government of the United States retained the sovereignty over the mandated territories conferred upon them by the Peace Treaties terminating the first World War. In the future peace treaty, Japan will be in a position to dispose of her rights regarding the islands formerly under her mandate, whatever these rights may be. If it is assumed that Japan had the right—alone or together with other states—to dispose of the territory formerly under her mandate, she might give—with retroactive force—her consent to the arrangement by which the islands were placed under the trusteeship system of the Charter, and thus legalise this procedure.

At the Hearing before the Committee on Foreign Relations of the United States Senate on July 7, 1947, the representative of the Department of State answered the question of a Senator concerning the title which the United States had with respect to the former Japanese Mandated Islands: 'We are perhaps not sovereign there in the sense of having title, but we can exercise all the prerogatives of sovereignty.' (Hearing before the Committee on Foreign Relations, United States Senate, Eightieth Congress, First Session on S.J. Res. 143, July 7, 1947, pp. 21 f.)

approval of a third party, means that the latter has to be a contracting party to this contract or treaty. The act termed in the Charter 'approval' of a trusteeship agreement is the act by which the Organisation concludes with one or more states a treaty placing a territory under trusteeship, that is to say, a treaty by which the terms of the trusteeship, especially the authority which shall exercise the administration of the trust territory and the authority which shall exercise the supervision of the administration, are determined. If the state which as contracting party to the trusteeship agreement places the territory under trusteeship is designated in the agreement as the administering authority, and no other state is recognised as 'directly concerned,' there can be a trusteeship 'agreement' only if by 'approving' the terms of the trusteeship the Organisation becomes a contracting party to the agreement. In such a case the Organisation does not really 'approve' an agreement established by two or more parties and submitted to the competent organ of the United Nations, but establishes the agreement together with the only state 'directly concerned.' This, however, is not compatible with the wording of Article 79 which evidently does not cover this case, although all the trusteeship agreements until now established—except that for Nauru—are of this type.

After the draft trusteeship agreement, submitted by the States directly concerned, has been approved by the General Assembly or the Security Council the agreement comes into force, unless it contains a provision determining another date. This was the case with the trusteeship agreement for the former Japanese mandated islands, which provides in Article 16 that it 'shall come into force when approved by the Security Council of the United Nations and by the Government of the United States after due constitutional process.'[1]

(*e*) Functions of Supervision

By establishing a trusteeship agreement the Organisation accepts the specific functions of 'supervision' and the administering authority assumes the specific obligations provided for within the trusteeship system of the Charter. But what are these functions and obligations?

Only Articles 83, 85 and 87 refer expressly to 'functions' of the Organisation within the trusteeship system; and only Articles 87 and 88 expressly confer upon the Organisation the power to take definite measures in order to exercise the supervision referred to in Article 75. Whether the basic 'objectives of the trusteeship system' laid down in Article 76 mean functions of the Organisation, or obligations of the

[1] The trusteeship agreement for the former Japanese mandated islands was approved by the Security Council on April 2, 1947, and came into force on July 18, 1947, the day on which the President of the United States, authorised by a joint resolution of Congress passed by both Houses, approved the agreement. (Congressional Record, Vol. 93, pp. 8905–7, 9027.)

administering authorities, or both, is doubtful. If Article 76 is to be interpreted to mean that the Organisation is authorised to pursue these objectives by actions of the General Assembly, the Security Council, or the Trusteeship Council, these actions must be determined in other Articles of the Charter. Article 83, paragraph 1, stipulates:

> All functions of the United Nations relating to strategic areas, including the approval of the terms of the trusteeship agreements and of their alteration or amendment, shall be exercised by the Security Council.

And Article 85, paragraph 1, stipulates:

> The functions of the United Nations with regard to trusteeship agreements for all areas not designated as strategic, including the approval of the terms of the trusteeship agreements and of their alteration or amendment, shall be exercised by the General Assembly.

In both paragraphs the approval of the terms of the trusteeship agreements is characterised as 'function' of the Organisation relating to trust territories. However, the so-called approval of the trusteeship agreements is not exactly a trusteeship function of the Organisation. The approval is the entering of the Organisation into the agreement by which a territory is placed under the trusteeship system. It is an act which, together with the corresponding acts of the other contracting parties, makes the functioning of the trusteeship system altogether possible. If states would not voluntarily place territories under the trusteeship system of the United Nations—no state is obliged to do so—by concluding an agreement with the United Nations determining the terms of trusteeship, the Organisation would actually have no trusteeship functions at all. The function which the Organisation has to exercise with respect to the administration of the trust territory is an essential, even the most important, element of the terms of trusteeship under which the trust territory is to be administered. Since according to Article 77, paragraph 2, these terms are to be determined by the trusteeship agreement and since Article 81 expressly provides that 'the trusteeship agreement shall in each case include the terms under which the trust territory will be administered,' the functions of the Organisation and the obligations of the administering authority must be stipulated in the agreement. Their determination by the Charter only means that the Organisation, if the agreement does not confer upon it the functions and does not stipulate the obligations of the administering authority determined in the Charter, must not approve the agreement. Non-approval of a trusteeship agreement that does not correspond to the provisions of the Charter is the only means at the disposal of the Organisation to guarantee that the principles laid down in Chapters XII and XIII of the Charter will be actually applied to the territories which the states entitled to dispose of them are willing to place under the trusteeship system. This is not a very effective means, since the Organisation cannot force the states concerned to enter into trusteeship agreements; and if there is no voluntary agreement upon the terms of trusteeship there is no trusteeship.

In addition to the general provisions of Article 77, paragraph 2, and Article 81, the Charter stipulates with regard to some particular actions of the Organisation expressly that they shall be provided for in the trusteeship agreement. Thus the performance of certain functions of the Security Council is determined in Article 83, paragraph 3, with the restriction 'subject to the provisions of the trusteeship agreements'; and some functions of the General Assembly in Article 87, with the restriction 'in conformity with the terms of the trusteeship agreements.' If the 'objectives' laid down in Article 76 imply 'functions' of the Organisation, those indicated in clause (*b*) of that Article are stipulated with the restriction: 'as may be provided by the terms of each trusteeship agreement'; and those indicated in clause (*d*), with the restriction: 'subject to the provisions of Article 80,' which contains the phrase 'except as may be agreed upon in individual trusteeship agreements.' The Rules of Procedure for the Trusteeship Council in regulating competences conferred upon the Trusteeship Council refer to the trusteeship agreements only with respect to some of these competences, and even not to all competences of which the Charter itself expressly provides that they must be stipulated in the trusteeship agreements. Thus Article 87 (*d*) of the Charter provides that the General Assembly and—under its authority—the Trusteeship Council shall take all actions referred to in Article 87, clauses (*a*), (*b*) and (*c*), 'in conformity with the terms of the trusteeship agreements.' But the Rules of Procedure for the Trusteeship Council refer to the trusteeship agreements only with respect to those determined in Article 87, clause (*c*) (periodic visits), not to those determined in clause (*a*) (consider reports). As to the action mentioned in clause (*b*) (accept and examine petitions) the Rules of Procedure refer only to the trusteeship agreements regarding strategic areas. The general rules laid down in Article 77, paragraph 2, and Article 81, that the terms of the trusteeship under which a territory is to be placed shall be a matter of agreement, or that all terms under which a trust territory is to be administered shall be included in the agreement, are completely ignored by the Rules of Procedure for the Trusteeship Council.

First to lay down a general rule that all terms of trusteeship shall be determined in the trusteeship agreements, and then to provide with respect to some—not to all—functions of the Organisation (and obligations of the administering authorities) expressly that they shall be stipulated in the trusteeship agreements, is highly misleading. For this technique might lead to the interpretation that only those functions of the Organisation (and obligations of the administering authorities) are to be provided for in the trusteeship agreements which the Charter expressly designates for this purpose; whereas the other functions (and obligations) are to be exercised by the Organisation (and fulfilled by the administering authorities) even without being provided for in the agreements. Such interpretation, however, is incompatible with the general rules laid down in Articles 77 (2) and 81, according to which all terms under which the trust territory is to be administered shall be included in the trusteeship agreement. The fact that only certain functions of the Organisation (and obligations of the administering authority) are stipulated with the express restriction: 'subject to the provisions of the trusteeship agreements' (Article 83, paragraph 3), or: 'in conformity with the terms of the trusteeship agreements' (Article 87 (*d*)), or: 'as may be agreed upon in individual trusteeship agreements' (Articles 76 (*d*), 80) might also be interpreted to mean that the provisions of the Charter concerning these functions and obligations do not constitute *jus cogens*, but only *jus dispositivum*, so that the Organisation may approve a trusteeship agreement even if it does not confer these functions upon the Organisation and does not impose these obligations upon the administering authority. It is, however, doubtful whether this interpretation corresponds to the intention of those who drafted the Charter, since there is no recognisable reason for a differentiation between mandatory and not-mandatory provisions of the trusteeship system laid down in the Charter.[2]

[2] At the 23rd meeting of the Fourth Committee of the General Assembly the delegate of the United Kingdom 'urged that it was not necessary to repeat in the trusteeship agreements provisions which were already in the Charter.' (Summary Record of Meetings of Fourth Committee, November 1–December 12, 1946, p. 138.) This statement is hardly compatible with the clear provisions of Article 77, paragraph 2, and Article 81. It is of course not necessary to repeat literally the provisions of the Charter in the text of the trusteeship agreements; reference to these provisions is sufficient. At the 24th meeting of the Fourth Committee the representative of Australia 'felt it unnecessary to repeat obligations included in the provisions of the Charter, to which reference had already been made in the draft agreement.' (p. 149.) This statement is correct. At the 124th meeting of the Security Council the delegate of the United States stated with respect to Article 77: 'That Article of the Charter relates not merely to the definition and description of the territory, but also to the terms upon which this territory shall be brought within the trusteeship system, and there can be no terms that are not agreed to by the Administering Authority.' (Official Records of the Security Council, 2nd Year, No. 31, p. 650.) But at the 116th meeting he stated with reference to the trusteeship agreement concerning the former Japanese mandated islands: 'It is the Charter that defines the duties, the powers, and the responsibilities of the Security Council, which is one party to this agreement; but it is this agreement which is necessary in order to define the powers that the United States may have if it becomes the trustee under the agreement.' (*Ibid.*, No. 23, p. 476.) If all terms of trusteeship must be agreed upon by the Organisation and the administering authority (being the only state directly concerned), then the trusteeship agreement has to define not only the powers of the administering authority, but also the powers of the Organisation as supervising authority.

The Organisation must not approve a trusteeship agreement which does not confer upon the Organisation the functions, and does not impose upon the administering authority the obligations, determined in the Charter. But the Organisation is not bound to approve a trusteeship agreement if it provides only for those, and not for other functions and obligations. The Organisation may make its approval dependent on being vested in the trusteeship agreement with functions and the administering authority being subjected to obligations not expressly determined in the Charter.[3] This results from the general rule that the terms of trusteeship are to be agreed upon by the Organisation and the states which place the territory under trusteeship; and from the special rule which is stipulated with respect to the functions of the General Assembly in Article 87, where after an enumeration of some actions of the Assembly in relation to non-strategic trust territories, it is said: the General Assembly may 'take these and other actions in conformity with the terms of the trusteeship agreements.'[4] The functions of the Organisation and the obligations of the administering authority determined in the Charter represent only the minimum which must be stipulated in the

[3] The statement which the representative of India made at the 23rd meeting of the Fourth Committee: 'that there was no restriction on what could be inserted in the trusteeship agreements' (Summary Record of Meetings of Fourth Committee, November 1–December 12, 1946, p. 146) goes certainly too far.

[4] Paragraph 12, Section B, of the Working Paper, which corresponds to Article 87 of the Charter, runs as follows:

> The General Assembly, and under its authority, the Trusteeship Council, in carrying out their functions, should be empowered to consider reports submitted by the administering state to accept petitions and examine them in consultation with the administering state, to make periodic visits to the respective territories at times agreed upon with the administering state, and to take other action in conformity with the Trusteeship arrangements. (U.N.C.I.O. Doc. 323, II/4/12, p. 3.)

The words 'and to take other action' evidently mean: actions in addition to those enumerated in this paragraph. The text of paragraph 12 was revised by inserting a comma after the word 'action.' This revision made it clear that the actions enumerated in paragraph 12, as well as 'other actions' shall be taken in conformity with the trusteeship agreement. The finally adopted text corresponds to the intention of this revision: 'take these [the enumerated] and other actions in conformity with the terms of the trusteeship agreements.' That also the actions enumerated in Article 87, clauses (*a*), (*b*) and (*c*), shall be taken 'in conformity with the trusteeship agreements' results from the provisions of Articles 77 and 79 according to which all terms of trusteeship shall be agreed upon by the states directly concerned and approved by the Organisation, which means that all terms of trusteeship, including those provided for in the Charter, shall be determined in the trusteeship agreements. The trusteeship status is, according to the clear wording of the Charter, to be established entirely on a contractual basis. There is no sufficient reason to assume that the words 'and other actions' in Article 87 mean: other actions than those enumerated in Article 87, but provided for in other Articles of the Charter.

trusteeship agreement in order to be approvable by the Organisation.[5] However, by the terms of a trusteeship agreement neither the organisation of the agencies competent to deal with trusteeship matters nor their mutual relations as laid down in the Charter can be changed. Thus, *e.g.*, no trusteeship agreement can be constitutionally

[5] As a matter of fact, the trusteeship agreements approved by the Organisation confer upon the latter all functions and impose upon the administering authorities all obligations provided for in the Charter. This is effected by general references to the Charter and by repetition of special provisions of Chapters XII and XIII in the text of the trusteeship agreements. The trusteeship agreements for New Guinea and Nauru contain in their respective Articles 3 the clause: 'The Administering Authority undertakes to administer the Territory in accordance with the provisions of the Charter'; they do not contain express provisions corresponding to Article 76 (*d*) of the Charter: 'to ensure equal treatment . . . for all Members of the United Nations, etc.'. Such provisions were unnecessary in view of Article 3 of the Agreements (cf. discussion in the Fourth Committee, Journal of the United Nations, No. 60, Suppl. No. 4 A/C.4/86, pp. 104 ff.). The trusteeship agreements for French Cameroons and French Togoland, in their respective Articles 2 contain the clause: 'The French Government, in its capacity of Administering Authority . . . undertakes to exercise therein the duties of trusteeship as defined in the . . . Charter;' and in their respective Articles 4 (A 1) the provision that the Administering Authority 'shall have full powers of legislation, administration and jurisdiction in the Territory and shall administer it in accordance with French law as an integral part of French territory, subject to the provisions of the Charter and of this Agreement.' If the administering authority is obliged to administer the territory 'subject to the provisions of the Charter' all provisions of the Charter regarding tursteeship are recognised as binding upon the administering authority. But it might be doubted whether the addition: 'and of this Agreement' does not constitute a restriction of the preceding general reference to the provisions of the Charter. Does, in case the Agreement is not in conformity with the Charter, the latter or the former prevail? Both interpretations are possible. But under Article 2 (preamble) of the agreement, the Charter prevails. The trusteeship agreements for Western Samoa (Article 3), British Togoland (Article 5a), British Cameroons (Article 5a), Tanganyika (Article 5a), and Ruanda-Urundi (Article 5 (1)) contain only the ambiguous formula that the administering authority 'shall have full powers of administration, legislation and jurisdiction over the Territory, subject to the provisions of this Agreement, and of the Charter of the United Nations' (or: 'subject to the provisions of the United Nations Charter and of this Agreement'). The trusteeship agreement for the former Japanese mandated islands provides in Article 3 that 'the administering authority shall have full powers of administration, legislation, and jurisdiction over the territory subject to the provisions of this agreement' (no addition: and of the Charter); but in Article 4: 'The administering authority, in discharging the obligations of trusteeship in the trust territory, shall act in accordance with the Charter of the United Nations, and the provisions of this agreement.' In addition to these general references to the Charter, the trusteeship agreements contain repetitions of particular provisions of the Charter or references to them. The agreement for Western Samoa contains as an Annex even the complete text of Chapters XII and XIII of the Charter and thus recognises all provisions of the Charter regarding trusteeship as binding upon the administering authority.

The trusteeship agreement for the former Japanese mandated islands, designated as strategic area in Article 1, confers upon the Organisation functions and imposes upon the administering authority obligations which the Charter does not provide in relation to strategic areas, namely the function determined in Article 87 and the obligation stipulated in Article 88. Cf. *infra*, pp. 616, 625, 629, 682.

approved if it confers functions of supervision of a strategic area to the General Assembly or of a non-strategic area to the Security Council (Articles 83, 85, of the Charter).[6]

The Charter distinguishes between ' all functions of the United Nations relating to strategic areas (Article 83, paragraph 1) and ' the functions of the United Nations with regard to trusteeship agreements for all areas not designated as strategic ' (Article 85, paragraph 1). It is not easy to understand why in the one case the Charter speaks of ' all ' functions and of functions relating to the ' areas,' whereas in the other case the Charter speaks of ' the ' functions and of functions relating to the ' trusteeship agreements.' It seems that ' all ' the functions of the Organisation, characterised as ' supervision ' in Article 75, can relate only to the trust areas or their administration, not to the trusteeship agreements which are the legal basis of these functions.

The approval of the terms of the trusteeship agreements for territories which have not the character of strategic areas and all functions of the United Nations relating to these areas, including alteration or amendment of the terms of trusteeship, are within the competence of the General Assembly. The approval of the terms of trusteeship agreements for territories which have the character of strategic areas and all functions of the United Nations relating to these areas, including alteration or amendment of the terms of trusteeship, are within the competence of the Security Council. To designate an area as strategic is one of the objectives of the trusteeship agreement. In this respect Article 82 stipulates:

> There may be designated, in any trusteeship agreement, a strategic area or areas which may include part or all of the trust territory to which the agreement applies, without prejudice to any special agreement or agreements made under Article 43.

According to this Article either the whole territory to be placed under the trusteeship system or part of it may be designated

[6] Cf. *infra*, p. 625. The Chinese delegation proposed to insert into the trusteeship agreement for Western Samoa a provision to the effect that disputes relating to the interpretation or application of the provisions of the agreement shall be submitted to the Trusteeship Council (instead of to the International Court of Justice as the draft agreement provided) (Doc. A/C.4/Sub.1/10). During the discussion in Sub-committee 1 of the Fourth Committee the representative of Belgium expressed the view ' that since the Trusteeship Council was a consultative organ, it could not exercise the juridical function which would be granted to it under the Chinese proposal.' (Summary Records of Meetings of Sub-Committee 1, November 15–December 10, 1946, p. 86, p. 240.) This view is correct only in so far as the minimum provisions of the Charter are concerned. But the Charter does not preclude the Organisation from approving a trusteeship agreement which confers upon the Trusteeship Council functions which are not provided for in the Charter but refer to trust territories and are within the scope of supervision of trusteeship administration. Cf. *infra*, pp. 684 ff.

in the agreement as a strategic area. If only a part of the territory is designated a strategic area, one and the same trusteeship agreement refers to strategic and non-strategic areas. Who is competent to 'approve' this agreement? Probably both the Assembly and the Council. The Charter itself does not provide for this case.[7] Neither for the case that the established status of a non-strategic trust territory is to be changed into the status of a strategic trust territory, that is to say if the administering authority of a non-strategic trust territory wants to designate all or part of the territory as a strategic area. In so far as this change implies an alteration of the existing trusteeship agreement, Article 85, paragraph 1, applies; consequently the General Assembly is competent to approve or to refuse to approve such alteration. But, since Article 83, paragraph 1, provides that the terms of a trusteeship agreement for strategic areas shall be approved by the Security Council, the latter, too, may be considered competent to approve or refuse to approve such change. Hence it may be assumed that the change requires approval of both, the Assembly and the Council. The trusteeship agreements for French Togoland (Article 11), the French Cameroons (Article 11), and for Ruanda-Urundi (Article 17), reserve to the administering authority 'the right . . . to propose at any future date the designation of the whole or part of the territory as a strategic area in accordance with Articles 82 and 83 of the Charter.' Since Article 85 is not referred to, the provision may be interpreted to mean that only the approval of the Security Council is required for the change to be proposed under the respective Articles of the Agreements. The trusteeship agreements for British Togoland (Article 17), the British Cameroons (Article 17), and Tanganyika (Article 17), reserve to the administering authority 'the right . . . to propose, at any future date, the amendment of this Agreement for the purpose of designating the whole or part of

[7] In the trusteeship agreement for the former Japanese mandated islands this territory is designated as a strategic area (Article 1). Article 13 of the agreement provides that Articles 87 and 88 of the Charter shall be applicable to the trust territory, although Article 87 stipulates only functions of the General Assembly relating to non-strategic areas, and Article 88 only obligations of administering authorities of such territories. But the application of the two Articles of the Charter to the trust territory is restricted by the condition: 'provided that the administering authority may determine the extent of their applicability to any areas which may from time to time be specified by it as closed for security reasons.' Thus within a strategic area a 'closed area' may be established, a category not provided for in the Charter. But a 'closed area' under Article 13 of the agreement is only that part of the strategic trust territory for which the agreement confers upon the Organisation (represented by the Security Council) no other functions than those provided for by the Charter with respect to strategic areas, and imposes upon the administering authority no other obligations than those imposed by the Charter upon administering authorities of such areas. Consequently only the 'closed area' is a strategic area in the strict sense of the term; as to the non-closed area no essential difference exists between this area and a non-strategic area. Cf. *infra*, pp. 649 f.

[the territory] as strategic area or for any other purpose not inconsistent with the basic objectives of the international trusteeship system.' Since the change is expressly characterised as an ' amendment ' of the agreement and no particular Article of the Charter is referred to, the provision may be interpreted to mean that Article 85 applies, that is to say that at least the approval of the General Assembly is required for the change to be proposed by the administering authority under the respective Articles of the trusteeship agreements.

If only part of the trust territory has the character of a strategic area, the supervision of the administration is within the competence of the General Assembly with respect to the non-strategic area under Article 85, paragraph 1, and within the competence of the Security Council with respect to the strategic area under Article 83, paragraph 1.

The wording of Article 83, paragraph 1, and Article 85, paragraph 1, seems to presuppose that the ' functions of the United Nations ' in its capacity as supervisor of the administration of the trust territories are determined by some other Article of the Charter. The only Article which can be interpreted to confer functions upon the Organisation is Article 76, setting forth the ' basic objectives of the trusteeship system.' If this Article is not interpreted in this way, Article 83 and 85 would refer to functions not determined by the Charter. If the ' basic objectives ' set forth in Article 76 imply ' functions ' of the Organisation, the Security Council shall exercise these functions relating to strategic areas under Article 83, paragraph 1, the General Assembly those relating to non-strategic areas under Article 85, paragraph 1, since nothing to the contrary is stipulated in the Charter. Article 83, paragraph 1, and Article 85, paragraph 1, add to the functions stipulated by Article 76: ' the approval of the terms of the trusteeship agreements and of their alteration or amendment.' Article 83, paragraph 2, expressly provides that ' the basic objectives set forth in Article 76 shall be applicable to the people of each strategic area.' The formulation ' to the people of each strategic area,' instead of ' to each strategic area,' is not quite understandable. The objectives set forth in clauses (*a*) and (*c*) of Article 76 are, by their very nature, not applicable to the ' people ' of the trust territory. Clause (*a*): ' to further international peace and security ' is applicable directly only to the administering authority, and only indirectly to the people in so far as this objective is also in the interest of this people. Clause (*d*): ' to ensure equal treatment, etc.' is applicable to the other Members of the United Nations and their nationals; only the restriction: ' without prejudice to the attainment of the foregoing objectives ' applies to the people of the trust territory in so far as the objectives set forth in clauses (*b*) and (*c*) apply to it. It is not very likely that the formulation of Article 83, paragraph 2, ' to the people of each strategic area ' was intended to restrict the application of the basic objectives to those set forth in clauses (*b*) and (*c*) of Article 76.[8] It probably means the same as 'to each strategic area.' In so far as the objectives of Article 76 imply 'functions,' the provision of paragraph 2 of Article 83 is superfluous because already included in the provision of paragraph 1. As a matter of fact, the Charter does not contain a provision analogous to that of Article 83, paragraph 2, with respect to the people of each non-strategic area. Nevertheless, the General Assembly has to pursue the basic objectives set forth in Article 76, relating to non-strategic areas, at least to the same extent as has the Security Council relating to strategic areas.

However, as pointed out, Article 76 does not provide the specific means, that is to say, the acts of the competent organs of the United Nations, by which the 'objectives' are to be achieved; Article 83, paragraph 1, and Article 85, paragraph 1, determine only the organs of the United Nations by which such acts, if provided, are to be performed. Such acts are provided with respect to non-strategic areas to be performed by the General Assembly and, under its authority, by the Trusteeship Council, in Article 87, which runs as follows:

> The General Assembly and, under its authority, in carrying out their functions, may:
>
> (*a*) consider reports submitted by the administering authority;
>
> (*b*) accept petitions and examine them in consultation with the administering authority;
>
> (*c*) provide for periodic visits to the respective trust territories at times agreed upon with the administering authority; and
>
> (*d*) take these and other actions in conformity with the terms of the trusteeship agreements.

This Article does not determine 'functions' of the General Assembly, but specific means by which the Assembly (and under its authority, the Trusteeship Council) may carry out functions which the Charter, in other Articles, has conferred upon the Organisation. As pointed out, the functions conferred upon the Organisation are those set forth as basic objectives in Article 76 and 'the approval of the terms of the trusteeship agreements and of their alteration or amendment' as provided in Articles 83 (1) and 85 (1). Article 85, paragraph 1, stipulates that the functions of the Organisation including the approval of the terms of the trusteeship agreements and of their alteration or amendment, in so far as they refer to non-strategic areas, are within the competence of the General Assembly; Article 87 determines the acts by which the Assembly may exercise the functions conferred upon it. It is evident that the approval of the terms of the trusteeship agreements, although characterised by Article 85, paragraph 1, as a

[8] Cf. *infra*, p. 636.

'function,' cannot be included in the functions referred to in Article 87. For the actions determined in Article 87 by which the 'functions' are to be carried out, such as: consider reports, accept and examine petitions, provide for periodic visits, have evidently no relation to the act of approving the trusteeship agreements. This, as pointed out, is not a true 'function' of the Organisation within the trusteeship system; it is the condition under which the trusteeship system works.

The action of the Organisation determined in clause (*a*) of Article 87, to 'consider reports submitted by the administering authority,' depends on the administering authority submitting such reports. The Charter provides only that the administering authority shall make 'annual' reports. In this respect Article 88 stipulates:

> The Trusteeship Council shall formulate a questionnaire on the political, economic, social, and educational advancement of the inhabitants of each trust territory, and the administering authority for each trust territory within the competence of the General Assembly shall make an annual report to the General Assembly upon the basis of such questionnaire.

To formulate the questionnaire referred to in Article 88 seems to be a measure which the Organisation shall take for all trust territories. The provision refers expressly to 'each' trust territory. But Article 88 is in close connection with Article 87 which speaks of the Trusteeship Council as an auxiliary organ of the General Assembly, competent only for non-strategic trust territories. Also the other Articles of Chapter XIII do not refer to the Trusteeship Council in its relation to the Security Council which is not mentioned in this Chapter. Hence an interpretation is not excluded according to which Article 88 establishes only a function of the Trusteeship Council to be exercised under the authority of the General Assembly, and that means a function which refers to non-strategic territories only. This interpretation could be supported by the second part of Article 88 providing that only the administering authorities of non-strategic trust territories shall make annual reports to the General Assembly on the basis of the questionnaire formulated by the Trusteeship Council. Why should the Trusteeship Council formulate a questionnaire for strategic trust territories, if the administering authorities of these territories are not bound to reply?

The Rules of Procedure for the Trusteeship Council are not clearer in this respect than Article 88 of the Charter. They contain the following provisions concerning the questionnaires:

> RULE 68
>
> Upon the coming into effect of each Trusteeship agreement, the Trusteeship Council shall transmit to the Administering Authority concerned, through the Secretary-General, such

questionnaire as it shall have formulated, in accordance with Article 88 of the Charter, on the political, economic, social and educational advancement of the inhabitants of the Trust Territory involved.

RULE 69

The Trusteeship Council may modify the questionnaires at its discretion.

RULE 70

When, in accordance with Article 91 of the Charter, the Trusteeship Council considers it appropriate to avail itself of the assistance of the Economic and Social Council or of any specialised agency in the preparation of questionnaires, the President of the Trusteeship Council shall transmit through the Secretary-General to the Economic and Social Council or to the specialised agency concerned those sections of the questionnaires with regard to which its advice may be desired.

RULE 71

1. The questionnaire shall be communicated to each Administering Authority at least six months before the expiration of the year covered by the first annual report, and shall remain in force, without specific renewal, from year to year.

2. Any subsequent modifications shall be communicated to the Administering Authority concerned at least six months before the date fixed for the presentation of the first annual report which is to be based on the modified questionnaire.

It should be noted that Article 87, clause (*a*) confers upon the General Assembly and, under its authority, on the Trusteeship Council the power to 'consider' reports submitted by the administering authority. This implies the power to discuss the reports but not the power to make recommendations concerning the administration of the territory. Whether and under what conditions the General Assembly is authorised by Article 10 to make recommendations on trusteeship matters shall be discussed later. To interpret the term 'consider' in Article 87 (*a*) as implying to make recommendations is hardly possible. The Charter—in Article 11, paragraph 1—uses the term 'consider' in the narrower sense in phrasing: '. . . consider . . . and . . . make recommendations.' In any case, the power to make recommendations may be conferred upon the General Assembly or the Trusteeship Council in the trusteeship agreement. The Rules of Procedure for the Trusteeship Council contain special provisions concerning the annual reports and their examination, which shall be quoted later.[9]

[9] Cf. *infra*, pp. 673 f.

By ' petitions ' referred to in clause (*b*), not only petitions of the inhabitants of the trust territories are meant. The Charter does not provide that petitions must be submitted through the administering authority. Hence petitions may be submitted by the inhabitants of the trust territory directly to the Organisation. The administering authority is obliged not to prevent such petitions and, if submitted to it, to forward them to the Organisation. The Rules of Procedure for the Trusteeship Council contain special provisions in this respect, which will be presented later.[1] The restriction ' in consultation with the administering authority ' may be interpreted not to mean that consent of the administering authority is necessary in order to examine petitions. Rule 92 of the Rules of Procedure provides that the administering authority concerned is entitled to be represented in the examination of petitions. Although the function of the Assembly and of the Trusteeship Council is limited to ' examination,' Rule 93 of the Rules of Procedure presuppose the possibility of actions taken by the Trusteeship Council on petitions.[2]

The most important function of the Organisation is determined in clause (*c*): to ' provide for periodic visits to the respective trust territories.' This gives the Organisation the power to inspect the trust territory, *i.e.*, to make inquiries and to get information on the spot. It should be noted that the Charter does not confer upon the General Assembly and, under its authority upon the Trusteeship Council, the power to make investigations on the trust territories. The right to make periodic visits, as provided in Article 87, clause (*c*), is different from the power to ' investigate ' conferred upon the Security Council in Article 34. But the power to make investigations, including the power to get not only voluntary information, may be conferred upon the Organisation by the trusteeship agreement. Rule 97 of the Rules of Procedure for the Trusteeship Council stipulates that ' special investigations or enquiries ' may be conducted ' in agreement with the Administering Authority.'

The power of the General Assembly and, under its authority, of the Trusteeship Council, to provide for periodic visits to the respective trust territories is restricted in so far as the time of the visits must be

1 Cf. *infra*, pp. 674 f.

2 Cf. *infra*, p. 678. At its first session the Trusteeship Council received a petition from the leaders and representatives of the trust territory of Western Samoa, requesting *inter alia* that Western Samoa be granted self-government. On the proposal of the representative of the administering authority—the Government of New Zealand—the Trusteeship Council established a special three-member mission for the purpose of visiting Western Samoa in order to investigate the subject of the petition. ' The clear intention of the Trusteeship Council was that this visit should not be considered a " periodic " visit under Article 87 (*c*) of the Charter, but a special one to investigate a petition.' *Yearbook of the United Nations*, 1946–47, p. 579.) It is important to note that this action has been taken with the consent, even at the proposal, of the administering authority.

agreed upon with the administering authority; and since the time is as essential an element as the space where the function is to be performed, its performance needs the consent of the administering power. That means: the trusteeship agreement may stipulate that the time for each visit shall be agreed upon with the administering authority. This particular agreement is different from the general agreement relating to all functions of the Organisation and all obligations of the administering authority, provided for in Article 77, paragraph 2, and Article 81; this general agreement is identical with the trusteeship agreement referred to in Article 87, clause (*d*) providing that the actions referred to in clauses (*a*) to (*c*) ' and other actions ' shall be taken ' in conformity with the terms of the trusteeship agreements.' This provision means that the Organisation can discharge the functions determined in Article 87 only if they are conferred upon it by the trusteeship agreements. In this way also other functions may be conferred upon the Organisation, as clause (*d*) expressly admits. The functions of the United Nations with regard to non-strategic trust territories are only those conferred upon it by the trusteeship agreements. The matter referred to in Article 88: formulation of a questionnaire on the political, economic, social, and educational advancement of the inhabitants of each trust territory seems to be an exception, since Article 88 does not refer—as does Article 87, clause (*d*)—to the terms of the trusteeship agreements. But, as pointed out, to all functions of the Organisation the provisions of Articles 77 (2) and 81 apply: that the terms upon which a territory is to be brought under trusteeship and the terms under which the trust territory will be administered, must be determined in the trusteeship agreement.

The Charter is dealing with the trusteeship system not only in Chapters XII and XIII, but also in Chapter IV. Article 10 confers upon the General Assembly the power to discuss any matter within the scope of the Charter and to make recommendations to the Members of the United Nations or to the Security Council or to both on any such matters. Article 18, paragraph 2, mentions among the decisions which require a two-thirds majority, decisions on ' the election of members of the Trusteeship Council ' and on ' questions relating to the operation of the trusteeship system.' Article 16 provides:

> The General Assembly shall perform such functions with respect to the international trusteeship system as are assigned to it under Chapters XII and XIII, including the approval of the trusteeship agreements for areas not designated as strategic.

In view of Article 85 of the Charter, Article 16 is technically superfluous and even misleading. It might be interpreted to constitute a restriction of Article 10, excluding from the matters which may be discussed by the General Assembly and on which the General Assembly may make recommendations those dealt with in Chapters XII and XIII.

This interpretation, however, is not in conformity with a provable intention of the legislator; and the other interpretation is more plausible that Article 16 was inserted into Chapter IV only to show that in drafting this Chapter, dealing with the General Assembly, the functions assigned to this body in Chapters XII and XIII were not ignored. Hence the General Assembly is competent to discuss trusteeship matters and to make recommendations on these matters under Article 10.[3]

Now, the question arises whether this function, too, must be conferred upon the General Assembly in the trusteeship agreements in accordance with the provisions of Articles 77 (2) and 81, in order that the Assembly be competent to exercise this function with respect to a definite trust territory; or whether the Assembly is competent to discuss matters relating to a definite trust territory and make recommendations on them even without being authorised to do so in the agreement by which the territory has been placed under the trusteeship system. That the General Assembly under Article 10 is competent to discuss trusteeship matters in general, not with respect to a definite trust territory, and to make recommendations, is beyond doubt. Another question is, whether the Assembly is competent under Article 10 to discuss matters and make recommendations on them only if they relate to a non-strategic territory, since, according to Article 85, only non-strategic areas are within the competence of the General Assembly, or to discuss questions and make recommendations on them also if they relate to strategic territories, since both territories are under the trusteeship system and the trusteeship system as a whole is within the scope of the Charter.

As to the first question, both interpretations indicated are possible. It may be argued that the range of Article 10 is restricted with respect to questions relating to definite trust territories by the provisions of Articles 77 (2) and 81, since the competence of the General Assembly to discuss such questions and make recommendations on them is an element of the terms upon which the territory is to be brought under the trusteeship system and under which it is to be administered. A question concerning a definite trust territory is 'within the scope of the Charter' only in so far as it has been brought—by the trusteeship agreement— within this scope. But it is possible also to argue that the provisions of Articles 77 (1) and 81 refer only to those functions of the Organisation which are determined in Chapters XII and XIII. If the first interpretation is accepted, the General Assembly is competent to discuss matters and make recommendations on them only with respect to trust territories for which the trusteeship agreement concerned has conferred upon the Assembly such competence. This may be also a trusteeship agreement relating to a strategic area and approved by the Security Council. If the second interpretation is

[3] Cf. *infra*, pp. 650 ff.

accepted, the General Assembly may apply Article 10 without regard to the provisions of the trusteeship agreements. The question as to whether the Assembly under Article 10 is authorised to discuss matters relating to non-strategic as well as to strategic areas and to make recommendations on them, may be answered in one as well as in another way. Taken literally, the function conferred upon the Assembly by Article 10 is a function of the United Nations relating to strategic as well as to non-strategic areas. Article 10 is obviously in conflict with Article 83, paragraph 1, which provides that 'all functions of the United Nations relating to strategic areas' shall be exercised by the Security Council. Hence Article 83, paragraph 1, may be interpreted to be restricted by Article 10, or Article 10 to be restricted by Article 83, paragraph 1. If the first interpretation were accepted, the meaning of Article 83, paragraph 1, would be: all functions of the United Nations relating to strategic areas except those expressly conferred upon the General Assembly . . . In conformity with this interpretation the General Assembly has an important competence with respect to all strategic areas, whereas the Security Council has no competence with respect to non-strategic areas. If the second interpretation is accepted, the meaning of Article 10 is: the General Assembly may discuss any question or any matter within the scope of the present Charter except those exclusively reserved to the Security Council . . . This interpretation is in conformity with the tendency prevailing in Chapters XII and XIII: to place strategic areas under the supervision of the Security Council and non-strategic areas under the supervision of the General Assembly.

If in trusteeship matters the competence of the General Assembly under Article 10 is considered to be dependent on the provisions of the trusteeship agreements recognising this competence, no trusteeship agreement must be approved by the General Assembly which does not confer upon it the function to discuss matters relating to the non-strategic trust territory and make recommendations on them to the administering authority. Whether the same holds with respect to trusteeship agreements relating to strategic areas, depends upon the just mentioned interpretation of Article 10. Finally, it should be noted that according to the wording of Article 10 the General Assembly is authorised to make recommendations only to administering authorities which are Members of the United Nations. The administering authority may according to Article 81 be a non-member state, since this Article refers to 'states,' not to Members. However, the wording of Article 10 does not prevent the Organisation form making the approval of a trusteeship agreement in which a non-member is designated as the administering authority dependent upon a provision in the agreement by which the General Assembly is authorised to make recommendations to the non-member state in its capacity as the administering authority.

As to the functions with regard to strategic trust territories,[4] the Charter does not contain a provision analogous to that of Article 87. If it is, under Articles 76 and 83, a function of the Security Council to pursue the basic objectives in the strategic trust areas, the Charter does not determine the actions by which the Security Council may exercise this function. But a trusteeship agreement for a territory designated as strategic area may confer upon the Security Council the same functions as those determined in Article 87.[5] Then there is no essential difference between the functions of the General Assembly relating to non-strategic areas and the functions of the Security Council relating to strategic areas. As to the functions of the Security Council relating to strategic areas the Charter contains only a provision concerning the assistance the Trusteeship Council may give to the Security Council in this respect. Article 83, paragraph 3, provides:

> The Security Council shall, subject to the provisions of the trusteeship agreements and without prejudice to security considerations, avail itself of the assistance of the Trusteeship Council to perform those functions of the United Nations under the trusteeship system relating to political, economic, social, and educational matters in the strategic areas.

The direct purpose of this provision is not to determine functions of the Security Council with respect to strategic areas, but to determine the relationship between the Security Council and the Trusteeship

[4] During the discussion of Section B, paragraph 8, of the Working Paper, which corresponds to Article 83 of the Charter, 'the opinion was expressed that the powers of the Trusteeship Council concerning strategic areas were not clearly indicated in the working paper.' (Summary Report of 9th meeting of Committee II/4, U.N.C.I.O. Doc. 552, II/4/23, p. 4.)

[5] As pointed out, Article 13 of the trusteeship agreement for the former Japanese mandated islands provides that 'the provisions of Articles 87 and 88 of the Charter shall be applicable to the trust territory,' which is designated as strategic area and hence placed under the jurisdiction of the Security Council. Since Article 87 establishes competences of the General Assembly, Article 13 of the trusteeship agreement, taken literally, confers functions with respect to a strategic area upon the General Assembly, which is incompatible with Articles 83 and 85 of the Charter. In order to be constitutional, Article 13 must be interpreted to mean that the Security Council shall exercise with respect to the trust territory the same functions as the General Assembly has under Article 87 with respect to non-strategic areas. The function of the Trusteeship Council established in Article 88 to formulate a questionnaire may be interpreted to refer to all trust territories, but the obligation to make annual reports to the General Assembly on the basis of this questionnaire is imposed only on administering authorities of non-strategic areas. Taken literally, Article 13 of the trusteeship agreement imposes upon the administering authority of a strategic area the obligation to make annual reports on the basis of the questionnaire, formulated by the Trusteeship Council, to the General Assembly; which, also, is incompatible with Articles 83 and 85 of the Charter. In order to be constitutional Article 13 must be interpreted to mean that the administering authority shall make annual reports to the Security Council on the basis of the questionnaire formulated by the Trusteeship Council.

Council. The Security Council shall avail itself of the assistance of the Trusteeship Council only without prejudice to security considerations and only in the performance of definite functions. These functions are characterised as 'relating to political, economic, social, and educational matters in the strategic areas.' That the Security Council has—or shall be, by the trusteeship agreements, vested with these and other functions in the strategic areas is presupposed by this provision of the Charter.

The functions referred to in Article 83, paragraph 3, correspond to certain 'objectives of the trusteeship system' set forth in Article 76. Clause (*b*) of this Article determines as basic objectives 'to promote the political, economic, social, and educational advancement of the inhabitants of the trust territories, and their progressive development towards self-government or independence . . .' The question arises whether the functions of the Security Council referred to in Article 83, paragraph 3, correspond only to the objectives mentioned in the first part of clause (*b*) of Article 76, or whether they correspond also to the second part: 'progressive development towards self-government or independence.' Since the latter is a 'political matter,' the answer may be in the affirmative; but since the wording of Article 83, paragraph 3, corresponds only to the wording of the first part of clause (*b*) of Article 76, the answer may be in the negative. In the first case the functions referred to in Article 83, paragraph 3, may be considered to be relating also to the objectives determined in clause (*c*) of Article 76: 'to encourage respect for human rights and for fundamental freedoms, etc.', but hardly to those determined in clauses (*a*) and (*d*). If the matters referred to in Article 83, paragraph 3, were identical with all the basic objectives set forth in Article 76, the wording of paragraph 3 of Article 83 should be: The Security Council shall, subject to . . . and without prejudice to security considerations, avail itself of the assistance of the Trusteeship Council to perform the functions referred to in paragraph 1 of this Article. The wording of paragraph 3 supports the interpretation that the functions of the Security Council referred to in that paragraph correspond only to some, not to all basic objectives. In performing the functions conferred upon it in relation to the objectives set forth in Article 76, clause (*b*), first part (or clauses (*b*) and (*c*)), the Security Council shall avail itself of the assistance of the Trusteeship Council. But, as pointed out, the Charter does not determine the actions to be taken by the Council in exercising these functions. The Security Council can exercise functions relating to the objectives set forth in Article 76 only if the trusteeship agreement concerning a strategic area confers upon it not only the function to pursue the basic objectives but also the power to take definite actions in order to exercise these functions, for instance, the power to take the actions which the General Assembly is authorised to take under Article 87.

This is possible although the Charter does not provide it. For the provisions of the Charter concerning the functions of the Organisation within the trusteeship system represent, as pointed out, only the minimum of competence the trusteeship agreement must confer upon the Organisation in order to be approved. The fact that the Charter provides the actions determined in Article 87 only for the General Assembly, not for the Security Council, has merely the consequence that a trusteeship agreement that does not confer upon the General Assembly the power to act in conformity with Article 87 must not be approved by the Assembly, while the Security Council, without violating the Charter, may approve a trusteeship agreement that does not confer upon it the power to perform the actions determined in Article 87 or any other actions to exercise functions relating to the objectives set forth in Article 76. If Article 83 in connection with Article 76 is interpreted to mean that the Charter confers upon the Security Council the function to pursue the objectives set forth in Article 76, with respect to strategic areas, and that means that the Security Council must not approve a trusteeship agreement which does not confer upon it this function, it is not very consistent to allow the Council to approve a trusteeship agreement which does not give it the necessary means to exercise this function.

The provision of Article 83, paragraph 3, that the Security Council shall avail itself of the assistance of the Trusteeship Council in performing the functions referred to in this paragraph, is subjected to an important restriction: 'without prejudice to security considerations.' According to the wording of this provision, the restriction refers to the Security Council's duty to avail itself of the assistance of the Trusteeship Council, not to the performance of the functions referred to in this paragraph; according to its wording, security considerations may justify the elimination of the Trusteeship Council from the functions of the Security Council referred to in this paragraph, but not restriction or exclusion of these functions. The provision of Article 83, paragraph 3, is expressly subjected 'to the provisions of the trusteeship agreements.' But even without this clause, the meaning of Article 83, paragraph 3—in accordance with the general rules laid down in Articles 77 (2) and 81—is that the Security Council may approve a trusteeship agreement concerning a strategic area in which the Security Council, on the ground of security considerations, is not allowed to avail itself of the assistance of the Trusteeship Council in the performance of its functions referred to in that paragraph. But the Security Council must not approve a trusteeship agreement concerning a strategic area in which—for security considerations—these functions are not conferred upon the Security Council.

It is rather strange that 'security considerations' in the administration of strategic areas are recognised by the Charter only with respect to the assistance of the Trusteeship Council. To designate a trust territory as a strategic area can hardly have another reason than 'security considerations.' This term is ambiguous. It may mean considerations of the collective security which under the Charter is to be administered by the Security Council; and it might be assumed that this was the reason why the supervision of the administration of strategic areas was conferred upon the Security Council. But the security considerations which justify the designation of a trust territory as strategic area may refer to the national security of the state exercising the function of an administering authority;[6] and it might be assumed that with regard to this national rather than collective security the distinction between strategic and non-strategic trust territories was made and the competence of the Security Council with respect to the former established. For if the Security Council is the supervising authority and the administering authority is a permanent member of the Security Council, it is in a much better position as to its own security than it would be as a member of the General Assembly; provided that the supervising authority were competent to make decisions binding upon the administering authority. But the Charter does not confer upon the Security Council or the General Assembly in their respective capacities as supervising authorities such a power. Hence the fact that permanent members of the Security Council have no veto right as members of the Trusteeship Council is no sufficient reason to restrict the Security Council in its right to avail itself of the assistance of the Trusteeship

[6] At the Hearing before the Committee on Foreign Relations of the United States Senate on July 7, 1947, the Chairman of the Committee asked: 'I would like to have your opinion as to whether there is anything in your opinion which in any degree handicaps or restrains our freedom of action in the use of these islands for security purposes.' The Secretary of State answered: 'I think the terms of the agreement have been so carefully drafted from the security point of view that there is no doubt in my mind that our security and our responsibility for general security are fully provided for. I refer the members of the committee to articles 3, 5 and 13, of the agreement. I believe all our interests are fully conserved.' Then the Chairman asked: 'So far as the use of these islands for security purposes is concerned, in what degree do we have less authority than we would have if we continued to run them the way they are being run now?' Whereupon the Secretary of State answered: 'I think under the terms of this trusteeship agreement we are not limited at all. I might put it this way: We must observe certain forms, but we have provisions in the agreement which allow us almost complete liberty of action.' The Chairman: 'So that you would say, as I understand you, that under the terms of the trusteeship agreement we have the same freedom of action on behalf of national security as we would have if we were continuing the administration of the islands under our present exclusive control?' The answer was: 'I think that is correct.' (Hearing before the Committee on Foreign Relations, United States Senate. Eightieth Congress, First Session on S.J. Res. 143. July 7, 1947, p. 5.)

Council. Security considerations would justify a restriction of the substantive functions of the Security Council in its capacity as supervising authority much more than they justify the elimination of the Trusteeship Council from these functions. Hence it may be doubted whether the phrase ' without prejudice to security considerations ' was not intended to refer also to the functions of the Security Council referred to in Article 83, paragraph 3, so that, contrary to the wording, security considerations may be the ground to exclude or restrict these functions. If this interpretation is accepted, the meaning of the formula ' functions of the United Nations under the trusteeship system relating to political, economic, social, and educational matters ' is of the greatest importance, and the question arises to what extent the basic objectives of the trusteeship system are actually applicable to strategic areas. If paragraph 3 of Article 83 would be interpreted to mean that security considerations justify not to confer, or to confer only under limitations, upon the Security Council in a trusteeship agreement concerning a strategic area the functions which correspond to the basic objectives set forth in Article 76, clause (*b*), first part, or even clauses (*b*) and (*c*), the said paragraph would constitute a remarkable restriction of paragraph 2 of Article 83, providing that the basic objectives are applicable to each strategic area. Then it would be difficult to understand why the phrase ' without prejudice to security considerations ' was not inserted in paragraph 2. That it was inserted in paragraph 3 is a strong argument against this interpretation and for the literal interpretation of paragraph 3, according to which this paragraph has no other intention but to permit the elimination of the Trusteeship Council from the functions referred to.[7]

[7] The trusteeship agreement designating the former Japanese mandated islands as a strategic area recognises in principle all basic objectives as obligations of the administering authority and even declares the provisions of Articles 87 and 88 of the Charter applicable to the trust territory (Article 13). But with respect to the obligation corresponding to the objective set forth in Article 76 (*d*) of the Charter, Article 8, paragraph 1, of the agreement, makes an exception, mentioned below, in favour of the administering authority. This exception is justified in the first sentence of Article 8, paragraph 1, as follows: ' In discharging its obligations under Article 76 (*d*) of the Charter, as defined by Article 83 (2) of the Charter, the administering authority, subject to the requirements of security, and the obligation to promote the advancement of the inhabitants, shall . . . ' In defending the exception against objections on the part of the delegate of the United Kingdom (cf. *infra*, p. 639), the delegate of the United States stated *inter alia*: ' The proposal made by my Government is for the designation of the former Japanese mandated islands as a strategic area. In such an area the security objective must be an overriding consideration.' (Official Records of the Security Council, 2nd Year, No. 31, p. 664.) The principle that security considerations are of decisive importance in strategic areas, is quite understandable, but, strange as it may be, it is not stipulated in the Charter. ' Security considerations ' are recognised only in Article 83, paragraph 3, and only in respect to the duty of the Security Council to avail itself of the assistance of the Trusteeship Council in the performance of certain functions determined in this paragraph. As pointed out, the function of the Organisation—and consequently also the obligation of the

As pointed out, the supervision of the trusteeship administration is exercised by actions of the Organisation determined—with respect to those within the competence of the General Assembly and the Trusteeship Council—by Articles 87 and 88 of the Charter. What is the nature of these actions relating to the administering authority? Do they have the character of mere recommendations or are the unilateral acts binding upon the administering authority? Chapters XII and XIII do not contain a provision referring to this question which can be answered only in accordance with the trusteeship agreement by which the respective competence is conferred upon the Organisation. The principle that the Assembly is competent only to make recommendations whereas the Security Council, under Article 25, has the power to adopt by majority vote decisions binding upon the Members, does not apply, because within the trusteeship system the Security Council has only the competences conferred upon it by the respective trusteeship agreements.[8]

administering authority—corresponding to the objective set forth in Article 76 (*d*) can hardly be considered as being among those referred to in Article 83, paragraph 3. As a matter of fact, the delegate of the United States did not refer to Article 83, paragraph 3, but to Article 76 (*d*) and Article 83, paragraph 2. Article 76 (*d*) contains the formula: 'without prejudice to the attainment of the foregoing objectives'; 'one of which is'—as the delegate of the United States emphasised—'the furtherance of international peace and security.' But the 'security' to which Article 76 (*a*) refers is international security, not the security of the trust territory and of the state exercising the function of administering authority, in whose favour the exception of Article 8, paragraph 1, of the trusteeship agreement is made. In Article 83, paragraph 2, there is no reference to security considerations. Cf. *infra*, p. 639.

8 The trusteeship agreements concerning British Togoland, British Cameroons, and Tanganyika contain in their Article 3 the provision that the Administering Authority 'undertakes to collaborate fully with the General Assembly of the United Nations and the Trusteeship Council in the discharge of all their functions as defined in Article 87 of the United Nations Charter, and to facilitate any periodic visits to . . . which they may deem necessary, at times to be agreed upon with the Administering Authority.' And in their Article 7: 'The Administering Authority undertakes to apply, in . . . the provisions of any international conventions and recommendations already existing or hereafter drawn up by the United Nations or by the specialised agencies referred to in Article 57 of the Charter, which may be appropriate to the particular circumstances of . . . and which would conduce to the achievement of the basic objectives of the international trusteeship system.'

The trusteeship agreements concerning French Togoland and the French Cameroons contain in their Article 2 the provision that the French Government undertakes 'to collaborate fully with the General Assembly and the Trusteeship Council in the discharge of their functions as defined in Articles 87 and 88 . . . ; To facilitate such periodic visits to . . . as the General Assembly or the Trusteeship Council may decide to arrange; to decide jointly with these bodies the dates on which such visits shall take place, and also to agree with them on all questions concerned with the organisation and accomplishment of these visits; To render general assistance to the General Assembly or to the Trusteeship Council in the application of these arrangements, and of such other arrangements as those bodies may make in accordance with the terms of the present Agreement.' Article 6 contains the provision that the administering authority undertakes to apply in the

(*f*) Obligations of Administration

(*aa*)—*Obligations of the administering authority under Chapter* XI

As to the obligations of the administering authority, the first question which arises is whether the obligations laid down in Chapter XI of the Charter with respect to non-self-governing territories are to be considered to be obligations of the authorities administering trust territories. The Charter does not contain an express provision concerning the relationship which exists between Chapter XI, that is

respective trust territories ' any conventions and recommendations made by the United Nations or the specialised agencies referred to in Article 57 of the Charter, the application of which would be in the interests of the population and consistent with the basic objectives of the trusteeship system and the terms of the present Agreement.'

The trusteeship agreement concerning Ruanda-Urundi contains in Article 3 the provision that the administering authority ' undertakes to collaborate fully with the General Assembly of the United Nations and with the Trusteeship Council in the discharge of all their functions as defined in Article 87 of the United Nations Charter.—It likewise undertakes to facilitate such periodic visits to the Trust Territory as the General Assembly or the Trusteeship Council may decide to arrange, to decide jointly with these organs the dates on which such visits shall take place and also to agree jointly with them on all questions concerned with the organisation and accomplishment of these visits.'

The trusteeship agreement concerning New Guinea contains in Article 8, the agreement for Nauru in Article 5, and the agreement for Western Samoa in Article 14 the provision that the administering authority ' will (shall) co-operate with the Trusteeship Council in the discharge of all the Council's functions under (in accordance with) Articles 87 and 88 of the Charter.' (The General Assembly is not mentioned.)

The trusteeship agreement for Western Samoa contains in Article 7 the provision that ' the Administering Authority undertakes to apply in Western Samoa the provisions of any international conventions and recommendations as drawn up by the United Nations or its specialised agencies which are, in the opinion of the Administering Authority, appropriate to the needs and conditions of the Trust Territory, and conducive to the achievement of the basic objectives of the international trusteeship system '; the trusteeship agreements for New Guinea (Article 6) and for Nauru (Article 6) contain analogous provisions.

The trusteeship agreement concerning the former Japanese mandated islands contains only, in Article 4, a general clause to the effect that ' The administering authority, in discharging the obligations of trusteeship in the Trust Territory, shall act in accordance with the Charter of the United Nations, and the provisions of this agreement,' and in Article 8 (4), the provision: ' The administering authority may negotiate and conclude commercial and other treaties and agreements with Members of the United Nations and other States, designed to attain for the inhabitants of the Trust Territory treatment by the Members of the United Nations and other States no less favourable than that granted by them to the nationals of other States. The Security Council may recommend, or invite other organs of the United Nations to consider and recommend, what rights the inhabitants of the trust territory should acquire in consideration of the rights obtained by Members of the United Nations in the Trust Territory.'

None of the trusteeship agreements establishes a strict obligation of the administering authority to comply with a unilateral decision of an organ of the United Nations.

the 'Declaration regarding Non-self-governing Territories,' and Chapters XII and XIII, dealing with the trusteeship system. The answer to the question as to the relationship between these two groups of norms must be found by an analysis of their contents. The provisions of Chapter XI refer to 'territories whose peoples have not yet attained a full measure of self-government' (Article 73). The territories to which the provisions of Chapters XII and XIII refer are not directly characterised by the Charter as non-self-governing territories. But, as pointed out, it may be concluded from the provisions of Article 76, clause (*b*), that only territories whose peoples have not yet attained 'self-government or independence' may be placed under the trusteeship system of the United Nations. And it may be assumed that when self-government or independence is granted to the people of a trust territory, the trusteeship status terminates.[9] Consequently all trust territories are 'non-self-governing' territories. From this point of view the provisions of Chapter XI refer also to trust territories.

The obligations laid down in Chapter XI are directly and unconditionally imposed upon the Members. They do not depend—as the obligations of authorities administering trust territories do—upon an agreement stipulating the obligations concerned. If the obligations laid down in Chapter XI are also obligations of the administering authorities of trust territories, they need not be stipulated in the trusteeship agreements.

The obligations laid down in Chapter XI are imposed only upon the Members of the United Nations (Articles 73, 74). Under Article 81, not only Member states but 'states' in general and the Organisation itself may become the administering authority of a trust territory. The question as to the obligations of the Organisation in its capacity as administrator of a trust territory shall be discussed later. To non-member states as administering authorities the obligations of the Members stipulated in Chapter XI do not apply, except they are considered to be extended to non-members by Article 2, paragraph 6.

The interpretation that the obligations laid down in Chapter XI are also obligations of Member states in their capacity as administering authorities of trust territories becomes questionable if the fact is taken into consideration that the content of the obligations stipulated in Article 73 is very similar to that of the 'objectives' of the trusteeship system, partly even literally identical. Thus, for instance, Article 73, clause (*c*) and Article 76, clause (*a*) ('to further international peace and security'). Article 73, clause (*a*) stipulates as an obligation of the Members 'to ensure, with due respect for the culture of the peoples concerned, their political, economic, social, and educational advancement . . .' Article 76, clause (*b*) determines as an objective of the trusteeship system 'to promote the political,

[9] Cf. *infra*, pp. 653 ff.

economic, social, and educational advancement of the inhabitants of the trust territories . . . ' But Article 73, clause (*a*) establishes the obligation to ensure 'just treatment' of the peoples concerned and 'their protection against abuses,' which is not declared in Article 76 as a basic objective of the trusteeship system. In so far as the 'obligations' established in Article 73 are substantially identical with the 'objectives' as laid down in Article 76, it may be argued that Article 76, but not Article 73, applies to the administering authorities of trust territories, since otherwise the formulation of the content of an obligation of Article 73 as an objective of Article 76 was superfluous. But if the obligations established in Article 73 go beyond the objectives laid down in Article 76, Article 73 might be interpreted to apply also to trust territories.[1] On the other hand, the content of some obligations established in Article 73 is not quite consistent with the content of some objectives laid down in Article 76. Thus Article 76, clause (*b*) establishes the objective 'to promote political, economic, social, and educational advancement, etc.,' under the condition that it 'may be provided by the terms of each trusteeship agreement,'[2] whereas Article 73, clause (*a*) stipulates the corre-

[1] Article 6 of the Trusteeship Agreement for Western Samoa is evidently not only in conformity with Article 76 (*b*) but also an implementation of the provision of Article 73 (*a*) of the Charter concerning abuses. It runs as follows:

> In pursuance of its undertakings to promote the social advancement of the inhabitants of the Trust Territory, and without in any way limiting its obligations thereunder, the Administering Authority shall:
>
> 1. Prohibit all forms of slavery and slave-trading;
> 2. Prohibit all forms of forced or compulsory labour, except for essential public works and services as specifically authorised by the local administration and then only in times of public emergency, with adequate remuneration and adequate protection of the welfare of the workers;
> 3. Control the traffic in arms and ammunition;
> 4. Control, in the interest of the inhabitants, the manufacture, importation and distribution of intoxicating spirits and beverages; and
> 5. Control the production, importation, manufacture, and distribution of opium and narcotic drugs.

[2] At the 13th meeting of Committee II/4 (U.N.C.I.O. Doc. 877, II/4/35), 'The Delegate for Egypt moved that the words at the end of sub-paragraph (*b*) [Article 76, clause (*b*)] "and as may be provided by the trusteeship arrangement" be deleted. In favour of the motion, it was said that retention of the words in question would detract from the value of the insertion of the word "independence"; and that the decision whether a given territory should be eligible for self-government only or for independence should be determined not at the time of the conclusion of the trusteeship arrangement but at a later period in accordance with the development of the territory. Against the motion, it was asserted that the language in question implemented rather than qualified the reference to "self-government or independence"; and was a recognition of the individuality of each territory to be placed under trusteeship. Some of these territories would evidently be eligible for independence while others evidently would not. The trusteeship arrangements would necessarily have to be adjusted to fit the needs of each territory. The Committee decided to retain the words "and as may be provided by the trusteeship arrangement" by a vote of 35 in favour and 3 against.'

sponding obligation unconditionally. In case of trust territories, only Article 76, clause (*b*)—not Article 73, clause (*a*)—does apply as far as the two provisions refer to the same matter. Article 73, clause (*b*) stipulates unconditionally as an obligation of Members: 'to develop self-government, to take due account of the political aspirations of the peoples, and to assist them in the progressive development of their free political institutions, according to the particular circumstances of each territory and its peoples and their varying stages of advancement.' Article 76, clause (*b*), however, declares as an objective of the trusteeship system 'as may be provided by the terms of each trusteeship agreement,': 'to promote . . . their [inhabitants of the trust territories] progressive development towards self-government *or independence*, as may be appropriate to the particular circumstances of each territory and its peoples and the free expressed wishes of the peoples concerned . . .' It is an unconditional obligation of Members which have or assume responsibility for the administration of territories referred to in Article 73 'to develop self -government.' But it is a conditional objective of the trusteeship system to promote 'development towards self-government *or independence*.' The—conditional—'objectives' of Article 76 obviously go much farther than the—unconditional—'obligations' of Article 73. In so far as the content of the 'obligations' differs from that of the 'objectives,' it must be argued that only Article 76, not Article 73, applies to powers which assume responsibility for the administration of trust territories.

There is one obligation stipulated in Article 73, clause (*e*) which is expressly restricted to non-trust territories: it is the obligation to transmit regularly to the Secretary-General certain information relating to economic, social, and educational conditions in the territories 'other than those territories to which Chapters XII and XIII apply.' Since the obligation established in Article 73 (*e*) is expressly restricted to non-trust territories, it might be concluded by *argumentum a contrario* that the obligations stipulated in clauses (*a*) to (*d*), not expressly restricted to non-trust territories, apply also to the administering authorities of trust areas unless the provisions of Chapters XII and XIII differ from those of Chapter XI. But the *argumentum a contrario* does not absolutely exclude another interpretation, especially if the latter is justifiable by the reasons presented above. With respect to the relationship between Chapter XI and Chapters XII and XIII the text of the Charter is highly ambiguous.[3]

[3] During the discussion of the Working Paper in the 6th meeting of Committee II/4 (U.N.C.I.O. Doc. 404, II/4/17) it was suggested that 'since Section A of the Working Paper (corresponding to Chapter XI) applies to all dependent territories and not merely to those placed under trusteeship' a certain amendment should more properly be placed in Section B instead of Section A. In its report to the General Assembly of December 12, 1946 (Doc. A/258, p. 4 f.), the Fourth Committee included the following statements, made in the deliberations of the

(bb)—Obligations of the administering authority under Article 76

In stipulating the basic objectives of the trusteeship system, the Charter may intend to establish principles determining the activity of the

sub-committee appointed to examine the trusteeship agreements submitted to the Assembly for approval: ' The Sub-Committee was in unanimous agreement with the view expressed by the Delegation of the Netherlands that the principle set forth in Article 73 of the Charter of the United Nations that the interests of the inhabitants of the Non-Self-Governing Territories are paramount, and the general obligations accepted in Articles 73 and 74 of the Charter, apply also to the Trust Territories, due account being given to the terms of the Trusteeship agreements and the different status of the two categories of Non-Self-Governing Territories.' At the 113th meeting of the Security Council the delegate of the United States declared with respect to the trusteeship agreement for the former Japanese mandated islands which the Government of the United States submitted to the Security Council for approval: ' In preparing this draft trusteeship agreement, the Government of the United States bore constantly in mind Article 73 of the Charter.' After quoting the first sentence of this Article, he declared: ' the United States Government believes that the draft trusteeship agreement now before you conforms fully to this principle in its provisions for the political, economic, social and educational advancement of the inhabitants of the trust territory.' (Official Records of the Security Council, 2nd Year, No. 20, p. 411 f.) ' To promote the political, economic, social, and educational advancement of the inhabitants of the trust territory ' is an objective of the trusteeship system expressly set forth in Article 76 (b). It is to this Article that the respective provisions of the trusteeship agreement (Article 6) refer, not to Article 73. Article 73 (*a*) reads: ' to ensure, with due respect for the culture of the peoples concerned, their political, economic, social, and educational advancement . . . ' Although the provisions of Chapter XI—if they apply to trust territories—are binding upon the administering authority even without being adopted in the trusteeship agreement, some of the agreements approved by the General Assembly contain express stipulation of obligations established by Artilce 73. Thus for instance, the trusteeship agreement concerning Western Samoa provides in its Article 5: ' The Administering Authority shall promote the development of free political institutions suited to Western Samoa,' which corresponds to Article 73 (*b*) ' . . . to assist them in the progressive development of their free political institutions, according to the particular circumstances of each territory and its peoples and their varying stages of advancement '—a provision to which nothing in Article 76 corresponds; and in Article 6 the Agreement stipulates: ' the Administering Authority shall: (1) Prohibit all forms of slavery and slave-trading; (2) Prohibit all forms of forced or compulsory labour, except for essential public works and services as specifically authorised by the local administration and then only in times of public emergency, with adequate remuneration and adequate protection of the welfare of the workers; (3) Control the traffic in arms and ammunition; (4) Control, in the interest of the inhabitants, the manufacture, importation and distribution of intoxicating spirits and beverages; and (5) Control the production, importation, manufacture, and distribution of opium and narcotic drugs.' This Article corresponds to Article 73 (*a*) of the Charter: ' to ensure . . . their protection against abuses,' which has no counterpart in Article 76. During the discussion of the draft trusteeship agreement for Western Samoa, the representative of the United Kingdom ' while agreeing that the obligations of Chapter XI applied to Trust Territories, observed that since Chapters XII and XIII were a self-contained unit, there would be an advantage in not referring, in the draft agreement, to Articles 73 and 74 of the Charter. Since the draft agreement did not conflict with the Charter, it was not necessary to confirm, in the text, obligations to which all Members of the United Nations had

Organisation as supervisor and of the states as administering authorities. That means that the ' objectives ' imply—in relation to the administering authorities—obligations. It should be pointed out, however, that this is not the only possible interpretation. It may be argued that the Charter in using the term ' objectives,' instead of ' obligations ' as used in Chapter XI, does not intend to prevent the Organisation from approving a trusteeship agreement which does not impose upon the administering authority the obligation to act in conformity with the ' objectives.' Against such interpretation it may be argued that the Charter expressly stipulates obligations of the administering authority only in Article 88, providing that annual reports shall be made on the basis of the questionnaires formulated by the Trusteeship Council, and in Article 84, providing that the trust territory shall play its part in the maintenance of international peace. If there shall be other and more important obligations, the objectives set forth in Article 76 must be interpreted to imply not only functions of the Organisation but also obligations of the administering authorities. Hence Article 83, paragraph 2, providing that the basic objectives shall be applicable to the people of each strategic area, stipulates also obligations of the administering authorities of the strategic areas.[4] As pointed out in discussing the question as to whether the objectives of Article 76 imply functions of the Organisation, there is no provision analogous to that of Article 83, paragraph 2, with respect to the non-strategic areas. If in setting forth basic objectives of the trusteeship system the Charter intends to establish not only functions of the Organisation but also obligations of the administering authorities, a special provision to the effect that the basic objectives are applicable to the trust territories is superfluous. If the basic objectives laid down in Article 76 imply obligations of the administering authorities, not only the Security Council but also the General Assembly must not, within their respective competence, approve a trusteeship agreement, which does not impose upon the administering authority all the obligations which correspond to the basic objectives of the trusteeship system. As a matter of fact, all trusteeship agreements until now approved by the Organisation establish obligations of the administering authorities corresponding to all basic objectives set forth in Article 76.[5]

already subscribed.' And the representative of Belguim declared that ' to include specific mention of Chapter XI in the draft agreement would imply that Chapter XI did not of itself have binding force. Furthermore, a reference to part of Chapter XI would weaken the effect of the remainder.' (Summary Records of Meetings of Sub-committee 1, November 15–December 10, 1946, p. 47 f.)

[4] Article 4 of the Trusteeship Agreement for the former Japanese mandated islands, designated as strategic area, expressly stipulates the obligation of the administering authority to ' apply the objectives of the international trusteeship system, as set forth in Article 76 of the Charter, to the people of the trust terirtory.'

[5] Cf. *supra*, p. 629. All trusteeship agreements contain a general provision that the administering authority undertakes to administer the trust territory in such a manner as to achieve the basic objectives set forth in Article 76; the trusteeship

Not all obligations implied in the ' basic objectives of the trusteeship system ' laid down in Article 76 are specific obligations of states administering a trust territory; and not all of them are obligations the administering authority has in relation to the inhabitants of the trust territory. The objective formulated in clause (*a*) ' to further international peace and security ' constitutes an extension of the purpose of the United Nations—determined in Article 1, paragraph 1: ' to maintain international peace and security '—to the trust territories and, in so far as this objective implies an obligation of the administering authority, an extension of the provisions of Article 2, paragraphs 3 and 4 and Chapter VI to the states in their capacity as administering authorities.

agreement for Western Samoa repeats in addition to this provision—in Article 4—the text of the clauses *a* to *d* of Article 76 of the Charter. The trusteeship agreement concerning the former Japanese mandated islands devotes four separate Articles (5 to 8), each for the stipulation of an obligation corresponding to the four clauses of Article 76 respectively.

The trusteeship agreement for New Guinea stipulates in Article 3 that the administering authority shall administer the territory ' in such a manner as to achieve in the Territory the basic objectives of the international trusteeship system, which are set forth in Article 76 of the Charter '; and in Article 8, that the administering authority shall

(*a*) take into consideration the customs and usages of the inhabitants of New Guinea and respect the rights and safeguard the interests, both present and future, of the indigenous inhabitants of the Territory; and in particular ensure that no rights over native land in favour of any person not an indigenous inhabitant of New Guinea may be created or transferred except with the consent of the competent public authority;

(*b*) promote, as may be appropriate to the circumstances of the Territory, the educational and cultural advancement of the inhabitants;

(*c*) assure to the inhabitants of the Territory, as may be appropriate to the particular circumstances of the Territory and its peoples, a progressively increasing share in the administrative and other services of the Territory;

(*d*) guarantee to the inhabitants of the Territory, subject only to the requirements of public order, freedom of speech, of the press, of assembly and of petition, freedom of conscience and worship and freedom of religious teaching.

Clause *a* has no equivalent in Article 76 of the Charter; clauses *b* and *c* correspond, by and large, to clause *b* of Article 76; clause *d* specifies only the provision of Article 76 (*c*) concerning ' fundamental freedoms,' but with a restriction not contained in Article 76 (*c*): subject to ' the requirements of public order,' and without using the formula contained in Article 76 (*c*): ' without distinction as to race, sex, language, or religion.' In so far as Article 8 of the trusteeship agreement lags behind Article 76 of the Charter, its provisions are of no legal importance, since Article 3 of the agreement recognises Article 76 of the Charter as binding upon the administering authority.

The trusteeship agreement for Nauru contains in Articles 3 and 5 provisions identical with those of Articles 3 and 8 of the agreement for New Guinea. The only difference is that clause *c* of Article 5 (corresponding to clause *c* of Article 8 of the agreement for New Guinea) contains the additional provision: ' and take all appropriate measures with a view to the political advancement of the inhabitants in accordance with Article 76 *b* of the Charter.'

The objective laid down in clause (*c*) (first sentence) ' to encourage respect for human rights, etc.' applies, it is true, to the people of the trust territory. But this objective is identical with the principle laid down in Article 1, paragraph 3 (second part) and applicable to the peoples of all states Members of the United Nations. This objective seems not to imply an obligation of the administering authority, but only a function of the Organisation. For the duty of the administering authority cannot be ' to encourage ' respect for human rights, but to establish and then to respect in its administration the human rights of the inhabitants. The Organisation may encourage respect for human rights by not approving a trusteeship agreement which does not impose this obligation upon the administering authority. But the approval of a trusteeship agreement which does not impose upon the administering authority a strict obligation to confer upon the inhabitants definite human rights and fundamental freedoms, is not unconstitutional, no such obligation being imposed by the Charter upon the Members in relation to the inhabitants of the metropolitan areas. The second sentence of Article 76 (*c*) ' to encourage recognition of the interdependence of the peoples of the world,' is a very vague formula without any legal importance. The objective laid down in clause (*d*) implies, it is true, a specific obligation of states administering trust territories; but it is an obligation towards other states, Members of the United Nations, and their nationals, not an obligation towards the inhabitants of the trust territory. The content of the obligation to ' ensure equal treatment in social, economic and commercial matters for all Members of the United Nations and their nationals ' is not very clear. The formula allows contradictory answers to important questions, such as the admissibility of monopolies.[6] Its value is also

[6] The trusteeship agreements submitted by Great Britain and Belgium contain provisions according to which the administering authority shall be free ' to creat monopolies of a purely fiscal character in order to provide . . . [the trust territory] with the fiscal resources which seem best suited to local requirements, or otherwise to serve the interests of the inhabitants of ' the trust territory, and, where interests of the economic advancement of the inhabitants of the trust territories may require, ' to establish, or permit to be established, for specific purposes, other monopolies or undertakings having in them an element of monopoly, under conditions of proper public control; provided that, in the selection of agencies to carry out the purposes of this paragraph, other than agencies controlled by the Government or those in which the Government participates, the Administering Authority shall not discriminate on grounds of nationality against Members of the United Nations or their nationals.' (Article 10 of the Trusteeship Agreements for Tanganyika, British Cameroons, British Togoland, Ruanda-Urundi). A report to the Fourth Committee (Doc. A/258, p. 6) contains the following statement: ' With regard to the provisions in the draft Trusteeship agreements concerning equality for Members of the United Nations in economic matters, it was the view of the sub-committee that the Trusteeship Council should watch year by year the grant of any monopolies, other than those controlled by the Government or in which the Government participates, with a view to ensuring their compatibility with Article 76, and, if necessary, in the light of changing circumstances and practical

impaired by the restriction 'without prejudice to the attainment of the foregoing objectives.' Referring to the objectives laid down in clauses (*a*) and (*b*), a trusteeship agreement may establish privileges of the state administering the trust territory and of its nationals, and such agreement may be approved by the Organisation without violating the Charter.[7]

The only obligations implied in the 'basic objectives' which are specific trusteeship obligations of the administering authorities and at the same time obligations towards the inhabitants of the trust territory are those stipulated in clause (*b*). This clause establishes two obligations: first, to 'promote the political, economic, social, and educational advancement of the inhabitants of the trust territories'; and, second, to promote 'their progressive development towards self-government or independence.' The second obligation may be considered to be only a specification of the first one, since promoting

experience,should formulate its views on the conditions under which such rights should be granted. In this connection the sub-committee was invited by the Delegations of Belguim and the United Kingdom to take notice of the following declaration of the intentions of their two Governments: (*a*) The Governments of Belgium and the United Kingdom have no intention of using the grant of private monopolies in Trust Territories as a normal instrument of policy; (*b*) Such private monopolies would be granted only when this was essential in order to enable a particular type of desirable economic development to be undertaken in the interest of the inhabitants; (*c*) In those special cases where such private monopolies were granted they would be granted for limited periods, and would be promptly reported to the Trusteeship Council.'

[7] The trusteeship agreement for the former Japanese mandated islands designating the United States of America as the administering authority contains in Article 8 the provision that the administering authority 'shall accord to nationals of each Member of the United Nations and to companies and associations organised in conformity with the laws of such Member, treatment in the Trust Territory no less favourable than that accorded therein to nationals, companies and associations of any other United Nation except the administering authority.' At the 124th meeting of the Security Council the delegate of the United Kingdom suggested the omission of the last words 'except the administering authority.' He stated: 'These words would seem to give a preferential position to the United States, which does not seem to be in strict accordance with Articles 83, paragraph 2, and 76 (*d*) of the Charter. From these two Articles, taken in conjunction, it is clear that, according to the Charter, there should be equal treatment in social, economic, and commercial matters for all Members of the United Nations and their nationals in the strategic area as in any other territory under trusteeship. Article 76 enumerates the basic objectives of the Trusteeship System, and paragraph *d* thereof says: "to ensure equal treatment in social, economic, and commercial matters for all Members of the United Nations and their nationals . . .'" The delegate of the United States rejected the suggestion referring, *inter alia*, to the phrase of Article 76 (*d*) 'without prejudice to the attainment of the foregoing objectives.' (Official Records of the Security Council, 2nd Year, No. 31, pp. 644 ff.) He also argued: 'Article 83, paragraph 2, provides for the manner in which Article 76 shall be carried out in a strategic area by stating that the provisions of Article 76 shall be applicable to the people of the Territory rather than to the people outside' (p. 665). Cf. also Summary Record of Meetings of Fourth Committee, November 1–December 12, 1946, pp. 263 ff., 299 ff.

'the political advancement' implies promoting 'progressive development towards self-government or independence.' The latter obligation is restricted by the clause 'as may be appropriate to the particular circumstances of each territory and its peoples.' (Whether this clause refers also to the first obligation is doubtful.) The 'particular circumstances' may justify to grant to the people of the trust territory only self-government, not independence. The wording 'self-government *or* independence should not be ignored.[8] To decide whether such circumstances exist and to what extent they prevent or retard the development towards self-government or independence is within the competence of the administering authority, which in this respect is also under the obligation: to afford the people of the trust territory opportunity to express freely its wishes with respect to the development towards self-government or independence. Since the basic objectives imply also functions of the Organisation, the administering authority, in fulfilling its obligation stipulated by clause (*b*) of Article 76 and especially its obligation to promote development towards self-government or independence as may be appropriate to the circumstances, is under the supervision of the General Assembly or the Security Council How this function is to be exercised has been discussed in connection with the functions of the Organisation.

The obligation—or, at least the second obligation—implied in the objectives set forth in Article 76, clause (*b*), is expressly conditioned by the phrase 'as may be provided by the terms of each trusteeship agreement.' Since the obligations of the administering authority are, just as the functions of the Organisation, an essential element of the terms of upon which a territory is brought under the trusteeship system and the terms upon which it is to be administered, all obligations of the administering authority must be stipulated in the trusteeship agreement according to the general rules laid down in Articles 77 (2) and 81. What has been said in this respect of the functions of the Organisation applies also to the obligations of the administering authorities. The obligations directly determined in the Charter are mandatory, that is to say, a trusteeship agreement which does not stipulate these obligations must not be approved by the Organisation; yet the agreement may impose upon the administering authority obligations in addition to those expressly stipulated by the Charter.[9]

[8] At the 20th meeting of the Fourth Committee of the General Assembly the delegate of Syria stated: 'The Charter envisaged no solution other than trusteeship and later independence.' (Journal of the United Nations, No. 34: Suppl. No. 4–A/C. 4/61, p. 64). In view of the wording of Article 76 (*b*): 'self-government *or* independence' this statement is not correct.

[9] The trusteeship agreements which contain a general clause to the effect that the administration of the trust territory shall be carried out in conformity with the Charter (cf. *supra*, p. 614), thereby adopt not only the provisions of the Charter concerning the functions of the Organisation but also those concerning the obligations of the administering authority. These agreements contain also express

(*cc*)—*Other Obligations of the Administering Authority*

Apart from Article 76, there are other provisions which establish, directly or indirectly, obligations of the administering authorities. Article 84 provides:

> It shall be the duty of the administering authority to ensure that the trust territory shall play its part in the maintenance of international peace and security. To this end the administering authority may make use of volunteer forces, facilities, and assistance from the trust territory in carrying out the obligations towards the Security Council undertaken in this regard by the administering authority, as well as for local defence and the maintenance of law and order within the trust territory.

The wording of the first sentence, establishing an obligation of the administering authority for each trust territory, is very vague: 'the trust territory shall play its part in the maintenance of international peace and security.' What part? This provision requires specification. This seems to be the purpose of the second sentence. This sentence, however, is not formulated in terms of obligation but in terms of right or power: 'the administering authority *may* make use, etc.' To fulfil its duty stipulated in the first sentence, the administering authority is authorised—not obliged—to make use of volunteer forces,

provisions imposing upon the administering authority particular obligations as determined in the Charter. The other agreements contain only provisions of the second kind. Some agreements, but not all, stipulate obligations determined by the Rules of Procedure for the Trusteeship Council, but not stipulated in the Charter. Thus Article 2 of the trusteeship agreements for French Togoland and for the French Cameroons stipulates: 'The French Government undertakes . . . to appoint a representative and, where necessary, qualified experts to attend the meetings of the Trusteeship Council or of the General Assembly at which the said [annual] reports . . . will be examined'; and 'to appoint a representative and, when necessary, qualified experts to participate, in consultation with the General Assembly or the Trusteeship Council, in the examination of petitions received by these bodies.' These provisions refer to Rules 74 and 75 of the Rules of Procedure for the Trusteeship Council concerning the examination of the annual reports, and to Rule 92 concerning petitions. The trusteeship agreements for British Togoland, the British Cameroons and Tanganyika contain only (in Article 16) the provision: 'The administering authority shall designate an accredited representative to be present at the sessions of the Trusteeship Council at which the reports of the administering authority with regard to . . . are considered.' The trusteeship agreements for Ruanda-Urundi (Article 16) and for Western Samoa (Article 14) contain the same provision.

Some trusteeship agreements impose upon the administering authority obligations not stipulated in the Charter or the Rules of Procedure. Thus all agreements, except those for New Guinea, Nauru, and for the former Japanese mandated islands, provide that disputes between the administering authority and another Member of the United Nations relating to the interpretation or the application of the trusteeship agreement, if they cannot be settled by negotiation or other means, shall be submitted to the International Court of Justice. Cf. *supra*, pp. 519 f.

facilities, and assistance from the trust territory. As far as ' volunteer ' forces from the trust territory are concerned, the administering authority can hardly be under an obligation to make use of them. For the fulfilment of such obligation would depend on the fact that there are ' volunteers '; and if there are not volunteers the obligation cannot be fulfilled. But it would be quite possible to impose upon the administering authority the obligation to make use of the ' facilities, and assistance from the trust territory.' If this is intended by Article 84, why is it stipulated that the administering authority ' may ' make use of them? Does the phrase ' the administering authority may make use of volunteer forces . . . from the trust territory ' mean that the administering authority is not allowed to establish compulsory military service in the trust territory, and that a trusteeship agreement which does not impose upon the administering authority the prohibition to establish compulsory military service, must not be approved by the Organisation? This is probably the intention of Article 84. If so, why does the second sentence of Article 84 not read as follows: To this end the administering authority shall make use of the facilities and assistance, but only of volunteer forces from the trust territory? If, however, the second sentence of Article 84 means only that the administering authority is authorised, but not obliged, to use the trust territory and its inhabitants for military purposes, how can—in the first sentence—a ' duty ' be imposed upon the administering authority to ensure that ' the trust territory ' shall play its part in the maintenance of international peace and security?

The second sentence of Article 84 begins with the words ' To this end.' These words refer to the ' duty ' imposed upon the administering authority in the first sentence ' to ensure that the trust territory shall play its part in the maintenance of international peace and security.' In order to fulfil this duty the latter ' may make use, etc.' However, the second sentence continues, ' in carrying out the obligations towards the Security Council undertaken in this regard by the administering authority, etc.' What is the relation between the ' duty ' imposed upon the administering authority in the first sentence and the ' obligations ' towards the Security Council referred to in the second sentence? To what obligations does this sentence refer? The ' duty ' stipulated in the first sentence is not necessarily an obligation towards the Security Council. The use, in the second sentence, of the words ' forces, facilities and assistance ' allows the assumption that this sentence refers to the obligation established by Article 43 of the Charter which provides that the Members, ' in order to contribute to the maintenance of international peace and security,' shall ' make available to the Security Council, on its call and in accordance with a special agreement or agreements, armed forces, assistance, and facilities . . . ' If this interpretation is accepted, Article 84 means that the administering authority, as a Member of the United Nations, shall fulfil its obligation under Article 43 not only by making available to the Security Council armed forces, assistance, and facilities from its metropolitan area but also from the trust territory, but—as far as the ' forces ' are concerned, only ' volunteer forces ' shall be used. However, since Article 43 is not expressly referred to, the sentence ' in carrying out the obligations towards the Security Council ' might be interpreted to refer to other obligations which the administering authority of a strategic area has towards the Security Council, provided that the trusteeship agreement stipulates such obligations.[1] In favour of such interpretation it might be argued that the use of the trust territory and its inhabitants for military purposes is justifiable only if the territory has a strategic character and hence falls under the jurisdiction of the Security Council. And, further, that the ' obligations towards the Security Council ' mentioned in Article 84 could not be the obligations under Article 43 because Article 84 speaks of obligations ' undertaken . . . by the administering authority.' The obligations under Article 43 are not undertaken by the administering authority, but by states in their capacity as Members of the United Nations, not in their capacity as administering authorities within the trusteeship system. Obligations undertaken by administering authorities towards the Security Council could only be obligations with respect to strategic trust territories. Consequently only an administering authority which is a Member of the United Nations could have the duty to ensure that the trust territory shall play its part in the maintenance of international peace and security by making use of volunteer forces, facilities, and assistance from the trust territory in carrying out the obligations towards the Security Council. If the administering authority is not a Member, if it is the Organisation itself or a non-member, there are no ' obligations towards the Security Council ' under Article 43.

This interpretation, although not excluded by the wording of Article 84, does hardly correspond to the intention of those who drafted the Charter. Article 84 provides that all trust territories shall play their part in the maintenance of peace, and that to this end all administering authorities may carry out their duties towards the

[1] This interpretation of Article 84 was advocated by the representative of the Soviet Union who at the 9th meeting of sub-committee 1 of the Fourth Committee stated with reference to the words ' obligations to the Security Council ' in Article 84: ' In the Soviet view, those " obligations " could refer only to the designation of strategic areas under Articles 82 and 83 of the Charter . . ' He declared that the authority to establish military bases in a trust-territory ' could be derived only from the reference in Article 84 to " obligations towards the Security Council,' " which—according to his view—were obligations of an administering authority of a strategic trust-territory. (Summary Records of (Summary Records of Meetings of Sub-Committee 1, November 15–December 10, 1946, p. 60)

Security Council by making use of the territory and its inhabitants. If this were possible only in case the territory is a strategic area, all trust territories would have to be established as strategic areas. This is evidently not the intention of the Charter. Hence the interpretation according to which the phrase 'obligations towards the Security Council' refers to the obligations under Article 43, may be considered as the most plausible one. That means that the duty established by Article 84 to ensure that the trust territory shall play its part in the maintenance of international peace and security can be fulfilled only within the obligation a Member has towards the Security Council under Article 43 of the Charter. Since this obligation is specified by the special agreement to which Article 43 refers, and since this Article provides that the agreement 'shall govern the number and types of forces, their degree of readiness and general location, and the nature of the facilities and assistance to be provided,' it is not impossible to argue that the special agreement which a Member state administering a trust territory concludes with the United Nations under Article 43, shall govern also the voluntary forces, facilities and assistance from the trust territory referred to in Article 84. Consequently only an administrating authority which is a Member of the United Nations, neither a non-member nor the Organisation itself as administering authority, can be under the duty established by Article 84.

As all obligations of the administering authority, also the obligation laid down in the first sentence of Article 84 must be stipulated in the trusteeship agreement, it must be stipulated whether the trusteeship agreement concerns a non-strategic or a strategic area. With respect to the fulfilment of this duty of the administering authority, also non-strategic areas are within the jurisdiction of the Security Council. The obligations must be carried out towards the Security Council. Yet the Council does not act in its capacity as supervisor within the trusteeship system, but as authority within the general system of collective security of the Charter.[2]

[2] The memorandum prepared by the Secretariat on the Question of Fortifications and Volunteer Forces in Trust Territories (Article 84) contains the following extracts of the Verbatim Records of the 10th meeting of Committee II/4 of the San Francisco Conference (not published in the Records of this meeting: U.N.C.I.O. Doc. 580, II/4/24), referring to Section B (9) of the Working Paper, Corresponding to Article 84 of the Charter. The delegate of the United States declared: 'I think it is very clear but I might point out specifically that, from some of the earlier discussions, we have here before us in the Paper the very specific provision that it must be volunteer forces, for one thing; in the second instance, that the purpose must be either (1) to carry out obligations undertaken by the state for the Security Council—and you are all familiar with the clauses under which each state makes certain agreements to the Security Council to carry out its obligations; (2) for local defense; or (3) for law and order within the territory. Those are the three purposes and, in any event, for any of the three purposes it must be volunteer forces.' The delegate of Egypt suggested that the phrase in the Working Paper

According to the wording of Article 84, the administering authority—to the end of fulfilling its duty to ensure that the trust territory shall play its part in the maintenance of international peace

B (9): ' To this end the state shall be empowered to make use of volunteer forces, facilities and assistance from the territory, etc.' be amended by the instertion of the words ' under the control of the Security Council " following the word ' empowered.' In introducing this amendment, the Egyptian representative declared: ' The first part of this paragraph recognises the duty of the state administering any trusteeship; the second part empowers that state with certain powers but these powers, according to this paragraph, seem to be absolutely without any control or restriction whatsoever. If the first part relating to these powers is to make use of volunteer forces—and that is a limitation, that there would be no compulsory service—then the second part relating to facilities and assistance can only be determined by the state administering the territory itself. It is in view of not recognising an absolute right to the state administering the territory that there should be an addition. These powers relating to facilities and assistance should not be within the exclusive jurisdiction of the state administering the territory. There should be some control on the state by the Security Council because these facilities and assistance can only be decided on by the territory itself or its population—it does amount to the exercise of some administrative authority in the territory and this administrative authority can only be exercised by the state administering the territory. " Volunteer forces " is quite understandable by itself because no forces can be taken by compulsory service. That would result from the word " volunteer." But these facilities and assistance by the government can only be decided by the state which exercises administration in the trust territory. In order that its power shall not be absolute, I submit that there should be added " under the control of the Security Council." '

In reply to the Egyptian statement, the delegate for the United States made a statement as follows: ' I think he is bringing the Security Council in a place which no one in this Conference has suggested that it should be in and would want it to be in. He is bringing the Security Council in in the matter of local defence and the maintenance of law and order within the territory, whereas it is the function of the Security Council to maintain international peace and security and not to get drawn into the policing job within a territory. There are three parts, as I explained. One part is to carry out the obligation for the Security Council and that is definitely under the Security Council now. The second part is for local defence and that does not come under the Security Council and should not come under it. The third part is the law and order within the territory, the policing function, and that should not be the job of the Security Council, but in all of these things it is all supervised by either one or the other of the bodies of our Organisation. It is either under the Security Council if it affects international peace and security or under the Assembly if it is a matter that affects the territory and properly comes under the Assembly or under the Trusteeship Council acting for the Assembly. One or the other of those three bodies is always supervising and there is no gap in between. This amendment would tend to make it only the Security Council that would come in and take away part of the jurisdiction of the Assembly and a part of the jurisdiction of the Trusteeship Council, which I do not feel it is wise to do, and I think that the way it is worded here with the obligations for international peace and security under the Security Council and the other two left as described in 10 (paragraph 10 of the Working Paper) for the General Assembly and the Trusteeship Council. I really believe it is the wisest division of supervision and authority and we should not take that power away from the Assembly and the Trusteeship Council and give it to the Security Council.' The proposed Egyptian amendment was defeated. (Doc. A/C. 4/40. p. 4 ff.)

and security—may make use of volunteer forces, facilities, and assistance from the trust territory not only in carrying out the obligations towards the Security Council, but also ' for local defence and the maintenance of law and order within the trust territory.' It may be doubted that ' maintenance of law and order within the trust territory ' is essentially connected with the maintenance of ' international ' peace and security, and that to maintain law and order within the trust territory, not only the use of voluntary forces but also the use of ' facilities and assistance,' provided for in Article 43 relating to a military action of the Organisation, is necessary. The probable meaning of the last sentence of Article 84 is that the administering authority ' shall ' make use only of voluntary forces from the trust territory, and shall make use of these forces and of facilities and assistance from the trust territory only for the purpose of fulfilling its obligations towards the Security Council under Article 43, or for the purpose of local defence and the maintenance of law and order within the trust territory. The words ' for local defence ' seem to mean that the use of volunteer forces, etc., referred to in this Article, on the part of the administering authority for the defence of the metropolitan territory (except in fulfilment of obligations towards the Security Council) is prohibited. That is to say that, if the trusteeship agreement does not contain this restriction, it must not be approved by the Organisation.

Article 84 of the Charter constitutes a remarkable difference as compared with Article 22 of the Covenant which stipulated in paragraph 5 (relating to so-called B Mandates) that the mandated territory shall be administered under conditions which will guarantee, among others, ' the prevention of the establishment of fortifications or military and naval bases and of military training of the natives for other than police purposes and the defence of the territory.' Neither Article 84 nor any other Article of the Charter prohibits establishment of fortifications or military and naval bases, or stationing and employing of military forces, recruited from the metropolitan area of the administering authority, on the trust territory; the duty of the administering authority stipulated in Article 84, ' to ensure that the trust territory shall play its part in the maintenance of international peace and security ' at least implies this possibility; and this possibility is not restricted by the provision of Article 84 that ' the administering authority may make use of volunteer forces, facilities, and assistance from the trust territory in carrying out the obligations towards the Security Council,' in strategic areas. Such restriction could be assumed only if the phrase ' in carrying out the obligations towards the Security Council ' were interpreted to refer to obligations of the administering authority of a strategic area which, as pointed out, is not in conformity with the intention of the Charter. Nothing in the Charter prevents the administering authority from using and training native military forces—if voluntary—not only for internal purposes of the trust territory but also in the service of collective security. That means that trusteeship agreements stipulating these powers of the administering authority or not excluding them—whether with respect to strategic or non-strategic areas—may be approved by the Organisation in conformity with the Charter.[3]

[3] As a matter of fact, all trusteeship agreements approved by the Organisation contain such provisions. Thus, for instance, Article 5 of the trusteeship agreements concerning British Togoland, British Cameroons, Tanganyika provides: 'the Administering Authority . . . shall be entitled to establish naval, military and air bases, to erect fortifications, to station and employ his own forces in the Territory and to take all such other measures as are, in his opinion, necessary for the defence of the territory and for ensuring that it plays its part in the maintenance of international peace and security.' Other trusteeship agreements contain similar provisions. The agreements concerning New Guinea and Nauru contain in Article 7 a general clause: 'The Administering Authority may take all measures in the Territory which it considers desirable to provide for the defence of the Territory and for maintenance of international peace and security.'

At the 23rd meeting of the Fourth Committee the delegate of the Soviet Union advocated the view that according to Article 83 of the Charter, the establishment of military, naval and air bases, is permissible only on trust territories designated as strategic areas, and consequently only with the approval of the Security Council. He stated: 'Articles 76 and 84 of the Charter provided for the participation of the Trust Territories in the maintenance of international peace and security. But the use of the territories for that purpose was limited by the provision of Article 84 concerning "volunteer" forces, facilities and assistance and by the reference in that Article to the obligations toward the Security Council undertaken by the administering authority. If bases should be required for purposes other than those stated in Article 84, the administering authorities could take advantage of Articles 82 and 83 of the Charter. If the administering Powers were to build fortifications in the Trust Territories they would transform them into strategic areas which should be put under the control of the Security Council. This was necessary, moreover, in order to avoid the use of the Trust Territories for military purposes to satisfy narrow national interests in contradiction with the aims stated in the Charter of the United Nations. That misuse of the Trust Territories would create a situation worse than that existing under the mandates system, which did not permit fortification of mandated territories.' (Summary Record of Meetings of Fourth Committee, November 1–December 12, 1946, p. 140). At the 62nd meeting of the General Assembly he declared: 'if conditions require the establishment of military bases and the maintenance of the armed forces of the Administering Authorities in the Trust Territories, then we will have the situation provided for in Articles 82 and 83 because the erection of fortifications and the establishment of military bases in trust territories by the Administering Authority will thus transform these territories into strategic regions.' (Official Records of the Second Part of the First Session of the General Assembly, Plenary Meetings, p. 1279.) This view presupposes that the phrase 'in carrying out their obligations towards the Security Council' in Article 84 refers to the obligations of the administering authority of a strategic trust territory, and that the establishment of military bases, fortifications and the like in a trust territory is possible only under Article 84 in carrying out the obligations of an administering authority of a strategic trust territory. The first mentioned assumption has the consequence that all trust territories are to be established as strategic areas; the second is possible only if the establishment of military bases, fortifications and the like in the trust territory falls within the meaning of making use of facilities and assistance from the trust territory.

Article 87, clause (*b*), in authorising the General Assembly and, under its authority, the Trusteeship Council to accept petitions and examine them, stipulates the obligation of the administering authority not to prevent petitions addressed by the inhabitants of the trust territories directly to the Organisation, and to forward such petitions if submitted to the administering authority. Rule 83 of the Rules of Procedure for the Trusteeship Council provides in this respect:

> Written petitions submitted to the Administering Authority for transmission shall be communicated promptly to the Secretary-General, with or without comments by the Administering Authority, at its discretion, or with an indication that such comments will follow in due course.

Article 87, clause (*c*), in authorising the General Assembly to provide for periodic visits, stipulates the corresponding obligation of the administering authority to permit such visits. The provisions of Article 87 refer only to non-strategic trust territories. But nothing in the Charter prevents inserting into trusteeship agreements concerning strategic areas a rule providing for periodic visits.

Article 84 of the Charter constitutes a limitation of the powers of the administering authority in so far as the latter, in fulfilling its obligations as a Member of the United Nations towards the Security Council under Article 43, and for the purposes of the defence of the territory and the maintenance of order in it, is not permitted to impose upon the inhabitants of the trust territory compulsory military service. Article 84 does not refer to the establishment of fortifications, military, naval, or air bases, nor to the use of other than native forces in the trust territory. The delegate of Belgium correctly stated: 'While Article 84 implied that administering authorities had no right to impose conscription on the populations of trust territories, it did not limit the measures which administering states might take for their own security.' (Summary Records of Meetings of Fourth Committee, November 1–December 12, 1946, p. 143.) At the 11th meeting of Sub-Committee 1 of the Fourth Committee the representative of Belgium stated that the Charter ' did not attempt to ensure demilitarization of the Trust Territories, as had been the case under the Mandates System.' (Summary Records of Meetings of Sub-Committee 1, November 15–December 10, 1946, p. 73.) Nothing in the Charter allows to differentiate between strategic and non-strategic areas in this respect. At the 10th meeting of Sub-Committee 1 during the discussion of the draft trusteeship agreement for Western Samoa, the representative of New Zealand stated: ' The concept of strategic areas had not been adopted in order to give to the Administering Authorities the powers necessary for defence of the Trust Territories. That right was inherent and was provided also in Article 84. The idea of strategic areas was intended to permit the Great Powers, who enjoyed the right of veto in the Security Council, to ensure that there would be no unnecessary interference in Territories where such interference could not be tolerated. Such a restriction on full supervision was not required in Western Samoa' (p. 69). It is certainly true that the veto right of the permanent members of the Security Council has the actual effect of restricting any function of this organ and consequently also the supervision of the administration of trust territories. But it is doubtful whether the anticipation of this effect led to the provision of Articles 82 and 83 of the Charter establishing the jurisdiction of the Security Council for strategic areas.

Article 88 stipulates the obligations of the administering authorities of non-strategic trust territories to ' make an annual report to the General Assembly ' upon the basis of the questionnaire formulated by the Trusteeship Council. In this respect the Rules of Procedure for the Trusteeship Council provide, in Rule 72, paragraph 1:

> The annual report of an Administering Authority prepared on the basis of the questionnaire formulated by the Trusteeship Council shall be submitted to the Secretary-General within four months from the termination of the year to which it refers;

and in Rule 73:

> The Administering Authorities shall furnish to the Secretary-General four hundred copies of each report for a Trust Territory. Copies of each such report shall at the same time be sent directly by the Administering Authority to the members of the Trusteeship Council as a means of expediting the work of the Council.

These provisions are not quite in conformity with Article 88 of the Charter which obligates the administering authorities to make the annual reports to the General Assembly, not to the Secretary-General or to the members of the Trusteeship Council.

Apart from Article 76, setting forth the basic objectives, the Charter does not stipulate specific obligations of the administering authorities in strategic areas. In this respect only the trusteeship agreements may or may not establish appropriate provisions.

(*g*) Differences between Strategic and Non-Strategic Trust Territories

What is the difference between a trust territory which has, and a trust territory which has not the character of a strategic area with respect to the functions of the Organisation and the obligations of the administering authority? The differences which the Charter itself makes in this respect are:

1. Whereas the supervision of the administration of non-strategic areas is according to Article 85 within the competence of the General Assembly, the supervision of the administration of strategic areas is according to Article 83 within the competence of the Security Council. Consequently, if the state administering a strategic trust territory is a permanent member of the Security Council, it can, by exercising its veto right, prevent any decision of the Council to be taken in its capacity as supervising authority.

2. Whereas in non strategic areas the assistance of the Trusteeship Council is obligatory in the performance of all functions of the Organisation, its assistance in strategic areas is obligatory only in the performance of the functions relating to political, economic, social,

and educational matters, and only without prejudice to security considerations (Article 83, paragraph 3). In case Article 83, paragraph 3, is interpreted to mean that on the ground of security considerations not only the assistance of the Trusteeship Council may be eliminated but also the functions of the Organisation referred to in this paragraph be restricted or not conferred at all on the Organisation, the administration of strategic areas differs from that of non-strategic areas also in that no such restriction of the functions of the Organisation is admissable in non-strategic areas.

3. Only in relation to non-strategic areas the competence of the Organisation to take the measures determined in Article 87, clauses (*a*) to (*d*) is obligatory.

4. Only the administering authorities of non-strategic areas must be obliged by the trusteeship agreements to permit petitions of the inhabitants and periodic visits by organs of the Organisation and to make annual reports (Articles 87, 88).

Since (apart from recommendations made by the General Assembly under Article 10) the actions determined in Article 87, clauses (*a*) to (*d*) are the only means provided in the Charter by which the Organisation can carry out its function of supervision, the decisive difference between strategic and non-strategic areas consists in that no effective supervision of the former is obligatory. It may be established by the trusteeship agreements, conferring upon the Security Council the powers which the Assembly has under Articles 87 and 88;[4] but a trusteeship agreement which does not establish supervision to be carried out by the means provided in Articles 87 and 88, may be approved by the Security Council in conformity with the Charter. In this case the realisation of the basic objectives of the trusteeship system, though also applicable to strategic areas, depends on the good will of the administering authority.[5]

4 Cf. *supra*, pp. 616, 625.

5 At the 23rd meeting of the Fourth Committee the delegate of Beglium declared: 'The only difference between strategic areas and ordinary trust territories was that the administering authorities would be bound by a simple majority or a two-thirds majority of the General Assembly. The acquiescence of the administering authorities would be required for all decisions concerning strategic areas.' (Journal of the United Nations, No. 60: Suppl. No. 4–A/C. 4/81, p. 96). This statement is not very clear. If it means that within the trusteeship system laid down in Chapters XII and XIII of the Charter the administering authority of a non-strategic area is bound by decisions of the General Assembly whereas the administering authority of a strategic area is not bound by decisions of the Security Council, it has no basis in the Charter. The Assembly as well as the Council is competent to exercise supervision of the administration of trust territories only on the basis of the respective trusteeship agreements, and that means, with the acquiescence of the administering authority in its capacity as contracting party to the agreement. The Charter does not provide for decisions of the General Assembly binding upon the administering authority without or against its will. All actions taken under Article 87 are to be taken 'in conformity with the terms

(*h*) The Organisation as Administering Authority

According to the express provision of Article 81, the trusteeship agreement may designate the Organisation itself as 'the authority which will exercise the administration of the trust territory.' But in this case most of the other provisions of the trusteeship system are hardly applicable. For the essential element of the system is the supervision of the administration of the trust territory by the Organisation. If the Organisation itself is the administering authority, no supervision in the true sense of the term is possible. It would be meaningless to impose upon the Organisation to make reports to the Organisation and to confer upon the Organisation the right to make periodic visits to the trust territory administered by the same Organisation, even if the organ of the United Nations vested with the exercise of the administration would be not identical with the organ to which the reports are to be made and which has the right to make the visits at times determined by an agreement concluded by the Organisation with itself. The application of Article 84 is more than problematical, for the Organisation can not have 'the obligations towards the Security Council' referred to in this Article. If the Organisation itself is the administering authority, the designation of the trust territory as strategic area is out of the question, since the difference between strategic and non-strategic territories consists in the different degree of supervision and in this case no true supervision can take place. If the Organisation itself is the administering authority and at the same time the territorial sovereign, the objective cannot be, as Article 76 (*b*) provides, self-government *or* independence, but only independence. For when the objective is achieved the status of trusteeship is to be terminated, and if the Organisation is the administering authority, this status cannot be terminated by granting self-government to the territory, since the Organisation is not authorised by the Charter to exercise sovereignty over a territory which has not the legal status of a trust territory.

If an agreement is to be made by which the Organisation itself is to be designated as administering authority the question arises which organ of the United Nations is competent to 'approve' this agreement; and in this case approval by the Organisation evidently means conclusion, on the part of the Organisation, of the trusteeship agreement with the state (or states) competent to dispose of the territory. Since the distinction between strategic and non-strategic areas is not applicable and the Charter does not contain a provision for this case, any organ competent under the Charter to deal with trusteeship matters may be

of the trusteeship agreements.' But a trusteeship agreement may confer upon the General Assembly, as well as on the Security Council the power to adopt, by a unilateral act, decisions binding upon the administering authority. As to the competence of the General Assembly in trusteeship matters under Article 10, cf. *supra*, pp. 622 ff.

considered as entitled to conclude this agreement. But it may also be argued that if the agreement does not designate the territory as a strategic area Article 85 is applicable and hence the General Assembly is competent to ' approve ' such agreement.

If in an agreement entered into under Article 81 a territory is placed under the direct administration of the Organisation, the legal status of this territory is quite different from that of a trust territory administered by a state under the supervision of the United Nations; and the agreement concerned must contain provisions different from those of a normal trusteeship agreement. Since the Charter itself contains no provision referring to the case of direct administration by the Organisation, especially no provision determining the organ of the United Nations competent to exercise the administration of the territory, the agreement by which the territory is placed under the administration of the Organisation must determine this organ. This organ may be the General Assembly, the Security Council, or the Trusteeship Council, authorised by the General Assembly. Since neither of them is fit for administration purposes, a special organ may be established by the General Assembly under Article 22 or by the Security Council under Article 29. An ordinary trusteeship agreement restricts itself to stipulate the obligations of the administering authority and the functions of the supervising Organisation. But an agreement by which the Organisation is designated as administering authority may contain the constitution organising the legislative, administrative and judicial powers to be exercised in this territory. But it is possible and even advisable to organise the administration of the territory by a unilateral act of the United Nations, *e.g.*, by a decision of the General Assembly or the Security Council This is legally possible because the Charter confers in Article 81 upon the Organisation the power to administer a territory. This power implies the competence of the Organisation to organise the administration of this territory by decisions of the organs concerned. The advantage of this way of organising the administration of the territory is that the establishment as well as changes of the constitution are independent from the consent of the state (or states) placing the territory under the administration of the United Nations. The only provisions of the trusteeship system as laid down in the Charter, which the trusteeship agreement designating the Organisation itself as administering authority must contain, are the provisions of Article 76 setting forth the basic objectives of the trusteeship system, especially the provisions of clauses (*b*) and (*d*). The United Nations must assume—in relation to the state (or states) placing the territory under the trusteeship administration of the Organisation—the obligations to promote in accordance with clause (*b*) the progressive development of the inhabitants of the trust territory towards self-government or independence and to ensure equal treatment for all Members of the United Nations and their nationals in accordance with clause (*d*). It is due to these obligations that the direct administration of a territory by the Organisation under Article 81—in spite of all differences as compared with the administration under the supervision of the Organisation—is still a trusteeship.[6]

The question may arise whether a stateless territory can be placed under the trusteeship system. Since no state is competent to dispose of such territory, the further question arises whether the United Nations is competent to establish a trusteeship over such a territory by a unilateral act, designating itself as administering authority. The Charter does not confer upon the Organisation such power, although direct administration by the Organisation might be particularly advisable in case of a territory which for some reason or other is not yet, or no more, under the effective control of a government in the sense of international law.[7]

B. *Alteration and Termination of the Trusteeship Status*

Article 79 provides that any ' alteration or amendment ' of the terms of trusteeship shall be agreed upon by ' the states directly concerned ' and shall be approved by the Organisation. Since,

[6] The draft trusteeship agreement for Palestine (Cf. *supra*, p. 592) contained in its preamble the provisions according to which it should be approved by the General Assembly. Article 2 provided: ' The United Nations, acting through the Trusteeship Council, is hereby designated as the Administering Authority.' But the administration would have been exercised by a Governor General to be appointed by the Trusteeship Council (Article 11). It is doubtful whether the General Assembly can transfer its power to establish subsidiary organs under Article 22 to the Trusteeship Council upon which the Charter does not confer such power. The draft agreement contained a complete constitution for Palestine; but also the provision: ' The Administering Authority undertakes to administer Palestine in such a manner as to achieve the basic objectives of the international trusteeship system laid down in Article 76 of the Charter.' (Article 4, paragraph 1). Article 42 of the draft agreement stipulated: ' 1. The Governor General shall collaborate fully with the General Assembly of the United Nations and the Trusteeship Council in the discharge of all their functions as defined in Article 87 of the Charter of the United Nations, and to facilitate any periodic visits to Palestine which they may deem necessary. 2. The Governor General shall make to the Trusteeship Council of the United Nations an annual report on the basis of a questionnaire drawn up by the Trusteeship Council in accordance with Article 88 of the Charter of the United Nations . . .' What could be the use of visits of the Trusteeship Council to a territory administered by this Council? Reports of the Governor General, acting as organ of the Trusteeship Council to this Council, are not the reports provided for by Article 88; the latter are reports of a government to an international organisation as its supervisory authority. The former are internal administrative measures.

[7] At the moment the government of the United Kingdom withdrew from Palestine, this territory was in a legal status of statelessness until the new state of Israel was established and recognised by other states. That part of Palestine which is not under the control of the new government legally will be a stateless territory until a recognised government will be established there.

legally, any amendment is an alteration and an alteration an amendment—the connotation of the latter term: improvement, constitutes a subjective value judgment without relevance—one of the two words is superfluous. Articles 83 and 85 provide that the approval of an alteration of the terms of trusteeship shall be within the competence of the Security Council and the General Assembly respectively. Under general international law the terms of a treaty can be altered only with the consent of all contracting parties, unless the text of the treaty provides for another way to alter its terms. Is the Organisation authorised by the Charter to approve a trusteeship agreement which contains the provision that alteration of its terms requires only the consent of some of the states which, as 'states directly concerned,' participated in the conclusion of the trusteeship agreement (provided that not only the state designated as administering authority participated in the conclusion), or a provision that the Organisation, through its competent organ, may modify the terms of trusteeship unilaterally at its discretion? The answer to this question depends on the meaning of the words of Article 79: 'The terms of trusteeship for each territory . . . including any alteration or amendment, shall be agreed upon . . . and shall be approved . . . ' These words may mean that the terms of the trusteeship agreements must include provisions concerning alteration and that these terms—including the provisions concerning alteration—after having been agreed upon by the states directly concerned shall be approved by the Organisation. As to the content of these provisions regarding alteration, Article 79 says nothing. The Organisation may approve—without violating the Charter—any such provision, even a provision conferring upon the states directly concerned the power to alter the terms of trusteeship without the consent of the Organisation. But the wording of Articles 83 and 85 concerning alteration or amendment is different from that of Article 79. The latter reads: 'The terms of trusteeship . . . including any alteration or amendment shall be agreed upon by the states directly concerned, . . . and shall be approved . . . ' Articles 83 and 85 speak of 'approval of the terms of the trusteeship agreements and of their alteration or amendment . . . ' That is to say, Articles 83 and 85 provide that the Security Council and the General Assembly shall approve the terms of the trusteeship agreements *and* their alterations or amendment. Hence the Organisation must not approve a trusteeship agreement which excludes the approval of the alteration of the agreement by the Organisation. But it may approve a trusteeship agreement which confers upon the Organisation exclusively the right to alter the terms of the trusteeship. However, Article 79 may also be interpreted to mean that not only the terms of trusteeship but also any alteration of these terms must be agreed upon by the states directly concerned and be approved by the Organisation. This interpretation may be confirmed by the wording of Articles 83 and 85 which provide for 'approval' of the alteration or amendment of the terms of the trusteeship agreements; and such alteration or amendment can be ' approved ' by the Organisation only if it has been suggested by the states directly concerned. This interpretation has the strange effect that a trusteeship agreement which confers the right to alter its terms exclusively on the Organisation, must not be approved by the latter; which is not in conformity with the principle that the provisions of the Charter concerning the trusteeship powers of the Organisation constitute only a minimum of competence which must be conferred upon the Organisation by the trusteeship agreements. If the states directly concerned in their capacity as contracting parties, or if the administering authority as the only state directly concerned in its capacity as contracting party, are willing to confer upon the Organisation the power to alter the terms of the trusteeship agreement by a unilateral act, there is no reason why the Organisation should not be allowed to approve it. Hence a more reasonable interpretation of Articles 79, 83 and 85, is that the consent of the states directly concerned to alteration or amendment of the terms of trusteeship (in addition to the approval by the Organisation) may or may not be stipulated by the trusteeship agreement.[8] Are the states, which, as states directly concerned, have to conclude the trusteeship agreement, identical with those which have to consent to its alteration? As pointed out, this question may be answered in the affirmative or in the negative.[9] If Article 79 is interpreted to mean that the states which are considered to be directly concerned in the conclusion of the trusteeship agreement are not necessarily identical with those directly concerned in its alteration, then it depends finally upon the Organisation to decide which states, in addition to those determined

[8] The Soviet delegation proposed to insert into the text of the trusteeship agreements the provision that the agreement ' shall remain in force for a period of . . . years and thereafter shall be reviewed and modified according to the degree of attainment of the purposes set forth in Article 76 of the Charter of the United Nations.' (Doc. A/258, p. 3.) If a periodic revision of the trusteeship agreement is to be effected by an agreement between the Organisation and the states directly concerned, the provision concerning such periodic revision has little value, since such revision depends on the consent of these states. It is effective only if the revision is to be brought about by a unilateral act of the Organisation. It seems that this was the intention of the Soviet proposition. For the delegate of Belgium observed ' that the U.S.S.R. proposal, in contradiction to Article 79 of the Charter, provided for the obligatory revision of the trusteeship agreements, without the approval of the mandatory States.' (Summary Records of Meetings of Fourth Committee, November 1–December 12, 1946, p. 146.) The statement that it is contrary to Article 79 to confer in a trusteeship agreement, upon the Organisation the power to revise, by a unilateral act, the terms of the agreement is not the only possible interpretation of the Articles concerned. The Organisation could—according to another interpretation—approve such a provision without violating the Charter. Only a provision to the effect that a revision of the trusteeship agreement may be made without the approval of the Organisation is at any rate incompatible with Article 83 and 85.

[9] Cf. *supra*, pp. 582 ff.

by general international law and the terms of the trusteeship agreement, have to participate in the alteration, by making its approval dependent on the consent of these states to the alteration. In any case, no trusteeship agreement must be approved which deprives the Organisation of its right to approve any alteration of its terms.[1]

[1] All trusteeship agreements approved by the Organisation except the agreements for New Guinea and Nauru, contain provisions concerning alteration or amendment of the terms of the agreement. If Article 79 is interpreted to mean that the trusteeship agreements shall contain provisions concerning alteration or amendment of the terms of trusteeship, the approval of an agreement which does not contain such a provision is not constitutional. If there is no such provision in the text of the agreement, alteration (or amendment) is possible with the consent of all contracting parties to the agreement, including the Organisation.

The provisions contained in the trusteeship agreements (except those contained in the agreement concerning the former Japanese mandated islands) are a mere reference to the provisions of the Charter concerning alteration or amendment (Articles 79, 83, 85—the trusteeship agreement concerning Western Samoa refers only to Article 79). Article 15 of the trusteeship agreement concerning the former Japanese mandated islands reads as follows: ' The terms of the present agreement shall not be altered, amended or terminated without the consent of the administering authority.' This is not a satisfactory formulation. Article 15 of the agreement does not provide for the consent of the Organisation to alteration, amendment, and termination of the trusteeship status, probably because it presupposed it as self-evident that the provision of Article 83, paragraph 1, of the Charter according to which the Security Council has the power to approve alteration or amendment of the terms of trusteeship agreements relating to strategic areas, applies. The delegate of the United States expressly stated at the 116th meeting of the Security Council that Article 15 of the draft agreement did not attempt to define the responsibilities of the Security Council in respect to the alterations since they were already defined in the Charter. (Official Records of the Security Council, 2nd Year, No. 23, p. 476.) But if a trusteeship agreement contains a provision concerning alteration or amendment at all, this provision should determine the complete procedure for alteration or amendment. As a matter of fact, the delegate of the United States declared to be willing to accept the following text of Article 15: ' The terms of the present agreement shall not be altered, amended or terminated, except by agreement of the administering authority and the Security Council.' (*Ibid.*) This formulation was more correct than the one finally accepted. The delegate of the Soviet Union suggested the following text: ' The terms of the present agreement may be altered, supplemented or terminated by decision of the Security Council.' (*Ibid.*, No. 20, p. 415.) The delegate of the United States refused to accept this suggestion as incompatible with the Charter. He interpreted Article 79 of the Charter to mean that alteration or amendment of the terms of trusteeship require the consent of all the contracting parties. In the course of the discussion he made the statement: ' We cannot grant to the Security Council powers that the Charter does not grant.' (*Ibid.*, No. 23, p. 475.) This statement is certainly not correct; it constitutes too far-going a generalisation. The provisions of the Charter concerning the powers of the Organisation within the trusteeship system constitute, as pointed out, the minimum of competence that must be recognised in the trusteeship agreements in order to be approved. As a matter of fact, the agreement concerning the former Japanese mandated islands grants to the Organisation powers that the Charter does not grant. At the 113th meeting of the Security Council the delegate of the United States stated: ' . . . the United States draft agreement goes beyond the requirements of the Charter in strategic areas. It provides that Articles 87 and 88, relating to

A special alteration of the terms of trusteeship is the designation of another administering authority. If the trusteeship agreement does not confer upon the Organisation the power to replace the administering authority designated in that agreement, by a unilateral act—and it is doubtful whether such a provision is in conformity with the Charter—a change of the administering authority is possible only by an agreement of the Organisation and the states which are entitled to participate in an alteration of the terms of trusteeship; among which there will probably always be the actual administering authority. It stands to reason that the state which shall replace the latter cannot be designated without its consent.

The Charter contains no express provision concerning the termination of the status of trusteeship. But Article 76, clause (*b*), may be interpreted to refer indirectly to it. If it is a basic objective of the trusteeship system to promote the development of the inhabitants of the trust territories 'towards self-government or independence,' the status of trusteeship must terminate as soon as the people of the trust territory has reached the political status of self-government or independence. No other interpretation seems to be possible, at least in case the trust territory obtains 'independence.' For this legal status is incompatible with that of trusteeship. However, a termination of the status of trusteeship is legally not possible against the will of the administering authority.[2] If termination of the trusteeship status is considered to be an alteration of the terms of trusteeship, any termination requires also the approval of the Organisation, even in case the status of trusteeship is to be terminated by granting independence to the people of the trust territory. If termination is not considered to fall within 'alteration' of the terms of trusteeship, the situation is different according to whether the trusteeship agreement does, or does not, contain provisions concerning the termination of the trusteeship status. As to the first case, the question arises what provisions of a trusteeship agreement concerning

reports, petitions, visits and questionnaires in non-strategic trusteeship areas, shall be applicable to the whole of this trust territory . . . ' (*Ibid.*, No. 20, p. 412). The delegate of Belgium rejected the Soviet Russian proposal for the following reason: 'One of the least contested principles of international law is that an agreement cannot be modified without the consent of the contracting parties. The Administering Authority is a party to the Trusteeship Agreement. Its consent is thus required for any modification or amendment of such an agreement or for its termination.' (*Ibid.*, No. 31, pp. 671.) But this rule applies only if the international agreement does not provide another way for its alteration.

[2] At the 14th meeting of Committee II/4 at the San Francisco Conference (U.N.C.I.O. Doc. 1018, II/4/38, p. 5) the delegate for Egypt suggested to insert into the Charter the principle 'That in all trust territories, within its competence, the General Assembly shall have the power to terminate the status of trusteeship, and declare the territory to be fit for full independence, either at the instance of the Administering Authority, or upon the recommendation of any member of the Assembly.' He later withdrew his motion.

termination of the trusteeship status may be or must not be approved by the Organisation. It may be argued: Since the states entitled to place a territory under trusteeship are not obliged to do so, a provision by which trusteeship is established only for a limited period of time by fixing a certain date for its end, or by establishing a resolutive condition, or by stipulating the right of withdrawal from the trusteeship system by notice at least on the part of the states, or state, directly concerned, seems not to be incompatible with the Charter. In this case the status of trusteeship terminates automatically or by withdrawal, and even before the objective referred to in Article 76 (*b*) has been reached. But the interpretation is not excluded that in view of the objective to promote the development of the people of the trust territory towards self-government or independence, an objective which has to be recognised in the trusteeship agreements, the Organisation must not approve an agreement which provides for a termination of the trusteeship status before this objective is achieved.

The trusteeship agreement may or may not contain provisions concerning the termination of the trusteeship status by granting the people of the trust territory self-government or independence. If there is such express provision in the agreement, the trusteeship status terminates in conformity with this provision. Even if there is in the agreement no provision concerning termination by achievement of the objectives, or no provision concerning termination at all, it may be argued that the achievement of the objectives referred to in Article 76 (*b*) terminates the binding force of the trusteeship agreement, since this is the meaning of the provision of this Article and consequently also of the trusteeship agreement. But the question whether the objectives have actually been achieved in a concrete case cannot be decided unilaterally by the administering authority. An agreement of the latter and the Organisation in its capacity as supervising authority is necessary. Hence also in this case termination of the trusteeship status requires the approval of the Organisation.[3]

[3] The trusteeship agreements approved by the General Assembly do not contain express provisions concerning the termination of the status of trusteeship. The Fourth Committee adopted the above mentioned proposal of the delegation of the Soviet Union to insert into each agreement the provision that the agreement 'shall remain in force for a period of ten years and thereafter shall be reviewed and modified according to the degree of attainment of the purposes set forth in Article 76 of the Charter of the United Nations.' (Doc. A/258, p. 3; Journal of the United Nations, No. 60: Suppl. No. 4–A/C. 4/81, p. 99 f.) The states which submitted the draft agreements to the Assembly declared this proposal as not acceptable (Doc. A/258, p. 4). At the 23rd meeting of the Fourth Committee the delegate of France declared that he considered the decision of the Committee to approve the Soviet proposal 'contrary to the Charter' (Journal of the United Nations, No. 60: Suppl. No. 4–A/C. 4/81, p. 100). If this meant that the General Assembly would violate the Charter in approving a trusteeship agreement containing the proposed clause, the statement has no basis in the Charter. During the discussion of the Fourth Committee the delegation of India stated that it 'regarded

Withdrawal or expulsion from the Organisation of the state which exercises the function of administering authority has not the effect of terminating the status of trusteeship. For membership is not an essential condition for the exercise of this function. Under Article 81 non-members may become the administering authority of a trust territory. Hence a state which has lost its membership remains under the obligations of the trusteeship agreement to which it is a contracting party in its capacity as administering authority, except for the obligation established by Article 84. For as a non-member state it has no obligation towards the Security Council under Article 43 of the Charter, and it is within this obligation that the 'duty of the administering authority to ensure that the trust territory shall play its part in the maintenance of international peace and security' is to be fulfilled.[4]

as fundamental and essential for the speedy attainment of independence by the people of the trust territories that there should be an appropriate time limit for independence set out in each of the agreements.' (Doc. A/258, p. 24.)

The only trusteeship agreement that contains an express provision concerning termination of the trusteeship status is the agreement for the former Japanese mandated islands, approved by the Security Council, which in the above quited Article 15, provides that the terms of the agreement shall not terminate 'without the consent of the administering authority.' Cf. *supra*, p. 656.

[4] At the 14th meeting of Committee II/4 of the San Francisco Conference (U.N.C.I.O. Doc. 1018, II/4/38, p. 5) the delegate for Egypt suggested to insert into the Charter the principle: 'That whenever there is any violation of the terms of the trusteeship arrangements by the administering authority, or when the administering power has ceased to be a Member of the United Nations, or has been suspended from membership, the Organisation shall take the necessary steps for the transfer of the territory under trusteeship to another administering authority . . .' He later withdrew his motion.

The Report of Rapporteur of Committee II/4 of the San Francisco Conference (U.N.C.I.O. Doc. 1115, II/4/44 (1) (*a*), p. 14 f.) contains as Annex C a Joint Statement by the Delegates of the United Kingdom and the United States, concerning the effect of an act of aggression commited by the administering authority and the effect of withdrawal and expulsion of the state exercising the function of administering authority. The statement concerning the second point runs as follows: 'If a State withdraws from the United Nations Organisation and continues to hold a trust territory under the Charter, how is the Organisation to continue to exercise its responsibilities with respect to the administration of that trust territory? If a State withdraws for reasons which reflect no discredit upon it, and if it declares its willingness to continue to abide by the terms of the Trusteeship system, although itself ceasing to be a member of the General Assembly or Trusteeship Council, there should be no reason for transferring the trust territory. There is no inherent reason why the system of annual reports, petitions, periodic visits, etc. could not continue in such circumstances and the Administering Authority could be given the opportunity (though not compelled) to attend meetings of the Trusteeship Council when matters affecting its Trust Territories are under consideration. Moreover, if after ceasing to be a Member of the United Nations, the Administering Authority committed violations of the Trust, any measures which are provided elsewhere in the Charter against Member States could be invoked equally against the State in question. If, however, the State were allowed to withdraw for other reasons, or were expelled, and did not voluntarily consent

If the *clausula rebus sic stantibus* is considered to be a rule of positive international law, it applies also to trusteeship agreements.

The most important question is how the objective can be achieved: to promote the development of the inhabitants of the trust territory towards self-government or independence. Certainly by establishing the trust territory and its population as an independent state. This is the only way to promote the development of the inhabitants of the trust territory towards independence. 'Independence,' as pointed out, does not necessarily imply self-government in the sense of a political self-determination of the people. Since the objective is formulated: self-government 'or' independence, it is also achieved when the trust territory is established as a sovereign state under a constitution which has no democratic character. It is not very likely that the Organisation will approve the termination of the trusteeship status in such a case; but approval is compatible with the Charter, which, besides, does not even make a democratic form of government a condition for membership.

Since the objective of the trusteeship system is self-government *or* independence, it is achieved also by granting the people of the trust territory, not independence, but only self-government. That means that the status of trusteeship may be terminated not only by placing the trust territory under its own sovereignty, but also by leaving the territory under the sovereignty exercised over it during the period of trusteeship, provided that the political status of self-government is guaranteed to the inhabitants of the trust territory. This may be done by granting to the people of the trust territory as an organised body a special status of self-government, or, without maintaining its political individuality, by extending the political status of the people of the metropolitan area to the inhabitants of the trust territory, provided that this is a status of self-government. Although the framers of the Charter probably had in mind only the first way in using the term self-government, the second way is not excluded by the

to the transfer of the Trust to another authority, the resulting situation could only be judged by the General Assembly and the Security Council on its merits in the light of all the circumstances prevailing at the time. It is impossible to make provision in advance for such a situation.'

At the 116th meeting of the Security Council the delegate of Syria expressed the wish to see the following principle adopted in the Security Council: 'When a trustee or a mandatory Power withdraws from the United Nations, or is expelled from it, its rights to that trust or to that mandate would not persist, and the General Assembly of the United Nations should be free to deprive it of that right for as long as it is not a Member.' (Official Records of the Security Council, 2nd Year, No. 23, p. 470.) On the basis of the present Charter this principle could apply only if inserted into the text of the trusteeship agreement and approved by the Organisation. To former mandated territories, not placed under trusteeship, only Chapter XI applies in so far as the territory concerned is a 'non-self-governing territory' and only as long as the former mandatory power is a Member of the United Nations.

wording of Article 76 (*b*). Whether it does or does not imply incorporation of the trust territory in the territory of the administering authority, depends on whether the administering authority is or is not the sovereign over the trust territory. If it is the sovereign, no such incorporation of the trust territory is legally possible, since the trust territory is already part of the territory of the administering authority. If the administering authority is not the territorial sovereign, incorporation of the trust territory by granting its people the status of self-government under the sovereignty of the administering authority is possible only with the consent of the territorial sovereign. This may be the Organisation or another state 'directly concerned,' and as such contracting party to the trusteeship agreement.

The objective of Article 76 (*b*) may be achieved also by placing, or leaving, the trust territory under the sovereignty of a state other than the administering authority on the condition that a political status of self-government is guaranteed to the people of the trust territory, either by extending to it the political status of self-government that the people of the state enjoys under whose sovereignty the trust territory is placed or left; or by granting to the people of the trust territory as a separate political body a special status of self-government under the sovereignty of the state under whose sovereignty the territory is placed or left. In case the Organisation is the administering authority and at the same time the territorial sovereign, the trusteeship status can be terminated—as pointed out—only by granting independence to the territory, not by granting only self-government. For the Organisation is not authorised by the Charter to exercise sovereignty over a territory which has not the legal status of a trust territory. Finally, the status of trusteeship may terminate by the fact that the United Nations—as supervising or administering authority—or the state exercising the function of administering authority, ceases to exist. In the first case a situation would arise quite similar to that created by the dissolution of the League of Nations, implying the abolishment of the mandate system. The legal status of the trust territories in such a situation depends on the question where the sovereignty over the trust territory lies. In case the state which has exercised the function of administering authority ceases to exist, another state can be designated as administering authority only by a new trusteeship agreement entered into by the Organisation and the state which has or assumes sovereignty over the territory.

C. *The Trusteeship Council*

(*a*) Organisation and Procedure

A striking difference between the mandate and the trusteeship system consists in that under the Covenant (Article 22, paragraph 9) the special organ of the system was a 'permanent commission' the members of which were experts appointed by the Council, not representatives of governments; whereas under the Charter a Council is established composed of Member states and designated, in Article 7 of the Charter, as a principle organ of the United Nations.

The composition of the Trusteeship Council is determined by Article 86, which runs as follows:

> 1. The Trusteeship Council shall consist of the following Members of the United Nations:
>
> (*a*) those Members administering trust territories;
>
> (*b*) such of those Members mentioned by name in Article 23 as are not administering trust territories; and
>
> (*c*) as many other Members elected for three-year terms by the General Assembly as may be necessary to ensure that the total number of members of the Trusteeship Council is equally divided between those Members of the United Nations which administer trust territories and those which do not.
>
> 2. Each member of the Trusteeship Council shall designate one specially qualified person to represent it therein.

Only Members of the United Nations can be members of the Trusteeship Council; and all Members which administer trust territories are, under Article 86, paragraph 1, clause (*a*), automatically members of the Trusteeship Council. According to Article 81—at least according to its wording—not only a Member of the United Nations but also another 'state' may become the administering authority of a trust territory, but it cannot become a member of the Trusteeship Council.

Under Article 86, paragraph 1, clauses (*a*) and (*b*), all permanent members of the Security Council are, at the same time, members of the Trusteeship Council; under clause (*a*), if they administer a trust territory; under clause (*b*), if they do not administer a trust territory. The other Members of the United Nations cease to be members of the Trusteeship Council when they lose their position as administering authority of the trust territory; or, in case they are elected members of the Trusteeship Council, when their term of office expires. The permanent members of the Security Council are permanent members of the Trusteeship Council whether they are or are not administering authorities, under Article 81. They are permanent members of the Trusteeship Council, but they have no veto right.

The third group of members (Article 86, paragraph 1 (*c*)) are those Members of the United Nations which are elected by the General Assembly for a term of three years, re-election not being precluded. Their number shall be equal to the number of the members of this Council administering trust territories (clause (*a*)) minus the number of permanent members of the Security Council not administering trust territories (clause (*b*)). This number is variable. In case the number of members administering trust territories is equal or less than the number of permanent members of the Security Council not administering trust territories, no Member of the United Nations can be elected a member of the Trusteeship Council. In this case, Article 86, paragraph 1, clause (*c*), is not applicable. In case the number of members administering trust territories is less than the number of permanent members not administering trust territories the total number of members of the Trusteeship Council is not equally divided between those Members of the United Nations which administer trust territories and those which do not. The number of those which do not administer trust territories is greater than the number of those which do. Also in case a Member of the United Nations administering a trust territory loses its position as a member of the Trusteeship Council—for instance, because the trust territory which it administers attains complete independence—the number of the members of the Trusteeship Council not administering a trust territory is greater than that of the members administering trust territories, until the term of office of one elected member expires. If, for the reason just mentioned, a permanent member of the Security Council ceases to be a member of the Trusteeship Council under clause (*a*), but continues to be a member of this Council under clause (*b*), the number of the members not administering a trust territory surpasses even by two the number of the members administering trust territories. In case the number of the members administering trust territories increases during the three-year term of the elected members, additional election has to take place. Thus the number of members which do not administer a trust territory in spite of the provision of Article 86, paragraph 1, clause (*c*), may be greater, but never can be smaller, than the number of those which do. The administering members can have no majority.

The members of the Trusteeship Council are states represented by individuals appointed by the competent organs of the respective states entitled to be represented on the Trusteeship Council. Each member is to be represented only by one person and has, under Article 89, paragraph 1, one vote. The appointment of the representative is determined, to a certain extent, by Article 86, paragraph 2, providing that 'each member of the Trusteeship Council shall designate one specially qualified person to represent it therein.' Who has to decide the question as to whether the person is 'specially qualified,' that is to say, an expert in the field of the competence of the Trusteeship Council? It is not impossible to interpret Article 86, paragraph 2, to mean that the Trusteeship Council may refuse to recognise a person as representative of a member for the reason that he does not fulfil the requirements of this paragraph. It is, however, not very likely that this interpretation will be accepted by the majority of the Council, so that it will be upon the member itself to decide whether a person is 'specially qualified.' Then the restriction imposed upon the members by Article 86, paragraph 2, is legally not very important.

The application of Article 86, and hence the establishment of the Trusteeship Council altogether, presupposes the coming into force of a minimum of trusteeship agreements referred to in Chapter XII. At its 63rd meeting the General Assembly adopted the following resolution:[5]

> The General Assembly approved, on December 13, 1946, in accordance with Article 85 of the Charter, the terms of the Trusteeship Agreements for New Guinea, Ruanda-Urundi, Cameroons under French administration and Togoland under French administration, Western Samoa, Tanganyika, Cameroons under British administration and Togoland under British administration.
>
> In these agreements, Australia, Belgium, France, New Zealand and the United Kingdom have been designated as Administering Authorities.
>
> The conditions necessary for the constitution of the Trusteeship Council can thus be fulfilled.
>
> In accordance with Article 86 (*a*), Australia, Belgium, France, New Zealand and the United Kingdom will be members of the Trusteeship Council.
>
> By application of Article 86 (*b*), China, the United States of America and the Union of Soviet Socialist Republics, being such of the members mentioned by name in Article 23 of the Charter as are not administering Trust Territories, will also be members of the Trusteeship Council.
>
> In accordance with Article 86 (*c*) it is necessary, in order to ensure that the total number of members of the Trusteeship Council is equally divided between those Members of the United Nations which administer Trust Territories and those which do not, that two members should be elected by the General Assembly.
>
> Therefore, The General Assembly,
>
> 1. Elects Mexico and Iraq as members of the Trusteeship Council for a term of three years;
>
> 2. Directs the Secretary-General to convoke the first session of the Trusteeship Council not later than March 15, 1947, and to draw up and communicate to each member of the Council the provisional agenda for that session at least thirty days in advance of the date of the session.

[5] Doc. A/64/Add. 1., pp. 122 f.

When this resolution was adopted, the trusteeship agreements concerning the former Japanese mandated islands (with the United States as administering authority) and that concerning Nauru, with Australia, New Zealand and the United Kingdom, as administering authority, were not yet in force.[6] Hence, the Trusteeship Council came into being with ten members. Five of its members were administering authorities: Australia, Belgium, France, New Zealand, the United Kingdom. Three of its members, namely, China, the United States and the Soviet Union, were members, in accordance with Article 86 (*b*) of the Charter, in their capacity as permanent members of the Security Council. The other two members were Mexico and Iraq, elected by the General Assembly at its 63rd meeting in accordance with Article 86 (*c*) of the Charter. At this meeting the delegate of the Soviet Union declared: ' The USSR delegation thinks that the agreements for trusteeship of the ex-mandated territories of Togoland, Tanganyika, Ruanda-Urundi, the Cameroons, New Guinea and Western Samoa are in contradiction to the terms of the Charter. . . . In view of these circumstances, the USSR delegation cannot participate in the election of members of the Trusteeship Council.'[7] In accordance with Article 86, paragraph 2, nine members of the Trusteeship Council designated their representatives in the Council. But the Soviet Union refused to designate a representative.[8] Hence the actual composition of the Trusteeship Council was not in conformity with Article 86, paragraph 2, providing: that each member of the Trusteeship Council ' shall ' designate one person to represent it therein. It may be doubted whether the proceedings of the Trusteeship Council were legal until the Soviet Union—at the beginning of the third part of the second session of this Council (from April 21 to May 4, 1948) designated its representative in conformity with Article 86, paragraph 2.[9] Another question is

[6] After having been approved by the Security Council at its 124th meeting on April 2, 1947, the trusteeship agreement concerning the former Japanese mandated islands came into force in accordance with its Article 16, by the approval of the Government of the United States authorised by a joint resolution of the Congress, Public Law 204, 80th Congress, 1st session July 18, 1947. The trusteeship agreement for Nauru came into force after having been approved by the General Assembly on November 1, 1947.

[7] Journal of the United Nations, No. 63: Suppl. No. A–A/P.V/63, pp. 670 f.

[8] *Yearbook*, pp. 577 f.

[9] In the *Department of State Bulletin* the opinion was expressed that the continued absence of the Soviet Union did not affect the legality of the proceedings of the Council inasmuch as Article 89 of the Charter provides that decisions of the Trusteeship Council ' shall be made by a majority of the members present and voting,' and both the provisional and final rules of procedure provide that ' at any meeting of the Council two-thirds of the members shall constitute a quorum.' (*Department of State Bulletin*, June 8, 1947, p. 1090.) The legality of the proceedings of a collegiate body does not depend only upon compliance with the provisions concerning the quorum and the voting procedure, but also—and in the first place—upon compliance with the provisions concerning its composition. The situation

whether the Trusteeship Council was and still is illegally constituted if—as the delegation of the Soviet Union contended—the trusteeship agreements were approved by the Organisation although not in conformity with the Charter. This question must be answered in the negative. In conferring upon the General Assembly and the Security Council the power to approve the trusteeship agreements, the Charter authorises the two organs to interpret the provisions relating to the content and conclusion of these agreements. Hence the agreements approved by the competent organs are to be considered as legal.[1]

The Rules of Procedure for the Trusteeship Council provide:

> RULE 12
>
> Members of the United Nations which are not members of the Trusteeship Council but which have proposed items on the agenda of that Council shall be invited to have present at the appropriate meetings of the Council, representatives who shall be entitled to participate, without vote, in the deliberations on those items.
>
> RULE 13
>
> Representatives of specialised agencies shall be invited to attend meetings of the Trusteeship Council and to participate, without vote, in its deliberations in the circumstances indicated in the respective agreements between the United Nations and the specialised agencies.
>
> RULE 18
>
> Each representative on the Trusteeship Council may be accompanied by such alternates and advisors as he may require. An alternate or an advisor may act as a representative when so designated by the representative.

These provisions have no basis in the Charter.[2]

Article 90 of the Charter authorises the Trusteeship Council to determine 'the method of selecting its President.' The Rules of Procedure provide in this respect:

in the Trusteeship Council was not correctly characterised by the term 'continued absence of the Soviet Union.' Such absence would have been possible even if the Government of the Soviet Union had designated a representative in accordance with Article 86, paragraph 2, of the Charter. The decisive fact is that no such representative had been designated and that consequently the Trusteeship Council was not composed in conformity with Article 86.

[1] At the 63rd meeting of the General Assembly the President declared that the General Assembly had approved the trusteeship agreements submitted to it by an overwhelming majority, and that elections to the Trusteeship Council would therefore be perfectly regular. (Official Records of the Second Part of the First Session of the General Assembly, p. 1321.)

[2] Cf. *supra*, pp. 84 f.

RULE 19

The Trusteeship Council, by secret and separate ballots, shall elect, at the beginning of its regular session in June, a President and a Vice-President from among the representatives of the members of the Trusteeship Council.

RULE 20

The President and Vice-President shall hold office until their respective successors are elected, and shall not be eligible for immediate re-election.

RULE 21

In the absence of the President, the Vice-President shall act as President. In the event that the President for any reason is no longer able to act in that capacity, the Vice-President shall serve as President during the unexpired term. In both cases the Vice-President shall have the same powers and duties as the President.

RULE 22

The President may appoint one of his alternates or advisors to participate in the proceedings and to vote in the Trusteeship Council. In such a case the President shall not exercise his right to vote.

The Charter provides only for a President, not for a Vice-President; hence the constitutionality of Rules 19 to 22 is doubtful. Since Rule 19 stipulates that the President and Vice-President are to be elected 'from among the representatives of the members of the Trusteeship Council,' it may be assumed that both officers are not able to perform their functions if they cease to be representatives of a member of the Council. This is expressly stipulated in Rule 21 of the Rules of Procedure of the Economic and Social Council, but not in the Rules of Procedure for the Trusteeship Council. Hence the opposite interpretation is not excluded.

As to the procedure of the Trusteeship Council, Article 89 of the Charter provides that each member shall have one vote, and that decisions of this body 'shall be made by a majority of the members present and voting.' As to the *quorum*, Rule 50 provides:

> At any meeting of the Trusteeship Council two-thirds of the members shall constitute a quorum.

As to the voting, the Rules of Procedure provide:

RULE 37

Decisions or recommendations of the Trusteeship Council shall be made by a majority of the members present and voting.

Members who abstain in particular votes shall not in those instances be counted as voting.

RULE 38

If a vote other than for an election is equally divided, a second vote shall be taken at the next meeting or, by decision of the Trusteeship Council, following a brief recess. Unless at the second vote there is a majority in favour of the proposal, it shall be deemed to be lost.

RULE 41

All elections and all decisions relating to the tenure of office of an individual shall be taken by secret ballot.

RULE 42

When only one person or member is to be elected and no candidate obtains in the first ballot the majority required, a second ballot shall be taken, which shall be confined to the two candidates obtaining the largest number of votes. If in the second ballot the votes are equally divided, the President shall decide between the candidates by drawing lots.

RULE 43

When two or more elective places are to be filled at one time under the same conditions, those candidates obtaining in the first ballot the majority required shall be elected. If the number of candidates obtaining such majority is less than the number of persons or members to be elected, there shall be additional ballots to fill the remaining places, the voting being restricted to the candidates obtaining the greatest number of votes in the previous ballot, the number of candidates being not more than twice as many as the places remaining to be filled.

As to the sessions of the Trusteeship Council, Article 90, paragraph 2, of the Charter, stipulates:

> The Trusteeship Council shall meet as required in accordance with its rules, which shall include provision for the convening of meetings on the request of a majority of its members.

The Rules of Procedure provide:

RULE 1

The Trusteeship Council shall meet in two regular sessions each year. The first of such sessions shall be convened during the latter half of June and the second shall be convened during the latter half of November.

RULE 2

Special sessions shall be held as and where occasion may require, by decision of the Trusteeship Council, or at the request of a majority of its members, or at the request of the General Assembly, or at the request of the Security Council acting in pursuance of the relevant provisions of the Charter.

RULE 3

A request for a special session may be made by the Economic and Social Council or by any member of the Trusteeship Council, and shall be addressed to the Secretary-General of the United Nations, who without delay shall communicate the request to the other members of the Trusteeship Council. On notification by the Secretary-General that the majority of the members have concurred, the President of the Trusteeship Council shall request the Secretary-General to call a special session.

(*b*) Relationship of the Trusteeship Council to the General Assembly, the Security Council, and other Organs of the United Nations.

The Trusteeship Council is intended to be an auxiliary organ of the General Assembly as well as of the Security Council. It does not have more authority in trusteeship matters than the two organs which it has to assist. Hence the Trusteeship Council—except if the Organisation is itself the administering authority—participates only in the supervision of the administration of the trust territories, not in their administration. The relation of the Trusteeship Council to the Assembly is determined by Article 85, paragraph 2, and Article 87. Article 85, paragraph 2, provides that the Trusteeship Council shall assist the Assembly in carrying out the functions of the United Nations with regard to trust territories which have not the character of strategic areas; it expressly states that the Trusteeship Council in assisting the Assembly operates 'under the authority of the General Assembly.' Article 87 determines the actions by which the General Assembly may exercise its functions of supervision, and repeats the provision that the Council shall act 'under the authority' of the Assembly in performing these actions. Article 88 seems to confer a particular competence—the formulation of a questionnaire—only upon the Trusteeship Council, authorising the Council to perform this function under its own authority, not under the authority of the General Assembly.[3] But this interpretation is incompatible with

[3] At the 9th meeting, 3rd session of the Trusteeship Council, the representative of China stated that the Trusteeship Council was the sole organ empowered to perform the functions set forth in Articles 87 and 88. (Doc. T/S.R. 82, p. 13.) At the 10th meeting the representative of the Philippines stated: 'From Article 16 of the Charter it was apparent that not all functions with respect to trusteeship were

Article 85 which provides that all functions of the United Nations with regard to trusteeship agreements for all areas not designated as strategic shall be exercised by the General Assembly. This provision applies also to the function determined in Article 88 in so far as this Article refers to non-strategic areas. Consequently, the Trusteeship Council in carrying out all its functions relating to non-strategic areas, also the function determined in Article 88, shall operate under the authority of, and in assistance to, the General Assembly.

The relationship between the Trusteeship Council and the Security Council is determined in Article 83, paragraph 3, by the formula: The Security Council 'shall avail itself of the assistance of the Trusteeship Council . . .' Whereas the Trusteeship Council is authorised to assist the General Assembly in all functions which this body has within the trusteeship system, the Security Council shall avail itself of the assistance of the Trusteeship Council only to perform the functions referred to in Article 83, paragraph 3, and this only without prejudice to security considerations. Since Article 83, paragraph 3, expressly provides: The Security Council 'shall' avail itself of the assistance of the Trusteeship Council, this assistance may be considered as obligatory.[4] But since the provision is restricted by

to be exercised by the General Assembly. Those functions not assigned to the General Assembly could be performed only by the Trusteeship Council or the Security Council. Moreover, Article 88 directly vested in the Trusteeship Council the power to formulate a questionnaire, a power not granted either to the General Assembly or to the Security Council.' (Doc. T/S.R. 83, p. 9.) Article 16 of the Charter does not exclude the General Assembly from the function determined in Article 88. Article 16 can not be interpreted without taking into consideration Article 85 which confers all functions of the United Nations with regard to non strategic trusteeships upon the General Assembly. Cf. *supra*, pp. 622 f.

[4] It seems that in this respect the Russian text of the Charter differs from the three others. At the 324th meeting of the Security Council, the delegate of the Soviet Union declared that the Russian text of Article 83 reads as follows: 'The Security Council, subject to the provisions of the Trusteeship Agreements and without prejudice to security considerations, avails itself of the assistance of the Trusteeship Council to perform those functions . . .' He added: 'There is no element of obligation in the words ". . . avails itself of the assistance of the Trusteeship Council to perform those functions . . ." The Security Council is not compelled to avail itself of the assistance of the Trusteeship Council, to say nothing of continuous assistance. The Charter does not impose any such obligation.' (Official Records of the Security Council, 3rd Year, No. 87, p. 12). Since the Russian text of the Charter is as authentic as the others, the interpretation of Article 83 of the Soviet delegate is as possible as the one based on the English text.

During the discussion of the question of the relationship between the Security Council and the Trusteeship Council as determined by Article 83, paragraph 3, the representative of the Soviet Union expressed the view that, since Article 83 paragraph 3, did not impose upon the Security Council an obligation to avail itself of the assistance of the Trusteeship Council, this assistance was dependent 'on the condition that express mention of it was made in the Trusteeship agreement.' The Australian delegate considered that under Article 83, paragraph 3, the Security Council was required to avail itself of the assistance of the Trusteeship Council except 'if such assistance were excluded by the terms of the Trusteeship agreement.'

the clause 'without prejudice to security considerations,' its effect is almost the same as if it had been formulated: The Security Council 'may' . . .' As to other trusteeship functions than those determined in Article 83, paragraph 3, the assistance of the Trusteeship Council is not obligatory in this sense. It is even doubtful whether the Security Council is allowed to avail itself of the Trusteeship Council in the exercise of Trusteeship functions other than those determined in Article 83, paragraph 3. For this is the only provision of the Charter referring to the relation between the Security Council and the Trusteeship Council. In Chapter XIII, the Security Council is not mentioned at all. At any rate, the Trusteeship Council can act with regard to strategic areas only as assistant to the Security Council. If Article 88 is interpreted to mean that the Trusteeship Council shall formulate a questionnaire on the political, economic, social, and educational advancement of the inhabitants not only of non-strategic, but also of strategic, trust territories, then Article 83, paragraph 3, applies, according to which the Security Council shall avail itself of the assistance of the Trusteeship Council in the performance of this function; which means that the Trusteeship Council, in formulating a questionnaire for strategic areas, can act only as assistant to the Security Council. Within the trusteeship system as laid down in the Charter the Trusteeship Council—although designated in Article 7, paragraph 1, of the Charter, as a 'principal' organ of the United Nations side by side with the General Assembly and the Security Council—is in all its functions only an auxiliary organ of the General Assembly or of the Security Council.[5]

(Doc. S/642 pp. 1 f.) The interpretation of the Soviet delegate ignores that all functions of the organisation—whether stipulated in the Charter as mandatory or not—must be provided for in the trusteeship agreement, since Article 77, paragraph 2, and Article 81 prescribe that the terms of the trusteeship shall be determined in the trusteeship agreement. If Article 83, paragraph 3, would read: the Security Council 'may' avail itself (instead of 'shall' avail itself), the Security Council could approve a trusteeship agreement by which the Security Council was not authorised to avail itself of the assistance of the Trusteeship Council. Since Article 83, paragraph 3, makes the assistance obligatory, no trusteeship agreement shall be approved by the Security Council which is not in conformity with this provision of the Charter. The application of Article 83, paragraph 3, shows how misleading the legislative technique of the Charter is, which on the one hand provides that all functions of the Organisation (and obligations of the administering authority) shall be determined by the trusteeship agreement, but on the other hand refers with respect to a particular function (or obligation) to the provisions of the trusteeship agreement. This inconsistency makes the interpretation of the Soviet delegate possible. The same is true with respect to the interpretation of the Australian delegate, which is based on the formula 'subject to the provisions of the trusteeship agreements.' If Article 77 (2) and 81 are not taken into consideration, Article 83, paragraph 3, may indeed be interpreted as the Australian delegate suggested.

5 At the 10th meeting, 3rd session, of the Trusteeship Council, the delegate of the Philippines emphasised 'that it was a mistake to regard the Trusteeship Council as a subsidiary organ either of the Security Council or of the General Assembly. While in some respects it played a subordinate role, it was an independent organ,

The Trusteeship Council in assisting the General Assembly shall act 'under the authority' of the latter, whereas its assistance to the Security Council is not characterised in this way. The meaning of the phrase 'under the authority of the General Assembly' is not clear. It may mean that the Trusteeship Council needs a special authorisation of the General Assembly in order to assist the latter in exercising a concrete function (except the function determined in Article 88 which is directly conferred upon the Trusteeship Council by the Charter). Then the Trusteeship Council can operate as assistant to

with its own functions, assigned to it directly by the Charter rather than delegated to it by another organ, and with its own task to perform in furthering the aims of the United Nations, paramount among which was the promotion of international peace and security.' (Doc. T/S.R. 83, p. 9.) This view has no basis in the Charter. The same is true of the arguments advanced by the representative of Argentina at the 324th meeting of the Security Council against the view of the Soviet delegate that it was impossible to put the Security Council and the Trusteeship Council on an equal footing. He quoted Article 7 of the Charter and stated: 'And all those organs are placed on the same level; there is no mention of any one organ being above another; on the contrary, it is understood that all of them exist in order to work together toward the fulfilment of the purposes and principles of the United Nations Charter.' (Official Records of the Security Council, 3rd Year, No. 87, pp. 13 f.) It is true that Article 7, paragraph 1, places all the organs mentioned there on the same level. But other provisions of the Charter establish relations of subordination and superordination among them.

At the 9th meeting, 3rd session of the Trusteeship Council, the representative of New Zealand maintained that the Trusteeship Council, in assisting the Security Council, 'could determine the terms on which it would give such assistance and could refuse it if the terms laid down by the Security Council seemed unacceptable.' (Doc. T/S.R 82, p. 12.) If a trusteeship agreement for a strategic area confers upon the Organisation—as the agreement for the former Japanese mandated Islands does—the same functions as the Organisation has under Articles 87 and 88 with respect to non-strategic areas, the Trusteeship Council can act only as assistant to the Security Council. Hence it cannot determine the terms on which it would give its assistance to the Security Council and certainly can not refuse its assistance if the terms laid down by the Security Council seems unacceptable.

At the same meeting of the Trusteeship Council the delegate of Belgium stated: 'It should be realised, however, that the Trusteeship Council's position in regard to the Security Council was not the same as it was in regard to the General Assembly. The Security Council's authority in relation to the Trusteeship Council, as far as strategic areas were concerned, was far greater than that of the General Assembly in relation to the Trusteeship Council as far as non-trust territories [should probably read: non strategic trust territories] were concerned. Article 83of the Charter made that clear' (p. 10). Article 83 provides that the Trusteeship Council shall give assistance to the Security Council. Article 85, referring to the relation between General Assembly and Trusteeship Council in all functions of the United Nations with regard to non-strategic trust territories provides exactly the same: the Trusteeship Council shall 'assist' the General Assembly. The only difference made in the Charter is that according to Articles 85 and 87 the Trusteeship Council shall operate 'under the authority' of the General Assembly, whereas there is no provision to the effect that the Trusteeship Council shall act under the authority of the Security Council. But this is rather in favour of the authority of the General Assembly in its relation to the Trusteeship Council, than in favour of the authority of the Security Council.

the General Assembly only if asked for its assistance. But the Assembly is bound to avail itself of this assistance in performing all trusteeship functions conferred upon it, whereas the Security Council only in performing the functions referred to in Article 83, paragraph 3. However, since the Charter provides that the Trusteeship Council shall assist the General Assembly in carrying out all its trusteeship functions, it may be argued that no special authorisation is necessary, that all trusteeship functions conferred upon the Assembly are to be carried out by the Trusteeship Council, the Assembly having the power to reserve to itself—by an express act—a particular function (except the one determined in Article 88) and to direct all the activities of the Trusteeship Council. This interpretation may be supported by the fact that Article 87, determining the actions by which the supervisory function of the General Assembly is to be carried out, is placed in Chapter XIII, entitled 'Trusteeship Council,' and by the wording of this Article: 'The General Assembly *and* . . . the Trusteeship Council, in carrying out *their* functions, may . . . '.

As to the relationship between Security Council and Trusteeship Council, Article 83, paragraph 3, may be interpreted to mean that the Trusteeship Council can act as assistant to the Security Council only if it is requested to act in a concrete case. Whether the Security Council may authorise the Trusteeship Council in a general way to perform the functions determined in Article 83, paragraph 3, with respect to strategic areas (subject to the provisions of the trusteeship agreements), is doubtful. In view of the fact that the Charter does not contain a provision concerning the relationship between Security Council and Trusteeship Council analogous to that of Article 87 concerning the relation between General Assembly and Trusteeship Council, the answer may be in the negative. But the wording of Article 83, paragraph 3, does not exclude an affirmative answer.

The Rules of Procedure which the Trusteeship Council adopted, seem to presuppose that no special authorisation by the General Assembly is necessary to enable the Trusteeship Council to carry out the trusteeship functions conferred by the Charter upon the Assembly. These functions are treated in the Rules of Procedure as if they were conferred only upon the Trusteeship Council, as if there were no difference between these functions and those conferred in Article 88 of the Charter directly upon the Trusteeship Council. Article 87, clause (*a*) confers upon the Assembly the power to consider reports submitted by the administering authority (to the Assembly, according to Article 88). The Rules of Procedure provide:

RULE 72

1. . . .

2. Each report of an Administering Authority shall be considered by the Trusteeship Council at the first regular

session following the expiration of six weeks from the receipt of the report by the Secretary-General.

3. The Secretary-General shall transmit these reports without delay to the members of the Trusteeship Council.

RULE 74

In the examination of all annual reports the Administering Authority concerned shall be entitled to designate and to have present a special representative who should be well informed on the territory involved.

RULE 75

The special representative of the Administering Authority may participate without vote in the examination and discussion of a report, except in a discussion directed to specific conclusions concerning it.

Article 87, clause (*b*), of the Charter, authorises the General Assembly to 'accept petitions and examine them in consultation with the administering authority.' In the Rules of Procedure regulating this matter, the Trusteeship Council is the only organ of the United Nations competent to perform the action determined by Article 87, clause (*b*):

XV. PETITIONS

RULE 76

Petitions may be accepted and examined by the Trusteeship Council if they concern the affairs of one or more Trust Territories or the operation of the International Trusteeship System as laid down in the Charter, except that with respect to petitions relating to a strategic area the functions of the Trusteeship Council shall be governed by Article 83 of the Charter and the terms of the relevant Trusteeship agreements.

RULE 77

Petitioners may be inhabitants of Trust Territories or other parties.

RULE 78

Petitions may be presented in writing in accordance with Rules 79 to 86, or orally in accordance with Rules 87 to 91.

RULE 79

A written petition may be in the form of a letter, telegram, memorandum or other document concerning the affairs of one or more Trust Territories or the operation of the International Trusteeship System as laid down in the Charter.

RULE 80

The Trusteeship Council may hear oral presentations in support or elaboration of a previously submitted written petition. Oral presentations shall be confined to the subject-matter of the petition as stated in writing by the petitioners. The Trusteeship Council, in exceptional cases, may also hear orally petitions which have not been previously submitted in writing, provided that the Trusteeship Council and the Administering Authority concerned have been previously informed with regard to their subject-matter.[6]

RULE 80 *bis*

The President of the Council shall be authorised between sessions of the Council, through the Secretary-General, to inform any petitioner who requests an opportunity for an oral presentation or petition under Rule 80, that the Council will grant him a hearing at such time and place as the President may name. Before communicating such information to the petitioner, the President shall enquire of the Administering Authority or Authorities concerned as to whether there are substantial reasons why the matter should first be discussed in the Council. If the Administering Authority is of the opinion that such substantial reasons exist, the President shall defer action until the matter has been decided by the Council.

RULE 81

Normally petitions shall be considered inadmissible if they are directed against judgments of competent courts of the Administering Authority or if they lay before the Council a dispute with which the courts have competence to deal. This rule shall not be interpreted so as to prevent consideration by the Trusteeship Council of petitions against legislation on the grounds of its incompatibility with the provisions of the Charter of the United Nations or of the Trusteeship agreement, irrespective of whether decisions on cases arising under such legislation have previously been given by the courts of the Administering Authority.

RULE 82

Written petitions may be addressed directly to the Secretary-General or may be transmitted to him through the Administering Authority.

[6] At the 3rd meeting, 3rd session, of the Trusteeship Council, the representative of the United States correctly interpreted Rule 80 of the Rules of Procedure to establish 'a privilege, and not an obligation.' (Doc. T/S.R. 76, p. 9.)

Rule 83

Written petitions submitted to the Administering Authority for transmission shall be communicated promptly to the Secretary-General, with or without comments by the Administering Authority, at its discretion, or with an indication that such comments will follow in due course.

Rule 84

Representatives of the Trusteeship Council engaged in periodic visits to Trust Territories or on other official missions authorised by the Council, may accept written petitions, subject to such instructions as may have been received from the Trusteeship Council. Petitions of this kind shall be transmitted promptly to the Secretary-General for circulation to the members of the Council. A copy of each such petition shall be communicated to the competent local authority. Any observations which the visiting representatives may wish to make on the petitions, after consultation with the local representative of the Administering Authority, shall be submitted to the Trusteeship Council.

Rule 85

The Secretary-General shall circulate promptly to the members of the Trusteeship Council all written petitions received by him, except those which are manifestly inconsequential, a list of which, with a summary of their contents, shall be communicated to the members of the Trusteeship Council. The original documents shall be made available to the Trusteeship Council for final disposition.

With respect to petitions relating to a strategic area, the functions of the Trusteeship Council shall be governed by Article 83 of the Charter and the terms of the relevant Trusteeship Agreement.

Rule 86

1. Written petitions will normally be placed on the agenda of a regular session provided that they shall have been received by the Administering Authority concerned either directly or through the Secretary-General at least two months before the date of the next following regular session.

2. Any observations on petitions which the Administering Authority desires to have circulated to members of the Trusteeship Council should, wherever possible, be transmitted to the Secretary-General not less than fourteen days before the opening of the session at which such petitions will be considered.

3. The date of receipt of a petition shall be considered as being:

(*a*) in respect of a petition which is presented through the Administering Authority, the date on which the petition is received by the competent local authority in the territory or the metropolitan Government of the Administering Authority, as the case may be, and

(*b*) in respect of a petition not presented through the Administering Authority, the date on which the petition is received by the Administering Authority through the Secretary-General. The Administering Authority concerned shall immediately notify the Secretary-General of the date of receipt of all such petitions.

4. In cases where the Administering Authority may be prepared to consider a written petition at shorter notice than is prescribed by the foregoing rules, or where, in exceptional cases, as a matter of urgency, it may be so decided by the Trusteeship Council in consultation with the Administering Authority concerned, such written petition may be placed on the agenda of a regular session notwithstanding that it has been presented after the due date, or it may be placed on the agenda of a special session.

RULE 87

Requests to present petitions orally or to make oral presentations in support or elaboration of written petitions, in accordance with Rule 80, may be addressed directly to the Secretary-General or may be transmitted to him through the Administering Authority. In the latter case the Administering Authority concerned shall communicate such requests promptly to the Secretary-General.

RULE 88

The Secretary-General shall promptly notify the members of the Trusteeship Council of all requests for oral petitions or oral presentations received by him, except for petitions relating to a strategic area with respect to which the functions of the Trusteeship Council shall be governed by Article 83 of the Charter and the terms of the relevant Trusteeship agreement.

RULE 89

Representatives of the Trusteeship Council engaged in periodic visits to the Trust Territories or on other official missions authorised by the Council may receive oral presentations or petitions, subject to such instructions as may have been received from the Trusteeship Council. Such oral presentations or petitions shall be recorded by the visiting mission, and the record shall be transmitted promptly to the

Secretary-General for circulation to the members of the Council and to the Administering Authority for comment. A copy of each such record shall be communicated to the competent local authority. Any observations which the visiting representatives may wish to make on the oral presentations or petitions, after consultation with the local representative of the Administering Authority, shall be submitted to the Trusteeship Council.

RULE 90

The Trusteeship Council, at the beginning of each session which includes the consideration of petitions on its agenda, may appoint an *ad hoc* committee on petitions whose membership shall be evenly divided between representatives of members administering Trust Territories and representatives of members having no administering responsibilities. The *ad hoc* committee on petitions shall be empowered to undertake a preliminary examination of the petitions on the agenda. No appraisal of the substance of the petitions shall be made by the *ad hoc* committee.

RULE 91

The Trusteeship Council may designate one or more of its representatives to accept oral petitions the subject-matter of which has been previously communicated to the Trusteeship Council and to the Administering Authority concerned. Oral petitions and oral presentations may be examined either in public or in private, as may be determined, in accordance with Rule 44.

RULE 92

In the examination of all petitions the Administering Authority concerned shall be entitled to designate and to have present a special representative who should be well informed on the territory involved.

RULE 93

The Secretary-General shall inform the Administering Authorities and the petitioners concerned of the actions taken by the Trusteeship Council on each petition, and shall transmit to them the official records of the public meetings at which the petitions were examined.

Article 87, clause (*c*), confers upon the General Assembly the power to 'provide for periodic visits to the respective trust territories.' The Rules of Procedure stipulate:

XVI. VISITS TO TRUST TERRITORIES

RULE 94

The Trusteeship Council, in accordance with the provisions of Article 87 (*c*) and Article 83, paragraph 3, of the Charter, as the case may be, and with the terms of the respective Trusteeship agreements, shall make provision for periodic visits to each Trust Territory with a view to achieving the basic objectives of the International Trusteeship System.

RULE 95

The Trusteeship Council, acting in conformity with the terms of the respective Trusteeship agreements, shall define the terms of reference of each visiting mission and shall issue to each mission such special instructions as it may consider appropriate.

RULE 96

The Trusteeship Council shall select the members of each visiting mission who shall preferably be one or more of the representatives on the Council. Each mission may be assisted by experts and by representatives of the local administration. A mission and the individual members thereof shall, while engaged in a visit, act only on the basis of the instructions of the Council and shall be responsible exclusively to it.

RULE 97

The Trusteeship Council may, in agreement with the Administering Authority, conduct special investigations or enquiries when it considers that conditions in a Trust Territory make such action desirable.[7]

RULE 98

All expenses of periodic visits, special investigations and enquiries, including the travel expenses of the visiting missions, shall be borne by the United Nations.

RULE 99

Each visiting mission shall transmit to the Trusteeship Council a report on its visit, a copy of which shall be promptly and, as a general rule, simultaneously transmitted to the Administering Authority and to each other member of the Trusteeship Council by the Secretary-General. The mission may authorise the Secretary-General to release its report in

[7] The constitutionality of this provision is doubtful. It is not covered by Article 87, which does not confer upon the General Assembly and Trusteeship Council the power to conduct ' special investigations or inquiries,' in addition to the periodic visits referred to in clause (*c*). Article 87 (*d*) of the Charter provides that the General Assembly and, under its authority, the Trusteeship Council may take actions other than those determined in clauses (*a*)–(*c*) : ' in conformity with the terms of the trusteeship agreements,' not—as Rule 97 stipulates—' in agreement with the Administering Authority.' According to the wording of Article 87 the power to conduct investigations must be established in the text of the trusteeship agreements.

such form and at such date as it may deem appropriate. The report and the decisions or observations of the Council with respect to each such report, as well as the comments made by the Administering Authority concerned, may be published in such form and at such date as the Council may determine.

The Rules of Procedure adopted by the Trusteeship Council further confer upon this body the following functions not, or not expressly, provided by the Charter:

XVII. Reports of the Trusteeship Council

Rule 100

The Trusteeship Council shall present annually to the General Assembly a general report on its activities and on the discharge of its responsibilities under the International Trusteeship System. Each such report shall include an annual review of the conditions in each Trust Territory.

Rule 101

1. The sections of the general reports of the Trusteeship Council to the General Assembly relating to conditions in specific Trust Territories, referred to in Rule 100, shall take into account the annual reports of the Administering Authorities, and such other sources of information as may be available, including petitions, reports of visiting missions, and any special investigations or enquiries, as provided for in Rule 97.

2. The general reports shall include, as appropriate, the conclusions of the Trusteeship Council regarding the execution and interpretation of the provisions of Chapters XII and XIII of the Charter and of the Trusteeship agreements, and such suggestions and recommendations concerning each Trust Territory as the Council may decide.

Rule 102

The reports of the Trusteeship Council to the General Assembly provided for in Rules 100 and 101 shall be transmitted through the Secretary-General at least thirty days before the opening of the regular session of the General Assembly.

Rule 103

The Trusteeship Council may designate the President, the Vice-President or another of its members to represent it during the consideration of its reports by the General Assembly.

XVIII. Other Functions

Rule 104

> The Trusteeship Council shall perform such other functions as may be provided for in the Trusteeship Agreements, and, in pursuance of the duty imposed upon it by Article 85 of the Charter, may submit to the General Assembly recommendations concerning the functions of the United Nations with regard to Trusteeship agreements, including the approval of the terms of the Trusteeship agreements and of their alteration or amendment. With regard to strategic areas, the Trusteeship Council may similarly perform such functions in so far as it may be requested to do so by the Security Council.

The provision of the Charter that the Trusteeship Council is only an assistant to the General Assembly (operating under the latter's authority) is completely ignored by the Rules of Procedure adopted by the Trusteeship Council. It might be argued that the Trusteeship Council was authorised by the General Assembly to regulate its competence in this way. For the Assembly adopted at its 27th meeting the following resolution:[8]

> The General Assembly requests the Secretary-General to transmit the ' Provisional rules of procedure of the Trusteeship Council ' (section 2 of Chapter IV of the Preparatory Commission's Report) to the Trusteeship Council as soon as it is constituted.

The ' Provisional rules of procedure of the Trusteeship Council ' recommended by the Preparatory Commission are, by and large, identical with the Rules of Procedure adopted by the Trusteeship Council. The resolution of the General Assembly might be interpreted to be a general authorisation of the Trusteeship Council to perform the functions conferred by the Charter upon the General Assembly, so that the Council, in performing these functions in conformity with its Rules of Procedure, acts ' under the authority of the General Assembly.'

As to the relationship to the Security Council, the Rules of Procedure carefully respect the provisions of the Charter. Rule 76 expressly provides that ' with respect to petitions relating to a stratgeic area the functions of the Trusteeship Council shall be governed by Article 83 of the Charter and the terms of the relevant Trusteeship agreements.' Analogous provisions are contained in Rule 85, concerning the Secretary-General's duty to circulate to the members of the Trusteeship Council the written petitions; in Rule 88, concerning the Secretary General's duty to notify the members of the requests for oral petitions; and in Rule 94, concerning periodic

[8] Resolutions adopted by the General Assembly, Doc. A/64, p. 13.

visits. As to functions other than those expressly determined in the Rules of Procedure, Rule 104 stipulates that 'with regard to strategic areas' the Trusteeship Council may perform such functions only 'in so far as it may be requested to do so by the Security Council.'

Under Article 83, paragraph 3, of the Charter, the Security Council shall avail itself of the assistance of the Trusteeship Council to perform functions relating to 'political, economic, social, and educational matters in the strategic areas.' Article 88 provides that the Trusteeship Council shall formulate a questionnaire on the 'political, economic, social, and educational advancement of the inhabitants of each trust territory.' The questionnaire refers to the same matters as those referred to in Article 83, paragraph 3. If Article 88 is interpreted to establish a function of the Organisation for all trust territories, the Security Council shall avail itself of the assistance of the Trusteeship Council in the performance of the function determined in Article 88, that is the formulation of a questionnaire on the political, economic, social, and educational advancement of the inhabitants of the strategic trust territory under the supervision of the Security Council. The function determined in Article 88 is a function of the Trusteeship Council under the Authority of the General Assembly (Article 85) with regard to non-strategic areas, and a function of the Trusteeship Council as assistant to the Security Council (Article 83, paragraph 3) with respect to strategic trust territories. If Article 88 is interpreted to mean that the Trusteeship Council (under the authority of the General Assembly) shall formulate a questionnaire only for non-strategic trust territories, the question of the relation between Security Council and Trusteeship Council regarding the formulation of the questionnaire arises only in case a trusteeship agreement for a strategic trust territory confers upon the Organisation the function determined in Article 88 and upon the administering authority the obligation established in this Article.[9]

[9] The question of the relationship between the Security Council and the Trusteeship Council with regard to the supervision of strategic trust territories arose as result of the entry into force of the trusteeship agreement for the former Japanese mandated islands, which in Article 13 provides that Articles 87 and 88 of the Charter shall be applicable to the trust territory. If this provision is interpreted to mean that the Security Council and the Trusteeship Council shall have the same functions with regard to the trust territory as the General Assembly and the Trusteeship Council have under Articles 87 and 88 with regard to non-strategic trust territories and the administering authority the same obligations as the administering authorities of non-strategic areas under Articles 87 and 88, then the relationship between the Security Council and the trusteeship Council in applying Articles 87 and 88 to the territory under the trusteeship administration of the United States is the same as the relationship between the General Assembly and the Trusteeship Council in applying these Articles to non-strategic territories. Hence the Security Council may authorise the Trusteeship Council in a general way to perform, subject to the provisions of the trusteeship agreement, the functions determined in Articles 87 and 88 with respect to the trust territory. On January 12, 1948, the Committee of experts submitted to the Security Council a report on the respective functions

The matters referred to in Article 83, paragraph 3, are—with the exception of ' political ' matters—the typical objects of economic and social co-operation, placed by the Charter within the competence of the Economic and Social Council. They are, according to Article 62, paragraph 1, ' international economic, social, cultural, educational, health, and related matters.' Under Article 65, the Economic and Social Council ' shall assist the Security Council upon its request ' evidently only in matters which are within the competence of the former. Under Article 83, paragraph 3, the Security Council shall avail itself of the assistance of the Trusteeship Council in matters which, to a great extent, are within the competence of the Economic and Social Council; under Article 65, the Security Council may

of the Security Council and the Trusteeship Council with regard to the Trusteeship System as applied to strategic areas. The majority of the Committee recommended to the Security Council the adoption of the following draft resolution:

Whereas Article 83, paragraph 3, of the Charter, provides that—

> ' The Security Council shall, subject to the provisions of the trusteeship agreements and without prejudice to security considerations, avail itself of the assistance of the Trusteeship Council to perform those functions of the United Nations under the trusteeship system relating to political, economic, social and educational matters in the strategic areas,'

The Security Council resolves:

> 1. That the Trusteeship Council be requested, subject to the provisions of trusteeship agreements or parts thereof in respect of strategic areas, and subject to the decisions of the Security Council made having regard to security considerations from time to time, to perform in accordance with its own procedures, on behalf of the Security Council, the functions specified in Articles 87 and 88 of the Charter relating to the political, economic, social and educational advancement of the inhabitants of such strategic areas.
>
> 2. That the Trusteeship Council be requested to send to the Security Council, one month before forwarding to the Administering Authority, a copy of the questionnaire formulated in accordance with Article 88 of the Charter and any amendments to such questionnaire which may be made from time to time by the Trusteeship Council.
>
> 3. That the Secretary-General be requested to advise the Security Council of all reports and petitions received from or relating to strategic areas under trusteeship, and to send copies thereof, as soon as possible after receipt, to the Trusteeship Council for examination and report to the Security Council.
>
> 4. That the Trusteeship Council be requested to submit to the Security Council its reports and recommendations on political, economic and educational matters affecting strategic areas under trusteeship. (Doc. T/173.)

' The matter was taken up by the Trusteeship Council at the 9th and 10th meetings of its 3rd session, on June 25 and 28, 1948, when a majority of the members expressed general satisfaction with the arrangements envisaged in the draft resolution, subject to certain reservations. The minority view was that the arrangements envisaged in the draft resolution were contrary to the principles laid down in Article 83, paragraph 1, of the Charter, according to which the main responsibility for strategic areas rested with the Security Council.' (Report of the Trusteeship Council governing its Second and Third Sessions, April 29, 1947–August 5, 1948, p. 3.) The view of the minority has no basis in the Charter.

request the assistance of the Economic and Social Council in these matters. But Article 91 provides:

> The Trusteeship Council shall, when appropriate, avail itself of the assistance of the Economic and Social Council and of the specialised agencies in regard to matters with which they are respectively concerned.

Under this provision, the assistance of the Economic and Social Council may be requested by the Trusteeship Council; under Article 65, the assistance of the Economic and Social Council may be requested by the Security Council.

Rule 105 of the Rules of Procedure for the Trusteeship Council repeats and extends—without basis in the Charter—the provision of Article 91:

> RULE 105
>
> 1. The Trusteeship Council shall, when appropriate, avail itself of the assistance of the Economic and Social Council, of the specialised agencies and of appropriate intergovernmental regional bodies which may be separately established, relating to matters with which they may be concerned.
>
> 2. The Secretary-General shall promptly communicate to these bodies the annual reports of the Administering Authorities and such reports and other documents of the Trusteeship Council as may be of special concern to them.

The Trusteeship Council at its first session, and the Economic and Social Council at its fourth session, 'adopted resolutions providing for the appointment of separate representative committees of three members each, for the purpose of entering into consultation regarding arrangements for co-operation between the two Councils with regard to matters of common concern.—At its first session the Trusteeship Council, in response to an invitation extended by the President of the Economic and Social Council, also took action resulting in the appointment of a committee of two members to join with representatives of the Economic and Social Council in any future negotiations with intergovernmental organisations to be brought into relationship with the United Nations, with respect to such clauses of the agreements as might concern the Trusteeship Council.'[1]

(*c*) Competence of the Trusteeship Council outside the scope of the Trusteeship system.

According to Articles 83, paragraph 3, 85, paragraph 2, and 87, the Trusteeship Council is an auxiliary organ of the General Assembly and the Security Council with the task of assisting these agencies in the performance of their trusteeship functions. No provision of the

[1] *Yearbook of the United Nations*, 1946–47, p. 581.

Charter confers upon the Trusteeship Council other functions than those relating to trust territories. Neither the General Assembly nor the Security Council has the power to confer upon the Trusteeship Council functions which are outside of the trusteeship system. The fact that the Charter does not expressly preclude the General Assembly or the Security Council from delegating to the Trusteeship Council the performance of special tasks not included in the trusteeship system does not justify such delegation. The principle: what is not forbidden is permitted, may apply to the relationship of a subject to the legal order; it does not apply to the competence of the organs of the community constituted by this legal order. Organs of a community are permitted to perform only those acts which the legal order authorises the organs to perform. Otherwise, any constitution of a national as well as of an international community would be meaningless. To confer upon the Trusteeship Council functions outside of the trusteeship system is unconstitutional even if these functions have some similarity to the trusteeship functions. Such similarity can not be substituted for the missing authorisation by the Charter. If the General Assembly or the Security Council is competent to perform a function which is not a trusteeship function, but similar to it, and if it needs an auxiliary organ to perform this function, it may under Articles 22 or 29 establish a subsidiary organ for this purpose. But this possibility does not justify the use of the Trusteeship Council instead.[2] This Council is not a subsidiary organ within the meaning of Article 7, paragraph 2.

As a matter of fact however, the General Assembly delegated to the Trusteeship Council functions which evidently were beyond its competence. After having refused to place the former mandated territory of South West Africa under the trusteeship system, the government of the Union of South Africa informed the United Nations in a letter of July 23, 1947,[3] that it had decided to continue to administer the territory in the spirit of the mandate and to submit reports on its administration for the information of the United Nations, whereupon the General Assembly, at its 105th meeting on November 1, 1947, adopted a resolution authorising the Trusteeship Council 'to examine the report on South West Africa recently submitted by the Government of the Union of South Africa and to submit its observations thereon to the General Assembly.'[4] Pursuant to this resolution the Trusteeship Council at its 15th meeting on December 12, 1947, adopted a resolution to the effect 'that the report in certain particulars appears to be incomplete and that opportunity should therefore be

[2] At the 18th meeting of the Fourth Committee the representative of Australia correctly stated: 'The supervisory function of the Trusteeship Council was confined to the territories under trusteeship . . . ' (Summary Record of Meetings of Fourth Committee, November 1–December 12, 1946, p. 94.)

[3] Doc. A/334.

[4] Resolutions adopted by the General Assembly, Doc. A/519, p. 48.

taken of the offer of the Government of the Union of South Africa to transmit, if desired, further available data; that the Government of the Union of South Africa be invited to supply supplementary information before the month of June, 1948, on the questions attached hereto in order that the Council may be able to submit its observations to the General Assembly at its next session.'[5]

In its resolution on the future government of Palestine adopted at its 128th meeting on November 29, 1947, the General Assembly laid down that the City of Jerusalem should be established as a *corpus separatum* under a special international regime. The Trusteeship Council was designated 'to discharge the responsibilities of the administering authority on behalf of the United Nations.' By this resolution the Trusteeship Council was requested to 'elaborate and approve a detailed Statute for the City.'[6] In pursuance of this resolution, the Trusteeship Council at its 36th meeting (third part of the second session) adopted a statute for the City of Jerusalem which in Article 3 provided: 'the Trusteeship Council, by virtue of the authority conferred upon it by the resolution of the General Assembly of the United Nations of November 29, 1947, shall discharge the

[5] Resolutions adopted by the Trusteeship Council during its Second Session from November 20, 1947, to May 4, 1948, Doc. T/179, pp. 15 f.—If South West Africa was considered to be a dependent, *i.e.*, non-self-governing territory, Article 73 (*e*) of the Charter and its implementation by the resolutions of the General Assembly apply (cf. *supra*, pp. 561 ff.). During the discussion of the problems of Chapter XI in Sub-Committee 2 of the Fourth Committee several delegates expressed the view that the Trusteeship Council was not competent to examine the information to be transmitted by the members administering non-self-governing territories. This was the reason why an *ad hoc* committee was established for this purpose. Cf. Summary Records of Meetings of Sub-Committee 2 of Fourth Committee, November 16–December 5, 1946, pp. 22 ff. and Summary Record of Meetings of Fourth Committee, November 1–December 12, 1946, Annex 19, p. 273. The latter Document (A/C. 4/52) contains the statement: 'In particular, the Trusteeship Council is not given powers or functions in respect of the Territories only covered by Chapter XI.' At the 31st meeting of its 3rd session the Trusteeship Council discussed the report of the Government of the Union of South Africa concerning South West Africa, together with the replies which this government had transmitted pursuant to the Council's request. During this discussion the representative of the Soviet Union 'drew the Council's attention to the fact that under Article 87 of the Charter it could consider reports submitted by the Administering Authorities; the Union of South Africa, however, was not an Administering Authority, nor was South West Africa a territory placed under trusteeship. Furthermore, paragraph (*e*) of Article 73 dealt with information concerning territories other than those mentioned in Chapters XII and XIII of the Charter, that is, Non-Self-Governing Territories, and South West Africa did not fall within this category. Under the Charter, therefore, the Council lacked any juridical basis to act in the matter and should put forward that as its reason for refusing to consider the report on South West Africa.' The U.S.S.R. proposal for non-consideration of the report submitted by the government of South Africa was rejected. (Doc. T/S.R. 104, pp. 6 f.)

[6] Resolutions adopted by the General Assembly, Doc. A/519, pp. 146 f.

responsibilities of the United Nations for the administration of the City in accordance with this Statute.' [7]

Since the legal status of Jerusalem to be established in accordance with the resolution of the General Assembly was not a trusteeship, the Trusteeship Council was neither competent to adopt the Statute nor would it have been competent to perform the function of an administering authority on behalf of the United Nations. [8]

At its 132nd meeting on April 26, 1948, the General Assembly adopted a resolution asking ' the Trusteeship Council to study, with the Mandatory Power and the interested parties, suitable measures for the protection of the city [of Jerusalem] and its inhabitants, and to submit within the shortest possible time proposals to the General Assembly to that effect.' [9] In pursuance of this resolution the Trusteeship Council, on May 5, 1948, submitted to the General Assembly a report in which the Council recommended to the General Assembly that it inform the Mandatory Power of its full agreement with the intention of the latter to appoint a Special Municipal Commissioner who shall carry out the functions hitherto performed by the Municipal Commission. [1] This recommendation did not

[7] Official Records of the Trusteeship Council, Second Session, Third Part, Annex, pp. 4 ff.

[8] The Report of the Working Committee on Jerusalem, established in accordance with a resolution of the Trusteeship Council passed at the 6th meeting of its 2nd session, on December 1, 1947 (Doc. T/122), contains the following statements: ' Although the General Assembly of the United Nations vested the Trusteeship Council with power to define, to constitute and to administer the international regime of the City of Jerusalem, it is obvious that the City is not a trust territory and that the provisions of Chapters XII and XIII of the Charter are not generally applicable to the case. Therefore the Committee tried to avoid any arbitrary resemblance to the Trusteeship system; it considered rather that the legal status of this territory was a new one; Jerusalem would come, as it were, directly under the authority of the United Nations and it would be governed on behalf of the community of nations. Such would be the entirely original sense which might suitably be given to the term: Special International Regime. In this matter, therefore, the Trusteeship Council will be carrying out a special duty on behalf of the United Nations. This will be its authority for assuming first the constituent and later the supreme administrative authority over the City of Jerusalem. The Assembly Resolution will be the text on which it will have to base its action in this matter . . . The reason for this juridical innovation may be found in the obligation laid upon the United Nations to ensure the protection of a City which is a holy place for three great religions ' (pp. 3–4). At the 19th meeting of the Trusteeship Council (2nd session, 2nd part) the representative of Iraq declared with respect to the statute for the City of Jerusalem: ' Should it be said that the plan represented a special arrangement, which was not intended to fit within the Trusteeship System, the answer must be that if the Trusteeship Council was not acting under Chapter XII of the Charter, it could not legally act in the matter at all.' (Doc. T/S.R. 46, p. 7.)

[9] Official Records of the Trusteeship Council, Second Session, Third Part Annex, p. 1.

[1] *Ibid.*, p. 3.

refer to a trust territory and, consequently, was not within the competence of the Trusteeship Council.

D. *Sovereignty*

Where does sovereignty over the trust territories lie? Since a territory can be placed under trusteeship only by the state which is the territorial sovereign, the question means whether the state which places a territory under trusteeship does, or does not, by so doing transfer the sovereignty over the territory to the Organisation as supervising authority or to the administering authority. If the state which places the territory under trusteeship is identical with the administering authority, the only question is whether placing a territory under trusteeship does, or does not, imply transfer of sovereignty to the Organisation as the supervising authority. This is the question with respect to all territories placed until now under the trusteeship system of the United Nations. These territories were formerly under mandate and their placement under the trusteeship system was carried out under the assumption that the states which placed them under the trusteeship system were not the territorial sovereigns. This, however, was a legal fiction incompatible with the rule of international law, that a territory can be disposed of only by the territorial sovereign or with its authorisation. By 'sovereignty' we mean the usual amount of powers which a government, independent from other governments, exercises under international law over a territory and its population. These powers are limited by general international law and may be limited by international agreements, conferring powers with respect to the territory concerned upon other international persons (states or international organisations). To what extent such limitation of the powers of a government is possible without the sovereignty passing from this government to another authority, is a question of degree. Within the trusteeship system as established under the Charter the legal power over the trust territory and its population is divided between the administering authority and the Organisation as the supervising authority. By far the greatest part of this power is—according to the Charter—with the administering authority, the Organisation as supervising authority having only those powers which are expressly conferred upon it by the trusteeship agreement in accordance with the Charter. It may be that by such an agreement an amount of legal power is transferred to the United Nations as supervising authority which might justify the view that the Organisation is the sovereign over the trust territory. But this is not a condition of the approval prescribed by the Charter. The minimum of competence which a trusteeship agreement must confer upon the Organisation in order to be approved by the latter does not suffice to justify the view that the state which in its capacity as territorial sovereign has placed the territory under trusteeship and has become the administering authority, has given up its sovereignty by ceding the territory to the United Nations; especially in case the trust territory is designated in the trusteeship agreement as strategic area. The attempt to consider the Organisation as the sovereign over the trust territories can hardly be based on the Charter, which, in this respect, is less satisfactory than the Covenant of the League of Nations, which in Article 22, paragraph 2, stipulates that the tutelage of the peoples for which the mandatory system is established should be exercised by the nations to which it is entrusted 'as mandatories on behalf of the League.' According to this statement the legal position of the League was analogous to that of the principal or *mandans* in case of private mandate. To this position corresponds in international law that of the territorial sovereign. This interpretation is confirmed by the provision of paragraph 8 of Article 22 that 'the degree of authority, control or administration to be exercised by the Mandatory shall, if not previously agreed upon by the Members of the League, be explicitly defined in each case by the Council.' According to the wording of this provision, it was the League, acting through its Members or through the Council, which was competent to define the duties and rights of the mandatory. Hence an interpretation was possible according to which the League of Nations was the sovereign in relation to the mandated territories.

In the text of the Charter, however, there is no provision that the administering authority should exercise the administration of the trust territory 'on behalf' of the United Nations; neither is there a provision that the terms of trusteeship shall be defined by the Organisation through its Members or through one of its organs. The Charter does not even say that the territories concerned shall be placed under the authority of the United Nations. The formula used in the Charter is that the territories may be placed under the trusteeship system. Only of this 'system,' that is a set of rules regulating trusteeship, is it said in Article 75 that it is to be established under the authority of the United Nations, which means that these rules are established in the Charter of the United Nations or shall be established in accordance with the Charter. The terms of the individual trusteeship are to be defined by agreements concluded by the states directly concerned; by any states directly concerned, not necessarily Members of the Organisation. If they are Members, they do not conclude the trusteeship agreements in this capacity. The Members are not obliged to enter such agreements; and if they cease to be Members, they remain administering authorities, and as such they are under the obligations of the trusteeship agreements. The Organisation, it is true, has to approve the trusteeship agreements—but this approval is part of the conclusion of a treaty to which the Organisation becomes a contracting party; whereas—at least according to the wording of Article 22, paragraph 8, of the Covenant—the Council had the power to define in each case by a unilateral act the degree of authority, control or administration to be exercised by the Mandatory (if this was not previously agreed upon by the Members of the League).[2] The interpretation that the Organisation itself is the sovereign, could be based only on the fact that as long as the trusteeship exists any disposition of the trust territory requires the approval of the Organisation. But since it requires also the consent of the administering authority as a contracting party to the trusteeship agreement, this argument is in favour of both. Hence the view is possible that the state, which in its capacity as territorial sovereign places a territory under trusteeship and becomes the administering authority, retains its sovereignty, though restricted by the trusteeship agreement, unless there is a contrary provision in the agreement.[3]

[2] As a matter of fact all the mandates 'defined' by the Council of the League of Nations constituted agreements entered into by the Principal Allied and Associated Powers, the mandatory power and the League of Nations represented by the Council.

[3] The texts of the trusteeship agreements until now approved by the Organisation do not allow the interpretation that the states which placed the territories under trusteeship have conferred upon the United Nations the sovereignty over the respective trust territories. On the contrary, the agreements contain provisions which support the interpretation that the states exercising the function of administering authority are the territorial sovereigns.

Firstly, all agreements, except the one concerning the former Japanese mandated islands, present the state which is designated as administering authority as the power which disposes of the territory by placing it voluntarily under the trusteeship system; which presupposes that this state was entitled to do so, and that means, that this state was, at the moment the trusteeship agreement was concluded, the territorial sovereign. The agreement concerning the former Japanese mandated islands does not contain such a statement; but, as a matter of fact, the United States of America, designated as administering authority, placed this territory under the trusteeship system, just as the United Kingdom, France, Belgium, Australia and New Zealand placed territories formerly under their mandates under trusteeship.

Secondly, all trusteeship agreements (except that for New Guinea) stipulate that the state exercising the function of administering authority shall have 'full powers of administration, legislation and jurisdiction' in the trust territory. In the agreement concerning New Guinea, submitted by Australia, the formula is used: 'The administering authority . . . will have the same powers of legislation, administration and jurisdiction in and over the Territory as if it were an integral part of Australia,' which also means full state power. Also the other agreements, except those for the former Japanese mandated islands, Tanganyika, Western Samoa, and Nauru, stipulate that the trust territory shall be administered as an 'integral part' of the territory of the state exercising the function of administering authority. This formula, however, is of secondary importance since it expresses only a consequence of the fact that the administering authority is in possession of full state power over the trust territory. Of secondary importance, because also a consequence of full state power, is: that the administering authority—according to all agreements except those for Western Samoa and Nauru—is entitled to constitute the trust territory into a customs, fiscal or administrative union or federation with other territories under the sovereignty (or 'jurisdiction') of the administering authority.

Thirdly, full state power over the trust territory conferred upon or retained

In case the agreement by which the territorial sovereign places a territory under trusteeship designates another state or the Organisation itself as administering authority, the most adequate interpretation is

by the administering state is, according to all trusteeship agreements, restricted only by the obligations expressly assumed in the trusteeship agreements; and these obligations constitute a relatively small limitation of that power. The Organisation, on the other hand, has only that—relatively small—amount of power which corresponds to the obligations expressly assumed by the administering authority.

Fourthly, no further restriction of the full state power which the administering authority possesses is legally possible, nor can the latter be legally deprived of it, without its consent. It is true that during the discussions of the trusteeship agreements submitted to the General Assembly by the United Kingdom and Australia, the delegates declared that the words 'integral part' of the territory of the administering authority as used in the trusteeship agreements do not imply the idea of sovereignty over the trust territory; and that the delegates of France and of Belgium declared that these words 'were necessary as matter of administrative convenience and were not considered as granting to the Governments of Belgium and France the power to diminish the political individuality of the Trust Territories.' (Doc. A/258, pp. 5, 6, 18.) But these declarations have hardly any legal importance since they are not made in the trusteeship agreements and are inconsistent with the decisive stipulations of the latter that the administering authority possesses 'full powers of administration, legislation and jurisdiction'; which means nothing else but sovereignty. At the 18th meeting of the Fourth Committee the delegate of the Soviet Union stated that the draft agreements submitted to the General Assembly 'attempted to transform the trust territories into an integral part of the administering nation on a basis of inequality with the parent country and on a basis of colonial possession. That tendency was specifically embodied in the Articles investing the trustee Power with full legislative, administrative, and judicial authority . . .' The last statement is correct in so far as it means that these provisions imply the sovereignty of the administering authority. But the statement of the Soviet delegate that these provisions 'violated . . . the main principles of Chapter XII' is not correct. (Journal of the United Nations, No. 30: Suppl. No. 4–A/C. 4/54, p. 39.) At the 62nd meeting of the General Assembly the delegate of the Soviet Union proposed a resolution by which the Assembly should reject the draft agreements submitted for approval 'as being inconsistent with the Charter' for three reasons, the second of which was: 'The draft agreements include the provision whereby the territory in trust shall be administered as an integral part of those States which are administering authorities which, in fact, amounts to annexation of the territories in trust by the said States, whereas Article 76 of the Charter provides that the Trusteeship System shall promote the progressive development of the Trust Territories towards self-government or independence.' (*Ibid.*, No. 62: Suppl. A–A/P.V./62, p. 632.) That the terms of the trusteeship agreements amount in fact to annexation, is correct. But the provision referred to is not in contradiction to Article 76 of the Charter.

In view of the provisions of the trusteeship agreements conferring upon the administering authority full state power (or recognising it), it is impossible to interpret the agreements as having conferred sovereignty over the trust territories upon the Organisation. Hence, according to the agreements, no other power but the administering authority can be considered as the territorial sovereign.

The Fourth Committee adopted a proposal of the delegation of India to insert into the trusteeship agreements to be approved by the General Assembly the following provision: 'The administering authority shall administer the Trust Territory on behalf and solely for the benefit of and in the interest of its people, and on the termination of the trusteeship, all the powers of the authority shall

that if the state placing the territory under trusteeship does not expressly retain its sovereignty in the trusteeship agreement, this sovereignty is transferred to the administering authority, and if this authority is the Organisation, to the United Nations.

The question of the sovereignty over the trust territory is of

cease and it shall surrender the territory, together with all public property then existing, whether movable or immovable, to the peoples whose right to sovereignty and independence shall always be recognised.' (Doc. A/258, p. 3.) This proposal was rejected by the states which had submitted the draft agreements to the General Assembly. The principle advocated by the delegate of India that 'sovereignty resided in the peoples of the territories which were still dependent' (Journal of the United Nations, No. 25: Suppl. No. 4–A/C. 4/45, p. 13), that is the principle of popular sovereignty, constitutes the political postulate of a democratic form of government to be established after the status of trusteeship has terminated, and has nothing to do with the principle of state sovereignty, which is involved in the question whether the administering state is or is not the sovereign over the trust territory. Hence the statement that sovereignty resided in the peoples of the territories which were still dependent, has no basis in the Charter. Even if the administering authority were obliged to grant to the people of the trust territory independence and a democratic form of government (which, after independence is attained, might immediately be replaced by an autocratic form of government), the administering authority could be the territorial sovereign during the period of trusteeship.

At the 5th meeting of the Fourth Committee, on January 25, 1946, the delegate of China declared: 'The essence of both the mandate system and the trusteeship system was that the title of a territory under trust belonged to its people. The ownership rested with the people themselves. The rights of the administering countries, whatever might be technically provided, morally extended only so far as the rights of guardians administering in the interest of the people.' (Journal of the General Assembly, No. 14: Suppl. No. 4–A/C. 4/6, p. 16). If the words 'title of a territory' and 'ownership' mean the legal power under international law to dispose of a territory, subject of such right can only be a state or an international organisation having the character of a juristic person, not a 'people' and certainly not the people inhabiting a trust territory.

At the 2nd meeting of Sub-Committee 1 of the Fourth Committee the representive of Iraq remarked 'that the draft agreement for Western Samoa should: (1) Incorporate a statement to the effect that sovereignty over the Territory was a natural right of its people; (2) Establish that the Administering Authority was an agent of the United Nations in promoting the political, economic, social and educational advancement of the people . . .' (Summary Records of Meetings of Sub-Committee 1, November 15–December 10, 1946, p. 7.) The administering authority may be conceived of as an organ (or agent) of the United Nations, the term 'organ' (or agent) taken in a broad sense. But the relationship of this organ to the United Nations is of a contractual character, which does not exclude the administering authority from sovereignty over the trust territory; just as the states in their capacity as Members may be conceived of as 'organs' of the United Nations without being deprived of their sovereignty. As pointed out the Charter, in contradistinction to the Covenant, does not provide that the administering authority exercises its function 'on behalf' of the Organisation. At the 22nd meeting of the Trusteeship Council the representative of Australia, in rejecting the view that the administering authority is an agent of the Trusteeship Council emphasised that "the Charter establishes the administering authority as an authority in its own right' and that 'neither the Charter nor the agreements use the phrase "on behalf of the United Nations.". (Doc. T/P.V. 95, pp. 87 f.).

importance in case of war and in case the trusteeship status terminates. In case the administering authority is in a state of war this status extends automatically to the trust territory only if this territory is under the sovereignty of the administering authority. However, even if the territory is not under the sovereignty of the administering authority, it is not very likely that actually it will not be involved in the belligerency of the administering power. In spite of the fact that the mandated territories—according to the prevailing interpretation—were not under the sovereignty of the belligerent mandatory powers, they were, as a matter of fact, treated during the Second World War as involved in a state of belligerency.

Should the status of trusteeship terminate before the objective determined in Article 76 (*b*), namely self-government or independence of the trust territory, has been achieved, the case that the administering authority is the territorial sovereign must be distinguished from the case that the sovereignty over the trust territory lies with another state (contracting party to the trusteeship agreement) or with the Organisation. In the first case, the administering authority continues to administer the territory, but is released from the obligations of trusteeship. In the second case, the administering authority has to place the territory at the disposal of the territorial sovereign. If, in this case, the Organisation is the territorial sovereign, a situation is created not covered by the Charter. The latter does not authorise the Organisation to exercise sovereignty over a territory not under trusteeship. The Organisation can not establish itself as administering authority or confer the trusteeship administration upon a state by a unilateral act. Even the possibility of a trusteeship agreement concluded only by the Organisation as territorial sovereign and a state designated as administering authority is not provided for by the Charter. Consequently, the Organisation, being the territorial sovereign, must not approve termination of the trusteeship status unless independence is granted to the trust territory. If the status of trusteeship terminates by granting independence to the trust territory, sovereignty over the territory is transferred to the new state thus established. If the status of trusteeship terminates by granting only self-government to the population of this trust territory, and neither the Organisation nor the administering authority is the territorial sovereign, any arrangement by which the territory is not left under the territorial sovereign which had placed it under trusteeship, needs the consent of the latter in addition to the consent of the Organisation and of the administering authority.

If the status of trusteeship terminates by the fact that the Organisation ceases to exist, the administering authority, if it is the sovereign, continues to administer the territory under its unrestricted authority. If another state in placing the territory under trusteeship has retained its sovereignty, the administering authority has to place the territory at the disposal of this state. If the Organisation was the administering authority and at the same time the sovereign, the territory assumes the legal status of statelessness.

If the trusteeship status terminates by the fact that the administering state ceases to exist, the legal status of the former trust territory depends on whether this state was also the territorial sovereign or another state, contracting party to the trusteeship agreement, has retained its sovereignty over the territory. In the first case the territory becomes stateless; in the second case the territorial sovereign, that is the state which had placed the territory under trusteeship without becoming the administering authority, may take over the administration and dispose of the territory at its discretion, since it is no longer bound by the trusteeship agreement. If the Organisation is the territorial sovereign and the state exercising the function of the administering authority ceases to exist, the above-mentioned situation, not covered by the Charter, arises. Under the Charter the Organisation can not dispose of the territory in a constitutional way.

E. *Sanctions*

Does the Charter provide any specific reaction of the Organisation against non-fulfilment of obligations imposed upon ' Members of the United Nations which have or assume responsibilities for the administration of territories whose peoples have not yet attained a full measure of self-government ' (Article 73) and in particular of the obligations imposed upon those which ' exercise the administration of the trust territory ' (Article 81)? As to the obligations stipulated by Articles 73 and 74, Article 6 of the Charter is applicable providing for expulsion in case of persistent violation of the Principles, one of which is to ' fulfil in good faith the obligations assumed . . . in accordance with the present Charter ' (Article 2, paragraph 2). It is possible, but not necessary, to interpret the phrase ' Obligations assumed in accordance with the present Charter ' to mean also obligations assumed by trusteeship agreements approved by the Organisation. However, the sanction of expulsion is applicable only to Members, and trusteeship obligations may be imposed upon a non-member state, since—as pointed out—not only a Member but also a non-member state may become the administrative authority of a trust territory. To expel a Member from the Organisation has not the effect to divest it of its position as administering authority of a trust territory. Nor has expulsion the effect to divest a state of the legal power it has over a non-self-governing territory referred to in Article 73 (not placed under trusteeship). The same is true with respect to voluntary withdrawal from the Organisation. The Charter does not confer upon the Organisation the power to divest a state of its function as administering authority of a trust territory as sanction for violations of its obligations under the trusteeship system or for violations of other obligations under the Charter, as for instance, the threat or use of force.[4] But the application of enforcement measures referred to in Articles 41 and 42 is not excluded. This, however, is possible only under the conditions determined by Article 39, that is to say, when the Security Council considers the non-fulfilment of the obligations relating to the administration of non-self-governing or trust territories a threat to, or breach of, the peace. There can be little doubt that the improper administation of a territory referred to in Chapter XI or of a trust territory can only exceptionally constitute a threat to the peace, that is to say, the probability of an actual conflict between the adminstering authority and another state. Consequently the measures provided for by Chapter VII cannot serve as normal means to enforce the principles of Chapters XI, XII and XIII.

[4] The above quoted ' Joint Statement by the Delegates of the United Kingdom and the United States (U.N.C.I.O. Doc. 1115, II/4/44 (1) (*a*), p. 14) contains the following passage: ' If a State administering a trust territory commits an act of aggression, what consequences will follow in relation to its trust? The powers of the Security Council as defined in Chapter VIII of the Charter are not limited to dealing with acts of aggression. The Security Council may investigate any situation which may lead to international friction or give rise to a dispute, in order to determine whether its continuance is likely to endanger the maintenance of international peace and security. Any Member of the United Nations may bring any such situation to the attention of the General Assembly or of the Security Council. If the Security Council should in any particular case decide that the continuance of the situation is in fact likely to endanger the maintenance of international peace and security it may recommend appropriate procedures or methods of adjustment. In this way a Trustee State which showed signs of aggressive intentions or had committed an aggression could be dealt with, whether it were still a member of the Organisation or not. In general, however, the same considerations apply as are explained in reply to Question 2, namely that the action to be taken in such a case can only be decided upon at the time and in the light of all relevant circumstances.'

Chapter 17

REGISTRATION AND PUBLICATION OF TREATIES

1. The Obligation of the Members to submit all Treaties to Registration

Article 102, paragraph 1, stipulates:—

> ' Every treaty and every international agreement entered into by any Member of the United Nations after the present Charter comes into force shall as soon as possible be registered with the Secretariat and published by it.'

This provision corresponds to that of Article 18 of the Covenant that ' every treaty or international engagement entered into hereafter by any Member of the League shall be forthwith registered with the Secretariat and shall as soon as possible be published by it.' Article 102 of the Charter differs from Article 18 of the Covenant in so far as the former refers to ' every treaty and international agreement ' whereas the latter to ' every treaty or international engagement.' An ' international engagement ' may be a unilateral act, and hence different from an agreement, which is a bilateral act. But there is no legal difference between a treaty and an international agreement from the point of view of international law.[1]

The obligation to register treaties with the Secretariat is incumbent upon the Members of the United Nations although this is not expressly provided for.[2] It is not stipulated; the Members shall submit to registration . . . , but: every treaty entered into by a Member shall be registered. If a treaty is concluded between two Members, are both obliged to effect registration ? The wording of Article 102 does

[1] The report of the rapporteur of Committee IV/2 (U.N.C.I.O. Doc. 933, IV/2/42 (2), pp. 3 f.) contains the following statement relating to paragraph 1 of Article 102: ' The proposed text is general in terms but is not intended to preclude appropriate regulations defining its application. The Committee has proposed the adoption of the term " agreement " in preference to the term " engagement " which may fall outside the strict meaning of the word " agreement ". The word " agreement " must be understood as including unilateral engagements of an international character which have been accepted by the state in whose favour such an engagement has been entered into.—Members of the Organisation are obliged to register. Furthermore, non-member states may submit treaties and agreements concluded by them with a view to their registration; and this was moreover the procedure followed by the League of Nations.—In spite of the opinion expressed by some delegations, the proposed text limits the obligation of registration to treaties or international agreements concluded after the Charter comes into effect.' If an ' unilateral engagement ' in favour of another state has been ' accepted ' by this state, this transaction may be characterised as international ' agreement ' or as ' treaty ' as well.

[2] Although Article 18 of the Covenant expressly referred only to Members of the League, non-members were actually permitted to register treaties with the Secretariat.

not release the one if the other has fulfilled its obligation under Article 102, paragraph 1. It is not clear whether only treaties submitted to registration by a party are to be registered, or whether the Secretary-General may *ex officio* register treaties, if not submitted by a party. Both interpretations are possible. Article 102 refers to all treaties concluded by Members, also to treaties concluded by Members with non-members (states or international organisations). Are non-members, too, under the obligation to register treaties concluded with Members, or are non-members (states or international organisations) authorised to submit treaties concluded with Members to registration ? According to the wording of Article 102, paragraph 1, there is no difference in this respect between Members and non-members; and paragraph 2 of Article 102 too, stipulating the sanction for non-compliance with paragraph 1, refers to the parties to non-registered treaties without differentiation between Members and non-members[2]. Under general international law as it existed at the moment the Charter came into force, non-members could not be bound by provisions of the Charter. But Article 2, paragraph 6, of the Charter may be interpreted to mean that the obligation established by Article 102, paragraph 1, extends to non-members, since the registration of treaties is necessary for the maintenance of international peace and security.

The obligation stipulated by Article 102 refers to all, and not to certain types of, treaties concluded by Members of the United Nations. The *Report to the President*, however, contains the following statement: '. . . should the obligation to register cover every international agreement or only certain ones ? Experience had indicated that the registration of every international agreement is unnecessary because many of them are of minor importance and of temporary effect. Such, for example, are numerous agreements between governments for the purchase and sale of commodities and the regulation of financial transactions. A more serious problem was the question whether military agreements concluded with the Security Council for the purpose of carrying out its duties under

[3] The Report of Rapporteur of Committee IV/2 (U.N.C.I.O. Doc. 933, IV/2/42 (2), p. 4) contains the following statement with respect to paragraph 2 of Article 102: 'This paragraph formulates sanctions concerning the obligation imposed in paragraph one. The Committee has preferred to depart from the formula used in Article 18 of the Covenant of the League of Nations which states that non-registered treaties shall have no obligatory force. It has confined itself to a sanction which has reference to the faculty of the parties to invoke the international treaty or agreement before the Organisation, which sanction, while giving all the efficacy desired by the obligation imposed in paragraph one, will not give rise in practice to difficulties of interpretation or application.—This provision also covers treaties and agreements to which both members and non-members are parties. It is open to the latter to have such treaties or agreements registered. Moreover, it is necessary that they should be able to do so, seeing that their right to invoke the treaty or agreement before an organ of the Organisation is made subject to registration.' Cf. *infra*, pp. 721 ff.

Chapter VII of the Charter should be registered. There was a realisation of the fact that detailed arrangements about the disposition of forces at a time when security measures were actually being taken could not be made public. Accordingly, although the obligation to register is stated in general terms, it was contemplated that regulations would be worked out in practice by the General Assembly concerning the registration or non-registration of particular types of agreements.' [4] There can be no doubt that the last sentence has no basis in the Charter. The Organisation is not competent to work out regulations by which the obligation stipulated by Article 102 is restricted to certain types of international agreements entered into by Members.

2. The Function of the Organisation of Registering and Publishing Treaties

The function of the Organisation of registering and publishing treaties as established in paragraph 1 of Article 102, is within the competence of the Secretary-General, in spite of the wording, which refers to the 'Secretariat.' The Secretariat, as pointed out, is not organised as a body able to act as a unit on behalf of the United Nations.

Article 102 provides only for registration and publication of treaties concluded by Members and only of treaties entered into by Members after the Charter has come into force. Treaties entered into by Members before this date, treaties concluded by the United Nations or specialised agencies with non-member states, and treaties concluded by non-member states with non-member states are not included. Nor are included legal transactions which, though not having the character of treaties, may have essential effect on treaties registered and published under Article 102, paragraph 1, such as adhesion to treaties or unilateral withdrawal from treaties. The Charter does not authorise the Secretary-General to register and publish treaties other than those entered into by Members after the coming into force of the Charter, or legal transactions not having the character of treaties entered into by a Member of the United Nations after the coming into force of the Charter.

At its 28th meeting on February 10, 1946, the General Assembly adopted a resolution [5] by which it instructed the Secretary-General:

> 1. To submit to the General Assembly proposals for detailed regulations and other measures designed to give effect to the provisions of Article 102 of the Charter;
>
> 2. To invite the governments of Members of the United Nations to transmit to the Secretary-General for filing and publication, treaties and international agreements entered into in recent years, but before the date of entry into force of the Charter, which had not been included in the League of Nations

[4] *Report to the President*, p. 154.

[5] Resolutions adopted by the General Assembly, Doc. A/64, p. 34.

treaty series, and to transmit for registration and publication treaties and international agreements entered into after the date of the entry into force of the Charter.

3. To receive, from the governments of non-member States, treaties and international agreements entered into both before and after the date of entry into force of the Charter, which have not been included in the League of Nations treaty series and which they may voluntarily transmit for filing and publication; and to dispose of them in accordance with the foregoing provisions, and subject to such detailed regulations and other measures as may hereafter be adopted.

The constitutionality of this resolution is doubtful. Under Article 98 of the Charter the General Assembly is certainly competent to 'instruct' the Secretary-General, that is to say, to order him to perform certain functions. But this provision does not apply to functions which are placed by the Charter within the exclusive competence of the Secretary-General, as the registration and publication of treaties. The constitutionality of the resolution is doubtful also for the reason that the General Assembly authorised the Secretary-General to register and publish treaties not included in the category of treaties which the Charter itself authorises the Secretary-General to register and publish.

Pursuant to the instruction of the General Assembly the Secretary-General submitted to it draft regulations for the registration and publication of treaties, and the Assembly adopted, at its 65th meeting,[6] the following Regulations to give effect to Article 102 of the Charter.

Part One

Registration

Article 1

1. Every treaty or international agreement, whatever its form and descriptive name, entered into by one or more Members of the United Nations after October 24, 1945, the date of the coming into force of the Charter, shall as soon as possible be registered with the Secretariat in accordance with these regulations.

2. Registration shall not take place until the treaty or international agreement has come into force between two or more of the parties thereto.

3. Such registration may be effected by any party or in accordance with article 4 of these regulations.

4. The Secretariat shall record the treaties and international

[6] Resolutions adopted by the General Assembly, Doc. A/64/Add.1, pp. 189–194.

agreements so registered in a Register established for that purpose.

ARTICLE 2

1. When a treaty or international agreement has been registered with the Secretariat, a certified statement regarding any subsequent action which effects a change in the parties thereto, or the terms, scope or application thereof, shall also be registered with the Secretariat.

2. The Secretariat shall record the certified statement so registered in the Register established under article 1 of these regulations.

ARTICLE 3

1. Registration by a party, in accordance with article 1 of these regulations, relieves all other parties of the obligation to register.

2. Registration effected in accordance with article 4 of these regulations relieves all parties of the obligation to register.

ARTICLE 4

1. Every treaty or international agreement subject to article 1 of these regulations shall be registered *ex officio* by the United Nations in the following cases:—

(*a*) Where the United Nations is a party to the treaty or agreement;

(*b*) Where the United Nations has been authorised by the treaty or agreement to effect registration.

2. A treaty or international agreement subject to article 1 of these regulations may be registered with the Secretariat by a specialized agency in the following cases:

(*a*) Where the constituent instrument of the specialized agency provides for such registration;

(*b*) Where the treaty or agreement has been registered with the specialized agency pursuant to the terms of its constituent instrument;

(*c*) Where the specialized agency has been authorized by the treaty or agreement to effect registration.

ARTICLE 5

1. A party or specialized agency, registering a treaty or international agreement under article 1 or 4 of these regula-

tions, shall certify that the text is a true and complete copy thereof and includes all reservations made by parties thereto.

2. The certified copy shall reproduce the text in all the languages in which the treaty or agreement was concluded and shall be accompanied by two additional copies and by a statement setting forth, in respect of each party:

(*a*) The date on which the treaty or agreement has come into force;

(*b*) The method whereby it has come into force (for example: by signature, by ratification or acceptance, by accession, et cetera).

ARTICLE 6

The date of receipt by the Secretariat of the United Nations of the treaty or international agreement registered shall be deemed to be the date of registration, provided that the date of registration of a treaty or agreement registered *ex officio* by the United Nations shall be the date on which the treaty or agreement first came into force between two or more of the parties thereto.

ARTICLE 7

A certificate of registration signed by the Secretary-General or his representative shall be issued to the registering party or agency and also to all signatories and parties to the treaty or international agreement registered.

ARTICLE 8

1. The Register shall be kept in the five official languages of the United Nations. The Register shall comprise, in respect of each treaty or international agreement, a record of :

(*a*) The serial number given in the order of registration;

(*b*) The title given to the instrument by the parties;

(*c*) The names of the parties between whom it was concluded;

(*d*) The dates of signature, ratification or acceptance, exchange of ratification, accession, and entry into force;

(*e*) The duration;

(*f*) The language or languages in which it was drawn up;

(*g*) The name of the party or specialized agency which registers the instrument and the date of such registration;

(*h*) Particulars of publication in the treaty series of the United Nations.

2. Such information shall also be included in the Register in regard to the statements registered under article 2 of these regulations.

3. The texts registered shall be marked "*ne varietur*" by the Secretary-General or his representative, and shall remain in the custody of the Secretariat.

Article 9

The Secretary-General, or his representative, shall issue certified extracts from the Register at the request of any Member of the United Nations or any party to the treaty or international agreement concerned. In other cases he may issue such extracts at his discretion.

Part Two

Filing and Recording

Article 10

The Secretariat shall file and record treaties and international agreements, other than those subject to registration under article 1 of these regulations, if they fall in the following categories:

(*a*) Treaties or international agreements entered into by the United Nations or by one or more of the specialized agencies;

(*b*) Treaties or international agreements transmitted by a Member of the United Nations which were entered into before the coming into force of the Charter, but which were not included in the treaty series of the League of Nations;

(*c*) Treaties or international agreements transmitted by a party not a Member of the United Nations which were entered into before or after the coming into force of the Charter which were not included in the treaty series of the League of Nations, provided, however, that this paragraph shall be applied with full regard to the provisions of the resolution of the General Assembly of 10 February 1946 set forth in the Annex to these regulations.

Article 11

The provisions of articles 2, 5, and 8 of these regulations shall apply, *mutatis mutandis*, to all treaties and international agreements filed and recorded under article 10 of these regulations.

PART THREE

Publication

ARTICLE 12

1. The Secretariat shall publish as soon as possible in a single series every treaty or international agreement which is registered, or filed and recorded, in the original language or languages, followed by a translation in English and in French. The certified statements referred to in article 2 of these regulations shall be published in the same manner.

2. The Secretariat shall, when publishing a treaty or agreement under paragraph 1 of this article, include the following information: the serial number in order of registration or recording; the date of registration, or recording; the name of the party or specialized agency which registered it or transmitted it for filing; and in respect of each party the date on which it has come into force and the method whereby it has come into force.

ARTICLE 13

The Secretariat shall publish every month a statement of the treaties and international agreements registered, or filed and recorded, during the preceding month, giving the dates and numbers of registration and recording.

ARTICLE 14

The Secretariat shall send to all Members of the United Nations the series referred to in article 12 and the monthly statement referred to in article 13 of these regulations.

These Regulations have the character of general rules of law and their enactment is a legislative act. The rules go far beyond the provisions of Article 102. The resolution by which the General Assembly established these rules has no basis in the Charter. Only the Secretary-General is competent to issue such regulations, and he is competent to issue such regulations only within the framework of Article 102. The rules are not—as it is said in the preamble of the resolution—established 'for the application of Article 102 of the Charter'; the Regulations adopted by the Assembly are substituted for the provision of Article 102, paragraph 1, which the Assembly, quite rightly, considered to be insufficient.

The Regulations go beyond the framework of Article 102 by the following provisions:

1. The Regulations differentiate between 'registration' on the one hand and 'filing and recording' on the other hand, whereas Article 102 provides only for registration. Since, according to article 11 of the Regulations the provisions of articles 2, 5 and 8 of the Regulations apply also to 'filing and recording,' and the treaties

filed and recorded, according to article 12 of the Regulations, are to be published in the same series as the 'registered' treaties, there seems to be no essential difference between 'registration' and 'filing and recording.' The said differentiation is in connection with the following difference between the Regulations and Article 102.

2. Whereas under Article 102 the Secretary-General is authorised only to 'register' treaties entered into by Members after the Charter has come into force, Article 10 of the Regulations obliges the Secretary-General to 'file and record' treaties other than those subject to registration under Article 102, namely: treaties entered into by the United Nations or by one or more of the specialised agencies with non-members; treaties entered into by Members before the Charter came into force and submitted for registration; and treaties entered into by non-members with non-members submitted for filing and recording. Excluded from the last-mentioned category are treaties entered into by Spain. For the resolution of the General Assembly referred to in article 10, clause (*c*) of the Regulations contains in its preamble the following statement:

> It is desirable, as a matter of practical convenience, that arrangements should be made for the publication of any treaties or international agreements which non-member States may voluntarily transmit and which have not been included in the treaty series of the League of Nations. These arrangements should not, however, extend to treaties or international agreements transmitted by any non-member State such as Spain, the Government of which has been founded with the support of the Axis Powers and does not, in view of its origin, its nature, its record and its close association with the aggressor States, possess qualifications necessary to justify membership in the United Nations under the provisions of the Charter.

3. Article 2 of the Regulations stipulates an obligation of the parties to registered treaties, not established by Article 102 of the Charter, to register with the Secretary-General a certified statement of any subsequent action which effects a change in the parties to the treaty, its terms, scope or application, and a corresponding obligation of the Secretary-General.

4. Article 1, paragraph 3, of the Regulations, expressly authorises any party to a treaty subject to registration under Article 102, and consequently also non-member states parties to such treaties, to effect registration; which excludes another, possible, interpretation of the Charter, according to which only Members are authorised to register treaties with the Secretary-General.

5. Article 4 of the Regulations provides for *ex officio* registration, not expressly provided for by Article 102.

6. Article 3 of the Regulations releases parties to treaties subject to registration from this obligation in case the treaty has been brought to registration by the other party or has been registered *ex officio*; which is not provided for in Article 102.[7]

The provisions of Article 102, paragraph 2, dealing with the legal consequences of non-registration shall be discussed in the chapter on sanctions.

[7] The Report by the Secretary-General on Registration and Publication of Treaties and International Agreements (Doc. A/380) contains the following statement: '. . . Steps have been taken for the *ex officio* registration of instruments of accession transmitted to the Secretary-General by new Members of the United Nations in pursuance of Rule 116 of the Provisional Rules of Procedure of the General Assembly. The Secretariat considers that such instruments constitute an international agreement in accordance with the definition contained in the report of Committee IV/2 of the United Nations Conference on International Organisation held at San Francisco (U.N.C.I.O. Report of Committee IV/2, Doc. 733, p. 715 [misprint; correct: Doc. 933, p. 705]) The statements made by the States parties to the Statute of the International Court of Justice, recognising the Court's jurisdiction as compulsory (Article 36, paragraph 2, of the Statute) are likewise registered *ex officio* by the Secretariat as constituting international undertakings. This solution, moreover, is in conformity with the practice followed by the League of Nations in the same connection.'

A declaration made under Article 36, paragraph 2, of the Statute is a unilateral act; it is, possibly, part of a —general, not special—agreement but, by itself, not an international agreement. It may be characterised as an 'international undertaking.' But neither Article 102 of the Charter nor the Regulations approved by the General Assembly on December 14, 1946, refer to 'international undertakings.' They refer only to 'treaties and international agreements.'

Chapter 18

SANCTIONS

1. The Concept of 'Sanction'

Law is, by its very nature, a coercive order. A coercive order is a system of rules prescribing certain patterns of behaviour by providing coercive measures, as sanctions, to be taken in case of contrary behaviour, or, what amounts to the same, in case of violation of the law. 'Violation' is a figurative and sometimes misleading expression. The term 'delict' (wrong, illegal act) more correctly designates any kind of behaviour which is made the condition of a sanction because it is considered to be undesirable.

Sanctions have the character of forcible deprivation of certain possessions, such as life, freedom, economic or other values. They are coercive in so far as they are to be taken even against the will of the subject to whom they are applied, if necessary by the employment of force. This is the way in which the law protects life, freedom, economic and other interests against delicts. Hence, sanctions are forcible interference in the sphere of interests normally protected by the law. They apply only on the condition that a delict has been committed or, what amounts to the same, that an obligation established by the law has been disregarded, and only against the delinquent or individuals who are in a legally determined relation to the delinquent, that is to the one who by his own behaviour has committed the delict. Sanctions are the specific reactions of the community, constituted by the legal order, against delicts.

The fundamental legal concepts: delict, obligation, and responsibility are corollaries of the concept of sanction. A certain behaviour is a delict if it is a condition of a sanction. A certain behaviour is the content of a legal obligation if the contrary behaviour is a condition of a sanction and as such a delict. If the sanction is directed against the delinquent, individual responsibility, that is, responsibility for an individual's own behaviour, is established. If the sanction is directed against an individual or individuals other than the delinquent, responsibility for the behaviour of another or others is established. If the sanction is directed against the individuals who belong to the same community—family, tribe, state—as the delinquent, collective responsibility is established.

International law is law in the true sense of the term, for its rules regulating the mutual behaviour of states provide sanctions to be directed against the state which has committed an international delict, or, what amounts to the same, has disregarded its obligations towards another state and thus violated the right of the other state. The specific sanctions provided by general international law are: reprisals and war. Both are coercive acts, the former a limited, the latter an unlimited interference in the sphere of interests of a state. The distinction between reprisals and war rests upon the degree of interference: whether the enforcement action undertaken against the state is aimed solely at the violation of certain interests of this state, or is directed towards its complete submission or total annihilation and consequently performed by the armed forces of the opponent.

It is a generally accepted principle of international law that a limited interference in the sphere of interests of one state by another is allowed only as a reaction against a delict, that is to say, as a sanction. But, is this principle applicable also to an unlimited interference in the sphere of interests of another state, to war? As far as the answer to this question is concerned, two opposite views exist. According to one opinion, war is neither a delict nor a sanction; any state that is not bound by special treaty to refrain from warring upon another state or to resort to war only under certain definite conditions may wage war against any other state on any ground, without violating general international law. The opposite opinion, however, holds that according to general international law war is in principle forbidden; it is permitted only as a reaction against an international delict and only when directed against the state responsible for this delict. Like reprisals, war has to be a sanction if it is not to be considered as a delict. This is the doctrine of *bellum justum*, just war.

If the doctrine of *bellum justum* is correct, then under general international law the employment of force on the part of one state against another is in principle forbidden as a delict; but it is exceptionally allowed as a reaction against a delict, that is to say, as a sanction. Only if it is possible to interpret so-called international law in this way can that order be considered as law in the true sense of the term.

General international law is characterised by a high degree of decentralisation. The community constituted by this law has no central government, no court, no administrative organs. The far-going decentralisation of general international law manifests itself in particular in the fact that no special organs exist to execute the sanctions against the delinquent. The international person whose right has been violated is authorised to react with reprisals or war against the international person who is responsible for the delict. Within general international law there are no courts competent to ascertain in an impartial way whether a delict has been committed and whether, therefore, a sanction should be directed against the delinquent. General international law is characterised by the principle of self help. In this respect it is primitive law.

The primitive technique of self-help prevailing in general international law almost completely frustrates the application of the *bellum justum* principle. For, as long as there is not established a central and impartial organ to decide whether or not a state has committed an international delict and thus violated the right of another state, this matter can be settled only by an agreement between the two states concerned. Since such agreement by which a state recognises to have violated the right of another state is likely to be reached only by a peace treaty imposed by the victor upon the vanquished state, the decisive question and hence also the question whether a war waged by one against another state is a just or an unjust war, remains unanswerable.

The question as to whether general international law forbids war except as a reaction against a delict has lost some of its importance since, in the period between the two World Wars, treaties have been concluded by almost all the states of the world for the purpose of outlawing war. The most important of these treaties are: the Covenant of the League of Nations (1919), the General Treaty for the Renunciation of War called the Briand-Kellogg Pact (1928), and the Charter of the United Nations (1945). The Covenant of the League of Nations did not forbid war under all circumstances. The Members of the League were allowed to resort to war against one another under certain circumstances, but only 'for the maintenance of right and justice.' The Briand-Kellogg Pact outlawed war as an instrument of national policy; consequently, war as an instrument of international policy and especially a war waged by one state against a state which has violated the Pact was not forbidden.

The Charter of the United Nations goes much farther than its predecessors. It obligates the Members of the United Nations not only not to resort to war against each other but to refrain from the threat or use of force and to settle their disputes by peaceful means (Article 2, paragraphs 3 and 4). The use of force—so-called enforcement action—is allowed by the Charter in principle only as a reaction of the Organisation against a threat to the peace or a breach of the peace (Articles 39, 41, 42); as action of the Members it is permitted only, exceptionally, in the exercise of self-defence (Article 51) or as action against a state which during the Second World War has been an enemy of the signatories of the Charter (Articles 107, 53). If the enforcement actions provided for by Articles 39, 41 and 42, of the Charter, are true sanctions, the Charter is—at least in principle—in conformity with the *bellum justum* doctrine.

Not all the states of the world are contracting parties to the treaty constituting the United Nations and hence members of this international community. But the Charter claims, in Article 2, paragraph 6, to apply also to states not Members of the United Nations so far as may be necessary for the maintenance of international peace and security. As pointed out, this provision is not in conformity with general international law as prevailing at the moment the Charter came into force. Whether the provision of Article 2, paragraph 6, will obtain general recognition remains to be seen. If so, the Charter of the

United Nations will assume the character of general international law. Then the sanctions provided for by the Charter, in so far as they apply to all states, are to be considered as sanctions under general international law. The procedure for the application of these sanctions is completely centralised, and thus self-help, at least in principle, eliminated.

In interpreting a legal instrument it is sometimes difficult to answer the question what behaviour constitutes a delict, that is to say, what behaviour is the condition of a sanction. For, according to the usually employed legal technique, the legislator stipulates the obligations he intends to impose upon the subjects separately from the sanctions he provides. He expresses his intention to establish an obligation usually by characterising a certain behaviour as desirable or undesirable by formulating a prescription or a prohibition, using the terms ' ought,' ' shall,' ' duty,' ' obligation ' and the like. Only exceptionally the intention of the legislator to establish an obligation is expressed merely by the fact that a coercive measure is attached to a certain conduct, which thus is to be considered as a delict without being expressly forbidden; and its omission an obligation without being expressly prescribed.

If a legislator declares a certain pattern of behaviour as contrary to what he desires by providing that the subjects ' shall ' not behave in this way, or that they ' ought ' or are ' obliged ' to behave in the contrary way, and if he expressly attaches coercive measures not only to the acts, or not to all the acts, which he has determined in this way as delicts, doubts may arise as to his intentions. Hence it may be difficult to answer the questions: which conduct is to be considered as a delict in the sense of conditioning a sanction, and which coercive measures are intended as true sanctions. From the point of view of a correct legal technique it is advisable to qualify a conduct as a delict and the contrary conduct as the content of an obligation only by attaching to it coercive measures as sanction, or by attaching sanctions only to a conduct qualified in an unambiguous way as content of an obligation. If a treaty providing for enforcement measures is to be interpreted as being in conformity with general international law, the conduct which constitutes the condition of an enforcement measure must be considered to be a delict and the contrary conduct the contents of an obligation, even if it is not expressly stipulated as obligation. This undoubtedly holds as to enforcement measures which have the character of reprisals; for reprisals are generally considered to be permissible only as reactions against delicts. As to enforcement measures which have the character of war (since they involve the employment of armed force) the above statement is correct only if the *bellum justum* principle is presupposed as part of positive international law. Otherwise, a treaty establishing the constitution of an international organisation may, in conformity with general international law, provide enforcement measures involving the use of armed force as reaction against a conduct of states which need not necessarily be considered as a delict or, what amounts to the same, as the violation of an obligation imposed upon the states by the constitution of the international organisation. Just as war, according to the doctrine rejecting the *bellum justum* principle, collective enforcement measures involving the use of armed force provided by the constitution of an international organisation need not necessarily have the character of sanctions. They may be actions, neither forbidden nor prescribed by general international law, but authorised or prescribed by the constitution of the international organisation.

2. Expulsion from the Organisation

The Charter of the United Nations does not use the term ' sanction ' and contains only two provisions that clearly stipulate sanctions. The one is Article 6, the other is Article 19. Article 6 runs as follows:

> A Member of the United Nations which has persistently violated the Principles contained in the present Charter may be expelled from the Organisation by the General Assembly upon the recommendation of the Security Council.

Expulsion from the Organisation is an enforcement measure in so far as it is an action taken against the will of the state concerned. Expulsion is enforced upon a Member, in contradistinction to voluntary withdrawal. It is an enforcement measure although the Charter uses the latter term only with reference to actions taken under Articles 39, 41 and 42. Expulsion from the Organisation is undoubtedly a sanction; for it is expressly directed against violations of the Charter or, more exactly, against a Member which has persistently violated the Principles contained in the Charter.

It may seem as if expulsion from the Organisation is not a sanction attached to all kinds of violations of the Charter; only the Principles laid down in Article 2 are referred to. But one of these Principles (Article 2, paragraph 2) is formulated: ' All Members . . . shall fulfil . . . the obligations assumed by them in accordance with the present Charter.' Hence, the persistent violation of any obligation established by the Charter may entail expulsion as its sanction. The question is only what conduct of the Members must be considered to be an ' obligation.' This question may easily be answered where the Charter uses the words: the Members shall do something, as in Article 2, paragraphs 2–5, or the Members agree to do something, as in Article 25, or the formula: the Members accept the obligation, as in Article 73, and the like. But there are provisions of the Charter (which shall be discussed later) in respect of which it is doubtful whether they constitute an ' obligation ' in the sense that their violation entails a sanction.

Since Article 6 speaks of ' Principles ' in the plural, not of ' any Principle,' it is not quite clear whether the persistent violation of one Principle is sufficient to justify expulsion, or whether the persistent violation of several Principles is necessary, and with respect to Principle 2, whether the persistent violation of one or of several obligations referred to in this Principle is required in order to justify expulsion. The decision of these questions as well as the interpretation of the term ' persistent ' is incumbent on the organs which have to apply Article 6: the Security Council and the General Assembly. The decision of the Security Council by which it ' recommends ' the expulsion of a Member to the General Assembly, requires, in conformity with Article 27, paragraph 3, affirmative vote of seven members including the concurring votes of the permanent members; the decision of the General Assembly requires, in conformity with Article 18, paragraph 2, a two-thirds majority of the members present and voting. Both decisions are necessary to bring about the expulsion of the Member. The General Assembly is not bound by a recommendation of the Security Council to expel a Member; but the Assembly cannot expel a Member without a previous recommendation of the Council to do so. The possibility of interpreting the formula ' upon the recommendation of the Security Council ' to mean that the Council may make a positive or a negative recommendation to the Assembly and that the latter, even in case the Council recommends not to expel the Member, may decide to expel the Member, has been discussed in the chapter on Membership.[1]

The Security Council and the General Assembly are not bound by the Charter to inflict the sanction stipulated in Article 6 upon a Member which has committed the delict determined in this Article. The Charter only authorises the two organs to do so; they ' may ' expel a Member found guilty by them of having persistently violated the Principles contained in the Charter. But they may, for some reason or other, refuse to exercise this function.

To ascertain whether a Member has violated its obligations under the Charter is to answer a legal question. Bodies such as the Security Council and the General Assembly are certainly not the proper organs to fulfil this task. There was no sufficient reason not to confer it upon the International Court of Justice and to restrict the function of the Security Council and the General Assembly, or of one of them, to apply for a decision of the Court and to act in conformity with it.

It may be doubtful whether expulsion from an organisation whose purpose is the maintenance of peace is an adequate sanction at all. This is certainly not the case if by expulsion the Member gets rid of the obligations which it has violated and thus has shown that it considers these obligations as an unwelcome burden. Expulsion has the effect of a sanction, that is to say, of an evil, only in so far as it deprives the

[1] Cf. *supra*, pp. 61 ff.

state of its rights as a Member. This effect, however, can be realised without releasing the guilty Member from its obligations.

3. Suspension from the Exercise of the Rights of Membership

The Charter provides for such a possibility in Article 5, which runs as follows:

> A Member of the United Nations against which preventive or enforcement action has been taken by the Security Council may be suspended from the exercise of the rights and privileges of membership by the General Assembly upon the recommendation of the Security Council. The exercise of these rights and privileges may be restored by the Security Council.

This Article introduces as a valuable innovation suspension from the exercise of the rights of membership. The addition 'and privileges' is superfluous since privileges are rights. If by 'privilege' is meant a particular right, a right constituting an advantage as compared with the rights of others, the Charter grants privileges only to the five powers which are permanent members of the Security Council.

By 'rights' all benefits may be understood which a state has in its capacity as Member of the United Nations, as, for instance: to be represented on the General Assembly and the three Councils; to be elected member of these Councils; to be invited to participate in the discussions of the Security Council under Articles 31, 32, 44; to bring to the attention of the Security Council or of the General Assembly disputes and other situations under Article 35, paragraph 1. The right to administer a trust territory is not a right of membership since, as pointed out, this is not a right which a state has in his capacity as a 'Member of the United Nations.' In conformity with Article 81, a non-member may be the administering authority on the basis of a trusteeship agreement. Hence the exercise of this right cannot be suspended under Article 5. But, as pointed out, the term 'membership' may be understood in a wider and in a narrower sense: membership in the Organisation comprising, or not comprising, the judicial community. If the term 'membership,' as used in Article 5, means membership in the Organisation comprising the judicial community, suspension from the exercise of the rights of membership includes suspension from the exercise of the rights established by the Statute of the International Court of Justice. In so far as these rights are to be exercised in the General Assembly or the Security Council, as the right to participate in the election of the judges of the Court (Article 4 of the Statute) or in the procedure for the amendment of the Statute (Article 69 of the Statute), their exercise is suspended also in case the term 'membership' is interpreted in the narrower sense. But the right to have access to the Court is established only by the Statute. It is a right of membership in the judicial community, a right which states have when they are parties to the Statute, whether they are or are not ' Members of the United Nations ' in the narrower sense of the term, and, under certain conditions, even if they are not parties to the Statute. Although the wording of Article 5 does not exclude the interpretation according to which also the exercise of this right, established by the Statute, is suspended, it is not very likely that this effect of Article 5 was intended by the framers of the Charter. It is probable that the term ' membership ' in Article 5 means only membership in the Organisation not comprising the judicial community. If this interpretation is accepted, Article 5 is applicable only to Members of the United Nations in the narrower sense, not to states which are parties to the Statute without being ' Members of the United Nations ' (Article 93 of the Charter) and not to states to which the Court is open without their being ' parties to the Statute ' (Article 35, paragraph 2 of the Statute).

That under Article 5 a Member of the United Nations (in the narrower sense of the term) is suspended from the exercise of its rights, does not mean that it may exercise the rights which a non-member state has under the Charter (not comprising the Statute). The suspended Member remains a ' Member ' and has to fulfil all the obligations of membership. The provisions of the Charter referring to non-members are not applicable to it. Hence it is not entitled to bring to the attention of the Security Council or the General Assembly a dispute under Article 35, paragraph 2, or to be invited to participate in the discussion of the Security Council under Article 32. Suspension from the exercise of the rights of membership does not mean to be treated as a non-member. Hence suspension from the exercise of the membership rights may—at least temporarily—place the Member concerned in a position worse than that of a non-member. It is regrettable that an interpretation of Article 5 excluding such effect has no basis in the wording of the Article.

It is significant that the General Assembly participates only in the action by which the exercise of the rights of membership is to be suspended, not in the action by which the exercise of the rights is to be restored. This can be done only by the Security Council.[2] The Charter does not provide that the Security Council must restore the exercise of the rights suspended according to Article 5 as soon as a preventive or enforcement action is terminated; nor does the wording of Article 5 allow the intrepretation that the suspension automatically terminates at that moment. Such a provision would not be advisable

[2] The *Report to the President*, pp. 57 f., contains the following statement: ' It is not necessary, however, for the General Assembly to participate in the decision to restore the rights and privileges of a suspended Member. The last point was made, not to detract from the powers of the General Assembly, but rather as a means of facilitating the operation of security measures and to speed the return to full participation in the Organisation of a Member which alters its behaviour for the better as a consequence of enforcement measures taken against it.'

because the question as to when the preventive or enforcement action is terminated may not be self-evident. Only the Security Council is competent to decide this question.

Suspension of the rights of membership, as stipulated in Article 5, is not—at least not directly—intended as a sanction. It is an additional measure taken against a Member subjected to 'preventive or enforcement action.' If the enforcement action (including a preventive enforcement action) is a sanction, suspension of the rights of membership—it is true—may be considered as an additional sanction. If, however, the enforcement action itself has not the character of a sanction, the suspension of the rights of membership cannot have this character either. The main purpose of this measure is to prevent a Member which is not expelled but against which enforcement action is in operation from exercising the rights of a Member. That a Member against whom enforcement action is taken may exercise his rights of a Member is indeed a most unsatisfactory situation. It was possible under the Covenant. Under the Charter this inconvenience is avoided.

What is the meaning of the term 'preventive or enforcement action' used in Article 5? As pointed out, probably enforcement action for the prevention or suppression of a breach of the peace taken under Articles 39, 41 and 42. It is possible to apply Article 5 also in case of an enforcement action taken under Article 94, paragraph 2, to give effect to a judgment of the International Court of Justice. But it is hardly possible to interpret the term preventive action as used in Article 5 to mean a provisional measure taken under Article 40 'in order to prevent an aggravation of the situation.' Otherwise the Charter would certainly go too far. For, to suspend the exercise of the rights of membership of a state which has been 'called upon' to comply with provisional measures is hardly justifiable, not only because the state may be the aggressor as well as its victim; but also because it is—as we shall see later—doubtful whether the states are obliged under Article 40 to comply with the 'call' of the Security Council.

4. The Effect of Expulsion

Suspension of the exercise of the rights of membership could be an appropriate sanction against any violation of obligations of a Member. It is regrettable that the Charter has not established this measure as a sanction instead of expulsion from the Organisation. The latter measure is all the more problematical as the Charter—if correctly interpreted—does not confer upon the Members the right of withdrawal from the Organisation.[3] Where such possibility exists, expulsion has, in contradistinction to voluntary withdrawal, the visible stigma of a moral discrimination. Where no voluntary withdrawal

[3] Cf. *supra*, pp. 122 ff.

is possible at all, a state that wishes to leave the burden of membership to the other members of the organisation might be induced to reach this goal by creating a situation which may lead to its expulsion.

This, however, is not quite feasible under the Charter which claims to be applicable not only to Members but also to non-members. Expulsion from the United Nations, in contradistinction to the same sanction under the Covenant of the League, has not the effect of getting rid of the obligations established by the Charter. For, as pointed out, according to Article 2, paragraph 6, the Organisation is authorised to insure that states which are not Members of the United Nations, and consequently also a state which has been expelled from the Organisation, act in accordance with the Principles of the Charter. Viewed in the light of Article 2, paragraph 6, the provision of Article 6 does not exactly constitute expulsion from the Organisation, but rather forfeiture of the rights of membership, and even not of all rights. One of the most important rights is the one stipulated in Article 2, paragraph 7: to be exempt from any intervention on the part of the Organisation ' in matters which are essentially within the domestic jurisdiction.' This right is conferred upon ' any state,' not only upon Members, and consequently, is not affected by expulsion from the Organisation. Another important right is the one stipulated in Article 32: A Member which is not a member of the Security Council, if it is a party to a dispute under consideration by the Security Council shall be invited to participate, without voting, in the discussion relating to the dispute. But the same right is conferred by this Article on non-members, so that, when a Member has been ' expelled' under Article 6, it retains this right as a non-member. Strange as it may seem, this right which cannot be lost by expulsion, may be—at least temporarily—lost by the suspension from the exercise of the rights of membership under Article 5. Hence the value of so-called expulsion under Article 6 is very problematical.[4]

[4] At the San Francisco Conference, expulsion and suspension gave rise to a lengthy exchange of views, and a special sub-committee was entrusted with the examination of these questions. ' On May 25, the sub-committee recommended that reference to expulsion be omitted from the Charter. The sub-committee also recommended that, if Committee I/2 sustained the view of the majority of the sub-committee on expulsion, then the Committee should change the draft of paragraph 3, Section B, Chapter V concerning suspension along the following lines: ' The Organisation may at any time suspend from the exercise of the rights or privileges of membership any member of the Organisation against which preventive or enforcement action shall have been taken by the Security Council, or which shall have violated the principles of the Charter in a grave or persistent fashion. The exercise of these rights and privileges may be restored in accordance with the procedure laid down in Chapter ..., paragraph ....' (U.N.C.I.O. Doc. 606, I/2/43).

' When this question was brought before the whole Committee, the members in favour of expulsion explained that the primary purposes of the Organisation were peace and security, not universality. Expulsion would only apply to Member states which were admittedly incorrigible and which violated the principles

This all the more as the decision of the Security Council to recommend to the General Assembly the expulsion of a Member requires, according to Article 27, paragraph 3, an affirmative vote of seven members including the concurring votes of the permanent members. Hence the sanction of expulsion can hardly be applied against one of the five great powers. The same is true with respect to the suspension from the exercise of the rights of membership. This measure, too, can be taken only by the General Assembly upon recommendation of the Security Council, and to the decision of the Security Council the veto right of the five big powers applies. In this point the Charter constitutes a regrettable setback as compared with the Covenant. Article 16, paragraph 4, provides that a Member of the League which has violated the Covenant may be 'declared to be no longer a Member of the League'—this is an euphemistic expression for 'expelled from the League'—'by a vote of the Council concurred in by the Representatives of all the other Members of the League represented thereon.' The Member which is to be expelled has no vote. This was the way

contained in the Charter in a grave or persistent manner. So far as such states were concerned, the attitude which would be adopted towards them by the Organisation would have to be stated quite plainly. In the case of a state the exercise of whose rights and privileges was suspended, to maintain its status as a member might prevent the Organisation from taking sufficiently severe action against it; and, failing the power of expulsion, a Member state might be able to take concerted action with a non-member state in order to impede the working of the Organisation. It was wrong to say that expulsion, as opposed to suspension, would release a state from all obligations imposed on Member states. In point of fact, by virtue of the principles contained in the Charter, it would still be bound by various obligations devolving upon non-member states in so far as such obligations affected the maintenance of peace. It was likewise wrong to say that such a measure was irremediable. Expulsion, though conclusive in character, could not be an obstacle to subsequent re-admittance if this were justified by circumstances. Those in favour of omitting any reference to expulsion in the Charter maintained that this would be incompatible with the concept of universality, which pre-supposed that all states would eventually be admitted to membership in the Organisation. It would entail more drawbacks for the Organisation itself than for the state concerned. It would set up a centre in opposition to the Organisation around which other discontented states would rally. It would force Member states to break off all relations, diplomatic and otherwise, with the state which had been expelled. It would prevent any reconciliation between the Organisation and the state expelled, and, whatever might be said, its results would be less severe than those of suspension.' . . . 'At the meeting of Committee I/2 held on May 25th, a proposal providing for inclusion of expulsion in the Charter was approved by a simple majority, but failed to obtain the support of two-thirds of the delegates present and voting.' The committee was left to reconsider this decision, and the final vote concluded with the inclusion in the Charter of the clause on expulsion as stipulated in Article 6. Consequently also the provision concerning suspension as stipulated in Article 5 was adopted. Cf. (U.N.C.I.O. Doc. 1160, I/2/76 (1), pp. 7 ff.).

It is worth noting that the delegate of the Soviet Union, which had been expelled from the League of Nations for having violated the Covenant, 'urged that the reference to expulsion be included with the Charter.' (U.N.C.I.O. Doc. 859, EX/21; cf. U.N.C.I.O. Doc. 941, I/2/62).

in which the Soviet Union had been expelled from the League. Such expulsion cannot happen under the Charter.

5. Suspension of the Right of Voting in the General Assembly

The Charter allows not only to deprive a Member of most of its rights of membership as a sanction for persistent violation of the Principles and to suspend a Member against which preventive or enforcement action has been taken from the exercise of all its rights; it allows also to suspend a Member from the exercise of a special right in case of non-fulfilment of a special obligation. It is the obligation stipulated in Article 17, paragraph 2, to bear the expenses of the Organisation as apportioned by the General Assembly. Article 19 provides:

> A Member of the United Nations which is in arrears in the payment of its financial contributions to the Organisation shall have no vote in the General Assembly if the amount of its arrears equals or exceeds the amount of the contributions due from it for the preceding two full years. The General Assembly may, nevertheless, permit such a Member to vote if it is satisfied that the failure to pay is due to conditions beyond the control of the Member.

The right to vote in the General Assembly is only one of the rights of membership. It includes the right to participate in elections since the act of election is composed of acts of voting.[5] A Member who, according to Article 19, has lost the exercise of its right to vote in the General Assembly may still exercise all the other rights of membership, expecially the right to participate in the deliberations of the General Assembly, the right to be elected member of the Security Council, and, if it is a member of the Security Council, to vote in the Security Council. That a Member may be excluded from voting in the General Assembly but not from voting in the Security Council is indeed a strange consequence of the wording of Article 19.[6]

This provision does not stipulate loss of the right to vote but temporary suspension of the exercise of this right. The suspension shall last only as long as the Member 'is in arrears in the payment of its financial contributions to the Organisation.'[7] The suspension of the

[5] Committee 1 to Commission II of the San Francisco Conference recommended that states failing to fulfill their financial obligations should be deprived of 'all' voting rights in the Assembly. (U.N.C.I.O. Doc. 570, II/1/26, p. 3).

[6] At the San Francisco Conference the delegate of the Netherlands made the following suggestion: 'A member of the Organisation which has not in due time paid its portion of the expenses loses its right to vote in the Assembly, *and, if a member of the Security Council, forfeits its seat thereon.*' (U.N.C.I.O. Doc. 1133, St./19.)

[7] Committee 1 to Commission II recommended 'that each member state shall have one vote in the General Assembly. It recommends also that states failing to fulfill their financial obligations should be deprived of all voting rights in the Assembly as long as they are in arrears. In its discussions of this matter, the experience of the League of Nations was cited as indicating the need for such a penalty.' (U.N.C.I.O. Doc. 666, II/1/26 (1) (*a*), p. 3).

right may be prevented by a decision of the General Assembly. The object of this decision is to permit a Member to vote. This decision may be taken if the General Assembly ascertains that the failure to pay is due to conditions beyond the control of the Member. If the subject matter of this decision is considered to be 'an important question' the decision is to be made according to Article 18, paragraph 2, by a two-thirds majority. The subject matter is not expressly mentioned in this Article; but it may be subsumed under 'budgetary questions.' However, it may be argued that the decision by which the General Assembly permits a Member to vote under Article 19, requires only a simple majority, since this matter, in contradistinction to 'suspension of the rights and privileges of membership' is not among those enumerated in Article 18, paragraph 2. The question as to whether this enumeration is exhaustive, may be answered in different ways.[8]

The General Assembly may, by decision, permit the Member which is in arrears in its payments to vote. But who has to decide that the Member is in arrears and that, consequently, it has 'no vote in the General Assembly' or—which is more exact—that the exercise of its right to vote is suspended? And who has to decide that a Member which was in arrears in the payment of its financial contributions and consequently suspended from the exercise of its right to vote has made up for the fulfilment of its obligations and that the exercise of its right to vote is to be restored? Article 19 says only that the Member 'shall have no vote' if it is 'in arrears.' It does not determine the procedure in which this condition or the fact that this condition has ceased to exist and the consequence of these facts are to be established, although it does so with respect to the permission to vote. An authentic establishment of the fact that a Member is in arrears in its payments is all the more necessary as the conditions under which a Member shall lose the exercise of its right to vote in the General Assembly are rather complex and open to disputes between the Member and the Organisation. The amount of its arrears must equal or exceed the amount of the contributions due from it for the preceding two full years. The same is true with respect to the fact that a Member which was in arrears has subsequently paid its financial contribution.

Probably it has been presupposed as self-evident that the General Assembly shall establish the fact that a Member is in arrears in its payments or the fact that it has subsequently paid its contributions and that the General Assembly, after having ascertained the one or the other fact, may suspend or restore the exercise of its right to vote by a decision to be made in conformity with Article 18. The question as to whether a decision by which the Assembly suspends the exercise of the right to vote requires a simple or a two-thirds majority, is to be

[8] Cf. *supra*, pp. 180 ff.

answered in the same way as the same question relating to the decision by which the Member is permitted to vote. Among the ' important questions ' enumerated in Article 18, paragraph 2, ' the suspension of the rights and privileges of membership ' is mentioned. The wording of this formula applies also to the decision by which the exercise of the right to vote in the General Assembly is suspended. But according to its intention the formula probably refers only to the suspension of the rights and privileges of membership provided for in Article 5. Article 19 does not speak of a ' suspension ' of the right—or the exercise of the right—to vote, although it provides for such suspension.

When the General Assembly, by a decision not expressly provided for in Article 19, establishes the fact that a Member is in arrears in the payment of its financial contributions to the Organisation and declares the exercise of the right of this Member to vote in the General Assembly suspended then the other decision, expressly provided for in Article 19, by which the General Assembly permits the Member to exercise its right to vote is excluded. For the first mentioned decision can be made only if the General Assembly is not satisfied that the failure to pay is due to conditions beyond the control of the Member. What is meant in Article 19, but formulated in a technically insufficient way, is this: If a Member is in arrears in the payment of its financial contributions to the Organisation, the General Assembly shall ascertain whether the failure to pay is due to conditions beyond the control of the Member and, if this is not the case, suspend the Member of the exercise of its right to vote in the General Assembly. The exercise of the right to vote shall be restored by the General Assembly as soon as the latter is in a position to ascertain that the Member has paid all the contributions due from it according to Article 17, paragraph 2.[9]

Suspension of the exercise of the right to vote in the General Assembly as provided for in Article 19 may be interpreted as a sanction of the violation of the special obligation laid down in Article 17, paragraph 2, in spite of the fact that Article 19, in contradistinction to Article 6, does not refer expressly to a ' violation ' of a Member's ' obligation ' but to the ' payment of its financial contributions.' However, the payment of the financial contributions to the Organisation as stipulated in Article 17, paragraph 2, is an obligation of the Members. Here it is said: The expenses of the Organisation ' shall ' be borne by the Members. That the suspension of the exercise of the right to vote is intended as a sanction, that is to say, as a reaction against the violation of an obligation, may be concluded also from the

[9] The Rules of Procedure of the General Assembly only provide in Rule 149 that the Committee on Contributions, to be appointed under Rules 147 and 148, shall advise the General Assembly ' on the action to be taken with regard to the application of Article 19 of the Charter.'

fact that this reaction shall not take place if the Member is not guilty, if it cannot be made responsible for the failure to pay since this failure is due to conditions ' beyond the control of the Member.' In the discussion of Committee 1 to Commission II of the San Francisco Conference the provision of Article 19 has frequently been characterised as ' penalty.'[1] Since the Security Council has no competence with respect to the suspension of the right to vote in the General Assembly, this is a sanction—the only one—which may be imposed even upon one of the states which are permanent members of the Security Council.

That a Member which is in arrears in the payment of its financial contributions to the Organisation has been suspended from the exercise to vote in the General Assembly does not exclude the possibility of expelling this Member from the Organisation for having persistently violated its obligation to bear the expenses of the Organisation as apportioned by the General Assembly.

6. The Sanction for Non-Compliance with a Judgment of the International Court of Justice.

Article 94, paragraph 1, of the Charter provides: ' Each Member of the United Nations undertakes to comply with the decision of the International Court of Justice in any case to which it is a party.' That means that each Member shall comply with the decision of the Court. The wording of the provision expresses the intention of the Charter to impose upon the Members an obligation. Non-compliance with the decision of the Court constitutes—according to the intention of the Charter—a violation of an obligation. Paragraph 2 of Article 94 expressly refers to the provision of paragraph 1 as to an ' obligation ' and provides for a reaction against a conduct which constitutes a failure to perform this obligation: the Security Council may ' decide upon measures to be taken to give effect to the judgment.' The wording of paragraph 2 is not quite consistent with the wording of paragraph 1. Paragraph 1 speaks of ' the decision ' of the Court; paragraph 2 of a ' judgment '. The Court may render various decisions; not every decision of the Court has the character of a ' judgment.' But paragraph 1 speaks of ' decision ' in the singular. Hence it may be assumed that the ' decision ' referred to in paragraph 1 is the ' judgment ' referred to in paragraph 2; and hence Article 94 may be interpreted to establish only an obligation to comply with the ' judgments ' of the Court, not an obligation to comply with all its decisions. Yet it is not excluded to interpret paragraph 1 to refer to all decisions of the Court. However, the provision of paragraph 2 determining a possible reaction against a violation of the obligation stipulated in paragraph 1 refers only to a ' judgment ' of

[1] Cf. U.N.C.I.O. Doc. 414, II/1/17, p. 2; 454, II/1/21, p. 1; 570, II/1/26, p. 3.

the Court, not to all its decisions. The Security Council is authorised to take measures only to give effect to a 'judgment' of the Court. If these measures have the character of enforcement measures, they may be interpreted to be sanctions. As pointed out in a previous chapter, enforcement measures taken by the Security Council under Article 94, paragraph 2, need not necessarily be enforcement measures under Article 39. The Security Council in order to give effect to a judgment of the Court may apply Article 41 without applying Article 39,[2] that is to say, without having previously determined the existence of a threat to, or breach of, the peace. But the Security Council may take all enforcement measures referred to in Article 39 in case of non-compliance with any decision of the Court, also with a decision which has not the character of a 'judgment,' after it has determined that such non-compliance constitutes a threat to, or breach of, the peace.

7. The Sanction for Non-Registration of Treaties

There is still another provision of the Charter which seems to have the character of a special sanction for the violation of a special obligation. It is the obligation stipulated in Article 102, paragraph 1: to register treaties with the Secretariat.

There can be little doubt that there is intended by this provision an obligation of the Members to bring every treaty entered into by them after the Charter has come into force to registration with the Secretariat. Every treaty 'shall' be registered. This presupposes that each Member submits the text of the treaty to the Secretariat for the purpose of registration. 'As soon as possible': this requirement can be fulfilled only by the Member concerned and by the Secretariat. It would have been better to have formulated the provision of Article 102, paragraph 1, by saying: Every Member shall . . . instead of: Every treaty shall . . . Article 102, paragraph 1, refers to 'every' treaty entered into by a Member, that is to say, not only to treaties concluded by a Member with another Member but also to treaties concluded by Members with non-members or international organisations.

What is the consequence if a Member violates its obligation under Article 102, paragraph 1, by not submitting a treaty entered into by it to the Secretariat for registration? To this question paragraph 2 of Article 102 gives the following answer:

> No party to any such treaty or international agreement which has not been registered in accordance with the provisions of paragraph 1 of this Article may invoke that treaty or agreement before any organ of the United Nations.

[2] Cf. *supra*, pp. 541 ff.

In this context we shall discuss only the effect of this provision on the Member which has not fulfilled its obligation under paragraph 1. That this Member cannot invoke a non-registered treaty before any organ of the United Nations means that the treaty is to be considered by the competent organ of the United Nations as non-valid in relation to the Member which invokes the treaty before that organ. The wording of Article 102, paragraph 2, does not preclude an organ of the United Nations, especially the International Court of Justice, from applying a non-registered treaty not invoked by a party; and a party may not invoke a treaty in case the treaty is less favourable to that party than to the other party. Then the other party is interested in the treaty; but Article 102, paragraph 2—according to its wording—applies also to that party. That the organ of the United Nations may apply a non-registered treaty *ex officio* whether the treaty is or is not invoked by a party, is more than doubtful. If a treaty may not be invoked by the parties before an international authority, that authority cannot apply the treaty. Hence the effect of the provision that no party to a non-registered treaty may invoke the treaty before any organ of the United Nations is the invalidation of the treaty within the legal sphere of the United Nations. It is a relative, not an absolute invalidation of the unregistered treaty. The parties to the unregistered treaty are not precluded from invoking the treaty before authorities different from the organs of the United Nations, and these authorities are not precluded from applying such a treaty.

In this respect Article 102 of the Charter differs from Article 18 of the Covenant which provided that no 'treaty or international engagement shall be binding until so registered.' That means that a treaty concluded by a Member state with another Member—or non-member state—shall be considered as absolutely non-valid. This provision has been found to go too far, especially with respect to treaties concluded with non-members for which the Covenant was not binding. It seems that this experience has led to the formation of Article 102, paragraph 2, of the Charter, restricting the invalidation of unregistered treaties to the legal realm of the Organisation. But Article 102, paragraph 2, applies not only to treaties concluded by Members but also to treaties concluded by Members with non-members. This might be justified by the assumption that the obligation to register treaties is, under Article 2, paragraph 6, to be considered as an obligation imposed—indirectly—also upon non-members. If so, the restriction of the rule laid down in Article 102, paragraph 2, to organs of the United Nations seems not to be necessary. For, then there exists no difference between a Member and a non-member with respect to the obligation to register treaties. If, however, Article 2, paragraph 6, is not interpreted to mean that the obligation to register treaties is incumbent also upon non-members, the provision of paragraph 2 of Article 102 that 'no party,' non-members included, may invoke the unregistered treaty before an organ of the United Nations is highly problematical. How can a sanction be inflicted upon a non-member for not having registered a treaty, if this state is not obliged to register? And how can an organ of the United Nations refuse to apply a non-registered treaty to which a non-member is a party, if the treaty, under general international law, is valid?

It is doubtful whether international authorities other than organs of the United Nations will recognise Article 2, paragraph 6, of the Charter as a rule imposing obligations upon non-members. If a dispute between a Member and a non-member is to be decided by an international tribunal of arbitration established by the parties to the dispute, it is quite possible that this tribunal will not consider the non-member as bound by the Charter and declare a treaty concluded by the parties as valid for both, even if not registered with the Secretariat. Hence, the restriction of Article 102, paragraph 2, is quite understandable. It shows how problematic Article 2, paragraph 6, is.

The effect of Article 102, paragraph 2, is that a Member forfeits the rights which the unregistered treaty confers upon it. So far the provision of Article 102, paragraph 2, has the effect of a sanction.[3] But since paragraph 2 of Article 102 provides that 'no party' to a non-registered treaty may invoke that treaty before any organ of the United Nations, the relative invalidation of the treaty has the effect that also the obligations imposed by the treaty on the Member guilty of non-registration cannot be maintained against it. This is not quite in the line of a sanction, especially in the case that the treaty has been concluded by a Member with a non-member and is more to the benefit of the latter than the former. The Member has the possibliity of frustrating the undesired effect of the treaty by not fulfilling its duty of registration. On the other hand, if the treaty has been brought to registration by the other party—and this is possible even if the other party is a non-member—the provision of Article 102, paragraph 2, does not work against the Member which disregards its duty under paragraph 1.

As a matter of fact, the Regulations established by the General Assembly for the Application of Article 102 provide in Article 1, paragraph 3, that registration may be effected by any party to a treaty, and in Article 4, even for an *ex officio* registration by the Secretary-General. According to Article 3 of the Regulations, registration by one party relieves all other parties, and *ex officio* registration all the parties of the obligation to register.

[3] The Report of Rapporteur of Committee IV/2 (U.N.C.I.O. Doc. 933, IV/2/42 (2), p. 4) expressly characterises the provision of Article 102, paragraph 2, as 'sanctions concerning the obligation imposed in paragraph one.'

Hence it may be doubtful whether the relative invalidation of treaties provided for by Article 102, paragraph 1, may properly be interpreted as a sanction for the violation of the obligation stipulated in that paragraph. Even if it is a sanction, the ' persistent violation ' of that obligation still remains under the general sanction of Article 6 of the Charter.

8. Enforcement Measures

The most important sanctions provided by the Charter are considered to be the enforcement measures determined in Chapter VII. The Charter lays particular stress on these measures in proclaiming in Article 1, paragraph 1, as the first Purpose of the United Nations ' to take effective collective measures for the prevention and removal of threats to the peace, and for the suppression of acts of aggression and other breaches of the peace.' The ' collective measures ' referred to in Article 1, paragraph 1, are specified in Articles 41, 42 and 45. There are two kinds of such measures: measures not involving the use of armed force, and measures involving the use of armed force. Both are ' enforcement measures ' or ' enforcement actions ' as they are sometimes called in the Charter (' measures ': Article 2, paragraph 7, Article 50; ' action ': Article 5, Article 53), although only the measures determined in Articles 42 to 47 involve the use of ' armed ' force. The measures determined in Article 41 are especially: ' complete or partial interruption of economic relations and of rail, sea, air, postal, telegraphic, radio, and other means of communication, and the severance of diplomatic relations.' This purpose is defined in Article 41 as follows: ' to give effect to its [the Security Council's] decisions '; that means to enforce the decision upon a recalcitrant state. Hence these measures, too, may be considered to be ' enforcement measures ' or ' enforcement actions ' referred to in various Articles of the Charter.

It has already been pointed out that it is doubtful whether the enforcement measures provided for by the Charter may be properly characterised as sanctions.

The economic and military enforcement actions stipulated by Article 16, paragraphs 1 and 2, of the Covenant of the League of Nations, had evidently the character of sanctions (although they were not designated as such in the Covenant), since they were expressly directed against a specific violation of the Covenant. Article 16, paragraph 1, dealing with the enforcement measure not involving the use of armed force, stated: ' Should any Member of the League resort to war in disregard of its covenants under Articles 12, 13 or 15 it shall *ipso facto* be deemed to have committed an act of war against all other Members of the League which hereby undertake immediately to subject it to . . . ' And paragraph 2 of Article 16, dealing with enforcement action involving the use of armed force, stipulated: ' It shall be the duty of the Council in such case '—that is to say, in case a Member resorts to war in disregard of its obligations under the Covenant—' to recommend to the several Governments concerned what effective military, naval or air force the Members of the League shall severally contribute to the armed forces to be used to protect the covenants of the League.' The use of armed force as an enforcement measure was expressly destined for the protection of the Covenant, that is for the defence of the particular law of the League.

The Charter, however, does not prescribe that the enforcement actions provided for in Chapter VII shall be taken exclusively against a Member which has violated its obligations; and the conditions under which the Security Council is authorised to take these actions are determined in a way different from that in which the obligations of the Members are formulated.[4]

Article 39, the first of Chapter VII dealing with the enforcement actions, runs as follows:

> The Security Council shall determine the existence of any threat to the peace, breach of the peace, or act of aggression and shall make recommendations, or decide what measures shall be taken in accordance with Articles 41 and 42, to maintain or restore international peace and security.

One of the most striking differences between Article 39 of the Charter and Article 16 of the Covenant is that under the Charter action can be taken only by a central organ, the Security Council, and only after the Council has determined the existence of a threat to, or breach of, the peace. The Covenant, however, according to its wording, provided an automatic reaction on the part of the Members. This seems to result from the provision that an illegal resort to war shall ' *ipso facto* '

[4] In the discussions at the San Francisco Conference the measures under Chapter VII were frequently designated as ' sanctions.' Cf. U.N.C.I.O. Doc. 134, III/3/3, pp. 10 ff.; 231, III/3/9; 231, III/3/9 (1); 320, III/3/15; 577, III/3/28. *The Report to the President* contains (p. 42) the following statement with reference to the obligation of the Members to refrain from giving assistance to any state against which the United Nations is taking preventive or enforcement action (Article 2, paragraph 5): ' It constitutes a general pledge not to strengthen the hand of a state which has violated its obligations under the Charter to the point where preventive or enforcement action has become necessary.' Here the *Report* presupposes that enforcement action is to be directed only against a state ' which has violated its obligations under the Charter,' which means that the enforcement action is considered to be a sanction.

At the *Hearings*, p. 252, the representative of the Department of State said in the discussion of Article 14: ' Sanction is provided only for breaches of the peace or threats to peace.' This refers to the enforcement measures of Chapter VII. That sanctions are provided ' only ' for breaches of the peace or threats to peace, or, in other terms, that these enforcement measures are the only sanctions provided for by the Charter is certainly not true. Expulsion is—according to Article 6—a sanction provided for persistent violation of any obligation imposed upon Members by the Charter.

be deemed to be an act of aggression against the Members, which were obliged to resort ' immediately ' to the economic sanctions determined in Article 16, paragraph 1. However, no sanction is possible as an automatic reaction against the violator of the law. As a sanction, such reaction can take place only after the violation of the law has been ascertained by an authority determined by the law. This may be the one competent to take the enforcement action. And this is indeed the only possible interpretation of Article 16: that it was upon each Member of the League to decide for itself whether the violation of the Covenant referred to in Article 16, paragraph 1, had been committed; and that the Member was obliged to take economic measures provided for in this paragraph only if it decided the question in the affirmative. The Council, too, could, under paragraph 2 of Article 16, recommend military measures only after having determined the existence of a breach of the Covenant. Hence there is no difference between the Covenant and the Charter as to the automatic character of the sanctions. But there is an essential difference between them as to the organ by which, and the conditions under which, the enforcement actions are to be taken.

As to the first point it has already been pointed out that the enforcement actions under Article 16 of the Covenant were almost completely decentralized, whereas the enforcement measures to be taken under Article 39 of the Charter are strictly centralised. As to the second point, it is important to note that none of the various obligations imposed upon the Members by the Charter is formulated as obligation to refrain from ' any threat to the peace, breach of the peace, or act of aggression.' The obligation the content of which comes nearest to this is the one constituted by Principle 4 in Article 2:

> All Members shall refrain in their international relations from the threat or use of force against the territorial integrity or political independence of any state, or in any other manner inconsistent with the Purposes of the United Nations.

The phrase ' or in any other manner inconsistent with the Purposes of the United Nations ' is an addition to the words ' against the territorial integrity, etc.' The meaning is: the Members shall refrain from the threat or use of force not only against the territorial integrity and political independence of any state; they shall refrain from the threat or use of force also in any other manner inconsistent with the Purposes of the United Nations, that is to say: with the provisions of Article 1 of the Charter. The main import of the obligation of the Members, established by Article 2, paragraph 4: ' to refrain from the threat or use of force ' is not affected by the reference to Article 1 of the Charter determining the main function of the Organisation. This function is defined—not exactly by the same, but almost by the same, formula as that used in Article 39. Article 39 speaks of ' threat to the peace, breach of peace, or act of aggression,' whereas Article 1, paragraph 1—more correctly—of ' threats to the peace,' ' acts of aggression or other breaches of the peace.' ' Breaches of the peace ' include ' acts of aggression.' It is superfluous to mention ' acts of aggression ' in addition to ' breaches of the peace '; this all the more as the Charter does not define the very problematical concept ' act of aggression.'

Hence the meaning of Article 2, paragraph 4 is: All Members shall refrain in their international relations from the threat or use of force, not only against the territorial integrity or political independence of any state, but also in a manner which is inconsistent with the function of the Organisation to prevent or suppress threats to the peace, acts of aggression or other breaches of the peace. If the intention was to establish—in conformity with the function of the Organisation—an obligation of the Members to refrain from threats to the peace, acts of aggression and other breaches of the peace, it is not understandable why Article 2, paragraph 4, stipulates: ' All Members shall refrain . . . from the threat or use of force . . . ' For there can be little doubt that the formula: ' threat to the peace, breach of the peace, or act of aggression ' as used in Article 39, has not the same meaning as the formula ' threat or use of force ' adopted in Article 2, paragraph 4.[5] As ' act of aggression ' an act may be considered which is not a ' threat or use of force.' In the definition of aggression laid down, *e.g.*, in the Geneva Protocol the refusal to submit a dispute to the procedure of peaceful settlement is declared an act of ' aggression.' The same is true regarding the term ' breach of the peace.' Any serious violation of international law and especially the violation of almost any obligation imposed upon the Members by the Charter—and not only a violation of the obligation to refrain from the threat or use of force—could be interpreted as breach of the peace. The scope of Article 39 of the Charter is much wider than that of Article 16 of the Covenant which limits the application of enforcement measures to illegal resort to war. Of the utmost importance is the difference between the meaning of ' threat of force ' used in Article 2, paragraph 4, and that of ' threat to the peace ' used in Article 39. It is completely within the discretion of the Security Council to decide what constitutes a ' threat to the peace.'[6] If a state refuses to execute

[5] At the 363rd meeting of the Security Council during the discussion of the conflict between the United States, the United Kingdom and France with the Soviet Union concerning the so-called blockade of Berlin (*cf. supra*, p. 443) the representative of the United States interpreted Article 39 as follows: ' What constitutes a " threat to the peace " as that term is used in Article 39 of the Charter ? A threat to the peace is created when a State uses force or the threat of force to secure compliance with its demands.' (Official Records of the Security Council, 3rd year, No. 115, p. 4.) This interpretation does not correspond to the wording of Article 39.

[6] In the Spanish question the sub-committee appointed by the Security Council on April 29, 1946, rejected Poland's proposal to apply Article 41, on the ground that the activities of the Franco regime did not constitute ' an existing threat to the peace within the meaning of Article 39.' Against this statement the representative

the decisión of the International Court of Justice (Article 94 of the Charter) or of another international tribunal, or to comply with the recommendations of a commission of conciliation, its conduct may be characterised as a ' threat to the peace,' but not as a ' threat of force ' as long as its conduct does not allow the conclusion that the state intends to resort to force. As a ' threat to the peace ' and, consequently, as a condition of enforcement action according to Article 39 may be interpreted: non-acceptance of the ' plans ' submitted under Article 26 by the Security Council to the Members of the United Nations for the establishment of a system for the regulation of armaments; non-compliance with the provision of Article 33, to seek a solution of a dispute by peaceful means; non-compliance with a call of the Security Council to settle a dispute by means of the own choice of the parties in accordance with Article 33, paragraph 2; non-compliance with the prescription of Article 37, paragraph 1, to refer a non-settled dispute to the Security Council; non-compliance with one of the various recommendations made by the General Assembly or the Security Council under Article 10, Article 11, paragraph 2, Article 14, Article 36, paragraph 1, Article 37, paragraph 2, Article 38, even if all these acts are not considered to be violations of obligations expressly stipulated in the Charter.[7] The

of Poland advanced the following view: ' The Security Council is free within the purposes and principles of the Organisation to determine whether a situation is a threat to the peace in the sense of Article 39. The Charter does not demand that such a situation, in order to be recognised as a threat to the peace, be an immediate danger of a breach of peace or act of aggression within the next few days, weeks or even months. Potential as well as imminent dangers can be construed as a threat to the peace in the sense of Article 39. To affirm otherwise would mean that no actions by the Security Council are possible in situations like that of Mussolini before the imminent invasion of Abyssinia or that of Hitler before the first bombs were dropped on Polish cities. Unless threats to the peace are taken care of by the Security Council at an early stage while they are still potential and easy to remove, the United Nations may find themselves in face of situations beyond their power to control. The enumeration in Article 41 of steps such as interruption of postal, telegraphic and radio communication and the severance of diplomatic relations indicates clearly that potential threats to the peace are also covered by Article 39. If only imminent threats to the peace were envisaged in Article 39, measures short of economic and military sanctions would be meaningless.' (Doc. S/75, pp. 14 ff.)

In the Greek question the delegate of the United States proposed a resolution finding that ' Albania, Bulgaria, and Yugoslavia have given assistance and support to the guerillas fighting against the Greek Government ' and determining ' that such assistance and support to the guerillas by Albania, Bulgaria, and Yugoslavia constitutes a threat to the peace within the meaning of Chapter VII of the Charter ' (Doc. S/486). Although 9 members voted in favour of this proposal it was not adopted because of the negative vote of one permanent member (Doc. S/P.V. 188).

7 The Report of Rapporteur on Chapter VIII, Section B (of the Dumbarton Oaks Proposals, corresponding to Chapter VII of the Charter) (U.N.C.I.O. Doc. 881, III/3/46, pp. 3 f.) contains the following statements: ' A number of amendments referring to paragraphs 1 and 2 were directed at limiting the very great freedom which, in the Dumbarton Oaks Proposals, is left to the Council in determining

Charter does not prescribe that the enforcement actions referred to in Articles 39, 41, and 42, shall be directed only against a Member which has violated one of the obligations stipulated by the Charter, especially the obligation to refrain from the threat or use of force; it does not even prescribe that the enforcement measures shall be directed only against a Member guilty of a threat to, or breach of, the peace. Even if Article 2, paragraph 4, should be interpreted to mean that the Members are obliged to refrain from any threat to the peace, breach of the peace, or other act of aggression, Article 39 need not be interpreted to mean that enforcement action shall be taken only against a Member which has violated this obligation. The Charter simply authorises the Security Council to take enforcement measures after having determined the existence of any threat to, or breach of, the peace, without binding the Council with respect to the persons against whom these measures shall be directed.[8] It is true that Article 24, paragraph 2, of the Charter stipulates that the Security

what action, if any, to take. Some of these amendments were designed to make more precise the Council's obligation to act in accordance with the purposes and principles of the Organisation and the provisions of the Charter. The Committee considered that, since such specifications were already stated in Chapter VI defining the powers of the Council, it was unnecessary to make special mention of them in the present chapter. The Committee similarly put aside a proposal which would have obligated the Council to aid any party submitting to judicial settlement. It believed that this unduly restricted the Council's freedom of action and that cases might arise where a party refusing to submit to a judicial settlement might not necessarily be at fault. A more protracted discussion developed in the Committee on the possible insertion in paragraph 2, Section B, Chapter VIII, of the determination of acts of aggression. Various amendments proposed on this subject recalled the definitions written into a number of treaties concluded before this war but did not claim to specify all cases of aggression. They proposed a list of eventualities in which intervention by the Council would be automatic. At the same time they would have left to the Council the power to determine the other cases in which it should likewise intervene. Although this proposition evoked considerable support, it nevertheless became clear to a majority of the Committee that a preliminary definition of aggression went beyond the possibilities of this Conference and the purpose of the Charter. The progress of the technique of modern warfare renders very difficult the definition of all cases of aggression. It may be noted that, the list of such cases being necessarily incomplete, the Council would have a tendency to consider of less importance the acts not mentioned therein; those omissions would encourage the aggressor to distort the definition or might delay action by the Council. Furthermore, in the other cases listed, automatic action by the Council might bring about a premature application of enforcement measures. The Committee therefore decided to adhere to the text drawn up at Dumbarton Oaks and to leave to the Council the entire decision as to what constitutes a threat to peace, a breach of the peace, or an act of aggression.'

8 *The Report to the President*, p. 92, stresses that the action on the part of the Security Council is not 'automatic'; previous determination of the existence of a threat to the peace, breach of the peace, or act of aggression is necessary. The Report states that it has been intentionally conferred upon the Security Council 'ample authority to decide what constitutes a threat to the peace, a breach of peace, or an act of aggression, and to decide also which of the disputing parties has been mainly at fault.' However, a decision of the Security Council with respect to the

Council in discharging its duties shall act in accordance with the Purposes and Principles of the United Nations, among which 'conformity with the principles of justice and international law (Article 1, paragraph 1) is established. This postulate, however, refers only to the Organisation's Purpose to bring about settlement of disputes or adjustment of situations, not to the enforcement actions,[9] and only the Members are obliged by Article 2, paragraph 3, to settle their disputes in a way that 'justice' is not endangered. However, even if the Security Council were bound to conform its enforcement actions with the principles of justice and international law, it would have the choice between justice and law, which are not identical. Consequently it might consider it to be just to direct enforcement action against a Member which legally, that is, from the point of view of international law, is not wrong, since it has not violated any obligation expressly imposed upon it by the text of the Charter.[1]

On the other hand, the fact that a Member, contrary to Article 2, paragraph 4, threatens to use force or actually uses force, has not necessarily as its consequence an enforcement action taken by the Security Council under Article 39. The Security Council may decide that such conduct is neither a threat to the peace nor a breach of the peace, and consequently the Council is not entitled to take enforcement measures.

According to the wording of Article 39, the Security Council may take enforcement measures not only against a Member of the United

question which of the parties is right and which is wrong, is not at all mentioned in the Charter. The Security Council is not bound to decide this question at all. Cf. note [1] on this page.

[9] Cf. *supra*, pp. 16 ff.

[1] At the *Hearings* (p. 282) the representative of the Department of State interpreted Article 39 to mean: 'the Council does not have to wait until there is a determination of who is right and who is wrong. The problem is to stop the fighting or to remove the threat to the peace as soon as possible.'

In the Palestine question the representative of the United Kingdom spoke against an application of Article 39 arguing, *inter alia*, that his government 'would fear that a search for the aggressor would land us in interminable and probably unprofitable wrangles' (Official Records of the Security Council, 3rd Year, No. 69, p. 4). The delegate of the United States objected: 'We do not have to determine, as suggested by the representative of the United Kingdom, who is the aggressor, who is at fault, if both parties are at fault, or which one is more at fault than the other. But as the guardians of the peace of the world, it is our primary duty to find out, under Article 39, whether there exists any threat to the peace' (p. 9). According to the wording of Article 39, the Security Council is not bound to determine the aggressor. But if the enforcement measure to be taken under this Article shall have the character of a sanction it must not be directed against a state which is not guilty of a violation of its obligations. If the violation consists in an act of aggression, the enforcement action as a true sanction must be directed against the aggressor. If Article 39 is interpreted to provide for sanctions, the Security Council is bound to determine who is the aggressor.

Nations but also against a state which is not a Member and hence subjected to the Charter only insofar as Article 2, paragraph 6, applies. The enforcement action may even be taken in relation to a territory which is no state's land (for instance Palestine immediately after the withdrawal of Great Britain). That means that the Security Council may intervene with enforcement measures in a conflict which takes place on such territory between two groups of the population or between a state and a group of the population of this territory. The enforcement action may be directed against the state or against a group of the population not having the character of a state, or against both. This view might be supported by the wording of Article 39 which makes the application of the enforcement measures dependent upon the existence of ' any threat to the peace, breach of the peace or act of aggression.' In contradistinction to other provisions of the Charter, Article 39 does not speak of a threat to, or breach of, ' international ' peace. Hence the peace referred to in this passage need not necessarily be a status in the relation between states. However, the purpose of the enforcement action to be taken under Article 39 is determined as the maintenance of restoration of ' international peace and security.' Hence the wording: ' any ' threat to the peace, etc., instead of : ' threat to international peace,' etc. cannot justify a forcible intervention of the Security Council in a conflict taking place on a stateless territory between two groups of the population of this territory or between a state and one of these groups. Such an intervention is possible under Article 39 because this Article leaves it to the Security Council to determine what facts constitute a threat to, or breach of, ' international ' peace and against whom the enforcement action for the maintenance or restoration of the international peace is to be directed. The Security Council may very well decide that a situation which has not the character of a conflict between two states is a threat to international peace and take enforcement action against a state or a group of people involved in this situation, though the state is not in conflict with another state and the group has not the character of a state. [2]

[2] In the Indonesian question the representative of the Netherlands maintained that Article 39 of the Charter was not applicable to the situation since there was no threat to, or breach of, ' international ' peace, for the conflict between the government of the Netherlands and Indonesia was not a conflict between two sovereign states, Indonesia not being a sovereign state. (Official Records of the Security Council, 2nd year, No. 67, pp. 1645 ff.; cf. *supra*, pp. 226, 365, 440.)

At its 173rd meeting the Security Council adopted a decision ' noting with concern the hostilities in progress between the armed forces of the Netherlands and the Republic of Indonesia ' and calling upon the parties ' (*a*) to cease hostilities forthwith, and (*b*) to settle their disputes by arbitration or by other peaceful means and keep the Security Council informed about the progress of the settlement.' (*Ibid.* No. 68, pp. 1702 f.) The Security Council did not determine under Article 39 that the ' hostilities ' noted in the decision constituted a threat to, or breach of, the peace. The call ' to settle their dispute, etc.' may be considered

9. Sanctions or Political Measures ?

The enforcement measures taken by the Security Council under Article 39 may be interpreted in a twofold manner. It may be

to be made under Chapter VI (Articles 33, paragraph 2); but the call ' to cease hostilities ' could be made only under Chapter VII, which was not possible without applying Article 39. Cf. *infra*, pp. 739 ff.

In the Palestine question the Security Council adopted at its 277th meeting a resolution noting ' with grave concern the increasing violence and disorder in Palestine,' without determining this situation as constituting a threat to, or breach of, the peace. In this decision the Council expressed the belief that ' it is of the utmost urgency that an immediate truce be effected in Palestine ' and called upon ' Arab and Jewish armed groups in Palestine to cease acts of violence immediately.' (Official Records of the Security Council, 3rd year, No. 52, p. 33.) The call to cease acts of violence, too, is possible only under Chapter VII.—At the 269th meeting of the Security Council in the course of the discussion of the Palestine question the representatives of the United Kingdom declared to be against an enforcement action under Article 39, because this Article required the existence of a threat to, or breach of, ' international ' peace. He stated: ' I may be wrong, but I think that in all other passages in the Charter where peace and security are mentioned, these words are qualified by the adjective " international," which does not figure in the first part of this Article 39. Certainly, that adjective does appear in the cases of Articles 33, 34 and 37. I believe that the omission of the word " international," in the first part of Article 39, may be due to an oversight. This belief is strengthened by the fact that that same Article 39 goes on to prescribe what may be done " to maintain or restore international peace and security." If that is so, what the Security Council has to do, under this Article, is to determine that there is a threat to, or breach of, international peace and security . . . ' (*Ibid.*, 3rd Year, No. 69, p. 2.) The representative of the United States did not agree with this interpretation. He denied that the omission of the word ' international ' in the first part of Article 39 was due to an oversight. He stated: ' How can that be when another very significant word was substituted for it; namely, the word " any " ? " Any " includes " international " and includes all other kinds of threats to the peace, breaches of the peace, or acts of aggression. I would claim that that word was substituted with great care and with full understanding of its importance, so that the Security Council, having found " any threat to the peace," might be able to proceed to the inquiry with respect to the application of remedies, or a prevention of that further step of extension of the conflagration into a breach of international peace, for this Article further says " and shall make recommendations . . . "; then we strike something astonishing— the distinctive " or "—" or decide what measure shall be taken in accordance with Articles 41 and 42, to maintain or restore international peace and security " ' (p. 7). The representative of Syria supported the view expressed by the representative of the United Kingdom, and denied that there existed a threat to, or breach of, international peace in Palestine. He declared: ' The position is that the international status of Palestine should be studied to ascertain whether or not international peace is being disturbed. It would be disturbed, for example, by a dispute between two or more States fighting over a certain situation; but such is not the case in Palestine and Article 39 does not apply.' (*Ibid.*, No. 70, p. 9.) At its 338th meeting the Security Council adopted a decision determining ' that the situation in Palestine constitutes a threat to the peace within the meaning of Article 39 of the Charter.' This was the first case where the Council in applying Article 39 determined a threat to, or breach of, the peace. But in this case the Council did not take enforcement measures under Article 41 or 42, but provisional measures under Article 40. It ordered the

argued that the enforcement measures determined in Articles 39, 41 and 42 are no ' sanctions ' since they are not established as reaction against a violation of obligations established by the Charter. The only genuine sanctions provided for by the Charter are expulsion from the Organisation according to Article 6, suspension from the right of voting in the General Assembly according to Article 19, and enforcement measures taken by the Security Council under Article 94, paragraph 2, to give effect to a judgment of the Court. The enforcement actions taken under Article 39 are purely political measures, that is to say, measures which the Security Council may apply at its discretion for the purpose to maintain or restore international peace. This interpretation may be confirmed by the fact that according to Article 39, the first Article of Chapter VII, the Security Council, after having determined the existence of a threat to the peace, breach of the peace, or act of aggression, may not only resort to enforcement action but may ' make recommendations.'[3] It has the choice between

Governments and authorities concerned ' to desist from further military action, etc.' (Official Records of the Security Council, 3rd Year, No. 97, pp. 43 ff.) Thus the order was directed not only at ' Governments.' Cf. *supra*, pp. 286 ff., and *infra*, pp. 740 ff.

[3] Committee 3 to Commission III of the San Francisco Conference decided that the text of Articles 39 and 40 should be interpreted in accordance with the scope of the following observations, the inclusion of which in the Report of the Rapporteur was unanimously approved by the Committee. ' In using the word " recommendations " in Section B [Chapter VII of the Charter] as already found in paragraph 5, Section A [Article 36, paragraph 1 of the Charter] the Committee has intended to show that the action of the Council so far as it relates to the peaceful settlement of a dispute or to situations giving rise to a threat of war, a breach of the peace, or aggression, should be considered as governed by the provisions contained in Section A [Chapter VI of the Charter]. Under such an hypothesis, the Council would in reality pursue simultaneously two distinct actions, one having for its object the settlement of the dispute or the difficulty, and the other the enforcement or provisional measures, each of which is governed by an appropriate section in Chapter VIII [Chapters VI and VII of the Charter].' Report of the Rapporteur on Chapter VIII, Section B (U.N.C.I.O. Doc. 881, III/3/46, p. 6). It is difficult to understand how the Security Council can ' pursue simultaneously ' action under Article 36, paragraph 1, and Article 37, paragraph 2, that is to say, recommend appropriate procedures or methods of adjustment or terms of settlement, and action under Article 39, that is to say, recommendations under this Article. Recommendations under Article 39 need not necessarily be different from recommendations made under Article 36, paragraph 1 or Article 37, paragraph 2. In this respect the actions are not ' distinct.' It seems that, according to the intentions of the Charter, the conditions under which recommendations under Article 36, paragraph 1, or Article 37, paragraph 2, and those under which recommendations under Article 39 may be made, are different. Recommendations under Article 36, paragraph 1 and Article 37, paragraph 2, may be made if the continuance of the situation or the dispute is likely to endanger the maintenance of international peace and security; recommendations under Article 39 may be made if there exists a threat to the peace. If these two conditions are really distinguishable, then action under Article 36, paragraph 1, or Article 37, paragraph 2, may be taken in one case and action under Article 39 in another case. Then it is impossible to ' pursue simultaneously ' both. If, however, there is no difference

the two different measures of which only the former could have the character of a sanction. Since the Council has the choice between recommendations and enforcement measures, it is not possible to maintain that it is under an obligation to take enforcement measures after it has determined the existence of a threat to, or breach of, the peace. The Security Council ' shall ' do the one *or* the other. The fact that the Charter in Chapter VII, entitled ' Action with respect to threats to the Peace, Breaches of the Peace, and Acts of Aggression, ' does not only provide enforcement action but also the making of recommendations, may allow the conclusion that this Chapter is not intended to deal particularly with sanctions. The Charter does not determine what kind of recommendation the Security Council may make under Article 39. Hence any kind of recommendation is permissible; and if the Security Council has determined the existence of a threat to the peace involved in a dispute, it may make under Article 39 the same recommendations as those it is authorised to make under Article 37, paragraph 2, after having determined that the continuance of the dispute is likely to endanger the maintenance of international peace.[4] Besides, it is hardly adequate to authorise the Security Council to make recommendations after it has determined the existence of a threat to, or breach of, the peace. Such recommendation may be justifiable in case of a threat to the peace if the Security Council had no opportunity of making recommendations in an earlier stage of affairs, when the continuance of the situation or the dispute was only ' likely to endanger ' the peace (Article 34). In case of an act of aggression or another breach of the peace, however, only enforcement action seems to be appropriate.[5] Under the Charter

between a situation being a threat to the peace and the continuance of a situation (including disputes) being likely to endanger peace, the Security Council has the choice between making recommendations under Article 36, paragraph 1, or Article 37, paragraph 2, and making recommendations under Article 39: the choice between two actions, not the possibility of pursuing simultaneously both. Action under Article 36, paragraph 1 and Article 37, paragraph 2, is different from action under Article 39 in so far as the rule excluding members of the Security Council parties to a dispute from voting applies to the former but not to the latter.

[4] During the discussion of the Palestine question the representative of Belgium declared to be against the proposal of the United States to apply Article 39. He stated: ' The United States resolution thus invokes Chapter VII of the Charter, which provides for the application of measures of coercion. The Belgian delegation, on the contrary, thinks that we must keep within the framework of Chapter VI of the Charter, which deals with the pacific settlement of disputes.' (Official Records of the Security Council, 3rd Year, No. 69, p. 10.) This statement seems to presuppose that Chapter VII provides only for enforcement measures and does not authorise the Security Council to settle a dispute by peaceful means. This view is not in conformity with Article 39.

[5] The Commentary to Articles 39 and 40 adopted by Committee 3 of Commission III of the San Francisco Conference contains also the following statement: ' It is the Committee's view that the power given to the Council under paragraphs 1 and 2 [Articles 39 and 40 of the Charter] not to resort to the measures contemplated in paragraphs 3 and 4 [Articles 41 and 42 of the Charter], or to resort to them only

the Security Council may act in this way; but the Charter does not prescribe this course of action.

To interpret enforcement measures taken in accordance with Article 39 not as sanctions, but as measures to be used by the Security Council at its discretion, would be in conformity with the general tendency which prevailed in drafting the Charter; the predominance of the political over the legal approach. This interpretation, however, leads to the consequence that with respect to enforcement measures there is no difference between a Member which has violated its obligations under the Charter, and a Member which is not guilty of any such violation. The latter, as well as the former, may be subjected to enforcement action if the Security Council deems it necessary for the maintenance or restoration of peace. An enforcement action is an evil much harder than the severest sanction applicable to a violator of the Charter, namely, expulsion from the Organisation.

However, the interpretation according to which the enforcement actions are merely political measures is not the only possible one. It may be argued that, in accordance with general international law, a forcible interference in the sphere of interest of a state, that is reprisals or war, is permitted only as a reaction against a violation of law, that is to say as sanction. Since the enforcement actions determined by Articles 39, 41 and 42 of the Charter constitute forcible interference in the sphere of a state, they must be interpreted as sanctions if the Charter is supposed to be in conformity with general international law. No other interpretation is possible with respect to the enforcement measures not involving the use of armed force as determined in Article 41. These measures have the character of reprisals; and according to a generally accepted opinion, reprisals are permissible only as reaction against a violation of international law, that is to say, as sanctions. Only as to enforcement action involving the use of armed force as determined in Article 42, it is disputed whether such action is permitted by general international law only as reaction against a delict, that is to say, as sanction, or whether such action is always possible without constituting a violation of general international law. If the first of the two interpretations of general international law is accepted, Chapter VII of the Charter is in conformity with general international law only under the assumption that both kinds of measures, those under Article 41, as well as those under

after having sought to maintain or restore peace by inviting the parties to consent to certain conservatory measures, refers above all to the presumption of a threat of war. The Committee is unanimous in the belief that, on the contrary, in the case of flagrant aggression imperilling the existence of a member of the Organisation, enforcement measures should be taken without delay, and to the full extent required by circumstances, except that the Council should at the same time endeavour to persuade the aggressor to abandon its venture, by the means contemplated in Section A and by prescribing conservatory measures.' (U.N.C.I.O. Doc. 881, III/3/46, p. 6.)

Article 42, have the character of true sanctions. If the enforcement actions are sanctions, then any conduct against which the Security Council is authorised by the Charter to react with enforcement actions must have the character if a violation of the Charter. Consequently the Members of the Organisation have not only the obligations expressly formulated in the text of the Charter, but also the obligation to refrain from any conduct which the Security Council under Article 39 declares to be a threat to, or breach of, the peace. For the Security Council is authorised by the Charter to take enforcement measures against a state responsible for such conduct, and these measures have the character of sanctions. By declaring the conduct of a state, which does not constitute a violation of an obligation expressly stipulated in the Charter, to be a threat to, or breach of, the peace, the Security Council establishes an obligation to refrain from this conduct. But, in order to be in conformity with general international law, the Security Council is allowed to direct its action only against the state responsible for the threat to, or breach of, the peace, in spite of the wording of Article 39 authorising the Council to take enforcement action against any state whatever after having determined the existence of any threat to, or breach of, the peace. Since the Security Council is completely free in its determination of what is a threat to the peace or breach of the peace, it may determine as such any conduct of a state without regard to whether this conduct constitutes the violation of an obligation stipulated by pre-existing law. By declaring the conduct of a state to be a threat to, or breach of, the peace, the Security Council may create new law.[6] Under Article 39, the Security Council may especially determine as threat to, or breach of, the peace, the non-compliance with any act of the Security Council or the General Assembly, whether it is called 'decision,' 'recommendation,' 'call,' or 'plan.'[7] The act of the General Assembly or the Security Council may by itself not intend to constitute an obligation; but compliance with it may become an obligation by a decision of the Security Council determining non-compliance with it as a threat to, or breach of, the peace. Hence the Security Council, after having determined under Article 39 that a definite conduct of a state constitutes a threat to, or breach of, the peace, may not only 'recommend' but also order the state to refrain from this conduct. The decision by which such an 'order' is issued by the Security Council is legally binding upon the state concerned not only in accordance with Article 25, but also because, and insofar as, the order is issued under a sanction provided for in Article 39. Since the Security Council under Article 39, after having determined the existence of a threat to, or breach of, the peace, may make a mere recommendation, its decision should be formulated in a way that there

[6] Cf. *supra*, pp. 293 ff.

[7] Cf. *supra*, pp. 95 ff.

could be no doubt whether it is intended as a recommendation or as an order.[8]

Since it is difficult to forseee whether the Security Council will consider in a concrete case non-compliance with a recommendation of an organ of the United Nations or any other conduct of a state as a threat to, or breach of, the peace and hence as a condition of enforcement measures, a highly unsatisfactory state of uncertainty exists with respect to the obligations of the Member. Such undesirable effect would have been avoided by using in Article 39 the same formula as in Article 2, paragraph 4. Besides, the formula ' threat or use of force ' designates an objectively determinable conduct, whereas the words ' threat to the peace, breach of the peace ' allow a highly subjective interpretation. To use in Article 39 the phrase ' threat or use of force ' instead of ' threat to the peace, breach of the peace ' would also have had the advantage that the enforcement actions authorised by Article 39 had been without any doubt conditioned by the violation of an obligation expressly imposed upon the Members in Article 2, paragraph 4, so that the Security Council would have had no power to create new law.

As pointed out, according to the wording of Article 39, enforcement measures may be taken by the Security Council also against non-member states. If Article 2, paragraph 6, is interpreted to mean that non-member states are legally bound by the Principles of the Charter, and if Article 39 constitutes an obligation to refrain from any conduct which the Security Council may determine as threat to, or breach of, the peace, non-member states, too, are under this obligation, and an enforcement measure taken against them under Article 39 may be interpreted to be a sanction. Enforcement action taken in relation to the population of a territory which is no state's land is not prohibited by general international law. Hence Article 39 may be interpreted to authorise the Security Council to take such action without violating international law.

The difference between the interpretation of Article 39 according to which this Article provides for true sanctions and the interpretation according to which the enforcement actions taken under this Article are political measures, is rather of theoretical than of practical importance. Both interpretations, however, reveal the extraordinary power which the Charter has conferred upon the Security Council. The latter, having the choice between making recommendations and the measures to be taken in accordance with Articles 41 and 42, is not bound, it is only authorised, to take enforcement action under the conditions determined in Article 39. It may, for political reasons, not be willing or, due to its voting procedure, not be able to act.

[8] Cf. *infra*, pp. 740 ff.

10. Collective or Individual Responsibility

The sanctions provided for by the Charter are—as a rule—to be directed against states as such, not against individuals. This in spite of the fact that under the Charter individuals may be appointed or elected with the effect of being directly organs of the United Nations; as, for instance, the Secretary-General and the members of the staff of the Secretariat. Sanctions to be directed against states as such constitute collective, not individual, responsibility. The Charter does establish only collective responsibility of states for violations of the Charter, not responsibility of the individuals who—in their capacity as organs of a state or in their capacity as organs of the United Nations—have constituted by their own conduct the violation of the Charter. This is of particular importance in respect to those violations of the Charter which have the character of an illegal use of force. In this respect the Charter remains far behind the Agreement concluded on August 8, 1945, at London for the Prosecution of European Axis War Criminals. This treaty established individual criminal responsibility for 'crimes against peace' committed by persons acting whether as individuals or as heads of state or as responsible officials in government departments (Articles 6 and 7 of the Charter of the International Military Tribunal, annexed to the Agreement). The individual criminal responsibility of the persons concerned was established by the Agreement which authorised an International Military Tribunal to impose upon these individuals, on conviction, death or such other punishment as shall be determined by it to be just (Article 27 of the Charter annexed to the Agreement).

The Agreement of London applied only to subjects and organs of the vanquished European Axis Powers, not to subjects or organs of the states Members of the United Nations. Hence individual criminal responsibility for violation of the rules prohibiting war, as established by the Agreement, without the consent of the vanquished states will hardly be recognised as a principle of a new international law. To achieve this effect it would have been necessary to insert the principle into the Charter as a general rule applicable to the subjects and organs of all the Members of the United Nations and—through Article, 2, paragraph 6—to all the other states of the world. This is possible only by an amendment to the Charter. The resolution adopted by the General Assembly at its 55th meeting[9] is not equivalent to such an amendment. The resolution runs as follows:—

> The General Assembly, Recognises the obligation laid upon it by Article 13, paragraph 1, sub-paragraph *a* of the Charter, to initiate studies and make recommendations for the purpose of encouraging the progressive development of international law and its codification; takes note of the Agreement for

[9] Resolutions adopted by the General Assembly, Doc. A/64/Add. 1. p. 188.

the establishment of an International Military Tribunal for the prosecution and punishment of the major war criminals of the European Axis signed in London on August 8, 1945, and of the Charter annexed thereto, and of the fact that similar principles have been adopted in the Charter of the International Military Tribunal for the trial of the major war criminals in the Far East, proclaimed at Tokyo on January 19, 1946.

Therefore Affirms the principles of international law recognised by the Charter of the Nuremberg Tribunal and the judgment of the Tribunal; Directs the Committee on the codification of international law established by the resolution of the General Assembly of December 11, 1946, to treat as a matter of primary importance plans for the formulation, in the context of a general codification of offences against the peace and security of mankind, or of an International Criminal Code, of the principles recognised in the Charter of the Nuremberg Tribunal and in the judgment of the Tribunal.

11. Provisional Measures

Enforcement actions under Article 39 may be preceded by 'provisional measures.' Article 40 stipulates—

> In order to prevent an aggravation of the situation, the Security Council may, before making the recommendations or deciding upon the measures provided for in Article 39, call upon the parties concerned to comply with such provisional measures as it deems necessary or desirable. Such provisional measures shall be without prejudice to the rights, claims, or position of the parties concerned. The Security Council shall duly take account of failure to comply with such provisional measures.

The 'situation' referred to in Article 40 is probably the same as the one to which Article 39 applies: a situation of which the Security Council has determined that it constitutes a threat to, or breach of, the peace. This does not result from the wording of Article 40 but from the fact that the provision is placed between Article 39 and the other Articles of Chapter VII dealing with 'action with respect to threats to the peace . . .' If this interpretation is accepted, the Security Council can call upon the parties to comply with provisional measures only after having determined, in accordance with Article 39, the existence of a threat to the peace, breach of the peace, or act of aggression. Then the Security Council has first to decide upon the provisional measures that it deems necessary or desirable, whereupon it may 'call' upon the parties concerned to comply with them. The practice of the Security Council, however, does not conform to this interpretation. There are cases where the Security Council has called upon the parties to comply with measures, such as to cease hostilities, or to achieve a truce, which could be understood only as provisional measures within the meaning of Article 40, without having previously determined the existence of a threat to, or breach of, the peace, and without expressly referring to Article 40.[1]

In the *Report to the President*[2] it has been pointed out that it is not the Security Council which takes the provisional measures, as it takes enforcement action. It is the parties themselves which are to take the provisional measures in accordance with the 'call' of the Security Council. This interpretation, however, is correct only if the 'call' of the Security Council is not binding upon the Members. Whether the 'call' is an act constituting an obligation of the parties concerned or a simple 'recommendation' depends on the intention of the Security Council and especially on the consequences which it attaches to a failure to comply with the call (or, as Article 40 says: with the provisional measures). The Council may make the call without intending to bind legally the parties concerned, and especially without intending to react against non-compliance with an enforcement action. Then the call is a mere recommendation. But the Council may make the call by a decision within the meaning of Article 25, especially with the expressed intention to take enforcement action in case of non-compliance. This possibility is provided for in Article 40, which stipulates that the Security Council 'shall duly take account' of failure to comply with the call. That can mean only that failure to comply with the call shall influence the action which the Council is to take according to Article 39; especially its choice between recommendations and enforcement actions, and its decision against which of the parties and what kind of enforcement action shall be taken. Hence the 'call' made under Article 40 may itself be a simple recommendation of provisional measures and the Council may make such a 'recommendation' if it deems these measures only 'advisable.' But the 'call' may also be an 'order' legally binding upon the parties because issued under the sanction provided for in Article 39,[3] and it will be an 'order' if the Council deems the

[1] For instance, the resolution adopted at the 173rd meeting in the Indonesian case (cf. *supra*, pp. 403, 440 ff.) and the resolutions adopted at the 277th, 302nd and 310th meetings in the Palestine case. Cf. *supra*, pp. 288 ff.

[2] The *Report to the President*, p. 92, says: 'the disputing parties will be asked to undertake themselves upon recommendation of the Security Council' the provisional measures. These measures 'are therefore not to be regarded as preliminary sanctions.' It is interesting that the *Report* characterises the 'call' referred to in Article 40 as 'recommendation' ignoring the possibility of taking such call as a binding decision, and that it emphasises that the provisional measures are not 'sanctions.' But are the enforcement measures 'sanctions'? To this question the *Report* gives no clear answer.

[3] At the 277th meeting of the Security Council the representative of the United States interpreted the resolution by which the Security Council, without determining the situation in Palestine as constituting a threat to, or breach of, the peace,

provisional measures 'necessary.' If the Security Council not merely recommends to the parties to take provisional measures but

'called' upon Arab and Jewish armed groups to cease acts of violence (cf. *supra*, p. 289) as follows: 'This resolution, if passed, would impose an obligation under the Charter upon every Member of the United Nations to carry out the decision made in it.' (Official Records of the Security Council, 3rd Year, No. 52, p. 31.) At the 293rd meeting of the Security Council, during the discussion of the Palestine question the representative of the United States submitted the following draft resolution:

> The Security Council,
>
> Taking into consideration that previous resolutions of the Security Council in respect to Palestine have not been complied with and that military operations are taking place in Palestine, Determines that the situation in Palestine constitutes a threat to the peace and a breach of the peace within the meaning of Article 39 of the Charter;
>
> Orders all Governments and authorities to cease and desist from any hostile military action and to that end to issue a cease-fire and stand-fast order to their military and para-military forces to become effective within thirty-six hours after the adoption of this resolution;
>
> Directs the Truce Commission established by the Security Council by its resolution of April 23, 1948 (document S/727) to report to the Security Council on the compliance with these orders. (*Ibid.*, No. 67, p. 2.)

At the 297th meeting of the Security Council the delegate of Syria objected 'that the third paragraph of the United States draft resolution states that the Security Council "orders all Governments and authorities to cease and desist . . ." and so on. I do not know whether there is any justification for the use of the word "orders." In the first place, it does not appear in the Charter at all. The Charter always refers to the Security Council's "making recommendations" or "calling upon." Certainly those who drafted the Charter paid attention to the point that it would not be consistent with the sovereignty of the States to address orders to them. I do not know whether the use of this phrase in the present instance was an oversight or whether it was intentional, but I think that "calls upon" or "recommends" would be more in keeping with the terms of the Charter.' (*Ibid.*, No. 70, p. 9.) It is true that the Charter does not use the word 'order' referring to acts of the Security Council. But Article 25 provides that the decisions, or certain decisions, of the Security Council are legally binding upon the Members; and among these decisions is certainly a decision adopted under Article 39 for the purpose to remove a threat to the peace or to suppress a breach of the peace (Article 1, paragraph 1) the existence of which has been determined by the Council, provided that the decision does not present itself as a mere 'recommendation.' It may present itself as an 'order'; then it is binding. The respresentative of the United States declared that the Security Council should issue the order he suggested 'as a provisional measure under Article 40.' And at its 338th meeting on July 15, 1948, the Security Council indeed adopted a resolution providing:

> The Security Council, taking into consideration that the Provisional Government of Israel has indicated its acceptance in principle of a prolongation of the truce in Palestine; that the States members of the Arab League have rejected successive appeals of the United Nations Mediator and of the Security Council in its resolution of July 7, 1948, for the prolongation of the truce in Palestine; and that there has consequently developed a renewal of hostilities in Palestine;
>
> Determines that the situation in Palestine constitutes a threat to the peace within the meaning of Article 39 of the Charter;

' orders ' these measures, it is the Security Council itself which takes these measures.

The provisional measures are characterised as preventive; their purpose is to ' prevent ' an aggravation of the situation. This does not mean that the enforcement actions to be taken after the call to comply with provisional measures may not have a ' preventive ' character. It has already been explained in a previous chapter of this study[4] why the provisional measures taken under Article 40, in spite of their preventive character, can hardly be interpreted to be the ' preventive actions ' referred to in Article 5 (or Article 2, paragraph 5, and Article 50). Hence suspension from the exercise of

> Orders the Governments and authorities concerned, pursuant to Article 40 of the Charter of the United Nations, to desist from further military action and to this end to issue cease-fire orders to their military and para-military forces, to take effect at a time to be determined by the Mediator, but in any event not later than three days from the date of the adoption of this resolution;
>
> Declares that failure by any of the Governments or authorities concerned to comply with the preceding paragraph of this resolution would demonstrate the existence of a breach of the peace within the meaning of Article 39 of the Charter requiring immediate consideration by the Security Council with a view to such further action under Chapter VII of the Charter as may be decided upon by the Council. (*Ibid.*, No. 97, pp. 43 ff.)

After having determined that the situation in Palestine constituted a threat to the peace, the Council under Article 39 was certainly competent to issue orders legally binding upon all authorities concerned. Article 40 referred to in the resolution, it is true, authorises the Security Council to ' call ' upon the parties concerned to comply with the provisional measures taken by the Council. But this call has the character of an ' order ' if the Council declares that non-compliance with the call constitutes a threat to, or breach of, the peace and hence the condition of a sanction provided for by Article 39.

In a resolution adopted at its 381st meeting on November 16, 1948 (Doc. S/1080), the Security Council reaffirmed ' its previous resolutions concerning the establishment and implementation of the Truce in Palestine and, recalling particularly its Resolution of July 15, 1948, which determined that the situation in Palestine constitutes a threat to the peace within the meaning of Article 39 of the Charter,' decided that ' an armistice shall be established in all sectors of Palestine,' and called upon the ' parties directly involved in the conflict in Palestine, as a further provisional measure under Article 40 of the Charter, to seek agreement forthwith, by negotiations conducted either directly or through the Acting Mediator on Palestine, with a view to the immediate establishment of the Armistice including: (*a*) the delineation of permanent armistice demarcation lines beyond which the armed forces of the respective parties shall not move; (*b*) such withdrawal and reduction of their armed forces as will ensure the maintenance of the armistice during the transition to permanent peace in Palestine.'

In its resolution adopted on August 26, 1947, in the Indonesian case, the Security Council reminded the Governments of the Netherlands and of the Indonesia Republic of its resolution of August 1, 1947, by which it ' called ' upon them to cease hostilities (which the Council characterised as ' cease fire order '), and called upon the two governments to adhere strictly to the ' recommendations ' of the Security Council of August 1, 1947. (Doc. S/P.V. 195.)

[4] Cf. *supra*, pp. 92 f.

the rights of membership in conformity with Article 5 is not applicable to a Member upon which the Security Council has called under Article 40 to comply with the provisional measures which it deems necessary or desirable. This results especially from the principle that ' provisional measures ' taken under Article 40 ' shall be without prejudice to the rights, claims, or position of the parties concerned.' The application of Article 5 certainly constitutes a prejudice to the rights of the party concerned, if this party is a Member of the United Nations. Since Article 40 refers not only to ' rights ' but also to ' claims, or position ' of the parties concerned, it might be doubtful whether under this Article any measure disadvantageous to a party could be recommended or ordered by the Security Council. But such an interpretation would deprive this Article of any value.[5] As to other measures taken under Chapter VII of the Charter no provision analogous to that of the second sentence of Article 40 exists. Hence it is permitted to assume that enforcement measures, except those with which the Security Council may threaten the parties which do not comply with the provisional measures ordered under Article 40, may be prejudicial to the rights of the parties concerned. By taking

[5] The preamble of the resolution adopted on May 29, 1948, at the 310th meeting of the Security Council in the Palestine question contains the following statement: ' Desiring to bring about a cessation of hostilities in Palestine without prejudice to the rights, claims, and position of either Arabs or Jews . . . ' These are the words used in Article 40 of the Charter. But the resolution does not expressly refer to this Article. In a note sent on June 7, 1948, to the Arab States and the Provisional Government of Israel the United Nations Mediator in Palestine stated: ' The clear intent of the truce as envisaged in the Security Council resolution of May 29 is to bring about the cessation of hostilities without prejudice to the rights, claims and position of either Jews or Arabs, and to ensure that no military advantage shall accrue to either side as a result of the application of the truce.' (Doc. S/829.)

In the Indonesian case it was proposed to call upon the parties to the conflict to withdraw their troops to the positions which they occupied before the beginning of military operations. At the 209th meeting of the Security Council the representative of the United States declared: ' The United States delegation assumes that this proposal is also made under Article 40; that is, that it is made in consideration of the Security Council taking into account failure to comply with the provisional measure, the order to cease fire . . . We must first see what authority we have for passing such a resolution . . . It is noticed that Article 40 has a provision in it as follows: '' Such provisional measures shall be without prejudice to the rights, claims, or position of the parties concerned.'' At once, the question arises as to whether the Security Council has adequate evidence that the finding proposed here and the action, if carried out, would affect the rights, claims, or position of the parties concerned. Unless that foundation is laid, I believe the Security Council should not, in law or in reason, pass this resolution.' (Doc. S/P.V. 209, p. 11.) But the representative of Poland declared at the 210th meeting: ' It is quite clear that the second sentence [of Article 40] means that no matter what steps should be taken, they shall not pre-judge the future attitude of any commission or body which shall participate in the solution of the problem. The only prejudging which is to take place is described in the third sentence of Article 40.' (Doc. S/P.V. 210, p. 16.)

enforcment measures the Security Council—as pointed out in another connection[6]—may create new law. If so, these measures may assume the character of legislative acts and are 'political' actions—like any legislative act—only when viewed from the angle of the law existing prior to their enactment.

12. The Execution of the Enforcement Measures

The Charter, as pointed out, establishes two kinds of enforcement measures: measures not involving, and measures involving the use of armed force. Measures not involving the use of armed force may, according to Article 41, 'include complete or partial interruption of economic relations and of rail, sea, air, postal, telegraphic, radio, and other means of communication, and the severance of diplomatic relations.' Article 41 authorises the Security Council to 'call upon the Members of the United Nations to apply such measures.' The measures involving the use of armed force are characterised in Article 42 as 'action by air, sea, or land forces'; and 'may include demonstrations, blockade, and other operations by air, sea, or land forces of Members of the United Nations.' This action may have the character of ordinary military measures. According to Article 43, paragraph 1, 'All Members of the United Nations' are obliged 'to make available to the Security Council, on its call and in accordance with a special agreement or agreements, armed forces, assistance, and facilities, including rights of passage, necessary for the purpose of maintaining international peace and security.' Article 45 stipulates: 'In order to enable the United Nations to take urgent military measures, Members—it is not said as in Article 43: "all" Members—shall hold immediately available national air-force contingents for combined international enforcement action.'

What is the nature of the act by which the Security Council takes an enforcement measure determined in Articles 41, 42, and 45? It is a 'decision.' According to Article 39, the Security Council shall 'decide' what measures shall be taken in accordance with Articles 41 and 42. According to Article 41, the Security Council may 'decide' what measures not involving the use of armed force are to be employed to give effect to its decisions. Article 42 says only the Security Council may 'take such action by air, sea, or land forces as may be necessary, etc.', without expressly authorising the Security Council to adopt a 'decision.' But Article 44 says: 'When the Security Council has decided to use force,' etc.; and Article 48, with reference to all enforcement actions, speaks of the action required to carry out the 'decisions' of the Security Council and stipulates: Such 'decisions' shall be carried out, etc. They are decisions to which Article 27, paragraph 3, of the Charter applies; they shall be made by an affirmative vote of seven Members including

[6] Cf. *supra*, p. 736.

the concurring votes of the permanent Members. Since they are not made under Chapter VI or under paragraph 3 of Article 52, but under Article 39 (Chapter VII), the rule excluding a party to a dispute determined by the Security Council as a threat to, or breach of, the peace, does not apply.

After having made a decision to take enforcement measures, the Security Council first is to ' determine ' by which Members of the United Nations the required action shall be carried out. Article 48, stipulates:

> 1. The action required to carry out the decision of the Security Council for the maintenance of international peace and security shall be taken by all the Members of the United Nations or by some of them, as the Security Council may determine.
>
> 2. Such decisions shall be carried out by the Members of the United Nations directly and through their action in the appropriate international agencies of which they are members.

After having determined by which Members the action shall be carried out, the Security Council ' calls ' upon the Members either ' to apply ' measures not involving the use of armed force according to Article 41, or—as formulated in Article 44—' to provide armed forces in fulfilment of the obligations assumed under Article 43.' The Security Council may call upon different Members to carry out different actions. If ' urgent military measures ' are to be taken the Security Council calls upon some Members to provide the national air force contingent in fulfilment of the obligations assumed under Article 45. This is not expressly provided by the Charter, but may be inferred by analogy.

These ' calls ' constitute obligations of the Members concerned since they are based on ' decisions ' of the Security Council, and the Members are—according to Article 25—obliged to accept and carry out the decisions of the Security Council. These obligations may be in conflict with obligations a Member has assumed in a treaty concluded previously with the State against which the enforcement action is to be directed. In this case, according to Article 103, the obligations under the Charter prevail.

If the Member of the United Nations called upon to carry out a decision of the Security Council under Article 48, paragraph 1, is a member of a specialised agency referred to in Article 57 of the Charter, it is obliged under paragraph 2 of Article 48 to carry out the decision of the Council not only ' directly ' but also through its action in this agency. It is not the agency as such which is bound to carry out the decision of the Council; it is the Member of the United Nations which as a member of the agency has to try to bring the agency, in conformity with the constitution, to action complementing the decision of the Security Council.

There exists a striking difference between the Charter of the United Nations and the Covenant of the League of Nations. The latter is characterised by a complete decentralisation of the procedure for the application of enforcement measures. Article 16 of the Covenant leaves it to the Members of the League to decide whether another Member has violated its obligations under the Covenant and whether enforcement measures not involving the use of armed force shall be applied. With respect to these measures no intervention of the Council is provided for. With respect to the measures involving the use of armed force, the Covenant does not impose upon the Members any obligation. It only authorises the Council to make recommendations. It is to be considered a great progress that the Charter has centralised both the decision as tc the question whether there exists a threat to the peace, breach of the peace, or act of aggression and the decision as tc the application of the enforcement measure whether involving or not involving the use of armed force, and has imposed upon the Members the obligation to carry out this decision.

Since the Member which by a call of the Security Council is obliged to participate in enforcement measures of the one or other kind may not be a member of the Security Council, the question arises whether such Member may or shall be invited to participate in the discussion or decision of the Security Council with respect to the enforcement measure. In this respect two Articles of the Charter apply: Article 31 and Article 44. In case the Security Council has decided to employ measures not involving the use of armed force, Article 31 applies, which has been analysed in other parts of this study.[7] In case the Council decides to employ measures involving the use of armed force, Article 44 applies, which runs as follows:—

> When the Security Council has decided to use force it shall, before calling upon a Member not represented on it to provide armed forces in fulfilment of the obligations assumed under Article 43, invite that Member, if the Member so desires, to participate in the decisions of the Security Council concerning the employment of contingents of that Member's armed forces.

Since Article 44 actually refers only to the case that the Security Council decides to employ armed force, the wording: ' When the Security Council has decided to use force ' is not correct. ' Force ' and ' armed force ' are not identical. Also measures not involving the use of armed force are enforcement measures. Only if the Security Council calls upon a Member which is not represented on it to provide armed forces in fulfilment of the obligations assumed under Article 43 or Article 45, it shall—according to Article 44— ' invite that Member, if the Member so desires, to participate in the decisions of the Security Council concerning the employment of contingents of that Member's armed forces.'

[7] Cf. *supra*, pp. 222 ff.

It is not very clear what is meant by the words 'decisions of the Security Council concerning the employment of contingents of that Member's armed forces.' It cannot mean that the Member is allowed to participate in the decision by which it is 'called', according to Article 43, 'to make available to the Security Council armed forces, assistance, and facilities'; for Article 44 refers expressly to the 'obligations assumed under Article 43.' If the Member is under 'obligation' to comply with the 'call' to make available to the Security Council armed forces, etc., it cannot participate in the decision 'to provide armed forces' as formulated in Article 44, since it cannot have the right to vote against such decision. The right to participate can only refer to decisions concerning the manner in which the contingents of armed forces, made available to the Security Council by that Member, are to be employed. Since Article 44 refers only to decisions 'concerning the employment of contingents' of the Member, the latter is not entitled to participate in decisions not concerning the 'armed forces' but other kinds of 'assistance, and facilities, including rights of passage,' made available to the Security Council by the Member according to Article 43, paragraph 1.[8]

[8] The Report of Rapporteur on Chapter VIII, Section B (Dumbarton Oaks Proposals, corresponding to Chapter VII of the Charter) (U.N.C.I.O. Doc. 881, III/3/46, p. 3) contains the following statement with reference to Article 44: 'This supplementary paragraph takes into account the concern very vigorously expressed by many powers that the military forces put at the disposition of the Security Council by the special agreements might be used without the contributing nation having had a voice in the Council meetings where it is decided to use these forces. Henceforth, every member not represented on the Council may participate, with the right of voting, in the deliberations of the Council when it is a question of the utilisation of its armed forces. To repeat a well-chosen expression of the Delegate of the Netherlands, the principle of "no military action without representation" was accepted by the Committee.—This decision is of such a nature as to reassure, in large measure, the middle and small powers, which might otherwise have feared that they were giving *carte blanche* to the Council in the particularly serious domain of the utilisation of their military forces outside their national frontiers. It has not appeared possible to extend the conception of *ad hoc* representation on the Council to include those instances wherein the latter discusses, not the utilisation of armed forces, but rather the use *of facilities and assistance* to be furnished by a state not a member of the Council. As a matter of fact, it was recognised that the adoption of such a formula might unduly increase the number of Council members and delay its decisions. Furthermore, the desire to take into consideration the well-founded observations of the Egyptian Delegation on this subject led the Committee to approve the explanations furnished by the Delegations of Great Britain, the U.S.S.R., France, and Greece. Accordingly, it was recognised that the question "of facilities and assistance" was already covered by the special agreements contemplated in paragraph 5, Section B, Chapter VIII. Paragraph 9 of the said chapter contemplates, on the other hand, that a state not represented on the Military Staff Committee should be invited to be associated with it should the need arise. Finally, paragraph 4 of Section D, Chapter VI, formally provides for the participation in the Council discussions of any member of the Organisation whose interests may be particularly affected. In the light of these assurances, which covered its point of view, the Delegation of Egypt withdrew its amendment.'

The decisions of the Security Council concerning the employment of contingents of the Member invited to participate in this decision under Article 44 require, according to Article 27, paragraph 3, an affirmative vote of seven members including the concurring votes of the permanent members. In case Article 44 is applied, twelve representatives instead of eleven may participate in the vote, so that a majority of seven opposes a minority of five instead of four. The question as to whether the vote of the Member invited under Article 44 is to be counted in determining the majority of seven, has been discussed in a previous chapter of this study.[9] The Member invited to participate in the decision may be outvoted.

The armed forces to be employed by the Security Council are to be made available to it by the Members. In this respect, Article 43, paragraph 1, provides:

> All Members of the United Nations, in order to contribute to the maintenance of international peace and security, undertake to make available to the Security Council, on its call and in accordance with a special agreement or agreements, armed forces, assistance, and facilities, including rights of passage, necessary for the purpose of maintaining international peace and security.

The wording of this provision is not very clear. The Members shall make available armed forces to the Security Council 'on its call and in accordance with a special agreement or agreements.' What is the relation of this 'call' to the agreements? Are the armed forces to be made available by the 'agreements' or by the 'call'? The most plausible interpretation is that first an agreement shall be concluded by which a Member places at the disposal of the Security Council armed forces, assistance, etc., and then the Council may call upon this Member to make available, for an action decided by the Council, the armed forces agreed upon. The 'call' shall be in accordance with the agreements.[1] As to the contents of the agreements, Article 43, paragraph 2, provides:

> Such agreement or agreements shall govern the numbers and types of forces, their degree of readiness and general

[9] Cf. *supra*, pp. 230 ff.

[1] This was the interpretation of Article 43 given by the representative of Belgium at the 142nd meeting of the Security Council. He declared: 'It seems to me that, under the terms of Article 43 of the Charter, in order that armed forces should be placed at the disposal of the Security Council, a request to that effect would first have to be made by the Council. I, therefore, envisage two stages: the first stage is that of the special agreements under which forces would be placed in reserve for use as needed; in the second stage, these forces could be used to deal with a concrete case, if called upon by the Security Council.' The President of the Council, however, was not of this opinion; he declared: 'According to my interpretation, this Article appears to mean that the Security Council, on the basis of special agreements entered into at its suggestion by a number of countries, would be able

> location, and the nature of the facilities and assistance to be provided.

By the call referred to in Article 43, paragraph 1, the Security Council may also summon a Member to make available the special air-force contingents referred to in Article 45, which runs as follows:—

> In order to enable the United Nations to take urgent military measures, Members shall hold immediately available national air-force contingents for combined international enforcement action. The strength and degree of readiness of these contingents and plans for their combined action shall be determined, within the limits laid down in the special agreement or agreements referred to in Article 43, by the Security Council with the assistance of the Military Staff Committee.

The second sentence of this Article is not quite consistent with Article 43, paragraph 2. According to the general rule laid down in that provision ' the numbers and types of forces, their degree of readiness and general location ' shall be determined by the special agreements, to which Article 45 expressly refers. But this Article provides that ' the strength and degree of readiness ' of the air-force contingents shall be determined by the Security Council with the assistance of the Military Staff Committee, with the proviso, it is true, 'within the limits laid down in the special agreement or agreements . . . ' But if the strength and degree of readiness is already determined in the agreements, there is nothing left to the Security Council to determine in this respect. The term ' strength ' in Article 45 is probably intended to mean the same as the words ' numbers (and types) of forces ' in Article 43, paragraph 2. The change of terminology and the omission of any reference to the ' general location ' in Article 45 is not very fortunate. This Article provides with respect to the strength and readiness of the air-force contingents the same as with respect to the plans ' for their combined action.' But Article 43, paragraph 2, does not leave to the special agreements to govern the plans for the action of the armed forces.

to determine in advance what forces would be at its disposal, should the necessity arise. In order to make use of these forces, the Security Council would have to pronounce a decision in each separate instance; a decision, and not an invitation. As the agreements would have been concluded in advance, I think that a decision of the Security Council would be sufficient. . . . Therefore, my interpretation of Article 43, at least of the expression " on its call ", is not the same as that of the Belgian representative. According to Mr. van Langenhove's interpretation, indeed, the Security Council would have to make a fresh call before the forces at the disposal of the United Nations could be used. In my opinion, this is not so. As I understand it, Article 43 of the Charter determines beforehand the forces which might be placed at the Security Council's disposal, and which, according to Mr. van Langenhove, would be only forces kept in reserve.' (Official Records of the Security Council, 2nd Year, No. 47, p. 1033.)

If, however, the intention of Article 45 was to restrict the scope of Article 43, paragraph 2, and to confer upon the Security Council with respect to the air-force contingents held ' immediately available ' for the purpose of ' urgent military measures ' a power which the Council has not with respect to the ordinary armed forces made available to it under Article 43, the intention was not clearly expressed.[2]

The special agreements referred to in Article 43 do not refer to the question as to whether or not the Member shall provide armed forces and especially national air-force contingents; they refer only to the question how these obligations established by the Charter itself shall be fulfilled on the part of the Member. They especially do not refer to the question as to how the Security Council shall or may use the armed forces placed at its disposal by the Member state. They shall

[2] The report of the Military Staff Committee on General Principles Governing the Organisation of the Armed Forces Made Available to the Security Council by Member Nations of the United Nations (*Yearbook*, pp. 424 ff.) seems to interpret Article 45 to mean that the provision of Article 43, paragraph 2, shall apply also to the air-force contingents referred to in Article 45. Article 16 of the General Principles as accepted by the Chinese, French, United Kingdom and United States delegations, runs as follows:

> The strength and composition of national air force contributions made available to the Security Council shall be determined as set forth in Article 12 above taking into account the obligations arising from Article 45 of the Charter.

Article 12 provides:

> The size and composition of contributions of individual Member Nations will be determined on the initiative of the Security Council, and on the advice of the Military Staff Committee, in the process of negotiations with each Member Nation in accordance with Article 43 of the Charter.

Article 16 of the General Principles as accepted by the Soviet Union delegation runs as follows:

> The strength and composition of national air force contingents made available to the Security Council by Member Nations for action envisaged in Article 45 of the Charter are determined by the Security Council, with the assistance of the Military Staff Committee, within the limits of a Special Agreement or Agreements referred to in Article 43 of the Charter.

At the 139th meeting of the Security Council the delegate of the Soviet Union interpreted Article 45, in its relation to Article 43, as follows: ' As for Article 45, its examination can take place only after the study of Article 43 of the Charter has been completed, and after the conclusion of special agreements on the contribution of armed forces. After the conclusion of such agreements the Security Council, with the assistance of the Military Staff Committee, will determine in accordance with Article 45 of the Charter what proportion of the overall strength of the national air-force contingents placed at the disposal of the Security Council under the agreements will be held immediately available for the fulfilment, in case of necessity, of urgent military measures.' (Official Records of the Security Council, 2nd Year, No. 44, p. 979.) Neither the text of Article 16 of the General Principles as suggested by the Soviet Union, nor the text of this Article as accepted by the other members of the Military Staff Committee leaves it to the special agreements to determine, in anv respect, the action of the air-force contingents.

govern, it is true, the ' general location ' of the armed forces to be made available to the Security Council by the Member. The words ' general location ' which have been added to the text of the corresponding provision of the Dumbarton Oaks Proposals (Chapter VIII, Section B, paragraph 5) are not very clear. They probably refer to the time when the armed forces are not employed by the Security Council.[3] But they might be misinterpreted to refer to the time during which the armed forces are employed by the Security Council, so that a special agreement may determine the territories where the Council is authorised to employ the contingent placed at its disposal

[3] In this way the report of the Military Staff Committee on General Principles interprets Article 43, paragraph 2. Article 32 of the General Principles (accepted by the Chinese, United Kingdom, and United States delegations) runs as follows:

> Armed forces made available to the Security Council by Member Nations when not employed by the Security Council will, within the terms of Special Agreements referred to in Article 43 of the Charter, be based at the discretion of Member Nations in any territories or waters to which they have legal right of access.

The text of Article 32 as accepted by the French delegation, reads as follows:

> When they are not employed by the Security Council, the Armed Forces which the Member Nation undertakes to make available to the Security Council, on its call, are stationed in the general locations governed by the Special Agreement or Agreements concluded between the Security Council and the Member Nation under Article 43 of the Charter:
>
> 1. either within the national borders of the Member Nation or the territories or waters under its jurisdiction;
>
> 2. or within the territory or waters of ex-enemy nations under Article 107 of the Charter or under the terms of the Peace Treaties;
>
> 3. or within the territory or waters of other Nations where Armed Forces have access under international agreements registered with the United Nations Secretariat and published by it in accordance with Article 102 of the Charter;
>
> 4. or in certain strategic areas specified by the Security Council and which have been the subject of specific agreements between the Security Council and the Member Nation under Articles 82 and 83 of the Charter.

At the 139th meeting of the Security Council the delegate of the Soviet Union declared: ' It is necessary to decide where the armed forces which are to be made available to the Security Council by the States under special agreements should be stationed. Should they be stationed in their own territories, or may they be stationed outside their own territories, in the territories and territorial waters of other States ? It is clear that the difference between the two possible solutions of this problem is of paramount importance. It is necessary to bear this in mind when discussing the question in the Security Council.—The proposal of the Union of Soviet Socialist Republics on the question of the location of armed forces provides that these forces should be stationed in their own territories and only in their own territories. This proposal states: " Armed forces made available to the Security Council by Member Nations of the United Nations shall be garrisoned within the frontiers of the contributing Member Nations' own territories or territorial waters except in cases envisaged in Article 107 of the Charter ".' (Official Records of the Security Council, 2nd Year, No. 44, p. 972.)

by the Member.[4] In addition to 'the numbers and types of forces, their degree of readiness and general location' the special agreements shall determine also 'the nature of the facilities and assistance to be provided.' This is a very broad formula which certainly allows inserting into the special agreements provisions concerning military bases necessary for the operation of the armed forces made available to the Security Council.[5] The determination of all the matters

[4] At the *Hearings* (pp. 651 ff.) a Senator asked one of the advisers to the United States delegation at San Francisco the question: 'Speaking of the agreement or agreements which are to govern the numbers and types of forces and the degree of readiness and general location and the nature of the facilities and assistance to be provided, as set out in Article 43, sub-section 2, is it your opinion that the United States in making available to the Council military contingents could restrict the place of the use of the forces—aside from the question of whether we could want to?' Whereupon the answer was: 'There is no doubt in my mind but what we can do that.' In reply to the question of another Senator the advisor made the following statement: 'In my opinion, . . . the phrase that they are "to be made available in accordance with a special agreement or agreements" enables the states to make any conditions which they want to attach, and I would think it quite probable that even the great powers, while they would probably want to make some forces available for use anywhere, that there would be some understanding whereby they would at least supply the preponderant force in the areas of their proximity.' If it was intended to leave to the special agreements to determine where the contingents placed at the disposal of the Security Council may be used by the latter, that is to say, to restrict the use of these forces, the words 'their general location' were certainly not adequate to express this idea. But in reply to a question, the advisor made the following statement: 'If restricted use of our military contingent were desired, Senator, I would think the wise thing to do would be to make provision for that in your basic military agreement which will come before the Senate for ratification.' Then a Senator asked: 'But aside from where it should be made, it is your opinion that a limitation of that kind could be, consistently with the obligations assumed under the Charter, inserted?' Whereupon the advisor stated: 'There is no doubt in my mind whatever as to that. Many of the smaller member states already are clear in their own minds that they will not agree to make contingents available except for use in relatively near areas. Whether or not a great power wants to do that is a question of policy. As to the fact that it may do it, there is no doubt whatever in my mind.'

As to the question whether the armed forces placed at the disposal of the Security Council shall be used exclusively by the Council, Article 18 of the General Principles provides:

> The Armed Forces made available to the Security Council by Member Nations of the United Nations will be employed, in whole or in part, only by the decision of the Security Council and only for the period necessary for the fulfilment of the tasks envisaged in Article 42 of the Charter.

But Article 17, accepted only by the Chinese and French delegations, runs as follows:

> In case of self-defence (Article 51 of the Charter) and of national emergencies Member Nations will have the right to make use of Armed Forces, which they have made available to the Security Council in conformity with the terms of special agreements. They undertake, however, to assume anew all of their obligations within the shortest possible space of time.

[5] Article 26 of the General Principles laid down in the report of the Military Staff Committee as accepted by the Chinese, United Kingdom, and United States delegations provides for 'bases as are required by armed forces operating under the

referred to in Article 43, paragraph 2, is left to agreement by the Organisation and the Members concerned, without any direction given in this respect by the Charter. This holds especially with regard to the proportion in which various Members shall contribute armed forces. Any solution adopted in this respect by the Security Council in its negotiations with the Members is in conformity with Charter.[6] Besides, the provision concerning the contents of the

Security Council.' The text of this Article as accepted by the French delegation contains an analogous provision. But at the 139th meeting of the Security Council the delegate of the Soviet Union declared: 'The proposals on bases cannot be accepted, in the first place, for the reason that the provision of bases is envisaged neither in Article 43 nor in the United Nations Charter in general. The Charter does not even mention bases. It speaks of armed forces, assistance and facilities, including rights of passage, but not bases.' He further stated: 'The provision of bases inevitably affects the sovereignty of nations.' (Official Records of the Security Council, 2nd Year, No. 44, pp. 969 f.) Neither the first nor the second contention is in conformity with the Charter. Military bases fall within 'facilities and assistance,' and an obligation assumed by an international agreement cannot be interpreted as an infringement on the sovereignty of the contracting party as recognised by the Charter.

[6] At the 139th meeting of the Security Council the delegate of the Soviet Union declared: 'The Soviet Union insists on the preservation of the equal position of all the permanent members of the Security Council in the contribution of armed forces. This equal position will be secured if all the permanent members contribute armed forces in accordance with the principle of equality.' He stated further: 'that the five Powers shall make available to the Security Council armed forces not only of equal overall strength, but also of the same composition, that is, an equal number of land, sea and air forces.' This attitude of the Soviet Union was in opposition to that of other members of the Military Staff Committee, which put forward the principles of so-called 'comparable contributions'. In accordance with this principle the five permanent members of the Security Council would make only comparatively equal contributions. The delegate of the Soviet Union declared: 'The acceptance of the principle of comparable contributions would mean the creation of a situation in which some nations would enjoy a predominant position as compared to others, in respect of armed forces to be made available to the Security Council. The acceptance of this principle might lead to the organisation of the armed forces being used in the interests of individual powerful states and to the detriment of the legitimate interests of other countries.' He tried to justify the principle of equality as follows: 'The principle of equality in the contribution of armed forces by the five permanent members of the Security Council, the principle proposed by the representatives of the Union of Soviet Socialist Republics, is based on the provisions of the United Nations Charter which place the main responsibility for the maintenance of international peace upon these States, which is in accordance with the equality of their position in the Security Council. This principle preserves the equal status of the permanent members in respect of the decision on this important question. It does not permit any preferential position for any one of the permanent members in the contribution of armed forces by them.' (Official Records of the Security Council, 2nd Year, No. 44, pp. 965 ff.) These statements are not correct. The Charter places the main responsibility for the maintenance of international peace not upon the five permanent members of the Security Council but on the Security Council (Article 24); and this principle does not prevent to conclude with the different permanent members different agreements under Article 43.

special agreements is of problematical value. The Members cannot be compelled to conclude agreements and, thus, are in a position to make their consent dependent upon conditions not provided by the Charter.

Article 43, paragraph 3, stipulates—

> The agreement or agreements shall be negotiated as soon as possible on the initiative of the Security Council. They shall be concluded between the Security Council and Members or between the Security Council and groups of Members and shall be subject to ratification by the signatory states in accordance with their respective constitutional processes.

These agreements are international treaties. Contracting parties to such a treaty are: on the one side the United Nations, represented by the Security Council, on the other side Members or 'groups of Members.' That means that the United Nations represented by the Security Council is supposed to be a juristic person of international law. It is not quite correct to state—as Article 43, paragraph 3, does—that the agreements concerned shall be concluded between the Security Council and Members, etc. The Security Council cannot be an international personality because it is only the organ of an international union of states which, through its Charter, has the quality of a person of international law. Contracting party to the agreement can be only the United Nations, represented by the Security Council. And the Security Council is able to fulfil this function through its President under Rule 19 of its Rules of Procedure, which provides that the President shall 'represent' the Security Council 'in its capacity as an organ of the United Nations.'

If a 'group' of Members is to be a contracting party to the agreement it is supposed to be a juristic person too. But this is possible only if it is an organised group endowed with an organ competent to represent the 'group' in relation to other persons of international law. According to Article 52, paragraph 1, the Members are authorised to establish 'regional arrangements or agencies' and according to Article 53, paragraph 1, the Security Council 'shall, where appropriate, utilise such regional arrangements or agencies for enforcement action under its authority.' If by the 'regional arrangement' an organised union (confederacy) of states is established with an agency (organ) competent to represent this union or confederacy of states in relation to the Security Council, the provision of Article 43, paragraph 3, according to which the agreement is to be concluded between the Security Council and a 'group' of Members, is applicable. If, however, the 'group' of Member is not organised in this manner, the agreement can be concluded only between the Security Council and the individual Members of the 'group.' If not organised, the group has no legal personality and cannot conclude—as a 'group'—international agreements.

An international agreement may or may not be subject to ratification, *i.e.* to an act different from the signing of the text of the agreement by the plenipotentiaries of the contracting parties. Such an act may be necessary, according to the constitution of the signatory. Article 43, paragraph 3, stipulates that the agreement or agreements referred to in paragraphs 1 and 2 of this Article shall be subject to ratification in accordance with the respective constitutional processes. But this provision refers only to the 'signatory states,' not to the United Nations represented by the Security Council. The Charter does not prescribe a specific procedure for the conclusion of treaties by the United Nations. The organ competent to conclude the treaty on behalf of the United Nations has to express its consent by a decision adopted in conformity with the respective rules of the Charter. If the Security Council is the competent organ, a decision adopted by a majority of seven members including the concurring votes of the permanent members is required. In case of an agreement concluded with a Member which is represented on the Council, this Member participates in the conclusion of the agreement on both sides. Until now, no special agreement has been concluded.[7]

[7] At the *Hearings* (pp. 645 f.) the conclusion of the special agreement on the part of the United States was discussed. The Chairman of the Committee on Foreign Relations interpreted the term 'constitutional processes' in Article 43, paragraph 3, to mean that the special agreement is to be concluded under the Constitution of the United States as a 'treaty,' not as an executive agreement: which means that the agreement must be concluded by the President with the advice and consent of the Senate, provided two-thirds of the Senators present concur. He declared: 'Our constitutional process is for us here at home to decide. There is no question in my mind that that means that the agreements must be ratified just like treaties are ratified, because they are with foreign countries. They are vital, they affect our military establishment, so they would have to be ratified by the United States Senate. . . . there was no question ever raised, so far as I know, in the Conference to that effect.' But a few months later, the phrase 'constitutional processes' has been interpreted in a different way by an Act of Congress. Section 6 of the Act of Congress (Public Law 264–79th Congress, Chapter 583–1st session, S. 1580), approved December 20, 1945, provides:

> The President is authorised to negotiate a special agreement or agreements with the Security Council which shall be subject to the approval of the Congress by appropriate Act or joint resolution, providing for the numbers and types of armed forces, their degree of readiness and general location, and the nature of facilities and assistance, including rights of passage, to be made available to the Security Council on its call for the purpose of maintaining international peace and security in accordance with Article 43 of said Charter. The President shall not be deemed to require the authorisation of the Congress to make available to the Security Council on its call in order to take action under Article 42 of said Charter and pursuant to such special agreement or agreements the armed forces, facilities, or assistance provided for therein; Provided, that nothing herein contained shall be construed as an authorisation to the President by the Congress to make available to the Security Council for such purpose armed

It seems that according to the intention of the framers of the Charter the Security Council is authorised to take enforcement action involving the use of armed force only through the armed forces made available to it by the special agreements concluded in conformity with Article 43. But the wording of Articles 39, 42, 47 and 48 does not exclude the possibility of a decision of the Security Council to the effect that Members which have not concluded a special agreement under Article 43 shall take a definite enforcement action, or that Members which have concluded special agreements shall provide armed forces in excess of those which they have placed at the disposal of the Council in their special agreements. The wording of Articles 39 and 42 does not even exclude the possibility of the establishment of an armed force of the Organisation different from and independent of the armed forces placed at the disposal of the Security Council by the Members. Article 42 refers to 'air, sea, or land forces' without providing that these forces must be armed forces placed at the disposal of the Security Council by the Members. But Article 48 expressly provides that the action required to carry out the decisions of the Security Council (concerning enforcement action) shall be taken by the Members. And Article 106 provides for a 'joint action' of the five Great Powers, permanent members of the Security Council, as an action different from an action of the Security Council 'pending the coming into force of such special agreements referred to in Article 43 as in the opinion of the Security Council enable it to begin the exercise of its responsibilities under Article 42.' Article 106 evidently presupposes that the Security Council cannot take an enforcement action involving the use of armed force if not a sufficient number of special agreements referred to in Article 43 have been concluded. The Report of Rapporteur on Chapter VIII, Section B of the Dumbarton Oaks Proposals (corresponding to Chapter VII of the Charter) contains the following statement: 'assurance was sought by the Canadian Delegation that members would not be required to provide forces in excess of those which had already been promised in the special agreements mentioned in paragraph 5. This interpretation was forthcoming from the Delegate of the United Kingdom, speaking on behalf of the sponsoring governments.'[8]

13. The Joint Action under Article 106

A treaty presupposes the voluntary co-operation of all the parties to the treaty. There is no obligation to conclude a treaty, and the

> forces, facilities, or assistance in addition to the forces, facilities, and assistance provided for in such special agreement or agreements.

It is important to note that according to this Act of Congress the employment by the Security Council of the armed forces made available by the United States is not to be considered as an act of war, the declaration of which requires, under Article 1, Section 8, of the Constitution, an act of Congress.

[8] U.N.C.I.O. Doc. 881, III/3/46, p. 7. Cf. the last sentence of the above quoted Section 6 of the Act of Congress of December 20, 1945.

Members of the United Nations are certainly not under any obligation to conclude with the Security Council the agreements referred to in Articles 43 and 45. If such agreements cannot be brought about, the provisions of Chapter VII concerning the employment of measures involving the use of armed force are not applicable. How, then, can the Purpose of the United Nations be fulfilled which the Charter places before all other Purposes: to take effective collective measures for the prevention and removal of threats to the peace, and for the suppression of acts of aggression, as long as the agreements referred to in Article 43 have not come into force? To this question Article 106 gives an answer—

> Pending the coming into force of such special agreements referred to in Article 43 as in the opinion of the Security Council enable it to begin the exercise of its responsibilities under Article 42, the parties to the Four-Nation Declaration signed at Moscow, October 30, 1943, and France, shall, in accordance with the provisions of paragraph 5 of the Declaration, consult with one another and as occasion requires with other Members of the United Nations with a view to such joint action on behalf of the Organisation as may be necessary for the purpose of maintaining international peace and security.

Paragraph 5 of the Four Power Declaration runs as follows:—

> The Governments of the United States of America, the United Kingdom, the Soviet Union and China: . . . jointly declare . . . . 5. That for the purpose of maintaining international peace and security pending the re-establishment of law and order and the inauguration of a system of general security, they will consult with one another and as occasion requires with other Members of the United Nations with a view to joint action on behalf of the community of nations.

During the period between the coming into force of the Charter and the establishment of the special agreements referred to in Article 43 the Security Council will fulfil its functions under Chapter VI and Articles 39, 40, 41 of Chapter VII, in so far as their application does not presuppose the establishment of the special agreements. The Report of Committee III/3 of the San Francisco Conference contains the following statement: 'The Security Council would refrain from the performance of its responsibilities only with respect to those functions the exercise of which is suspended until the conclusion of the special agreements indicated above' [Article 43].[9]

[9] U.N.C.I.O. Doc. 1095, III/3/50, p. 3. In the course of the discussion of the Palestine question the delegate of the United States declared at the 253rd meeting of the Security Council: 'If the Security Council should decide that it is necessary to use armed force to maintain international peace in connection with Palestine, the United States would be ready to consult under the Charter with a view to such

During this period the function of the Organisation determined in Article 42 may be exercised by the five Great Powers determined in Article 106. They are identical with the Powers having permanent seats in the Security Council. Article 106 authorises these Powers to take 'joint action on behalf of the Organisation' only as long as the Security Council has not expressed the opinion that enough special agreements have come into force to enable it to begin the exercise of its responsibilities under Article 42. As soon as the Security Council declares that it is able to exercise these responsibilities, the authorisation of Article 106 ceases to be valid. Is it valid as long as the Security Council does not make such a declaration, or is any joint action under Article 106 possible only if the Security Council positively declares not yet to be able to exercise its responsibilities under Article 42 ?[1] Both interpretations are possible. What majority is required for the decision that sufficient agreements have come into force to enable the Security Council to exercise its responsibilities under Article 42 ? Since this decision does not refer to a procedural matter, Article 27, paragraph 3, is applicable. That means that each of the five Great Powers which are authorised to take joint action and at the same time permanent members of the Security Council may prevent such a decision, and, if such a decision is required to terminate the authorisation of Article 106, to prolong this authorisation *ad libitum*.[2]

action as may be necessary to maintain international peace. Such consultation would be required in view of the fact that agreement has not yet been reached making armed forces available to the Security Council under the terms of Article 43.' (Doc. S/P.V. 253, p. 48.) This statement means that the United States was ready to apply Article 106 of the Charter.

[1] The Security Council may decide to invite the five Powers to apply Article 106. Such a decision would imply the expression of the opinion that the Security Council is not yet able to begin the exercise of its responsibilities under Article 42. In the Palestine question the representative of Columbia proposed at the 254th meeting of the Security Council the following resolution: 'Having received the First Special Report of the United Nations Palestine Commission on the Problem of Security in Palestine, and considering . . . that Articles 39 and 41 of the Charter, referred to in recommendations (*b*) and (*c*) of the General Assembly's Resolution of November 29, 1947, envisage measures to be taken in the case of conflicts or disputes between States, but do not authorise the Security Council to create special forces for the purposes indicated by the United Nations Palestine Commission, the Security Council, 1. According to Article 106 of the Charter, invites the parties to the Four-Nation Declaration signed at Moscow, October 30, 1943, and France, to consult with one another with a view to such joint action on behalf of this Organisation as may be necessary to prevent or remove any threat to the peace, breach of the peace, or act of aggression arising from the implementation of the General Assembly's Resolution of November 29, 1947 . . .' (Doc. S/684).

[2] The corresponding provision of the Dumbarton Oaks Proposals, Chapter XII, paragraph 1, runs as follows:—

> Pending the coming into force of the special agreement or agreements referred to in Chapter VIII, Section B, paragraph 5, and in accordance

The Charter does not directly authorise the five Powers to take joint action. Just as paragraph 5 of the Four-Power Declaration, Article 106 of the Charter stipulates only that the Powers shall 'consult' with one another and, if necessary with other Members of the United Nations, 'with a view to such joint action.' Such 'joint action'[3] is not obligatory and could not be made obligatory by the Charter, since such action is possible only if an agreement is reached with respect to the action. If is not very clear whether an agreement of all the five Great Powers is necessary in order that the 'joint action' can be taken, or whether two or three or four of them may take such 'joint action' even if the other or the others do not agree. That an agreement of the five Powers suffices, seems to be certain, and since the 'joint action' is to be taken 'on behalf of the Organisation' the interpretation which seems to be most plausible is that all five Powers must agree in order to make a 'joint action' possible. By such an agreement only one, or some, of the five Powers may be authorised to carry out the action agreed upon by all the five. Such agreement has no less voluntary character than the special agreements referred to in Article 43. If it cannot be reached, the

> with the provisions of paragraph 5 of the Four-Nation Declaration, signed at Moscow, October 30, 1943, the States parties to that Declaration should consult with one another and as occasion arises with other members of the Organisation with a view to such joint action on behalf of the Organisation as may be necessary for the purpose of maintaining international peace and security.

The Summary Report of Meetings of Sub-committee 3/A, to Consider Redraft of Chapter XII (Dumbarton Oaks Proposals), contains the following interpretation: 'The decision to turn over the military enforcement responsibilities of the signatories of the Moscow Declaration and of France to the Security Council should be the responsibility of the signatory powers and of France and not of the Security Council.' (U.N.C.I.O. Doc. WD 68, III/3/A2.) This sentence was later changed to read as follows: 'The decision to turn over to the Security Council the responsibilities for the maintenance of peace assumed by the signatories of the Moscow Declaration and by France should be the responsibility of the signatory powers and of France.' (U.N.C.I.O. Doc. 765, III/3/39, p. 3.) According to this interpretation of Chapter XII, paragraph 1, of the Dumbarton Oaks Proposals, which in this point is not essentially different from Article 106, it is upon the five Powers determined in Article 106 to decide when the authority conferred upon them by Article 106 terminates.

[3] The Report of Committee 3 to Commission III on Chapter XII (Dumbarton Oaks Proposals, corresponding to Chapter XVII of the Charter), (U.N.C.I.O. Doc. 1095, III/3/50, p. 3) contains the following statements: 'Several Delegations, especially those of Canada, Egypt and Belgium, have requested the Delegations submitting the amendment to make a declaration explaining the meaning of the words "joint action on behalf of the Organisation." The Delegate of the United Kingdom pointed out that it was impossible to define such an action, since the powers of the Security Council would gradually develop in proportion to the forces which would be put at its disposal. The Delegate of the United States, for his part, explained that the meaning of the words "joint action," might be deduced without difficulty from the first part of the paragraph, which referred to the special agreements mentioned in Chapter VIII, Section B, paragraph 5.'

most important function of the Organisation, the function which forms the core of the Charter, cannot be performed by measures involving the use of armed force.

But Article 106 authorises the five Powers not only to take an action involving the use of armed force. Any action which these Powers deem 'necessary for the purpose of maintaining international peace and security' is covered by this provision. Those who drafted Article 106 had probably only a military action in mind, for they inserted this Article into Chapter XVII under the heading 'Transitional Security Arrangements' and the transitional period is characterised in Article 106 as the time during which the Security Council is not able to take enforcement measures involving the use of armed force referred to in Article 42. But the wording of Article 106 does not restrict the 'joint action' to a military action.

To take the military enforcement action referred to in Article 42 is—according to Article 39—permissible only after the Security Council, by a vote of seven members including the concurring votes of the permanent members, has determined the existence of a threat to the peace or breach of the peace. Article 106, however, authorises the five Powers, which are the permanent members of the Security Council, to take joint action, including enforcement action, on behalf of the Organisation without obliging them to determine beforehand the existence of a threat to, or breach of, the peace. Article 106 may be interpreted to authorise the five Powers to take a 'joint action' involving the use of armed force only after the Security Council has determined the existence of a threat to, or breach of, the peace and decided that an enforcement action involving the use of armed force is necessary. The fact that the special agreements referred to in Article 43 are not yet in force is no reason to suspend the just-mentioned functions of the Security Council with respect to the military enforcement action to be taken by the five Powers designated in Article 106. But its wording does not exclude the interpretation according to which the five Powers in taking their joint action are completely independent of the Security Council, and their action is limited only in so far as it is, in their opinion, necessary for the purpose of maintaining international peace and security.[4]

[4] At the 262nd meeting of the Security Council during the discussion of the Palestine question, the representative of Syria stated: 'If we refer to Article 106, we find that action by the permanent members under that Article will always be in order when the Security Council decides that a situation exists which endangers international peace and security, when other methods and means have been tried and proved to be inadequate, and when action under Article 42 of the Charter is necessary. Then, as long as Article 43 is not implemented, the five permanent members would convene to determine what action to take. Article 106 refers to Article 42. Article 42 reads: "Should the Security Council consider that measures provided for in Article 41 would be inadequate or have proved to be inadequate, it may take such action by air, sea, or land forces," and so forth. When it is decided to

Since the joint action under Article 106 is an action ' on behalf of the Organisation,' and that means that it is to be considered as an action of the United Nations, Article 2, paragraph 5 applies. Hence all Members are obliged to give the joint action taken under Article 106 every assistance and to refrain from giving assistance to any state against which the joint action is directed. The question as to against whom the joint action referred to in Article 106 may be directed is not answered by this Article. The answer is left to the five Powers. Hence it may be directed against a state which has not violated an obligation expressly stipulated in the Charter. If the ' joint action ' is an enforcement action, it can be interpreted to be a sanction only if it is assumed that under the Charter all states are obliged to refrain from any conduct which, in the opinion of the five Powers referred to in Article 106, makes such joint action necessary. In view of the difficulties to implement Article 43 of the Charter, Article 106 confers upon the five permanent members of the Security Council, provided they agree with respect to the application of this Article, an almost unlimited power for an indefinite period of time.[5]

apply this Article, then Article 106 will be in force and the permanent members of the Security Council can convene among themselves and consult as to the action to be taken.' (Doc. S/P.V. 262, pp. 86–95.) According to this interpretation, the ' joint action ' referred to in Article 106 is only an action involving the use of armed force, and may be taken only if the Security Council has decided that Article 42 should be applied. At its 263rd meeting the Security Council adopted a resolution calling upon the five permanent members to consult and make recommendations regarding guidance and instructions for the Palestine Commission, the results of their consulations to be reported back to the Council within ten days. (United Nations Bulletin, Vol. IV, p. 213.) This resolution cannot be interpreted to be a recommendation made to the five powers referred to in Article 106 of the Charter, to apply this Article. The question as to whether the Security Council is competent to make such a recommendation after having determined the existence of a threat to, or breach of, the peace, may be answered in the affirmative.

5 The *Report to the President*, pp. 161 ff., contains the following statements with respect to Article 106: ' Nowhere more clearly than in the Chapter on transitional security arrangements is there manifested the intelligent realism of the architects of the United Nations. From the outset these men faced squarely the fact that the Charter could not create an Organisation which would spring into being possessed from the start of full power to maintain international peace and security. They knew that if it was to succeed it must not be burdened at the outset with responsibilities which it could not immediately fulfil. They knew that it must be given time to become firmly established.' ' Armed force is the ultimate sanction in the enforcement of peace. The United Nations will have no armed force at its disposal until at least some of the agreements envisaged in Article 43 become effective. This difficulty is taken care of by Article 106, the first of the two which comprise this short Chapter. During the indefinite time which must elapse before the Security Council decides that enough of the agreements are effective for it to begin the exercise of its responsibilities for military enforcement action, the five great powers which are to be the permanent members of the Security Council undertake to exercise on behalf of the Organisation, jointly and with other Members of the United Nations, such security functions as may be necessary.' The text of Article 106 ' makes it clear that not all the special arrangements for the provision of armed forces have to be ratified—a process which might take years—before the

14. International Police Force?

One of the most important questions concerning the enforcement action involving the use of armed force is the question as to the power the Charter has conferred upon the Security Council with regard to the armed forces which the Members are obliged to make available to the Security Council according to Article 43, and especially the national air-force contingents which certain Members are obliged to hold immediately available for urgent military measures according to Article 45. It is the question whether there is established by the Charter an armed force of the United Nations distinct from the armed

Security Council can take military enforcement action. Only such agreements as the Security Council itself deems sufficient for the purpose need be in effect. Article 106 does not, as some delegates wished it to, define precisely the functions of the Security Council during the interim period, nor the limits of the joint action which the five powers may take. Had it done so it would have established a fixed and frozen division of responsibility, and thus defeated its own purpose, which is to provide for the orderly growth of the Security Council's functions, to permit it to take successively larger bites of responsibility. This flexibility is accomplished in two ways. First, only the power to take military enforcement action is withheld from the Security Council and that only temporarily. Secondly, the five powers which will be permanent members of the Security Council are granted authority to fill the temporary vacuum to the extent necessary by taking action on behalf of the Organisation. It should be emphasised, however, that this five-power action must be joint and that consultation with other Members of the United Nations is provided for. In other words, while this action may, in a formal sense, be outside the framework of the Organisation, it is to be completely within the spirit of the Charter.' According to this interpretation of Article 106, the 'joint action' must be a military enforcement action taken by the five permanent members of the Security Council, and the power conferred upon them ends only when the Security Council has decided that enough of the agreements referred to in Article 43 of the Charter are effective to begin the exercise of its responsibilities for military enforcement action.

The Report of Committee 3 to Commission III on Chapter XII (of the Dumbarton Oaks Proposals corresponding to Chapter XVII of the Charter) (U.N.C.I.O. Doc. 1095, III, 3/50, p. 2) contains the following statement: 'The Delegations have not questioned the necessity, during the transitional period, of the collective responsibility of the Five Powers which derives from the obligations which they have assumed during the course of hostilities. But some delegations, particularly the Canadian Delegation, called attention to the fact that paragraph 1 would grant temporary authority to the Five Powers for a period which might be very long, and this authority was qualified only by the phrase, "joint action on behalf of the Organisation." They, therefore, asked that paragraph 1 further specify the powers granted to the Five Powers during the interim period, especially with respect to responsibility for the peaceful settlement of disputes according to Section A, Chapter VIII, and the matter of ascertaining which special agreements would need to become effective before the Security Conucil assumes its full responsibility.' The only difference between Chapter XII, paragraph 1 of the Dumbarton Oaks Proposals and Article 106 of the Charter is that France has been added to the four Powers of the Moscow Declaration, and that the Security Council has been authorised to decide the question whether sufficient agreements have come into force to enable it to exercise its responsibilities under Article 43. The powers granted to the five Powers are no more specified in Article 106 than they were in the Dumbarton Oaks Proposals.

forces of the Members or whether the military enforcement action provided for by the Charter is to be executed by the Members through their own armed forces.

There can be no doubt that the armed forces which—to have recourse to an expression used by Article 47, paragraphs 1 and 3—are ' placed at the disposal of the Security Council ' are composed of the contingents of the armed forces of several Members. Article 42 says that the military action taken by the Security Council may include ' operations by air, sea, or land forces of Members of the United Nations.' Article 48 expressly states that the action required to carry out the decisions of the Security Council shall be taken by the Members of the United Nations and that the decisions of the Council shall be carried out by the Member ' directly.' The provision that the decisions of the Security Council with regard to enforcement action shall be carried out by the Members ' directly ' seems to indicate that the enforcement action involving the use of armed force is according to the Charter decentralised to the same extent as it was according to the Covenant. But there are other provisions of the Charter which have no equivalent in the Covenant and which are not consistent with the principle stipulated in Article 48, paragraph 2, that the enforcement actions shall be carried out by the Members of the United Nations ' directly.' The provisions confer upon the Security Council the right to ' dispose ' of the armed forces made available to it by the Members.

We have already mentioned the fact that the Charter expressly uses this term in Article 47. In the same direction points the formula: the Members shall ' make available to the Security Council ' armed forces (Article 43, paragraph 1). The Charter expressly states in Article 42 that the Security Council ' may take such action by air, sea, or land forces as may be necessary to maintain or restore international peace and security.' The Covenant of the League of Nations carefully avoided speaking of an action of the Council or the League. Article 16, paragraph 2, only authorised the Council to ' recommend to the several Governments concerned what effective military, naval or air forces the Members of the League shall severally contribute to the armed forces to be used to protect the covenants of the League.' It did not say: to the armed forces of the League, or to be used by the Council. The armed forces contributed by the Members of the League were not ' at the disposal ' of the Council. The Security Council, however, is authorised by Article 46 to make ' plans for the application of armed force ' which can mean only: for the armed forces made available to it by the Members. Finally, the Charter attaches a Military Staff Committee as an auxiliary organ to the Security Council. This indicates that the Security Council is supposed to exercise—directly or indirectly—the function of a commander-in-chief of the armed forces placed at its disposal. Article 47, paragraphs 1 and 2, stipulate:

> 1. There shall be established a Military Staff Committee to advise and assist the Security Council on all questions relating to the Security Council's military requirements for the maintenance of international peace and security, the employment and command of forces placed at its disposal, the regulation of armaments, and possible disarmament.
>
> 2. The Military Staff Committee shall consist of the Chiefs of Staff of the permanent members of the Security Council or their representatives. Any Member of the United Nations not permanently represented on the Committee shall be invited by the Committee to be associated with it when the efficient discharge of the Committee's responsibilities requires the participation of that Member in its work.

In view of the fact that enforcement action involving the use of armed force is a function of the Security Council, not a function of its five permanent members (as is the joint action under Article 106), the composition of the Military Staff Committee is not quite consistent with the organisation of the Security Council.[6]

[6] At the San Francisco Conference the delegate of the Phillippine Commonwealth proposed that the Military Staff Committee should be composed of the Chiefs of Staffs of all the members of the Security Council. His proposal was not accepted for the following reasons justifying the limitation of membership on the Military Staff Committee to the permanent members: '1. Paragraph 9 provided that members not permanently represented should be asked to join when appropriate. 2. The initiative for expanding the membership to meet a particular situation should be left to the Military Staff Committee; otherwise it might become as large as the Council itself. 3. If the forces of a country were used there was no question but that the military staff of that country would be consulted. 4. Because of the complex duties of the Committee, it was essential that its composition should be limited to the permanent Council members in order to avoid a committee with constantly changing membership. 5. Allied military machinery in this war was of the same type as that proposed in paragraph 9. 6. As a Chief of Staff, the Military Staff Committee's function would be to make decisions, and therefore, it should be a small group. The function of command was a different matter. No committee, large or small, could exercise command; and the selection of individuals for this purpose would be decided upon later. 7. The limitation of membership on the Military Staff Committee to the permanent members of the Council did not conflict with the pending Canadian amendment regarding representation of non-members in Council decisions.' (U.N.C.I.O. Doc. 628, III/3/33, pp. 3 f.)

At the 139th meeting of the Security Council the delegate of Australia made the following complaint: 'For over a year, the Military Staff Committee has been meeting in secret and, apart from brief *communiques* which indicated little beyond the fact that there were disagreements among members, no information has been available to the non-permanent members of the Council as to the matters under discussion. The Australian Government believes that it is impossible under these conditions for the non-permanent members to discharge their obligations under the Charter, and that they should be associated with the Military Staff Committee during their term of office.' (Security Council, Official Records, 2nd Year, No. 44, p. 983.)

Paragraph 3 of Article 47 stipulates:

> The Military Staff Committee shall be responsible under the Security Council for the strategic direction of any armed forces placed at the disposal of the Security Council. Questions relating to the command of such forces shall be worked out subsequently.

It is not expressly said that the ' command ' and the ' strategic direction ' are to be exercised by the Security Council. This interpretation, however, is not only a possible but the most adequate one in view of the fact that the forces are placed at the Security Council's ' disposal.'

There can be no doubt that a body composed of eleven members, whose decisions require an affirmative vote of seven members, including the concurring votes of the permanent members, is not a proper organ to work as a commander-in-chief of armed forces. But according to Article 29, ' the Security Council may establish such subsidiary organs as it deems necessary for the performance of its functions.' In conformity with this Article, the Security Council may very well appoint a commander-in-chief.[7] Whether such a commander-in-chief is appointed by the Security Council or whether the command and strategic direction of the armed forces placed at

[7] Chapter X of the General Principles laid down in the report of the Military Staff Committee contains the following provisions:—

ARTICLE 36

> The armed forces which Member Nations of the United Nations agree to make available to the Security Council shall be under the exclusive command of the respective contributing Nations, except when operating under the Security Council.

ARTICLE 37

> When these forces are called upon for the fulfilment of measures envisaged in Article 42 of the Charter, they shall come under the control of the Security Council.

ARTICLE 38

> During the period these armed forces are employed by the Security Council, the Military Staff Committee shall be responsible, under the Security Council, for their strategic direction. The time and place at which the Military Staff Committee will assume or relinquish strategic direction will be designated by the Security Council.

ARTICLE 39

> The command of national contingents will be exercised by Commanders appointed by the respective Member Nations. These contingents will retain their national character and will be subject at all times to the discipline and regulations in force in their own national armed forces.

ARTICLE 40

> The Commanders of national contingents will be entitled to communicate directly with the authorities of their own country on all matters.

the disposal of the Security Council is exercised directly by this body, the contingents of the armed forces of the various Members are united under a unified command and may properly be characterised as the armed force of the United Nations.[8] With reference to the 'urgent military measures' to be taken according to Article 45, the Charter speaks of 'combined international enforcement action.' Since the Security Council is an organ of the United Nations, any instrument used in such action is an instrument of the United Nations, 'To take effective collective measures for the prevention and removal of threats to the peace, and for the suppression of acts of aggression or other breaches of the peace'—which means enforcement actions—is declared by Article 1, paragraph 1, of the Charter as one of the Purposes of the United Nations. Article 24, paragraph 1, speaks of 'prompt and effective action by the United Nations.' It is, therefore, as pointed out,[9] not consistent and, in addition, not correct, if this paragraph states that in order to ensure such action by the United Nations 'its Members confer on the Security Council primary responsibility for the maintenance of international peace and security, and agree that in carrying out its duties under this responsibility the Security Council acts on their behalf.' It is not the Members that confer on the Security Council any responsibility; it is the Charter that constitutes all duties, rights, and responsibilities of the Members as well as of the organs of the United Nations; and its

Article 41 as accepted by the Chinese, Soviet Union, and United States delegations runs as follows:—

ARTICLE 41

> An overall Commander or overall Commanders of armed forces made available to the Security Council may be appointed by the latter, on the advice of the Military Staff Committee, for the period of employment of these forces by the Security Council.

The same Article as accepted by the French and British delegations reads as follows:—

> A supreme Commander or supreme Commanders of armed forces made available to the Security Council may be appointed by the latter, on the advice of the Military Staff Committee, for the period of employment of these forces by the Security Council.
>
> Commanders-in-Chief of land, sea or air forces acting under the supreme Commander or Commanders mentioned above may be appointed by the Security Council on the advice of the Military Staff Committee.

8 At the 140th meeting of the Security Council the delegate of Brazil stated: 'The United Nations does not constitute a super-State. The Charter is merely a treaty between sovereign Powers. Thus, the establishment of an international force is the result of agreements to be concluded which are subject also to the constitutional process of ratification. This signifies that the United Nations does not dispose of a power of its own, but only of a borrowed power which issues from and is nourished by the Member nations and their industrial structures.' (Official Records of the Security Council, 2nd Year, No. 45, pp. 990 f.) This statement is not quite correct. The armed forces placed at the disposal of the Security Council may very well be characterised as the 'own' power of the United Nations.

9 Cf. *supra*, p. 280.

organs, especially the Security Council, do not act on behalf of the Members but on behalf of the Organisation. This becomes particularly clear when an enforcement action involving the use of armed force is taken by a majority decision of the Security Council adopted against the vote of members the armed forces of which are to be employed in this action. That the Organisation has an international character is the consequence of the fact that it is established by an international treaty and that its centralisation does not exceed a certain degree. Even if ' international,' it is usual to consider it as an entity different from its Members especially when it has—as the United Nations have—the character of an international person capable of concluding international treaties. Any action and in particular the enforcement action of an international organisation is an ' international ' action. That the ' urgent military measures ' to be taken by the United Nations are characterised in Article 45 as ' combined international enforcement action ' is quite compatible with designating the armed forces placed at the disposal of the Security Council as ' armed forces of the United Nations.' The action is a ' combined ' action if the armed forces placed at the disposal of the Security Council are composed of the contingents of several Members; but it is an international action, and the armed forces are armed forces of the United Nations even if the action is performed by the Security Council through the contingent of one Member only. Article 48, however, stipulates that the action of the Security Council for the maintenance of international peace and security ' shall be taken by all the Members of the United Nations or by some of them, as the Security Council may determine.' According to the wording of this provision, the Security Council seems not to be authorised to call upon one Member only to apply measures not involving the use of armed force according to Article 41; or to provide armed forces in fulfilment of the obligations assumed under Article 43; or a national air-force contingent in accordance with Article 45; so that the enforcement action will always be a ' combined ' international action although the Charter uses this term with reference only to urgent military measures.

The result of the preceding analysis is that the above raised question whether the Charter establishes an armed force of the United Nations distinct from the armed forces of the Members, or whether the enforcement actions provided for by the Charter are to be executed by the Members through their own armed forces, cannot be answered simply in one or in the other way. The Charter has created a type which is in the midst between two extremes. Regarding their composition, the armed forces, by which the action of the Security Council for the maintenance or restoration of peace is performed, are the combined armed forces of all or of several Members. In this respect there is no armed force of the United Nations distinct from the armed forces of the Members. However, the armed forces of the Members are unified by being placed at the disposal and under the command and the strategic direction of a single body, the Security Council, assisted by a Military Staff Committee. By virtue of this unitary command the United Nations has its own armed force although it is composed of the armed forces of its Members.[1]

[1] In his statement at the opening meeting of Committee III/3 of the San Francisco Conference the Rapporteur (delegate of the French Republic) said: ' Theoretically, the international force can be conceived in several forms: A permanent army of an international nature over and above the national armies or even replacing them; national contingents under international command, which presupposes control by permanent international military staff; national contingents at the disposal of an international body, but remaining under the command of their national army.' The type of armed force chosen by the Charter corresponds, according to the Rapporteur, to the second of the three plans he exposed. He declared, that ' the question of command is not settled in advance ' by the Dumbarton Oaks Proposals, ' it is merely provided that the Military Staff Committee is responsible under the Security Council for the strategic direction of any armed forces placed at the disposal of the Security Council, and that questions of command of forces be worked out subsequently.' (U.N.C.I.O. Doc. 134, III/3/3.) The Rapporteur seems to have overseen that Chapter VIII, Section B, paragraph 9 of the Dumbarton Oaks Proposals which is identical with Article 47, paragraph 1, of the Charter expressly provides that the Military Staff Committee shall ' advise and assist the Security Council on all questions relating to . . . the employment and command of forces placed at its disposal.' In view of this provision the sentence in Article 47, paragraph 3, ' Questions relating to the command of such forces shall be worked out subsequently,' may be interpreted to refer to the details in the exercise of a function conferred, in principle, upon the Security Council by Article 47, paragraph 1.

At the *Hearings* (p. 301) a Senator asked: ' Under the provisions in this Charter, is it contemplated that there be any standing force called for by the Security Council,' and another Senator added: ' Do you mean an international police force ? ' To these questions the representative of the State Department answered: ' No; there would be national contingents availabe for combined action.' This answer does not take into consideration the military command under which the national contingents are placed. The term ' international police force ' is quite applicable to the armed forces under the command of the Security Council, if the term is taken literally, meaning that the armed forces have an international character and are not the instrument of a superstate.

Chapter 19

LIMITATIONS ON THE FUNCTIONS OF THE ORGANISATION

(Article 2, Paragraph 7, Articles 51, 53, and 107)

The general provisions of the Charter conferring functions upon the Organisation and obligations upon the Members are subject to important restrictions established by Article 2, paragraph 7, concerning matters of domestic jurisdiction, Article 51 concerning the right of self-defence, and Articles 53 and 107 concerning action in relation to former enemy states.

1. Domestic Jurisdiction (Article 2, paragraph 7)

Article 2, paragraph 7 runs as follows:

> Nothing contained in the present Charter shall authorise the United Nations to intervene in matters which are essentially within the domestic jurisdiction of any state or shall require the Members to submit such matters to settlement, under the present Charter; but this principle shall not prejudice the application of enforcement measures under Chapter VII.

This paragraph[1] comprises two different rules. One prohibits intervention on the part of the Organisation in matters which are essentially within the domestic jurisdiction of any state; another

[1] In a statement on Article 2, paragraph 7 (U.N.C.I.O. Doc. 929, I/1/37) the delegate of Norway said: 'It is tantamount to imposing on the working of the system of international investigation and conciliation very severe limitations and thus to exposing the peace of the world to dangers, the extent of which it is difficult to assess in advance. One is reminded of the caustic remark of Elihu Root: "The people of the State of New York are in favour of prohibition, but against the application of it."' At the 17th meeting of Committee I/1 (U.N.C.I.O. Doc. 1019, I/1/42, p. 1) the delegate of the United States in his exposition of the intent of Article 2, paragraph 7, emphasised that this provision deals with domestic jurisdiction 'as a basic principle, and not, as had been the case in the original Dumbarton Oaks Proposals and in Article 15 of the Covenant of the League of Nations, as a technical and legalistic formula designed to deal with the settlement of disputes by the Security Council. This change in concept had been caused, he explained, by the change in the character of the Organisation as planned in the discussions at San Francisco. The scope of the Organisation was now broadened to include functions which would enable the Organisation to eradicate the underlying causes of war as well as to deal with crises leading to war. Under the Economic and Social Council the Organisation would deal with economic and social problems. This broadening of the scope of the Organisation constituted a great advance, but it also engendered special problems.' The Summary Report of the 16th meeting of Committee I/1 (U.N.C.I.O. Doc. 976, I/1/40, p. 1) contains the following statement with reference to Article 2, paragraph 7: 'Nearly all speakers

releases the Members from submitting such matters to settlement under the Charter. The first rule establishes a restriction of the competence of the Organisation, the second a restriction of the obligations of the Members. By the first rule intervention on the part of ' the United Nations ' is prohibited, this term meaning the Organisation, not the individual Members to whom the second rule refers. An obligation of the Members to refrain from intervention in domestic matters of other states is not expressly stipulated by the Charter but is implied in the obligation established by Article 2, paragraph 4. Under general international law, illegal intervention is a dictatorial interference by a state in the affairs of another state, affecting the latter's political independance or territorial integrity. This is just what Article 2, paragraph 4 does prohibit.[2]

The essential content of Article 2, paragraph 7 has been taken over from Article 15, paragraph 8, of the Covenant of the League of Nations, which runs as follows:—

> If the dispute between the parties is claimed by one of them, and is found by the Council to arise out of a matter which by international law is solely within the domestic jurisdiction of that party, the Council shall so report, and shall make no recommendation as to its settlement.

That means that the Council shall have no jurisdiction in the case of a dispute which arises out of a matter which is solely within the domestic jurisdiction of a party to the dispute. The idea underlying the exclusion of the Council from an intervention in these affaris was probably that there exist certain matters which, by their very nature, are solely within the domestic jurisdiction of the states and that a dispute which arises out of a matter which is solely within the jurisdiction of a state is an internal or domestic, that is a national, not an international, affair, and the relation between the contesting states no ' international ' relation. Consequently there is no reason to confer upon an international agency the competence to intervene in the dispute.

Article 15, paragraph 8 was one of the most discussed provisions of the Covenant. There can be little doubt that its basic idea: the

agreed in recognising that the object of the paragraph was to uphold two principles: (1) Explicit recognition of the rule that there should not be undue interference with the domestic jurisdiction of the several states; and (2) that the performance by the Security Council of its functions for the maintenance of peace and security should be assured.'

[2] In the discussion of the Greek question the delegate of the Ukrainian Republic said at the 60th meeting of the Security Council: ' Article 2, paragraph 7, of the United Nations Charter denies other Governments the right to intervene in the internal affairs of a foreign country. In that case, however, this Article and paragraph are directed against the British authorities who have violated the Article.' (Official Records of the Security Council, 1st Year, 2nd Series, No. 8, p. 209.) This interpretation of Article 2, paragraph 7, has no basis in the Charter.

existence of matters which, by their very nature, are solely within the domestic jurisdiction of a state, is erroneous. There is no matter that cannot be regulated by a rule of customary or contractual international law; and if a matter is regulated by a rule of international law it is no longer 'solely within the domestic jurisdiction' of the state concerned. Solely within the domestic jurisdiction of a state are only matters which, for the time being, are not regulated by a rule of inter national law. That a matter is not regulated by a rule of international law, that is to say that there is no rule of international law referring to that matter, does not mean that the matter is not regulated at all by international law. For, if there is no rule of international law imposing in a certain matter an obligation upon a state to behave in a definite way, this state is, under international law, free to behave in this matter as it pleases or, in other terms, this state has under international law the right—and the other states the obligation not to prevent the former—to behave according to its discretion; which implies that no other state has a right to claim a definite behaviour in that matter from the state concerned. Consequently, when a dispute between two states arises out of a matter which according to the opinion of one of the parties is solely within its domestic jurisdiction, this dispute is an international dispute, just as any other dispute between two states; and there is no reason that can be deduced from the nature of the dispute, for eliminating the jurisdiction of an international agency. Even if this agency be only competent to decide the question whether or not the matter out of which the dispute has arisen is solely within the domestic jurisdiction of the party which makes the claim, that is to say, to decide whether or not the matter is regulated by a rule of customary or contractual international law, the decision is the settlement of a true international dispute. For, if the decision is in the affirmative, its meaning is that the state which claims the matter to be within its exclusive domestic juridsiction is, according to existing international law, right; and the other party is, according to this law, wrong when asking for a certain conduct on the part of the former with respect to the matter. If the decision is in the negative, its meaning is that the state which opposes its domestic jurisdiction to the other party's claim is, according to international law, wrong, at least in so far as its objection against the other party's claim is not justified. Since the decisive question is a question of international law—Article 15, paragraph 8, of the Covenant correctly speaks 'of a matter which *by international law* is solely within the domestic jurisdiction'—both decisions may properly be rendered by an international agency. The paradoxical result of Article 15, paragraph 8 of the Covenant was that the Council was competent to decide the question as to whether the matter out of which the dispute had arisen was solely within the domestic jurisdiction of the party which made the claim; and this act of the

Council implied the decision of the dispute. But the Council was forbidden to make recommendations, that is to say, to intervene in the dispute in the normal way (although it might take action under Article 11).[3] The original intention of those who drafted Article 15, paragraph 8, to eliminate the jurisdiction of the Council, has not been realised by the wording they were compelled to give this provision.

Article 2, paragraph 7 of the Charter does not refer expressly to disputes, as Article 15, paragraph 8, of the Covenant did;[4] and it prohibits not only—as Article 15, paragraph 8, of the Covenant did—recommendations by the Council but any kind of intervention by any organ of the United Nations (except the case referred to in the second sentence of Article 2, paragraph 7). By the term 'to intervene' any activity of the Organisation may be understood. The *Report to the President* correctly states: 'The proviso with reference to domestic jurisdiction becomes a limitation upon all activities of the Organisation rather than merely a limitation upon the action of the Security Council under Chapter VI of the Charter.'[5] If, however, the question as to whether a matter is or is not essentially within the domestic jurisdiction of a state is to be decided by an organ of the United Nations, discussion[6] and investigation of the matter must be considered to be an activity not prohibited by Article 2, paragraph 7. Especially investigation may be necessary to decide whether a matter is essentially within the domestic jurisdiction of a state. But the

[3] At the 17th meeting of Committee III/1 (U.N.C.I.O. Doc. 922, III/1/44) the Norwegian delegate pointed out 'that the provision which prevented the Security Council from dealing with any matter of domestic jurisdiction was a backward step, for under Article 11 of the Covenant of the League of Nations the League Council had had power to take such matter into consideration in arriving at a possible conciliation.'

[4] In this respect Article 2, paragraph 7, differs essentially from the corresponding provision of the Dumbarton Oaks Proposals, which in Chapter VIII, Section A: 'Pacific Settlement of Disputes,' stipulated:

> 7. The provisions of paragraph 1 to 6 of Section A should not apply to situations or disputes arising out of matters which by international law are solely within the domestic jurisdiction of the state concerned.

[5] *Report to the President*, p. 43.

[6] In the case of treatment of Indians in the Union of South Africa, brought before the General Assembly by the Government of India, the delegate of South Africa contended that the case referred to a matter essentially within the domestic jurisdiction of the Union. At the 1st meeting of the joint first and sixth Committee of the General Assembly, November 21, 1946, he declared 'he could not agree that recommendation by the General Assembly would not be an intervention. . . . Without admitting the right of the United Nations to intervene in the matter, he had no objection to the case being freely discussed.' (Journal of the United Nations, No. 40, Suppl. No. 1 and 6–A/C. 1 and 6/1, p. 4.) The General Assembly did not formally decide the question as to whether the matter was essentially within the domestic jurisdiction of the Union of South Africa, but actually intervened by

power to make investigations is expressly conferred only upon the Security Council and only for the purpose to determine whether the continuance of a dispute or situation is likely to endanger international peace and security, not for the purpose to determine whether a matter is essentially within the domestic jurisdiction of a state.

The general prohibition to intervene in matters of domestic jurisdiction may be of great importance with respect to the functions of the Organisation under Chapters IX and X. Article 55 authorises the United Nations to promote—

> (*a*) higher standards of living, full employment, and conditions of economic and social progress and development;
>
> (*b*) solutions of international economic, social, health, and related problems; and international cultural and educational co-operation; and
>
> (*c*) universal respect for, and observance of, human rights and fundamental freedoms for all without distinction as to race, sex, language, or religion.

Article 62 stipulates:

> 1. The Economic and Social Council may make or initiate studies and reports with respect to international, economic, social, cultural, educational, health, and related matters and may make recommendations with respect to any such matters to the General Assembly, to the Members of the United Nations, and to the specialised agencies concerned.
>
> 2. It may make recommendations for the purpose of promoting respect for, and observance of, human rights and fundamental freedoms for all.

It is hardly possible to fulfil these functions without intervening in matters of domestic jurisdiction, meaning matters with respect to which the states have no international obligations. Under Article 56 the Members are obliged 'to take joint and separate action in co-operation with the Organisation for the achievement of the purposes set forth in Article 55.' This provision might be interpreted to mean that the Members are obliged to permit intervention on the part of the Organisation in matters referred to in Article 55, even if these matters are within their domestic jurisdiction. This provision is hardly consistent with Article 2, paragraph 7.[7]

That Article 2, paragraph 7, refers also to disputes results from the fact that it releases the Members from the obligation 'to submit such

adopting a resolution at its 52nd plenary meeting, December 8, 1946, which did not contain a recommendation but the statement of a fact, the expression of an opinion and the request to report. (Resolutions adopted by the General Assembly, Doc. A/64/Add. 1, p. 69.) Cf. *supra*, pp. 30 f.

[7] The Report of Rapporteur of Committee II/3 of the San Francisco Conference (U.N.C.I.O. Doc. 861, II/3/55 (1), pp. 3 f.) contains the following statement: 'There were some misgivings that the statement of purposes now recommended

matters [of domestic jurisdiction] to settlement under the present Charter.' It is in the first place disputes which are submitted to

implied that the Organisation might interfere in the domestic affairs of member countries. To remove all possible doubt, the Committee agreed to include in its records the following statement: " The members of Committee 3 of Commission II are in full agreement that nothing contained in Chapter IX [Chapters IX and X of the Charter] can be construed as giving authority to the Organisation to intervene in the domestic affairs of member states ".' This means that the provisions of Chapters IX and X of the Charter are to be interpreted as restricted by Article 2, paragraph 7. But the interpretation that the provision of Article 2, paragraph 7, is restricted by the provisions of Chapters IX and X of the Charter is not excluded.

At the *Hearings* (p. 307) the representative of the Department of State made the following statement: 'The language of Chapter IX [of the Dumbarton Oaks Proposals] is very strong and very far-reaching; and questions were raised in the discussion as to whether or not the language used could in any way be interpreted as meaning interference in the domestic affairs of the Member States. It was quite clear that the principle regarding domestic jurisdiction already inserted in the Charter would be governing.' Then he referred to the above quoted statement in the Report of Committee II/3. Later a Senator asked (pp. 309 f.): 'I notice several reiterations of the thought of the Charter that the Organisation shall not interfere with domestic affairs of any country. How can you get into these social questions and economic questions without conducting investigations and making inquiries in the various countries?' and later: 'Might the activities of the Organisation concern themselves with, for example, wage rates and working conditions in different countries?' To this the representative of the State Department answered: 'The question of what matters the Organisation would be concerned with would depend upon whether or not they had international repercussions. . . . International problems may arise out of all sorts of circumstances.' At a later stage of the discussion the Senator asked (p. 311 f.): 'This Organisation, you said, concerns itself with the international aspects of these various matters. Is there any international aspect of any of these matters that operates entirely within its own vacuum that does not originate within domestic jurisdiction?', whereupon the representative of the State Department answered: 'I suppose we can say that there is no such thing as an international problem that is not related to national problems, because the word " international " itself means that there are nations involved. What domestic jurisdiction relates to here, I should say, as it does in all of these matters, is that there are certain matters which are handled internally by nations which do not affect other nations or may not affect other nations. On the other hand, there are certainly many matters handled internally which do affect other nations and which by international law are considered to be of concern to other nations.' The discussion continued: The Senator: 'For example, let me ask you if this would be true. It is conceivable that there are racial questions on the southern shores of the Mediterranean that might have very explosive effects under some circumstances; but they originate locally, do they not?' The representative: 'Yes.' The Senator: 'And because they might have explosive effects, this Organisation might concern itself with them; is that correct?' The representative: 'It might, if somebody brings them to the attention of the Organisation.' The Senator: 'And by the same token, am I correct in this, that any racial matter, any of these matters we are talking about, that originate in one country domestically and that has the possibility of making international trouble, might be subject to the investigation and recommendations of the Organisation?' The representative: 'I should think so, because the Organisation is created for that.'

This discussion shows clearly that the principle of non-intervention in domestic affairs—however this concept may be defined—is hardly compatible with the functions the Charter confers upon the Organisation in Chapters IX and X.

'settlement'. The Charter uses the term 'settlement' especially, but not exclusively, with reference to 'disputes.' In Article 1, paragraph 1, we read: 'adjustment or settlement of international disputes or situations . . .' Article 2, paragraph 7, applies not only to disputes; it applies to 'matters,' including situations not having the character of disputes.[8] It differs from Article 15, paragraph 8, of the Covenant in that it prohibits intervention in matters which are 'essentially,' not as Article 15, paragraph 8 said 'solely,' within the domestic jurisdiction of a state; and Article 2, paragraph 7 of the

In the case of treatment of Indians in the Union of South Africa, the delegate of the Union of South Africa admitted at the 1st meeting of the joint first and sixth Committee of the General Assembly that an exception to the rule of domestic jurisdiction 'might be sought in the direction of human rights and fundamental freedoms, such as the right to exist, the right to freedom of conscience and freedom of speech, and the right of free access to the courts.' He denied, however, that the Union of South Africa had in any way infringed any of these elementary human rights. (Journal of the United Nations, No. 40: Suppl. Nos. 1 and 6—A/C1 and 6/1, p. 4.) At the 51st meeting of the General Assembly, the delegate of Panama stated: 'Are human rights essentially within the domestic jurisdiction of the State? My answer is no, and a hundred times no. I submit that by the San Francisco Charter human rights have been taken out of the province of domestic jurisdiction and placed within the realm of international law.' (*Ibid.*, No. 54, Suppl. A-P.V./51, p. 368.)

In the Indonesian case some members of the Security Council (the Soviet Russian and the Egyptian delegates) tried to justify an intervention by the United Nations (sending a commission of investigation on the spot) in spite of the claim of the delegate of the Netherlands that the relationship between the Dutch Government and the Indonesians was essentially within the domestic jurisdiction of the Netherlands, by referring to Article 1, paragraph 2, of the Charter, stipulating as a Purpose of the United Nations 'to develop friendly relations among nations based on respect for the principle of . . . self-determination of peoples.' (Journal of the Security Council 1st Year, No. 11, p. 207; No. 12, p. 213.) Whether this provision applies at all to peoples which have not or not yet the character of states, is here of no importance. Interesting is only that Article 2, paragraph 7, is interpreted as being restricted by a provision of the Charter which does not even establish an obligation of the Members.

[8] In the case of the treatment of Indians in the Union of South Africa the delegate of India declared at the 19th meeting of the General Committee that his Government did not bring the case before the General Assembly as a 'dispute' but as a 'question.' He said: 'The delegation of India did not call upon the Assembly to intervene in a dispute arising out of the treatment of Indians in South Africa; it insisted that the question should be discussed by the Assembly.' (Journal of the United Nations, No. 15: Suppl. B-A/BUR/35, p. 6.) He tried to avoid the case being qualified a 'dispute' in order to meet the objection of the other party, the Union of South Africa, that the case, arising out of a matter essentially within the domestic jurisdiction of the South African Union, was not required by the Charter to be submitted to settlement under the Charter. According to the interpretation of Article 2, paragraph 7, by the Indian delegate, the provision, 'Nothing contained in the Charter . . . shall require the Members to submit such matters to settlement under the present Charter,' refers only to 'disputes.' This is certainly a too restrictive interpretation. The term 'settlement' as used in the Charter, *e.g.*, in the title of Chapter VI, sometimes refers not only to disputes but also to other situations.

Charter does not contain—as Article 15, paragraph 8 of the Covenant did—the words: 'by international law.' But one state's claim that a matter is within its domestic jurisdiction may be contested by another state with reference to positive international law; and then there exists an international dispute that can be settled only by agreement of the contesting states or by the decision of an international agency. Article 2, paragraph 7, does not prevent a state, in conflict with another state claiming the matter out of which the conflict arises to be essentially within its domestic jurisdiction, from contesting this claim and from bringing the case before the Organisation.[9]

The fact that Article 2, paragraph 7 of the Charter does not speak of matters which are 'solely,' but of matters which are 'essentially' within the domestic jurisdiction of a state, is no improvement. Just as there are no matters which, by their very nature, are 'solely' within the domestic jurisdiction, there are no matters which are 'essentially' within the domestic jurisdiction of a state. Even matters such as form of government, acquisition or loss of citizenship, treatment of minorities, questions of tariff or immigration, may be the object of an international agreement. The fact that these matters are, normally, not regulated by a rule of international law is no reason to assume that they are 'essentially' within the domestic jurisdiction of the states. The only question is whether the matter out of which a dispute between two states or another situation arises, is, or is not, regulated by a rule of customary international law or by a treaty to which the parties to the dispute or the states involved in the situation are contracting parties. If the matter is not regulated by a rule of customary or contractual international law, that is to say, if international law does not impose any obligation upon a state with respect to this matter, then, and only then the matter is solely—but never essentially—within the domestic jurisdiction of the state;[1] and it is

[9] In the discussion of the case of the treatment of Indians in the Union of South Africa the delegate of the Soviet Union, at the 52nd meeting of the General Assembly, called the attention of the Assembly to the fact that Article 2, paragraph 7, stipulates only that nothing contained in the Charter 'shall' require the Members to submit such matters to settlement under the Charter. This means—according to his interpretation—that the Members are not obliged, but that they are not forbidden, to submit such matters to settlement under the Charter. 'In other words, it leaves it absolutely up to the complainant state. If India therefore wishes to use this body as the hearing body for its complaint it has the absolute right to do so in accordance with this particular Article of the Charter, and it is quite obvious that the complaint of the Indian delegation is of an international character within the competence of the United Nations, and more specifically of the General Assembly.' (Journal of the United Nations, No. 55: Suppl. A–A/P.V./52, p. 387.)

[1] The Permanent Court of International Justice interpreted Article 15, paragraph 8, of the Covenant of the League of Nations as follows: 'The words "solely within the domestic jurisdiction" seem rather to contemplate certain matters which, though they may very closely concern the interests of more than one State, are not,

solely within the domestic jurisdiction of this state ' by international law.' The question whether a matter is solely within the domestic jurisdiction of a state can be decided only by examining the status of international law with respect to this question, that is to say, it can be decided only ' by international law.' It is, therefore, no improvement either, that Article 2, paragraph 7 of the Charter omits the reference to international law made by Article 15, paragraph 8 of the Covenant.

The replacement of the term ' solely ' by the term ' essentially '[2]

in principle, regulated by international law. As regards such matters, each State is sole judge. The question whether a certain matter is or is not solely within the jurisdiction of a State is an essentially relative question; it depends upon the development of international relations. . . . it may well happen that, in a matter which . . . is not, in principle, regulated by international law, the right of a State to use its discretion is nevertheless restricted by obligations which it may have undertaken towards other States. In such a case, jurisdiction which, in principle, belongs solely to the State, is limited by rules of international law. Article 15, paragraph 8, then ceases to apply as regards those States which are entitled to invoke such rules . . . (Publications of the Court, Series B, Advisory Opinion No. 4.) Hence, in spite of the formula used by the Court it is of no importance whether the matter is or is not, ' in principle,' regulated by international law. The only point is: whether the matter is, or is not, regulated by international law.

At the 17th meeting of Committee I/1 (U.N.C.I.O. Doc. 1019, I/1/42, p. 5) the Belgian delegate said that an international treaty does not bring automatically its substance into the realm of international law: ' For example, nationality was a common subject for treaties, but these treaties did not bring nationality *ipso facto* under international law. This still remained within domestic jurisdiction and fell under international law only so far as treaties specifically so provided.' Interpreting the opinion No. 37 of the Permanent Court of International Justice the Belgian delegate finally stated that ' nationality remained within the reserved domain and that each state was the sole judge if the matter did not clearly fall under international agreement.'

[2] During the discussion of Article 2, paragraph 7, at the 17th meeting of Committee I/1 (U.N.C.I.O. Doc. 1019, I/1/42, pp. 5 f.) the delegate of Australia declared with regard to the substitution of the word 'essentially ' for ' solely,' he agreed with the opinion, expressed previously by the delegate of the United States, ' that matters *solely* within domestic jurisdiction were constantly contracting. For example international agreement to promote full employment would have been unheard of a few years ago and even now, although this matter remained within domestic jurisdiction. It was not " solely " within domestic jurisdiction. It was, however, " essentially " within domestic jurisdiction and that was a better criterion to apply.' Consequently: in spite of the fact that a dispute refers to the obligation assumed by an international treaty, an intervention in this dispute on the part of the Organisation is excluded if the international obligation refers to a subject matter which is ' essentially ' within the domestic jurisdiction. Since this can be said of almost every subject matter, Article 2, paragraph 7, may be used as an instrument to paralyse an important part of the activity of the Organisation.

The *Report to the President* (p. 45) justifies the replacement of the term ' solely ' (which Chapter VIII, Section A, paragraph 7, of the Dumbarton Oaks Proposals, had taken over from Article 15, paragraph 8 of the Covenant) by the term ' essentially ' as follows: ' It seemed more appropriate to look to what was the essence, the heart of the matter, rather than to be compelled to determine that a certain matter was " solely " domestic in character.' Neither by its very nature nor for the

may have very undesirable consequences. It may be interpreted to mean that intervention of the Organisation and the obligation to submit the matter to settlement under the Charter is excluded even if the matter is regulated by a rule of international law, that is to say if the state concerned is with respect to the matter under an international obligation, even under an obligation established by the Charter, and hence the matter is not 'solely' within the domestic jurisdiction of the state concerned: provided that it is 'essentially' within its domestic jurisdiction.[3] A state may admit to be with respect to a certain matter under an obligation imposed upon it by an international treaty to which the state is a party, and nevertheless assert that this matter is 'essentially' within its domestic jurisdiction; which means that the state is not obliged to submit conflicts which arise out of this obligation to settlement under the Charter and to accept intervention on the part of the Organisation. The fact that a matter is 'essentially'—though not 'solely'—within the domestic jurisdiction of a state

reason that international law does not establish certain obligations with respect to it, a matter is 'essentially' domestic in character. As far as the reference to 'international law' is concerned, which Chapter VIII, Section A, paragraph 7, of the Dumbarton Oaks Proposals, had also taken over from Article 15, paragraph 8, of the Covenant, but which in the text of Article 2, paragraph 7, of the Charter, has been dropped, the *Report to the President* (p. 44 f.) states: 'This deletion was supported by the argument that the body of international law on this subject is indefinite and inadequate. To the extent that the matter is dealt with by international practice and by text writers, the conceptions are antiquated and not of a character which ought to be frozen into the new Organisation.' As to the question whether a rule of general customary international law or a treaty imposes upon the state which considers a matter to be within its domestic jurisdiction, a definite obligation with respect to this matter, 'the body of international law' is neither 'indefinite' nor 'inadequate.' This question as to whether a state is under an obligation imposed upon it by international law is to be answered in almost any dispute. If the 'body of international law' were really so 'indefinite and inadequate' that it would be justifiable to ignore it, no dispute could be decided in accordance with international law.

[3] If it is assumed that a matter is not or not only within the domestic jurisdiction of a state when the latter is, with respect to this matter, under an international obligation, then there is a clear line between matters which are within domestic, that is national, and matters which are within international jurisdiction. The opinion advocated by the Australian delegate in the discussion of the Spanish question that 'the line between what is of international concern and what is of domestic concern, is not fixed' (Journal of the Security Council, 1st Year, No. 29, p. 578) can be maintained only under the supposition that the domestic character of a matter does not depend upon its being regulated or not regulated by a rule of international law, but upon its own nature, so that a matter, even if regulated by a rule of international law, may be considered to be within the domestic jurisdiction of a state and hence exempt from the jurisdiction of any international agency. The statement that there is no fixed line between domestic and international matters means that it must be left to the discretion of the authority concerned—a state or an international agency—to decide the question as to whether a matter is within the domestic jurisdiction of a state and hence beyond the jurisdiction of an international agency.

may be interpreted to mean that the state concerned is with respect to this matter only under national or general international law, and if there is a treaty referring to this matter, under that treaty, but not under the law of the Charter. And it may be assumed that a matter is 'essentially' within the domestic jurisdiction of a state if it is essential to its sovereignty. Consequently a state may refuse to submit a matter to settlement under the Charter and deny the right of the Organisation to intervene if such submission or intervention is incompatible with its sovereignty.[4]

If, according to the idea underlying Article 15, paragraph 8 of the Covenant and Article 2, paragraph 7 of the Charter, disputes concerning a matter which is within the domestic jurisdiction of a state are not 'international' disputes and therefore the relation between the contesting states is not an 'international' relation,[5]

[4] At the 4th meeting of the joint first and sixth Committee of the General Assembly, in the discussion of the case of treatment of Indians in the Union of South Africa, the delegate of Peru declared: 'Article 2, paragraph 7, was a guarantee of the independence and sovereignty of Member states . . .' (Journal of the United Nations, No. 46: Suppl. No. 1 and 6–A/C.1 and 6/13, p. 36.) At the 51st meeting of the General Assembly, in the discussion of the same case, the delegate of Mexico said of Article 2, paragraph 7: 'It is an active principle of incalculable value to the relations of the States with each other, whose sovereignty and juridical equality is consecrated by the Charter in Article 2, paragraph 1.' (*Ibid.*, No. 54, Suppl. A–/P.V./51, p. 366.)

At the 115th meeting of the Security Council during the discussion of international control of atomic energy the representative of the Soviet Union declared 'that the proposal to grant to an international control organ the right to possess establishments for the production of atomic energy, and unlimited power to carry out other important functions connected with the ownership and management of the establishments and with the disposition of their production, would lead to interference by the control organ in the internal affairs and internal life of States and eventually would lead to arbitrary action by the control organ in the solution of such problems as fall completely within the domestic jurisdiction of a State. I deem it necessary to emphasise that the granting of broad rights and powers of such a kind to the control organ is incompatible with State sovereignty. Therefore, such proposals are unacceptable and must be rejected as unjustifiable.' (Official Records of the Security Council, 2nd Year, No. 22, p. 452.) If the statement that the problems concerned 'fall completely within the domestic jurisdiction of the state' was a reference to Article 2, paragraph 7, of the Charter, it was out of place. The control measures in question were intended to be stipulated by an international agreement; Article 2, paragraph 7, does not prevent the Members to restrict their sovereignty by such agreements.

[5] With reference to Article 2, paragraph 7, the delegate of Australia expressed at the San Francisco Conference the opinion that an organisation 'that is genuinely *international* in character,' should not be permitted 'to intervene in those domestic matters in which, by definition, international law permits each state entire liberty of action.' (U.N.C.I.O. Doc. 969, I/1/39, p. 2.) He spoke of 'a matter of legitimate "international" and not merely of "domestic" concern' (p. 4). Thus he interpreted the term 'domestic' to mean the opposite of 'international.' During the discussion of the Spanish question in the Security Council the Australian delegate formulated the following question: 'Is the existence of the Franco regime a matter of international concern and not one essentially within the jurisdiction of

then the obligation of the Members established in Article 2, paragraph 4 of the Charter: to refrain from threat or use of force 'in their international relations' seems not to apply to a case where the dispute arises out of a matter which is within the domestic jurisdiction of one of the parties to the dispute. Article 2, paragraph 7 of the Charter expressly stipulates that in matters which are within the domestic jurisdiction of a state, the Members are not obliged to submit such disputes 'to settlement under the present Charter.' It is not said: to submit such matters to settlement through organs of the United Nations. That the Members are not obliged to submit disputes which arise out of domestic matters 'to settlement under the present Charter,' might be interpreted to mean that they are not only not obliged to refer such disputes to the Security Council according to Article 37, paragraph 1, and not obliged to accept intervention in such disputes on the part of the General Assembly under Article 10 or 11, or of the Security Council under Article 33, paragraph 2, Articles 34, 36, or even of the International Court of Justice under Article 36, paragraphs 2 to 6 of the Statute.[6] But it might be interpreted to mean

Spain?' (Journal of the Security Council, 1st Year, No. 31, pp. 602 f.) At the same meeting of the Security Council the delegate of the Netherlands said with respect to the term 'international concern': 'We should not introduce in such an incidental way notions which do not find support in the Charter.' (p. 610.) In the Report of the Sub-committee on the Spanish Question, appointed by the Security Council (Doc. S/75), it is stated that the question is 'of international concern,' not 'of essential local or domestic concern.' A working group set up by the Commission on Human Rights discussed the question whether or not the Declaration (Convention) on Human Rights should include an express statement to the effect that the matters dealt with in it are of international concern. 'The Group studied the bearing of Article 2, paragraph 7, of the Charter of the United Nations, on the future Declaration or Convention. The proposed clause seemed to it unnecessary. The "domestic jurisdiction" of States, to which the above-mentioned article referred, if rightly interpreted, only covered questions which had not become international in one way or another. Once States agreed that such questions should form the subject of a Declaration or Convention, they clearly placed them outside their "domestic jurisdiction" and Article 2, paragraph 7, became inapplicable.' (Doc. E/CN.4/53, p. 5.)

[6] At the 17th meeting of Committee I/1 (U.N.C.I.O. Doc. 1019, I/1/42, p. 3) the delegate of Greece declared 'that the basic issue was one of determining what was domestic jurisdiction; his Delegation felt that the International Court was the body which should determine this matter.' He suggested the following amendment: 'It should be left to the International Court of Justice at the request of a party *to decide* whether or not such situation or dispute arises out of matters that under international law, fall within the domestic jurisdiction of the State concerned.' In reply to the arguments advanced in favour of the Greek amendment, the representative of the United States commented 'that disputes involving interpretation were not peculiar to Article 8, and that it was unnecessarily limited to place the proposed revision in one article. For example, Article 5 of Chapter II stated that the "Organisation shall give every assistance," but there might be a question as to what constituted "every assistance" or whether a state was giving "every assistance." Shall it be the Court or the Council? Some body would have to determine questions such as this. The committees of Commission IV had been

that they are not obliged to settle the dispute in accordance with the Principle laid down in Article 2, paragraph 3 of the Charter: to settle disputes by peaceful means. The idea that the Members are not obliged to settle a dispute arising out of a matter of domestic jurisdiction by peaceful means might be considered as being in conformity with the wording of Article 2, paragraph 3, which obligates the Members to settle by peaceful means only their 'international' disputes; which implies that there exist disputes between states which are not 'international' disputes: the disputes which arise out of a matter of domestic jurisdiction. It is true that in Chapter VI entitled 'Pacific Settlement of Disputes,' Articles 33 to 38 refer to 'disputes,' and not to 'international disputes.' This, however, may be explained by the fact that after Chapter I in the Articles establishing the Purposes and Principles has determined the kind of disputes which are to be settled by peaceful means—namely, 'international' disputes in the sense of Article 2, paragraph 7—it has been deemed superflous to repeat in the subsequent Chapters the adjective 'international.' It may be considered as self-evident that the disputes referred to in the subsequent Chapters and especially in Chapter VI are the same as those referred to in Chapter I.

If the Members are expressly released from their obligation to settle their disputes by peaceful means in case the dispute concerns a matter which is within the domestic jurisdiction of one of the parties, they might consider themselves to be free to settle the dispute by threat or use of force. There exists an essential relation between the obligation to settle disputes by peaceful means and the obligation to refrain from threat or use of force. The one has no meaning without the other because they present only the positive and the negative

studying this very type of problem, but they were not prepared to say that all matters of this kind should be referred to the International Court for settlement. It would hardly seem possible or desirable to introduce into Chapter II the principle of "compulsory jurisdiction" for the Court when another branch of the Conference had rejected this principle as impractical of adoption at the present time.' At the same meeting the delegate of Belgium suggested to formulate Article 2, paragraph 7, as follows: 'Nothing contained in this Charter shall authorise the Organisation to intervene in matters which *in the judgment of the Organisation are according to international law exclusively* (or *solely*) within the domestic jurisdiction of any State or shall require the members to submit such matters under this Charter . . . ' Neither the Greek nor the Belgian suggestion have been accepted.

At the 3rd meeting of Commission I (U.N.C.I.O. Doc. 1167, I/10, p. 3) the delegate of Uruguay said with reference to the fact that no organ of the Organisation is authorised to decide the question whether a matter is or is not within the domestic jurisdiction of a state: 'With the rule now proposed a great jump backwards will be taken: the definition of the question according to domestic law made by the interested member itself, made according to a political criterion, and not according to a juridical criterion. The Delegation of Uruguay therefore voted in favour of the proposal made by the Delegation of Greece and later voted for the proposal made by the Delegation of Belgium.'

aspect of one and the same obligation. The fact that the Members are not obliged to settle certain disputes by peaceful means could easily be interpreted to imply the authorisation to settle these disputes by the threat or use of force. This interpretation finds confirmation in the wording of Article 2, paragraph 4. If the obligation to settle their ' international ' disputes by peaceful means does not refer to disputes arising out of matters which are essentially within the domestic jurisdiction of one of the contesting states, then the obligation to refrain from threat or use of force ' in their international relations ' does not refer to the relations between states in disputes arising out of a matter which is essentially within the domestic jurisdiction of one of the contesting states. It might be assumed that the word ' international ' has the same significance in paragraphs 3 and 4 of Article 2: ' International ' in contradistinction to ' domestic.'

One of the textual deficiencies of the Covenant of the League of Nations was that Article 15, paragraph 8, could be interpreted in two contradictory ways. The question as to whether the states are allowed to resort to war against one another in case the dispute arose out of a matter which was solely within the domestic jurisdiction of one party could be answered in the affirmative as well as in the negative. It was possible to argue: since the Covenant does not expressly forbid the resort to war—as it does in Article 15, paragraph 6—the parties are allowed to resort to war. But it was also possible to argue: since the Covenant does not expressly allow to resort to war—as it does in Article 15, paragraph 7—the parties are forbidden to resort to war. For the latter interpretation the argument could be advanced that a matter is to be considered as being solely within the domestic jurisdiction of one party only if the claim of this party has been confirmed by the Council. The party which claims the matter to be within its domestic jurisdiction is, normally, the defendant. The decision of the Council that the claim is justified implies the decision that this party is right and the other party is wrong. For a matter is solely within the domestic jurisdiction of a state if there exists no international obligation of that state with respect to the matter in question. Consequently, the other party has no right to demand anything from the former with respect to the matter. It would be absurd if the Covenant had authorised a Member to resort to war against another Member whose right has been recognised by a decision of the Council.

The Charter of the United Nations does not offer the possibility of such contradictory interpretation. It does not—as the Covenant did—forbid war in some cases and allow war in other cases. The Charter contains—in Article 2, paragraph 4—a general prohibition on the threat or use of force. Consequently, the use of force may be considered as allowed only if an exception to this rule is expressly stipulated. Article 2, paragraph 7, first sentence, might be interpreted as establishing such an exception with respect to disputes arising out of matters which are essentially within the domestic jurisdiction of a state. This consequence of the wording of Article 2, paragraph 7, however, seems to be excluded in so far as by the second sentence of that paragraph the Organisation is authorised to intervene with enforcement measures in case there exists a threat to, or breach of, the peace, determined by the Security Council. Thus Article 2, paragraph 7, cannot be interpreted as a restriction of the obligation established by Article 2, paragraph 4; but the obligation established by Article 2, paragraph 3: settlement of international disputes by peaceful means, is not beyond the restricting effect of the domestic jurisdiction clause. If a matter is essentially within the domestic jurisdiction of a state, the latter may consider itself not obliged to settle a dispute, arising out of this matter, by peaceful means; but, on the other hand, the state is not allowed to settle it in a way which, according to the opinion of the Security Council, constitutes a threat to, or breach of, the peace, provided that Article 39 imposes upon the Members the obligation to refrain from conduct which, in the judgment of the Security Council, constitutes a threat to, or breach of, the peace.

The importance of Article 2, paragraph 7, depends to a great extent on the answer to the question as to who is competent to decide whether a matter is essentially within the domestic jurisdiction of a state. Under Article 15, paragraph 8 of the Covenant the question as to whether a matter was or was not within the domestic jurisdiction of the state concerned was to be decided by the Council. But Article 2, paragraph 7 of the Charter does not contain a provision conferring such power on the Security Council or any other organ of the United Nations. Consequently the provision that a Member is not obliged to submit matters which are essentially within its domestic jurisdiction to settlement under the Charter may be interpreted to mean that the Member itself has to decide whether the matter is essentially within its domestic jurisdiction. If the matter is the subject of a conflict with another state and the latter, too, considers the matter to be essentially within its domestic jurisdiction, both are in the same legal position. But if the other state contests the claim of the former and asserts that the matter out of which the conflict arose is within the jurisdiction of the Organisation, the restriction of the obligations of a Member established by Article 2, paragraph 7 would apply only to that party to the conflict which claims that the matter is essentially within its domestic jurisdiction, not to the other. This is one of the absurd consequences of the interpretation, compatible with the wording of the Charter, that it is upon the state concerned to decide for itself whether a matter is essentially within its domestic jurisdiction. If this claim is contested by the other state party to the conflct, the case may be brought before an organ of the United Nations. If the matter is brought before the Security Council or the General Assembly under Articles 35, 37, 11, or in any other way, or before the International Court of Justice under the Statute, and the competence of the Organisation or of the Court is contested with reference to Article 2, paragraph 7, the Council or the Assembly or the Court has to decide the question. The decision of the Council is certainly substantive in the sense of Article 27, paragraph 3; the decision of the Assembly may be considered to refer to an ' important question ' in the sense of Article 18, paragraph 3. The decision of the Court falls under Article 36, paragraph 6 of the Statute. Then the question arises whether the organ of the United Nations is bound by the statement of the party concerned that the matter is essentially within its domestic jurisdiction or whether the organ has the power to decide this question independently of the party. In view of the fact that Article 2, paragraph 7 does not expressly confer upon organs of the United Nations the competence to decide the question, both interpretations are possible. If the second of the two interpretations is accepted and if the Security Council decides that the matter is not within the domestic jurisdiction of the party, the latter is bound under Article 25 to accept this decision, provided that the party considers it as ' in accordance with the Charter,'—and provided that it is upon the party to decide whether the decision of the Security Council is ' in accordance with the Charter.'[7] This formula used in Article 25 may play a highly undesirable role in case a conflict arises between a party and the Security Council as to the domestic character of a matter under consideration by the Council. If there exists such a conflict between a party and the General Assembly, the former is not bound to accept the decision of the Assembly. There is no provision analogous to that of Article 25 referring to decisions of the General Assembly.

A state may refuse to comply with a recommendation made by the General Assembly because the state considers it as an intervention in a matetr which is essentially within its domestic jurisdiction. This, however, is of minor importance since recommendations of the Assembly have at any rate no binding force. In case the Court decides under Article 36, paragraph 6 of the Statute that a matter is not within the domestic jurisdiction of a party and hence rejects the objection against its competence, the party is, under Article 94, paragraph 1 of the Charter, obliged to comply with this decision. But the interpretation is not excluded that the Court in its decision under Article 36, paragraph 6 of the Statute is bound by the declaration of a party that the matter out of which the dispute before the Court arose is essentially within the party's domestic jurisdiction.[8]

[7] Cf. *supra*, pp. 95 f.

[8] The wording of Article 2, paragraph 7, does not prevent a state, which has declared under Article 36, paragraph 2, of the Statute of the International Court of Justice, to recognise as compulsory the jurisdiction of the Court in the legal disputes

As to the interpretation of the formula 'essentially within the domestic jurisdiction' of a state, the party as well as the organs of the United Nations are not bound by any provision of the Charter. It is quite natural that the state concerned will be inclined to interpret it in an extensive, the organs of the United Nations in a restrictive way.[9] If it is assumed that a matter is 'essentially within the domestic jurisdiction' of a state only if the latter is under no international obligation with respect to this matter[1] and that this question is to

referred to in this paragraph, from declining the jurisdiction of the Court by claiming that the dispute arises out of a matter which is essentially within the domestic jurisdiction of that state. The only question is whether, in case the other party contradicts this view and the Court under Article 36, paragraph 6, decides the question of its jurisdiction, the Court is, or is not, bound by the statement of the party which claims that the matter is within its domestic jurisdiction. As pointed out, both interpretations are possible.

The Resolution 196 adopted by the United States Senate on August 2, 1946 (*Congressional Record*, Vol. 92, No. 154, p. 10850) authorising the President of the United States to deposit with the Secretary-General of the United Nations a declaration under paragraph 2 of Article 36 of the Statute of the International Court of Justice, contains the provision 'that the declaration shall not apply to "disputes with regard to matters which are essentially within the jurisdiction of the United States as determined by the United States".' This provision is in conformity with the wording of Article 2, paragraph 7, of the Charter. In this case the Court is certainly bound to recognise a matter to be essentially within the domestic jurisdiction of the United States, and hence the Court has no jurisdiction, if the United States in a case before the Court, in opposition to the other party to the case, declares the matter to be essentially within its domestic jurisdiction. Cf. *supra*, pp. 527 ff.

9 In the Spanish question the General Assembly acted under the presupposition that the political regime established within a state is not a matter essentially within the domestic jurisdiction of that state. In its resolution adopted at the 59th meeting the Assembly even recommended, among others, 'that all Members of the United Nations immediately recall from Madrid their Ambassadors and Ministers plenipotentiary, accredited there'; which is a measure short of enforcement action under Article 41. (Doc. A/64/Add. 1, p. 64.)

In the discussion of the Indonesian situation at the 14th meeting of the Security Council the delegate of the Soviet Union made the following statement with reference to Article 2, paragraph 7: 'There are matters, however, which, though formally comprised in the domestic jurisdiction of a given state, border upon external political relations, threatening the peace and security of peoples. Such matters cannot be left to be settled by the State itself, notwithstanding the principle of sovereignty.' (Journal of the Security Council, 1st Year, No. 11, p. 208.) The statement that in case of matters 'threatening the peace and security' intervention on the part of the Organisation is allowed, is in conformity with the second sentence of paragraph 7 of Article 2. But the statement that such intervention is permissible also in case of matters which 'though formally comprised in the domestic jurisdiction of a given state, border upon external political relations,' has no basis in the wording of the Charter. There is practically no matter 'comprised in the domestic jurisdiction' which does not, in some way or other, 'border upon external political relations.'

1 In the discussion of the treatment of Indians in South Africa at the 19th meeting of the General Committee the delegate of the Soviet Union as well as the delegate of the Ukrainian Republic expressed the view that the treatment of Indians by the Government of the Union of South Africa cannot be a matter essentially within the

be decided by organs of the United Nations, the possible effect of the prohibition of intervention stipulated by the first sentence of Article 2, paragraph 7 is considerably reduced.

After having excluded, in a categorical manner, any intervention on the part of the United Nations in matters which are essentially within the domestic jurisdiction of any state, paragraph 7 of Article 2 declares: 'but this principle shall not prejudice the application of enforcement measures under Chapter VII.' The enforcement measures under Chapter VII are certainly methods—the most radical methods—of intervening in matters of the Members. Hence the prohibition of intervention proclaimed in the first sentence must be interpreted as restricted by the second sentence. This sentence authorises the Organisation to intervene even in a matter which is essentially within the domestic jurisdiction of a state.

The second sentence of Article 2, paragraph 7 does not allow any kind of intervention. Only enforcement measures are allowed in case the matter is essentially within the domestic jurisdiction of a state. If enforcement measures are to be taken under Article 39, the question as to whether the matter with respect to which these measures are to be taken, is or is not within the domestic jurisdiction of the state concerned, is of no importance. The only question is whether there exists a threat to, or breach of, the peace.

Are 'enforcement measures' only measures involving the use of armed force as determined in Article 42; or also measures taken in accordance with Article 41, not involving the use of armed force?

domestic jurisdiction of the Union, since this treatment constituted a violation of treaty obligations. The delegate of the Ukraine referred also to terms of the Preamble of the Charter affirming the inviolability of treaties. (Journal of the United Nations, No. 15: Suppl. B–A/Bur/35, pp. 6 f.)

The delegate of the Union of South Africa recognised at the 1st meeting of the joint first and sixth Committee that an 'exception to the rule of non-interference in domestic affairs was to be found in treaty obligations.' But he denied that there existed such treaty obligations of the Union with respect to the treatment of Indians. (*Ibid.*, No. 40: Suppl. Nos. 1 and 6 A/C.1 and 6/1, p. 3.)

At the 51st meeting of the General Assembly the delegate of Mexico, interpreting Article 2, paragraph 7, said: 'let us not pretend, at every opportunity, to invoke the provisions in Article 2, paragraph 7, in order to evade complying with our fundamental obligations. Let us not invoke it as a clause frustrating other principles contained in the Charter of the United Nations.' (*Ibid.*, No. 54: Suppl. A–/P.V./51, p. 367.)

In the discussion of the treatment of Indians in South Africa the opinion prevailed that a matter ceases to be essentially within the domestic jurisdiction of a state if the matter is regulated by the Charter or another international agreement to which the state is a contracting party. This interpretation of Article 2, paragraph 7, is probably the tacit presupposition of the statement in the resolution which—in spite of the objection of the Union of South Africa, invoking this paragraph—the General Assembly adopted in the case, and which runs as follows: 'The General Assembly . . . is of the opinion that the treatment of Indians in the Union should be in conformity with the international obligations under agreements concluded between the two Governments and the relevant provisions of the Charter.' (Resolutions adopted by the General Assembly, Doc. A/64/Add.1, p. 69.)

It is probable that the latter interpretation corresponds to the intention of those who drafted the Charter. If so, in case of domestic jurisdiction, the following acts of intervention on the part of the United Nations are excluded by Article 2, paragraph 7: recommendations of the General Assembly referred to in Article 10, Article 11, paragraph 2, and Article 14,; calling upon the parties on the part of the Security Council to settle their dispute by peaceful means of their own choice under Article 33, paragraph 2; investigation of the dispute or situation by the Security Council referred to in Article 34; determination by the Security Council whether the continuation of the dispute or situation is likely to endanger the maintanence of international peace and security under the same Article; recommendation of appropriate procedures or methods of adjustment by the Security Council under Article 36, paragraph 1, or Article 37, paragraph 2; recommendation of terms of settlement by the Security Council under Article 37, paragraph 2; further: recommendations of the Security Council referred to in Article 39;[2] ' provisional measures ' taken by the Security Council under Article 40 if not taken as ' enforcement ' measures, that is to say, under the sanction provided for in Article 39.[3] There can be no doubt that the continuance of a dispute arising out of a matter which according to the opinion of one of the contesting parties is essentially within its

[2] According to the amendment suggested by the sponsoring governments at the San Francisco Conference the second sentence of Article 2, paragraph 7, should read as follows: ' but this principle shall not prejudice the application of Chapter VIII, Section B [of the Dumbarton Oaks Proposals, Chapter VII of the Charter].' Under this provision recommendations under Article 39 were possible. In order to exclude such recommendations, upon a motion of the Australian Delegation, the words ' application of Chapter VIII, Section B ' were replaced by the words: ' enforcement measures under Chapter VIII, Section B.' Cf. the Memorandum of the Australian Delegation to Proposed paragraph 8 of Chapter II (Principles), U.N.C.I.O. Doc. 969, I/1/39. The Supplement to Report of Rapporteur, Committee I/1 to Commission I (U.N.C.I.O. Doc. 1070, I/1/34 (1) (*d*), p. 3) contains the statement that the Committee answered the question whether Article 2, paragraph 7, authorises the Security Council to make such recommendations as provided for in Article 39 of the Charter negatively. The *Report to the President*, p. 44, contains the statement that the provision prohibiting the intervention of the Organisation is so phrased 'as to exclude the inference that the Security Council might make a recommendation to a state concerning the way in which a domestic question should be settled.'

As to the privileged position of the five permanent members of the Security Council with respect to the intervention permitted by Article 2, paragraph 7, second sentence, the Australian delegation made the following statement: ' They [the sponsoring governments] can assure their legislatures that these drastic powers of intervention in domestic matters [as suggested by the amendment of the sponsoring powers] can never be put into operation against themselves. What is the position, however, of the remaining members of the Organisation—those forty-five members who have no veto ? The very argument which justifies acceptance of this proposed paragraph by the sponsoring governments destroys the case for its acceptance by the rest.' (U.N.C.I.O. Doc. 969, I/1/39, pp. 3 f.)

[3] Cf. *supra*, pp. 739 ff.

domestic jurisdiction may endanger the maintenance of international peace and security. But, according to the wording of Article 2, paragraph 7, the Security Council is not allowed to investigate such dispute and to determine whether its continuance is likely to endanger the maintenance of international peace and security under Article 34 of the Charter, since this is not an enforcement measure. But the Council may decide to take enforcement action according to Article 39. This Article must be interpreted to mean that to ' make recommendations, or decide what measures shall be taken in accordance with Articles 41 and 42, to maintain or restore international peace and security ' is possible only after the Security Council has determined ' the existence of a threat to the peace, a breach of the peace, or an act of aggression.' This determination has about the same character as the action of the Security Council provided in Article 34 by the terms ' to determine whether the continaunce of the dispute or situation is likely to endanger the maintenance of international peace and security.' The latter action is forbidden by Article 2, paragraph 7 as an intervention which has not the character of an enforcement measure under Chapter VII. To determine the existence of a threat to the peace, breach of the peace, or act of aggression, is certainly a measure under Chapter VII; but it is in itself no enforcement measure under Chapter VII. If Article 2, paragraph 7 is taken literally, the Security Council is not allowed to determine, in a domestic matter, the existence of a threat to the peace, breach of the péace, or act of aggression. Such interpretation however, is hardly possible since Article 39 authorises the Security Council to take enforcement measures only after having determined the existence of a threat to, or breach of, the peace, and since intervention by enforcement measures under Chapter VII is not forbidden in matters which are within the domestic jurisdiction of a state, probably because such intervention is intended as a reaction against a threat to, or breach of, the peace; and if a matter of domestic jurisdiction constitutes a threat to, or breach of, the peace, the principle of non-intervention is considered as not justifiable. It will be, therefore, hardly possible to interpret the second sentence of Article 2, paragraph 7, literally. If intervention by enforcement measures under Chapter VII in matters of domestic jurisdiction is allowed, then intervention by determining the existence of a threat to the peace, breach of the peace, or act of aggression in such matter of domestic jurisdiction must be allowed as well. Then it is not understandable why the Security Council just in domestic jurisdiction matters should be allowed to determine the existence of a threat to the peace, but not allowed to investigate a dispute and to determine whether its continuance is likely to endanger the maintenance of international peace and security; why the Security Council should be allowed to take enforcement actions but not recommend procedure or methods of adjustment and terms of settlement, and how it can take such enforcement measures without investigating the dispute and determining its dangerous character. A reasonable application of the second sentence of Article 2, paragraph 7, is possible only if it is interpreted to mean that the principle laid down in the first sentence shall not prejudice the application of Chapter VII (instead of application of ' enforcement measures under Chapter VII ').[4]

The enforcement measures under Chapter VII are probably intended to be ' sanctions ' to be directed against a state violating its obligations under the Charter. If so, the Members are obliged to refrain from a conduct which, according to the opinion of the Security Council, constitutes a threat to, or breach of, the peace. This obligation goes further than the one stipulated by Article 2, paragraph 4: to refrain from the threat or use of force. Then this provision is not restricted by Article 2, paragraph 7. But, as pointed out,[5] the enforcement actions may be considered to be political measures, not legal sanctions in the strict sense of that term to be directed only against a delinquent state. If this interpretation is accepted, and if Article 2, paragraph 7 is interpreted to restrict the obligations established in Article 2, paragraphs 3 and 4, a Member which, in a conflict arising out of a matter of domestic jurisdiction, does not submit the matter to settlement under the Charter, that is to say, to settlement by peaceful means, but tries to settle the conflict by threat or use of force or in another way that may be considered by the Security Council as threat to, or breach of, the peace, does not violate an obligation imposed upon it by the Charter; but nevertheless exposes itself to enforcement action taken by the Security Council—not as a sanction but as a political measure.

Under Article 2, paragraph 7, as well as under Article 39, the Organisation is authorised, not obliged, to intervene with enforcement measures in a matter of domestic jurisdiction in case of a threat to, or breach of, the peace. Consequently, the Security Council may—for some reason or another—refrain from intervening even in case of threat to, or breach of, the peace. If the Members are not obliged to refrain from threat to, or breach of, the peace (including threat

[4] In the Indonesian question the representative of the Netherlands denied the competence of the Security Council to intervene because according to the opinion of his government the conflict with Indonesia was a matter essentially within the domestic jurisdiction of the Netherlands. (Official Records of the Security Council, 2nd Year, No. 67, p. 1645.) This opinion was shared by the representative of the United Kingdom (*Ibid.*, No. 68, p. 1656). The representative of India interpreted the second sentence of Article 2, paragraph 7, to mean ' that it would be within the jurisdiction of the Security Council to treat of and take the necessary action on even matters which are essentially within the domestic jurisdiction of a State, if those matters have a bearing upon international peace and security. Accordingly, even if, for argument's sake, we agreed with the representative of the United Kingdom that this is a domestic matter, the Security Council would, in the light of the circumstances prevailing today, be justified in taking action under Article 39 of the Charter.' (*Ibid.*, p. 1684.)

[5] Cf. *supra*, pp. 732 ff.

or use of force) in matters which are essentially within their domestic jurisdiction, their situation is different from that which otherwise exists in case the Security Council is not willing or not able to reach a decision under Article 39: In general, inactivity of the Security Council does not justify the parties to a conflict to resort to self-help. Under Article 51 they are allowed to do so only as reaction against an 'armed attack'; self-help is permissible only as self-defence. If, however, the conflict arises out of a matter which is within the domestic jurisdiction of a state and if Article 2, paragraph 7, in connection with Article 39, would be interpreted to establish a restriction of Article 2, paragraph 4, the state within whose domestic jurisdiction the matter is, could resort to force as a means of self-help even when not attacked, without violating the Charter.[6]

The wording of Article 2, paragraph 7, goes probably much farther than the intention of those who drafted it. It is very likely that the authors of the Charter did not intend to release by Article 2, paragraph 7, any Member from the obligation to refrain from the threat or use of force, in the settlement of a conflict arising out of a matter which, in the opinion of that Member, is essentially within its domestic jurisdiction. Probably it was only intended to release the Member from its obligation under Article 2, paragraph 3; although this intention has not been expressed in the text of the Article. The consequence of such interpretation is that conflicts which arise out of a matter of domestic jurisdiction may remain unsettled. If a Member refuses to settle a dispute under Article 33, paragraph 1, claiming the matter to be essentially within its domestic jurisdiction, and if the other party nevertheless refers the dispute under Article 37, paragraph 1, to the Security Council, the latter can intervene only if it assumes the power to decide the question whether the matter actually is essentially within the domestic jurisdiction of the Member making this claim. This the Security Council can do in spite of Article 2, paragraph 7. If the Security Council could not assume this power, any Member could block the intervention of the Organisation in any dispute by pleading domestic jurisdiction. If the enforcement measures provided in Chapter VII are intended to be true 'sanctions' one may assume that the Members are not only under the

[6] The *Report to the President* (p. 45) states: 'It is quite conceivable that there might be an international dispute with reference to such matters as tariff, immigration, or the like, but where such a dispute relates to matters which are essentially domestic in character, settlement through international processes should not be required.' Even if a treaty imposes upon one party to the dispute a definite obligation with respect to the tariff or immigration matter which is the object of the dispute? If the dispute is 'international,' why should settlement through international processes not be required? Besides, Article 2, paragraph 7, does not only forbid 'settlement.' The Report continues: 'It would of course remain true that under the fourth principle, neither party to the dispute would be justified in resorting to force.' This is a possible but not a necessary conclusion from Article 2, paragraph 7.

obligation established in Article 2, paragraph 4, to 'refrain from the threat or use of force' but also under the obligation to refrain from 'any threat to the peace, breach of the peace, or act of aggression'—the conditions of enforcement measures established in Article 39. The latter obligation would be broader than the former and not restricted to 'international relations' in contradistinction to 'domestic matters.' The consequence of such interpretation would be that even in a matter of domestic jurisdiction the obligation to refrain from any threat to the peace, breach of the peace or act of aggression would prevail. If it is further assumed that the Security Council, in spite of the wording of Article 2, paragraph 7, is authorised to determine the violation of this obligation also in case of a dispute arising out of a matter of domestic jurisdiction, the Security Council may consider the refusal to settle the conflict by pacific means under Article 33, paragraph 1, as a 'threat to the peace' and take enforcement action against the Member concerned. It is obvious that this interpretation would completely paralyse the effect of the first sentence of Article 2, paragraph 7.

2. Self-Defence (Article 51)

Although the right of self-defence is supposed to be established by a rule of general international law which has the character of *jus cogens* so that it cannot be affected by any treaty, it has been considered not as superfluous to stipulate this right expressly in the Charter. Neither the Covenant of the League of Nations nor the Pact of Paris[7] contained an analogous provision.

Article 51 of the Charter runs as follows:—

> Nothing in the present Charter shall impair the inherent right of individual or collective self-defence if an armed attack occurs against a Member of the United Nations, until the Security Council has taken the measures necessary to maintain international peace and security. Measures taken by Members in the exercise of this right of self-defence shall be immediately reported to the Security Council and shall not in any way affect the authority and responsibility of the Security Council under the present Charter to take at any time such action as it deems necessary in order to maintain or restore international peace and security.

This provision presupposes the existence of the right of self-defence as established, not by positive international law, but by natural law, for it speaks of an 'inherent' right. This is a theoretical opinion

[7] In his speech of March 15, 1928, before the Council on Foreign Relations, New York (published as Special Supplement to *Foreign Affairs*, Vol. 6, No. 3) Mr. Kellogg declared: 'This right [of self-defence] is so inherent and universal that it was not deemed necessary even to insert it expressly in the treaty.'

of the legislator which has no legal importance. The effect of Article 51 would not change if the term 'inherent' were dropped. In declaring that nothing in the Charter shall impair the inherent right of self-defence, the Charter confers such right upon the Members, whether positive general international law or natural law establishes it or not. The right of self-defence means in this connection: the authorisation of the Members to use force in order to defend themselves against an armed attack. This right constitutes an important restriction of the obligation of the Members to refrain from the threat or use of force (Article 2, paragraph 4) and of the provision of Article 53, paragraph 1, that 'no enforcement action shall be taken under regional arrangements or by regional agencies without the authorisation of the Security Council.' The Charter does not maintain very consistently the presupposed idea of an 'inherent' right of self-defence, which implies that this right exists independently from positive law and hence cannot be altered by it. For the Charter extends this right in one respect and limits it in the other.

The right of self-defence, according to the natural-law doctrine, is the right of an individual, or a state, to defend his person, property, or honour against a real or imminent attack. It is a right of the attacked or threatened individual or state, and of no other individual or state. Article 51 confers the right to use force not only upon the attacked state but also upon other states which unite with the attacked state in order to assist it in its defence. This is probably the meaning of the term 'collective self-defence.' If so, the term 'collective self-defence' is not quite correct. It is certainly collective 'defence,' but not collective 'self'-defence. Collective defence exists if two or more states organise their defence against attack from third states by concluding a treaty obliging or authorising the contracting parties to assist one another in case one of them is attacked by a third state. The action on the part of the states which are not attacked, but only assist the attacked state against its aggressor, is not exactly 'self'-defence.

According to Article 51, treaties of assistance for the purpose of collective defence are allowed. The action characterised by Article 51 as 'collective self-defence' may be a collective action organised by such treaties of assistance, a collective enforcement action to be taken against the state guilty of an armed attack against one of the contracting parties to the treaty of assistance. Such enforcement action may be very similar to the enforcement action which the Security Council—within the system of collective security—is authorised to take against aggressors under Article 39.

According to its wording, Article 51 establishes a right of Members. The first sentence refers only to an armed attack 'against a Member'; and the second sentence refers only 'to measures taken by Members in the exercise of this right of self-defence.' Hence the term

' collective self-defence ' may be interpreted to cover only assistance given by Members to attacked Members and only defence treaties concluded by Members. However, if Article 2, paragraph 6, is to be interpreted to mean that the obligation to refrain from threat and use of force is imposed also upon non-member states, it may be assumed that the right of self-defence as stipulated in Article 51 cannot be denied to non-members, and that the Security Council is authorised to ensure that non-members act in accordance with the second sentence of Article 51, that is to say, to report to the Security Council the measures they have taken in the exercise of this right. For this is certainly ' necessary for the maintenance of international peace and security.' Then, there is no reason to deny the Members the right to assist non-members in their defence against an armed attack and to conclude defence treaties with non-members.

Such defence treaties may be regional arrangements referred to in Article 52.[8] If so, the rule of Article 53, paragraph 1: ' no

[8] Such a regional arrangement is the Inter-American Treaty of Reciprocal Assistance signed at the Inter-American Conference for the Maintenance of Continental Peace and Security at Rio de Janeiro on September 2, 1947. Articles 3–8 of this Treaty read as follows:

ARTICLE 3

1. The High Contracting Parties agree that an armed attack by any state against an American State shall be considered as an attack against all the American States and, consequently, each one of the said Contracting Parties undertakes to assist in meeting the attack in the exercise of the inherent right of individual or collective self-defence recognised by Article 51 of the Charter of the United Nations.

2. On the request of the State or States directly attacked and until the decision of the Organ of Consultation of the Inter-American System, each one of the Contracting Parties may determine the immediate measures which it may individually take in fulfilment of the obligation contained in the preceding paragraph and in accordance with the principle of continental solidarity. The Organ of Consultation shall meet without delay for the purpose of examining those measures and agreeing upon the measures of a collective character that should be taken.

3. The provisions of this Article shall be applied in case of any armed attack which takes place within the region described in Article 4 or within the territory of an American State. When the attack takes place outside of the said areas, the provisions of Article 6 shall be applied.

4. Measures of self-defence provided for under this Article may be taken until the Security Council of the United Nations has taken the measures necessary to maintain international peace and security.

ARTICLE 4

The region to which this Treaty refers is bounded as follows: beginning at the North Pole; thence due south to a point 74 degrees north latitude, 10 degrees west longitude; thence by a rhumb line to a point 47 degrees 30 minutes north latitude, 50 degrees west longitude; thence by a rhumb line to a point 35 degrees north latitude, 60 degrees west longitude; thence

enforcement-action shall be taken under regional arrangements or by regional agencies without the authorisation of the Security Council' must be interpreted not to refer to enforcement actions taken under

due south to a point in 20 degrees north latitude; thence by a rhumb line to a point 5 degrees north latitude, 24 degrees west longitude; thence due south to the South Pole; thence due north to a point 30 degrees south latitude, 90 degrees west longitude; thence by a rhumb line to a point on the Equator at 97 degrees west longitude; thence by a rhumb line to a point 15 degrees north latitude, 120 degrees west longitude; thence by a rhumb line to a point 50 degrees north latitude, 170 degrees east longitude; thence due north to a point in 54 degrees north latitude; thence by a rhumb line to a point 65 degrees 30 minutes north latitude, 168 degrees 58 minutes 5 seconds west longitude; thence due north to the North Pole.

Article 5

The High Contracting Parties shall immediately send to the Security Council of the United Nations, in conformity with Articles 51 and 54 of the Charter of the United Nations, complete information concerning the activities undertaken or in contemplation in the exercise of the right of self-defence or for the purpose of maintaining inter-American peace and security.

Article 6

If the inviolability or the integrity of the territory or the sovereignty or political independence of any American State should be affected by an aggression which is not an armed attack or by an extra-continental or intra-continental conflict, or by any other fact or situation that might endanger the peace of America, the Organ of Consultation shall meet immediately in order to agree on the measures which must be taken in case of aggression to assist the victim of the aggression or, in any case, the measures which should be taken for the common defence and for the maintenance of the peace and security of the Continent.

Article 7

In the case of a conflict between two or more American States, without prejudice to the right of self-defence in conformity with Article 51 of the Charter of the United Nations, the High Contracting Parties, meeting in consultation shall call upon the contending States to suspend hostilities and restore matters to the *statu quo ante bellum*, and shall take in addition all other necessary measures to re-establish or maintain inter-American peace and security and for the solution of the conflict by peaceful means. The rejection of the pacifying action will be considered in the determination of the aggressor and in the application of the measures which the consultative meeting may agree upon.

Article 8

For the purposes of this Treaty, the measures on which the Organ of Consultation may agree will comprise one or more of the following: recall of chiefs of diplomatic missions; breaking of diplomatic relations; breaking of consular relations; partial or complete interruption of economic relations or of rail, sea, air, postal, telegraphic, telephonic, and radiotelephonic or radiotelegraphic communications; and use of armed force.

Another regional arrangement containing provisions for an implementation of Article 51 of the Charter is the treaty signed by Belgium, France, Luxembourg,

Article 51; so that the exception mentioned in Article 53: ' measures against enemy states ' is not the only exception to the rule just mentioned.

It is doubtful whether the term ' collective ' self-defence necessarily means that the defence must be organised prior to the

the Netherlands, and Great Britain, at Brussels on March 17, 1948. It contains the following provisions:

ARTICLE 4

If any of the High Contracting Parties should be the object of an armed attack in Europe, the other high contracting parties will, in accordance with the provisions of Article 51 of the Charter of the United Nations, afford the party so attacked all military and other aid and assistance in their power.

ARTICLE 5

All measures taken as a result of the preceding article shall be immediately reported to the Security Council. They shall be terminated as soon as the Security Council has taken the measures necessary to maintain or restore international peace and security.

The present treaty does not prejudice in any way the obligations of the high contracting parties under the provisions of the Charter of the United Nations. It shall not be interpreted as affecting in any way the authority and responsibility of the Security Council under the Charter to take at any time such action as it deems necessary in order to maintain or restore international peace and security.

An international agreement concluded exclusively for the implementation of Article 51 is the North Atlantic Treaty, signed at Washington on April 4, 1949. It contains the following provisions:

PREAMBLE

The parties to this treaty reaffirm their faith in the purposes and principles of the Charter of the United Nations and their desire to live in peace with all peoples and all governments.

They are determined to safeguard the freedom, common heritage and civilisation of their peoples, founded on the principles of democracy, individual liberty and the rule of law.

They seek to promote stability and well-being in the North Atlantic area.

They are resolved to unite their efforts for collective defence and for the preservation of peace and security.

They therefore agree to this North Atlantic treaty:

ARTICLE 1

The parties undertake, as set forth in the Charter of the United Nations, to settle any international disputes in which they may be involved by peaceful means in such a manner that international peace and security, and justice, are not endangered, and to refrain in their international relations from the threat or use of force in any manner inconsistent with the purposes of the United Nations.

ARTICLE 2

The parties will contribute toward the further development of peaceful and friendly international relations by strengthening their free institutions, by bringing about a better understanding of the principles upon which these institutions are founded, and by promoting conditions of stability and well-being. They will seek to eliminate conflict in their international

aggression by an international treaty. It is not impossible to interpret the term to mean that any Member is authorised to assist an attacked Member in its self-defence without having previously concluded with the attacked state a treaty of assistance.

economic policies and will encourage economic collaboration between any or all of them.

ARTICLE 3

In order more effectively to achieve the objectives of this treaty, the parties, separately and jointly, by means of continuous and effective self-help and mutual aid, will maintain and develop their individual and collective capacity to resist armed attack.

ARTICLE 4

The parties will consult together whenever, in the opinion of any of them, the territorial integrity, political independence or security of any of the parties is threatened.

ARTICLE 5

The parties agree that an armed attack against one or more of them in Europe or North America shall be considered an attack against them all; and consequently they agree that, if such an armed attack occurs, each of them, in exercise of the right of individual or collective self-defence recognised by Article 51 of the Charter of the United Nations, will assist the party or parties so attacked by taking forthwith, individually and in concert with the other parties, such action as it deems necessary, including the use of armed force, to restore and maintain the security of the North Atlantic area.

Any such armed attack and all measures taken as a result thereof shall immediately be reported to the Security Council. Such measures shall be terminated when the security council has taken the measures necessary to restore and maintain international peace and security.

ARTICLE 6

For the purpose of Article 5 an armed attack on one or more of the parties is deemed to include an armed attack on the territory of any of the parties in Europe or North America, on the Algerian departments of France, on the occupation forces of any party in Europe, on the islands under the jurisdiction of any party in the North Atlantic area north of the Tropic of Cancer or on the vessels or aircraft in this area of any of the parties.

ARTICLE 7

This treaty does not affect, and shall not be interpreted as affecting, in any way the rights and obligations under the Charter of the parties which are members of the United Nations, or the primary responsibility of the Security Council for the maintenance of international peace and security.

ARTICLE 8

Each party declares that none of the international engagements now in force between it and any other of the parties or any third state is in conflict with the provisions of this treaty, and undertakes not to enter into any international engagement in conflict with this treaty.

ARTICLE 9

The parties hereby establish a council, on which each of them shall be represented, to consider matters concerning the implementation of this

It is hardly possible to consider the right or the duty of a non-attacked state to assist an attacked state as an ' inherent ' right, that is to say, a right established by natural law. On the other hand, the Charter restricts the right of self-defence by stipulating that the right applies only against ' an armed attack,' and only as long as the Security Council ' has not taken the measures necessary to maintain international peace and security.' It is of importance to note that Article 51 does not use the term ' aggression ' but the much narrower concept of ' armed attack,' which means that a merely ' imminent ' attack or any act of aggression which has not the character of an attack involving

treaty. The council shall be so organised as to be able to meet promptly at any time. The council shall set up such subsidiary bodies as may be necessary; in particular, it shall establish immediately a defence committee, which shall recommend measures for the implementation of Articles 3 and 5.

ARTICLE 10

The parties may, by unanimous agreement, invite any other European state in a position to further the principles of this treaty and to contribute to the security of the North Atlantic area to accede to this treaty. Any state so invited may become a party to the treaty by depositing its instrument of accession with the Government of the United States of America. The Government of the United States of America will inform each of the parties of the deposit of each such instrument of accession.

ARTICLE 11

This treaty shall be ratified and its provisions carried out by the parties in accordance with their respective constitutional processes. The instruments of ratification shall be deposited as soon as possible with the Government of the United States of America, which will notify all the other signatories of each deposit. The treaty shall enter into force between the states which have ratified it as soon as the ratifications of the majority of the signatories, including the ratifications of Belgium, Canada, France, Luxembourg, the Netherlands, the United Kingdom and the United States, have been deposited and shall come into effect with respect to other states on the date of the deposit of their ratifications.

ARTICLE 12

After the treaty has been in force 10 years, or at any time thereafter, the parties shall, if any of them so requests, consult together for the purpose of reviewing the treaty, having regard for the factors then affecting peace and security in the North Atlantic area, including the development of universal, as well as regional, arrangements under the charter of the United Nations for the maintenance of international peace and security.

ARTICLE 13

After the treaty has been in force for 20 years, any party may cease to be a party one year after its notice of denunciation has been given to the Government of the United States of America, which will inform the governments of the other parties of the deposit of each notice of denunciation.

ARTICLE 14

This treaty, of which the English and French texts are equally authentic, shall be deposited in the archives of the Government of the United States of America. Duly certified copies thereof will be transmitted by that Government to the Governments of the other signatories.

the use of armed force does not justify resort to force as an exercise of the right established by Article 51.[9] The ' armed attack ' against which the use of force as individual or collective self-defence is permitted, is not restricted to aggressive actions undertaken by Members. The right of self-defence applies also to armed attacks by non-members. However competent to interpret the term ' armed attack ' and to ascertain that an armed attack has occured in a concrete case is the state which considers itself as being attacked, and the other states which are willing to assist it in its defence. These states may understand by ' armed attack ' not only the fact that a state has resorted to war against another state, but also the fact that a state has interfered in the civil war taking place within another state by arming or otherwise assisting the revolutionary group in its fight against the legitimate government.[1] But the state against which the

[9] It is therefore hardly possible to interpret Article 51 to mean that it does not affect the validity of the Monroe doctrine, a provision expressly inserted in the Covenant of the League (Article 21). At the *Hearings* (pp. 649 f.) a Senator asked about the relation of the Monroe Doctrine to the Charter. In answering this question one of the chief official advisers of the United States delegation at San Francisco made the following statement: ' The Monroe Doctrine is a doctrine originally enunciated and pursued as a doctrine of self-defence. The words, as I recall, of the declaration state that the United States would look upon any attempt by a foreign power—a continental power—to extend either its colonial empire or its political system into this hemisphere as a threat to our peace and security. In other words, for 125 years we have sustained the proposition that for a European power to extend its colonial system or its political system to South America is a threat to our national safety. That view has over that period of 125 years been acquiesced in by all the nations of the world. Now, there is nothing whatever in the Charter which impairs a nation's right of self-defence. The prohibition against the use of force is a prohibition against the use of force for purposes inconsistent with the purposes of the Charter. Among the purposes of the Charter is security.—So it is my view—and I so expressed it to the United States Delegation—that there is nothing whatsoever in this Charter that impairs the Monroe Doctrine as a doctrine which has been proclaimed, sustained, and recognised by the world as a doctrine of self-defence.' Even if interpreted as a doctrine of self-defence the Monroe Doctrine is more than a principle proclaiming self-defence against ' armed attack.' In so far as it goes beyond this limit it is not maintained by Article 51. The advisor made also the following statement: ' . . . Of course, you realise that so far as this hemispheric matter is concerned, the Security Council cannot act in this hemisphere without the consent of the United States, so that it virtually is optional to the United States by virtue of its position as a permanent member of the Security Council to determine whether or not action in this hemisphere will be taken in the first instance through the Security Council, or whether we will vote against action by the Security Council, thereby automatically leaving it to the hemispheric defence to act.' The United States, as a permanent member of the Security Council, is certainly in a position to block any action on the part of the Council. But under Article 51 the hemisphere defence can work only as reaction against an ' armed attack,' which is certainly less than the Monroe Doctrine, even in its most restrictive interpretation, implies.

[1] It seems that according to the opinion of the Government of the United States Article 51 was applicable to the relation between Greece on the one hand and Yugoslavia, Bulgaria and Albania, on the other. At the 82nd meeting of the General Assembly on September 17, 1947, the representative of the United States

right of self-defence as established in Article 51 is exercised has the same competence to interpret Article 51; and it is very probable that it will deny to be guilty of an 'armed attack,' especially by interpreting this term in another way than its opponent. Then, the state against which Article 51 is applied might declare this action not

referred to the Investigation Commission established by the Security Council in the Greek case and the fact that 'that Commission and its Subsidiary Group, by large majorities, have attributed the disturbances [in Greece] principally to the illegal assistance and support furnished by Yugoslavia, Albania and Bulgaria to guerrilla forces fighting against the Greek Government.' He declared: 'The extent or effectiveness of such assistance to the Greek guerrillas is not the point at issue here. It is a universally accepted principle of international law that for one nation to arm or otherwise assist rebellious forces against another government is a hostile and aggressive act. Not only has this principle been upheld in a number of famous cases in international law, but it has also found expression in international agreements . . . This Assembly cannot stand by as a mere spectator while a Member of the United Nations is endangered by attacks from abroad. If the United Nations should fail to protect the integrity of one small state, the security of all small states would be placed in jeopardy. The inability of the Security Council to take effective action in this case passes on a grave responsibility to the General Assembly.' At the 86th meeting of the General Assembly, the delegate of Greece stated that 'Albania, Bulgaria and Yugoslavia are sending arms and munitions across the Greek frontier with the object of destroying the political independence and territorial integrity of a Member State of the United Nations,' that his country is being 'attacked' in this way. He characterised the activity of the three neighbour states as 'an aggression against Greece' and as an 'international crime.' He again expressly referred to this act of aggression as to an 'attack' against Greece. (Official Records of the Second Session of the General Assembly, Plenary Meetings, Vol. I, pp. 20, 146 ff.)

On September 25, 1947, the representative of the United States submitted to the Political and Security Committee of the General Assembly a draft resolution which contained the following provision: the General Assembly of the United Nations 'Finds that Albania, Bulgaria and Yugoslavia, in contravention of principles of the Charter of the United Nations, have given assistance and support to the guerrillas fighting against the Greek Government; Calls upon Albania, Bulgaria and Yugoslavia to cease and desist from rendering any further assistance or support in any form to the guerrillas fighting against the Greek Government . . . ' (United Nations Weekly Bulletin, Vol III, No. 15, p. 454.) The purpose of the proposal, which was not accepted, was evidently to substitute for the blocked Security Council the General Assembly. If the Assembly would 'find' that Yugoslavia, Bulgaria and Albania were responsible for an action which in the opinion of Greece and other Members willing to assist Greece, was an armed attack within the meaning of Article 51, then the state of uncertainty which—as pointed out—prevails in the application of Article 51 until the Security Council intervenes, could be—if not avoided, so at least reduced. Neither Yugoslavia—a Member state, nor Bulgaria and Albania—non-member states, would be bound by such a 'finding' of the General Assembly, and Yugoslavia, if Greece and her allies would resort to war against that state, could claim to exercise herself, the right of self-defence under Article 51. But Greece and her allies, applying Article 51, were morally backed in their contention to exercise self-defence against an armed attack. It is, however, more than doubtful whether in a case of individual or collective self-defence the General Assembly is competent to 'find' the facts, which according to Article 51 condition the exercise of this right. This is a prerogative of the Security Council.

as legitimate self-defence but as an illegal attack, against which it considers itself entitled to exercise self-defence. In such case the question as to which state exercises the right of self-defence and which state is guilty of an illegal attack, remains undecided until the only organ of the United Nations competent to decide whether an armed attack occurred and who is responsible for it, the Security Council, intervenes. As soon as the Security Council takes the measures necessary to restore peace, the competence to interpret the term 'armed attack' and to ascertain whether an armed attack has occurred in a concrete case, is transferred to this organ. The Member states acting under Article 51 are, according to Article 25 of the Charter, obliged 'to accept and carry out the decisions of the Security Council' in this respect. Under Article 51, the state which according to the opinion of the Security Council is the victim of the armed attack and the states assisting it in its defence are obliged to stop the use of force as soon as the Council has taken the necessary measures, provided these measures do not involve enforcement action ordered by the Council to be taken by the attacked state or its allies.

Collective self-defence under Article 51 must be distinguished from the system of collective security as established by the Charter in Article 1, paragraph 1, Article 24, paragraph 1, and Articles 39, 41, and 42. Collective self-defence under Article 51 is certainly an 'effective collective measure,' but not the collective 'measure' referred to in Articles 1, 24, 39, 41, and 42. The difference between collective self-defence under Article 51 and the measures of collective security taken under Articles 39, 41, or 42, is that the latter are actions of the Organisation whereas the former are actions of individual Members of the United Nations; that, consequently, the question as to whether there exists an act of aggression is to be decided in the first case by a central organ of the United Nations whereas in the latter case—at least provisionally—by each Member acting under Article 51; and, finally, that enforcement action taken by the Security Council as a measure of collective security is the ordinary and by the Charter intended reaction against a breach of the peace committed by an act of aggression, whereas the collective self-defence under Article 51 is purposed by the Charter as a provisional measure permitted only 'until the Security Council has taken the measures necessary to maintain international peace and security.' That is to say: Individual and collective self-defence are admitted only 'until' the machinery of collective security is put into action. The use of the term 'until' and the obligation imposed on the Members to report immediately to the Security Council the measures taken under Article 51 show that the application of this Article is intended by the Charter only as a temporary measure; not as a substitute for the collective security to be realised by the Organisation. Until the Council intervenes there exists, as pointed out, a state of uncertainty regarding the question which state is exercising its right of self-defence in the armed conflict to which Article 51 refers, and which state is responsible for an armed attack. An unambiguous application of Article 51 is possible only when the Security Council has taken the measures necessary to restore peace. It must be admitted, however, that the wording of Article 51 does not exclude its application—by both parties to the armed conflict—in case the system of collective security is blocked because the Security Council is, for some reason or another, not able to fulfil its function with respect to an armed attack actually undertaken against a Member of the United Nations.

In order to enable the Security Council to take on time the measures necessary to maintain international peace and security, ' measures taken by Members in the exercise of this right of self-defence shall be immediately reported to the Security Council.' Reported by whom ? Probably by the states which have taken the measures. If this is the intended meaning of the sentence, it would have been correct to say: The states which exercise this right of self-defence shall immediately report the measures taken by them to the Security Council, for it is obviously intended to establish an obligation of the Members (and through Article 2, paragraph 6 of non-member states) to report to the Security Council.

The obligation to stop the exercise of the right of self-defence is conditioned by the fact that the Security Council ' has taken the measures necessary to maintain international peace and security.' It is significant that Article 51 does not provide: until the Security Council has taken enforcement action against the state guilty of an armed attack. The Security Council may take any ' measures necessary to maintain international peace and security,' ' to maintain,' and not as it is usually formulated: ' to maintain or to restore international peace and security,' although in case an ' armed attack ' has occurred and thus peace has been broken, only ' to restore ' and not to ' maintain ' peace seems to be possible. It may be doubted whether enforcement measures for the purpose of restoring the peace, broken by an armed attack within the meaning of Article 51, must be taken under Article 39, that is to say, that the Security Council before taking such measures must determine the existence of an act of aggression. For Article 39 is not referred to in Article 51. However, Article 51 is placed in Chapter VII, and Article 39 stipulates that the Security Council shall determine the existence of ' any ' threat to the peace, breach of the peace or act of aggression; and an armed attack is an act of aggression. [2] Hence it may be assumed that any action taken by the Security Council under Article 51 is to be one of the measures referred to in Articles 39, 41, and 42. These measures need not necessarily be enforcement measures. They may be

[2] Cf. *supra*, p. 542.

'recommendations' made under Article 39. They may be enforcement measures not involving the use of armed force. If they are enforcement measures involving the use of armed force, the Council may, under Article 48, decide that the Member or Members exercising the right of individual or collective self-defence under Article 51 shall continue to act against the aggressor, but that they shall do so in execution of the decision the Security Council has taken in this case for the maintenance of peace. That is to say, the Security Council may call upon the Member or Members exercising the right of self-defence to make available to the Council the armed forces held in reserve in accordance with the special agreements which they have concluded under Article 43 for the enforcement action decided by the Council in this case. Then, the action of the Member or Members, which began as the exercise of the right of self-defence, is transformed into an action of the United Nations for the restoration of peace.[8] If it is assumed that the Security Council can take under Article 51 only the measures referred to in Article 39, enforcement action involving the use of armed force under Article 51 is possible only after the agreements referred to in Article 43 of the Charter have come into force.

Who is competent to decide the question whether the Security Council has taken the measures 'necessary' to maintain international peace and security? The Security Council itself exclusively, or the state or states exercising the right of self defence? The Charter does not say in the first sentence of Article 51—as it says in the last sentence:—measures which the Council deems necessary. An interpretation of the first sentence is not excluded according to which a state is not obliged to cease to exercise its right of self-defence when it has reported to the Security Council and the Council has taken measures which, according to the opinion of the state, are not the measures 'necessary to maintain international peace and security.'

[8] Article 17 of the General Principles Governing the Organisation of the Armed Forces Made Available to the Security Council by Member Nations of the United Nations (*Yearbook*, p. 425) laid down in the report of the Military Staff Committee as accepted by the Chinese and French delegations provides:

> In case of self-defence (Article 51 of the Charter) and of national emergencies, Member Nations will have the right to make use of armed forces, which they have made available to the Security Council in conformity with the terms of special agreements. They undertake, however, to assume anew all of their obligations within the shortest possible space of time.

This provision is not accepted by the Soviet Union, the United Kingdom, and the United States. At the 139th meeting of the Security Council the delegate of the Soviet Union declared with respect to this provision: 'The inclusion of such a provision in the General Principles might be utilised in some cases to evade fulfilment of the obligations undertaken by States under the agreements. This could be done on the pretext that it was necessary to use the armed forces contributed for other purposes having nothing in common with the tasks of maintaining international security, and carrying out international measures to this end.' (Official Records of the Security Council, 2nd Year, No. 44, p. 978.)

This interpretation may be confirmed by the doctrine that the right of self-defence is conferred upon the states by a rule of general international law which has the character of *jus cogens* and consequently cannot be altered by treaty provisions. The opinion of the state victim of the illegal attack may be quite different from the opinion of the Security Council about the measures which are 'necessary' in the case concerned. It was probably not the intention of the legislator to confer upon the attacked state the power to decide whether the measures taken by the Security Council are adequate. His idea was probably that a state is allowed to exercise its right of self-defence until the Security Council has taken the measures which the Security Council deems necessary to restore peace. But this idea is not unambiguously expressed in Article 51.[4]

Any decision of the Security Council to take measures necessary for the maintenance or restoration of peace, and especially the decision to take enforcement measures requires, according to Article 27, paragraph 3, an affirmative vote of seven members including the concurring votes of the permanent members. This provision makes it possible that even in case of armed attack, referred to in Article 51, no decision of the Security Council can be reached. If in case of an armed attack within the meaning of Article 51 enforcement measures are necessary to restore the peace, the Security Council, as pointed out, must first of all determine under Article 39, the existence of an act of aggression. What is the consequence if the voting on this question does not result in an affirmative decision ? Does it mean that no armed attack exists and that the State which claims to exercise its right of self-defence has to stop its action ? Certainly not. For the fact that the Security Council does not take a decision is not equivalent to the condition under which the exercise of the right of self-defence must cease, namely that the 'Security

The British Commentary on the Charter of the United Nations, Presented by the Secretary of State for Foreign Affairs to Parliament by Command of His Majesty, Comd. 6666, London, 1945, p. 9, states with reference to Article 51: 'It will be for the Security Council to decide whether these measures have been taken and whether they are adequate for the purpose. In the event of the Security Council failing to take any action, or if such action as it does take is clearly inadequate, the right of self-defence could be invoked by any Member or group of Members as justifying any action they thought fit to take.' If it is for the Security Council to decide whether the measures taken by it are adequate, it is not very likely that an action taken by the Security Council will be declared by this body as 'clearly inadequate.' It seems as if the Commentary supposes that the Member concerned is entitled to decide whether the action taken by the Security Council is 'clearly inadequate,' whereas the Council has to decide whether it is adequate. This is hardly consistent. The question of adequacy must always be decided by someone. 'Clearly' perhaps means: self-evident, no decision necessary. But such a situation does not exist in law. There are no facts in itself, only facts established by the competent authorities. The question: who is the competent authority, can never be avoided.

Council has taken the necessary measure to maintain international peace and security.' The opinion of the Security Council that no armed attack exists which would justify the use of force on the part of the state which claims to exercise a right of self-defence, must be expressed by a positive decision by which the Security Council declares the action of the state (or states) which claims to exercise the right of self-defence as an act of aggression. But in order to exercise the right of self-defence under Article 51, the state or states concerned need not wait until the Security Council by a decision has determined the existence of an act of aggression.[5] The action of the Security Council under Article 51 is by its very nature subsequent to the action by which a Member exercises its right of self-defence. In case a state which has a permanent seat in the Security Council or a state protected by a permanent member is the aggressor, the action of the Council is practically excluded. Hence the right of individual and collective self-defence as established by Article 51 may play a greater role than it might be expected to play within an organisation whose main purpose is to make the exercise of this right superfluous.[6] The provision of the second sentence of Article 51: that measures taken by Members in the exercise of the right of self-defence 'shall not in any way affect the authority and responsibility of the Security Council under the present Charter to take at any time such action as it deems necessary in order to maintain or restore international peace and security,' is difficult to understand. How can an action taken by a Member affect the competence of the Security Council, especially if this action must stop at the very moment the Security Council is taking the measures which it deems necessary to maintain or restore international peace and security? If the meaning of the sentence is that the right of self-defence of the Members shall not affect the competence of the Council, the sentence seems to be superfluous. That the Security Council is authorised in case of an armed attack 'to take at any time such action as it deems necessary in order to

5 In Sub-Committee 3 of the Interim Committee of the General Assembly during the discussion of the problem of voting in the Security Council the representative of Turkey stated that the decision by which the Security Council determines the existence of a threat to the peace, breach of the peace, or act of aggression, should not be subject to the unanimity rule. (Doc. A/AC.18/62, p. 24.) At the 16th meeting of the Interim Committee on July 7, 1948, he referred to this statement and declared: 'If the principle of unanimity were applied to that category of decision, the victim of aggression might be deprived of the rights conferred upon it by the Charter.' 'His proposal was intended to prevent beyond all doubt that a victim of aggression should be denied its right under Article 51.' (Doc. A/AC.18/SR.16, pp. 8, 9.) However, the exercise of the right of self-defence does not presuppose a decision of the Security Council under Article 39.

6 At the 20th meeting of Committee III/1 of the San Francisco Conference (U.N.C.I.O. Doc. 967, III/1/48), the delegate of the United States observed 'that if a major power became the aggressor the Council had no power to prevent war. In such case the inherent right of self-defence applied, and the nations of the world must decide whether or not they would go to war.'

maintain or restore international peace and security,' follows already from the first sentence of Article 51. It could be objected that the first sentence refers only to the 'authority,' not to the 'responsibility' of the Security Council to take at any time such action as it deems necessary. But, the 'responsibility' of the Security Council to take such action is sufficiently established by other provisions of the Charter, *e.g.*, Articles 24 and 39.

3. Action in Relation to Former Enemy States (Articles 53, 107)

Article 107 constitutes an important restriction on the obligations of the Members, especially on their obligation to refrain from the threat or use of force, as well as on the functions of the Organisation. This Article runs as follows:—

> Nothing in the present Charter shall invalidate or preclude action, in relation to any state which during the Second World War has been an enemy of any signatory to the present Charter, taken or authorised as a result of that war by the Governments having responsibility for such action.

The Article refers in the first place to actions directed against ex-enemy states. Any action, especially action taken by force, forbidden by the Charter, is not forbidden if directed against an ex-enemy state. This action is limited in so far only as it should be 'a result' of the Second World War and 'taken or authorised by the Governments having responsibility for such action.' But what does it mean that an action is a 'result' of the war, and which Governments have responsibility for such action? The most reasonable answer to these questions would be: actions authorised by armistice—surrender—or peace treaties, actions for which the states parties to these arrangements have responsibility. But such restriction of the action referred to in Article 107 is not stipulated.[7] The Report of Committee 3 to Commission III on Chapter XII (Dumbarton Oaks Proposals, corresponding to Chapter XVII of the Charter) contains the following statement of the delegate of the United Kingdom: 'It would be impossible to limit this action, as proposed by the Australian Delegate, to that decided upon in an armistice, a peace treaty, or a joint declaration like the Declaration of Moscow, because responsibility, as envisaged in paragraph 2 [of Chapter XII of the Dumbarton Oaks Proposals corresponding to Article 107 of the Charter] could fall

[7] At the 17th meeting of Committee III/3 of the San Francisco Conference the delegate of Canada declared that the text of paragraph 2, Chapter XII of the Dumbarton Oaks Proposals (corresponding to Article 107 of the Charter) 'was so unlimited as to time and scope that it could exempt practically anything from Council action. He agreed that the Council should have no responsibility for military measures to be taken against Germany and Japan, but he reluctantly stated that he would vote against the two paragraphs as they stood.' (U.N.C.I.O. Doc. 765, III/3/39.)

upon a state which is party to none of these acts.'[8] Another document of Committee III/3 contains the following statement: 'The United Kingdom Delegate . . . said that it would be unwise to limit the definition of the expression "Governments having responsibility for such action" to governments parties to armistice terms, peace treaties, and the Moscow Declaration. It was conceivable that in some cases there would be no peace treaty and that a government which had not been a party either to the Moscow Declaration or to an instrument of surrender might be called upon to assume some degree of responsibility for action in regard to an enemy state.'[9]

The result of the negotiations in Committee III/3 of the San Francisco Conference was that no formula limiting the action referred to in Article 107, or the governments responsible for such action, has been inserted in the text of the Article. According to its wording, any action against ex-enemy states is permitted to any government if the action can be justified as a result of World War II. Since Article 107 does not restrict the action to action authorised by any special agreement and since no special authority is designated to decide the question as to whether an action is to be considered as 'a result of the Second World War,' the decision of this question is left to the government which takes the action or authorises another government to take it.[1] That means that the formula 'as a result of that war' does not imply any serious restriction. The wording of Article 107: 'action in relation to any state which . . .' includes not only actions against ex-enemy states but also actions taken with the consent of an ex-enemy state, such as treaties especially peace treaties with these states, and actions of a Member state taking place on the territory of an ex-enemy state occupied by Member states. If it was the intention of Article 107 to leave the conclusion of the peace treaties to the Member states which have been at war with the ex-enemy states, the provision was superfluous. The Charter does not and cannot prevent that the peace treaties will be concluded by those who—under general international law—are competent to conduct these legal transactions: by the belligerents. The Charter could only provide that the peace treaties should not contain provisions inconsistent with the Charter. But the Charter did not impose upon the Members such obligation. The contents of the peace treaties with the states which have been enemies to any signatory of the Charter

[8] U.N.C.I.O. Doc. 1095, III/3/50, p. 4.

[9] U.N.C.I.O. Doc. 1161, III/3/53.

[1] As to the meaning of the expression 'action taken or authorised' the delegate of the United Kingdom declared 'that, in his opinion, the distinction is made between "positive" and "negative" action; that is to say, between action with respect to enemy States by the governments responsible for this action, and the action which the responsible governments had authorised other governments to take.' (Report of Committee III/3 on Chapter XII [Dumbarton Oaks Proposals, corresponding to Chapter XVII of the Charter] (U.N.C.I.O. Doc. 1095, III/3/50, p. 4).)

during the Second World War is not restricted by the Charter. Article 103 of the Charter providing that in case of a conflict between the obligations of the Member states under the Charter and their obligations under any other international agreement, their obligations under the Charter shall prevail, does not apply to treaties with ex-enemy states, especially not to the peace treaties. This is an important consequence of Article 107. But that does not mean that the Organisation has no competence at all with respect to questions which are to be settled by the peace treaties. The competence of the Organisation is restricted by Article 107 only in so far as no organ of the United Nations has the power to 'invalidate or preclude,' by its act, action taken or authorised by a responsible government as a result of World War II in relation to an ex-enemy state. Hence discussion and mere recommendations of action in relation to former enemy states are not excluded from the competence of the General Assembly or the Security Council, since they do not imply invalidation or preclusion of such action.[2] The term 'action in relation to' an ex-enemy state might be interpreted to include also action by one Member state against another if this action has any relation to a former enemy state. But this was probably not the intention of those who drafted Article 107. This results from another provision of the Charter which expressly refers to Article 107,

[2] During the discussion of the problem of Korean independence in the First Committee of the General Assembly, the delegate of the Ukrainian Soviet Socialist Republic pointed out 'that questions connected with the conclusion of peace treaties and their subsequent execution did not fall within the competence of the United Nations.' Also the delegate of the Soviet Union declared 'that the problem of Korea was not within the competence of the United Nations.' But the delegate of Australia pointed out 'that Article 107 of the Charter did not preclude examination of this question by the United Nations, since the General Assembly had the necessary competence to recommend if not to carry out measures.' (A/C.1/SR. 87.) At the 112th meeting of the General Assembly the representative of Poland declared that the problem of Korea 'belonged to the questions of the liquidation of the consequences of the war—problems which similar to the problems of peace treaties and others, are not within the province of our Organisation and for the consideration of which other organs have been created.' Also the delegate of Norway stated that 'the problem of the peace settlement with ex-enemy states of which this question of the independence of Korea is a part, does not at first hand belong to the matters to be dealt with by our Organisation. (Doc. A/P.V. 112.) At the 90th meeting of the General Assembly the delegate of the Soviet Union stated: 'The Charter clearly leaves no doubt that under Article 107 questions such as that of the Peace Treaty with Italy are not subject to discussion by the General Assembly.' But the delegate of Australia stated: 'All those who took part in the drafting of the Charter at San Francisco know the exact purpose for the inclusion of that Article. It was simply to make it clear that the belligerent countries responsible for the defeat of the enemies in the Second World War, shall have the right to proceed to make the treaty. There is nothing in the Charter that stops it, but neither is there anything in the Charter which prevents situations created by any treaty from being brought before the General Assembly for discussion.' (Official Records of the Second Session of the General Assembly, Plenary Meetings, Vol. I, pp. 277, 280.)

namely Article 53, paragraph 1, which speaks of ' measures against any enemy state . . . provided for pursuant to Article 107 . . . '[3] The intention of Article 107 is to exclude the enemy states from the protection granted by the Charter to all other states; and this protection consists in the obligations of the Members to refrain in their international relations from the threat or use of force, and to settle their international disputes by peaceful means, and in the power of the Organisation to react against violations of these obligations. Article 107 is not intended to apply to conflicts between Members of the United Nations, even if these conflicts are in some relation to former enemy states.[4]

[3] At the 16th meeting of Committee III/3 of the San Francisco Conference the delegate of the United States stated that ' in respect to paragraph 2 of Chapter XII [of the Dumbarton Oaks Proposals, corresponding to Article 107 of the Charter] he felt that the Organisation had no responsibility in respect to surrender terms or peace settlements, and that no steps should be taken in the Charter to hinder action against the enemy on the part of the victors in the war.' (U.N.C.I.O. Doc. 704, III/3/36, p. 4.) In a statement submitted to Commission III, the Australian delegation interpreted paragraph 2 of Chapter XII to mean ' that certain Governments will have special responsibility to take action or to authorise action against enemy states as a result of the present war.' (U.N.C.I.O. Doc. 1150, III/12, p. 35.)

[4] In the conflict between the United States, Great Britain and France on the one hand and the Soviet Union on the other, which had arisen as the result of the imposition by the Soviet Government of restrictions on transport and communications between the western zones of occupation in Germany and Berlin, brought before the Security Council by a letter of the three first mentioned powers to the Secretary-General dated September 29, 1948 (cf. *supra*, p. 443), the delegate of the Soviet Union, at the 361st meeting of the Security Council, denied the jurisdiction of the Security Council referring to Article 107. This denial of the Council's jurisdiction was based on an interpretation of Article 107 according to which this provision referred to any action having any relation whatever to an ex-enemy state, even if such action constituted a conflict between two Member states and as such a threat to the peace. The representative of the Soviet Union declared: ' There can be no question that the situation in Berlin is not closely bound up with the question of Germany as a whole and that any separation of the question of the situation in Berlin from the problem of Germany as a whole would be completely artificial and would merely lead to erroneous and unpractical decision. To refer the Berlin question to the Security Council would be a direct violation of Article 107 of the United Nations Charter. According to Article 107 of the United Nations Charter, the Berlin question, forming as it does a part of the question of Germany as a whole, belongs to the competence of those Governments which are responsible for the occupation of Germany, and consequently, it is not a matter which can be considered by the Security Council. In fact, as regards Germany in general and in (?)Berlin in particular, there exists a whole series of important international agreements and treaties signed by the four Powers. . . . in view of the special international agreements and treaties signed by the great Powers, the whole problem of Germany, including the Berlin question, is a matter to be settled by the Governments which bear the responsibility for the occupation of Germany; this problem cannot, therefore, be allowed to come up for consideration before any other body than that defined in the international agreements under which are the signatures of the great Powers. That, in short, is the principle proclaimed in Article 107 of the United Nations Charter, which makes it clear that the responsibility for conditions in the territories of enemy countries controlled by allied Governments devolves

Action against former enemy states may be taken not only under Article 107, but also under Article 53 which provides:

> 1. The Security Council shall, where appropriate, utilise such [as referred to in Article 52] regional arrangements or

on those same Governments. It follows, therefore, that all questions arising in connection with such control, including the question of the situation in Berlin, have to be decided through direct negotiations between the Governments responsible under the above international agreements for the state of things in Germany as a whole and in any of its parts or sectors, and particularly, of course, in Berlin, its capital.' The delegate of the United States, in order to justify the competence of the Security Council, made the following statements: 'Article 107 of the Charter was not designed to prevent any disputes among the victorious Powers from coming to the Security Council, but to prevent interference by the former enemy States in any action taken by the victorious Powers within the agreed realm of their responsibility. In other words, Article 107, while precluding appeals to United Nations organs by defeated enemy States concerning action taken against them during the period of military occupation by the responsible allied Powers, does not prevent one of the allied Powers from bringing its differences with other allied Powers to the attention of United Nations organs for consideration according to the provisions of Chapters IV, VI or VII of the Charter; much less would it preclude consideration by the Security Council of action by a Member of the United Nations constituting a threat to the peace . . . Furthermore, the language of Article 107 refers to action in relation to former enemy States; it does not refer to action by a victorious Power in the territory of former enemy States against or in relation to another Member of the United Nations. This sense of the Article is specifically evident from the language of Article 53, paragraph 1, where the Charter refers to: ". . . measures against any enemy State . . . provided for pursuant to Article 107 . . .".' After having referred to the discussions of Article 107 in Committee 3 of Commission III of the San Francisco Conference, he concluded: 'Thus it is apparent that there is nothing in the Charter that prevents the Security Council or the General Assembly from assuming jurisdiction over matters that involve the enemy States, when necessary to remove a threat to the peace created by the action of one of the Members of the United Nations against three other Members.' (Official Records of the Security Council, 3rd year, No. 113, pp. 10 ff, 19 ff.) The representative of the United Kingdom declared that the sole object of Article 107 was 'to leave the hands of the Allied Powers free as regards any action they might think it necessary to take in relation to one of the enemy States, either in the continuance of actual hostilities or as regards post-hostility action, such as the occupation of enemy territory, the enforcement of transfers of territory under a peace treaty, exacting reparations, and so on. But for a provision of this kind, much of the action which the Allies might legitimately wish to take and might have to take in relation to the enemy States might have been technically inconsistent with the purposes and principles of the Charter—for instance, the principle of not using force. Further, the hands of the Allies might have been tied completely as regards their post hostility dealings with the enemy States and as regards the eventual peace treaties or arrangements.' As to the terms of Article 107, he stated 'that the only case that comes under Article 107 is one of action taken—these are the words—" in relation to " an enemy State. The U.S.S.R. action, of which the Western Powers are complaining, has not however been taken in relation to Germany. It is essentially action taken in relation to the Western Powers themselves by cutting off their communications with a part of Germany where they have the right to be and by attempting to deny them access to it or to compel their withdrawal. That the locale of this action is Germany and that the population of Berlin is affected by it does not suffice to

agencies for enforcement action under its authority. But no enforcement action shall be taken under regional arrangements or by regional agencies without the authorisation of the Security Council, with the exception of measures against any enemy state, as defined in paragraph 2 of this Article, provided for pursuant to Article 107 or in regional arrangements directed against renewal of aggressive policy on the part of any such state, until such time as the Organisation may, on request of the Governments concerned, be charged with the responsibility for preventing further aggression by such a state.

2. The term enemy state as used in paragraph 1 of this Article applies to any state which during the Second World War has been an enemy of any signatory of the present Charter.

This Article authorises regional agencies and states under regional arrangements to act against ex-enemy states[5] as they are authorised to act by Article 107. In addition to this, it authorises regional agencies and states under regional arrangements to resort to force against ex-enemy states for a purpose which is defined by the terms ' against renewal of aggressive policy ' That means: prevent the renewal of aggressive policy, as well as react against an actual attempt to renew aggressive policy. This authorisation is not restricted, as the one established by Article 107, to ' the Governments having responsibility for such action.' Any Member of the United Nations party to a regional arrangement may take enforcement action against renewal of aggressive policy on the part of a state which during the Second World War has been an enemy of any signatory of the Charter (Article 53, paragraph 2) if such action is provided for in the regional arrangement. The enforcement action under Article 53, paragraph 1, need not be—as the enforcement action under Article 107—' taken or authorised as a result of that war.' Any enforcement action is permissible if it is directed against the renewal of aggressive policy on the part of an enemy state. The question as to whether these circumstances exist

constitute it as action taken in relation to Germany or to bring it under Article 107. The term used, as I have said, is " . . . in relation to "—not affecting or concerning—and in the context " . . . in relation to " is clearly intended to mean action of which the enemy State is the object and not merely the subject, the occasion or the locale. The object of the U.S.S.R. action in the case of Berlin is clearly the three Western Powers and their position, and it is inherently in relation to them and not in relation to Germany that it is being taken' (pp. 28 f.). In paragraph 2 of the Article the term ' enemy state ' is defined in the same way as in Article 107. Technically it would have been more correct to refer in Article 53 to the definition in Article 107 than to define the term twice. With respect to the concept of ' enemy state ' the delegate of the United Kingdom gave the following explanation : ' 1. *Enemy States* are those which, on the day of the signature of the Charter, are still at war with any one of the United Nations. 2. *The present war* is to be understood as a series of wars which began on or before September 3, 1939, and which are still in progress. (U.N.C.I.O. Doc. 1095, III/3/50, p. 4.)

has to be decided by the regional agency or the individual states acting under a regional arrangement. Such regional arrangement frees the states from the restriction established by the terms of Article 107: ' as a result of that war '; unless action against ' renewal of aggressive policy on the part of any such ex-enemy state ' is considered to be always ' a result of that war.'

There seems to be, however, a temporal restriction established by the statement: ' until such time as the Organisation may . . . be charged with the responsibility for preventing further aggression by such state.' But this restriction is deprived of any effect by the provision that the Organisation shall be charged with the responsibility for preventing further aggression by the enemy state ' on the request of the Governments concerned.' Such ' request ' must be accepted by the Organisation. It is an ' offer ' made by the ' Governments concerned ' to the United Nations to take over the responsibility referred to in Article 53, paragraph 1. The Members, parties to a regional arrangement directed against the renewal of aggressive policy on the part of any enemy state, may maintain the authorisation established in Article 53, paragraph 1, as long as they please. The Organisation has no power to terminate this authorisation; it may only accept the offer on the part of the Governments concerned to take over the responsibility determined in Article 53, paragraph 2. That means that the Organisation is authorised by the Charter to enter into a treaty by which some states renounce the power conferred upon them by Article 53, paragraph 1, in favour of the Organisation. Since this power is conferred by Article 53, paragraph 2, only on states in their capacity as parties to a regional arrangement, the ' Governments concerned ' which have to make the ' request ' referred to in Article 53, paragraph 1, are all the states parties to the regional arrangement directed against the renewal of aggressive policy. If a state is bound by a regional arrangement with respect to measures against enemy states, it is not free to request the Organisation to take over the function determined by the regional arrangement. The ' request ' must be made on the basis of an agreement of the states, parties to the regional arrangement, unless the regional arrangement provides for another possibility. If the regional arrangement expires, the authorisation of Article 53, paragraph 1, relating to the enforcement action against renewal of aggressive policy on the part of enemy states terminates.

The acceptance of the responsibility referred to in Article 53, paragraph 1, on the part of the Organisation has the effect that the competence of the Organisation to take enforcement action is somewhat increased in relation to the enemy state concerned, as compared with the competence established by Article 39. Under Article 39, the Organisation may take enforcement action only in case the Security Council has determined the existence of a threat to the peace, breach of the peace, or act of aggression. After having accepted the responsibility referred to in Article 53, paragraph 1, the Organisation may take enforcement action ' for preventing further aggression ' by the enemy state, against the aggressive policy of which the regional arrangement was directed. The formula ' for preventing further aggression ' goes farther than the formula ' threat to the peace, breach of the peace, or act of aggression.' Enforcement action ' for preventing further aggression ' is possible even without an actual threat to the peace.

Article 53, paragraph 1, authorises the Organisation to accept the offer made on the part of Members, parties to a regional arrangement, to assume the responsibility for preventing further aggression by the enemy state against which the regional arrangement was directed. No other offer, especially not an offer only to share this responsibility with the parties to the regional arrangement, can be accepted. But the Charter does not determine the organ through which this offer is to be accepted and the responsibility to be discharged. The general structure of the Organisation permits the interpretation that this organ is the Security Council. As to the possibility of a request by the ' Governments concerned ' that the Organisation be charged with the responsibility for preventing further aggression by the enemy states, Article 53, paragraph 1, differs from Article 107. This Article does not provide for an analogous transfer of the right to take action against the enemy states by ' the Governments having responsibility for such action,' to the Organisation.[6]

[6] The *Report to the President*, pp. 164, states with respect to Article 107: ' Like Paragraph 1 [of Chapter XII of the Dumbarton Oaks Proposals corresponding to Article 106 of the Charter], however, it was criticised on the ground that it lacked precision and clarity, but in this case the five powers did not feel it advisable to offer or accept any significant change, although they were agreeable to a slight modification in phraseology.' The text of Chapter XII, paragraph 2, of the Dumbarton Oaks Proposals (corresponding to Article 107 of the Charter) reads as follows: ' No provision of the Charter should preclude action taken or authorised in relation to enemy states as a result of the present war by Governments having responsibility for such action.' There is no essential difference between this text and that of Article 107 of the Charter. The Report says: ' There is one fact about Article 107 which should be noted. While no limitation can be imposed by the Organisation on action taken for the control of the present enemy, the Organisation itself is not barred by any language in the Charter from acting in this field, so that the responsible governments may, whenever and in whatever degree they wish, transfer responsibilities of this character to it.' Article 107 does not confer any power upon the Organisation; it only releases the Members and non-members (with respect to Article 2, paragraph 6) from obligations in relation to ex-enemy states. At the *Hearings* (p. 322) the representative of the Department of State declared that the situation referred to in Article 107, ' will continue until this phase of security work is turned over by the Governments concerned to the Organisation and the Security Council becomes responsible for it.' The Organisation cannot accept responsibilities transferred to it by a Member or a non-member, except if the Charter authorises the Organisation to do so. Such authorisation is given to the Organisation in Article 53 with respect to regional organisations. Article 107 does not contain such authorisation.

The fact that the states, parties to a regional arrangement directed against the renewal of aggressive policy of a definite enemy state, have made the request referred to in Article 53, paragraph 1, and that this request has been accepted by the Organisation does not establish a monoply of the Organisation for enforcement action. The authorisation of Article 53, paragraph 1, may still work for the same states parties to another regional arrangement and directed against another enemy state or for other states parties to a regional arrangement directed against the same or another enemy state.

Within the problematic restrictions established by Articles 107 and 53, the Members of the United Nations are not obliged by the Charter to refrain from the threat or use of force in relation to ex-enemy states and, consequently, not to settle by peaceful means their disputes with ex-enemy states. The ex-enemy states have all the obligations which Article 2, paragraph 6, imposes upon non-member states, but the Member states have no substantial obligations in relation to the ex-enemy states. In this respect, the ex-enemy states are, in principle, outside of the law of the Charter. This outlawry is permanent; for, according to the wording of Article 107, it is not terminated by the admission of an ex-enemy state to the Organisation. The definition of the term ' enemy state ' in Article 53, paragraph 2, applies also to states after they have become Members of the United Nations.[7] All this was probably not intended and is

[7] At the *Hearings* (p. 303) the question arose as to whether the exception established by Article 53, paragraph 1, would apply in case a former enemy state would become a Member of the United Nations. The representative of the Department of State answered this question as follows: ' Presumably when any one of these nations becomes a Member of the Organisation, this exception would no longer apply to it.' Then a Senator remarked: ' But it still says that it applies to any state which has been an enemy.' Whereupon the answer was : ' That is right.' Then the Senator stated: ' You cannot change the fact that it has been an enemy.' To the renewed question whether the exception would apply to a Member which has been an enemy, the representative of the State Department answered: ' Presumably it would not, because a nation which joined the Organisation would be on a basis of complete equality with all the other Members of the Organisation.' The principle of sovereign equality does not prevent the Charter from conferring rights upon certain Members without conferring these rights upon other Members. Later the representative declared : ' I should say that this would mean that with respect to that particular nation the governments concerned would have agreed to hand over to the Security Council the function of seeing to it that that nation did not again become an aggressor.' However, a former enemy state may be admitted to the Organisation against the vote of a Member which has no permanent seat in the Security Council, and the decision of the General Assembly by which a state is admitted to membership does not confer upon the Security Council or any other organ of the United Nations any function which is not conferred upon it by the ' present Charter.'

The British Commentary on the Charter, p. 9, contains the following statement: ' It might, however, be assumed that if any such state [enemy state] were to be admitted to the Organisation, the necessity for making special arrangements to prevent aggression on its part would disappear, since it could only be admitted if

politically hardly justifiable; but the text of the Charter does not correspond to the probably more reasonable intention of its authors.[8]

The outlawry of former enemy states has some exceptions, in so far as the Charter confers certain rights upon non-member states without excluding former enemy states. These rights are: to be exempt from intervention by the Organisation in matters of domestic jurisdiction, established by Article 2, paragraph 7; the right to bring before the General Assembly or the Security Council a dispute to which

all the permanent members of the Security Council and two thirds of the members of the General Assembly were convinced that it qualified under Article 4. On the other hand it is not to be excluded that such state might be required, in return for admission, to agree to the continuance of certain conditions.' Legally, such agreement between the Organisation and the former enemy state is hardly possible under the Charter. Besides, it is not necessary. The provisions of Articles 53 and 107 are, according to the wording of these Articles, applicable to ex-enemy states also after their admission to the Organisation.

8 Article 32 of the General Principles as accepted by the French delegation, provides that the armed forces made available by a Member to the Security Council under Article 43 may, when not employed by the Council, be stationed 'within the territory or waters of ex-enemy nations under Article 107 of the Charter or under the terms of the Peace Treaties.' The same Article as accepted by the Soviet delegation contains a similar provision.

9 The Report of Committee 3 to Commission III on Chapter XII (Dumbarton Oaks Proposals, corresponding to Chapter XVII of the Charter) (U.N.C.I.O. Doc. 1905, III/1/150, pp. 3 f.) contains the following statement: 'The Greek Delegation proposed an amendment which would prevent present enemy States from having recourse to the Security Council or the Assembly, and Committee 2 of Commission III had decided, by a vote of 34–0, to refer this amendment to Committee 3, stating that it approved the amendment in principle in so far as it applied to Section A of Chapter VIII. After modification of the text, and although the Delegates who had taken the floor had expressed their agreement on the principle of the proposal, the Committee rejected, by a vote of 17–5, the insertion of the Greek amendment into the Charter. However, on the proposal of the United States Delegate, the Committee voted unanimously to insert the following text into the report: "It is understood that the enemy states in this war shall not have the right of recourse to the Security Council or the General Assembly before the Security Council grants them this right."' This resolution of Committee III/3 has no basis in the text of the Charter. The Charter in Article 11, paragraph 2, Article 35, paragraph 2, Articles 32 and 50 confers upon states which are not Members of the United Nations rights which imply recourse to the Organisation. These Articles do not differentiate between states which during the Second World War have been enemies of any signatory to the Charter and other states not Members of the United Nations. The resolution of Committee III/1 has not the character of an authentic interpretation of the Charter. The *Report to the President*, p. 164, contains the following statement relating to the Greek amendment: 'The Committee rejected this amendment believing that its intent was adequately covered in other places of the Charter and that the right of recourse should not be emphasised.' The only places in the Charter where the intent of the Greek amendment could be covered are Articles 53 and 107. Their wordings refer only to actions directed against enemy states, not to acts of these states, and especially not to acts by which these states might have recourse to the General Assembly or the Security Council. But, as pointed out, Articles 107 and 53 restrict the competence of these organs in case former enemy states have recourse to them.

the enemy state is a party, established by Article 11, paragraph 2, and Article 35, paragraph 2; the right to be invited to participate in the discussion of a dispute to which the enemy state is a party when the dispute is under consideration by the Security Council, established by Article 32; and the right to consult the Security Council in case the enemy state finds itself confronted with special economic problems arising from the carrying out of preventive or enforcement measures taken by the Security Council against any other state, established by Article 50. The provisions of Articles 107 and 53 have not the effect of excluding former enemy states from the exercise of these rights. But if such a state brings a dispute with a Member state before the Security Council or the General Assembly, the competence of these organs is restricted by Articles 107 and 53, in so far as they are not permitted to invalidate or preclude, by their decisions, action taken under Article 107 or to react against an enforcement action taken under Article 53, paragraph 1.[9]

As to the right of collective self-defence, the situation of former enemy states is doubtful. It may be argued that if the action against a former enemy state has the character of an armed attack, Article 51 applies, which provides that 'nothing in the present Charter shall impair' this right. Hence, Members are authorised to assist a former enemy state in its defence against an armed attack, even if the attack is covered by Article 107 or 53, and therefore to conclude defence treaties with former enemy states; provided that Article 51 applies to attacks against non-members. If this interpretation is accepted, Articles 107 and 53 are restricted by Article 51. However, Article 107, too, provides: 'Nothing in the present Charter shall invalidate or preclude action . . .' Hence, the interpretation is not excluded that the right to take action against a former enemy state under Article 107 restricts the right to assist such state against an armed attack covered by Article 107. The wording of Article 53 does not exclude the right to defend a former enemy state against an action taken under Article 53, if this action has the character of an armed attack. But regional arrangements for the implementation of Article 51, concluded with, and consequently in favour of, former enemy states, are hardly compatible with the spirit of Article 53 which authorises regional arrangements directed against former enemy states.

[9] For note see facing page.

Chapter 20

AMENDMENTS

1. Amendments to the Charter in the narrower sense of the term

UNDER general international law amendments to a treaty are to be made by another treaty entered into by the same contracting parties, unless the original treaty contains provisions instituting a particular amendment procedure. The Charter does contain such provisions, conferring upon certain organs and a qualified majority of the Members of the United Nations the power to amend the Charter.

There are two different sets of rules concerning amendments. The first one is Chapter XVIII of the Charter (in the narrower sense) containing Articles 108 and 109. The second is Chapter V of the Statute of the International Court of Justice containing Articles 69 and 70; and the Statute forms an integral part of the Charter (in the wider sense).

Chapter XVIII of the Charter in the narrower sense refers to amendments to the 'present Charter.' This term may mean the Charter in the narrower sense not including the Statute of the International Court of Justice, or the Charter in a wider sense including the Statute. In Chapter XIX, dealing with 'Ratification and Signature,' the term 'present Charter' certainly means the Charter in the wider sense, since the Statute has no special rules concerning this subject. Since the Statute contains special provisions concerning its amendments, it is probable that Chapter XVIII of the Charter in the narrower sense was intended to refer only to amendments of the Charter not including the Statute. But another interpretation according to which the term 'present Charter' in Articles 108 and 109 has the same meaning as in Articles 110 and 111, namely: the Charter including the Statute, is not excluded, so that the Statute of the International Court of Justice may be amended not only by the procedure stipulated in Articles 69 and 70 of the Statute but also by the procedures stipulated in Articles 108 and 109 of the Charter in the narrower sense of the term. It is regrettable that the wording of Chapter XVIII is not accommodated to the dual meaning of the term in question.

In Chapter XVIII of the Charter in the narrower sense of the term two different amendment procedures are provided, an ordinary and an extraordinary one. The ordinary procedure is stipulated in Article 108:

> Amendments to the present Charter shall come into force for all Members of the United Nations when they have been adopted by a vote of two thirds of the members of the General Assembly and ratified in accordance with their respective

constitutional processes by two-thirds of the Members of the United Nations, including all the permanent members of the Security Council.

The extraordinary procedure is stipulated in Article 109:

> 1. A General Conference of the Members of the United Nations for the purpose of reviewing the present Charter may be held at a date and place to be fixed by a two-thirds vote of the members of the General Assembly and by a vote of any seven members of the Security Council. Each Member of the United Nations shall have one vote in the conference.
>
> 2. Any alteration of the present Charter recommended by a two-thirds vote of the conference shall take effect when ratified in accordance with their respective constitutional processes by two-thirds of the Members of the United Nations including all the permanent members of the Security Council.
>
> 3. If such a conference has not been held before the tenth annual session of the General Assembly following the coming into force of the present Charter, the proposal to call such a conference shall be placed on the agenda of that session of the General Assembly, and the conference shall be held if so decided by a majority vote of the members of the General Assembly and by a vote of any seven members of the Security Council.

This Article is the result of an attempt to establish an amendment procedure different from and easier than that of Article 108.[1] But there is hardly any essential difference between the procedure of Article 108 and that of Article 109. The General Conference referred to in Article 109 is composed in the same way as the General Assembly referred to in Article 108; each Member is represented and has one vote. The only difference: that the number of representatives in the General Assembly is limited to five whereas there is no such restriction with respect to the representation of the Members in the General Conference, is of no importance. The text of the amendment which is the object of the ratifications is to be adopted by the General Conference in the same way as by the General Assembly, namely, by a two-thirds vote of the members of the respective bodies.

[1] In Committee I/2 (U.N.C.I.O. Doc. 991, I/2/66) the delegate of Belgium stated 'that in view of the number of anomalies in the Charter, it might be difficult to secure public support for the Charter without . . . a specific provision for revision.' The specific provision for revision is laid down in Article 109, providing for a general conference for the purpose of reviewing the Charter. The delegate of the Soviet Union declared in Committee I/2 (U.N.C.I.O. Doc. 1052, I/2/71) 'that his delegation was opposed to facilitating the convocation of such a conference for which there might be no need in the future.' He explained the attitude of his delegation by 'the desire expressed by many delegations to use such a conference to destroy the veto power. He believed that such a conference would also be used to threaten the unanimity of the major powers.'

In contradistinction to decisions of the General Assembly on important matters made under Article 18, paragraph 2, the decision made under Article 108 does not require a two-thirds majority of the members 'present and voting,' but of all the members of the Assembly. The same principle applies to the decision made by the General Conference under Article 109, paragraph 2. That the Conference, according to Article 109, paragraph 2, has to 'recommend' 'alterations' of the Charter whereas the Assembly, according to Article 108, has to 'adopt' 'amendments,' makes no legal difference in the function of the two bodies. The alterations recommended by the General Conference come into force under the same conditions as the amendments adopted by the General Assembly, namely, by ratification on the part of two-thirds of the Members of the United Nations including all the permanent members of the Security Council. The amendment, whether adopted by the General Assembly under Article 108 or recommended by the General Conference under Article 109, paragraph 2, after being ratified by two-thirds of the Members comes into force for all Members, also for those which through their representatives voted against the amendment in the Assembly or the Conference, or did not ratify it.[2]

There is no reason to believe that a two-thirds majority of the Members can be reached more easily in the General Conference than in the General Assembly. If such a two-thirds majority of the Members is possible at all, the ordinary procedure of Article 108 will sooner reach its aim than the extraordinary procedure of Article 109. For the General Assembly is an established body, whereas the General Conference must first be convoked, which under Article 109, paragraph 1, is possible only on the basis of a two-thirds vote of the members of the General Assembly and a vote of any seven members of the Security Council, or, in the case referred to in Article 109, paragraph 3, on the basis of a majority vote of the members of the General Assembly and a vote of any seven members of the Security Council. This disadvantage is not completely compensated by the fact that no permanent member of the Security Council can prevent the convocation of the General Conference under Article 109,

[2] The Covenant of the League of Nations provided in Article 26:—

> 1. Amendments to this Covenant will take effect when ratified by the Members of the League whose Representatives compose the Council and by a majority of the Members of the League whose Representatives compose the Assembly.
>
> 2. No such amendments shall bind any Member of the League which signifies its dissent therefrom, but in that case it shall cease to be a Member of the League.

Although the Charter does not contain a similar provision, Commission I of the San Francisco Conference adopted an interpretation according to which a Member has the right of withdrawal from the Organisation in case an amendment comes into force 'in which it has not concurred and which it finds itself unable to accept.' (U.N.C.I.O. Doc. 1178, I/2/76 (2), p. 6.) Cf. *supra*, pp. 122 ff.

paragraph 1, or under Article 109, paragraph 3. The purpose of the latter provisions is to guarantee that the question of calling a General Conference shall be at least discussed in the General Assembly after a certain period of time during which the Charter has been in force.[3] The calling of a General Conference under Article 109, just as the admission of a new Member under Article 4 or the expulsion of a Member under Article 6, is within the common competence of the General Assembly and the Security Council. But the co-operation of the two bodies is regulated in Article 109 in a way different from that in Articles 4 and 6. Whereas under the two last-mentioned Articles the General Assembly is authorised to take the measure concerned 'upon the recommendation of the Security Council,' under Article 109 'a two-thirds [or 'a majority'] vote of the members of the General Assembly' and 'a vote of any seven members of the Security Council' is necessary for the convocation of a General Conference. In the procedure determined by Article 4 and by Article 6 the decision of the Security Council must precede the decision of the General Assembly, and the Assembly can admit a new Member or expel a Member only after the Council has 'recommended' such action to the Assembly. Under Article 109, the General Assembly may proceed independently from the Security Council, and the Security Council independently from the General Assembly.

It is difficult to understand why Article 109, paragraph 3 prescribes that the proposal to call the General Conference shall be placed on the agenda of a certain session of the General Assembly, but not on the agenda of a session of the Security Council. The decisions of the latter is as essential for the convocation of the General Conference as that of the former. The Security Council may or may not place the proposal on its agenda. It is not bound to do so even when the General Assembly has adopted a decision that the General Conference shall be called. But the Assembly may discuss the proposal without reaching a decision by which the proposal is adopted.

3 The Report of the Rapporteur of Committee I/2 on Chapter XI (Dumbarton Oaks Proposals) (U.N.C.I.O. Doc. 1154, I/2/73 (2), p. 4) contains the following statements: 'The members of the Committee favouring a specific time limit for the calling of the conference felt that if the Organisation were to endure, it should be scrutinized after a number of years and modified, if necessary, in the light of its experience and the situation then prevailing. It was emphasized that provision for a special conference did not mean that the Organisation established now would be temporary but, on the contrary, that in order to be an effective and lasting mechanism it should be inspected and revised in those parts which had not proved efficient.' With respect to the question as to how the item of calling the Conference should be placed on the agenda of the General Assembly, the Report states: 'It was explained that the Secretary-General would place the item on the agenda and the Assembly would act in accordance with the procedures prescribed in the Charter.' 'It was pointed out, however, that a special provision was not needed for an item to be placed on the agenda, since any member state has the right at any time to have such a subject included' (p. 6).

Hence the value of the provision that the proposal shall be placed on the agenda of a session of the Assembly is doubtful. Article 109, paragraph 3 speaks of a ' proposal ' to call a conference, but it does not specify whose proposal it shall be and by whom the proposal shall be placed on the agenda of a session of the General Assembly. Such a provision is necessary since the placing on the agenda is, according to the wording of paragraph 3, obligatory. In this respect, Rules 11 and 12 of the Rules of Procedure of the General Assembly may apply, which provide that ' the provisional agenda for a regular session shall be drawn up by the Secretary-General,' and that the provisional agenda of a regular session shall include *inter alia* ' all items which the Secretary-General deems it necessary to put before the General Assembly.' Hence the Secretary-General is obliged under Article 109, paragraph 3 of the Charter to place on the provisional agenda of the tenth annual session of the General Assembly the proposal to call a General Conference, provided such a general conference has not been held previously.

The condition on which the proposal to call a General Conference shall be placed on the agenda of a session of the General Assembly is not adequately formulated: ' If such a conference has not been held before the tenth annual session of the General Assembly following the coming into force of the present Charter.' The intention probably was that the review of the Charter should be discussed when the Charter has been ten years in force without having been amended. If the problem of reviewing the Charter has been discussed in the Security Council and the General Assembly in conformity with Article 108, with the result that an amendment has come into force ' before the tenth annual session of the General Assembly following the coming into force of the present Charter ' (that is June 26, 1946), there is no reason for compulsorily placing the proposal to call a General Conference on the agenda of the General Assembly. The obligatory initiation of this procedure is not justified in case no General Conference was held; it is justified only in case no review of the Charter or no amendment has taken place within a certain period of time.

If there is a two-thirds majority in the General Assembly for a certain amendment, but if the ratifications required by Article 108 cannot be obtained, it is useless to resort to the procedure of Article 109, since the two-thirds majority in the General Conference is equivalent to that in the General Assembly and Article 109 requires exactly the same ratifications as Article 108.[4]

[4] The original idea was to establish another voting procedure in the General Conference than that provided in Article 108 for the General Assembly, and another ratification procedure than that provided in the same Article. The delegate of Australia declared in Committee I/2 (U.N.C.I.O. Doc. 1022, I/2/69) ' that the

Although the decision by which the General Assembly adopts, under Article 108, an amendment, and the decision by which it fixes, under Article 109, paragraph 1, the date when and the place where the General Conference shall be held, are not among the important questions enumerated in Article 18, paragraph 2, they must be rendered by a two-thirds majority, not of ' the members present and voting.' but of ' the members of the General Assembly.' Consequently, Rule 60 of the Rules of Procedure according to which a majority of the members of the General Assembly shall constitute a quorum, cannot apply to decisions under Articles 108 and 109, paragraph 1. In contradistinction to decisions made under Article 18, paragraph 3, by a majority of the members present and voting, a resolution by which the General Assembly, under Article 109, paragraph 3, decides that a General Conference shall be held, requires a majority of all the members. Whether in this case Rule 60 of the Rules of Procedure applies, is doubtful.

Although the decision by which the Security Council under Article 109, paragraph 1, fixes the date when and the place where the General Conference shall take place and the decision by which it adopts under Article 109, paragraph 3, the proposal that a General Conference shall be held, have not a procedural character, they may be adopted by a vote of any seven members of the Council. It is difficult to understand why under paragraph 1 of Article 109 the General Assembly and the Security Council are authorised only to

voting procedure at the Special Conference and for the ratification of amendments proposed by the Conference should be left to the good sense and widsom of the members of that Conference. He stated his belief that this matter was more important than that of the veto on conciliation or on enforcement by the Security Council. If the veto is applied to the process of ratification, he contended, it will be necessary to examine the possibilities of the right of withdrawal from the Organisation. The Report of the Rapporteur of Committee I/2 on Chapter XI (Dumbarton Oaks Proposals) (U.N.C.I.O. Doc. 1154, I/2/73 (2), p. 8) contains the following statement: ' The discussions of the Sub-committee and the Committee on the method of ratification of amendments proposed by the special conference centered on the contention of those delegates who opposed the sponsoring governments that this matter should be left to the Conference itself to decide. It was argued by the delegates that the provision in the Charter for voting procedure in the Security Council would render ratification of the Charter by the parliaments of their countries difficult and even questionable, but that ratification would be facilitated if assurance were given that a special conference to revise the Charter could itself decide on the method of ratification of such amendments as it might suggest. If such an arrangement were not possible, then it might be necessary to provide for withdrawal from the Organisation.—In answer to this position, representatives of the sponsoring governments declared that these powers could not enter upon the great responsibilities and obligations of membership which they were prepared to accept if forced to take the risk that these responsibilities might be increased without their consent.' As soon as it became impossible to establish for the extraordinary amendments another voting and ratification procedure than that established for ordinary amendments, the former lost their specific meaning.

decide when and where a General Conference shall be held, under paragraph 3 only whether a General Conference shall be held.

It should be noted that the Charter contains no provision concerning the convocation of the first meeting of the General Conference and its organisation and procedure. The General Assembly and the Security Council are only authorised to decide, under Article 109, paragraph 1, where and when, under Article 109, paragraph 3, whether a General Conference shall be held, but not by whom its first meeting shall be summoned and who shall preside over it. Neither is the General Conference authorised to adopt its own rules of procedure.

Since, in order to bring the amendment into force, the two thirds of the Members of the United Nations which have to ratify the amendment must include all permanent members of the Security Council, no amendment is possible against the veto of one of these permanent members.[5] By non-ratifying an amendment adopted by the General Assembly or recommended by the General Conference, any permanent Member of the Security Council can prevent its coming into force even if all the other Members of the United Nations have ratified it.

The Charter does not prescribe a certain period of time within which an amendment adopted by the General Assembly or recommended by the General Conference must be ratified and that non-ratification within this period is equivalent to refusal of ratification. Lack of such provision might have undesirable consequences. The fact that an amendment duly accepted by the Assembly or Conference fails to secure the necessary ratifications is considered to be a legitimate reason for withdrawal from the Organisation.[6] But when is a state entitled to assume that an amendment has failed to secure the necessary ratifications?

The Charter expressly prescribes that the ratifications of amendments shall be in accordance with the respective constitutional processes (Articles 108, 109, paragraph 2). Hence the same problem arises as the one discussed in connection with Article 110, paragraph 1, concerning the ratification of the Charter: Who is competent to

[5] *The Report on the Conference held at San Francisco, April 25–June 26, 1945*, by the Chairman of the New Zealand Delegation (Department of External Affairs, Wellington, 1945, Publ. No. 11) contains the following statement (p. 39): 'The unreason of maintaining for ever the dead hand of the five Powers on amendment was particularly apparent when one considered the changes which inevitably took place in the Power relations of States. Who could say if all five Powers would be truly Great Powers in ten years' time? Were they all truly Great Powers even now? If the Conference could not agree that the desire of three or even four Great Powers sufficed to bring into effect amendments agreed to at the special Conference and ratified by a sufficient number of other Powers, would it not be possible to leave the whole question of ratification open to be decided by the Conference when it met?'

[6] Cf. *supra*, p. 124.

decide the question as to whether the concrete ratification of an amendment is in accordance with the constitution of the ratifying state? As far as the ratification of the Charter is concerned, a possible answer to this question is furnished by the provision of Article 110, paragraph 2—that the ratification shall be deposited with the Government of the United States and that this Government shall notify all the signatory states and the Secretary-General of each deposit. But there is no analogous provision relating to the ratifications of amendments. The Members of the United Nations which have ratified an amendment are not obliged to deposit the ratification with the Government of the United States or with any other organ of the Organisation. How shall the Organisation be informed of the fact that a Member has ratified an amendment? Who is competent to declare in an authentic way that an amendment has obtained the necessary ratifications and hence has come into force? This question has the same importance as the question whether the Charter has received the necessary ratifications. It is possible and probable that the Secretary-General will invite the Members to deposit the ratifications of amendments with the Secretariat in order to ascertain whether the amendment has come into force under Articles 108 or 109. However, in so doing the Secretary-General will not exercise a function expressly conferred upon him by the Charter. Therefore he has certainly not the authority to decide for himself whether the ratification of the amendment was constitutional or not. Since no other organ of the United Nations is directly or indirectly authorised to make such a decision, only the government of the ratifying state is competent in this respect. Hence the express prescription of the constitutionality of amendment ratifications has no specific effect.

2. Amendments to the Statute of the International Court of Justice

Relating to amendments to the Statute of the International Court of Justice, Article 69 of the Statute stipulates:

> Amendments to the present Statute shall be affected by the same procedure as is provided by the Charter of the United Nations for amendments to that Charter, subject however to any provisions which the General Assembly upon recommendation of the Security Council may adopt concerning the participation of states which are parties to the present Statute but are not Members of the United Nations.

Article 70 runs as follows:—

> The Court shall have power to propose such amendments to the present Statute as it may deem necessary, through written communications to the Secretary-General, for consideration in conformity with the provisions of Article 69.

The wording of Article 69 ' by the same procedure as is provided by the Charter of the United Nations for amendments to that Charter ' is not very clear since the Charter provides two different procedures, an ordinary and an extraordinary. Are both applicable in amending the Statute or is only one, and if only one, which one? Any answer is possible; but the intended meaning of the words ' the same procedure ' in Article 69 is probably: the procedure of Article 108 of the Charter.

This procedure if applied to amendments to the Statute is modified in two points. First, not only Members of the United Nations but also states which, according to Article 93 of the Charter, are parties to the Statute but not Members of the United Nations, may participate in the amendment procedure. It is significant that participation of these states is not obligatory. The General Assembly, upon recommendation of the Security Council, may—or may not—adopt provisions concerning the participation of states which are parties to the Statute but not Members of the United Nations, and these provisions may or may not place the non-members on an equal footing with Members. In case non-member states parties to the Statute are not admitted to the amendment procedure, the question arises as to whether they are bound by the amendment. The answer to this question depends upon the conditions on which the state has become a party to the Statute, which conditions have to be determined according to Article 93, paragraph 2 of the Charter by the General Assembly upon recommendation of the Security Council, and accepted by the state concerned. Switzerland became a party to the Statute on the condition that it accepted the provisions of the Statute (Resolution of the General Assembly of December 11, 1946, clause *a*). Switzerland in accepting this condition recognised the provision of Article 69 of the Statute concerning amendments and, consequently, is bound by any amendment, whether it does or does not participate in the amendment procedure.[7]

The second modification of the procedure of Article 108 as applied to amendments to the Statute concerns the power of the Court to propose amendments according to Article 70 of the Statute.

[7] After Switzerland became a party to the Statute, the representative of Belgium, in a letter dated August 12, 1948 (Doc. S/969), called the attention of the Security Council to the recommendations to be made under Article 4, paragraph 3 (participation in the election of the members of the Court), and Article 69 (participation in the amendment procedure). He stated, however, that ' circumstances do not necessitate an examination at this time of the recommendations mentioned in Article 69.' Consequently he submitted to the Security Council, and the Council adopted, only the text of a resolution concerning the conditions under which a state, a party to the Statute, but not a Member of the United Nations, may participate in the elections of the members of the Court. Cf. *supra*, p. 516.

CHAPTER 21

THE ASSURANCE OF THE INTEGRITY AND INDEPENDENCE OF TRIESTE AND THE GOVERNMENT OF THIS COMMUNITY AS FUNCTIONS OF THE UNITED NATIONS

1. THE FUNCTIONS CONFERRED UPON THE UNITED NATIONS BY THE PEACE TREATY WITH ITALY

As pointed out in a previous connection,[1] functions not conferred upon the Organisation by the Charter may be conferred upon it by treaties concluded by the United Nations.

The Peace Treaty concluded by the Allied and Associated Powers and Italy stipulates in Article 21, paragraph 3, that the Free Territory of Trieste, constituted by this Treaty, 'shall be governed in accordance with an instrument for a provisional regime drafted by the Council of Foreign Ministers and approved by the Security Council. This Instrument shall remain in force until such date as the Security Council shall fix for the coming into force of the Permanent Statute which shall have been approved by it. The Free Territory shall thenceforth be governed by the provisions of such Permanent Statute. The texts of the Permanent Statute and of the Instrument for the Provisional Regime are contained in Annexes VI and VII.' The Annexes form integral parts of the Peace Treaty (Article 84). The provisions of Annexes VI and VII confer important functions upon the Security Council of the United Nations. There is a third Annex (VIII), the Instrument for the Free Port of Trieste, which likewise contains a provision conferring functions upon the Security Council (approval of amendments to this Instrument). The Peace Treaty itself (not comprising the Annexes) does not provide for approval by the Security Council of Annex VIII, but Article 34 of the Permanent Statute of the Free Territory (Annex VI) stipulates that the Instrument for the Free Port of Trieste (Annex VIII) shall be approved by the Security Council.

If a treaty provides for approval of some of its provisions by a third party, these provisions can come into force only after they have been approved by the third party. Such approval by a third party amounts to accession, not to the treaty as a whole, but to parts of it. According to Article 90 the Peace Treaty with Italy 'shall come into force immediately upon the deposit of ratifications by the Union of Soviet Socialist Republics, by the United Kingdom of Great Britain and Northern Ireland, by the United States of America, and by France.'[2]

[1] Cf. *supra*, p. 330.

[2] Article 90 of the Treaty, which in its preamble is presented as a treaty of peace, provides that it shall be ratified by the Allied and Associated Powers and also by

But Annex VII, the Instrument for the Provisional Regime of the Free Territory of Trieste, can come into force only after the deposit of the ratifications by the above-mentioned four Powers and the approval by the Security Council, provided for by Article 21 of the Treaty. The same is true with respect to Annex VI, the Permanent Statute of the Free Territory of Trieste. But the latter can come into force—according to Article 21 of the Treaty—only after the Instrument for the Provisional Regime has ceased to be in force. Annex VIII, the Instrument for the Free Port of Trieste, can come into force only after the Permanent Statute has come into force, since it can come into force only after its approval by the Security Council, and the Security Council can approve it only on the basis of the Permanent Statute.

The provision of Article 21 of the Treaty that the Permanent Statute shall come into force after the Instrument for the Provisional Regime had ceased to be in force, seems to be incompatible with the fact that the Instrument for the Provisional Regime confers important functions upon the Governor, and the Governor is to be appointed by the Security Council under Article 11, paragraph 1, of the Permanent Statute. This presupposes that the Permanent Statute comes into force before the Provisional Regime is established, for this Regime cannot function without the Governor. This is in direct opposition to Article 21 of the Treaty. Now, Article 2 of the Instrument for the Provisional Regime stipulates: 'The Governor and the Provisional Council of Government shall exercise their functions in the manner laid down in the provisions of the Permanent Statute, as and when these provisions prove to be applicable and in so far as they are not superseded by the present Instrument. Likewise, all other provisions of the Permanent Statute shall be applicable during the period of the Provisional Regime as and when these provisions prove to be applicable and in so far as they are not superseded by the present Instrument.' That means that all provisions of the Permanent Statute shall be applicable during the period of the Provisional Regime as and when these provisions prove to be applicable and in so far as they are not superseded by the Instrument for the Provisional Regime. However, how can the provisions of the Permanent Statute 'prove to be applicable' during the period of the Provisional Regime if the Permanent Statute—according to Article 21 of the Treaty—comes into force only after this Regime has ceased to exist? How can the Instrument for the Provisional Regime 'supersede' provisions of the Permanent Statute if the latter is preceded by the former? It is the

Italy. But the Treaty shall come into force immediately upon the deposit of ratifications by the Soviet Union, the United Kingdom, the United States, and France. With respect to each Allied or Associated Power whose instrument of ratification is thereafter deposited, the Treaty shall come into force upon the date of deposit. That means that the Peace Treaty could come into force in relation to Italy without ratification by that state. If so, why was ratification by Italy required?

previous law that may be ' superseded ' by the subsequent law, not *vice versa*. In order to make sense, Article 2 of the Instrument of the Provisional Regime must be interpreted to mean: the provisions of the Permanent Statute which are compatible with the provisions of the Instrument for the Provisional Regime shall come into force together with the latter. Hence, the date to be fixed, according to Article 21 of the Peace Treaty, by the Security Council for the coming into force of the Permanent Statute, must be interpreted to refer only to those provisions of this Statute which are not compatible with the provisions of the Instrument. Only if this interpretation of Article 21, though hardly in conformity with its wording, is accepted, can the provision of Article 11 of the Permanent Statute, concerning the appointment of the Governor, be applied by the Security Council prior to the date fixed for the coming into force of the Statute, and a Governor appointed immediately after the approval of the Instrument for the Provisional Regime: which approval must be combined with the approval of the Permanent Statute, in order to comply with the provision of Article 21 that the provisions of the Permanent Statute shall have been approved by the Security Council before being applied. If this interpretation is accepted, then also the approval by the Security Council of the Instrument for the Free Port of Trieste is possible before the coming into force of the Permanent Statute.[3]

If a treaty provides for approval of parts of it by a third party, this provision implies—if nothing to the contrary is stipulated—that neither changes nor ablishment of these parts are possible without the consent of the third party. As to the Instrument for the Provisional Regime, the Peace Treaty only stipulates that it shall cease to be valid when the Permanent Statute comes into force. The Treaty does not contain a provision concerning amendments to this Instrument. They can be made only in the way in which amendments to the Peace Treaty are to be made: by the consent of all contracting parties plus the consent of the Security Council. As to the Permanent Statute, Article 37 of this Statute provides that amendments can be made only by the Security Council. As to a complete abolishment of the Permanent Statute (implying the termination of the legal status of the Free Territory of Trieste as established by the Peace Treaty), two interpretations are possible. If the abolishment of the Statute is

[3] As a matter of fact, the Security Council approved at its 91st meeting, on January 10, 1947, all three annexes by one and the same resolution, even before the Peace Treaty with Italy was in force. (Official Records of the Security Council, 2nd Year, No. 3, p. 61.) Cf. *infra*, p. 835. At the 143rd meeting, the question of the appointment of the Governor of the Free Territory was discussed. The representative of Australia stated among other things that it seemed clear that: (1) it was not necessary for the Permanent Statute to come into force before the appointment of the Governor; and (2) it was necessary for the Instrument for the Provisional Regime to come into force before the Governor was formally appointed. (Official Records of the Security Council, 2nd Year, No. 48, p. 1048.)

considered to be an act of amendment, only the Security Council is competent to perform such act. If abolishment of the Statute is not considered to be an act of amendment, the principles of general international law apply.

The Instrument for the Free Port of Trieste provides in Article 25 that amendments to this Instrument can come into force only if approved by the Security Council and on the date determined by it.

The Free Territory of Trieste, if constituted in accordance with the Peace Treaty, will have a population living on a definite territory (Article 22 of the Peace Treaty) under a government which, according to the provisions of that treaty, will be 'independent.' To guarantee the independence of the community called Free Territory of Trieste (and its integrity), is a function conferred upon the United Nations (Article 21 of the Peace Treaty, Article 2 of Annex VI). According to the Permanent Statute (Annex VI), the organs of government shall be a Governor, a Council of Government, a Popular Assembly elected by the people, and a Judiciary (Article 9). The Governor shall be appointed by the Security Council of the United Nations after consultation with the governments of Yugoslavia and Italy (Article 11). He shall exercise the functions conferred upon him in his capacity as 'representative of the Security Council' (Article 17). He is bound by the instructions given to him by the Security Council (Article 25) and responsible only to this body which has the power to suspend or to dismiss him from his office (Articles 11 and 17). It is the Security Council which, through its representative, the Governor, exercises the functions conferred upon the latter. Hence the Security Council is to be considered as an organ of the government of the Free Territory of Trieste.

The Permanent Statute confers highly important powers upon the Governor, and that means upon the Security Council, such as: to prevent the entry into force of provisions of the Constitution proposed by the Constituent Assembly, or any subsequent amendment thereto, in contradiction to the Statute (Article 10); to be present at all meetings of the Council of Government and to express his views on all questions affecting his responsibilities (Article 13); to appoint the Judiciary and to investigate, at the request of the Popular Assembly, any charge brought against a member of the Judiciary which, if proved, would warrant that member's suspension or removal (Article 16); to supervise the observance of the Statute, including the protection of the basic human rights of the inhabitants, and to ensure that public order and security are maintained by the government of the Territory in accordance with the Statute, the constitution and the laws of the Territory (Article 17); to initiate legislation in matters which in his view affect the responsibilities of the Security Council; to return, with his comments and recommendations, to the Popular Assembly any legislation which in his opinion is in contradiction to the Statute

(Article 19); to require the Council of Government to suspend certain administrative measures and, should the Council of Government object, to suspend these measures; to propose to the Council of Government the adoption of certain administrative measures (Article 20); to order directly and require the execution of certain measures in case of emergency and, in such circumstances, to assume control of the security services (Article 22); to exercise the power of pardon and reprieve (Article 23); to ensure that the foreign relations of the Territory shall be conducted in conformity with the Statute, the constitution and laws of the Territory, and to this end, to prevent the entry into force of treaties affecting foreign relations which in his judgment conflict with the Statute, constitution or laws of the Territory; to sign, together with a representative of the Council of Government, treaties, exequaturs and consular commissions (Article 24).

There are functions of government conferred by the Permanent Statute directly upon the Security Council, to be exercised by decisions of that body. It has already been mentioned that the Security Council has the power to appoint, suspend or dismiss the Governor. If the Governor prevents the entry into force of a provision of the constitution proposed by the Constituant Assembly or any subsequent amendment thereto, and if the Assembly does not accept his views and recommendations, he has to refer the matter to the Security Council which has the power of final decision (Article 10); if the Governor has returned to the Assembly an act of legislation and the Assembly makes manifest its refusal to withdraw this legislation or to amend it in conformity with his comments or recommendations, the Governor shall, unless he is prepared to withdraw his comments or recommendations, report the matter to the Security Council which has the power of final decision (Article 19); if the Governor suspends administrative measures of the Council of Government, both may refer the question to the Security Council for decision; if the Governor proposes to the Council of Government the adoption of administrative measures and the Council does not accept such proposals, the Governor may refer the matter to the Security Council for decision (Article 20); the Popular Assembly may petition the Security Council concerning any exercise by the Governor of his emergency powers (Article 22).

In exercising the powers conferred—directly or indirectly—upon the Security Council the United Nations shall perform functions of government with respect to a community different from the United Nations itself. But there is a function conferred by the Peace Treaty upon the United Nations which has not the character of a function within the government of the Free Territory. It is determined in Article 2 of the Permanent Statute, which runs as follows—

The integrity and independence of the Free Territory shall

be assured by the Security Council of the United Nations Organisation. This responsibility implies that the Council shall:

(*a*) ensure the observance of the present Statute and in particular the protection of the basic human rights of the inhabitants;

(*b*) ensure the maintenance of public order and security in the Free Territory.

The integrity and independence of the Free Territory of Trieste may be endangered by external aggression or by internal disturbances. Article 2 may be interpreted to mean that the United Nations is bound to assure the integrity and independence of the Territory in both directions. The provisions of clauses *a* and *b*—it is true—refer only to the case that the integrity and independence are endangered by internal disturbances; to ensure the observance of the present Statute and in particular the protection of the basic human rights of the inhabitants as well as the maintenance of public order and security, is implied in the governmental function which the Security Council, through the Governor, has to perform in conformity with Articles 17 and 22 of the Statute. But, according to the wording of Article 2, the fulfilment of the functions determined in clauses *a* and *b* is ' implied ' in the responsibiilty of the Security Council to assure the integrity and independence of the territory. Hence, to protect the integrity and independence against external aggression is not excluded from this responsibility. It is in the first place against external aggression that the integrity and independence of a country is to be protected. Article 10 of the Covenant of the League of Nations expressly stipulated the obligation of the Members ' to respect and preserve as against external aggression the territorial integrity and existing political independence of all Members of the League.' Besides, it is difficult to understand how the integrity and independence of the Free Territory of Trieste can be endangered by non-observance of the provisions concerning the basic human rights of the inhabitants. The protection by the United Nations of the integrity and independence of the Free Territory against external aggression is all the more necessary as Article 3 of the Permanent Statute provides:—

1. The Free Territory shall be demilitarised and declared neutral.

2. No armed forces, except upon direction of the Security Council, shall be allowed in the Free Territory.

3. No para-military formations, exercises or activities shall be permitted within the Free Territory.

4. The government of the Free Territory shall not make or discuss any military arrangements or undertakings with any state.

In assuring the integrity and independence of the Free Territory the Security Council does not act as an organ of the government of that community, but as the organ of an international organisation different from it. [4]

As to the legal status of the Free Territory two different interpretations are possible. It may be argued that the community called Free Territory of Trieste after being constituted in conformity with the Italian Peace Treaty will have all the elements of a state in the sense of international law: a population living on a definite territory under a government the independence of which is guaranteed by the United Nations, so that it may be considered to be a new state. According to Article 21, paragraph 1 of the Peace Treaty, 'the Free Territory of Trieste is recognised by the Allied and Associated Powers and Italy.' Such recognition is usually granted to a community as a state. Also the above-mentioned demilitarisation and neutralisation are, as a rule, imposed only upon states. A particularity of the new state is that its head is not a physical, but a juristic person: the United Nations represented by the Security Council. The governmental functions conferred upon the United Nations with respect to the Free Territory are indeed functions usually conferred upon a head of state.

If, however, the requirement of an independent government is understood to mean a government not only independent from the governments of other states in the exercise of its functions, but also in its establishment, then a community the government of which is to be established by the governments of other states or by an international organisation cannot be considered to be a state in the sense of international law. It may have the character of an international personality, but this personality cannot be considered to be sovereign. If this view is accepted, the Free Territory is, in spite of its

[4] Other functions are conferred upon the United Nations by the Peace Treaty with Italy regarding the Free Territory of Trieste, which are not within the competence of the Organisation as government of the Territory. According to Article 36 of the Permanent Statute and Article 24 of the Instrument of the Free Port of Trieste, the Secretary-General may be requested to appoint, in case of a dispute relating to the interpretation or execution of the Statute or the Instrument, a third member of an arbitral tribunal, provided that the parties to the dispute fail to agree upon the appointment of that member. Similar functions not relating to the Free Territory are conferred upon the Secretary-General of the United Nations by Articles 83 and 87 of the Peace Treaty. Annexe XI, paragraph 3 provides that in case the Governments of the Soviet Union, Great Britain, the United States, and France should be unable to agree upon the disposal of Italy's territorial possessions in Africa 'the matter shall be referred to the General Assembly of the United Nations for a recommendation, and the Four Powers agree to accept the recommendation and to take the appropriate measures for giving effect to it.' No approval of these provisions on the part of the United Nations is required by the Peace Treaty; nor has the Organisation actually accepted these functions conferred on it by the Peace Treaty, but not established in the Charter.

'independence' guaranteed by the United Nations, not a state but a state-like community under the sovereignty of the United Nations.[5]

2. The Competence of the United Nations to Assume and Carry out the Functions conferred on it by the Peace Treaty with Italy

The first question that arises is whether the Charter of the United Nations authorises the Organisation to 'approve' the Annexes VI, VII, and VIII of the Peace Treaty with Italy and, by approving these instruments, to assume the functions conferred upon the Organisation by these Annexes. The second question is whether the Security Council is the competent organ of the United Nations for approving the Annexes VI, VII, and VIII of the Peace Treaty with Italy and for exercising the functions conferred upon it by these instruments. It stands to reason that both questions can be answered only on the basis of the Charter, not on the basis of the Peace Treaty. An international agreement, even if entered into by all Members of the United Nations—the Peace Treaty with Italy is concluded only by some of the Members—cannot establish competences of the United Nations or of particular organs of it. As pointed out in a previous connection, the Charter does not contain a provision authorising the United Nations to enter into other international agreements than those expressly mentioned in the Charter. Especially, to 'approve' international agreements the Organisation is authorised only by Article 63 of the Charter with respect to agreements entered into by the Economic and Social Council with specialised agencies, and by Articles 79, 83, and 85 with respect to trusteeship agreements. For the approval of the Annexes VI, VII, and VIII of the Peace Treaty with Italy there is no legal basis in the Charter and in particular no basis for the approval of these instruments by the Security Council. Among the many technical insufficiences of the Charter one of the

[5] The Peace Treaty with Italy imposes obligations (*e.g.*, demilitarisation and neutralisation) and confers rights (*e.g.*, in Annex IX) upon the Free Territory of Trieste, although this community is not and cannot be a contracting party to the Peace Treaty, since Trieste, a new state or statelike community, can come into existence only after the Peace Treaty has come into force. Article 24, paragraph 5 of Annex VI (Permanenent Statute of the Free Territory of Trieste), it is true, contains the following provision:

> The Free Territory of Trieste shall recognise the full force of the Treaty of Peace with Italy, and shall give effect to the applicable provisions of that Treaty. The Free Territory shall also recognise the full force of the other agreements or arrangements which have been or will be reached by the Allied and Associated Powers for the restoration of peace.

To recognise the Peace Treaty with Italy is an obligation imposed upon the Free Territory of Trieste by a treaty to which Trieste was not a contracting party when this treaty came into force. The other obligations imposed and the rights conferred upon the Free Territory by the Peace Treaty do not depend on the fulfilment of the obligation to 'recognise the full force of the Treaty of Peace with Italy.'

worst is the lack of a general authorisation of the Organisation to enter into international agreements.

An interpretation to the effect that the Organisation is competent to enter into any international agreement because this corresponds to the intention though not to the wording of the Charter, is all the more problematical as by such agreements an amendment to the Charter may be effected, and the amendment procedure, precisely determined by Articles 108 and 109, is very different from the procedure provided for by the Peace Treaty for the approval of Annexes VI, VII, and VIII. The latter consists in nothing else but a decision of the Security Council. The assumption of the functions conferred upon the Organisation by the Peace Treaty with Italy certainly constitutes an essential amendment to the Charter. For these functions are totally different from those conferred upon the Organisation by the Charter. After the Permanent Statute of the Free Territory of Trieste has come into force, the United Nations is obliged to assure the integrity and independence of a community which is not a Member of the United Nations and of which it is doubtful whether it can become a Member at all; yet the Charter even does not impose—at least not by an express provision—upon the Organisation the function to guarantee the integrity and independence of the Members. How can the United Nations carry out the function of assuring the integrity and independence of the Free Territory of Trieste? If it is against an external aggression, only by taking enforcement measures. This is possible under the Charter in conformity with Articles 39, 41, and 42, and the enforcement measures are to be executed by the Members called upon by the Security Council under Article 41 or 43. This call is to be made by a decision, which the Members are obliged to accept and carry out in conformity with Article 25. But Article 25 refers only to decisions 'in accordance with the present Charter'; and it is more than doubtful whether a decision of the Security Council to take enforcement measures in order to assure the integrity and independence of the Free Territory of Trieste, is 'in accordance with the present Charter,' which neither establishes this function nor authorises the Organisation to assume it by a treaty.

After the Instrument for the Provisional Regime and the Permanent Statute are approved by the Security Council, the latter has to appoint the Governor. Does Article 29 of the Charter apply to this appointment? The Governor is certainly an organ of the Security Council, but he is certainly not a 'subsidiary organ' within the meaning of Article 29. When the Permanent Statute comes into force, the Council has to exercise—partly directly, partly through the Governor—functions usually conferred upon a head of a state, which functions have nothing in common with anything the Council has to do under the Charter, except in case the Organisation itself is established as administering authority of a trust territory under Article 81. This is the only case where the United Nations is authorised by the Charter to exercise the rights of sovereignty over a territory. But the Free Territory of Trieste is certainly not a trust territory.

As far as the competence of the Security Council in particular is concerned, Article 24 of the Charter applies. Even the most extensive interpretation of this Article cannot justify an act by which the Council assumes the functions determined in Annexes VI, VII, and VIII. As pointed out in another connection,[6] the wording of Artice 24 cannot be interpreted to mean that the Council is authorised to take any action whatever if it considers it appropriate for the maintenance of peace; even an extensive interpretation of this Article can go no further than to the assumption that the Council is authorised to maintain peace by exercising the powers granted to it by other Articles of the Charter and the Statute of the International Court or by treaties constitutionally concluded by the Organisation (and not only the powers granted by Chapters VI, VII, VIII, and XII of the Charter, as paragraph 2 of Article 24 provides).

There is no provision in the Charter authorising especially the Security Council to assure the integrity and independence of a state or a statelike community. There is certainly no provision in the Charter that empowers especially the Security Council to exercise the functions of the head of a state or statelike community. If Article 24 could be interpreted to mean that the Security Council is competent to take any action whatever for the maintenance of peace, it would, perhaps, be possible to justify the Council's decision to assure the integrity and independence of the Free Territory, since it is not absolutely excluded to consider this function as a means for the maintenance of peace. But it would hardly be possible to justify in this way the assumption of the headship of a state or statelike community.[7]

[6] Cf. *supra*, pp. 279 ff.

[7] At the 89th and 91st meetings of the Security Council the Australian delegate denied the competence of the Council to approve the Annexes VI, VII, and VIII of the Peace Treaty with Italy and thus to assume the functions conferred upon it by these instruments. He stated: 'Chapter V of the Charter contains the general powers and functions of the Security Council, and it is further stated in Article 24, paragraph 2, that specific powers granted to the Council for the discharge of its duty to maintain international peace and security are laid down in Chapter VI, VII, VIII, and XII.' None of these Chapters authorise the Council to assume the functions determined in the Annexes VI, VII, and VIII of the Treaty. The Australain delegate particularly stated that the Charter did not authorise the Council to accept the responsibility of assuring the integrity and independence of the Free Territory, and he reminded the Council that 'at San Francisco, the question of including in the Charter of the United Nations a general guarantee of territorial integrity was discussed; but, as members of the Security Council will know, the proposals for such a guarantee were deliberately rejected.' (Official Records of the Security Council, 2nd year, No. 1, pp. 5 f.)

In order to justify the approval by the Security Council of the three Annexes, the Secretary-General submitted to the Security Council a statement in which he

The United Nations has not the legal, but it has certainly the actual power to assume for the Security Council the functions conferred upon it by the Peace Treaty with Italy. As a matter of fact, the Security Council, at its 91st meeting, adopted the following resolution:—

> The Security Council, having reached and examined the Annexes to the proposed Peace Treaty with Italy relating to the creation and government of the Free Territory of Trieste (including an arrangement for the Free Port), hereby records its approval of the three following documents:—
>
> 1. The instrument for the provisional regime of the Free Territory of Trieste;
> 2. The permanent Statute for the Free Territory of Trieste;
> 3. The instrument for the Free Port of Trieste; and its acceptance of the responsibilities developing upon it under the same.[8]

Whether the Security Council will be able to perform under its rules of procedure the functions which it has assumed by this resolution,

declared that the provision of Article 24 of the Charter by which primary responsibility for the maintenance of international peace and security is conferred upon the Council, constitutes 'a grant of power sufficiently wide to enable the Security Council to approve the documents in question and to assume the responsibilities arising therefrom.' 'The only limitations [of the responsibility of the Council for the maintenance of peace] are the fundamental principles and purposes found in Chapter I of the Charter.' (*Ibid.*, No. 3, pp. 44 f.) Cf. *supra*, pp. 284 f.

With reference to the statement of the Secretary-General the Australian delegate declared: 'Let us assume for our present purpose that Article 24 does confer a general responsibility for the maintenance of international peace and security over and above the specific powers listed in Chapters VI, VII, VIII and XII of the Charter. This general authority would not, in our view, authorise the assumption by the Council of the functions assigned to it in the Trieste Statute. The reasons for taking this view are the following: 1. The functions to be assigned to the Council by the Statute are not necessarily limited to the maintenance of international peace and security. 2. The giving of a categorical guarantee of the integrity and independence of the Free Territory goes farther than is warranted by the purposes and principles of the United Nations, and the Security Council is specifically required by Article 24 to act in accordance with such purposes and principles.' (*Ibid.*, No. 3, pp. 56 f.) The Australian delegate argued also that the Security Council was not authorised to assume the responsibility of gauranteeing the integrity and independence of the Free Territory because such responsibility would imply the obligations of those Members of the United Nations who happened to be members of the Security Council at any particular time. This would be incompatible with the Charter since 'there is no obligation on Members, under the Charter, to ensure the integrity and independence of any territory, and this omission is deliberate' (p. 57). This argument is not convincing. A responsibility of the Council is not an obligation of the Members represented on the Council. If the Council has a function it performs it by taking decisions, and all Members are, under Article 25, obliged to carry out these decisions.

[8] Official Records of the Security Council, 2nd year, No. 3, p. 60.

remains to be seen. Till now, the Council has not been able to appoint a Governor for the Free Territory of Trieste, which is an indispensable condition for the application of most of the provisions of the Instrument for the Provisional Regime and for the working of the Permanent Statute.[9]

[9] By a letter dated July 28, 1948, the Government of Yugoslavia charged that the United States and the United Kingdom had violated the terms of the Peace Treaty with Italy in their administration of their Zone of Trieste by various agreements with the Italian Government concerning the free circulation of the Italian lira in Trieste and other financial matters (Doc. S/927). At the 354th meeting of the Security Council a proposal to declare these agreements as null and void was defeated. Then the Security Council voted on the following draft resolution, submitted by the representative of the Ukranian Republic:

> The Security Council
>
> Having considered the note of the Government of the Federal People's Republic of Yugoslavia and
>
> Considering that the question of the appointment of a Governor of the Free Territory of Trieste has not yet been settled, and that the delay is making it difficult to implement other provisions of the Peace Treaty with Italy and decisions of the Council of Ministers of Foreign Affairs of April 22, 1947,
>
> Considers that it is urgently necessary to settle the question of the appointment of a Governor of the Free Territory of Trieste.

Only four members voted in favour; six members abstained from voting; one member did not take part in the voting. Hence the proposed resolution was not adopted. (Official Records of the Security Council, 3rd year, No. 107. pp. 36 f.)

APPENDICES

Appendix 1

CHARTER OF THE UNITED NATIONS

We the peoples of the united Nations determined

to save succeeding generations from the scourge of war, which twice in our lifetime has brought untold sorrow to mankind, and

to reaffirm faith in fundamental human rights, in the dignity and worth of the human person, in the equal rights of men and women and of nations large and small, and

to establish conditions under which justice and respect for the obligations arising from treaties and other sources of international law can be maintained, and

to promote social progress and better standards of life in larger freedom,

and for these ends

to practice tolerance and live together in peace with one another as good neighbours, and

to unite our strength to maintain international peace and security, and

to ensure, by the acceptance of principles and the institution of methods, that armed force shall not be used, save in the common interest, and

to employ international machinery for the promotion of the economic and social advancement of all peoples,

have resolved to combine our efforts to accomplish these aims.

Accordingly, our respective Governments, through representatives assembled in the city of San Francisco, who have exhibited their full powers found to be in good and due form, have agreed to the present Charter of the United Nations and do hereby establish an international organisation to be known as the United Nations.

Chapter I

PURPOSES AND PRINCIPLES

Article 1

The purposes of the United Nations are:

1. To maintain international peace and security, and to that end: to take effective collective measures for the prevention and removal of threats to the peace, and for the suppression of acts of aggression or other breaches of the peace, and to bring about by peaceful means, and in conformity with the principles of justice and international law,

adjustment or settlement of international disputes or situations which might lead to a breach of the peace;

2. To develop friendly relations among nations based on respect for the principle of equal rights and self-determination of peoples, and to take other appropriate measures to strengthen universal peace;

3. To achieve international co-operation in solving international problems of an economic, social, cultural, or humanitarian character, and in promoting and encouraging respect for human rights and for fundamental freedoms for all without distinction as to race, sex, language, or religion; and

4. To be a centre for harmonising the actions of nations in the attainment of these common ends.

Article 2

The Organisation and its Members, in pursuit of the Purposes stated in Article 1, shall act in accordance with the following Principles.

1. The Organisation is based on the principle of the sovereign equality of all its Members.

2. All Members, in order to ensure to all of them the rights and benefits resulting from membership, shall fulfil in good faith the obligations assumed by them in accordance with the present Charter.

3. All Members shall settle their international disputes by peaceful means in such a manner that international peace and security, and justice, are not endangered.

4. All Members shall refrain in their international relations from the threat or use of force against the territorial integrity or political independence of any state, or in any other manner inconsistent with the Purposes of the United Nations.

5. All Members shall give the United Nations every assistance in any action it takes in accordance with the present Charter, and shall refrain from giving assistance to any state against which the United Nations is taking preventive or enforcement action.

6. The Organisation shall ensure that states which are not Members of the United Nations act in accordance with these Principles so far as may be necessary for the maintenance of international peace and security.

7. Nothing contained in the present Charter shall authorise the United Nations to intervene in matters which are essentially within the domestic jurisdiction of any state or shall require the Members to submit such matters to settlement under the present Charter; but this principle shall not prejudice the application of enforcement measures under Chapter VII.

Chapter II

MEMBERSHIP

Article 3

The original Members of the United Nations shall be the states which, having participated in the United Nations Conference on International Organisation at San Francisco, or having previously signed the Declaration by United Nations of January 1, 1942, sign the present Charter and ratify it in accordance with Article 110.

Article 4

1. Membership in the United Nations is open to all other peace-loving states which accept the obligations contained in the present Charter and, in the judgment of the Organisation, are able and willing to carry out these obligations.

2. The admission of any such state to membership in the United Nations will be effected by a decision of the General Assembly upon the recommendation of the Security Council.

Article 5

A Member of the United Nations against which preventive or enforcement action has been taken by the Security Council may be suspended from the exercise of the rights and privileges of membership by the General Assembly upon the recommendation of the Security Council. The exercise of these rights and privileges may be restored by the Security Council.

Article 6

A Member of the United Nations which has persistently violated the Principles contained in the present Charter may be expelled from the Organisation by the General Assembly upon the recommendation of the Security Council.

Chapter III

ORGANS

Article 7

1. There are established as the principal organs of the United Nations: a General Assembly, a Security Council, an Economic and Social Council, a Trusteeship Council, an International Court of Justice, and a Secretariat.

2. Such subsidiary organs as may be found necessary may be established in accordance with the present Charter.

Article 8

The United Nations shall place no restrictions on the eligibility of men and women to participate in any capacity and under conditions of equality in its principal and subsidiary organs.

Chapter IV

THE GENERAL ASSEMBLY

Composition

Article 9

1. The General Assembly shall consist of all the Members of the United Nations.

2. Each Member shall have not more than five representatives in the General Assembly.

Functions and Powers

Article 10

The General Assembly may discuss any questions or any matters within the scope of the present Charter or relating to the powers and functions of any organs provided for in the present Charter, and except as provided in Article 12, may make recommendations to the Members of the United Nations or to the Security Council or to both on any such questions or matters.

Article 11

1. The General Assembly may consider the general principles of co-operation in the maintenance of international peace and security, including the principles governing disarmament and the regulation of armaments, and may make recommendations with regard to such principles to the Members or to the Security Council or to both.

2. The General Assembly may discuss any questions relating to the maintenance of international peace and security brought before it by any Member of the United Nations, or by the Security Council, or by a state which is not a Member of the United Nations in accordance with Article 35, paragraph 2, and, except as provided in Article 12, may make recommendations with regard to any such questions to the state or states concerned or to the Security Council or to both. Any such question on which action is necessary shall be referred to the Security Council by the General Assembly either before or after discussion.

3. The General Assembly may call the attention of the Security Council to situations which are likely to endanger international peace and security.

4. The powers of the General Assembly set forth in this Article shall not limit the general scope of Article 10.

Article 12

1. While the Security Council is exercising in respect of any dispute or situation the functions assigned to it in the present Charter, the General Assembly shall not make any recommendation with regard to that dispute or situation unless the Security Council so requests.

2. The Secretary-General, with the consent of the Security Council, shall notify the General Assembly at each session of any matters relative to the maintenance of international peace and security which are being dealt with by the Security Council and shall similarly notify the General Assembly, or the Members of the United Nations if the General Assembly is not in session, immediately the Security Council ceases to deal with such matters.

Article 13

1. The General Assembly shall initiate studies and make recommendations for the purpose of:

(*a*) promoting international co-operation in the political field and encouraging the progressive development of international law and its codification;

(*b*) promoting international co-operation in the economic, social, cultural, educational, and health fields, and assisting in the realisation of human rights and fundamental freedoms for all without distinction as to race, sex, language, or religion.

2. The further responsibilities, functions, and powers of the General Assembly with respect to matters mentioned in paragraph 1 (*b*) above are set forth in Chapters IX and X.

Article 14

Subject to the provisions of Article 12, the General Assembly may recommend measures for the peaceful adjustment of any situation, regardless of origin, which it deems likely to impair the general welfare or friendly relations among nations, including situations resulting from a violation of the provisions of the present Charter setting forth the Purposes and Principles of the United Nations.

Article 15

1. The General Assembly shall receive and consider annual and special reports from the Security Council; these reports shall include an account of the measures that the Security Council has decided upon or taken to maintain international peace and security.

2. The General Assembly shall receive and consider reports from the other organs of the United Nations.

Article 16

The General Assembly shall perform such functions with respect to the international trusteeship system as are assigned to it under Chapters XII and XIII, including the approval of the trusteeship agreements for areas not designated as strategic.

Article 17

1. The General Assembly shall consider and approve the budget of the Organisation.

2. The expenses of the Organisation shall be borne by the Members as apportioned by the General Assembly.

3. The General Assembly shall consider and approve any financial and budgetary arrangements with specialised agencies referred to in Article 57 and shall examine the administrative budgets of such specialised agencies with a view to making recommendations to the agencies concerned.

VOTING

Article 18

1. Each member of the General Assembly shall have one vote.

2. Decisions of the General Assembly on important questions shall be made by a two-thirds majority of the members present and voting. These questions shall include: recommendations with respect to the maintenance of international peace and security, the election of the non-permanent members of the Security Council, the election of the members of the Economic and Social Council, the election of members of the Trusteeship Council in accordance with paragraph 1 (*c*) of Article 86, the admission of new Members to the United Nations, the suspension of the rights and privileges of membership, the expulsion of Members, questions relating to the operation of the trusteeship system, and budgetary questions.

3. Decisions on other questions, including the determination of additional categories of questions to be decided by a two-thirds majority, shall be made by a majority of the members present and voting.

Article 19

A Member of the United Nations which is in arrears in the payment of its financial contributions to the Organisation shall have no vote in the General Assembly if the amount of its arrears equals or exceeds the amount of the contributions due from it for the preceding two full years. The General Assembly may, nevertheless, permit such a Member to vote if it is satisfied that the failure to pay is due to conditions beyond the control of the Member.

PROCEDURE

Article 20

The General Assembly shall meet in regular annual sessions and in such special sessions as occasion may require. Special sessions shall be convoked by the Secretary-General at the request of the Security Council or of a majority of the Members of the United Nations.

Article 21

The General Assembly shall adopt its own rules of procedure. It shall elect its President for each session.

Article 22

The General Assembly may establish such subsidiary organs as it deems necessary for the performance of its functions.

Chapter V

THE SECURITY COUNCIL

Composition

Article 23

1. The Security Council shall consist of eleven Members of the United Nations. The Republic of China, France, the Union of Soviet Socialist Republics, the United Kingdom of Great Britain and Northern Ireland, and the United States of America shall be permanent members of the Security Council. The General Assembly shall elect six other Members of the United Nations to be non-permanent members of the Security Council, due regard being specially paid, in the first instance to the contribution of Members of the United Nations to the maintenance of international peace and security and to the other purposes of the Organisation, and also to equitable geographical distribution.

2. The non-permanent members of the Security Council shall be elected for a term of two years. In the first election of the non-permanent members, however, three shall be chosen for a term of one year. A retiring member shall not be eligible for immediate re-election.

3. Each member of the Security Council shall have one representative.

Functions and Powers

Article 24

1. In order to ensure prompt and effective action by the United Nations, its Members confer on the Security Council primary responsibility for the maintenance of international peace and security, and agree that in carrying out its duties under this responsibility the Security Council acts on their behalf.

2. In discharging these duties the Security Council shall act in accordance with the Purposes and Principles of the United Nations. The specific powers granted to the Security Council for the discharge of these duties are laid down in Chapters VI, VII, VIII, and XII.

3. The Security Council shall submit annual and, when necessary, special reports to the General Assembly for its consideration.

Article 25

The Members of the United Nations agree to accept and carry out the decisions of the Security Council in accordance with the present Charter.

Article 26

In order to promote the establishment and maintenance of international peace and security with the least diversion for armaments of the world's human and economic resources, the Security Council shall be responsible for formulating, with the assistance of the Military Staff Committee referred to in Article 47, plans to be submitted to the Members of the United Nations for the establishment of a system for the regulation of armaments.

VOTING

Article 27

1. Each member of the Security Council shall have one vote.

2. Decisions of the Security Council on procedural matters shall be made by an affirmative vote of seven members.

3. Decisions of the Security Council on all other matters shall be made by an affirmative vote of seven members including the concurring votes of the permanent members; provided that, in decisions under Chapter VI, and under paragraph 3 of Article 52, a party to a dispute shall abstain from voting.

PROCEDURE

Article 28

1. The Security Council shall be so organised as to be able to function continuously. Each member of the Security Council shall for this purpose be represented at all times at the seat of the Organisation.

2. The Security Council shall hold periodic meetings at which each of its members may, if it so desires, be represented by a member of the government or by some other specially designated representative.

3. The Security Council may hold meetings at such places other than the seat of the Organisation as in its judgment will best facilitate its work.

Article 29

The Security Council may establish such subsidiary organs as it deems necessary for the performance of its functions.

Article 30

The Security Council shall adopt its own rules of procedure, including the method of selecting its President.

Article 31

Any Member of the United Nations which is not a member of the Security Council may participate, without vote, in the discussion of any question brought before the Security Council whenever the latter considers that the interests of that Member are specially affected.

Article 32

Any Member of the United Nations which is not a member of the Security Council or any state which is not a Member of the United Nations, if it is a party to a dispute under consideration by the Security Council, shall be invited to participate, without vote, in the discussion relating to the dispute. The Security Council shall lay down such conditions as it deems just for the participation of a state which is not a Member of the United Nations.

CHAPTER VI

PACIFIC SETTLEMENT OF DISPUTES

Article 33

1. The parties to any dispute, the continuance of which is likely to endanger the maintenance of international peace and security, shall, first of all, seek a solution by negotiation, enquiry, mediation, conciliation, arbitration, judicial settlement, resort to regional agencies or arrangements, or other peaceful means of their own choice.

2. The Security Council shall, when it deems necessary, call upon the parties to settle their dispute by such means.

Article 34

The Security Council may investigate any dispute, or any situation which might lead to international friction or give rise to a dispute, in order to determine whether the continuance of the dispute or situation is likely to endanger the maintenance of international peace and security.

Article 35

1. Any Member of the United Nations may bring any dispute, or any situation of the nature referred to in Article 34, to the attention of the Security Council or of the General Assembly.

2. A state which is not a Member of the United Nations may bring to the attention of the Security Council or of the General Assembly any dispute to which it is a party if it accepts in advance, for the purposes of the dispute, the obligations of pacific settlement provided in the present Charter.

3. The proceedings of the General Assembly in respect of matters brought to its attention under this Article will be subject to the provisions of Articles 11 and 12.

Article 36

1. The Security Council may, at any stage of a dispute of the nature referred to in Article 33 or of a situation of like nature, recommend appropriate procedures or methods of adjustment.

2. The Security Council should take into consideration any procedures for the settlement of the dispute which have already been adopted by the parties.

3. In making recommendations under this Article the Security Council should also take into consideration that legal disputes should as a general rule be referred by the parties to the International Court of Justice in accordance with the provisions of the Statute of the Court.

Article 37

1. Should the parties to a dispute of the nature referred to in Article 33 fail to settle it by the means indicated in that Article, they shall refer it to the Security Council.

2. If the Security Council deems that the continuance of the dispute is in fact likely to endanger the maintenance of international peace and security, it shall decide whether to take action under Article 36 or to recommend such terms of settlement as it may consider appropriate.

Article 38

Without prejudice to the provisions of Articles 33 to 37, the Security Council may, if all the parties to any dispute so request, make recommendations to the parties with a view to a pacific settlement of the dispute.

Chapter VII

ACTION WITH RESPECT TO THREATS TO THE PEACE, BREACHES OF THE PEACE, AND ACTS OF AGGRESSION

Article 39

The Security Council shall determine the existence of any threat to the peace, breach of the peace, or act of aggression and shall make recommendations, or decide what measures shall be taken in accordance with Articles 41 and 42, to maintain or restore international peace and security.

Article 40

In order to prevent an aggravation of the situation, the Security Council may, before making the recommendations or deciding upon the measures provided for in Article 39, call upon the parties concerned to comply with such provisional measures as it deems necessary or desirable. Such provisional measures shall be without prejudice to the rights, claims, or position of the parties concerned. The Security Council shall duly take account of failure to comply with such provisional measures.

Article 41

The Security Council may decide what measures not involving the use of armed force are to be employed to give effect to its decisions, and it may call upon the Members of the United Nations to apply such measures. These may include complete or partial interruption of economic relations and of rail, sea, air, postal, telegraphic, radio, and other means of communication, and the severance of diplomatic relations.

Article 42

Should the Security Council consider that measures provided for in Article 41 would be inadequate or have proved to be inadequate, it may take such action by air, sea, or land forces as may be necessary to maintain or restore international peace and security. Such action may include demonstrations, blockade, and other operations by air, sea, or land forces of Members of the United Nations.

Article 43

1. All Members of the United Nations, in order to contribute to the maintenance of international peace and security, undertake to make available to the Security Council, on its call and in accordance with a special agreement or agreements, armed forces, assistance, and facilities, including rights of passage, necessary for the purpose of maintaining international peace and security.

2. Such agreement or agreements shall govern the numbers and types of forces, their degree of readiness and general location, and the nature of the facilities and assistance to be provided.

3. The agreement or agreements shall be negotiated as soon as possible on the initiative of the Security Council. They shall be concluded between the Security Council and Members or between the Security Council and groups of Members and shall be subject to ratification by the signatory states in accordance with their respective constitutional processes.

Article 44

When the Security Council has decided to use force it shall, before calling upon a Member not represented on it to provide armed forces in fulfilment of the obligations assumed under Article 43, invite that Member, if the Member so desires, to participate in the decisions of the Security Council concerning the employment of contingents of that Member's armed forces.

Article 45

In order to enable the United Nations to take urgent military measures, Members shall hold immediately available national air-force contingents for combined international enforcement action. The strength and degree of readiness of these contingents and plans for their combined action shall be determined, within the limits laid down in the special agreement or agreements referred to in Article 43, by the Security Council with the assistance of the Military Staff Committee.

Article 46

Plans for the application of armed force shall be made by the Security Council with the assistance of the Military Staff Committee.

Article 47

1. There shall be established a Military Staff Committee to advise and assist the Security Council on all questions relating to the Security Council's military requirements for the maintenance of international peace and security, the employment and command of forces placed at its disposal, the regulation of armaments, and possible disarmament.

2. The Military Staff Committee shall consist of the Chiefs of Staff of the permanent members of the Security Council or their representatives. Any Member of the United Nations not permanently represented on the Committee shall be invited by the Committee to be associated with it when the efficient discharge of the Committee's responsibilities requires the participation of that Member in its work.

3. The Military Staff Committee shall be responsible under the Security Council for the strategic direction of any armed forces placed at the disposal of the Security Council. Questions relating to the command of such forces shall be worked out subsequently.

4. The Military Staff Committee, with the authorisation of the Security Council and after consultation with appropriate regional agencies, may establish regional sub-committees.

Article 48

1. The action required to carry out the decisions of the Security Council for the maintenance of international peace and security shall be taken by all the Members of the United Nations or by some of them, as the Security Council may determine.

2. Such decisions shall be carried out by the Members of the United Nations directly and through their action in the appropriate international agencies of which they are members.

Article 49

The Members of the United Nations shall join in affording mutual assistance in carrying out the measures decided upon by the Security Council.

Article 50

If preventive or enforcement measures against any state are taken by the Security Council, any other state, whether a Member of the United Nations or not, which finds itself confronted with special economic problems arising from the carrying out of those measures shall have the right to consult the Security Council with regard to a solution of those problems.

Article 51

Nothing in the present Charter shall impair the inherent right of individual or collective self-defence if an armed attack occurs against a Member of the United Nations, until the Security Council has taken the measures necessary to maintain international peace and security. Measures taken by Members in the exercise of this right of self-defence shall be immediately reported to the Security Council and shall not in any way affect the authority and responsibility of the Security Council under the present Charter to take at any time such action as it deems necessary in order to maintain or restore international peace and security.

CHAPTER VIII

REGIONAL ARRANGEMENTS

Article 52

1. Nothing in the present Charter precludes the existence of regional arrangements or agencies for dealing with such matters relating to the maintenance of international peace and security as are appropriate for regional action, provided that such arrangements or agencies and their activities are consistent with the Purposes and Principles of the United Nations.

2. The Members of the United Nations entering into such arrangements or constituting such agencies shall make every effort to achieve pacific settlement of local disputes through such regional arrangements or by such regional agencies before referring them to the Security Council.

3. The Security Council shall encourage the development of pacific settlement of local disputes through such regional arrangements or by such regional agencies either on the initiative of the states concerned or by reference from the Security Council.

4. This Article in no way impairs the application of Articles 34 and 35.

Article 53

1. The Security Council shall, where appropriate, utilise such regional arrangements or agencies for enforcement action under its authority. But no enforcement action shall be taken under regional arrangements or by regional agencies without the authorisation of the Security Council, with the exception of measures against any enemy state, as defined in paragraph 2 of this Article, provided for pursuant to Article 107 or in regional arrangements directed against renewal of aggressive policy on the part of any such state, until such time as the Organisation may, on request of the Governments concerned, be charged with the responsibility for preventing further aggression by such a state.

2. The term enemy state as used in paragraph 1 of this Article applies to any state which during the Second World War has been an enemy of any signatory of the present Charter.

Article 54

The Security Council shall at all times be kept fully informed of activities undertaken or in contemplation under regional arrangements or by regional agencies for the maintenance of international peace and security.

Chapter IX

INTERNATIONAL ECONOMIC AND SOCIAL CO-OPERATION

Article 55

With a view to the creation of conditions of stability and well-being which are necessary for peaceful and friendly relations among nations based on respect for the principle of equal rights and self-determination of peoples, the United Nations shall promote:

(*a*) higher standards of living, full employment, and conditions of economic and social progress and development;

(*b*) solutions of international economic, social, health, and related problems; and international cultural and educational co-operation; and

(*c*) universal respect for, and observance of, human rights and fundamental freedoms for all without distinction as to race, sex, language, or religion.

Article 56

All Members pledge themselves to take joint and separate action in co-operation with the Organisation for the achievement of the purposes set forth in Article 55.

Article 57

1. The various specialised agencies, established by intergovernmental agreement and having wide international responsibilities, as defined in their basic instruments, in economic, social, cultural, educational, health, and related fields, shall be brought into relationship with the United Nations in accordance with the provisions of Article 63.

2. Such agencies thus brought into relationship with the United Nations are hereinafter referred to as specialised agencies.

Article 58

The Organisation shall make recommendations for the co-ordination of the policies and activities of the specialised agencies.

Article 59

The Organisation shall, where appropriate, initiate negotiations among the states concerned for the creation of any new specialised agencies required for the accomplishment of the purposes set forth in Article 55.

Article 60

Responsibility for the discharge of the functions of the Organisation set forth in this Chapter shall be vested in the General Assembly and, under the authority of the General Assembly, in the Economic and Social Council, which shall have for this purpose the powers set forth in Chapter X.

Chapter X

THE ECONOMIC AND SOCIAL COUNCIL

Composition

Article 61

1. The Economic and Social Council shall consist of eighteen Members of the United Nations elected by the General Assembly.

2. Subject to the provisions of paragraph 3, six members of the Economic and Social Council shall be elected each year for a term of three years. A retiring member shall be eligible for immediate re-election.

3. At the first election, eighteen members of the Economic and Social Council shall be chosen. The term of office of six members so chosen shall expire at the end of one year, and of six other members at the end of two years, in accordance with arrangements made by the General Assembly.

4. Each member of the Economic and Social Council shall have one representative.

Functions and Powers

Article 62

1. The Economic and Social Council may make or initiate studies and reports with respect to international economic, social, cultural, educational, health, and related matters and may make recommendations with respect to any such matters to the General Assembly, to the Members of the United Nations, and to the specialised agencies concerned.

2. It may make recommendations for the purpose of promoting respect for, and observance of, human rights and fundamental freedoms for all.

3. It may prepare draft conventions for submission to the General Assembly, with respect to matters falling within its competence.

4. It may call, in accordance with the rules prescribed by the United Nations, international conferences on matters falling within its competence.

Article 63

1. The Economic and Social Council may enter into agreements with any of the agencies referred to in Article 57, defining the terms on which the agency concerned shall be brought into relationship with the United Nations. Such agreements shall be subject to approval by the General Assembly.

2. It may co-ordinate the activities of the specialised agencies through consultation with and recommendations to such agencies and through recommendations to the General Assembly and to the Members of the United Nations.

Article 64

1. The Economic and Social Council may take appropriate steps to obtain regular reports from the specialised agencies. It may make arrangements with the Members of the United Nations and with the specialised agencies to obtain reports on the steps taken to give effect to its own recommendations and to recommendations on matters falling within its competence made by the General Assembly.

2. It may communicate its observations on these reports to the General Assembly.

Article 65

The Economic and Social Council may furnish information to the Security Council and shall assist the Security Council upon its request.

Article 66

1. The Economic and Social Council shall perform such functions as fall within its competence in connection with the carrying out of the recommendations of the General Assembly.

2. It may, with the approval of the General Assembly, perform services at the request of Members of the United Nations and at the request of specialised agencies.

3. It shall perform such other functions as are specified elsewhere in the present Charter or as may be assigned to it by the General Assembly.

VOTING

Article 67

1. Each member of the Economic and Social Council shall have one vote.

2. Decisions of the Economic and Social Council shall be made by a majority of the members present and voting.

PROCEDURE

Article 68

The Economic and Social Council shall set up commissions in economic and social fields and for the promotion of human rights, and such other commissions as may be required for the performance of its functions.

Article 69

The Economic and Social Council shall invite any Member of the United Nations to participate, without vote, in its deliberations on any matter of particular concern to that Member.

Article 70

The Economic and Social Council may make arrangements for representatives of the specialised agencies to participate, without vote, in its deliberations and in those of the commissions established by it, and for its representatives to participate in the deliberations of the specialised agencies.

Article 71

The Economic and Social Council may make suitable arrangements for consultation with non-governmental organisations which are concerned with matters within its competence. Such arrangements may be made with international organisations and, where appropriate, with national organisations after consultation with the Member of the United Nations concerned.

Article 72

1. The Economic and Social Council shall adopt its own rules of procedure, including the method of selecting its President.

2. The Economic and Social Council shall meet as required in accordance with its rules, which shall include provision for the convening of meetings on the request of a majority of its members.

CHAPTER XI

DECLARATION REGARDING NON-SELF-GOVERNING TERRITORIES

Article 73

Members of the United Nations which have or assume responsibilities for the administration of territories whose peoples have not yet attained a full measure of self-government recognise the principle that the interests of the inhabitants of these territories are paramount, and accept as a sacred trust the obligation to promote to the utmost, within the system of international peace and security established by the present Charter, the well-being of the inhabitants of these territories, and, to this end:

(*a*) to ensure, with due respect for the culture of the peoples concerned, their political, economic, social, and educational advancement, their just treatment, and their protection against abuses;

(*b*) to develop self-government, to take due account of the political aspirations of the peoples, and to assist them in the progressive development of their free political institutions, according to the particular circumstances of each territory and its peoples and their varying stages of advancement;

(*c*) to further international peace and security;

(*d*) to promote constructive measures of development, to encourage research, and to co-operate with one another and, when and where appropriate, with specialised international bodies with a view to the practical achievement of the social, economic, and scientific purposes set forth in this Article; and

(*e*) to transmit regularly to the Secretary-General for information purposes, subject to such limitation as security and constitutional considerations may require, statistical and other information of a technical nature relating to economic, social, and educational conditions in the territories for which they are respectively responsible other than those territories to which Chapters XII and XIII apply.

Article 74

Members of the United Nations also agree that their policy in respect of the territories to which this Chapter applies, no less than in respect of their metropolitan areas, must be based on the general principle of good neighbourliness, due account being taken of the interests and well-being of the rest of the world, in social, economic, and commercial matters.

Chapter XII

INTERNATIONAL TRUSTEESHIP SYSTEM

Article 75

The United Nations shall establish under its authority an international trusteeship system for the administration and supervision of such territories as may be placed thereunder by subsequent individual agreements. These territories are hereinafter referred to as trust territories.

Article 76

The basic objectives of the trusteeship system, in accordance with the Purposes of the United Nations laid down in Article 1 of the present Charter, shall be:

(*a*) to further international peace and security;

(*b*) to promote the political, economic, social, and educational advancement of the inhabitants of the trust territories, and their progressive development towards self-government or independence as may be appropriate to the particular circumstances of each territory and its peoples and the freely expressed wishes of the peoples concerned, and as may be provided by the terms of each trusteeship agreement;

(*c*) to encourage respect for human rights and for fundamental freedoms for all without distinction as to race, sex, language, or religion, and to encourage recognition of the interdependence of the peoples of the world; and

(*d*) to ensure equal treatment in social, economic, and commercial matters for all Members of the United Nations and their nationals, and also equal treatment for the latter in the administration of justice, without prejudice to the attainment of the foregoing objectives and subject to the provisions of Article 80.

Article 77

1. The trusteeship system shall apply to such territories in the following categories as may be placed thereunder by means of trusteeship agreements:

(*a*) territories now held under mandate;

(*b*) territories which may be detached from enemy states as a result of the Second World War; and

(*c*) territories voluntarily placed under the system by states responsible for their administration.

2. It will be a matter for subsequent agreement as to which territories in the foregoing categories will be brought under the trusteeship system and upon what terms.

Article 78

The trusteeship system shall not apply to territories which have become Members of the United Nations, relationship among which shall be based on respect for the principle of sovereign equality.

Article 79

The terms of trusteeship for each territory to be placed under the trusteeship system, including any alteration or amendment, shall be agreed upon by the states directly concerned, including the mandatory power in the case of territories held under mandate by a Member of the United Nations, and shall be approved as provided for in Articles 83 and 85.

Article 80

1. Except as may be agreed upon in individual trusteeship agreements, made under Articles 77, 79, and 81, placing each territory under the trusteeship system, and until such agreements have been concluded, nothing in this Chapter shall be construed in or of itself to alter in any manner the rights whatsoever of any states or any peoples or the terms of existing international instruments to which Members of the United Nations may respectively be parties.

2. Paragraph 1 of this Article shall not be interpreted as giving grounds for delay or postponement of the negotiation and conclusion of agreements for placing mandated and other territories under the trusteeship system as provided for in Article 77.

Article 81

The trusteeship agreement shall in each case include the terms under which the trust territory will be administered and designate the authority which will exercise the administration of the trust territory. Such authority, hereinafter called the administering authority, may be one or more states or the Organisation itself.

Article 82

There may be designated, in any trusteeship agreement, a strategic area or areas which may include part or all of the trust territory to which the agreement applies, without prejudice to any special agreement or agreements made under Article 43.

Article 83

1. All functions of the United Nations relating to strategic areas, including the approval of the terms of the trusteeship agreements and of their alteration or amendment, shall be exercised by the Security Council.

2. The basic objectives set forth in Article 76 shall be applicable to the people of each strategic area.

3. The Security Council shall, subject to the provisions of the trusteeship agreements and without prejudice to security considerations, avail itself of the assistance of the Trusteeship Council to perform those functions of the United Nations under the trusteeship system relating to political, economic, social, and educational matters in the strategic areas.

Article 84

It shall be the duty of the administering authority to ensure that the trust territory shall play its part in the maintenance of international peace and security. To this end the administering authority may make use of volunteer forces, facilities, and assistance from the trust territory in carrying out the obligations towards the Security Council undertaken in this regard by the administering authority, as well as for local defence and the maintenance of law and order within the trust territory.

Article 85

1. The functions of the United Nations with regard to trusteeship agreements for all areas not designated as strategic, including the approval of the terms of the trusteeship agreements and of their alteration or amendment, shall be exercised by the General Assembly.

2. The Trusteeship Council, operating under the authority of the General Assembly, shall assist the General Assembly in carrying out these functions.

CHAPTER XIII

THE TRUSTEESHIP COUNCIL

COMPOSITION

Article 86

1. The Trusteeship Council shall consist of the following Members of the United Nations:

(*a*) those Members administering trust territories;

(*b*) such of those Members mentioned by name in Article 23 as are not administering trust territories; and

(*c*) as many other Members elected for three-year terms by the General Assembly as may be necessary to ensure that the total number of members of the Trusteeship Council is equally divided between those Members of the United Nations which administer trust territories and those which do not.

2. Each member of the Trusteeship Council shall designate one specially qualified person to represent it therein.

FUNCTIONS AND POWERS

Article 87

The General Assembly and, under its authority, the Trusteeship Council, in carrying out their functions, may:

(*a*) consider reports submitted by the administering authority;

(*b*) accept petitions and examine them in consultation with the administering authority;

(*c*) provide for periodic visits to the respective trust territories at times agreed upon with the administering authority; and

(*d*) take these and other actions in conformity with the terms of the trusteeship agreements.

Article 88

The Trusteeship Council shall formulate a questionnaire on the political, economic, social, and educational advancement of the inhabitants of each trust territory, and the administering authority for each trust territory within the competence of the General Assembly shall make an annual report to the General Assembly upon the basis of such questionnaire.

VOTING

Article 89

1. Each member of the Trusteeship Council shall have one vote.

2. Decisions of the Trusteeship Council shall be made by a majority of the members present and voting.

PROCEDURE

Article 90

1. The Trusteeship Council shall adopt its own rules of procedure, including the method of selecting its President.

2. The Trusteeship Council shall meet as required in accordance with its rules, which shall include provision for the convening of meetings on the request of a majority of its members.

Article 91

The Trusteeship Council shall, when appropriate, avail itself of the assistance of the Economic and Social Council and of the specialised agencies in regard to matters with which they are respectively concerned.

CHAPTER XIV

THE INTERNATIONAL COURT OF JUSTICE

Article 92

The International Court of Justice shall be the principal judicial organ of the United Nations. It shall function in accordance with the annexed Statute, which is based upon the Statute of the Permanent Court of International Justice and forms an integral part of the present Charter.

Article 93

1. All members of the United Nations are *ipso facto* parties to the Statute of the International Court of Justice.

2. A state which is not a Member of the United Nations may become a party to the Statute of the International Court of Justice on conditions to be determined in each case by the General Assembly upon the recommendation of the Security Council.

Article 94

1. Each Member of the United Nations undertakes to comply with the decision of the International Court of Justice in any case to which it is a party.

2. If any party to a case fails to perform the obligations incumbent upon it under a judgment rendered by the Court, the other party may have recourse to the Security Council, which may, if it deems necessary, make recommendations or decide upon measures to be taken to give effect to the judgment.

Article 95

Nothing in the present Charter shall prevent Members of the United Nations from entrusting the solution of their differences to other tribunals by virtue of agreements already in existence or which may be concluded in the future.

Article 96

1. The General Assembly or the Security Council may request the International Court of Justice to give an advisory opinion on any legal question.

2. Other organs of the United Nations and specialised agencies, which may at any time be so authorised by the General Assembly, may also request advisory opinions of the Court on legal questions arising within the scope of their activities.

CHAPTER XV

THE SECRETARIAT

Article 97

The Secretariat shall comprise a Secretary-General and such staff as the Organisation may require. The Secretary-General shall be appointed by the General Assembly upon the recommendation of the Security Council. He shall be the chief administrative officer of the Organisation.

Article 98

The Secretary-General shall act in that capacity in all meetings of the General Assembly, of the Security Council, of the Economic and Social Council, and of the Trusteeship Council, and shall perform such other functions as are entrusted to him by these organs. The Secretary-General shall make an annual report to the General Assembly on the work of the Organisation.

Article 99

The Secretary-General may bring to the attention of the Security Council any matter which in his opinion may threaten the maintenance of international peace and security.

Article 100

1. In the performance of their duties the Secretary-General and the staff shall not seek or receive instructions from any government or

from any other authority external to the Organisation. They shall refrain from any action which might reflect on their position as international officials responsible only to the Organisation.

2. Each Member of the United Nations undertakes to respect the exclusively international character of the responsibilities of the Secretary-General and the staff and not to seek to influence them in the discharge of their responsibilities.

Article 101

1. The staff shall be appointed by the Secretary-General under regulations established by the General Assembly.

2. Appropriate staffs shall be permanently assigned to the Economic and Social Council, the Trusteeship Council, and, as required, to other organs of the United Nations. These staffs shall form a part of the Secretariat.

3. The paramount consideration in the employment of the staff and in the determination of the conditions of service shall be the necessity of securing the highest standards of efficiency, competence, and integrity. Due regard shall be paid to the importance of recruiting the staff on as wide a geographical basis as possible.

Chapter XVI

MISCELLANEOUS PROVISIONS

Article 102

1. Every treaty and every international agreement entered into by any Member of the United Nations after the present Charter comes into force shall as soon as possible be registered with the Secretariat and published by it.

2. No party to any such treaty or international agreement which has not been registered in accordance with the provisions of paragraph 1 of this Article may invoke that treaty or agreement before any organ of the United Nations.

Article 103

In the event of a conflict between the obligations of the Members of the United Nations under the present Charter and their obligations under any other international agreement, their obligations under the present Charter shall prevail.

Article 104

The Organisation shall enjoy in the territory of each of its Members such legal capacity as may be necessary for the exercise of its functions and the fulfilment of its purposes.

Article 105

1. The Organisation shall enjoy in the territory of each of its Members such privileges and immunities as are necessary for the fulfilment of its purposes.

2. Representatives of the Members of the United Nations and officials of the Organisation shall similarly enjoy such privileges and immunities as are necessary for the independent exercise of their functions in connection with the Organisation.

3. The General Assembly may make recommendations with a view to determining the details of the application of paragraphs 1 and 2 of this Article or may propose conventions to the Members of the United Nations for this purpose.

Chapter XVII

TRANSITIONAL SECURITY ARRANGEMENTS

Article 106

Pending the coming into force of such special agreements referred to in Article 43 as in the opinion of the Security Council enable it to begin the exercise of its responsibilities under Article 42, the parties to the Four-Nation Declaration, signed at Moscow, October 30, 1943, and France, shall, in accordance with the provisions of paragraph 5 of that Declaration, consult with one another and as occasion requires with other Members of the United Nations with a view to such joint action on behalf of the Organisation as may be necessary for the purpose of maintaining international peace and security.

Article 107

Nothing in the present Charter shall invalidate or preclude action, in relation to any state which during the Second World War has been an enemy of any signatory to the present Charter, taken or authorised as a result of that war by the Governments having responsibility for such action.

Chapter XVIII

AMENDMENTS

Article 108

Amendments to the present Charter shall come into force for all Members of the United Nations when they have been adopted by a vote of two thirds of the members of the General Assembly and ratified in accordance with their respective constitutional processes by two thirds of the Members of the United Nations, including all the permanent members of the Security Council.

Article 109

1. A General Conference of the Members of the United Nations for the purpose of reviewing the present Charter may be held at a date and place to be fixed by a two-thirds vote of the members of the General Assembly and by a vote of any seven members of the Security Council. Each Member of the United Nations shall have one vote in the conference.

2. Any alteration of the present Charter recommended by a two-thirds vote of the conference shall take effect when ratified in accordance with their respective constitutional processes by two thirds of the Members of the United Nations including all the permanent members of the Security Council.

3. If such a conference has not been held before the tenth annual session of the General Assembly following the coming into force of the present Charter, the proposal to call such a conference shall be placed on the agenda of that session of the General Assembly, and the conference shall be held if so decided by a majority vote of the members of the General Assembly and by a vote of any seven members of the Security Council.

Chapter XIX

RATIFICATION AND SIGNATURE

Article 110

1. The present Charter shall be ratified by the signatory states in accordance with their respective constitutional processes.

2. The ratifications shall be deposited with the Government of the United States of America, which shall notify all the signatory states of each deposit as well as the Secretary-General of the Organisation when he has been appointed.

3. The present Charter shall come into force upon the deposit of ratifications by the Republic of China, France, the Union of Soviet Socialist Republics, the United Kingdom of Great Britain and Northern Ireland, and the United States of America, and by a majority of the other signatory states. A protocol of the ratifications deposited shall thereupon be drawn up by the Government of the United States of America which shall communicate copies thereof to all the signatory states.

4. The states signatory to the present Charter which ratify it after it has come into force will become original Members of the United Nations on the date of the deposit of their respective ratifications.

Article 111

The present Charter, of which the Chinese, French, Russian, English, and Spanish texts are equally authentic, shall remain deposited in the archives of the Government of the United States of America. Duly certified copies thereof shall be transmitted by that Government to the Governments of the other signatory states.

IN FAITH WHEREOF the representatives of the Governments of the United Nations have signed the present Charter.

DONE at the city of San Francisco the twenty-sixth day of June, one thousand nine hundred and forty-five.

APPENDIX 2

STATUTE OF THE INTERNATIONAL COURT OF JUSTICE

Article 1

THE INTERNATIONAL COURT OF JUSTICE established by the Charter of the United Nations as the principal judicial organ of the United Nations shall be constituted and shall function in accordance with the provisions of the present Statute.

CHAPTER I

ORGANISATION OF THE COURT

Article 2

The Court shall be composed of a body of independent judges, elected regardless of their nationality from among persons of high moral character, who possess the qualifications required in their respective countries for appointment to the highest judicial offices, or are juris-consults of recognised competence in international law.

Article 3

1. The Court shall consist of fifteen members, no two of whom may be nationals of the same state.

2. A person who for the purposes of membership in the Court could be regarded as a national of more than one state shall be deemed to be a national of the one in which he ordinarily exercises civil and political rights.

Article 4

1. The members of the Court shall be elected by the General Assembly and by the Security Council from a list of persons nominated by the national groups in the Permanent Court of Arbitration, in accordance with the following provisions.

2. In the case of Members of the United Nations not represented in the Permanent Court of Arbitration, candidates shall be nominated by national groups appointed for this purpose by their governments under the same conditions as those prescribed for members of the Permanent Court of Arbitration by Article 44 of the Convention of The Hague of 1907 for the pacific settlement of international disputes.

3. The conditions under which a state which is a party to the present Statute but is not a Member of the United Nations may participate in electing the members of the Court shall, in the absence of a special agreement, be laid down by the General Assembly upon recommendation of the Security Council.

Article 5

1. At least three months before the date of the election, the Secretary-General of the United Nations shall address a written request to the members of the Permanent Court of Arbitration belonging to the states which are parties to the present Statute, and to the members of the national groups appointed under Article 4, paragraph 2, inviting them to undertake, within a given time, by national groups, the nomination of persons in a position to accept the duties of a member of the Court.

2. No group may nominate more than four persons, not more than two of whom shall be of their own nationality. In no case may the number of candidates nominated by a group be more than double the number of seats to be filled.

Article 6

Before making these nominations, each national group is recommended to consult its highest court of justice, its legal faculties and schools of law, and its national academies and national sections of international academies devoted to the study of law.

Article 7

1. The Secretary-General shall prepare a list in alphabetical order of all the persons thus nominated. Save as provided in Article 12, paragraph 2, these shall be the only persons eligible.

2. The Secretary-General shall submit this list to the General Assembly and to the Security Council.

Article 8

The General Assembly and the Security Council shall proceed independently of one another to elect the members of the Court.

Article 9

At every election, the electors shall bear in mind not only that the persons to be elected should individually possess the qualifications required, but also that in the body as a whole the representation of the main forms of civilisation and of the principal legal systems of the world should be assured.

Article 10

1. Those candidates who obtain an absolute majority of votes in the General Assembly and in the Security Council shall be considered as elected.

2. Any vote of the Security Council, whether for the election of judges or for the appointment of members of the conference envisaged in Article 12, shall be taken without any distinction between permanent and non-permanent members of the Security Council.

3. In the event of more than one national of the same state obtaining an absolute majority of the votes both of the General Assembly and of the Security Council, the eldest of these only shall be considered as elected.

Article 11

If, after the first meeting held for the purpose of the election, one or more seats remain to be filled, a second and, if necessary, a third meeting shall take place.

Article 12

1. If, after the third meeting, one or more seats still remain unfilled, a joint conference consisting of six members, three appointed by the General Assembly and three by the Security Council, may be formed at any time at the request of either the General Assembly or the Security Council, for the purpose of choosing by the vote of an absolute majority one name for each seat still vacant, to submit to the General Assembly and the Security Council for their respective acceptance.

2. If the joint conference is unanimously agreed upon any person who fulfils the required conditions, he may be included in its list, even though he was not included in the list of nominations referred to in Article 7.

3. If the joint conference is satisfied that it will not be successful in procuring an election, those members of the Court who have already been elected shall, within a period to be fixed by the Security Council, proceed to fill the vacant seats by selection from among those candidates who have obtained votes either in the General Assembly or in the Security Council.

4. In the event of an equality of votes among the judges, the eldest judge shall have a casting vote.

Article 13

1. The members of the Court shall be elected for nine years and may be re-elected; provided, however, that of the judges elected at the first election, the terms of five judges shall expire at the end of three years and the terms of five more judges shall expire at the end of six years.

2. The judges whose terms are to expire at the end of the above-mentioned initial periods of three and six years shall be chosen by lot to be drawn by the Secretary-General immediately after the first election has been completed.

3. The members of the Court shall continue to discharge their duties until their places have been filled. Though replaced, they shall finish any cases which they may have begun.

4. In the case of the resignation of a member of the Court, the resignation shall be addressed to the President of the Court for

transmission to the Secretary-General. This last notification makes the place vacant.

Article 14

Vacancies shall be filled by the same method as that laid down for the first election, subject to the following provision: the Secretary-General shall, within one month of the occurrence of the vacancy, proceed to issue the invitations provided for in Article 5, and the date of the election shall be fixed by the Security Council.

Article 15

A member of the Court elected to replace a member whose term of office has not expired shall hold office for the remainder of his predecessor's term.

Article 16

1. No member of the Court may exercise any political or administrative function, or engage in any other occupation of a professional nature.

2. Any doubt on this point shall be settled by the decision of the Court.

Article 17

1. No member of the Court may act as agent, counsel, or advocate in any case.

2. No member may participate in the decision of any case in which he has previously taken part as agent, counsel, or advocate for one of the parties, or as a member of a national or international court, or of a commission of enquiry, or in any other capacity.

3. Any doubt on this point shall be settled by the decision of the Court.

Article 18

1. No member of the Court can be dismissed unless, in the unanimous opinion of the other members, he has ceased to fulfil the required conditions.

2. Formal notification thereof shall be made to the Secretary-General by the Registrar.

3. This notification makes the place vacant.

Article 19

The members of the Court, when engaged on the business of the Court, shall enjoy diplomatic privileges and immunities.

Article 20

Every member of the Court shall, before taking up his duties, make a solemn declaration in open court that he will exercise his powers impartially and conscientiously.

Article 21

1. The Court shall elect its President and Vice-President for three years; they may be re-elected.

2. The Court shall appoint its Registrar and may provide for the appointment of such other officers as may be necessary.

Article 22

1. The seat of the Court shall be established at The Hague. This, however, shall not prevent the Court from sitting and exercising its functions elsewhere whenever the Court considers it desirable.

2. The President and the Registrar shall reside at the seat of the Court.

Article 23

1. The Court shall remain permanently in session, except during the judicial vacations, the dates and duration of which shall be fixed by the Court.

2. Members of the Court are entitled to periodic leave, the dates and duration of which shall be fixed by the Court, having in mind the distance between The Hague and the home of each judge.

3. Members of the Court shall be bound, unless they are on leave or prevented from attending by illness or other serious reasons duly explained to the President, to hold themselves permanently at the disposal of the Court.

Article 24

1. If, for some special reason, a member of the Court considers that he should not take part in the decision of a particular case, he shall so inform the President.

2. If the President considers that for some special reason one of the members of the Court should not sit in a particular case, he shall give him notice accordingly.

3. If in any such case the member of the Court and the President disagree, the matter shall be settled by the decision of the Court.

Article 25

1. The full Court shall sit except when it is expressly provided otherwise in the present Statute.

2. Subject to the condition that the number of judges available to constitute the Court is not thereby reduced below eleven, the Rules of the Court may provide for allowing one or more judges, according to circumstances and in rotation, to be dispensed from sitting.

3. A quorum of nine judges shall suffice to constitute the Court.

Article 26

1. The Court may from time to time form one or more chambers, composed of three or more judges as the Court may determine, for

dealing with particular categories of cases; for example, labour cases and cases relating to transit and communications.

2. The Court may at any time form a chamber for dealing with a particular case. The number of judges to constitute such a chamber shall be determined by the Court with the approval of the parties.

3. Cases shall be heard and determined by the chambers provided for in this Article if the parties so request.

Article 27

A judgment given by any of the chambers provided for in Articles 26 and 29 shall be considered as rendered by the Court.

Article 28

The chambers provided for in Articles 26 and 29 may, with the consent of the parties, sit and exercise their functions elsewhere than at The Hague.

Article 29

With a view to the speedy despatch of business, the Court shall form annually a chamber composed of five judges which, at the request of the parties, may hear and determine cases by summary procedure. In addition, two judges shall be selected for the purpose of replacing judges who find it impossible to sit.

Article 30

1. The Court shall frame rules for carrying out its functions. In particular, it shall lay down rules of procedure.

2. The Rules of the Court may provide for assessors to sit with the Court or with any of its chambers, without the right to vote.

Article 31

1. Judges of the nationality of each of the parties shall retain their right to sit in the case before the Court.

2. If the Court includes upon the Bench a judge of the nationality of one of the parties, any other party may choose a person to sit as judge. Such person shall be chosen preferably from among those persons who have been nominated as candidates as provided in Articles 4 and 5.

3. If the Court includes upon the Bench no judge of the nationality of the parties, each of these parties may proceed to choose a judge as provided in paragraph 2 of this Article.

4. The provisions of this Article shall apply to the case of Articles 26 and 29. In such cases, the President shall request one or, if necessary, two of the members of the Court forming the chamber to give place to the members of the Court of the nationality of the parties concerned, and, failing such, or if they are unable to be present, to the judges specially chosen by the parties.

5. Should there be several parties in the same interest, they shall, for the purpose of the preceding provisions, be reckoned as one party only. Any doubt upon this point shall be settled by the decision of the Court.

6. Judges chosen as laid down in paragraphs 2, 3, and 4 of this Article shall fulfil the conditions required by Articles 2, 17 (paragraph 2), 20, and 24 of the present Statute. They shall take part in the decision on terms of complete equality with their colleagues.

Article 32

1. Each member of the Court shall receive an annual salary.

2. The President shall receive a special annual allowance.

3. The Vice-President shall receive a special allowance for every day on which he acts as President.

4. The judges chosen under Article 31, other than members of the Court, shall receive compensation for each day on which they exercise their functions.

5. These salaries, allowances, and compensation shall be fixed by the General Assembly. They may not be decreased during the term of office.

6. The salary of the Registrar shall be fixed by the General Assembly on the proposal of the Court.

7. Regulations made by the General Assembly shall fix the conditions under which retirement pensions may be given to members of the Court and to the Registrar, and the conditions under which members of the Court and the Registrar shall have their travelling expenses refunded.

8. The above salaries, allowances, and compensation shall be free of all taxation.

Article 33

The expenses of the Court shall be borne by the United Nations in such a manner as shall be decided by the General Assembly.

Chapter II

COMPETENCE OF THE COURT

Article 34

1. Only states may be parties in cases before the Court.

2. The Court, subject to and in conformity with its Rules, may request of public international organisations information relevant to cases before it, and shall receive such information presented by such organisations on their own initiative.

3. Whenever the construction of the constituent instrument of a public international organisation or of an international convention

adopted thereunder is in question in a case before the Court, the Registrar shall so notify the public international organisation concerned and shall communicate to it copies of all the written proceedings.

Article 35

1. The Court shall be open to the states parties to the present Statute.

2. The conditions under which the Court shall be open to other states shall, subject to the special provisions contained in treaties in force, be laid down by the Security Council, but in no case shall such conditions place the parties in a position of inequality before the Court.

3. When a state which is not a Member of the United Nations is a party to a case, the Court shall fix the amount which that party is to contribute towards the expenses of the Court. This provision shall not apply if such state is bearing a share of the expenses of the Court.

Article 36

1. The jurisdiction of the Court comprises all cases which the parties refer to it and all matters specially provided for in the Charter of the United Nations or in treaties and conventions in force.

2. The states parties to the present Statute may at any time declare that they recognise as compulsory *ipso facto* and without special agreement, in relation to any other state accepting the same obligation, the jurisdiction of the Court in all legal disputes concerning:

(*a*) the interpretation of a treaty;

(*b*) any question of international law;

(*c*) the existence of any fact which, if established, would constitute a breach of an international obligation;

(*d*) the nature or extent of the reparation to be made for the breach of an international obligation.

3. The declarations referred to above may be made unconditionally or on condition of reciprocity on the part of several or certain states, or for a certain time.

4. Such declarations shall be deposited with the Secretary-General of the United Nations, who shall transmit copies thereof to the parties to the Statute and to the Registrar of the Court.

5. Declarations made under Article 36 of the Statute of the Permanent Court of International Justice and which are still in force shall be deemed, as between the parties to the present Statute, to be acceptances of the compulsory jurisdiction of the International Court of Justice for the period which they still have to run and in accordance with their terms.

6. In the event of a dispute as to whether the Court has jurisdiction, the matter shall be settled by the decision of the Court.

Article 37

Whenever a treaty or convention in force provides for reference of a matter to a tribunal to have been instituted by the League of Nations, or to the Permanent Court of International Justice, the matter shall, as between the parties to the present Statute, be referred to the International Court of Justice.

Article 38

1. The Court, whose function is to decide in accordance with international law such disputes as are submitted to it, shall apply:

(*a*) international conventions, whether general or particular, establishing rules expressly recognised by the contesting states;

(*b*) international custom, as evidence of a general practice accepted as law;

(*c*) the general principles of law recognised by civilised nations;

(*d*) subject to the provisions of Article 59, judicial decisions and the teachings of the most highly qualified publicists of the various nations, as subsidiary means for the determination of rules of law.

2. This provision shall not prejudice the power of the Court to decide a case *ex aequo et bono*, if the parties agree thereto.

Chapter III

PROCEDURE

Article 39

1. The official languages of the Court shall be French and English. If the parties agree that the case shall be conducted in French, the judgment shall be delivered in French. If the parties agree that the case shall be conducted in English, the judgment shall be delivered in English.

2. In the absence of an agreement as to which language shall be employed, each party may, in the pleadings, use the language which it prefers; the decision of the Court shall be given in French and English. In this case the Court shall at the same time determine which of the two texts shall be considered as authoritative.

3. The Court shall, at the request of any party, authorise a language other than French or English to be used by that party.

Article 40

1. Cases are brought before the Court, as the case may be, either by the notification of the special agreement or by a written application

addressed to the Registrar. In either case the subject of the dispute and the parties shall be indicated.

2. The Registrar shall forthwith communicate the application to all concerned.

3. He shall also notify the Members of the United Nations through the Secretary-General, and also any other states entitled to appear before the Court.

Article 41

1. The Court shall have the power to indicate, if it considers that circumstances so require, any provisional measures which ought to be taken to preserve the respective rights of either party.

2. Pending the final decision, notice of the measures suggested shall forthwith be given to the parties and to the Security Council.

Article 42

1. The parties shall be represented by agents.

2. They may have the assistance of counsel or advocates before the Court.

3. The agents, counsel, and advocates of parties before the Court shall enjoy the privileges and immunities necessary to the independent exercise of their duties.

Article 43

1. The procedure shall consist of two parts: written and oral.

2. The written proceedings shall consist of the communication to the Court and to the parties of memorials, counter-memorials and, if necessary, replies; also all papers and documents in support.

3. These communications shall be made through the Registrar, in the order and within the time fixed by the Court.

4. A certified copy of every document produced by one party shall be communicated to the other party.

5. The oral proceedings shall consist of the hearing by the Court of witnesses, experts, agents, counsel, and advocates.

Article 44

1. For the service of all notices upon persons other than the agents, counsel, and advocates, the Court shall apply direct to the government of the state upon whose territory the notice has to be served.

2. The same provision shall apply whenever steps are to be taken to procure evidence on the spot.

Article 45

The hearing shall be under the control of the President or, if he is unable to preside, of the Vice-President; if neither is able to preside, the senior judge present shall preside.

Article 46

The hearing in Court shall be public, unless the Court shall decide otherwise, or unless the parties demand that the public be not admitted.

Article 47

1. Minutes shall be made at each hearing and signed by the Registrar and the President.

2. These minutes alone shall be authentic.

Article 48

The Court shall make orders for the conduct of the case, shall decide the form and time in which each party must conclude its arguments, and make all arrangements connected with the taking of evidence.

Article 49

The Court may, even before the hearing begins, call upon the agents to produce any document or to supply any explanations. Formal note shall be taken of any refusal.

Article 50

The Court may, at any time, entrust any individual, body, bureau, commission, or other organisation that it may select, with the task of carrying out an enquiry or giving an expert opinion.

Article 51

During the hearing any relevant questions are to be put to the witnesses and experts under the conditions laid down by the Court in the rules of procedure referred to in Article 30.

Article 52

After the Court has received the proofs and evidence within the time specified for the purpose, it may refuse to accept any further oral or written evidence that one party may desire to present unless the other side consents.

Article 53

1. Whenever one of the parties does not appear before the Court, or fails to defend its case, the other party may call upon the Court to decide in favour of its claim.

2. The Court must, before doing so, satisfy itself, not only that it has jurisdiction in accordance with Articles 36 and 37, but also that the claim is well founded in fact and law.

Article 54

1. When, subject to the control of the Court, the agents, counsel, and advocates have completed their presentation of the case, the President shall declare the hearing closed.

2. The Court shall withdraw to consider the judgment.

3. The deliberations of the Court shall take place in private and remain secret.

Article 55

1. All questions shall be decided by a majority of the judges present.

2. In the event of an equality of votes, the President or the judge who acts in his place shall have a casting vote.

Article 56

1. The judgment shall state the reasons on which it is based.

2. It shall contain the names of the judges who have taken part in the decision.

Article 57

If the judgment does not represent in whole or in part the unanimous opinion of the judges, any judge shall be entitled to deliver a separate opinion.

Article 58

The judgment shall be signed by the President and by the Registrar. It shall be read in open court, due notice having been given to the agents.

Article 59

The decision of the Court has no binding force except between the parties and in respect of that particular case.

Article 60

The judgment is final and without appeal. In the event of dispute as to the meaning or scope of the judgment, the Court shall construe it upon the request of any party.

Article 61

1. An application for revision of a judgment may be made only when it is based upon the discovery of some fact of such a nature as to be a decisive factor, which fact was, when the judgment was given, unknown to the Court and also to the party claiming revision, always provided that such ignorance was not due to negligence.

2. The proceedings for revision shall be opened by a judgment of the Court expressly recording the existence of the new fact, recognising that it has such a character as to lay the case open to revision, and declaring the application admissible on this ground.

3. The Court may require previous compliance with the terms of the judgment before it admits proceedings in revision.

4. The application for revision must be made at latest within six months of the discovery of the new fact.

5. No application for revision may be made after the lapse of ten years from the date of the judgment.

Article 62

1. Should a state consider that it has an interest of a legal nature which may be affected by the decision in the case, it may submit a request to the Court to be permitted to intervene.

2. It shall be for the Court to decide upon this request.

Article 63

1. Whenever the construction of a convention to which states other than those concerned in the case are parties is in question, the Registrar shall notify all such states forthwith.

2. Every state so notified has the right to intervene in the proceedings; but if it uses this right, the construction given by the judgment will be equally binding upon it.

Article 64

Unless otherwise decided by the Court, each party shall bear its own costs.

Chapter IV

ADVISORY OPINIONS

Article 65

1. The Court may give an advisory opinion on any legal question at the request of whatever body may be authorised by or in accordance with the Charter of the United Nations to make such a request.

2. Questions upon which the advisory opinion of the Court is asked shall be laid before the Court by means of a written request containing an exact statement of the question upon which an opinion is required, and accompanied by all documents likely to throw light upon the question.

Article 66

1. The Registrar shall forthwith give notice of the request for an advisory opinion to all states entitled to appear before the Court.

2. The Registrar shall also, by means of a special and direct communication, notify any state entitled to appear before the Court or international organisation considered by the Court, or, should it not be sitting, by the President, as likely to be able to furnish information on the question, that the Court will be prepared to receive, within a time limit to be fixed by the President, written statements, or to hear, at a public sitting to be held for the purpose, oral statements relating to the question.

3. Should any such state entitled to appear before the Court have failed to receive the special communication referred to in paragraph 2

of this Article, such state may express a desire to submit a written statement or to be heard; and the Court will decide.

4. States and organisations having presented written or oral statements or both shall be permitted to comment on the statements made by other states or organisations in the form, to the extent, and within the time limits which the Court, or, should it not be sitting, the President, shall decide in each particular case. Accordingly, the Registrar shall in due time communicate any such written statements to states and organisations having submitted similar statements.

Article 67

The Court shall deliver its advisory opinions in open court, notice having been given to the Secretary-General and to the representatives of Members of the United Nations, of other states and of international organisations immediately concerned.

Article 68

In the exercise of its advisory functions the Court shall further be guided by the provisions of the present Statute which apply in contentious cases to the extent to which it recognises them to be applicable.

CHAPTER V

AMENDMENT

Article 69

Amendments to the present Statute shall be effected by the same procedure as is provided by the Charter of the United Nations for amendments to that Charter, subject however to any provisions which the General Assembly upon recommendation of the Security Council may adopt concerning the participation of states which are parties to the present Statute but are not Members of the United Nations.

Article 70

The Court shall have power to propose such amendments to the present Statute as it may deem necessary, through written communications to the Secretary-General, for consideration in conformity with the provisions of Article 69.

REFERENCES TO ARTICLES OF THE CHARTER OF THE UNITED NATIONS

REFERENCES TO ARTICLES OF THE STATUTE OF THE INTERNATIONAL COURT OF JUSTICE

INDEX

RECENT TRENDS IN THE LAW OF THE UNITED NATIONS

RECENT TRENDS
IN
THE LAW
OF
THE UNITED NATIONS

BY

HANS KELSEN

A Supplement to
'THE LAW OF THE UNITED NATIONS'

Published under the auspices of
THE LONDON INSTITUTE OF WORLD AFFAIRS

TEXT

First Edition	1950
Second Impression	1951
Third Impression	1954
Fourth Impression (Bound in Supplement)	1964

SUPPLEMENT

First Edition	1951
Second Impression	1954

Published in 1964 *in Great Britain by Stevens & Sons Ltd of* 11 *New Fetter Lane, E.C.*4 *in the City of London*

Published in 1964 *in the United States of America by Frederick A. Praeger Inc. of* 111 *Fourth Ave., New York* 3, *N.Y., U.S.A.*

Printed in the United States of America

CONTENTS

INTRODUCTION

In view of the legally relevant events which have occurred since the completion of *The Law of the United Nations*, a revision has become necessary. This is earlier than expected, and before it is possible to prepare a new edition. At the suggestion of the Publishers it has been decided to publish a Supplement dealing only with the principal cases where the application of the Charter and its interpretation might be of outstanding importance.

The problems discussed in this Supplement are: the organisation of collective self-defence through the North Atlantic Treaty; the action in Korea; the re-appointment of the Secretary-General; and the resolution of the General Assembly 'Uniting for Peace.' The North Atlantic Treaty has been referred to in the first impression as a regional arrangement for the organisation of collective self-defence. But this Treaty has since assumed paramount political importance, and its conformity with the Charter as well as its character as a regional arrangement has been challenged. Hence it seems desirable to re-examine the Treaty in connection with the analysis of the other topics of this Supplement.

This analysis does not in every respect affirm the constitutionality of the actions under consideration. The author, however, is fully aware of the fact that the law of a community—national or international—and especially its constitution or constituent treaty, may be changed not only by formal amendments carried out in accordance with the procedure laid down for this purpose in the law itself. It may be modified also by its actual application based on an interpretation which, more or less consistent with the letter of the law, is not in conformity with the ascertainable intention of its authors. This is the way the law adapts itself to changing circumstances if it is too difficult or impossible to put in operation the amendment procedure. This is the case with the amendment procedure prescribed in the Charter of the United Nations. Since the rule of unanimity among the five great Powers having permanent seats in the Security Council applies to this procedure, amendments to the Charter are practically impossible.

Lack of unanimity of the five great Powers has paralyzed the system of collective security established in the Charter, and has prevented, or at least hampered, the exercise of other important functions of the Organisation, such as the admission of new Members. The actions analysed in this Supplement are all attempts to find a way out of the impasse in which the unfortunate rule of unanimity has led the United Nations. Viewed retrospectively with regard to the

Charter (the view necessarily presented in this Supplement), these actions may, in some of their aspects, be considered unconstitutional. But directing our view towards the future, we may see them as the first steps in the development of a new law of the United Nations.

In the main work the author has frequently emphasized that the principle *ex injuria jus non oritur*—law cannot originate in an illegal act—has important exceptions. There are certainly cases where a new law originates in the violation of an old law. If and in so far as the organisation of collective self-defence through the North Atlantic Treaty, the action in Korea, the re-appointment of the Secretary-General, and the resolution 'Uniting for Peace' are inconsistent with the old law of the United Nations, they, perhaps, constitute one of these cases of which we may say *ex injuria jus oritur*.

Chapter 1 of this Supplement is partly identical with an article the author published under the title 'Is the North Atlantic Treaty in Conformity with the Charter of the United Nations?' in *The University of Kansas City Law Review*, vol. 19; chapter 4 is partly identical with an article the author published under the title 'Is the Acheson Plan Constitutional?' in *The Western Political Quarterly*, University of Utah, vol. III.

HANS KELSEN.

February, 1951.

Chapter 1

ORGANISATION OF COLLECTIVE SELF-DEFENCE

1. Collective Self-Defence as Distinguished from its Preparation

The North Atlantic Treaty signed at Washington on April 4, 1949, is an agreement concluded by twelve states of which ten are Members of the United Nations and two non-Members, one of them (Italy) being a former enemy state within the meaning of Article 107 of the Charter of the United Nations. Its main purpose is laid down in Article 5 which provides:—

> The Parties agree that an armed attack against one or more of them in Europe or North America shall be considered an attack against them all; and consequently they agree that, if such an armed attack occurs, each of them, in exercise of the right of individual or collective self-defence recognised by Article 51 of the Charter of the United Nations, will assist the Party or Parties so attacked by taking forthwith, individually and in concert with the other Parties, such action as it deems necessary, including the use of armed force, to restore and maintain the security of the North Atlantic area.
>
> Any such armed attack and all measures taken as a result thereof shall immediately be reported to the Security Council. Such measures shall be terminated when the Security Council has taken the measures necessary to restore and maintain international peace and security.

This Article constitutes an organisation of the collective self-defence provided for by Article 51 of the Charter which reads as follows:—

> Nothing in the present Charter shall impair the inherent right of individual or collective self-defence if an armed attack occurs against a Member of the United Nations, until the Security Council has taken the measures necessary to maintain international peace and security. Measures taken by Members in the exercise of this right of self-defence shall be immediately reported to the Security Council and shall not in any way affect the authority and responsibility of the Security Council under the present Charter to take at any time such action as it deems necessary in order to maintain or restore international peace and security.

In referring to an 'inherent' right (in the French text: 'droit naturel') this provision seems to claim a merely declaratory not a constitutive character. According to its wording Article 51 only recognises the right of self-defence as established independently of the Charter by natural law. This Article of the Charter presupposes the natural-law doctrine. But it does not and cannot stipulate an obligation of the Members to accept this doctrine. For those who do not accept it Article 51 has, in spite of its wording, a constitutive character. It is this Article which establishes the right of self-defence ; and this right, as a right which states have in their capacity as Members of the United Nations, has no other content than the one determined by Article 51. If one accepts the natural-law doctrine the validity of Article 51 becomes highly problematical. For this Article extends as well as restricts the right of self-defence as it is usually presented by the followers of the natural-law doctrine. According to this doctrine, natural law does not establish, as Article 51 does, a right of collective self-defence; and the right of self-defence may be exercised under natural law not only as long as an international organisation does not intervene. Referring to its ' inherent ' or ' natural ' right a state may, in opposition to the provision of Article 51, continue to exercise self-defence after the Security Council has taken the measures determined in Article 51. An interpretation of this Article in accordance with its wording leads to its self-destruction.[1]

The wording of Article 51 is objectionable also in other respects. The statement that nothing in the Charter shall impair the right of self-defence ' *if* an armed attack occurs,' means, if taken literally, that this right is not impaired by other provisions of the Charter under the condition only that, and consequently *after* the moment when, an armed attack occurs. But the right may be impaired by other provisions of the Charter as long as no such armed attack occurs. This, however, is impossible because the right of self-defence exists only *if*, and that implies *after* an armed attack occurs. It is the right of self-defence and not its being not impaired by provisions of the Charter which is conditioned by the occurrence of an armed attack. What is meant by the first sentence of Article 51 is probably: that nothing in the Charter (the word ' present ' is superfluous and even misleading because it might exclude provisions established by an amendment to the Charter) shall impair the right of self-defence to be exercised against armed attack. Perhaps the wording ' *if* an armed attack occurs ' has been chosen in order to spare the word ' against ' for the specification of the armed attack as directed ' against ' a Member.

The defective wording of the first sentence of Article 51 makes an interpretation possible according to which the conclusion of a treaty organising collective self-defence is permissible only ' if,' and that means, after an armed attack occurs. If this interpretation is accepted the North Atlantic Treaty as well as the two other treaties

[1] Cf. *The Law of the United Nations*, pp. 791 ff., 794 ff.

concluded for the organisation of collective self-defence, the Rio de Janeiro and the Brussels Treaties, are unconstitutional. But this interpretation is based not only on an obvious error in the wording of Article 51 but also on the assumption that the conclusion of a treaty for the organisation of collective self-defence is an act by which the right of collective self-defence is exercised and, hence, possible only ' if,' and that implies after, an armed attack occurs. This assumption, however, is erroneous, or at least, not the only possible one. The exercise of the right of self-defence consists in actions, especially enforcement actions (meaning actions involving the use of force) directed against the aggressor after an armed attack has occurred. The right of self-defence is an essential restriction of the obligation established by Article 2, Paragraph 4, of the Charter to refrain from the use of force, especially from the use of armed force, which is a possible if not an essential element of the exercise of the right of self-defence against an armed attack. The conclusion of a treaty for the organisation of collective self-defence may be considered not as exercise of the right of self-defence but as preparation of the exercise of this right. Then it is not incompatible with Article 51 which does not refer to such preparation, just as armament for the purpose of preparing self-defence is not incompatible with Article 51.

If the term ' collective self-defence ' has any meaning at all it means defence of the attacked state exercised not only by this state itself but also by other states coming to its assistance. With respect to the latter states the term ' self '-defence is another mistake in the wording of Article 51. What is meant by collective ' self '-defence is collective ' defence ' against an armed attack. ' Collective ' defence implies organised defence; and such organisation is effective only if prepared before an armed attack occurs. The interpretation of Article 51 according to which a defence treaty must not be concluded before an armed attack occurs has the effect to make collective self-defence almost illusory.

If the conclusion of a defence treaty for the organisation of collective defence is not the exercise of the right of self-defence, it is not a measure to be reported to the Security Council according to the second sentence of Article 51. Nor is any other preparatory measure, taken in fulfillment of a defence treaty prior to the armed attack, under the obligation established by the second sentence of Article 51. Such measures are those taken under Article 3 of the North Atlantic Treaty stipulating the obligation of the parties to maintain and develop their individual and collective capacity to resist armed attack by means of continuous and effective self-help and mutual aid; those taken under Article 4 stipulating the obligation of the parties to consult together whenever in the opinion of any of them the territorial integrity, political independence or security of any of the parties is threatened; and those taken under Article 9 stipulating the obligation to establish a council and a defence committee, as well as the activities of these organs. The constitutionality of these provisions of the North Atlantic Treaty does not depend on their conformity with Article 51 of the Charter which refers to the exercise of the right of self-defence not to its preparation.

2. Collective Self-Defence of Non-Members

More serious than the question as to the constitutionality of the conclusion of a defence treaty prior to the occurrence of an armed attack, is the question as to whether by such a treaty an obligation may be imposed upon Members of the United Nations to defend a non-Member and especially a former enemy state against an armed attack. According to its wording Article 51 stipulates a right to be exercised only in favour of Members of the United Nations. The Article refers in its first sentence expressly to an armed attack 'against a Member of the United Nations'; and in its second sentence only to measures 'taken by Members' in the exercise of the right of individual or collective self-defence. If the right of self-defence exists only in case of an armed attack against a Member, Article 51 establishes only a defence right of Members. If Article 51 is taken literally the obligation of the Members established by Article 2, paragraph 4, of the Charter to refrain from the use of force is restricted by Article 51 only insofar as force may be used against a state attacking a Member of the United Nations, not against a state attacking a non-Member. If Article 51 is interpreted literally an obligation assumed by a Member to assist, by using force, an attacked non-Member is not covered by the right of collective self-defence as established by Article 51. The provision of Article 5 of the North Atlantic Treaty: 'the Parties agree that an armed attack against one or more of them in Europe or North America shall be considered an attack against them all' is not an authentic interpretation of Article 51 of the Charter and, hence, cannot confer upon Members the right which they have not under the Charter, the right to use force against a state attacking a non-Member. The formula used in the first sentence of Article 5 of the North Atlantic Treaty is nothing but a legal fiction. No legal norm can change the fact that an attack directed against one state only is not an attack directed against another state. The fiction that an attack against one contracting party of the North Atlantic Treaty is to be considered an attack against them all, can even not justify the use of the term 'self'-defence in case a state uses force against a state attacking a third state. If Article 51 of the Charter is taken literally the obligation established by Article 5 of the North Atlantic Treaty to assist an attacked party by taking action 'including the use of armed force,' as an obligation of a Member to assist an attacked non-Member, is in conflict with the obligation of a Member under Article 2, paragraph 4, of the Charter. In such case Article 103 of the Charter applies. That means that the obligation under the Charter prevails. Members of the United Nations must not fulfill their obligation under the North Atlantic Treaty in relation to non-Members. But the non-Members, parties to the Treaty, are not released of their obligation to assist an attacked Member, contracting party to the Treaty.

The restriction of the right of individual and collective self-defence to Members of the United Nations is hardly consistent with the provision of Article 2, paragraph 6 of the Charter which provides:

> The Organisation shall ensure that states which are not Members of the United Nations act in accordance with these Principles so far as may be necessary for the maintenance of international peace and security.

This provision may be interpreted to mean that the Organisation is authorised to take enforcement measures against a non-Member which acts contrary to the Principles laid down in Article 2 of the Charter. That means that the main obligation of the Members, especially the obligation stipulated in Article 2, paragraph 4: to refrain from the threat or use of force, is extended to non-Members. If the provision of Article 2, paragraph 4, applies also to non-Members it can only apply with the restriction established by Article 51, because it is with this restriction that Article 2, paragraph 4, applies to Members. Hence, Article 51 may, in spite of its wording, be interpreted to confer the right of individual and collective self-defence also upon non-Members. If this interpretation is accepted the obligation of the Members to refrain from the use of force under Article 2, paragraph 4, is restricted by Article 51 not only in case of an armed attack directed against a Member but also in case of an armed attack directed against a non-Member. Only if this interpretation of Article 51—which is in open contradiction to its wording—is accepted the North Atlantic Treaty does not establish an obligation of the Members of the United Nations in conflict with their obligations under the Charter.

3. Collective Self-Defence of Former Enemy States

If the non-Member is a state which during the Second World War has been an enemy of any signatory to the Charter, Article 107 of the Charter applies, which provides that ' nothing in the present Charter shall invalidate or preclude action in relation ' to such state ' taken or authorised as a result of that war by the governments having responsibility for such action.' Such action may be an enforcement action involving the use of armed force. The obligation of the Members established by Article 2, paragraph 4, to refrain from the threat and use of force is restricted not only by Article 51 but also by Article 107. An action under Article 107 may have the character of an armed attack against a former enemy state. If the armed attack against a former enemy state is covered by Article 107, Members of the United Nations are not permitted to come to the assistance of the attacked state under Article 51; for Article 107 provides that nothing in the present Charter, hence also not the right of collective self-defence as established in the Charter, shall invalidate or preclude an action taken under Article 107. Hence, Article 51 may be interpreted to be restricted by Article 107. But this is only a possible not a necessary interpretation. For, Article 51, too, begins with the formula: 'Nothing in the present Charter shall impair. . . .' Hence, Article 107 may be interpreted to be restricted by Article 51. Both interpretations, one excluding the other, are according to the wording of the two Articles possible. If the first-mentioned interpretation is accepted the obligation assumed by Members to assist a former enemy state in case of an armed attack covered by Article 107 is in conflict with the obligation under Article 2, paragraph 4, not restricted, in this case, by Article 51. The right of Members to take under Article 107 an enforcement action against a former enemy state does not cease to exist after a peace treaty has been concluded with a former enemy state. According to its wording Article 107 applies also after the conclusion of a peace treaty. In the peace treaty Members may renounce the right which they have under Article 107 to take enforcement action against the former enemy state. As a matter of fact, Articles 83, 86, and 87 of the Peace Treaty with Italy providing for peaceful settlement of disputes concerning the interpretation and execution of the Peace Treaty, may be interpreted to mean that the Members of the United Nations contracting parties to the Peace Treaty with Italy have renounced their right under Article 107 to take enforcement action against Italy, insofar as there is a dispute concerning the interpretation and execution of the treaty. But the provisions of the Peace Treaty do not change the legal situation which exists under the Charter since they have not the effect of an amendment to Article 107. By an attack against a former enemy state covered by Article 107 the Member may violate the Peace Treaty but it does not violate the Charter; and, hence, the Peace Treaty cannot change the effect Article 107 has on Article 51 of the Charter.

4. Collective Self-Defence and Regional Arrangements

The constitutionality of the North Atlantic Treaty depends not only on its conformity with Article 51 but also on the answer to the question as to whether the Treaty is a regional arrangement within the meaning of Chapter VIII of the Charter.[2] If the answer is in the affirmative the North Atlantic Treaty and the contracting parties to this Treaty must conform with certain provisions of Chapter VIII of the Charter.

[2] Cf. *The Law of the United Nations*, pp. 319 ff.

Article 52, paragraph 1 of the Charter, the first provision of Chapter VIII, runs as follows:

> Nothing in the present Charter precludes the existence of regional arrangements or agencies for dealing with such matters relating to the maintenance of international peace and security as are appropriate for regional action, provided that such arrangements or agencies and their activities are consistent with the Purposes and Principles of the United Nations.

Article 52, paragraph 1, is not the only provision of the Charter which opens with a statement: 'Nothing in the present Charter precludes . . .' or a similar formula. Article 2, paragraph 7, Article 51, and Article 107 start in the same way.[3] But in contradistinction to the provisions of these Articles, Article 52, paragraph 1, does not constitute a restriction of other norms stipulated by the Charter. For the Charter does not contain any provision prohibiting the Members to enter into agreements of any kind whatever. Taken literally, the statement that regional arrangements are not precluded by the Charter is superfluous. Even if it were not inserted into the Charter the existence of regional arrangements as characterised in Article 52, paragraph 1, would not be precluded. In order to avoid the view that the statement concerned is superfluous it should be interpreted to mean that *only* regional arrangements are permitted, all other arrangements among Members prohibited. This, however, was evidently not the intention of the framers of Chapter VIII. The Charter does not contain a definition of the concept 'regional arrangement.' The meaning of this term must be derived from the text of Article 52. Technically it would have been more correct to formulate a positive definition of the 'regional arrangements' to which the other provisions of Chapter VIII refer, instead of leaving such definition to the interpretation of Article 52.

A regional arrangement within the meaning of Article 52, paragraph 1, is probably an international agreement or treaty. It is difficult to understand why the term 'arrangement' and not the term 'agreement' (as in Article 43: 'special agreement,' or in Chapter XII: 'trusteeship agreement') has been chosen. If the 'arrangement' is not an agreement, it is of no legal importance.

In accordance with Article 52, paragraph 1, a regional arrangement must deal with 'matters relating to the maintenance of international peace and security.' An agreement dealing with other matters is not a regional arrangement within the meaning of Chapter VIII. That an agreement is a 'regional' arrangement means that not all the Members of the United Nations but only some

[3] Article 2, paragraph 7, of the Charter begins: 'Nothing contained in the present Charter shall authorise the United Nations. . . .' As to the introductory phrases of Articles 51 and 107, cf. *ibid.*, p. 815.

of them are contracting parties, that is to say, that the community constituted by such an agreement is a partial international community, in contradistinction to the total international community constituted by the Charter. In order to be a 'regional' arrangement the activity of the organisation constituted by the agreement must be limited to a definite area, a 'region.' Article 52, paragraph 1, speaks of arrangements 'dealing with such matters relating to the maintenance of international peace and security as are appropriate for regional action.' 'Regional action' is action restricted to a region. Hence, the area to which the activity of the regional organisation, that is the regional actions, are limited must be determined in the agreement which is to be considered as a 'regional' arrangement. It is not necessary that the contracting parties to the agreement are geographically neighbours. It suffices that they have a common interest in an activity relating to the maintenance of international peace and security and restricted to a definite area.

Another question is whether such regional arrangements may be entered into only by Members or also by Members and non-Members. In this respect, Article 52 of the Charter allows two contradictory interpretations. Paragraph 1 of Article 52 does not restrict regional arrangements to treaties concluded by Members. But paragraph 2, dealing with the regional arrangements mentioned in paragraph 1, expressly refers only to 'Members of the United Nations' entering into such arrangements. Hence, in interpreting paragraph 1, one may have regard to paragraph 2 and assume that the regional arrangements referred to in paragraph 1 are agreements to which only Members of the United Nations may be contracting parties. It is, however, not excluded to interpret paragraph 2 to mean that the obligation established by this paragraph concerning settlement of disputes is incumbent only upon those parties to the regional arrangement which are Members of the United Nations.

5. The North Atlantic Treaty as a Regional Arrangement

According to the interpretation just presented, the North Atlantic Treaty fulfils all the requirements of a regional arrangement. It is a treaty entered into by some, not by all, Members of the United Nations, and the most important function of the organisation established by this treaty—the exercise of collective self-defence, is restricted to a definite area determined in Article 6 of the Treaty, the 'North Atlantic area' as it is expressly characterised in this and other Articles of the Treaty. The North Atlantic Treaty deals with a matter relating to international peace and security. The main purpose of the Treaty, the organisation of collective self-defence, is certainly such a matter. In view of the fact that the system of collective security established by Chapter VII of the Charter did not work, collective self-defence was the only means for the maintenance of international security provided by the Charter. The North Atlantic Treaty has been initiated by a resolution adopted by the Senate of the United States of America (80th Congress, Second Session, 1948). The Senate resolved that the Government should pursue 'Progressive development of regional and other collective arrangements for individual and collective self-defence in accordance with the purposes, principles and provisions of the Charter.' According to this resolution of the Senate, development of collective self-defence by regional arrangements is at least possible. The North Atlantic Treaty is admittedly patterned on the Rio de Janeiro Treaty, which presents itself expressly as a regional arrangement.

It has been argued that the North Atlantic Treaty is not a regional arrangement because its main purpose, the organisation of collective self-defence, is not referred to in Chapter VIII of the Charter dealing with regional arrangements. Regional arrangements may provide for enforcement actions to be taken only with the authorisation of the Security Council (with the exception of certain enforcement actions directed against former enemy states). The enforcement action taken under a regional arrangement is to be distinguished from the action taken against an aggressor in the exercise of the right of self-defence stipulated in Article 51 of the Charter. 'Enforcement action,' according to this interpretation, means action decided on or approved by the Security Council for the purpose of the restoration of peace. The use of force in the exercise of the right of self-defence under Article 51 takes place prior to an 'enforcement action' in the specific sense of the term, that is to say, an action involving the use of armed or non-armed force taken by the Security Council.

It is true that the Charter uses the term 'enforcement action' and 'enforcement measure' in Article 2, paragraphs 5 and 7, and Article 50 in order to designate the enforcement action taken by the Security Council under Chapter VII. And even in the first sentence of Article 53, paragraph 1, the term 'enforcement action' has this meaning. But in the second sentence of that paragraph the term cannot have the same meaning. The paragraph reads:—

> The Security Council shall, where appropriate, utilize such regional arrangements or agencies for enforcement action under its authority. But no enforcement action shall be taken under regional arrangements or by regional agencies without the authorisation of the Security Council, with the exception of measures against any enemy state, as defined in paragraph 2 of this Article, provided for pursuant to Article 107 or in regional arrangements directed against renewal of aggressive policy on the part of any such state, until. . . .

According to the wording of this paragraph, action taken against a former enemy state under Article 107 or against renewal of aggressive policy on the part of any such state is, if such action involves the use of force, an enforcement action, and as such permitted, although it is neither decided on or approved by the Security Council, but taken by Members of the United Nations.

It is true that enforcement action in the exercise of the right of self-defence is not mentioned among the enforcement actions which may be taken under a regional arrangement without the authorisation of the Security Council. The explanation may be that the framers of the Charter considered it superfluous to refer expressly to the exercise of self-defence as an exception to the rule that no enforcement action shall be taken without the authorisation of the Security Council. For Article 51 provides that nothing in the Charter, hence also not the provision of Article 53 that no enforcement action shall be taken without the authorisation of the Security Council, shall impair the right of individual and collective self-defence, that is the right to take enforcement action against a state guilty of an armed attack prior to any intervention on the part of the Security Council. But it may also be that the framers of the Charter did not take into consideration the possibility of organising collective self-defence through regional arrangements, since they recognised the right of self-defence only as a provisional measure to be taken within the short period of time between the occurrence of an armed attack and the putting into operation the machinery of collective security by the Security Council. The framers of the Charter did not anticipate that the system of collective security laid down in the Charter will not work at all, and they certainly did not intend collective self-defence as a substitute for collective security. But the wording of the Charter does not exclude organisation of collective self-defence through regional arrangements even as a substitute for the paralysed system of collective security. It may be not in conformity with the intention of the framers of the Charter to organise collective self-defence by a treaty; but if a treaty is concluded by some Members of the United Nations for the purpose of organising collective self-defence, restricted to a certain area, this treaty is a regional arrangement; and the rule of Article 53 that no enforcement action shall be taken without the authorisation of the Security Council, does not apply to the exercise of the right of collective self-defence organised in the regional arrangement, because this rule is restricted by Article 51.

Hence, there is no cogent reason to assume that the North Atlantic Treaty is not a regional arrangement because it regulates the organisation of collective self-defence, and because the organisation of collective self-defence is no subject-matter of a regional arrangement, the enforcement action taken in the exercise of collective self-defence being different from the enforcement action which may be taken under a regional arrangement.

The only difference which exists between an enforcement action in the specific sense of this term, that is to say, within the meaning of Article 2, paragraphs 5 and 7, Article 50, Article 53, paragraph 1, first sentence, and enforcement action taken in the exercise of the right of self-defence or in conformity with Article 53, paragraph 1, second sentence, is that the enforcement action in the specific sense is an action involving the use of force taken by the Security Council, whereas enforcement action in a non-specific sense is an action involving the use of force not taken by the Security Council.

The assumption that the enforcement action taken in the exercise of the right of collective self-defence organised by a treaty must be directed against a state which does not belong to the organisation established by the treaty, whereas the enforcement action to be taken under a regional arrangement is to be directed against a state member of the regional organisation, and that, consequently, the North Atlantic Pact is no regional arrangement because it does not contemplate that, if a party violates the peace, the other parties should be the medium of taking enforcement action against it, has no basis, neither in the Charter nor in the North Atlantic Treaty. That regional arrangements may provide for enforcement action against states not parties to the regional arrangement, is not only not excluded by the wording of Articles 52 and 53; Article 53 expressly refers to enforcement actions against former enemy states, whether these states are or are not members of the regional organisation. It is more than probable that the framers of the Charter did not suppose that former enemy states will be members of a regional organisation within the meaning of Chapter VIII. The original idea was that regional arrangements will be concluded *against* former enemy states.

As to collective self-defence stipulated in Article 51, nothing in the wording of this Article can be interpreted to mean that the enforcement action taken in the exercise of collective self-defence must not be directed against an aggressor which is a party to the treaty organising the collective self-defence. Nor does the wording of the North Atlantic Treaty exclude the application of its Article 5 against an aggressor who is a contracting party to the Treaty. It is true that the Treaty is concluded in the first place as a defence against a possible aggressor who is not a party to the Treaty. But, for good reasons, in the wording of the Treaty everything has been avoided that could betray this intention. Under Article 10 of the Treaty, it is even not excluded to invite this state to accede to the Treaty.

Hence it is hardly possible to deny the possibility of interpreting the North Atlantic Treaty as a regional arrangement within the meaning of Chapter VIII of the Charter. This seems to be the most plausible, but it is not the only possible interpretation. Since the Charter does not define the concept of regional arrangement and especially since the exercise of collective self-defence is not expressly referred to in Article 53, it is not impossible to consider a treaty for the implementation of Article 51 as an agreement different from a regional arrangement. As in so many cases, the Charter allows contradictory interpretations. If the North Atlantic Treaty is interpreted to be a regional arrangement its constitutionality depends on its conformity to the provisions of Chapter VIII of the Charter, applying to treaties which have the character of regional arrangements.

According to paragraph 1 of Article 52 a regional arrangement ought to be consistent with the Purposes and Principles of the United Nations. There can be no doubt that the purposes of the North Atlantic Treaty, especially the organisation of collective self-defence, is consistent with the Principles and Purposes of the United Nations. According to paragraph 2 of Article 52 the Members of the United Nations parties to a regional arrangement 'shall make every effort to achieve pacific settlement of local disputes through such regional arrangements . . .' This implies that the regional arrangements must contain some provisions concerning the pacific settlement of local disputes, that is to say, disputes between parties to the regional arrangement. The provision of Article 52, paragraph 2, is evidently inconsistent with the provision of paragraph 1 according to which regional arrangements may be entered into for purposes which have nothing to do with disputes between the parties to the arrangement, as, for instance, a regional arrangement for economic co-operation or a regional arrangement for collective self-defence, both dealing with matters relating to the maintenance of international peace and security and both consistent with the Purposes and Principles of the United Nations.

It is obvious that the provisions of Article 1 of the North Atlantic Treaty establishing the obligation of the parties to settle international disputes by peaceful means—an obligation which has nothing to do with collective self-defence—has been inserted into the Treaty in order to comply with Article 52, paragraph 2, of the Charter, which applies only to regional arrangements. It is, however, doubtful whether a mere repetition of the provisions of the Charter concerning peaceful settlement of disputes suffices to fulfil the requirement of Article 52, paragraph 2: that settlement of local disputes shall be achieved 'through' the regional arrangement (or by a regional agency if such agency is established by the arrangement). Settlement of local disputes 'through' a regional arrangement may be interpreted to mean that the arrangement must contain provisions concerning a special procedure for the settlement of local disputes by the regional organisation constituted by the arrangement. A mere repetition of the provisions of the Charter does not suffice because such repetition is superfluous. The obligation concerned exists even if not repeated in the regional arrangement. Article 52, paragraph 2, should not be interpreted to provide something which is already provided in Article 33, paragraph 1, of the Charter.

Except Article 1—of which as pointed out, it might be doubtful whether it fully complies with Article 52, paragraph 2, of the Charter—the North Atlantic Treaty does not contain provisions incompatible with Chapter VIII of the Charter.

6. The North Atlantic Treaty in Relation to Italy

Article 53, paragraph 1, expressly authorises enforcement action to be taken under regional arrangements not only pursuant to Article 107 but also directed against renewal of aggressive policy on the part of a former enemy state. If a former enemy state is a party to a regional arrangement for the organisation of collective self-defence and if under another regional arrangement, entered into by Members of the United Nations, an enforcement action is directed against the renewal of aggressive policy of this state, the question arises whether the Members of the United Nations, parties to the first-mentioned regional arrangement, may fulfil their obligation to assist the attacked former enemy state without violating Article 53, paragraph 1. In this case the interpretation according to which Article 53, paragraph 1, is restricted by the right of collective self-defence as established by Article 51, and, consequently, the application of this Article to any enforcement action directed against a former enemy state in case this action constitutes an armed attack, is problematical. For the right of the Members to assist non-Members in the defence against an armed attack is not expressly stipulated in Article 51 and it is doubtful whether regional arrangements may be concluded with non-Members; and especially because according to the intention expressed in Article 53, regional arrangements are to be entered into *against* former enemy states, not in favour of such states. The interpretation that Members have under Article 51 of the Charter the right to defend a former enemy state against an armed attack even if this attack is an enforcement action against renewal of aggressive policy (which may be assumed, *e.g.*, in case the former enemy state begins to rearm) almost completely abolishes the right which the Members of the United Nations have in relation to former enemy states under Article 53, paragraph 1.

The question to what extent the obligation imposed by Article 5 of the North Atlantic Treaty upon Members of the United Nations, parties to this treaty, may be fulfilled in relation to Italy as a former enemy state, is not a question of the constitutionality of the North Atlantic Treaty, which provides in Article 7 expressly that it ' does not affect, and shall not be interpreted as affecting, in any way the rights and obligations under the Charter of the parties which are Members of the United Nations.' It is the question how to apply the North Atlantic Treaty in conformity with the Charter. This holds true also with respect to the question as to the applicability of Article 54 of the Charter which provides that ' the Security Council shall at all times be kept fully informed of activities undertaken or in contemplation under regional arrangements or by regional agencies for the maintenance of international peace and security.' If the North Atlantic Treaty is a regional arrangement the contracting parties to this Treaty are obliged to inform the Security Council of any action they undertake or contemplate under the Treaty. That such an obligation is not established by the North Atlantic Treaty itself, is of no importance. It need not be established by the regional arrangement; for it is established directly by the Charter.

A treaty concluded by some Members of the United Nations for dealing with matters relating to the maintenance of international peace and security, providing for regional action may also contain provisions which do not deal with matters relating to the maintenance of international peace and security and which do not provide for regional action. Then the treaty has only partly the character of a regional arrangement and the provisions of Article 52, paragraph 1, last part, and Articles 52, paragraphs 2 to 4, 53 and 54 apply only insofar as the treaty is a regional arrangement. One provision of the North Atlantic Treaty may be considered not to belong to a regional arrangement. It is Article 4 which provides: 'The parties will consult together whenever, in the opinion of one of them, the territorial integrity, political independence, or security of any of the parties is threatened.' This provision, it is true, deals with a matter relating to the maintenance of international peace and security but it does not provide for a regional action. The consultation referred to in Article 4 is not restricted to situations within the area determined in Article 6. Hence, the parties to the North Atlantic Treaty are, with respect to such consultation, not under the obligation of Article 54 to report to the Security Council.

Chapter 2

THE ACTION IN KOREA

On June 25, 1950, the representative of the United States on the Security Council transmitted to the Secretary-General of the United Nations a message which his Government had received from the United States Ambassador to the Republic of Korea, informing the Department of State that 'according to Korean Army reports which are partly confirmed by Korean Military Advisory Group field advisor reports North Korean forces invaded Republic of Korea territory at several points this morning (June 25)'.[1] He asked the Secretary-General to bring the message to the immediate attention of the President of the United Nations Security Council. At the same time, the United Nations Commission on Korea reported to the Secretary-General: 'Government of Republic of Korea states that about 04.00 hrs., June 25, attacks were launched in strength by North Korean forces all along the 38th parallel.' The Commission wished 'to draw attention of Secretary-General to serious situation developing which is assuming character of full-scale war and may endanger the maintenance of international peace and security. It suggests that he consider possibility of bringing matter to notice of Security Council.'[2] At the meeting of the Security Council on June 25, the representative of the United States introduced a draft resolution which the Security Council, after some amendment and revision, adopted. It is the first of three resolutions adopted by the Security Council in the Korean affair.

1. The Resolution of June 25, 1950

In the resolution adopted on June 25, 1950,[3] the Security Council *notes* 'with grave concern the armed attack upon the Republic of Korea by forces from North Korea.' Then it '*determines* that this action constitutes a breach of the peace' and '*calls* for immediate cessation of hostilities; and *calls* upon the authorities of North Korea to withdraw forthwith their armed forces to the thirty-eighth parallel.' Finally, the Security Council '*calls* upon all Members to render every assistance to the United Nations in the execution of this resolution and to refrain from giving assistance to the North Korean authorities.'

The fact that the Security Council noted that an 'armed attack' occurred seems to indicate that the Security Council intended to act under Article 51, which is the only Article of the Charter in which the term 'armed attack' is used. This interpretation of the decision

1 *United States Policy in the Korean Crisis.* Department of State Publication 3922. Far Eastern Series 34 (1950), p. 11.

2 U.N. Doc. S/1496.

3 U.N. Doc. S/1501.

of the Security Council implies that South Korea was in a state of self-defence within the meaning of Article 51, and that the Security Council interpreted this Article to apply not only to Members of the United Nations—as it might be assumed in conformity with its wording[4]—but also to non-Members. If the Security Council in adopting this resolution acted under Article 51, its action terminated the exercise of the right of—individual or collective—self-defence, and South Korea as well as the Members of the United Nations were allowed under the Charter to act only in conformity with the measures which the Security Council took under Article 51 as the 'measures necessary to maintain international peace and security.' The measures taken by the Security Council by its resolution of June 25, 1950, were: a call 'for the immediate cessation of hostilities'; a call 'upon the authorities of North Korea to withdraw forthwith their armed forces to the thirty-eighth parallel'; a call 'upon all Members to render every assistance to the United Nations in the execution of this resolution and to refrain from giving assistance to the North Korean authorities.' The call for the immediate cessation of hostilities may be interpreted as being directed at both parties to the armed conflict in Korea; the call for withdrawal of their armed forces to the thirty-eighth parallel is directed only at the authorities of North Korea. As to the call directed at all Members to assist the United Nations in the execution of the resolution, it is evident that the Members could not assist in the execution of this resolution in so far as the Council 'noted' an armed attack or 'determined' a breach of the peace. And it is difficult to understand how Members of the United Nations not yet involved in the armed conflict in Korea could assist in the execution of the resolution in so far as the Council called for 'immediate cessation of hostilities' or in so far as it called upon the North Korean authorities 'to withdraw forthwith their armed forces to the thirty-eighth parallel.' The call 'to refrain from giving assistance to the North Korean authorities' seems superfluous in view of the call for 'immediate cessation of hostilities.' The formulation of the call 'upon all Members' is an almost literary repetition of Article 2, paragraph 5 of the Charter. But the prohibition laid down in this paragraph refers to assistance given 'to any state against which the United Nations is taking preventive or enforcement action.' North Korea was in the opinion of the Security Council no 'State.' The Council intentionally avoided to speak of a North Korean State, it spoke only of 'forces from North Korea' and 'authorities of North Korea.'

In the first part of the resolution of June 25, 1950, the Security Council referred to the resolution of the General Assembly of October 21, 1949, in which the Assembly declared that the Government of the Republic of Korea 'having effective control and jurisdiction' over South Korea is 'the only such ("lawfully established") govern-

[4] Cf. *supra*, p. 920.

ment in Korea.' This may mean that the Security Council considered this government as the legitimate government of the whole of Korea, in spite of the fact that this government had no effective control over North Korea. But it may also mean that the Security Council considered the ' government in Korea ' only as the government of South Korea, and North Korea—since there was no legitimate government—as a stateless territory. But the formula ' Government of the Republic of Korea ' used in contradistinction to the formula ' authorities of *North* Korea,' seems to indicate that the first of the two interpretations corresponds to the intentions of the Security Council. If the ' Government of the Republic of Korea ' was to be considered as the legitimate government of the whole of Korea, the ' armed forces from North Korea ' were revolutionary forces, and the ' authorities of North Korea ' insurgents, not—or not yet—recognised by the Government of the Republic of Korea or by the Security Council as a belligerent power.

By its resolution of June 25, 1950, the Security Council did not take an enforcement action against the authorities of North Korea. The Council did not, or not expressly, authorise or order the Government of the Republic of Korea to continue hostilities in case the authorities of North Korea should not comply with the call for immediate cessation of hostilities and the call for withdrawal to the thirty-eighth parallel. Under Article 51, the Security Council could issue such order or authorisation. Then, and only then, the action of the Government of the Republic of Korea could be interpreted—not as the continuation of the exercise of the right of individual self-defence, since this right can be exercised only until the Security Council has interfered—but as an enforcement action performed in compliance with a measure taken by the Council under Article 51. And then the call directed at ' all Members to render every assistance to the United Nations in the execution of this resolution,' too, could be interpreted as such a measure. It may be that the Council was of the opinion that its call for immediate cessation of hostilities implied an order or an authorisation given to the Government of the Republic of Korea to continue hostilities against the authorities of North Korea in case the latter did not cease hostilities and not withdraw their armed forces to the thirty-eighth parallel. If so, the wording of the resolution did not express this intention. Hence, the call for immediate cessation of hostilities and the call upon the North Korean authorities to withdraw their armed forces to the thirty-eighth parallel can hardly be interpreted as an enforcement action taken by the United Nations within the meaning of Article 2, paragraph 5. But they may be interpreted as ' preventive ' measures taken by the Security Council under Article 40 of the Charter, in so far as the ' provisional measures ' referred to in this Article are to be taken ' in order to *prevent* an aggravation of the situation.'[5] Such

[5] Cf. *The Law of the United Nations*, pp. 92 ff.

measures may be taken not exclusively against states, since Article 40 speaks of ' parties,' not of states. Under Article 40, the Council is authorised to ' call ' upon the parties concerned to comply with such provisional measures as it deems necessary or desirable. This, also, indicates that the two ' calls ' of the resolution are provisional measures under Article 40. If the calls to cease hostilities and to withdraw to the thirty-eighth parallel are provisional measures taken by the Council under Article 40, the resolution must be considered in the light of Article 39. For a provisional measure under Article 40 cannot be taken without a previous determination of the existence of a threat to, or breach of, the peace, as stipulated in Article 39. In its resolution the Security Council expressly ' determines that this action [the armed attack upon the Republic of Korea by forces from North Korea] constitutes a breach of the peace.' Only by Article 39 the Security Council is authorised to ' determine the existence of any threat to the peace, breach of the peace, or act of aggression.'

The Charter distinguishes between ' threat to the peace ' and ' breach of the peace,' an ' act of aggression ' being, as it is correctly formulated in Article 1, paragraph 1, only a special case of a breach of the peace. This distinction is of great importance. Peace or, as the Charter says, ' international peace ' is a relation between states. Hence a ' breach of the peace ' can be committed only by a state in its relation to another state. If the ' forces form North Korea ' are not the armed forces of a state and the ' North Korean authorities ' not the government of a state but a revolutionary group or insurgents, and, consequently, the war in Korea a civil war, then the Council could not determine the existence of a breach of the peace; it could only determine a threat to the peace. It may be doubted whether the action of insurgents against the legitimate government can be an ' armed attack ' within the meaning of Article 51. It may be argued that an ' armed attack ' exists only in case one state attacks another state with its armed forces. But if the Council considers the action of insurgents against the legitimate government as an armed attack and if it thinks necessary to apply Article 39, it can declare this armed attack only as a threat to the peace, and that means a threat to the international peace, and not as a breach of the international peace, that is the peace between states, not the peace within one and the same state. It is true that Article 39 does not speak of a threat to the international peace, but only of a threat to the peace. But that by ' threat to the peace ' a threat to the international peace is meant, follows from the provision of the same Article 39 that the enforcement measures referred to in this Article shall be taken ' to maintain or restore international peace and security.'[6]

[6] That the war in Korea was a civil, not an international, war, was maintained by the representative of the Soviet Union at the 482nd meeting of the Security Council (U.N. Doc. S/P.V. 482, pp. 10, 12). He also stated that ' the concept of aggression is not applicable to civil war ' (U.N. Doc. S/P.V. 489, p. 4).

It may be that the members of the Security Council who voted for the resolution of June 25, 1950, were of the opinion that the 'armed forces from North Korea' and the 'authorities of North Korea' were only the instrument of the Government of the Soviet Union, and, hence, the armed conflict in Korea an international war between two states. But none of the resolutions adopted by the Security Council in the case of Korea expressed this opinion. Hence, this opinion cannot be accepted as basis of an interpretation of the action in Korea.

Under Article 39 the Security Council may make recommendations or take enforcement measures in accordance with Articles 41 and 42. But in its resolution of June 25, the Security Council did neither make a recommendation nor did it take an enforcement measure. It merely applied Article 40, that is to say, it called upon the parties concerned to comply with the provisional measures it deemed necessary.

On June 27, 1950, the President of the United States 'ordered United States air and sea forces to give the Korean Government troops cover and support';[7] this action was justified as an assistance to the United Nations in the execution of the Security Council's resolution of June 25, 1950. Only after this order was issued by the United States President the Security Council adopted a resolution by which an armed intervention by a Member of the United Nations against North Korea could indeed be justified.

2. The Resolution of June 27, 1950

It is the resolution of June 27, 1950,[8] in which the Security Council '*recommends* that the Members of the United Nations furnish such assistance to the Republic of Korea as may be necessary to repel the armed attack and to restore international peace and security in the area.' It seems as if this resolution was adopted as a measure necessary to maintain international peace, referred to in Article 51, since the Council recommended that the Members assist the Republic of Korea in repelling the 'armed attack.' Even if so, it cannot be interpreted as a recommendation to exercise the right of collective self-defence since, as pointed out, this right cannot be exercised after the Security Council has taken the measures necessary to maintain international peace and security. It may be doubted whether the Security Council under Article 51 can take enforcement measures other than those provided for in Articles 39, 41 and 42. But if the measures taken by the Security Council under Article 51 in case of an armed attack are not the enforcement measures referred to in Articles 39, 41 and 42, the Council need not previously determine the existence of a threat to the peace, breach of the peace, or act of aggression, as

[7] Statement by the President, June 27, 1950, *United States Policy in the Korean Crisis*, p. 18.

[8] U.N. Doc. S/1511.

provided for in Article 39. However, in its resolution of June 27, the Security Council expressly refers to its resolution of June 25, in which it 'determines that this action [the armed attack upon the Republic of Korea by forces from North Korea] constitutes a breach of the peace.' That indicates that the Security Council intended to act under Article 39 and to take the measures (not necessarily enforcement measures) provided for in this Article.

The recommendation made in the resolution of June 27 implies the recommendation of an enforcement action involving the use of armed force. Article 39, it is true, authorises the Security Council, after it has determined the existence of a threat to, or breach of, the peace, to 'make recommendations,' without restricting the content of these recommendations. But it is doubtful whether a recommendation of an enforcement action corresponds to the intention of those who framed the Charter. Article 39 distinguishes between 'recommendations' and 'measures . . . taken in accordance with Articles 41 and 42,' which Articles provide enforcement measures involving or not involving the use of armed force. Making recommendations and taking enforcement measures are, within the meaning of Article 39, two different functions of the Security Council. If the Security Council, after having determined under Article 39 the existence of a threat to, or breach of, the peace, is of the opinion that enforcement measures are necessary to maintain or restore international peace, the Council must take these measures itself by acting under Article 41 or 42, that is to say, by ordering Members to apply certain measures determined in Article 41, or, in conformity with Article 42, by ordering Members to use the contingents of their armed forces placed at the disposal of the Security Council in conformity with the special agreements referred to in Article 43. That means that enforcement measures under Article 39 can only be ordered by the Security Council, but not recommended. Only if they are ordered by the Security Council, that is to say, if there is a decision of the Security Council binding upon the Members within the meaning of Articles 25 and 48, are they the enforcement measures referred to in Article 39. Only in this way, that is to say 'in accordance with Articles 41 and 42,' can the Security Council take the enforcement measures stipulated in Chapter VII. If the Council wants to make recommendations under Article 39, it cannot recommend enforcement measures; it can recommend only peaceful means for the adjustment of a situation which the Council has declared to be a threat to, or breach of, the peace.

This seems to be the interpretation of the Charter which was at the basis of the United Nations Participation Act adopted by the 79th Congress of the United States in 1945.[9] For this Act authorises the President of the United States to apply the measures not involving

79th Congress, 1st Session, Public Law, 246.

the use of armed force decided upon by the Security Council in conformity with Article 41 of the Charter; and to make available to the Security Council, on its call, without authorisation of the Congress, the armed forces provided in the special agreements entered into by the President and the Security Council with the approval of an Act of Congress or a Joint Resolution, that is to say, to apply measures involving the use of armed force decided upon by the Security Council in conformity with Article 42. The United Nations Participation Act did not authorise the President to apply enforcement measures merely recommended by the Security Council; probably because the Government of the United States at that time considered enforcement actions taken by the Security Council in conformity with Article 41 or Article 42 as the only enforcement actions of the United Nations in which a Member was supposed to participate under the Charter. The Act did not authorise the President to participate in an enforcement action merely recommended by the Security Council probably because the Government of the United States did not consider such an enforcement action as provided for by the Charter. However, it must be admitted that the wording of Article 39 does not exclude an interpretation according to which the Security Council may, under this Article, recommend to Members to use force and especially to use armed force. Only if this interpretation is accepted is the resolution of the Security Council of June 27 constitutional.

If the Security Council recommends under Article 39 the use of force and especially the use of armed force, the same question arises as in the case the Security Council decides under Article 39 to take enforcement measures in accordance with Articles 41 and 42: May the enforcement action be directed only against Members or also against non-Member states, and even against groups of individuals which have not the character of a state, especially revolutionary forces, insurgents. Article 39, as pointed out,[1] does not restrict the Security Council to direct the enforcement measures taken under Articles 41 and 42 only against Members; they may be directed against non-Member states and even against groups which have not the character of states, *e.g.*, a people living on a stateless territory, or a community not recognised as a state, or insurgents not recognised as belligerent power. If the Security Council is authorised by Article 39 to recommend to Members the use of force and especially the use of armed force, it may recommend to take these measures against Members, non-Members, or groups not having the character of states. That means that Article 39 authorises the Council to interfere by enforcement measures in a civil war. In its resolution of June 27, the Council recommended to Members to use armed force against North Korea, which, as pointed out, the Council did not consider to be a state.

[1] Cf. *The Law of the United Nations*, p. 19.

As pointed out, the Security Council can interfere in a civil war under Article 39 only if it has determined the existence of a threat to the international peace, not the existence of a breach of the international peace, insofar as a civil war is not an international war and, hence, does not constitute a breach of international peace. Consequently, in such a case the enforcement measures are to be taken under Article 39 not to 'restore,' but to 'maintain' international peace. If the armed conflict in Korea was a civil war, the resolution of June 27 should not have recommended that the Members of the United Nations furnish assistance to the Republic of Korea 'to restore international peace and security in the area,' but 'to maintain international peace and security.' International peace is not a status which exists within the area of one state—this is internal peace—but in the relations among two or more states. The formula used in the resolution of June 27 is justified only if the Security Council was of the opinion that the armed conflict in Korea—at least before the Council recommended military intervention by Members of the United Nations—was an international war between the Republic of Korea and another state. But this opinion, as pointed out, has not been expressed in the language of the resolutions adopted by the Security Council in the Korean affair.

Another question is whether the use of force recommended by the Security Council under Article 39 can be considered as a sanction. This question may be answered in the same way as the analogous question arising in case of an enforcement action taken by the Council in accordance with Articles 41 and 42: If the Member states as well as the non-Member states are supposed to be under an obligation to refrain from conduct which the Security Council considers to be a threat to, or breach of, the peace, then an enforcement measure taken against a state guilty of a violation of that obligation is a true sanction because it is a reaction against an international delict, whether this measure is ordered or only recommended by the Security Council. If, as in the Korean case, a state assists another state with its armed forces, and that implies, assists the government of another state in its fight against insurgents not recognised as a belligerent power, then the enforcement action of the assisting state has the same character as that of the assisted state. It is participation in a civil war on the side of the legitimate government. This is an internal affair of the assisted state, its reaction against a violation of its law, *i.e.*, the illegal use of force against the legitimate government. Since the participation of a state in a civil war within another state on the side of the legitimate government is legally possible only with the—express or tacit—consent of this state, the enforcement action of the assisting state is, in the last analysis, an action of the assisted state, because authorised by its government.

It is, however, more than paradoxical to consider such an action, carried out by the armed forces of two or more states on the basis of an express or tacit international agreement, not as war in the sense of international law. It might be not impossible to assume that in case of participation of one state in the civil war within another state on the side of the latter's government on the basis of an international agreement, the civil war assumes the character of an international war. Participation of a state, with its armed forces, in the civil war within another state on the side of the insurgents is certainly international war in the relationship between the two states concerned. If it is assumed that general international law permits the states to assist with their armed forces the government of a state in its fight against an insurrection, and if it is admitted that in such a case the civil war assumes the character of international war, insurrection is not only a delict under national, but also under international law; then the use of armed force by the assisting state against the insurgents has the character of an international sanction, and then the participation of a state with its armed forces in a civil war on the side of the insurgents is illegal from the point of view of general international law.

3. The Resolution of July 7, 1950

On July 7, 1950, the Security Council adopted a resolution[2] in which the Council '1. *Welcomes* the prompt and vigorous support which governments and peoples of the United Nations have given to its Resolutions of June 25 and 27, 1950, to assist the Republic of Korea in defending itself against armed attack and thus to restore international peace and security in the area; 2. *Notes* that Members of the United Nations have transmitted to the United Nations offers of assistance for the Republic of Korea; 3. *Recommends* that all Members providing military forces and other assistance pursuant to the aforesaid Security Council resolutions make such forces and other assistance available to a unified command under the United States; 4. *Requests* the United States to designate the commander of such forces; 5. *Authorises* the unified command at its discretion to use the United Nations flag in the course of operations against North Korean forces concurrently with the flags of the various nations participating; 6. *Requests* the United States to provide the Security Council with reports as appropriate on the course of action taken under the unified command.'

In paragraph 1 of this resolution not only the resolution of June 27, but also the resolution of June 25, is interpreted as recommendation to assist the Republic of Korea in its defence against an armed attack, although the wording of the resolution of June 25 does not justify such interpretation. As to this resolution, the interpretation is an *ex post facto* justification of the action which the United States of America took subsequent to the resolution of June 25, but prior

[2] UN. Doc. S/1588.

to the resolution of June 27. The resolution of July 7 interprets the action of the Members of the United Nations in Korea as assistance to the Republic of Korea ' defending itself against armed attack,' that is to say, as the exercise of the right of collective self-defence on the part of the Members concerned. Such interpretation is, as pointed out, not possible after the intervention of the Security Council has taken place.[3]

4. Action in Korea as Action of the United Nations

It seems that in paragraphs 3 to 5 of the resolution the Security Council considers the action in Korea as an action of the United Nations, for it authorises the use of the United Nations flag. At the 476th meeting of the Security Council on July 7,[4] the President of the Council expressly declared with respect to the action in Korea recommended by the Security Council: ' This is a United Nations action.' If the action taken by Members of the United Nations in conformity with a recommendation made by the Security Council under Article 39 is an action of the United Nations, it cannot be the exercise of the right of collective self-defence. For collective self-defence is provided by the Charter only for the period of time during which no action of the United Nations, *i.e.*, action by the Security Council, takes place.

Although it is not possible to consider the action undertaken by the Members in conformity with the resolutions of the Security Council of June 25 and 27, 1950, as the exercise of the right of collective self-defence, since it was entered upon after the Council had taken the measures necessary to maintain international peace and security, it is doubtful whether the action taken by Members can be considered as an action of the United Nations. It may be argued that an action of the United Nations is an act performed by an organ of the United Nations in the exercise of a function conferred upon the Organisation by the Charter. The United Nations can act directly only by decisions taken by its organs. But it may act indirectly if the function conferred upon the Organisation can be performed only through the action of a Member or Members. If a function conferred upon the Organisation can be performed only through the action of a Member or Members, the competent organ must have the power to impose by its decision upon a Member or Members an obligation to take the action. Only an action taken by Members of the United Nations in fulfilment of an obligation imposed upon them by a decision of an organ of the United Nations can have the character of an action of the United Nations, not an action performed in compliance with a

[3] At the 285th Plenary Meeting of the General Assembly, the representative of Sweden declared: ' Both the action of the United States and the decisions of other countries to assist South Korea are solidly based upon provisions of Article 51 of the Charter concerning collective self-defence.'

[4] U.N. Doc. S/P.V. 476, pp. 3–5.

mere recommendation. Only if a Member acts in fulfilment of an obligation imposed upon it by the decision of an organ of the United Nations to the effect of performing a function of the Organisation, the United Nations is acting through the Member. As a matter of fact, only the Security Council can adopt decisions binding upon the Members (Articles 24, 48). If, *e.g.*, in case of a dispute between two Members before the Security Council, one party in compliance with a recommendation made by the Security Council for the settlement of the dispute, withdraws from a certain territory, this action is certainly not an action of the United Nations. The decision by which the Security Council makes a recommendation for the settlement of the dispute is an action of the United Nations, an action by which the Council exercises a function conferred upon it by the Charter. But the action of the Member complying with the recommendation is not an action of the United Nations, it is an action of the Member. If it is assumed that the Security Council under Article 39 may recommend to Members to use force and especially armed force, the enforcement action taken by the Members in compliance with this recommendation is not an action of the United Nations, in contradistinction to enforcement measures taken by the Security Council under Article 39 in accordance with Articles 41 and 42. These are enforcement measures which the Security Council can take only through the Members. Article 48, paragraph 1 provides with respect to these actions:

> The action required to carry out the decisions of the Security Council for the maintenance of international peace and security shall be taken by all the Members of the United Nations or by some of them, as the Security Council may determine.

The Members are obliged to carry out the decisions of the Security Council, and the ' decisions ' of the Security Council are the decisions which the Security Council under Article 39 adopts concerning the measures to be taken in accordance with Articles 41 and 42, not the recommendations the Security Council may make under Article 39. Hence it may be doubted whether an action taken by Members in compliance with a recommendation made by the Security Council under Article 39 is an ' action of the United Nations,' especially whether it is the ' prompt and effective action by the United Nations' for which Article 24 imposes primary responsibility upon the Security Council. However, since the Charter does not define the concept of ' action of (or by) the United Nations,' it is not excluded to consider an action performed by a Member in conformity with a recommendation of an organ of the United Nations, especially an action performed in conformity with a recommendation made by the Security Council under Article 39, as an ' action of (or by) the United Nations,' this term used in a wider sense; especially if Article 39 is interpreted to mean that the Security Council may recommend to Members also the taking of enforcement action involving or not involving the use of armed force in order to maintain or restore international peace and security.

5. The Use of the United Nations Flag

The authorisation to use the United Nations flag is based on the resolution 167 (II), adopted by the General Assembly at its 96th meeting on October 20, 1947,[5] by which the Secretary-General was authorised to adopt a Flag Code, that is to say, given the power to issue general rules regulating the use of the flag, binding upon the Member states. It implies the power to authorise the use of the flag in concrete cases. This is a legislative function. By Article 98, the General Assembly, the Security Council, and the other Councils of the United Nations are authorised to entrust the Secretary-General with the performance of functions other than that of acting as the chief administrative officer of the Organisation in all meetings of these organs. But it may be doubted whether these organs can entrust the Secretary-General with powers which they themselves do not have; and the General Assembly does not have the power to issue general norms concerning the use of the flag of the United Nations, binding upon the Members. As long as the use of the flag was not regulated, no use of the flag could be considered as illegal. But on December 19, 1947, the Secretary-General issued a Flag Code, which stipulated in Pt. 8: 'The flag shall not be used except in accordance with this Flag Code and any regulations made pursuant thereto'; and in Pt. 11: 'Any violation of this Flag Code shall be penalised in accordance with the law of the Country in which such violation takes place.' The Code did not contain a special provision authorising the use of the flag in military operations. Such use of the flag was covered only by the provision of Pt. 4, par. 2: 'The flag shall be used by any unit acting on behalf of the United Nations such as the Military Staff Committee, and any Committee or Commission or other entity established by the United Nations in such circumstances not covered in this Code as may become necessary in the interests of the United Nations.' It is more than doubtful whether the use of the flag in a military operation of the armed forces of Members and of a state not a Member of the United Nations (the Republic of Korea), even if the operation was performed in compliance with a recommendation of the Security Council, was in accordance with the Flag Code in force at the time the Security Council made that recommendation. But shortly after the resolution of the Security Council of July 7, 1950, namely, on July 28, 1950, the Secretary-General issued a new Flag Code, which in Pt. 6, under the heading 'Use of Flag in Military Operations,' stipulates: 'The flag

[5] Cf. *The Law of the United Nations*, p. 194.

may be used in military operations only upon express authorisation to that effect by a competent organ of the United Nations.'[6]

According to the resolution 167 (II) of the General Assembly, the only organ of the United Nations competent to authorise the use of the flag was the Secretary-General, and the new Code did not confer this power on other organs of the United Nations. But the Secretary-General was probably of the opinion that the General Assembly and the Security Council are competent to authorise the use of the flag. This opinion has no basis neither in the Charter nor in the resolution 167 (II) of the General Assembly. The effect of the provision of Pt. 6 is that the Secretary-General conferred the power to authorise the use of the flag on other organs of the United Nations which have competence with respect to military operations. Thus the provision of Pt. 6 of the new Flag Code is an *ex post facto* justification of the resolution by which the Security Council authorised the use of the flag of the United Nations in the military operation recommended by the Council.

6. The Unified Command

If the Security Council has, under Article 39, the power to recommend to Members to take enforcement action involving the use of armed force, it may also recommend to Members 'to make such forces and other assistance available to a unified command' under a

[6] Other important provisions of the amended Flag Code are:—

'2. Dignity of Flag. The flag shall not be subjected to any indignity.

4. Use of Flag by the United Nations. (1) The flag shall be flown (a) from all buildings, offices and other property occupied by the United Nations; (b) from any official residence when such residence has been so designated by regulation. (2) The flag shall be used by any unit acting on behalf of the United Nations such as any Committee or Commission or other entity established by the United Nations, in such circumstances not covered in this Code as may become necessary in the interests of the United Nations.

5. Use of Flag generally. The flag may be used in accordance with this Flag Code by Governments, organisations and individuals to demonstrate support of the United Nations and to further its principles and purposes. The manner and circumstances of display shall conform, insofar as appropriate, to the laws and customs applicable to the display of the national flag of the country in which the idsplay is made.

7. Prohibition. The flag shall not be used in any manner inconsistent with this Code or with any regulations made pursuant thereto. On no account shall the flag or a replica thereof be used for commercial purposes or in direct association with an article of merchandise.

10. Violation. Any violation of this Flag Code may be punished in accordance with the law of the country in which such violation takes place.

11. Regulations. (1) The Secretary-General may delegate his authority under this Code. (2) The Secretary-General or his duly authorised representative is the only person empowered to make regulations under this Code. Such regulations may be made for the purposes indicated in this Code and generally for the purpose of implementing or clarifying any provision of this Code whenever the Secretary-General or his duly authorised representative considers such implementation or clarification necessary.'

definite Member, and request, that is to say, recommend to that Member to designate the commander. But the commander is not an organ of the United Nations within the meaning of Article 7 of the Charter. He would be a subsidiary organ of the United Nations if established in conformity with Article 29 of the Charter, that is to say, appointed by a decision of the Security Council; which is probably possible only in case of an enforcement action taken by the Security Council under Article 42. The unification of the armed forces of the Members taking action in compliance with the recommendation of the Security Council is the effect of a voluntary agreement of these Members, and the commander of the unified forces is the common organ of these Members.

7. Absence of the Soviet Union from the Security Council

The three resolutions of the Security Council have been adopted in the absence of one of the permanent members, the Soviet Union. Hence the question arises whether the Security Council can adopt a valid decision in case not all the eleven Members which under Article 23 are to be represented on the Council are present, and especially in case the representative of a permanent member is not present. It may be argued, as pointed out,[7] that neither the Charter nor the Rules of Procedure of the Security Council contain a provision concerning the *Quorum*;[8] and if the constitution of a collegiate body does not contain a provision concerning the *Quorum*, all members of the body must be present in order to enable it to adopt a valid decision.[9] But the wording of Article 27 of the Charter, regulating

7 Cf. *The Law of the United Nations*, pp. 244 ff.

8 In contradistinction to the Rules of Procedure of the Security Council the Rules of Procedure of the General Assembly provide in Rule 68: 'A majority of the Members of the General Assembly shall constitute a quorum.'

9 At the 482nd meeting of the Security Council (U.N. Doc. S/P.V. 482, p. 15) the representative of the Soviet Union declared: 'It goes without saying that the Security Council can function normally and fulfill the noble mission entrusted to it—the maintenance of peace and pacific settlement—only if it functions with its full lawful membership in compliance with the requirements of the United Nations Charter, namely with the participation of the representative of the U.S.S.R. and of the Chinese People's Republic. Only if all its five permanent members participate will the decisions it adopts be lawful, authoritative and irrefutable from the standpoint of the United Nations Charter and of generally accepted international standard. . . .' He said of the resolutions adopted by the Security Council in the Korean affair: 'The resolutions adopted by the Security Council under the dictate of the United States delegation and in breach of the United Nations Charter have no legal force.' At the 487th meeting of the Security Council (U.N. Doc. S/P.V. 487, p. 20) the representative of France expressed the opinion that the Soviet Union violated its obligation under the Charter by the absence of its representative from the meetings of the Security Council. He declared: 'The absence was certainly contrary to the spirit and, in our opinion, also to the letter of the Charter.' The representative of the Soviet Union objected: 'The Charter does not require from each member of the Council obligatory participation in its meetings in all circumstances. . . . The refusal of the

the procedure in the Security Council, does not exclude an interpretation according to which the presence of all the members of the Security Council is not required for a valid decision of that organ. For Article 27 provides that decisions of the Security Council shall be made by an affirmative vote of seven members. Consequently the Security Council can adopt a valid decision even when only seven members are present. This rule of Article 27 may be interpreted to imply an indirect provision concerning the *Quorum*. If this was not the intention of the framers of the Charter—and it probably was not—their true intention was not expressed in a satisfactory way. As to the effect of the absence of a member, there is no difference between the absence of a permenent and of a non-permanent member. The absence of a permanent member in case of a decision on a non-procedural matter implies the question whether a decision on a non-procedural matter requires the concurring votes of all the permanent members, or only the concurring votes of the permanent members present and voting. As pointed out,[1] both answers are equally possible.

8. The Representation of China

The unconstitutionality of the resolutions adopted by the Security Council in the Korean affair has been asserted also for the reason that the Chinese Republic, which according to Article 23 of the Charter is a permanent member of the Security Council, was not represented when the Council adopted the resolutions concerned. In a cablegram dated June 29, 1950, to the Secretary-General concerning the Security Council resolution of June 27, 1950,[2] the Deputy Minister of Foreign Affairs of the Soviet Union stated that this resolution 'has no legal force' because it has been adopted in the

Government of the U.S.S.R. to take part in the meetings of the Security Council cannot therefore be regarded as a violation of established procedure' (*ibid.*, p. 26). This interpretation of the Charter is possible in view of its wording.

[1] Cf. *The Law of the United Nations*, pp. 240 ff. As pointed out, the wording of the English text of Article 27, paragraph 3: 'including the concurring votes of the permanent members' (not: *all* the permanent members) does not exclude the interpretation that a valid decision on a non-procedural matter requires only the concurring votes of the permanent members present and voting; but the French text reads: 'les voix de tous les membres permanents'; and the other texts of Article 27, paragraph 3, have the same wording. There can be no doubt that according to the intention of the framers of the Charter the concurring votes of all the permanent members are required. This intention is not only expressed in the non-English texts of the Charter and in the Statement of the Delegations of the Four Sponsoring Powers on Voting Procedure in the Security Council of June 7, 1945 (cf. *ibid.*, pp. 249 ff.), but also in the Statement by the Acting Secretary of State Josef C. Grew (*Hearings before the Committee on Foreign Relations United States Senate on the Charter of the United Nations*, Washington, 1945, p. 213) and in the *Report to the President by the Secretary of State on the Results of the San Francisco Conference*, Department of State, Publication 2349, Conference Series 71, p. 71.

[2] U.N. Doc. S/1517.

absence of the representatives of two permanent members, the U.S.S.R. and China. At the 480th meeting of the Security Council the delegate of the Soviet Union in his capacity as President of the Security Council, ruled 'that the representative of the Kuomintang group seated in the Security Council does not represent China and cannot therefore take part in the meetings of the Security Council.' The President's ruling was rejected by the Security Council.[3]

The President announced: 'The results of the voting are as follows: 7 against the President's ruling and 3 in favour of the ruling. I am not counting the vote of the representative of the Kuomintang group.' The representative of the United States protested against this announcement. He was of the opinion that the vote of the person whom the President of the Council designated as the 'representative of the Kuomintang group' was to be counted as the vote of the representative of China. Later the President changed his announcement by stating 'that 8 votes were cast against the President's ruling including the vote of the representative of the Kuomintang group . . ." (U.N. Doc. S/P.V. 480, Rev. 1, pp. 36–40, 42–47). Although the Security Council rejected the view that the nationalist Government has ceased to be the legitimate government and that the communist Government is the legitimate government of China, and hence also competent to appoint the representative of China on the Security Council undr Rule 39 of the Rules of Procedure, the Security Council invited the communist Government of China, that is the Central People's Government of the People's Republic of China, to send a representative to participate in certain meetings of the Council.

At its 506th meeting the Security Council adopted the following resolution concerning the complaint of armed invasion of Taiwan (Formosa) (U.N. Doc. S/1836):—

"The Security Council—

Considering that it is its duty to investigate any situation likely to lead to international friction or to give rise to a dispute, in order to determine whether the continuance of such dispute or situation may endanger international peace and security, and likewise to determine the existence of any threat to the peace;

Considering that, in the event of a complaint regarding situations or facts similar to those mentioned above, the Council may hear the complainants;

Considering that, in view of the divergency of opinion in the Council regarding the representation of China and without prejudice to this question, it may, in accordance with Rule 39 of the Rules of Procedure, invite representatives of the Central People's Government of the People's Republic of China to provide it with information or assist it in the consideration of these matters;

Having noted the declaration of the People's Republic of China regarding the armed invasion of the Island of Taiwan (Formosa);

Decides—

(a) to defer consideration of this question until the first meeting of the Council held after November 15, 1950;

(b) to invite a representative of said Government to attend the meetings of the Security Council held after November 15, 1950, during the discussion of that Government's declaration regarding an armed invasion of the Island of Taiwan (Formosa).'

At its 520th meeting (U.N. Doc. S/P.V. 519, p. 91; 520, p. 37) the Security Council adopted a resolution by which it decided 'to invite, in accordance with Rule 39 of the Rules of Procedure, a representative of the Central Government

The view that the resolutions of the Security Council are unconstitutional because China was not represented on the Council, may be based on the fact that the national Government which signed the credentials of the person acting as the representative of China, has lost its effective control over the Chinese territory and its people. Consequently, under general international law, it has ceased to be the government of the Republic of China, and credentials signed by it are no longer valid. The only government of the Republic of China under general international law is the communist government which is in effective control of the territory of China and its people. But no representative of China armed with credentials signed by the communist government of the Republic of China is admitted to the Security Council. Hence the Chinese Republic is not represented in the Security Council; that means that the Security Council is not composed in accordance with the Charter. Only if constitutionally composed, the Security Council can adopt valid decisions. This is certainly a possible interpretation of the Charter, which does not contain provisions concerning the appointment of the representatives of the Members in the General Assembly, the Security Council, and the other Councils of the United Nations. If one of these bodies

of the People's Republic of China to be present during discussion by the Council of the special Report of the United Nations Command in Korea, document S/1884.'

At the 277th Plenary Meeting of the General Assembly, on September 19, 1950, the representative of India submitted a draft resolution 'recognising that the Central Government of the People's Republic of China is the only such government functioning in the Republic of China as now constituted.' The General Assembly rejected this suggestion as well as two other draft resolutions submitted by the representative of the Soviet Union. According to one, the General Assembly should decide 'that the representatives of the Kuomintang group cannot take part in the work of the General Assembly and its organs because they are not the representatives of China'; according to the other, the Assembly should decide 'to invite the representatives of the People's Government to take part in the work of the General Assembly.' The General Assembly adopted a resolution establishing 'a Special Committee consisting of the President of the Assembly and six other representatives selected by the President to consider the question of Chinese representation and report back, with recommendations, to the present session of the General Assembly. . . .' This resolution contains also the statement 'that pending a decision of the General Assembly on the report of this Special Committee, the representatives of the National Government of China shall be seated in the General Assembly with the same rights as other representatives.' The representative of the Soviet Union declared: 'The U.S.S.R. delegation considers that the decision which has just been taken to reject the draft resolutions of the U.S.S.R. and the Indian delegation is wrong and illegal,' and 'that the decision just taken against that proposal is both wrong and illegal.'

At the 281st Plenary Meeting of the General Assembly the chairman of the Credentials Committee reported that the Committee has rejected a proposal of the representative of the Soviet Union not to recognise as valid the credentials of the representatives of the National Government of China. At the same meeting the Assembly rejected a proposal of the representative of the Soviet Union to the effect 'that the credentials of the representative of the Government of Nationalist China should not be recognised as valid.'

has to decide the question whether a certain person is the representative of a Member state—and that means whether his credentials are signed by the Government of the Member state or whether he is himself a member of the Government and as such entitled to represent the state—it is bound by the rule of general international law that the government of a state is the individual, or the body of individuals, who is, or are, in effective control of the territory and population concerned. However, it is not excluded to argue that the Charter confers upon the Security Council the power to decide the question as to whether a certain person is the representative of a Member state in conformity with general international law, and consequently also the power to apply and interpret international law in this respect. As long as the Security Council does not decide that a person whom the Security Council has recognised as the representative of a member of the Council has lost this quality—because the government which had signed his credentials or of which he is a member has lost effective control over the territory and people concerned—this person is, within the meaning of the Charter, the representative of the Member state.

9. Representation of Members in Case of a Revolutionary Change of Government

At the 480th meeting of the Security Council the representative of Great Britain challenged the ruling of the President that the representative of the Kuomintang group did not represent China and therefore could not take part in the meetings of the Security Council, referring to Rule 17 of the Rules of Procedure of the Security Council, which runs as follows:—'Any representative on the Security Council, to whose credentials objection has been made within the Security Council, shall continue to sit with the same rights as other representatives until the Security Council has decided the matter.' The wording of this Rule is certainly in favour of the view that the representative whose credentials have been issued by the national Government of China has the right to be seated in the Security Council until the Council—and not the President—has decided the question as to whether he is or is not the representative of China. But it is doubtful whether this Rule was intended to apply to the case that, as a result of civil war within a Member state, two governments claim the right to issue the credentials of the representative of that state. That the Rules of Procedure do not anticipate this case results from the fact that according to the wording of Chapter III of the Rules of Procedure (Representation and Credentials) the representatives appointed by each of the two governments shall be seated in the Security Council. Rule 13 stipulates that each member of the Security Council, and that means, each state which according to the Charter is a member of the

Security Council, shall be represented by an accredited representative, and that the credentials shall be communicated to the Secretary-General not less than twenty-four hours before he takes his seat on the Council. The Secretary-General has according to the wording of Rule 15, only the function to examine the credentials and to submit a report to the Security Council; he has not the power to make a—provisional—decision concerning the validity of the credentials, this decision being reserved to the Security Council. For Rule 16 provides: 'Pending the approval of the credentials of a representative on the Security Council in accordance with Rule 15, such representative shall be seated provisionally with the same rights as other representatives.' If two persons present credentials issued by two different authorities claiming to be the government of one and the same Member state, both—according to the wording of this Rule—shall be provisionally seated in the Security Council, even if the Secretary-General in his report to the Council suggests to approve only one of the two credentials. Such a situation was hardly foreseen by the framers of the Rules of Procedure. That one Member is represented, even only provisionally, by two representatives, is incompatible with Article 27, paragraph 1, of the Charter. That the Rules of Procedure do not apply to the case of two governments claiming the right to represent one and the same Member state follows also from Rule 13, which provides: 'The Head of Government or Minister of Foreign Affairs of each member of the Security Council shall be entitled to sit on the Security Council without submitting credentials.' In this case the Secretary-General has no function at all; and nothing in the Rules of Procedure could prevent the Head or Minister of Foreign Affairs of the communist government of China to take a seat in the Security Council and take part in its meetings, together with the representatives accredited by the national government of China. The Rules of Procedure do not even provide for the possibility of making objection to the participation in the meetings by the Head or Minister of Foreign Affairs of a revolutionary government established in a state member of the Security Council. Rule 17 provides only for the possibility of making objection to the credentials of a representative. But according to Rule 13, the Head or Minister of Foreign Affairs of a government do not need credentials.

The Rules of Procedure of the General Assembly do not expressly provide—as do the Rules of Procedure of the Security Council in Rule 13 for the members of the Council—that each member of the General Assembly shall be represented 'by an accredited representative.' They only stipulate in Rule 27, that 'the credentials of representatives, and the names of members of a delegation shall be submitted to the Secretary-General' and that 'the credentials shall be issued either by the Head of the State or Government or by the Minister of Foreign Affairs.' The Credentials Committee, established according to Rule 28, has only the power to examine the credentials and to report to the General Assembly. Rule 29 provides: 'Any representative to whose admission a Member has made objection shall be seated provisionally with the same rights as other representatives, until the Credentials Committee has reported and the General Assembly has given its decision.' Under this provision, objection may be made not—as under Rule 17 of the Rules of Procedure of the Security Council—to the credentials of a representative, but to the admission of the representative; so that a person may be seated as representative of a Member in the General Assembly without credentials, *e.g.*, a Minister of Foreign Affairs of a Member. The Rules of Procedure of the General Assembly do not contain provisions by which, in case of two authorities claiming to be the government of a Member state, it could be prevented that the Heads or Foreign Ministers of both governments or the representatives accredited by each of the two governments—in contradiction to the provisions of the Charter—participate, at least provisionally, in the meetings of the General Assembly.

10. Approval of Credentials: Procedural or Non-Procedural Matter

The approval by the Security Council of the credentials of the representative of a member of the Council is, according to the practice of the Security Council, a decision on a procedural matter. But if in case of a revolutionary change of government the credentials signed by the new government are to be approved, the approval implies the recognition of the new government and, consequently, the decision that the person who hitherto has represented the Member state ceases to be its representative. It may be doubted whether the approval of the credentials in this case, too, is a decision on a merely procedural matter, for it implies the recognition on the part of the Security Council, and hence on the part of the United Nations, of a new government.[4] But the view that it is a decision on a non-

[4] In a memorandum on the legal aspects of the problem of representation in the United Nations (U.N. Doc. S/1466), the Secretary-General advocated the doctrine that admission of a community to the United Nations by the General Assembly on the recommendation of the Security Council is a collective act, distinctly separate from the individual act of recognition of that community as a state by a Member; and, second, that the approval of the credentials of a representative by the General Assembly, the Security Council, and other Councils of the United Nations is a collective act distinctly separate from the individual act of recognition of a new government by a Member. The memorandum stated: 'The Members have therefore made clear by an unbroken practice that (1) a Member could properly vote to accept a representative of a government which it did not recognise, or with which it had no diplomatic relations, and (2) that such a vote did not imply recognition or a readiness to assume diplomatic relations.' Insofar as by 'recognition' of a community as a state by the government of another state is meant that the latter ascertains the fact that the community in question is a state

procedural matter leads to the absurd consequence that the person still acting as a representative of the Member state, if this state has a permanent seat in the Security Council, may prevent the approval of the credentials signed by the new government by exercising the veto right of the permanent member.

in the sense of international law, and that consequently international law is applicable to the relation between the recognising state and the recognised community, it can hardly be denied that admission to the United Nations of a community not yet recognised by a Member means that the United Nations, through the Security Council and the General Assembly, has recognised this community as a state, since according to Article 4 of the Charter only ' states ' can be admitted to membership. If a community is admitted to the United Nations, all other Members—also those which have not yet recognised this community as a state and even those of them which have voted against its admission—are under definite obligations, and have defined rights in relation to this community as a state. This implies that they are obliged by the Charter to consider this community as a state. They would certainly violate the Charter if they would refuse to fulfil their obligations in relation to this community on the ground that it is no state and hence not a subject of international law. Consequently, admission of a community not yet recognised by some Members necessarily implies that these Members must consider the community as a state, which is the essential function of the legal act of recognition. But, admission of a community not yet recognised by some Members does not imply the obligation of these Members to enter into the normal diplomatic, political and economic relations with the community admitted to the United Nations. The Charter, according to its wording, does not impose upon the Members such obligation. If by ' recognition ' of a state the expression of the willingness of the recognising state is understood to enter into the normal relations with the recognised state, then admission of a community to the United Nations does not imply such recognition on the part of the Members. But this is recognition, not in a legal, but in a merely political sense.

Approval of the credentials of a representative by the General Assembly or the Security Council or any other Council of the United Nations necessarily implies that the General Assembly or the respective Council considers the government which issued the credentials as the legitimate government of the Member state to be represented in the Assembly or the respective Council. If in case of a revolutionary change of government within a Member state the General Assembly or a Council approves the credentials of the representatives issued by the new government, all members of the approving body are bound by this decision, since the Charter may be interpreted to confer upon the General Assembly and the Councils the power to approve the credentials of the representatives of their members, which necessarily implies the power to recognise the government issuing the credentials, in case it becomes doubtful who is the legitimate government of a Member competent to issue the credentials of its representatives. In this case the approval of the credentials is a legal act binding upon the members of the approving body. Hence the states, members of the body which has approved the credentials issued by the new government, violate their obligations under the Charter if they refuse to consider the government recognised by the organ of the United Nations, the member of which they are, as the legitimate government of the Member concerned; at least insofar as decisions of the organ referring to that Member are concerned. If recognition of a government means the ascertainment of the fact that an individual, or a group of individuals, is the legitimate government of a state, then approval by a collegiate organ of the United Nations of the credentials of a representative issued by a new (revolutionary) government of a Member state implies the recognition of this government by the members of the collegiate organ. But it

Another inconvenience may result from the fact that the Charter does not provide a uniform procedure for the approval of the credentials of the person by which a Member state is to be represented in the various organs of the United Nations. Since these organs have the power to approve the credentials of the representatives of their members independently of one another, it might occur that in the case of revolutionary change of government the credentials signed by the new government may be approved by the one, but not by the other, and thus the new government recognised by some, but not by other organs of the United Nations. A unification of the various procedures for the approval of credentials by conferring this function on one and the same organ (*e.g.*, the Secretary-General) is highly desirable.

11. Change of Name of a Permanent Member of the Security Council

The communist government of China calls itself the 'Central People's Government of the People's Republic of China.' This indicates that China under this government has adopted a name different from that under which it became an original Member of the United Nations in conformity with Article 3, and a permanent member of the Security Council in conformity with Article 23, paragraph 1 of the Charter. This name was 'Republic of China,' the new name is 'People's Republic of China.' At the 302nd Plenary Meeting of the General Assembly, the representative of Canada stated that a resolution proposed by the delegate of the Soviet Union to the effect that the General Assembly shall 'recommend to the permanent members of the Security Council, namely, the People's Republic of China, France, the Union of the Soviet Socialist Republics, the United Kingdom and the United States of America . . .' attempted 'to re-write paragraph 1 of Article 23 of the Charter.' He asked: 'Would that, by any chance, be a violation of the Charter ? ' The representative of Great Britain explained his voting against the proposal of the Soviet Union by saying that 'the form in which the proposal is put, is, in effect, a re-writing of the Charter. It seems to my delegation that it is not open to anyone to define who are the permanent members of the Security Council in any way different from the way in which that definition is given in the Charter itself.' If that means that the change of the name of a permanent member of

does not imply political recognition of the new government on the part of the members of the collegiate organ, that is to say, the members may refuse to enter into the normal relations with the new government.

It must, however, be admitted, that this is only a possible interpretation of the Charter with respect to the legal effect of the approval of credentials of representatives, and that another interpretation according to which such approval has no legal effect on the Members, is not excluded—in spite of its absurd consequences.

the Security Council requires an amendment to Article 23 of the Charter, the statement is not correct. Under general international law a state has the right to change its name, and the Charter does not restrict this right of a Member state of the United Nations, even if this state is a permanent member of the Security Council mentioned under a definite name in Article 23 of the Charter. Change of such name is one of the changes of the Charter that can be brought about outside the amendment procedure laid down in Articles 108 and 109, as, *e.g.*, the determination of additional categories of questions to be decided by the General Assembly by a two-thirds majority under Article 18, paragraph 3, by which Article 18, paragraph 2 is amended;[5] or the withdrawal from the United Nations of a permanent member of the Security Council, provided that such withdrawal is considered to be legally possible. Such withdrawal has the legal effect that the state concerned ceases to be a permanent member of the Security Council, in spite of the fact that its name remains in the text of Article 23, paragraph 1, that is to say, the legal effect of an amendment to that provision. The same effect has the change of name of a state which is a permanent member of the Security Council. If the communist government of China should be recognised by the United Nations as the government of China, China will be a Member of the United Nations and a permanent member of the Security Council under its new name ' People's Republic of China,' no ' re-writing of the Charter ' being necessary.

12. Action in Korea by the General Assembly

As soon as the representative of the Soviet Union again participated in the meetings of the Security Council, no further action of this organ in the Korean crisis was possible because of lack of unanimity among the permanent members. Hence the General Assembly, in conformity with the resolution ' Uniting for Peace,' took up the question of aggression in Korea. The action taken by the General Assembly shall be discussed in the chapter dealing with the Resolution ' Uniting for Peace.'[6]

[5] Cf. *The Law of the United Nations*, p. 183.

[6] Cf. *infra*, pp. 986 ff.

Chapter 3

APPOINTMENT OF THE SECRETARY-GENERAL

At the 298th Plenary Meeting on November 1, 1950, the General Assembly, by 46 votes in favour, 5 votes against, and with 8 abstentions, adopted a resolution to the effect to continue the present Secretary-General in office for three years. He had been appointed on February 1, 1946, for a term of five years. The resolution of November 1, 1950, was adopted without a recommendation by the Security Council, since the majority of seven members including the concurring votes of the permanent members, required for such recommendation by Article 27 of the Charter, could not be obtained.

The only provision of the Charter applying to this case is that of Article 97, which reads as follows: 'The Secretary-General shall be appointed by the General Assembly upon the recommendation of the Security Council.' In conformity with this provision, Rule 140 of the Rules of Procedure of the General Assembly stipulates: 'When the Security Council has submitted its recommendation on the appointment of the Secretary-General, the General Assembly shall consider the recommendation and vote upon it by secret ballot in private meeting.' Since the first Secretary-General was appointed for a term of five years, an extension of his term of office was possible under the Charter only as an 'appointment' of the same individual to the office of Secretary-General. The Charter does not provide two different procedures for the case that the individual to be appointed to the function of Secretary-General is the same as the one who previously had been appointed to this function, and the case that another individual is to be appointed. The Charter does not differentiate re-appointment from appointment. At the 296th Plenary Meeting the representative of France quite correctly stated: 'There is no ambiguity in Article 97 of the Charter. The appointment of a Secretary-General by the General Assembly presupposes a recommendation by the Security Council. It was specified in 1945 (*Report of the Preparatory Commission of the United Nations*) that this provision applies equally to a reappointment and a first appointment. It is therefore clear that in the absence of a recommendation the Assembly can neither appoint a new Secretary-General nor reappoint the present one.' He declared that his delegation regarded the suggested resolution as an 'interim measure' which would be effective for a certain length of time; there is no use pretending that it was provided for by the Charter. On the other hand, 'there is nothing in the Charter to forbid it.' As pointed out in another connection,[1] the principle: What is not forbidden is permitted,

[1] Cf. *The Law of the United Nations*, p. 685.

does not apply to the competence of the organs of a community, determined by its constitution. The General Assembly—as any other organ of the United Nations—is not permitted to do what it is not forbidden to do; it is permitted to do only what it is authorised to do by the Charter of the United Nations. The representative of China stated that the most honest interpretation of the situation would be that the suggested resolution was 'extra-legal . . . but not expressly against any provision of law.' The representative of Ecuador stated: 'It was Resolution 11 (I) of January 24, 1946, which fixed that term at five years. The Assembly has retained and, in fact, still has the right to alter its own resolutions and thereby to extend the term of office.' The representative of Uruguay interpreted Article 97 to mean that 'the responsibility for deciding the term of office of the Secretary-General was entrusted to the General Assembly.' However, the Charter of the United Nations does not distinguish between the 'appointment' of the Secretary-General and the determination of his term of office; and, consequently, not only the 'appointment' but also the determination of the term of office must be established by a co-operation of the Security Council and the General Assembly. The Charter knows only appointment including determination of the term of office.

The representative of Uruguay referred to the discussion of the text of Article 97 at Committee I/2 of the San Francisco Conference, in order to prove that according to the intentions of the framers of the Charter 'the Assembly is the sovereign body of the United Nations which is competent to settle the present problem,' that is to say, to extend, without a recommendation by the Security Council, the term of office of the Secretary-General. However, the records of the San Francisco Conference show just the contrary. At the 29th meeting of Committee I/2,[2] the delegate for the Netherlands suggested that, if appointment of the Secretary-General should require a decision of the Security Council adopted by a vote of seven members including the concurring votes of the permanent members, 'to leave the terms of the appointment to be worked out in the light of experience.' He meant that the terms of appointment should not be determined by the Charter itself, but left to the decision of the appointing organs. The delegate for New Zealand 'also supported the Netherlands motion. He pointed out if it were carried, the terms of the Secretary-General's appointment would be worked out by agreement between the Security Council and the General Assembly. The delegate for the United States was assured before the vote was taken, that when these terms came up for settlement, the principle of unanimity among the permanent members of the Security Council would be observed.' The Report of the Rapporteur (General) of Committee I/2 on Chapter X (The Secretariat)[3] contains the statement that the delegate for the Netherlands, supported by the

[2] U.N.C.I.O. Doc. 1087, I/2/78, *Documents*, Vol. VII, pp. 279 ff.

[3] U.N.C.I.O. Doc. 1155, I/2/74 (2), *Documents*, Vol. VII, pp. 388 ff.

delegate for New Zealand, ' suggested that the determination of the term of office might be left as a matter of later agreement between the Security Council and the General Assembly. It was understood by the Committee that the unanimity of the permanent members would be required in the decision of the Security Council on this matter.'

That the term of office of the Secretary-General is to be determined not unilaterally by the General Assembly but by an agreement between the General Assembly and the Security Council, results also from the resolution of the General Assembly concerning Terms of Appointment of the Secretary-General, adopted at the 17th Plenary Meeting on January 24, 1946. This resolution contains the following statements: ' 3. The first Secretary-General shall be appointed for five years, the appointment being open at the end of that period for a further five-year term. 4. The following observations contained in paragraphs 18-21 of section 2, Chapter VIII of the Preparatory Commission's Report be noted and approved: (a) There being no stipulation on the subject in the Charter, the General Assembly and the Security Council are free to modify the term of office of future Secretaries-General in the light of experience.' That means that an agreement between the General Assembly and the Security Council is required to modify the term of office of the future Secretary-General. But the representative of Uruguay interpreted this passage as if it would read: The General Assembly *or* the Security Council are free to modify etc. It is true that the Security Council in its decision concerning the appointment of the first Secretary-General, adopted at its 4th (private) meeting on January 29, 1946, did not refer to the term of office. But this cannot constitute a precedent to the effect of depriving the Security Council of a power conferred upon it by the Charter. The representative of Peru tried to justify the constitutionality of the resolution by which the first Secretary-General has been continued in office without a recommendation of the Security Council, as ' a dynamic interpretation of the Charter.' But the representative of Syria openly declared: ' It seems that there is practically a revolt in the General Assembly against the Security Council.' Syria was among the eight members of the General Assembly which abstained from voting. Also Australia was among them; its representative explained the abstention of his state by declaring that the adopted resolution might create a precedent, both as regards Article 97 and certain other Articles of the Charter, with which Australia would find it difficult to agree.

At the 296th Plenary Meeting of the General Assembly the representative of the Soviet Union declared that if the Secretary-General would be reappointed without a recommendation by the Security Council, the Government of the Soviet Union ' will refuse to regard him as the Secretary-General.'

CHAPTER 4

UNITING FOR PEACE

1. THE RESOLUTION ADOPTED BY THE GENERAL ASSEMBLY ON NOVEMBER 3, 1950

AT its 302nd Plenary Meeting on November 3, 1950, the General Assembly adopted the following three resolutions:

RESOLUTION A

UNITING FOR PEACE

THE GENERAL ASSEMBLY,

Recognising that the first two stated Purposes of the United Nations are:

> 'To maintain international peace and security, and to that end: To take effective collective measures for the prevention and removal of threats to the peace, and for the suppression of acts of aggression or other breaches of the peace, and to bring about by peaceful means, and in conformity with the principles of justice and international law, adjustment or settlement of international disputes or situations which might lead to a breach of the peace,' and
>
> 'To develop friendly relations among nations based on respect for the principle of equal rights and self-determination of peoples, and to take other appropriate measures to strengthen universal peace,'

Reaffirming that it remains the primary duty of all Members of the United Nations, when involved in an international dispute, to seek settlement of such a dispute by peaceful means through the procedures laid down in Chapter VI of the Charter, and recalling the successful achievements of the United Nations in this regard on a number of previous occasions,

Finding that international tension exists on a dangerous scale,

Recalling its resolution 290 (IV) entitled 'Essentials of Peace,' which states that disregard of the Principles of the Charter of the United Nations is primarily responsible for the continuance of international tension, and desiring to contribute further to the objectives of that resolution,

Reaffirming the importance of the exercise by the Security Council of its primary responsibility for the maintenance of international peace and security, and the duty of the permanent members to seek unanimity and to exercise restraint in the use of the veto,

Reaffirming that the initiative in negotiating the agreements for armed forces provided for in Article 43 of the Charter belongs to the Security Council and desiring to ensure that, pending the conclusion of such agreements, the United Nations has at its disposal means for maintaining international peace and security,

Conscious that failure of the Security Council to discharge its responsibilities on behalf of all the Member states, particularly those responsibilities referred to in the two preceding paragraphs, does not relieve Member states of their obligations or the United Nations of its responsibility under the Charter to maintain international peace and security.

Recognising, in particular, that such failure does not deprive the General Assembly of its rights or relieve it of its responsibilities under the Charter in regard to the maintenance of international peace and security,

Recognising that discharge by the General Assembly of its responsibilities in these respects calls for possibilities of observation which would ascertain the facts and expose aggressors; for the existence of armed forces which could be used collectively; and for the possibility of timely recommendation by the General Assembly to Members of the United Nations for collective action which, to be effective, should be prompt;

[A]

1. *Resolves* that if the Security Council, because of lack of unanimity of the permanent members, fails to exercise its primary responsibility for the maintenance of international peace and security in any case where there appears to be a threat to the peace, breach of the peace, or act of aggression, the General Assembly shall consider the matter immediately with a view to making appropriate recommendations to Members for collective measures, including in the case of a breach of the peace or act of aggression the use of armed force when necessary, to maintain or restore international peace and security. If not in session at the time, the General Assembly may meet in emergency special session within twenty-four hours of the request therefor. Such emergency special session shall be called if requested by the Security Council on the vote of any seven members, or by a majority of the Members of the United Nations;

2. *Adopts* for this purpose the amendments to its rules of procedure set forth in the annex to this resolution ;

[B]

3. *Establishes* a Peace Observation Commission, which for the calendar years 1951 and 1952 shall be composed of fourteen Members, namely: China, Colombia, Czechoslovakia, France, India, Iraq, Israel, New Zealand, Pakistan, Sweden, the Union of Soviet Socialist Republics, the United Kingdom of Great Britain and Northern Ireland, the United States of America and Uruguay, and which could observe and report on the situation in any area where there exists international tension the continuance of which is likely to endanger the maintenance of international peace and security. Upon the invitation or with the consent of the state into whose territory the Commission would go, the General Assembly, or the Interim Committee when the Assembly is not in session, may utilise the Commission if the Security Council is not exercising the functions assigned to it by the Charter with respect to the matter in question. Decisions to utilise the Commission shall be made on the affirmative vote of two-thirds of the members present and voting. The Security Council may also utilise the Commission in accordance with its authority under the Charter;

4. *The Commission shall have* authority in its discretion to appoint subcommissions and to utilise the services of observers to assist it in the performance of its functions;

5. *Recommends* to all Governments and authorities that they co-operate with the Commission and assist it in the performance of its functions;

6. *Requests* the Secretary-General to provide the necessary staff and facilities, utilising, where directed by the Commission, the United Nations panel of field observers envisaged in Resolution 297 B (IV);

[C]

7. *Invites* each Member of the United Nations to survey its resources in order to determine the nature and scope of the assistance it may be in a position to render in support of any recommendations of the Security Council or of the General Assembly for the restoration of international peace and security;

8. *Recommends* to the states Members of the United Nations that each Member maintain within its national armed forces elements so trained, organised and equipped that they could promptly be made available, in accordance with its constitutional processes, for service as a United Nations unit or units, upon recommendation by the Security Council or General Assembly, without prejudice to the use of such

elements in exercise of the right of individual or collective self-defence recognised in Article 51 of the Charter;

9. *Invites* the Members of the United Nations to inform the Collective Measures Committee provided for in paragraph 11 as soon as possible of the measures taken in implementation of the preceding paragraph;

10. *Requests* the Secretary-General to appoint, with the approval of the Committee provided for in paragraph 11, a panel of military experts who could be made available, on request, to Member states wishing to obtain technical advice regarding the organisation, training, and equipment for prompt service as United Nations units of the elements referred to in paragraph 8;

[D]

11. *Establishes* a Collective Measures Committee consisting of fourteen Members, namely: Australia, Belgium, Brazil, Burma, Canada, Egypt, France, Mexico, Philippines, Turkey, the United Kingdom of Great Britain and Northern Ireland, the United States of America, Venezuela, and Yugoslavia, and directs the Committee, in consultation with the Secretary-General and with Member states as the Committee finds appropriate, to study and make a report to the Security Council and the General Assembly, not later than September 1, 1951, on methods, including those in Section C of the present resolution, which might be used to maintain and strengthen international peace and security in accordance with the Purposes and Principles of the Charter, taking account of collective self-defence and regional arrangements (Articles 51 and 52 of the Charter);

12. *Recommends* to all Member states that they co-operate with the Committee and assist it in the performance of its functions;

13. *Requests* the Secretary-General to furnish the staff and facilities necessary for the effective accomplishment of the purposes set forth in Sections C and D of this resolution;

[E]

14. *THE GENERAL ASSEMBLY,*

In adopting the proposals set forth above, is fully conscious that enduring peace will not be secured solely by collective security arrangements against breaches of international peace and acts of aggression, but that a genuine and lasting peace depends also upon the observance of all the Principles and Purposes established in the Charter of the United Nations, upon the implementation of the resolutions of the Security Council, the General Assembly, and other principal organs of the United Nations intended to achieve the maintenance of international peace and security, and especially upon respect for and observance of human rights and fundamental freedoms for all and on the establishment and maintenance of conditions of economic and social well-being in all countries; and accordingly

15. *Urges* Member states to respect fully, and to intensify, joint action, in co-operation with the United Nations, to develop and stimulate universal respect for and observance of human rights and fundamental freedoms, and to intensify individual and collective efforts to achieve conditions of economic stability and social progress, particularly through the development of under-developed countries and areas.

Annex

The rules of procedure of the General Assembly are amended in the following repects:

1. The present text of Rule 8 shall become paragraph (A) of that rule, and a new paragraph (B) shall be added to read as follows: 'Emergency special sessions pursuant to resolution . . . (V) shall be convened within twenty-four hours of the receipt by the Secretary-General of a request for such a session from the Security Council, on the vote of any seven members thereof, or of a request from a majority of the Members of the United Nations expressed by vote in the Interim Committee or otherwise, or of the concurrence of a majority of Members as provided in Rule 9.'

2. The present text of Rule 9 shall become paragraph (A) of that rule and a new paragraph (B) shall be added to read as follows: 'This rule shall apply also to a request by any Member for an emergency special session pursuant to resolution . . . (V). In such a case the Secretary-General shall communicate with other Members by the most expeditious means of communication available.'

3. Rule 10 is amended by adding at the end thereof the following: 'In the case of an emergency special session convened pursuant to Rule 8 (B), the Secretary-General shall notify the Members of the United Nations at least twelve hours in advance of the opening of the session.'

4. Rule 16 is amended by adding at the end thereof the following: 'The provisional agenda of an emergency special session shall be communicated to the Members of the United Nations simultaneously with the communication summoning the session.'

5. Rule 19 is amended by adding at the end thereof the following: 'During an emergency special session additional

items concerning the matters dealt with in resolution . . . (V) may be added to the agenda by a two-thirds majority of the members present and voting.'

6. There is added a new rule to precede Rule 65 to read as follows: 'Notwithstanding the provisions of any other rule and unless the General Assembly decides otherwise, the Assembly, in case of an emergency special session, shall convene in plenary session only and proceed directly to consider the item proposed for consideration in the request for the holding of the session, without previous reference to the General Committee or to any other Committee; the President and Vice-Presidents for such emergency special sessions shall be, respectively, the Chairman of those delegations from which were elected the President and Vice-Presidents of the previous session.'

Resolution B

For the purpose of maintaining international peace and security, in accordance with the Charter of the United Nations, and, in particular, with Chapters V, VI and VII of the Charter,

THE GENERAL ASSEMBLY,

Recommends to the Security Council: That it should take the necessary steps to ensure that the action provided for under the Charter is taken with respect to threats to the peace, breaches of the peace, or acts of aggression and with respect to the peaceful settlement of disputes or situations likely to endanger the maintenance of international peace and security;

That it should devise measures for the earliest application of Articles 43, 45, 46 and 47 of the Charter of the United Nations regarding the placing of armed forces at the disposal of the Security Council by the states Members of the United Nations and the effective functioning of the Military Staff Committee.

The above dispositions should in no manner prevent the General Assembly from fulfilling its functions under resolution A.

Resolution C

THE GENERAL ASSEMBLY,

Recognising that the primary function of the United Nations Organisation is to maintain and promote peace, security, and justice among all nations,

Recognising the responsibility of all Member states in promoting the cause of international peace in accordance with their obligations as provided in the Charter,

Recognising that the Charter charges the Security Council with the primary responsibility for maintaining international peace and security,

Reaffirming the importance of unanimity among the permanent members of the Security Council on all problems which are likely to threaten world peace,

Recalling General Assembly resolution 190 (III) entitled ' Appeal to the great powers to renew their efforts to compose their differences and establish a lasting peace,'

Recommends to the permanent members of the Security Council that:

(A) They meet and discuss, collectively or otherwise, and, if necessary, with other states concerned, all problems which are likely to threaten international peace and hamper the activities of the United Nations, with a view to their resolving fundamental differences and reaching agreement in accordance with the spirit and letter of the Charter;

(B) They advise the General Assembly and, when it is not in session, the Members of the United Nations, as soon as appropriate, of the results of their consultations.

2. Interpretation of Article 10 in Relation to Article 11 of the Charter

The constitutionality of Resolution A (Uniting for Peace), which was questioned in the discussions of the First Committee and the General Assembly, depends on the interpretation of Articles 10, 11, 14 and 106. The first question is whether the General Assembly is authorised by the Charter to recommend to Members collective measures ' and especially the ' use of armed force ' as it is provided for in Section A, paragraph 1 of Resolution A (Uniting for Peace).

This Resolution does not yet recommend to Members the use of force. In Section A, paragraph 1 the General Assembly only ' resolves ' that the General Assembly, under certain conditions ' shall consider ' a certain matter ' with a view to making appropriate recommendations to Members for collective measures, including . . . the use of armed force.' This provision of the Resolution could be based only on Chapter IV of the Charter. The functions which the General Assembly has under Chapter IV are: to ' consider ' principles (Article 11, paragraph 1), reports (Article 15), the budget and budgetary and financial arrangements (Article 17); to ' discuss ' questions or matters (Articles 10; 11, paragraph 2); to ' initiate studies ' (Article 13); to ' make recommendations ' (Articles 10; 11, paragraph 2; 12, paragraph 1; 13; 14; 17); to ' refer ' questions to the Security Council (Article 11, paragraph 2); to ' call the attention of the Security Council to situations . . ' (Article 11, paragraph 3);

to ' approve ' the budget and financial and budgetary arrangements (Article 17); to ' adopt ' its rules of procedure (Article 21); to ' establish ' subsidiary organs (Article 22). By adopting Section A, paragraph 1 of Resolution A, the Assembly exercised none of these functions. It resolved to exercise some of these functions, namely, to ' consider ' matters and to ' recommend ' measures, later and under certain conditions. If strictly interpreted, the Charter authorises the General Assembly to consider matters or to recommend measures (but not to resolve that it ' shall ' consider certain matters or 'shall' recommend certain measures under certain conditions). A provision to the effect that an organ of the United Nations ' shall ' do something is conferring upon this organ a definite power or function. The General Assembly is not authorised by the Charter to confer upon itself a certain power or function. If the General Assembly possesses this power or function already under the Charter, a resolution to the effect that it shall exercise the power or function is, at least, superfluous. If the General Assembly has not the power or function under the Charter, the resolution amounts to an attempt to amend the Charter in a way different from that prescribed by Articles 108 and 109. If it is doubtful whether the General Assembly has under the Charter the power or function in question, such a resolution amounts to an attempt to interpret the Charter. The General Assembly—as any organ of the United Nations—is certainly competent to interpret the Charter, but only in connection with an act by which the organ applies the Charter. Application of the law necessarily implies interpretation of the law. In considering the matter and in making the recommendation referred to in Section A, paragraph 1 of the resolution, the Assembly could interpret the Charter as conferring upon it the power to consider this matter and make this recommendation. That is to say, the interpretation of the Charter could be implied in the act applying the Charter; it should not be pronounced in an act different from the act by which the General Assembly takes the matter concerned into consideration and makes the respective recommendation. But it might also be argued that if the General Assembly is competent to consider a matter and to make a definite recommendation, the General Assembly does not violate the Charter when it resolves that it will, in the future, or that it ' shall ' consider the matter and make the recommendation.

Is the General Assembly competent to consider the matter and to make the recommendations referred to in Section A, paragraph 1 of the Resolution called ' Uniting for Peace ' ? Article 10 of the Charter which determines the competence of the General Assembly in the most general way, does not authorise the General Assembly to ' consider,' but only to ' discuss ' questions or matters within the scope of the Charter. Article 11, paragraph 1 authorises the General Assembly to ' consider ' general principles of co-operation, etc., not a concrete matter; and Article 11, paragraph 2 confers upon the Assembly the power to ' discuss,' not to ' consider,' any questions relating to the maintenance of international peace and security brought before it by any Member, etc. If it is assumed that the power to ' discuss ' a matter includes the power to ' consider ' it,[1] then the General Assembly has under Article 10 as well as under Article 11, paragraph 2, the power to consider the matter referred to in Section A, paragraph 1; for the maintenance of international peace and security in any case where there appears to be a ' threat to the peace, breach of the peace, or act of aggression ' is certainly a matter within the scope of the Charter (Article 10), as well as a question ' relating to the maintenance of international peace and security ' (Article 11). If the matter referred to in Section A, paragraph 1—according to the wording of this provision—is considered to be a ' question relating to the maintenance of international peace and security,' it can be discussed (and by being discussed, ' considered ') by the General Assembly only if it is brought before it by any Member of the United Nations, or by the Security Council, or by a state which is not a Member in accordance with Article 35, paragraph 2. But this restriction is not made in Article 10 authorising the General Assembly to discuss all questions ' within the scope of the present Charter '—and questions relating to the maintenance of international peace and security are within the scope of the Charter, in whatever way they are brought before the General Assembly. Here the question arises whether Article 11 restricts the scope of Article 10, or *vice versa*. But the same question arises also with respect to the recommendation to be made according to Section A, paragraph 1 of Resolution A, and shall be discussed in that connection.

The only restriction which Article 10 imposes upon the power of the General Assembly to make recommendations is the one stipulated in Article 12, to which Article 10, as well as Article 11, paragraph 2, refer: that the Assembly shall not make a recommendation with regard to a dispute or other situation while the Security Council is exercising in respect of this dispute or situation the functions assigned to it in the Charter. The different interpretations of this provision have been discussed in a previous connection.[2]

Article 10 does not restrict the content of the recommendations the General Assembly may make on questions which are within the scope of the Charter. The main recommendation which the General Assembly shall make according to the Resolution called ' Uniting for Peace,' namely the recommendation to Members to apply collective measures, including the use of armed force, in order to maintain or restore international peace and security, is certainly a recommendation on a question within the scope of the Charter.

[1] Cf. *The Law of the United Nations*, pp. 201, 255 ff., 620.
[2] Cf. *ibid.*, pp. 216 ff.

It is also, and even more precisely, a question on which the General Assembly is authorised by the first sentence of Article 11, paragraph 2 to make recommendations, namely a question relating to the maintenance of international peace and security. Under this provision the General Assembly is authorised to make recommendations to 'the state or states concerned.' The Assembly may make recommendations to states, whether or not they are Members of the United Nations, provided the question on which the recommendation is made concerns them. Under Article 10, the General Assembly may make recommendations only to Members. In this respect the power of the Assembly to make recommendations under Article 11, paragraph 2 is wider than its power under Article 10. But this difference is of no importance, since the Resolution 'Uniting for Peace' authorises the General Assembly only to make recommendations to Members. Insofar the Resolution is in conformity with Article 10 as well as Article 11, paragraph 2.

However, the second sentence of Article 11, paragraph 2 provides: 'Any such question on which action is necessary shall be referred to the Security Council by the General Assembly either before or after discussion.' As pointed out in a previous connection,[3] it is difficult to understand how the General Assembly can refer a question 'on which action is necessary' to the Security Council before having discussed the question. But the provision that the Assembly shall refer such question 'either before or after discussion' to the Security Council can hardly be interpreted in another way but that the General Assembly shall not make a recommendation on such a question. Doubtful is only the meaning of the term 'action.' As pointed out,[4] it may be understood in a wide sense, comprising any kind of action, *e.g.*, also a recommendation. In this sense, the term 'action' is, *e.g.*, used in Article 37, where the words 'to take action under Article 36' mean: to make a recommendation of appropriate means for the adjustment of a dispute or other situation. If by 'action' also recommendations were to be understood, the General Assembly could make no recommendations at all, and that would mean that Article 11, paragraph 2 would deprive the Assembly of the most important function conferred upon it by the same Article and by other Articles of the Charter. Hence it is hardly possible to interpret the term 'action' in Article 11 in an extensive way. In order to avoid absurd consequences, the term must be interpreted in a restrictive way. It may be interpreted to mean: enforcement action, *i.e.*, any use of force, especially any use of armed force. If the General Assembly is of the opinion that on a question under its consideration the use of force is necessary, it must refer this question to the Security Council, without making a recommendation on that

[3] Cf. *The Law of the United Nations*, pp. 200 ff.
[4] Cf. *ibid.*

question. This was probably the intention of the framers of the Charter.

At the 358th meeting of the First Committee during the discussion of the Resolution 'Uniting for Peace,' the Canadian delegate stated: 'the action referred to in Article 11, paragraph 2 was that which the Security Council could take under the chapter of the Charter which defined its functions. That action was not, therefore, to be confused with the recommendations which the Assembly was empowered to make to Member states under the provisions of the same Article 11, paragraph 2.'[5] That means that by 'action' not any kind of enforcement action, but only enforcement action to be taken by the Security Council under Chapter VII (Articles 39, 41 and 42) may be understood. Consequently, Article 11, paragraph 2 might be interpreted as follows: If the General Assembly thinks it necessary that the Security Council take enforcement action under Articles 39, 41, or 42, it shall refer the question to the Security Council; but the Assembly is not bound to do so if it deems that another enforcement action is necessary, *e.g.*, an enforcement action involving the use of armed force taken by Members on the recommendation of the General Assembly.[6] It must be admitted that this

[5] At the 364th meeting of the First Committee, the Australian delegate stated that 'the Assembly was under no obligation to transmit to the Council every question, regardless of what kind of action it required, for there were many Articles of the Charter authorising action on the part of the Assembly in the sphere of maintenance of international peace and security. Thus Articles 55, 56, 59 and 60 referred to joint action under the authority of the General Assembly with a view to assuring friendly and peaceful relations in the sphere of economic and social co-operation, a question which was directly related to the maintenance of international peace and security. Articles 73, 76, 85 and 87 also referred to action by the General Assembly for the maintenance of international peace and security in the case of Non-Self-Governing or Trust Territories. . . . It was therefore evident that the exception set forth in Article 11, paragraph 2, did not refer to all actions which might be taken by the United Nations. . . . The correct reading of the word "necessary" in Article 11, paragraph 2, was: necessary to be taken under the Charter. . . .'

[6] At the 354th meeting of the First Committee the delegate of the United States declared: 'Obviously, a recommendation by the General Assembly had not the force of a decision of the Security Council taken under the terms of Chapter VII of the Charter. But the history of the Korean question had shown that the voluntary response to a recommendation could be even more effective than obedience to an order; although the Security Council had not exercised its powers of action, fifty-three Members were carrying out its recommendation.' That means that a recommendation of the General Assembly is not an 'action,' in contradistinction to a decision taken by the Security Council under Chapter VII. By taking such a decision the Council exercises 'its powers of action.' If the statement of the United States delegate was intended to interpret the meaning of the term 'action' as used in the provision of Article 11, paragraph 2, that the General Assembly shall refer to the Security Council questions on which action is necessary, it should be noted that the decisive question is not whether under Article 11, paragraph 2, the General Assembly is authorised to make recommendations, but whether it is authorised to recommend 'action.' Even if it is admitted

interpretation is not excluded by the wording of the second sentence of Article 11, paragraph 2. But it is not very plausible. If the General Assembly is of the opinion that on a question under its consideration an enforcement action of the Security Council is necessary, the Assembly can hardly do anything else but refer this question to the Security Council. No special provision to this effect is needed. And the Assembly can refer the question to the Council under the more general provision of Article 11, paragraph 3, which stipulates that the Assembly 'may call the attention of the Security Council to situations which are likely to endanger international peace and security,' provided that the situation is not yet under the consideration of the Security Council. Moreover, it is already difficult to restrict the meaning of the term 'action' to the meaning 'any enforcement action whatever'; but still more difficult to restrict the meaning of the term by excluding from it every enforcement action taken in any other way than by the Security Council under Chapter VII. If such a specific and far-reaching restriction of the meaning of the term 'action' had been intended, the framers of the Charter had probably expressed their intention in some way or another, and had not chosen the simple word 'action.' But since a restrictive interpretation of the term is necessary anyway, a more restrictive interpretation than the one according to which 'action' means any enforcement action whatever, is not excluded.[7] If the

that the provision of Article 11, paragraph 2, does not prohibit the Assembly from making recommendations in general, the question still remains whether this provision prohibits the Assembly from making a definite recommendation: the recommendation to use force, especially to use armed force. At the 364th meeting of the First Committee the representative of the United Kingdom stated: 'His delegation recognised that the Charter did not give the General Assembly the power to take coercive action. The General Assembly could only make recommendations'; but he added: 'experience had shown that the recommendations of the General Assembly carried great force, in the same way as the Security Council recommendations had done on the Korean question in virtue of Article 39.' But according to the wording of Article 11, paragraph 2, the Charter gives to the General Assembly not only not the power to 'take action' but also not the power to 'recommend' action. Besides, if a recommendation of the General Assembly carries so great a force as the representative of the United Kingdom asserted, there is no essential difference between taking action and recommending action. A similar interpretation was advocated by the representative of Pakistan at the 363rd meeting of the First Committee. He stated: 'Action in the sense of enforcement action, was in the domain of the Council alone. Recommendations could, nevertheless, be made by the Assembly.' He meant that a 'recommendation' is not an 'action.' But if 'action' in Article 11, paragraph 2, means any enforcement action whatever, Article 11, paragraph 2 precludes recommendations of enforcement actions. Although the representative of Pakistan stressed that 'action' did not include 'recommendations,' he finally declared: 'where the Council was unable to take action, the General Assembly had a responsibility to act under Article 10.'; that is to say, to 'act' by making a recommendation.

7 At the 364th meeting of the First Committee the representative of the United Kingdom suggested to interpret Article 11, paragraph 2, as follows: 'action'

more restrictive interpretation is accepted, then Article 11, paragraph 2 does not prohibit the General Assembly from recommending to Members the use of armed force. But if the interpretation is accepted according to which 'action' in Article 11, paragraph 2 means any enforcement action whatever, the provision of this Article may be considered as constituting a restriction of the competence of the General Assembly, generally established by Article 10, to make recommendations of any kind on all questions within the scope of the Charter.

However, this effect of the provision of Article 11, paragraph 2, that the General Assembly shall refer any question on which action is necessary to the Security Council, without making recommendations on such question, is, as pointed out in a previous connection,[8] questionable in view of Article 11, paragraph 4, which stipulates: 'The powers of the General Assembly set forth in this Article [Article 11] shall not limit the general scope of Article 10.' The wording of this provision is rather strange. If Article 11—as this provision says—does set forth powers of the General Assembly, it can be only additional powers, powers set forth in addition to those set forth in Article 10. If so, the powers set forth in Article 11 could not limit—they could only extend the general scope of Article 10. This is, as pointed out, indeed the case with respect to the first sentence of Article 11, paragraph 2, authorising the General Assembly to make recommendations not only—as under Article 10—to Members but also to non-Members. But the second sentence of Article 11, paragraph 2, according to the most plausible interpretation, restricts the powers of the General Assembly set forth in Article 10. Taken literally, paragraph 4 of Article 11 is meaningless. But it

means any kind of enforcement action; the General Assembly is bound to refer to the Security Council a question on which any kind of enforcement action is necessary. However, 'if the Security Council did not make use of its powers, Article 11 would not in any way preclude the General Assembly from exercising, in respect of such a situation, the powers conferred on it by Article 10.' This interpretation can hardly be accepted. It may be assumed that Article 10 restricts the scope of Article 11, paragraph 2; but there is no provision in the Charter that Article 10 does restrict Article 11, paragraph 2 only under the condition that the Security Council does not make use of its powers.

A similar interpretation was suggested at the 359th meeting of the First Committee by the representative of Pakistan. He stated: 'If that sentence [the second sentence of Article 11, paragraph 2] were designed to ensure that before the General Assembly exercised its residuary powers it should refer the matter to the Security Council to enable the Council to take adequate, appropriate and effective action, then, if the Security Council failed to act effectively, those words would not bar the Assembly from exercising its residuary powers.' But he added, 'But it was possible, on the other hand, that that sentence was designed to ensure that the General Assembly, if it were of the view that action would have to be taken, would refer the matter to the Security Council because that was the only organ vested with the power to take action.'

[8] Cf. *The Law of the United Nations*, p. 207.

might be interpreted to mean: the provisions of Article 11 (not the powers set forth in Article 11) shall not restrict the scope of Article 10. If this is supposed to be the meaning of paragraph 4, none of the other provisions of Article 11 can restrict the competence of the General Assembly determined in Article 10. Then, the provision of paragraph 2 of Article 11: that the General Assembly shall refer any question on which action is necessary to the Security Council, insofar as it is interpreted to restrict the competence of the Assembly established in Article 10, is to be considered as non-valid, as if it were not inserted in the Charter. But the contrary interpretation is by no means excluded. It may be argued: Since it is not possible to consider a clear provision of the Charter—such as the provision that the General Assembly shall refer to the Security Council any question on which action (meaning any enforcement action whatever) is necessary—as non-existent, Article 10 must be interpreted as being restricted by that provision; and Article 11, paragraph 4, which, taken literally, is meaningless, must be considered as non-applicable.[9]

[9] At the 359th meeting of the First Committee the representative of Syria declared that the resolution 'Uniting for Peace' was based on an interpretation of the Charter according to which the General Assembly had 'the power to act under Chapter VII of the Charter concerning the use of armed force for the purpose of maintaining international peace and security. Such an interpretation might be questioned. It had not occurred to any delegation at San Francisco that the Assembly was entitled to use armed force in such circumstances.' Nevertheless, he expressed 'his satisfaction that such a large majority of the Members had given a positive interpretation to the Charter which would enable the Assembly to act when the Council was unable to function. . . . He wondered, however, why the Member states had not arrived at such interpretation long before when the Council had failed to act.' He 'thought that it would be difficult to justify, from a legal point of view, the position that the Assembly could take back and act upon powers which it had delegated to the Council. However, if the Charter were considered as a treaty of Alliance, it would follow that each Member would be expected to come to the aid of any of its allies when aggression took place against that ally. Such a principle would provide the basis for collective action by all Members in doing whatever might be necessary in a given situation. Although the draft resolution did not clearly state it in that manner, such an interpretation might be given to enable the Assembly to take action on that basis.' Such an interpretation is hardly possible. It is not the General Assembly which had delegated to the Security Council its powers, it is the Charter of the United Nations which confers upon the Council definite powers, in spite of the wording of Article 24 according to which the 'Members confer on the Security Council primary responsibility. . . .' The right of the Members to come to the aid of any other Member whenever aggression takes place, is stipulated in Article 51 of the Charter, which does not confer upon the Assembly any power. As to the relation of the Resolution 'Uniting for Peace' to Article 51 of the Charter, cf. *infra*, pp. 979 ff.

At the 361st meeting of the First Committee the representative of Sweden declared: Regarding 'the competence of the General Assembly to recommend the use of armed forces for enforcement action, it must be recognised that there was some doubt. Article 11, paragraph 2, stated in categorical terms that any question involving the maintenance of peace and security on which action was required must

If one and the same legal instrument contains two contradictory provisions—as (according to a certain interpretation) Article 11, paragraph 2 and Article 11, paragraph 4, it is always possible to interpret the one as abolished by the other, or *vice versa*. If one and the same legal instrument contains two partly contradictory provisions —as Article 10 and Article 11, paragraph 2—and if one provision, as Article 10, has a more general, the other, as Article 11, paragraph 2, a more particular character, the latter may be considered to have the precedence of the former.[1] But this is only a possible, not an obligatory principle of interpretation, unless it is laid down as rule of law. If this is not the case, as under the Charter which contains no rules of interpretation, it is possible to interpret the particular provision (of Article 11, paragraph 2) as restricted by the general provision (Article 10), or *vice versa*. Even if Article 11, paragraph 4 did not exist, it would be possible to maintain that Article 10 permits the Assembly to recommend the use of armed force, whereas Article 11, paragraph 2 prohibits the Assembly from making such recommendation. Hence it is possible to interpret Article 10 as restricted by Article 11, or Article 11 as restricted by Article 10.

The interpretation according to which the competence of the General Assembly determined in Article 10 is restricted by the

be referred to the Security Council, either before or after discussion by the Assembly. The argument that the Article did not extend to the mere making of recommendations by the Assembly was certainly debatable. Moreover, Swedish experts who had been given the task of submitting their opinion on the Charter to the Swedish Government before its entry into the Organisation, had pronounced themselves in the opposite sense. On the other hand, it had been noted during the past few years that the General Assembly had had the tendency of extending its competence beyond the limits indicated in the Articles of the Charter. The Assembly had, for instance, adopted a resolution [39 (I)] in connection with the question of Franco Spain recommending a type of diplomatic boycott. That action was tantamount to an enforcement measure. In another resolution [193 A (III)] the General Assembly had recommended that Member states should not permit the export of raw materials to the states neighbours to Greece. That again was a recommendation calling for action. That tendency to bolster the position of the General Assembly in the security field by extending its competence was quite natural. The same development had taken place in the League of Nations. The letter of the Charter had, therefore, been exceeded in practice, but this was a felicitous and a happy development of the Organisation. Its Charter, like all other constitutions, must develop so that it would not become a dead letter.'

1 At the 365th meeting of the First Committee, the representative of India stated: ' Article 10 being the general provision applying to any matter within the scope of the Charter, and Article 11 being the particular provision applying to questions relating to the maintenance of international peace. However, according to the canon of interpretation, the particular provision applied in preference to the general one, and the general provisions did not derogate from special provisions. Hence, also the matter had to be dealt with under Article 11 rather than under Article 10.'

second sentence of Article 11, paragraph 2, that the General Assembly shall refer to the Security Council any question on which action, *i.e.*, any enforcement action whatever, is necessary, may be supported by the Report which the Secretary of State of the United States made to the President on the results of the San Francisco Conference.[2] The Report is highly indicative of the intentions of those who framed the Charter. For, among them the United States played the most important role. In this Report, the provision of Article 11, paragraph 2, that the Assembly shall refer to the Security Council any question on which action is necessary, is not considered to be invalidated or in some way restricted by the provision of Article 11, paragraph 4 or by the wording of Article 10. The Report twice refers to the provision of Article 11, paragraph 2. It states that the General Assembly 'must' refer questions on which action is necessary to the Security Council, and speaks of the 'responsibility' of the General Assembly to refer such questions to the Security Council.[3] That by 'action' any enforcement action whatever, especially enforcement action involving the use of armed force is meant, results from the fact that the Report characterises the General Assembly as 'a forum for discussion and debate,'[4] in contradistinction to the Security Council which is characterised as 'an enforcement agency'; and that the Report emphasises that the General Assembly 'cannot invade the functions which have been specifically assigned in security matters to the Security Council.'[5]

The same interpretation of Article 11, paragraph 2 in relation to Article 10 has been advocated by the representative of the Department of State in the *Hearings Before the Committee on Foreign Relations of the United States Senate.*[6] The representative of the Department of State declared before the Committee that 'those who worked on the Dumbarton Oaks document and those who worked on the same subject in San Francisco were very definitely of the opinion that experience had shown that it was well to separate the functions' of the General Assembly from those of the Security Council[7]—in contradistinction to the Covenant of the League of Nations which conferred upon the Assembly and the Council the same functions. Among the functions of the Security Council, but not among the functions of the General Assembly, he mentioned: 'removing threats to the peace' and suppressing breaches of the peace.'[8] As to Article 11, he declared:

2 *Report to the President on the Results of the San Francisco Conference by the Secretary of State.* Department of State. Publication 2349. Conference Series 71. Washington, 1945.

3 *Ibid.*, p. 62.

4 *Ibid.*, p. 14.

5 *Ibid.*, p. 65.

6 Cf. *The Law of the United Nations*, pp. 209 f.

7 *Hearings*, p. 243.

8 *Ibid.*, p. 243.

' In its [the General Assembly's] activities with regard to such questions [relating to the maintenance of international peace and security] there are two limitations imposed on the General Assembly. One is that since primary responsibility for action with respect to the maintenance of international peace and security is placed in the Security Council, the Assembly, when it deals with a question on which action might be necessary, should refer this question to the Security Council either before or after its own discussion of it.'[9] The representative of the State Department did not say that ' action ' meant only a specific, not every enforcement action whatever. On the contrary. He emphasized that ' the right of the General Assembly to discuss, consider and debate any question relating to the maintenance of international peace and security is absolute '; but he did not say the same concerning the right of the General Assembly to make recommendations.[1] In the *Hearings*, the question as to whether the General Assembly has the power to recommend the use of force was circumstantially discussed. A Senator asked: ' Does the General Assembly have any power to recommend measures for the forcible adjustment of any situation ? ' To this question the answer of the representative of the Department of State was: ' No. The General Assembly has no such power.'[2] Later, another Senator asked: ' Is the Assembly free to recommend that the Council take action and, if so, can it make any recommendations as to kind or character of action to be taken ? '[3] He meant whether the General Assembly may recommend to the Security Council to take enforcement action. To this question the representative of the State Department—modifying his first answer—replied: ' It could do that. It probably would not.' That the General Assembly under any circumstances could recommend to *Members* the use of force, was not mentioned. But there can be

[9] *Ibid.*, p. 246.

[1] It is characteristic that in the discussion of Article 10 at the San Francisco Conference and especially in the discussion of the formula ' within the scope of the present Charter ' emphasis was laid almost exclusively on the right of the General Assembly to ' discuss ' matters. Thus, *e.g.*, at the 4th meeting of Commission II (U.N.C.I.O. Doc. 1151, II/17, *Documents*, Vol. VIII, p. 208), the Australian delegate declared: ' the text that is now put before the Commission means, in our view, the clear right of the Assembly to discuss any question or any matter within the scope of this Charter. That scope will include every aspect of the Charter, everything contained in it and everything covered by it. It will include the Preamble of the Charter, the great purposes and principles embodied in it, the activities of all its organs; and the right of discussion will be free and untrammelled and will range over that tremendous area.' It is in this connection that he referred to the General Assembly as the ' Town Meeting of the United Nations of the World.' It is true that he said in his speech also that ' there is no limit on the power of recommendation save the one mentioned in the text [of Article 10].' But he probably would not have denied the limitation established by Article 11, paragraph 2, if somebody had called his attention to this provision.

[2] *Hearings*, p. 252.

[3] *Ibid.*, p. 254.

hardly any doubt that the representative of the State Department would have answered a question to this effect decidedly in the negative.

However, none of these arguments in favour of one interpretation can absolutely exclude the other. Both interpretations are, in spite of the fact that they contradict each other, possible in view of the wording of the Charter.

3. Force Monopoly of the Security Council?

The answer to the question as to whether the General Assembly has the power under the Charter to recommend to Members collective measures including the use of armed force does not only depend on whether the Assembly is bound by Article 11, paragraph 2, to refer to the Security Council any question on which action is necessary, without making recommendations on such question, that is to say, on the relation between Article 10 and Article 11; but also on the answer to the question as to the relationship between Article 10 and Article 2, paragraph 4. This provision imposes upon the Members the obligation to refrain in their international relations from the 'use of force' in a manner 'inconsistent with the Purposes of the United Nations.' One of the most important Purposes of the United Nations is laid down in Article 1, paragraph 1 of the Charter: 'to take effective collective measures for the prevention and removal of threats to the peace, and for the suppression of acts of aggression or other breaches of the peace.' By 'effective collective measures' the measures may be understood which the Charter provides in Chapter VII, that is to say, enforcement measures to be taken by the Security Council under Articles 39, 41 and 42. In other terms, the Charter may be interpreted to allow the use of force only as a collective action (the cases of self-defence (Article 51) and of action against former enemy states (Articles 107, 53) excepted), and that means as an action of the United Nations, that the Charter establishes a force monopoly of the Organisation to be exercised by the Security Council and only by the Security Council.

It may be doubtful whether the 'effective collective measures' referred to in Article 1 paragraph 1, are only the measures to be taken by the Security Council under Articles 41 and 42, that is to say, enforcement measures involving or not involving the use of armed force, or also recommendations to use force made by the Security Council under Article 39. It may be argued, as pointed out, that Article 39 distinguishes between recommendations and enforcement measures, that by 'recommendations' only recommendations of measures of peaceful settlement are meant; that consequently the Security Council can only take enforcement measures itself, but not recommend enforcement measures to be taken by Members, that is to say, cannot recommend to Members to use force. Force can be used only by the Security Council under Articles 41 and 42 (and perhaps also under Article 94, paragraph 2).[4] But the wording of Article 39 does certainly not exclude another interpretation, according to which the Security Council may recommend to Members the use of armed force, as the Security Council actually did in the Korean affair.[5] If such recommendation may be considered to constitute an ' effective collective measure ' within the meaning of Article 1, paragraph 1, it is because it is a measure taken by the Security Council for the maintenance or restoration of international peace and security. To maintain or restore peace by the use of force is a function conferred by the Charter upon the Organisation as a collective body. The Charter does not establish (as it seems to be assumed in the Preamble of the Resolution ' Uniting for Peace ') an obligation of the individual Members to maintain or restore international peace and security.[6] In all Articles of the Charter referring to the maintenance or restoration of international peace and security this function is dealt with as with a task to be fulfilled by the Organisation. Only in Article 73 (c) international peace and security is mentioned in connection with an obligation of Members having responsibilities for the administration of non-self-governing territories; but the obligation is not to maintain or restore, but to ' further ' international peace and security. If the ' basic objectives ' of the trusteeship system, laid down in Article 76, constitute obligations of the Members acting under the trusteeship system,[7] then Article 76 (a) too, establishes an obligation of these Members to ' further,' not to maintain or restore, international peace and security.

If by ' effective collective measures ' referred to in Article 1, paragraph 1, only the measures are to be understood which the Charter provides in Chapter VII, that is measures to be taken exclusively by the Security Council, then the General Assembly is not authorised to recommend to Members the use of armed force. For such a use of force would constitute a violation of Article 2, paragraph 4, namely, a use of force inconsistent with the purposes of the United Nations. The General Assembly cannot recommend to Members to violate their obligation under Article 2, paragraph 4; provided Article 11, paragraph 2, is interpreted to mean that the Assembly shall refer to the Security Council any question relating to the maintenance of peace on which action is necessary—action meaning any enforcement action whatever, that is to say, any use of force, without making itself a recommendation to use force.

[4] Cf. *The Law of the United Nations*, pp. 541, 721. [5] Cf. *supra*, p. 932.

[6] The passage in the Preamble reads as follows: ' Conscious that failure of the Security Council to discharge its responsibilities on behalf of all the Member states, particularly those responsibilities referred to in the two preceding paragraphs [*i.e.*, the members of the Security Council] does not relieve *Member states of their obligations* or the United Nations of its responsibility under the Charter to *maintain international peace and security*.' (Italics added.)

[7] Cf. *The Law of the United Nations*, pp. 633 ff.

The view that the General Assembly is not competent to recommend to Members measures involving the use of force and especially involving the use of armed force, is also consistent with the wording of Article 14, which is the only provision of the Charter referring to 'measures' to be recommended by the General Assembly. Article 14 reads as follows:—

> Subject to the provisions of Article 12, the General Assembly may recommend measures for the peaceful adjustment of any situation, regardless of origin, which it deems likely to impair the general welfare or friendly relations among nations, including situations resulting from a violation of the provisions of the present Charter setting forth the Purposes and Principles of the United Nations.

This Article may be interpreted to mean that the only 'measures' which the General Assembly is competent to recommend are 'measures for the *peaceful* adjustment' of situations, even if the situation results from a violation of Articles 1 and 2 of the Charter; and the situation to which the recommendation provided for in Sectio.. A, paragraph 1, of the Resolution 'Uniting for Peace' refers, namely, 'breach of the peace or act of aggression,' includes certainly a violation of Article 2, paragraph 4: illegal use of force.[8]

[8] At the *Hearings* before the Senate Committee on Foreign Relations, the representative of the Department of State interpreted Article 14 of the Charter as follows: 'Article 14 gives the General Assembly the function and the power of recommending measures for the peaceful adjustment of any situation regardless of origin which it deems likely to impair the general welfare or friendly relations among nations' (p. 249). And when a Senator, referring to the wording 'measures for the peaceful adjustment . . .' asked: 'Therefore, is it [the power to make recommendations] not limited ?' the representative did not reply that this power was unlimited, but declared: 'Article 14 relates to those situations which do not involve a possible violation or possible impairment of international peace or security' (p. 253). This is not quite consistent with the wording of Article 14 (' including situations resulting from a violation of the provisions of the present Charter setting forth the Purposes and Principles of the United Nations'). In his answer, the representative evidently tried to justify the provision of Article 14, restricting the power of the General Assembly to recommendations of 'peaceful adjustment.' Later, the representative declared: 'that so far as situations which are referred to in Article 14 are concerned, so long as they arise out of conditions which are likely to impair the general welfare and friendly relations among nations and are not deemed to be a threat to international peace and security, there is no authority in the Charter for any forcible measures. If those same situations became transformed or aggravated in such a way that it became possible for the Organisation—and in this case, the Security Council—to determine that a situation like that is of such a nature that its continuance may threaten the peace, the Organisation still has no power to take forcible action. It is only when the Security Council determines that an actual threat to the peace exists or that a breach of the peace has occurred, that the Organisation has the right to take forcible action' (p. 253). At the 368th meeting of the First Committee, the representative of Bolivia stated that the resolution 'Uniting for Peace' 'was based on Articles 10 and 14 of the Charter, and in them it found ample justification.' Article 14 is certainly no basis for the resolution.

The interpretation according to which the 'effective collective measures' referred to in Article 1, paragraph 1, are enforcement measures to be taken only by the Security Council and only under Article 39, may be confirmed by the fact that in Article 24 the Charter, 'in order to ensure prompt and effective action by the United Nations,' confers upon the Security Council 'primary responsibility for the maintenance of international peace and security.' This provision may be interpreted to mean that a 'prompt and effective action by the United Nations,' that is an action of the United Nations as an 'effective collective measure,' can be taken only by the Security Council. This interpretation may be further confirmed by the fact that Article 1, paragraph 1, specifies these 'effective collective measures' as to be taken 'for the prevention and removal of threats to the peace, and for the suppression of acts of aggression or other breaches of the peace,' and that the determination of 'the existence of any threat to the peace, breach of the peace, or act of aggression' is a function conferred in Article 39 upon the Security Council and only upon the Security Council, upon no other organ of the United Nations, especially not upon the General Assembly.

Finally, it should be noted that some provisions of the Charter can be satisfactorily explained only if it is presupposed that enforcement measures can be taken exclusively by the Security Council. Thus, Article 5 provides that a Member of the United Nations 'against which preventive or enforcement action has been taken by the Security Council' may be suspended from the exercise of the rights and privileges of membership by the General Assembly upon the recommendation of the Security Council. If an enforcement action could be taken against a Member also upon a recommendation by the General Assembly, there would be no reason to restrict suspension from the exercise of the rights of membership to the case where enforcement action is taken by the Security Council. Under Article 50, any state has the right to consult the Security Council with regard to economic problems arising from the carrying out of enforcement measures 'taken by the Security Council' against any other state. If enforcement measures could be taken on the recommendation of the General Assembly, the state carrying out these measures would be confronted with the same economic problems which may arise from the carrying out of enforcement measures taken by the Security Council. But for the case of carrying out enforcement measures on the recommendation of the General Assembly the Charter does not establish an analogous right of consultation.[9] Article 53,

[9] At the 363rd meeting of the First Committee, the representative of Pakistan admitted that 'preventive or enforcement action, the issuance of directives or orders, could only be taken by the Security Council, no matter how grave the emergency. Articles 5 and 50 clearly stated that enforcement action could only be taken by the Council.'

paragraph 1, provides that no enforcement action shall be taken under regional arrangements or by regional agencies without the authorisation of the Security Council, because the Charter—according to the intention of its authors—confers only upon the Security Council the power to take enforcement action. Article 99 authorises the Secretary-General to bring to the attention of the Security Council any matter which in his opinion may threaten the maintenance of international peace and security. But why does the Charter not authorise the Secretary-General to bring such matter to the attention of the General Assembly? Probably because the framers of the Charter were of the opinion that in case of a threat to the peace only the Security Council, and not the General Assembly, was competent to take the necessary measures.

4. The 'Primary' Responsibility of the Security Council for the Maintenance of Peace

However, in his address made at the 279th Plenary Meeting of the General Assembly, the Secretary of State of the United States advocated another interpretation of the Charter. He declared: 'Article 24 of the Charter gives the Security Council primary responsibility for the maintenance of peace. This is the way it should be. But if the Security Council is not able to act because of the obstructive tactic of a permanent member, the Charter does not leave the United Nations impotent. The obligation of all Members to take action to maintain or restore peace does not disappear. The Charter, in Articles 10, 11, and 14, also vests in the General Assembly authority and responsibility for matters affecting international peace. The General Assembly can and should organise itself to discharge its responsibility promptly and decisively if the Security Council is prevented from acting.' And at the 354th meeting of the First Committee the representative of the United States declared 'The United States delegation considered the responsibility for maintaining peace was not the monopoly of the great Powers' (meaning: the Security Council) and that 'the General Assembly, should therefore take "effective collective measures for the prevention and removal of threats to the peace" (Article 1, paragraph 1).'

It must be admitted that the wording of the provisions concerned does not exclude the interpretation that by 'effective collective measures' also measures recommended by the General Assembly may be understood. This interpretation may be supported by the fact that the Charter speaks in Article 24 of a 'primary,' not of an exclusive, responsibility of the Security Council,[1] and hence does not

[1] This interpretation of Article 24 of the Charter was advocated, *e.g.*, by the representative of the United Kingdom at the 360th meeting of the First Committee. He stated: 'Article 24 spoke of primary responsibility; that implied a secondary

prevent the General Assembly from assuming a secondary responsibility for the maintenance of international peace and security, in order to ensure prompt and effective action by the United Nations within its competence determined by Articles 10 and 11. Then, a recommendation made by the General Assembly to Members to use force could not be considered as a recommendation of a use of force inconsistent with the purposes of the United Nations.

5. The Secondary Responsibility of the General Assembly for the Maintenance of Peace

If this interpretation is accepted, the question arises under what conditions the General Assembly may assume the responsibility for the maintenance of international peace and security through prompt and effective action. The answer might be: If the Security Council is not able to fulfil the functions for which this body is primarily responsible. This answer, however, meets with a serious difficulty. Article 106 provides:

> Pending the coming into force of such special agreements referred to in Article 43 as in the opinion of the Security Council enable it to begin the exercise of its responsibilities under Article 42, the parties to the Four-Nation Declaration, signed at Moscow, October 30, 1943, and France, shall, in accordance with the provisions of paragraph 5 of that Declaration, consult with one another and as occasion requires with other Members of the United Nations with a view to such joint action on behalf of the Organisation as may be necessary for the purpose of maintaining international peace and security.

This provision may be interpreted to mean that *as long* as the Security Council cannot take enforcement measures involving the use of armed force because it has not yet at its disposal the armed forces referred to in Article 43, the only ' effective collective measure ' or ' prompt and effective action by the United Nations ' as an action involving the use of armed force that can be taken as an action ' on behalf of the Organisation,' is the ' joint action ' provided in Article 106; and not an action recommended by the General Assembly. The phrase ' Pending the coming into force, etc.,' taken literally, means a certain period of time, not a certain condition. This interpretation may be supported by the fact that Article 106 is the first Article of Chapter XVII entitled ' Transitional Security Arrangements,' which indicates that, according to the intention of the framers of the Charter, the provisions of this Chapter shall be

responsibility, which under other Articles, such as Articles 10, 11 and 12, was laid upon the General Assembly.' The same argument was used by the representative of the Philippines at the 299th and the representative of Cuba at the 301st Plenary Meeting of the General Assembly.

applied during a transitional period. During that period of time the use of armed force by the United Nations shall be possible only through the 'joint action' of the five Great Powers. Since the special agreements referred to in Article 106 (43) are not yet in force, the General Assembly has not, or at least not yet, the power to recommend an enforcement action involving the use of armed force different from the joint action stipulated in Article 106. However, it can hardly be doubted that by 'transitional' measures the framers of the Charter meant measures to be taken during a very short period of time, and that they did not anticipate that five years after the coming into force of the Charter the special agreements referred to in Article 43 would not yet be concluded. Hence, Article 106 might be interpreted to mean: Only *if* the Security Council cannot take enforcement measures involving the use of armed force because it has not yet at its disposal the armed forces referred to in Article 106 (43), and only under this condition, the 'joint action' shall take place. Then, another enforcement action can be taken if the Security Council cannot act *on account of another reason*, for instance because its action is blocked by the exercise of the veto right. If this interpretation is accepted, it might be argued: Since Article 106 provides the 'joint action' only for the case that the Security Council cannot take enforcement measures involving the use of armed force because it has not yet at its disposal the armed forces referred to in Article 43—and not for the case that the Security Council is unable to act because of the exercise of the veto right, the secondary responsibility of the General Assembly for the maintenance of international peace and security through prompt and effective action comes into consideration in case the Security Council cannot act because of the exercise of the veto right. Indeed, the Resolution 'Uniting for Peace' provides that the General Assembly shall recommend the use of armed force only 'if the Security Council, because of lack of unanimity of the permanent members, fails to exercise its primary responsibility for the maintenance of international peace and security.' This is consistent with Article 106 only if the provision of this Article, in contradiction to its wording, is interpreted to provide the joint action not for a definite period of time, but only under a definite condition.

Whatever interpretation of Article 106 may be accepted, the restriction laid down in it does not appear in Article 10, which does not refer to Article 106, as it does not refer to Article 11. Hence the interpretation is not excluded that it is not Article 10 which is restricted by Article 106, but that Article 106 is restricted by Article 10. Consequently it may be argued: The power of the General Assembly to recommend the use of armed force can be based only on Article 10 of the Charter, and the only restriction which this Article stipulates is the one laid down in Article 12, that the General

Assembly shall not make any recommendation with regard to a dispute or situation while the Security Council is exercising in respect of that dispute or situation the functions assigned to it in the Charter. If the General Assembly has the power to recommend the use of armed force at all, it may make such a recommendation even if the Security Council does not fail to exercise its primary responsibility for the maintenance of international peace and security because of lack of unanimity of the permanent members, and even if the Security Council has decided by an affirmative vote of seven members including the concurring votes of all permanent members that in a certain matter no threat to the peace, breach of the peace, or act of aggression exists or that no enforcement measure is necessary, and consequently has recommended only specific means of peaceful settlement, provided that the Security Council has ceased to deal with the matter. The interpretation according to which the General Assembly has the power to recommend the use of armed force may lead to serious conflicts between the General Assembly and the Security Council in security matters.

Under Section A of the Resolution 'Uniting for Peace' the General Assembly, it is true, is authorised to recommend to Members collective measures, and especially the use of armed force, only 'if the Security Council, because of lack of unanimity of the permanent members, fails to exercise its primary responsibility for the maintenance of international peace and security.' But this formula covers not only the case where one permanent member of the Council has voted against all the other permanent and three or more non-permanent members, which was probably the only case the framers of the resolution had in mind. The wording of the formula covers also the case where a decision of the Security Council to be taken under Article 39 could not be achieved because among the majority of seven (or more) votes were only the concurring votes of one or two or three permanent members. That means that by Section A of the Resolution 'Uniting for Peace' the General Assembly is authorised to recommend to Members the use of armed force, although two, three, or even four permanent members of the Council have voted against taking an enforcement measure because they were of the opinion that no threat to, or breach of, the peace existed. In such a case too, the Assembly may, according to the wording of Section A, of the resolution, by a two-thirds majority declare that there exists a threat to the peace, that the Security Council has failed to exercise its primary responsibility for the maintenance of international peace and security, and then recommend to Members collective measures, including enforcement measures not involving the use of armed force; and if the Assembly is of the opinion that there exists a breach of the peace, it may even recommend the use of armed force. It may be doubted whether the formula covers also the case where no voting at all has taken place in the Security Council on a situation ' where there appears to be a threat to the peace, breach of the peace, or act of aggression.' But the question may be answered in the affirmative, since according to the wording of the formula it is for the General Assembly to decide whether there exists a threat to the peace, breach of the peace, or act of aggression, and whether the Security Council, ' because of lack of unanimity of the permanent members,' has failed to exercise its primary responsibility. The Assembly may decide that the Security Council failed to exercise its primary responsibility because of lack of unanimity of its permanent members, although no voting has taken place in the Security Council.[2]

The Resolution ' Uniting for Peace ' provides that the General Assembly shall recommend the use of armed force only ' in the case of a breach of the peace or act of aggression.' Hence, in order to recommend the use of armed force the General Assembly must determine the existence of a breach of the peace or act of aggression. In the preamble, the General Assembly declares that discharge of its responsibilities in respect to the maintenance of international peace and security ' calls for possibilities of observation which would ascertain the facts and expose aggressors.' That means that the Resolution ' Uniting for Peace ' confers upon the General Assembly the power to determine the existence of a breach of the peace or act of aggression. Article 39 of the Charter confers this power only on the Security Council. It provides: ' The Security Council shall determine the existence of *any* threat to the peace, breach of the peace, or act of aggression. . . .' No Article of the Charter does confer upon the General Assembly such power. However, Article 10 does not provide that the General Assembly may make recommendations on questions within the scope of the Charter only if there exists a definite situation. The power of the General Assembly to make recommendations—in contradistinction to the power of the Security Council to make recommendations or take enforcement action under Article 39—is not conditioned by the existence of a threat to the peace, breach of the peace, or act of

[2] At the 359th meeting of the First Committee the representative of India stated: ' The phrase " because of lack of unanimity of the permanent members" was not precise. For example, would a draft resolution on which there had not been unanimity among the five permanent members of the Council come within the meaning of that phrase if, besides dividing the permanent members, it failed to obtain the bare majority of seven votes—in other words, if four or more of the six non-permanent members voted against the proposal ? Also, was it intended that Section A should become operative upon the objection of a single draft resolution in the Security Council, regarding a conflict as, for instance, in regard to the use of armed forces, or would the Security Council have the necessary time in which to adopt an alternative resolution providing for a solution by mediation or by the application of economic sanctions ? Decisions taken after due consideration often turned out to be more satisfactory.'

aggression. Hence, in order to make a recommendation to use armed force, the Assembly under the Charter need not determine the existence of a breach of the peace or act of aggression. If the Assembly has the power to recommend the use of armed force at all, it may make such recommendation whenever it considers such recommendation appropriate. No previous determination of the existence of a breach of the peace or act of aggression is required. In order to avoid the objection that the Charter authorises only the Security Council, and not the General Assembly, to determine the existence of a breach of the peace or act of aggression, any reference to these circumstances should have been omitted in the text of the resolution.

6. Uniting for Peace and Collective Self-Defence

Some Members o the United Nations tried to justify the constitutionality of the resolution as a kind of implementation of Article 51 of the Charter. Thus, *e.g.*, the representative of Colombia stated at the 361st meeting of the First Committee: 'Under Article 51, nations could take measures for collective defence against an aggressor until such time as the Security Council reached a decision. That was, after all, what was proposed in the seven-Power draft.' And the representative of the United Kingdom declared at the 360th meeting of the First Committee: 'It would be absurd if the letter of the Charter, which recognised the right of collective self-defence and the pooling of forces, failed to permit the United Nations to approve the effectiveness, morality and constitutionality of action taken by the Member states along those lines.' At the 364th meeting, he said: 'There was no violation of the Charter when the General Assembly, acting within its power, recommended to governments that they should exercise their right of self-defence, and the latter complied.' It seems that if the General Assembly has the power to recommend to Members the use of armed force, it has also the power to recommend to Members the use of armed force in the exercise of their right of individual or collective self-defence. But a resolution by which the General Assembly recommends to Members to exercise their right of individual or collective self-defence by using armed force against a definite state, implies that the Assembly determines the existence of an armed attack, which is an act of aggression, and that the Assembly determines that the state against which it recommends the use of armed force is the aggressor. This is a function which the Charter does not confer upon the General Assembly, but—in Articles 39 and 51—exclusively upon the Security Council. As a matter of fact, Section A of the Resolution 'Uniting for Peace' does not authorise the General Assembly to recommend to Members to exercise their right of self-defence. Nor do the references to Article 51 in Section C, paragraph 8 and Section D, paragraph 11, imply such an authorisation.

7. The Armed Forces to be Made Available as United Nations Units

Another question is whether the General Assembly has under the Charter the power to recommend to the Members of the United Nations—as provided in Section C, paragraph 8 of the Resolution—' that each Member maintain within its national armed forces elements so trained, organised, and equipped that they could promptly be made available, in accordance with their respective constitutional processes, for service as a United Nations unit or units, upon recommendation by the Security Council or General Assembly . . .' and—as provided in Section C, paragraph 10—to ' request the Secretary-General to appoint . . . a panel of military experts who could be made available, upon request, to Member states which wish to obtain technical advice regarding the organisation, training, and equipment for prompt service as United Nations units of the elements referred to in Paragraph 8.' It might be argued that the General Assembly is not authorised by the Charter to make such a recommendation, because the Charter regulates the matter to which that recommendation refers in a totally different way. It provides in Article 43 that ' all Members of the United Nations, in order to contribute to the maintenance of international peace and security ' shall make available ' to the Security Council '—and not to the General Assembly—armed forces in accordance with ' special agreements,' concluded between the United Nations represented by the Security Council and the Members concerned; and establishes in Article 47 the Military Staff Committee, composed of the Chiefs of Staff of the permanent members of the Security Council, for such technical purposes as referred to in Section C, paragraph 10, of the Resolution. It might be argued that the Charter does not authorise the General Assembly to substitute for this method of organising an armed force of the United Nations any other method. This interpretation probably corresponds to the intention of those who framed the Charter, who, as the *Report to the President* states, thought of the Security Council as of the only ' enforcement agency of the United Nations.' But, again, the wording of the Charter does not exclude an interpretation which does not correspond to this intention. If an interpretation of the Charter is possible according to which the General Assembly has the power to recommend to Members the use of armed force, it can hardly be denied that the General Assembly may also recommend to the Members to maintain within their national armed forces elements available for carrying out the recommendation of the Assembly to use armed force,[3] and to establish, under Article 22, a panel of

[3] At the 356th meeting of the First Committee the representative of Peru interpreted Article 43: ' It would, however, be an erroneous interpretation of Article 43 to claim that the obligation of Member states to contribute to the armed forces of the United Nations was subject to the invitation by the Security Council and to the special agreements provided for in Article 43. It was true that, in principle,

military experts as a subsidiary organ for the performance of its functions exercised by the just-mentioned recommendation, or, under Article 98, to entrust the Secretary-General with the function of appointing such a panel of experts.

In Section C of the Resolution ' Uniting for Peace,' the General Assembly recommends to the Members that each Member maintain elements of its armed forces which could be ' made available . . . for service as a United Nations unit or units, upon recommendation by the Security Council or General Assembly.' It is not expressly said to whom these elements shall be made available, in contradistinction to the provision of Article 43 according to which the contingents of the Members' armed forces shall be made 'available to the Security Council.'[4] According to the wording of Section C, paragraph 8 of the resolution, the ' elements ' of the armed forces of the Members shall be made available ' upon recommendation by the Security Council or General Assembly.' That may be interpreted to mean: available to the Security Council or the General Assembly. The General Assembly is not authorised by the Charter to confer upon the

it was for the Council to act in that field. But if the Security Council, the mandatary organ, failed in the task entrusted to it by the mandating authority, the obligation of Member states would not disappear or be suspended.' This interpretation of Article 43 is correct. But the obligation of the Members established by Article 43 is an obligation ' to make available to the Security Council '—not to the General Assembly—' on its call and in accordance with a special agreement or agreements,' concluded with the United Nations represented by the Security Council, and not by the General Assembly, ' armed forces, etc.' As long as these special agreements are not in force, the obligation of the Members under Article 43 cannot be fulfilled. The representative of Peru said further: ' That obligation of every Member was recalled in Article 45; and undoubtedly when the joint draft resolution referred to the forces which each state should place at the disposal of the United Nations, the forces mentioned in Article 45 were meant. The adoption of that draft resolution would therefore simply mean the application of the Article in spirit and letter.' The forces to which the resolution refers cannot be the forces mentioned in Article 45. For Article 45 expressly stipulates that ' the strength and degree of readiness of these contingents and plans for their combined action shall be determined, within the limits laid down in the special agreement or agreements referred to in Article 43, by the Security Council with the assistance of the Military Staff Committee '—not by recommendation by the General Assembly with the assistance of a committee established by the General Assembly. The Resolution ' Uniting for Peace ' is certainly not the application of Article 45.

[4] At the 366th meeting of the First Committee the representative of the Soviet Union declared that the provision of the Resolution ' Uniting for Peace ' concerning elements of the armed forces of the Members was in contradiction to Article 43 of the Charter, according to which contingents of the armed forces of the Members are to be placed at the disposal of the Security Council. That contradiction, he stated, ' could not be denied by asserting that, according to the former text, the armed forces would not be placed at the disposal of the General Assembly . . . if armed forces were organised by the Member states with a view to action recommended by the General Assembly, that would clearly show that such armed forces were at the disposal of that body.'

Security Council the power to dispose of armed forces made available to the Security Council on a recommendation of the Assembly, even if it is only the power to dispose of these armed forces by mere recommendation.

The General Assembly can dispose of these elements only by recommendation, that is to say, the General Assembly—provided it has the power of recommending to Members the use of armed force—may recommend to Members to use these elements in a certain way, especially against a definite state. Hence it may be doubted whether these elements of the national armed forces may properly be called a 'United Nations unit' or 'United Nations units,' even if the Assembly would recommend to the Members to make these elements available to a unified command under a definite Member and request that Member to designate the commander, and if the Members would actually comply with such recommendation.[5] As a 'unit of the United Nations' only armed forces may be considered which are placed at the disposal of an organ of the United Nations competent to dispose of these forces by decisions binding upon the Members. But this is a terminological question which, from a legal point of view, is of minor importance.[6]

8. The Peace Observation Commission and The Collective Measures Committee

The establishment of the Peace Observation Commission in Section B, paragraph 1 of the Resolution 'Uniting for Peace' is based on Article 22 of the Charter, authorising the General Assembly to 'establish such subsidiary organs as it deems necessary for the performance of its functions.' Insofar as the function for the performance of which the Commission is established is to determine the existence of a situation likely to endanger the maintenance of international peace and security and specially the existence of a breach of the peace or act of aggression, the establishment of the Commission can hardly be considered as constitutional. For—as pointed out—the determination of these facts is not a function

5 Such a recommendation was made in the Korean affair by the Security Council in its resolution adopted on July 7, 1950.

6 At the 302nd Plenary Meeting of the General Assembly the representative of Canada, one of the sponsors of the resolution, declared: 'this resolution does not set up an international force. It recommends that Members place national contingents at the disposal of the United Nations to carry out obligations and recommendations which those Members accept. These contingents must be equipped, trained and ready to join in international police action, so that, if a June 27, 1950, occurs again, the United Nations will have forces from many of its Members ready to meet aggression . . . that will be the test of the effectiveness of this new effort to put international force behind the collective will for peace of the United Nations.' No 'international force,' but an 'international police action' and an 'international force' behind the collective will for peace ?

conferred upon the General Assembly by the Charter. If the determination of the facts is not a function conferred by the Charter upon the General Assembly, the latter cannot authorise the Interim Committee to utilise the Commission for the performance of this function. According to the provision of Section B, paragraph 3, that ' the Security Council may also utilise the Commission in accordance with its authority under the Charter,' the Commission is a subsidiary organ not only of the General Assembly but also of the Security Council. But under Article 22 the General Assembly has only the power to establish subsidiary organs for the performance of its own functions—not for the performance of functions of the Security Council.

If it is assumed that the General Assembly has the power to recommend to Members the use of armed force, it has also the power to establish the Collective Measures Committee referred to in Section D, paragraphs 11, 12, and 13, and to instruct this Committee, as a subsidiary organ of the General Assembly, to make reports to the latter; but hardly to make reports to the Security Council. If the Assembly has the power to recommend to Members the use of armed force, it has, as pointed out, also the power to request the Secretary-General to appoint a panel of military experts, as stipulated in Section C, paragraph 10 of the Resolution, and to invite the Members of the United Nations to inform the Collective Measures Committee of the measures taken in implementation of the recommendation to maintain within their national armed forces elements available for service as United Nations units.[7]

9. The Emergency Special Session of the General Assembly

The Annex to the Resolution ' Uniting for Peace ' contains an amendment to the Rules of Procedure of the General Assembly, which is based on Article 21 of the Charter conferring upon the Assembly the power to regulate its own procedure within the framework of the Charter. The provision that ' emergency special sessions ' shall be convened is covered by Article 20 of the Charter which provides for ' special sessions ' in addition to the ' regular annual sessions ' of the General Assembly. That an emergency session ' shall be convened within twenty-four hours . . .' is within the framework of Article 20. But the provision that the emergency sessions shall be convened at the request of the Security Council ' on the vote of any seven members thereof,' may be considered as

[7] At the 367th meeting of the First Committee the representative of the Soviet Union objected that the Members would report to the Collective Measures Committee, not to the Security Council, which is a violation of Article 51. This objection has no basis in the Resolution ' Uniting for Peace,' which does not prevent the Members exercising their right of collective self-defence from fulfilling their obligation under Article 51.

unconstitutional. It may be argued that the General Assembly has not the power to decide a question of procedure of the Security Council. What kind of majority is required for a decision of the Council requesting a special session of the Assembly, is—in conformity with Article 27 of the Charter—exclusively for the Security Council to decide.[8] But it may also be argued that under Article 10 the General Assembly has the power to discuss any question 'relating to the powers and functions of any organs provided for in the present Charter' and to make recommendations on such questions, and that the request to convoke a special session of the General Assembly is a function of the Security Council. Consequently, the General Assembly may under Article 10 make recommendations to the Security Council concerning the exercise of this function. The formula 'Emergency special sessions . . . shall be convened within twenty-four hours of the receipt . . . of a request for such a session from the Security Council, on the vote of any seven members' may be interpreted as intending not to bind the Security Council, but to recommend to the Council under Article 10 to make the request by a majority of any seven members; or to mean only that an emergency session shall be called if requested by the Security Council on the vote of any seven members, provided the Council has decided to make such a request by a majority of any seven members. The formula may be considered to be superfluous, but not unconstitutional.

Such contradictory interpretations are possible also with respect to the provision that an emergency special session shall be convened at the request of 'a majority of the Members of the United Nations expressed by vote in the Interim Committee.' This provision means that a special session of the General Assembly shall be convoked at the request of the Interim Committee, which is not in conformity with the wording of Article 20, providing that a special session shall be convoked at the request 'of a majority of the Members of the United Nations,' not at the request of a committee of the General Assembly. But it might also be argued that the Charter does not prescribe the procedure by which the request of the majority of the Members is to be expressed; consequently any such procedure is constitutional.[9]

[8] At the 364th meeting of the First Committee the representative of Syria stated: 'The Council was the master of its own procedure and it was not for the General Assembly, through the intermediary of the First Committee, to decide whether the convening of special sessions was a question of procedure or a question of substance. Furthermore, the revised joint draft resolution provided that a special session of the General Assembly could be called at the request of the Security Council on the vote of any seven members. Such a provision was a violation of Article 20 of the Charter and prejudged the Security Council's right to decide for itself whether or not the votes of the five permanent members should be included in the affirmative vote of seven of its members.'

[9] At the 364th meeting of the First Committee the representative of the Soviet Union argued: A special emergency session for the purpose to consider a threat

10. The Resolution 'Uniting for Peace' and the Covenant of the League of Nations

However the question may be answered as to whether and to what extent the Resolution 'Uniting for Peace' is consistent with the wording of the Charter, it can hardly be denied that the United Nations under this Resolution assumes the character of an international organisation very different from that which the framers of the Charter had in mind. The system of collective security established by this Resolution is much nearer to that established by the Covenant of the League of Nations than to that intended by the framers of the Charter. In some respects it even lags behind that of the Covenant, which imposed upon the Members the obligation to take enforcement measures not involving the use of armed force against an aggressor, but left to their discretion the taking of enforcement measures involving the use of armed force. Under the Resolution 'Uniting for Peace,' however, both kinds of enforcement measures are not obligatory, since they can be only recommended by the General Assembly. In other respects the Resolution goes beyond the Covenant. The power to decide whether the conditions exist under which enforcement measures may be taken, is not left to the Members as under the Covenant; it is the General Assembly, an organ of the United Nations, which, under the Resolution 'Uniting for Peace'—but not under the Charter—has the power to determine the existence of a breach of the peace or act of aggression; and, last but not least, the General Assembly can adopt its resolutions by a majority vote, whereas in the League of Nations the principle of unanimity of all the Members prevailed. But the force monopoly of the Security Council, the radical centralisation of the collective security system, that great progress that the framers of the Charter intended to achieve above and beyond the Covenant, is abandoned; and had to

to the peace, breach of the peace, or act of aggression, cannot be convened by a simple majority of Members of the United Nations, because a decision of the General Assembly determining the existence of a threat to or breach of the peace is an important question, and consequently can be adopted—according to Article 18 of the Charter—only by a two-thirds majority. This argument is not convincing. Under Article 20, a special session can be convoked at the request of a majority of the Members which are of the opinion that a threat to or breach of the peace exists; but it may be that in the General Assembly thus convoked, a two-thirds majority for a resolution determining the existence of a threat to or breach of the peace cannot be obtained. The provision of Article 20, concerning convocation of the General Assembly, is independent of the provision of Article 18, concerning the voting procedure. At the 365th meeting of the First Committee, the representative of the Byelorussian Soviet Socialist Republic maintained that the word 'majority' in Article 20 of the Charter meant 'two-thirds of the Member states.' This is hardly a possible interpretation. When a two-thirds majority is meant, the Charter expressly so provides. 'Majority' means always simple majority; especially in Article 18, regulating the voting procedure of the General Assembly.

be abandoned because the rule of unanimity of the permanent members did not work.

This relapse to a state of a more decentralised system of collective security within which no veto right of privileged Members prevails, implies, on the other hand, the possibility—not anticipated by the framers of the Charter[1]—of taking enforcement action against an aggressor, even if the aggressor is a permanent member of the Security Council or a state protected by it.

11. The First Application of the Resolution 'Uniting for Peace'

The new system of collective security has been applied the first time by a resolution of the General Assembly adopted on February 1, 1951.

The report of the United Nations Command in Korea, dated November 5, 1950, that Chinese communist military units are deployed for action against the forces of the United Nations in Korea, led to a joint draft resolution submitted by Cuba, Equador, France, Norway, the United Kingdom, and the United States, to the Security Council on November 10, 1950.[2] In this draft resolution the Security Council '*calls upon* all states and authorities, and in particular those responsible for the action noted above [*i.e.*, the action of the Chinese communist military units], to refrain from assisting or encouraging the North Korean authorities, to prevent their nationals or individuals or units of their armed forces from giving assistance to North Korean forces and to cause the immediate withdrawal of any such nationals, individuals, or units which may presently be in Korea; *affirms* that it is the policy of the United Nations to hold the Chinese frontier with Korea inviolate and fully to protect legitimate Chinese and Korean interests in the frontier zone; *calls attention* to the grave danger which continued intervention by Chinese forces in Korea would entail for the maintenance of such a policy; . . .' On November 30, 1950, this draft resolution was rejected in the Security Council by a vote of 9 members against 1, the vote of the Soviet Union. Four days later the sponsors of the rejected draft resolution asked the General Assembly to take up, as an important and urgent question, the intervention of the Central

1 In the *Hearings* before the Senate Committee on Foreign Relations (p. 215), the Secretary of State declared: 'The question is asked: What would happen if one of the five permanent members used the unanimity rule to veto enforcement action against itself ? The answer is plain. If one of these nations ever embarked upon a course of aggression, a major war would result, no matter what the membership and voting provisions of the Security Council might be. The Charter does not confer any power upon the great nations which they do not already possess in fact. Without the Charter the power of these nations to make or break the peace would still exist.'

2 U.N. Doc. S/1894.

People's Government of the People's Republic of China. On February 1, 1951, the General Assembly adopted the above-mentioned resolution, which reads as follows:—

THE GENERAL ASSEMBLY

Noting that the Security Council, because of lack of unanimity of the permanent members, has failed to exercise its primary responsibility for the maintenance of international peace and security in regard to Chinese Communist intervention in Korea;

Noting that the Central People's Government of the People's Republic of China has not accepted United Nations proposals to bring about a cessation of hostilities in Korea with a view to peaceful settlement, and that its armed forces continue their invasion of Korea and their large-scale attacks upon United Nations forces there;

1. *Finds* that the Central People's Government of the People's Republic of China, by giving direct aid and assistance to those who were already committing aggression in Korea and by engaging in hostilities against United Nations forces there, has itself engaged in aggression in Korea;

2. *Calls upon* the Central People's Government of the People's Republic of China to cause its forces and nationals in Korea to cease hostilities against the United Nations forces and to withdraw from Korea;

3. *Affirms* the determination of the United Nations to continue its action in Korea to meet the aggression;

4. *Calls upon* all states and authorities to continue to lend every assistance to the United Nations action in Korea;

5. *Calls upon* all states and authorities to refrain from giving any assistance to the aggressors in Korea;

6. *Requests* a committee composed of the members of the Collective Measures Committee as a matter of urgency to consider additional measures to be employed to meet this aggression and to report thereon to the General Assembly, it being understood that the committee is authorised to defer its report if the Good Offices Committee, referred to in the following paragraph, reports satisfactory progress in its efforts;

7. *Affirms* that it continues to be the policy of the United Nations to bring about a cessation of hostilities in Korea and the achievement of United Nations objectives in Korea by peaceful means, and requests the President of the General Assembly to designate forthwith two persons who would meet with him at any suitable opportunity to use their good offices to this end.

The statement 'that the Security Council, because of lack of unanimity of the permanent members, has failed to exercise its primary responsibility for the maintenance of international peace and security in regard to Chinese Communist intervention in Korea,' refers evidently to the fact that the Soviet Union has vetoed the above-mentioned draft resolution.

The most important content of the resolution of February 1, 1951, is that the General Assembly 'finds that the Central People's Government of the People's Republic of China . . . has itself engaged in aggression in Korea.' That means, expressed in terms of the Charter, that the General Assembly determines the existence of an act of aggression for which the government of China is declared to be responsible. To 'determine the existence of any . . . act of aggression' is a function which the Charter in Article 39 confers upon the Security Council and which the resolution 'Uniting for Peace' has conferred upon the General Assembly in case the Security Council did not exercise this function. That the General Assembly in its resolution of February 1, 1951, does not use the words of Article 39 but says that it 'finds that the Central People's Government of the People's Republic of China . . . has itself engaged in aggression,' is legally of no importance, since it can be no other function but that stipulated in the first part of Article 39 which the General Assembly exercised in its resolution of February 1, 1951.

The state which this resolution declared responsible for an act of aggression is the Republic of China, Member of the United Nations and permanent member of the Security Council. No other state could be referred to in this resolution. It is important to note that the General Assembly designated this state as the 'People's Republic of China,' that is the name this state has adopted in the course of the communist revolution. The General Assembly referred to the 'Central People's Government,' guilty of an act of aggression in Korea, as to the government of China, now called the 'People's Republic of China.' The General Assembly considered the Central People's Government as the government of China although China was and is not represented in the General Assembly by a delegation appointed by this government, but by a delegation appointed by the so called National Government of China. That implies that the General Assembly considered two governments as the governments of China; which is hardly compatible with the principle of general international law that a state can have only one government responsible for acts imputable to this state.

The actions to be taken by the General Assembly under the resolution 'Uniting for Peace' in case of a threat to the peace, breach of the peace or act of aggression are 'recommendations to Members for collective measures, including in the case of a breach of the peace or act of aggression the use of armed force when necessary.' In its resolution of February 1, 1951, the General Assembly did not make 'recommendations'; at least, the Assembly did not use this term. It calls ' upon the Central People's Government of the People's Republic of China ' and ' upon all states and authorities.' The term ' call ' is ambiguous.[3] It may mean a mere recommendation; but it may also mean a binding order. Interpreted in accordance with the resolution ' Uniting for Peace,' the term ' call ' used in the resolution of February 1, 1951, may be interpreted to mean recommendation; but this interpretation is only a possible, not a necessary one.

Under the resolution ' Uniting for Peace,' the General Assembly is authorised to make recommendations to Members only. But in the resolution of February 1, 1951, the General Assembly makes recommendations—provided ' calls ' means recommendations—also to non-Members, just as the Security Council may, under Article 40 of the Charter, ' call upon the parties concerned,' and not only upon Members, to comply with certain measures decided upon by the Council. The call ' upon all states and authorities to continue to lend every assistance to the United Nations action in Korea ' is addressed not only to the Members involved in this action but also to the Republic of Korea, a non-Member; and the call ' upon all states and authorities to refrain from giving any assistance to the aggressors in Korea ' is addressed to all Members and non-Members. As to the call ' upon the Central People's Government of the People's Republic of China to cause its forces and nationals in Korea to cease hostilities against the United Nations forces and to withdraw from Korea,' it may be interpreted to be a recommendation to a Member; but it is not a recommendation for ' collective measures.' Nor is the call ' upon all states and authorities to refrain from giving any assistance to the aggressors in Korea ' a recommendation for ' collective measures.' Such a recommendation is certainly the call ' upon all states and authorities to continue to lend every assistance to the United Nations action in Korea.' Since this action is an enforcement action involving the use of armed force, the call is—at least—a recommendation for a collective measure including the use of armed force within the meaning of the resolution ' Uniting for Peace.' Since the intervention of Communist China in the war in Korea, determined by the General Assembly as an act of aggression, the United Nations action in Korea is in fact directed not only against the ' forces from North Korea ' but also against the People's Republic of China. Hence the call of the General Assembly to ' lend every assistance to the United Nations action in Korea ' is a recommendation for collective measures including the use of armed force, to be directed not only against the ' authorities of North Korea ' but also against the People's Republic of China insofar as military units of the People's Republic of China are engaged in the aggression. The statement of the resolution of February 1, 1951, that the General Assembly

[3] Cf. *The Law of the United Nations*, p. 96.

'affirms the determination of the United Nations to continue its action in Korea to meet the aggression,' may also be interpreted to mean that the General Assembly recommends to the states involved in the action in Korea to continue to take enforcement measures involving the use of armed force against the aggressors, among which, according to the resolution of February 1, 1951, there is now also the People's Republic of China.

Hence the opinion that the General Assembly in its resolution of February 1, 1951, did not yet recommend sanctions against Communist China is not quite correct, provided that enforcement action, directed, upon a recommendation of the General Assembly, against a state declared by the Assembly to be an aggressor, has the character of a sanction at all.

By making recommendations (under the name of 'calls') to a Member for an action which has not the character of a 'collective measure' and by making recommendations to non-Members for collective measures including the use of armed force, the resolution of February 1, 1951, goes beyond the resolution 'Uniting for Peace'; but the last two paragraphs do not exceed the framework of the resolution 'Uniting for Peace.'

INDEX

CPSIA information can be obtained
at www.ICGtesting.com
Printed in the USA
BVOW09*0004121116
R7606900001B/R76069PG466907BVX2B/1/P

9 781584 770770